Copyright © 2023 by Barchart.com, Inc. All rights reserved.

Published by Barchart.com, Inc., Chicago, Illinois

No part of this publication may be reproduced, stored in a retrieval system, or transmitted in any form or by any means, electronic, mechanical, photocopying, recording, scanning, or otherwise, except as permitted under Section 107 or 108 of the 1976 United States Copyright Act, without either the prior written permission of the Publisher, or authorization through payment of the appropriate per-copy fee to the Copyright Clearance Center, Inc., 222 Rosewood Drive, Danvers, MA 01923, (978) 750-8400, fax (978) 646-8600, or on the web at www.copyright.com. Requests to the Publisher for permission should be addressed to the Permissions Department, Barchart.com, 209 West Jackson Boulevard, Suite 200, Chicago, IL 60606, (312) 554-8122, fax (312) 939-4135

Limit of Liability/Disclaimer of Warranty: While the publisher and author have used their best efforts in preparing this book, they make no representations or warranties with respect to the accuracy or completeness of the contents of this book and specifically disclaim any implied warranties of merchantability or fitness for a particular purpose. No warranty may be created or extended by sales representatives or written sales materials. The advice and strategies contained herein may not be suitable for your situation. You should consult with a professional where appropriate. Neither the publisher nor author shall be liable for any loss of profit or any other commercial damages, including but not limited to special, incidental, consequential, or other damages.

For general information on our other products and services or for technical support, please contact our Customer Support Department within the United States at (800) 238-5814 outside the United States at (312) 554-8122 or fax (312) 939-4135.

ISBN 978-0-910418-23-2

Printed in the United States of America

10  9  8  7  6  5  4  3  2  1


Barchart believes that the information and opinions contained herein are reliable, but Barchart does not make any warranties whatsoever, expressed or implied, and Barchart assumes no liability for reliance on or use of information and opinion contained herein.

cmdty Editorial Board

| President | Editor | Contributing Author |
|---|---|---|
| Eero A. Pikat | Christopher J. Lown | Richard W. Asplund |

Barchart.com
209 W. Jackson Blvd, 2nd Floor
Chicago, Illinois 60606
Phone: 877.247.4394
Fax: 312.939.4135
Website: www.barchart.com/cmdty
Email: commodities@barchart.com

# Table of Contents

PAGE  8T   Commodity Indexes
      18T  Markets Retrench as Inflation and Rate-hikes Take Center Stage
      20T  Conversion Factors

| PAGE | | | | |
|---|---|---|---|---|
| | 1 | Aluminum | 187 | Lithium |
| | 5 | Antimony | 188 | Lumber and Plywood |
| | 6 | Apples | 193 | Magnesium |
| | 7 | Arsenic | 194 | Manganese |
| | 8 | Barley | 196 | Meats |
| | 13 | Bauxite | 200 | Mercury |
| | 14 | Bismuth | 201 | Milk |
| | 15 | Broilers | 207 | Molybdenum |
| | 18 | Butter | 208 | Nickel |
| | 21 | Cadmium | 209 | Oats |
| | 22 | Canola (Rapeseed) | 213 | Olive Oil |
| | 26 | Cattle and Calves | 214 | Onions |
| | 35 | Cement | 215 | Oranges and Orange Juice |
| | 36 | Cheese | 218 | Palm Oil |
| | 44 | Chromium | 220 | Paper |
| | 45 | Coal | 221 | Peanuts and Peanut Oil |
| | 51 | Cobalt | 225 | Pepper |
| | 52 | Cocoa | 266 | Petroleum |
| | 57 | Coconut Oil and Copra | 232 | Platinum-Group Metals |
| | 59 | Coffee | 237 | Potatoes |
| | 64 | Coke | 241 | Rice |
| | 65 | Copper | 244 | Rubber |
| | 75 | Corn | 246 | Rye |
| | 82 | Corn Oil | 248 | Salt |
| | 83 | Cotton | 249 | Sheep and Lambs |
| | 91 | Cottonseed and Products | 251 | Silk |
| | 94 | Currencies | 252 | Silver |
| | 102 | Diamonds | 257 | Soybean Meal |
| | 103 | Eggs | 261 | Soybean Oil |
| | 107 | Electric Power | 266 | Soybeans |
| | 110 | Ethanol | 273 | Stock Index Futures, U.S. |
| | 113 | Fertilizers (Nitrogen, Phosphate & Potash) | 281 | Stock Index Futures, Worldwide |
| | 115 | Fish | 286 | Sugar |
| | 118 | Flaxseed and Linseed Oil | 292 | Sulfur |
| | 121 | Fruits | 293 | Sunflowerseed and Oil |
| | 127 | Gas | 297 | Tallow and Greases |
| | 130 | Gasoline | 299 | Tea |
| | 135 | Gold | 300 | Thorium |
| | 140 | Grain Sorghum | 301 | Tin |
| | 142 | Hay | 305 | Titanium |
| | 143 | Heating Oil | 307 | Tobacco |
| | 148 | Hides and Leather | 310 | Tungsten |
| | 150 | Hogs | 311 | Turkeys |
| | 157 | Honey | 314 | Uranium |
| | 159 | Hops | 317 | Vanadium |
| | 160 | Interest Rates, U.S. | 318 | Vegetables |
| | 171 | Interest Rates, Worldwide | 328 | Wheat and Flour |
| | 177 | Iron and Steel | 341 | Wool |
| | 182 | Lard | 343 | Zinc |
| | 183 | Lead | | |

# cmdtyView®

## advanced charting, tools, and data from a modern web-based platform

**barchart**

barchart.com/cmdty
commodities@barchart.com
877.247.4394

### Charting
View any instrument - cash, crush, futures, indexes - in seasonal or interactive charts

### Futures Trading
Access your trading account from any device with connectivity to 50+ brokers

### Forward Curves
Prebuilt curves or customize for your needs. Create, edit, chart, and go

### Local Cash Bids
Find the best price in your area or identify basis trends with our data and tools

### Grain Indexes
Our indexes ensure that the price you're buying or selling is the fair market price

### Newswires
Actionable news, market analysis, and proprietary content delivered in real-time

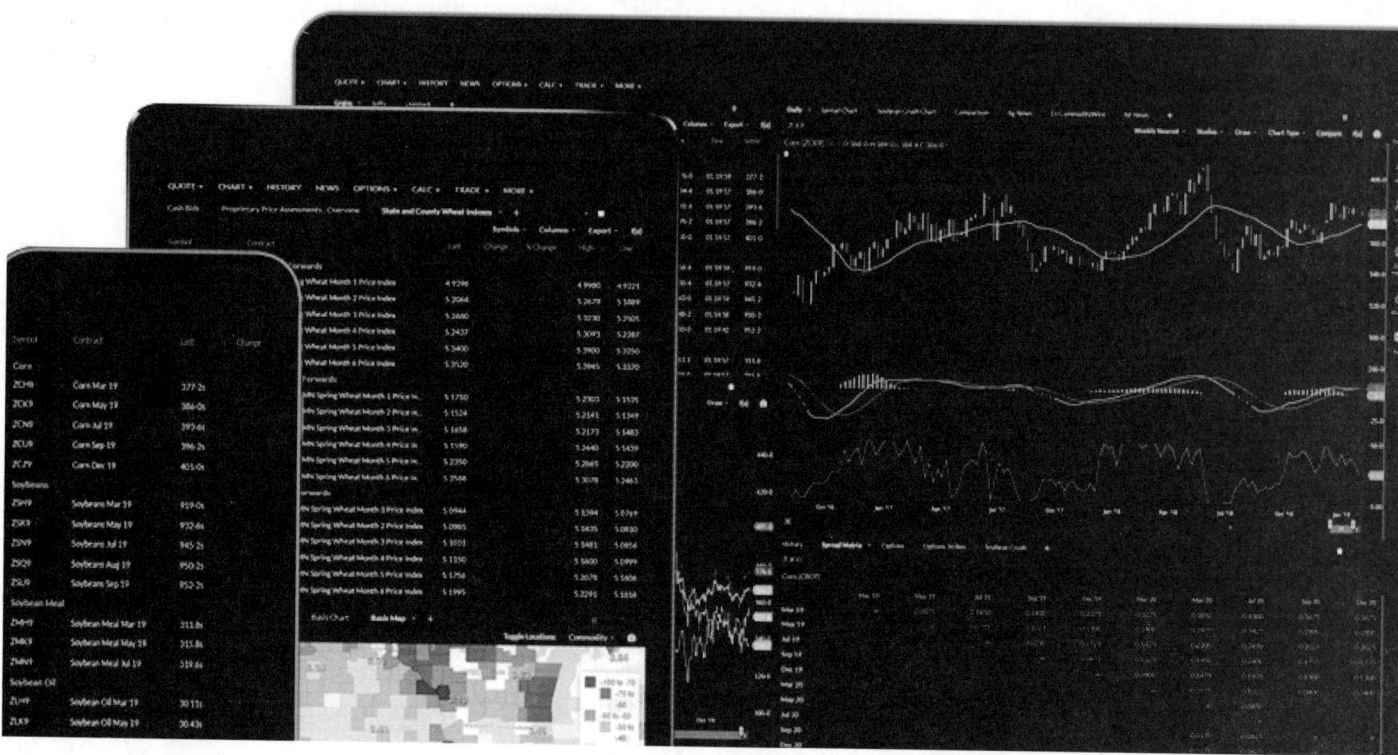

# barchart

# Commodity Fundamentals & Statistics

The premier solution for economic data, commodity statistics, and fundamentals - **all available in cmdtyView, over API, or in cmdtyView for Excel**

**Energy Data**  **Agriculture Data**  **Metals Data**  **Economic Data**

## Available Reports Include

- Advance Economic Indicators
- Advance Monthly Sales for Retail and Food Services
- Advance Report on Durable Goods Manufacturers Shipments, Inventories, and Orders
- Agricultural Prices
- Cattle on Feed
- Cold Storage
- Commitments of Traders
- Construction Spending
- Consumer Price Index
- Crop Production

- Crop Progress
- Dairy Products
- Domestic Product and Income
- Employment Situation
- Fats and Oils
- Futures Activity
- Grain Stocks
- Hogs and Pigs
- Livestock Slaughter
- Manufacturers Shipments, Inventories and Orders
- Manufacturing and Trade Inventories and Sales

- Meat Animals Production, Disposition, and Income
- Monthly Wholesale Trade
- New Residential Construction
- New Residential Sales
- Personal Income and Outlays
- Petroleum Marketing Monthly
- Petroleum Supply Monthly
- Producer Price Index
- WASDE
- Weekly Natural Gas Storage Report
- Weekly Petroleum Status Report

### Access a World of Data at your Fingertips

barchart.com/cmdty
commodities@barchart.com
877.247.4394

# cmdtyView for Excel

**barchart**

Power your research and analysis with better tools. With futures prices, physical data, and fundamentals at your fingertips - **the possibilities are endless.**

## Global Market Data

cmdtyView for Excel has access to all the global exchange data that is available through the cmdtyView terminal. Delayed and historical data is included - with real-time commodity prices available from our global exchange partners

## Physical & Fundamenta Data

Our Excel Add-in is packed with all of our exclusive cash pricing and global fundamental data on commodities. When you combine fundamental data with global market data and cash prices the sky is the limit.

## Built for Analysis

Sometimes you can't do everything you need to in software. cmdtyView for Excel was designed for analysis and research that can help you automate and improve your workflows. Take your research and analysis to the next level.

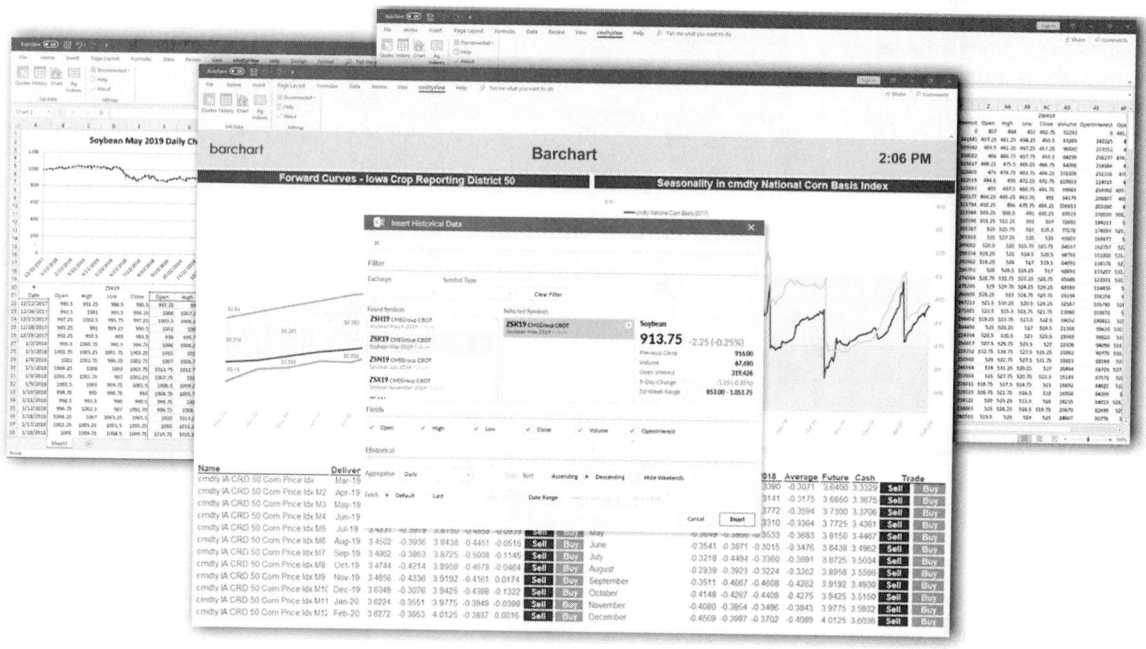

barchart.com/cmdty
commodities@barchart.com
877.247.4394

# barchart

# Barchart OnDemand
## Market Data APIs

Our flexible cloud-based APIs make getting powerful data into your applications, workflows and products simple.

## Power your business with Barchart OnDemand

 Construct dynamic apps and tools

 Integrate market data into your website

 Simplify your current data strategy

 Power charts with real-time or historical data

 Get to market faster with built-in scale

### Scale Your Business

Data is served through AWS ensuring reliability, redundancy, and built-in security that scales dynamically as your business grows

### Always Compatible

Barchart OnDemand works with any operating system or programming language allowing you to start building in minutes

### Reliable Performance

We embrace the cloud but also maintain physical data centers allowing us to cater to low latency requirements and provide a true physical back-up

## Data Coverage

- Exchange Price Data
- Index Price Data
- Commodities
- Technical Data
- OTC & Cash Markets
- Economic Data
- News
- Weather
- Equities
- ETFs & Mutual Funds
- Forex
- Corporate Actions

**Barchart Solutions**
solutions@barchart.com
312.566.9235

# Commodity Indexes

The Refinitiv/Core Commodity CRB® Index (ticker symbol CRY) in early 2022 extended the rally that began in early 2020 to post a new 11-year high in June 2022, but then moved modestly lower during the remainder of the year, closing the year up +19.5% yr/yr. That added to the sharp gain of +39.4% seen in 2021.

Commodity prices in the early stages of the pandemic in early-2020 plunged on the sharp drop in demand caused by the widespread economic shutdowns across the globe. However, commodity prices then staged a massive come-back starting in mid-2020 on the economic boom and strong commodity demand resulting from the massive global monetary and fiscal stimulus. Commodity prices also spiked higher on commodity supply constraints caused by production and transportation disruptions. Those bullish trends continued in early 2022. However, commodity prices began to fall back in the latter half of 2022 due to rising interest rates and a sharply higher dollar.

Five of the six commodity sub-sectors closed higher in 2022, while one sub-sector closed lower. The ranked returns in 2022 were as follows: Energy +20.3%, Grains +10.5%, Livestock +9.6%, Softs +6.1%, Precious Metals +4.7%, and Industrials -20.3%.

## Energy

The Energy sub-sector includes Crude Oil, Heating Oil, and Natural Gas. The Energy sub-sector in 2022 rallied sharply by an average of +20.3%, adding to 2021's extraordinary rally of +54.5%. On a nearest-futures basis, crude oil in 2022 closed up +6.7%, gasoline closed up +10.4%, heating oil closed up +44.3%, and natural gas closed up by +20.3%. Crude oil prices and petroleum products rallied in 2022 due to (1) sanctions on Russian oil and gas tied to the Ukraine invasion, and (2) continued support from production cuts by the OPEC+ cartel.

## Grains

The Grains and Oilseeds sub-sector includes Corn, Soybeans, and Wheat. The Grains and Oilseeds sub-sector in 2022 closed higher by an average of +10.5%, adding to 2021's gain of +14.6% and marking the fifth consecutive year of gains. On a nearest-futures basis, soybeans in 2022 rose by +14.3%, corn rose by +14.4%, and wheat rose by +2.8%.

## Industrials

The Industrials sub-sector includes Copper and Cotton. The Industrials sub-sector in 2022 fell by an average of -20.3%, reversing part of 2021's sharp gain of +35.5%. Copper in 2022 fell by -14.6%, reversing part of the +26.8% gain seen in 2021. Cotton in 2022 fell by -26.0%, reversing part of the +44.1% surge seen in 2021.

## Livestock

The Livestock sub-sector includes Live Cattle and Lean Hogs. The Livestock sub-sector in 2022 closed higher by an average of +9.6%, adding to the +19.5% gain seen in 2021. On a nearest-futures basis, live cattle futures in 2022 closed up +11.5%, adding to the 2021 gain of +23.0%. Lean hog futures in 2022 closed up +7.6%, adding to the 2021 gain of +15.9%.

## Precious Metals

The Precious Metals sub-sector includes Gold, Platinum, and Silver. The Precious Metals sub-sector in 2022 closed mildly higher by +4.7%, recovering of the 2021 decline of -8.5%. In 2022, gold fell by -0.1%, silver rose by +2.9%, and platinum rose by +11.3%.

## Softs

The Softs sub-sector includes Cocoa, Coffee, Orange Juice, and Sugar #11. The Softs sub-sector in 2022 closed higher by an average of +6.1%, adding to the +28.4% gain seen in 2021. In 2022, coffee closed down -26.0%, sugar closed up +6.1%, orange juice closed up +41.1%, and cocoa closed up +3.2%.

# CMDTY INDEXES

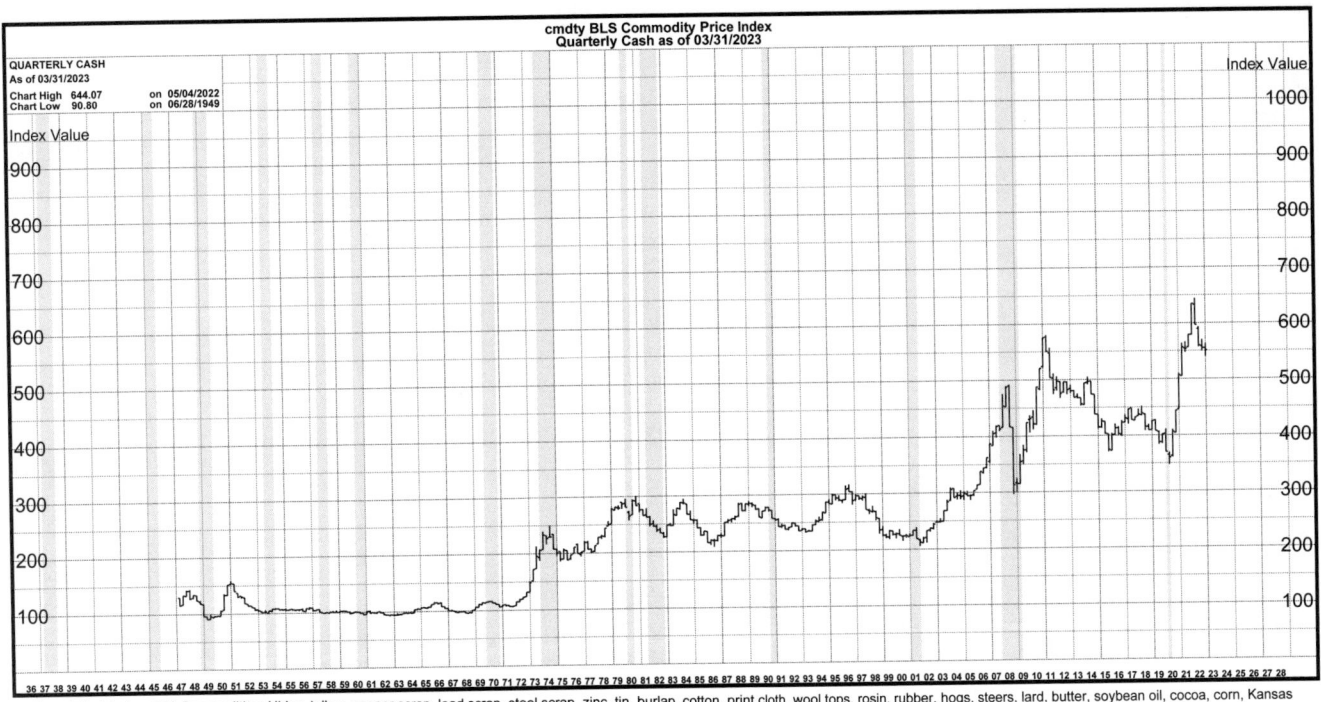

Unweighted Index of 23 Commodities: Hides, tallow, copper scrap, lead scrap, steel scrap, zinc, tin, burlap, cotton, print cloth, wool tops, rosin, rubber, hogs, steers, lard, butter, soybean oil, cocoa, corn, Kansas City wheat, Minneapolis wheat, and sugar. Shaded areas indicate US recessions.

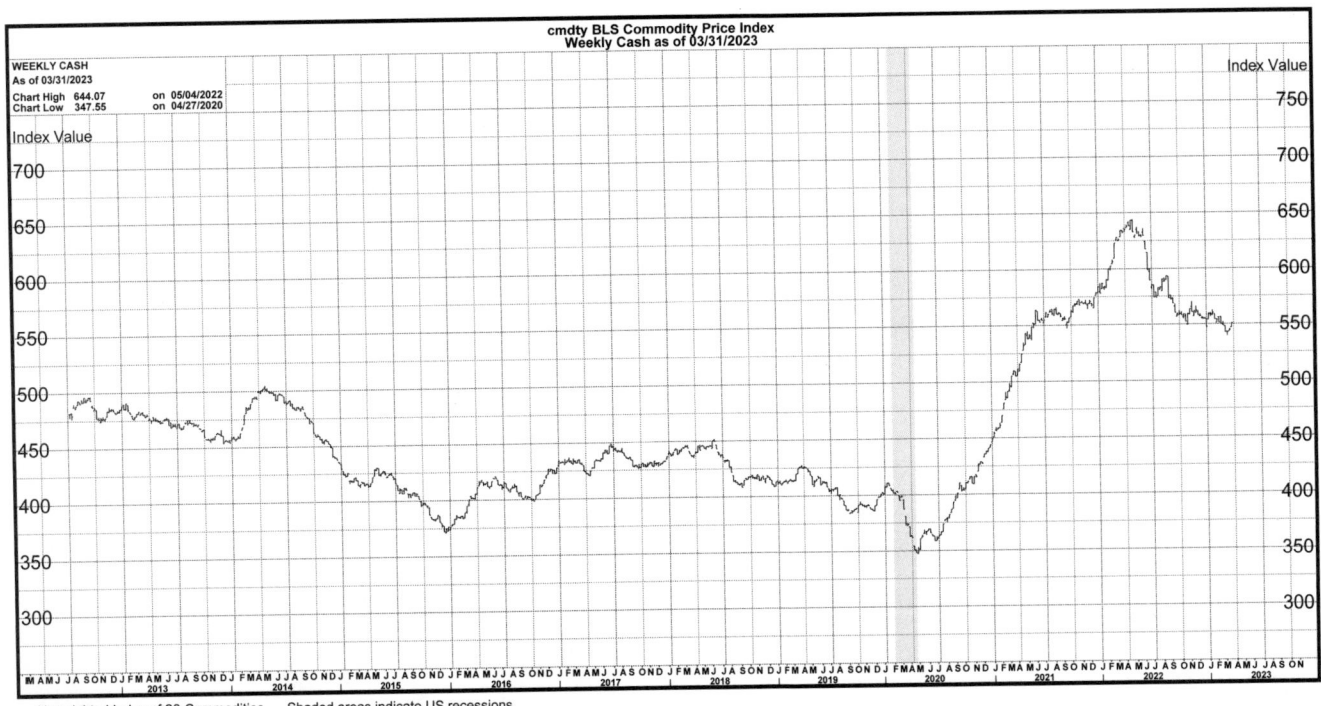

Unweighted Index of 23 Commodities. Shaded areas indicate US recessions.

## cmdty BLS Commodity Price Index (1967=100)

| Year | Jan. | Feb. | Mar. | Apr. | May | June | July | Aug. | Sept. | Oct. | Nov. | Dec. | Average |
|---|---|---|---|---|---|---|---|---|---|---|---|---|---|
| 2013 | 485.62 | 481.97 | 481.13 | 477.55 | 474.67 | 474.05 | 469.75 | 471.23 | 470.60 | 462.25 | 458.57 | 459.56 | 472.25 |
| 2014 | 457.25 | 465.09 | 487.18 | 497.58 | 500.90 | 495.60 | 491.20 | 484.78 | 479.78 | 465.82 | 455.62 | 445.75 | 477.21 |
| 2015 | 429.10 | 420.06 | 416.96 | 415.41 | 425.99 | 424.32 | 416.08 | 408.18 | 405.50 | 397.38 | 385.58 | 379.17 | 410.31 |
| 2016 | 377.44 | 385.09 | 396.03 | 410.34 | 413.55 | 416.74 | 411.76 | 409.65 | 402.79 | 401.09 | 411.91 | 424.17 | 405.05 |
| 2017 | 431.01 | 433.68 | 433.15 | 423.76 | 431.69 | 440.28 | 444.10 | 439.00 | 430.79 | 428.83 | 430.05 | 430.49 | 433.07 |
| 2018 | 438.94 | 441.96 | 442.40 | 441.42 | 444.86 | 445.13 | 434.09 | 417.91 | 412.39 | 416.93 | 415.79 | 413.91 | 430.48 |
| 2019 | 412.09 | 413.25 | 419.52 | 424.52 | 414.57 | 412.09 | 405.07 | 395.48 | 385.93 | 390.23 | 389.27 | 395.16 | 404.77 |
| 2020 | 406.45 | 401.38 | 394.37 | 347.43 | 362.02 | 364.77 | 368.33 | 383.96 | 402.56 | 410.48 | 419.93 | 435.95 | 391.47 |
| 2021 | 454.27 | 473.30 | 498.71 | 518.14 | 540.48 | 555.37 | 558.51 | 561.32 | 554.25 | 564.60 | 569.46 | 570.96 | 534.95 |
| 2022 | 583.18 | 598.12 | 627.49 | 637.85 | 633.50 | 618.54 | 579.83 | 587.38 | 567.58 | 557.75 | 560.41 | 557.79 | 592.45 |

Average. *Source: cmdty by Barchart*

# CMDTY INDEXES

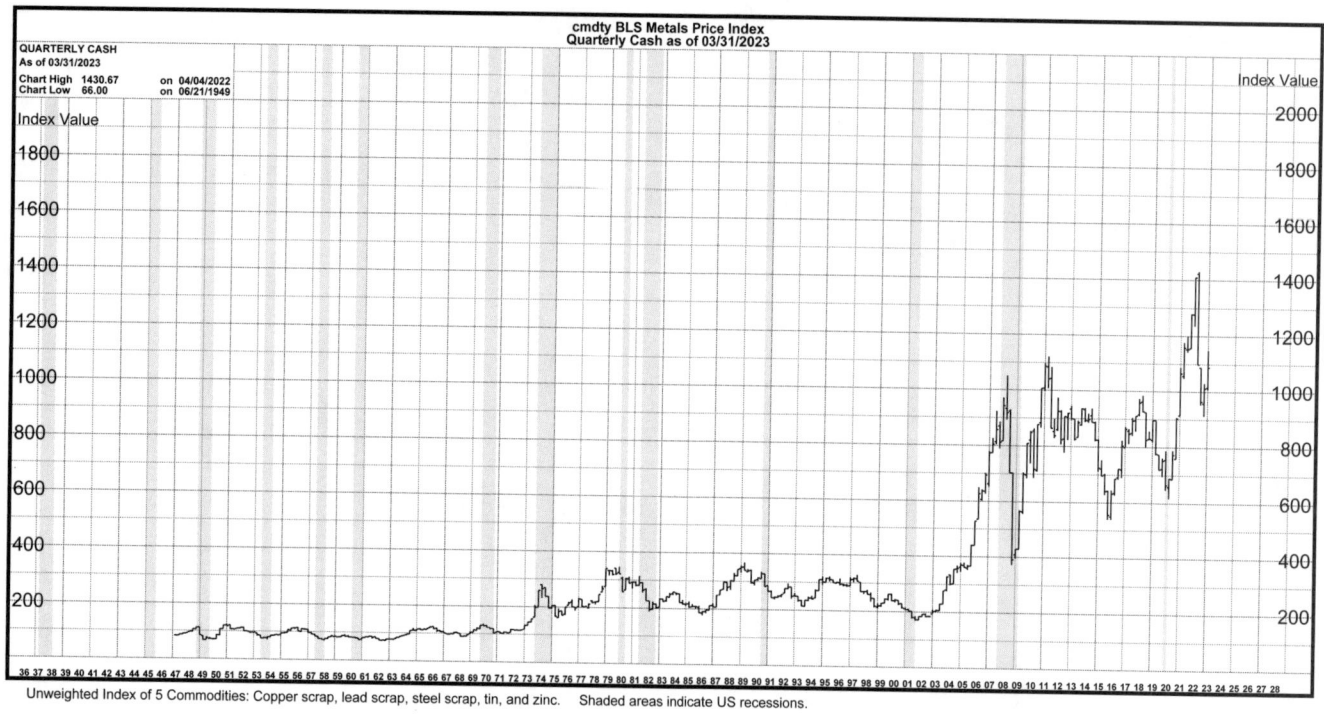

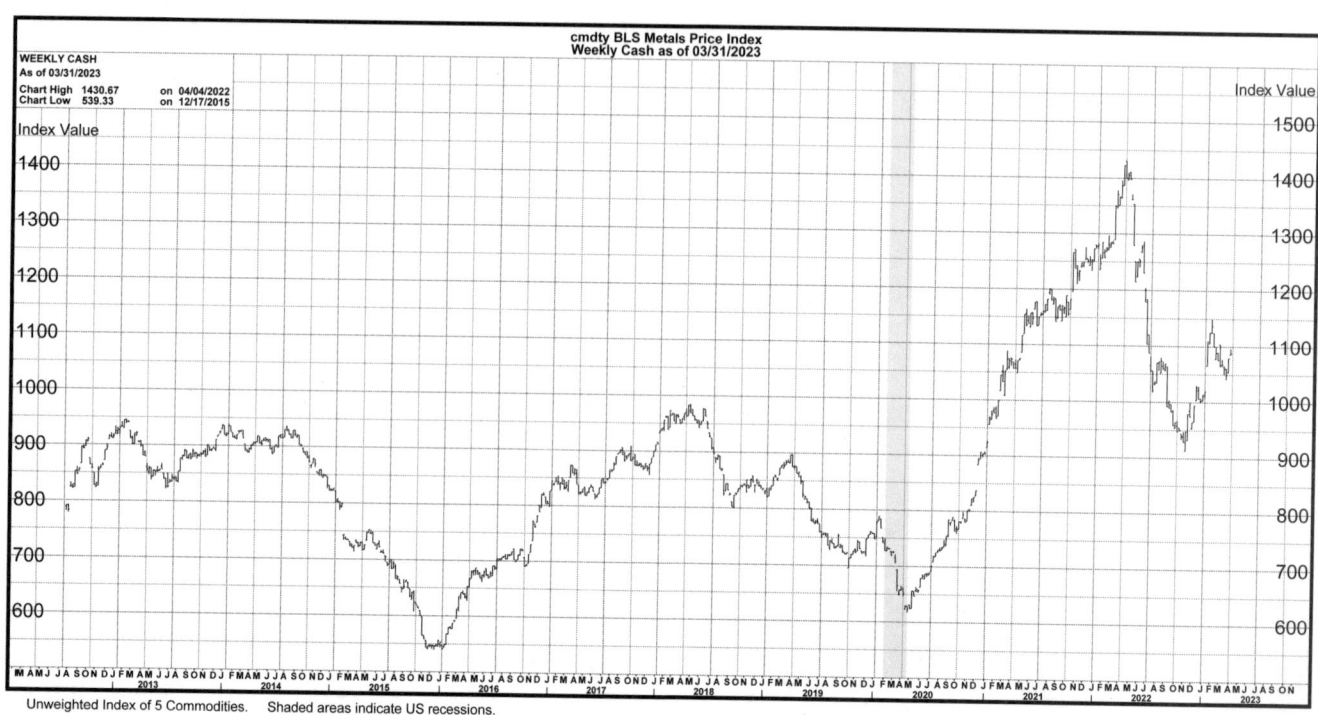

## cmdty BLS Metal Price Index (1967=100)

| Year | Jan. | Feb. | Mar. | Apr. | May | June | July | Aug. | Sept. | Oct. | Nov. | Dec. | Average |
|---|---|---|---|---|---|---|---|---|---|---|---|---|---|
| 2013 | 929.61 | 930.76 | 908.99 | 870.31 | 850.59 | 841.39 | 838.54 | 875.10 | 881.56 | 883.73 | 891.08 | 919.04 | 885.06 |
| 2014 | 925.99 | 920.45 | 900.88 | 905.67 | 908.51 | 897.46 | 921.84 | 922.59 | 903.65 | 876.01 | 856.97 | 836.99 | 898.08 |
| 2015 | 808.63 | 753.27 | 725.64 | 726.61 | 741.70 | 717.50 | 693.73 | 662.74 | 649.72 | 619.91 | 560.90 | 546.74 | 683.92 |
| 2016 | 549.39 | 582.24 | 628.81 | 662.38 | 675.30 | 676.25 | 698.07 | 709.14 | 710.14 | 705.02 | 762.46 | 807.03 | 680.52 |
| 2017 | 834.55 | 840.10 | 854.85 | 833.46 | 828.55 | 825.47 | 849.85 | 882.09 | 891.55 | 884.15 | 871.25 | 885.11 | 856.75 |
| 2018 | 938.18 | 960.91 | 957.84 | 970.72 | 955.27 | 954.43 | 896.38 | 848.71 | 816.40 | 837.13 | 842.37 | 840.64 | 901.58 |
| 2019 | 833.16 | 861.27 | 882.86 | 872.14 | 822.84 | 783.29 | 756.30 | 737.84 | 731.65 | 718.48 | 729.26 | 749.17 | 789.86 |
| 2020 | 766.00 | 732.19 | 688.18 | 636.00 | 651.04 | 680.58 | 713.15 | 739.13 | 775.25 | 780.54 | 806.50 | 886.86 | 737.95 |
| 2021 | 960.01 | 1,010.63 | 1,057.85 | 1,074.57 | 1,141.44 | 1,155.92 | 1,170.18 | 1,172.74 | 1,163.57 | 1,216.13 | 1,243.58 | 1,258.00 | 1,135.39 |
| 2022 | 1,266.43 | 1,279.96 | 1,365.47 | 1,398.48 | 1,262.43 | 1,197.29 | 1,046.36 | 1,061.52 | 981.39 | 946.24 | 960.10 | 1,010.85 | 1,148.04 |

Average. *Source: cmdty by Barchart*

# CMDTY INDEXES

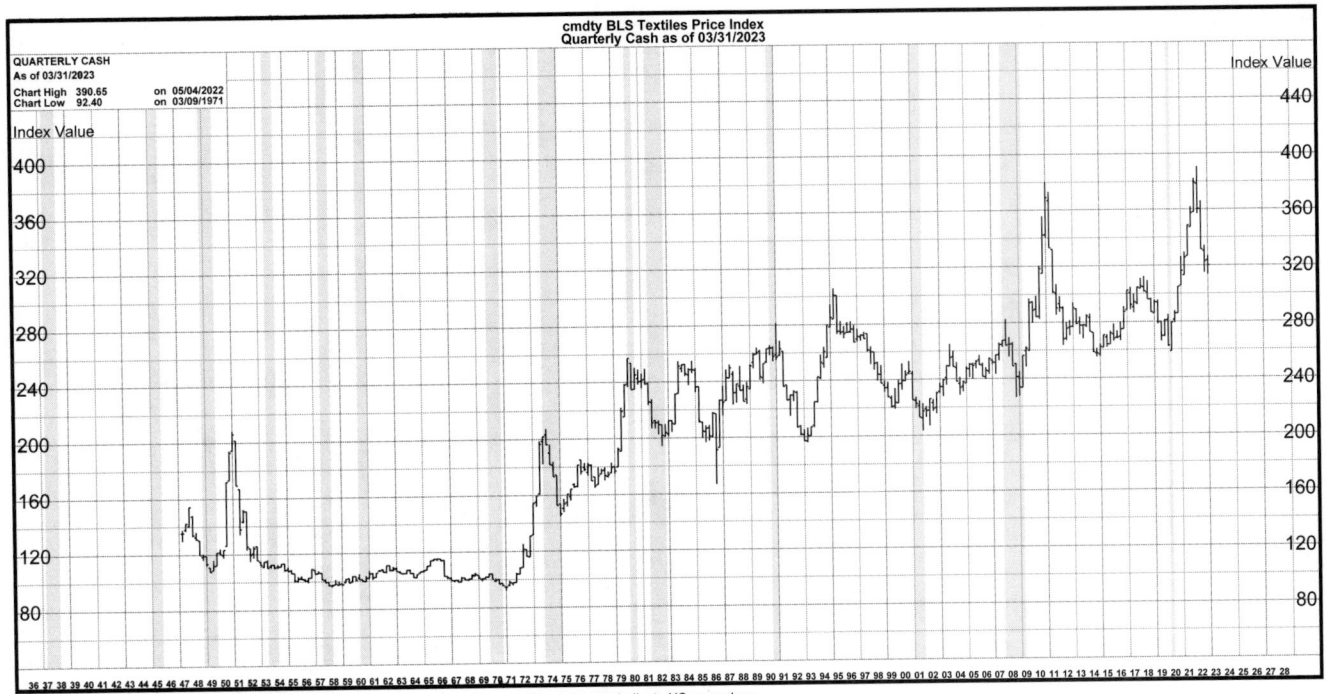

Unweighted Index of 4 Commodities: Burlap, cotton, print cloth, and wool tops.   Shaded areas indicate US recessions.

Unweighted Index of 4 Commodities.   Shaded areas indicate US recessions.

## cmdty BLS Textiles Price Index   (1967=100)

| Year | Jan. | Feb. | Mar. | Apr. | May | June | July | Aug. | Sept. | Oct. | Nov. | Dec. | Average |
|---|---|---|---|---|---|---|---|---|---|---|---|---|---|
| 2013 | 279.44 | 283.14 | 289.79 | 286.96 | 286.20 | 283.33 | 278.59 | 278.23 | 275.03 | 274.73 | 269.70 | 275.78 | 280.08 |
| 2014 | 278.29 | 278.84 | 283.25 | 283.66 | 283.35 | 277.98 | 268.12 | 262.53 | 262.02 | 259.07 | 257.53 | 258.34 | 271.08 |
| 2015 | 257.16 | 260.85 | 261.80 | 265.21 | 265.95 | 267.24 | 267.42 | 267.46 | 263.78 | 266.74 | 268.72 | 271.68 | 265.33 |
| 2016 | 275.67 | 273.67 | 268.32 | 271.13 | 270.18 | 270.66 | 274.89 | 272.29 | 271.23 | 279.05 | 286.95 | 287.39 | 275.12 |
| 2017 | 292.60 | 296.28 | 299.77 | 300.52 | 299.68 | 293.69 | 290.06 | 292.93 | 295.83 | 293.56 | 295.50 | 301.02 | 295.95 |
| 2018 | 308.00 | 305.82 | 307.44 | 304.71 | 305.47 | 306.44 | 305.15 | 303.14 | 299.06 | 295.34 | 291.57 | 291.47 | 301.97 |
| 2019 | 288.81 | 288.83 | 292.65 | 293.47 | 284.62 | 281.83 | 275.44 | 268.15 | 269.65 | 271.96 | 273.52 | 277.23 | 280.51 |
| 2020 | 283.37 | 282.02 | 270.53 | 266.59 | 271.63 | 277.34 | 282.17 | 284.87 | 285.48 | 291.03 | 295.42 | 300.70 | 282.60 |
| 2021 | 308.57 | 317.15 | 319.60 | 320.76 | 323.43 | 326.35 | 331.00 | 334.13 | 337.65 | 351.79 | 359.31 | 353.65 | 331.95 |
| 2022 | 362.31 | 367.39 | 371.60 | 379.59 | 384.06 | 374.64 | 352.60 | 358.12 | 344.57 | 325.61 | 325.75 | 323.76 | 355.83 |

Average.   *Source: cmdty by Barchart*

11T

# CMDTY INDEXES

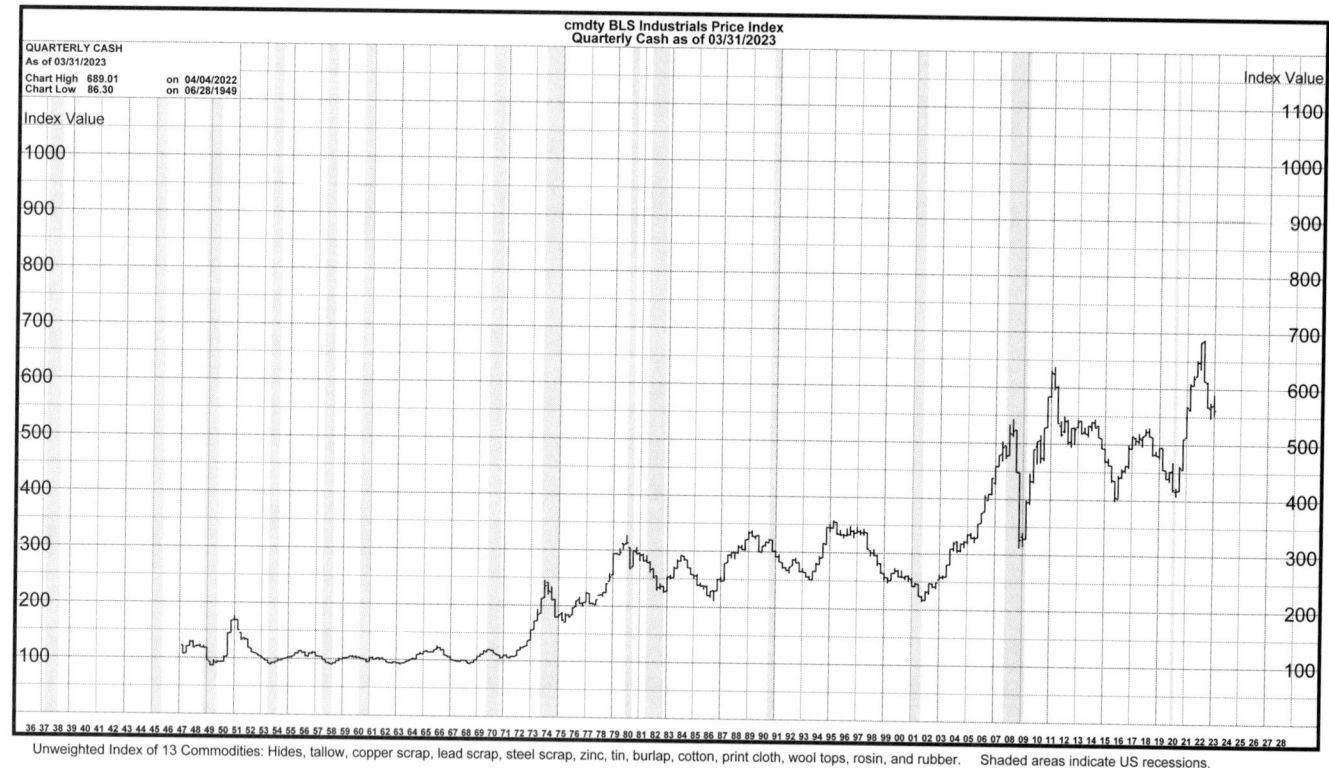

Unweighted Index of 13 Commodities: Hides, tallow, copper scrap, lead scrap, steel scrap, zinc, tin, burlap, cotton, print cloth, wool tops, rosin, and rubber.   Shaded areas indicate US recessions.

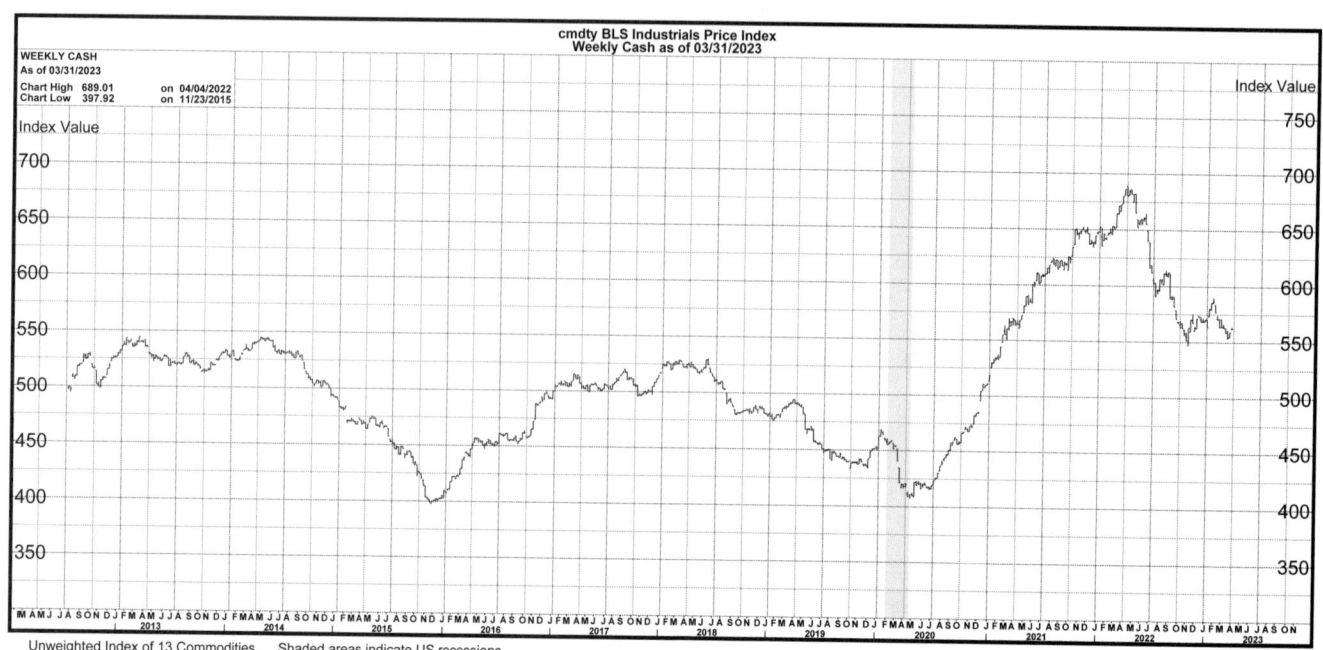

Unweighted Index of 13 Commodities.   Shaded areas indicate US recessions.

## cmdty BLS Industrials Price Index   (1967=100)

| Year | Jan. | Feb. | Mar. | Apr. | May | June | July | Aug. | Sept. | Oct. | Nov. | Dec. | Average |
|---|---|---|---|---|---|---|---|---|---|---|---|---|---|
| 2013 | 534.06 | 538.69 | 539.87 | 532.46 | 524.75 | 523.74 | 520.86 | 525.30 | 521.20 | 514.92 | 519.98 | 529.58 | 527.12 |
| 2014 | 528.48 | 527.92 | 535.44 | 541.50 | 542.77 | 534.33 | 532.02 | 529.81 | 520.65 | 506.18 | 504.60 | 497.80 | 525.13 |
| 2015 | 485.52 | 474.22 | 470.13 | 467.83 | 471.58 | 466.96 | 451.80 | 443.96 | 439.86 | 424.27 | 403.04 | 401.58 | 450.06 |
| 2016 | 409.74 | 421.84 | 436.56 | 450.36 | 452.52 | 451.96 | 457.45 | 456.93 | 456.68 | 460.60 | 484.07 | 494.37 | 452.76 |
| 2017 | 503.07 | 506.20 | 510.83 | 505.47 | 504.70 | 502.57 | 504.42 | 511.92 | 513.67 | 502.70 | 499.14 | 506.88 | 505.96 |
| 2018 | 522.93 | 524.51 | 525.49 | 524.02 | 519.13 | 522.01 | 509.95 | 496.98 | 483.37 | 483.58 | 484.68 | 485.14 | 506.82 |
| 2019 | 479.23 | 482.58 | 490.35 | 490.65 | 471.54 | 458.61 | 449.63 | 445.49 | 442.17 | 438.31 | 438.36 | 446.51 | 461.12 |
| 2020 | 461.10 | 457.03 | 434.96 | 413.57 | 418.55 | 418.45 | 426.77 | 444.66 | 457.42 | 465.93 | 475.68 | 502.37 | 448.04 |
| 2021 | 527.24 | 546.05 | 563.14 | 569.68 | 586.71 | 605.53 | 613.90 | 619.74 | 618.97 | 640.13 | 648.37 | 640.69 | 598.35 |
| 2022 | 645.69 | 648.80 | 671.38 | 682.65 | 661.92 | 642.27 | 599.13 | 607.90 | 580.53 | 560.64 | 563.83 | 570.90 | 619.64 |

Average.   *Source: cmdty by Barchart*

# CMDTY INDEXES

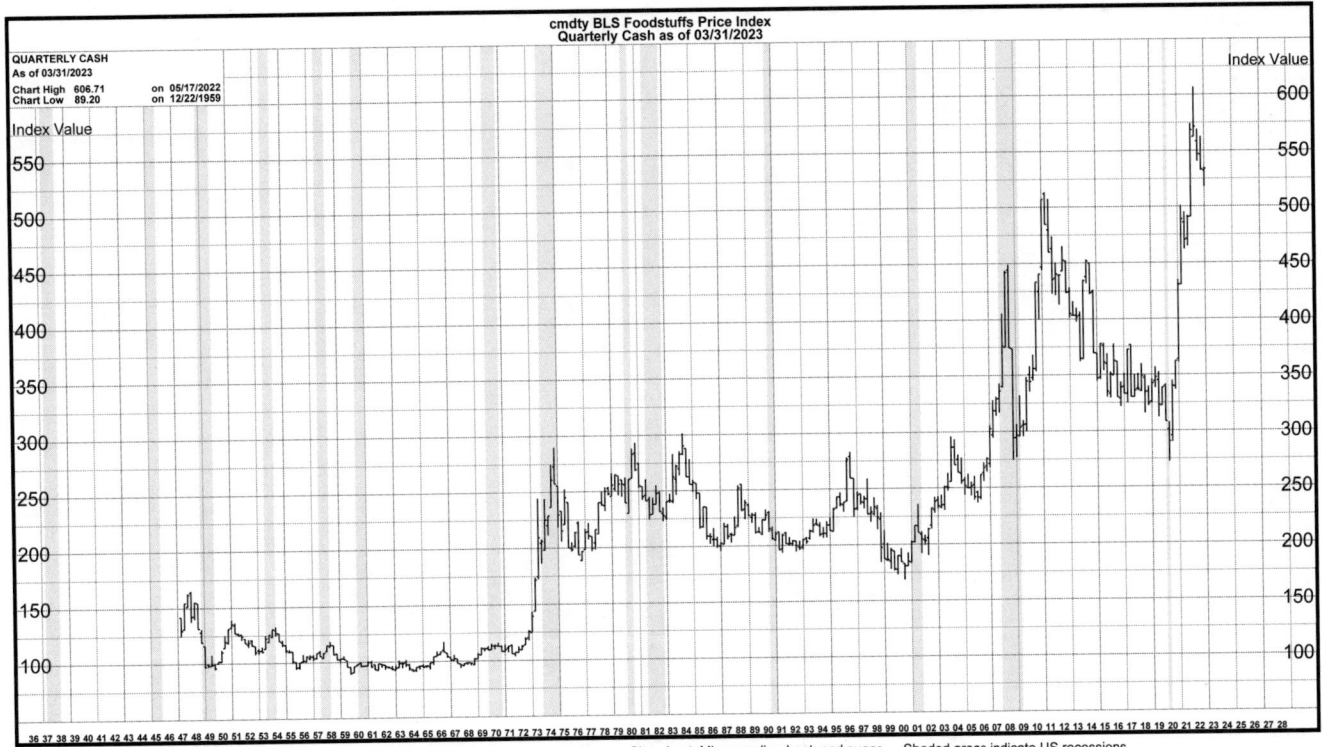

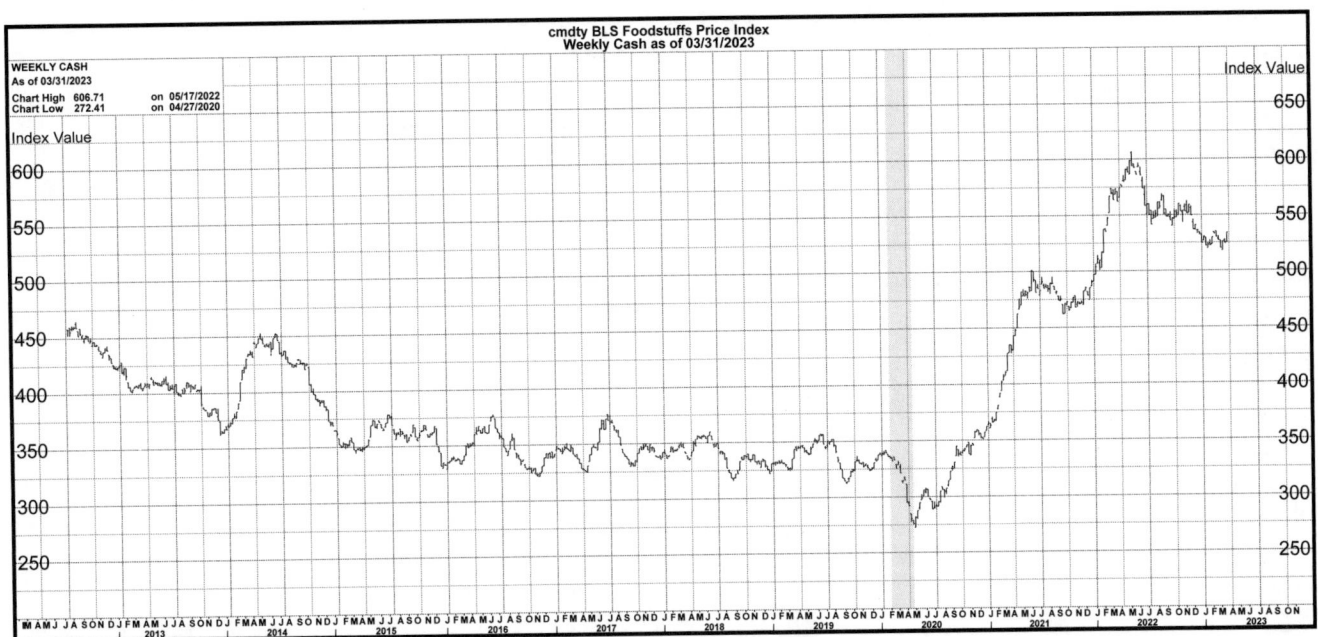

## cmdty BLS Foodstuffs Price Index   (1967=100)

| Year | Jan. | Feb. | Mar. | Apr. | May | June | July | Aug. | Sept. | Oct. | Nov. | Dec. | Average |
|------|------|------|------|------|------|------|------|------|------|------|------|------|---------|
| 2013 | 422.99 | 410.14 | 407.07 | 407.78 | 410.33 | 410.17 | 404.33 | 402.51 | 405.75 | 395.29 | 382.14 | 374.23 | 402.73 |
| 2014 | 370.69 | 387.03 | 424.76 | 440.01 | 445.70 | 444.24 | 437.38 | 426.08 | 426.02 | 412.87 | 392.84 | 379.75 | 415.61 |
| 2015 | 358.69 | 352.29 | 350.34 | 349.61 | 367.54 | 369.24 | 369.14 | 361.25 | 360.32 | 361.29 | 361.42 | 348.87 | 359.17 |
| 2016 | 334.98 | 337.31 | 343.78 | 358.46 | 362.83 | 370.40 | 353.47 | 349.64 | 335.73 | 328.19 | 326.03 | 339.73 | 345.05 |
| 2017 | 344.49 | 346.60 | 341.09 | 328.23 | 344.21 | 363.46 | 369.20 | 351.43 | 333.86 | 340.67 | 346.50 | 339.79 | 345.79 |
| 2018 | 340.59 | 344.84 | 344.76 | 344.32 | 355.67 | 353.36 | 343.73 | 325.14 | 327.65 | 336.27 | 332.96 | 328.82 | 339.84 |
| 2019 | 331.10 | 330.08 | 334.65 | 344.14 | 343.99 | 352.85 | 348.13 | 332.80 | 316.85 | 329.71 | 327.67 | 330.97 | 335.25 |
| 2020 | 338.49 | 332.49 | 320.43 | 284.57 | 293.39 | 298.94 | 297.53 | 310.40 | 334.49 | 341.57 | 350.47 | 354.96 | 321.48 |
| 2021 | 366.06 | 384.70 | 418.16 | 451.53 | 479.68 | 489.80 | 486.85 | 486.15 | 472.21 | 470.62 | 471.75 | 483.05 | 455.05 |
| 2022 | 503.07 | 531.47 | 568.68 | 577.88 | 594.19 | 585.39 | 552.61 | 558.94 | 548.99 | 553.22 | 555.09 | 538.98 | 555.71 |

Average.   Source: cmdty by Barchart

13T

# CMDTY INDEXES

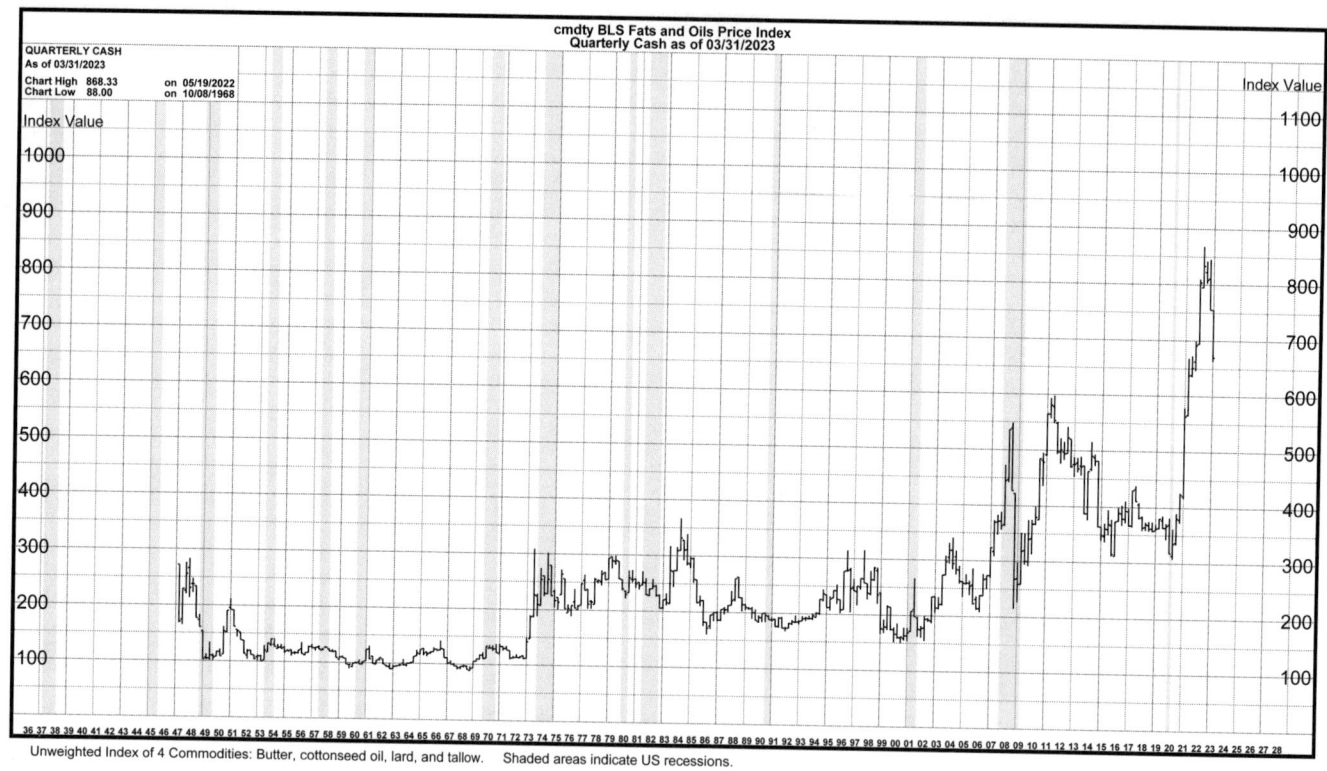

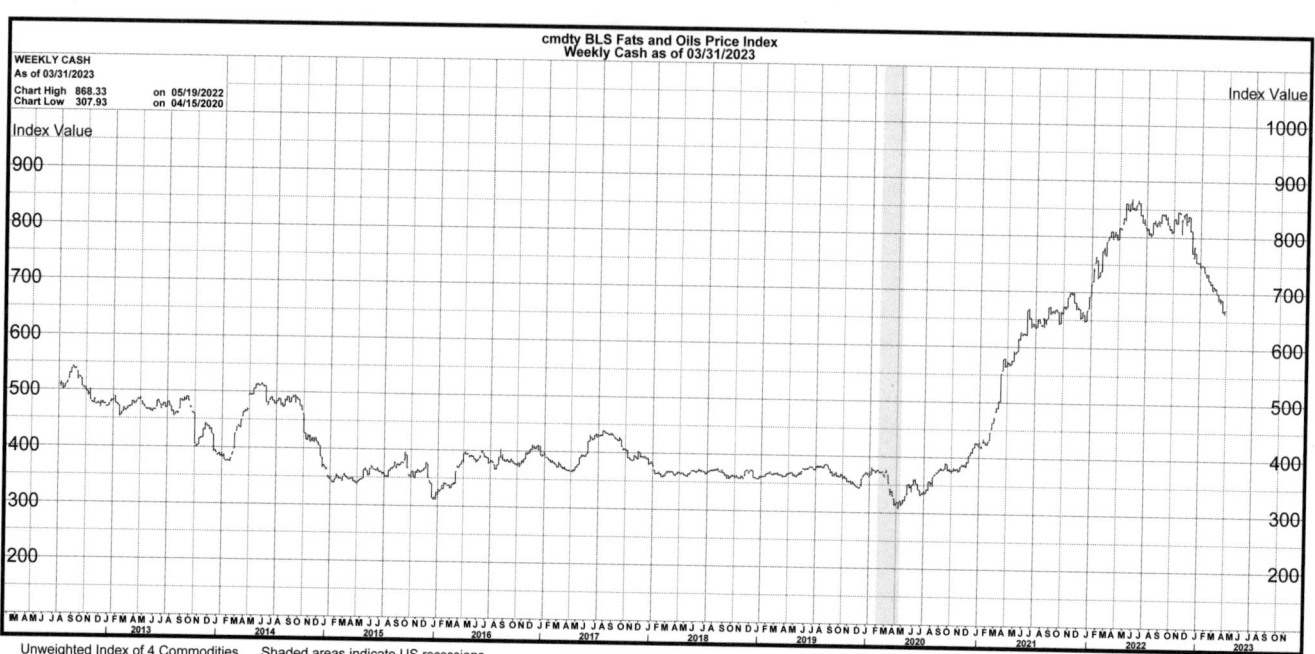

## cmdty BLS Fats and Oils Price Index (1967=100)

| Year | Jan. | Feb. | Mar. | Apr. | May | June | July | Aug. | Sept. | Oct. | Nov. | Dec. | Average |
|---|---|---|---|---|---|---|---|---|---|---|---|---|---|
| 2013 | 478.78 | 463.85 | 472.83 | 480.48 | 466.32 | 473.86 | 473.76 | 463.55 | 484.31 | 435.85 | 427.75 | 414.70 | 461.34 |
| 2014 | 383.34 | 388.71 | 444.35 | 482.96 | 511.46 | 492.95 | 483.40 | 482.99 | 488.24 | 444.49 | 416.67 | 383.76 | 450.28 |
| 2015 | 345.69 | 348.02 | 348.93 | 342.31 | 357.64 | 363.99 | 355.78 | 368.38 | 378.59 | 356.58 | 362.48 | 345.06 | 356.12 |
| 2016 | 325.81 | 337.32 | 352.31 | 387.99 | 386.67 | 491.94 | 378.62 | 384.16 | 381.65 | 376.69 | 394.32 | 405.54 | 383.59 |
| 2017 | 390.86 | 379.46 | 372.45 | 367.41 | 387.20 | 417.41 | 431.12 | 432.99 | 422.43 | 398.69 | 392.43 | 390.23 | 398.56 |
| 2018 | 372.28 | 362.23 | 365.82 | 365.04 | 364.99 | 368.91 | 368.71 | 370.93 | 360.64 | 360.00 | 365.24 | 363.08 | 365.66 |
| 2019 | 362.32 | 366.62 | 364.16 | 366.46 | 368.12 | 377.58 | 378.90 | 379.58 | 366.11 | 360.90 | 350.84 | 358.63 | 366.69 |
| 2020 | 372.49 | 371.78 | 349.23 | 315.98 | 339.57 | 347.49 | 342.96 | 368.86 | 380.44 | 377.46 | 385.37 | 413.22 | 363.74 |
| 2021 | 424.74 | 446.78 | 523.90 | 574.71 | 609.44 | 641.69 | 641.84 | 655.41 | 659.00 | 678.44 | 681.08 | 662.18 | 599.93 |
| 2022 | 732.60 | 760.02 | 803.67 | 818.63 | 855.02 | 848.92 | 811.05 | 828.36 | 826.21 | 831.71 | 833.34 | 776.71 | 810.52 |

Average.   Source: cmdty by Barchart

# CMDTY INDEXES

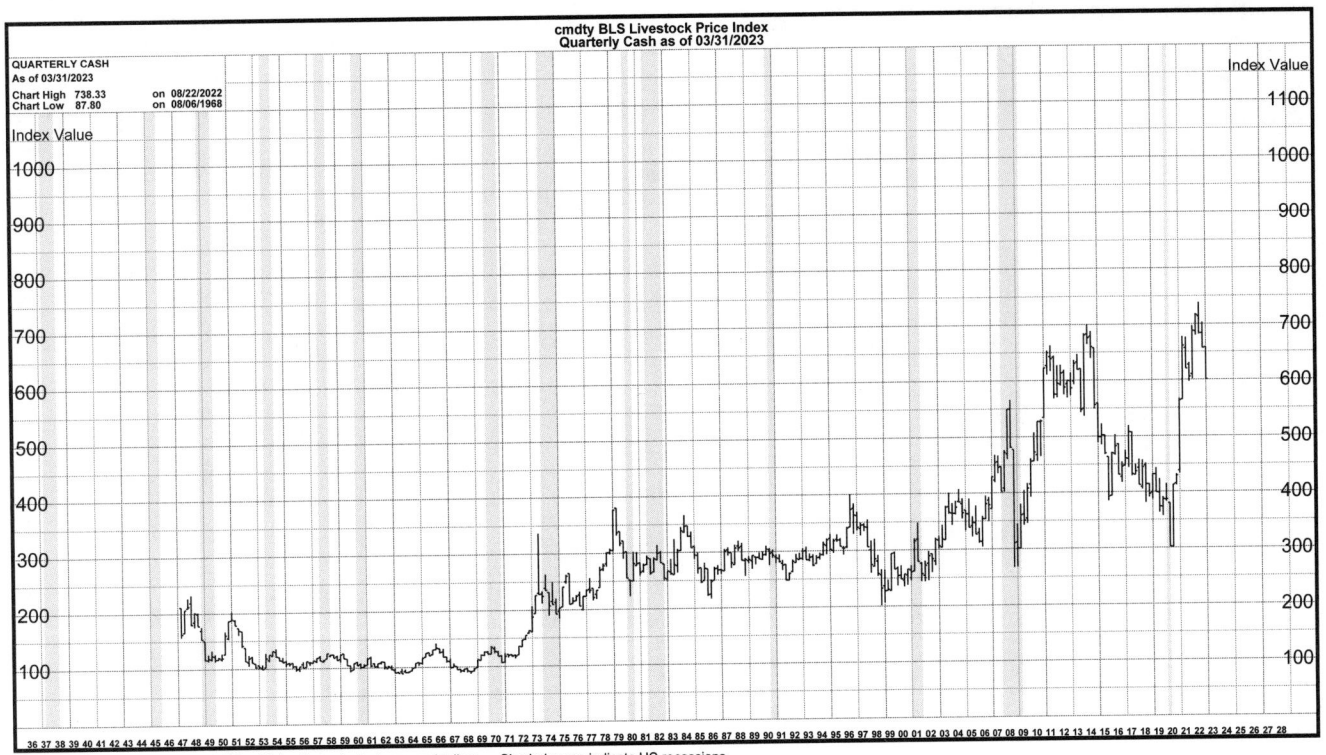

Unweighted Index of 5 Commodities: Hides, hogs, lard, steers, and tallow.    Shaded areas indicate US recessions.

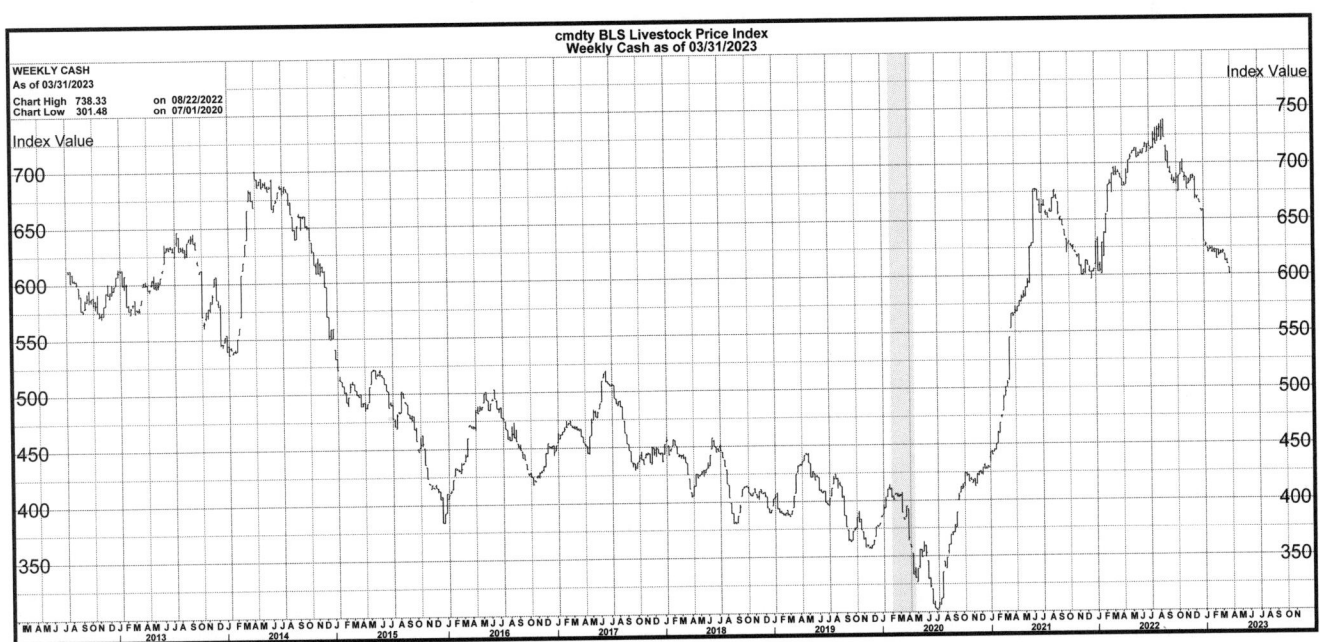

Unweighted Index of 5 Commodities.    Shaded areas indicate US recessions.

## cmdty BLS Livestock Price Index    (1967=100)

| Year | Jan. | Feb. | Mar. | Apr. | May | June | July | Aug. | Sept. | Oct. | Nov. | Dec. | Average |
|------|------|------|------|------|-----|------|------|------|-------|------|------|------|---------|
| 2013 | 606.27 | 584.54 | 580.26 | 598.17 | 601.26 | 626.31 | 634.54 | 630.72 | 637.72 | 591.03 | 583.70 | 571.43 | 603.83 |
| 2014 | 543.02 | 557.63 | 645.13 | 685.62 | 689.00 | 676.46 | 683.71 | 661.15 | 656.18 | 639.12 | 613.66 | 573.26 | 635.33 |
| 2015 | 523.85 | 500.96 | 503.91 | 491.27 | 517.22 | 513.03 | 484.28 | 490.90 | 477.86 | 452.68 | 419.99 | 404.96 | 481.74 |
| 2016 | 410.40 | 432.01 | 453.40 | 479.17 | 491.47 | 491.94 | 473.49 | 461.17 | 443.34 | 423.46 | 428.92 | 449.89 | 453.22 |
| 2017 | 459.17 | 470.78 | 466.97 | 452.02 | 478.49 | 506.82 | 500.73 | 478.13 | 439.94 | 438.59 | 442.67 | 443.87 | 464.85 |
| 2018 | 450.12 | 447.67 | 433.39 | 415.52 | 427.78 | 447.09 | 441.73 | 410.57 | 401.17 | 409.82 | 406.81 | 396.83 | 422.84 |
| 2019 | 399.14 | 388.75 | 407.21 | 437.39 | 426.55 | 409.36 | 408.37 | 410.57 | 370.18 | 379.01 | 360.20 | 373.81 | 397.55 |
| 2020 | 400.48 | 404.58 | 394.37 | 347.43 | 351.93 | 319.36 | 318.49 | 358.55 | 396.49 | 419.00 | 418.06 | 427.44 | 379.68 |
| 2021 | 442.88 | 470.67 | 524.44 | 573.09 | 592.29 | 659.71 | 658.18 | 665.79 | 643.40 | 625.72 | 608.99 | 605.67 | 589.24 |
| 2022 | 618.76 | 657.61 | 690.72 | 687.49 | 708.61 | 711.95 | 718.04 | 728.27 | 691.62 | 690.80 | 685.48 | 669.79 | 688.26 |

Average.    *Source: cmdty by Barchart*

15T

# CMDTY INDEXES

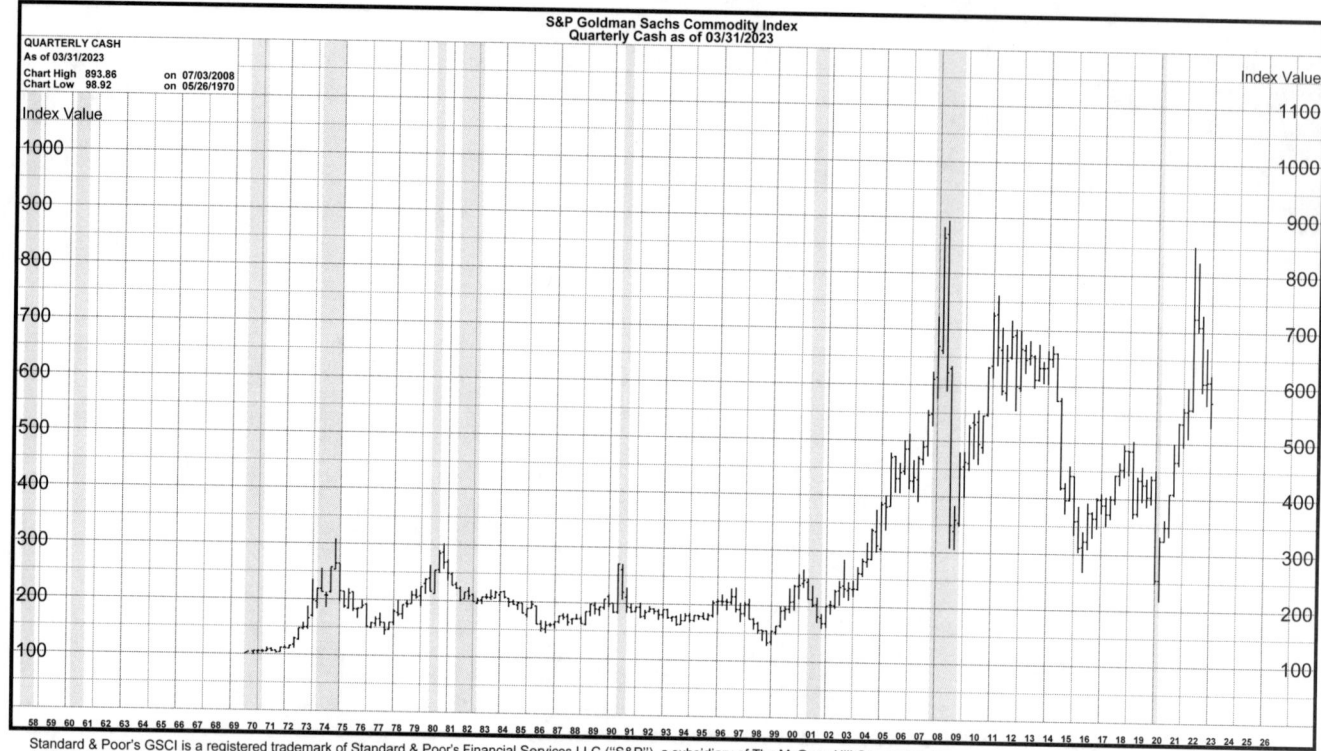

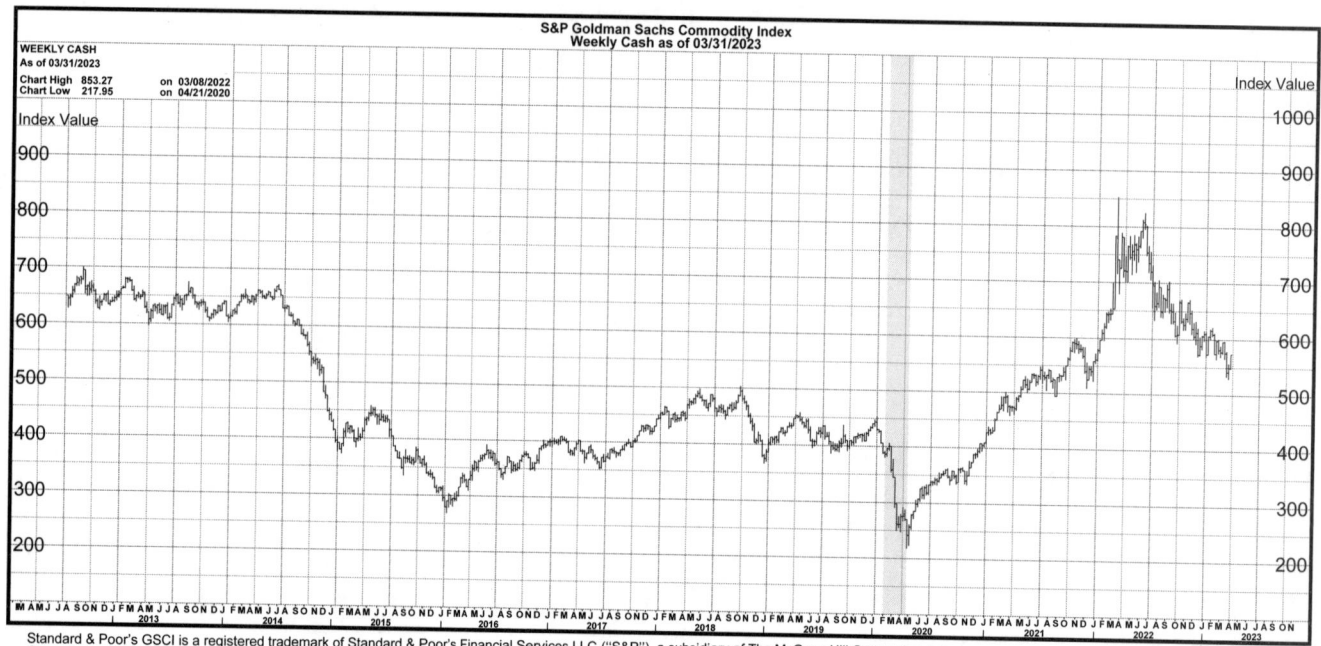

## S&P GSCI Index   (12/31/1969=100)

| Year | Jan. | Feb. | Mar. | Apr. | May | June | July | Aug. | Sept. | Oct. | Nov. | Dec. | Average |
|------|------|------|------|------|-----|------|------|------|-------|------|------|------|---------|
| 2013 | 658.10 | 669.41 | 648.20 | 624.14 | 627.04 | 622.56 | 639.34 | 645.98 | 645.31 | 633.40 | 614.88 | 631.12 | 638.29 |
| 2014 | 617.20 | 640.25 | 645.88 | 653.19 | 652.42 | 657.64 | 636.14 | 609.55 | 588.76 | 548.78 | 521.86 | 449.57 | 601.77 |
| 2015 | 388.27 | 412.87 | 403.39 | 423.64 | 443.38 | 436.70 | 402.75 | 360.85 | 362.48 | 364.45 | 345.91 | 315.98 | 388.39 |
| 2016 | 289.97 | 293.46 | 324.99 | 337.79 | 361.37 | 377.36 | 354.83 | 353.51 | 353.18 | 372.96 | 359.92 | 391.89 | 347.60 |
| 2017 | 396.61 | 402.05 | 385.28 | 390.60 | 381.04 | 364.63 | 374.75 | 380.46 | 394.88 | 401.99 | 425.01 | 425.39 | 393.56 |
| 2018 | 452.52 | 444.49 | 446.07 | 463.57 | 484.33 | 472.75 | 465.94 | 459.42 | 470.55 | 479.81 | 428.86 | 396.52 | 455.40 |
| 2019 | 401.35 | 417.75 | 430.35 | 449.24 | 434.87 | 412.23 | 421.95 | 398.31 | 410.88 | 405.91 | 417.71 | 428.12 | 419.06 |
| 2020 | 420.61 | 386.88 | 297.14 | 258.35 | 284.90 | 320.86 | 338.20 | 353.55 | 348.00 | 354.70 | 368.28 | 396.92 | 344.03 |
| 2021 | 428.99 | 464.45 | 478.68 | 485.80 | 516.16 | 528.92 | 530.65 | 520.37 | 538.90 | 583.89 | 573.46 | 545.64 | 516.33 |
| 2022 | 596.98 | 645.02 | 746.61 | 740.08 | 764.01 | 773.66 | 677.38 | 668.93 | 631.62 | 638.30 | 632.79 | 594.99 | 675.86 |

Average.   Source: CME Group; Chicago Mercantile Ezchange

# CMDTY INDEXES

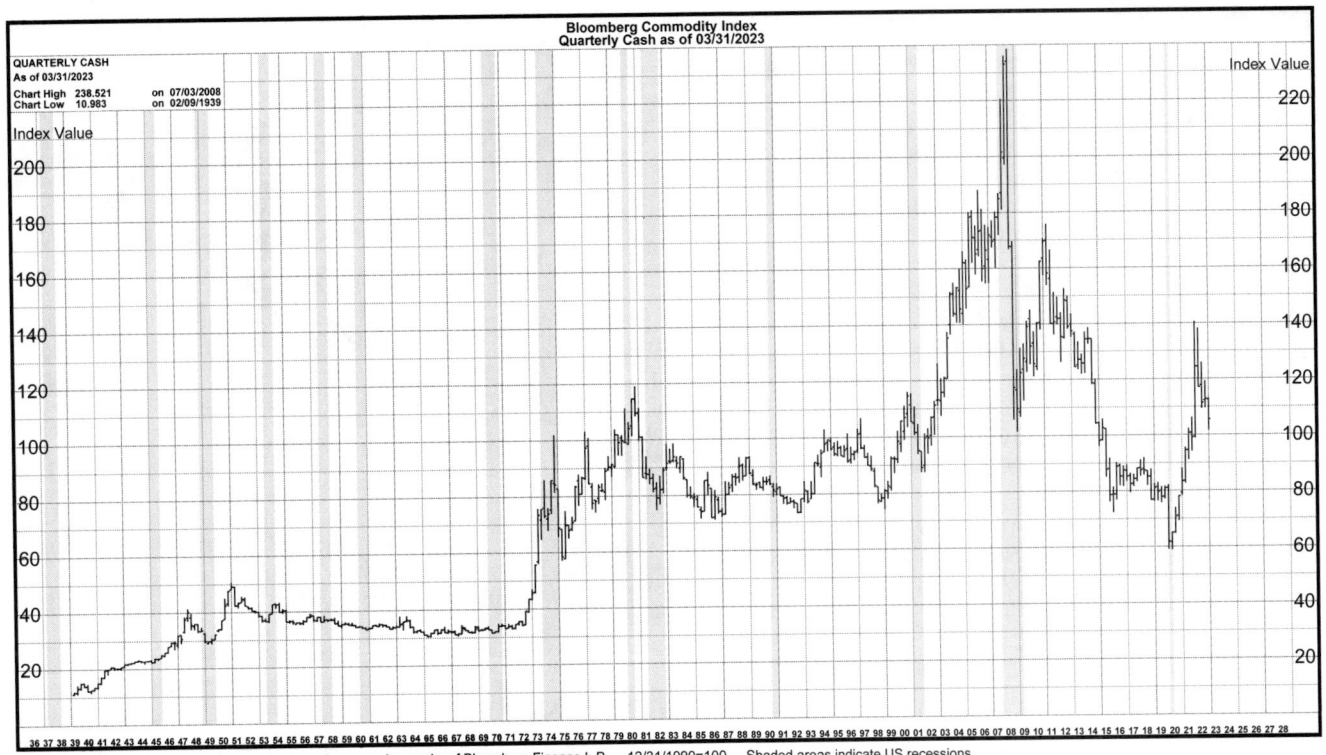

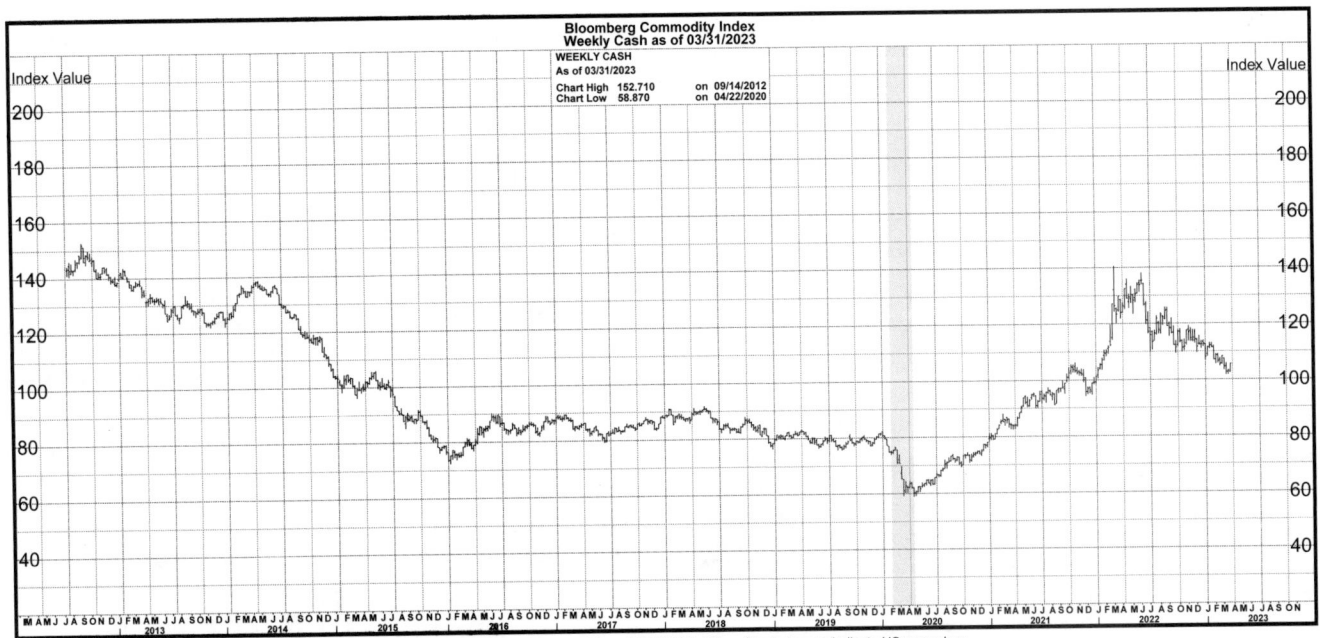

## Bloomberg Commodity Index   (12/31/1990=100)

| Year | Jan. | Feb. | Mar. | Apr. | May | June | July | Aug. | Sept. | Oct. | Nov. | Dec. | Average |
|---|---|---|---|---|---|---|---|---|---|---|---|---|---|
| 2013 | 140.01 | 139.55 | 137.44 | 132.99 | 132.04 | 129.38 | 127.65 | 128.32 | 128.98 | 127.48 | 123.20 | 126.25 | 131.11 |
| 2014 | 125.24 | 130.97 | 134.71 | 136.56 | 135.81 | 134.75 | 130.44 | 126.39 | 121.57 | 117.97 | 116.95 | 109.39 | 126.73 |
| 2015 | 102.09 | 102.74 | 99.64 | 100.95 | 103.32 | 100.92 | 96.70 | 89.46 | 88.43 | 88.72 | 83.31 | 78.74 | 94.58 |
| 2016 | 75.41 | 75.36 | 79.16 | 81.15 | 84.40 | 88.25 | 85.82 | 84.51 | 84.08 | 85.97 | 83.99 | 87.30 | 82.95 |
| 2017 | 87.80 | 88.15 | 85.30 | 84.99 | 83.53 | 81.21 | 83.04 | 83.40 | 85.03 | 85.16 | 86.78 | 85.14 | 84.96 |
| 2018 | 89.02 | 88.02 | 87.59 | 88.72 | 90.37 | 88.31 | 84.53 | 83.90 | 83.50 | 85.94 | 83.10 | 80.58 | 86.13 |
| 2019 | 79.75 | 80.90 | 81.35 | 81.88 | 79.22 | 78.20 | 79.38 | 76.81 | 78.81 | 78.54 | 79.05 | 79.49 | 79.45 |
| 2020 | 79.01 | 74.65 | 65.70 | 61.54 | 62.23 | 64.17 | 67.10 | 71.48 | 71.66 | 72.55 | 73.68 | 75.75 | 69.96 |
| 2021 | 80.12 | 84.29 | 84.74 | 86.53 | 92.29 | 93.34 | 94.57 | 94.54 | 97.88 | 103.57 | 102.23 | 97.27 | 92.61 |
| 2022 | 103.83 | 111.11 | 125.48 | 128.54 | 130.12 | 128.91 | 116.02 | 121.45 | 116.22 | 113.81 | 115.71 | 112.65 | 118.65 |

Average. Bloomberg and Bloomberg Indices are trademarks or service marks of Bloomberg Finance L.P. Formerly the Dow Jones-UBS Commodity Index. *Source: CME Group; Chicago Board of Trade*

# MARKETS RETRENCH AS INFLATION AND RATE-HIKES TAKE CENTER STAGE

The markets in 2022 retrenched as the Covid pandemic abated and life began to return to normal. The Covid pandemic began in the U.S. and Europe in early 2020, but vaccines quickly became available by late 2020 and helped slow the spread of the disease. By March 2022, the Covid surge in the U.S. had largely ended, and many social distancing and mask requirements were dropped.

U.S. GDP took a hit of -2.8% in 2020 due to the initial shock from the pandemic, but the U.S. economy quickly recovered due to the massive U.S. fiscal and monetary stimulus-response. Congress quickly swung into action by providing around $5 trillion of stimulus programs, which succeeded in helping unemployed persons and plugging the massive GDP hole caused by the economic shutdowns. The Fed cut interest rates to nearly zero, injected massive liquidity into the financial system with bond buying, and launched a wide range of rescue programs. That stimulus allowed U.S. GDP in 2021 to recover sharply to +5.9%, which was the strongest annual growth rate since 1984.

However, the booming economy caused a severe inflation outbreak and the Federal Reserve by 2022 was forced to respond with a sharp increase in interest rates. The U.S. consumer price index (CPI) peaked at a 40-year high of 9.1% yr/yr in June 2022, and remained high at 6.5% by December 2022. The U.S. core CPI (excluding food and energy) peaked at +6.6% yr/yr in September 2022 and remained high at +5.7% yr/yr by December 2022.

The inflation surge was caused by the booming global economy, high commodity and raw material costs, supply chain disruptions that caused shortages in many industries, and excess liquidity in the financial system. In addition, energy prices surged in early 2022 after Russia invaded Ukraine, and much of the developed world responded with sanctions against Russian oil and natural gas.

The Federal Reserve was forced into raising interest rates sharply by a total of 4.25 percentage points during 2022. The Fed raised its federal funds rate target range from the 0.00%/0.25% level that prevailed during the pandemic to 4.25%/4.50% by December 2022. That was the sharpest annual interest rate hike since 2006. Moreover, Fed officials at the end of 2022 were forecasting that they would need to raise the federal funds rate further to 5.10% by the end of 2023.

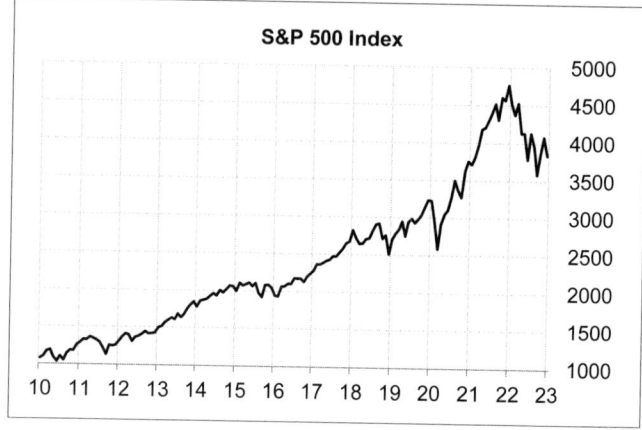

Despite the Fed's sharp interest rate hike, the U.S. economy held its own during 2022 with a GDP increase of +2.2%. Moreover, the U.S. labor market remained very strong, with the unemployment rate in December 2022 at a record low of 3.5%.

The 10-year T-note yield in 2022 surged from 1.51% at the beginning of the year to a 15-year high of 4.34% by October 2022. The surge in the T-note yield was due to the inflation surge and the Fed's sharp interest rate hikes.

The 10-year T-note yield was then able to ease to 3.87% by the end of 2022 after the U.S. inflation statistics cooled and the Fed slowed its rate-hike regime. Also, the markets were looking forward to a weak economy in 2023.

The dollar surged during 2022 as the Federal Reserve raised interest rates much faster than other major global central banks. The dollar index rallied by 20% to a 20-year high in September 2022. However, the dollar index then fell back in late 2022 as U.S. interest rates cooled, and the dollar index finished the year up +8.2% at 103.522.

The Federal Reserve led the world with its 4.25 percentage point rate hike in 2022, which produced a sharp improvement in the dollar's interest rate differentials. The European Central Bank, by contrast, did not start raising interest rates until July 2022 and implemented an overall hike of only 2.50 percentage points of its main refinancing rate during 2022 to 2.50%. Meanwhile, the Bank of Japan maintained its zero interest rate policy all during 2022 and did not even curtail its quantitative easing program.

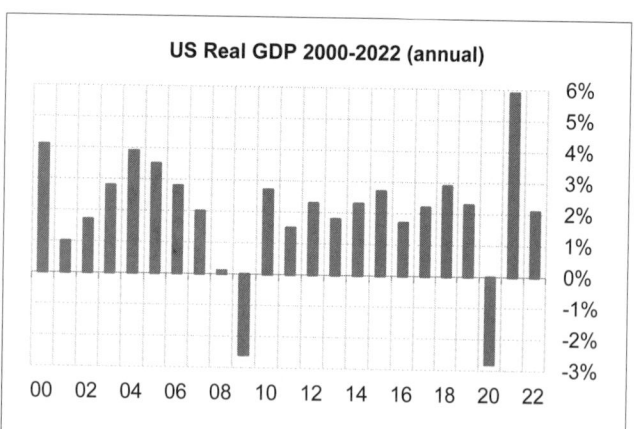

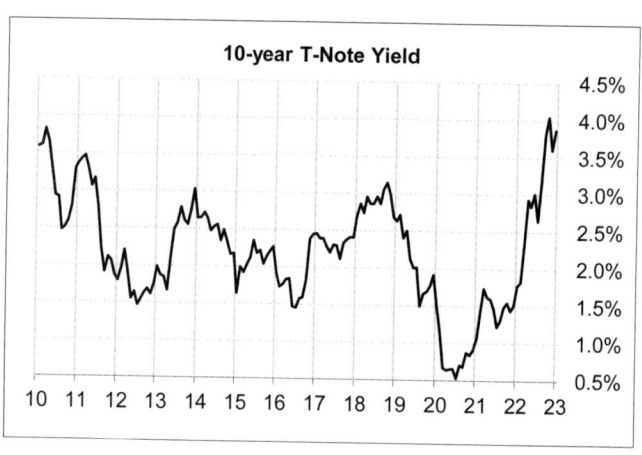

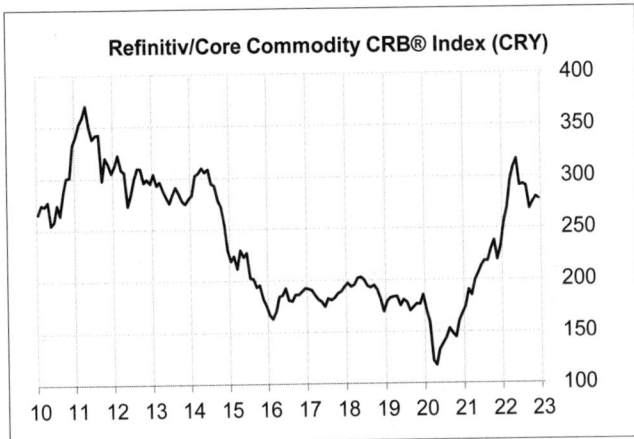

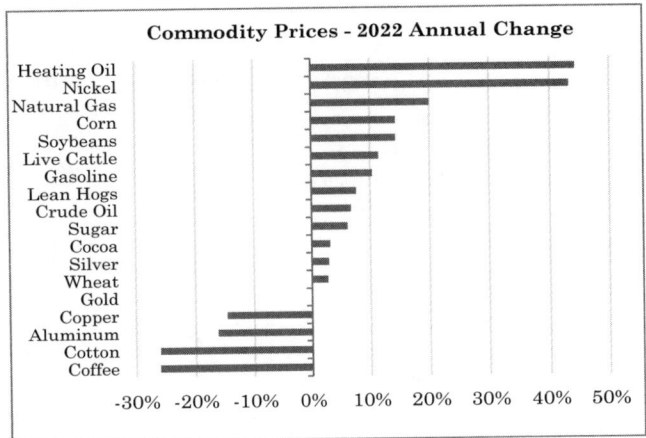

The U.S. stock market stumbled in 2022 after the extraordinary rally that began in early 2020 when the U.S. government launched its massive fiscal and monetary stimulus programs. The S&P index topped out at a record high in January 2022 and then entered a choppy downward trend through the rest of the year. The S&P 500 index ended 2022 down -19.4%, and the tech-heavy Nasdaq 100 index ended the year down -33.0%.

The U.S. stock market was hit with heavy selling as U.S. economic growth and earnings cooled and as the markets absorbed the Fed's sharp interest rate hikes. Earnings growth for the S&P 500 companies fell to a lackluster +5% yr/yr in 2022 after the post-pandemic 2021 growth spurt of +52% yr/yr.

Commodity prices in the first half of 2022 extended the historic rally that began in early 2020 as the booming global economy boosted demand for most commodities. However, commodity prices then traded lower during the second half of 2022 as the global economy cooled, interest rates rose, and the dollar rallied. The Refinitiv/CoreCommodity CRB Index® in 2022 still closed the year higher by +19.5%, adding to the +38.5% rally seen in 2021.

Gold prices saw a sharp rally during 2020 due to the massive amount of monetary policy stimulus provided by the Fed and other global central banks in the early stages of the pandemic. However, gold prices then turned sideways during 2021. Gold prices saw an upward blip in early 2022 but then turned lower on the sharp increase in the dollar and global interest rates. Nearest-futures gold prices during 2022 closed the year little changed, while silver closed mildly higher by +2.9%.

Crude oil prices rallied sharply in early 2022 after Russia invaded Ukraine. The U.S. and Europe responded with heavy sanctions on Russia that restricted Russia's ability to export oil and natural gas, thus pushing global oil and natural gas prices sharply higher.

Oil prices also saw support during 2022 as the OPEC+ cartel continued to artificially restrict supply with production cuts. Oil supply was also suppressed during 2022 as the U.S. kept heavy sanctions on Iran for its nuclear program, thus preventing Iran from exporting any significant quantity of oil.

The U.S. macroeconomic outlook shifted in March 2023 due to the failure of Silicon Valley Bank, one of the 20 largest U.S. banks. That failure sparked a run on other regional U.S. banks and also brought down NY-based Signature Bank.

The run on Silicon Valley Bank was caused by the fact that its balance sheet had a big hole after it had loaded up on Treasury notes and bonds that lost value when the Fed raised interest rates sharply during 2022. The markets were worried that other large financial institutions might be in a similar predicament.

Due to the banking system problems, the markets in early 2023 shifted to the view that the Fed might be forced to cut interest rates by late 2023 due to the increased chances of a recession.

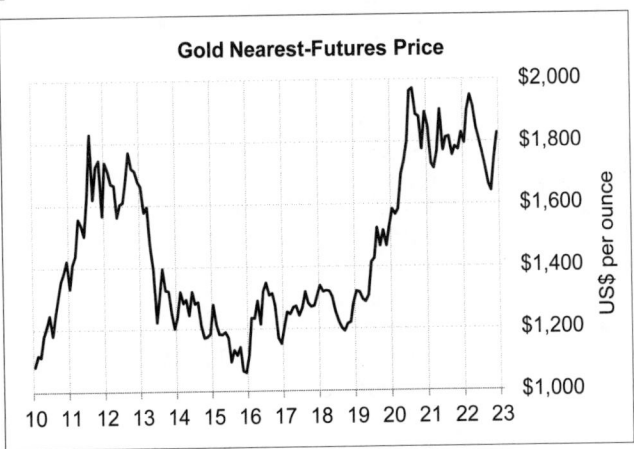

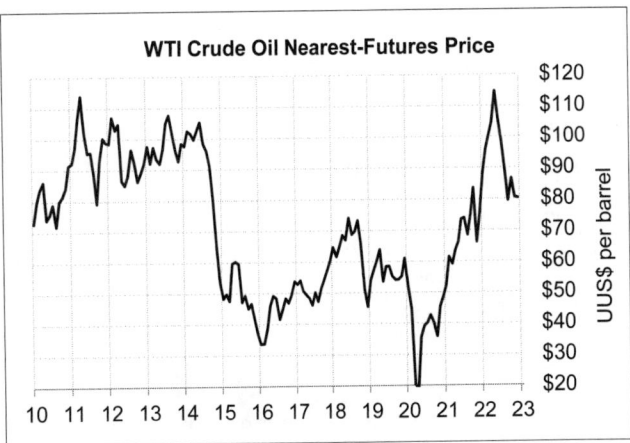

# Conversion Factors

## Commonly Used Agricultural Weights and Measurements

**Bushel Weights:**
Corn, Sorghum and Rye = 56 lbs.
Wheat and Soybeans = 60 lbs.
Canola = 50 lbs.
Barley Grain = 48 lbs.
Barley Malt = 34 lbs.
Oats = 32 lbs.

**Bushels to tonnes:**
Corn, Sorghum and Rye = bushels x 0.0254
Wheat and Soybeans = bushels x 0.027216
Barley Grain = bushels x 0.021772
Oats = bushels x 0.014515

**1 tonne (metric ton) equals:**
2204.622 lbs.
1,000 kilograms
22.046 hundredweight
10 quintals

**Ethanol**
1 bushel Corn = 2.75 gallons Ethanol = 18 lbs Dried Distillers Grain
1 tonne Corn = 101.0 gallons Ethanol = 661 lbs Dried Distillers Grain
1 tonne Sugar = 149.3 gallons Ethanol

**1 tonne (metric ton) equals:**
39.3679 bushels of Corn, Sorghum or Rye
36.7437 bushels of Wheat or Soybeans
22.046 hundredweight
45.9296 bushels of Barley Grain
68.8944 bushels of Oats
4.5929 Cotton bales (the statistical bale used by the USDA and ICAC contains a net weight of 480 pounds of lint)

**Area Measurements:**
1 acre = 43,560 square feet = 0.040694 hectare
1 hectare = 2.4710 acres = 10,000 square meters
640 acres = 1 square mile = 259 hectares

**Yields:**
Rye, Corn: bushels per acre x 0.6277 = quintals per hectare
Wheat: bushels per acre x 0.6725 = quintals per hectare
Barley Grain: bushels per acre x 0.538 = quintals per hectare
Oats: bushels per acre x 0.3587 = quintals per hectare

## Commonly Used Weights

The troy, avoirdupois and apothecaries' grains are identical in U.S. and British weight systems, equal to 0.0648 gram in the metric system. One avoirdupois ounce equals 437.5 grains. The troy and apothecaries' ounces equal 480 grains, and their pounds contain 12 ounces.

**Troy weights and conversions:**
24 grains = 1 pennyweigh
20 pennyweights = 1 ounce
12 ounces = 1 pound
1 troy ounce = 31.103 grams
1 troy ounce = 0.0311033 kilogram
1 troy pound = 0.37224 kilogram
1 kilogram = 32.1507 troy ounces
1 tonne = 32,151 troy ounces

**Avoirdupois weights and conversions:**
27 11/32 grains = 1 dram
16 drams = 1 ounce
16 ounces = 1 lb.
1 lb. = 7,000 grains
14 lbs. = 1 stone (British)
100 lbs. = 1 hundredweight (U.S.)
112 lbs. = 8 stone = 1 hundredweight (British)
2,000 lbs. = 1 short ton (U.S. ton)
2,240 lbs. = 1 long ton (British ton)
160 stone = 1 long ton
20 hundredweight = 1 ton
1 lb. = 0.4536 kilogram
1 hundredweight (cwt.) = 45.359 kilograms
1 short ton = 907.18 kilograms
**1 long ton = 1,016.05 kilograms**

**Metric weights and conversions:**
1,000 grams = 1 kilogram
100 kilograms = 1 quintal
1 tonne = 1,000 kilograms = 10 quintals
1 kilogram = 2.204622 lbs.
1 quintal = 220.462 lbs.
1 tonne = 2204.6 lbs.
1 tonne = 1.102 short tons
1 tonne = 0.9842 long ton

**U.S. dry volumes and conversions:**
1 pint = 33.6 cubic inches = 0.5506 liter
2 pints = 1 quart = 1.1012 liters
8 quarts = 1 peck = 8.8098 liters
4 pecks = 1 bushel = 35.2391 liters
1 cubic foot = 28.3169 liters

**U.S. liquid volumes and conversions:**
1 ounce = 1.8047 cubic inches = 29.6 milliliters
1 cup = 8 ounces = 0.24 liter = 237 milliliters
1 pint = 16 ounces = 0.48 liter = 473 milliliters
1 quart = 2 pints = 0.946 liter = 946 milliliters
1 gallon = 4 quarts = 231 cubic inches = 3.785 liters
1 milliliter = 0.033815 fluid ounce
1 liter = 1.0567 quarts = 1,000 milliliters
1 liter = 33.815 fluid ounces
1 imperial gallon = 277.42 cubic inches = 1.2 U.S. gallons = 4.546 liters

# Energy Conversion Factors

U.S. Crude Oil (average gravity)
1 U.S. barrel = 42 U.S. gallons
1 short ton = 6.65 barrels
1 tonne = 7.33 barrels

## Barrels per tonne for various origins

| | |
|---|---|
| Abu Dhabi | 7.624 |
| Algeria | 7.661 |
| Angola | 7.206 |
| Australia | 7.775 |
| Bahrain | 7.335 |
| Brunei | 7.334 |
| Canada | 7.428 |
| Dubai | 7.295 |
| Ecuador | 7.580 |
| Gabon | 7.245 |
| Indonesia | 7.348 |
| Iran | 7.370 |
| Iraq | 7.453 |
| Kuwait | 7.261 |
| Libya | 7.615 |
| Mexico | 7.104 |
| Neutral Zone | 6.825 |
| Nigeria | 7.410 |
| Norway | 7.444 |
| Oman | 7.390 |
| Qatar | 7.573 |
| Romania | 7.453 |
| Saudi Arabia | 7.338 |
| Trinidad | 6.989 |
| Tunisia | 7.709 |
| United Arab Emirates | 7.522 |
| United Kingdom | 7.279 |
| United States | 7.418 |
| Former Soviet Union | 7.350 |
| Venezuela | 7.005 |
| Zaire | 7.206 |

## Barrels per tonne of refined products:

| | |
|---|---|
| aviation gasoline | 8.90 |
| motor gasoline | 8.50 |
| kerosene | 7.75 |
| jet fuel | 8.00 |
| distillate, including diesel | 7.46 |
| (continued above) | |
| residual fuel oil | 6.45 |
| lubricating oil | 7.00 |
| grease | 6.30 |
| white spirits | 8.50 |
| paraffin oil | 7.14 |
| paraffin wax | 7.87 |
| petrolatum | 7.87 |
| asphalt and road oil | 6.06 |
| petroleum coke | 5.50 |
| bitumen | 6.06 |
| LPG | 11.6 |

## Approximate heat content of refined products:

(Million Btu per barrel, 1 British thermal unit is the amount of heat required to raise the temperature of 1 pound of water 1 degree F.)

| Petroleum Product | Heat Content |
|---|---|
| asphalt | 6.636 |
| aviation gasoline | 5.048 |
| butane | 4.326 |
| distillate fuel oil | 5.825 |
| ethane | 3.082 |
| isobutane | 3.974 |
| jet fuel, kerosene | 5.670 |
| jet fuel, naptha | 5.355 |
| kerosene | 5.670 |
| lubricants | 6.065 |
| motor gasoline | 5.253 |
| natural gasoline | 4.620 |
| pentanes plus | 4.620 |

## Petrochemical feedstocks:

| | |
|---|---|
| naptha less than 401*F | 5.248 |
| other oils equal to or greater than 401*F | 5.825 |
| still gas | 6.000 |
| petroleum coke | 6.024 |
| plant condensate | 5.418 |
| propane | 3.836 |
| residual fuel oil | 6.287 |
| special napthas | 5.248 |
| unfinished oils | 5.825 |
| unfractionated steam | 5.418 |
| waxes | 5.537 |

*Source: U.S. Department of Energy*

# Natural Gas Conversions

Although there are approximately 1,031 Btu in a cubic foot of gas, for most applications, the following conversions are sufficient:

| Cubic Feet | | | MMBtu | | |
|---|---|---|---|---|---|
| 1,000 | (one thousand cubic feet) | = | 1 Mcf | = | 1 |
| 1,000,000 | (one million cubic feet) | = | 1 MMcf | = | 1,000 |
| 10,000,000 | (ten million cubic feet) | = | 10 MMcf | = | 10,000 |
| 1,000,000,000 | (one billion cubic feet) | = | 1 Bcf | = | 1,000,000 |
| 1,000,000,000,000 | (one trillion cubic feet) | = | 1 Tcf | = | 1,000,000,000 |

# Acknowledgments

*The editors wish to thank the following for source material:*

Agricultural Marketing Service (AMS)

Agricultural Research Service (ARS)

American Bureau of Metal Statistics, Inc. (ABMS)

American Metal Market (AMM)

Bureau of the Census

Bureau of Economic Analysis (BEA)

Bureau of Labor Statistics (BLS)

Chicago Board of Trade (CBT)

Chicago Mercantile Exchange (CME / IMM / IOM)

Commodity Credit Corporation (CCC)

Commodity Futures Trading Commision (CFTC)

Economic Research Service (ERS)

Farm Service Agency (FSA)

Federal Reserve Bank of St. Louis

Food and Agriculture Organization of the United Nations (FAO)

Foreign Agricultural Service (FAS)

Futures Industry Association (FIA)

ICE Futures U.S, Canada, Europe (ICE)

International Cotton Advisory Committee (ICAC)

International Cocoa Organization (ICCO)

Minneapolis Grain Exchange (MGEX)

National Agricultural Statistics Service (NASS)

New York Mercantile Exchange (NYMEX)

Oil World

The Organisation for Economic Co-Operation and Development (OECD)

The Silver Institute

United Nations (UN)

United States Department of Agriculture (USDA)

Wall Street Journal (WSJ)

# Aluminum

Aluminum (atomic symbol Al) is a silvery, lightweight metal that is the most abundant metallic element in the earth's crust. Aluminum was first isolated in 1825 by a Danish chemist, Hans Christian Oersted, using a chemical process involving a potassium amalgam. A German chemist, Friedrich Woehler, improved Oersted's process by using metallic potassium in 1827. He was the first to show aluminum's lightness. In France, Henri Sainte-Claire Deville isolated the metal by reducing aluminum chloride with sodium and established a large-scale experimental plant in 1854. He displayed pure aluminum at the Paris Exposition of 1855. In 1886, Charles Martin Hall in the U.S. and Paul L.T. Heroult in France simultaneously discovered the first practical method for producing aluminum through electrolytic reduction, which is still the primary method of aluminum production today.

By volume, aluminum weighs less than a third as much as steel. This high strength-to-weight ratio makes aluminum a good choice for the construction of aircraft, railroad cars, and automobiles. Aluminum is used in cooking utensils and the pistons of internal-combustion engines because of its high heat conductivity. Aluminum foil, siding, and storm windows make excellent insulators. Because it absorbs relatively few neutrons, aluminum is used in low-temperature nuclear reactors. Aluminum is also useful in boat hulls and various marine devices due to its resistance to corrosion in saltwater.

Futures and options on Primary Aluminum and Aluminum Alloy are traded on the London Metal Exchange (LME). Aluminum futures are traded on the Multi Commodity Exchange of India, and the Shanghai Futures Exchange (SHFE). The London Metals Exchange aluminum futures contracts are priced in terms of dollars.

**Supply** – World production of aluminum in 2022 rose by +2.2% yr/yr to a new record high of 69 million metric tons. The world's largest producers of aluminum in 2022 were China with 58.0% of world production, Russia with 5.4%, Canada with 4.3%, and Australia with 2.2%. U.S. production of primary aluminum in 2021 fell by -3.3% yr/yr to 860,000 metric tons.

**Demand** – U.S. consumption of aluminum in 2022 rose by +25.0% yr/yr to 5.100 million metric tons.

**Trade** – U.S. aluminum exports in 2022 rose by +5.0% yr/yr to 3.100 million metric tons, below the 2012 record high of 3.480 million metric tons. U.S. imports of aluminum in 2022 rose by +18.7% yr/yr to 6.540 million metric tons. The U.S. was a net importer of aluminum in 2022 and relied on imports for 31.7% of its consumption.

### World Production of Primary Aluminum    In Thousands of Metric Tons

| Year | Australia | Brazil | Canada | China | France | Germany | Norway | Russia | Spain | United Kingdom | United States | Venezuela | World Total |
|---|---|---|---|---|---|---|---|---|---|---|---|---|---|
| 2013 | 1,777 | 1,304 | 2,967 | 26,500 | 346 | 492 | 1,155 | 3,601 | 235 | 44 | 1,946 | 186 | 52,100 |
| 2014 | 1,704 | 962 | 2,858 | 28,300 | 360 | 531 | 1,250 | 3,300 | 350 | 42 | 1,710 | 138 | 54,100 |
| 2015 | 1,646 | 772 | 2,880 | 31,400 | 420 | 541 | 1,225 | 3,529 | 350 | 47 | 1,590 | 119 | 57,800 |
| 2016 | 1,635 | 793 | 3,209 | 32,698 | 425 | 547 | 1,247 | 3,561 | 350 | 48 | 818 | 147 | 59,400 |
| 2017 | 1,487 | 802 | 3,212 | 32,273 | 429 | 550 | 1,253 | 3,583 | 350 | 47 | 741 | 144 | 59,500 |
| 2018 | 1,574 | 659 | 2,923 | 35,802 | 380 | 529 | 1,295 | 3,627 | 350 | 44 | 891 | 86 | 63,600 |
| 2019 | 1,570 | 650 | 2,854 | 35,044 | 430 | 540 | 1,300 | 3,637 | 220 | 39 | 1,090 | 8 | 62,900 |
| 2020 | 1,582 | 684 | 3,119 | 37,080 | 430 | 550 | 1,330 | 3,639 | 200 | 48 | 1,012 | 20 | 65,200 |
| 2021[1] | 1,570 | | 3,140 | 38,900 | | | 1,400 | 3,640 | | | 889 | | 67,500 |
| 2022[2] | 1,500 | | 3,000 | 40,000 | | | 1,400 | 3,700 | | | 860 | | 69,000 |

[1] Preliminary.   [2] Estimate.   Source: U.S. Geological Survey (USGS)

### Production of Primary Aluminum (Domestic and Foreign Ores) in the U.S.    In Thousands of Metric Tons

| Year | Jan. | Feb. | Mar. | Apr. | May | June | July | Aug. | Sept. | Oct. | Nov. | Dec. | Total |
|---|---|---|---|---|---|---|---|---|---|---|---|---|---|
| 2013 | 171 | 155 | 172 | 167 | 171 | 165 | 168 | 163 | 157 | 154 | 149 | 154 | 1,946 |
| 2014 | 153 | 139 | 153 | 143 | 147 | 140 | 143 | 143 | 136 | 137 | 134 | 141 | 1,710 |
| 2015 | 142 | 130 | 143 | 138 | 142 | 133 | 134 | 135 | 128 | 128 | 121 | 113 | 1,587 |
| 2016 | 106 | 96 | 77 | 63 | 64 | 62 | 64 | 62 | 61 | 62 | 61 | 63 | 841 |
| 2017 | 62 | 56 | 63 | 60 | 64 | 61 | 63 | 63 | 60 | 63 | 61 | 64 | 741 |
| 2018 | 66 | 61 | 71 | 71 | 73 | 63 | 68 | 76 | 76 | 84 | 88 | 95 | 892 |
| 2019 | 95 | 87 | 93 | 92 | 94 | 91 | 92 | 90 | 87 | 91 | 89 | 91 | 1,092 |
| 2020 | 92 | 88 | 95 | 92 | 96 | 89 | 82 | 80 | 72 | 75 | 74 | 77 | 1,012 |
| 2021 | 78 | 69 | 75 | 72 | 75 | 72 | 73 | 73 | 72 | 76 | 75 | 79 | 889 |
| 2022[1] | 82 | 75 | 84 | 82 | 84 | 78 | 64 | 61 | 61 | 64 | 62 | 64 | 861 |

[1] Preliminary.   Source: U.S. Geological Survey (USGS)

# ALUMINUM

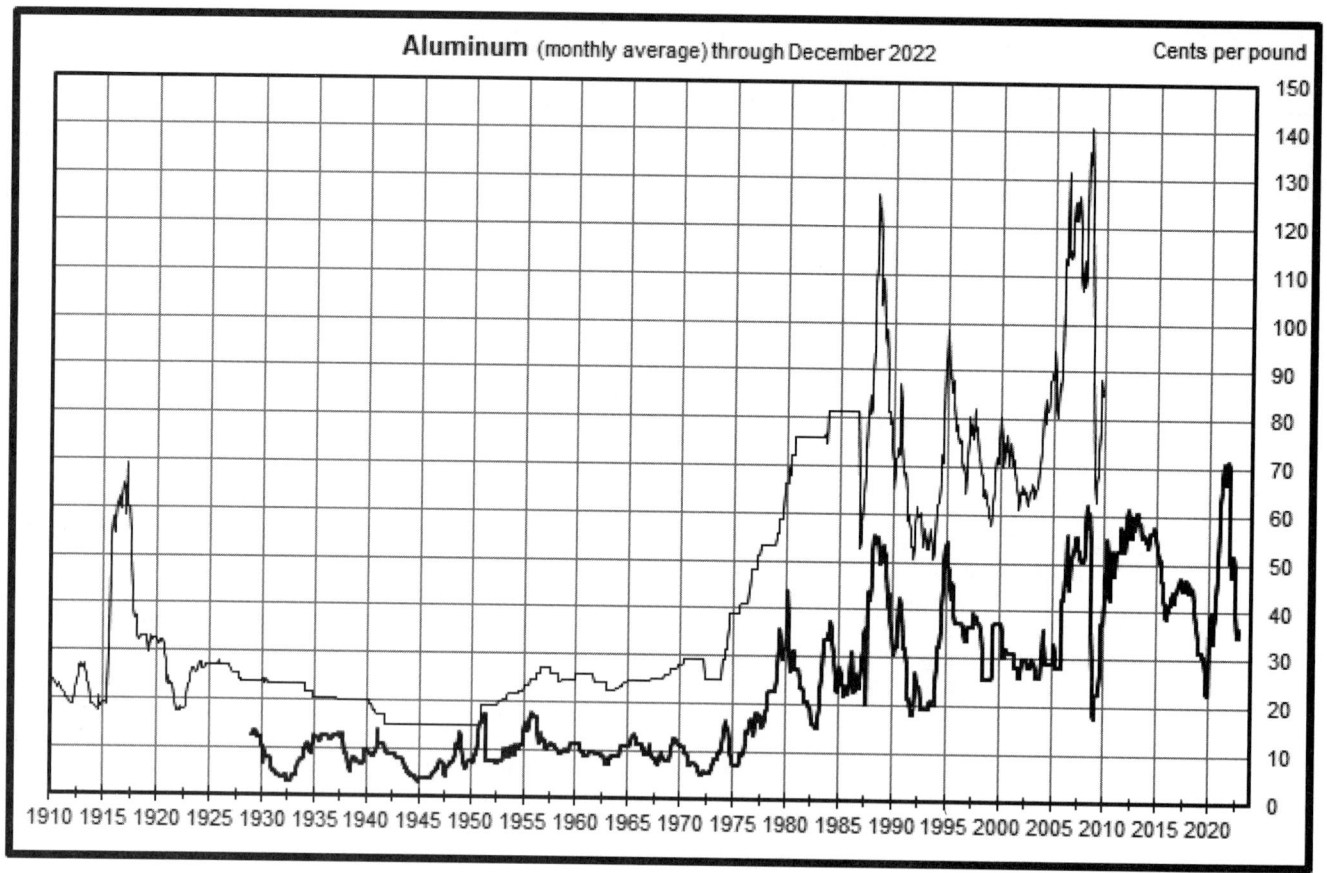

## Salient Statistics of Aluminum in the United States    In Thousands of Metric Tons

| Year | Net Import Reliance as a % of Apparent Consump | Production Primary | Secondary | Primary Shipments | Recovery from Scrap Old | New | Apparent Consumption | Plate, Sheet, Foil | Rolled Structural Shapes[3] | Extruded Shapes[4] | All | Permanent Mold | Die | Sand | Total All Net Shipments |
|---|---|---|---|---|---|---|---|---|---|---|---|---|---|---|---|
| 2013 | 21 | 1,946 | 3,410 | 9,920 | 1,630 | 1,790 | 4,520 | 4,830 | 914 | 1,950 | 7,694 | 604 | 1,240 | 132 | 2,000 | 9,694 |
| 2014 | 33 | 1,710 | 3,640 | 9,960 | 1,690 | 1,870 | 5,070 | 5,020 | 887 | 2,100 | 8,007 | 563 | 1,330 | 214 | 2,120 | 10,127 |
| 2015 | 41 | 1,587 | 3,380 | 10,400 | 1,560 | 2,000 | 5,300 | 5,220 | 629 | 2,460 | 8,309 | 526 | 1,470 | 295 | 2,300 | 10,609 |
| 2016 | 53 | 818 | 3,580 | 10,600 | 1,570 | 2,010 | 5,090 | 5,330 | 626 | 2,490 | 8,446 | 505 | 1,550 | 284 | 2,350 | 10,796 |
| 2017 | 59 | 741 | 3,630 | 11,000 | 1,590 | 2,050 | 5,680 | 5,580 | 708 | 2,580 | 8,868 | 645 | 1,400 | 237 | 2,290 | 11,158 |
| 2018 | 50 | 891 | 3,710 | 11,200 | 1,570 | 2,140 | 4,900 | 5,760 | 669 | 2,710 | 9,139 | 517 | 1,410 | 272 | 2,220 | 11,359 |
| 2019 | 47 | 1,093 | 3,470 | 11,200 | 1,540 | 1,920 | 4,980 | 5,840 | 659 | 2,600 | 9,099 | 494 | 1,300 | 352 | 2,150 | 11,249 |
| 2020 | 38 | 1,012 | 3,050 | 9,810 | 1,420 | 1,630 | 3,930 | 5,230 | 646 | 2,280 | 8,156 | 435 | 1,140 | 210 | 1,790 | 9,946 |
| 2021 | 41 | 889 | 3,300 | | 1,520 | 1,780 | 4,080 | | | | | | | | | |
| 2022[1] | 54 | 860 | 3,400 | | 1,500 | 1,900 | 5,100 | | | | | | | | | |

[1] Preliminary.  [2] To domestic industry.  [3] Also rod, bar & wire.  [4] Also rod, bar, tube, blooms & tubing.  [5] Consists of total shipments less shipments to other mills for further fabrication.    *Source: U.S. Geological Survey (USGS)*

## Supply and Distribution of Aluminum in the United States    In Thousands of Metric Tons

| Year | Apparent Consumption | Production Primary | From Old Scrap | Imports | Exports | Inventories - December 31 - Private | Government[3] | Year | Apparent Consumption | Production Primary | From Old Scrap | Imports | Exports | Inventories - December 31 - Private | Government[3] |
|---|---|---|---|---|---|---|---|---|---|---|---|---|---|---|---|
| 2011 | 3,570 | 1,986 | 1,440 | 3,710 | 3,420 | 1,060 | ---- | 2017 | 5,680 | 741 | 1,590 | 6,920 | 2,900 | 1,470 | ---- |
| 2012 | 3,950 | 2,070 | 1,630 | 4,349 | 3,480 | 1,140 | ---- | 2018 | 4,900 | 891 | 1,570 | 6,245 | 3,070 | 1,570 | ---- |
| 2013 | 4,520 | 1,946 | 1,630 | 4,725 | 3,390 | 1,130 | ---- | 2019 | 4,980 | 1,093 | 1,540 | 5,876 | 2,970 | 1,600 | ---- |
| 2014 | 5,070 | 1,710 | 1,690 | 4,849 | 3,240 | 1,280 | ---- | 2020 | 3,930 | 1,012 | 1,420 | 4,802 | 2,746 | 1,490 | ---- |
| 2015 | 5,300 | 1,587 | 1,560 | 5,081 | 3,010 | 1,350 | ---- | 2021[1] | 4,080 | 889 | 1,520 | 5,510 | 2,951 | 1,870 | ---- |
| 2016 | 5,090 | 818 | 1,570 | 6,019 | 2,820 | 1,400 | ---- | 2022[2] | 5,100 | 860 | 1,500 | 6,540 | 3,100 | 2,000 | ---- |

[1] Preliminary.  [2] Estimate.  [3] National Defense Stockpile.   *Source: U.S. Geological Survey (USGS)*

# ALUMINUM

## Aluminum Products Distribution of End-Use Shipments in the United States    In Thousands of Metric Tons

| Year | Containers & Packaging | Building & Construction | Trans-portation | Electrical | Consumer Durables | Machinery & Equipment | Other Markets | Total to Domestic Users | Exports | Total |
|---|---|---|---|---|---|---|---|---|---|---|
| 2011 | 2,160 | 1,110 | 2,820 | 798 | 631 | 682 | 322 | 8,520 | 1,700 | 10,200 |
| 2012 | 2,110 | 1,180 | 3,220 | 861 | 672 | 696 | 343 | 9,080 | 1,690 | 10,800 |
| 2013 | 2,090 | 1,310 | 3,430 | 867 | 700 | 726 | 332 | 9,450 | 1,720 | 11,200 |
| 2014 | 2,090 | 1,390 | 3,810 | 807 | 748 | 768 | 343 | 9,960 | 1,620 | 11,600 |
| 2015 | 2,140 | 1,420 | 4,180 | 800 | 741 | 768 | 327 | 10,400 | 1,620 | 12,000 |
| 2016 | 2,160 | 1,470 | 4,220 | 836 | 794 | 784 | 318 | 10,600 | 1,410 | 12,000 |
| 2017 | 2,130 | 1,530 | 4,370 | 919 | 860 | 841 | 333 | 11,000 | 1,340 | 12,300 |
| 2018 | 2,170 | 1,570 | 4,520 | 880 | 860 | 852 | 356 | 11,200 | 1,550 | 12,800 |
| 2019 | 2,220 | 1,530 | 4,540 | 871 | 832 | 837 | 347 | 11,200 | 1,300 | 12,500 |
| 2020[1] | 2,250 | 1,450 | 3,450 | 876 | 725 | 753 | 312 | 9,810 | 1,250 | 11,100 |

[1] Preliminary.    Source: U.S. Geological Survey (USGS)

## Salient Statistics of Recycling Aluminum in the United States

| Year | Percent Recycled | New Scrap[1] | Old Scrap[2] | Recycled Metal[3] | Apparent Supply | New Scrap[1] | Old Scrap[2] | Recycled Metal[3] | Apparent Supply |
|---|---|---|---|---|---|---|---|---|---|
|   |   | ---------------------- In Metric Tons ---------------------- | | | | ---------------- Value in Thousands of Dollars ---------------- | | | |
| 2011 | 1,670,000 | 1,440,000 | 3,110,000 | 5,210,000 | 60.0 | 4,280,000 | 3,690,000 | 7,970,000 | 13,300,000 |
| 2012 | 1,750,000 | 1,620,000 | 3,380,000 | 5,880,000 | 57.0 | 3,900,000 | 3,620,000 | 7,510,000 | 13,100,000 |
| 2013 | 1,790,000 | 1,630,000 | 3,410,000 | 6,310,000 | 54.0 | 3,710,000 | 3,380,000 | 7,090,000 | 13,100,000 |
| 2014 | 1,930,000 | 1,700,000 | 3,640,000 | 7,010,000 | 52.0 | 4,450,000 | 3,920,000 | 8,380,000 | 16,200,000 |
| 2015 | 1,910,000 | 1,470,000 | 3,380,000 | 7,120,000 | 47.0 | 3,710,000 | 2,850,000 | 6,560,000 | 13,900,000 |
| 2016 | 2,010,000 | 1,570,000 | 3,580,000 | 7,100,000 | 50.0 | 3,560,000 | 2,790,000 | 6,350,000 | 12,600,000 |
| 2017 | 2,050,000 | 1,590,000 | 3,630,000 | 7,730,000 | 47.0 | 4,430,000 | 3,440,000 | 7,870,000 | 16,700,000 |
| 2018 | 2,140,000 | 1,570,000 | 3,710,000 | 7,040,000 | 53.0 | 5,410,000 | 3,970,000 | 9,280,000 | 17,800,000 |
| 2019 | 1,920,000 | 1,540,000 | 3,470,000 | 6,910,000 | 50.0 | 4,220,000 | 3,380,000 | 7,600,000 | 15,200,000 |
| 2020 | 1,630,000 | 1,420,000 | 3,050,000 | 5,620,000 | 54.0 | 3,230,000 | 2,800,000 | 6,030,000 | 11,100,000 |

[1] Scrap that results from the manufacturing process.    [2] Scrap that results from consumer products.    [3] Metal recovered from new plus old scrap.
Source: U.S. Geological Survey (USGS)

## Producer Prices for Aluminum Used Beverage Can Scrap    In Cents Per Pound

| Year | Jan. | Feb. | Mar. | Apr. | May | June | July | Aug. | Sept. | Oct. | Nov. | Dec. | Average |
|---|---|---|---|---|---|---|---|---|---|---|---|---|---|
| 2013 | 79.03 | 79.19 | 75.69 | 76.25 | 75.18 | 73.08 | 71.02 | 72.27 | 68.95 | 69.74 | 68.16 | 68.76 | 73.11 |
| 2014 | 73.24 | 76.75 | 77.52 | 82.43 | 79.62 | 80.41 | 83.80 | 85.33 | 85.93 | 85.92 | 91.17 | 88.64 | 82.56 |
| 2015 | 83.85 | 81.13 | 75.14 | 71.00 | 61.70 | 56.09 | 57.86 | 58.00 | 60.24 | 59.30 | 56.84 | 59.89 | 65.09 |
| 2016 | 60.63 | 61.60 | 59.87 | 60.71 | 59.90 | 60.36 | 61.30 | 61.52 | 60.02 | 63.00 | 67.15 | 67.81 | 61.99 |
| 2017 | 70.30 | 72.37 | 73.35 | 71.55 | 68.27 | 67.23 | 67.05 | 70.98 | 73.12 | 74.09 | 72.88 | 69.95 | 70.93 |
| 2018 | 75.57 | 75.66 | 75.59 | 81.81 | 84.41 | 85.29 | 77.40 | 73.37 | 65.87 | 63.50 | 59.35 | 58.12 | 73.00 |
| 2019 | 54.98 | 57.58 | 59.60 | 59.48 | 57.00 | 54.12 | 54.00 | 53.18 | 51.50 | 51.59 | 53.24 | 53.12 | 54.95 |
| 2020 | 53.40 | 51.66 | 50.02 | 40.79 | 39.80 | 44.77 | 47.45 | 48.40 | 50.93 | 52.18 | 56.55 | 62.82 | 49.90 |
| 2021 | 65.00 | 67.50 | 73.00 | 75.50 | 74.13 | 70.88 | 71.40 | 77.63 | 83.30 | 87.50 | 84.00 | 85.70 | 76.30 |
| 2022 | 99.38 | 111.63 | 129.30 | 122.38 | 106.25 | 93.70 | 76.88 | 77.50 | 72.80 | 73.00 | 72.38 | 79.30 | 92.88 |

Source: American Metal Market (AMM)

## Average Price of Cast Aluminum Scrap (Crank Cases) in Chicago[1]    In Cents Per Pound

| Year | Jan. | Feb. | Mar. | Apr. | May | June | July | Aug. | Sept. | Oct. | Nov. | Dec. | Average |
|---|---|---|---|---|---|---|---|---|---|---|---|---|---|
| 2013 | 60.50 | 60.45 | 59.50 | 59.00 | 58.50 | 58.35 | 55.50 | 56.00 | 55.90 | 55.54 | 55.55 | 54.50 | 57.44 |
| 2014 | 54.50 | 53.50 | 53.50 | 55.00 | 56.50 | 56.50 | 56.50 | 56.55 | 57.40 | 56.50 | 56.50 | 55.45 | 55.70 |
| 2015 | 53.40 | 52.50 | 51.32 | 50.50 | 51.00 | 46.50 | 46.41 | 43.88 | 42.45 | 41.41 | 38.97 | 38.64 | 46.42 |
| 2016 | 39.97 | 40.50 | 41.50 | 41.50 | 43.45 | 43.05 | 44.05 | 43.46 | 41.93 | 43.50 | 44.50 | 44.50 | 42.66 |
| 2017 | 45.60 | 45.97 | 46.93 | 47.00 | 45.95 | 44.95 | 44.50 | 44.65 | 46.50 | 46.50 | 45.95 | 44.00 | 45.71 |
| 2018 | 45.40 | 46.03 | 44.50 | 44.02 | 45.05 | 44.98 | 41.93 | 39.93 | 37.45 | 36.50 | 34.50 | 34.00 | 41.19 |
| 2019 | 31.50 | 31.50 | 31.50 | 31.50 | 30.50 | 30.50 | 29.91 | 27.41 | 25.50 | 22.93 | 22.50 | 22.50 | 28.15 |
| 2020 | 37.07 | 39.24 | 39.95 | 34.17 | 33.80 | 35.77 | 37.20 | 39.60 | 43.60 | 47.00 | 51.76 | 57.50 | 41.39 |
| 2021 | 63.00 | 65.50 | 68.50 | 70.50 | 71.00 | 68.75 | 67.40 | 66.63 | 67.60 | 71.25 | 70.00 | 50.50 | 68.34 |
| 2022 | 51.50 | 50.00 | 47.50 | 50.00 | 51.50 | 49.00 | 39.50 | 35.00 | 35.00 | 35.00 | 35.00 | 36.50 | 42.96 |

[1] Dealer buying prices.    Source: American Metal Market (AMM)

# ALUMINUM

**Aluminum Exports of Crude Metal and Alloys from the United States**  In Thousands of Metric Tons

| Year | Jan. | Feb. | Mar. | Apr. | May | June | July | Aug. | Sept. | Oct. | Nov. | Dec. | Total |
|---|---|---|---|---|---|---|---|---|---|---|---|---|---|
| 2013 | 27.5 | 29.4 | 31.1 | 32.9 | 30.0 | 29.8 | 26.5 | 33.7 | 31.0 | 32.3 | 32.3 | 25.9 | 362.4 |
| 2014 | 31.1 | 25.6 | 30.5 | 30.7 | 33.0 | 31.0 | 28.7 | 31.5 | 30.0 | 33.7 | 26.9 | 28.2 | 360.9 |
| 2015 | 26.5 | 26.0 | 25.2 | 25.0 | 26.9 | 29.5 | 26.7 | 27.2 | 25.2 | 26.1 | 22.9 | 22.8 | 310.0 |
| 2016 | 25.7 | 24.5 | 25.3 | 22.1 | 22.7 | 18.7 | 19.4 | 20.1 | 23.6 | 21.7 | 21.2 | 17.1 | 262.1 |
| 2017 | 24.9 | 20.5 | 23.7 | 22.3 | 22.4 | 24.5 | 22.8 | 27.7 | 21.0 | 23.9 | 22.5 | 18.9 | 275.1 |
| 2018 | 25.6 | 28.4 | 23.6 | 25.5 | 25.3 | 22.8 | 24.9 | 27.5 | 23.0 | 25.5 | 22.2 | 18.1 | 292.4 |
| 2019 | 22.2 | 18.6 | 20.9 | 21.8 | 20.9 | 19.0 | 18.3 | 19.2 | 17.4 | 18.6 | 18.4 | 17.5 | 232.8 |
| 2020 | 16.6 | 19.0 | 20.3 | 10.0 | 9.1 | 15.9 | 14.6 | 14.8 | 16.8 | 15.5 | 15.3 | 14.4 | 182.2 |
| 2021 | 15.7 | 15.3 | 19.5 | 17.7 | 16.1 | 18.3 | 14.8 | 14.2 | 13.0 | 13.7 | 14.4 | 12.6 | 185.3 |
| 2022[1] | 17.3 | 17.8 | 19.2 | 19.1 | 26.2 | 22.8 | 23.0 | 24.6 | 25.5 | 31.0 | 27.8 | 23.6 | 277.9 |

[1] Preliminary.  Source: U.S. Geological Survey (USGS)

**Aluminum General Imports of Crude Metal and Alloys into the United States**  In Thousands of Metric Tons

| Year | Jan. | Feb. | Mar. | Apr. | May | June | July | Aug. | Sept. | Oct. | Nov. | Dec. | Total |
|---|---|---|---|---|---|---|---|---|---|---|---|---|---|
| 2013 | 248.0 | 220.0 | 283.0 | 457.0 | 314.0 | 267.0 | 273.0 | 271.0 | 242.0 | 219.0 | 299.0 | 220.0 | 3,313.0 |
| 2014 | 253.0 | 221.0 | 439.0 | 291.0 | 290.0 | 294.0 | 237.0 | 270.0 | 253.0 | 271.0 | 213.0 | 270.0 | 3,302.0 |
| 2015 | 273.0 | 245.0 | 312.0 | 322.0 | 299.0 | 301.0 | 301.0 | 251.0 | 283.0 | 270.0 | 267.0 | 259.0 | 3,383.0 |
| 2016 | 362.0 | 270.0 | 385.0 | 350.0 | 336.0 | 401.0 | 346.0 | 345.0 | 349.0 | 316.0 | 392.0 | 381.0 | 4,233.0 |
| 2017 | 459.0 | 394.0 | 476.0 | 434.0 | 411.0 | 410.0 | 411.0 | 379.0 | 338.0 | 358.0 | 358.0 | 400.0 | 4,828.0 |
| 2018 | 333.0 | 374.0 | 555.0 | 381.0 | 349.0 | 297.0 | 332.0 | 292.0 | 313.0 | 306.0 | 294.0 | 306.0 | 4,132.0 |
| 2019 | 298.0 | 284.0 | 312.0 | 314.0 | 287.0 | 315.0 | 91.2 | 73.8 | 53.9 | 65.1 | 302.0 | 317.0 | 2,713.0 |
| 2020 | 347.0 | 208.0 | 246.0 | 338.0 | 316.0 | 262.0 | 253.0 | 270.0 | 214.0 | 231.0 | 241.0 | 229.0 | 3,155.0 |
| 2021 | 250.0 | 243.0 | 308.0 | 324.0 | 313.0 | 294.0 | 299.0 | 319.0 | 285.0 | 339.0 | 338.0 | 316.0 | 3,628.0 |
| 2022[1] | 343.0 | 262.0 | 341.0 | 331.0 | 404.0 | 460.0 | 345.0 | 360.0 | 317.0 | 322.0 | 279.0 | 388.0 | 4,152.0 |

[1] Preliminary.  Source: U.S. Geological Survey (USGS)

**Average Price of Aluminum (Cash) in London**  In U.S. Dollars per Metric Ton

| Year | Jan. | Feb. | Mar. | Apr. | May | June | July | Aug. | Sept. | Oct. | Nov. | Dec. | Average |
|---|---|---|---|---|---|---|---|---|---|---|---|---|---|
| 2013 | 2,036.5 | 2,053.6 | 1,911.3 | 1,861.1 | 1,832.6 | 1,814.6 | 1,769.6 | 1,816.3 | 1,761.3 | 1,814.6 | 1,748.0 | 1,739.8 | 1,846.6 |
| 2014 | 1,727.4 | 1,695.2 | 1,705.4 | 1,810.7 | 1,751.1 | 1,839.0 | 1,948.3 | 2,030.5 | 1,990.4 | 1,946.2 | 2,055.6 | 1,909.5 | 1,867.4 |
| 2015 | 1,814.7 | 1,817.8 | 1,773.9 | 1,819.2 | 1,804.0 | 1,687.7 | 1,639.5 | 1,548.1 | 1,589.6 | 1,516.5 | 1,467.9 | 1,497.2 | 1,664.7 |
| 2016 | 1,481.1 | 1,531.3 | 1,531.0 | 1,571.2 | 1,550.6 | 1,593.5 | 1,629.1 | 1,639.3 | 1,592.4 | 1,665.9 | 1,737.1 | 1,727.7 | 1,604.2 |
| 2017 | 1,791.2 | 1,860.8 | 1,901.5 | 1,921.2 | 1,913.0 | 1,885.3 | 1,903.0 | 2,030.3 | 2,096.5 | 2,131.5 | 2,097.4 | 2,080.5 | 1,967.7 |
| 2018 | 2,209.7 | 2,182.4 | 2,070.8 | 2,254.7 | 2,299.7 | 2,237.6 | 2,082.2 | 2,051.5 | 2,026.5 | 2,029.9 | 1,938.5 | 1,920.4 | 2,108.7 |
| 2019 | 1,853.7 | 1,863.0 | 1,871.2 | 1,845.5 | 1,781.3 | 1,756.0 | 1,797.0 | 1,740.7 | 1,753.5 | 1,726.0 | 1,774.8 | 1,771.4 | 1,794.5 |
| 2020 | 1,773.1 | 1,688.1 | 1,610.9 | 1,459.9 | 1,466.4 | 1,568.6 | 1,643.8 | 1,737.3 | 1,743.8 | 1,806.1 | 1,935.3 | 2,014.7 | 1,704.0 |
| 2021 | 2,004.0 | 2,078.6 | 2,190.5 | 2,319.4 | 2,433.5 | 2,446.7 | 2,497.6 | 2,603.0 | 2,834.6 | 2,934.4 | 2,636.5 | 2,695.5 | 2,472.8 |
| 2022 | 3,006.0 | 3,245.8 | 3,498.4 | 3,244.4 | 2,837.8 | 2,563.4 | 2,408.4 | 2,430.8 | 2,224.1 | 2,255.5 | 2,350.7 | 2,401.7 | 2,705.6 |

Contract Size = 25 Metric Tons  Source: London Metal Exchange (LME)

**Average Price of Aluminum (3-Month) in London**  In U.S. Dollars per Metric Ton

| Year | Jan. | Feb. | Mar. | Apr. | May | June | July | Aug. | Sept. | Oct. | Nov. | Dec. | Average |
|---|---|---|---|---|---|---|---|---|---|---|---|---|---|
| 2013 | 2,073.3 | 2,094.8 | 1,950.5 | 1,893.3 | 1,864.5 | 1,854.9 | 1,814.3 | 1,863.4 | 1,808.0 | 1,860.5 | 1,793.5 | 1,784.6 | 1,888.0 |
| 2014 | 1,771.7 | 1,738.5 | 1,748.5 | 1,848.0 | 1,792.4 | 1,873.3 | 1,968.9 | 2,040.1 | 2,022.0 | 1,962.2 | 2,043.7 | 1,927.5 | 1,894.7 |
| 2015 | 1,827.3 | 1,835.0 | 1,781.7 | 1,809.7 | 1,836.8 | 1,726.6 | 1,680.2 | 1,576.4 | 1,605.3 | 1,541.0 | 1,482.0 | 1,497.9 | 1,683.3 |
| 2016 | 1,481.5 | 1,525.0 | 1,537.7 | 1,581.1 | 1,564.5 | 1,602.1 | 1,641.0 | 1,651.6 | 1,606.4 | 1,671.3 | 1,735.3 | 1,720.4 | 1,609.8 |
| 2017 | 1,786.8 | 1,870.7 | 1,912.3 | 1,933.4 | 1,917.1 | 1,892.1 | 1,921.1 | 2,036.7 | 2,122.6 | 2,150.6 | 2,114.8 | 2,096.7 | 1,979.6 |
| 2018 | 2,217.8 | 2,171.0 | 2,088.9 | 2,251.8 | 2,298.7 | 2,233.9 | 2,065.6 | 2,074.9 | 2,058.1 | 2,040.8 | 1,950.8 | 1,922.8 | 2,114.6 |
| 2019 | 1,867.4 | 1,888.2 | 1,895.1 | 1,865.0 | 1,809.6 | 1,782.9 | 1,819.4 | 1,770.2 | 1,779.4 | 1,733.7 | 1,767.6 | 1,781.9 | 1,813.3 |
| 2020 | 1,792.8 | 1,713.2 | 1,633.6 | 1,497.1 | 1,498.3 | 1,590.6 | 1,677.4 | 1,774.5 | 1,781.3 | 1,822.6 | 1,948.7 | 2,026.6 | 1,729.7 |
| 2021 | 2,005.1 | 2,084.8 | 2,211.3 | 2,328.9 | 2,454.3 | 2,455.7 | 2,509.9 | 2,595.0 | 2,849.6 | 2,951.1 | 2,639.6 | 2,695.4 | 2,481.7 |
| 2022 | 3,002.5 | 3,215.8 | 3,509.7 | 3,263.4 | 2,864.6 | 2,585.8 | 2,414.4 | 2,423.9 | 2,235.9 | 2,261.2 | 2,373.0 | 2,434.7 | 2,715.4 |

Contract Size = 25 Metric Tons  Source: London Metal Exchange (LME)

# Antimony

Antimony (atomic symbol Sb) is a lustrous, extremely brittle and hard crystalline semi-metal that is silvery-white in its most common allotropic form. Antimony is a poor conductor of heat and electricity. In nature, antimony has a strong affinity for sulfur and such metals as lead, silver, and copper. Antimony is primarily a byproduct of the mining, smelting, and refining of lead, silver, and copper ores. There is no longer any mine production of antimony in the U.S.

The most common use of antimony is in antimony trioxide, a chemical that is used as a flame retardant in textiles, plastics, adhesives, and building materials. Antimony trioxide is also used in battery components, ceramics, bearings, chemicals, glass, and ammunition.

**Prices** – Antimony prices in 2022 surged by +17.5% yr/yr to a 10-year high of 585.87 cents per pound, remaining below the record high of 671.10 posted in 2011.

**Supply** – World mine production of antimony in 2022 fell by -1.8% yr/yr to 110,000 metric tons, a 23-year low. China accounted for 54.5% of world antimony production in 2022. After China, the only significant antimony producers were Russia with 18.2% and Tajikistan with 15.5%. U.S. secondary production of antimony in 2022 fell by -1.2% yr/yr to 4,200 metric tons.

**Demand** – U.S. industrial consumption of antimony in 2019 fell by -7.2% yr/yr to 5,810 metric tons, the lowest since the data series began in 1943. Regarding consumption of antimony in the U.S. in 2019, 36.1% was used for metal products, 41.8% was used for flame-retardants, and 22.2% was used for non-metal products.

**Trade** – The gross weight of U.S. imports of antimony oxide in 2022 fell by -0.5% yr/yr to 19,000 metric tons. U.S. exports of antimony oxide in 2021 rose by +37.3% yr/yr to 2,100 metric tons.

### World Mine Production of Antimony (Content of Ore)  In Metric Tons

| Year | Australia | Bolivia | Canada | China | Kyrgyzstan | Russia | South Africa | Tajikistan | Turkey | World Total |
|---|---|---|---|---|---|---|---|---|---|---|
| 2017 | 3,115 | 2,700 | ---- | 98,000 | ---- | 14,400 | 1,200 | 14,000 | 2,000 | 140,000 |
| 2018 | 2,170 | 3,110 | ---- | 89,600 | ---- | 30,000 | ---- | 15,200 | 2,400 | 147,000 |
| 2019 | 2,030 | 3,000 | ---- | 89,000 | ---- | 30,000 | ---- | 28,000 | 2,400 | 162,000 |
| 2020 | 3,900 | 2,600 | 2 | 61,000 | ---- | 25,000 | ---- | 13,000 | 1,330 | 111,000 |
| 2021[1] | 4,000 | 2,600 | 2 | 61,000 | ---- | 20,000 | ---- | 1,800 | 1,300 | 112,000 |
| 2022[2] | 4,000 | 2,500 | 2 | 60,000 | ---- | 20,000 | ---- | 17,000 | 1,300 | 110,000 |

[1] Preliminary.  [2] Estimate.  [3] Less than 1/2 unit.  Source: U.S. Geological Survey (USGS)

### Salient Statistics of Antimony in the United States  In Metric Tons

| Year | Avg. Price Cents/lb. C.i.F. U.S. Ports | Production[3] Primary[2] Mine | Production[3] Smelter | Secondary (Alloys)[2] | Imports for Consumption Ore Gross Weight | Imports for Consumption Ore Antimony Content | Oxide (Gross Weight) | Exports (Oxide) | Industry Stocks, Dec 31[3] Metallic | Oxide | Sulfide | Other | Total |
|---|---|---|---|---|---|---|---|---|---|---|---|---|---|
| 2018 | 381.00 | ---- | W | 4,090 | ---- | 96 | 19,200 | 1,750 | | | ---- | | 1,400 |
| 2019 | 304.00 | ---- | W | 4,140 | ---- | 121 | 17,200 | 1,570 | | | ---- | | |
| 2020 | 267.00 | ---- | W | 4,250 | ---- | 105 | 15,000 | 1,230 | | | ---- | | |
| 2021[1] | 531.00 | ---- | W | 4,250 | ---- | 31 | 19,100 | 1,530 | | | ---- | | |
| 2022[2] | 630.00 | ---- | W | 4,200 | ---- | 30 | 19,000 | 2,100 | | | ---- | | |

[1] Preliminary.  [2] Estimate.  [3] Antimony content.  [4] Including primary antimony residues & slag.  W = Withheld proprietary data.
Source: U.S. Geological Survey (USGS)

### Industrial Consumption of Primary Antimony in the United States  In Metric Tons (Antimony Content)

| Year | Ammunition | Antimonial Lead[3] | Sheet & Pipe[4] | Bearing Metal & Bearings | Solder | Products | Flame Retardants Plastics | Total | Ceramics & Glass | Pigments | Plastics | Total | Grand Total |
|---|---|---|---|---|---|---|---|---|---|---|---|---|---|
| 2015 | W | W | W | 20 | 19 | 2,450 | 2,200 | 2,860 | W | 808 | W | 2,960 | 8,270 |
| 2016 | W | W | W | 9 | 15 | 2,840 | 2,290 | 2,790 | W | 703 | W | 2,770 | 8,400 |
| 2017 | W | W | W | 8 | 14 | 2,410 | 2,420 | 2,810 | W | W | W | 1,330 | 6,550 |
| 2018 | W | W | W | 8 | 13 | 2,380 | 2,030 | 2,470 | W | W | W | 1,330 | 6,260 |
| 2019[1] | W | W | W | 7 | 17 | 2,100 | 1,900 | 2,430 | W | W | W | 1,290 | 5,810 |

[1] Preliminary.  [2] Estimated coverage based on 77% of the industry.  W = Withheld proprietary data.  Source: U.S. Geological Survey (USGS)

### Average Price of Antimony[1] in the United States  In Cents Per Pound

| Year | Jan. | Feb. | Mar. | Apr. | May | June | July | Aug. | Sept. | Oct. | Nov. | Dec. | Average |
|---|---|---|---|---|---|---|---|---|---|---|---|---|---|
| 2018 | 373.63 | 388.62 | 394.60 | 382.37 | 373.58 | 373.25 | 362.83 | 375.06 | 388.05 | 382.06 | 371.23 | 362.88 | 377.34 |
| 2019 | 360.51 | 358.34 | 345.38 | 325.66 | 317.62 | 294.82 | 276.95 | 272.52 | 269.13 | 282.44 | 283.66 | 275.56 | 305.22 |
| 2020 | 267.17 | 283.95 | 288.74 | 267.92 | 257.79 | 247.65 | 240.97 | 248.91 | 263.84 | 271.59 | 284.21 | 299.81 | 268.55 |
| 2021 | 351.73 | 415.61 | 524.16 | 486.10 | 451.19 | 458.07 | 489.00 | 543.32 | 568.13 | 602.02 | 596.48 | 601.02 | 507.24 |
| 2022 | 605.84 | 612.50 | 666.41 | 675.68 | 620.92 | 606.66 | 626.22 | 598.14 | 579.90 | 552.25 | 515.15 | 490.77 | 595.87 |

[1] Prices are for antimony metal (99.65%) merchants, minimum 18-ton containers, c.i.f. U.S. Ports.  Source: American Metal Market (AMM)

# Apples

The apple tree is the common name of trees from the rose family, Rosaceae, and the fruit that comes from them. The apple tree is a deciduous plant and grows mainly in the temperate areas of the world. The apple tree is believed to have originated in the Caspian and Black Sea area. Apples were the favorite fruit of the ancient Greeks and Romans. The early settlers brought apple seeds with them and introduced them to America. John Champman, also known as Johnny Appleseed, was responsible for the extensive planting of apple trees in the Midwestern United States.

Futures on apples are traded in the Zhengzhou Commodity Exchange.

**Prices** – The average monthly price of apples received by growers in the U.S. in 2022 rose by +4.1% yr/yr to 76.65 cents per pound.

**Supply** – World apple production in the 2022-23 marketing year fell by -4.7% yr/yr to 78.760 million metric tons. The world's largest apple producers in 2022/23 were China (with 52.1% of world production), the European Union (16.2%), Turkey (6.1%), and the U.S. (5.7%). U.S. apple production in 2022/23 rose by +3.7% to 4.494 million metric tons, which would be well above the 3-decade low of 3.798 million metric tons posted in 2002-03.

**Demand** – The utilization breakdown of the 2017 apple crop showed that 67.4% of apples were for fresh consumption, 12.1% for juice and cider, 10.1% for canning, 3.2% for dried apples and 1.1% for frozen apples. U.S. per capita apple consumption in 2021 was 15.75 pounds.

## World Production of Apples, Fresh (Dessert & Cooking)   In Thousands of Metric Tons

| Crop Year | Argentina | Brazil | Chile | China | European Union | India | Japan | Russia | South Africa | Turkey | Ukraine | United States | World Total |
|---|---|---|---|---|---|---|---|---|---|---|---|---|---|
| 2015-16 | 600 | 1,055 | 1,335 | 38,900 | 12,453 | 2,520 | 765 | 1,311 | 924 | 2,570 | 1,099 | 4,546 | 74,114 |
| 2016-17 | 560 | 1,308 | 1,310 | 40,393 | 12,479 | 2,258 | 735 | 1,509 | 902 | 2,926 | 1,076 | 5,010 | 76,698 |
| 2017-18 | 560 | 1,203 | 1,330 | 41,390 | 9,798 | 1,920 | 756 | 1,360 | 836 | 3,032 | 1,462 | 5,085 | 75,191 |
| 2018-19 | 550 | 1,223 | 1,210 | 33,000 | 14,810 | 2,371 | 702 | 1,611 | 894 | 3,600 | 1,154 | 4,479 | 71,849 |
| 2019-20 | 600 | 983 | 1,124 | 42,425 | 11,480 | 2,370 | 720 | 1,779 | 991 | 3,620 | 1,115 | 4,852 | 78,581 |
| 2020-21 | 550 | 983 | 1,099 | 44,066 | 11,935 | 2,300 | 720 | 1,540 | 1,164 | 4,300 | 1,115 | 4,505 | 80,683 |
| 2021-22[1] | 427 | 983 | 1,046 | 45,973 | 12,277 | 2,300 | 720 | 1,540 | 1,170 | 4,493 | 1,115 | 4,336 | 82,643 |
| 2022-23[2] | 535 | 983 | 1,040 | 41,000 | 12,772 | 2,350 | 720 | 1,540 | 1,100 | 4,770 | 1,115 | 4,494 | 78,760 |

[1] Preliminary.  [2] Estimate.  Source: Foreign Agricultural Service, U.S. Department of Agriculture (FAS-USDA)

## Salient Statistics of Apples[2] in the United States

| | Production | | Growers Prices | | Utilization of Quantities Sold (Processed[5]) | | | | | | Avg. Farm Price Cents/lb. | Foreign Trade[4] Domestic | | | | Fresh Per Capita Consumption Lbs. |
|---|---|---|---|---|---|---|---|---|---|---|---|---|---|---|---|---|
| Year | Total | Utilized | Fresh Cents/lb. | Processing $/ton | Fresh | Canned | Dried | Frozen | Juice & Cider | Other[3] | | Farm Value Million $ | Exports Fresh | Imports Fresh Dried[5] & Dried[5] Metric Tons | | |
| 2014 | 11,863 | 11,270 | 32.7 | 178.0 | 7,909 | 1,135 | 171 | 251 | 1,480 | 60 | 25.6 | 2,870.7 | 1,057.9 | 26.1 | 209.5 | 18.7 |
| 2015 | 10,103 | 10,023 | 44.1 | 201.0 | 6,928 | 1,110 | 179 | 188 | 1,329 | 187 | 33.6 | 3,350.1 | 747.3 | 28.0 | 233.6 | 17.5 |
| 2016 | 11,495 | 11,046 | 40.5 | 214.0 | 7,745 | 1,211 | 339 | 138 | 1,342 | 137 | 31.6 | 3,492.6 | 867.5 | ---- | 171.1 | 19.2 |
| 2017 | 11,554 | 11,210 | 40.7 | 248.0 | 7,816 | 1,162 | 370 | 123 | 1,395 | 180 | 32.1 | 3,601.4 | 1,007.3 | ---- | 134.3 | 18.1 |
| 2018 | 10,240 | 9,874 | 38.7 | 207.0 | 6,827 | ---- | ---- | ---- | ---- | ---- | 29.9 | 2,954.2 | 742.3 | ---- | 146.4 | 16.9 |
| 2019 | 11,086 | 10,696 | 32.7 | 200.0 | 7,456 | ---- | ---- | ---- | ---- | ---- | 25.8 | 2,762.3 | 862.2 | ---- | 107.8 | 17.6 |
| 2020 | 10,285 | 9,932 | 38.4 | 203.0 | 6,827 | ---- | ---- | ---- | ---- | ---- | 29.6 | 2,937.5 | 775.3 | ---- | 108.9 | 16.2 |
| 2021[1] | 9,849 | 9,559 | 39.6 | 279.0 | 6,613 | ---- | ---- | ---- | ---- | ---- | 31.7 | | 723.4 | ---- | 105.6 | 15.8 |

[1] Preliminary.  [2] Commercial crop.  [3] Mostly crushed for vinegar, jam, etc.  [4] Year beginning July.  [5] Fresh weight basis.
Source: Economic Research Service, U.S. Department of Agriculture (ERS-USDA)

## Price of Apples Received by Growers (for Fresh Use) in the United States   In Cents Per Pound

| Year | Jan. | Feb. | Mar. | Apr. | May | June | July | Aug. | Sept. | Oct. | Nov. | Dec. | Average |
|---|---|---|---|---|---|---|---|---|---|---|---|---|---|
| 2015 | 31.6 | 29.2 | 27.8 | 25.9 | 24.3 | 20.7 | 19.0 | 30.3 | 44.3 | 41.6 | 40.1 | 44.7 | 31.6 |
| 2016 | 44.7 | 44.7 | 45.9 | 45.1 | 39.1 | 38.0 | 40.6 | 46.1 | 53.0 | 45.2 | 39.9 | 39.6 | 43.5 |
| 2017 | 39.7 | 36.9 | 35.8 | 35.3 | 36.0 | 36.3 | 37.0 | 42.6 | 59.1 | 45.9 | 39.9 | 39.7 | 40.4 |
| 2018 | 37.5 | 35.0 | 33.6 | 32.7 | 29.6 | 28.6 | 31.1 | 29.6 | 45.2 | 39.6 | 38.7 | 40.1 | 35.1 |
| 2019 | 39.7 | 37.9 | 37.7 | 38.1 | 38.3 | 37.2 | 38.8 | 40.2 | 48.9 | 39.1 | 33.3 | 33.6 | 38.6 |
| 2020 | 31.3 | 58.3 | 57.7 | 57.7 | 57.9 | 58.6 | 60.0 | 64.2 | 70.7 | 69.1 | 69.7 | 70.2 | 60.5 |
| 2021 | 72.3 | 73.7 | 73.5 | 73.7 | 72.1 | 71.8 | 73.5 | 76.1 | 81.4 | 72.6 | 71.5 | 71.6 | 73.7 |
| 2022[1] | 74.6 | 75.9 | 76.1 | 74.6 | 73.7 | 72.0 | 69.0 | 71.5 | 78.4 | 81.0 | 84.1 | 88.9 | 76.7 |

[1] Preliminary.  NQ = No quote.  Source: Economic Research Service, U.S. Department of Agriculture (ERS-USDA)

# Arsenic

Arsenic (atomic symbol As) is a silver-gray, extremely poisonous, semi-metallic element. Arsenic, which is odorless and flavorless, has been known since ancient times, but it wasn't until the Middle Ages that its poisonous characteristics first became known. Metallic arsenic was first produced in the 17th century by heating arsenic with potash and soap. Arsenic is rarely found in nature in its elemental form and is typically recovered as a by-product of ore processing. Recently, small doses of arsenic have been found to put some types of cancer into remission. It can also help thin blood. Homoeopathists have successfully used undetectable amounts of arsenic to cure stomach cramps.

The U.S. does not produce any arsenic and instead imports all its consumption needs for arsenic metals and compounds. More than 95 percent of the arsenic consumed in the U.S. is in compound form, mostly as arsenic trioxide, which in turn is converted into arsenic acid. Production of chromated copper arsenate, a wood preservative, accounts for about 90% of the domestic consumption of arsenic trioxide. Three companies in the U.S. manufacture chromate copper arsenate. Another company used arsenic acid to produce an arsenical herbicide. Arsenic metal is used to produce nonferrous alloys, primarily for lead-acid batteries.

One area where there is increased consumption of arsenic is in the semiconductor industry. Very high-purity arsenic is used in the production of gallium arsenide. High-speed and high-frequency integrated circuits that use gallium arsenide have better signal reception and lower power consumption. An estimated 30 metric tons per year of high-purity arsenic is used in the production of semiconductor materials.

In the early 2000s, as much as 88% of U.S. arsenic production was used for wood preservative treatments, so the demand for arsenic was closely tied to new home construction, home renovation, and deck construction. However, the total demand for arsenic in 2004 dropped by 69% from 2003. Due to arsenic's toxicity and tighter environmental regulation, only 65% of that much smaller amount was used for wood preservative treatments.

**Supply** – World production of white arsenic (arsenic trioxide) in 2022 rose by +1.7% yr/yr to 61,000 metric tons. The world's largest producer in 2022 was Peru with 45.9% of world production, followed by China with 39.3% of world production, Morocco with 11.3%, and both Belgium and Russia with 1.6%. The U.S. supply of arsenic in 2022 fell by -3.7% yr/yr to 5,390 metric tons.

**Demand** – U.S. demand for arsenic in 2022 fell by -3.6% to 5,400 metric tons. Arsenic is mainly used in wood preservatives, with smaller usage levels in non-ferrous alloys, electrical, and glass.

**Trade** – U.S. imports of trioxide arsenic in 2021 fell by -38.6%% yr/yr to 6,140 metric tons. U.S. exports of trioxide arsenic in 2022 rose by +6.9% yr/yr to 31 metric tons, far below the record high of 3,270 metric tons in 2005.

### World Production of White Arsenic (Arsenic Trioxide)    In Metric Tons

| Year | Belgium | Bolivia | Chile | China | Japan | Mexico | Morocco | Namibia | Peru | Russia | World Total |
|---|---|---|---|---|---|---|---|---|---|---|---|
| 2015 | 1,000 | 33 | ---- | 25,000 | 45 | ---- | 7,566 | 1,960 | ---- | 1,500 | 37,200 |
| 2016 | 1,000 | 38 | ---- | 25,000 | 45 | ---- | 7,600 | 1,900 | 33,000 | 1,500 | 70,100 |
| 2017 | 1,000 | 20 | ---- | 24,000 | 45 | ---- | 6,879 | 700 | 32,000 | 1,500 | 66,500 |
| 2018 | 1,000 | 238 | ---- | 24,000 | 45 | ---- | 5,578 | ---- | 29,000 | ---- | 59,900 |
| 2019 | 1,000 | 120 | ---- | 24,000 | 40 | ---- | 5,055 | ---- | 35,000 | 2,226 | 67,400 |
| 2020 | 1,000 | 100 | ---- | 24,000 | 40 | ---- | 7,694 | ---- | 27,000 | 500 | 60,300 |
| 2021[1] | 1,000 | 120 | ---- | 24,000 | 40 | ---- | 6,883 | ---- | 27,000 | 1,000 | 60,000 |
| 2022[2] | 1,000 | 140 | ---- | 24,000 | 45 | ---- | 6,900 | ---- | 28,000 | 1,000 | 61,000 |

[1] Preliminary.   [2] Estimate.   [3] Output of Tsumeb Corp. Ltd. only.   [4] Includes low-grade dusts that were exported to the U.S. for further refining.
*Source: U.S. Geological Survey (USGS)*

### Salient Statistics of Arsenic in the United States   (In Metric Tons -- Arsenic Content)

| | Supply | | Distribution | | Estimated Demand Pattern | | | | | | Average Price Trioxide Metal | | | |
|---|---|---|---|---|---|---|---|---|---|---|---|---|---|---|
| | Imports | | Industry Stocks | | Industry Stocks | Agricultural Chem- | | Wood Preserv- | Non-Ferrous Alloys & | | | Mexican Chinese | Imports | |
| Year | Metal | Compounds | Jan. 1 | Total | Apparent Demand | Dec. 31 | icals | Glass | atives | lectric | Other | Total | -- Cents/Pound -- | Trioxide[3] | Exports |
| 2015 | 514 | 5,920 | ---- | 6,434 | 6,430 | ---- | ---- | ---- | ---- | ---- | ---- | 6,430 | ---- | 2 | 7,810 | 1,670 |
| 2016 | 793 | 5,320 | ---- | 6,113 | 6,120 | ---- | ---- | ---- | ---- | ---- | ---- | 6,120 | ---- | 2 | 7,000 | 1,760 |
| 2017 | 942 | 5,980 | ---- | 6,922 | 6,920 | ---- | ---- | ---- | ---- | ---- | ---- | 6,920 | ---- | 2 | 7,900 | 698 |
| 2018 | 929 | 5,540 | ---- | 6,469 | 6,470 | ---- | ---- | ---- | ---- | ---- | ---- | 6,470 | ---- | 1 | 7,320 | 107 |
| 2019 | 391 | 7,050 | ---- | 7,441 | 7,440 | ---- | ---- | ---- | ---- | ---- | ---- | 7,440 | ---- | 2 | 9,130 | 56 |
| 2020 | 522 | 7,750 | ---- | 8,272 | 8,270 | ---- | ---- | ---- | ---- | ---- | ---- | 8,270 | ---- | 2 | 10,000 | 29 |
| 2021[1] | 835 | 4,760 | ---- | 5,595 | 5,600 | ---- | ---- | ---- | ---- | ---- | ---- | 5,600 | ---- | 1 | 6,140 | 31 |
| 2022[2] | 790 | 4,600 | ---- | 5,390 | 5,400 | ---- | ---- | ---- | ---- | ---- | ---- | 5,300 | ---- | | | 100 |

[1] Preliminary.   [2] Estimate.   [3] For Consumption.   *Source: U.S. Geological Survey (USGS)*

# Barley

Barley is the common name for the genus of cereal grass and is native to Asia and Ethiopia. Barley is an ancient crop and was grown by the Egyptians, Greek, Romans, and Chinese. Barley is now the world's fourth-largest grain crop, after wheat, rice, and corn. Barley is planted in the spring in most of Europe, Canada and the United States. The U.S. barley crop year begins June 1. It is planted in the autumn in parts of California, Arizona, and along the Mediterranean Sea. Barley is hardy and drought resistant and can be grown on marginal cropland. Salt-resistant strains are being developed for use in coastal regions. Barley grain, along with hay, straw, and several by-products are used for animal feed. Barley is used for malt beverages and for cooking. Barley, like other cereals, contains a large proportion of carbohydrate (67%) and protein (12.8%).

Barley futures are traded on ASX 24 exchange and National Commodity & Derivatives Exchange (NCDEX).

**Prices** – The monthly average price for all barley received by U.S. farmers in the 2021/22 marketing year rose by +13.3% yr/yr to $5.40 per bushel.

**Supply** – World barley production in the 2022/23 marketing year is forecasted to rise by +2.7% yr/yr to 149.465 million metric tons. The world's largest barley crop of 179.038 million metric tons occurred in 1990/91. The world's largest barley producers in 2022/23 are expected to be the European Union with 34.4% of world production, Russia with 14.1%, Australia with 9.0%, Canada with 6.7%, Turkey with 5.0%, and Ukraine with 4.1%.

U.S. barley production in the 2022/23 marketing year is expected to rise by +45.2% yr/yr to 174.333 million bushels, which would be far below the record U.S. barley crop of 608.532 million bushels seen in 1986/87. U.S. farmers are expected to harvest +22.3% yr/yr more acres in 2022/23 to 2.433 million acres. Ending stocks for the 2022/23 marketing year are expected to rise by +45.9% to 61.490 million bushels.

**Demand** – U.S. total barley disappearance in 2022/23 is expected to rise by +3.6% yr/yr to 170.000 million bushels. About 76.2% of barley is used for food and alcoholic beverages, 21.2% for animal feed and residual, and 2.6% for seed.

**Trade** – World exports of barley in 2022/23 are expected to fall by -8.4% yr/yr to 29.695 million metric tons. The largest world exporters of barley in 2022/23 are expected to be Australia with 25.3% of the world exports, the European Union with 20.2%, Russia with 18.5%, and Ukraine with 8.1%. The largest importers of barley in 2022/23 are expected to be China with 30.5% and Saudi Arabia with 15.9% of the world's imports.

## World Production of Barley   In Thousands of Metric Tons

| Crop Year | Argentina | Australia | Canada | Ethiopia | European Union | Iran | Kazakhstan | Morocco | Russia | Turkey | Ukraine | United States | World Total |
|---|---|---|---|---|---|---|---|---|---|---|---|---|---|
| 2013-14 | 4,750 | 9,174 | 10,282 | 1,908 | 59,674 | 3,000 | 2,539 | 2,723 | 15,389 | 7,300 | 7,561 | 4,719 | 144,412 |
| 2014-15 | 2,900 | 8,646 | 7,117 | 1,953 | 60,609 | 3,200 | 2,412 | 1,638 | 20,026 | 4,000 | 9,450 | 3,953 | 141,657 |
| 2015-16 | 4,940 | 8,993 | 8,257 | 2,047 | 62,095 | 3,200 | 2,675 | 3,397 | 17,083 | 7,400 | 8,751 | 4,750 | 149,543 |
| 2016-17 | 3,300 | 13,506 | 8,839 | 2,221 | 53,211 | 3,724 | 3,231 | 620 | 17,547 | 4,750 | 9,874 | 4,353 | 147,216 |
| 2017-18 | 3,740 | 9,254 | 7,891 | 1,960 | 51,482 | 3,100 | 3,305 | 2,466 | 20,211 | 6,400 | 8,695 | 3,119 | 143,123 |
| 2018-19 | 4,635 | 8,819 | 8,380 | 1,749 | 49,470 | 2,800 | 3,971 | 2,919 | 16,737 | 7,000 | 7,604 | 3,343 | 139,598 |
| 2019-20 | 3,615 | 10,127 | 10,383 | 2,378 | 55,180 | 3,600 | 3,830 | 1,161 | 19,939 | 7,900 | 9,528 | 3,756 | 158,360 |
| 2020-21 | 4,035 | 14,649 | 10,741 | 2,261 | 54,234 | 3,600 | 3,659 | 640 | 20,629 | 8,100 | 7,947 | 3,719 | 160,905 |
| 2021-22[1] | 5,300 | 13,906 | 6,959 | 2,350 | 52,046 | 2,700 | 2,367 | 2,780 | 17,505 | 4,500 | 9,923 | 2,615 | 145,469 |
| 2022-23[2] | 4,200 | 13,400 | 9,987 | 2,400 | 51,450 | 3,000 | 2,700 | 700 | 21,000 | 7,400 | 6,100 | 3,796 | 149,465 |

[1] Preliminary.  [2] Estimate.   Source: Foreign Agricultural Service, U.S. Department of Agriculture (FAS-USDA)

## World Consumption of Barley   In Thousands of Metric Tons

| Crop Year | Australia | Belarus | Canada | China | European Union | Iran | Morocco | Russia | Saudi Arabia | Turkey | Ukraine | United States | World Total |
|---|---|---|---|---|---|---|---|---|---|---|---|---|---|
| 2013-14 | 2,800 | 1,800 | 7,718 | 6,300 | 53,400 | 4,700 | 2,300 | 12,700 | 8,625 | 6,950 | 5,100 | 4,775 | 141,421 |
| 2014-15 | 3,000 | 2,000 | 6,471 | 11,400 | 51,000 | 4,600 | 2,650 | 14,100 | 8,525 | 5,350 | 5,500 | 4,235 | 143,322 |
| 2015-16 | 3,300 | 1,850 | 7,040 | 7,500 | 51,400 | 5,200 | 3,200 | 13,700 | 10,225 | 6,900 | 5,500 | 4,235 | 143,322 |
| 2016-17 | 3,500 | 1,400 | 6,680 | 9,200 | 47,800 | 5,200 | 2,400 | 14,700 | 9,825 | 5,500 | 4,300 | 4,408 | 145,410 |
| 2017-18 | 3,700 | 1,450 | 6,805 | 9,300 | 46,900 | 6,000 | 2,800 | 14,500 | 8,525 | 6,700 | 4,900 | 4,375 | 148,448 |
| 2018-19 | 5,000 | 1,150 | 6,508 | 7,000 | 45,600 | 6,200 | 2,900 | 12,200 | 7,025 | 7,500 | 4,500 | 3,466 | 146,584 |
| 2019-20 | 6,000 | 1,300 | 8,108 | 8,000 | 49,500 | 6,400 | 2,500 | 15,400 | 7,025 | 8,500 | 4,200 | 3,537 | 140,092 |
| 2020-21 | 6,500 | 1,450 | 7,747 | 13,000 | 48,250 | 6,900 | 1,160 | 14,400 | 7,025 | 8,990 | 4,600 | 3,922 | 156,507 |
| 2021-22[1] | 5,700 | 1,050 | 5,413 | 11,400 | 45,450 | 4,700 | 3,120 | 14,300 | 7,025 | 7,400 | 4,100 | 3,753 | 161,626 |
| 2022-23[2] | 6,000 | 1,150 | 6,900 | 11,100 | 47,300 | 5,500 | 1,720 | 15,400 | 4,925 | 7,700 | 3,800 | 3,593 | 149,716 |

[1] Preliminary.  [2] Estimate.   Source: Foreign Agricultural Service, U.S. Department of Agriculture (FAS-USDA)

# BARLEY

## World Exports of Barley   In Thousands of Metric Tons

| Crop Year | Argentina | Australia | Canada | Ethiopia | European Union | Iran | Kazakhstan | Morocco | Russia | Turkey | Ukraine | United States | World Total |
|---|---|---|---|---|---|---|---|---|---|---|---|---|---|
| 2013-14 | 2,891 | 6,217 | 1,561 | 5,741 | 441 | 416 | 2,709 | 28 | 6 | 2,476 | 311 | 34 | 22,857 |
| 2014-15 | 1,552 | 5,219 | 1,517 | 9,547 | 431 | 483 | 5,348 | 21 | 9 | 4,456 | 311 | 43 | 29,030 |
| 2015-16 | 3,077 | 5,745 | 1,195 | 10,834 | 81 | 804 | 4,241 | 54 | 3 | 4,412 | 235 | 42 | 30,823 |
| 2016-17 | 2,556 | 9,190 | 1,546 | 5,672 | 1 | 682 | 2,951 | 26 | 129 | 5,354 | 95 | 114 | 29,492 |
| 2017-18 | 2,399 | 5,662 | 2,021 | 5,934 | 1 | 1,347 | 5,884 | 53 | 147 | 4,289 | 111 | 7 | 29,099 |
| 2018-19 | 3,237 | 3,687 | 2,296 | 4,898 | 6 | 1,820 | 4,661 | 68 | 148 | 3,561 | 107 | 62 | 25,537 |
| 2019-20 | 2,421 | 3,324 | 2,244 | 7,767 | 1 | 1,366 | 4,470 | 52 | 2 | 4,984 | 125 | 45 | 28,951 |
| 2020-21 | 2,336 | 8,342 | 3,534 | 7,399 | 2 | 1,085 | 6,259 | 117 | 60 | 4,187 | 300 | 241 | 36,281 |
| 2021-22[1] | 3,900 | 8,007 | 1,981 | 7,331 | 2 | 427 | 3,300 | 120 | 173 | 5,705 | 162 | 262 | 32,413 |
| 2022-23[2] | 2,700 | 7,500 | 3,000 | 6,000 | 5 | 600 | 5,500 | 150 | 300 | 2,400 | 109 | 100 | 29,695 |

[1] Preliminary.   [2] Estimate.   Source: Foreign Agricultural Service, U.S. Department of Agriculture (FAS-USDA)

## World Imports of Barley   In Thousands of Metric Tons

| Crop Year | Algeria | Brazil | China | Iran | Japan | Jordan | Kuwait | Libya | Saudi Arabia | Tunisia | United Arab Emirates | United States | World Total |
|---|---|---|---|---|---|---|---|---|---|---|---|---|---|
| 2013-14 | 511 | 318 | 4,891 | 900 | 1,294 | 1,009 | 436 | 681 | 9,000 | 646 | 468 | 408 | 23,223 |
| 2014-15 | 876 | 484 | 9,859 | 2,200 | 1,097 | 891 | 412 | 1,001 | 8,200 | 483 | 393 | 513 | 29,925 |
| 2015-16 | 837 | 547 | 5,869 | 1,700 | 1,155 | 796 | 511 | 1,324 | 11,200 | 561 | 668 | 405 | 28,638 |
| 2016-17 | 635 | 691 | 8,104 | 1,200 | 1,197 | 838 | 569 | 1,084 | 8,100 | 584 | 501 | 210 | 28,764 |
| 2017-18 | 528 | 547 | 8,144 | 3,200 | 1,253 | 907 | 521 | 438 | 8,000 | 604 | 263 | 199 | 30,243 |
| 2018-19 | 325 | 656 | 5,181 | 3,100 | 1,158 | 1,017 | 434 | 884 | 6,500 | 558 | 352 | 128 | 24,763 |
| 2019-20 | 560 | 664 | 5,969 | 2,900 | 1,253 | 389 | 500 | 895 | 6,700 | 613 | 434 | 154 | 28,647 |
| 2020-21 | 834 | 501 | 12,049 | 3,500 | 1,132 | 548 | 507 | 1,043 | 7,000 | 995 | 453 | 142 | 36,077 |
| 2021-22[1] | 772 | 637 | 8,282 | 1,600 | 1,184 | 1,278 | 551 | 535 | 4,200 | 909 | 337 | 320 | 30,131 |
| 2022-23[2] | 400 | 500 | 9,000 | 2,500 | 1,200 | 900 | 450 | 750 | 4,700 | 650 | 450 | 327 | 29,503 |

[1] Preliminary.   [2] Estimate.   Source: Foreign Agricultural Service, U.S. Department of Agriculture (FAS-USDA)

## World Exports of Barley   In Thousands of Metric Tons

| Crop Year | Argentina | Australia | Canada | Ethiopia | European Union | Iran | Kazakhstan | Morocco | Russia | Turkey | Ukraine | United States | World Total |
|---|---|---|---|---|---|---|---|---|---|---|---|---|---|
| 2013-14 | 2,891 | 6,217 | 1,561 | 5,741 | 441 | 416 | 2,709 | 28 | 6 | 2,476 | 311 | 34 | 22,857 |
| 2014-15 | 1,552 | 5,219 | 1,517 | 9,547 | 431 | 483 | 5,348 | 21 | 9 | 4,456 | 311 | 43 | 29,030 |
| 2015-16 | 3,077 | 5,745 | 1,195 | 10,834 | 81 | 804 | 4,241 | 54 | 3 | 4,412 | 235 | 42 | 30,823 |
| 2016-17 | 2,556 | 9,190 | 1,546 | 5,672 | 1 | 682 | 2,951 | 26 | 129 | 5,354 | 95 | 114 | 29,492 |
| 2017-18 | 2,399 | 5,662 | 2,021 | 5,934 | 1 | 1,347 | 5,884 | 53 | 147 | 4,289 | 111 | 7 | 29,099 |
| 2018-19 | 3,237 | 3,687 | 2,296 | 4,898 | 6 | 1,820 | 4,661 | 68 | 148 | 3,561 | 107 | 62 | 25,537 |
| 2019-20 | 2,421 | 3,324 | 2,244 | 7,767 | 1 | 1,366 | 4,470 | 52 | 2 | 4,984 | 125 | 45 | 28,951 |
| 2020-21 | 2,336 | 8,342 | 3,534 | 7,399 | 2 | 1,085 | 6,259 | 117 | 60 | 4,187 | 300 | 241 | 36,281 |
| 2021-22[1] | 3,900 | 8,007 | 1,981 | 7,331 | 2 | 427 | 3,300 | 120 | 173 | 5,705 | 162 | 262 | 32,413 |
| 2022-23[2] | 2,700 | 7,500 | 3,000 | 6,000 | 5 | 600 | 5,500 | 150 | 300 | 2,400 | 109 | 100 | 29,695 |

[1] Preliminary.   [2] Estimate.   Source: Foreign Agricultural Service, U.S. Department of Agriculture (FAS-USDA)

## Barley Acreage and Prices in the United States

| Crop Year Beginning June 1 | Acreage 1,000 Acres Planted | Acreage 1,000 Acres Harvested for Grain | Yield Per Harvested Acre -- Bushels -- | Seasonal Prices Received by Farmers[3] All (Dollars per Bushel) | Seasonal Prices Received by Farmers[3] Feed[4] | Seasonal Prices Received by Farmers[3] Malting[4] | Portland No. 2 Western | Gov't Price Support National Average Loan Rate | Gov't Price Support Target Price | Gov't Price Support Put Under Support (mil. Bu.) | Gov't Price Support Percent of Production |
|---|---|---|---|---|---|---|---|---|---|---|---|
| 2013-14 | 3,528 | 3,040 | 71.3 | 6.06 | 4.22 | 6.49 | ---- | 1.95 | 2.63 | 4.2 | 1.9 |
| 2014-15 | 3,031 | 2,497 | 72.7 | 5.22 | 3.20 | 5.77 | ---- | 1.95 | 4.95 | 3.9 | 2.1 |
| 2015-16 | 3,623 | 3,158 | 69.1 | 5.46 | 3.11 | 5.78 | ---- | 1.95 | 4.95 | 8.3 | 3.8 |
| 2016-17 | 3,059 | 2,565 | 77.9 | 4.97 | 2.73 | 5.26 | ---- | 1.95 | 4.95 | 9.3 | 4.6 |
| 2017-18 | 2,486 | 1,962 | 73.0 | 4.47 | 3.00 | 4.67 | ---- | 1.95 | 4.95 | 4.5 | 3.1 |
| 2018-19 | 2,548 | 1,982 | 77.5 | 4.64 | 3.25 | 4.80 | ---- | 1.95 | 4.95 | 5.1 | 3.3 |
| 2019-20 | 2,772 | 2,221 | 77.7 | 4.69 | 3.37 | 4.85 | ---- | 2.50 | 4.95 | 6.1 | 3.6 |
| 2020-21 | 2,726 | 2,214 | 77.2 | 4.77 | 3.42 | 4.94 | ---- | 2.50 | | | |
| 2021-22[1] | 2,708 | 1,990 | 60.3 | 5.40 | 5.39 | 5.40 | ---- | 2.50 | | | |
| 2022-23[2] | 2,945 | 2,433 | 71.7 | 7.23 | 6.23 | 7.32 | ---- | 2.50 | | | |

[1] Preliminary.   [2] Estimate.   [3] Excludes support payments.   Source: Economic Research Service, U.S. Department of Agriculture (ERS-USDA)

# BARLEY

## Salient Statistics of Barley in the United States     In Millions of Bushels

| Crop Year Beginning June 1 | Beginning Stocks | Production | Imports | Total Supply | Food & Alcohol Beverage | Seed | Feed & Residual | Total | Exports | Total Disappearance | Gov't Owned | Privately Owned | Total Stocks |
|---|---|---|---|---|---|---|---|---|---|---|---|---|---|
| 2013-14 | 80.4 | 216.7 | 18.7 | 315.9 | 148.3 | 5.1 | 65.9 | 219.4 | 14.3 | 233.6 | ---- | 82.3 | 82.3 |
| 2014-15 | 82.3 | 181.5 | 23.6 | 287.4 | 154.3 | 5.9 | 34.4 | 194.5 | 14.3 | 208.8 | ---- | 78.6 | 78.6 |
| 2015-16 | 78.6 | 218.2 | 18.6 | 315.3 | 153.1 | 5.2 | 44.2 | 202.4 | 10.8 | 213.2 | ---- | 102.1 | 102.1 |
| 2016-17 | 102.1 | 199.9 | 9.6 | 311.7 | 151.6 | 4.2 | 45.2 | 200.9 | 4.4 | 205.3 | ---- | 106.4 | 106.4 |
| 2017-18 | 106.4 | 143.3 | 9.1 | 258.8 | 147.5 | 4.3 | 7.4 | 159.2 | 5.1 | 164.3 | ---- | 94.5 | 94.5 |
| 2018-19 | 94.5 | 153.5 | 5.9 | 253.9 | 143.7 | 4.7 | 14.0 | 162.4 | 4.9 | 167.4 | ---- | 86.5 | 86.5 |
| 2019-20 | 86.5 | 172.5 | 7.1 | 266.1 | 137.2 | 4.6 | 38.4 | 180.1 | 5.7 | 185.9 | ---- | 80.3 | 80.3 |
| 2020-21 | 80.3 | 170.8 | 6.5 | 257.6 | 142.1 | 4.6 | 25.7 | 172.4 | 13.8 | 186.2 | ---- | 71.4 | 71.4 |
| 2021-22[1] | 71.4 | 120.1 | 14.7 | 206.2 | 132.0 | 4.9 | 19.7 | 156.6 | 7.4 | 164.0 | ---- | 42.2 | 42.2 |
| 2022-23[2] | 42.2 | 174.3 | 15.0 | 231.5 | 125.7 | 4.3 | 35.0 | 165.0 | 5.0 | 170.0 | ---- | 61.5 | 61.5 |

[1] Preliminary.  [2] Estimate.  [3] Uncommitted inventory.  [4] Includes quantity under loan & farmer-owned reserve.  [5] Included in Food & Alcohol.
Source: Economic Research Service, U.S. Department of Agriculture (ERS-USDA)

## Stocks of Barley in the United States     In Thousands of Bushels

| Year | On Farms Mar. 1 | June 1 | Sept. 1 | Dec. 1 | Off Farms Mar. 1 | June 1 | Sept. 1 | Dec. 1 | Total Stocks Mar. 1 | June 1 | Sept. 1 | Dec. 1 |
|---|---|---|---|---|---|---|---|---|---|---|---|---|
| 2013 | 35,180 | 15,840 | 105,620 | 81,340 | 81,897 | 64,557 | 90,470 | 88,063 | 117,077 | 80,397 | 196,090 | 169,403 |
| 2014 | 43,830 | 19,110 | 97,820 | 74,510 | 77,734 | 63,145 | 81,997 | 81,625 | 121,564 | 82,255 | 179,817 | 156,135 |
| 2015 | 41,990 | 20,940 | 135,840 | 96,670 | 76,247 | 57,639 | 83,132 | 83,738 | 118,237 | 78,579 | 218,972 | 180,408 |
| 2016 | 57,910 | 27,740 | 130,600 | 99,100 | 79,832 | 74,370 | 99,737 | 93,408 | 137,742 | 102,110 | 230,337 | 192,508 |
| 2017 | 56,490 | 27,050 | 90,400 | 74,340 | 88,211 | 79,314 | 89,283 | 84,528 | 144,701 | 106,364 | 179,683 | 158,868 |
| 2018 | 48,540 | 26,420 | 91,350 | 72,070 | 81,491 | 68,061 | 83,456 | 80,561 | 130,031 | 94,481 | 174,806 | 152,631 |
| 2019 | 46,180 | 22,870 | 116,720 | 87,630 | 75,216 | 63,653 | 73,112 | 69,756 | 121,396 | 86,523 | 189,832 | 157,386 |
| 2020 | 51,580 | 25,100 | 108,980 | 85,190 | 63,760 | 55,153 | 70,484 | 63,437 | 115,340 | 80,253 | 179,464 | 148,627 |
| 2021 | 55,850 | 21,390 | 77,680 | 43,120 | 64,628 | 50,028 | 57,716 | 54,103 | 120,478 | 71,418 | 135,396 | 97,223 |
| 2022[1] | 25,250 | 9,760 | 121,370 | 63,690 | 47,591 | 32,397 | 44,234 | 51,681 | 72,841 | 42,157 | 165,604 | 115,371 |

[1] Preliminary.  Source: National Agricultural Statistics Service, U.S. Department of Agriculture (NASS-USDA)

## Production of Barley in the United States, by State     In Thousands of Bushels

| Crop Year | Arizona | California | Colorado | Idaho | Minnesota | Montana | North Dakota | Oregon | Pennsylvania | Virginia | Washington | Wyoming | Total |
|---|---|---|---|---|---|---|---|---|---|---|---|---|---|
| 2013 | 8,142 | 3,150 | 7,714 | 57,660 | 5,175 | 43,160 | 46,080 | 3,500 | 4,080 | 3,608 | 14,040 | 6,052 | 216,745 |
| 2014 | 4,000 | 1,825 | 6,696 | 51,700 | 3,120 | 44,660 | 35,845 | 1,900 | 3,550 | 2,212 | 6,300 | 7,276 | 181,542 |
| 2015 | 1,920 | 1,595 | 8,190 | 56,260 | 9,240 | 44,720 | 67,200 | 1,924 | 2,600 | 1,200 | 5,040 | 8,170 | 218,187 |
| 2016 | 2,048 | 4,500 | 9,675 | 62,060 | 5,214 | 46,800 | 42,880 | 2,144 | 2,850 | 804 | 7,161 | 7,872 | 199,914 |
| 2017 | 2,227 | 1,450 | 8,976 | 48,450 | 5,168 | 28,815 | 26,000 | 2,356 | 3,150 | 803 | 4,505 | 6,426 | 143,258 |
| 2018 | 1,100 | 1,794 | 7,685 | 53,530 | 5,092 | 33,600 | 28,490 | 1,378 | 2,079 | 630 | 4,891 | 5,100 | 153,527 |
| 2019 | 1,890 | 3,102 | 7,176 | 55,120 | 3,685 | 44,840 | 32,040 | 2,730 | 1,750 | 455 | 5,880 | 7,062 | 172,499 |
| 2020 | 976 | 1,551 | 6,815 | 55,000 | 2,350 | 49,770 | 28,980 | 2,160 | 2,280 | 441 | 6,390 | 6,432 | 170,813 |
| 2021 | 2,000 | 819 | 5,217 | 44,500 | 1,870 | 24,700 | 21,930 | 672 | 2,240 | 525 | 2,660 | 6,552 | 120,090 |
| 2022[1] | 1,995 | 1,045 | 4,440 | 59,940 | 3,960 | 34,440 | 48,180 | 1,045 | 1,340 | 602 | 5,040 | 5,394 | 174,333 |

[1] Preliminary.  Source: National Agricultural Statistics Service, U.S. Department of Agriculture (NASS-USDA)

## Average Price Received by Farmers for All Barley in the United States     In Dollars Per Bushel

| Crop Year | June | July | Aug. | Sept. | Oct. | Nov. | Dec. | Jan. | Feb. | Mar. | Apr. | May | Average |
|---|---|---|---|---|---|---|---|---|---|---|---|---|---|
| 2013-14 | 6.35 | 6.38 | 6.15 | 5.88 | 5.94 | 6.20 | 6.11 | 6.04 | 5.94 | 5.94 | 5.90 | 5.94 | 6.06 |
| 2014-15 | 6.01 | 5.62 | 5.60 | 5.31 | 5.24 | 5.09 | 5.16 | 4.86 | 5.22 | 5.94 | 4.94 | 4.75 | 5.22 |
| 2015-16 | 5.04 | 5.19 | 5.59 | 5.49 | 5.54 | 5.55 | 5.88 | 5.47 | 5.51 | 5.43 | 5.29 | 5.59 | 5.46 |
| 2016-17 | 5.39 | 5.00 | 4.89 | 4.54 | 4.85 | 4.97 | 5.12 | 4.91 | 5.08 | 4.97 | 4.87 | 5.05 | 4.97 |
| 2017-18 | 4.47 | 4.54 | 4.52 | 4.32 | 4.44 | 4.60 | 4.38 | 4.45 | 4.58 | 4.46 | 4.44 | 4.45 | 4.47 |
| 2018-19 | 4.62 | 4.52 | 4.54 | 4.49 | 4.25 | 4.78 | 4.64 | 4.57 | 4.65 | 4.88 | 4.80 | 4.90 | 4.64 |
| 2019-20 | 4.81 | 4.69 | 4.74 | 4.56 | 4.58 | 4.74 | 4.51 | 4.67 | 4.68 | 4.89 | 4.64 | 4.76 | 4.69 |
| 2020-21 | 4.57 | 4.66 | 4.60 | 4.76 | 4.74 | 4.78 | 4.79 | 4.67 | 4.97 | 4.90 | 4.83 | 4.92 | 4.77 |
| 2021-22 | 4.86 | 5.02 | 5.04 | 5.11 | 5.38 | 5.22 | 5.41 | 5.59 | 5.43 | 5.69 | 6.00 | 6.07 | 5.40 |
| 2022-23[1] | 6.46 | 6.60 | 7.44 | 7.43 | 7.47 | 7.24 | 7.48 | 7.26 | 7.65 | | | | 7.23 |

[1] Preliminary.  Source: National Agricultural Statistical Service, U.S. Department of Agriculture (NASS-USDA)

# BARLEY

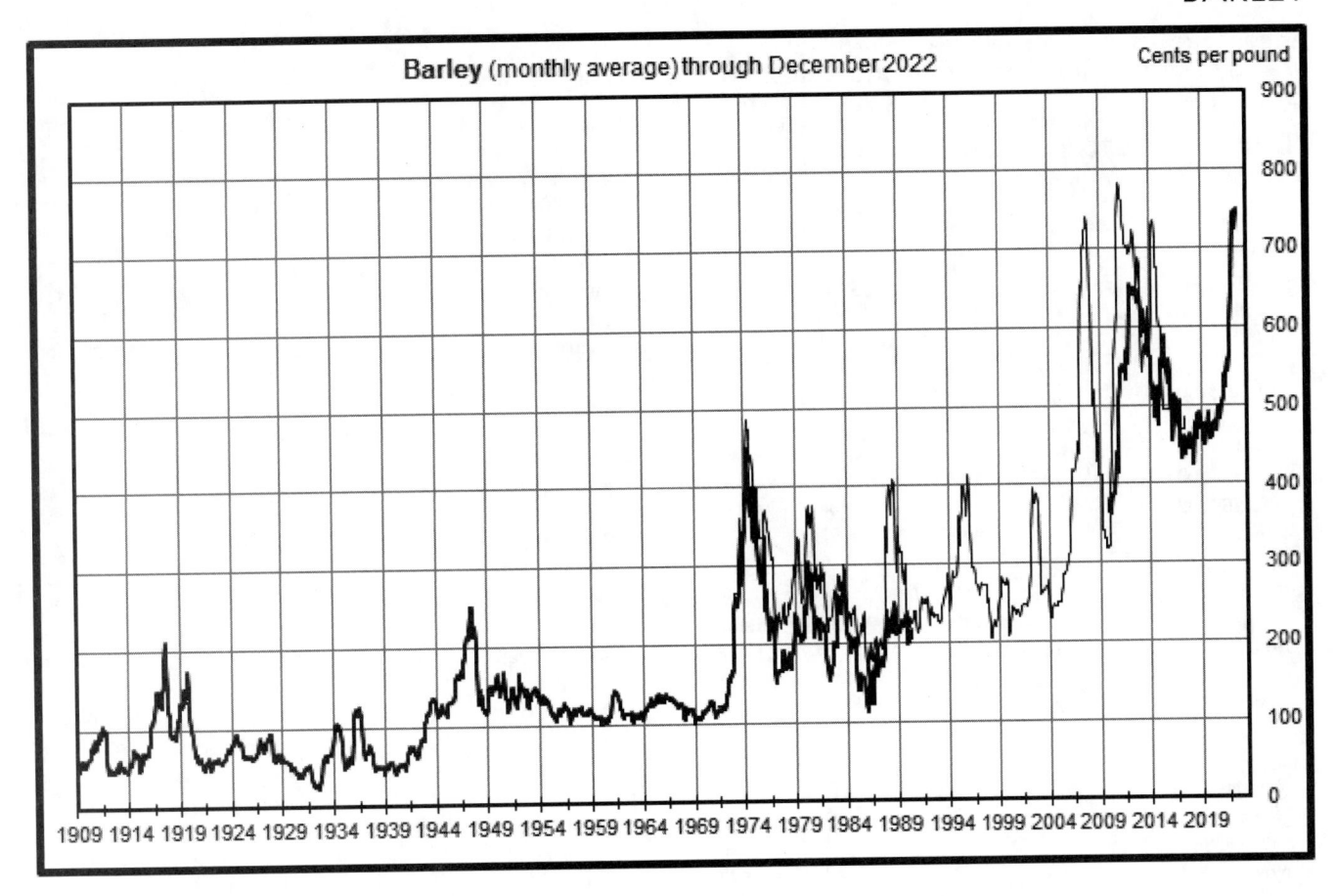

Barley (monthly average) through December 2022 — Cents per pound

## Average Price Received by Farmers for Feed Barley in the United States — In Dollars Per Bushel

| Crop Year | June | July | Aug. | Sept. | Oct. | Nov. | Dec. | Jan. | Feb. | Mar. | Apr. | May | Average |
|---|---|---|---|---|---|---|---|---|---|---|---|---|---|
| 2013-14 | 5.75 | 5.17 | 4.42 | 4.25 | 4.10 | 3.63 | 3.65 | 4.21 | 3.77 | 3.81 | 3.77 | 4.15 | 4.22 |
| 2014-15 | 4.32 | 3.85 | 3.31 | 2.97 | 3.13 | 2.84 | 2.99 | 2.99 | 2.94 | 3.08 | 3.05 | 2.90 | 3.20 |
| 2015-16 | 3.55 | 2.97 | 3.00 | 3.24 | 2.97 | 3.03 | 3.11 | 3.14 | 3.07 | 2.79 | 2.82 | 3.67 | 3.11 |
| 2016-17 | 3.38 | 3.18 | 2.75 | 2.39 | 2.52 | 2.49 | 2.87 | 2.61 | 2.75 | 2.50 | 2.64 | 2.69 | 2.73 |
| 2017-18 | 3.47 | 3.04 | 2.97 | 2.62 | 3.07 | 2.80 | 2.85 | 3.01 | 2.83 | 2.90 | 3.08 | 3.33 | 3.00 |
| 2018-19 | 3.79 | 3.41 | 3.12 | 3.07 | 2.97 | 3.23 | 3.06 | 3.11 | 3.23 | 3.23 | 3.39 | 3.44 | 3.25 |
| 2019-20 | 4.32 | 3.89 | 3.43 | 3.18 | 3.10 | 2.81 | 3.32 | 3.27 | 3.16 | 3.55 | 3.16 | 3.20 | 3.37 |
| 2020-21 | 3.25 | 3.37 | 3.04 | 3.11 | 3.28 | 3.32 | 3.01 | 3.20 | 3.50 | 3.82 | 3.91 | 4.21 | 3.42 |
| 2021-22 | 4.33 | 3.98 | 4.62 | 4.98 | 5.37 | 5.56 | 5.51 | 5.76 | 6.05 | 6.12 | 6.34 | 6.08 | 5.39 |
| 2022-23[1] | 6.73 | 6.70 | 5.98 | 5.65 | 5.70 | 6.14 | 6.15 | 6.36 | 6.64 | | | | 6.23 |

[1] Preliminary. *Source: National Agricultural Statistical Service, U.S. Department of Agriculture (NASS-USDA)*

## Average Price Received by Farmers for Malting Barley in the United States — In Dollars Per Bushel

| Crop Year | June | July | Aug. | Sept. | Oct. | Nov. | Dec. | Jan. | Feb. | Mar. | Apr. | May | Average |
|---|---|---|---|---|---|---|---|---|---|---|---|---|---|
| 2013-14 | 6.68 | 6.56 | 6.56 | 6.44 | 6.49 | 6.61 | 6.52 | 6.52 | 6.43 | 6.30 | 6.45 | 6.37 | 6.49 |
| 2014-15 | 6.30 | 5.90 | 6.11 | 5.91 | 5.76 | 5.69 | 5.63 | 5.47 | 5.67 | 5.39 | 5.75 | 5.62 | 5.77 |
| 2015-16 | 5.68 | 5.73 | 5.91 | 5.74 | 5.78 | 5.80 | 5.99 | 5.68 | 5.70 | 5.64 | 5.71 | 6.03 | 5.78 |
| 2016-17 | 5.70 | 5.33 | 5.31 | 5.13 | 5.17 | 5.21 | 5.32 | 5.19 | 5.20 | 5.13 | 5.13 | 5.27 | 5.26 |
| 2017-18 | 4.66 | 4.78 | 4.70 | 4.64 | 4.64 | 4.81 | 4.51 | 4.60 | 4.77 | 4.60 | 4.73 | 4.58 | 4.67 |
| 2018-19 | 4.88 | 4.79 | 4.68 | 4.72 | 4.42 | 4.85 | 4.78 | 4.71 | 4.75 | 5.02 | 4.92 | 5.03 | 4.80 |
| 2019-20 | 4.88 | 4.83 | 4.89 | 4.78 | 4.77 | 4.84 | 4.81 | 4.82 | 4.78 | 5.07 | 4.74 | 4.98 | 4.85 |
| 2020-21 | 4.95 | 4.92 | 4.77 | 4.92 | 4.98 | 5.00 | 4.86 | 4.82 | 5.02 | 5.04 | 5.04 | 5.00 | 4.94 |
| 2021-22 | 4.99 | 5.18 | 5.10 | 5.16 | 5.38 | 5.17 | 5.39 | 5.54 | 5.33 | 5.59 | 5.90 | 6.07 | 5.40 |
| 2022-23[1] | 6.41 | 6.59 | 7.54 | 7.65 | 7.63 | 7.38 | 7.61 | 7.34 | 7.77 | | | | 7.32 |

[1] Preliminary. *Source: National Agricultural Statistical Service, U.S. Department of Agriculture (NASS-USDA)*

# BARLEY

## Weekly Outstanding Export Sales and Cumulative Exports of U.S. Barley        In Thousands of Metric Tons

| Marketing Year 2021/2022 Week Ending | Weekly Exports | Accumulated Exports | Net Sales | Outstanding Sales | Marketing Year 2022/2023 Week Ending | Weekly Exports | Accumulated Exports | Net Sales | Outstanding Sales |
|---|---|---|---|---|---|---|---|---|---|
| Jun 03, 2021 | 20 | 20 | 2,551 | 24,747 | Jun 02, 2022 | | | | 13,768 |
| Jun 10, 2021 | | 20 | | 24,747 | Jun 09, 2022 | 964 | 964 | | 12,804 |
| Jun 17, 2021 | 1,033 | 1,053 | 11 | 23,725 | Jun 16, 2022 | 473 | 1,437 | 1,600 | 13,931 |
| Jun 24, 2021 | | 1,053 | | 23,725 | Jun 23, 2022 | 728 | 2,165 | -1,688 | 11,515 |
| Jul 01, 2021 | 300 | 1,353 | 300 | 23,725 | Jun 30, 2022 | 32 | 2,197 | 1,830 | 13,313 |
| Jul 08, 2021 | | 1,353 | | 23,725 | Jul 07, 2022 | 513 | 2,710 | | 12,800 |
| Jul 15, 2021 | 249 | 1,602 | | 23,476 | Jul 14, 2022 | | 2,710 | | 12,800 |
| Jul 22, 2021 | 403 | 2,005 | -65 | 23,008 | Jul 21, 2022 | | 2,710 | | 12,800 |
| Jul 29, 2021 | 263 | 2,268 | | 22,745 | Jul 28, 2022 | 42 | 2,752 | | 12,758 |
| Aug 05, 2021 | | 2,268 | | 22,745 | Aug 04, 2022 | 1,015 | 3,767 | | 11,743 |
| Aug 12, 2021 | 619 | 2,887 | -125 | 22,001 | Aug 11, 2022 | | 3,767 | | 11,743 |
| Aug 19, 2021 | 1,018 | 3,905 | 440 | 21,423 | Aug 18, 2022 | | 3,767 | | 11,743 |
| Aug 26, 2021 | | 3,905 | -68 | 21,355 | Aug 25, 2022 | 154 | 3,921 | | 11,589 |
| Sep 02, 2021 | | 3,905 | -100 | 21,255 | Sep 01, 2022 | | 3,921 | | 11,589 |
| Sep 09, 2021 | 768 | 4,673 | | 20,487 | Sep 08, 2022 | | 3,921 | | 11,589 |
| Sep 16, 2021 | | 4,673 | -31 | 20,456 | Sep 15, 2022 | | 3,921 | | 11,589 |
| Sep 23, 2021 | | 4,673 | 5,000 | 25,456 | Sep 22, 2022 | | 3,921 | | 11,589 |
| Sep 30, 2021 | 978 | 5,651 | | 24,478 | Sep 29, 2022 | | 3,921 | | 11,589 |
| Oct 07, 2021 | | 5,651 | | 24,478 | Oct 06, 2022 | | 3,921 | | 11,589 |
| Oct 14, 2021 | 722 | 6,373 | -20 | 23,736 | Oct 13, 2022 | | 3,921 | | 11,589 |
| Oct 21, 2021 | 822 | 7,195 | | 22,914 | Oct 20, 2022 | | 3,921 | | 11,589 |
| Oct 28, 2021 | 65 | 7,260 | | 22,849 | Oct 27, 2022 | | 3,921 | -1,516 | 10,073 |
| Nov 04, 2021 | | 7,260 | -18 | 22,831 | Nov 03, 2022 | | 3,921 | | 10,073 |
| Nov 11, 2021 | 165 | 7,425 | -61 | 22,605 | Nov 10, 2022 | | 3,921 | | 10,073 |
| Nov 18, 2021 | | 7,425 | | 22,605 | Nov 17, 2022 | 331 | 4,252 | -2,364 | 7,378 |
| Nov 25, 2021 | 1,028 | 8,453 | | 21,577 | Nov 24, 2022 | 770 | 5,022 | | 6,608 |
| Dec 02, 2021 | 514 | 8,967 | 444 | 21,507 | Dec 01, 2022 | 514 | 5,536 | | 6,094 |
| Dec 09, 2021 | 884 | 9,851 | | 20,623 | Dec 08, 2022 | | 5,536 | | 6,094 |
| Dec 16, 2021 | 893 | 10,744 | | 19,730 | Dec 15, 2022 | 921 | 6,457 | | 5,173 |
| Dec 23, 2021 | 749 | 11,493 | | 18,981 | Dec 22, 2022 | | 6,457 | | 5,173 |
| Dec 30, 2021 | | 11,493 | | 18,981 | Dec 29, 2022 | | 6,457 | | 5,173 |
| Jan 06, 2022 | | 11,493 | | 18,981 | Jan 05, 2023 | 288 | 6,745 | | 4,885 |
| Jan 13, 2022 | 1,027 | 12,520 | | 17,954 | Jan 12, 2023 | | 6,745 | | 4,885 |
| Jan 20, 2022 | | 12,520 | | 17,954 | Jan 19, 2023 | 445 | 7,190 | | 4,440 |
| Jan 27, 2022 | 875 | 13,395 | | 17,079 | Jan 26, 2023 | | 7,190 | | 4,440 |
| Feb 03, 2022 | 1,299 | 14,694 | -2,007 | 13,773 | Feb 02, 2023 | | 7,190 | | 4,440 |
| Feb 10, 2022 | | 14,694 | | 13,773 | Feb 09, 2023 | | 7,190 | | 4,440 |
| Feb 17, 2022 | | 14,694 | | 13,773 | Feb 16, 2023 | 771 | 7,961 | 264 | 3,933 |
| Feb 24, 2022 | | 14,694 | | 13,773 | Feb 23, 2023 | | 7,961 | | 3,933 |
| Mar 03, 2022 | | 14,694 | | 13,773 | Mar 02, 2023 | | | | |
| Mar 10, 2022 | | 14,694 | | 13,773 | Mar 09, 2023 | | | | |
| Mar 17, 2022 | | 14,694 | 132 | 13,905 | Mar 16, 2023 | | | | |
| Mar 24, 2022 | | 14,694 | -8,187 | 5,718 | Mar 23, 2023 | | | | |
| Mar 31, 2022 | | 14,694 | | 5,718 | Mar 30, 2023 | | | | |
| Apr 07, 2022 | 22 | 14,716 | 136 | 5,832 | Apr 06, 2023 | | | | |
| Apr 14, 2022 | | 14,716 | | 5,832 | Apr 13, 2023 | | | | |
| Apr 21, 2022 | | 14,716 | -92 | 5,740 | Apr 20, 2023 | | | | |
| Apr 28, 2022 | 66 | 14,782 | | 5,674 | Apr 27, 2023 | | | | |
| May 05, 2022 | | 14,782 | | 5,674 | May 04, 2023 | | | | |
| May 12, 2022 | 493 | 15,275 | | 5,181 | May 11, 2023 | | | | |
| May 19, 2022 | | 15,275 | | 5,181 | May 18, 2023 | | | | |
| May 26, 2022 | | 15,275 | | 5,181 | May 25, 2023 | | | | |
| Jun 02, 2022 | | 15,275 | | 5,181 | Jun 01, 2023 | | | | |

*Source: Foreign Agricultural Service, U.S. Department of Agriculture (FAS-USDA)*

# Bauxite

Bauxite is a naturally occurring, heterogeneous material comprised of one or more aluminum hydroxide minerals plus various mixtures of silica, iron oxide, titanium, alumina-silicates, and other impurities in trace amounts. Bauxite is an important ore of aluminum and forms by the rapid weathering of granite rocks in warm, humid climates. It is easily purified and can be converted directly into either alum or metallic aluminum. It is a soft mineral with hardness varying from 1 to 3, and specific gravity from 2 to 2.55. Bauxite is dull in appearance and may vary in color from white to brown. It usually occurs in aggregates in pea-sized lumps.

Bauxite is the only raw material used in the production of alumina on a commercial scale in the United States. Bauxite is classified according to the intended commercial application, such as abrasive, cement, chemical, metallurgical, and refractory. Of all the bauxite mined, about 95 percent is converted to alumina to produce aluminum metal with some smaller amounts going to nonmetal uses as various forms of specialty alumina. Small amounts are used in non-metallurgical bauxite applications. Bauxite is also used to produce aluminum chemicals and is used in the steel industry.

**Supply** – World production of bauxite in 2022 fell by -1.0% yr/yr to 380.000 million metric tons. The world's largest producer of bauxite in 2022 was Australia, with 26.3% of the world's production, followed by China with 23.7%, Guinea with 22.6%, Brazil with 8.7%, India with 4.5%, Russia with 1.3%, and Jamaica with 1.0%.

**Demand** – U.S. consumption of bauxite in 2022 rose by +3.9% yr/yr to 2.900 million metric tons, but still well below the record high of 15.962 million metric tons seen in 1980.

**Trade** – The U.S. relies on imports for almost 100% of its bauxite consumption needs. Domestic ore, which provides less than 1 percent of the U.S. requirement for bauxite, is mined by one company from surface mines in the states of Alabama and Georgia. U.S. imports of bauxite in 2022 fell by -7.2% yr/yr to 3.600 million metric tons, the lowest since 1952. U.S. exports of bauxite in 2020 remain unchanged at 3.22 million metric tons.

## World Production of Bauxite    In Thousands of Metric Tons

| Year | Australia | Brazil | China | Greece | Guinea | Guyana[3] | Hungary | India | Jamaica[3] | Russia[3] | Sierra Leone | Suriname | World Total |
|---|---|---|---|---|---|---|---|---|---|---|---|---|---|
| 2015 | 80,909 | 37,057 | 60,790 | 1,832 | 16,303 | 1,498 | 8 | 27,757 | 9,629 | 5,900 | 1,334 | 1,600 | 294,000 |
| 2016 | 83,517 | 39,244 | 68,620 | 1,880 | 31,500 | 1,480 | 17 | 23,886 | 8,540 | 5,431 | 1,369 | ---- | 286,000 |
| 2017 | 89,421 | 38,072 | 68,390 | 1,927 | 46,160 | 1,482 | 4 | 22,803 | 8,245 | 5,523 | 1,788 | ---- | 307,000 |
| 2018 | 95,948 | 32,377 | 77,170 | 1,559 | 57,000 | 1,924 | 5 | 23,229 | 10,058 | 5,651 | 1,938 | ---- | 340,000 |
| 2019 | 105,544 | 31,938 | 105,000 | 1,492 | 67,000 | 1,900 | ---- | 22,321 | 9,022 | 5,574 | 1,884 | ---- | 387,000 |
| 2020 | 104,328 | 31,000 | 92,700 | 1,500 | 86,000 | 900 | ---- | 20,200 | 7,546 | 5,570 | 1,342 | ---- | 391,000 |
| 2021[1] | 103,000 | 33,000 | 90,000 | | 86,000 | | ---- | 17,400 | 5,950 | 5,680 | | ---- | 384,000 |
| 2022[2] | 100,000 | 33,000 | 90,000 | | 86,000 | | ---- | 17,000 | 3,900 | 5,000 | | ---- | 380,000 |

[1] Preliminary.  [2] Estimate.  [3] Dry Bauxite equivalent of ore processed.  Source: U.S. Geological Survey (USGS)

## Salient Statistics of Bauxite in the United States    In Thousands of Metric Tons

| Year | Net Import Reliance as a % of Apparent Consump | Average Price F.O.B. Mine $ per Ton | Consumption by Industry Total | Alumina | Abrasive | Chemical | Refractory | Dry Equivalent Imports[4] | Exports[3] | Consumption | Stocks, December 31 Producers & Consumers | Gov't Owned | Total |
|---|---|---|---|---|---|---|---|---|---|---|---|---|---|
| 2015 | >75 | ---- | 9,660 | 9,340 | ---- | ---- | ---- | 10,400 | 3 | 11,200 | W | ---- | W |
| 2016 | >75 | ---- | 5,360 | 5,080 | ---- | ---- | ---- | 4,930 | 5 | 6,630 | W | ---- | W |
| 2017 | >75 | ---- | 4,330 | 2,340 | ---- | ---- | ---- | 4,350 | 5 | 4,330 | W | ---- | W |
| 2018 | >75 | ---- | 4,460 | 2,800 | ---- | ---- | ---- | 3,980 | 4 | 4,460 | W | ---- | W |
| 2019 | >75 | ---- | 3,680 | 3,470 | ---- | ---- | ---- | 4,620 | 3 | 3,680 | W | ---- | W |
| 2020 | >75 | ---- | 3,330 | 3,120 | ---- | ---- | ---- | 3,760 | 3 | 3,330 | W | ---- | W |
| 2021[1] | >75 | ---- | 2,790 | 2,580 | ---- | ---- | ---- | 3,880 | | | W | ---- | W |
| 2022[2] | >75 | ---- | 2,900 | 2,900 | ---- | ---- | ---- | 3,600 | | | W | ---- | W |

[1] Preliminary.  [2] Estimate.  [3] Including concentrates.  [4] For consumption.  W = Withheld.  Source: U.S. Geological Survey (USGS)

## World Production of Alumina    In Thousands of Metric Tons

| Year | Australia | Brazil | China | Germany | India | Ireland | Jamaica | Kazakhstan | Russia | Suriname | Ukraine | United States | World Total |
|---|---|---|---|---|---|---|---|---|---|---|---|---|---|
| 2013 | 20,097 | 10,452 | 58,978 | 1,910 | 5,512 | 1,983 | 1,865 | 1,448 | 2,593 | 748 | 1,481 | 4,550 | 119,000 |
| 2016 | 20,681 | 10,886 | 61,034 | 1,900 | 6,028 | 1,967 | 1,865 | 1,500 | 2,682 | ---- | 1,510 | 2,360 | 121,000 |
| 2017 | 20,486 | 11,061 | 69,017 | 1,900 | 6,055 | 1,937 | 1,782 | 1,509 | 2,822 | ---- | 1,676 | 1,430 | 129,000 |
| 2018 | 20,062 | 8,258 | 72,531 | 1,900 | 6,430 | 1,874 | 2,484 | 1,481 | 2,763 | ---- | 1,715 | 1,570 | 131,000 |
| 2019 | 20,192 | 8,700 | 72,474 | 1,900 | 6,690 | 1,893 | 2,173 | 1,500 | 2,755 | ---- | 1,690 | 1,410 | 133,000 |
| 2020 | 20,800 | 10,300 | 73,100 | 1,900 | 6,560 | 1,880 | 1,620 | 1,400 | 2,870 | ---- | 1,730 | 1,340 | 136,000 |
| 2021[1] | 20,400 | 12,000 | 75,200 | 900 | 7,000 | 1,880 | 1,160 | 1,400 | 3,050 | ---- | 1,770 | 1,180 | 139,000 |
| 2022[2] | 20,000 | 11,000 | 76,000 | 750 | 7,400 | 1,800 | 480 | 1,400 | 3,100 | ---- | 740 | 1,200 | 140,000 |

[1] Preliminary.  [2] Estimate.  Source: U.S. Geological Survey (USGS)

# Bismuth

Bismuth (symbol Bi) is a rare metallic element with a pinkish tinge. Bismuth has been known since ancient times, but it was confused with lead, tin, and zinc until the middle of the 18th century. Among the elements in the earth's crust, bismuth is ranked about 73rd in natural abundance. This makes bismuth about as rare as silver. Most industrial bismuth is obtained as a by-product of ore extraction.

Bismuth is useful for castings because of the unusual way that it expands after solidifying. Some of bismuth's alloys have unusually low melting points. Bismuth is one of the most difficult of all substances to magnetize. It tends to turn at right angles to a magnetic field. Because of this property, it is used in instruments for measuring the strength of magnetic fields.

Bismuth finds a wide variety of uses such as pharmaceutical compounds, ceramic glazes, crystal ware, and chemicals and pigments. Bismuth is found in household pharmaceuticals and is used to treat stomach ulcers. Bismuth is opaque to X-rays and can be used in fluoroscopy. Bismuth has also found new use as a nontoxic substitute for lead in various applications such as brass plumbing fixtures, crystal ware, lubricating greases, pigments, and solders. There has been environmental interest in the use of bismuth as a replacement for lead used in shot for waterfowl hunting and in fishing sinkers. Another use has been for galvanizing to improve drainage characteristics of galvanizing alloys. Zinc-bismuth alloys have the same drainage properties as zinc-lead without being as hazardous.

**Prices** – The average price of bismuth (99.99% pure) in the U.S. in 2022 rose by +4.3% yr/yr to $3.90 per pound, well below the 2007 record high of $14.07 per pound.

**Supply** – World refinery production of bismuth in 2021 rose by +0.5% to 19,000 metric tons. China had 84.2% of production, Japan had 3.2%, Kazakhstan had 1.3%, and Mexico had +0.1%. The U.S. does not have any significant domestic refinery production of bismuth.

**Demand** – U.S. consumption of bismuth in 2022 rose by +0.5% yr/yr to 600 metric tons. In 2020 the consumption uses of bismuth were 59.5% for chemicals and 16.4% for fusible alloys.

**Trade** – U.S. imports of bismuth in 2020 fell by -29.5% yr/yr to 1.650 million metric tons, the fewest since 2010. In 2020, 1.5% of U.S. imports came from Belgium and 0.2% from Mexico. U.S. exports of bismuth and alloys in 2022 fell by -33.7% yr/yr to 670 metric tons, well below the 2010 record high of 1,040 metric tons.

## World Production of Bismuth   In Metric Tons (Mine Output=Metal Content)

| Year | Bolivia | Canada | China | Mexico | Russia | World Total | Belgium | China | Japan | Kazakhstan[3] | Mexico | Peru | World Total |
|---|---|---|---|---|---|---|---|---|---|---|---|---|---|
| 2015 | 10 | 3 | 7,400 | 700 | 40 | 10,200 | ---- | 16,013 | 632 | 220 | 603 | ---- | 19,400 |
| 2016 | ---- | ---- | ---- | ---- | ---- | ---- | ---- | 15,643 | 428 | 270 | 539 | ---- | 19,700 |
| 2017 | ---- | ---- | ---- | ---- | ---- | ---- | ---- | 14,813 | 525 | 270 | 513 | ---- | 19,800 |
| 2018 | ---- | ---- | ---- | ---- | ---- | ---- | ---- | 15,537 | 571 | 280 | 333 | ---- | 20,700 |
| 2019 | ---- | ---- | ---- | ---- | ---- | ---- | ---- | 16,000 | 570 | 230 | 300 | ---- | 19,200 |
| 2020[1] | ---- | ---- | ---- | ---- | ---- | ---- | ---- | 16,000 | 570 | 230 | 10 | ---- | 18,900 |
| 2021[2] | | | | | | | ---- | 16,000 | 600 | 240 | 10 | ---- | 19,000 |

[1] Preliminary.  [2] Estimate.  Source U.S. Geological Survey (USGS)

## Salient Statistics of Bismuth in the United States   In Metric Tons

| Year | Metallurgical Additives | Other Alloys & Uses | Fusible Alloys | Chemicals[3] | Total Consumption | Consumer Stocks Dec. 31 | Exports of Metal & Alloys | Belgium | Mexico | Preu | Total | Dealer Price $ Per Pound |
|---|---|---|---|---|---|---|---|---|---|---|---|---|
| 2015 | W | W | 84 | 416 | 621 | 456 | 519 | 155.0 | 16.4 | ---- | 1,950 | 6.43 |
| 2016 | W | W | 99 | 453 | 651 | 513 | 431 | 130.0 | 161.0 | ---- | 2,190 | 4.53 |
| 2017 | W | W | 99 | 439 | 694 | 489 | 392 | 141.0 | 176.0 | 0.1 | 2,820 | 4.94 |
| 2018 | W | W | 96 | 314 | 570 | 346 | 653 | 143.0 | 205.0 | ---- | 2,510 | 4.61 |
| 2019 | W | W | 118 | 305 | 548 | 443 | 636 | 116.0 | 195.0 | ---- | 2,340 | 3.18 |
| 2020[1] | W | W | 84 | 305 | 513 | 271 | 699 | 24.2 | 3.3 | ---- | 1,650 | 2.72 |
| 2021[2] | W | W | | | 500 | 200 | 840 | | | ---- | | 3.65 |

[1] Preliminary.  [2] Estimate.  [3] Includes pharmaceuticals.  Source: U.S. Geological Survey (USGS)

## Average Price of Bismuth (99.99%) in the United States   In Dollars Per Pound

| Year | Jan. | Feb. | Mar. | Apr. | May | June | July | Aug. | Sept. | Oct. | Nov. | Dec. | Average |
|---|---|---|---|---|---|---|---|---|---|---|---|---|---|
| 2016 | 4.41 | 4.40 | 4.46 | 4.46 | 4.54 | 4.48 | 4.28 | 4.36 | 4.60 | 4.72 | 4.64 | 4.63 | 4.50 |
| 2017 | 4.72 | 4.63 | 4.70 | 4.84 | 4.93 | 4.87 | 4.85 | 4.87 | 5.17 | 5.20 | 5.20 | 5.25 | 4.94 |
| 2018 | 5.22 | 5.21 | 5.28 | 5.22 | 5.04 | 4.68 | 4.55 | 4.35 | 4.27 | 4.17 | 3.80 | 3.69 | 4.62 |
| 2019 | 3.68 | 3.94 | 3.68 | 3.57 | 3.42 | 3.19 | 2.92 | 2.84 | 2.74 | 2.75 | 2.81 | 2.66 | 3.18 |
| 2020 | 2.58 | 2.58 | 2.63 | 2.57 | 2.59 | 2.60 | 2.61 | 2.67 | 2.91 | 2.98 | 2.98 | 2.98 | 2.72 |
| 2021 | 3.00 | 3.16 | 3.59 | 3.83 | 3.85 | 3.87 | 3.79 | 3.84 | 3.87 | 3.94 | 4.06 | 4.08 | 3.74 |
| 2022 | 4.00 | 3.97 | 4.01 | 3.91 | 3.88 | 3.84 | 3.83 | 3.85 | 3.76 | 3.93 | 3.98 | 3.87 | 3.90 |

Source: American Metal Market (AMM)

# Broilers

Broiler chickens are raised for meat rather than for eggs. The broiler industry was started in the late 1950s when chickens were selectively bred for meat production. Broiler chickens are housed in massive flocks, mainly between 20,000 and 50,000 birds, with some flocks reaching over 100,000 birds. Broiler chicken farmers usually rear five or six batches of chickens per year.

After just six or seven weeks, broiler chickens are slaughtered (a chicken's natural lifespan is around seven years). Chickens marketed as pouissons, or spring chickens, are slaughtered after four weeks. A few are kept longer than seven weeks to be sold as the larger roasting chickens.

**Prices** – The average monthly price received by farmers for broilers (live weight) in 2022 rose by +51.0% yr/yr to 84.6 cents per pound. The average monthly price of wholesale broilers (ready-to-cook) in 2022 rose by +39.0% to 140.64 cents per pound, above the 2014 record high of 104.88 cents per pound.

**Supply** – Total production of broilers in 2022 rose by +2.7% yr/yr to 46.095 billion pounds. The number of broilers raised for commercial production in 2022 was up +2.5% yr/yr to 9.437 billion birds, up from last year's record high. The average live weight per bird rose by +0.3% to 6.48 pounds, which was a new record high and was about 79% heavier than the average bird weight of 3.62 pounds seen in 1970, attesting to the increased efficiency of the industry.

**Demand** – U.S. per capita consumption of broilers in 2022 rose by +2.5% to 99.0 pounds (ready-to-cook) per-person per-year, up from last year's record high. U.S. consumption of chicken has more than doubled in the past four decades, up from 47.0 pounds in 1980, as consumers have increased their consumption of chicken because of the focus on low-carb diets and because chicken is a leaner and healthier meat than either beef or pork.

## Broiler Supply and Prices in the United States

| Years and Quarters | Number (Million) | Average Weight (Pounds) | Liveweight Pounds (Mil. Lbs.) | Certified RTC[3] Weight (Mil. Lbs.) | Total Production RTC[3] (Mil. Lbs.) | Per Capita Consumption RTC[3] Basis (Mil. Lbs.) | Farm | Georgia Dock[4] |
|---|---|---|---|---|---|---|---|---|
| 2017 | 8,916 | 6.20 | 55,313 | 41,661 | 41,662 | 90.8 | 54.58 | ---- |
| 2018 | 8,984 | 6.25 | 56,185 | 42,328 | 43,905 | 92.4 | 56.83 | ---- |
| 2019 | 9,135 | 6.31 | 57,641 | 43,426 | 43,905 | 95.1 | 48.18 | ---- |
| 2020 | 9,139 | 6.43 | 58,599 | 44,163 | 44,583 | 95.8 | 36.42 | ---- |
| 2021 | 9,151 | 6.45 | 59,019 | 44,540 | 44,899 | 96.5 | 56.02 | ---- |
| 2022[1] | 9,331 | 6.47 | 60,370 | 45,588 | 46,201 | 98.9 | 84.73 | ---- |
| I | 2,295 | 6.45 | 14,798 | 11,170 | 11,170 | 23.8 | 80.97 | ---- |
| II | 2,328 | 6.42 | 14,942 | 11,279 | 11,279 | 24.2 | 105.77 | ---- |
| III | 2,328 | 6.42 | 14,942 | 11,279 | 11,896 | 25.7 | 81.00 | ---- |
| IV | 2,380 | 6.59 | 15,689 | 11,861 | 11,857 | 25.2 | 71.17 | ---- |

[1] Preliminary. [2] Estimate. [3] Total production equals federal inspected slaughter plus other slaughter minus cut-up & further processing condemnation. [4] Ready-to-cook basis. *Source: Economic Research Service, U.S. Department of Agriculture (ERS-USDA)*

## Salient Statistics of Broilers in the United States

| Year | Commercial Production Number (Mil. Lbs.) | Commercial Production Liveweight (Mil. Lbs.) | Average Liveweight Per Bird (Mil. Lbs.) | Average Price (cents Lb.) | Value of Production (Mil. $) | Production Federally Inspected | Production Other Chickens | Total | Storage Stocks January 1 | Exports | Broiler Feed Ratio (pounds) | Consumption Total (Mil. Lbs.) | Per Capita[4] (Pounds) |
|---|---|---|---|---|---|---|---|---|---|---|---|---|---|
| 2016 | 8,768 | 54,037 | 6.16 | 50.4 | 25,936 | 40,692 | | 40,692 | 840 | 6,803 | 4.7 | 34,194 | 90.90 |
| 2017 | 8,916 | 55,313 | 6.20 | 54.6 | 30,232 | 41,661 | | 41,661 | 786 | 6,910 | 5.4 | 34,895 | |
| 2018 | 9,032 | 56,518 | 6.26 | 56.8 | 31,750 | 42,583 | | 42,583 | | | | | |
| 2019 | 9,221 | 58,266 | 6.32 | 48.2 | 28,314 | 43,889 | | 43,889 | | | | | |
| 2020 | 9,230 | 59,146 | 6.41 | 36.4 | 21,267 | 44,582 | | 44,582 | | | | | |
| 2021[1] | 9,209 | 59,473 | 6.46 | 56.0 | 31,520 | 44,890 | | 44,890 | | | | | |
| 2022[2] | 9,430 | 61,181 | 6.49 | 84.7 | | 46,206 | | 46,206 | | | | | |

Preliminary. [2] Estimate. [3] Ready-to-cook. [4] Retail weight basis. *Source: Economic Research Service, U.S. Department of Agriculture (ERS-USDA)*

## Average Wholesale Broiler[2] Prices RTC (Ready-to-Cook)   In Cents Per Pound

| Year | Jan. | Feb. | Mar. | Apr. | May | June | July | Aug. | Sept. | Oct. | Nov. | Dec. | Average |
|---|---|---|---|---|---|---|---|---|---|---|---|---|---|
| 2014 | 96.45 | 92.45 | 106.26 | 110.11 | 117.59 | 113.40 | 107.16 | 99.69 | 107.05 | 106.68 | 103.68 | 98.07 | 104.88 |
| 2015 | 99.62 | 92.56 | 98.88 | 104.79 | 106.71 | 101.17 | 91.01 | 82.61 | 77.40 | 74.09 | 75.37 | 82.05 | 90.52 |
| 2016 | 87.90 | 81.52 | 84.46 | 88.41 | 93.72 | 96.93 | 88.62 | 79.71 | 76.68 | 70.73 | 79.28 | 84.04 | 84.33 |
| 2017 | 85.58 | 85.07 | 94.49 | 96.91 | 108.97 | 109.02 | 103.80 | 92.47 | 88.38 | 84.84 | 86.06 | 87.33 | 93.58 |
| 2018 | 94.00 | 91.08 | 101.97 | 108.73 | 117.59 | 118.92 | 110.60 | 87.33 | 83.13 | 83.56 | 86.91 | 89.75 | 97.80 |
| 2019 | 98.90 | 89.78 | 93.33 | 97.61 | 100.89 | 94.63 | 88.24 | 80.88 | 76.92 | 78.86 | 78.30 | 84.63 | 88.58 |
| 2020 | 90.56 | 80.64 | 79.35 | 53.52 | 73.75 | 73.60 | 70.41 | 66.08 | 63.58 | 67.70 | 76.80 | 82.47 | 73.21 |
| 2021 | 82.29 | 82.97 | 86.68 | 101.50 | 105.41 | 106.39 | 105.75 | 104.80 | 105.75 | 102.95 | 105.47 | 124.40 | 101.20 |
| 2022[1] | 131.40 | 125.79 | 148.04 | 166.89 | 169.67 | 165.83 | 153.31 | 130.40 | 124.70 | 121.94 | 124.66 | 123.69 | 140.53 |

[1] Preliminary. [2] 12-city composite wholesale price. *Source: Economic Research Service, U.S. Department of Agriculture (ERS-USDA)*

# BROILERS

## Certified Federally Inspected Chicken Slaughter in the United States    In Thousand Head

| Year | Jan. | Feb. | Mar. | Apr. | May | June | July | Aug. | Sept. | Oct. | Nov. | Dec. | Total |
|---|---|---|---|---|---|---|---|---|---|---|---|---|---|
| 2013 | 734,639 | 649,727 | 679,303 | 719,688 | 743,372 | 679,881 | 748,385 | 742,973 | 694,243 | 768,507 | 655,869 | 687,463 | 8,504,050 |
| 2014 | 704,432 | 664,590 | 689,189 | 711,014 | 712,142 | 712,605 | 743,158 | 709,909 | 731,821 | 770,431 | 644,637 | 728,499 | 8,545,000 |
| 2015 | 724,764 | 654,077 | 741,648 | 725,427 | 704,517 | 747,484 | 762,580 | 740,789 | 748,689 | 743,126 | 674,127 | 720,679 | 8,688,700 |
| 2016 | 699,346 | 699,896 | 760,432 | 707,069 | 745,305 | 754,657 | 708,391 | 793,503 | 745,766 | 731,963 | 712,780 | 709,319 | 8,768,427 |
| 2017 | 749,302 | 679,696 | 771,634 | 690,347 | 782,516 | 763,000 | 725,770 | 809,566 | 728,356 | 782,869 | 728,303 | 704,485 | 8,915,844 |
| 2018 | 772,266 | 693,759 | 742,817 | 731,026 | 794,062 | 744,471 | 775,038 | 823,156 | 719,006 | 817,500 | 729,068 | 689,771 | 9,031,940 |
| 2019 | 788,098 | 697,844 | 730,928 | 758,037 | 803,158 | 738,489 | 814,385 | 804,355 | 766,832 | 849,010 | 712,323 | 757,769 | 9,221,228 |
| 2020 | 820,185 | 716,853 | 810,686 | 752,639 | 732,106 | 773,413 | 786,204 | 771,711 | 790,691 | 787,752 | 719,240 | 768,071 | 9,229,551 |
| 2021 | 745,452 | 676,811 | 832,145 | 762,423 | 738,961 | 804,545 | 769,481 | 799,282 | 794,794 | 771,627 | 749,916 | 763,139 | 9,208,576 |
| 2022[1] | 755,990 | 714,577 | 824,227 | 738,353 | 780,516 | 809,283 | 758,278 | 862,696 | 806,793 | 809,586 | 793,686 | 776,509 | 9,430,494 |

[1] Preliminary.    Source: National Agricultural Statistics Service (NASS)


## Average Live Weight of Chickens Slaughtered in the United States    In Pounds

| Year | Jan. | Feb. | Mar. | Apr. | May | June | July | Aug. | Sept. | Oct. | Nov. | Dec. | Average |
|---|---|---|---|---|---|---|---|---|---|---|---|---|---|
| 2013 | 5.92 | 5.91 | 5.87 | 5.90 | 5.87 | 5.88 | 5.84 | 5.90 | 5.95 | 6.01 | 6.01 | 5.99 | 5.92 |
| 2014 | 6.00 | 6.01 | 5.98 | 5.99 | 5.97 | 5.99 | 5.95 | 5.98 | 5.99 | 6.07 | 6.07 | 5.99 | 6.01 |
| 2015 | 6.12 | 6.09 | 6.07 | 6.12 | 6.11 | 6.09 | 6.05 | 6.12 | 6.18 | 6.19 | 6.07 | 6.10 | 6.12 |
| 2016 | 6.19 | 6.17 | 6.16 | 6.19 | 6.17 | 6.14 | 6.09 | 6.09 | 6.15 | 6.20 | 6.17 | 6.14 | 6.16 |
| 2017 | 6.20 | 6.16 | 6.16 | 6.18 | 6.18 | 6.16 | 6.14 | 6.18 | 6.25 | 6.29 | 6.21 | 6.20 | 6.20 |
| 2018 | 6.26 | 6.23 | 6.24 | 6.27 | 6.25 | 6.22 | 6.21 | 6.28 | 6.30 | 6.32 | 6.27 | 6.27 | 6.26 |
| 2019 | 6.25 | 6.21 | 6.20 | 6.29 | 6.33 | 6.32 | 6.32 | 6.34 | 6.30 | 6.32 | 6.29 | 6.22 | 6.32 |
| 2020 | 6.41 | 6.33 | 6.32 | 6.45 | 6.48 | 6.48 | 6.33 | 6.38 | 6.38 | 6.41 | 6.38 | 6.39 | 6.42 |
| 2021 | 6.43 | 6.39 | 6.39 | 6.44 | 6.46 | 6.47 | 6.46 | 6.42 | 6.50 | 6.48 | 6.40 | 6.41 | 6.46 |
| 2022[1] | 6.47 | 6.45 | 6.42 | 6.40 | 6.42 | 6.44 | 6.43 | 6.47 | 6.56 | 6.64 | 6.57 | 6.56 | 6.49 |

[1] Preliminary.    Source: National Agricultural Statistics Service (NASS)


## Live Weight of Chickens Slaughtered in the United States    In Millions of Pounds

| Year | Jan. | Feb. | Mar. | Apr. | May | June | July | Aug. | Sept. | Oct. | Nov. | Dec. | Total |
|---|---|---|---|---|---|---|---|---|---|---|---|---|---|
| 2013 | 4,349.5 | 3,838.9 | 3,992.3 | 4,252.2 | 4,366.8 | 4,000.6 | 4,370.3 | 4,383.3 | 4,128.9 | 4,615.2 | 3,941.0 | 4,117.7 | 50,356.9 |
| 2014 | 4,226.5 | 3,992.5 | 4,120.1 | 4,260.1 | 4,254.3 | 4,266.0 | 4,418.5 | 4,244.3 | 4,385.4 | 4,680.1 | 3,911.1 | 4,445.7 | 51,378.7 |
| 2015 | 4,433.9 | 3,982.6 | 4,501.6 | 4,436.6 | 4,303.9 | 4,551.0 | 4,609.9 | 4,533.9 | 4,623.3 | 4,600.6 | 4,159.2 | 4,428.1 | 53,376.2 |
| 2016 | 4,330.5 | 4,321.1 | 4,683.2 | 4,379.8 | 4,602.0 | 4,632.7 | 4,313.7 | 4,829.1 | 4,584.4 | 4,536.0 | 4,429.1 | 4,395.6 | 54,037.1 |
| 2017 | 4,644.2 | 4,185.8 | 4,756.9 | 4,267.0 | 4,838.3 | 4,702.1 | 4,456.9 | 4,999.9 | 4,554.7 | 4,920.9 | 4,568.1 | 4,418.2 | 55,313.2 |
| 2018 | 4,832.5 | 4,322.8 | 4,633.5 | 4,586.6 | 4,964.0 | 4,629.8 | 4,813.7 | 5,168.3 | 4,532.2 | 5,164.3 | 4,583.2 | 4,287.6 | 56,518.5 |
| 2019 | 4,929.0 | 4,331.4 | 4,529.2 | 4,766.2 | 5,080.0 | 4,666.0 | 5,146.8 | 5,101.5 | 4,889.0 | 5,439.3 | 4,544.5 | 4,842.7 | 58,265.7 |
| 2020 | 5,254.1 | 4,539.9 | 5,124.8 | 4,785.5 | 4,725.2 | 5,012.0 | 4,973.3 | 4,955.1 | 5,141.0 | 5,102.7 | 4,605.5 | 4,926.7 | 59,145.7 |
| 2021 | 4,790.0 | 4,322.9 | 5,315.0 | 4,907.0 | 4,776.2 | 5,208.1 | 4,971.0 | 5,170.9 | 5,203.5 | 5,061.3 | 4,859.4 | 4,887.8 | 59,472.9 |
| 2022[1] | 4,893.4 | 4,611.1 | 5,293.5 | 4,722.8 | 5,007.4 | 5,211.4 | 4,872.6 | 5,584.7 | 5,295.6 | 5,379.0 | 5,215.9 | 5,094.0 | 61,181.3 |

[1] Preliminary.    Source: National Agricultural Statistics Service (NASS)


## Total Chilled and Frozen Pounds Certified[2] in the United States    In Millions of Pounds

| Year | Jan. | Feb. | Mar. | Apr. | May | June | July | Aug. | Sept. | Oct. | Nov. | Dec. | Total |
|---|---|---|---|---|---|---|---|---|---|---|---|---|---|
| 2013 | 3,266.8 | 2,877.3 | 2,999.0 | 3,194.2 | 3,270.1 | 3,002.0 | 3,278.8 | 3,296.2 | 3,107.4 | 3,474.1 | 2,967.2 | 3,093.3 | 37,826.5 |
| 2014 | 3,175.9 | 3,008.8 | 3,098.6 | 3,210.9 | 3,201.2 | 3,205.6 | 3,331.1 | 3,197.6 | 3,306.6 | 3,525.2 | 2,939.9 | 3,348.5 | 38,549.8 |
| 2015 | 3,328.8 | 3,000.7 | 3,387.9 | 3,345.7 | 3,246.1 | 3,428.4 | 3,469.0 | 3,417.4 | 3,486.3 | 3,465.4 | 3,135.4 | 3,334.5 | 40,045.7 |
| 2016 | 3,256.8 | 3,256.5 | 3,525.9 | 3,302.1 | 3,466.4 | 3,484.8 | 3,246.2 | 3,633.1 | 3,454.8 | 3,417.1 | 3,337.0 | 3,311.5 | 40,691.9 |
| 2017 | 3,496.9 | 3,153.9 | 3,582.2 | 3,216.3 | 3,647.9 | 3,542.5 | 3,357.6 | 3,763.0 | 3,429.9 | 3,709.0 | 3,437.3 | 3,324.8 | 41,661.3 |
| 2018 | 3,639.0 | 3,256.7 | 3,489.7 | 3,456.2 | 3,738.0 | 3,490.9 | 3,629.5 | 3,892.3 | 3,417.8 | 3,893.4 | 3,450.7 | 3,228.7 | 42,583.0 |
| 2019 | 3,711.3 | 3,263.1 | 3,409.8 | 3,587.4 | 3,827.9 | 3,518.1 | 3,874.9 | 3,841.6 | 3,680.5 | 4,100.1 | 3,427.1 | 3,647.4 | 43,889.2 |
| 2020 | 3,957.1 | 3,418.5 | 3,861.2 | 3,600.3 | 3,559.4 | 3,780.0 | 3,745.8 | 3,733.9 | 3,878.4 | 3,848.9 | 3,478.0 | 3,720.1 | 44,581.6 |
| 2021 | 3,613.0 | 3,271.7 | 4,008.8 | 3,696.4 | 3,611.5 | 3,923.6 | 3,750.3 | 3,902.0 | 3,928.5 | 3,827.8 | 3,665.3 | 3,690.8 | 44,889.5 |
| 2022[1] | 3,690.3 | 3,484.5 | 3,995.0 | 3,564.9 | 3,778.9 | 3,934.9 | 3,684.8 | 4,211.0 | 4,000.5 | 4,068.5 | 3,940.9 | 3,851.6 | 46,205.8 |

[1] Preliminary.    [2] Ready-to-cook weights.    Source: National Agricultural Statistics Service (NASS)

# BROILERS

**Average Price Received by Farmers for Broilers (Liveweight)**   In U.S. Cents per Pound

| Year | Jan. | Feb. | Mar. | Apr. | May | June | July | Aug. | Sept. | Oct. | Nov. | Dec. | Average |
|---|---|---|---|---|---|---|---|---|---|---|---|---|---|
| 2013 | 61.0 | 61.0 | 66.0 | 66.0 | 68.0 | 67.0 | 60.0 | 54.0 | 55.0 | 53.0 | 56.0 | 56.0 | 60.3 |
| 2014 | 58.0 | 55.0 | 65.0 | 68.0 | 73.0 | 70.0 | 66.0 | 60.0 | 66.0 | 65.0 | 63.0 | 58.0 | 63.9 |
| 2015 | 60.0 | 54.0 | 59.0 | 64.0 | 65.0 | 62.0 | 51.0 | 47.0 | 43.0 | 41.0 | 42.0 | 47.0 | 52.9 |
| 2016 | 51.0 | 46.0 | 48.0 | 51.0 | 56.0 | 86.5 | 51.0 | 44.0 | 42.0 | 37.0 | 44.0 | 48.0 | 50.4 |
| 2017 | 49.0 | 48.0 | 55.0 | 57.0 | 66.0 | 66.0 | 62.0 | 54.0 | 51.0 | 48.0 | 49.0 | 50.0 | 54.6 |
| 2018 | 53.0 | 52.0 | 59.0 | 65.0 | 72.0 | 73.0 | 67.0 | 49.0 | 46.0 | 46.0 | 49.0 | 51.0 | 56.8 |
| 2019 | 56.0 | 49.0 | 51.0 | 55.0 | 57.0 | 54.0 | 48.7 | 42.1 | 39.1 | 41.0 | 40.3 | 44.9 | 48.2 |
| 2020 | 49.4 | 41.9 | 43.0 | 22.6 | 34.5 | 36.6 | 34.5 | 30.9 | 29.2 | 31.5 | 39.1 | 43.8 | 36.4 |
| 2021 | 43.2 | 43.8 | 43.1 | 54.8 | 59.3 | 60.0 | 59.3 | 58.7 | 59.5 | 57.8 | 59.2 | 73.5 | 56.0 |
| 2022[1] | 79.0 | 74.7 | 89.2 | 104.5 | 107.7 | 105.1 | 94.7 | 76.5 | 71.8 | 69.5 | 71.4 | 72.6 | 84.7 |

[1] Preliminary.   Source: Economic Research Service, U.S. Department of Agriculture (ERS-USDA)


**Average Wholesale Price of Broilers (Breast, boneless)**   In U.S. Cents per Pound

| Year | Jan. | Feb. | Mar. | Apr. | May | June | July | Aug. | Sept. | Oct. | Nov. | Dec. | Average |
|---|---|---|---|---|---|---|---|---|---|---|---|---|---|
| 2013 | 136.51 | 140.00 | 147.19 | 160.62 | 194.87 | 189.21 | 179.72 | 178.90 | 149.30 | 132.25 | 126.32 | 126.15 | 155.09 |
| 2014 | 125.77 | 126.49 | 145.25 | 171.76 | 184.99 | 198.77 | 197.87 | 183.78 | 187.48 | 170.11 | 143.92 | 132.86 | 164.09 |
| 2015 | 135.47 | 139.97 | 140.74 | 153.47 | 163.91 | 146.67 | 137.30 | 140.20 | 130.32 | 110.48 | 105.98 | 103.33 | 133.99 |
| 2016 | 107.12 | 108.40 | 108.79 | 116.62 | 123.79 | 115.07 | 129.21 | 142.84 | 133.84 | 116.06 | 99.01 | 98.16 | 116.58 |
| 2017 | 101.00 | 108.90 | 125.94 | 129.90 | 151.42 | 163.80 | 156.62 | 145.98 | 133.97 | 112.69 | 103.93 | 103.52 | 128.14 |
| 2018 | 106.20 | 105.20 | 123.32 | 136.36 | 127.05 | 117.65 | 127.09 | 112.51 | 95.41 | 91.25 | 85.30 | 88.72 | 109.67 |
| 2019 | 100.86 | 107.06 | 113.96 | 127.65 | 120.11 | 115.97 | 110.99 | 105.06 | 93.37 | 86.91 | 88.86 | 98.00 | 105.73 |
| 2020 | 92.18 | 88.69 | 112.78 | 91.12 | 137.50 | 124.01 | 114.82 | 115.20 | 98.94 | 89.21 | 89.61 | 94.15 | 104.02 |
| 2021 | 108.84 | 132.75 | 141.28 | 171.92 | 212.97 | 203.54 | 182.75 | 188.22 | 208.42 | 186.50 | 182.55 | 200.58 | 176.69 |
| 2022[1] | 230.98 | 264.45 | 277.55 | 301.94 | 352.06 | 332.13 | 282.36 | 227.75 | 185.42 | 118.07 | 98.16 | 95.77 | 230.55 |

[1] Preliminary.   Source: Economic Research Service, U.S. Department of Agriculture (ERS-USDA)


**Average Wholesale Price of Broilers (Breast, with ribs)**   In U.S. Cents per Pound

| Year | Jan. | Feb. | Mar. | Apr. | May | June | July | Aug. | Sept. | Oct. | Nov. | Dec. | Average |
|---|---|---|---|---|---|---|---|---|---|---|---|---|---|
| 2013 | 109.57 | 116.28 | 120.50 | 123.79 | 135.85 | 143.99 | 141.46 | 134.50 | 124.74 | 116.71 | 112.99 | 108.82 | 124.10 |
| 2014 | 109.57 | 103.23 | 103.27 | 115.54 | 127.95 | 135.96 | 134.97 | 130.79 | 129.09 | 129.51 | 119.74 | 119.52 | 121.60 |
| 2015 | 118.30 | 117.58 | 117.01 | 118.87 | 119.00 | 122.59 | 117.76 | 103.97 | 97.40 | 90.27 | 92.00 | 92.60 | 108.95 |
| 2016 | 97.38 | 101.37 | 102.38 | 104.93 | 112.84 | 114.15 | 108.53 | 101.41 | 103.81 | 102.72 | 100.76 | 103.25 | 104.46 |
| 2017 | 100.81 | 101.66 | 110.51 | 121.96 | 134.85 | 144.42 | 143.53 | 131.87 | 120.05 | 103.34 | 103.21 | 102.51 | 118.23 |
| 2018 | 114.34 | 117.06 | 121.50 | 131.82 | 132.40 | 136.01 | 131.90 | 119.48 | 110.71 | 104.91 | 109.29 | 111.90 | 120.11 |
| 2019 | 119.97 | 122.42 | 120.11 | 119.81 | 118.40 | 116.42 | 118.68 | 114.13 | 103.35 | 100.33 | 104.20 | 103.78 | 113.47 |
| 2020 | 104.40 | 99.49 | 109.63 | 92.34 | 98.84 | 104.10 | 106.44 | 105.38 | 97.83 | 102.77 | 104.43 | 106.38 | 102.67 |
| 2021 | 107.56 | 108.29 | 112.97 | 120.92 | 124.60 | 124.60 | 118.25 | 117.16 | 117.40 | 117.07 | 118.32 | 128.77 | 117.99 |
| 2022[1] | 133.08 | 135.61 | 154.45 | 173.80 | 203.64 | 211.55 | 210.71 | 201.21 | 163.63 | 144.79 | 114.68 | 114.01 | 163.43 |

[1] Preliminary.   Source: Economic Research Service, U.S. Department of Agriculture (ERS-USDA)


**Average Wholesale Price of Broilers (Legs, whole)**   In U.S. Cents per Pound

| Year | Jan. | Feb. | Mar. | Apr. | May | June | July | Aug. | Sept. | Oct. | Nov. | Dec. | Average |
|---|---|---|---|---|---|---|---|---|---|---|---|---|---|
| 2013 | 66.91 | 67.53 | 67.69 | 72.29 | 73.35 | 75.21 | 71.78 | 70.72 | 72.22 | 64.26 | 58.96 | 59.64 | 68.38 |
| 2014 | 59.54 | 59.04 | 61.56 | 66.97 | 68.62 | 67.86 | 65.94 | 57.58 | 54.78 | 55.48 | 56.61 | 54.57 | 60.71 |
| 2015 | 51.17 | 44.64 | 44.83 | 48.08 | 41.35 | 37.95 | 35.24 | 36.62 | 36.15 | 32.13 | 32.40 | 30.76 | 39.28 |
| 2016 | 33.41 | 36.40 | 38.49 | 40.85 | 41.07 | 48.14 | 41.94 | 44.04 | 47.45 | 44.16 | 39.51 | 39.18 | 41.22 |
| 2017 | 39.31 | 40.51 | 44.61 | 50.24 | 51.86 | 53.12 | 52.53 | 52.53 | 48.50 | 41.93 | 44.80 | 42.63 | 46.88 |
| 2018 | 46.50 | 49.13 | 50.64 | 50.78 | 50.87 | 48.56 | 46.07 | 45.66 | 41.30 | 41.41 | 42.12 | 41.68 | 46.23 |
| 2019 | 51.52 | 50.32 | 59.34 | 59.38 | 59.50 | 62.03 | 61.34 | 61.66 | 60.83 | 58.85 | 56.26 | 64.53 | 58.80 |
| 2020 | 64.93 | 63.61 | 64.75 | 54.83 | 48.61 | 44.29 | 39.80 | 39.88 | 43.72 | 38.46 | 42.08 | 47.88 | 49.40 |
| 2021 | 39.25 | 44.83 | 49.36 | 58.70 | 61.98 | 59.85 | 60.00 | 60.10 | 61.49 | 56.35 | 54.34 | 52.06 | 54.86 |
| 2022[1] | 51.58 | 50.69 | 51.94 | 56.57 | 67.91 | 86.39 | 82.81 | 77.95 | 60.59 | 43.62 | 43.95 | 40.59 | 59.55 |

[1] Preliminary.   Source: Economic Research Service, U.S. Department of Agriculture (ERS-USDA)

# Butter

Butter is a dairy product produced by churning the fat from milk, usually cow's milk, until it solidifies. In some parts of the world, butter is also made from the milk of goats, sheep, and even horses. Butter has been in use since at least 2,000 BC. Today butter is used principally as a food item, but in ancient times it was used more as an ointment, medicine, or illuminating oil. Butter was first churned in skin pouches thrown back and forth over the backs of trotting horses.

It takes about 10 quarts of milk to produce 1 pound of butter. The manufacture of butter is the third largest use of milk in the U.S. California is generally the largest producing state, followed closely by Wisconsin, with Washington as a distant third. Commercially finished butter is comprised of milk fat (80% to 85%), water (12% to 16%), and salt (about 2%). Although the price of butter is highly correlated with the price of milk, it also has its own supply and demand dynamics.

The consumption of butter has dropped in recent decades because pure butter has a high level of animal fat and cholesterol that have been linked to obesity and heart disease. The primary substitute for butter is margarine, which is produced from vegetable oil rather than milk fat. U.S. per capita consumption of margarine has risen from 2.6 pounds in 1930 to recent levels near 8.3 pounds, much higher than U.S. butter consumption.

Butter Futures and options are traded on the CME Group. The CME's butter futures contract calls for the delivery of 20,000 pounds of butter and is priced in cents per pound. Futures on butter are traded on the European Energy Exchange and the Singapore Exchange.

**Prices** – The average monthly price of butter at the CME in 2022 rose by +66% yr/yr to $2.87/pound, which was a new record annual average high.

**Supply** – World production of butter in 2023 is forecasted to rise by +1.6% yr/yr to 11.584 million metric tons, a new record high. The world's largest producers of butter for 2023 are forecasted to be India with 57.8% of the world production, the European Union with 17.6%, the U.S. with 8.4%, New Zealand with 4.1%, and Russia with 2.4%. Production of creamery butter by U.S. factories in 2022 fell by -1.6% yr/yr to 2.038 billion pounds.

**Demand** – Total commercial use of creamery butter in the U.S. fell by -6.8% yr/yr to 1.994 million pounds in 2022. Cold storage stocks of creamery butter in the U.S. on January 1, 2022, fell by -27.3 yr/yr to 199.056 million pounds.

**Trade** – World imports of butter in 2023 are expected to remain unchanged at 626,000 metric tons. U.S. imports of butter in 2023 are expected to fall by -8.6% to 74,000 metric tons. World exports of butter in 2023 are expected to fall by -4.8% yr/yr to 1.032 million metric tons. U.S exports in 2023 are expected to fall by -11.9% yr/yr to 74,000 metric tons, far below the 1993 record high of 145,000 metric tons.

## Supply and Distribution of Butter in the United States    In Millions of Pounds

| Year | Production | Cold Storage Stocks[3] Jan. 1 | Imports | Total Supply | Domestic Disappearance Total | Per Capita (Pounds) | Exports | USDA Stocks[4] Jan. 1 | USDA Stocks[4] Dec 31 | Removed by USDA Programs | Total Use | 93 Score AA Wholesale Price $ per Pound |
|---|---|---|---|---|---|---|---|---|---|---|---|---|
| 2014 | 1,855.3 | 112,467 | 46.297 | 2,015 | 1,746 | 5.5 | 163 | ---- | ---- | ---- | 1,909 | 2.1643 |
| 2015 | 1,849.5 | 104,728 | 83.775 | 2,039 | 1,834 | 5.6 | 51 | ---- | ---- | ---- | 1,885 | 2.0886 |
| 2016 | 1,839.4 | 155,082 | 103.616 | 2,097 | 1,872 | 5.7 | 60 | ---- | ---- | ---- | 1,931 | 2.0815 |
| 2017 | 1,847.5 | 166,043 | 90.389 | 2,103 | 1,872 | 5.7 | 64 | ---- | ---- | ---- | 1,936 | 2.3278 |
| 2018 | 1,891.0 | 168,787 | 130.071 | 2,266 | 1,980 |  | 108 | ---- | ---- | ---- | 2,088 | 2.2503 |
| 2019 | 1,977.0 | 179,333 | 145.504 | 2,319 | 2,072 |  | 57 | ---- | ---- | ---- | 2,130 | 2.2302 |
| 2020 | 2,145.9 | 189,655 | 154.322 | 2,489 | 2,156 |  | 60 | ---- | ---- | ---- | 2,216 | 1.5782 |
| 2021[1] | 2,071.7 | 273,805 | 160.936 | 2,524 | 2,172 |  | 132 | ---- | ---- | ---- | 2,304 | 1.7325 |
| 2022[2] | 2,057.4 | 199,056 | 160.936 | 2,564 | 2,229 |  | 119 | ---- | ---- | ---- | 2,348 | ---- |

[1] Preliminary.  [2] Estimates.  [3] Includes butter-equivalent.  [4] Includes butteroil.  [5] Includes stocks held by USDA.
Source: Economic Research Service, U.S. Department of Agriculture (ERS-USDA)

## Quarterly Commercial Disappearance of Creamery Butter in the United States    In Millions of Pounds

| Year | First Quarter | Second Quarter | Third Quarter | Fourth Quarter | Total | Year | First Quarter | Second Quarter | Third Quarter | Fourth Quarter | Total |
|---|---|---|---|---|---|---|---|---|---|---|---|
| 2011 | 387.0 | 372.0 | 426.3 | 494.5 | 1,679.7 | 2017 | 412.9 | 428.8 | 463.5 | 550.5 | 1,855.8 |
| 2012 | 402.5 | 403.6 | 435.6 | 491.3 | 1,733.0 | 2018 | 429.0 | 421.6 | 468.5 | 576.2 | 1,895.3 |
| 2013 | 412.3 | 372.2 | 434.2 | 517.8 | 1,736.5 | 2019 | 442.7 | 427.2 | 472.9 | 594.2 | 1,937.0 |
| 2014 | 380.9 | 433.5 | 433.6 | 508.5 | 1,756.4 | 2020 | 461.4 | 514.2 | 485.7 | 611.1 | 2,072.4 |
| 2015 | 417.3 | 403.2 | 468.4 | 509.5 | 1,798.4 | 2021 | 504.8 | 470.9 | 540.5 | 623.9 | 2,140.2 |
| 2016 | 447.6 | 406.3 | 457.7 | 546.4 | 1,857.9 | 2022[1] | 483.0 | 468.0 | 491.0 | 552.0 | 1,994.0 |

[1] Preliminary.  Source: Economic Research Service, U.S. Department of Agriculture (ERS-USDA)

# BUTTER

## World Production of Butter[3]   In Thousands of Metric Tons

| Year | Argentina | Australia | Brazil | Canada | European Union | India | Japan | Mexico | New Zealand | Russia | Ukraine | United States | World Total |
|---|---|---|---|---|---|---|---|---|---|---|---|---|---|
| 2014 | 52 | 125 | 85 | 88 | 2,250 | 4,887 | 61 | 207 | 580 | 252 | 115 | 842 | 9,748 |
| 2015 | 46 | 120 | 83 | 91 | 2,335 | 5,035 | 65 | 216 | 594 | 260 | 103 | 839 | 9,999 |
| 2016 | 37 | 110 | 82 | 93 | 2,021 | 5,200 | 66 | 217 | 570 | 246 | 103 | 834 | 9,938 |
| 2017 | 30 | 103 | 83 | 109 | 2,031 | 5,400 | 60 | 223 | 525 | 270 | 109 | 838 | 10,161 |
| 2018 | 33 | 93 | 85 | 116 | 2,069 | 5,600 | 60 | 228 | 550 | 256 | 106 | 893 | 10,452 |
| 2019 | 33 | 70 | 85 | 112 | 2,125 | 5,850 | 62 | 231 | 525 | 268 | 89 | 905 | 10,775 |
| 2020 | 34 | 75 | 82 | 118 | 2,173 | 6,100 | 72 | 233 | 500 | 282 | 89 | 973 | 11,153 |
| 2021 | 41 | 70 | 82 | 122 | 2,141 | 6,300 | 71 | 235 | 470 | 270 | 72 | 940 | 11,256 |
| 2022[1] | 40 | 60 | 81 | 120 | 2,080 | 6,500 | 75 | 236 | 500 | 275 | 60 | 933 | 11,397 |
| 2023[2] | 40 | 50 | 82 | 125 | 2,040 | 6,700 | 77 | 245 | 475 | 280 | 55 | 975 | 11,584 |

[1] Preliminary.   [2] Forecast.   [3] Factory (including creameries and dairies) & farm.   NA = Not available.
*Source: Foreign Agricultural Service, U.S. Department of Agriculture (FAS-USDA)*

## World Consumption of Butter   In Thousands of Metric Tons

| Year | Argentina | Australia | Brazil | Canada | European Union | India | Japan | Mexico | Russia | Taiwan | Ukraine | United States | World Total |
|---|---|---|---|---|---|---|---|---|---|---|---|---|---|
| 2014 | 38 | 89 | 80 | 99 | 2,161 | 4,876 | 75 | 236 | 376 | 22 | 116 | 792 | 9,217 |
| 2015 | 37 | 94 | 84 | 106 | 2,150 | 5,032 | 77 | 249 | 350 | 25 | 97 | 832 | 9,373 |
| 2016 | 32 | 102 | 89 | 117 | 1,810 | 5,196 | 72 | 267 | 353 | 24 | 93 | 849 | 9,411 |
| 2017 | 28 | 115 | 88 | 121 | 1,862 | 5,387 | 72 | 264 | 357 | 24 | 82 | 849 | 9,701 |
| 2018 | 21 | 117 | 91 | 124 | 1,898 | 5,577 | 78 | 250 | 346 | 23 | 76 | 898 | 9,944 |
| 2019 | 19 | 104 | 89 | 141 | 1,900 | 5,803 | 83 | 277 | 384 | 24 | 80 | 940 | 10,315 |
| 2020 | 14 | 106 | 85 | 141 | 1,909 | 6,081 | 79 | 266 | 402 | 22 | 83 | 978 | 10,680 |
| 2021 | 10 | 95 | 88 | 147 | 1,927 | 6,289 | 81 | 256 | 393 | 22 | 72 | 985 | 10,897 |
| 2022[1] | 10 | 91 | 86 | 150 | 1,890 | 6,456 | 84 | 270 | 389 | 25 | 55 | 935 | 10,990 |
| 2023[2] | 10 | 92 | 88 | 155 | 1,845 | 6,645 | 85 | 273 | 400 | 25 | 60 | 985 | 11,209 |

[1] Preliminary.   [2] Forecast.   *Source: Foreign Agricultural Service, U.S. Department of Agriculture (FAS-USDA)*

## World Exports of Butter   In Thousands of Metric Tons

| Year | Argentina | Australia | Brazil | Canada | European Union | India | Mexico | New Zealand | Russia | Ukraine | United Kingdom | United States | World Total |
|---|---|---|---|---|---|---|---|---|---|---|---|---|---|
| 2014 | 14 | 44 | 6 | 2 | 143 | 10 | 8 | 560 | 4 | 5 | ---- | 74 | 928 |
| 2015 | 9 | 35 | 1 | 1 | 183 | 9 | 10 | 552 | 3 | 11 | ---- | 23 | 908 |
| 2016 | 6 | 30 | ---- | 1 | 302 | 9 | 15 | 554 | 4 | 9 | 65 | 27 | 1,100 |
| 2017 | 4 | 16 | ---- | 1 | 255 | 15 | 8 | 476 | 3 | 28 | 56 | 29 | 966 |
| 2018 | 11 | 17 | ---- | 2 | 247 | 33 | 11 | 501 | 3 | 29 | 65 | 49 | 1,048 |
| 2019 | 15 | 18 | 1 | 2 | 302 | 47 | 13 | 509 | 2 | 16 | 73 | 26 | 1,094 |
| 2020 | 21 | 16 | ---- | 5 | 316 | 20 | 9 | 471 | 3 | 9 | 65 | 27 | 1,032 |
| 2021 | 31 | 22 | 1 | 1 | 265 | 11 | 2 | 436 | 3 | 9 | 55 | 58 | 974 |
| 2022[1] | 30 | 20 | 1 | 1 | 260 | 44 | 1 | 500 | 3 | 10 | 50 | 84 | 1,084 |
| 2023[2] | 30 | 15 | 1 | 1 | 265 | 55 | 2 | 450 | 3 | 5 | 50 | 74 | 1,032 |

[1] Preliminary.   [2] Forecast.   *Source: Foreign Agricultural Service, U.S. Department of Agriculture (FAS-USDA)*

## World Imports of Butter   In Thousands of Metric Tons

| Year | Australia | Brazil | Canada | European Union | India | Japan | Mexico | New Zealand | Russia | Taiwan | Ukraine | United States | World Total |
|---|---|---|---|---|---|---|---|---|---|---|---|---|---|
| 2014 | 23 | 1 | 11 | 52 | 1 | 11 | 37 | 1 | 137 | 22 | 11 | 21 | 417 |
| 2015 | 22 | 2 | 17 | 27 | 6 | 16 | 43 | 1 | 90 | 25 | 1 | 38 | 363 |
| 2016 | 30 | 7 | 27 | 64 | 6 | 13 | 65 | 2 | 106 | 24 | 1 | 47 | 555 |
| 2017 | 35 | 5 | 22 | 62 | 2 | 8 | 49 | 1 | 99 | 24 | 1 | 41 | 525 |
| 2018 | 42 | 6 | 22 | 76 | 1 | 16 | 33 | 1 | 88 | 23 | 1 | 59 | 566 |
| 2019 | 40 | 5 | 25 | 77 | ---- | 25 | 59 | 1 | 117 | 24 | 4 | 66 | 608 |
| 2020 | 43 | 3 | 24 | 52 | 1 | 18 | 42 | 1 | 128 | 22 | 10 | 70 | 611 |
| 2021 | 37 | 7 | 28 | 51 | ---- | 12 | 23 | 1 | 122 | 22 | 10 | 69 | 576 |
| 2022[1] | 35 | 6 | 32 | 70 | ---- | 9 | 35 | 2 | 120 | 25 | 1 | 81 | 626 |
| 2023[2] | 40 | 7 | 30 | 70 | ---- | 9 | 30 | 1 | 125 | 25 | 10 | 74 | 626 |

[1] Preliminary.   [2] Forecast.   *Source: Foreign Agricultural Service, U.S. Department of Agriculture (FAS-USDA)*

# BUTTER

## World Ending Stocks of Butter    In Thousands of Metric Tons

| Year | Argentina | Australia | Canada | European Union | India | Japan | New Zealand | Russia | United States | World Total |
|---|---|---|---|---|---|---|---|---|---|---|
| 2014 | 4 | 64 | 9 | 22 | 8 | 15 | 53 | 19 | 48 | 251 |
| 2015 | 4 | 77 | 10 | 51 | 8 | 19 | 72 | 16 | 70 | 332 |
| 2016 | 3 | 85 | 12 | 25 | 9 | 26 | 62 | 11 | 75 | 314 |
| 2017 | 2 | 92 | 21 | ---- | 9 | 22 | 84 | 20 | 76 | 333 |
| 2018 | 3 | 93 | 33 | ---- | ---- | 20 | 105 | 15 | 81 | 359 |
| 2019 | 2 | 81 | 27 | ---- | ---- | 24 | 93 | 14 | 86 | 333 |
| 2020 | 1 | 77 | 23 | ---- | ---- | 35 | 93 | 19 | 124 | 385 |
| 2021 | 1 | 67 | 25 | ---- | ---- | 37 | 97 | 15 | 90 | 346 |
| 2022[1] | 1 | 51 | 26 | ---- | ---- | 37 | 67 | 18 | 85 | 295 |
| 2023[2] | 1 | 34 | 25 | ---- | ---- | 38 | 61 | 20 | 75 | 264 |

[1] Preliminary.   [2] Forecast.   Source: Foreign Agricultural Service, U.S. Department of Agriculture (FAS-USDA)

## Production of Creamery Butter in Factories in the United States    In Thousands of Pounds

| Year | Jan. | Feb. | Mar. | Apr. | May | June | July | Aug. | Sept. | Oct. | Nov. | Dec. | Total |
|---|---|---|---|---|---|---|---|---|---|---|---|---|---|
| 2013 | 188,037 | 173,335 | 181,421 | 166,658 | 163,785 | 140,124 | 132,746 | 134,370 | 132,232 | 145,886 | 142,192 | 161,730 | 1,862,516 |
| 2014 | 184,030 | 166,097 | 166,626 | 167,730 | 166,285 | 140,391 | 137,788 | 129,092 | 131,802 | 151,201 | 144,518 | 169,755 | 1,855,315 |
| 2015 | 173,634 | 155,976 | 167,816 | 165,457 | 169,409 | 143,692 | 135,525 | 128,072 | 133,652 | 148,414 | 152,323 | 175,549 | 1,849,519 |
| 2016 | 170,746 | 168,272 | 174,916 | 171,210 | 166,178 | 147,705 | 135,169 | 123,523 | 135,283 | 139,858 | 143,086 | 163,453 | 1,839,399 |
| 2017 | 178,060 | 161,013 | 177,021 | 161,956 | 163,397 | 139,200 | 135,625 | 131,152 | 134,552 | 144,671 | 149,721 | 171,105 | 1,847,473 |
| 2018 | 182,143 | 167,669 | 181,847 | 175,216 | 170,122 | 142,122 | 134,564 | 133,571 | 135,041 | 148,896 | 149,428 | 170,388 | 1,891,007 |
| 2019 | 189,642 | 164,525 | 180,694 | 172,371 | 170,044 | 154,848 | 150,705 | 141,323 | 144,334 | 162,921 | 161,852 | 183,774 | 1,977,033 |
| 2020 | 204,948 | 194,756 | 200,052 | 227,212 | 172,353 | 149,145 | 152,958 | 150,931 | 150,721 | 161,991 | 172,909 | 207,926 | 2,145,902 |
| 2021 | 222,262 | 188,833 | 199,574 | 182,991 | 183,041 | 156,965 | 147,112 | 147,053 | 143,640 | 164,296 | 155,987 | 179,962 | 2,071,716 |
| 2022[1] | 194,034 | 183,462 | 201,940 | 181,179 | 180,139 | 160,162 | 151,731 | 143,438 | 140,789 | 161,803 | 170,955 | 187,799 | 2,057,431 |

[1] Preliminary.   Source: Economic Research Service, U.S. Department of Agriculture (ERS-USDA)

## Cold Storage Holdings of Creamery Butter in the United States, on First of Month    In Millions of Pounds

| Year | Jan. | Feb. | Mar. | Apr. | May | June | July | Aug. | Sept. | Oct. | Nov. | Dec. |
|---|---|---|---|---|---|---|---|---|---|---|---|---|
| 2013 | 153,027 | 207,075 | 238,342 | 254,991 | 309,719 | 321,954 | 318,893 | 295,751 | 263,928 | 233,031 | 181,799 | 121,627 |
| 2014 | 112,467 | 143,890 | 171,773 | 191,755 | 186,914 | 209,430 | 199,248 | 180,834 | 172,789 | 152,361 | 147,956 | 107,566 |
| 2015 | 104,728 | 148,885 | 179,003 | 184,373 | 232,372 | 265,198 | 256,000 | 254,347 | 212,189 | 187,528 | 178,834 | 132,740 |
| 2016 | 155,082 | 192,101 | 235,559 | 243,134 | 295,771 | 324,942 | 328,149 | 332,848 | 318,774 | 269,125 | 228,158 | 161,203 |
| 2017 | 166,043 | 221,556 | 269,857 | 272,500 | 292,284 | 313,593 | 310,158 | 307,359 | 280,194 | 255,839 | 217,918 | 159,258 |
| 2018 | 168,787 | 226,694 | 265,756 | 273,955 | 307,325 | 338,492 | 336,625 | 318,325 | 209,851 | 282,379 | 231,223 | 154,366 |
| 2019 | 179,333 | 211,168 | 243,511 | 269,697 | 290,820 | 313,822 | 326,297 | 329,595 | 304,368 | 290,649 | 234,507 | 180,637 |
| 2020 | 189,655 | 247,376 | 301,820 | 309,587 | 372,598 | 375,777 | 362,452 | 371,467 | 371,519 | 343,948 | 299,731 | 251,820 |
| 2021 | 273,805 | 331,912 | 354,595 | 355,784 | 390,145 | 413,926 | 414,654 | 396,474 | 362,708 | 324,395 | 278,772 | 210,473 |
| 2022[1] | 199,056 | 219,353 | 263,028 | 282,821 | 298,334 | 321,579 | 330,844 | 315,100 | 278,303 | 267,339 | 239,658 | 199,778 |

[1] Preliminary.   Source: Agricultural Statistics Board, U.S. Department of Agriculture (ASB-USDA)

## Average Price of Butter at Chicago Mercantile Exchange    In Cents Per Pound

| Year | Jan. | Feb. | Mar. | Apr. | May | June | July | Aug. | Sept. | Oct. | Nov. | Dec. | Average |
|---|---|---|---|---|---|---|---|---|---|---|---|---|---|
| 2013 | 1.4933 | 1.5713 | 1.6421 | 1.7197 | 1.5997 | 1.5105 | 1.4751 | 1.4013 | 1.5233 | 1.5267 | 1.6126 | 1.5963 | 1.5560 |
| 2014 | 1.7756 | 1.8047 | 1.9145 | 1.9357 | 2.1713 | 2.2630 | 2.4624 | 2.5913 | 2.9740 | 2.3184 | 1.9968 | 1.7633 | 2.1643 |
| 2015 | 1.5714 | 1.7293 | 1.7166 | 1.7937 | 1.9309 | 1.9065 | 1.9056 | 2.1542 | 2.6690 | 2.4757 | 2.8779 | 2.3318 | 2.0886 |
| 2016 | 2.1214 | 2.0840 | 1.9605 | 2.0563 | 2.0554 | 2.2640 | 2.2731 | 2.1776 | 1.9950 | 1.8239 | 1.9899 | 2.1763 | 2.0815 |
| 2017 | 2.2393 | 2.1534 | 2.1392 | 2.0992 | 2.2684 | 2.5688 | 2.6195 | 2.6473 | 2.4370 | 2.3293 | 2.2244 | 2.2078 | 2.3278 |
| 2018 | 2.1587 | 2.1211 | 2.2011 | 2.3145 | 2.3751 | 2.3270 | 2.2361 | 2.3009 | 2.2545 | 2.2600 | 2.2480 | 2.2071 | 2.2503 |
| 2019 | 2.2481 | 2.2659 | 2.2773 | 2.2635 | 2.3366 | 2.3884 | 2.3897 | 2.2942 | 2.1690 | 2.1071 | 2.0495 | 1.9736 | 2.2302 |
| 2020 | 1.8813 | 1.7913 | 1.7235 | 1.1999 | 1.4710 | 1.8291 | 1.6925 | 1.5038 | 1.5163 | 1.4550 | 1.3941 | 1.4806 | 1.5782 |
| 2021 | 1.4548 | 1.3586 | 1.5898 | 1.7814 | 1.8107 | 1.7934 | 1.7401 | 1.6998 | 1.7725 | 1.7746 | 1.9503 | 2.0641 | 1.7325 |
| 2022 | 2.6130 | 2.6668 | 2.7260 | 2.7694 | 2.7360 | 2.9232 | 2.9461 | 2.9792 | 3.1156 | 3.1911 | 2.9560 | 2.7759 | 2.8665 |

Source: Economic Research Service, U.S. Department of Agriculture (ERS-USDA)

# Cadmium

Cadmium (atomic symbol Cd) is a soft, bluish-white, metallic element that can easily be shaped and cut with a knife. Cadmium melts at 321 degrees Celsius and boils at 765 degrees Celsius. Cadmium burns brightly in air when heated, forming the oxide CdO. In 1871, the German chemist Friedrich Stromeyer discovered cadmium in incrustations in zinc furnaces.

Rare greenockite is the only mineral-bearing cadmium. Cadmium occurs most often in small quantities associated with zinc ores, such as sphalerite. Electrolysis or fractional distillation is used to separate the cadmium and zinc. About 80% of world cadmium output is a by-product of zinc refining. The remaining 20% comes from secondary sources and the recycling of cadmium products. Cadmium recycling is practical only from nickel-cadmium batteries and from some alloys and dust from electric-arc furnaces.

Cadmium is used primarily for metal plating and coating operations in transportation equipment, machinery, baking enamels, photography, and television phosphors. It is also used in solar modules, pigments and lasers, and in nickel-cadmium and solar batteries.

**Supply** – World cadmium production in 2022 fell by -2.8% yr/yr at 24,000 metric tons, moderately below the 2018 record high of 27,000 metric tons. The largest producer was China, with 41.7% of total world production, followed by South Korea with 16.7%, Japan with 7.9%, and Canada with 7.5%.

**Trade** – In 2022 the U.S. imports fell by -76.4% yr/yr to 57 metric tons. U.S. exports of cadmium in 2021 fell by -65.7% yr/yr to 92 metric tons.

## World Refinery Production of Cadmium    In Metric Tons

| Year | Australia | Canada | China | Germany | India | Japan | Kazakh-stan | Korea, South | Mexico | Nether-lands | Russia | United States[3] | World Total |
|---|---|---|---|---|---|---|---|---|---|---|---|---|---|
| 2014 | 350 | 1,187 | 8,201 | 400 | 116 | 1,829 | 1,633 | 5,645 | 1,409 | 620 | 1,200 | W | 25,100 |
| 2015 | 380 | 1,159 | 8,162 | 400 | 130 | 1,959 | 1,475 | 5,600 | 1,283 | 1,100 | 1,200 | W | 25,100 |
| 2016 | 352 | 2,305 | 8,222 | 400 | 21 | 1,988 | 1,500 | 5,273 | 1,244 | 1,000 | 1,200 | W | 25,600 |
| 2017 | 388 | 1,802 | 8,411 | 500 | 61 | 2,142 | 1,500 | 4,960 | 1,142 | 890 | 1,200 | W | 25,300 |
| 2018 | 342 | 1,857 | 10,349 | 500 | ---- | 1,979 | 1,500 | 4,905 | 1,357 | 960 | 1,150 | W | 27,000 |
| 2019 | 174 | 1,803 | 10,000 | 500 | ---- | 1,783 | 1,500 | 4,400 | 1,395 | 860 | 1,000 | W | 25,500 |
| 2020 | 348 | 1,800 | 10,000 | 450 | ---- | 1,880 | 1,500 | 3,000 | 978 | 880 | 1,000 | W | 24,000 |
| 2021[1] | 402 | 1,800 | 10,000 | 417 | ---- | 1,900 | 1,200 | 4,000 | 859 | 854 | 1,000 | 241 | 24,700 |
| 2022[2] | 400 | 1,800 | 10,000 | 420 | | 1,900 | 1,200 | 4,000 | 1,200 | 500 | 1,000 | 250 | 24,000 |

[1] Preliminary.   [2] Estimate.   [3] Primary and secondary metal.   *Source: U.S. Geological Survey (USGS)*

## Salient Statistics of Cadmium in the United States    In Metric Tons of Contained Cadmium

| Year | Net import Reliance As a % of Apparent Consumption | Production (Metal) | Producer Shipments | Cadmium Sulfide Production | Production Other Compounds | Imports of Cadmium Metal[3] | Exports[4] | Apparent Consumption | Industry Stocks Dec. 31[5] | New York Dealer Price $ Per Lb. |
|---|---|---|---|---|---|---|---|---|---|---|
| 2014 | E | W | W | ---- | ---- | 139 | 270 | W | W | .88 |
| 2015 | E | W | W | ---- | ---- | 326 | 596 | W | W | .67 |
| 2016 | <25 | W | W | ---- | ---- | 292 | 540 | W | W | .61 |
| 2017 | <25 | W | W | ---- | ---- | 296 | 428 | W | W | .79 |
| 2018 | <75 | W | W | ---- | ---- | 294 | 139 | W | W | 1.31 |
| 2019 | <75 | W | W | ---- | ---- | 492 | 122 | W | W | 1.21 |
| 2020 | <75 | W | W | ---- | ---- | 375 | 486 | W | W | 1.04 |
| 2021[1] | <50 | W | W | ---- | ---- | 242 | 268 | W | W | 1.16 |
| 2022[2] | <25 | W | W | ---- | ---- | 57 | 92 | W | W | 1.50 |

[1] Preliminary.   [2] Estimate.   [3] For consumption.   [4] Cadmium metal, alloys, dross, flue dust.   [5] Metallic, Compounds, Distributors.   [6] Sticks & Balls in 1 to 5 short ton lots of metal (99.95%).   E = Net exporter.   *Source: U.S. Geological Survey (USGS)*

## Average Price of Cadmium (99.95%) in the United States    In Dollars Per Pound

| Year | Jan. | Feb. | Mar. | Apr. | May | June | July | Aug. | Sept. | Oct. | Nov. | Dec. | Average |
|---|---|---|---|---|---|---|---|---|---|---|---|---|---|
| 2014 | 82.98 | 82.50 | 80.71 | 80.00 | 80.00 | 80.00 | 80.00 | 81.90 | 85.00 | 85.00 | 83.06 | 80.00 | 81.76 |
| 2015 | 79.90 | 73.82 | 64.61 | 54.91 | 50.25 | 44.66 | 41.97 | 39.16 | 35.50 | 36.11 | 39.33 | 42.83 | 50.25 |
| 2016 | 46.79 | 52.36 | 58.74 | 68.79 | 73.00 | 71.64 | 64.29 | 54.30 | 50.77 | 54.05 | 63.89 | 67.50 | 60.51 |
| 2017 | 67.50 | 70.75 | 74.20 | 77.90 | 78.35 | 74.32 | 70.69 | 70.50 | 71.64 | 90.86 | 104.55 | 102.14 | 79.45 |
| 2018 | 101.00 | 121.85 | 152.50 | 155.43 | 143.46 | 130.83 | 129.66 | 127.50 | 127.50 | 127.50 | 127.50 | 126.50 | 130.94 |
| 2019 | 125.30 | 135.88 | 138.00 | 137.66 | 131.11 | 123.10 | 113.22 | 109.09 | 108.57 | 110.00 | 108.10 | 116.38 | 121.37 |
| 2020 | 119.15 | 119.75 | 121.50 | 116.67 | 107.50 | 105.00 | 97.30 | 94.25 | 91.61 | 89.56 | 89.75 | 93.89 | 103.83 |
| 2021 | 96.22 | 110.38 | 24.56 | 129.50 | 129.50 | 116.17 | 104.94 | 96.25 | 104.28 | 118.33 | 130.25 | 131.90 | 107.69 |
| 2022 | 132.50 | 134.38 | 144.95 | 154.67 | 158.13 | 156.67 | 154.34 | 150.67 | 157.33 | 166.88 | 172.45 | 180.00 | 155.25 |

*Source: American Metal Market (AMM)*

# Canola (Rapeseed)

Canola is a genetic variation of rapeseed that was developed by Canadian plant breeders specifically for its nutritional qualities and its low level of saturated fat. The term *Canola* is a contraction of "Canadian oil." The history of canola oil begins with the rapeseed plant, a member of the mustard family. The rape plant is grown both as feed for livestock and birdfeed. For 4,000 years, the oil from the rapeseed was used in China and India for cooking and as lamp oil. During World War II, rapeseed oil was used as a marine and industrial lubricant. After the war, the market for rapeseed oil plummeted. Rapeseed growers needed other uses for their crops, and that stimulated the research that led to the development of canola. In 1974, Canadian plant breeders from the University of Manitoba produced canola by genetically altering rapeseed. Each canola plant produces yellow flowers, which then produce pods. The tiny round seeds within each pod are crushed to produce canola oil. Each canola seed contains approximately 40% oil. Canola oil is the world's third-largest source of vegetable oil, accounting for 13% of world vegetable oils, following soybean oil at 32%, and palm oil at 28%. The rest of the seed is processed into canola meal, which is used as high-protein livestock feed.

The climate in Canada is especially suitable for canola plant growth. Today, over 13 million acres of Canadian soil are dedicated to canola production. Canola oil is Canada's leading vegetable oil. Due to strong demand from the U.S. for canola oil, approximately 70% of Canada's canola oil is exported to the U.S. Canola oil is used as a salad oil, cooking oil, and for margarine as well as in the manufacture of inks, biodegradable greases, pharmaceuticals, fuel, soap, and cosmetics.

Canola futures and options are traded on the ICE Futures U.S. exchange. The futures contract calls for the delivery of 20 metric tons of canola and 5 contracts are together called a "1 board lot." The futures contract is priced in Canadian dollars per metric ton.

**Prices** – ICE canola prices on the nearest-futures chart (Barchart.com symbol code RS) in 2022 fell by -15.2% yr/yr to CD $858.40 per metric ton. The average monthly wholesale price of canola oil in the Midwest in 2022 rose by +13.2% yr/yr to 89.59 cents per pound. The average monthly wholesale price of canola meal (delivery Pacific Northwest) in the 2021/22 crop year rose by +24.8% to $439.10 per short ton.

**Supply** – World canola production in the 2022/23 marketing year is forecasted to rise by +14.2% yr/yr to 84,786 million metric tons, a new record high from 2017/2018. The world's largest canola producers in 2022/23 are expected to be the European Union with 23.0% of world production, Canada with 22.4%, China with 17.3%, and India with 13.6%. U.S. production of canola in 2022/23 is expected to rise by +40.0% yr/yr to 1.742 million metric tons. U.S. production of canola oil in 2022/23 is expected to rise by +28.9% to 866,000 metric tons, forecasted to be a new record high. World production of canola meal in 2022/23 is expected to rise by +7.6% to 44.987 million metric tons.

**Demand** – World crush demand for canola in 2022/23 is expected to rise by +8.5% yr/yr to 77.802 million metric tons. World consumption of canola meal in 2022/23 is expected to rise by +7.3% yr/yr to 44.598 million metric tons. World consumption of canola oil in 2022/23 is expected to rise by +6.0% to 31.207 million metric tons.

**Trade** – World canola exports in 2022/23 are expected to rise by +24.8% to 18,249 million metric tons becoming the new record high. World canola oil exports are expected to rise by +27.1% to 6.697 million metric tons, becoming a new record high since 2020/21. World canola meal exports are expected to rise by +6.3% yr/yr to 8.121 million metric tons, resulting in 2020/21 remaining the record high. World canola imports in 2022/23 are expected to rise by +21.8% to 16.914 million metric tons, world canola oil imports are expected to rise by +28.3% to 6.600 million metric tons, and world canola meal imports are expected to rise by +5.9% to 8.018 million metric tons. Regarding U.S. canola trade, U.S. canola imports in 2022/23 are expected to rise by +24.4% to 612,000 metric tons, and U.S. exports are expected to rise by +42.2% to 182,000 metric tons.

## World Production of Canola (Rapeseed)   In Thousands of Metric Tons

| Year | Australia | Bangla-desh | Belarus | Canada | China | European Union | India | Kazakh-stan | Pakistan | Russia | Ukraine | United States | World Total |
|---|---|---|---|---|---|---|---|---|---|---|---|---|---|
| 2013-14 | 3,832 | 230 | 676 | 18,551 | 13,523 | 21,306 | 6,650 | 242 | 220 | 1,259 | 2,352 | 1,000 | 70,630 |
| 2014-15 | 3,540 | 230 | 730 | 16,410 | 13,914 | 24,587 | 5,080 | 241 | 211 | 1,324 | 2,200 | 1,138 | 70,429 |
| 2015-16 | 2,775 | 230 | 382 | 18,377 | 13,859 | 21,997 | 5,920 | 138 | 200 | 1,001 | 1,744 | 1,305 | 68,840 |
| 2016-17 | 4,313 | 230 | 260 | 19,599 | 13,128 | 18,763 | 6,620 | 170 | 181 | 997 | 1,250 | 1,405 | 69,570 |
| 2017-18 | 3,893 | 230 | 603 | 21,458 | 13,274 | 20,017 | 7,100 | 279 | 225 | 1,497 | 2,217 | 1,394 | 75,287 |
| 2018-19 | 2,366 | 230 | 456 | 20,724 | 13,281 | 18,048 | 7,500 | 394 | 302 | 1,989 | 2,850 | 1,644 | 72,886 |
| 2019-20 | 2,299 | 230 | 578 | 19,912 | 13,485 | 15,252 | 7,400 | 241 | 488 | 2,040 | 3,465 | 1,553 | 69,635 |
| 2020-21[1] | 4,756 | 230 | 731 | 19,485 | 14,049 | 16,732 | 8,500 | 153 | 337 | 2,567 | 2,750 | 1,575 | 73,892 |
| 2021-22[2] | 7,050 | 230 | 500 | 13,757 | 14,714 | 17,216 | 11,000 | 146 | 470 | 2,775 | 3,015 | 1,244 | 74,240 |
| 2022-23[3] | 7,300 | 230 | 550 | 19,000 | 14,700 | 19,500 | 11,500 | 160 | 490 | 3,900 | 3,200 | 1,742 | 84,786 |

[1] Preliminary.   [2] Estimate.   [3] Forecast.   Source: Economic Research Service, U.S. Department of Agriculture (ERS-USDA); The Oil World

# CANOLA

**World Supply and Distribution of Canola**  In Thousands of Metric Tons

| Crop Year | Production | Imports | Total | Exports | Crush | Consumption | Ending Stocks |
|---|---|---|---|---|---|---|---|
| 2013-14 | 70,630 | 15,550 | 91,686 | 15,100 | 66,232 | 68,819 | 7,767 |
| 2014-15 | 70,429 | 14,316 | 92,512 | 15,105 | 67,092 | 70,084 | 7,323 |
| 2015-16 | 68,840 | 14,106 | 90,269 | 14,399 | 66,697 | 69,618 | 6,252 |
| 2016-17 | 69,570 | 15,795 | 91,674 | 16,145 | 67,421 | 70,339 | 5,190 |
| 2017-18 | 75,287 | 15,719 | 96,196 | 16,595 | 68,450 | 71,561 | 8,040 |
| 2018-19 | 72,886 | 14,635 | 95,561 | 14,678 | 68,044 | 71,081 | 9,802 |
| 2019-20 | 69,635 | 15,711 | 95,148 | 15,982 | 68,490 | 71,600 | 7,566 |
| 2020-21[1] | 73,892 | 16,662 | 98,120 | 18,106 | 71,194 | 73,717 | 6,297 |
| 2021-22[2] | 74,240 | 13,883 | 94,420 | 14,626 | 71,680 | 75,317 | 4,477 |
| 2022-23[3] | 84,786 | 16,914 | 106,177 | 18,249 | 77,802 | 81,173 | 6,755 |

Crop year beginning June 1.   [1] Preliminary.   [2] Estimate.   [3] Forecast.   *Source: Economic Research Service, U.S. Department of Agriculture (USDA)*

**World Supply and Distribution of Canola Meal**  In Thousands of Metric Tons

| Crop Year | Production | Imports | Total | Exports | Consumption | Ending Stocks |
|---|---|---|---|---|---|---|
| 2013-14 | 38,317 | 6,502 | 45,809 | 6,357 | 38,516 | 936 |
| 2014-15 | 38,715 | 6,008 | 45,659 | 6,068 | 38,593 | 998 |
| 2015-16 | 38,592 | 5,691 | 45,281 | 5,695 | 38,456 | 1,130 |
| 2016-17 | 38,802 | 6,176 | 46,287 | 6,255 | 38,608 | 1,424 |
| 2017-18 | 39,417 | 6,465 | 47,306 | 6,675 | 39,115 | 1,516 |
| 2018-19 | 39,202 | 7,135 | 47,853 | 7,217 | 39,363 | 1,273 |
| 2019-20 | 39,533 | 7,966 | 48,772 | 7,722 | 39,602 | 1,448 |
| 2020-21[1] | 41,101 | 8,299 | 50,848 | 8,222 | 41,333 | 1,293 |
| 2021-22[2] | 41,803 | 7,570 | 50,666 | 7,641 | 41,554 | 1,471 |
| 2022-23[3] | 44,987 | 8,018 | 54,476 | 8,121 | 44,598 | 1,757 |

Crop year beginning June 1.   [1] Preliminary.   [2] Estimate.   [3] Forecast.   *Source: Economic Research Service, U.S. Department of Agriculture (USDA)*

**World Supply and Distribution of Canola Oil**  In Thousands of Metric Tons

| Crop Year | Production | Imports | Total | Exports | Consumption | Ending Stocks |
|---|---|---|---|---|---|---|
| 2013-14 | 27,050 | 3,809 | 35,802 | 3,829 | 25,701 | 6,272 |
| 2014-15 | 27,449 | 3,948 | 37,669 | 4,066 | 26,945 | 6,658 |
| 2015-16 | 27,373 | 4,123 | 38,154 | 4,171 | 28,284 | 5,699 |
| 2016-17 | 27,602 | 4,548 | 37,801 | 4,638 | 28,958 | 4,205 |
| 2017-18 | 28,133 | 4,828 | 37,166 | 4,834 | 28,961 | 3,371 |
| 2018-19 | 27,800 | 5,177 | 36,348 | 5,263 | 28,139 | 2,946 |
| 2019-20 | 28,136 | 5,798 | 36,880 | 5,874 | 28,184 | 2,822 |
| 2020-21[1] | 29,114 | 6,319 | 38,255 | 6,411 | 28,461 | 3,383 |
| 2021-22[2] | 29,068 | 5,143 | 37,594 | 5,271 | 29,439 | 2,884 |
| 2022-23[3] | 31,800 | 6,600 | 41,284 | 6,697 | 31,207 | 3,380 |

Crop year beginning June 1.   [1] Preliminary.   [2] Estimate.   [3] Forecast.   *Source: Economic Research Service, U.S. Department of Agriculture (USDA)*

**Salient Statistics of Canola in the United States**  In Thousands of Metric Tons

| Crop Year | Beginning Stocks | Imports | Imports | Total | Exports | Crush | Consumption |
|---|---|---|---|---|---|---|---|
| 2013-14 | 81 | 1,000 | 927 | 2,008 | 159 | 1,685 | 2,008 |
| 2014-15 | 129 | 1,138 | 777 | 2,044 | 160 | 1,737 | 2,044 |
| 2015-16 | 110 | 1,305 | 359 | 1,774 | 176 | 1,542 | 1,774 |
| 2016-17 | 161 | 1,405 | 697 | 2,263 | 118 | 2,003 | 2,263 |
| 2017-18 | 109 | 1,394 | 651 | 2,154 | 154 | 1,765 | 2,154 |
| 2018-19 | 88 | 1,644 | 564 | 2,296 | 181 | 1,722 | 2,296 |
| 2019-20 | 139 | 1,553 | 563 | 2,255 | 183 | 1,834 | 2,255 |
| 2020-21[1] | 219 | 1,575 | 440 | 2,234 | 156 | 2,080 | 2,234 |
| 2021-22[2] | 214 | 1,244 | 492 | 1,950 | 128 | 1,658 | 1,950 |
| 2022-23[3] | 110 | 1,742 | 612 | 2,464 | 182 | 2,004 | 2,464 |

Crop year beginning June 1.   [1] Preliminary.   [2] Estimate.   [3] Forecast.   *Source: Economic Research Service, U.S. Department of Agriculture (USDA)*

# CANOLA

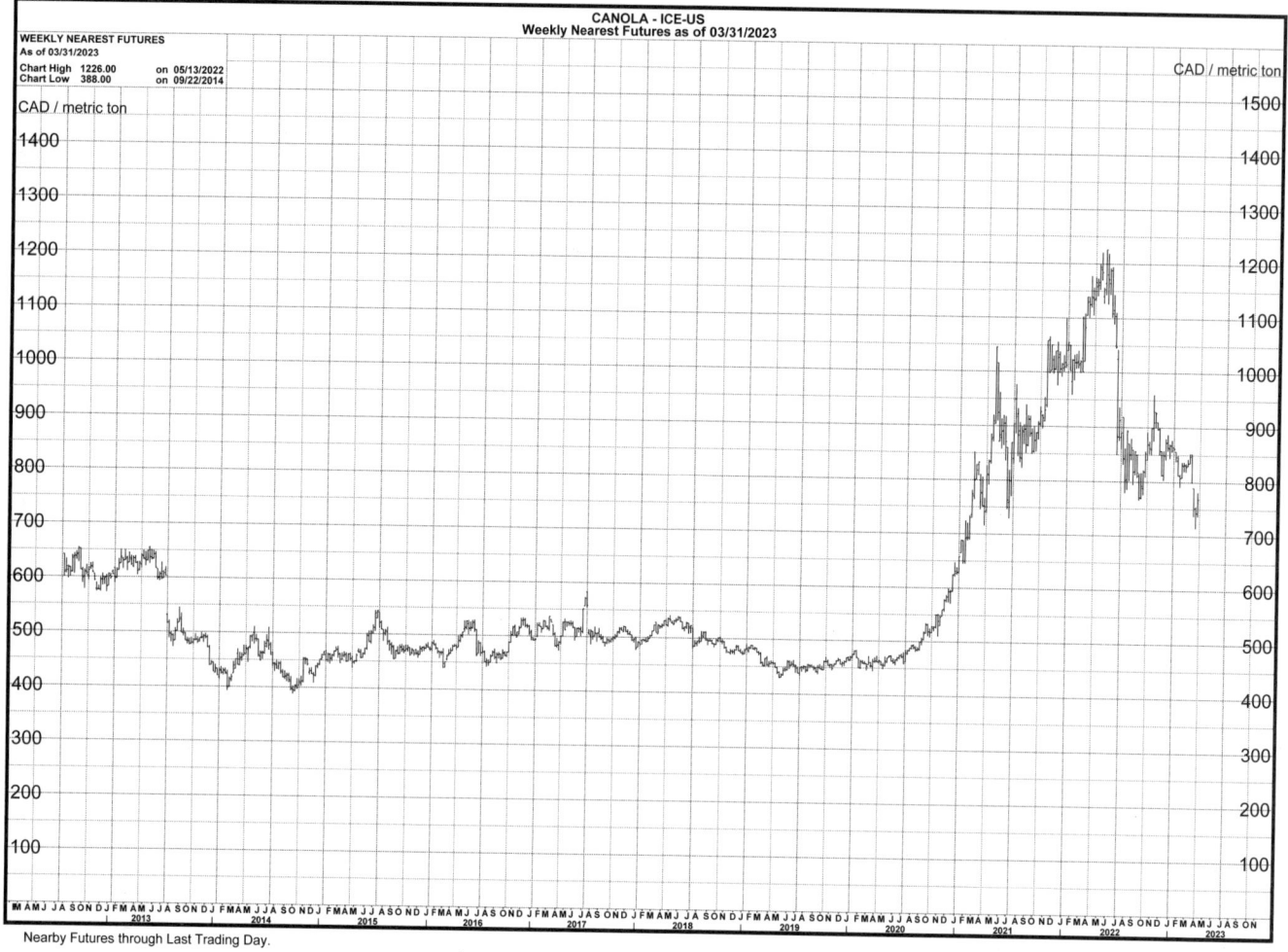

**CANOLA - ICE-US**
Weekly Nearest Futures as of 03/31/2023

WEEKLY NEAREST FUTURES
As of 03/31/2023
Chart High 1226.00 on 05/13/2022
Chart Low 388.00 on 09/22/2014

CAD / metric ton

Nearby Futures through Last Trading Day.

## Volume of Trading of Canola Futures in Winnipeg   In 20 Metric Ton Units

| Year | Jan. | Feb. | Mar. | Apr. | May | June | July | Aug. | Sept. | Oct. | Nov. | Dec. | Total |
|---|---|---|---|---|---|---|---|---|---|---|---|---|---|
| 2013 | 413,545 | 558,269 | 295,056 | 489,741 | 355,341 | 347,609 | 276,608 | 381,094 | 523,431 | 654,471 | 479,983 | 716,539 | 5,491,687 |
| 2014 | 536,669 | 570,465 | 454,015 | 552,959 | 369,170 | 424,087 | 331,748 | 298,308 | 486,457 | 615,158 | 479,983 | 716,539 | 5,491,687 |
| 2015 | 489,637 | 486,854 | 400,209 | 447,467 | 327,911 | 644,971 | 335,432 | 365,804 | 447,279 | 624,741 | 346,000 | 568,886 | 5,553,922 |
| 2016 | 408,059 | 641,600 | 441,094 | 619,493 | 518,643 | 644,052 | 358,823 | 385,481 | 407,031 | 702,156 | 403,539 | 585,625 | 5,559,469 |
| 2017 | 397,507 | 549,415 | 508,671 | 521,424 | 344,251 | 530,093 | 331,900 | 298,854 | 390,755 | 625,937 | 490,671 | 627,053 | 6,244,156 |
| 2018 | 349,016 | 530,467 | 351,802 | 541,694 | 324,795 | 561,388 | 269,381 | 251,140 | 260,732 | 537,386 | 381,367 | 511,181 | 5,391,355 |
| 2019 | 368,405 | 516,738 | 415,251 | 588,285 | 438,572 | 513,703 | 275,852 | 296,384 | 435,966 | 767,539 | 333,575 | 516,654 | 4,828,030 |
| 2020 | 496,090 | 575,177 | 481,171 | 426,406 | 297,740 | 508,999 | 409,940 | 425,008 | 661,995 | 702,630 | 323,919 | 671,042 | 5,611,656 |
| 2021 | 664,635 | 538,933 | 550,593 | 480,895 | 434,674 | 457,399 | 389,025 | 369,036 | 543,404 | 578,551 | 505,482 | 729,352 | 6,219,990 |
| 2022 | 483,771 | 457,952 | 391,689 | 383,358 | 333,590 | 535,822 | 344,636 | 514,163 | 684,010 | 728,966 | 696,913 | 546,626 | 6,101,496 |

Contract size = 20 tonnes.   Source: ICE Futures Canada (ICE)

## Average Open Interest of Canola Futures in Winnipeg   In 20 Metric Ton Units

| Year | Jan. | Feb. | Mar. | Apr. | May | June | July | Aug. | Sept. | Oct. | Nov. | Dec. |
|---|---|---|---|---|---|---|---|---|---|---|---|---|
| 2013 | 155,134 | 189,913 | 178,763 | 164,200 | 143,013 | 129,283 | 118,115 | 145,257 | 186,811 | 177,248 | 200,975 | 226,220 |
| 2014 | 230,796 | 224,847 | 230,852 | 219,844 | 168,705 | 165,651 | 147,462 | 165,501 | 173,282 | 159,986 | 142,371 | 139,732 |
| 2015 | 170,492 | 217,729 | 205,075 | 168,204 | 151,739 | 189,500 | 180,410 | 173,734 | 172,828 | 186,334 | 174,098 | 187,855 |
| 2016 | 187,904 | 177,999 | 171,820 | 162,225 | 173,204 | 172,984 | 155,301 | 173,698 | 195,884 | 190,086 | 208,329 | 210,792 |
| 2017 | 181,938 | 181,007 | 185,572 | 185,411 | 178,603 | 159,381 | 117,599 | 128,345 | 180,168 | 173,585 | 192,341 | 171,325 |
| 2018 | 171,262 | 180,496 | 184,370 | 210,695 | 207,565 | 200,361 | 172,198 | 173,769 | 178,603 | 147,365 | 168,872 | 175,750 |
| 2019 | 179,931 | 175,601 | 186,451 | 182,587 | 181,226 | 149,724 | 145,360 | 160,362 | 191,328 | 189,443 | 178,886 | 185,330 |
| 2020 | 187,307 | 189,665 | 177,355 | 173,681 | 178,525 | 171,799 | 165,281 | 199,313 | 230,858 | 205,153 | 220,330 | 210,429 |
| 2021 | 208,767 | 214,023 | 215,803 | 200,943 | 189,813 | 197,136 | 205,549 | 215,315 | 210,134 | 205,707 | 194,497 | 184,288 |
| 2022 | 173,223 | 157,954 | 146,356 | 143,578 | 140,476 | 141,374 | 132,475 | 157,169 | 204,760 | 218,705 | 232,219 | 231,568 |

Contract size = 20 tonnes.   Source: ICE Futures Canada (ICE)

# CANOLA

### Production of Canola in the United States, by States — In Thousands of Pounds

| Year | Idaho | Kansas | Minnesota | Montana | North Dakota | Oklahoma | Oregon | Washington | Other | Total |
|---|---|---|---|---|---|---|---|---|---|---|
| 2012 | 65,700 | ---- | 43,365 | 59,400 | 2,007,900 | 139,650 | 14,145 | 26,100 | 35,350 | 2,391,610 |
| 2013 | 79,550 | ---- | 32,175 | 106,260 | 1,665,300 | 208,600 | 19,360 | 61,200 | 38,060 | 2,210,505 |
| 2014 | 61,200 | ---- | 22,275 | 84,180 | 2,142,000 | 96,100 | 15,000 | 56,400 | 33,840 | 2,510,995 |
| 2015 | 37,800 | ---- | 40,420 | 93,940 | 2,492,000 | 131,100 | 3,240 | 37,400 | 42,570 | 2,878,470 |
| 2016 | 45,100 | 46,560 | 46,750 | 100,200 | 2,668,000 | 101,500 | 8,880 | 62,000 | ---- | 3,078,990 |
| 2017 | 37,910 | 62,040 | 71,760 | 117,820 | 2,496,000 | 168,000 | 11,160 | 90,720 | ---- | 3,055,410 |
| 2018 | 88,200 | 33,600 | 92,700 | 129,920 | 3,096,800 | 46,640 | 7,650 | 119,930 | ---- | 3,615,440 |
| 2019 | ---- | 20,710 | 110,095 | 200,100 | 2,898,000 | 29,610 | ---- | 142,350 | ---- | 3,400,865 |
| 2020 | ---- | 5,012 | 75,360 | 241,380 | 2,920,400 | 10,710 | ---- | 200,200 | ---- | 3,453,062 |
| 2021[1] | ---- | 7,800 | 104,550 | 144,900 | 2,304,800 | 15,500 | ---- | 143,000 | ---- | 2,720,550 |

[1] Preliminary. Source: Economic Research Service, U.S. Department of Agriculture (ERS-USDA)

### Average Price Received by Farmers for Canola in the United States — In U.S. Dollars per cwt.

| Year | Jan. | Feb. | Mar. | Apr. | May | June | July | Aug. | Sept. | Oct. | Nov. | Dec. | Average |
|---|---|---|---|---|---|---|---|---|---|---|---|---|---|
| 2013 | 26.80 | 27.80 | 27.30 | 27.50 | 28.00 | 27.40 | 26.20 | 22.20 | 20.70 | 21.00 | 20.30 | 20.70 | 24.66 |
| 2014 | 19.80 | 18.50 | 18.40 | 19.50 | 21.70 | 20.80 | 20.70 | 17.80 | 16.20 | 15.80 | 17.10 | 16.60 | 18.58 |
| 2015 | 17.80 | 17.20 | 16.60 | 16.30 | 16.70 | 17.80 | 18.10 | 15.60 | 15.10 | 14.80 | 15.10 | 14.90 | 16.33 |
| 2016 | 13.80 | 15.30 | 15.10 | 16.10 | W | 18.80 | 16.60 | 15.60 | 15.50 | 15.80 | 16.20 | 17.10 | 15.99 |
| 2017 | 17.30 | 17.40 | 17.60 | 18.00 | 16.80 | 17.40 | 17.80 | 17.70 | 17.30 | 16.60 | 17.20 | 16.70 | 17.32 |
| 2018 | 17.70 | 18.30 | 18.20 | 17.50 | 18.50 | 17.20 | 17.10 | 15.30 | 15.20 | 15.60 | 16.10 | 16.30 | 16.92 |
| 2019 | 16.70 | 16.20 | 15.80 | 15.80 | 15.20 | 14.90 | 14.80 | 14.50 | 14.20 | 14.20 | 14.30 | 14.70 | 15.11 |
| 2020 | 16.10 | 16.10 | 15.70 | 15.20 | 14.40 | 15.20 | 15.60 | 15.10 | 16.40 | 16.30 | 18.10 | 17.20 | 15.95 |
| 2021 | 18.80 | 20.40 | 22.00 | 23.80 | 26.10 | 26.00 | 27.70 | 30.90 | 28.70 | 29.60 | 31.70 | 32.50 | 26.52 |
| 2022[1] | 33.70 | 37.50 | 39.10 | 41.30 | 42.90 | 45.60 | 42.70 | 40.00 | 28.10 | 28.10 | 29.20 | 29.20 | 36.45 |

[1] Preliminary. Source: Economic Research Service, U.S. Department of Agriculture (ERS-USDA)

### Wholesale Price of Canola Oil in Midwest — In Cents Per Pound

| Year | Jan. | Feb. | Mar. | Apr. | May | June | July | Aug. | Sept. | Oct. | Nov. | Dec. | Average |
|---|---|---|---|---|---|---|---|---|---|---|---|---|---|
| 2013 | 57.19 | 59.38 | 58.95 | 60.44 | 60.45 | 57.50 | 53.25 | 48.05 | 46.00 | 44.88 | 45.05 | 42.63 | 52.81 |
| 2014 | 39.75 | 42.56 | 45.75 | 47.63 | 47.50 | 46.00 | 43.63 | 40.10 | 38.94 | 39.45 | 38.94 | 39.25 | 42.46 |
| 2015 | 38.80 | 38.94 | 35.69 | 37.19 | 38.55 | 40.19 | 38.30 | 35.13 | 33.31 | 34.20 | 33.63 | 36.50 | 36.70 |
| 2016 | 34.06 | 34.63 | 35.55 | 36.80 | 35.06 | 35.10 | 33.55 | 36.94 | 37.25 | 38.94 | 39.25 | 40.20 | 36.44 |
| 2017 | 38.69 | 37.25 | 37.30 | 36.13 | 37.06 | 37.85 | 39.75 | 41.19 | 41.15 | 39.06 | 39.69 | 38.65 | 38.65 |
| 2018 | 38.31 | 37.44 | 37.10 | 37.31 | 38.25 | 37.75 | 38.69 | 38.75 | 38.19 | 38.94 | 37.45 | 36.75 | 37.91 |
| 2019 | 37.13 | 37.75 | 36.15 | 35.44 | 34.10 | 34.63 | 34.56 | 35.25 | 35.00 | 36.31 | 36.15 | 38.06 | 35.88 |
| 2020 | 37.90 | 35.50 | 32.88 | 32.38 | 32.40 | 36.63 | 40.50 | 47.81 | 47.94 | 44.35 | 49.50 | 51.65 | 40.79 |
| 2021 | 53.31 | 58.94 | 71.31 | 79.55 | 94.06 | 93.50 | 92.30 | 81.00 | 76.00 | 82.30 | 84.38 | 82.95 | 79.13 |
| 2022[1] | 88.56 | 85.88 | 92.00 | 103.15 | 108.69 | 102.25 | 87.90 | 91.31 | 76.85 | 80.13 | 84.38 | 74.05 | 89.59 |

[1] Preliminary. Source: Economic Research Service, U.S. Department of Agriculture (ERS-USDA)

### Average Wholesale Price of Canola Meal, 36% Pacific Northwest — In Dollars Per Short Ton

| Crop Year | Oct. | Nov. | Dec. | Jan. | Feb. | Mar. | Apr. | May | June | July | Aug. | Sept. | Average |
|---|---|---|---|---|---|---|---|---|---|---|---|---|---|
| 2013-14 | 334.95 | 342.86 | 373.60 | 365.48 | 384.21 | 383.68 | 398.39 | 407.14 | 387.65 | 317.81 | 303.74 | 316.94 | 359.70 |
| 2014-15 | 301.75 | 356.31 | 349.31 | 311.56 | 296.21 | 279.54 | 261.35 | 274.60 | 305.85 | 328.03 | 285.83 | 264.01 | 301.20 |
| 2015-16 | 257.69 | 248.98 | 240.64 | 231.76 | 224.34 | 228.87 | 247.53 | 329.01 | 345.14 | 306.03 | 255.35 | 231.00 | 262.20 |
| 2016-17 | 225.05 | 234.78 | 243.30 | 267.41 | 276.90 | 276.33 | 270.66 | 279.64 | 281.66 | 307.73 | 289.45 | 262.33 | 267.94 |
| 2017-18 | 257.73 | 255.74 | 266.53 | 270.20 | 315.95 | 334.58 | 332.16 | 336.93 | 302.75 | 279.84 | 274.55 | 266.86 | 291.15 |
| 2018-19 | 279.40 | 279.16 | 291.42 | ---- | ---- | ---- | ---- | 259.55 | 278.76 | 265.45 | ---- | 253.03 | 272.40 |
| 2019-20 | 267.90 | ---- | ---- | ---- | 253.67 | 274.75 | 274.53 | 276.25 | 270.03 | 271.11 | 281.09 | 296.60 | 273.99 |
| 2020-21 | 327.24 | 333.89 | 338.55 | 387.53 | 376.08 | 365.14 | 377.58 | 391.45 | 345.90 | 326.68 | 329.45 | 322.96 | 351.87 |
| 2021-22 | 322.83 | 350.22 | 382.97 | 410.88 | 454.63 | 487.04 | 470.78 | 454.50 | 478.18 | 501.18 | 521.53 | 434.54 | 439.10 |
| 2022-23[1] | 409.18 | 403.00 | 437.10 | 474.03 | 501.03 | | | | | | | | 444.87 |

[1] Preliminary. Source: Economic Research Service, U.S. Department of Agriculture (ERS-USDA)

# Cattle and Calves

The beef cycle begins with the cow-calf operation, which breeds the new calves. Most ranchers breed their herds of cows in summer, thus producing the new crop of calves in spring (the gestation period is about nine months). This allows the calves to be born during the milder weather of spring and provides the calves with ample forage through the summer and early autumn. The calves are weaned from the mother after 6-8 months, and most are then moved into the "stocker" operation. The calves usually spend 6-10 months in the stocker operation, growing to near full-sized by foraging for summer grass or winter wheat. When the cattle reach 600-800 pounds, they are typically sent to a feedlot and become "feeder cattle." In the feedlot, the cattle are fed with a special food mix to encourage rapid weight gain. The mix includes grain (corn, milo, or wheat), a protein supplement (soybean, cottonseed, or linseed meal), and roughage (alfalfa, silage, prairie hay, or an agricultural by-product such as sugar beet pulp). The animal is considered "finished" when it reaches full weight and is ready for slaughter, typically at around 1,200 pounds, which produces a dressed carcass of around 745 pounds. After reaching full weight, the cattle are sold for slaughter to a meatpacking plant. Futures and options on live cattle and feeder cattle are traded at the CME Group. Both the live and feeder cattle futures contracts trade in terms of cents per pound.

**Prices** – CME live cattle futures prices (Barchart.com symbol LE) started 2022 strong and climbed to a 7-year high in April of $1.4423 a pound. Tighter cattle supplies pushed prices higher in early 2022. Abnormally dry conditions in the northern U.S. plains in 2021 squeezed supplies of hay and feed for cattle, prompting some ranchers to slaughter cattle usually held for breeding. The USDA's biannual cattle inventory report in January showed the U.S. cattle herd dropped to 91.9 million head, the smallest herd since 2016. Cattle prices then sold off through May to a 1-year low of $1.323 a pound as soaring beef prices undercut consumer demand, with ground beef prices surging to a record high of $4.19 a pound in April. Sinking demand pushed beef supplies in U.S. cold storage up to 520 million pounds in May, an all-time high for the month of May. However, cattle prices then trended higher the remainder of the year and posted a 7-1/2 year high of $1.5893 a pound in December. Extreme weather in the U.S. Plains in mid-2022 killed thousands of cattle. That also led to lighter cattle weights and smaller beef supplies as the average cattle slaughter weight fell to a 3-year low in late June. A plunge in beef packer profit margins to record lows prompted cattle ranchers to send fewer cattle to slaughter as October cattle-on-feed placements tumbled -6.1% yr/yr to 2.108 million head, the lowest in 10 years. Cattle prices finished 2022 up +13.7% yr/yr at $1.5790 per pound.

**Supply** – The number of world cattle as of January 1, 2023, rose by +0.1% to 941.1 million head. As of January 1, 2023, the number of cattle on farms in India (the world's largest herd) rose by +0.3% to 307.550 million head, and on Brazilian farms (the world's second-largest herd) rose by +0.3% to 194.365 million head. As of January 1, 2022, the number of cattle and calves on U.S. farms fell by -2.0% yr/yr to 91.902 million head. The USDA reported that U.S. commercial production of beef in 2022 rose by +1.7% yr/yr to 28.417 billion pounds.

**Demand** – The federally-inspected slaughter of cattle in the U.S., a measure of cattle consumption, rose by +1.4% yr/yr to 33.664 million head in 2022, well above the 5-decade low of 28.296 million head in 2015.

**Trade** – U.S. imports of live cattle in 2022 fell by -11.1% yr/yr to 1.578 million head. U.S. imports of beef in 2022 rose by +0.9% to 3.350 billion pounds. U.S. exports of beef in 2022 rose by +3.5% yr/yr to a record 3.090 billion pounds.

## World Cattle and Buffalo Numbers as of January 1    In Thousands of Head

| Year | Argentina | Australia | Brazil | Canada | China | European Union | India | Mexico | New Zealand | Russia | United States | Uruguay | World Total |
|---|---|---|---|---|---|---|---|---|---|---|---|---|---|
| 2012 | 50,714 | 28,506 | 184,041 | 12,230 | 93,840 | 87,054 | 300,000 | 20,090 | 10,021 | 19,901 | 91,160 | 11,232 | 954,742 |
| 2013 | 52,201 | 28,418 | 184,464 | 12,240 | 91,373 | 87,106 | 299,600 | 18,521 | 10,180 | 19,680 | 90,095 | 11,384 | 949,549 |
| 2014 | 52,396 | 29,291 | 184,988 | 12,050 | 89,858 | 87,619 | 300,200 | 17,760 | 10,183 | 19,273 | 88,243 | 11,903 | 946,084 |
| 2015 | 52,168 | 29,102 | 187,474 | 11,640 | 90,073 | 88,383 | 300,600 | 17,120 | 10,368 | 18,920 | 89,173 | 12,053 | 929,251 |
| 2016 | 53,118 | 27,413 | 190,062 | 11,610 | 90,558 | 79,303 | 301,000 | 16,615 | 10,033 | 18,528 | 91,888 | 12,016 | 929,707 |
| 2017 | 54,163 | 24,971 | 187,285 | 11,535 | 88,345 | 79,698 | 301,400 | 16,490 | 10,152 | 18,248 | 93,625 | 11,864 | 925,578 |
| 2018 | 54,793 | 26,176 | 186,245 | 11,670 | 90,386 | 79,010 | 301,900 | 16,584 | 10,146 | 18,195 | 94,298 | 11,744 | 929,055 |
| 2019 | 55,008 | 25,699 | 187,290 | 11,670 | 89,153 | 77,840 | 302,700 | 16,699 | 10,107 | 18,050 | 94,805 | 11,396 | 928,341 |
| 2020 | 54,461 | 23,655 | 190,026 | 11,540 | 91,383 | 77,161 | 303,200 | 16,900 | 10,151 | 18,022 | 93,793 | 11,436 | 929,581 |
| 2021 | 53,540 | 23,021 | 193,195 | 11,515 | 95,621 | 76,499 | 305,500 | 17,000 | 10,083 | 17,953 | 93,790 | 11,966 | 937,639 |
| 2022[1] | 53,400 | 23,944 | 193,780 | 11,505 | 98,172 | 75,655 | 306,700 | 17,314 | 10,150 | 17,798 | 91,902 | 11,646 | 940,098 |
| 2023[2] | 52,770 | 25,710 | 194,365 | 11,195 | 101,500 | 74,620 | 307,550 | 17,850 | 10,071 | 17,435 | 89,000 | 11,636 | 941,392 |

[1] Preliminary.  [2] Forecast.    Source: Foreign Agricultural Service, U.S. Department of Agriculture (FAS-USDA)

# CATTLE AND CALVES

## Cattle Supply and Distribution in the United States    In Thousands of Head

| Year | Cattle & Calves on Farms Jan. 1 | Imports | Calves Born | Total Supply | Federally Inspected | Other[3] Commercial | All Commercial | Farm | Total Slaughter | Deaths on Farms | Exports | Total Disappearance |
|---|---|---|---|---|---|---|---|---|---|---|---|---|
| 2013 | 90,095 | 2,033 | 33,630 | 125,758 | 32,698 | 526 | 32,698 | 130 | 32,828 | 3,870 | 161 | 36,859 |
| 2014 | 88,243 | 2,358 | 33,522 | 124,123 | 30,242 | 494 | 30,242 | 124 | 30,366 | 3,850 | 108 | 34,323 |
| 2015 | 89,173 | 1,985 | 34,087 | 125,244 | 28,742 | 462 | 28,742 | 116 | 28,858 | 3,880 | 73 | 32,811 |
| 2016 | 91,888 | 1,708 | 35,063 | 128,659 | 30,602 | 472 | 30,602 | 123 | 30,725 | 3,875 | 69 | 34,670 |
| 2017 | 96,325 | 1,806 | 35,758 | 133,889 | 32,208 | 494 | 32,208 | 116 | 32,323 | 3,928 | 195 | 36,446 |
| 2018 | 94,298 | 1,900 | 36,313 | 132,510 | 33,090 | 495 | 33,090 | 119 | 33,208 | 3,991 | 240 | 37,439 |
| 2019 | 94,805 | 2,043 | 35,592 | 132,439 | 33,648 | 489 | 33,648 | 123 | 33,770 | 4,156 | 306 | 38,232 |
| 2020 | 93,793 | 2,114 | 35,496 | 131,403 | 32,599 |  | 32,599 | 123 | 32,722 | 3,940 | 321 | 36,983 |
| 2021[1] | 93,790 | 1,776 | 35,085 | 130,650 | 33,568 |  | 33,568 | 118 | 33,687 | 3,913 | 511 | 38,111 |
| 2022[2] | 91,902 | 1,628 | 34,600 | 128,130 | 34,028 |  | 34,028 |  | 34,028 |  | 422 | 34,450 |

[1] Preliminary.    [2] Estimate.    [3] Wholesale and retail.    *Source: Economic Research Service, U.S. Department of Agriculture (ERS-USDA)*

## Beef Supply and Utilization in the United States

| Years and Quarters | Beginning Stocks | Commercial (Production) | Total (Production) | Imports | Total Supply | Exports | Ending Stocks | Total Disappearance | Per Capita Disappearance - Carcass Weight | Per Capita Disappearance - Retail Weight Total |
|---|---|---|---|---|---|---|---|---|---|---|
| 2019 | ---- | 27,155 | 27,155 | 3,058 | 30,213 | 3,026 | ---- | ---- | ---- | 57.8 |
| I | ---- | 6,414 | 6,414 | 739 | 7,153 | 700 | ---- | ---- | ---- | 13.9 |
| II | ---- | 6,817 | 6,817 | 836 | 7,653 | 790 | ---- | ---- | ---- | 14.7 |
| III | ---- | 6,923 | 6,923 | 771 | 7,694 | 788 | ---- | ---- | ---- | 14.5 |
| IV | ---- | 7,001 | 7,001 | 712 | 7,713 | 749 | ---- | ---- | ---- | 14.7 |
| 2020 | ---- | 27,174 | 27,174 | 3,339 | 30,513 | 2,951 | ---- | ---- | ---- | 58.1 |
| I | ---- | 6,931 | 6,931 | 774 | 7,705 | 769 | ---- | ---- | ---- | 14.6 |
| II | ---- | 6,059 | 6,059 | 848 | 6,907 | 605 | ---- | ---- | ---- | 13.5 |
| III | ---- | 7,115 | 7,115 | 1,025 | 8,140 | 759 | ---- | ---- | ---- | 15.5 |
| IV | ---- | 7,069 | 7,069 | 693 | 7,762 | 819 | ---- | ---- | ---- | 14.5 |
| 2021 | ---- | 27,948 | 27,948 | 3,346 | 31,294 | 3,441 | ---- | ---- | ---- | 58.9 |
| I | ---- | 6,900 | 6,900 | 696 | 7,596 | 798 | ---- | ---- | ---- | 14.5 |
| II | ---- | 6,963 | 6,963 | 865 | 7,828 | 875 | ---- | ---- | ---- | 14.9 |
| III | ---- | 6,979 | 6,979 | 923 | 7,902 | 912 | ---- | ---- | ---- | 14.6 |
| IV | ---- | 7,106 | 7,106 | 863 | 7,969 | 856 | ---- | ---- | ---- | 14.8 |
| 2022[1] | ---- | 28,290 | 28,290 | 3,391 | 31,681 | 3,536 | ---- | ---- | ---- | 59.1 |
| I | ---- | 7,022 | 7,022 | 985 | 8,007 | 846 | ---- | ---- | ---- | 15.0 |
| II | ---- | 7,069 | 7,069 | 859 | 7,928 | 940 | ---- | ---- | ---- | 14.7 |
| III | ---- | 7,147 | 7,147 | 798 | 7,945 | 906 | ---- | ---- | ---- | 14.8 |
| IV | ---- | 7,053 | 7,053 | 750 | 7,803 | 844 | ---- | ---- | ---- | 14.6 |
| 2023[2] | ---- | 26,495 | 26,495 | 3,425 | 29,920 | 3,090 | ---- | ---- | ---- | 56.3 |
| I | ---- | 6,830 | 6,830 | 950 | 7,780 | 760 | ---- | ---- | ---- | 14.8 |
| II | ---- | 6,595 | 6,595 | 850 | 7,445 | 775 | ---- | ---- | ---- | 12.0 |
| III | ---- | 6,530 | 6,530 | 860 | 7,390 | 785 | ---- | ---- | ---- | 12.5 |
| IV | ---- | 6,540 | 6,540 | 765 | 7,305 | 770 | ---- | ---- | ---- | 13.7 |

[1] Preliminary.    [2] Forecast.    *Source: Economic Research Service, U.S. Department of Agriculture (ERS-USDA)*

## United States Cattle on Feed in 13 States    In Thousands of Head

| Year | Number on Feed[3] | Placed on Feed | Marketings | Other Disappearance | Year | Number on Feed[3] | Placed on Feed | Marketings | Other Disappearance |
|---|---|---|---|---|---|---|---|---|---|
| 2019 | 11,680 | 23,580 | 22,526 | 776 | 2021[1] | 11,967 | 23,294 | 22,522 | 697 |
| I | 11,680 | 5,839 | 5,370 | 196 | I | 11,967 | 5,713 | 5,609 | 174 |
| II | 11,953 | 5,666 | 5,941 | 198 | II | 11,897 | 5,404 | 5,827 | 179 |
| III | 11,480 | 5,692 | 5,693 | 191 | III | 11,295 | 5,999 | 5,572 | 172 |
| IV | 11,288 | 6,383 | 5,522 | 191 | IV | 11,550 | 6,178 | 5,514 | 172 |
| 2020 | 11,958 | 22,626 | 21,892 | 725 | 2022[2] | 12,042 | 22,937 | 22,591 | 702 |
| I | 11,958 | 5,228 | 5,716 | 173 | I | 12,042 | 5,862 | 5,598 | 176 |
| II | 11,297 | 5,282 | 4,943 | 198 | II | 12,105 | 5,302 | 5,868 | 199 |
| III | 11,438 | 6,177 | 5,728 | 170 | III | 11,340 | 5,964 | 5,689 | 162 |
| IV | 11,717 | 5,939 | 5,505 | 184 | IV | 11,454 | 5,809 | 5,436 | 165 |

[1] Preliminary.    [2] Estimate.    [3] Beginning of period.    *Source: Economic Research Service, U.S. Department of Agriculture (ERS-USDA)*

# CATTLE AND CALVES

### United States Cattle on Feed, 1000+ Capacity Feedlots, on First of Month — In Thousands of Head

| Year | Jan. | Feb. | Mar. | Apr. | May | June | July | Aug. | Sept. | Oct. | Nov. | Dec. |
|---|---|---|---|---|---|---|---|---|---|---|---|---|
| 2013 | 11,172 | 11,070 | 10,845 | 10,924 | 10,760 | 10,767 | 10,375 | 10,025 | 9,876 | 10,110 | 10,585 | 10,724 |
| 2014 | 10,523 | 10,678 | 10,716 | 10,792 | 10,554 | 10,497 | 10,043 | 9,752 | 9,719 | 9,985 | 10,571 | 10,816 |
| 2015 | 10,626 | 10,713 | 10,688 | 10,797 | 10,640 | 10,571 | 10,236 | 10,002 | 9,986 | 10,228 | 10,809 | 10,800 |
| 2016 | 10,575 | 10,709 | 10,770 | 10,853 | 10,783 | 10,804 | 10,356 | 10,165 | 10,135 | 10,256 | 10,665 | 10,652 |
| 2017 | 10,605 | 10,782 | 10,772 | 10,919 | 10,998 | 11,096 | 10,821 | 10,604 | 10,504 | 10,813 | 11,332 | 11,516 |
| 2018 | 11,489 | 11,630 | 11,715 | 11,729 | 11,558 | 11,553 | 11,287 | 11,093 | 11,125 | 11,400 | 11,692 | 11,739 |
| 2019 | 11,680 | 11,676 | 11,785 | 11,953 | 11,807 | 11,728 | 11,480 | 11,112 | 10,982 | 11,288 | 11,816 | 12,031 |
| 2020 | 11,958 | 11,928 | 11,811 | 11,297 | 11,200 | 11,671 | 11,438 | 11,284 | 11,394 | 11,717 | 11,973 | 12,036 |
| 2021 | 11,967 | 12,106 | 12,000 | 11,897 | 11,731 | 11,704 | 11,295 | 11,074 | 11,234 | 11,550 | 11,948 | 11,985 |
| 2022[1] | 12,042 | 12,209 | 12,193 | 12,105 | 11,967 | 11,841 | 11,340 | 11,224 | 11,282 | 11,454 | 11,696 | 11,673 |

[1] Preliminary. Source: Economic Research Service, U.S. Department of Agriculture (ERS-USDA)

### United States Cattle Placed on Feed, 1000+ Capacity Feedlots — In Thousands of Head

| Year | Jan. | Feb. | Mar. | Apr. | May | June | July | Aug. | Sept. | Oct. | Nov. | Dec. | Total |
|---|---|---|---|---|---|---|---|---|---|---|---|---|---|
| 2013 | 1,869 | 1,438 | 1,884 | 1,720 | 2,055 | 1,551 | 1,684 | 1,772 | 1,988 | 2,378 | 1,867 | 1,654 | 21,860 |
| 2014 | 2,014 | 1,658 | 1,801 | 1,623 | 1,909 | 1,468 | 1,559 | 1,725 | 2,014 | 2,368 | 1,794 | 1,537 | 21,470 |
| 2015 | 1,789 | 1,551 | 1,809 | 1,548 | 1,719 | 1,481 | 1,547 | 1,632 | 1,941 | 2,286 | 1,602 | 1,527 | 20,432 |
| 2016 | 1,779 | 1,710 | 1,892 | 1,664 | 1,889 | 1,525 | 1,572 | 1,879 | 1,895 | 2,171 | 1,843 | 1,785 | 21,604 |
| 2017 | 1,981 | 1,694 | 2,117 | 1,848 | 2,119 | 1,770 | 1,615 | 1,928 | 2,150 | 2,393 | 2,099 | 1,799 | 23,513 |
| 2018 | 2,068 | 1,817 | 1,921 | 1,695 | 2,124 | 1,798 | 1,742 | 2,070 | 2,051 | 2,248 | 1,996 | 1,757 | 23,287 |
| 2019 | 1,967 | 1,858 | 2,014 | 1,842 | 2,063 | 1,761 | 1,705 | 1,884 | 2,103 | 2,462 | 2,093 | 1,828 | 23,580 |
| 2020 | 1,955 | 1,716 | 1,557 | 1,432 | 2,052 | 1,798 | 1,893 | 2,057 | 2,227 | 2,192 | 1,903 | 1,844 | 22,626 |
| 2021 | 2,024 | 1,691 | 1,998 | 1,825 | 1,910 | 1,669 | 1,733 | 2,103 | 2,163 | 2,246 | 1,967 | 1,965 | 23,294 |
| 2022[1] | 2,004 | 1,868 | 1,990 | 1,809 | 1,864 | 1,629 | 1,764 | 2,115 | 2,085 | 2,100 | 1,925 | 1,784 | 22,937 |

[1] Preliminary. Source: Economic Research Service, U.S. Department of Agriculture (ERS-USDA)

### United States Cattle Marketings, 1000+ Capacity Feedlots[2] — In Thousands of Head

| Year | Jan. | Feb. | Mar. | Apr. | May | June | July | Aug. | Sept. | Oct. | Nov. | Dec. | Total |
|---|---|---|---|---|---|---|---|---|---|---|---|---|---|
| 2013 | 1,892 | 1,603 | 1,724 | 1,815 | 1,948 | 1,880 | 1,970 | 1,871 | 1,692 | 1,827 | 1,660 | 1,736 | 21,618 |
| 2014 | 1,788 | 1,549 | 1,660 | 1,778 | 1,865 | 1,847 | 1,787 | 1,692 | 1,683 | 1,685 | 1,475 | 1,655 | 20,464 |
| 2015 | 1,625 | 1,516 | 1,631 | 1,639 | 1,711 | 1,747 | 1,725 | 1,588 | 1,642 | 1,630 | 1,532 | 1,674 | 19,660 |
| 2016 | 1,589 | 1,591 | 1,747 | 1,658 | 1,794 | 1,912 | 1,713 | 1,868 | 1,732 | 1,705 | 1,787 | 1,777 | 20,873 |
| 2017 | 1,751 | 1,648 | 1,914 | 1,703 | 1,951 | 1,989 | 1,784 | 1,979 | 1,783 | 1,801 | 1,844 | 1,752 | 21,899 |
| 2018 | 1,858 | 1,675 | 1,840 | 1,803 | 2,056 | 2,006 | 1,873 | 1,983 | 1,719 | 1,887 | 1,869 | 1,741 | 22,310 |
| 2019 | 1,910 | 1,683 | 1,777 | 1,928 | 2,070 | 1,943 | 2,002 | 1,953 | 1,738 | 1,875 | 1,813 | 1,834 | 22,526 |
| 2020 | 1,931 | 1,775 | 2,010 | 1,459 | 1,515 | 1,969 | 1,990 | 1,892 | 1,846 | 1,873 | 1,779 | 1,853 | 21,892 |
| 2021 | 1,829 | 1,739 | 2,041 | 1,936 | 1,870 | 2,021 | 1,899 | 1,884 | 1,789 | 1,791 | 1,869 | 1,854 | 22,522 |
| 2022[1] | 1,773 | 1,825 | 2,000 | 1,893 | 1,914 | 2,061 | 1,825 | 2,004 | 1,860 | 1,804 | 1,891 | 1,741 | 22,591 |

[1] Preliminary. Source: Economic Research Service, U.S. Department of Agriculture (ERS-USDA)

### Quarterly Trade of Live Cattle in the United States — In Head

| | Imports | | | | | Exports | | | | |
|---|---|---|---|---|---|---|---|---|---|---|
| Year | First Quarter | Second Quarter | Third Quarter | Fourth Quarter | Total | First Quarter | Second Quarter | Third Quarter | Fourth Quarter | Total |
| 2013 | 595,623 | 474,806 | 309,404 | 653,290 | 2,033,123 | 30,707 | 50,454 | 38,259 | 41,258 | 160,678 |
| 2014 | 599,440 | 562,937 | 415,409 | 780,581 | 2,358,367 | 27,541 | 25,988 | 25,813 | 28,342 | 107,684 |
| 2015 | 564,315 | 534,024 | 413,354 | 472,875 | 1,984,568 | 12,576 | 23,575 | 15,664 | 20,744 | 72,559 |
| 2016 | 490,504 | 459,089 | 288,205 | 470,251 | 1,708,049 | 13,498 | 11,733 | 10,219 | 34,035 | 69,485 |
| 2017 | 517,913 | 439,901 | 317,584 | 530,501 | 1,805,899 | 31,987 | 32,447 | 34,867 | 95,332 | 194,633 |
| 2018 | 467,307 | 497,270 | 364,205 | 570,731 | 1,899,513 | 37,834 | 47,737 | 62,942 | 90,987 | 239,500 |
| 2019 | 567,085 | 562,871 | 330,188 | 582,609 | 2,042,753 | 61,985 | 49,821 | 68,007 | 125,937 | 305,750 |
| 2020 | 530,203 | 584,788 | 432,959 | 566,261 | 2,114,211 | 69,291 | 52,041 | 77,718 | 122,092 | 321,142 |
| 2021 | 478,802 | 423,336 | 355,851 | 517,513 | 1,775,502 | 124,620 | 132,925 | 126,313 | 127,620 | 511,478 |
| 2022[1] | 470,555 | 384,719 | 298,059 | 474,830 | 1,628,163 | 91,421 | 78,388 | 102,434 | 150,102 | 422,345 |

[1] Preliminary. Source: Economic Research Service, U.S. Department of Agriculture (ERS-USDA)

# CATTLE AND CALVES

## Federally Inspected Slaughter of Cattle in the United States — In Thousands of Head

| Year | Jan. | Feb. | Mar. | Apr. | May | June | July | Aug. | Sept. | Oct. | Nov. | Dec. | Total |
|---|---|---|---|---|---|---|---|---|---|---|---|---|---|
| 2013 | 2,785 | 2,315 | 2,545 | 2,689 | 2,823 | 2,693 | 2,856 | 2,778 | 2,568 | 2,851 | 2,527 | 2,518 | 31,947 |
| 2014 | 2,634 | 2,204 | 2,413 | 2,556 | 2,597 | 2,568 | 2,562 | 2,463 | 2,490 | 2,591 | 2,210 | 2,398 | 29,684 |
| 2015 | 2,377 | 2,135 | 2,342 | 2,346 | 2,345 | 2,430 | 2,459 | 2,288 | 2,435 | 2,469 | 2,259 | 2,414 | 28,296 |
| 2016 | 2,320 | 2,252 | 2,493 | 2,373 | 2,479 | 2,670 | 2,443 | 2,711 | 2,578 | 2,592 | 2,632 | 2,572 | 30,115 |
| 2017 | 2,533 | 2,330 | 2,726 | 2,425 | 2,713 | 2,821 | 2,577 | 2,903 | 2,655 | 2,753 | 2,726 | 2,543 | 31,704 |
| 2018 | 2,714 | 2,378 | 2,661 | 2,599 | 2,868 | 2,842 | 2,729 | 2,937 | 2,577 | 2,908 | 2,762 | 2,544 | 32,518 |
| 2019 | 2,786 | 2,416 | 2,609 | 2,789 | 2,900 | 2,769 | 2,903 | 2,887 | 2,635 | 2,926 | 2,737 | 2,713 | 33,069 |
| 2020 | 2,854 | 2,539 | 2,875 | 2,189 | 2,223 | 2,820 | 2,866 | 2,751 | 2,756 | 2,889 | 2,657 | 2,734 | 32,152 |
| 2021 | 2,691 | 2,473 | 2,947 | 2,794 | 2,645 | 2,897 | 2,801 | 2,834 | 2,732 | 2,794 | 2,805 | 2,772 | 33,184 |
| 2022[1] | 2,649 | 2,634 | 2,955 | 2,759 | 2,760 | 2,985 | 2,731 | 3,019 | 2,840 | 2,842 | 2,855 | 2,638 | 33,666 |

[1] Preliminary.  Source: National Agricultural Statistics Service, U.S. Department of Agriculture (NASS-USDA)

## Federally Inspected Slaughter of Calves and Vealers in the United States — In Thousands of Head

| Year | Jan. | Feb. | Mar. | Apr. | May | June | July | Aug. | Sept. | Oct. | Nov. | Dec. | Total |
|---|---|---|---|---|---|---|---|---|---|---|---|---|---|
| 2013 | 69.9 | 58.7 | 61.6 | 57.7 | 57.6 | 56.7 | 69.1 | 63.5 | 62.0 | 68.5 | 59.7 | 65.8 | 750.8 |
| 2014 | 62.0 | 51.5 | 52.9 | 48.0 | 45.9 | 44.6 | 47.8 | 43.0 | 41.8 | 42.6 | 35.2 | 42.2 | 557.5 |
| 2015 | 39.3 | 36.1 | 39.2 | 34.7 | 32.7 | 34.5 | 36.0 | 33.9 | 36.8 | 39.6 | 38.2 | 44.5 | 445.5 |
| 2016 | 41.2 | 37.8 | 41.3 | 34.2 | 34.9 | 37.0 | 37.1 | 40.3 | 41.8 | 47.6 | 46.6 | 48.1 | 487.9 |
| 2017 | 45.9 | 39.6 | 44.3 | 38.4 | 38.5 | 39.6 | 38.3 | 45.4 | 42.9 | 43.2 | 41.7 | 45.6 | 503.4 |
| 2018 | 48.4 | 40.4 | 43.0 | 42.1 | 45.7 | 44.6 | 47.0 | 51.6 | 47.8 | 52.9 | 54.9 | 53.0 | 571.4 |
| 2019 | 53.0 | 47.9 | 45.1 | 42.1 | 45.5 | 43.7 | 53.0 | 50.2 | 48.4 | 54.6 | 45.8 | 49.1 | 578.4 |
| 2020 | 49.2 | 39.1 | 42.5 | 32.6 | 31.7 | 35.9 | 40.3 | 33.4 | 31.6 | 36.3 | 34.4 | 40.0 | 447.0 |
| 2021 | 31.8 | 32.5 | 31.0 | 26.8 | 24.8 | 31.2 | 32.9 | 34.3 | 33.5 | 34.6 | 32.5 | 38.1 | 384.0 |
| 2022[1] | 31.7 | 29.8 | 31.9 | 27.4 | 26.8 | 28.6 | 28.9 | 33.3 | 30.9 | 29.7 | 30.7 | 32.4 | 362.1 |

[1] Preliminary.  Source: Crop Reporting Board, U.S. Department of Agriculture (CRB-USDA)

## Average Live Weight of Cattle Slaughtered Under Federal Inspection — In Pounds per Head

| Year | Jan. | Feb. | Mar. | Apr. | May | June | July | Aug. | Sept. | Oct. | Nov. | Dec. | Average |
|---|---|---|---|---|---|---|---|---|---|---|---|---|---|
| 2013 | 1,331 | 1,323 | 1,315 | 1,298 | 1,291 | 1,302 | 1,304 | 1,312 | 1,316 | 1,331 | 1,342 | 1,337 | 1,317 |
| 2014 | 1,338 | 1,334 | 1,321 | 1,308 | 1,302 | 1,309 | 1,322 | 1,332 | 1,347 | 1,359 | 1,367 | 1,367 | 1,334 |
| 2015 | 1,362 | 1,359 | 1,351 | 1,341 | 1,335 | 1,335 | 1,348 | 1,365 | 1,386 | 1,394 | 1,396 | 1,391 | 1,364 |
| 2016 | 1,385 | 1,375 | 1,373 | 1,351 | 1,335 | 1,337 | 1,347 | 1,354 | 1,373 | 1,385 | 1,387 | 1,384 | 1,366 |
| 2017 | 1,374 | 1,363 | 1,352 | 1,327 | 1,309 | 1,323 | 1,335 | 1,347 | 1,362 | 1,364 | 1,376 | 1,382 | 1,351 |
| 2018 | 1,380 | 1,370 | 1,360 | 1,336 | 1,317 | 1,322 | 1,332 | 1,346 | 1,361 | 1,366 | 1,372 | 1,370 | 1,353 |
| 2019 | 1,366 | 1,354 | 1,341 | 1,330 | 1,317 | 1,315 | 1,328 | 1,340 | 1,354 | 1,363 | 1,378 | 1,376 | 1,347 |
| 2020 | 1,378 | 1,379 | 1,371 | 1,357 | 1,371 | 1,368 | 1,366 | 1,368 | 1,382 | 1,389 | 1,391 | 1,392 | 1,376 |
| 2021 | 1,403 | 1,394 | 1,376 | 1,369 | 1,363 | 1,349 | 1,351 | 1,356 | 1,368 | 1,379 | 1,386 | 1,395 | 1,374 |
| 2022[1] | 1,401 | 1,398 | 1,388 | 1,376 | 1,353 | 1,342 | 1,343 | 1,351 | 1,368 | 1,379 | 1,387 | 1,388 | 1,373 |

[1] Preliminary.  Source: National Agricultural Statistics Board, U.S. Department of Agriculture (NASS-USDA)

## Beef Steer-Corn Price Ratio[1] in the United States

| Year | Jan. | Feb. | Mar. | Apr. | May | June | July | Aug. | Sept. | Oct. | Nov. | Dec. | Average |
|---|---|---|---|---|---|---|---|---|---|---|---|---|---|
| 2013 | 18.7 | 17.8 | 17.8 | 18.2 | 18.2 | 17.8 | 17.8 | 19.6 | 23.0 | 27.6 | 30.2 | 29.9 | 21.4 |
| 2014 | 31.7 | 33.3 | 33.2 | 31.8 | 31.2 | 32.9 | 38.7 | 43.8 | 45.3 | 45.7 | 46.9 | 43.8 | 38.2 |
| 2015 | 43.5 | 42.5 | 42.5 | 43.7 | 44.2 | 43.5 | 39.5 | 40.5 | 38.0 | 35.1 | 36.5 | 33.7 | 40.3 |
| 2016 | 36.1 | 37.4 | 38.5 | 37.4 | 35.1 | 33.2 | 33.3 | 36.8 | 33.9 | 31.0 | 32.7 | 34.0 | 35.0 |
| 2017 | 35.0 | 35.2 | 36.4 | 37.9 | 40.0 | 38.8 | 34.7 | 35.2 | 32.7 | 34.0 | 38.4 | 37.2 | 36.3 |
| 2018 | 37.4 | 37.6 | 36.2 | 34.1 | 33.2 | 31.6 | 32.3 | 33.3 | 32.4 | 32.7 | 33.7 | 33.6 | 34.0 |
| 2019 | 34.8 | 35.0 | 35.7 | 36.3 | 33.6 | 28.9 | 27.2 | 28.5 | 27.4 | 28.3 | 31.3 | 32.3 | 31.6 |
| 2020 | 33.0 | 32.3 | 31.0 | 33.7 | 34.7 | 34.8 | 30.5 | 33.3 | 30.8 | 29.9 | 28.8 | 28.0 | 31.7 |
| 2021 | 26.4 | 24.2 | 23.7 | 22.8 | 20.5 | 20.5 | 20.4 | 19.8 | 23.2 | 25.1 | 25.1 | 25.8 | 23.1 |
| 2022[1] | 24.9 | 23.2 | 21.6 | 20.1 | 19.8 | 19.3 | 19.9 | 19.9 | 20.5 | 22.8 | 23.7 | 24.0 | 21.6 |

[1] Bushels of corn equal in value to 100 pounds of steers and heifers.   [2] Preliminary.   Source: Economic Research Service, U.S. Department of Agriculture

# CATTLE AND CALVES

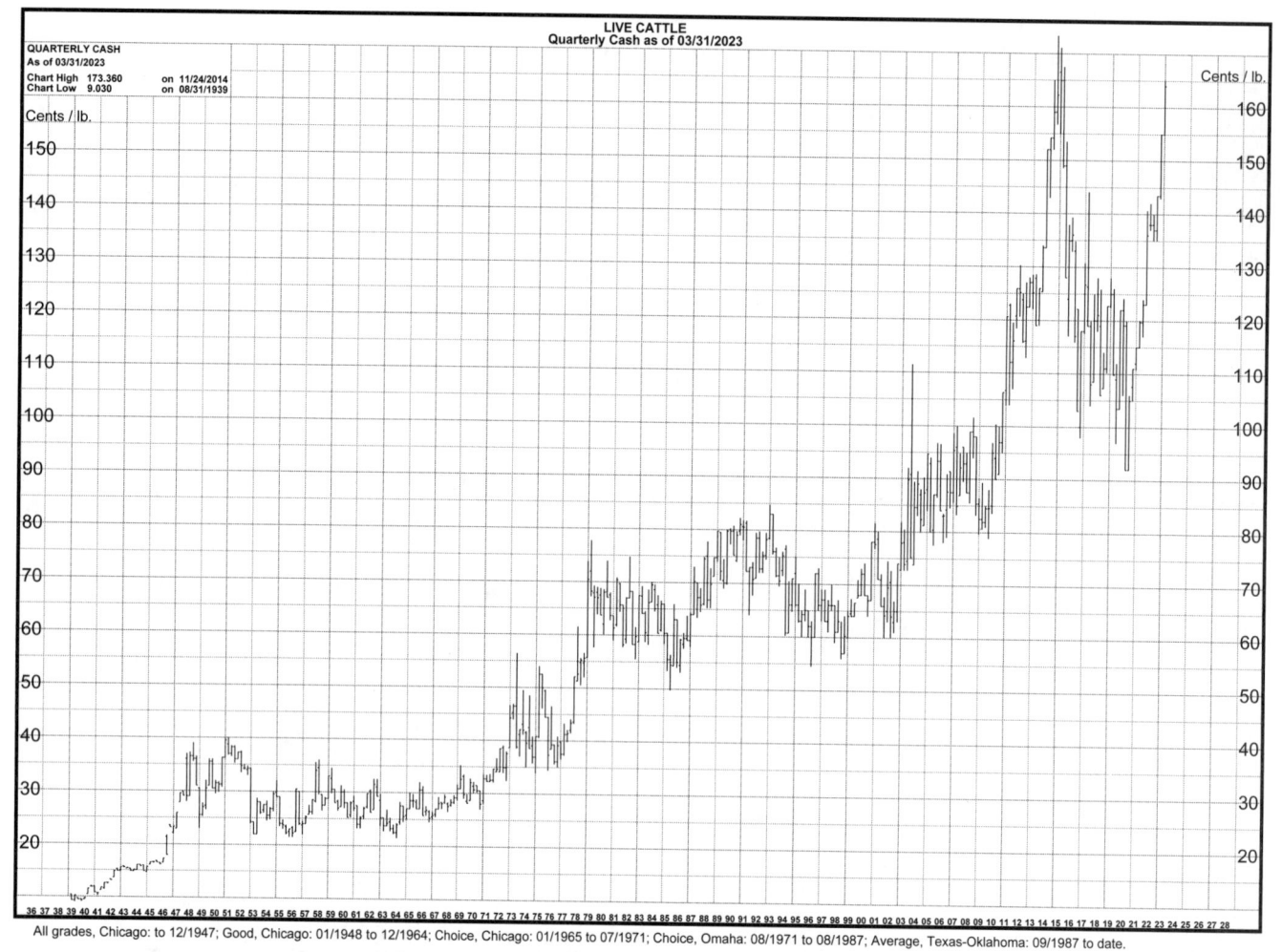

**LIVE CATTLE** — Quarterly Cash as of 03/31/2023

QUARTERLY CASH
As of 03/31/2023
Chart High 173.360 on 11/24/2014
Chart Low 9.030 on 08/31/1939

All grades, Chicago: to 12/1947; Good, Chicago: 01/1948 to 12/1964; Choice, Chicago: 01/1965 to 07/1971; Choice, Omaha: 08/1971 to 08/1987; Average, Texas-Oklahoma: 09/1987 to date.

## Average Price Received by Farmers for Beef Cattle in the United States — In Dollars Per 100 Pounds

| Year | Jan. | Feb. | Mar. | Apr. | May | June | July | Aug. | Sept. | Oct. | Nov. | Dec. | Average |
|---|---|---|---|---|---|---|---|---|---|---|---|---|---|
| 2013 | 126.00 | 123.00 | 125.00 | 125.00 | 126.00 | 122.00 | 120.00 | 121.00 | 122.00 | 127.00 | 130.00 | 130.00 | 124.75 |
| 2014 | 138.00 | 144.00 | 148.00 | 148.00 | 146.00 | 147.00 | 156.00 | 158.00 | 157.00 | 161.00 | 167.00 | 164.00 | 152.83 |
| 2015 | 164.00 | 159.00 | 160.00 | 162.00 | 160.00 | 155.00 | 149.00 | 148.00 | 139.00 | 128.00 | 129.00 | 122.00 | 147.92 |
| 2016 | 130.00 | 132.00 | 135.00 | 131.00 | 128.00 | 125.00 | 119.00 | 117.00 | 108.00 | 101.00 | 104.00 | 111.00 | 120.08 |
| 2017 | 117.00 | 119.00 | 125.00 | 128.00 | 136.00 | 132.00 | 120.00 | 114.00 | 105.00 | 109.00 | 119.00 | 118.00 | 120.17 |
| 2018 | 120.00 | 125.00 | 125.00 | 119.00 | 120.00 | 112.00 | 110.00 | 110.00 | 108.00 | 110.00 | 113.00 | 117.00 | 115.75 |
| 2019 | 121.00 | 123.00 | 126.00 | 125.00 | 120.00 | 114.00 | 112.00 | 111.00 | 103.00 | 107.00 | 113.00 | 118.00 | 116.08 |
| 2020 | 122.00 | 120.00 | 113.00 | 108.00 | 109.00 | 109.00 | 97.10 | 103.00 | 104.00 | 106.00 | 107.00 | 108.00 | 108.84 |
| 2021 | 110.00 | 112.00 | 113.00 | 118.00 | 118.00 | 121.00 | 122.00 | 123.00 | 124.00 | 123.00 | 129.00 | 137.00 | 120.83 |
| 2022[1] | 135.00 | 137.00 | 139.00 | 139.00 | 141.00 | 140.00 | 142.00 | 141.00 | 143.00 | 145.00 | 151.00 | 154.00 | 142.25 |

[1] Preliminary. *Source: National Agricultural Statistics Service, U.S. Department of Agriculture (NASS-USDA)*

## Average Price Received by Farmers for Calves in the United States — In Dollars Per 100 Pounds

| Year | Jan. | Feb. | Mar. | Apr. | May | June | July | Aug. | Sept. | Oct. | Nov. | Dec. | Average |
|---|---|---|---|---|---|---|---|---|---|---|---|---|---|
| 2013 | 168.00 | 170.00 | 163.00 | 159.00 | 157.00 | 152.00 | 162.00 | 178.00 | 200.00 | 190.00 | 192.00 | 197.00 | 174.00 |
| 2014 | 208.00 | 209.00 | 216.00 | 222.00 | 229.00 | 249.00 | 257.00 | 271.00 | 279.00 | 307.00 | 305.00 | 303.00 | 254.58 |
| 2015 | 288.00 | 277.00 | 290.00 | 288.00 | 288.00 | 292.00 | 275.00 | 273.00 | 241.00 | 234.00 | 217.00 | 193.00 | 263.00 |
| 2016 | 196.00 | 201.00 | 199.00 | 183.00 | 173.00 | 168.00 | 145.00 | 158.00 | 142.00 | 134.00 | 144.00 | 148.00 | 165.92 |
| 2017 | 152.00 | 151.00 | 159.00 | 164.00 | 171.00 | 164.00 | 157.00 | 163.00 | 173.00 | 177.00 | 177.00 | 174.00 | 165.17 |
| 2018 | 174.00 | 180.00 | 175.00 | 170.00 | 165.00 | 158.00 | 153.00 | 160.00 | 169.00 | 174.00 | 169.00 | 166.00 | 167.75 |
| 2019 | 169.00 | 170.00 | 170.00 | 174.00 | 148.00 | 149.00 | 144.00 | 142.00 | 144.00 | 154.00 | 158.00 | 159.00 | 156.75 |
| 2020 | 168.00 | 168.00 | 160.00 | 151.00 | 151.00 | 149.00 | 149.00 | 153.00 | 155.00 | 156.00 | 162.00 | 165.00 | 157.25 |
| 2021 | 165.00 | 167.00 | 163.00 | 168.00 | 159.00 | 159.00 | 165.00 | 175.00 | 173.00 | 175.00 | 174.00 | 181.00 | 168.67 |
| 2022[1] | 185.00 | 194.00 | 187.00 | 186.00 | 183.00 | 184.00 | 186.00 | 197.00 | 195.00 | 200.00 | 203.00 | 206.00 | 192.17 |

[1] Preliminary. *Source: National Agricultural Statistics Board, U.S. Department of Agriculture (NASS-USDA)*

# CATTLE AND CALVES

**CATTLE, LIVE - CME**
Weekly Selected Futures as of 03/31/2023

WEEKLY SELECTED FUTURES
As of 03/31/2023
Chart High 171.975 on 10/31/2014
Chart Low 81.450 on 04/24/2020

Nearby Futures through Last Trading Day.

## Volume of Trading of Live Cattle Futures Chicago   In Thousands of Contracts

| Year | Jan. | Feb. | Mar. | Apr. | May | June | July | Aug. | Sept. | Oct. | Nov. | Dec. | Total |
|------|------|------|------|------|------|------|------|------|-------|------|------|------|-------|
| 2013 | 1,484.1 | 1,069.5 | 1,249.3 | 977.9 | 1,189.7 | 831.3 | 1,020.8 | 884.5 | 972.5 | 1,040.2 | 986.9 | 756.2 | 12,463.0 |
| 2014 | 1,381.4 | 970.0 | 1,270.2 | 847.7 | 1,139.3 | 1,126.6 | 1,503.5 | 1,023.5 | 1,303.4 | 1,061.5 | 962.5 | 1,009.6 | 13,599.3 |
| 2015 | 1,282.2 | 918.7 | 1,163.5 | 959.6 | 1,139.1 | 955.3 | 1,166.5 | 901.6 | 1,344.2 | 1,222.5 | 1,213.9 | 1,173.9 | 13,440.9 |
| 2016 | 1,127.6 | 956.2 | 1,187.4 | 1,010.7 | 1,234.8 | 852.5 | 1,070.5 | 990.9 | 1,335.8 | 1,028.2 | 1,257.5 | 1,070.7 | 13,122.8 |
| 2017 | 1,300.9 | 958.4 | 1,552.2 | 1,260.5 | 2,164.7 | 1,201.2 | 1,487.1 | 1,155.8 | 1,364.4 | 1,228.1 | 1,501.6 | 990.4 | 16,165.2 |
| 2018 | 1,493.4 | 1,078.6 | 1,621.7 | 1,294.7 | 1,680.4 | 1,170.3 | 1,476.9 | 1,205.5 | 1,433.2 | 1,397.4 | 1,466.9 | 1,121.1 | 16,440.1 |
| 2019 | 1,657.5 | 1,139.7 | 1,778.9 | 1,440.6 | 1,760.8 | 1,132.9 | 1,321.6 | 1,338.6 | 1,539.7 | 1,154.9 | 1,488.3 | 965.6 | 16,719.1 |
| 2020 | 1,607.7 | 1,452.6 | 2,194.9 | 1,204.7 | 1,499.0 | 997.6 | 1,373.3 | 1,120.5 | 1,331.4 | 1,239.8 | 1,211.4 | 905.9 | 16,138.8 |
| 2021 | 1,419.5 | 1,040.4 | 1,341.3 | 1,143.1 | 1,179.2 | 1,017.1 | 1,201.6 | 1,115.8 | 1,366.8 | 888.8 | 1,274.1 | 955.3 | 13,943.1 |
| 2022 | 1,420.9 | 1,112.8 | 1,539.4 | 1,014.1 | 1,300.6 | 1,091.1 | 1,146.4 | 1,035.0 | 1,329.6 | 1,051.5 | 1,213.9 | 895.7 | 14,150.8 |

Contract size = 40,000 lbs.   Source: CME Group; Chicago Mercantile Exchange (CME)

## Average Open Interest of Live Cattle Futures in Chicago   In Contracts

| Year | Jan. | Feb. | Mar. | Apr. | May | June | July | Aug. | Sept. | Oct. | Nov. | Dec. |
|------|------|------|------|------|------|------|------|------|-------|------|------|------|
| 2013 | 329,529 | 330,784 | 335,436 | 325,462 | 315,201 | 290,113 | 275,925 | 289,980 | 295,826 | 314,058 | 333,154 | 323,189 |
| 2014 | 354,327 | 371,310 | 369,611 | 352,639 | 345,372 | 352,223 | 343,096 | 313,046 | 315,722 | 313,134 | 317,289 | 286,556 |
| 2015 | 261,167 | 243,091 | 259,858 | 273,309 | 296,935 | 287,815 | 241,553 | 236,485 | 258,984 | 258,122 | 271,979 | 256,669 |
| 2016 | 274,078 | 272,513 | 291,131 | 282,634 | 271,110 | 247,299 | 248,641 | 247,108 | 262,608 | 268,144 | 278,901 | 294,562 |
| 2017 | 333,745 | 332,286 | 360,860 | 404,610 | 421,183 | 403,152 | 372,623 | 320,894 | 327,393 | 334,666 | 380,212 | 341,419 |
| 2018 | 353,135 | 370,641 | 362,617 | 348,766 | 356,141 | 329,947 | 317,434 | 301,001 | 314,505 | 335,731 | 342,814 | 347,681 |
| 2019 | 386,607 | 393,106 | 437,825 | 440,940 | 384,191 | 357,676 | 331,025 | 324,793 | 338,349 | 308,578 | 362,444 | 381,270 |
| 2020 | 384,707 | 341,499 | 305,367 | 266,157 | 264,856 | 271,676 | 273,740 | 291,037 | 294,504 | 279,047 | 275,585 | 284,898 |
| 2021 | 315,035 | 330,683 | 336,111 | 333,141 | 318,494 | 300,080 | 300,394 | 295,926 | 297,788 | 284,484 | 302,468 | 309,096 |
| 2022 | 330,015 | 352,569 | 320,520 | 307,172 | 303,632 | 283,487 | 265,660 | 266,581 | 293,460 | 271,432 | 289,848 | 302,343 |

Contract size = 40,000 lbs.   Source: CME Group; Chicago Mercantile Exchange (CME)

# CATTLE AND CALVES

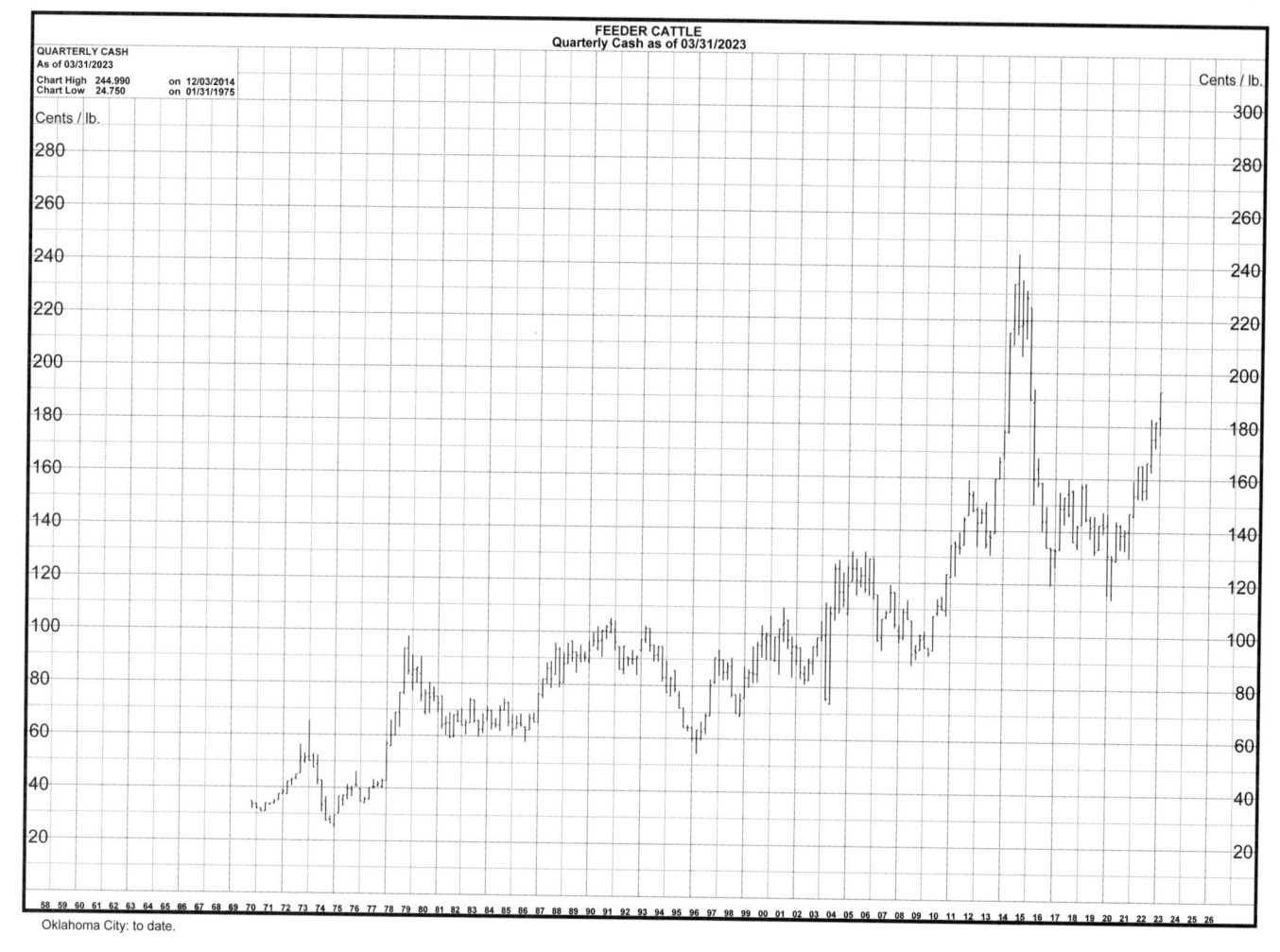

**FEEDER CATTLE**
Quarterly Cash as of 03/31/2023

Chart High 244.990 on 12/03/2014
Chart Low 24.750 on 01/31/1975

Oklahoma City: to date.

## Average Slaughter Steer Price, Choice 2-4, Nebraska Direct (1100-1300 Lb.) — In Dollars Per 100 Pounds

| Year | Jan. | Feb. | Mar. | Apr. | May | June | July | Aug. | Sept. | Oct. | Nov. | Dec. | Average |
|---|---|---|---|---|---|---|---|---|---|---|---|---|---|
| 2013 | 124.33 | 125.47 | 126.33 | 128.08 | 126.48 | 121.70 | 120.41 | 123.78 | 124.23 | 130.09 | 132.23 | 131.18 | 126.19 |
| 2014 | 143.33 | 146.45 | 151.93 | 149.01 | 146.19 | 149.55 | 158.57 | 158.35 | 159.86 | 164.91 | 170.04 | 163.09 | 155.11 |
| 2015 | 165.13 | 160.29 | 163.42 | 162.98 | 160.76 | 151.13 | 149.17 | 149.06 | 136.28 | 132.88 | 126.90 | 125.00 | 148.58 |
| 2016 | 133.15 | 133.85 | 137.83 | 129.52 | 129.90 | 122.95 | 117.10 | 116.91 | 106.22 | 101.76 | 106.23 | 115.24 | 120.70 |
| 2017 | 119.92 | 121.83 | 126.91 | 131.18 | 138.42 | 130.10 | 118.08 | 113.01 | 107.73 | 113.40 | 122.49 | 119.73 | 121.90 |
| 2018 | 124.35 | 127.93 | 124.97 | 121.11 | 116.14 | 110.10 | 112.39 | 109.98 | 110.69 | 111.53 | 115.28 | 120.34 | 117.07 |
| 2019 | 123.28 | 124.66 | 127.51 | 125.82 | 118.03 | 113.08 | 112.99 | 111.13 | 103.30 | 109.80 | 115.96 | 120.20 | 117.15 |
| 2020 | 123.86 | 117.31 | 111.06 | 105.18 | 103.14 | 99.98 | 97.72 | 105.51 | 103.28 | 106.36 | 109.39 | 110.00 | 107.73 |
| 2021 | 109.84 | 114.00 | 114.71 | 121.67 | 118.00 | 121.98 | 124.75 | 124.31 | 124.00 | 124.91 | 134.17 | 140.12 | 122.71 |
| 2022[1] | NA | 140.39 | 138.39 | 143.09 | 143.59 | 142.79 | 142.53 | 142.25 | 141.66 | 149.00 | 155.92 | 156.62 | 145.11 |

[1] Preliminary. Source: Economic Research Service, U.S. Department of Agriculture (ERS-USDA)

## Average Price of Feeder Steers in Oklahoma City — In Dollars Per 100 Pounds

| Year | Jan. | Feb. | Mar. | Apr. | May | June | July | Aug. | Sept. | Oct. | Nov. | Dec. | Average |
|---|---|---|---|---|---|---|---|---|---|---|---|---|---|
| 2013 | 147.99 | 142.75 | 136.98 | 136.75 | 133.75 | 135.73 | 144.26 | 152.68 | 156.92 | 161.92 | 165.05 | 166.20 | 148.41 |
| 2014 | 170.98 | 170.61 | 174.43 | 178.55 | 185.49 | 201.90 | 216.19 | 221.28 | 228.15 | 239.59 | 240.37 | 233.67 | 205.10 |
| 2015 | 224.57 | 210.18 | 212.80 | 218.29 | 219.14 | 226.34 | 219.98 | 215.14 | 200.97 | 188.55 | 181.41 | 159.43 | 206.40 |
| 2016 | 162.19 | 158.82 | 160.13 | 154.07 | 146.07 | 144.74 | 142.23 | 146.88 | 136.34 | 124.66 | 126.85 | 131.41 | 144.53 |
| 2017 | 132.65 | 127.78 | 129.29 | 136.04 | 144.23 | 150.36 | 149.39 | 146.20 | 149.54 | 155.21 | 157.93 | 152.81 | 144.29 |
| 2018 | 149.61 | 147.91 | 141.90 | 136.73 | 136.14 | 140.75 | 147.25 | 150.14 | 153.97 | 156.14 | 149.97 | 146.09 | 146.38 |
| 2019 | 144.00 | 141.23 | 139.72 | 143.93 | 135.89 | 132.53 | 138.02 | 139.56 | 138.44 | 144.50 | 146.22 | 144.35 | 140.70 |
| 2020 | 145.17 | 140.57 | 128.37 | 118.95 | 123.91 | 128.99 | 135.40 | 142.24 | 141.42 | 139.14 | 137.16 | 138.37 | 134.97 |
| 2021 | 134.97 | 137.08 | 135.59 | 139.20 | 133.29 | 141.79 | 151.35 | 156.62 | 155.27 | 154.31 | 156.42 | 161.21 | 146.42 |
| 2022 | 161.24 | 161.34 | 155.01 | 155.61 | 154.93 | 160.89 | 170.18 | 178.63 | 179.03 | 174.49 | 176.09 | 178.75 | 167.18 |

Source: Economic Research Service, U.S. Department of Agriculture (ERS-USDA)

# CATTLE AND CALVES

**CATTLE, FEEDER - CME**
Weekly Nearest Futures as of 03/31/2023

Weekly Nearest Futures As of 03/31/2023
Chart High 245.200 on 10/09/2014
Chart Low 103.950 on 04/06/2020

Nearby Futures through Last Trading Day using Selected contract months: February, April, June, August, October and December.

## Volume of Trading of Feeder Cattle Futures Chicago    In Contracts

| Year | Jan. | Feb. | Mar. | Apr. | May | June | July | Aug. | Sept. | Oct. | Nov. | Dec. | Total |
|---|---|---|---|---|---|---|---|---|---|---|---|---|---|
| 2013 | 160,605 | 164,860 | 175,594 | 187,666 | 116,948 | 83,548 | 128,070 | 140,792 | 125,003 | 151,256 | 112,137 | 122,805 | 1,669,284 |
| 2014 | 145,259 | 146,539 | 162,287 | 146,874 | 133,506 | 158,374 | 225,649 | 223,720 | 202,774 | 225,198 | 128,870 | 216,672 | 2,115,722 |
| 2015 | 238,256 | 194,105 | 223,149 | 200,013 | 163,686 | 157,044 | 213,709 | 216,119 | 221,822 | 242,183 | 192,224 | 230,741 | 2,493,051 |
| 2016 | 188,497 | 201,016 | 245,203 | 234,293 | 182,499 | 153,988 | 191,531 | 248,780 | 248,507 | 251,274 | 191,263 | 201,104 | 2,537,955 |
| 2017 | 203,909 | 229,093 | 303,851 | 355,689 | 337,360 | 257,443 | 300,121 | 383,206 | 319,319 | 328,842 | 248,101 | 274,899 | 3,541,833 |
| 2018 | 253,040 | 289,662 | 339,715 | 339,742 | 269,509 | 244,093 | 338,063 | 372,382 | 293,434 | 331,588 | 226,165 | 231,572 | 3,528,965 |
| 2019 | 259,892 | 265,244 | 369,642 | 367,089 | 337,636 | 278,936 | 305,091 | 363,903 | 301,660 | 281,320 | 234,331 | 243,802 | 3,608,546 |
| 2020 | 306,940 | 345,608 | 382,220 | 227,965 | 181,226 | 179,978 | 310,756 | 363,903 | 267,000 | 297,802 | 211,790 | 245,495 | 3,320,683 |
| 2021 | 233,141 | 194,993 | 290,080 | 286,614 | 201,385 | 217,986 | 260,875 | 314,469 | 342,624 | 253,647 | 234,357 | 237,760 | 3,067,931 |
| 2022 | 240,504 | 275,227 | 294,599 | 281,093 | 218,127 | 253,220 | 296,538 | 318,085 | 338,797 | 306,717 | 278,749 | 254,055 | 3,355,711 |

Contract size = 40,000 lbs.    Source: CME Group; Chicago Mercantile Exchange (CME)

## Average Open Interest of Feeder Cattle Futures in Chicago    In Contracts

| Year | Jan. | Feb. | Mar. | Apr. | May | June | July | Aug. | Sept. | Oct. | Nov. | Dec. |
|---|---|---|---|---|---|---|---|---|---|---|---|---|
| 2013 | 31,493 | 36,800 | 41,033 | 37,706 | 34,030 | 32,391 | 33,146 | 35,643 | 30,728 | 36,706 | 37,119 | 42,899 |
| 2014 | 50,558 | 48,154 | 49,331 | 44,614 | 45,889 | 48,933 | 49,843 | 44,856 | 44,339 | 45,027 | 45,056 | 42,924 |
| 2015 | 40,979 | 38,257 | 40,956 | 39,645 | 38,528 | 44,008 | 42,717 | 41,337 | 36,061 | 34,280 | 34,208 | 35,145 |
| 2016 | 36,524 | 39,140 | 41,160 | 41,481 | 41,159 | 40,322 | 43,402 | 43,468 | 42,550 | 43,049 | 43,052 | 44,837 |
| 2017 | 49,515 | 50,369 | 53,105 | 59,119 | 57,620 | 56,183 | 59,574 | 56,346 | 54,234 | 60,884 | 60,534 | 54,316 |
| 2018 | 52,654 | 56,500 | 53,852 | 49,675 | 45,338 | 44,834 | 50,036 | 50,612 | 52,540 | 54,729 | 48,850 | 49,150 |
| 2019 | 50,475 | 49,902 | 53,540 | 51,765 | 50,005 | 48,816 | 48,400 | 47,550 | 46,855 | 40,898 | 43,622 | 49,468 |
| 2020 | 53,349 | 56,346 | 41,760 | 32,784 | 29,922 | 33,428 | 40,400 | 44,587 | 42,971 | 43,704 | 37,461 | 42,381 |
| 2021 | 41,053 | 41,296 | 45,950 | 46,256 | 44,208 | 42,766 | 45,672 | 49,861 | 42,908 | 39,704 | 41,239 | 40,542 |
| 2022 | 44,876 | 47,112 | 43,989 | 42,282 | 44,958 | 44,609 | 39,808 | 43,167 | 43,734 | 48,734 | 47,473 | 45,983 |

Contract size = 40,000 lbs.    Source: CME Group; Chicago Mercantile Exchange (CME)

# CATTLE AND CALVES

## Imports of Live Cattle to the United States — In Head

| Year | Jan. | Feb. | Mar. | Apr. | May | June | July | Aug. | Sept. | Oct. | Nov. | Dec. | Total |
|---|---|---|---|---|---|---|---|---|---|---|---|---|---|
| 2013 | 160,736 | 208,773 | 226,114 | 217,212 | 155,817 | 101,777 | 90,688 | 89,256 | 129,460 | 162,914 | 222,059 | 268,317 | 2,033,123 |
| 2014 | 157,455 | 207,261 | 234,724 | 247,523 | 181,306 | 134,108 | 134,894 | 115,476 | 165,039 | 234,626 | 269,330 | 276,625 | 2,358,367 |
| 2015 | 135,659 | 194,466 | 234,190 | 207,189 | 162,677 | 164,158 | 147,554 | 119,789 | 146,011 | 167,165 | 150,282 | 155,428 | 1,984,568 |
| 2016 | 104,397 | 151,467 | 234,640 | 212,913 | 131,340 | 114,836 | 82,366 | 98,247 | 107,592 | 117,113 | 176,971 | 176,167 | 1,708,049 |
| 2017 | 132,418 | 168,473 | 217,022 | 153,851 | 158,767 | 127,283 | 118,288 | 98,361 | 100,935 | 139,922 | 206,296 | 184,283 | 1,805,899 |
| 2018 | 114,278 | 153,951 | 199,078 | 172,772 | 169,813 | 154,685 | 126,622 | 119,865 | 117,718 | 167,968 | 208,127 | 194,636 | 1,899,513 |
| 2019 | 142,628 | 189,372 | 235,085 | 222,429 | 190,006 | 150,436 | 121,463 | 98,408 | 110,317 | 165,526 | 204,458 | 212,625 | 2,042,753 |
| 2020 | 146,927 | 169,997 | 213,279 | 201,339 | 190,279 | 193,170 | 158,200 | 128,333 | 146,426 | 181,890 | 186,471 | 197,900 | 2,114,211 |
| 2021 | 133,149 | 155,017 | 190,636 | 179,484 | 121,792 | 122,060 | 113,284 | 121,055 | 121,512 | 148,223 | 183,674 | 185,616 | 1,775,502 |
| 2022[1] | 132,431 | 156,522 | 181,602 | 124,780 | 132,692 | 127,247 | 96,706 | 107,749 | 93,604 | 116,528 | 177,067 | 181,235 | 1,628,163 |

[1] Preliminary. Source: Economic Research Service, U.S. Department of Agriculture (ERS-USDA)

## Exports of Live Cattle to the United States — In Head

| Year | Jan. | Feb. | Mar. | Apr. | May | June | July | Aug. | Sept. | Oct. | Nov. | Dec. | Total |
|---|---|---|---|---|---|---|---|---|---|---|---|---|---|
| 2013 | 10,756 | 7,541 | 12,410 | 15,607 | 19,764 | 15,083 | 13,087 | 8,661 | 16,511 | 15,715 | 10,831 | 14,712 | 160,678 |
| 2014 | 8,824 | 7,740 | 10,977 | 9,351 | 11,531 | 5,106 | 9,438 | 10,303 | 6,072 | 10,932 | 7,871 | 9,539 | 107,684 |
| 2015 | 3,280 | 5,139 | 4,157 | 7,543 | 10,196 | 5,836 | 7,338 | 5,265 | 3,061 | 4,382 | 8,119 | 9,539 | 72,559 |
| 2016 | 3,331 | 5,010 | 5,157 | 3,893 | 3,365 | 4,475 | 3,332 | 3,309 | 3,578 | 7,072 | 8,119 | 8,243 | 69,485 |
| 2017 | 13,085 | 8,319 | 10,583 | 12,477 | 7,745 | 12,225 | 7,199 | 11,583 | 16,085 | 34,433 | 13,111 | 13,852 | 194,633 |
| 2018 | 7,797 | 14,893 | 15,144 | 15,122 | 14,746 | 17,869 | 17,312 | 19,387 | 26,243 | 44,207 | 36,655 | 24,244 | 239,500 |
| 2019 | 22,983 | 19,572 | 19,430 | 17,229 | 16,696 | 15,896 | 16,713 | 20,589 | 30,705 | 55,073 | 26,237 | 20,543 | 305,750 |
| 2020 | 31,438 | 24,628 | 13,225 | 16,355 | 19,271 | 16,415 | 21,581 | 18,384 | 37,753 | 43,842 | 43,253 | 27,611 | 321,142 |
| 2021 | 36,994 | 39,725 | 47,901 | 41,022 | 40,044 | 51,859 | 46,895 | 36,215 | 43,203 | 57,483 | 40,553 | 37,697 | 511,478 |
| 2022 | 35,762 | 28,594 | 27,065 | 31,488 | 24,594 | 22,306 | 22,763 | 30,521 | 49,150 | 59,240 | 49,604 | 41,258 | 422,345 |

[1] Preliminary. Source: Economic Research Service, U.S. Department of Agriculture (ERS-USDA)

## Federally Inspected Slaughter of Bison in the United States — In Thousands of Head

| Year | Jan. | Feb. | Mar. | Apr. | May | June | July | Aug. | Sept. | Oct. | Nov. | Dec. | Total |
|---|---|---|---|---|---|---|---|---|---|---|---|---|---|
| 2013 | 3.6 | 3.2 | 3.6 | 3.7 | 4.2 | 3.7 | 4.3 | 4.1 | 3.2 | 4.4 | 4.1 | 4.4 | 46.6 |
| 2014 | 4.8 | 3.9 | 4.7 | 4.2 | 4.6 | 4.5 | 4.4 | 3.9 | 4.1 | 4.4 | 3.8 | 4.4 | 51.7 |
| 2015 | 4.8 | 4.0 | 4.6 | 3.9 | 4.5 | 4.2 | 4.7 | 4.2 | 4.2 | 4.2 | 4.5 | 4.1 | 51.9 |
| 2016 | 4.2 | 4.3 | 4.9 | 4.3 | 4.8 | 4.9 | 4.3 | 4.4 | 4.1 | 4.1 | 4.5 | 3.9 | 52.7 |
| 2017 | 4.2 | 4.1 | 4.8 | 4.0 | 4.8 | 5.1 | 4.5 | 4.3 | 3.8 | 4.5 | 4.3 | 3.4 | 51.8 |
| 2018 | 3.8 | 3.7 | 4.6 | 4.2 | 4.7 | 5.0 | 4.6 | 4.4 | 3.5 | 4.4 | 4.4 | 3.7 | 51.0 |
| 2019 | 4.8 | 3.8 | 4.5 | 4.7 | 4.6 | 4.5 | 4.7 | 4.6 | 4.2 | 5.0 | 4.3 | 4.6 | 54.3 |
| 2020 | 4.9 | 4.4 | 5.8 | 5.4 | 5.7 | 5.2 | 5.6 | 5.0 | 4.8 | 5.5 | 5.0 | 5.4 | 62.7 |
| 2021 | 5.2 | 4.8 | 5.7 | 5.7 | 5.4 | 5.5 | 5.4 | 5.1 | 5.6 | 5.8 | 6.2 | 5.9 | 66.3 |
| 2022[1] | 6.1 | 5.9 | 6.3 | 5.4 | 5.9 | 6.4 | 5.6 | 6.4 | 5.5 | 6.0 | 6.3 | 6.4 | 72.2 |

[1] Preliminary. Source: Economic Research Service, U.S. Department of Agriculture (ERS-USDA)

## Other Slaughter of Bison in the United States — In Thousands of Head

| Year | Jan. | Feb. | Mar. | Apr. | May | June | July | Aug. | Sept. | Oct. | Nov. | Dec. | Total |
|---|---|---|---|---|---|---|---|---|---|---|---|---|---|
| 2013 | 1.0 | 1.0 | 0.9 | 0.9 | 0.9 | 0.8 | 0.9 | 0.9 | 0.8 | 0.8 | 0.8 | 0.9 | 10.6 |
| 2014 | 0.9 | 0.8 | 0.9 | 0.7 | 0.6 | 0.6 | 0.7 | 0.7 | 0.6 | 0.8 | 0.7 | 0.7 | 8.6 |
| 2015 | 0.8 | 0.8 | 1.1 | 0.7 | 0.6 | 0.8 | 0.6 | 0.6 | 0.7 | 0.7 | 0.7 | 0.7 | 8.8 |
| 2016 | 0.7 | 0.7 | 0.9 | 0.7 | 0.7 | 0.8 | 0.6 | 0.6 | 0.6 | 0.7 | 0.6 | 0.5 | 8.1 |
| 2017 | 0.6 | 0.6 | 1.2 | 0.4 | 0.4 | 0.4 | 0.4 | 0.5 | 0.6 | 0.7 | 0.5 | 0.4 | 6.7 |
| 2018 | 0.5 | 0.4 | 1.0 | 0.4 | 0.4 | 0.3 | 0.3 | 0.5 | 0.4 | 0.5 | 0.5 | 0.6 | 5.8 |
| 2019 | 0.6 | 0.5 | 0.6 | 0.5 | 0.4 | 0.4 | 0.3 | 0.4 | 0.4 | 0.5 | 0.4 | 0.5 | 5.5 |
| 2020 | 0.6 | 0.5 | 0.6 | 0.2 | 0.2 | 0.1 | 0.1 | 0.2 | 0.2 | 0.3 | 0.3 | 0.3 | 3.6 |
| 2021 | 0.4 | 0.2 | 0.3 | 0.2 | 0.2 | 0.3 | 0.2 | 0.3 | 0.3 | 0.4 | 0.3 | 0.3 | 3.4 |
| 2022 | 0.4 | 0.3 | 0.3 | 0.1 | 0.2 | 0.2 | 0.2 | 0.2 | 0.2 | 0.3 | 0.3 | 0.3 | 3.0 |

[1] Preliminary. Source: Economic Research Service, U.S. Department of Agriculture (ERS-USDA)

# Cement

Cement is made in a wide variety of compositions and is used in many ways. The best-known cement is *Portland cement*, which is bound with sand and gravel to create concrete. Concrete is used to unite the surfaces of various materials and to coat surfaces to protect them from various chemicals. Portland cement is almost universally used for structural concrete. It is manufactured from lime-bearing materials, usually limestone, together with clays, blast-furnace slag containing alumina and silica or shale. The combination is usually approximately 60 percent lime, 19 percent silica, 8 percent alumina, 5 percent iron, 5 percent magnesia, and 3 percent sulfur trioxide. Gypsum is often added to slow the hardening process. In 1924, the name "Portland cement" was coined by Joseph Aspdin, a British cement maker, because of the resemblance between concrete made from his cement and Portland stone. The United States did not start producing Portland cement in any great quantity until the 20th century. Hydraulic cements are those that set and harden in water. Clinker cement is an intermediate product in cement manufacture. The production and consumption of cement is directly related to the level of activity in the construction industry.

**Prices** – The average value (F.O.B. mill) of Portland cement in 2022 rose by +0.0% to $130 per metric ton, remaining at the record high since 2021.

**Supply** – World production of hydraulic cement in 2022 fell by -6.8% yr/yr to 4.100 billion metric tons. The world's largest hydraulic cement producers were China with 51.2% of world production in 2022, India with 9.0%, the U.S. with 2.3%, and Turkey with 2.1%.

U.S. production of cement in 2022 rose by +2.2% yr/yr to 95.00 million metric tons, but still below the 2005 record high of 99.319 million metric tons. U.S. shipments of cement from mills in the U.S. in 2022 rose by +0.9% to 110.000 million metric tons but remained below the 2005 record high of 128.000 million metric tons.

**Demand** – U.S. consumption of cement in 2021 rose by +5.8% yr/yr to 109.000 million metric tons, still well below the 2005 record high of 128.260 million metric tons.

**Trade** – The U.S. relied on imports for 16.7% of its cement consumption in 2022. The two main suppliers of cement to the U.S. were Canada and Mexico. U.S. exports of cement in 2022 fell by -4.3% yr/yr to 900 thousand metric tons.

## World Production of Hydraulic Cement   In Thousands of Short Tons

| Year | Brazil | China | France | Germany | India | Italy | Japan | Korea, South | Russia | Spain | Turkey | United States | World Total |
|---|---|---|---|---|---|---|---|---|---|---|---|---|---|
| 2015 | 65,283 | 2,359,000 | 15,600 | 31,150 | 260,000 | 20,800 | 54,827 | 52,044 | 62,104 | 15,000 | 71,419 | 84,940 | 4,060,000 |
| 2016 | 57,557 | 2,410,000 | 15,900 | 32,737 | 284,000 | 19,300 | 53,255 | 56,747 | 54,935 | 15,000 | 75,403 | 85,153 | 4,140,000 |
| 2017 | 54,004 | 2,331,000 | 16,900 | 33,991 | 308,000 | 19,300 | 55,195 | 57,400 | 54,721 | 14,500 | 80,552 | 86,799 | 4,130,000 |
| 2018 | 53,553 | 2,236,000 | 16,500 | 33,633 | 310,000 | 19,300 | 55,307 | 52,093 | 53,678 | 16,215 | 72,544 | 87,021 | 4,080,000 |
| 2019 | 56,611 | 2,350,000 | 16,500 | 34,200 | 334,000 | 19,200 | 53,462 | 50,000 | 57,679 | 16,998 | 56,966 | 87,710 | 4,190,000 |
| 2020 | 61,052 | 2,380,000 | 15,200 | 33,600 | 295,000 | 18,500 | 50,905 | 48,000 | 56,000 | 15,600 | 72,299 | 89,000 | 4,190,000 |
| 2021[1] | 66,000 | 2,400,000 | | | 350,000 | | 50,000 | 50,000 | 61,000 | | 82,000 | 93,000 | 4,400,000 |
| 2022[2] | 65,000 | 2,100,000 | | | 370,000 | | 50,000 | 50,000 | 62,000 | | 85,000 | 95,000 | 4,100,000 |

[1] Preliminary.   [2] Estimate.   *Source: U.S. Geological Survey (USGS)*

## Salient Statistics of Cement in the United States

| Year | Net Import Reliance as a % of Apparent Consump | Production Portland 1,000 Metric tons | Production Other[3] | Production Total | Capacity Used at Portland Mills % | Shipments From Mills Total (Mil. MT) | Shipments From Mills Value[4] (Mil. $) | Average Value (F.O.B. Mill) $ per MT | Stocks at Mills Dec. 31 | Exports | Apparent Consumption | Imports for Consumption[5] Canada | Japan | Mexico | Spain | Total |
|---|---|---|---|---|---|---|---|---|---|---|---|---|---|---|---|---|
| 2015 | 11 | 82,093 | 2,312 | 84,405 | 68.5 | 93,338 | 9,800 | 106.50 | 7,230 | 1,288 | 92,150 | 4,497 | 2 | 338 | 270 | 11,255 |
| 2016 | 13 | 82,181 | 2,514 | 84,695 | 69.5 | 94,300 | 10,500 | 111.00 | 7,420 | 1,283 | 95,150 | 4,512 | 1 | 466 | 389 | 13,238 |
| 2017 | 13 | 83,963 | 2,393 | 86,356 | 69.8 | 96,900 | 11,300 | 117.00 | 7,870 | 1,035 | 97,160 | 4,352 | 1 | 686 | 601 | 13,497 |
| 2018 | 14 | 84,000 | 2,400 | 86,400 | 69.9 | 98,500 | 11,900 | 121.00 | 8,580 | 919 | 98,500 | 5,326 | 1 | 1,024 | 429 | 14,660 |
| 2019 | 15 | 85,800 | 1,800 | 87,600 | 69.9 | 103,000 | 12,700 | 124.00 | 7,990 | 1,024 | 102,000 | 5,252 | 1 | 1,324 | 242 | 15,834 |
| 2020 | 15 | 87,400 | 1,900 | 89,300 | 71.3 | 103,000 | 12,900 | 125.00 | 7,180 | 884 | 105,000 | 5,031 | 1 | 1,705 | 123 | 16,735 |
| 2021[1] | 18 | | | 93,000 | | 109,000 | | 130.00 | 7,000 | 940 | 110,000 | | | | | |
| 2022[2] | 21 | | | 95,000 | | 110,000 | | 130.00 | 7,500 | 900 | 120,000 | | | | | |

[1] Preliminary.   [2] Estimate.   [3] Masonry, natural & pozzolan (slag-line).   [4] Value received F.O.B. mill, excluding cost of containers.   [5] Hydraulic & clinker cement for consumption.   [6] Less than 1/2 unit.   *Source: U.S. Geological Survey (USGS)*

## Shipments of Finished Portland Cement from Mills in the United States   In Thousands of Metric Tons

| Year | Jan. | Feb. | Mar. | Apr. | May | June | July | Aug. | Sept. | Oct. | Nov. | Dec. | Total |
|---|---|---|---|---|---|---|---|---|---|---|---|---|---|
| 2016 | 4,725.8 | 5,376.4 | 6,723.3 | 6,763.5 | 7,136.6 | 8,268.5 | 7,237.9 | 8,272.8 | 7,741.7 | 7,958.6 | 7,008.8 | 5,414.3 | 82,628.2 |
| 2017 | 4,869.2 | 5,398.2 | 6,687.5 | 6,673.6 | 7,738.1 | 8,236.3 | 7,507.0 | 8,497.2 | 7,606.4 | 8,222.6 | 7,253.1 | 5,515.0 | 84,204.1 |
| 2018 | 5,125.4 | 5,130.2 | 6,589.9 | 7,220.0 | 8,205.8 | 8,135.0 | 8,034.7 | 8,769.6 | 7,307.9 | 8,421.8 | 6,699.3 | 5,346.6 | 84,986.2 |
| 2019 | 5,565.0 | 5,013.8 | 6,386.3 | 7,550.0 | 7,941.0 | 7,791.7 | 8,653.3 | 8,910.4 | 8,162.9 | 8,656.2 | 6,830.7 | 5,809.9 | 87,271.2 |
| 2020 | 5,962.4 | 5,447.4 | 6,619.9 | 7,119.8 | 7,562.4 | 8,734.2 | 8,497.4 | 8,298.4 | 8,019.8 | 8,602.4 | 7,429.4 | 6,480.3 | 88,773.7 |
| 2021 | 5,728.0 | 4,791.9 | 7,555.3 | 8,239.3 | 7,755.9 | 8,568.3 | 8,154.1 | 8,562.8 | 8,296.0 | 8,299.4 | 8,036.2 | 6,936.1 | 90,923.3 |
| 2022[1] | 5,641.9 | 5,584.9 | 7,767.9 | 7,621.9 | 8,112.2 | 9,065.2 | 7,983.0 | 8,978.1 | 8,414.5 | 8,438.3 | 7,103.5 | 6,001.2 | 90,712.6 |

[1] Preliminary.   *Source: U.S. Geological Survey (USGS)*

# Cheese

Since prehistoric times, humans have been making and eating cheese. Dating back as far as 6,000 BC, archaeologists have discovered that cheese had been made from cow and goat milk and stored in tall jars. The Romans turned cheese-making into a culinary art, mixing sheep and goat milk and adding herbs and spices for flavoring. By 300 AD, cheese was being exported regularly to countries along the Mediterranean coast.

Cheese is made from the milk of cows and other mammals such as sheep, goats, buffalo, reindeer, camels, yaks, and mares. More than 400 varieties of cheese exist. There are three basic steps common to all cheese making. First, proteins in milk are transformed into curds, or solid lumps. Second, the curds are separated from the milky liquid (or whey) and shaped or pressed into molds. Finally, the shaped curds are ripened using a variety of aging and curing techniques. Cheeses are usually grouped according to their moisture content into fresh, soft, semi-soft, hard, and very hard. Many classifications overlap due to texture changes with aging.

Cheese is a multi-billion-dollar a year industry in the U.S. Cheddar cheese is the most common natural cheese produced in the U.S., accounting for 35% of U.S. production. Cheeses originating in America include Colby, cream cheese, and Monterey Jack. Varieties other than American cheeses, mostly Italian, now have had a combined level of production that easily exceeds American cheeses.

Futures and options on cheese are traded on the CME Group. The CME's cheese futures contract calls for the delivery of 20,000 pounds of cheese and is priced in Dollars per pound.

**Prices** – The average monthly price of American Cheese at the CME Group in 2022 rose by +21.1% yr/yr to $2.0958 per pound, below the 2014 record high of $2.1094 cents per pound.

**Supply** – World production of cheese in 2023 is expected to rise by +0.8% yr/yr to 22.353 million metric tons, which would be a new record high. The European Union is expected to be the world's largest producer of cheese, with 47.4% of the total world production in 2022. U.S. production was the next largest with 28.7% of the total. U.S. production of all cheese in 2022 rose by +1.7% to 13.903 billion pounds, which was a new record high.

## World Production of Cheese   In Thousands of Metric Tons

| Year | Argentina | Australia | Brazil | Canada | European Union | Japan | Korea, South | Mexico | New Zealand | Russia | Ukraine | United States | World Total |
|---|---|---|---|---|---|---|---|---|---|---|---|---|---|
| 2012 | 564 | 352 | 700 | 386 | 9,287 | 47 | 23 | 293 | 328 | 790 | 245 | 4,938 | 18,420 |
| 2013 | 549 | 318 | 722 | 388 | 9,368 | 49 | 22 | 316 | 311 | 713 | 247 | 5,036 | 18,227 |
| 2014 | 562 | 328 | 736 | 396 | 9,560 | 46 | 24 | 343 | 325 | 760 | 203 | 5,222 | 18,738 |
| 2015 | 566 | 343 | 754 | 419 | 9,740 | 46 | 23 | 363 | 355 | 861 | 190 | 5,367 | 19,276 |
| 2016 | 552 | 344 | 745 | 445 | 9,640 | 47 | 25 | 375 | 360 | 865 | 186 | 5,525 | 19,835 |
| 2017 | 514 | 348 | 771 | 497 | 9,796 | 46 | 35 | 396 | 386 | 951 | 190 | 5,733 | 20,390 |
| 2018 | 444 | 366 | 760 | 510 | 9,872 | 45 | 37 | 419 | 370 | 970 | 192 | 5,914 | 20,656 |
| 2019 | 523 | 364 | 770 | 515 | 10,155 | 44 | 40 | 437 | 365 | 983 | 187 | 5,959 | 21,128 |
| 2020 | 488 | 379 | 790 | 523 | 10,362 | 48 | 45 | 446 | 350 | 1,059 | 180 | 6,005 | 21,525 |
| 2021 | 530 | 385 | 790 | 522 | 10,550 | 49 | 45 | 448 | 380 | 1,075 | 182 | 6,217 | 22,051 |
| 2022[1] | 535 | 390 | 745 | 530 | 10,550 | 48 | 47 | 455 | 375 | 1,085 | 150 | 6,350 | 22,167 |
| 2023[2] | 535 | 395 | 770 | 540 | 10,600 | 50 | 45 | 465 | 360 | 1,100 | 145 | 6,425 | 22,353 |

[1] Preliminary.   [2] Forecast.   NA = Not available.   Source: Foreign Agricultural Service, U.S. Department of Agriculture (FAS-USDA)

## Production of Cheese in the United States   In Millions of Pounds

| Year | American Whole Milk | American Part Skim | American Total | Swiss, Including Block | Munster | Brick | Lim-burger | Cream & Neufchatel Cheese | Italian Varieties | Blue Mond | All Other Varieties | Total of All Cheese[2] | Cottage Cheese Lowfat | Curd[3] | Cream-ed[4] |
|---|---|---|---|---|---|---|---|---|---|---|---|---|---|---|---|
| 2013 | 4,420 | ---- | 4,420 | 294.5 | 163.2 | 9.3 | [5] | 842.3 | 4,735.5 | [5] | 151.9 | 11,102 | 370.3 | 389.4 | 307.4 |
| 2014 | 4,588 | ---- | 4,588 | 297.8 | 163.7 | 2.9 | [5] | 851.7 | 4,950.2 | [5] | 154.2 | 11,512 | 364.6 | 381.1 | 303.1 |
| 2015 | 4,694 | ---- | 4,694 | 312.0 | 177.5 | 3.4 | [5] | 876.3 | 5,081.8 | [5] | ---- | 11,831 | 363.0 | 400.6 | 317.5 |
| 2016 | 4,769 | ---- | 4,769 | 312.0 | 181.4 | 2.8 | [5] | 909.0 | 5,304.4 | [5] | ---- | 12,182 | 367.8 | 406.4 | 329.4 |
| 2017 | 5,072 | ---- | 5,072 | 316.7 | 189.2 | 2.4 | [5] | 918.1 | 5,395.2 | [5] | ---- | 12,640 | 344.4 | 390.4 | 330.5 |
| 2018 | 5,254 | ---- | 5,254 | 332.3 | 191.2 | 2.3 | [5] | 914.8 | 5,556.9 | [5] | ---- | 13,025 | 342.1 | 402.4 | 352.8 |
| 2019 | 5,211 | ---- | 5,211 | 338.3 | 196.9 | 2.0 | [5] | 931.6 | 5,668.1 | [5] | ---- | 13,107 | 324.9 | 388.0 | 353.5 |
| 2020 | 5,337 | ---- | 5,337 | 324.9 | 188.5 | 1.6 | [5] | 1,002.0 | 5,624.3 | [5] | ---- | 13,238 | 308.4 | 378.8 | 361.8 |
| 2021 | 5,563 | ---- | 5,563 | 330.2 | 191.5 | 2.0 | [5] | 1,034.9 | 5,750.6 | [5] | ---- | 13,695 | 302.5 | 358.4 | 348.2 |
| 2022[1] | 5,574 | ---- | 5,574 | 348.6 | | | [5] | 1,091.6 | 5,909.3 | [5] | ---- | 12,750 | 297.1 | 363.1 | 344.1 |

[1] Preliminary.   [2] Excludes full-skim cheddar and cottage cheese.   [3] Includes cottage, pot, and baker's cheese with a butterfat content of less than 4%.
[4] Includes cheese with a butterfat content of 4 to 19 %.   [5] Included in All Other Varieties.   NA = Not available.
Source: Economic Research Service, U.S. Department of Agriculture ERS-USDA)

# CHEESE

## World Consumption of Cheese   In Thousands of Metric Tons

| Year | Argentina | Australia | Brazil | Canada | European Union | Japan | Korea, South | Mexico | New Zealand | Russia | Ukraine | United States | World Total |
|---|---|---|---|---|---|---|---|---|---|---|---|---|---|
| 2014 | 507 | 265 | 754 | 407 | 8,884 | 278 | 118 | 438 | 40 | 1,043 | 197 | 4,977 | 18,092 |
| 2015 | 524 | 270 | 773 | 415 | 9,087 | 294 | 137 | 475 | 41 | 1,041 | 184 | 5,149 | 18,599 |
| 2016 | 508 | 275 | 785 | 458 | 8,616 | 304 | 136 | 496 | 42 | 1,069 | 187 | 5,379 | 19,252 |
| 2017 | 485 | 291 | 799 | 504 | 8,727 | 324 | 159 | 511 | 40 | 1,141 | 188 | 5,494 | 19,690 |
| 2018 | 380 | 293 | 785 | 536 | 8,790 | 329 | 155 | 526 | 38 | 1,200 | 198 | 5,675 | 19,958 |
| 2019 | 461 | 297 | 795 | 539 | 9,019 | 346 | 166 | 551 | 38 | 1,231 | 205 | 5,751 | 20,462 |
| 2020 | 420 | 305 | 817 | 555 | 9,183 | 335 | 188 | 549 | 38 | 1,338 | 222 | 5,745 | 20,768 |
| 2021 | 457 | 310 | 817 | 562 | 9,361 | 335 | 195 | 568 | 38 | 1,363 | 230 | 5,939 | 21,276 |
| 2022[1] | 435 | 320 | 774 | 571 | 9,365 | 332 | 193 | 594 | 39 | 1,390 | 185 | 6,029 | 21,288 |
| 2023[2] | 450 | 320 | 800 | 585 | 9,415 | 335 | 200 | 605 | 40 | 1,430 | 190 | 6,079 | 21,522 |

[1] Preliminary.   [2] Forecast.   NA = Not available.   Source: Foreign Agricultural Service, U.S. Department of Agriculture (FAS-USDA)

## World Exports of Cheese   In Thousands of Metric Tons

| Year | Argentina | Australia | Brazil | Canada | European Union | Japan | Korea, South | Mexico | New Zealand | Russia | Ukraine | United States | World Total |
|---|---|---|---|---|---|---|---|---|---|---|---|---|---|
| 2014 | 57 | 151 | 3 | 12 | 721 | 4 | 278 | 29 | 19 | 368 | 1,810 | 4,938 | 18,420 |
| 2015 | 43 | 171 | 3 | 12 | 719 | 4 | 327 | 24 | 11 | 317 | 1,815 | 5,367 | 19,276 |
| 2016 | 53 | 167 | 3 | 13 | 1,231 | 5 | 355 | 25 | 8 | 287 | 2,515 | 5,525 | 19,835 |
| 2017 | 44 | 171 | 4 | 13 | 1,275 | 7 | 343 | 25 | 9 | 340 | 2,589 | 5,733 | 20,390 |
| 2018 | 61 | 172 | 4 | 10 | 1,279 | 16 | 322 | 24 | 8 | 348 | 2,643 | 5,914 | 20,656 |
| 2019 | 61 | 160 | 3 | 12 | 1,348 | 7 | 335 | 26 | 7 | 357 | 2,767 | 5,959 | 21,128 |
| 2020 | 70 | 153 | 4 | 11 | 1,402 | 11 | 327 | 30 | 6 | 355 | 2,837 | 6,005 | 21,525 |
| 2021 | 78 | 157 | 5 | 8 | 1,385 | 12 | 358 | 35 | 7 | 402 | 2,902 | 6,217 | 22,051 |
| 2022[1] | 85 | 155 | 5 | 7 | 1,370 | 16 | 335 | 40 | 5 | 451 | 2,957 | 6,350 | 22,167 |
| 2023[2] | 90 | 165 | 5 | 8 | 1,375 | 15 | 335 | 45 | 5 | 469 | 3,005 | 6,425 | 22,353 |

[1] Preliminary.   [2] Forecast.   NA = Not available.   Source: Foreign Agricultural Service, U.S. Department of Agriculture (FAS-USDA)

## World Imports of Cheese   In Thousands of Metric Tons

| Year | Australia | Brazil | Canada | European Union | Japan | Korea, South | Mexico | Philippines | Russia | Taiwan | Ukraine | United States | World Total |
|---|---|---|---|---|---|---|---|---|---|---|---|---|---|
| 2014 | 80 | 21 | 26 | 77 | 232 | 97 | 99 | 19 | 320 | 26 | 12 | 127 | 1,223 |
| 2015 | 89 | 22 | 26 | 61 | 249 | 112 | 116 | 27 | 209 | 29 | 5 | 157 | 1,196 |
| 2016 | 99 | 43 | 27 | 195 | 258 | 110 | 126 | 30 | 223 | 32 | 7 | 165 | 1,909 |
| 2017 | 116 | 32 | 28 | 191 | 273 | 125 | 122 | 38 | 226 | 32 | 10 | 138 | 1,938 |
| 2018 | 98 | 29 | 31 | 197 | 286 | 124 | 123 | 38 | 250 | 32 | 14 | 138 | 1,998 |
| 2019 | 97 | 28 | 36 | 212 | 303 | 131 | 121 | 40 | 273 | 31 | 24 | 139 | 2,095 |
| 2020 | 98 | 31 | 41 | 223 | 292 | 148 | 114 | 41 | 311 | 34 | 47 | 128 | 2,139 |
| 2021 | 97 | 32 | 48 | 196 | 288 | 157 | 132 | 49 | 326 | 37 | 55 | 145 | 2,159 |
| 2022[1] | 90 | 34 | 50 | 185 | 280 | 150 | 155 | 50 | 345 | 35 | 40 | 146 | 2,128 |
| 2023[2] | 90 | 35 | 53 | 190 | 285 | 150 | 155 | 50 | 375 | 36 | 50 | 153 | 2,200 |

[1] Preliminary.   [2] Forecast.   NA = Not available.   Source: Foreign Agricultural Service, U.S. Department of Agriculture (FAS-USDA)

## World Ending Stocks of Cheese   In Thousands of Metric Tons

| Year | Argentina | Australia | Canada | Japan | Korea, South | New Zealand | Russia | Ukraine | United States | World Total |
|---|---|---|---|---|---|---|---|---|---|---|
| 2014 | 40 | 57 | 63 | 15 | 4 | 64 | 30 | 8 | 462 | 792 |
| 2015 | 40 | 48 | 81 | 15 | 2 | 59 | 35 | 8 | 520 | 850 |
| 2016 | 34 | 49 | 82 | 15 | 1 | 32 | 29 | 6 | 544 | 827 |
| 2017 | 23 | 51 | 90 | 9 | 2 | 46 | 40 | 9 | 581 | 876 |
| 2018 | 30 | 50 | 85 | 10 | 8 | 68 | 36 | 9 | 610 | 929 |
| 2019 | 33 | 54 | 85 | 10 | 13 | 73 | 35 | 8 | 600 | 923 |
| 2020 | 32 | 73 | 83 | 14 | 17 | 68 | 37 | 7 | 633 | 982 |
| 2021 | 30 | 88 | 83 | 15 | 23 | 63 | 40 | 7 | 654 | 1,014 |
| 2022[1] | 50 | 93 | 85 | 10 | 26 | 76 | 40 | 7 | 670 | 1,064 |
| 2023[2] | 50 | 93 | 85 | 9 | 20 | 73 | 40 | 7 | 700 | 1,090 |

[1] Preliminary.   [2] Forecast.   NA = Not available.   Source: Foreign Agricultural Service, U.S. Department of Agriculture (FAS-USDA)

# CHEESE

## Production of Cheese[2] in the United States    In Millions of Pounds

| Year | Jan. | Feb. | Mar. | Apr. | May | June | July | Aug. | Sept. | Oct. | Nov. | Dec. | Total |
|---|---|---|---|---|---|---|---|---|---|---|---|---|---|
| 2013 | 931.7 | 848.7 | 954.3 | 929.8 | 943.9 | 912.1 | 893.9 | 931.7 | 899.2 | 954.8 | 922.5 | 979.3 | 11,101.7 |
| 2014 | 962.4 | 859.4 | 976.0 | 967.3 | 977.2 | 951.0 | 965.0 | 935.6 | 943.0 | 987.8 | 965.2 | 1,022.1 | 11,512.1 |
| 2015 | 994.1 | 896.7 | 1,013.0 | 977.3 | 988.2 | 976.1 | 1,002.0 | 979.0 | 965.5 | 1,018.0 | 986.4 | 1,035.1 | 11,831.4 |
| 2016 | 1,025.7 | 947.5 | 1,028.6 | 1,003.2 | 1,010.7 | 998.4 | 1,020.8 | 1,006.8 | 991.4 | 1,052.2 | 1,029.2 | 1,067.0 | 12,181.5 |
| 2017 | 1,060.9 | 958.4 | 1,069.8 | 1,057.1 | 1,074.7 | 1,044.0 | 1,052.0 | 1,045.3 | 1,026.8 | 1,082.4 | 1,065.7 | 1,102.8 | 12,640.0 |
| 2018 | 1,098.7 | 992.8 | 1,108.0 | 1,078.1 | 1,085.2 | 1,066.0 | 1,087.1 | 1,087.0 | 1,059.1 | 1,154.2 | 1,096.0 | 1,112.4 | 13,024.6 |
| 2019 | 1,098.4 | 991.3 | 1,122.4 | 1,085.0 | 1,105.9 | 1,067.7 | 1,087.6 | 1,113.6 | 1,080.5 | 1,138.2 | 1,093.4 | 1,122.5 | 13,106.7 |
| 2020 | 1,110.5 | 1,031.7 | 1,121.4 | 1,052.0 | 1,101.2 | 1,121.6 | 1,110.1 | 1,091.5 | 1,104.2 | 1,136.9 | 1,102.3 | 1,154.5 | 13,237.9 |
| 2021 | 1,135.6 | 1,043.5 | 1,183.4 | 1,154.6 | 1,163.2 | 1,126.8 | 1,145.7 | 1,148.8 | 1,134.4 | 1,152.1 | 1,130.4 | 1,176.5 | 13,694.9 |
| 2022[1] | 1,172.0 | 1,105.3 | 1,210.1 | 1,158.7 | 1,184.1 | 1,152.5 | 1,151.2 | 1,150.4 | 1,140.0 | 1,171.0 | 1,153.7 | 1,194.6 | 13,943.7 |

[1] Preliminary.   [2] Excludes cottage cheese.   Source: National Agricultural Statistics Service, U.S. Department of Agriculture (NASS-USDA)

## Production of American Cheese[2] in the United States    In Thousands of Pounds

| Year | Jan. | Feb. | Mar. | Apr. | May | June | July | Aug. | Sept. | Oct. | Nov. | Dec. | Total |
|---|---|---|---|---|---|---|---|---|---|---|---|---|---|
| 2013 | 377,258 | 347,262 | 384,770 | 376,891 | 387,590 | 362,977 | 345,707 | 381,125 | 347,449 | 371,125 | 356,220 | 381,474 | 4,419,848 |
| 2014 | 388,420 | 345,464 | 387,071 | 385,322 | 399,239 | 374,373 | 385,175 | 376,203 | 369,843 | 393,414 | 383,500 | 399,999 | 4,588,023 |
| 2015 | 402,222 | 357,376 | 395,823 | 396,691 | 407,667 | 390,447 | 397,235 | 394,943 | 379,550 | 392,592 | 380,004 | 399,921 | 4,694,471 |
| 2016 | 402,377 | 368,000 | 402,001 | 398,750 | 403,040 | 392,166 | 401,815 | 393,459 | 379,456 | 403,397 | 400,983 | 423,444 | 4,768,888 |
| 2017 | 434,638 | 390,324 | 429,569 | 434,669 | 443,095 | 419,273 | 414,508 | 414,292 | 403,555 | 430,496 | 413,725 | 443,985 | 5,072,129 |
| 2018 | 448,124 | 406,189 | 443,185 | 444,287 | 442,968 | 429,076 | 440,937 | 435,388 | 424,032 | 457,122 | 434,185 | 443,985 | 5,253,833 |
| 2019 | 439,283 | 391,027 | 442,723 | 430,539 | 443,683 | 427,638 | 434,449 | 452,030 | 415,687 | 445,601 | 434,185 | 448,340 | 5,253,833 |
| 2020 | 437,451 | 418,605 | 446,423 | 446,525 | 441,148 | 431,782 | 453,096 | 445,137 | 432,114 | 460,217 | 432,438 | 456,378 | 5,211,476 |
| 2021 | 474,315 | 426,094 | 480,500 | 478,196 | 481,545 | 457,394 | 467,274 | 462,477 | 454,668 | 460,680 | 449,783 | 474,946 | 5,337,227 |
| 2022[1] | 471,650 | 442,683 | 473,724 | 467,510 | 481,173 | 461,140 | 466,434 | 453,081 | 441,832 | 469,466 | 462,954 | 482,701 | 5,574,348 |

[1] Preliminary.   [2] Includes Cheddar, Colby, Monterey, and Jack.   Source: National Agricultural Statistics Service, U.S. Department of Agriculture

## Production of Blue and Gorgonzola Cheese in the United States    In Thousands of Pounds

| Year | Jan. | Feb. | Mar. | Apr. | May | June | July | Aug. | Sept. | Oct. | Nov. | Dec. | Total |
|---|---|---|---|---|---|---|---|---|---|---|---|---|---|
| 2013 | 6,919 | 7,537 | 7,464 | 7,704 | 9,318 | 7,748 | 6,786 | 8,438 | 7,703 | 7,881 | 7,061 | 7,842 | 92,401 |
| 2014 | 7,272 | 6,611 | 8,028 | 8,329 | 7,917 | 7,819 | 8,687 | 8,231 | 7,966 | 7,464 | 6,884 | 7,637 | 92,845 |
| 2015 | 7,402 | 7,730 | 8,198 | 7,777 | 7,929 | 7,933 | 7,930 | 7,729 | 8,208 | 7,751 | 7,843 | 8,059 | 94,489 |
| 2016 | 6,994 | 7,289 | 8,046 | 7,010 | 8,685 | 8,083 | 7,284 | 8,195 | 6,980 | 7,493 | 7,704 | 7,109 | 90,872 |
| 2017 | 7,620 | 7,060 | 7,182 | 7,876 | 8,607 | 7,942 | 7,845 | 7,840 | 6,904 | 7,899 | 7,532 | 7,009 | 91,316 |
| 2018 | 7,459 | 7,115 | 8,151 | 7,863 | 7,994 | 7,246 | 7,890 | 8,027 | 8,339 | 8,379 | 7,442 | 8,743 | 94,648 |
| 2019 | 7,522 | 6,482 | 7,977 | 7,588 | 8,331 | 8,758 | 7,914 | 8,387 | 8,099 | 9,270 | 7,668 | 6,648 | 94,644 |
| 2020 | 7,120 | 7,035 | 7,230 | 3,131 | 4,434 | 6,966 | 7,710 | 8,646 | 6,677 | 6,530 | 5,646 | 4,918 | 76,043 |
| 2021 | 5,345 | 6,795 | 7,782 | 7,393 | 8,207 | 7,751 | 6,742 | 7,314 | 7,494 | 8,896 | 7,913 | 7,556 | 89,188 |
| 2022[1] | 8,197 | 8,170 | 7,102 | 7,883 | 7,380 | 7,959 | 7,422 | 7,391 | 7,519 | 7,466 | 7,701 | 6,571 | 90,761 |

[1] Preliminary.   Source: National Agricultural Statistics Service, U.S. Department of Agriculture (NASS-USDA)

## Production of Brick and Muenster Cheeses in the United States    In Thousands of Pounds

| Year | Jan. | Feb. | Mar. | Apr. | May | June | July | Aug. | Sept. | Oct. | Nov. | Dec. | Total |
|---|---|---|---|---|---|---|---|---|---|---|---|---|---|
| 2013 | 13,922 | 11,622 | 13,302 | 13,942 | 15,309 | 13,448 | 14,686 | 15,309 | 13,981 | 16,167 | 15,464 | 15,380 | 172,532 |
| 2014 | 13,079 | 11,606 | 13,757 | 13,698 | 15,174 | 13,951 | 14,862 | 14,726 | 13,309 | 14,520 | 13,738 | 14,172 | 166,592 |
| 2015 | 15,384 | 13,060 | 14,748 | 14,919 | 16,314 | 14,151 | 17,246 | 14,663 | 13,301 | 16,667 | 16,051 | 14,485 | 180,989 |
| 2016 | 14,898 | 14,227 | 14,075 | 15,955 | 16,252 | 15,053 | 16,390 | 15,165 | 15,161 | 16,958 | 15,634 | 14,431 | 184,199 |
| 2017 | 15,104 | 13,208 | 15,947 | 16,755 | 16,496 | 15,581 | 18,274 | 16,667 | 15,147 | 17,595 | 16,248 | 14,568 | 191,591 |
| 2018 | 15,282 | 14,089 | 15,117 | 16,133 | 17,079 | 16,235 | 18,151 | 16,169 | 15,964 | 18,514 | 16,100 | 14,690 | 193,523 |
| 2019 | 18,222 | 14,853 | 14,806 | 16,927 | 18,167 | 16,749 | 17,710 | 15,723 | 15,664 | 19,217 | 15,745 | 15,123 | 198,906 |
| 2020 | 15,036 | 14,760 | 16,684 | 13,573 | 18,188 | 17,343 | 16,319 | 14,535 | 16,252 | 16,842 | 16,755 | 13,785 | 190,072 |
| 2021 | 16,679 | 14,628 | 17,557 | 15,476 | 17,416 | 17,506 | 16,326 | 14,388 | 14,621 | 16,074 | 16,259 | 16,260 | 193,190 |
| 2022[1] | 16,494 | 15,009 | 16,449 | 17,868 | 15,963 | 16,631 | 16,140 | 14,876 | 15,510 | 16,560 | 15,819 | 15,370 | 192,689 |

[1] Preliminary.   Source: National Agricultural Statistics Service, U.S. Department of Agriculture (NASS-USDA)

# CHEESE

## Production of Cream and Neufchatel Cheeses in the United States    In Thousands of Pounds

| Year | Jan. | Feb. | Mar. | Apr. | May | June | July | Aug. | Sept. | Oct. | Nov. | Dec. | Total |
|---|---|---|---|---|---|---|---|---|---|---|---|---|---|
| 2013 | 64,296 | 56,575 | 63,072 | 63,998 | 64,764 | 66,889 | 66,186 | 75,979 | 79,670 | 81,298 | 81,582 | 77,955 | 842,264 |
| 2014 | 62,019 | 54,268 | 66,734 | 71,432 | 65,134 | 69,553 | 71,158 | 73,798 | 76,243 | 83,428 | 80,094 | 77,852 | 851,713 |
| 2015 | 64,490 | 59,747 | 71,231 | 61,357 | 61,071 | 68,551 | 74,875 | 82,070 | 83,438 | 96,108 | 81,217 | 72,131 | 876,286 |
| 2016 | 72,325 | 69,992 | 66,940 | 70,299 | 61,734 | 71,636 | 71,859 | 84,945 | 78,674 | 93,188 | 86,074 | 81,306 | 908,972 |
| 2017 | 73,848 | 64,164 | 63,346 | 69,644 | 70,934 | 69,356 | 78,631 | 86,692 | 89,137 | 84,929 | 83,126 | 84,264 | 918,071 |
| 2018 | 71,932 | 63,932 | 72,774 | 68,434 | 67,467 | 74,650 | 73,530 | 85,203 | 78,516 | 95,019 | 85,805 | 77,562 | 914,824 |
| 2019 | 72,842 | 60,192 | 79,212 | 70,516 | 72,309 | 71,339 | 79,986 | 85,171 | 86,328 | 89,440 | 85,127 | 79,176 | 931,638 |
| 2020 | 79,982 | 62,709 | 76,471 | 63,071 | 76,750 | 94,387 | 90,069 | 91,402 | 92,527 | 91,338 | 94,664 | 88,646 | 1,002,016 |
| 2021 | 78,479 | 72,787 | 82,298 | 81,648 | 93,185 | 86,574 | 82,130 | 94,946 | 92,398 | 86,516 | 90,978 | 92,979 | 1,034,918 |
| 2022[1] | 87,407 | 85,210 | 96,581 | 84,477 | 102,683 | 93,874 | 87,564 | 94,908 | 91,272 | 89,794 | 85,845 | 92,026 | 1,091,641 |

[1] Preliminary.    Source: National Agricultural Statistics Service, U.S. Department of Agriculture (NASS-USDA)

## Production of Swiss Cheese in the United States    In Thousands of Pounds

| Year | Jan. | Feb. | Mar. | Apr. | May | June | July | Aug. | Sept. | Oct. | Nov. | Dec. | Total |
|---|---|---|---|---|---|---|---|---|---|---|---|---|---|
| 2013 | 25,602 | 23,362 | 24,637 | 25,916 | 26,455 | 23,326 | 25,240 | 24,422 | 23,010 | 23,983 | 23,452 | 25,090 | 294,495 |
| 2014 | 26,055 | 23,148 | 25,699 | 25,550 | 26,690 | 25,092 | 25,734 | 22,695 | 22,599 | 23,350 | 23,763 | 27,427 | 297,802 |
| 2015 | 24,427 | 23,571 | 26,662 | 26,616 | 27,387 | 25,619 | 26,802 | 26,152 | 25,278 | 26,529 | 25,150 | 27,822 | 312,015 |
| 2016 | 27,434 | 24,429 | 26,020 | 24,257 | 26,336 | 27,140 | 27,001 | 25,403 | 25,034 | 26,017 | 25,883 | 27,023 | 311,977 |
| 2017 | 26,286 | 24,169 | 26,846 | 26,383 | 26,262 | 26,040 | 26,736 | 25,646 | 25,622 | 27,338 | 26,837 | 28,489 | 316,654 |
| 2018 | 28,183 | 26,350 | 28,685 | 26,828 | 28,816 | 27,763 | 28,195 | 27,884 | 26,414 | 27,390 | 27,888 | 27,907 | 332,303 |
| 2019 | 29,913 | 26,489 | 27,682 | 27,601 | 29,824 | 28,290 | 29,103 | 28,896 | 27,705 | 29,136 | 26,100 | 27,534 | 338,273 |
| 2020 | 28,525 | 26,640 | 27,396 | 25,754 | 24,242 | 26,314 | 26,340 | 28,424 | 27,438 | 28,070 | 27,985 | 27,793 | 324,921 |
| 2021 | 25,977 | 22,988 | 26,004 | 28,832 | 28,347 | 29,639 | 28,870 | 27,257 | 25,653 | 27,949 | 27,249 | 31,460 | 330,225 |
| 2022[1] | 31,137 | 28,209 | 31,525 | 30,290 | 30,659 | 29,021 | 27,247 | 28,032 | 26,211 | 26,353 | 29,438 | 30,517 | 348,639 |

[1] Preliminary.    Source: National Agricultural Statistics Service, U.S. Department of Agriculture (NASS-USDA)

## Production of Cheddar Cheese in the United States    In Thousands of Pounds

| Year | Jan. | Feb. | Mar. | Apr. | May | June | July | Aug. | Sept. | Oct. | Nov. | Dec. | Total |
|---|---|---|---|---|---|---|---|---|---|---|---|---|---|
| 2013 | 280,944 | 251,977 | 284,123 | 279,144 | 281,307 | 259,631 | 246,804 | 269,747 | 241,687 | 268,497 | 252,211 | 273,767 | 3,189,839 |
| 2014 | 283,595 | 254,140 | 283,494 | 290,713 | 293,923 | 274,257 | 274,163 | 265,918 | 262,230 | 277,835 | 266,025 | 290,745 | 3,317,038 |
| 2015 | 296,767 | 262,602 | 287,042 | 287,350 | 296,447 | 287,956 | 286,435 | 279,379 | 271,551 | 278,915 | 265,947 | 292,720 | 3,393,111 |
| 2016 | 297,480 | 258,530 | 286,426 | 300,166 | 293,238 | 280,220 | 284,607 | 281,932 | 271,561 | 284,058 | 286,571 | 309,709 | 3,434,498 |
| 2017 | 327,339 | 291,518 | 323,453 | 329,682 | 327,467 | 302,102 | 298,297 | 298,318 | 291,766 | 307,844 | 296,609 | 327,073 | 3,721,468 |
| 2018 | 331,985 | 301,256 | 320,257 | 319,153 | 318,665 | 312,869 | 325,217 | 311,974 | 297,632 | 323,213 | 314,170 | 326,117 | 3,802,508 |
| 2019 | 323,210 | 280,816 | 315,229 | 306,510 | 321,122 | 307,403 | 305,911 | 321,190 | 284,142 | 309,584 | 309,223 | 330,369 | 3,714,709 |
| 2020 | 319,240 | 302,408 | 314,114 | 330,119 | 315,704 | 302,960 | 322,775 | 323,153 | 303,253 | 325,354 | 321,553 | 349,162 | 3,829,795 |
| 2021 | 346,949 | 300,535 | 336,776 | 337,847 | 348,365 | 329,810 | 325,011 | 320,293 | 309,879 | 324,914 | 313,524 | 333,665 | 3,927,568 |
| 2022[1] | 332,479 | 308,061 | 327,246 | 319,950 | 334,615 | 336,594 | 331,613 | 314,380 | 301,273 | 336,106 | 320,259 | 340,005 | 3,902,581 |

[1] Preliminary.    Source: National Agricultural Statistics Service, U.S. Department of Agriculture (NASS-USDA)

## Production of Feta Cheese in the United States    In Thousands of Pounds

| Year | Jan. | Feb. | Mar. | Apr. | May | June | July | Aug. | Sept. | Oct. | Nov. | Dec. | Total |
|---|---|---|---|---|---|---|---|---|---|---|---|---|---|
| 2013 | 8,275 | 7,295 | 8,810 | 8,663 | 9,299 | 9,028 | 9,413 | 8,962 | 8,808 | 9,144 | 7,729 | 8,183 | 103,609 |
| 2014 | 7,957 | 8,142 | 9,201 | 9,681 | 9,672 | 9,743 | 10,214 | 8,459 | 8,842 | 8,610 | 7,209 | 7,892 | 105,622 |
| 2015 | 8,706 | 8,227 | 9,871 | 11,258 | 10,222 | 9,785 | 10,512 | 9,277 | 9,237 | 9,095 | 7,563 | 8,671 | 112,424 |
| 2016 | 11,927 | 9,183 | 11,212 | 11,113 | 10,959 | 10,234 | 10,185 | 11,071 | 10,518 | 11,504 | 10,506 | 8,437 | 126,849 |
| 2017 | 8,723 | 9,235 | 10,637 | 11,010 | 11,717 | 11,622 | 11,701 | 10,388 | 9,874 | 10,120 | 8,368 | 9,075 | 122,470 |
| 2018 | 9,667 | 9,692 | 11,187 | 12,036 | 12,706 | 11,959 | 12,603 | 10,564 | 10,018 | 12,507 | 8,411 | 8,473 | 129,823 |
| 2019 | 9,763 | 10,434 | 11,479 | 12,413 | 12,585 | 11,539 | 11,570 | 10,948 | 10,710 | 11,074 | 8,365 | 9,820 | 130,700 |
| 2020 | 10,193 | 9,400 | 12,930 | 7,473 | 10,090 | 11,372 | 14,479 | 13,765 | 13,477 | 12,583 | 8,274 | 8,938 | 132,974 |
| 2021 | 8,459 | 12,097 | 15,470 | 15,602 | 15,678 | 15,465 | 15,336 | 15,462 | 15,237 | 13,588 | 11,739 | 12,554 | 166,687 |
| 2022[1] | 9,606 | 11,942 | 12,025 | 15,158 | 11,931 | 11,812 | 11,746 | 13,076 | 14,335 | 14,492 | 13,043 | 9,356 | 148,522 |

[1] Preliminary.    Source: National Agricultural Statistics Service, U.S. Department of Agriculture (NASS-USDA)

# CHEESE

### Production of Gouda Cheese in the United States — In Thousands of Pounds

| Year | Jan. | Feb. | Mar. | Apr. | May | June | July | Aug. | Sept. | Oct. | Nov. | Dec. | Total |
|---|---|---|---|---|---|---|---|---|---|---|---|---|---|
| 2013 | 1,741 | 3,605 | 4,273 | 5,185 | 3,773 | 4,311 | 4,554 | 4,891 | 3,070 | 3,326 | 4,914 | 4,087 | 47,730 |
| 2014 | 5,735 | 5,391 | 4,941 | 3,638 | 5,334 | 7,578 | 7,089 | 5,692 | 2,258 | 2,436 | 3,038 | 2,781 | 55,911 |
| 2015 | 4,671 | 6,295 | 6,469 | 4,966 | 4,388 | 2,572 | 3,686 | 5,231 | 5,216 | 4,524 | 5,739 | 4,581 | 58,317 |
| 2016 | 4,327 | 4,737 | 5,689 | 3,761 | 6,356 | 2,031 | 4,045 | 5,592 | 5,988 | 6,732 | 5,412 | 3,931 | 58,601 |
| 2017 | 3,875 | 7,314 | 5,984 | 5,095 | 4,069 | 4,728 | 5,365 | 5,073 | 4,678 | 5,302 | 8,213 | 5,704 | 65,400 |
| 2018 | 5,121 | 3,457 | 5,924 | 4,513 | 6,123 | 6,243 | 5,509 | 7,001 | 4,871 | 6,132 | 6,369 | 3,989 | 65,252 |
| 2019 | 5,439 | 2,710 | 4,136 | 3,594 | 3,126 | 3,330 | 3,896 | 5,192 | 4,810 | 4,152 | 4,149 | 4,119 | 48,653 |
| 2020 | 4,559 | 4,927 | 4,242 | 3,231 | 2,703 | 3,674 | 3,918 | 2,939 | 2,838 | 3,810 | 4,058 | 3,864 | 44,763 |
| 2021 | 5,211 | 5,210 | 5,374 | 3,549 | 5,723 | 4,597 | 5,070 | 4,503 | 4,419 | 3,768 | 4,358 | 4,226 | 56,008 |
| 2022[1] | 5,957 | 5,340 | 6,881 | 5,308 | 5,567 | 6,053 | 4,906 | 4,286 | 4,034 | 3,515 | 5,195 | 5,011 | 62,053 |

[1] Preliminary.  Source: National Agricultural Statistics Service, U.S. Department of Agriculture (NASS-USDA)

### Production of Hispanic Cheese in the United States — In Thousands of Pounds

| Year | Jan. | Feb. | Mar. | Apr. | May | June | July | Aug. | Sept. | Oct. | Nov. | Dec. | Total |
|---|---|---|---|---|---|---|---|---|---|---|---|---|---|
| 2013 | 19,701 | 19,165 | 19,351 | 19,981 | 20,011 | 19,596 | 20,543 | 20,736 | 20,692 | 21,253 | 20,476 | 19,915 | 241,420 |
| 2014 | 19,519 | 17,945 | 22,557 | 19,677 | 20,898 | 20,671 | 21,306 | 22,101 | 21,007 | 22,417 | 19,873 | 21,608 | 249,579 |
| 2015 | 20,976 | 19,761 | 23,127 | 20,881 | 21,019 | 20,869 | 20,587 | 20,796 | 22,084 | 21,595 | 21,152 | 21,444 | 254,291 |
| 2016 | 20,407 | 21,975 | 22,698 | 21,429 | 20,735 | 22,588 | 21,781 | 22,619 | 22,850 | 22,729 | 22,592 | 22,538 | 264,941 |
| 2017 | 22,079 | 21,700 | 25,936 | 23,715 | 24,637 | 24,228 | 22,886 | 24,544 | 22,428 | 26,827 | 24,423 | 23,118 | 286,521 |
| 2018 | 24,032 | 21,791 | 25,611 | 24,115 | 26,245 | 25,727 | 24,709 | 27,013 | 25,193 | 30,134 | 27,373 | 29,973 | 311,916 |
| 2019 | 23,433 | 27,287 | 28,755 | 27,877 | 29,824 | 25,877 | 26,805 | 27,679 | 28,068 | 30,543 | 27,890 | 26,441 | 330,479 |
| 2020 | 27,247 | 26,821 | 31,839 | 28,953 | 29,871 | 30,969 | 29,475 | 28,119 | 29,938 | 29,092 | 26,589 | 27,561 | 346,474 |
| 2021 | 27,384 | 28,250 | 32,336 | 27,579 | 27,919 | 29,352 | 30,462 | 28,675 | 30,327 | 31,735 | 28,114 | 28,693 | 350,826 |
| 2022[1] | 26,340 | 28,836 | 31,747 | 28,946 | 29,865 | 31,454 | 32,127 | 33,901 | 31,546 | 32,614 | 32,628 | 32,018 | 372,022 |

[1] Preliminary.  Source: National Agricultural Statistics Service, U.S. Department of Agriculture (NASS-USDA)

### Production of Italian Cheese in the United States — In Thousands of Pounds

| Year | Jan. | Feb. | Mar. | Apr. | May | June | July | Aug. | Sept. | Oct. | Nov. | Dec. | Total |
|---|---|---|---|---|---|---|---|---|---|---|---|---|---|
| 2013 | 400,858 | 359,627 | 412,857 | 393,584 | 393,657 | 392,141 | 391,399 | 381,623 | 384,445 | 408,770 | 390,202 | 426,313 | 4,735,476 |
| 2014 | 420,216 | 374,469 | 426,306 | 417,452 | 415,297 | 410,340 | 409,723 | 392,972 | 406,080 | 417,600 | 413,496 | 446,284 | 4,950,235 |
| 2015 | 433,087 | 389,962 | 441,855 | 420,852 | 419,504 | 422,133 | 429,399 | 403,150 | 402,466 | 428,460 | 426,849 | 464,109 | 5,081,826 |
| 2016 | 451,589 | 415,039 | 458,663 | 438,996 | 443,594 | 436,333 | 447,386 | 426,222 | 431,888 | 449,808 | 439,889 | 464,948 | 5,304,355 |
| 2017 | 455,515 | 407,544 | 471,216 | 449,326 | 454,425 | 451,434 | 452,010 | 437,910 | 433,070 | 454,859 | 457,497 | 470,442 | 5,395,248 |
| 2018 | 473,913 | 428,100 | 483,095 | 460,768 | 460,817 | 450,929 | 462,769 | 453,431 | 450,964 | 483,852 | 469,207 | 479,005 | 5,556,850 |
| 2019 | 480,134 | 441,082 | 493,275 | 475,467 | 474,522 | 461,688 | 463,865 | 466,578 | 470,642 | 485,559 | 471,962 | 483,331 | 5,668,105 |
| 2020 | 485,398 | 448,190 | 485,546 | 447,648 | 482,323 | 485,761 | 454,998 | 445,538 | 469,823 | 473,294 | 454,904 | 490,878 | 5,624,301 |
| 2021 | 481,029 | 443,254 | 502,101 | 483,156 | 472,514 | 465,030 | 480,260 | 480,009 | 475,972 | 488,426 | 479,853 | 498,981 | 5,750,585 |
| 2022[1] | 503,643 | 466,287 | 517,561 | 489,492 | 486,776 | 482,456 | 486,412 | 488,719 | 494,141 | 496,883 | 488,712 | 508,181 | 5,909,263 |

[1] Preliminary.  Source: National Agricultural Statistics Service, U.S. Department of Agriculture (NASS-USDA)

### Production of Mozzarella Cheese in the United States — In Thousands of Pounds

| Year | Jan. | Feb. | Mar. | Apr. | May | June | July | Aug. | Sept. | Oct. | Nov. | Dec. | Total |
|---|---|---|---|---|---|---|---|---|---|---|---|---|---|
| 2013 | 311,837 | 278,522 | 323,187 | 302,643 | 307,092 | 307,964 | 307,910 | 296,420 | 301,973 | 318,997 | 307,484 | 335,960 | 3,699,989 |
| 2014 | 333,319 | 300,506 | 335,385 | 332,466 | 331,181 | 328,829 | 327,914 | 311,973 | 319,861 | 326,866 | 326,093 | 350,532 | 3,924,925 |
| 2015 | 341,183 | 305,421 | 344,459 | 330,958 | 333,451 | 331,196 | 338,554 | 316,045 | 316,408 | 332,824 | 335,210 | 363,227 | 3,988,936 |
| 2016 | 353,001 | 323,713 | 358,081 | 340,584 | 345,063 | 339,993 | 350,089 | 328,118 | 334,808 | 346,013 | 338,728 | 359,555 | 4,117,746 |
| 2017 | 353,165 | 315,534 | 362,560 | 348,680 | 352,115 | 350,106 | 351,858 | 336,517 | 332,291 | 347,484 | 351,563 | 365,619 | 4,167,492 |
| 2018 | 365,563 | 328,591 | 372,712 | 358,320 | 359,072 | 355,249 | 367,437 | 357,346 | 358,579 | 381,217 | 370,269 | 377,006 | 4,351,361 |
| 2019 | 379,627 | 347,234 | 391,166 | 372,686 | 374,770 | 370,364 | 368,167 | 370,384 | 375,726 | 384,612 | 375,266 | 383,976 | 4,493,978 |
| 2020 | 381,983 | 353,200 | 386,397 | 353,043 | 379,446 | 389,307 | 364,832 | 355,527 | 371,610 | 371,411 | 358,817 | 382,737 | 4,448,310 |
| 2021 | 374,948 | 345,504 | 392,656 | 377,151 | 371,087 | 364,385 | 374,441 | 374,517 | 369,882 | 378,302 | 375,299 | 388,985 | 4,487,157 |
| 2022[1] | 394,810 | 359,283 | 407,492 | 386,815 | 388,217 | 382,890 | 390,204 | 385,347 | 384,752 | 388,666 | 384,929 | 399,992 | 4,653,397 |

[1] Preliminary.  Source: National Agricultural Statistics Service, U.S. Department of Agriculture (NASS-USDA)

# CHEESE

**Production of Parmesan Cheese in the United States**    In Thousands of Pounds

| Year | Jan. | Feb. | Mar. | Apr. | May | June | July | Aug. | Sept. | Oct. | Nov. | Dec. | Total |
|---|---|---|---|---|---|---|---|---|---|---|---|---|---|
| 2013 | 30,487 | 25,205 | 25,993 | 30,039 | 28,116 | 30,003 | 28,960 | 26,969 | 24,883 | 25,416 | 18,769 | 24,901 | 319,741 |
| 2014 | 24,452 | 21,546 | 25,563 | 24,830 | 26,551 | 25,717 | 26,618 | 23,618 | 25,439 | 25,670 | 24,036 | 27,808 | 301,848 |
| 2015 | 30,754 | 27,711 | 30,742 | 28,762 | 28,369 | 29,611 | 29,656 | 25,168 | 23,607 | 27,644 | 25,501 | 31,478 | 339,003 |
| 2016 | 33,820 | 31,383 | 33,371 | 35,973 | 35,073 | 34,343 | 37,542 | 33,156 | 30,373 | 32,957 | 32,273 | 37,055 | 407,319 |
| 2017 | 38,697 | 32,553 | 39,191 | 38,242 | 38,033 | 38,418 | 39,411 | 36,612 | 34,641 | 37,766 | 37,886 | 39,190 | 450,640 |
| 2018 | 42,568 | 38,996 | 41,508 | 39,631 | 37,515 | 33,192 | 32,003 | 28,959 | 26,467 | 33,656 | 32,470 | 37,526 | 424,491 |
| 2019 | 37,840 | 35,654 | 37,118 | 38,548 | 38,170 | 32,682 | 33,174 | 32,410 | 30,153 | 32,349 | 30,314 | 33,962 | 412,374 |
| 2020 | 38,288 | 36,596 | 34,337 | 37,774 | 35,179 | 29,904 | 29,991 | 31,273 | 34,035 | 35,822 | 33,825 | 42,139 | 419,163 |
| 2021 | 40,967 | 37,301 | 41,629 | 40,900 | 40,065 | 39,627 | 41,960 | 37,738 | 38,861 | 40,503 | 39,024 | 44,605 | 483,180 |
| 2022[1] | 45,578 | 45,376 | 43,317 | 39,681 | 37,015 | 37,497 | 37,086 | 36,948 | 44,178 | 42,099 | 40,295 | 42,866 | 491,936 |

[1] Preliminary.   Source: National Agricultural Statistics Service, U.S. Department of Agriculture (NASS-USDA)

**Production of Provolone Cheese in the United States**    In Thousands of Pounds

| Year | Jan. | Feb. | Mar. | Apr. | May | June | July | Aug. | Sept. | Oct. | Nov. | Dec. | Total |
|---|---|---|---|---|---|---|---|---|---|---|---|---|---|
| 2013 | 27,717 | 27,143 | 29,490 | 34,043 | 30,827 | 29,594 | 29,094 | 29,251 | 28,698 | 31,273 | 30,313 | 32,626 | 360,069 |
| 2014 | 31,575 | 25,631 | 33,268 | 30,371 | 30,740 | 29,372 | 29,718 | 29,504 | 30,048 | 30,429 | 29,847 | 30,585 | 361,088 |
| 2015 | 30,169 | 28,261 | 31,522 | 31,975 | 31,620 | 31,796 | 32,427 | 32,387 | 32,591 | 32,875 | 31,175 | 32,518 | 379,316 |
| 2016 | 32,849 | 29,130 | 33,162 | 33,729 | 34,445 | 34,196 | 33,892 | 34,108 | 33,924 | 35,058 | 33,840 | 33,256 | 401,589 |
| 2017 | 31,434 | 28,740 | 34,517 | 32,669 | 32,456 | 34,090 | 34,139 | 34,184 | 33,438 | 34,101 | 32,535 | 31,489 | 393,792 |
| 2018 | 32,633 | 29,285 | 33,826 | 34,496 | 34,396 | 32,809 | 34,606 | 35,501 | 34,374 | 34,283 | 31,173 | 30,404 | 397,786 |
| 2019 | 30,472 | 29,682 | 30,873 | 33,053 | 32,436 | 31,166 | 33,498 | 33,216 | 33,468 | 34,272 | 30,150 | 30,084 | 382,370 |
| 2020 | 31,236 | 29,137 | 29,698 | 26,762 | 33,655 | 35,309 | 31,853 | 27,450 | 31,047 | 32,403 | 29,199 | 30,165 | 367,914 |
| 2021 | 31,245 | 28,052 | 30,776 | 32,804 | 32,232 | 31,032 | 34,310 | 34,156 | 31,888 | 31,708 | 29,589 | 27,563 | 375,355 |
| 2022[1] | 28,271 | 28,997 | 30,488 | 29,582 | 30,325 | 31,024 | 30,761 | 33,449 | 29,390 | 31,827 | 30,488 | 29,449 | 364,051 |

[1] Preliminary.   Source: National Agricultural Statistics Service, U.S. Department of Agriculture (NASS-USDA)

**Production of Ricota Cheese in the United States**    In Thousands of Pounds

| Year | Jan. | Feb. | Mar. | Apr. | May | June | July | Aug. | Sept. | Oct. | Nov. | Dec. | Total |
|---|---|---|---|---|---|---|---|---|---|---|---|---|---|
| 2013 | 21,401 | 19,049 | 22,752 | 17,724 | 18,566 | 15,695 | 17,012 | 19,224 | 19,496 | 22,579 | 24,048 | 23,571 | 241,117 |
| 2014 | 22,124 | 18,067 | 21,697 | 19,807 | 17,557 | 16,571 | 16,012 | 19,041 | 21,133 | 24,273 | 23,120 | 25,882 | 245,284 |
| 2015 | 20,273 | 17,646 | 23,689 | 17,440 | 15,215 | 17,914 | 17,789 | 19,500 | 20,722 | 24,234 | 24,100 | 24,942 | 243,464 |
| 2016 | 22,197 | 20,754 | 23,758 | 18,209 | 18,196 | 17,449 | 15,914 | 21,982 | 22,289 | 24,251 | 23,890 | 23,342 | 252,231 |
| 2017 | 21,050 | 19,046 | 23,083 | 18,102 | 19,000 | 17,300 | 15,963 | 20,568 | 21,857 | 24,226 | 23,327 | 22,390 | 245,912 |
| 2018 | 22,989 | 20,886 | 23,200 | 17,734 | 18,077 | 17,656 | 17,463 | 21,221 | 20,976 | 23,902 | 23,204 | 22,153 | 249,461 |
| 2019 | 21,577 | 18,614 | 22,352 | 19,824 | 18,244 | 16,645 | 17,800 | 19,418 | 20,130 | 23,459 | 23,973 | 22,905 | 244,941 |
| 2020 | 22,354 | 19,096 | 23,777 | 19,610 | 22,703 | 20,726 | 18,556 | 21,249 | 22,286 | 22,985 | 21,952 | 23,349 | 258,643 |
| 2021 | 22,547 | 21,646 | 24,556 | 19,813 | 16,005 | 16,478 | 16,188 | 20,747 | 22,070 | 23,161 | 22,621 | 22,492 | 248,324 |
| 2022[1] | 21,525 | 18,741 | 23,178 | 21,104 | 19,108 | 18,771 | 16,423 | 21,088 | 21,668 | 20,996 | 20,290 | 22,814 | 245,706 |

[1] Preliminary.   Source: National Agricultural Statistics Service, U.S. Department of Agriculture (NASS-USDA)

**Production of Romano Cheese in the United States**    In Thousands of Pounds

| Year | Jan. | Feb. | Mar. | Apr. | May | June | July | Aug. | Sept. | Oct. | Nov. | Dec. | Total |
|---|---|---|---|---|---|---|---|---|---|---|---|---|---|
| 2013 | 3,656 | 4,658 | 5,359 | 3,659 | 3,716 | 3,088 | 2,891 | 3,584 | 3,882 | 4,129 | 3,464 | 2,966 | 45,052 |
| 2014 | 3,270 | 3,003 | 3,785 | 3,822 | 3,666 | 3,889 | 4,003 | 3,184 | 3,470 | 4,198 | 4,011 | 4,720 | 45,021 |
| 2015 | 4,857 | 4,770 | 3,937 | 4,801 | 4,368 | 5,319 | 5,287 | 3,920 | 3,578 | 4,137 | 4,551 | 5,509 | 55,034 |
| 2016 | 3,626 | 4,341 | 4,428 | 4,971 | 4,407 | 4,462 | 4,452 | 3,918 | 4,017 | 4,844 | 4,565 | 4,417 | 52,448 |
| 2017 | 4,571 | 5,175 | 4,269 | 4,974 | 6,276 | 4,521 | 4,587 | 4,407 | 4,107 | 5,029 | 4,967 | 5,419 | 58,302 |
| 2018 | 4,611 | 4,653 | 5,432 | 4,678 | 5,086 | 5,195 | 5,176 | 4,223 | 3,840 | 4,537 | 5,104 | 5,523 | 58,058 |
| 2019 | 3,868 | 3,822 | 4,301 | 4,631 | 4,452 | 4,676 | 4,328 | 4,007 | 4,148 | 5,169 | 5,545 | 5,281 | 54,228 |
| 2020 | 4,728 | 4,265 | 4,598 | 5,307 | 4,768 | 4,420 | 4,413 | 3,926 | 3,976 | 3,950 | 4,458 | 5,707 | 54,516 |
| 2021 | 5,038 | 4,571 | 5,352 | 5,911 | 6,310 | 5,870 | 5,611 | 5,143 | 5,632 | 6,131 | 5,039 | 6,457 | 67,065 |
| 2022[1] | 5,507 | 6,586 | 4,635 | 4,400 | 4,181 | 4,171 | 4,519 | 4,617 | 5,848 | 5,351 | 4,807 | 4,355 | 58,977 |

[1] Preliminary.   Source: National Agricultural Statistics Service, U.S. Department of Agriculture (NASS-USDA)

# CHEESE

## Cold Storage of All Varieties of Cheese in the United States, on First of Month  In Thousands of Pounds

| Year | Jan. | Feb. | Mar. | Apr. | May | June | July | Aug. | Sept. | Oct. | Nov. | Dec. |
|---|---|---|---|---|---|---|---|---|---|---|---|---|
| 2013 | 1,023,102 | 1,032,196 | 1,068,756 | 1,105,725 | 1,121,293 | 1,150,039 | 1,149,377 | 1,146,131 | 1,100,351 | 1,070,697 | 1,019,716 | 996,609 |
| 2014 | 1,009,381 | 1,015,053 | 1,010,132 | 1,018,290 | 1,037,586 | 1,065,540 | 1,055,442 | 1,054,892 | 1,041,408 | 1,013,782 | 995,666 | 1,017,192 |
| 2015 | 1,017,936 | 1,048,243 | 1,067,060 | 1,068,645 | 1,085,909 | 1,111,854 | 1,142,241 | 1,161,796 | 1,167,393 | 1,152,446 | 1,146,191 | 1,148,060 |
| 2016 | 1,146,086 | 1,178,194 | 1,182,308 | 1,191,394 | 1,209,222 | 1,249,382 | 1,250,328 | 1,275,546 | 1,241,119 | 1,235,452 | 1,222,315 | 1,182,646 |
| 2017 | 1,198,334 | 1,192,166 | 1,226,457 | 1,262,244 | 1,303,328 | 1,308,929 | 1,316,698 | 1,369,506 | 1,333,551 | 1,308,072 | 1,267,950 | 1,258,630 |
| 2018 | 1,280,484 | 1,278,637 | 1,317,731 | 1,324,728 | 1,345,280 | 1,384,940 | 1,388,638 | 1,412,980 | 1,360,489 | 1,379,703 | 1,375,149 | 1,352,739 |
| 2019 | 1,344,794 | 1,369,236 | 1,366,937 | 1,384,366 | 1,397,974 | 1,385,616 | 1,380,784 | 1,360,510 | 1,364,830 | 1,373,856 | 1,341,695 | 1,322,482 |
| 2020 | 1,322,014 | 1,353,618 | 1,362,091 | 1,374,507 | 1,478,640 | 1,454,505 | 1,415,905 | 1,391,664 | 1,377,907 | 1,355,799 | 1,341,428 | 1,348,101 |
| 2021 | 1,396,311 | 1,408,243 | 1,436,246 | 1,468,976 | 1,448,762 | 1,458,368 | 1,435,146 | 1,449,523 | 1,432,852 | 1,457,850 | 1,448,595 | 1,422,271 |
| 2022[1] | 1,441,631 | 1,445,090 | 1,466,985 | 1,465,826 | 1,480,872 | 1,512,916 | 1,506,289 | 1,521,900 | 1,481,491 | 1,469,796 | 1,448,093 | 1,430,992 |

Quantities are given in "net weight."   [1] Preliminary.   Source: *National Agricultural Statistics Service, U.S. Department of Agriculture (NASS-USDA)*

## Cold Storage of Natural American Cheese in the United States, on First of Month  In Thousands of Pounds

| Year | Jan. | Feb. | Mar. | Apr. | May | June | July | Aug. | Sept. | Oct. | Nov. | Dec. |
|---|---|---|---|---|---|---|---|---|---|---|---|---|
| 2013 | 635,590 | 643,184 | 661,019 | 684,653 | 698,655 | 714,637 | 710,604 | 701,964 | 668,361 | 661,046 | 626,161 | 613,965 |
| 2014 | 618,265 | 630,820 | 628,679 | 639,067 | 648,900 | 656,446 | 655,239 | 660,438 | 648,784 | 631,279 | 623,336 | 635,776 |
| 2015 | 627,769 | 636,019 | 645,670 | 634,270 | 644,113 | 669,464 | 685,745 | 698,029 | 709,029 | 698,875 | 696,781 | 699,794 |
| 2016 | 701,073 | 716,370 | 716,357 | 725,837 | 734,121 | 757,530 | 756,950 | 769,705 | 742,497 | 742,804 | 736,017 | 713,231 |
| 2017 | 726,403 | 722,449 | 744,640 | 772,702 | 804,645 | 816,266 | 810,234 | 831,538 | 800,994 | 780,466 | 740,404 | 733,378 |
| 2018 | 746,846 | 741,772 | 762,770 | 766,628 | 780,256 | 804,075 | 800,379 | 823,342 | 787,435 | 803,750 | 811,593 | 798,970 |
| 2019 | 800,336 | 803,578 | 783,210 | 784,761 | 782,769 | 786,579 | 784,362 | 773,183 | 767,366 | 774,761 | 811,593 | 798,970 |
| 2020 | 749,886 | 779,672 | 778,265 | 776,360 | 834,295 | 820,018 | 793,026 | 785,521 | 789,594 | 772,362 | 743,621 | 740,367 |
| 2021 | 801,720 | 809,110 | 817,169 | 834,403 | 826,740 | 827,995 | 809,825 | 817,589 | 827,067 | 844,115 | 756,168 | 762,041 |
| 2022[1] | 842,869 | 837,609 | 831,198 | 828,449 | 835,747 | 857,893 | 846,773 | 860,017 | 841,536 | 843,113 | 831,213 | 816,099 |

Quantities are given in "net weight."   [1] Preliminary.   Source: *National Agricultural Statistics Service, U.S. Department of Agriculture (NASS-USDA)*

## Cold Storage of Swiss Cheese in the United States, on First of Month  In Thousands of Pounds

| Year | Jan. | Feb. | Mar. | Apr. | May | June | July | Aug. | Sept. | Oct. | Nov. | Dec. |
|---|---|---|---|---|---|---|---|---|---|---|---|---|
| 2013 | 31,747 | 30,401 | 30,130 | 30,589 | 28,503 | 29,051 | 31,347 | 32,715 | 32,006 | 29,975 | 27,923 | 26,102 |
| 2014 | 24,688 | 25,421 | 26,942 | 27,425 | 28,316 | 30,538 | 27,972 | 24,593 | 27,085 | 25,684 | 25,600 | 24,419 |
| 2015 | 21,282 | 22,411 | 23,587 | 24,573 | 23,986 | 21,424 | 20,841 | 21,591 | 22,203 | 22,037 | 21,404 | 22,665 |
| 2016 | 24,587 | 24,100 | 24,703 | 24,629 | 24,592 | 24,967 | 24,492 | 25,702 | 26,019 | 26,055 | 24,428 | 24,749 |
| 2017 | 24,200 | 23,930 | 26,999 | 26,053 | 26,962 | 26,242 | 25,495 | 27,009 | 26,831 | 25,408 | 24,277 | 24,933 |
| 2018 | 26,367 | 28,733 | 27,884 | 29,080 | 29,193 | 31,424 | 31,312 | 32,189 | 31,211 | 30,848 | 30,775 | 29,866 |
| 2019 | 29,775 | 29,353 | 31,047 | 31,487 | 28,176 | 24,685 | 27,417 | 27,179 | 27,340 | 26,392 | 26,144 | 24,540 |
| 2020 | 24,178 | 22,902 | 24,089 | 23,272 | 25,694 | 24,548 | 24,005 | 20,537 | 20,602 | 20,762 | 20,149 | 20,063 |
| 2021 | 19,851 | 21,344 | 21,692 | 22,661 | 21,160 | 21,877 | 22,623 | 22,768 | 22,475 | 21,879 | 21,363 | 20,669 |
| 2022[1] | 21,928 | 23,530 | 25,206 | 23,199 | 23,975 | 25,840 | 24,570 | 22,506 | 21,140 | 23,115 | 21,947 | 22,397 |

Quantities are given in "net weight."   [1] Preliminary.   Source: *National Agricultural Statistics Service, U.S. Department of Agriculture (NASS-USDA)*

## Cold Storage of Other Natural American Cheese in the United States, on First of Month  In Thousands of Lbs.

| Year | Jan. | Feb. | Mar. | Apr. | May | June | July | Aug. | Sept. | Oct. | Nov. | Dec. |
|---|---|---|---|---|---|---|---|---|---|---|---|---|
| 2013 | 355,765 | 358,611 | 377,607 | 390,483 | 394,135 | 406,351 | 407,426 | 411,452 | 399,984 | 379,676 | 365,632 | 356,542 |
| 2014 | 366,428 | 358,812 | 354,511 | 351,798 | 360,370 | 378,556 | 372,231 | 369,861 | 365,539 | 356,819 | 346,730 | 356,997 |
| 2015 | 368,885 | 389,813 | 397,035 | 409,802 | 417,810 | 420,966 | 435,655 | 442,176 | 436,161 | 431,534 | 428,006 | 425,601 |
| 2016 | 420,426 | 437,724 | 441,248 | 440,928 | 450,509 | 466,885 | 468,886 | 480,139 | 472,603 | 466,593 | 461,870 | 444,666 |
| 2017 | 447,731 | 445,787 | 454,818 | 463,489 | 471,721 | 466,421 | 480,969 | 510,959 | 505,726 | 502,198 | 503,269 | 500,319 |
| 2018 | 507,271 | 508,132 | 527,077 | 529,020 | 535,831 | 549,441 | 556,947 | 557,449 | 541,843 | 545,105 | 532,781 | 523,903 |
| 2019 | 514,683 | 536,305 | 552,680 | 568,118 | 587,029 | 574,352 | 569,005 | 560,148 | 570,124 | 572,703 | 571,930 | 557,575 |
| 2020 | 547,950 | 551,044 | 559,737 | 574,875 | 618,651 | 609,939 | 598,874 | 585,606 | 567,711 | 562,675 | 565,111 | 565,997 |
| 2021 | 574,740 | 577,789 | 597,385 | 611,912 | 600,862 | 608,496 | 602,698 | 609,166 | 583,310 | 591,859 | 583,885 | 566,827 |
| 2022[1] | 576,834 | 583,951 | 610,581 | 614,178 | 621,150 | 629,183 | 634,946 | 639,377 | 618,815 | 603,568 | 594,933 | 592,496 |

Quantities are given in "net weight."   [1] Preliminary.   Source: *National Agricultural Statistics Service, U.S. Department of Agriculture (NASS-USDA)*

# CHEESE

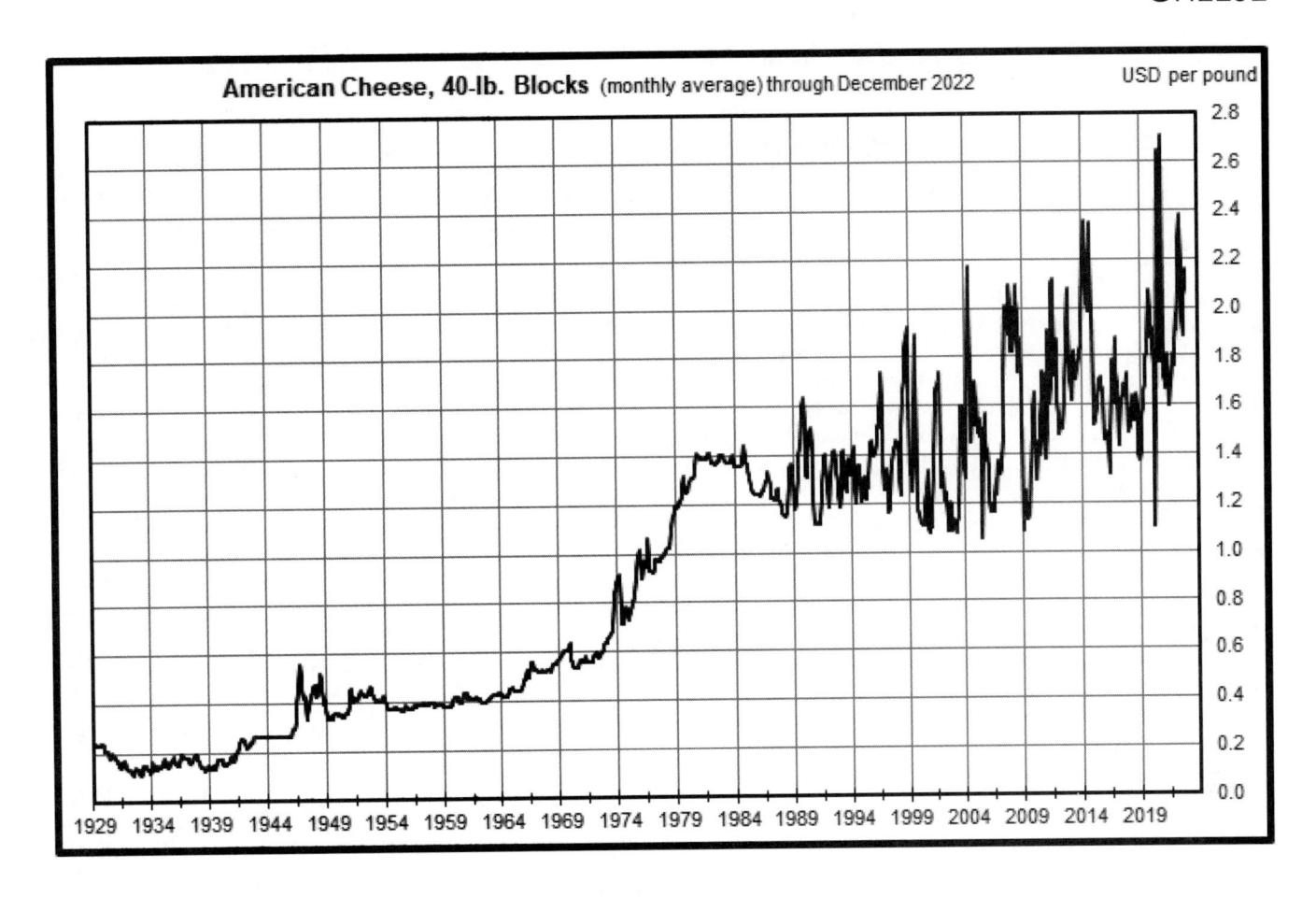

**American Cheese, 40-lb. Blocks** (monthly average) through December 2022  USD per pound

### Average Price of Cheese, 40-lb. Blocks, Chicago Mercantile Exchange  In U.S. Dollars Per Pound

| Year | Jan. | Feb. | Mar. | Apr. | May | June | July | Aug. | Sept. | Oct. | Nov. | Dec. | Average |
|---|---|---|---|---|---|---|---|---|---|---|---|---|---|
| 2013 | 1.6965 | 1.6420 | 1.6240 | 1.8225 | 1.8052 | 1.7140 | 1.7072 | 1.7493 | 1.7956 | 1.8236 | 1.8478 | 1.9431 | 1.7642 |
| 2014 | 2.2227 | 2.1945 | 2.3554 | 2.2439 | 2.0155 | 2.0237 | 1.9870 | 2.1820 | 2.3499 | 2.1932 | 1.9513 | 1.5938 | 2.1094 |
| 2015 | 1.5218 | 1.5382 | 1.5549 | 1.5890 | 1.6308 | 1.7052 | 1.6659 | 1.7111 | 1.6605 | 1.6674 | 1.6176 | 1.4616 | 1.6103 |
| 2016 | 1.4757 | 1.4744 | 1.4877 | 1.4194 | 1.3174 | 1.5005 | 1.6613 | 1.7826 | 1.6224 | 1.6035 | 1.8775 | 1.7335 | 1.5797 |
| 2017 | 1.6866 | 1.6199 | 1.4342 | 1.4976 | 1.6264 | 1.6022 | 1.6586 | 1.6852 | 1.6370 | 1.7305 | 1.6590 | 1.4900 | 1.6106 |
| 2018 | 1.4938 | 1.5157 | 1.5614 | 1.6062 | 1.6397 | 1.5617 | 1.5364 | 1.6341 | 1.6438 | 1.5874 | 1.3951 | 1.3764 | 1.5460 |
| 2019 | 1.4087 | 1.5589 | 1.5908 | 1.6619 | 1.6799 | 1.7906 | 1.8180 | 1.8791 | 2.0395 | 2.0703 | 1.9664 | 1.8764 | 1.7784 |
| 2020 | 1.9142 | 1.8343 | 1.7550 | 1.1019 | 1.6704 | 2.5620 | 2.6466 | 1.7730 | 2.3277 | 2.7103 | 2.5808 | 1.7708 | 2.0539 |
| 2021 | 1.7171 | 1.6870 | 1.6695 | 1.7918 | 1.8072 | 1.6058 | 1.5948 | 1.6902 | 1.7761 | 1.8070 | 1.7605 | 1.8633 | 1.7309 |
| 2022[1] | 1.9787 | 1.9091 | 2.0748 | 2.2759 | 2.3798 | 2.3214 | 2.1622 | 1.9484 | 1.8835 | 2.0453 | 2.0748 | 2.1594 | 2.1011 |

[1] Preliminary.   Source: Economic Research Service, U.S. Department of Agriculture (ERS-USDA)

### Average Price of American Cheese, Barrels, Chicago Mercantile Exchange  In U.S. Dollars Per Pound

| Year | Jan. | Feb. | Mar. | Apr. | May | June | July | Aug. | Sept. | Oct. | Nov. | Dec. | Average |
|---|---|---|---|---|---|---|---|---|---|---|---|---|---|
| 2013 | 1.6388 | 1.5880 | 1.5920 | 1.7124 | 1.7251 | 1.7184 | 1.6919 | 1.7425 | 1.7688 | 1.7714 | 1.7833 | 1.8651 | 1.7165 |
| 2014 | 2.1727 | 2.1757 | 2.2790 | 2.1842 | 1.9985 | 1.9856 | 1.9970 | 2.1961 | 2.3663 | 2.0782 | 1.9326 | 1.5305 | 2.0747 |
| 2015 | 1.4995 | 1.4849 | 1.5290 | 1.6135 | 1.6250 | 1.6690 | 1.6313 | 1.6689 | 1.5840 | 1.6072 | 1.5305 | 1.4638 | 1.5756 |
| 2016 | 1.4842 | 1.4573 | 1.4530 | 1.4231 | 1.3529 | 1.5301 | 1.7363 | 1.8110 | 1.5415 | 1.5295 | 1.7424 | 1.6132 | 1.5562 |
| 2017 | 1.5573 | 1.6230 | 1.4072 | 1.4307 | 1.4806 | 1.3972 | 1.4396 | 1.5993 | 1.5691 | 1.6970 | 1.6656 | 1.5426 | 1.5341 |
| 2018 | 1.3345 | 1.4096 | 1.5071 | 1.4721 | 1.5870 | 1.4145 | 1.3707 | 1.5835 | 1.4503 | 1.3152 | 1.3100 | 1.2829 | 1.4198 |
| 2019 | 1.2379 | 1.3867 | 1.4910 | 1.5925 | 1.6278 | 1.6258 | 1.7343 | 1.7081 | 1.7463 | 2.0224 | 2.2554 | 1.8410 | 1.6891 |
| 2020 | 1.5721 | 1.5470 | 1.4399 | 1.0690 | 1.5980 | 2.3376 | 2.4080 | 1.4937 | 1.6401 | 2.2213 | 2.2929 | 1.4944 | 1.7595 |
| 2021 | 1.5601 | 1.4841 | 1.5023 | 1.6011 | 1.8035 | 1.6506 | 1.5663 | 1.4371 | 1.4873 | 1.7011 | 1.7272 | 1.6263 | 1.5956 |
| 2022[1] | 1.7951 | 1.8746 | 2.0066 | 2.2759 | 2.4187 | 2.3472 | 2.2054 | 1.9698 | 1.9830 | 2.2210 | 2.0744 | 1.9293 | 2.0918 |

[1] Preliminary.   Source: Economic Research Service, U.S. Department of Agriculture (ERS-USDA)

# Chromium

Chromium (atomic symbol Cr) is a steel-gray, hard, and brittle, metallic element that can take on a high polish. Chromium and its compounds are toxic. Discovered in 1797 by Louis Vauquelin, chromium is named after the Greek word for color, *khroma*. Vauquelin also discovered that an emerald's green color is due to the presence of chromium. Many precious stones owe their color to the presence of chromium compounds.

Chromium is primarily found in chromite ore. The primary use of chromium is to form alloys with iron, nickel, or cobalt. Chromium improves hardness and resistance to corrosion and oxidation in iron, steel, and nonferrous alloys. It is a critical alloying ingredient in the production of stainless steel, making up 10% or more of the final composition. More than half of the chromium consumed is used in metallic products, and about one-third is used in refractories. Chromium is also used as a lustrous decorative plating agent, in pigments, leather processing, plating of metals, and catalysts.

**Supply** – World mine production of chromium in 2022 fell by -2.8%% yr/yr to 41.000 million metric tons. The world's largest producers of chromium in 2022 were South Africa with 43.9% of world production, Turkey with 16.8%, and Kazakhstan with 15.9%. South Africa's production in 2022 fell by -3.2% yr/yr to 18.000 million metric tons, which was below the record high of 19.084 million metric tons in 2019.

**Trade** – The U.S. relied on imports for 80% of its chromium consumption in 2021, well below the record high of 91% posted back in the 1970s. U.S. chromium imports in 2021 rose by +21.8% yr/yr to 367,170 metric tons. U.S. exports of chromium in 2021 rose by +36.7% yr/yr to 3,765 metric tons.

### World Mine Production of Chromium  In Thousands of Metric Tons (Gross Weight)

| Year | Albania | Brazil | Cuba | Finland | India | Iran | Kazakhstan | Madagascar | Philippines | South Africa | Turkey | Zimbabwe | World Total |
|---|---|---|---|---|---|---|---|---|---|---|---|---|---|
| 2015 | 646 | 527 | ---- | 1,952 | 2,666 | 392 | 5,383 | 148 | 16 | 15,656 | 8,301 | 267 | 37,000 |
| 2016 | 727 | 426 | ---- | 2,105 | 3,329 | 420 | 5,543 | 108 | 26 | 14,708 | 6,066 | 736 | 35,500 |
| 2017 | 808 | 450 | ---- | 1,954 | 3,478 | 292 | 6,313 | 208 | 21 | 18,680 | 7,850 | 1,674 | 43,000 |
| 2018 | 1,143 | 450 | ---- | 2,211 | 4,076 | 119 | 6,689 | 109 | 45 | 18,983 | 10,757 | 1,756 | 48,200 |
| 2019 | 1,288 | 199 | ---- | 2,415 | 4,139 | 122 | 7,019 | 76 | 32 | 19,084 | 8,666 | 1,550 | 46,400 |
| 2020 | 627 | 227 | ---- | 2,293 | 2,500 | 135 | 7,000 | 60 | 35 | 13,243 | 8,000 | 1,197 | 37,000 |
| 2021[1] | 650 | 200 | ---- | 2,274 | 4,250 | | 6,500 | | | 18,600 | 6,960 | | 42,200 |
| 2022[2] | | | ---- | 2,200 | 4,200 | | 6,500 | | | 18,000 | 6,900 | | 41,000 |

[1] Preliminary.  [2] Estimate.  Source: U.S. Geological Survey (USGS)

### World Production of Ferrochromium  In Thousands of Metric Tons (Gross Weight)

| Year | Albania | Brazil | China | Finland | Germany | India | Kazakhstan | Russia | South Africa | Sweden | Turkey | Zimbabwe | World Total |
|---|---|---|---|---|---|---|---|---|---|---|---|---|---|
| 2014 | 35 | 285 | 4,120 | 441 | 18 | 944 | 1,352 | 440 | 3,719 | 67 | 86 | 235 | 11,800 |
| 2015 | 44 | 173 | 3,940 | 457 | 17 | 944 | 1,414 | 363 | 3,685 | 90 | 83 | 116 | 11,400 |
| 2016 | 45 | 150 | 4,230 | 469 | 17 | 944 | 1,525 | 268 | 3,596 | 82 | 75 | 78 | 11,600 |
| 2017 | 51 | 172 | 4,940 | 416 | 29 | 944 | 1,640 | 436 | 3,485 | 92 | 84 | 143 | 12,600 |
| 2018 | 93 | 175 | 5,280 | 493 | 31 | 944 | 1,740 | 332 | 3,516 | 101 | 92 | 365 | 13,500 |
| 2019 | 66 | 137 | 6,030 | 505 | 26 | 930 | 1,858 | 384 | 3,248 | 118 | 82 | 312 | 14,000 |
| 2020[1] | 54 | 254 | 5,700 | 498 | 11 | 826 | 1,841 | 343 | 2,404 | 87 | 94 | 134 | 12,500 |
| 2021[2] | 110 | 214 | 5,900 | 515 | 12 | 1,090 | 1,705 | 350 | 3,700 | 115 | 101 | 307 | 14,500 |

[1] Preliminary.  [2] Estimate.  Source: U.S. Geological Survey (USGS)

### Salient Statistics of Chromite in the United States  In Thousands of Metric Tons (Gross Weight)

| Year | Net Import Reliance as a % of Apparent Consumpn | Production of Ferrochromium | Exports | Imports for Consumption | Reexports | Consumption by Primary Consumer Group - Total | Metallurgical & Chemical | Refractory | Government[5] Stocks, Dec. 31 Metallurgical & Chemical | Refractory | Total Stocks | $/Metric Ton South Africa[3] | Turkish[4] |
|---|---|---|---|---|---|---|---|---|---|---|---|---|---|
| 2015 | 64 | W | 10 | 329 | ---- | ---- | ---- | ---- | ---- | ---- | ---- | ---- | ---- |
| 2016 | 66 | W | 3 | 348 | ---- | ---- | ---- | ---- | ---- | ---- | ---- | ---- | ---- |
| 2017 | 71 | W | 7 | 399 | ---- | ---- | ---- | ---- | ---- | ---- | ---- | ---- | ---- |
| 2018 | 76 | W | 5 | 432 | ---- | ---- | ---- | ---- | ---- | ---- | ---- | ---- | ---- |
| 2019 | 74 | W | 3 | 365 | ---- | ---- | ---- | ---- | ---- | ---- | ---- | ---- | ---- |
| 2020 | 73 | W | 3 | 301 | ---- | ---- | ---- | ---- | ---- | ---- | ---- | ---- | ---- |
| 2021[1] | 81 | W | 4 | 367 | ---- | ---- | ---- | ---- | ---- | ---- | ---- | ---- | ---- |
| 2022[2] | 83 | W | | | ---- | ---- | ---- | ---- | ---- | ---- | ---- | ---- | ---- |

[1] Preliminary.  [2] Estimate.  [3] $Cr_2O_3$, 44% (Transvaal).  [4] 48% $Cr_2O_3$.  [5] Data through 1999 are for Consumer.  W = Withheld.
Source: U.S. Geological Survey (USGS)

# Coal

Coal is a sedimentary rock composed primarily of carbon, hydrogen, and oxygen. Coal is a fossil fuel formed from ancient plants buried deep in the Earth's crust over 300 million years ago. Historians believe coal was first used commercially in China for smelting copper and for casting coins around 1,000 BC. Almost 92% of all coal consumed in the U.S. is burned by electric power plants, and coal accounts for about 55% of total electricity output. Coal is also used in the manufacture of steel. The steel industry first converts coal into coke, then combines the coke with iron ore and limestone, and finally heats the mixture to produce iron. Other industries use coal to make fertilizers, solvents, medicine, pesticides, and synthetic fuels.

There are four types of mined coal: anthracite (used in high-grade steel production), bituminous (used for electricity generation and for making coke), sub-bituminous, and lignite (both used primarily for electricity generation).

Futures and options on coal trade at the ICE Futures Europe, New York Mercantile Exchange, and Singapore Exchange. Futures are traded on CME Group, Dalian Commodity Exchange, and Zhengzhou Commodity Exchange. The CME's contract trades in units of 1,550 tons and is priced in terms of dollars and cents per ton.

**Price** – In 2021, the average mine price rose by +16.0% to $36.45 per short ton.

**Supply** – U.S. production of bituminous coal in 2022 rose by +2.9% yr/yr to 592.066 million tons.

**Demand** – U.S. consumption of coal in 2021 rose by +14.5% to 545.610 million tons.

**Trade** – U.S. exports of coal in 2021 rose by +23.2% yr/yr to 85.115 million tons. The major exporting destinations for the U.S. are Europe and Asia. U.S. imports in 2021 rose by +4.9% yr/yr to 5.388 million tons.

### World Production of Primary Coal    In Thousands of Short Tons

| Year | Australia | China | Colombia | Germany | India | Indonesia | Kazakhstan | Poland | Russia | South Africa | Turkey | United States | World Total |
|---|---|---|---|---|---|---|---|---|---|---|---|---|---|
| 2012 | 486,118 | 4,348,754 | 98,207 | 217,144 | 608,792 | 425,577 | 132,858 | 158,197 | 363,058 | 285,031 | 77,458 | 1,016,458 | 8,877,767 |
| 2013 | 516,068 | 4,380,935 | 94,247 | 210,493 | 621,072 | 522,904 | 131,808 | 156,875 | 385,818 | 282,162 | 72,877 | 984,842 | 8,991,146 |
| 2014 | 548,559 | 4,270,260 | 97,640 | 205,597 | 659,542 | 504,965 | 125,647 | 150,374 | 393,765 | 287,196 | 71,911 | 1,000,049 | 8,903,921 |
| 2015 | 574,181 | 4,129,849 | 94,300 | 203,612 | 696,349 | 508,789 | 118,299 | 149,147 | 409,701 | 282,334 | 64,390 | 896,941 | 8,697,270 |
| 2016 | 560,423 | 3,759,538 | 99,772 | 193,593 | 720,040 | 502,871 | 113,620 | 143,996 | 423,095 | 281,986 | 80,473 | 728,364 | 8,170,406 |
| 2017 | 557,423 | 3,884,055 | 99,813 | 193,039 | 739,669 | 508,438 | 111,782 | 139,597 | 449,579 | 283,431 | 81,679 | 774,609 | 8,404,034 |
| 2018 | 541,744 | 4,076,056 | 92,907 | 186,311 | 788,582 | 614,839 | 118,660 | 134,432 | 476,919 | 281,553 | 92,524 | 756,167 | 8,737,724 |
| 2019 | 564,027 | 4,239,848 | 92,972 | 144,749 | 805,053 | 679,199 | 115,216 | 123,406 | 481,701 | 284,234 | 95,999 | 706,307 | 8,889,980 |
| 2020[1] | 550,889 | 4,300,747 | 54,378 | 118,363 | 793,418 | 621,403 | 113,920 | 110,638 | 442,475 | 272,392 | 82,356 | 535,434 | 8,473,550 |
| 2021[2] | 514,937 | 4,548,131 | 61,948 | 139,174 | 839,963 | 676,808 | 98,214 | 118,346 | 481,049 | 251,915 | 94,394 | 577,430 | 8,907,743 |

[1] Preliminary.  [2] Estimate.  NA = Not available.  *Source: United Nations*

### World Imports of Primary Coal    In Thousands of Short Tons

| Year | China | Germany | India | Italy | Japan | Korea, South | Netherlands | Russia | Taiwan | Turkey | United Kingdom | United States | World Total |
|---|---|---|---|---|---|---|---|---|---|---|---|---|---|
| 2012 | 273,638 | 48,275 | 176,647 | 28,526 | 204,117 | 138,380 | 45,630 | 26,293 | 72,460 | 32,182 | 49,401 | 7,272 | 1,388,770 |
| 2013 | 321,195 | 56,415 | 200,091 | 22,435 | 211,162 | 139,452 | 53,386 | 28,318 | 74,146 | 29,358 | 55,789 | 8,906 | 1,490,130 |
| 2014 | 267,667 | 63,239 | 247,369 | 21,570 | 207,700 | 144,440 | 59,917 | 27,693 | 73,959 | 32,868 | 46,545 | 11,350 | 1,508,004 |
| 2015 | 224,937 | 62,077 | 243,544 | 21,578 | 210,160 | 148,907 | 62,097 | 26,914 | 72,731 | 37,461 | 26,674 | 11,318 | 1,452,830 |
| 2016 | 281,695 | 60,802 | 217,086 | 19,041 | 209,162 | 148,170 | 57,458 | 24,433 | 72,343 | 40,050 | 9,363 | 9,846 | 1,463,710 |
| 2017 | 298,649 | 53,720 | 219,434 | 17,767 | 212,532 | 162,239 | 51,703 | 27,454 | 74,506 | 43,129 | 9,367 | 7,803 | 1,539,931 |
| 2018 | 310,120 | 49,852 | 247,125 | 16,324 | 208,700 | 163,935 | 48,835 | 27,801 | 73,318 | 42,295 | 11,116 | 5,954 | 1,598,904 |
| 2019 | 330,527 | 45,577 | 266,445 | 11,933 | 205,233 | 155,862 | 41,514 | 26,742 | 74,221 | 41,615 | 6,866 | 6,697 | 1,607,020 |
| 2020[1] | 335,177 | 33,000 | 238,732 | 8,608 | 191,439 | 136,127 | 23,469 | 26,399 | 69,735 | 44,364 | 4,995 | 5,137 | 1,483,981 |
| 2021[2] | 356,794 | 42,753 | 210,811 | 9,717 | 201,137 | 138,468 | 39,891 | 25,663 | 74,297 | 40,253 | 5,079 | 5,389 | 1,531,027 |

[1] Preliminary.  [2] Estimate.  *Source: Energy Information Administration, U.S. Department of Energy (EIA-DOE)*

### World Exports of Primary Coal    In Thousands of Short Tons

| Year | Australia | Canada | China | Colombia | Indonesia | Kazakhstan | Mongolia | Poland | Russia | South Africa | United States | Vietnam | World Total |
|---|---|---|---|---|---|---|---|---|---|---|---|---|---|
| 2012 | 340,924 | 38,367 | 10,218 | 87,494 | 383,163 | 30,348 | 19,290 | 7,958 | 147,917 | 83,885 | 124,586 | 22,377 | 1,383,355 |
| 2013 | 391,684 | 43,099 | 8,278 | 82,408 | 420,201 | 36,691 | 20,255 | 12,219 | 156,087 | 83,515 | 117,659 | 17,368 | 1,492,046 |
| 2014 | 426,338 | 37,821 | 6,327 | 96,035 | 421,052 | 31,400 | 21,262 | 10,241 | 167,419 | 83,555 | 97,257 | 10,262 | 1,508,232 |
| 2015 | 432,489 | 33,760 | 5,886 | 80,242 | 403,140 | 30,496 | 15,945 | 10,398 | 174,262 | 83,114 | 73,958 | 1,904 | 1,438,411 |
| 2016 | 429,130 | 33,602 | 9,689 | 91,881 | 406,630 | 27,733 | 29,097 | 10,340 | 187,614 | 83,935 | 60,271 | 1,252 | 1,469,912 |
| 2017 | 418,028 | 34,284 | 8,918 | 92,886 | 429,383 | 29,147 | 37,600 | 8,160 | 223,176 | 92,349 | 96,945 | 2,101 | 1,550,460 |
| 2018 | 421,021 | 35,647 | 5,445 | 92,366 | 449,757 | 28,356 | 39,950 | 5,781 | 233,963 | 88,521 | 116,244 | 1,922 | 1,589,875 |
| 2019 | 433,135 | 39,324 | 6,604 | 78,869 | 488,219 | 28,285 | 39,912 | 5,061 | 246,269 | 86,717 | 93,765 | 1,260 | 1,620,541 |
| 2020[1] | 409,335 | 34,875 | 3,487 | 74,775 | 451,520 | 27,260 | 31,611 | 5,193 | 244,312 | 82,573 | 69,067 | 982 | 1,491,047 |
| 2021[2] | 403,224 | 34,910 | 2,840 | 61,289 | 478,029 | 26,280 | 21,645 | 7,177 | 261,987 | 72,880 | 85,115 | 1,070 | 1,523,747 |

[1] Preliminary.  [2] Estimate.  *Source: Energy Information Administration, U.S. Department of Energy (EIA-DOE)*

# COAL

## World Consumption of Primary Coal — In Thousands of Short Tons

| Year | Australia | China | Germany | India | Japan | Kazakh-stan | Korea, South | Poland | Russia | South Africa | Turkey | United States | World Total |
|---|---|---|---|---|---|---|---|---|---|---|---|---|---|
| 2012 | 140,866 | 4,657,005 | 271,234 | 776,357 | 207,804 | 99,174 | 140,359 | 155,991 | 242,966 | 202,973 | 108,904 | 889,185 | 8,941,721 |
| 2013 | 129,023 | 4,733,478 | 272,161 | 807,223 | 219,371 | 98,451 | 139,556 | 158,229 | 218,386 | 202,731 | 92,719 | 924,442 | 9,012,667 |
| 2014 | 123,259 | 4,585,493 | 264,633 | 895,227 | 215,079 | 91,383 | 144,083 | 151,044 | 210,323 | 201,737 | 106,463 | 917,731 | 8,902,163 |
| 2015 | 128,732 | 4,407,410 | 264,188 | 885,134 | 212,558 | 84,313 | 148,403 | 149,679 | 234,110 | 197,530 | 101,722 | 798,115 | 8,622,022 |
| 2016 | 131,065 | 4,286,002 | 255,911 | 871,799 | 212,493 | 82,075 | 148,576 | 148,848 | 227,095 | 199,817 | 116,878 | 731,071 | 8,390,968 |
| 2017 | 126,611 | 4,314,474 | 245,811 | 922,488 | 214,393 | 79,863 | 152,392 | 150,121 | 229,361 | 199,901 | 122,959 | 716,856 | 8,477,170 |
| 2018 | 116,348 | 4,381,153 | 238,344 | 986,378 | 208,504 | 83,703 | 153,102 | 146,983 | 243,703 | 189,076 | 134,169 | 688,105 | 8,594,825 |
| 2019 | 112,009 | 4,430,349 | 188,825 | 978,482 | 206,517 | 83,259 | 146,355 | 131,484 | 247,454 | 208,987 | 137,176 | 586,543 | 8,468,123 |
| 2020[1] | 106,909 | 4,456,931 | 152,854 | 924,468 | 203,062 | 82,186 | 138,065 | 120,794 | 231,471 | 207,376 | 113,735 | 476,693 | 8,136,713 |
| 2021[2] | 109,921 | 4,675,321 | 181,467 | 987,859 | 201,875 | 83,303 | 139,458 | 128,278 | 244,725 | 195,429 | 120,818 | 547,386 | 8,576,843 |

[1] Preliminary.  [2] Estimate.  *Source: Energy Information Administration, U.S. Department of Energy (EIA-DOE)*

## Production of Bituminous & Lignite Coal in the United States — In Thousands of Short Tons

| Year | Alabama | Colorado | Illinois | Indiana | Kentucky | Montana | Ohio | Pennsylvania | Texas | West Virginia | Virginia | Wyoming | Total |
|---|---|---|---|---|---|---|---|---|---|---|---|---|---|
| 2013 | 18,620 | 24,236 | 52,147 | 39,102 | 80,380 | 42,231 | 25,113 | 54,009 | 42,851 | 16,619 | 112,786 | 387,924 | 984,842 |
| 2014 | 16,363 | 24,007 | 57,969 | 39,267 | 77,335 | 44,562 | 22,252 | 60,910 | 43,654 | 15,059 | 112,187 | 395,665 | 1,000,049 |
| 2015 | 13,191 | 18,879 | 56,101 | 34,295 | 61,425 | 41,864 | 17,041 | 50,031 | 35,918 | 13,914 | 95,633 | 375,773 | 896,941 |
| 2016 | 9,643 | 12,634 | 43,422 | 28,767 | 42,868 | 32,336 | 12,564 | 45,720 | 39,001 | 12,910 | 79,757 | 297,218 | 728,364 |
| 2017 | 12,613 | 15,047 | 48,128 | 31,418 | 42,608 | 35,232 | 9,336 | 49,065 | 36,338 | 13,205 | 92,733 | 316,454 | 774,118 |
| 2018 | 14,783 | 14,026 | 49,482 | 34,598 | 39,740 | 38,610 | 8,993 | 49,968 | 24,823 | 13,012 | 95,510 | 304,188 | 756,167 |
| 2019 | 14,124 | 12,868 | 45,853 | 31,559 | 36,006 | 34,468 | 7,779 | 50,053 | 23,307 | 12,297 | 93,279 | 276,912 | 706,309 |
| 2020 | 12,151 | 10,035 | 31,578 | 19,942 | 24,217 | 26,422 | 3,587 | 36,305 | 19,682 | 9,685 | 67,278 | 218,556 | 535,434 |
| 2021[1] | 9,444 | 11,875 | 36,848 | 19,470 | 26,426 | 28,580 | 2,759 | 42,422 | 17,250 | 10,902 | 78,620 | 238,773 | 575,320 |
| 2022[2] | 10,408 | 12,782 | 38,346 | 23,512 | 28,457 | 28,233 | 2,492 | 39,807 | 17,084 | 10,995 | 83,487 | 244,860 | 592,067 |

[1] Preliminary.  [2] Estimate.  *Source: Energy Information Administration, U.S. Department of Energy (EIA-DOE)*

## Production[2] of Bituminous Coal in the United States — In Thousands of Short Tons

| Year | Jan. | Feb. | Mar. | Apr. | May | June | July | Aug. | Sept. | Oct. | Nov. | Dec. | Total |
|---|---|---|---|---|---|---|---|---|---|---|---|---|---|
| 2013 | 82,529 | 77,414 | 84,381 | 78,724 | 83,075 | 80,841 | 84,344 | 90,013 | 82,707 | 80,435 | 80,408 | 77,827 | 982,699 |
| 2014 | 82,835 | 75,177 | 86,794 | 82,835 | 83,645 | 78,929 | 84,275 | 87,167 | 83,410 | 80,435 | 80,408 | 77,827 | 998,102 |
| 2015 | 86,548 | 72,210 | 81,430 | 74,704 | 69,942 | 66,484 | 76,618 | 82,777 | 77,868 | 75,705 | 68,613 | 63,036 | 895,936 |
| 2016 | 60,413 | 57,181 | 55,186 | 48,089 | 52,983 | 59,356 | 61,667 | 68,118 | 64,947 | 68,578 | 67,006 | 63,176 | 726,700 |
| 2017 | 68,236 | 64,221 | 64,167 | 58,598 | 61,950 | 66,053 | 62,834 | 70,434 | 62,759 | 66,201 | 64,184 | 63,061 | 772,697 |
| 2018 | 61,827 | 60,129 | 65,351 | 57,892 | 61,048 | 61,408 | 62,817 | 69,160 | 62,289 | 66,355 | 62,690 | 63,305 | 754,271 |
| 2019 | 65,644 | 58,145 | 55,505 | 60,981 | 61,627 | 56,491 | 58,862 | 63,571 | 58,392 | 57,405 | 54,139 | 52,936 | 703,698 |
| 2020 | 55,420 | 47,215 | 45,901 | 39,162 | 37,088 | 39,422 | 43,024 | 47,310 | 44,939 | 44,802 | 44,161 | 44,618 | 533,062 |
| 2021 | 48,318 | 40,668 | 50,632 | 45,144 | 48,446 | 48,611 | 48,307 | 49,868 | 49,590 | 48,747 | 48,619 | 48,371 | 575,320 |
| 2022[1] | 49,570 | 47,570 | 51,220 | 46,530 | 49,705 | 48,820 | 49,037 | 53,314 | 51,298 | 51,066 | 48,501 | 45,436 | 592,067 |

[1] Preliminary.  [2] Includes small amount of lignite.  *Source: Energy Information Administration, U.S. Department of Energy (EIA-DOE)*

## Production[2] of Pennsylvania Anthracite Coal — In Thousands of Short Tons

| Year | Jan. | Feb. | Mar. | Apr. | May | June | July | Aug. | Sept. | Oct. | Nov. | Dec. | Total |
|---|---|---|---|---|---|---|---|---|---|---|---|---|---|
| 2013 | 183 | 172 | 187 | 186 | 196 | 191 | 174 | 186 | 171 | 168 | 168 | 163 | 2,143 |
| 2014 | 157 | 143 | 165 | 147 | 148 | 140 | 174 | 180 | 172 | 176 | 168 | 177 | 1,947 |
| 2015 | 170 | 142 | 160 | 182 | 171 | 162 | 204 | 220 | 207 | 192 | 174 | 160 | 2,145 |
| 2016 | 156 | 147 | 142 | 128 | 141 | 157 | 117 | 129 | 123 | 147 | 144 | 135 | 1,665 |
| 2017 | 178 | 168 | 168 | 156 | 165 | 176 | 133 | 149 | 133 | 167 | 162 | 159 | 1,912 |
| 2018 | 144 | 140 | 152 | 155 | 163 | 164 | 151 | 166 | 149 | 177 | 167 | 169 | 1,896 |
| 2019 | 192 | 170 | 162 | 232 | 235 | 215 | 207 | 224 | 205 | 269 | 253 | 248 | 2,611 |
| 2020 | 247 | 210 | 205 | 185 | 175 | 186 | 194 | 213 | 202 | 186 | 184 | 186 | 2,372 |
| 2021 | 177 | 149 | 186 | 150 | 161 | 162 | 166 | 171 | 170 | 207 | 206 | 205 | 2,111 |
| 2022[1] | 211 | 203 | 218 | 193 | 206 | 203 | 198 | 216 | 207 | 233 | 222 | 208 | 2,519 |

[1] Preliminary.  [2] Represents production in Pennsylvania only.  *Source: Energy Information Administration, U.S. Department of Energy (EIA-DOE)*

# COAL

## Salient Statistics of Coal in the United States   In Thousands of Short Tons

| Year | Production | Imports | Consumption | Exports Brazil | Exports Canada | Exports Europe | Exports Asia | Exports Total | Total Ending Stocks[2] | Losses & Unaccounted For[3] |
|---|---|---|---|---|---|---|---|---|---|---|
| 2012 | 1,016,458 | 9,159 | 889,185 | 7,954 | 7,211 | 66,399 | 32,512 | 125,746 | 238,853 | 14,980 |
| 2013 | 984,842 | 8,906 | 924,442 | 8,610 | 7,110 | 60,755 | 27,245 | 117,659 | 200,335 | 1,451 |
| 2014 | 1,000,049 | 11,350 | 917,731 | 8,032 | 6,724 | 52,469 | 19,450 | 97,257 | 197,727 | 10,858 |
| 2015 | 896,941 | 11,318 | 798,115 | 6,339 | 5,958 | 37,894 | 17,544 | 73,958 | 238,431 | 5,331 |
| 2016 | 728,364 | 9,846 | 731,071 | 6,939 | 5,011 | 27,381 | 15,714 | 60,271 | 192,990 | 2,346 |
| 2017 | 774,609 | 7,803 | 716,856 | 7,563 | 5,286 | 39,561 | 32,841 | 96,945 | 166,956 | 5,029 |
| 2018 | 756,167 | 5,954 | 688,105 | 8,595 | 5,726 | 43,808 | 40,281 | 116,244 | 129,796 | 5,397 |
| 2019 | 706,309 | 6,697 | 586,543 | 7,591 | 5,118 | 33,370 | 33,148 | 93,765 | 165,334 | 5,238 |
| 2020 | 535,434 | 5,137 | 476,693 | 7,889 | 4,587 | 22,154 | 27,680 | 69,067 | 161,718 | 7,129 |
| 2021[1] | 577,431 | 5,388 | 545,610 | 6,201 | 4,587 | 22,078 | 42,622 | 85,115 | 124,403 | 4,223 |

[1] Preliminary.   [2] Producer & distributor and consumer stocks, excludes stocks held by retail dealers for consumption by the residential and commercial sector.   [3] Equals production plus imports minus the change in producer & distributor and consumer stocks minus consumption minus exports.
*Source: Energy Information Administraion, U.S. Department of Energy (EIA-DOE)*

## Consumption and Stocks of Coal in the United States   In Thousands of Short Tons

| | Consumption Electric Utilities Anthracite | Bituminous | Lignite | Total | Industrial Coke Plants | Industrial Other Industrial[2] | Residential and Commercial | Total | Stocks, Dec. 31 Consumer Electric Utilities | Coke Plants | Other Industrials | Producers and Distributors |
|---|---|---|---|---|---|---|---|---|---|---|---|---|
| Year | | | | | | | | | | | | |
| 2012 | ---- | ---- | ---- | 823,551 | 20,751 | 42,838 | 2,045 | 889,185 | 185,116 | 2,522 | 4,475 | 46,157 |
| 2013 | ---- | ---- | ---- | 857,962 | 21,474 | 43,055 | 1,951 | 924,442 | 147,884 | 2,200 | 4,097 | 45,652 |
| 2014 | ---- | ---- | ---- | 851,602 | 21,297 | 42,946 | 1,887 | 917,731 | 151,792 | 2,640 | 4,196 | 38,894 |
| 2015 | ---- | ---- | ---- | 738,444 | 19,708 | 38,459 | 1,503 | 798,115 | 195,912 | 2,236 | 4,382 | 35,871 |
| 2016 | ---- | ---- | ---- | 678,554 | 16,485 | 34,849 | 1,183 | 731,071 | 162,476 | 1,675 | 3,637 | 25,309 |
| 2017 | ---- | ---- | ---- | 664,993 | 17,538 | 33,264 | 1,061 | 716,856 | 137,721 | 1,718 | 3,242 | 23,999 |
| 2018 | ---- | ---- | ---- | 637,217 | 18,337 | 31,580 | 972 | 688,105 | 102,793 | 1,807 | 3,258 | 21,692 |
| 2019 | ---- | ---- | ---- | 538,606 | 17,967 | 29,095 | 876 | 586,543 | 128,102 | 2,333 | 3,258 | 31,320 |
| 2020 | ---- | ---- | ---- | 435,827 | 14,414 | 25,660 | 793 | 476,693 | 131,431 | 1,654 | 2,848 | 23,640 |
| 2021[1] | ---- | ---- | ---- | 501,366 | 17,589 | 25,845 | 811 | 545,610 | 91,884 | 1,658 | 2,624 | 19,013 |

[1] Preliminary.   [2] Including transportation.   [3] Excludes stocks held at retail dealers for consumption by the residential and commercial sector.
*Source: Energy Information Administration, U.S. Department of Energy (EIA-DOE)*

## Trends in Bituminous Coal, Lignite and Pennsylvania Anthracite in the United States   In Thousands of Short Tons

| | Bituminous Coal and Lignite Production Under-Ground | Surface | Total | Miners[1] Employd | Labor Productivity Under-Ground | Surface | Average -Short Tons Per Miner Per Hour- | Pennsylvania Anthracite Under-Ground | Surface | Total | Miners[1] Employed | Labor Productivity Short Tons Miner/Hr. | All Mines Labor Productivity Short Tons Miner/Hr. |
|---|---|---|---|---|---|---|---|---|---|---|---|---|---|
| Year | | | | | | | | | | | | | |
| 2012 | 342,387 | 674,072 | 1,016,458 | 89,838 | 2.84 | 8.97 | 5.19 | 120 | 2,215 | 2,335 | 1,146 | 1.02 | 5.19 |
| 2013 | 341,685 | 643,157 | 984,842 | 80,396 | 3.07 | 9.69 | 5.53 | 95 | 1,965 | 2,060 | 1,095 | 1.01 | 5.53 |
| 2014 | 354,704 | 645,345 | 1,000,049 | 74,931 | 3.35 | 10.42 | 5.95 | 93 | 1,740 | 1,833 | 956 | .98 | 5.96 |
| 2015 | 306,821 | 590,119 | 896,941 | 65,971 | 3.45 | 10.95 | 6.28 | 86 | 1,867 | 1,953 | 1,005 | .94 | 6.28 |
| 2016 | 252,106 | 476,258 | 728,364 | 51,795 | 3.83 | 10.73 | 6.61 | 91 | 1,409 | 1,500 | 952 | .83 | 6.61 |
| 2017 | 273,129 | 501,480 | 774,609 | 53,051 | 3.77 | 10.92 | 6.55 | 79 | 1,788 | 1,867 | 914 | 1.07 | 6.55 |
| 2018 | 275,361 | 480,806 | 756,167 | 53,583 | 3.68 | 10.36 | 6.24 | 72 | 1,739 | 1,811 | 900 | 1.03 | 6.23 |
| 2019 | 267,373 | 438,936 | 706,309 | 52,804 | 3.60 | 9.88 | 5.95 | 63 | 2,522 | 2,585 | 916 | 1.43 | 5.94 |
| 2020 | 195,530 | 339,905 | 535,434 | 42,159 | 3.60 | 10.24 | 6.12 | 63 | 2,352 | 2,415 | 902 | 1.44 | 6.12 |
| 2021 | 220,597 | 356,834 | 577,431 | 39,518 | 4.03 | 11.38 | 6.71 | 54 | 2,043 | 2,097 | 810 | 1.29 | 6.71 |

[1] Excludes miners employed at mines producing less than 10,000 tons.
*Source: Energy Information Administration, U.S. Department of Energy (EIA-DOE)*

## Average Prices of Coal in the United States   In Dollars Per Short Ton

| Year | End-Use Sector Electric Utilities | Coke Plants | Other Industrial[2] | Imports[3] | Exports Steam | Exports Metallurgical | Exports Total Average[3] | Year | End-Use Sector Electric Utilities | Coke Plants | Other Industrial[2] | Imports[3] | Exports Steam | Exports Metallurgical | Exports Total Average[3] |
|---|---|---|---|---|---|---|---|---|---|---|---|---|---|---|---|
| 2012 | ---- | 190.55 | 70.33 | 96.78 | 76.16 | 152.23 | 118.43 | 2017 | ---- | ---- | ---- | 79.53 | 58.29 | 134.55 | 102.09 |
| 2013 | ---- | 156.99 | 69.32 | 83.35 | 69.23 | 115.50 | 95.06 | 2018 | ---- | ---- | ---- | 82.39 | 64.60 | 138.98 | 104.63 |
| 2014 | ---- | ---- | ---- | 80.96 | 67.05 | 99.49 | 87.08 | 2019 | ---- | ---- | ---- | 80.04 | 63.76 | 137.44 | 105.34 |
| 2015 | ---- | ---- | ---- | 71.61 | 56.44 | 89.31 | 76.89 | 2020 | ---- | ---- | ---- | 71.79 | 62.51 | 104.55 | 88.08 |
| 2016 | ---- | ---- | ---- | 65.75 | 48.58 | 71.13 | 73.66 | 2021[1] | ---- | ---- | ---- | 91.48 | 63.81 | 158.27 | 114.07 |

[1] Preliminary.   [2] Manufacturing plants only.   [3] Based on the free alongside ship (F.A.S.) value.
*Source: Energy Information Administration, U.S. Department of Energy (EIA-DOE)*

# COAL

### Exports of Coal in the United States   In Thousands of Short Tons

| Year | Jan. | Feb. | Mar. | Apr. | May | June | July | Aug. | Sept. | Oct. | Nov. | Dec. | Total |
|---|---|---|---|---|---|---|---|---|---|---|---|---|---|
| 2013 | 9,572 | 8,627 | 13,637 | 9,754 | 10,478 | 9,194 | 9,125 | 10,073 | 9,391 | 9,855 | 8,511 | 9,443 | 117,659 |
| 2014 | 8,152 | 8,972 | 10,460 | 7,952 | 8,182 | 8,540 | 7,119 | 7,637 | 7,966 | 7,738 | 7,557 | 6,981 | 97,257 |
| 2015 | 7,871 | 6,496 | 7,612 | 7,216 | 6,761 | 5,789 | 5,117 | 6,409 | 5,388 | 5,744 | 4,709 | 4,846 | 73,958 |
| 2016 | 4,433 | 4,511 | 5,208 | 4,583 | 4,209 | 5,432 | 3,276 | 5,003 | 4,273 | 4,863 | 6,554 | 7,926 | 60,271 |
| 2017 | 7,403 | 7,062 | 8,075 | 7,132 | 7,200 | 7,504 | 7,154 | 8,592 | 8,825 | 9,130 | 9,049 | 9,818 | 96,945 |
| 2018 | 8,659 | 8,983 | 9,886 | 11,032 | 9,400 | 10,107 | 9,924 | 9,995 | 9,683 | 10,768 | 8,920 | 8,888 | 116,244 |
| 2019 | 9,329 | 6,752 | 9,132 | 8,642 | 8,979 | 8,308 | 6,469 | 7,749 | 7,742 | 6,590 | 7,582 | 6,491 | 93,765 |
| 2020 | 6,230 | 6,611 | 7,070 | 5,551 | 4,714 | 4,583 | 5,344 | 4,545 | 5,371 | 4,921 | 7,034 | 7,093 | 69,067 |
| 2021 | 6,021 | 6,990 | 7,728 | 6,843 | 7,482 | 7,692 | 6,446 | 7,353 | 6,796 | 7,516 | 6,834 | 7,413 | 85,115 |
| 2022[1] | 5,710 | 7,164 | 7,312 | 8,048 | 7,364 | 7,589 | 6,691 | 6,961 | 7,086 | 6,676 | 7,548 | 6,615 | 84,765 |

[1] Preliminary.   Source: Energy Information Administration, U.S. Department of Energy (EIA-DOE)

### Imports of Coal in the United States   In Thousands of Short Tons

| Year | Jan. | Feb. | Mar. | Apr. | May | June | July | Aug. | Sept. | Oct. | Nov. | Dec. | Total |
|---|---|---|---|---|---|---|---|---|---|---|---|---|---|
| 2013 | 654 | 385 | 390 | 672 | 870 | 1,213 | 874 | 710 | 815 | 707 | 850 | 766 | 8,906 |
| 2014 | 1,065 | 582 | 803 | 930 | 1,280 | 1,365 | 928 | 1,076 | 1,148 | 584 | 1,005 | 586 | 11,350 |
| 2015 | 1,293 | 866 | 850 | 879 | 919 | 842 | 1,091 | 970 | 904 | 854 | 882 | 969 | 11,318 |
| 2016 | 693 | 819 | 1,186 | 740 | 910 | 641 | 990 | 943 | 800 | 768 | 706 | 652 | 9,850 |
| 2017 | 743 | 612 | 560 | 493 | 1,053 | 651 | 956 | 839 | 513 | 582 | 368 | 408 | 7,777 |
| 2018 | 500 | 349 | 518 | 494 | 544 | 509 | 692 | 484 | 263 | 304 | 400 | 898 | 5,954 |
| 2019 | 625 | 358 | 706 | 537 | 408 | 660 | 511 | 519 | 651 | 742 | 466 | 515 | 6,697 |
| 2020 | 535 | 343 | 461 | 365 | 535 | 227 | 530 | 314 | 501 | 264 | 639 | 423 | 5,137 |
| 2021 | 525 | 309 | 241 | 509 | 512 | 509 | 564 | 368 | 202 | 526 | 436 | 689 | 5,388 |
| 2022[1] | 503 | 289 | 530 | 684 | 325 | 627 | 660 | 779 | 531 | 404 | 690 | 292 | 6,314 |

[1] Preliminary.   Source: Energy Information Administration, U.S. Department of Energy (EIA-DOE)

### Consumption of Coal in the United States   In Thousands of Short Tons

| Year | Jan. | Feb. | Mar. | Apr. | May | June | July | Aug. | Sept. | Oct. | Nov. | Dec. | Total |
|---|---|---|---|---|---|---|---|---|---|---|---|---|---|
| 2013 | 80,587 | 72,486 | 75,914 | 65,960 | 69,885 | 80,169 | 88,299 | 87,156 | 77,902 | 71,824 | 71,439 | 82,821 | 924,442 |
| 2014 | 89,063 | 81,581 | 77,685 | 63,210 | 69,185 | 79,487 | 86,802 | 86,357 | 74,294 | 66,494 | 70,155 | 73,419 | 917,731 |
| 2015 | 76,895 | 72,318 | 63,560 | 53,207 | 61,923 | 73,845 | 81,449 | 78,574 | 69,369 | 58,405 | 53,640 | 73,419 | 798,115 |
| 2016 | 66,662 | 55,211 | 44,575 | 43,384 | 49,343 | 67,551 | 78,569 | 78,175 | 66,615 | 58,953 | 52,533 | 69,501 | 731,071 |
| 2017 | 68,006 | 52,381 | 53,325 | 48,565 | 55,202 | 63,099 | 74,214 | 70,229 | 59,039 | 54,436 | 55,357 | 63,003 | 716,856 |
| 2018 | 69,254 | 50,025 | 48,870 | 44,793 | 51,574 | 60,240 | 68,083 | 67,976 | 58,159 | 52,811 | 56,170 | 60,149 | 688,105 |
| 2019 | 60,199 | 49,200 | 48,348 | 37,282 | 44,060 | 48,267 | 59,802 | 56,311 | 51,113 | 41,518 | 45,869 | 44,575 | 586,543 |
| 2020 | 40,771 | 36,012 | 32,843 | 26,754 | 29,784 | 39,798 | 52,852 | 53,610 | 41,828 | 37,393 | 37,874 | 47,175 | 476,693 |
| 2021 | 49,010 | 51,521 | 38,331 | 33,634 | 39,282 | 51,590 | 60,022 | 59,904 | 47,960 | 39,435 | 36,555 | 38,368 | 545,610 |
| 2022[1] | 52,345 | 43,422 | 37,939 | 34,262 | 38,495 | 45,135 | 52,835 | 51,693 | 40,618 | 35,051 | 35,810 | | 510,115 |

[1] Preliminary.   Source: Energy Information Administration, U.S. Department of Energy (EIA-DOE)

### Stocks of Coal in the United States   In Thousands of Short Tons

| Year | Jan. | Feb. | Mar. | Apr. | May | June | July | Aug. | Sept. | Oct. | Nov. | Dec. |
|---|---|---|---|---|---|---|---|---|---|---|---|---|
| 2013 | 233,054 | 230,219 | 226,848 | 228,796 | 233,626 | 228,246 | 216,276 | 209,959 | 207,221 | 208,449 | 210,232 | 200,335 |
| 2014 | 185,093 | 170,792 | 168,718 | 179,555 | 186,696 | 182,153 | 174,083 | 167,818 | 170,214 | 182,218 | 187,891 | 197,727 |
| 2015 | 200,117 | 195,189 | 200,119 | 213,690 | 219,265 | 212,713 | 204,074 | 200,714 | 205,997 | 219,276 | 232,337 | 238,431 |
| 2016 | 229,181 | 228,793 | 232,962 | 234,322 | 232,520 | 220,992 | 205,411 | 193,859 | 189,600 | 193,082 | 201,620 | 192,990 |
| 2017 | 186,622 | 190,868 | 191,964 | 194,162 | 192,045 | 186,694 | 176,606 | 170,839 | 168,490 | 170,338 | 172,472 | 166,956 |
| 2018 | 153,075 | 150,337 | 155,418 | 156,693 | 155,559 | 148,806 | 136,250 | 130,535 | 128,015 | 131,900 | 131,733 | 129,796 |
| 2019 | 125,763 | 127,331 | 126,150 | 136,039 | 145,314 | 146,872 | 141,511 | 142,445 | 144,192 | 154,104 | 158,921 | 165,334 |
| 2020 | 171,201 | 176,447 | 181,242 | 188,040 | 190,533 | 184,699 | 170,072 | 160,630 | 158,555 | 162,077 | 163,547 | 159,822 |
| 2021 | 150,115 | 134,839 | 136,555 | 142,474 | 144,939 | 135,727 | 121,063 | 106,398 | 101,149 | 105,479 | 112,806 | 115,356 |
| 2022[1] | 108,692 | 106,297 | 111,431 | 116,172 | 118,196 | 112,466 | 103,974 | 99,069 | 102,030 | 111,297 | 117,333 | |

[1] Preliminary.   Source: Energy Information Administration, U.S. Department of Energy (EIA-DOE)

# COAL

### Stocks of Coal, Producers and Distributors, in the United States    In Thousands of Short Tons

| Year | Jan. | Feb. | Mar. | Apr. | May | June | July | Aug. | Sept. | Oct. | Nov. | Dec. |
|---|---|---|---|---|---|---|---|---|---|---|---|---|
| 2013 | 46,907 | 47,665 | 48,422 | 48,991 | 49,560 | 50,129 | 49,131 | 48,133 | 47,135 | 47,061 | 46,987 | 45,652 |
| 2014 | 44,951 | 44,804 | 44,728 | 44,813 | 43,871 | 42,682 | 41,939 | 39,892 | 38,828 | 38,266 | 38,159 | 38,894 |
| 2015 | 38,817 | 39,581 | 39,610 | 40,226 | 39,817 | 39,399 | 38,993 | 37,353 | 36,213 | 36,233 | 36,509 | 35,871 |
| 2016 | 35,236 | 35,258 | 35,207 | 35,011 | 34,053 | 32,932 | 31,393 | 29,126 | 27,282 | 26,425 | 25,645 | 25,309 |
| 2017 | 24,974 | 25,170 | 25,190 | 25,169 | 24,350 | 23,430 | 25,465 | 24,226 | 23,430 | 23,459 | 23,705 | 23,999 |
| 2018 | 24,769 | 24,938 | 24,736 | 23,417 | 22,841 | 22,997 | 21,025 | 21,806 | 22,537 | 21,878 | 22,419 | 21,692 |
| 2019 | 21,391 | 23,551 | 24,160 | 22,767 | 24,273 | 24,529 | 25,240 | 26,441 | 27,714 | 29,683 | 30,717 | 31,320 |
| 2020 | 31,382 | 31,803 | 30,829 | 31,168 | 31,522 | 29,510 | 27,716 | 27,138 | 25,537 | 25,025 | 24,152 | 23,640 |
| 2021 | 21,805 | 22,682 | 22,629 | 22,532 | 22,444 | 22,361 | 21,420 | 19,986 | 19,042 | 19,026 | 19,022 | 19,013 |
| 2022[1] | 19,804 | 20,938 | 20,953 | 20,952 | 20,934 | 20,927 | 19,959 | 18,506 | 17,515 | 17,613 | 17,704 | |

[1] Preliminary.    Source: Energy Information Administration, U.S. Department of Energy (EIA-DOE)

### Stocks of Coal, Residential and Commercial, in the United States    In Thousands of Short Tons

| Year | Jan. | Feb. | Mar. | Apr. | May | June | July | Aug. | Sept. | Oct. | Nov. | Dec. |
|---|---|---|---|---|---|---|---|---|---|---|---|---|
| 2013 | 566 | 548 | 530 | 530 | 529 | 529 | 529 | 530 | 530 | 519 | 507 | 495 |
| 2014 | 465 | 435 | 405 | 413 | 421 | 429 | 440 | 451 | 462 | 458 | 454 | 449 |
| 2015 | 429 | 408 | 388 | 387 | 386 | 386 | 388 | 390 | 392 | 393 | 394 | 394 |
| 2016 | 373 | 353 | 332 | 334 | 336 | 337 | 348 | 359 | 370 | 367 | 364 | 360 |
| 2017 | 352 | 343 | 335 | 333 | 331 | 329 | 332 | 335 | 337 | 328 | 319 | 310 |
| 2018 | 298 | 287 | 275 | 268 | 262 | 256 | 257 | 259 | 260 | 256 | 251 | 247 |
| 2019 | 238 | 229 | 221 | 214 | 208 | 201 | 212 | 222 | 232 | 237 | 242 | 246 |
| 2020 | 235 | 223 | 212 | 212 | 212 | 213 | 220 | 227 | 234 | 239 | 245 | 250 |
| 2021 | 243 | 236 | 229 | 223 | 217 | 210 | 207 | 204 | 201 | 193 | 184 | 176 |
| 2022[1] | 170 | 163 | 157 | 158 | 158 | 158 | 168 | 177 | 187 | 188 | 186 | |

[1] Preliminary.    Source: Energy Information Administration, U.S. Department of Energy (EIA-DOE)

### Stocks of Coal, Coke Plants, in the United States    In Thousands of Short Tons

| Year | Jan. | Feb. | Mar. | Apr. | May | June | July | Aug. | Sept. | Oct. | Nov. | Dec. |
|---|---|---|---|---|---|---|---|---|---|---|---|---|
| 2013 | 2,417 | 2,312 | 2,207 | 2,305 | 2,402 | 2,500 | 2,516 | 2,531 | 2,546 | 2,431 | 2,315 | 2,200 |
| 2014 | 2,064 | 1,927 | 1,791 | 1,840 | 1,888 | 1,937 | 2,060 | 2,184 | 2,307 | 2,418 | 2,529 | 2,640 |
| 2015 | 2,471 | 2,303 | 2,135 | 2,299 | 2,463 | 2,627 | 2,756 | 2,884 | 3,013 | 2,754 | 2,495 | 2,236 |
| 2016 | 2,129 | 2,022 | 1,914 | 1,877 | 1,839 | 1,802 | 1,755 | 1,707 | 1,660 | 1,665 | 1,670 | 1,675 |
| 2017 | 1,579 | 1,483 | 1,388 | 1,467 | 1,547 | 1,626 | 1,641 | 1,655 | 1,670 | 1,686 | 1,702 | 1,718 |
| 2018 | 1,648 | 1,578 | 1,508 | 1,544 | 1,580 | 1,616 | 1,681 | 1,746 | 1,811 | 1,809 | 1,808 | 1,807 |
| 2019 | 1,873 | 1,939 | 2,005 | 2,102 | 2,199 | 2,296 | 2,352 | 2,407 | 2,463 | 2,420 | 2,376 | 2,333 |
| 2020 | 2,271 | 2,210 | 2,148 | 2,106 | 2,064 | 2,022 | 2,007 | 1,991 | 1,975 | 1,868 | 1,761 | 1,654 |
| 2021 | 1,618 | 1,581 | 1,545 | 1,648 | 1,750 | 1,853 | 1,833 | 1,814 | 1,794 | 1,749 | 1,704 | 1,658 |
| 2022[1] | 1,636 | 1,613 | 1,590 | 1,600 | 1,610 | 1,620 | 1,629 | 1,638 | 1,646 | 1,848 | 1,824 | |

[1] Preliminary.    Source: Energy Information Administration, U.S. Department of Energy (EIA-DOE)

### Stocks of Coal, Total End-Use Sectors, in the United States    In Thousands of Short Tons

| Year | Jan. | Feb. | Mar. | Apr. | May | June | July | Aug. | Sept. | Oct. | Nov. | Dec. |
|---|---|---|---|---|---|---|---|---|---|---|---|---|
| 2013 | 7,281 | 6,982 | 6,683 | 6,784 | 6,885 | 6,987 | 7,119 | 7,252 | 7,385 | 7,187 | 6,989 | 6,792 |
| 2014 | 6,438 | 6,083 | 5,729 | 5,817 | 5,904 | 5,992 | 6,274 | 6,557 | 6,840 | 6,988 | 7,136 | 7,285 |
| 2015 | 6,911 | 6,536 | 6,162 | 6,400 | 6,639 | 6,877 | 7,143 | 7,410 | 7,676 | 7,455 | 7,233 | 7,012 |
| 2016 | 6,742 | 6,472 | 6,202 | 6,126 | 6,050 | 5,973 | 5,899 | 5,825 | 5,751 | 5,724 | 5,698 | 5,672 |
| 2017 | 5,434 | 5,196 | 4,959 | 5,056 | 5,153 | 5,250 | 5,330 | 5,409 | 5,489 | 5,416 | 5,343 | 5,270 |
| 2018 | 5,072 | 4,873 | 4,674 | 4,705 | 4,736 | 4,768 | 4,876 | 4,985 | 5,094 | 5,166 | 5,239 | 5,312 |
| 2019 | 5,227 | 5,142 | 5,058 | 5,199 | 5,341 | 5,483 | 5,609 | 5,736 | 5,863 | 5,855 | 5,846 | 5,838 |
| 2020 | 5,685 | 5,533 | 5,380 | 5,338 | 5,296 | 5,253 | 5,208 | 5,162 | 5,116 | 4,994 | 4,873 | 4,751 |
| 2021 | 4,605 | 4,459 | 4,312 | 4,438 | 4,563 | 4,688 | 4,669 | 4,650 | 4,631 | 4,574 | 4,516 | 4,459 |
| 2022[1] | 4,356 | 4,252 | 4,149 | 4,150 | 4,152 | 4,153 | 4,223 | 4,293 | 4,363 | 5,595 | 5,553 | |

[1] Preliminary.    Source: Energy Information Administration, U.S. Department of Energy (EIA-DOE)

# COAL

## Stocks of Coal, Electric Power Sector[2], in the United States — In Thousands of Short Tons

| Year | Jan. | Feb. | Mar. | Apr. | May | June | July | Aug. | Sept. | Oct. | Nov. | Dec. |
|---|---|---|---|---|---|---|---|---|---|---|---|---|
| 2013 | 178,859 | 175,565 | 171,736 | 173,014 | 177,174 | 171,124 | 160,019 | 154,567 | 152,694 | 154,194 | 156,249 | 147,884 |
| 2014 | 133,705 | 119,904 | 118,260 | 128,925 | 136,921 | 133,479 | 125,870 | 121,369 | 124,546 | 136,964 | 142,595 | 151,548 |
| 2015 | 154,390 | 149,071 | 154,347 | 167,063 | 172,809 | 166,437 | 157,938 | 155,952 | 162,109 | 175,588 | 188,595 | 195,548 |
| 2016 | 187,203 | 187,064 | 191,553 | 193,185 | 192,417 | 182,086 | 168,119 | 158,908 | 156,567 | 160,932 | 170,277 | 162,009 |
| 2017 | 156,214 | 160,502 | 161,815 | 163,937 | 162,542 | 158,014 | 145,811 | 141,204 | 139,571 | 141,463 | 143,424 | 137,687 |
| 2018 | 123,235 | 120,526 | 126,008 | 128,571 | 127,982 | 121,041 | 110,348 | 103,744 | 100,384 | 104,855 | 104,075 | 102,793 |
| 2019 | 99,378 | 98,835 | 97,102 | 108,852 | 115,888 | 117,710 | 110,933 | 110,560 | 110,952 | 119,045 | 123,033 | 128,497 |
| 2020 | 134,134 | 139,112 | 145,034 | 151,534 | 153,716 | 149,935 | 137,149 | 128,330 | 127,902 | 132,058 | 134,522 | 131,431 |
| 2021 | 123,705 | 107,698 | 109,613 | 115,505 | 117,932 | 108,678 | 94,974 | 81,762 | 77,476 | 81,879 | 89,268 | 91,884 |
| 2022[1] | 84,533 | 81,106 | 86,328 | 91,070 | 93,110 | 87,386 | 79,792 | 76,271 | 80,152 | 88,089 | 94,076 | |

[1] Preliminary. [2] The electric power sector comprises electricity-only and combined-heat-and-power (CHP) plants within the NAICS 22 category whose primary business is to sell electricity, or electricity and heat, to the public. Source: Energy Information Administration, U.S. Department of Energy (EIA-DOE)

## Average Mine Prices of Coal in the United States — In Dollars Per Short Ton

| Year | Underground | Surface | Total | Lignite | Sub-bituminous | Bituminous | Anthracite[1] | Bituminous & Lignite FOB Mines[2] | Anthracite FOB Mines[2] | All Coal CIF[3] Electric Utility Plants |
|---|---|---|---|---|---|---|---|---|---|---|
| 2012 | 66.56 | 26.43 | 39.95 | 19.60 | 15.34 | 66.04 | 80.21 | 66.04 | 80.21 | 45.77 |
| 2013 | 60.98 | 24.50 | 37.24 | 19.96 | 14.86 | 60.61 | 87.82 | 60.61 | 87.82 | 45.03 |
| 2014 | 56.97 | 22.83 | 34.83 | 19.44 | 14.72 | 55.99 | 90.98 | 55.99 | 90.98 | 45.66 |
| 2015 | 52.20 | 21.47 | 31.83 | 22.36 | 14.63 | 51.57 | 97.91 | 51.57 | 97.91 | 42.58 |
| 2016 | 49.02 | 20.47 | 30.57 | 19.99 | 14.83 | 48.40 | 97.61 | 48.40 | 97.61 | 40.39 |
| 2017 | 56.99 | 20.95 | 33.72 | 19.51 | 14.29 | 55.60 | 93.17 | 55.60 | 93.17 | 33.72 |
| 2018 | 60.38 | 21.90 | 35.99 | 20.21 | 13.64 | 59.43 | 99.97 | 59.43 | 99.97 | 35.99 |
| 2019 | 58.68 | 22.47 | 36.07 | 19.86 | 14.01 | 58.93 | 102.22 | 58.93 | 102.22 | |
| 2020 | 49.80 | 20.67 | 31.41 | 22.16 | 14.43 | 50.05 | 90.68 | 50.05 | 90.68 | |
| 2021 | 60.49 | 21.32 | 36.45 | 20.10 | 14.18 | 61.68 | 107.08 | 61.68 | 107.08 | |

[1] Produced in Pennsylvania. [2] FOB = free on board. [3] CIF = cost, insurance and freight. W = Withheld data.
Source: Energy Information Administration, U.S. Department of Energy (EIA-DOE)

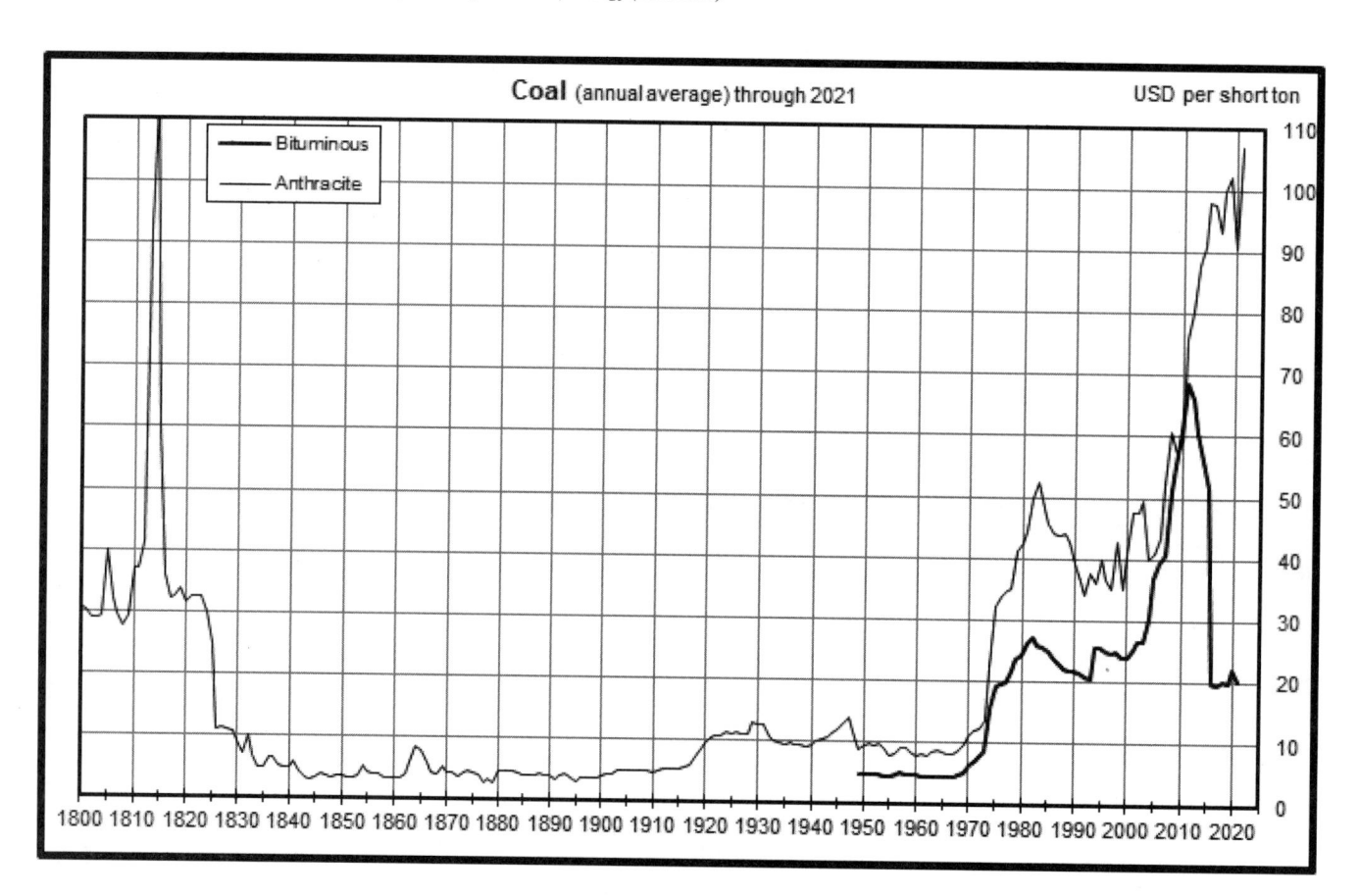

# Cobalt

Cobalt (atomic symbol Co) is a lustrous, silvery-white, magnetic, metallic element used chiefly for making alloys. Cobalt was known in ancient times and used by the Persians in 2250 BC to color glass. The name *cobalt* comes from the German word *kobalt* or *kobold*, meaning evil spirit. Miners gave cobalt its name because it was poisonous and troublesome since it polluted and degraded other mined elements, like nickel. In the 1730s, George Brandt first isolated metallic cobalt and was able to show that cobalt was the source of the blue color in glasses. In 1780, it was recognized as an element. Cobalt is generally not found in nature as a free metal and is instead found in ores. Cobalt is mainly produced as a by-product of nickel and copper mining.

Cobalt is used in a variety of applications: high-temperature steel alloys; fasteners in gas turbine engines; magnets and magnetic recording media; drying agents for paints and pigments; and steel-belted radial tires. Cobalt-60, an important radioactive tracer and cancer-treatment agent, is an artificially produced radioactive isotope of cobalt.

**Prices** – The price of cobalt in 2022 rose by +28.0% yr/yr to $31.00 per pound, well below the 2008 record high of $39.01 per pound.

**Supply** – World production of cobalt in 2022 rose by +15.2% yr/yr to 190,000 metric tons, a new record high. The world's largest cobalt mine producers in 2022 were the Congo with 68.4% of world production, Indonesia with 5.3%, and Russia with 4.7%.

The U.S. does not target cobalt for mining or refining, although some cobalt is produced as a byproduct of other mining operations. Imports, stock releases, and secondary materials comprise the U.S. cobalt supply. Secondary production includes extraction from superalloy scrap, cemented carbide scrap, and spent catalysts. In the U.S. there are two domestic producers of extra-fine cobalt powder. U.S. secondary production of cobalt in 2022 rose by +5.6% yr/yr to 1,900 metric tons.

**Demand** – U.S. consumption of cobalt in 2022 rose by +18.2% yr/yr to 7,800 metric tons. In 2019, the largest use of cobalt by far was for superalloys, with 33.8% of consumption. Other smaller-scaled applications for cobalt include cutting and wear-resistant materials at 6.4%.

**Trade** – U.S. imports of cobalt in 2022 rose by +12.2% to 11,000 metric tons, down from the 2019 record high of 13,900. In 2022, the U.S. relied on imports for 76% of its cobalt consumption, down from the 99% level seen in the early 1970s.

## World Mine Production of Cobalt    In Metric Tons (Cobalt Content)

| Year | Australia | Botswana | Brazil | Canada | China | Congo[3] (Kinshasa) | Cuba | Indonesia | Morocco | New Caledonia | Russia | Zambia | World Total |
|---|---|---|---|---|---|---|---|---|---|---|---|---|---|
| 2013 | 6,400 | 248 | 3,500 | 4,005 | 2,600 | 56,000 | 4,000 | 1,700 | 2,000 | 3,190 | 6,300 | 2,500 | 103,000 |
| 2014 | 6,201 | 196 | 3,828 | 3,907 | 2,800 | 65,000 | 3,300 | 1,300 | 1,400 | 4,040 | 6,300 | 2,300 | 115,000 |
| 2015 | 5,721 | 316 | 2,771 | 4,339 | 2,600 | 72,000 | 4,000 | 1,300 | 1,500 | 3,640 | 6,200 | 1,700 | 122,000 |
| 2016 | 5,140 | 248 | 852 | 4,126 | 2,300 | 68,000 | 3,900 | 1,200 | 1,600 | 3,390 | 5,500 | 600 | 112,000 |
| 2017 | 5,034 | ---- | 185 | 3,704 | 2,500 | 80,000 | 3,900 | 1,200 | 2,300 | 2,780 | 5,900 | 990 | 126,000 |
| 2018 | 4,878 | ---- | ---- | 3,279 | 2,000 | 104,000 | 3,500 | 1,200 | 2,300 | 2,100 | 6,100 | 835 | 148,000 |
| 2019 | 5,742 | ---- | 30 | 3,336 | 2,500 | 100,000 | 3,800 | 1,100 | 2,300 | 1,700 | 6,300 | 420 | 144,000 |
| 2020 | 5,630 | ---- | ---- | 3,690 | 2,200 | 98,000 | 3,800 | 1,100 | 2,300 | | 9,000 | | 142,000 |
| 2021[1] | 5,295 | ---- | ---- | 4,361 | 2,200 | 119,000 | 4,000 | 2,700 | 2,300 | | 8,000 | | 165,000 |
| 2022[2] | 5,900 | | | 3,900 | 2,200 | 130,000 | 3,800 | 10,000 | 2,300 | | 8,900 | | 190,000 |

[1] Preliminary.   [2] Estimate.   [3] Formerly Zaire.   Source: U.S. Geological Survey (USGS)

## Salient Statistics of Cobalt in the United States    In Metric Tons (Cobalt Content)

| Year | Net Import Reliance As a % of Apparent Consump | Cobalt Secondary Production | Processor and Consumer Stocks Dec. 31 | Imports for Consumption | Ground Coat Frit | Stainless & Heat Resisting | Catalysts | Superalloys | Tool Steel | Magnetic Alloys | Pigments | Drier in Paints, etc | Cutting & Wear-Resistant Material | Welding Materials | Total Apparent Uses | Price $ Per Pound[4] |
|---|---|---|---|---|---|---|---|---|---|---|---|---|---|---|---|---|
| 2013 | 75 | 2,160 | 1,070 | 10,400 | W | W | W | 3,770 | W | 303 | W | W | 705 | 397 | 8,660 | 12.89 |
| 2014 | 75 | 2,200 | 1,410 | 11,300 | ---- | ---- | ---- | 3,930 | ---- | 328 | ---- | ---- | 783 | 573 | 8,710 | 14.48 |
| 2015 | 73 | 2,750 | 1,070 | 11,400 | ---- | ---- | ---- | 3,960 | ---- | ---- | ---- | ---- | 726 | ---- | 10,300 | 13.44 |
| 2016 | 76 | 2,750 | 969 | 12,800 | ---- | ---- | ---- | 4,080 | ---- | ---- | ---- | ---- | 672 | ---- | 11,500 | 12.01 |
| 2017 | 69 | 2,750 | 1,020 | 11,900 | ---- | ---- | ---- | 4,240 | ---- | ---- | ---- | ---- | 753 | ---- | 8,950 | 26.97 |
| 2018 | 64 | 2,750 | 1,060 | 11,900 | ---- | ---- | ---- | 4,240 | ---- | ---- | ---- | ---- | 800 | ---- | 7,680 | 37.43 |
| 2019 | 78 | 2,750 | 1,090 | 13,900 | ---- | ---- | ---- | 4,220 | ---- | ---- | ---- | ---- | 799 | ---- | 12,500 | 16.95 |
| 2020 | 76 | 2,010 | 952 | 9,740 | | | | | | | | | | | 8,470 | 15.70 |
| 2021[1] | 73 | 1,800 | 1,010 | 9,800 | | | | | | | | | | | 6,600 | 24.21 |
| 2022[2] | 76 | 1,900 | 1,000 | 11,000 | | | | | | | | | | | 7,800 | 31.00 |

[1] Preliminary.   [2] Estimate.   [3] Or related usage.   [4] Annual spot for cathodes.   W = Withheld.   Source: U.S. Geological Survey (USGS)

# Cocoa

Cocoa is the common name for a powder derived from the fruit seeds of the cacao tree. The Spanish called cocoa "the food of the gods" when they found it in South America 500 years ago. Today, it remains a valued commodity. Dating back to the time of the Aztecs, cocoa was mainly used as a beverage. The processing of the cacao seeds, also known as cocoa beans, begins when the harvested fruit is fermented or cured into a pulpy state for three to nine days. The cocoa beans are then dried in the sun and cleaned in special machines before they are roasted to bring out the chocolate flavor. After roasting, they are put into a crushing machine and ground into cocoa powder. Cocoa has a high food value because it contains as much as 20 percent protein, 40 percent carbohydrate, and 40 percent fat. It is also mildly stimulating because of the presence of theobromine, an alkaloid that is closely related to caffeine. Roughly two-thirds of cocoa bean production is used to make chocolate and one-third to make cocoa powder.

Four major West African cocoa producers, the Ivory Coast, Ghana, Nigeria, and Cameroon, together account for about two-thirds of world cocoa production. Outside of West Africa, the major producers of cocoa are Indonesia, Brazil, Malaysia, Ecuador, and the Dominican Republic. Cocoa producers like Ghana and Indonesia have been making efforts to increase cocoa production while producers like Malaysia have been switching to other crops. Ghana has had an ongoing problem with black pod disease and the crop's smuggling into the neighboring Ivory Coast. Brazil was once one of the largest cocoa producers but has had problems with witches' broom disease. In West Africa, the main crop harvest starts in the September-October period and can be extended into the January-March period. Cocoa trees reach maturity in 5-6 years but can live to be 50 years old or more. The cocoa tree will produce thousands of flowers during a growing season, but only a few will develop into cocoa pods.

Cocoa futures and options are traded at the ICE Futures U.S. and ICE Futures Europe exchanges. The futures contracts call for the delivery of 10 metric tons of cocoa and the contract is priced in US dollars per metric ton.

**Prices** – ICE cocoa futures prices (Barchart.com symbol CC) rallied sharply in early-2022 and posted the high for the year in February at $2,790 per metric ton. Strength in global cocoa demand supported prices in early 2022. Europe ground 1.67 MMT of cocoa beans into butter and powder for confectionary products in 2021, up +6.1% y/y and the most in data that goes back to 1999. Also, weather concerns in West Africa supported cocoa prices as the seasonal Harmattan winds dried out cocoa farms in the Ivory Coast, the world's top cocoa producer. Cocoa prices then zigzagged lower into September when they posted a 2-1/2 year low of $2,192 per metric ton. The Federal Reserve's rate-hike campaign in 2022 boosted the dollar index to a 10-year high in September, undercutting most commodity prices, including cocoa. Also, beneficial growing conditions in the second half of 2022 improved West African cocoa crop prospects. The International Cocoa Organization (ICCO) projected that 2021/22 Ivory Coast cocoa production would be little changed at 2.4 MMT, and Ghana 2021/22 cocoa production would climb +24% y/y to 850,00 MT. Global cocoa production in 2020/21 had risen to a record 5.242 MMT, and the global cocoa market was in a surplus of +209,000 MT. Cocoa prices then moved higher into year-end on concern about the quality of some West African cocoa crops. Cocoa farmers continue to struggle with the lack of fertilizer and pesticides as the war in Ukraine has limited Russian exports of potash and other fertilizers worldwide. Also, chocolate consumption rebounded higher to pre-pandemic levels after countries around the world lifted pandemic restrictions. Cocoa prices finished 2022 up +3.2% yr/yr at $2,600 per metric ton.

**Supply** – The world's production of cocoa beans in the 2021/22 crop year fell by -3.5% to 5.580 million metric tons. The world's largest cocoa producer by far is the Ivory Coast, with 39.4% of the world's production, followed by Ghana with 14.7%, and Indonesia with 13.0%. Closing stocks of cocoa in the 2019/20 crop year rose by +2.4% yr/yr to 1.760 million metric tons.

**Demand** – World seasonal grindings of cocoa in 2019/20 fell by -3.1% yr/yr to 4.635 million metric tons. The European Union is by far the largest global consumer of cocoa, consuming about 33.7% of the global crop.

**Trade** – U.S. imports of cocoa and cocoa products in 2022 rose by +1.2% yr/yr to 1.553 million metric tons, a new record high.

### World Supply and Demand Cocoa    In Thousands of Metric Tons

| Crop Year Beginning Oct. 1 | Stocks Oct. 1 | Net World Production[4] | Total Availability | Seasonal Grindings | Closing Stocks | Stock Change | Stock/Consumption Ratio % |
|---|---|---|---|---|---|---|---|
| 2010-11 | 1,418 | 4,309 | 5,727 | 3,938 | 1,746 | 328 | 44.3 |
| 2011-12 | 1,746 | 4,095 | 5,841 | 3,972 | 1,828 | 82 | 46.0 |
| 2012-13 | 1,828 | 3,943 | 5,771 | 4,180 | 1,552 | -276 | 37.1 |
| 2013-14 | 1,552 | 4,370 | 5,922 | 4,335 | 1,543 | -9 | 35.6 |
| 2014-15 | 1,543 | 4,252 | 5,795 | 4,152 | 1,600 | 57 | 38.5 |
| 2015-16 | 1,600 | 3,994 | 5,594 | 4,127 | 1,427 | -173 | 34.6 |
| 2016-17 | 1,427 | 4,768 | 6,195 | 4,394 | 1,753 | 326 | 39.9 |
| 2017-18[1] | 1,753 | 4,648 | 6,401 | 4,585 | 1,770 | 17 | 38.6 |
| 2018-19[2] | 1,770 | 4,780 | 6,550 | 4,784 | 1,718 | -52 | 35.9 |
| 2019-20[3] | 1,718 | 4,724 | 6,442 | 4,635 | 1,760 | 42 | 38.0 |

[1] Preliminary.  [2] Estimate.  [3] Forecast.  [4] Obtained by adjusting the gross world crop for a one percent loss in weight.
Source: International Cocoa Organization (ICO

# COCOA

## World Production of Cocoa Beans   In Metric Tons

| Crop Year Beginning Oct. 1 | Brazil | Cameroon | Colombia | Côte d'Ivoire | Dominican Republic | Ecuador | Ghana | Indonesia | Malaysia | Mexico | Nigeria | Papau New Guinea | World Total |
|---|---|---|---|---|---|---|---|---|---|---|---|---|---|
| 2012-13 | 253,211 | 268,941 | 41,670 | 1,485,882 | 72,225 | 133,323 | 879,348 | 740,500 | 3,645 | 38,825 | 383,000 | 38,700 | 4,613,817 |
| 2013-14 | 256,186 | 275,000 | 46,739 | 1,448,992 | 68,021 | 128,446 | 835,466 | 720,900 | 2,809 | 33,284 | 367,000 | 41,200 | 4,486,252 |
| 2014-15 | 273,793 | 269,228 | 47,732 | 1,637,778 | 69,913 | 156,216 | 858,720 | 728,400 | 2,665 | 26,969 | 329,870 | 45,369 | 4,741,947 |
| 2015-16 | 278,299 | 310,000 | 54,798 | 1,796,000 | 75,500 | 180,192 | 858,720 | 593,331 | 1,729 | 28,007 | 302,066 | 36,100 | 4,817,460 |
| 2016-17 | 213,871 | 211,000 | 56,785 | 1,634,000 | 81,246 | 177,551 | 858,720 | 656,817 | 1,723 | 26,863 | 298,029 | 38,000 | 4,643,998 |
| 2017-18 | 235,809 | 246,200 | 89,282 | 2,034,000 | 86,599 | 205,955 | 969,300 | 590,684 | 1,012 | 27,287 | 250,000 | 36,900 | 5,159,325 |
| 2018-19 | 239,318 | 249,900 | 97,978 | 2,113,189 | 85,991 | 235,182 | 904,700 | 767,280 | 826 | 28,399 | 270,000 | 33,300 | 5,438,354 |
| 2019-20[1] | 259,451 | 280,000 | 102,154 | 2,235,043 | 76,113 | 283,680 | 811,700 | 734,795 | 1,017 | 28,452 | 250,000 | 35,700 | 5,492,530 |
| 2020-21[2] | 269,731 | 280,000 | 63,416 | 2,200,000 | 77,681 | 327,903 | 1,047,000 | 720,660 | 706 | 29,429 | 290,000 | 38,000 | 5,780,850 |
| 2021-22[3] | 302,157 | 290,000 | 65,164 | 2,200,000 | 70,631 | 302,094 | 822,000 | 728,046 | 537 | 28,106 | 280,000 | 42,000 | 5,580,432 |

[1] Preliminary.   [2] Estimate.   [3] Forecast.   Source: *Food and Agricultural Organization of the United Nations (FAO)*

## World Consumption of Cocoa[4]   In Thousands of Metric Tons

| Crop Year Beginning Oct. 1 | Canada | Côte d'Ivoire | Brazil | European Union | Ghana | Indonesia | Japan | Malaysia | Singapore | Turkey | United States | Russia | World Total |
|---|---|---|---|---|---|---|---|---|---|---|---|---|---|
| 2010-11 | 62 | 361 | 239 | 1,492 | 230 | 190 | 40 | 305 | 83 | 70 | 401 | 61 | 3,938 |
| 2011-12 | 60 | 431 | 243 | 1,383 | 212 | 270 | 40 | 297 | 83 | 75 | 387 | 63 | 3,972 |
| 2012-13 | 64 | 471 | 241 | 1,443 | 225 | 290 | 40 | 293 | 77 | 75 | 429 | 71 | 4,180 |
| 2013-14 | 67 | 519 | 240 | 1,461 | 234 | 340 | 44 | 259 | 79 | 88 | 446 | 62 | 4,335 |
| 2014-15 | 62 | 558 | 224 | 1,432 | 234 | 335 | 45 | 195 | 81 | 86 | 400 | 46 | 4,152 |
| 2015-16 | 62 | 492 | 225 | 1,483 | 202 | 382 | 47 | 194 | 81 | 84 | 398 | 49 | 4,127 |
| 2016-17 | 62 | 577 | 227 | 1,503 | 250 | 455 | 49 | 216 | 82 | 102 | 390 | 52 | 4,397 |
| 2017-18[1] | 62 | 559 | 231 | 1,575 | 310 | 483 | 55 | 236 | 90 | 99 | 385 | 55 | 4,596 |
| 2018-19[2] | 61 | 605 | 235 | 1,585 | 320 | 487 | 54 | 327 | 89 | 104 | 400 | 60 | 4,805 |
| 2019-20[3] | 58 | 615 | 222 | 1,560 | 333 | 512 | 57 | 360 | 95 | 111 | 400 | 60 | 4,861 |

[1] Preliminary.   [2] Estimate.   [3] Forecast.   [4] Figures represent the "grindings" of cocoa beans in each country.
Source: *International Cocoa Organization (ICO)*

## Imports of Cocoa Butter in Selected Countries   In Metric Tons

| Year | Australia | Austria | Belgium | Canada | France | Germany | Italy | Japan | Netherlands | Sweden | Switzerland | United Kingdom | United States |
|---|---|---|---|---|---|---|---|---|---|---|---|---|---|
| 2011 | 15,081 | 5,155 | 75,003 | 22,463 | 61,948 | 89,511 | 21,988 | 19,475 | 91,297 | 6,010 | 26,813 | 43,440 | 92,572 |
| 2012 | 15,971 | 5,090 | 75,402 | 24,090 | 71,043 | 92,370 | 25,999 | 26,566 | 72,416 | 6,219 | 26,430 | 51,541 | 72,085 |
| 2013 | 17,900 | 5,425 | 75,585 | 25,929 | 65,205 | 109,853 | 30,310 | 24,260 | 92,547 | 6,192 | 28,795 | 50,789 | 80,676 |
| 2014 | 16,074 | 4,912 | 79,049 | 26,250 | 68,073 | 124,839 | 28,364 | 27,351 | 82,319 | 6,400 | 28,767 | 47,171 | 97,774 |
| 2015 | 17,527 | 4,119 | 81,283 | 24,950 | 62,998 | 106,110 | 28,406 | 21,305 | 62,409 | 6,284 | 27,548 | 59,164 | 95,125 |
| 2016 | 16,293 | 4,970 | 93,024 | 26,218 | 64,443 | 130,642 | 28,150 | 22,362 | 77,969 | 6,247 | 27,545 | 53,109 | 82,678 |
| 2017 | 17,798 | 5,557 | 95,598 | 25,385 | 78,733 | 145,287 | 28,914 | 23,553 | 86,544 | 6,519 | 29,483 | 53,778 | 111,696 |
| 2018 | 18,548 | 4,363 | 94,139 | 23,912 | 74,686 | 143,417 | 31,726 | 26,584 | 96,183 | 5,752 | 29,087 | 60,147 | 108,329 |
| 2019 | 21,013 | 4,973 | 107,047 | 26,702 | 74,322 | 163,171 | 34,426 | 26,668 | 104,785 | 6,405 | 29,005 | 66,526 | 114,707 |
| 2020[1] | 21,952 | 6,004 | 118,700 | 23,432 | 91,512 | 129,604 | 37,560 | 21,676 | 99,212 | 7,936 | 24,004 | 66,456 | 126,264 |

[1] Preliminary.   Sources: *Food and Agricultural Organization of the United Nations (FAO)*

## Imports of Cocoa Liquor and Cocoa Powder in Selected Countries   In Metric Tons

| | Cocoa Liquor | | | | | | Cocoa Powder | | | | | | |
|---|---|---|---|---|---|---|---|---|---|---|---|---|---|
| Year | France | Germany | Japan | Netherlands | United Kingdom | United States | Belgium | France | Germany | Italy | Japan | Netherlands | United States |
| 2011 | 84,704 | 79,039 | 9,358 | 82,633 | 12,108 | 22,996 | 18,324 | 58,723 | 54,215 | 27,717 | 17,361 | 53,899 | 162,723 |
| 2012 | 83,905 | 82,605 | 9,351 | 74,125 | 14,907 | 20,461 | 16,226 | 53,499 | 52,762 | 25,370 | 17,201 | 45,494 | 161,081 |
| 2013 | 96,205 | 81,726 | 8,487 | 98,497 | 9,934 | 18,379 | 19,336 | 65,479 | 59,576 | 26,630 | 15,897 | 49,255 | 150,266 |
| 2014 | 94,219 | 77,645 | 9,829 | 112,010 | 9,238 | 22,302 | 18,833 | 59,356 | 69,838 | 28,444 | 17,705 | 56,878 | 154,294 |
| 2015 | 69,450 | 74,768 | 11,884 | 76,553 | 10,348 | 14,764 | 47,539 | 56,542 | 69,652 | 33,407 | 19,771 | 28,048 | 137,590 |
| 2016 | 73,167 | 78,359 | 12,215 | 79,963 | 16,134 | 32,559 | 46,881 | 46,516 | 69,627 | 33,500 | 19,768 | 30,216 | 180,582 |
| 2017 | 96,669 | 63,007 | 14,719 | 115,370 | 13,957 | 30,067 | 29,992 | 41,469 | 68,300 | 35,693 | 21,258 | 71,285 | 182,884 |
| 2018 | 85,741 | 61,730 | 16,307 | 148,578 | 15,848 | 34,418 | 23,502 | 46,315 | 70,963 | 37,269 | 19,976 | 79,249 | 156,978 |
| 2019 | 92,926 | 62,977 | 16,605 | 137,938 | 20,712 | 45,375 | 27,160 | 49,100 | 70,960 | 39,228 | 17,840 | 98,996 | 163,504 |
| 2020[1] | 100,056 | 78,620 | 12,572 | 160,004 | 12,708 | 91,412 | 25,972 | 50,395 | 187,478 | 40,161 | 21,244 | 80,228 | 177,571 |

[1] Preliminary.   Source: *Food and Agricultural Organization of the United Nations (FAO)*

# COCOA

## Imports of Cocoa and Products in the United States    In Metric Tons

| Year | Jan. | Feb. | Mar. | Apr. | May | June | July | Aug. | Sept. | Oct. | Nov. | Dec. | Total |
|---|---|---|---|---|---|---|---|---|---|---|---|---|---|
| 2013 | 118,129 | 125,897 | 119,255 | 106,917 | 136,359 | 88,132 | 112,058 | 94,986 | 93,586 | 91,863 | 90,006 | 126,702 | 1,303,889 |
| 2014 | 105,743 | 141,186 | 165,373 | 133,870 | 95,607 | 94,784 | 104,583 | 98,192 | 91,016 | 93,453 | 80,532 | 91,672 | 1,296,010 |
| 2015 | 109,669 | 121,573 | 132,182 | 138,943 | 115,781 | 124,700 | 107,942 | 88,465 | 101,383 | 105,487 | 87,698 | 105,521 | 1,339,343 |
| 2016 | 123,193 | 144,838 | 122,403 | 125,085 | 99,749 | 95,351 | 97,444 | 109,180 | 100,657 | 114,504 | 105,660 | 129,828 | 1,367,892 |
| 2017 | 143,196 | 143,358 | 175,485 | 162,652 | 129,538 | 111,460 | 108,712 | 100,961 | 90,012 | 95,449 | 95,478 | 99,473 | 1,455,775 |
| 2018 | 149,657 | 134,349 | 134,869 | 129,987 | 111,950 | 93,772 | 104,645 | 111,269 | 92,118 | 105,331 | 99,051 | 108,658 | 1,375,657 |
| 2019 | 129,159 | 139,778 | 126,889 | 139,919 | 130,856 | 104,081 | 112,192 | 105,572 | 103,153 | 106,925 | 86,189 | 112,285 | 1,396,996 |
| 2020 | 122,994 | 144,552 | 152,889 | 128,688 | 105,708 | 111,954 | 106,218 | 99,647 | 111,169 | 104,048 | 95,729 | 109,582 | 1,393,178 |
| 2021 | 144,402 | 122,963 | 187,430 | 154,240 | 129,183 | 131,072 | 100,701 | 107,233 | 119,621 | 110,146 | 117,616 | 109,737 | 1,534,343 |
| 2022[1] | 125,413 | 96,994 | 138,493 | 147,052 | 146,602 | 152,770 | 120,292 | 130,113 | 123,600 | 124,929 | 117,729 | 93,514 | 1,517,499 |

[1] Preliminary.    Source: Foreign Agricultural Service, U.S. Department of Agriculture (FAS-USDA)

## Visible Stocks of Cocoa in Port of Hampton Road Warehouses[1], at End of Month    In Thousands of Bags

| Year | Jan. | Feb. | Mar. | Apr. | May | June | July | Aug. | Sept. | Oct. | Nov. | Dec. |
|---|---|---|---|---|---|---|---|---|---|---|---|---|
| 2013 | 11.3 | 11.3 | 11.3 | 9.6 | 9.6 | 9.6 | 10.5 | 10.5 | 5.1 | 9.6 | 9.5 | 9.6 |
| 2014 | 9.6 | 9.6 | 9.6 | 9.6 | 9.6 | 9.6 | 9.6 | 9.6 | 9.6 | 9.6 | 9.6 | 9.6 |
| 2015 | 9.6 | 9.6 | 9.6 | 9.6 | 9.6 | 7.2 | 7.2 | 7.2 | 7.2 | 7.2 | 7.2 | 9.6 |
| 2016 | 7.2 | 7.2 | 7.2 | 7.2 | 7.2 | 7.2 | 7.2 | 7.2 | 7.2 | 7.2 | 7.2 | 7.2 |
| 2017 | 7.2 | 6.5 | 6.5 | 6.5 | 6.5 | 6.5 | 6.5 | 6.5 | 6.5 | 6.5 | 2.7 | 2.7 |
| 2018 | 2.4 | 2.4 | 2.0 | 2.0 | 1.9 | 1.9 | 1.4 | 1.4 | ---- | ---- | ---- | ---- |
| 2019 | ---- | ---- | ---- | ---- | ---- | ---- | ---- | ---- | ---- | ---- | ---- | ---- |
| 2020 | ---- | ---- | ---- | ---- | ---- | ---- | ---- | ---- | ---- | ---- | ---- | ---- |
| 2021 | ---- | ---- | ---- | ---- | ---- | ---- | ---- | 53.9 | 67.2 | 88.4 | 110.7 | 89.5 |
| 2022 | 87.5 | 87.4 | 87.4 | 88.1 | 88.4 | 93.3 | 94.4 | 106.7 | 113.2 | 119.2 | 116.5 | 110.1 |

[1] Licensed warehouses approved by ICE.    Source: ICE Futures U.S. (ICE)

## Visible Stocks of Cocoa in Philadelphia (Del. River) Warehouses[1], at End of Month    In Thousands of Bags

| Year | Jan. | Feb. | Mar. | Apr. | May | June | July | Aug. | Sept. | Oct. | Nov. | Dec. |
|---|---|---|---|---|---|---|---|---|---|---|---|---|
| 2013 | 3,070.3 | 3,690.7 | 3,924.4 | 3,884.4 | 4,110.6 | 4,035.9 | 3,945.1 | 3,897.9 | 3,583.0 | 3,170.0 | 2,921.9 | 3,050.1 |
| 2014 | 3,215.1 | 3,687.7 | 4,395.1 | 4,862.6 | 4,647.1 | 4,354.2 | 4,167.4 | 3,909.4 | 3,569.5 | 3,168.6 | 2,816.0 | 2,494.7 |
| 2015 | 2,640.6 | 2,953.7 | 3,044.0 | 3,700.4 | 3,780.4 | 4,166.1 | 4,013.1 | 3,788.7 | 3,568.2 | 3,286.3 | 3,146.1 | 2,956.1 |
| 2016 | 3,186.6 | 3,464.0 | 3,960.3 | 3,809.4 | 3,690.7 | 3,441.0 | 3,155.1 | 2,908.5 | 2,606.9 | 2,546.0 | 2,479.5 | 2,493.6 |
| 2017 | 2,961.9 | 3,695.8 | 4,460.4 | 5,117.8 | 5,394.3 | 5,245.8 | 4,992.7 | 4,669.1 | 4,318.8 | 3,834.3 | 3,462.8 | 3,147.5 |
| 2018 | 3,746.2 | 4,259.6 | 4,501.8 | 5,054.0 | 4,870.3 | 4,579.7 | 4,386.0 | 4,215.1 | 3,955.9 | 3,633.1 | 3,269.1 | 3,236.1 |
| 2019 | 3,344.6 | 3,701.7 | 3,901.5 | 4,104.4 | 4,281.1 | 4,171.4 | 3,958.4 | 3,706.2 | 3,461.9 | 3,112.4 | 2,808.2 | 2,550.9 |
| 2020 | 2,797.9 | 3,406.5 | 3,637.2 | 3,906.0 | 3,904.8 | 3,823.1 | 3,731.8 | 3,496.9 | 3,380.1 | 3,218.4 | 2,885.5 | 2,831.3 |
| 2021 | 3,030.6 | 3,514.0 | 4,141.7 | 4,430.4 | 5,153.9 | 5,467.4 | 5,379.2 | 5,186.7 | 5,103.7 | 4,952.8 | 4,697.6 | 4,307.3 |
| 2022 | 4,214.9 | 4,347.0 | 4,321.0 | 4,606.8 | 4,846.7 | 5,113.6 | 5,104.5 | 5,278.5 | 5,226.8 | 5,114.3 | 5,075.8 | 4,709.7 |

[1] Licensed warehouses approved by ICE.    Source: ICE Futures U.S. (ICE)

## Visible Stocks of Cocoa in New York Warehouses[1], at End of Month    In Thousands of Bags

| Year | Jan. | Feb. | Mar. | Apr. | May | June | July | Aug. | Sept. | Oct. | Nov. | Dec. |
|---|---|---|---|---|---|---|---|---|---|---|---|---|
| 2013 | 679.9 | 619.6 | 621.1 | 708.3 | 779.6 | 779.6 | 717.2 | 660.4 | 589.3 | 529.2 | 451.3 | 475.6 |
| 2014 | 391.0 | 386.7 | 364.5 | 482.6 | 619.3 | 566.5 | 505.4 | 435.9 | 419.3 | 380.9 | 317.1 | 308.3 |
| 2015 | 276.6 | 266.0 | 245.3 | 260.4 | 286.9 | 366.0 | 342.2 | 314.5 | 284.7 | 277.7 | 278.0 | 287.8 |
| 2016 | 283.3 | 353.2 | 412.3 | 388.1 | 317.4 | 302.9 | 299.7 | 311.3 | 312.4 | 289.8 | 250.2 | 274.9 |
| 2017 | 336.9 | 318.2 | 344.6 | 388.7 | 424.8 | 399.4 | 367.4 | 331.1 | 291.6 | 252.7 | 244.0 | 232.2 |
| 2018 | 271.1 | 281.8 | 288.4 | 315.4 | 278.3 | 264.7 | 265.4 | 240.5 | 224.6 | 206.8 | 197.7 | 230.7 |
| 2019 | 223.0 | 245.5 | 305.6 | 327.8 | 351.3 | 335.2 | 326.5 | 296.8 | 288.6 | 246.5 | 198.2 | 175.7 |
| 2020 | 250.2 | 310.0 | 336.6 | 375.0 | 358.1 | 323.2 | 305.2 | 289.6 | 266.7 | 237.2 | 224.5 | 228.8 |
| 2021 | 221.7 | 237.4 | 332.7 | 381.9 | 394.5 | 392.2 | 348.0 | 304.0 | 288.5 | 283.0 | 283.7 | 279.0 |
| 2022 | 265.9 | 271.1 | 313.6 | 331.3 | 348.0 | 342.5 | 338.2 | 342.2 | 323.2 | 313.6 | 316.0 | 322.4 |

[1] Licensed warehouses approved by ICE.    Source: ICE Futures U.S. (ICE)

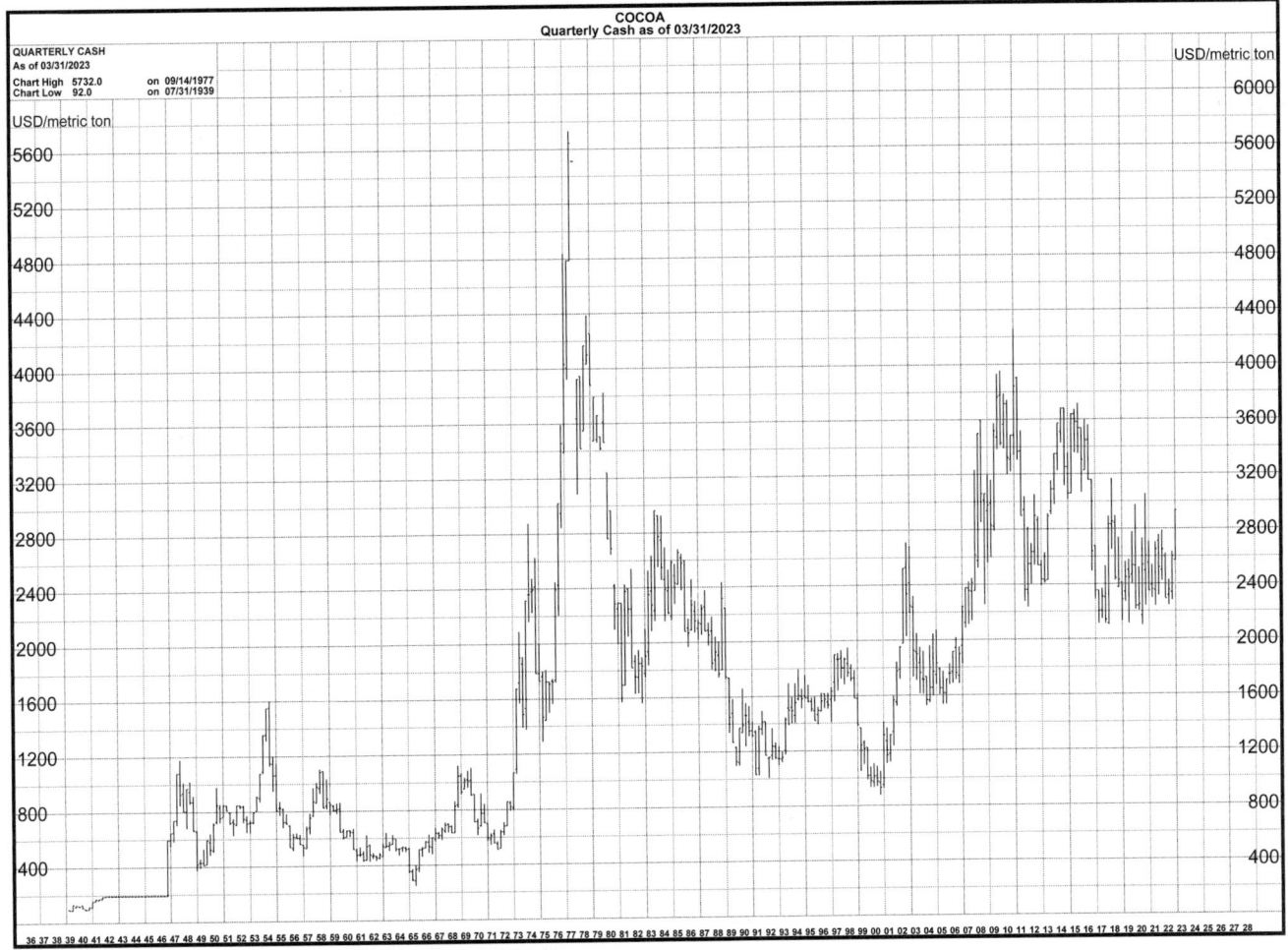

# COCOA

**COCOA**
Quarterly Cash as of 03/31/2023

QUARTERLY CASH
As of 03/31/2023
Chart High 5732.0 on 09/14/1977
Chart Low 92.0 on 07/31/1939

Exchange Standard: to 10/1946; ACCRA: 11/1946 to 09/1980; Ivory Coast: 10/1980 to date.

## Average Cash Price of Cocoa, Ivory Coast in New York    In Dollars Per Metric Ton

| Year | Jan. | Feb. | Mar. | Apr. | May | June | July | Aug. | Sept. | Oct. | Nov. | Dec. | Average |
|------|------|------|------|------|-----|------|------|------|-------|------|------|------|---------|
| 2013 | 2,519 | 2,455 | 2,428 | 2,492 | 2,566 | 2,494 | 2,521 | 2,672 | 2,819 | 2,988 | 2,996 | 3,099 | 2,671 |
| 2014 | 3,068 | 3,281 | 3,325 | 3,340 | 3,287 | 3,476 | 3,494 | 3,591 | 3,523 | 3,455 | 3,176 | 3,191 | 3,351 |
| 2015 | 3,170 | 3,181 | 3,181 | 3,129 | 3,331 | 3,493 | 3,590 | 3,424 | 3,546 | 3,434 | 3,630 | 3,632 | 3,395 |
| 2016 | 3,297 | 3,124 | 3,327 | 3,333 | 3,412 | 3,439 | 3,482 | 3,434 | 3,288 | 3,070 | 2,800 | 2,620 | 3,219 |
| 2017 | 2,493 | 2,379 | 2,381 | 2,214 | 2,200 | 2,235 | 2,195 | 2,256 | 2,231 | 2,354 | 2,411 | 2,190 | 2,295 |
| 2018 | 2,148 | 2,362 | 2,701 | 2,974 | 2,952 | 2,800 | 2,748 | 2,573 | 2,626 | 2,511 | 2,569 | 2,530 | 2,625 |
| 2019 | 2,304 | 2,251 | 2,205 | 2,380 | 2,369 | 2,483 | 2,458 | 2,199 | 2,370 | 2,471 | 2,610 | 2,531 | 2,386 |
| 2020 | 2,669 | 2,870 | 2,433 | 2,326 | 2,400 | 2,404 | 2,211 | 2,508 | 2,607 | 2,421 | 2,624 | 2,581 | 2,505 |
| 2021 | 2,524 | 2,571 | 2,521 | 2,400 | 2,444 | 2,358 | 2,345 | 2,530 | 2,626 | 2,633 | 2,453 | 2,482 | 2,491 |
| 2022 | 2,540 | 2,639 | 2,591 | 2,560 | 2,485 | 2,396 | 2,334 | 2,369 | 2,339 | 2,338 | 2,450 | 2,539 | 2,465 |

*Source: Economic Research Service, U.S. Department of Agriculture (ERS-USDA)*

## Total Visible Stocks of Cocoa in Warehouses[1], at End of Month    In Thousands of Bags

| Year | Jan. | Feb. | Mar. | Apr. | May | June | July | Aug. | Sept. | Oct. | Nov. | Dec. |
|------|------|------|------|------|-----|------|------|------|-------|------|------|------|
| 2013 | 3,814.6 | 4,416.3 | 4,653.7 | 4,690.9 | 4,987.5 | 4,966.3 | 4,745.1 | 4,632.7 | 4,232.5 | 3,754.5 | 3,436.3 | 3,574.1 |
| 2014 | 3,648.9 | 4,117.1 | 4,800.1 | 5,384.4 | 5,305.6 | 4,960.0 | 4,711.8 | 4,384.1 | 4,027.5 | 3,588.3 | 3,171.9 | 2,824.9 |
| 2015 | 2,939.1 | 3,241.1 | 3,310.7 | 3,978.6 | 4,085.2 | 4,546.7 | 4,369.9 | 4,117.8 | 3,867.5 | 3,578.7 | 3,438.3 | 3,255.3 |
| 2016 | 3,481.4 | 3,828.6 | 4,384.0 | 4,209.0 | 4,019.5 | 3,755.4 | 3,465.7 | 3,230.7 | 2,930.3 | 2,846.7 | 2,740.7 | 2,779.4 |
| 2017 | 3,309.3 | 4,023.4 | 4,814.4 | 5,515.9 | 5,828.5 | 5,654.6 | 5,369.5 | 5,009.6 | 4,617.9 | 4,096.9 | 3,714.4 | 3,386.7 |
| 2018 | 4,025.4 | 4,549.1 | 4,793.7 | 5,372.4 | 5,151.2 | 4,847.1 | 4,653.5 | 4,457.3 | 4,180.9 | 3,840.3 | 3,467.2 | 3,467.2 |
| 2019 | 3,568.1 | 3,947.6 | 4,207.5 | 4,432.2 | 4,632.3 | 4,506.6 | 4,284.9 | 4,003.0 | 3,750.5 | 3,358.8 | 3,006.4 | 2,726.6 |
| 2020 | 3,048.2 | 3,716.5 | 3,973.8 | 4,280.9 | 4,262.9 | 4,146.3 | 4,037.0 | 3,786.5 | 3,646.7 | 3,455.6 | 3,110.0 | 3,060.1 |
| 2021 | 3,252.3 | 3,751.4 | 4,474.4 | 4,812.3 | 5,548.4 | 5,859.6 | 5,727.1 | 5,544.6 | 5,459.4 | 5,324.2 | 5,092.0 | 4,675.8 |
| 2022 | 4,568.3 | 4,705.5 | 4,722.0 | 5,026.2 | 5,283.1 | 5,549.5 | 5,537.1 | 5,727.4 | 5,663.2 | 5,547.0 | 5,508.3 | 5,142.2 |

[1] Licensed warehouses approved by ICE.    *Source: ICE Futures U.S. (ICE)*

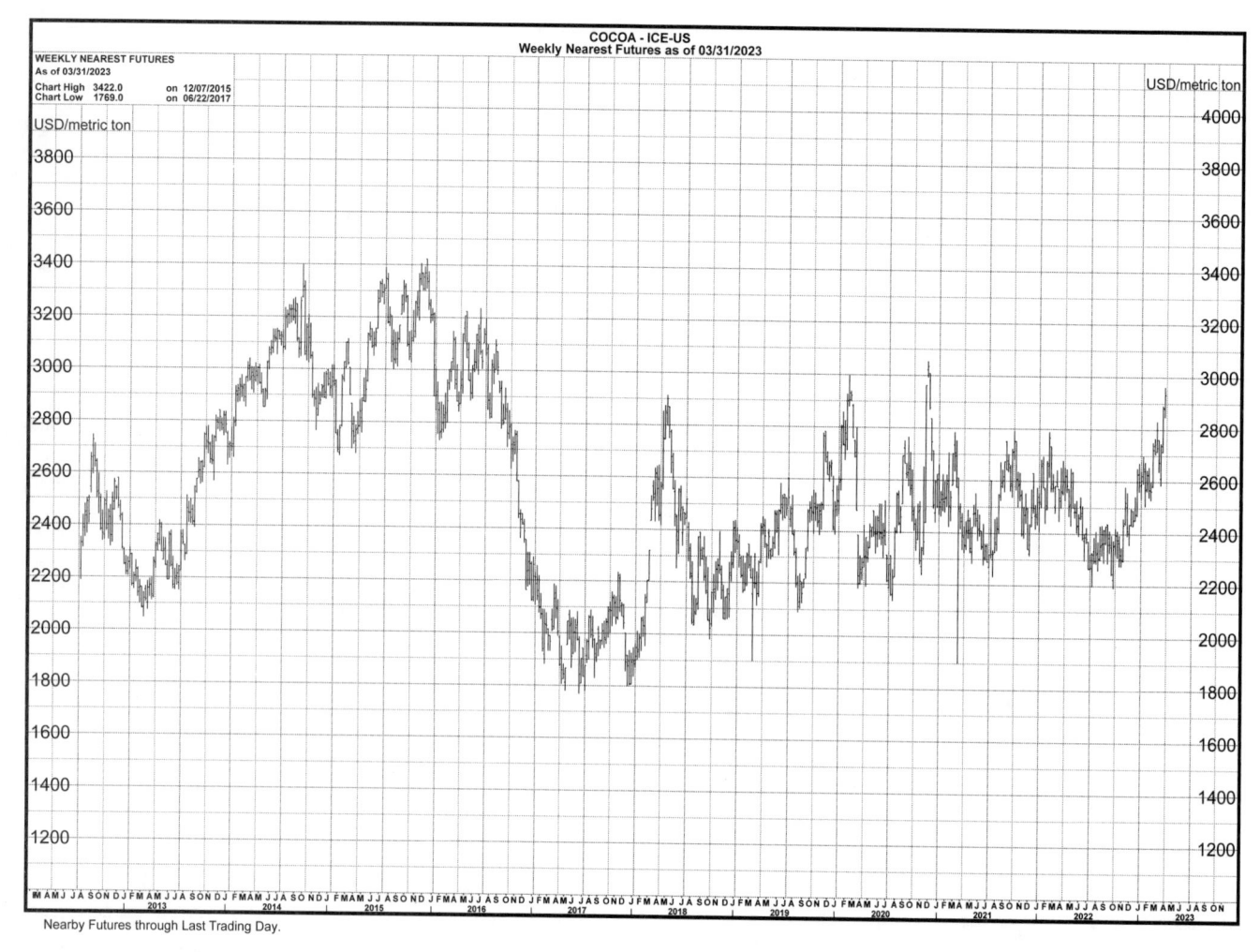

# COCOA

## Volume of Trading of Cocoa Futures in New York    In Thousands of Contracts

| Year | Jan. | Feb. | Mar. | Apr. | May | June | July | Aug. | Sept. | Oct. | Nov. | Dec. | Total |
|------|------|------|------|------|-----|------|------|------|-------|------|------|------|-------|
| 2012 | 505.6 | 598.3 | 425.5 | 752.3 | 541.0 | 792.1 | 504.9 | 646.1 | 379.5 | 484.4 | 621.7 | 332.2 | 6,583.7 |
| 2013 | 571.9 | 588.5 | 453.2 | 593.1 | 454.4 | 625.4 | 552.0 | 541.1 | 478.5 | 617.5 | 508.5 | 331.8 | 6,315.8 |
| 2014 | 586.6 | 679.4 | 694.1 | 739.8 | 520.0 | 710.6 | 531.4 | 801.8 | 602.1 | 770.4 | 775.6 | 501.3 | 7,913.0 |
| 2015 | 940.4 | 950.7 | 667.6 | 927.4 | 857.7 | 778.3 | 712.6 | 988.0 | 730.5 | 856.4 | 829.0 | 623.5 | 9,862.2 |
| 2016 | 797.5 | 929.4 | 906.3 | 974.0 | 927.0 | 1,095.5 | 790.4 | 1,116.9 | 660.7 | 1,066.3 | 1,049.7 | 747.9 | 11,061.6 |
| 2017 | 973.4 | 1,122.9 | 1,135.9 | 1,266.5 | 972.5 | 1,176.0 | 884.3 | 1,090.3 | 707.9 | 1,021.6 | 1,077.3 | 607.0 | 12,035.6 |
| 2018 | 959.8 | 1,002.6 | 902.9 | 1,276.7 | 972.2 | 973.9 | 855.8 | 1,253.7 | 1,031.8 | 1,059.9 | 1,171.3 | 789.2 | 12,249.9 |
| 2019 | 1,103.1 | 1,164.8 | 1,236.8 | 704.7 | 636.7 | 846.5 | 698.2 | 916.9 | 661.5 | 791.5 | 996.2 | 595.1 | 10,352.1 |
| 2020 | 697.1 | 910.7 | 893.6 | 955.7 | 841.4 | 937.1 | 863.8 | 1,177.2 | 744.9 | 955.2 | 1,140.5 | 713.4 | 10,830.5 |
| 2021 | 993.8 | 1,065.9 | 1,000.7 | 939.4 | 1,007.5 | 1,156.5 | 952.1 | 1,416.4 | 939.0 | 1,128.8 | 1,333.1 | 732.0 | 12,665.3 |

Source: ICE Futures U.S. (ICE)

## Average Open Interest of Cocoa Futures in New York    In Contracts

| Year | Jan. | Feb. | Mar. | Apr. | May | June | July | Aug. | Sept. | Oct. | Nov. | Dec. |
|------|------|------|------|------|-----|------|------|------|-------|------|------|------|
| 2013 | 197,848 | 192,704 | 200,696 | 199,773 | 220,741 | 196,543 | 176,618 | 183,556 | 201,739 | 219,812 | 212,717 | 213,685 |
| 2014 | 210,130 | 216,867 | 215,297 | 206,091 | 204,253 | 216,264 | 214,879 | 213,149 | 208,448 | 199,236 | 177,425 | 186,443 |
| 2015 | 200,884 | 193,672 | 211,199 | 199,675 | 208,637 | 215,736 | 219,497 | 182,777 | 200,200 | 216,932 | 232,054 | 234,884 |
| 2016 | 227,549 | 234,056 | 238,732 | 234,122 | 242,073 | 198,093 | 215,818 | 206,006 | 210,888 | 251,984 | 244,643 | 254,911 |
| 2017 | 275,443 | 265,621 | 285,852 | 284,418 | 296,408 | 257,541 | 273,750 | 244,093 | 258,013 | 253,440 | 241,566 | 251,261 |
| 2018 | 275,944 | 263,249 | 296,500 | 289,878 | 304,760 | 266,004 | 247,961 | 240,819 | 242,329 | 264,377 | 241,641 | 235,570 |
| 2019 | 251,715 | 236,101 | 255,428 | 244,996 | 251,723 | 265,064 | 281,033 | 265,389 | 284,179 | 304,661 | 316,902 | 314,178 |
| 2020 | 311,242 | 347,493 | 278,299 | 215,335 | 224,401 | 219,668 | 224,055 | 209,904 | 219,811 | 211,501 | 192,405 | 214,734 |
| 2021 | 225,150 | 215,702 | 200,366 | 195,012 | 203,638 | 220,400 | 256,845 | 232,266 | 233,303 | 250,609 | 239,954 | 237,002 |
| 2022 | 240,988 | 253,691 | 243,660 | 241,588 | 285,017 | 303,130 | 310,780 | 301,967 | 303,177 | 307,044 | 274,001 | 266,888 |

Source: ICE Futures U.S. (ICE)

# Coconut Oil and Copra

Coconut oil and copra come from the fruit of the coconut palm tree, which originated in Southeast Asia. Coconut oil has been used for thousands of years as cooking oil and is still a staple in the diets of many people living in tropical areas. Until shortages of imported oil developed during WWII, Americans also used coconut oil for cooking.

Copra is the meaty inner lining of the coconut. It is an oil-rich pulp with a light, slightly sweet, nutty flavor. Copra is used mainly as a source of coconut oil and is also used shredded for baking. High-quality copra contains about 65% to 72% oil, and oil made from the copra is called crude coconut oil. Crude coconut oil is processed from copra by expeller press and solvent extraction. It is not considered fit for human consumption until it has been refined, which consists of neutralizing, bleaching, and deodorizing it at high heat with a vacuum. The remaining oil cake obtained as a by-product is used for livestock feed.

Premium grade coconut oil, also called virgin coconut oil, is the oil made from the first pressing without the addition of any chemicals. Premium grade coconut oil is more expensive than refined or crude oil because the producers use only selected raw materials, and there is a lower production yield due to only one pressing.

Coconut oil accounts for approximately 20% of all vegetable oils used worldwide. Coconut oil is used in margarines, vegetable shortening, salad oils, confections, and sports drinks to boost energy and enhance athletic performance. It is also used in the manufacture of soaps, detergents, shampoos, cosmetics, candles, glycerin, and synthetic rubber. Coconut oil is very healthy, unless it is hydrogenated, and is easily digested.

**Supply** – World production of copra in 2022 rose by +9.0% at 4.897 million metric tons and remained below the record high of 5.662 million metric tons posted in 2001. The world's largest producers of copra in 2022 were the Philippines with 37.6% of world production, Indonesia with 28%, India with 12.7%, and Mexico with 4.9%. World production of coconut oil in the 2021/22 marketing year rose by +14.4% yr/yr to 3.029 million metric tons.

**Demand** – Virtually all the world's production of copra goes for crushing into coconut meal and oil (over 99%). World consumption of coconut oil in 2021/22 rose by +4.7% yr/yr to 2.968 million metric tons, but still below the 2009/10 record high of 3.574 million metric tons.

**Trade** – Copra is generally crushed in the country of origin, meaning that less than 4% of copra itself is exported; the rest is exported in the form of coconut oil. World exports of coconut oil in 2021/22 rose by +18.2 yr/yr to 2.164 million metric tons, but still below the 2009/10 record high of 2.406 million metric tons.

## World Production of Copra   In Thousands of Metric Tons

| Year | India | Indonesia | Ivory Coast | Malaysia | Mexico | Mozambique | Papua New Guinea | Philippines | Sri Lanka | Thailand | Vanuatu | Vietnam | World Total |
|---|---|---|---|---|---|---|---|---|---|---|---|---|---|
| 2013 | 640 | 1,470 | 29 | 79 | 207 | 50 | 80 | 2,300 | 90 | 49 | 25 | 57 | 5,392 |
| 2014 | 670 | 1,530 | 27 | 62 | 203 | 52 | 72 | 1,740 | 80 | 49 | 25 | 57 | 4,881 |
| 2015 | 620 | 1,540 | 28 | 64 | 209 | 54 | 95 | 1,680 | 83 | 49 | 18 | 57 | 4,812 |
| 2016 | 580 | 1,290 | 26 | 58 | 221 | 50 | 97 | 1,280 | 95 | 46 | 28 | 55 | 4,141 |
| 2017 | 420 | 1,180 | 28 | 67 | 231 | 52 | 114 | 1,370 | 90 | 46 | 27 | 56 | 4,001 |
| 2018 | 530 | 1,460 | 30 | 65 | 237 | 52 | 118 | 1,670 | 91 | 48 | 21 | 57 | 4,704 |
| 2019 | 580 | 1,320 | 30 | 78 | 236 | 53 | 85 | 1,820 | 107 | 50 | 21 | 60 | 4,756 |
| 2020[1] | 560 | 1,240 | 30 | 80 | 237 | 46 | 98 | 1,460 | 88 | 46 | 20 | 65 | 4,285 |
| 2021[2] | 610 | 1,310 | 28 | 85 | 239 | 50 | 88 | 1,530 | 96 | 48 | 19 | 66 | 4,491 |
| 2022[3] | 620 | 1,370 | 28 | 91 | 239 | 52 | 100 | 1,840 | 96 | 48 | 22 | 67 | 4,897 |

[1] Preliminary.   [2] Estimate.   [3] Forecast.   Source: The Oil World

## World Supply and Distribution of Coconut Oil   In Thousands of Metric Tons

| | Production | | | | | | | Consumption | | | | | | Ending Stocks | | |
|---|---|---|---|---|---|---|---|---|---|---|---|---|---|---|---|---|
| Crop Year | India | Indonesia | Malaysia | Philippines | World Total | World Exports | World Imports | European Union | India | Indonesia | Philippines | United States | World Total | Philippines | United States | World Total |
| 2012-13 | 380 | 850 | 51 | 1,654 | 3,471 | 2,078 | 2,086 | 716 | 381 | 193 | 564 | 521 | 3,423 | 80 | 80 | 436 |
| 2013-14 | 391 | 933 | 51 | 1,153 | 3,050 | 1,866 | 1,859 | 646 | 392 | 176 | 364 | 518 | 3,119 | 68 | 65 | 359 |
| 2014-15 | 377 | 937 | 51 | 1,093 | 2,968 | 1,964 | 1,953 | 537 | 389 | 161 | 233 | 531 | 2,893 | 69 | 61 | 424 |
| 2015-16 | 346 | 805 | 45 | 888 | 2,594 | 1,671 | 1,684 | 501 | 340 | 166 | 198 | 469 | 2,685 | 74 | 66 | 345 |
| 2016-17 | 270 | 691 | 45 | 953 | 2,481 | 1,698 | 1,673 | 457 | 262 | 181 | 119 | 439 | 2,464 | 58 | 52 | 338 |
| 2017-18 | 304 | 845 | 41 | 1,030 | 2,754 | 1,791 | 1,791 | 550 | 298 | 195 | 133 | 429 | 2,658 | 100 | 47 | 434 |
| 2018-19 | 344 | 802 | 43 | 1,226 | 2,958 | 2,171 | 2,111 | 613 | 340 | 228 | 87 | 439 | 2,819 | 65 | 41 | 512 |
| 2019-20[1] | 342 | 745 | 50 | 1,037 | 2,718 | 1,979 | 1,961 | 590 | 339 | 204 | 66 | 446 | 2,746 | 40 | 57 | 466 |
| 2020-21[2] | 361 | 766 | 52 | 913 | 2,648 | 1,832 | 1,916 | 553 | 352 | 216 | 70 | 426 | 2,836 | 59 | 51 | 361 |
| 2021-22[3] | 373 | 816 | 55 | 1,219 | 3,030 | 2,165 | 2,151 | 590 | 369 | 230 | 74 | 437 | 2,969 | 64 | 59 | 409 |

[1] Preliminary.   [2] Estimate.   [3] Forecast.   Source: The Oil World

# COCONUT OIL AND COPRA

## Supply and Distribution of Coconut Oil in the United States    In Millions of Pounds

| Crop Year | Rotterdam Copra Tonne $ U.S. | Rotterdam Coconut Oil, CIF $ U.S. | Imports For Consumption | Stocks Oct. 1 | Total Supply | Exports | Disappearance Total Domestic | Disappearance Edible Products | Disappearance Inedible Products | Production Total | Production Oct.-Dec. | Production Jan.-Mar. | Production April-June | Production July-Sept. |
|---|---|---|---|---|---|---|---|---|---|---|---|---|---|---|
| 2012-13 | 570 | 858 | 1,214 | 176 | 1,390 | 56 | 1,149 | NA | NA | NA | NA | NA | NA | NA |
| 2013-14 | 854 | 1,278 | 1,173 | 143 | 1,316 | 64 | 1,142 | ---- | ---- | ---- | ---- | ---- | ---- | ---- |
| 2014-15 | 749 | 1,128 | 1,261 | 134 | 1,395 | 99 | 1,171 | ---- | ---- | ---- | ---- | ---- | ---- | ---- |
| 2015-16 | 907 | 1,360 | 1,157 | 146 | 1,302 | 111 | 1,034 | ---- | ---- | ---- | ---- | ---- | ---- | ---- |
| 2016-17 | 1,076 | 1,620 | 1,036 | 115 | 1,151 | 98 | 968 | ---- | ---- | ---- | ---- | ---- | ---- | ---- |
| 2017-18 | 784 | 1,175 | 988 | 104 | 1,091 | 54 | 945 | ---- | ---- | ---- | ---- | ---- | ---- | ---- |
| 2018-19 | 483 | 724 | 996 | 90 | 1,086 | 42 | 967 | ---- | ---- | ---- | ---- | ---- | ---- | ---- |
| 2019-20 | 602 | 899 | 1,060 | 126 | 1,186 | 41 | 984 | ---- | ---- | ---- | ---- | ---- | ---- | ---- |
| 2020-21[1] | 993 | 1,483 | 979 | 113 | 1,093 | 52 | 940 | ---- | ---- | ---- | ---- | ---- | ---- | ---- |
| 2021-22[2] | 1,333 | 2,010 | 1,036 | 130 | 1,166 | 56 | 963 | ---- | ---- | ---- | ---- | ---- | ---- | ---- |

[1] Preliminary.   [2] Forecast.   Source: Bureau of Census, U.S. Department of Commerce

## Average Price of Coconut Oil (Crude) Tank Cars in New York    In Cents Per Pound

| Year | Jan. | Feb. | Mar. | Apr. | May | June | July | Aug. | Sept. | Oct. | Nov. | Dec. | Average |
|---|---|---|---|---|---|---|---|---|---|---|---|---|---|
| 2012 | 68.25 | 68.00 | 64.90 | 63.63 | 59.25 | 54.00 | 52.75 | 50.30 | 47.75 | 43.75 | 41.40 | 38.88 | 54.40 |
| 2013 | 39.38 | 41.25 | 39.30 | 38.00 | 38.20 | 40.75 | 41.50 | 41.50 | 46.00 | 45.00 | 59.30 | 61.00 | 44.26 |
| 2014 | 59.70 | 63.00 | 65.38 | 62.75 | 65.70 | 65.31 | 62.88 | 56.60 | 55.31 | 53.75 | 55.69 | 56.50 | 60.21 |
| 2015 | 56.30 | 54.94 | 52.94 | 49.50 | 52.25 | 53.19 | 52.30 | 51.56 | 50.75 | 51.05 | 50.31 | 52.20 | 52.27 |
| 2016 | 53.69 | 54.44 | 67.75 | 76.90 | 68.38 | 69.35 | 70.85 | 72.06 | 74.30 | 70.00 | 73.50 | 78.20 | 69.12 |
| 2017 | 83.63 | 90.00 | 73.90 | 82.81 | 84.00 | 83.60 | 81.00 | 85.88 | 86.63 | 68.50 | 72.25 | 72.10 | 80.36 |
| 2018 | 68.75 | 66.00 | 55.90 | 58.75 | 52.50 | 46.20 | 45.00 | 45.00 | 44.50 | 43.00 | 39.00 | 37.50 | 50.18 |
| 2019 | 39.00 | 37.25 | 35.30 | 33.50 | 33.00 | 32.00 | 32.00 | 33.20 | 34.50 | 34.00 | 35.60 | 44.50 | 35.32 |
| 2020 | 32.88 | 32.38 | 32.40 | 36.63 | 40.50 | 47.81 | 47.94 | 37.87 | 44.35 | 49.50 | 51.65 | 53.31 | 42.27 |
| 2021[1] | 68.75 | 66.00 | 52.13 | 72.60 | 78.00 | 80.00 | 80.00 | 80.00 | 80.00 | 85.00 | 92.50 | 87.00 | 76.83 |

[1] Preliminary.   Source: Economic Research Service, U.S. Department of Agriculture (ERS-USDA)

## Consumption of Coconut Oil in End Products (Edible and Inedible) in the United States    In Millions of Pounds

| Year | Jan. | Feb. | Mar. | Apr. | May | June | July | Aug. | Sept. | Oct. | Nov. | Dec. | Total |
|---|---|---|---|---|---|---|---|---|---|---|---|---|---|
| 2002 | 55.4 | 41.3 | 50.8 | 59.3 | 53.9 | 46.4 | 50.7 | 51.8 | 45.9 | 54.3 | 56.1 | 49.4 | 615.4 |
| 2003 | 51.2 | 49.3 | 56.8 | 50.6 | 52.3 | 46.7 | 48.9 | 49.6 | 50.3 | 47.8 | 41.8 | 38.5 | 583.7 |
| 2004 | 50.0 | 51.7 | 58.5 | 54.6 | 48.5 | 55.6 | 52.9 | 55.1 | 48.9 | 48.2 | 64.3 | 51.7 | 640.0 |
| 2005 | 46.7 | 52.0 | 47.9 | 48.8 | 51.4 | 55.5 | 47.2 | 58.1 | 49.2 | 52.8 | 53.4 | 58.1 | 621.1 |
| 2006 | 70.4 | 62.7 | 50.4 | 47.5 | 50.7 | 51.6 | 43.1 | 51.6 | 43.8 | 49.6 | 44.4 | 40.8 | 606.4 |
| 2007 | 49.8 | 48.5 | 47.0 | 51.2 | 53.7 | 60.3 | 60.3 | 74.2 | 67.5 | 71.8 | 71.3 | 62.7 | 718.3 |
| 2008 | 63.6 | 72.1 | 64.8 | 74.4 | 69.7 | 70.4 | 65.8 | 67.6 | 65.8 | 63.0 | 63.6 | 53.6 | 794.5 |
| 2009 | 67.9 | 62.8 | 60.2 | 66.9 | 66.9 | 27.6 | 36.5 | 28.1 | 29.4 | 32.8 | 32.1 | 30.6 | 541.8 |
| 2010 | 41.0 | 36.6 | 45.3 | 34.9 | 39.8 | 38.6 | 37.2 | 40.4 | 32.1 | 41.4 | 39.9 | 70.8 | 498.0 |
| 2011[1] | 34.6 | 37.0 | 40.6 | 38.0 | 39.0 | 37.0 | 26.7 | NA | NA | NA | NA | NA | 433.5 |

[1] Preliminary.   Source: Bureau of Census, U.S. Department of Commerce

## Stocks of Coconut Oil (Crude and Refined) in the United States, on First of Month    In Millions of Pounds

| Year | Jan. | Feb. | Mar. | Apr. | May | June | July | Aug. | Sept. | Oct. | Nov. | Dec. |
|---|---|---|---|---|---|---|---|---|---|---|---|---|
| 2002 | 245.9 | 238.8 | 249.6 | 251.3 | 233.5 | 231.6 | 303.3 | 301.6 | 245.8 | 226.5 | 273.8 | 264.1 |
| 2003 | 195.2 | 194.0 | 214.3 | 224.9 | 223.7 | 187.8 | 162.2 | 202.9 | 195.6 | 218.9 | 184.6 | 186.1 |
| 2004 | 167.2 | 160.3 | 192.6 | 181.7 | 131.4 | 108.7 | 90.6 | 132.8 | 149.2 | 131.3 | 147.7 | 182.5 |
| 2005 | 225.9 | 163.7 | 188.4 | 191.0 | 170.6 | 187.7 | 263.5 | 250.4 | 253.7 | 242.1 | 252.3 | 273.3 |
| 2006 | 268.3 | 236.9 | 224.5 | 227.3 | 260.2 | 229.1 | 213.8 | 214.4 | 204.7 | 224.5 | 179.2 | 180.2 |
| 2007 | 214.4 | 228.5 | 261.5 | 223.1 | 191.8 | 157.9 | 171.2 | 154.4 | 127.7 | 128.4 | 142.5 | 212.6 |
| 2008 | 205.6 | 192.9 | 180.9 | 191.9 | 223.9 | 203.9 | 187.8 | 181.5 | 180.4 | 182.2 | 163.3 | 174.6 |
| 2009 | 164.1 | 183.7 | 215.6 | 167.2 | 143.9 | 138.0 | 134.8 | 133.2 | 102.3 | 182.3 | 159.0 | 154.7 |
| 2010 | 220.2 | 204.5 | 172.1 | 144.6 | 119.3 | 120.3 | 172.2 | 179.3 | 197.1 | 185.8 | 166.7 | 167.2 |
| 2011[1] | 181.5 | 150.2 | 162.7 | 154.6 | 150.0 | 157.6 | 158.4 | 190.9 | NA | NA | NA | NA |

[1] Preliminary.   Source: Bureau of Census, U.S. Department of Commerce

# Coffee

Coffee is one of the world's most important cash commodities. Coffee is the common name for any type of tree in the genus madder family. Coffee is a tropical evergreen shrub that has the potential to grow 100 feet tall. The coffee tree grows in tropical regions between the Tropics of Cancer and Capricorn in areas with abundant rainfall, year-round warm temperatures averaging about 70 degrees Fahrenheit, and no frost. In the U.S., the only places that produce any significant amount of coffee are Puerto Rico and Hawaii. The coffee plant will produce its first full crop of beans at about five years old and then be productive for about 15 years. The average coffee tree produces enough beans to make about 1 to 1 ½ pound of roasted coffee per year. It takes approximately 4,000 handpicked green coffee beans to make a pound of coffee. Wine was the first drink made from the coffee tree using coffee cherries, honey, and water. In the 17th century, the first coffee house, also known as a "penny university" because of the price per cup, opened in London. The London Stock Exchange grew from one of these first coffee houses.

Coffee is generally classified into two types of beans: arabica and robusta. The most widely produced coffee is arabica, which makes up about 70 percent of total production. It grows mainly at high altitudes of 600 to 2,000 meters, with Brazil and Colombia being the largest producers. Arabic coffee is traded at the Intercontinental Exchange (ICE). The stronger of the two types is robusta. It is grown at lower altitudes, with the largest producers being Indonesia, West Africa, Brazil, and Vietnam. Robusta coffee is traded on the LIFFE exchange.

Ninety percent of the world coffee trade is in green (unroasted) coffee beans. Seasonal factors have a significant influence on the price of coffee. There is no extreme peak in world production at any one time of the year, although coffee consumption declines by 12 percent or more below the year's average in the warm summer months. Therefore, coffee imports and roasts both tend to decline in spring and summer and pick up again in fall and winter.

Meager prices for coffee can create serious long-term problems for coffee producers. When prices fall below production costs, there is little economic incentive to produce coffee, and coffee trees may be neglected or completely abandoned. When prices are low, producers cannot afford to hire the labor needed to maintain the trees and pick the crop at harvest. The result is that trees yield less due to reduced use of fertilizer and fewer employed coffee workers. One effect is a decline in the quality of the coffee that is produced. Higher quality Arabica coffee is often produced at higher altitudes, which entails higher costs. It is this coffee that is often abandoned. Although the pressure on producers can be severe, the market eventually comes back into balance as supply declines in response to low prices.

Coffee prices are subject to upward spikes in June, July, and August due to possible freeze scares in Brazil during the winter months in the Southern Hemisphere. The Brazilian coffee crop is harvested starting in May and extending for several weeks into the winter months in Brazil. A major freeze in Brazil occurs roughly every five years on average.

Coffee futures and options are traded at the ICE Futures U.S. and ICE Futures Europe exchanges, and the B3 Exchange (formerly BM&F/BOVESPA). Coffee futures are traded on the JSE Securities Exchange (JSE).

**Prices** – ICE Arabica coffee futures prices (Barchart.com symbol KC) raced higher in early 2022 and posted an 11-year high in February of 260.45 cents per pound. Coffee prices rallied sharply in early 2022 due to excessive dryness in Brazil, supply chain turmoil from the pandemic, and a limited amount of container ships that sent freight costs soaring. Concern about future coffee supplies prompted coffee roasters worldwide to tap ICE coffee inventories, which sent ICE stockpiles plummeting to a 22-year low in February. Coffee prices then drifted lower into early July on concern about global demand. The war in Ukraine upended Brazil's coffee exports after Cecafe reported Brazil's coffee exports to Russia and Ukraine were down 72% and 62%, respectively, in March from February. Also, the resurgence of Covid infections in China kept pandemic lockdowns in place that curbed the country's coffee consumption. Coffee prices then rebounded into late August as a La Nina weather pattern led to drier-than-normal conditions in Brazil and Colombia, the two largest arabica coffee producers. Brazil's 2021/22 arabica coffee production fell -26.7% yr/yr to 36.4 million bags, the lowest in 4 years, and Colombia's 2021/22 arabica production fell -12% yr/yr to 11.1 million bags. Coffee prices then tumbled to a 1-1/2 year low of 150.45 cents per pound in November as supply chain turmoil eased and freight costs dropped. Also, the Brazilian real tumbled to a 1-year low in November, which encouraged export selling by Brazil's coffee producers. In addition, weather conditions improved in Brazil, which prompted Conab to project that Brazil's 2023 arabica crop would rise +14.4% to 37.4 million bags. Coffee prices finished 2022 down -76% yr/yr at 167.30 cents per pound.

**Supply** – World coffee production in the 2022/23 marketing year (July-June) is expected to rise by +4.7% yr/yr to 174.950 million bags (1 bag equals 60 kilograms or 132.3 pounds). Coffee ending stocks in the 2022/23 marketing year are expected to rise by +6.3% yr/yr to 34.704 million bags. Brazil is the world's largest coffee producer by far with 36.8% of the world's supply followed by Vietnam with 17.7%.

**Demand** – World consumption of green coffee in 2020/21 remain unchanged yr/yr at 161.872 million bags.

**Trade** – World coffee exports in 2022/23 are forecasted to rise by +0.8% yr/yr to 141.564 million bags, down from the 2020/21 record high of 144.389 million bags. The world's largest exporters of coffee in 2021/22 were Brazil with 23.6% of world exports, Vietnam with 20.6%, and Columbia with 10.0%. U.S. coffee imports in 2021 fell by -4.0% yr/yr to 26.288 million bags, modestly below the 2019 record high of 29.216 million bags. The key countries from which the U.S. imported coffee in 2022 were Brazil with 28.2%, Columbia with 17.8%, Mexico with 6.2%, and Guatemala with 5.5%.

# COFFEE

### World Supply and Distribution of Coffee for Producing Countries   In Thousands of 60 Kilogram Bags

| Crop Year | Beginning Stocks | Production | Imports | Total Supply | Total Exports | Bean Exports | Rst/Grn Exports | Soluble Exports | Domestic Use | Ending Stocks |
|---|---|---|---|---|---|---|---|---|---|---|
| 2013-14 | 35,365 | 160,054 | 117,741 | 313,160 | 128,877 | 110,004 | 3,220 | 15,653 | 143,099 | 41,184 |
| 2014-15 | 41,184 | 153,796 | 118,255 | 313,235 | 123,630 | 103,721 | 3,523 | 16,386 | 146,473 | 43,132 |
| 2015-16 | 43,132 | 152,404 | 125,309 | 320,845 | 133,140 | 112,322 | 3,817 | 17,001 | 152,754 | 34,951 |
| 2016-17 | 34,951 | 161,129 | 128,103 | 324,183 | 132,946 | 112,675 | 4,087 | 16,184 | 154,784 | 36,453 |
| 2017-18 | 36,453 | 159,839 | 129,658 | 325,950 | 133,579 | 112,919 | 4,155 | 16,505 | 160,380 | 31,991 |
| 2018-19 | 31,991 | 175,956 | 137,571 | 345,518 | 142,865 | 121,273 | 4,390 | 17,202 | 165,530 | 37,123 |
| 2019-20 | 37,123 | 169,030 | 130,445 | 336,598 | 138,491 | 116,380 | 4,967 | 17,144 | 161,876 | 36,231 |
| 2020-21[1] | 36,231 | 176,361 | 131,333 | 343,925 | 144,389 | 121,160 | 5,457 | 17,772 | 161,872 | 37,664 |
| 2021-22[2] | 37,664 | 167,134 | 133,585 | 338,383 | 140,493 | 117,345 | 5,007 | 18,141 | 165,240 | 32,650 |
| 2022-23[3] | 32,650 | 174,950 | 135,708 | 343,308 | 141,564 | 118,210 | 5,012 | 18,342 | 167,040 | 34,704 |

[1] Preliminary.   [2] Estimate.   [3] Forecast.   132.276 Lbs. Per Bag   Source: Foreign Agricultural Service, U.S. Department of Agriculture (FAS-USDA)

### World Production of Green Coffee   In Thousands of 60 Kilogram Bags

| Crop Year | Brazil | Colombia | Costa Rica | Cote d'Ivoire | El Salvador | Ethiopia | Guatemala | India | Indonesia | Mexico | Uganda | Vietnam | World Total |
|---|---|---|---|---|---|---|---|---|---|---|---|---|---|
| 2013-14 | 57,200 | 12,075 | 1,450 | 1,675 | 550 | 6,345 | 3,515 | 5,075 | 11,900 | 3,950 | 3,850 | 29,833 | 160,054 |
| 2014-15 | 54,300 | 13,300 | 1,400 | 1,400 | 700 | 6,475 | 3,185 | 5,440 | 10,470 | 3,180 | 3,500 | 27,400 | 153,796 |
| 2015-16 | 49,400 | 14,000 | 1,625 | 1,600 | 560 | 6,510 | 3,295 | 5,800 | 12,100 | 2,300 | 3,550 | 28,930 | 152,404 |
| 2016-17 | 56,100 | 14,600 | 1,300 | 1,090 | 600 | 6,943 | 3,570 | 5,200 | 10,600 | 3,300 | 4,875 | 26,700 | 161,129 |
| 2017-18 | 52,100 | 13,825 | 1,525 | 1,250 | 660 | 7,055 | 3,780 | 5,266 | 10,400 | 4,000 | 4,600 | 29,300 | 159,839 |
| 2018-19 | 66,500 | 13,870 | 1,250 | 2,000 | 654 | 7,350 | 3,770 | 5,325 | 10,600 | 3,550 | 4,650 | 30,400 | 175,956 |
| 2019-20 | 60,500 | 14,100 | 1,466 | 1,725 | 510 | 7,475 | 3,645 | 4,967 | 10,700 | 3,700 | 5,475 | 31,300 | 169,030 |
| 2020-21[1] | 69,900 | 13,400 | 1,472 | 910 | 540 | 7,600 | 3,930 | 5,237 | 10,700 | 3,625 | 6,630 | 29,000 | 176,361 |
| 2021-22[2] | 58,100 | 13,000 | 1,275 | 800 | 590 | 8,150 | 3,830 | 5,530 | 10,580 | 3,840 | 6,250 | 31,600 | 167,134 |
| 2022-23[3] | 64,300 | 13,000 | 1,365 | 800 | 575 | 8,250 | 3,730 | 5,740 | 11,350 | 3,845 | 6,650 | 30,900 | 174,950 |

[1] Preliminary.   [2] Estimate.   [3] Forecast.   132.276 Lbs. Per Bag   Source: Foreign Agricultural Service, U.S. Department of Agriculture (FAS-USDA)

### World Exportable[4] Production of Green Coffee   In Thousands of 60 Kilogram Bags

| Crop Year | Brazil | Colombia | Cote d'Ivoire | Ethiopia | Guatemala | Honduras | India | Indonesia | Mexico | Peru | Uganda | Vietnam | World Total |
|---|---|---|---|---|---|---|---|---|---|---|---|---|---|
| 2013-14 | 34,146 | 11,040 | 1,570 | 3,285 | 3,175 | 3,940 | 5,013 | 10,380 | 2,725 | 4,100 | 3,600 | 28,289 | 128,877 |
| 2014-15 | 36,573 | 12,420 | 1,350 | 3,500 | 3,070 | 4,760 | 4,894 | 8,720 | 2,560 | 2,750 | 3,350 | 21,567 | 123,630 |
| 2015-16 | 35,543 | 12,390 | 1,540 | 3,405 | 3,044 | 5,000 | 5,693 | 9,896 | 2,340 | 3,300 | 3,300 | 29,065 | 133,140 |
| 2016-17 | 33,081 | 13,755 | 990 | 3,853 | 3,330 | 7,175 | 6,158 | 8,174 | 2,865 | 4,025 | 4,600 | 26,450 | 132,946 |
| 2017-18 | 30,454 | 12,725 | 1,150 | 3,893 | 3,465 | 7,225 | 6,148 | 8,010 | 3,220 | 4,185 | 4,300 | 29,907 | 133,579 |
| 2018-19 | 41,426 | 13,615 | 1,940 | 4,174 | 3,604 | 6,910 | 5,778 | 6,150 | 2,896 | 4,293 | 4,450 | 28,318 | 142,865 |
| 2019-20 | 40,256 | 12,980 | 1,665 | 4,135 | 3,220 | 4,900 | 5,185 | 7,152 | 2,986 | 3,720 | 5,350 | 27,326 | 138,491 |
| 2020-21[1] | 45,673 | 12,735 | 680 | 4,675 | 3,679 | 6,010 | 5,794 | 7,872 | 3,030 | 3,326 | 5,900 | 25,300 | 144,389 |
| 2021-22[2] | 33,220 | 14,040 | 1,400 | 4,600 | 3,689 | 6,500 | 5,905 | 7,550 | 3,100 | 3,900 | 5,800 | 28,900 | 140,493 |
| 2022-23[3] | 33,220 | 14,040 | 1,400 | 4,600 | 3,689 | 6,500 | 5,905 | 7,550 | 3,100 | 3,900 | 5,800 | 28,900 | 139,023 |

[1] Preliminary.   [2] Estimate.   [3] Forecast.   [4] Marketing year begins in October in some countries and April or July in others. Exportable production represents total harvested production minus estimated domestic consumption.   132.276 Lbs. Per Bag
Source: Foreign Agricultural Service, U.S. Department of Agriculture (FAS-USDA)

### Coffee Imports in the United States   In Thousands of 60 Kilogram Bags

| Year | Brazil | Colombia | Costa Rica | Republic | Ecuador | El Salvador | Ethiopia | Guatemala | Indonesia | Mexico | Peru | Venezuela | World Total |
|---|---|---|---|---|---|---|---|---|---|---|---|---|---|
| 2013 | 6,090 | 4,241 | 762 | 34 | 54 | 427 | 268 | 1,696 | 1,344 | 1,923 | 869 | 4 | 25,683 |
| 2014 | 7,326 | 4,611 | 671 | 23 | 71 | 205 | 293 | 1,390 | 1,117 | 1,393 | 873 | ---- | 26,221 |
| 2015 | 7,817 | 5,376 | 586 | 4 | 54 | 287 | 366 | 1,190 | 1,218 | 1,230 | 776 | ---- | 26,415 |
| 2016 | 6,704 | 5,253 | 648 | 4 | 52 | 217 | 292 | 1,011 | 1,212 | 1,030 | 1,112 | ---- | 27,502 |
| 2017 | 6,218 | 5,767 | 492 | 9 | 41 | 273 | 439 | 1,282 | 1,247 | 1,305 | 1,065 | ---- | 27,918 |
| 2018 | 6,347 | 5,701 | 603 | 7 | 4 | 248 | 425 | 1,380 | 969 | 1,366 | 1,052 | ---- | 27,217 |
| 2019 | 7,974 | 5,964 | 511 | 16 | 3 | 273 | 430 | 1,404 | 1,039 | 1,306 | 1,051 | 71 | 29,216 |
| 2020 | 7,839 | 5,062 | 584 | 10 | 12 | 200 | 409 | 1,185 | 930 | 1,290 | 958 | 52 | 26,543 |
| 2021 | 8,037 | 5,096 | 483 | 21 | 5 | 242 | 494 | 1,490 | 890 | 1,445 | 672 | 0 | 27,380 |
| 2022[1] | 7,426 | 4,689 | 498 | 70 | 18 | 248 | 456 | 1,448 | 1,056 | 1,624 | 936 | 72 | 26,288 |

[1] Preliminary.   132.276 Lbs. Per Bag   Source: Bureau of Census, U.S. Department of Commerce

# COFFEE

## Monthly Coffee Imports in the United States   In Thousands of 60 Kilogram Bags (132.276 Lbs. Per Bag)

| Year | Jan. | Feb. | Mar. | Apr. | May | June | July | Aug. | Sept. | Oct. | Nov. | Dec. | Total |
|---|---|---|---|---|---|---|---|---|---|---|---|---|---|
| 2013 | 2,200 | 1,933 | 2,090 | 2,154 | 2,629 | 2,283 | 2,459 | 2,184 | 1,875 | 1,933 | 1,828 | 2,115 | 25,683 |
| 2014 | 1,919 | 1,895 | 2,407 | 2,489 | 2,545 | 2,468 | 2,356 | 2,357 | 2,174 | 2,019 | 1,640 | 1,943 | 26,213 |
| 2015 | 1,780 | 1,708 | 2,430 | 2,255 | 2,489 | 2,407 | 2,338 | 2,265 | 2,269 | 2,120 | 2,154 | 2,194 | 26,410 |
| 2016 | 2,135 | 2,166 | 2,293 | 2,305 | 2,551 | 2,408 | 2,316 | 2,333 | 2,382 | 2,014 | 2,419 | 2,179 | 27,503 |
| 2017 | 2,349 | 2,362 | 2,681 | 2,280 | 2,476 | 2,532 | 2,350 | 2,437 | 2,109 | 2,119 | 1,992 | 2,235 | 27,921 |
| 2018 | 2,090 | 2,220 | 2,420 | 2,382 | 2,542 | 2,225 | 2,274 | 2,186 | 2,013 | 2,260 | 2,266 | 2,349 | 27,225 |
| 2019 | 2,472 | 2,216 | 2,495 | 2,519 | 2,942 | 2,640 | 2,625 | 2,628 | 2,299 | 2,128 | 1,988 | 2,259 | 29,211 |
| 2020 | 2,293 | 1,901 | 2,384 | 2,417 | 2,547 | 2,674 | 2,173 | 1,913 | 1,915 | 2,073 | 1,991 | 2,261 | 26,543 |
| 2021 | 2,006 | 2,096 | 2,253 | 2,269 | 2,612 | 2,464 | 2,492 | 2,663 | 2,021 | 2,435 | 1,877 | 2,209 | 27,398 |
| 2022[1] | 2,429 | 2,055 | 2,545 | 2,792 | 2,226 | 2,552 | 2,770 | 2,369 | 2,228 | 2,429 | 1,893 | 2,159 | 28,447 |

[1] Preliminary.  *Source: Bureau of the Census, U.S. Department of Commerce*

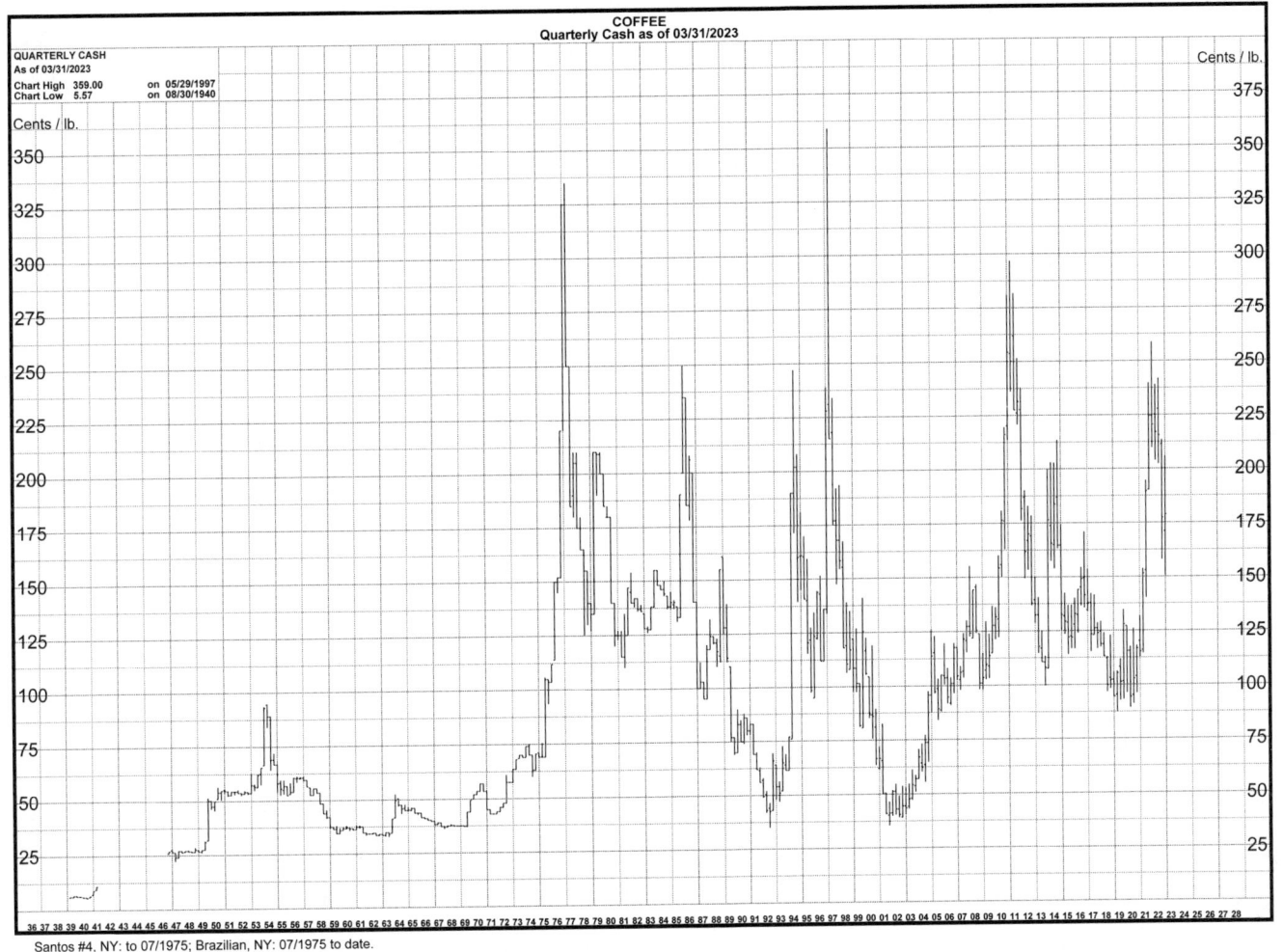

## Average Price of Brazilian[1] Coffee in New York   In Cents Per Pound

| Year | Jan. | Feb. | Mar. | Apr. | May | June | July | Aug. | Sept. | Oct. | Nov. | Dec. | Average |
|---|---|---|---|---|---|---|---|---|---|---|---|---|---|
| 2013 | 139.36 | 133.37 | 129.74 | 130.11 | 129.82 | 116.91 | 114.89 | 111.97 | 106.33 | 103.58 | 98.82 | 100.48 | 117.95 |
| 2014 | 107.49 | 142.75 | 174.89 | 182.89 | 170.89 | 154.02 | 154.00 | 171.99 | 168.11 | 181.58 | 169.10 | 157.87 | 161.30 |
| 2015 | 151.21 | 143.32 | 127.81 | 129.02 | 123.49 | 124.97 | 119.77 | 121.21 | 113.14 | 118.43 | 122.95 | 123.73 | 126.59 |
| 2016 | 121.21 | 122.24 | 130.38 | 128.10 | 129.05 | 138.38 | 144.76 | 141.41 | 149.80 | 153.15 | 157.72 | 137.14 | 137.78 |
| 2017 | 145.70 | 137.68 | 134.07 | 130.39 | 125.40 | 122.39 | 127.26 | 128.24 | 124.46 | 120.01 | 117.26 | 114.00 | 127.24 |
| 2018 | 115.60 | 114.19 | 112.99 | 112.56 | 113.34 | 110.44 | 107.20 | 102.41 | 98.17 | 111.21 | 109.59 | 100.61 | 109.03 |
| 2019 | 101.56 | 100.67 | 97.50 | 94.42 | 93.33 | 99.97 | 103.01 | 96.07 | 97.74 | 97.35 | 107.23 | 117.37 | 100.52 |
| 2020 | 106.89 | 102.00 | 109.05 | 108.91 | 104.45 | 99.05 | 103.66 | 114.78 | 116.25 | 105.85 | 109.70 | 114.74 | 107.94 |
| 2021 | 115.73 | 119.35 | 120.36 | 122.03 | 134.77 | 141.03 | 152.24 | 160.14 | 170.02 | 181.57 | 195.17 | 203.06 | 151.29 |
| 2022 | 204.29 | 210.89 | 194.78 | 198.43 | 193.71 | 202.46 | 190.82 | 200.11 | 199.63 | 178.54 | 156.66 | 157.19 | 190.63 |

[1] And other Arabicas.  *Source: Foreign Agricultural Service, U.S. Department of Agriculture (FAS-USDA)*

# COFFEE

### Average Monthly Retail[1] Price of Coffee in the United States — In Cents Per Pound

| Year | Jan. | Feb. | Mar. | Apr. | May | June | July | Aug. | Sept. | Oct. | Nov. | Dec. | Average |
|---|---|---|---|---|---|---|---|---|---|---|---|---|---|
| 2015 | 4.738 | 4.910 | 4.827 | 4.990 | 4.715 | 4.686 | 4.790 | 4.808 | 4.669 | 4.609 | 4.412 | 4.486 | 4.720 |
| 2016 | 4.498 | 4.447 | 4.405 | 4.428 | 4.443 | 4.481 | 4.428 | 4.316 | 4.372 | 4.309 | 4.306 | 4.281 | 4.393 |
| 2017 | 4.468 | 4.583 | 4.650 | 4.622 | 4.597 | 4.545 | 4.335 | 4.373 | 4.323 | 4.327 | 4.324 | 4.285 | 4.453 |
| 2018 | 4.291 | 4.267 | 4.343 | 4.313 | 4.294 | ---- | ---- | ---- | 4.306 | ---- | ---- | ---- | 4.302 |
| 2019 | ---- | ---- | ---- | ---- | ---- | ---- | ---- | ---- | ---- | 4.174 | 4.197 | 4.053 | 4.141 |
| 2020 | 4.174 | 4.250 | 4.334 | 4.396 | 4.466 | 4.517 | 4.536 | 4.504 | 4.487 | 4.522 | 4.485 | 4.520 | 4.433 |
| 2021 | 4.591 | 4.673 | 4.671 | 4.752 | 4.566 | 4.605 | 4.562 | 4.726 | 4.733 | 4.800 | 4.816 | 4.965 | 4.705 |
| 2022 | 5.135 | 5.247 | 5.410 | 5.529 | 5.835 | 5.793 | 6.112 | 6.235 | 6.170 | 6.408 | 6.356 | 6.465 | 5.891 |

[1] Roasted in 13.1 to 20 ounce cans. *Source: Foreign Agricultural Service, U.S. Department of Agriculture (FAS-USDA)*

### Average Price of Colombian Mild Arabicas[1] in the United States — In Cents Per Pound

| Year | Jan. | Feb. | Mar. | Apr. | May | June | July | Aug. | Sept. | Oct. | Nov. | Dec. | Average |
|---|---|---|---|---|---|---|---|---|---|---|---|---|---|
| 2015 | 182.32 | 171.68 | 151.94 | 157.06 | 150.19 | 152.02 | 144.52 | 146.96 | 135.55 | 143.10 | 138.63 | 139.89 | 151.16 |
| 2016 | 135.21 | 137.17 | 145.20 | 143.66 | 144.49 | 156.86 | 164.46 | 160.78 | 168.85 | 172.28 | 177.85 | 156.64 | 155.29 |
| 2017 | 164.96 | 163.67 | 158.40 | 154.97 | 151.41 | 146.12 | 152.51 | 155.15 | 151.47 | 144.26 | 144.09 | 141.62 | 152.39 |
| 2018 | 143.77 | 141.50 | 139.45 | 139.29 | 140.26 | 138.55 | 133.92 | 129.99 | 125.74 | 140.83 | 139.27 | 127.86 | 136.70 |
| 2019 | 129.28 | 127.93 | 125.23 | 124.42 | 124.40 | 133.49 | 137.63 | 129.20 | 131.90 | 132.09 | 146.12 | 161.50 | 133.60 |
| 2020 | 147.52 | 146.43 | 158.99 | 161.92 | 154.96 | 147.16 | 153.38 | 167.22 | 168.36 | 154.28 | 161.21 | 170.44 | 157.66 |
| 2021 | 173.42 | 176.96 | 177.49 | 181.70 | 198.99 | 206.53 | 218.66 | 225.40 | 240.38 | 258.87 | 279.56 | 290.57 | 219.04 |
| 2022 | 294.93 | 306.36 | 285.81 | 292.76 | 286.44 | 301.57 | 286.07 | 295.66 | 294.09 | 261.95 | 223.22 | 224.12 | 279.42 |

[1] ICO monthly and composite indicator prices on the New York Market, 1979 ICA Agreement basis. *Source: Foreign Agricultural Service, U.S. Department of Agriculture (FAS-USDA)*

### Average Price of Other Mild Arabicas[1] in the United States — In Cents Per Pound

| Year | Jan. | Feb. | Mar. | Apr. | May | June | July | Aug. | Sept. | Oct. | Nov. | Dec. | Average |
|---|---|---|---|---|---|---|---|---|---|---|---|---|---|
| 2015 | 190.90 | 179.94 | 160.02 | 164.00 | 158.48 | 159.76 | 154.45 | 156.92 | 146.15 | 153.25 | 147.98 | 148.66 | 160.04 |
| 2016 | 145.03 | 147.70 | 157.50 | 154.22 | 155.19 | 165.45 | 171.76 | 167.54 | 176.30 | 178.96 | 184.12 | 161.78 | 163.80 |
| 2017 | 168.61 | 166.35 | 160.15 | 155.40 | 150.00 | 143.22 | 149.66 | 149.88 | 146.56 | 140.71 | 140.90 | 137.42 | 150.74 |
| 2018 | 138.81 | 136.28 | 135.03 | 134.34 | 135.61 | 134.03 | 130.60 | 125.21 | 121.18 | 137.34 | 137.11 | 127.10 | 132.72 |
| 2019 | 128.46 | 128.45 | 123.89 | 121.13 | 120.55 | 129.73 | 135.47 | 126.23 | 128.89 | 126.99 | 140.98 | 157.11 | 130.66 |
| 2020 | 142.19 | 135.50 | 148.33 | 154.52 | 149.84 | 141.52 | 146.78 | 163.25 | 166.56 | 152.06 | 150.73 | 157.81 | 150.76 |
| 2021 | 160.69 | 166.43 | 167.05 | 168.65 | 186.46 | 192.45 | 204.29 | 216.24 | 225.54 | 241.06 | 258.95 | 267.71 | 204.63 |
| 2022 | 271.08 | 279.83 | 258.49 | 265.40 | 260.42 | 273.69 | 255.91 | 268.43 | 267.49 | 240.08 | 213.85 | 210.24 | 255.41 |

[1] ICO monthly and composite indicator prices on the New York Market, 1979 ICA Agreement basis. *Source: Foreign Agricultural Service, U.S. Department of Agriculture (FAS-USDA)*

### Average Price of Robustas 1976[1] in the United States — In Cents Per Pound

| Year | Jan. | Feb. | Mar. | Apr. | May | June | July | Aug. | Sept. | Oct. | Nov. | Dec. | Average |
|---|---|---|---|---|---|---|---|---|---|---|---|---|---|
| 2015 | 102.33 | 103.74 | 98.07 | 92.06 | 87.56 | 90.25 | 87.12 | 85.78 | 81.50 | 82.78 | 81.74 | 79.28 | 89.35 |
| 2016 | 74.71 | 74.04 | 75.60 | 80.18 | 83.93 | 85.94 | 90.82 | 91.79 | 96.88 | 103.65 | 103.72 | 101.85 | 88.59 |
| 2017 | 108.32 | 106.49 | 106.73 | 103.58 | 98.36 | 101.95 | 104.94 | 104.52 | 99.18 | 98.39 | 91.33 | 87.59 | 100.95 |
| 2018 | 88.65 | 89.24 | 88.18 | 88.31 | 88.74 | 86.07 | 84.42 | 80.74 | 76.70 | 85.32 | 83.52 | 77.57 | 84.79 |
| 2019 | 78.24 | 78.65 | 76.96 | 73.28 | 71.12 | 74.02 | 73.93 | 70.78 | 70.64 | 68.63 | 73.28 | 73.22 | 73.56 |
| 2020 | 70.55 | 68.07 | 67.46 | 63.97 | 64.53 | 64.62 | 67.69 | 72.68 | 72.77 | 68.36 | 72.38 | 72.04 | 68.76 |
| 2021 | 70.71 | 73.37 | 73.86 | 74.47 | 79.68 | 84.85 | 94.37 | 95.18 | 104.60 | 105.24 | 109.40 | 112.76 | 89.87 |
| 2022 | 109.71 | 109.44 | 103.82 | 103.96 | 103.10 | 103.81 | 100.44 | 109.65 | 111.36 | 103.01 | 92.59 | 93.76 | 103.72 |

[1] ICO monthly and composite indicator prices on the New York Market, 1979 ICA Agreement basis. *Source: Foreign Agricultural Service, U.S. Department of Agriculture (FAS-USDA)*

### Average Price of Composite 1979[1] in the United States — In Cents Per Pound

| Year | Jan. | Feb. | Mar. | Apr. | May | June | July | Aug. | Sept. | Oct. | Nov. | Dec. | Average |
|---|---|---|---|---|---|---|---|---|---|---|---|---|---|
| 2015 | 148.24 | 141.10 | 127.04 | 129.02 | 123.49 | 124.97 | 119.77 | 121.21 | 113.14 | 118.43 | 122.95 | 114.63 | 125.33 |
| 2016 | 110.89 | 111.75 | 117.83 | 117.93 | 119.91 | 127.05 | 132.98 | 131.00 | 138.22 | 142.68 | 145.82 | 131.70 | 127.31 |
| 2017 | 139.07 | 145.50 | 139.67 | 136.09 | 131.21 | 123.71 | 129.19 | 131.93 | 129.67 | 124.55 | 124.28 | 121.47 | 131.36 |
| 2018 | 123.67 | 120.83 | 119.80 | 118.76 | 119.57 | 115.10 | 110.54 | 104.46 | 99.87 | 115.59 | 113.27 | 102.10 | 113.63 |
| 2019 | 102.94 | 100.06 | 95.81 | 92.47 | 91.95 | 100.69 | 105.43 | 95.85 | 98.73 | 98.10 | 109.94 | 126.36 | 101.53 |
| 2020 | 110.73 | 102.62 | 112.87 | 111.22 | 101.69 | 92.56 | 97.96 | 111.79 | 113.81 | 100.37 | 106.41 | 114.96 | 106.42 |
| 2021 | 116.69 | 120.06 | 122.16 | 124.18 | 140.85 | 148.12 | 160.62 | 174.89 | 183.72 | 199.98 | 218.90 | 230.26 | 161.70 |
| 2022 | 233.80 | 245.05 | 222.03 | 226.23 | 217.84 | 230.40 | 214.80 | 221.91 | 219.59 | 192.27 | 166.54 | 169.00 | 213.29 |

[1] ICO monthly and composite indicator prices on the New York Market, 1979 ICA Agreement basis. *Source: Foreign Agricultural Service, U.S. Department of Agriculture (FAS-USDA)*

# COFFEE

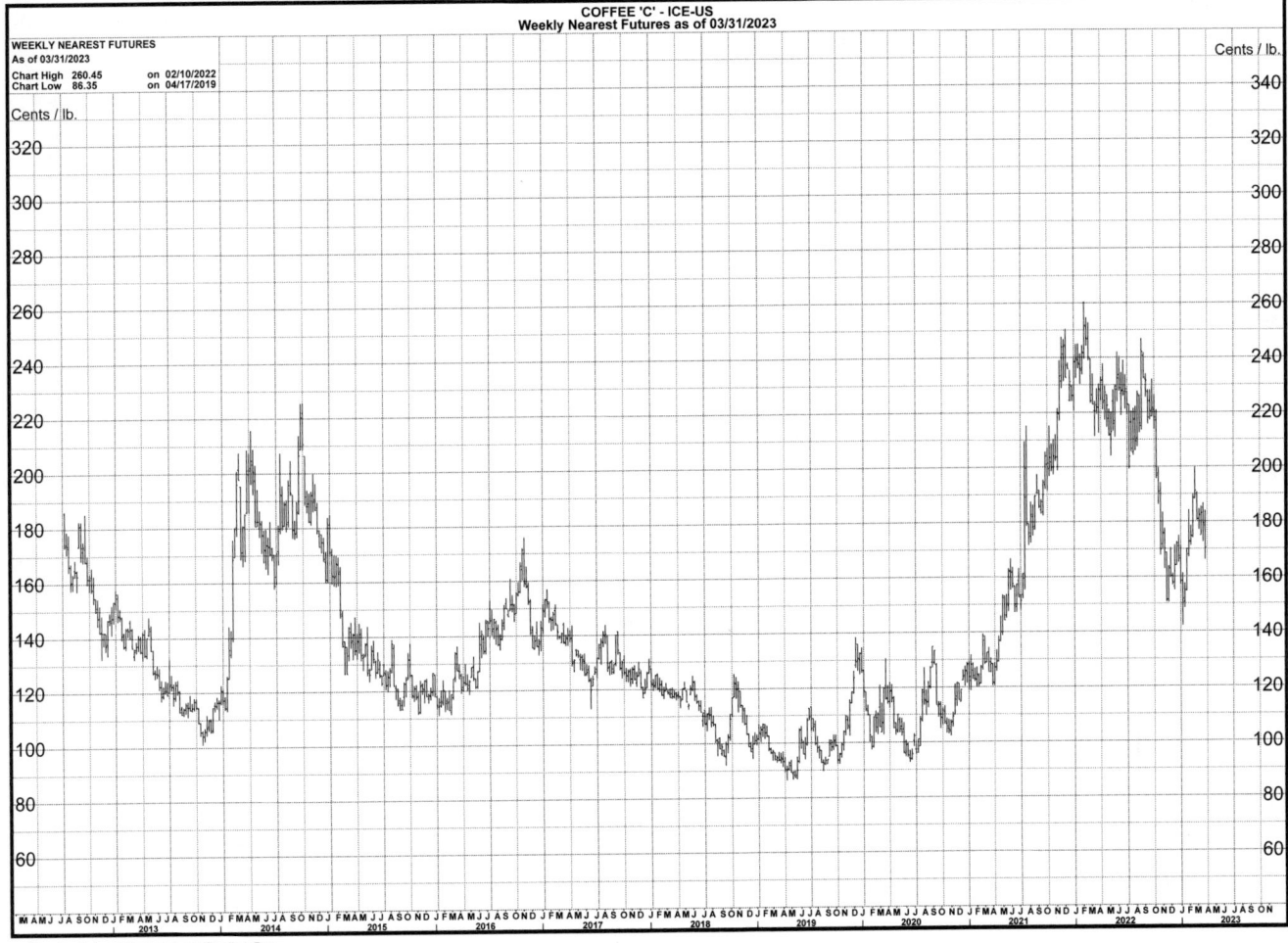

**COFFEE 'C' - ICE-US**
Weekly Nearest Futures as of 03/31/2023

WEEKLY NEAREST FUTURES
As of 03/31/2023
Chart High 260.45 on 02/10/2022
Chart Low 86.35 on 04/17/2019

Nearby Futures through Last Trading Day.

## Volume of Trading of Coffee "C" Futures in New York    In Thousands of Contracts

| Year | Jan. | Feb. | Mar. | Apr. | May | June | July | Aug. | Sept. | Oct. | Nov. | Dec. | Total |
|---|---|---|---|---|---|---|---|---|---|---|---|---|---|
| 2013 | 555.0 | 758.7 | 468.1 | 904.5 | 609.1 | 742.2 | 590.9 | 703.8 | 347.9 | 423.5 | 700.5 | 319.8 | 7,124.0 |
| 2014 | 567.6 | 1,140.9 | 597.0 | 736.5 | 458.7 | 596.7 | 404.4 | 619.6 | 395.0 | 583.3 | 610.8 | 341.8 | 7,052.2 |
| 2015 | 586.6 | 795.0 | 615.1 | 786.6 | 596.2 | 847.1 | 541.0 | 964.6 | 490.3 | 633.1 | 864.1 | 388.4 | 8,108.1 |
| 2016 | 665.2 | 983.2 | 863.9 | 1,009.1 | 777.4 | 1,181.7 | 554.0 | 908.3 | 600.7 | 695.4 | 1,092.8 | 524.6 | 9,856.3 |
| 2017 | 621.0 | 824.7 | 618.4 | 1,018.5 | 642.1 | 1,079.2 | 637.4 | 983.2 | 599.2 | 701.7 | 1,135.5 | 573.0 | 9,434.1 |
| 2018 | 931.7 | 1,202.8 | 818.5 | 1,357.2 | 937.4 | 1,313.8 | 939.8 | 1,698.4 | 734.9 | 1,493.0 | 1,342.6 | 617.5 | 13,387.7 |
| 2019 | 954.9 | 1,329.5 | 980.4 | 1,766.3 | 1,246.7 | 1,552.9 | 1,096.3 | 1,277.2 | 751.0 | 1,133.9 | 1,715.1 | 1,216.9 | 15,020.9 |
| 2020 | 1,060.2 | 1,556.0 | 1,401.1 | 884.6 | 716.1 | 1,157.4 | 916.7 | 1,259.8 | 1,001.2 | 829.1 | 1,139.7 | 635.7 | 12,557.5 |
| 2021 | 789.1 | 1,169.0 | 967.0 | 1,164.0 | 821.5 | 1,182.8 | 1,171.2 | 1,202.8 | 663.3 | 830.3 | 1,367.5 | 635.6 | 11,964.1 |
| 2022 | 850.1 | 1,080.8 | 864.4 | 891.5 | 722.2 | 933.4 | 677.3 | 965.0 | 569.7 | 983.0 | 907.8 | 546.9 | 9,991.9 |

Contract size = 37,500 lbs.    Source: ICE Futures U.S. (ICE)

## Average Open Interest of Coffee "C" Futures in New York    In Contracts

| Year | Jan. | Feb. | Mar. | Apr. | May | June | July | Aug. | Sept. | Oct. | Nov. | Dec. |
|---|---|---|---|---|---|---|---|---|---|---|---|---|
| 2013 | 151,087 | 161,116 | 170,696 | 168,341 | 164,440 | 167,032 | 153,493 | 151,666 | 154,791 | 160,797 | 159,934 | 146,729 |
| 2014 | 146,800 | 162,005 | 169,201 | 160,266 | 162,103 | 163,163 | 161,218 | 156,931 | 154,752 | 168,847 | 156,410 | 155,382 |
| 2015 | 166,609 | 172,443 | 195,176 | 190,207 | 190,814 | 183,516 | 186,782 | 178,827 | 187,577 | 188,355 | 188,664 | 169,129 |
| 2016 | 193,283 | 190,752 | 194,420 | 190,067 | 190,161 | 182,825 | 182,322 | 175,300 | 180,542 | 194,806 | 205,128 | 187,602 |
| 2017 | 184,650 | 177,790 | 184,499 | 200,509 | 210,358 | 220,709 | 222,738 | 197,922 | 197,826 | 225,779 | 216,415 | 211,636 |
| 2018 | 232,027 | 234,405 | 257,968 | 267,133 | 256,291 | 272,561 | 306,898 | 319,784 | 326,360 | 303,193 | 252,010 | 262,406 |
| 2019 | 289,302 | 298,522 | 330,681 | 339,589 | 340,252 | 289,964 | 266,503 | 269,809 | 265,338 | 297,591 | 288,911 | 280,314 |
| 2020 | 288,410 | 297,314 | 257,518 | 231,067 | 243,733 | 269,731 | 270,527 | 263,448 | 271,972 | 275,901 | 269,054 | 258,135 |
| 2021 | 268,082 | 267,944 | 279,077 | 280,999 | 288,427 | 280,142 | 286,325 | 288,914 | 289,185 | 305,743 | 292,093 | 261,912 |
| 2022 | 268,965 | 263,173 | 227,846 | 214,353 | 209,923 | 205,870 | 197,482 | 197,924 | 192,472 | 198,120 | 203,558 | 193,893 |

Contract size = 37,500 lbs.    Source: ICE Futures U.S. (ICE)

# Coke

Coke is the hard and porous residue left after certain types of bituminous coals are heated to high temperatures (up to 2,000 degrees Fahrenheit) for about 17 hours. It is blackish-gray and has a metallic luster. The residue is mostly carbon. Coke is used as a reducing agent in the smelting of pig iron and the production of steel. Petroleum coke is made from the heavy tar-like residue of the petroleum refining process. It is used primarily to generate electricity.

Futures on coke are traded on the Dalian Commodity Exchange.

**Supply** – Production of petroleum coke in the U.S. in 2022 rose by +5.6% yr/yr to 294.837 million barrels and remains below the U.S. production record of 369.305 million barrels posted back in 1957. U.S. stocks of coke at coke plants (Dec 31) in 2021 fell by -26.8% yr/yr to 352,000 tons.

**Trade** – U.S. coke exports in 2021 rose by +204.4% yr/yr to 2.081 million short tons, and 55.7% of that went to Canada. U.S. coke imports in 2021 fell by -27.6% yr/yr to 117,000 short tons. About 48.6% of U.S. imports were from Canada.

### Salient Statistics of Coke in the United States    In Thousands of Short Tons

| Year | Total Production | Coke Total | Breeze Total | Consumption[2] | Producer and Distributor Stocks: Dec. 31 | Exports | Imports |
|---|---|---|---|---|---|---|---|
| 2015 | 14,470 | 13,755 | 715 | 13,128 | 707 | 857 | 140 |
| 2016 | 12,416 | 11,855 | 561 | 11,212 | 579 | 1,000 | 229 |
| 2017 | 13,554 | 12,948 | 606 | 11,815 | 558 | 1,209 | 58 |
| 2018 | 14,507 | 13,806 | 701 | 12,976 | 354 | 1,151 | 117 |
| 2019 | 13,523 | 12,870 | 653 | 11,932 | 440 | 967 | 116 |
| 2020 | 10,860 | 10,353 | 507 | 9,791 | 481 | 684 | 162 |
| 2021[1] | 13,155 | 12,545 | 610 | 10,710 | 352 | 2,081 | 117 |

[1] Preliminary.   [2] Equal to production plus imports minus the change in producer and distributor stocks minus exports.
W = Withheld.   *Source: Energy Information Administration, U.S. Department of Energy (EIA-DOE)*

### Production of Petroleum Coke in the United States    In Thousands of Barrels

| Year | Jan. | Feb. | Mar. | Apr. | May | June | July | Aug. | Sept. | Oct. | Nov. | Dec. | Total |
|---|---|---|---|---|---|---|---|---|---|---|---|---|---|
| 2016 | 27,669 | 25,498 | 27,657 | 26,846 | 27,638 | 27,488 | 29,710 | 29,120 | 27,782 | 26,504 | 27,713 | 29,251 | 332,876 |
| 2017 | 28,715 | 24,498 | 26,747 | 27,709 | 29,018 | 28,113 | 29,113 | 28,358 | 24,187 | 26,703 | 27,286 | 28,556 | 329,003 |
| 2018 | 27,460 | 24,563 | 27,740 | 27,003 | 28,074 | 27,423 | 28,199 | 29,609 | 26,529 | 26,862 | 26,718 | 29,164 | 329,344 |
| 2019 | 26,971 | 22,775 | 25,638 | 24,593 | 24,422 | 25,582 | 28,008 | 27,677 | 24,694 | 24,956 | 26,196 | 28,599 | 310,111 |
| 2020 | 28,158 | 25,862 | 25,247 | 21,759 | 22,173 | 22,165 | 24,200 | 23,099 | 21,900 | 22,324 | 21,675 | 22,150 | 280,712 |
| 2021 | 22,350 | 17,560 | 21,734 | 22,152 | 24,707 | 25,056 | 24,927 | 25,168 | 23,212 | 23,057 | 23,614 | 25,621 | 279,158 |
| 2022[1] | 23,942 | 21,800 | 24,420 | 24,415 | 25,237 | 25,633 | 25,768 | 25,447 | 24,271 | 24,394 | 24,940 |  | 294,837 |

[1] Preliminary.   *Source: Energy Information Administration, U.S. Department of Energy (EIA-DOE)*

### Coke and Breeze Production at Coke Plants in the United States    In Thousands of Short Tons

| Year | Middle Atlantic | East North Central | East South Central | Other | U.S. Total | Coke Total | Breeze Total |
|---|---|---|---|---|---|---|---|
| 2015 | 4,722 | 7,562 | 1,270 | 916 | 14,470 | 13,755 | 715 |
| 2016 | 3,560 | 6,645 | 1,231 | 980 | 12,416 | 11,855 | 561 |
| 2017 | 4,066 | 7,181 | 1,238 | 1,069 | 13,554 | 12,948 | 606 |
| 2018 | 4,353 | 7,810 | 1,238 | 1,043 | 14,508 | 13,806 | 701 |
| 2019 | 4,017 | 7,278 | 1,376 | 852 | 13,523 | 12,870 | 653 |
| 2020 | 2,730 | 6,225 | 1,219 | 687 | 10,860 | 10,353 | 507 |
| 2021[1] | 4,013 | 7,262 | 1,235 | 645 | 13,155 | 12,545 | 610 |

[1] Preliminary.   W = Withheld.   *Source: Energy Information Administration, U.S. Department of Energy (EIA-DOE)*

### Coal Carbonized and Coke and Breeze Stocks at Coke Plants in the United States    In Thousands of Short Tons

| | Coal Carbonized at Coke Plants (By Census Division) | | | | | Stocks at Coke Plants, Dec. 31 (By Census Division) | | | | | | |
|---|---|---|---|---|---|---|---|---|---|---|---|---|
| Year | Middle Atlantic | East North Central | East South Central | Other | Total | Middle Atlantic | East North Central | East South Central | Other | Total | Coke Total | Breeze Total |
| 2015 | 6,219 | 10,584 | 1,204 | 1,701 | 19,708 | 797 | 1,172 | 197 | 70 | 2,236 | ---- | ---- |
| 2016 | 4,694 | 8,947 | 1,253 | 1,591 | 16,485 | 304 | 1,024 | 203 | 144 | 1,675 | ---- | ---- |
| 2017 | 5,347 | 9,295 | 1,308 | 1,588 | 17,538 | 355 | 1,042 | 145 | 176 | 1,718 | ---- | ---- |
| 2018 | 5,731 | 9,694 | 1,242 | 1,670 | 18,337 | 444 | 1,015 | 197 | 151 | 1,807 | ---- | ---- |
| 2019 | 5,505 | 9,772 | 978 | 1,712 | 17,967 | 446 | 1,371 | 286 | 230 | 2,333 | ---- | ---- |
| 2020 | 3,667 | 8,441 | 770 | 1,536 | 14,414 | 364 | 929 | 194 | 167 | 1,654 | ---- | ---- |
| 2021[1] | 5,292 | 9,847 | 752 | 1,698 | 17,589 | 442 | 886 | 98 | 232 | 1,658 | ---- | ---- |

[1] Preliminary.   W = Withheld.   *Source: Energy Information Administration, U.S. Department of Energy (EIA-DOE)*

# Copper

The word *copper* comes from the name of the Mediterranean island Cyprus that was a primary source of the metal. Dating back more than 10,000 years, copper is the oldest metal used by humans. From the Pyramid of Cheops in Egypt, archeologists recovered a portion of a water plumbing system that had copper tubing in serviceable condition after more than 5,000 years.

Copper is one of the most widely used industrial metals because it is an excellent conductor of electricity, has strong corrosion-resistance properties, and is very ductile. It is also used to produce the alloys of brass (a copper-zinc alloy) and bronze (a copper-tin alloy), both of which are far harder and stronger than pure copper. Electrical uses of copper account for about 75% of total copper usage, and building construction is the single largest market (the average U.S. home contains 400 pounds of copper). Copper is biostatic, meaning that bacteria will not grow on its surface, and it is therefore used in air-conditioning systems, food processing surfaces, and doorknobs to prevent the spread of disease.

Copper futures and options are traded on the London Metal Exchange (LME) and the CME Group. Copper futures are traded on the Shanghai Futures Exchange. The CME copper futures contract calls for the delivery of 25,000 pounds of Grade 1 electrolyte copper and is priced in terms of cents per pound.

**Prices** – CME copper futures prices (Barchart.com symbol HG) in Q1 of 2022 raced higher and posted an all-time high of $5.0100 per pound in March. Global copper supply concerns sent copper prices soaring after Russia invaded Ukraine, which rattled raw materials markets and prompted many countries to impose bans on Russian commodity exports. Demand for copper was already strengthening amid the global recovery from the pandemic. Copper prices then ratcheted lower and posted a 2-year low of $3.15 per pound in July on concern that record high fuel prices in Europe would push the Eurozone into a recession. In addition, a resurgence of Covid in China kept large swaths of the country locked down with its Covid-zero policy and curbed China's demand for industrial metals. Finally, interest rate hikes by most of the world's central banks during 2022 slowed global growth. Copper prices stabilized in Q4 and moved higher into year-end after China eased some of its Covid restrictions. Copper prices finished 2022 down -14.6% yr/yr at $3.8055 per pound.

**Supply** – World production of copper in 2022 rose by +3.8% yr/yr to a record 22.000 million metric tons. The largest producer of copper was Chile with 23.6% of the world's production, followed by Peru with 10.0%, China with 8.6%, the U.S. with 5.9%, and Russia with 4.5%. U.S. production of total new copper in 2022 rose by +4.1% yr/yr to 960,000 metric tons, far below the record U.S. production level of 2.140 million metric tons seen in 1998.

**Demand** – U.S. consumption of refined copper in 2022 rose by +1.7% yr/yr to 1.800 million metric tons. The primary users of copper in the U.S. are wire rod mills, followed by brass mills.

**Trade** – U.S. exports of refined copper in 2021 rose by +14.7% yr/yr to 47,570 metric tons. U.S. imports of copper in 2021 rose by +35.9% yr/yr to 918,900 metric tons, below the record high of 1.070 million metric tons in 2006.

## World Mine Production of Copper (Content of Ore)   In Thousands of Metric Tons

| Year | Australia | Canada[3] | Chile | China | Indonesia | Mexico | Peru | Poland | Russia | South Africa | United States[3] | Zambia | World Total[2] |
|---|---|---|---|---|---|---|---|---|---|---|---|---|---|
| 2013 | 1,001.0 | 631.9 | 5,776.0 | 1720 | 504.0 | 480.0 | 1,375.6 | 429.3 | 722 | 76.5 | 1,249 | 760.0 | 18,250 |
| 2014 | 970.0 | 673.0 | 5,749.6 | 1780 | 374.4 | 515.0 | 1,379.6 | 421.7 | 742 | 87.6 | 1,357 | 708.0 | 18,410 |
| 2015 | 971.0 | 697.0 | 5,764.0 | 1710 | 574.5 | 594.0 | 1,700.8 | 425.9 | 732 | 77.4 | 1,383 | 712.0 | 19,130 |
| 2016 | 948.0 | 693.1 | 5,552.6 | 1900 | 728.0 | 794.0 | 2,353.9 | 424.3 | 702 | 65.3 | 1,430 | 762.8 | 20,100 |
| 2017 | 856.0 | 595.0 | 5,503.5 | 1706 | 621.9 | 742.2 | 2,445.6 | 419.3 | 762 | 65.5 | 1,260 | 794.1 | 20,000 |
| 2018 | 920.0 | 542.9 | 5,831.6 | 1625 | 651.1 | 696.6 | 2,437.0 | 401.3 | 785 | 46.9 | 1,220 | 854.1 | 20,400 |
| 2019 | 934.0 | 572.7 | 5,787.4 | 1684 | 360.8 | 715.0 | 2,455.4 | 398.9 | 801 | 52.5 | 1,260 | 797.0 | 20,400 |
| 2020 | 885.0 | 585.0 | 5,730.0 | 1720 | 505.0 | 733.0 | 2,150.0 | 393.0 | 810 |  | 1,200 | 853.0 | 20,600 |
| 2021[1] | 813.0 | 550.0 | 5,620.0 | 1910 | 731.0 | 734.0 | 2,300.0 | 391.0 | 940 |  | 1,230 | 842.0 | 21,200 |
| 2022[2] | 830.0 | 530.0 | 5,200.0 | 1900 | 920.0 | 740.0 | 2,200.0 | 390.0 | 1,000 |  | 1,300 | 770.0 | 22,000 |

[1] Preliminary.   [2] Estimate.   [3] Recoverable.   *Source: U.S. Geological Survey (USGS)*

## Commodity Exchange Warehouse Stocks of Copper, on First of Month   In Short Tons

| Year | Jan. 1 | Feb. 1 | Mar. 1 | Apr. 1 | May 1 | June 1 | July 1 | Aug. 1 | Sept. 1 | Oct. 1 | Nov. 1 | Dec. 1 |
|---|---|---|---|---|---|---|---|---|---|---|---|---|
| 2013 | 70,712 | 74,111 | 75,025 | 76,241 | 85,562 | 79,838 | 71,733 | 64,565 | 36,518 | 31,099 | 26,347 | 19,076 |
| 2014 | 13,033 | 19,224 | 13,589 | 19,967 | 18,292 | 16,378 | 19,653 | 23,912 | 27,984 | 34,162 | 29,759 | 28,137 |
| 2015 | 26,157 | 21,289 | 18,034 | 26,864 | 23,316 | 22,518 | 30,120 | 37,283 | 36,860 | 40,153 | 53,517 | 72,749 |
| 2016 | 69,753 | 65,615 | 67,502 | 71,991 | 65,495 | 61,044 | 62,445 | 65,416 | 67,282 | 70,575 | 71,961 | 78,310 |
| 2017 | 88,902 | 102,072 | 125,849 | 144,120 | 155,295 | 157,922 | 163,072 | 171,314 | 181,926 | 196,210 | 206,099 | 209,143 |
| 2018 | 210,972 | 221,036 | 230,376 | 233,927 | 248,744 | 231,364 | 223,981 | 200,039 | 189,050 | 172,440 | 157,434 | 135,536 |
| 2019 | 110,086 | 85,970 | 57,629 | 42,692 | 34,300 | 31,637 | 33,886 | 40,110 | 43,829 | 39,719 | 36,285 | 40,097 |
| 2020 | 37,550 | 31,415 | 28,617 | 32,253 | 42,268 | 60,505 | 62,206 | 89,049 | 85,425 | 79,843 | 79,945 | 81,592 |
| 2021 | 77,599 | 74,238 | 69,556 | 71,435 | 66,536 | 60,708 | 49,345 | 45,885 | 50,811 | 56,467 | 57,235 | 58,671 |
| 2022 | 69,667 | 81,066 | 70,886 | 74,733 | 83,504 | 79,652 | 74,345 | 60,740 | 51,077 | 44,951 | 36,971 | 36,847 |

*Source: CME Group; Commodity Exchange (COMEX)*

# COPPER

## Salient Statistics of Copper in the United States    In Thousands of Metric Tons

| Year | Mines | Smelters | Refineries | From Foreign Ores | Total New | Secondary Recovery | Imports[5] Unmanufactured | Refined | Exports Ore, Concentrate[6] | Refined[7] | COMEX | Primary Producers (Refined) | Blister & Material in Solution | Apparent Consumption Refined Copper (Reported) | Primary & Old Copper[8] |
|---|---|---|---|---|---|---|---|---|---|---|---|---|---|---|---|
| 2013 | 1,250 | 516 | 518 | ---- | 993 | 166 | ---- | 734 | 348 | 111 | 15 | 259 | 13 | 1,830 | 1,760 |
| 2014 | 1,360 | 522 | 535 | ---- | 1,050 | 173 | ---- | 620 | 410 | 127 | 24 | 190 | 10 | 1,760 | 1,780 |
| 2015 | 1,380 | 527 | 503 | ---- | 1,090 | 166 | ---- | 687 | 392 | 86 | 63 | 209 | 14 | 1,810 | 1,820 |
| 2016 | 1,430 | 563 | 561 | ---- | 1,180 | 149 | ---- | 708 | 331 | 134 | 81 | 223 | 14 | 1,800 | 1,880 |
| 2017 | 1,260 | 470 | 482 | ---- | 1,040 | 146 | ---- | 813 | 237 | 94 | 191 | 265 | 13 | 1,800 | 1,860 |
| 2018 | 1,220 | 536 | 538 | ---- | 1,070 | 149 | ---- | 778 | 253 | 190 | 100 | 244 | 9 | 1,820 | 1,820 |
| 2019 | 1,260 | 464 | 457 | ---- | 985 | 150 | ---- | 663 | 356 | 125 | 34 | 110 | | 1,810 | 1,820 |
| 2020 | 1,200 | | | ---- | 874 | 150 | ---- | 676 | 383 | 41 | | 118 | | 1,810 | 1,820 |
| 2021[1] | 1,230 | | | ---- | 922 | 160 | ---- | 919 | 347 | 48 | | 117 | | 1,770 | 1,660 |
| 2022[2] | 1,300 | | | ---- | 960 | | ---- | 810 | 330 | 30 | | 120 | | 1,800 | 1,900 |

[1] Preliminary.    [2] Estimate.    [3] Also from matte, etc., refinery reports.    [4] From old scrap only.    [5] For consumption.    [6] Blister (copper content).
[7] Ingots, bars, etc.    [8] Old scrap only.    W = Withheld.    Source: U.S. Geological Survey (USGS)

## Consumption of Refined Copper[3] in the United States    In Thousands of Metric Tons

| Year | Cathodes | Wire Bars | Ingots and Ingot Bars | Cakes & Slabs | Billets | Other[4] | Wire Rod Mills | Brass Mills | Chemical Plants | Ingot Makers | Foundries | Miscellaneous[5] | Total Consumption |
|---|---|---|---|---|---|---|---|---|---|---|---|---|---|
| 2010 | 1,570.0 | W | 22.5 | 44.1 | W | 127.0 | 1,250.0 | 459.0 | 0.4 | 4.5 | 18.2 | 34.6 | 1,760.0 |
| 2011 | 1,580.0 | W | 2.5 | 43.8 | W | 136.0 | 1,270.0 | 430.0 | 1.5 | 5.0 | 17.7 | 37.5 | 1,760.0 |
| 2012 | 1,610.0 | W | 2.3 | 42.8 | W | 102.0 | 1,280.0 | 424.0 | 0.3 | 4.5 | 19.9 | 34.3 | 1,760.0 |
| 2013 | 1,680.0 | W | 2.1 | 43.5 | W | 103.0 | 1,310.0 | 457.0 | 0.2 | 4.5 | 18.5 | 36.2 | 1,830.0 |
| 2014 | 1,620.0 | ---- | 2.9 | 43.7 | ---- | 92.5 | 1,270.0 | 424.0 | 0.2 | W | 27.9 | 26.1 | 1,760.0 |
| 2015 | 1,670.0 | ---- | 3.0 | 42.3 | ---- | 99.4 | 1,320.0 | 422.0 | 6.6 | W | 32.8 | 26.0 | 1,810.0 |
| 2016 | 1,660.0 | ---- | 3.1 | 43.7 | ---- | 91.6 | 1,320.0 | 421.0 | 0.2 | 4.6 | 30.3 | 25.7 | 1,800.0 |
| 2017 | 1,660.0 | ---- | 4.8 | 43.9 | ---- | 91.4 | 1,320.0 | 420.0 | 0.2 | 4.6 | 32.1 | 25.6 | 1,800.0 |
| 2018[1] | 1,650.0 | ---- | 4.3 | 43.8 | ---- | 113.0 | 1,330.0 | 419.0 | 0.2 | 4.6 | 34.0 | 26.6 | 1,820.0 |
| 2019[2] | 1,650.0 | ---- | 3.9 | 43.9 | ---- | 111.0 | 1,330.0 | 413.0 | 0.2 | 8.7 | 30.7 | 23.9 | 1,810.0 |

[1] Preliminary.    [2] Estimate.    [3] Primary & secondary.    [4] Includes Wirebars and Billets.    [5] Includes iron and steel plants, primary smelters producing alloys other than copper, consumers of copper powder and copper shot, and other manufacturers.    W = Withheld.
Source: U.S. Geological Survey (USGS)

## Salient Statistics of Recycling Copper in the United States

| Year | New Scrap[1] | Old Scrap[2] | Recycled Metal[3] | Apparent Supply | Percent Recycled | New Scrap[1] | Old Scrap[2] | Recycled Metal[3] | Apparent Supply |
|---|---|---|---|---|---|---|---|---|---|
| | In Metric Tons | | | | | Value in Thousands of Dollars | | | |
| 2011 | 649,000 | 153,000 | 802,000 | 2,380,000 | 33.7 | 5,810,000 | 1,370,000 | 7,180,000 | 21,300,000 |
| 2012 | 642,000 | 164,000 | 807,000 | 2,400,000 | 34.0 | 5,200,000 | 1,330,000 | 6,530,000 | 19,400,000 |
| 2013 | 630,000 | 166,000 | 797,000 | 2,390,000 | 33.0 | 4,720,000 | 1,250,000 | 5,970,000 | 17,900,000 |
| 2014 | 672,000 | 173,000 | 845,000 | 2,450,000 | 35.0 | 4,710,000 | 1,210,000 | 5,930,000 | 17,200,000 |
| 2015 | 640,000 | 166,000 | 806,000 | 2,480,000 | 33.0 | 3,610,000 | 940,000 | 4,550,000 | 14,000,000 |
| 2016 | 690,000 | 149,000 | 838,000 | 2,570,000 | 33.0 | 3,420,000 | 737,000 | 4,160,000 | 12,800,000 |
| 2017 | 702,000 | 146,000 | 847,000 | 2,560,000 | 33.0 | 4,410,000 | 918,000 | 5,330,000 | 16,100,000 |
| 2018 | 712,000 | 141,000 | 853,000 | 2,530,000 | 34.0 | 4,690,000 | 926,000 | 5,620,000 | 16,700,000 |
| 2019 | 700,000 | 166,000 | 866,000 | 2,520,000 | 34.0 | 4,320,000 | 1,020,000 | 5,340,000 | 15,600,000 |
| 2020 | 697,000 | 160,000 | 858,000 | 2,360,000 | 36.0 | 4,410,000 | 1,010,000 | 5,420,000 | 14,900,000 |

[1] Scrap that results from the manufacturing process.    [2] Scrap that results from consumer products.    [3] Metal recovered from new plus old scrap.
Source: U.S. Geological Survey (USGS)

## Copper Refined from Scrap in the United States    In Metric Tons

| Year | Jan. | Feb. | Mar. | Apr. | May | June | July | Aug. | Sept. | Oct. | Nov. | Dec. | Total |
|---|---|---|---|---|---|---|---|---|---|---|---|---|---|
| 2013 | 3,870 | 3,660 | 4,550 | 4,770 | 4,910 | 4,910 | 4,680 | 3,800 | 3,780 | 3,990 | 3,970 | 4,450 | 46,900 |
| 2014 | 3,860 | 3,870 | 3,750 | 3,960 | 3,810 | 3,900 | 3,930 | 3,430 | 4,210 | 3,900 | 3,800 | 3,600 | 46,000 |
| 2015 | 4,030 | 3,810 | 4,150 | 4,180 | 4,360 | 3,310 | 3,570 | 3,890 | 4,200 | 5,010 | 4,250 | 4,050 | 48,800 |
| 2016 | 4,250 | 7,190 | 4,900 | 3,200 | 3,180 | 3,260 | 3,280 | 3,300 | 3,810 | 3,410 | 3,220 | 3,330 | 46,330 |
| 2017 | 3,240 | 4,090 | 3,240 | 3,230 | 3,380 | 3,280 | 3,220 | 3,340 | 3,310 | 3,280 | 3,240 | 3,250 | 40,100 |
| 2018 | 3,220 | 3,260 | 3,220 | 3,260 | 3,330 | 3,400 | 3,390 | 3,220 | 3,810 | 4,180 | 3,370 | 3,520 | 41,180 |
| 2019 | 3,770 | 3,330 | 3,950 | 3,600 | 3,470 | 3,480 | 3,860 | 5,860 | 3,360 | 3,220 | 3,240 | 3,240 | 44,380 |
| 2020 | 3,260 | 3,220 | 3,220 | 4,530 | 4,380 | 3,620 | 3,720 | 3,380 | 3,490 | 3,220 | 3,290 | 3,300 | 42,630 |
| 2021 | 3,220 | 4,060 | 3,460 | 5,190 | 4,560 | 5,060 | 3,340 | 3,750 | 4,590 | 3,540 | 3,990 | 4,060 | 48,820 |
| 2022[1] | 3,990 | 3,280 | 3,490 | 3,250 | 3,220 | 3,370 | 3,250 | 3,260 | 3,220 | 3,220 | 3,280 | 3,240 | 40,070 |

[1] Preliminary.    Source: U.S. Geological Survey (USGS)

# COPPER

### Imports of Refined Copper into the United States — In Metric Tons

| Year | Jan. | Feb. | Mar. | Apr. | May | June | July | Aug. | Sept. | Oct. | Nov. | Dec. | Total |
|---|---|---|---|---|---|---|---|---|---|---|---|---|---|
| 2013 | 86,800 | 64,600 | 88,200 | 55,600 | 83,600 | 69,200 | 70,000 | 50,200 | 42,800 | 40,300 | 33,900 | 48,500 | 734,000 |
| 2014 | 42,900 | 36,200 | 45,100 | 56,200 | 54,100 | 53,000 | 62,900 | 46,700 | 59,900 | 58,600 | 46,000 | 58,500 | 620,000 |
| 2015 | 70,900 | 50,300 | 68,700 | 60,500 | 56,100 | 64,500 | 78,500 | 47,400 | 47,800 | 51,700 | 44,200 | 45,400 | 686,000 |
| 2016 | 57,700 | 57,700 | 52,000 | 53,600 | 51,800 | 55,100 | 61,100 | 60,200 | 55,200 | 64,500 | 67,100 | 72,000 | 708,000 |
| 2017 | 72,600 | 59,600 | 84,800 | 51,900 | 63,500 | 66,100 | 72,500 | 55,200 | 86,800 | 76,500 | 65,200 | 58,400 | 813,100 |
| 2018 | 88,300 | 77,000 | 72,900 | 61,800 | 64,600 | 66,200 | 59,500 | 59,700 | 67,300 | 64,700 | 51,000 | 44,500 | 777,500 |
| 2019 | 57,300 | 37,800 | 40,500 | 65,400 | 52,400 | 55,200 | 68,200 | 50,600 | 60,700 | 69,300 | 49,000 | 59,500 | 665,900 |
| 2020 | 62,300 | 34,400 | 70,500 | 74,300 | 66,200 | 63,300 | 37,300 | 59,800 | 39,900 | 57,300 | 53,300 | 57,400 | 676,000 |
| 2021 | 42,400 | 73,000 | 99,700 | 85,200 | 66,600 | 69,600 | 57,100 | 105,000 | 90,700 | 92,300 | 60,000 | 77,300 | 918,900 |
| 2022[1] | 140,000 | 34,300 | 48,700 | 64,800 | 74,300 | 75,900 | 80,900 | 36,400 | 50,700 | 49,700 | 37,900 | 38,800 | 732,400 |

[1] Preliminary.  Source: U.S. Geological Survey (USGS)

### Exports of Refined Copper from the United States — In Metric Tons

| Year | Jan. | Feb. | Mar. | Apr. | May | June | July | Aug. | Sept. | Oct. | Nov. | Dec. | Total |
|---|---|---|---|---|---|---|---|---|---|---|---|---|---|
| 2013 | 3,540 | 5,300 | 5,110 | 5,380 | 5,740 | 4,890 | 8,270 | 17,100 | 14,900 | 10,300 | 15,200 | 17,700 | 113,000 |
| 2014 | 9,420 | 9,000 | 8,630 | 5,470 | 7,670 | 6,270 | 10,200 | 8,360 | 11,000 | 11,100 | 17,300 | 22,900 | 127,000 |
| 2015 | 5,860 | 8,490 | 10,100 | 6,620 | 7,190 | 9,400 | 5,870 | 6,430 | 4,490 | 6,110 | 8,690 | 7,270 | 86,500 |
| 2016 | 6,390 | 16,800 | 24,800 | 9,650 | 22,000 | 5,600 | 6,510 | 6,420 | 6,630 | 7,750 | 13,100 | 8,040 | 133,690 |
| 2017 | 12,300 | 9,100 | 9,760 | 12,200 | 9,230 | 6,140 | 7,140 | 6,680 | 7,190 | 5,210 | 4,400 | 4,810 | 94,160 |
| 2018 | 9,550 | 7,270 | 12,100 | 13,700 | 13,800 | 11,200 | 11,300 | 15,700 | 15,600 | 31,000 | 36,200 | 12,400 | 189,820 |
| 2019 | 12,600 | 13,100 | 10,200 | 13,500 | 11,000 | 13,800 | 9,810 | 6,960 | 8,410 | 8,530 | 9,510 | 7,830 | 125,250 |
| 2020 | 4,170 | 2,470 | 4,000 | 1,580 | 540 | 1,220 | 5,300 | 6,470 | 4,570 | 2,930 | 3,090 | 5,150 | 41,490 |
| 2021 | 4,350 | 2,970 | 3,360 | 5,280 | 5,580 | 6,880 | 5,270 | 1,830 | 2,300 | 3,490 | 2,630 | 3,630 | 47,570 |
| 2022[1] | 2,530 | 3,110 | 2,590 | 2,820 | 2,890 | 1,720 | 1,900 | 3,060 | 2,470 | 1,190 | 1,430 | 2,100 | 27,810 |

[1] Preliminary.  Source: U.S. Geological Survey (USGS)

### Production of Refined Copper in the United States — In Metric Tons

| Year | Jan. | Feb. | Mar. | Apr. | May | June | July | Aug. | Sept. | Oct. | Nov. | Dec. | Total |
|---|---|---|---|---|---|---|---|---|---|---|---|---|---|
| 2013 | 89,300 | 76,200 | 85,700 | 88,500 | 83,000 | 80,300 | 83,800 | 85,300 | 81,100 | 94,800 | 92,800 | 99,200 | 1,040,000 |
| 2014 | 96,600 | 87,300 | 88,400 | 95,500 | 99,600 | 98,400 | 103,000 | 101,000 | 91,600 | 80,900 | 70,000 | 82,300 | 1,090,000 |
| 2015 | 83,700 | 85,500 | 93,900 | 90,700 | 86,700 | 91,000 | 94,400 | 93,000 | 97,600 | 104,000 | 107,000 | 113,000 | 1,140,000 |
| 2016 | 110,000 | 99,200 | 110,000 | 100,000 | 103,000 | 97,500 | 100,000 | 101,000 | 103,000 | 105,000 | 98,500 | 94,100 | 1,221,300 |
| 2017 | 101,000 | 93,900 | 105,000 | 91,000 | 84,800 | 83,000 | 90,600 | 99,400 | 95,700 | 82,400 | 70,900 | 81,200 | 1,078,900 |
| 2018 | 92,800 | 92,300 | 98,000 | 85,200 | 90,900 | 88,000 | 95,300 | 97,100 | 87,000 | 93,400 | 96,400 | 94,700 | 1,111,100 |
| 2019 | 83,200 | 68,100 | 76,400 | 83,000 | 86,500 | 90,000 | 96,500 | 94,100 | 97,000 | 95,500 | W | W | 1,030,000 |
| 2020 | 77,900 | 74,800 | 78,100 | 69,100 | 72,600 | 71,900 | 78,400 | 77,500 | 74,200 | 70,900 | 80,400 | 81,700 | 907,500 |
| 2021 | 85,400 | 82,900 | 85,000 | 74,200 | 74,000 | 76,700 | 80,400 | 84,900 | 83,500 | 83,900 | 79,700 | 80,800 | 971,400 |
| 2022[1] | 84,400 | 78,600 | 87,000 | 78,200 | 82,300 | 79,900 | 85,800 | 85,000 | 85,000 | 76,800 | 72,900 | 76,200 | 972,100 |

Recoverable Copper Content.  [1] Preliminary.  Source: U.S. Geological Survey (USGS)

### Mine Production of Recoverable Copper in the United States — In Thousands of Metric Tons

| | Recoverable Copper | | | Contained Copper | | |
|---|---|---|---|---|---|---|
| Year | Arizona | Others[2] | Total | Electrowon | Concentrates[3] | Total |
| 2013 | 795.0 | 453.0 | 1,250.0 | 475.0 | 804.0 | 1,280.0 |
| 2014 | 893.0 | 464.0 | 1,360.0 | 514.0 | 871.0 | 1,380.0 |
| 2015 | 985.0 | 419.0 | 1,410.0 | 588.0 | 851.0 | 1,440.0 |
| 2016 | 968.5 | 461.2 | 1,431.0 | 614.5 | 848.9 | 1,464.0 |
| 2017 | 867.7 | 391.1 | 1,257.5 | 557.5 | 729.6 | 1,287.0 |
| 2018 | 801.2 | 420.8 | 1,223.1 | 532.0 | 715.7 | 1,247.3 |
| 2019 | 860.8 | 398.5 | 1,256.6 | 527.6 | 757.7 | 1,285.9 |
| 2020 | 880.4 | 317.8 | 1,198.7 | 559.1 | 664.8 | 1,224.3 |
| 2021 | 872.2 | 359.9 | 1,227.8 | 563.1 | 692.6 | 1,254.9 |
| 2022[1] | 854.9 | 377.9 | 1,234.4 | 557.1 | 701.6 | 1,258.8 |

[1] Preliminary.  [2] Includes production from Alaska, Idaho, Missouri, Montana, Nevada, New Mexico, and Utah.  [3] Includes copper content of precipitates and other metal concentrates.  Source: U.S. Geological Survey (USGS)

# COPPER

### Production of Recoverable Copper in Arizona — In Thousands of Metric Tons

| Year | Jan. | Feb. | Mar. | Apr. | May | June | July | Aug. | Sept. | Oct. | Nov. | Dec. | Total |
|---|---|---|---|---|---|---|---|---|---|---|---|---|---|
| 2013 | 65.7 | 57.7 | 66.5 | 64.1 | 70.7 | 64.6 | 68.2 | 65.1 | 66.6 | 68.5 | 65.9 | 71.3 | 795.0 |
| 2014 | 69.7 | 66.6 | 75.1 | 70.3 | 68.6 | 73.1 | 75.8 | 76.2 | 73.3 | 82.3 | 72.1 | 85.6 | 893.0 |
| 2015 | 78.4 | 70.5 | 80.5 | 75.9 | 76.5 | 77.2 | 81.3 | 84.1 | 83.9 | 89.3 | 85.7 | 90.3 | 985.0 |
| 2016 | 84.5 | 79.4 | 81.6 | 81.2 | 83.5 | 79.8 | 80.2 | 86.4 | 80.1 | 81.0 | 74.2 | 76.6 | 968.5 |
| 2017 | 71.0 | 64.2 | 77.5 | 72.5 | 75.1 | 71.9 | 73.5 | 71.2 | 75.0 | 66.9 | 72.8 | 76.1 | 867.7 |
| 2018 | 68.8 | 61.5 | 68.2 | 65.4 | 69.3 | 70.6 | 66.8 | 69.1 | 63.0 | 64.0 | 65.2 | 69.3 | 801.2 |
| 2019 | 67.9 | 63.6 | 74.0 | 69.7 | 71.5 | 73.4 | 79.2 | 77.3 | 74.0 | 72.3 | 66.0 | 71.9 | 860.8 |
| 2020 | 70.8 | 65.4 | 67.6 | 76.4 | 75.5 | 77.8 | 79.5 | 78.9 | 72.6 | 71.0 | 69.9 | 75.0 | 880.4 |
| 2021 | 71.6 | 70.6 | 76.2 | 66.9 | 68.4 | 74.2 | 68.2 | 76.0 | 78.4 | 73.1 | 73.5 | 75.1 | 872.2 |
| 2022[1] | 72.2 | 65.5 | 73.1 | 72.2 | 77.9 | 73.9 | 73.3 | 69.6 | 69.7 | 68.9 | 66.6 | 72.0 | 854.9 |

[1] Preliminary.   Source: U.S. Geological Survey (USGS)

### Production of Recoverable Copper in the United States — In Thousands of Metric Tons

| Year | Jan. | Feb. | Mar. | Apr. | May | June | July | Aug. | Sept. | Oct. | Nov. | Dec. | Total |
|---|---|---|---|---|---|---|---|---|---|---|---|---|---|
| 2013 | 110.0 | 89.8 | 102.0 | 92.2 | 105.0 | 103.0 | 107.0 | 104.0 | 105.0 | 113.0 | 105.0 | 113.0 | 1,250.0 |
| 2014 | 115.0 | 105.0 | 119.0 | 113.0 | 113.0 | 111.0 | 116.0 | 113.0 | 116.0 | 113.0 | 105.0 | 113.0 | 1,360.0 |
| 2015 | 111.0 | 105.0 | 121.0 | 111.0 | 109.0 | 109.0 | 121.0 | 119.0 | 117.0 | 112.0 | 99.3 | 121.0 | 1,410.0 |
| 2016 | 122.0 | 118.0 | 122.0 | 121.0 | 123.0 | 117.0 | 115.0 | 127.0 | 117.0 | 124.0 | 122.0 | 126.0 | 1,431.0 |
| 2017 | 110.0 | 98.7 | 114.0 | 109.0 | 107.0 | 109.0 | 104.0 | 102.0 | 117.0 | 125.0 | 112.0 | 112.0 | 1,257.5 |
| 2018 | 102.0 | 89.2 | 96.0 | 100.0 | 99.1 | 113.0 | 105.0 | 102.0 | 99.5 | 99.3 | 104.0 | 101.0 | 1,223.1 |
| 2019 | 97.8 | 97.1 | 108.0 | 101.0 | 105.0 | 106.0 | 117.0 | 114.0 | 108.0 | 99.8 | 101.0 | 103.0 | 1,256.6 |
| 2020 | 99.6 | 94.0 | 96.0 | 101.0 | 102.0 | 105.0 | 106.0 | 105.0 | 112.0 | 101.0 | 95.7 | 102.0 | 1,198.7 |
| 2021 | 96.7 | 96.4 | 104.0 | 95.5 | 99.0 | 103.0 | 99.2 | 105.0 | 97.9 | 96.5 | 95.7 | 100.0 | 1,227.8 |
| 2022[1] | 106.0 | 97.6 | 105.0 | 103.0 | 108.0 | 103.0 | 107.0 | 102.0 | 101.0 | 100.0 | 98.8 | 103.0 | 1,234.4 |

[1] Preliminary.   Source: U.S. Geological Survey (USGS)

### Production of Contained (Electrowon) Copper in the United States — In Thousands of Metric Tons

| Year | Jan. | Feb. | Mar. | Apr. | May | June | July | Aug. | Sept. | Oct. | Nov. | Dec. | Total |
|---|---|---|---|---|---|---|---|---|---|---|---|---|---|
| 2013 | 39.3 | 34.5 | 38.8 | 39.1 | 42.3 | 40.4 | 39.8 | 38.8 | 36.8 | 41.5 | 40.6 | 42.8 | 475.0 |
| 2014 | 42.9 | 38.5 | 41.3 | 41.1 | 41.4 | 41.6 | 43.0 | 43.0 | 43.3 | 47.3 | 42.9 | 47.2 | 514.0 |
| 2015 | 44.5 | 40.5 | 46.6 | 45.4 | 46.0 | 45.9 | 48.3 | 52.4 | 54.5 | 55.3 | 53.8 | 55.7 | 588.0 |
| 2016 | 54.5 | 48.5 | 51.4 | 49.7 | 51.7 | 50.7 | 54.0 | 52.7 | 51.4 | 53.3 | 48.7 | 47.9 | 614.5 |
| 2017 | 46.8 | 41.6 | 49.0 | 45.6 | 48.6 | 46.6 | 44.9 | 46.9 | 46.7 | 46.6 | 46.6 | 47.6 | 557.5 |
| 2018 | 46.8 | 40.5 | 44.3 | 43.2 | 46.0 | 44.9 | 46.0 | 45.4 | 43.0 | 43.1 | 43.0 | 45.8 | 532.0 |
| 2019 | 42.4 | 39.8 | 44.6 | 41.3 | 44.7 | 45.9 | 47.6 | 46.5 | 44.7 | 45.8 | 41.1 | 43.2 | 527.6 |
| 2020 | 44.6 | 41.0 | 44.9 | 44.6 | 48.2 | 48.3 | 49.6 | 49.1 | 45.7 | 47.6 | 47.1 | 48.4 | 559.1 |
| 2021 | 47.1 | 43.9 | 46.5 | 44.0 | 44.4 | 46.6 | 47.2 | 51.3 | 49.0 | 50.4 | 45.8 | 46.9 | 563.1 |
| 2022[1] | 45.4 | 40.3 | 48.5 | 44.9 | 49.1 | 46.5 | 47.6 | 46.8 | 46.8 | 48.6 | 44.6 | 48.0 | 557.1 |

[1] Preliminary.   Source: U.S. Geological Survey (USGS)

### Production of contained Copper (Concentrates[2]) in the United States — In Thousands of Metric Tons

| Year | Jan. | Feb. | Mar. | Apr. | May | June | July | Aug. | Sept. | Oct. | Nov. | Dec. | Total |
|---|---|---|---|---|---|---|---|---|---|---|---|---|---|
| 2013 | 73.2 | 57.2 | 65.9 | 55.3 | 64.8 | 64.6 | 70.4 | 67.6 | 70.8 | 73.9 | 67.1 | 72.8 | 804.0 |
| 2014 | 74.5 | 69.4 | 80.2 | 74.8 | 74.0 | 71.8 | 75.5 | 73.0 | 74.8 | 69.2 | 58.6 | 76.3 | 871.0 |
| 2015 | 69.0 | 67.0 | 77.4 | 68.1 | 65.9 | 65.2 | 76.1 | 69.8 | 67.4 | 71.3 | 70.9 | 73.1 | 851.0 |
| 2016 | 70.4 | 72.8 | 73.0 | 73.9 | 74.0 | 69.0 | 63.7 | 76.9 | 67.6 | 74.9 | 66.1 | 66.6 | 848.9 |
| 2017 | 66.9 | 59.4 | 67.9 | 66.0 | 60.9 | 64.7 | 61.6 | 57.0 | 55.0 | 54.8 | 59.7 | 55.7 | 729.6 |
| 2018 | 56.9 | 50.7 | 53.7 | 58.8 | 55.2 | 70.1 | 61.4 | 64.6 | 59.1 | 59.8 | 62.4 | 63.0 | 715.7 |
| 2019 | 57.6 | 59.5 | 65.7 | 62.3 | 62.8 | 62.1 | 72.3 | 70.5 | 69.8 | 57.0 | 56.7 | 61.4 | 757.7 |
| 2020 | 57.2 | 55.1 | 53.1 | 58.8 | 55.7 | 58.6 | 58.9 | 57.9 | 54.3 | 50.8 | 50.6 | 53.8 | 664.8 |
| 2021 | 51.7 | 54.7 | 59.9 | 53.6 | 56.8 | 59.0 | 54.1 | 58.8 | 60.8 | 57.9 | 62.3 | 63.0 | 692.6 |
| 2022[1] | 62.8 | 59.4 | 58.4 | 59.9 | 60.9 | 58.2 | 61.4 | 57.5 | 56.5 | 53.5 | 56.2 | 56.9 | 701.6 |

[1] Preliminary.   [2] Includes copper content of precipitates and other metal concentrates.   Source: U.S. Geological Survey (USGS)

# COPPER

### Production of Contained Copper in the United States   In Thousands of Metric Tons

| Year | Jan. | Feb. | Mar. | Apr. | May | June | July | Aug. | Sept. | Oct. | Nov. | Dec. | Total |
|---|---|---|---|---|---|---|---|---|---|---|---|---|---|
| 2013 | 113.0 | 91.8 | 105.0 | 94.4 | 107.0 | 105.0 | 110.0 | 106.0 | 108.0 | 115.0 | 108.0 | 116.0 | 1,280.0 |
| 2014 | 117.0 | 108.0 | 121.0 | 116.0 | 115.0 | 113.0 | 118.0 | 116.0 | 118.0 | 116.0 | 102.0 | 123.0 | 1,380.0 |
| 2015 | 113.0 | 108.0 | 124.0 | 114.0 | 112.0 | 111.0 | 124.0 | 122.0 | 122.0 | 127.0 | 125.0 | 129.0 | 1,440.0 |
| 2016 | 125.0 | 121.0 | 124.0 | 124.0 | 126.0 | 120.0 | 118.0 | 130.0 | 118.0 | 128.0 | 115.0 | 115.0 | 1,464.0 |
| 2017 | 114.0 | 101.0 | 117.0 | 112.0 | 109.0 | 111.0 | 107.0 | 104.0 | 102.0 | 101.0 | 106.0 | 103.0 | 1,287.0 |
| 2018 | 104.0 | 91.3 | 98.0 | 102.0 | 101.0 | 115.0 | 107.0 | 110.0 | 102.0 | 103.0 | 105.0 | 109.0 | 1,247.3 |
| 2019 | 99.9 | 99.2 | 110.0 | 104.0 | 108.0 | 108.0 | 120.0 | 117.0 | 114.0 | 103.0 | 97.8 | 105.0 | 1,285.9 |
| 2020 | 102.0 | 96.1 | 98.0 | 103.0 | 104.0 | 107.0 | 109.0 | 107.0 | 100.0 | 98.5 | 97.7 | 102.0 | 1,224.3 |
| 2021 | 98.8 | 98.5 | 106.0 | 97.6 | 101.0 | 106.0 | 101.0 | 110.0 | 110.0 | 108.0 | 108.0 | 110.0 | 1,254.9 |
| 2022[1] | 108.0 | 99.8 | 107.0 | 105.0 | 110.0 | 105.0 | 109.0 | 104.0 | 103.0 | 102.0 | 101.0 | 105.0 | 1,258.8 |

[1] Preliminary.   Source: U.S. Geological Survey (USGS)

### Production of Copper at Smelters in the United States   In Thousands of Metric Tons

| Year | Jan. | Feb. | Mar. | Apr. | May | June | July | Aug. | Sept. | Oct. | Nov. | Dec. | Total |
|---|---|---|---|---|---|---|---|---|---|---|---|---|---|
| 2013 | 39.0 | 46.6 | 44.8 | 39.8 | 41.2 | 22.7 | 41.8 | 42.3 | 46.1 | 51.3 | 49.9 | 51.0 | 516.5 |
| 2014 | 47.4 | 47.6 | 51.3 | 48.1 | 53.4 | 49.7 | 57.3 | 54.4 | 34.7 | 21.0 | 17.0 | 40.2 | 522.0 |
| 2015 | 47.8 | 42.8 | 45.7 | 34.9 | 40.7 | 42.6 | 41.8 | 40.3 | 39.6 | 48.7 | 46.5 | 55.1 | 527.0 |
| 2016 | 45.6 | 46.1 | 41.4 | 47.3 | 51.9 | 45.4 | 33.1 | 47.7 | 54.0 | 51.9 | 43.3 | 55.0 | 562.7 |
| 2017 | 48.9 | 47.8 | 52.2 | 40.7 | 20.1 | 37.1 | 45.8 | 47.2 | 49.0 | 29.3 | 14.5 | 37.8 | 470.4 |
| 2018 | 53.9 | 42.2 | 41.5 | 44.8 | 39.0 | 45.7 | 47.5 | 46.1 | 40.8 | 48.2 | 45.3 | 40.6 | 535.6 |
| 2019 | 34.7 | 17.7 | 37.0 | 32.9 | 54.1 | 51.8 | 34.5 | 49.2 | 43.2 | 43.8 | W | W | 464.0 |
| 2020 | 30.0 | 30.0 | 30.0 | 20.0 | 20.0 | 20.0 | 25.0 | 25.0 | 25.0 | 30.0 | 30.0 | 30.0 | 315.0 |
| 2021 | 35.0 | 35.0 | 35.0 | 25.0 | 25.0 | 25.0 | 30.0 | 30.0 | 30.0 | 30.0 | 30.0 | 30.0 | 360.0 |
| 2022[1] | 35.0 | 35.0 | 35.0 | 30.0 | 30.0 | 30.0 | 35.0 | 35.0 | 35.0 | 25.0 | 25.0 | 25.0 | 375.0 |

[1] Preliminary.   Source: U.S. Geological Survey (USGS)

### Production of Copper at Brass Mills in the United States   In Thousands of Metric Tons

| Year | Jan. | Feb. | Mar. | Apr. | May | June | July | Aug. | Sept. | Oct. | Nov. | Dec. | Total |
|---|---|---|---|---|---|---|---|---|---|---|---|---|---|
| 2013 | 78.4 | 77.9 | 80.1 | 82.6 | 81.3 | 80.3 | 80.0 | 80.8 | 78.9 | 76.6 | 76.1 | 75.0 | 948.0 |
| 2014 | 78.0 | 85.0 | 82.6 | 80.5 | 81.4 | 79.7 | 76.7 | 79.1 | 79.5 | 78.4 | 79.1 | 77.2 | 954.0 |
| 2015 | 77.8 | 78.9 | 76.9 | 74.3 | 73.8 | 75.0 | 72.7 | 74.1 | 74.6 | 74.2 | 72.5 | 72.7 | 891.0 |
| 2016 | 73.6 | 73.6 | 75.0 | 73.5 | 72.3 | 72.3 | 72.8 | 74.4 | 72.5 | 74.8 | 72.7 | 72.3 | 879.8 |
| 2017 | 73.5 | 72.8 | 74.2 | 72.2 | 74.7 | 73.3 | 73.0 | 75.0 | 74.0 | 74.1 | 72.5 | 72.1 | 881.4 |
| 2018 | 73.6 | 72.7 | 74.3 | 73.6 | 73.6 | 73.9 | 73.4 | 73.8 | 73.5 | 74.3 | 73.5 | 73.8 | 884.0 |
| 2019 | 74.2 | 73.5 | 74.2 | 73.7 | 73.8 | 73.6 | 70.3 | 73.8 | 73.2 | 73.9 | 73.2 | 72.7 | 880.1 |
| 2020 | 73.7 | 73.9 | 74.5 | 72.5 | 73.4 | 73.7 | 73.5 | 73.7 | 73.8 | 74.4 | 73.6 | 73.7 | 884.4 |
| 2021 | 73.9 | 74.1 | 74.7 | 75.0 | 73.2 | 74.2 | 74.6 | 76.0 | 74.0 | 74.6 | 74.5 | 74.4 | 893.2 |
| 2022[1] | 74.3 | 76.0 | 76.9 | 769.3 | 74.2 | 74.8 | 74.6 | 75.3 | 79.9 | 75.4 | 74.9 | 74.8 | 1,600.4 |

[1] Preliminary.   Source: U.S. Geological Survey (USGS)

### Production of Copper at Wire-rod Mills in the United States   In Thousands of Metric Tons

| Year | Jan. | Feb. | Mar. | Apr. | May | June | July | Aug. | Sept. | Oct. | Nov. | Dec. | Total |
|---|---|---|---|---|---|---|---|---|---|---|---|---|---|
| 2013 | 105.0 | 111.0 | 114.0 | 112.0 | 115.0 | 110.0 | 107.0 | 113.0 | 116.0 | 115.0 | 103.0 | 91.7 | 1,310.0 |
| 2014 | 115.0 | 104.0 | 102.0 | 110.0 | 111.0 | 110.0 | 115.0 | 113.0 | 104.0 | 118.0 | 99.9 | 78.8 | 1,280.0 |
| 2015 | 118.0 | 105.0 | 118.0 | 114.0 | 116.0 | 116.0 | 112.0 | 109.0 | 108.0 | 114.0 | 95.9 | 92.2 | 1,320.0 |
| 2016 | 112.0 | 109.0 | 117.0 | 109.0 | 110.0 | 115.0 | 98.5 | 118.0 | 107.0 | 115.0 | 112.0 | 94.3 | 1,316.8 |
| 2017 | 114.0 | 105.0 | 117.0 | 112.0 | 112.0 | 115.0 | 97.2 | 119.0 | 115.0 | 117.0 | 106.0 | 92.5 | 1,321.7 |
| 2018 | 114.0 | 107.0 | 115.0 | 103.0 | 115.0 | 118.0 | 99.3 | 124.0 | 110.0 | 114.0 | 113.0 | 97.7 | 1,330.0 |
| 2019 | 113.0 | 103.0 | 117.0 | 104.0 | 116.0 | 109.0 | 110.0 | 112.0 | 113.0 | 112.0 | 101.0 | 93.5 | 1,303.5 |
| 2020 | 110.0 | 110.0 | 108.0 | 94.6 | 95.3 | 89.4 | 108.0 | 104.0 | 105.0 | 108.0 | 106.0 | 101.0 | 1,239.3 |
| 2021 | 104.0 | 102.0 | 125.0 | 115.0 | 120.0 | 119.0 | 112.0 | 117.0 | 118.0 | 115.0 | 115.0 | 86.1 | 1,348.1 |
| 2022[1] | 117.0 | 103.0 | 118.0 | 117.0 | 112.0 | 111.0 | 117.0 | 112.0 | 116.0 | 115.0 | 94.8 | 82.2 | 1,315.0 |

[1] Preliminary.   Source: U.S. Geological Survey (USGS)

# COPPER

### Shipments of Copper at Brass Mills in the United States   In Thousands of Metric Tons

| Year | Jan. | Feb. | Mar. | Apr. | May | June | July | Aug. | Sept. | Oct. | Nov. | Dec. | Total |
|---|---|---|---|---|---|---|---|---|---|---|---|---|---|
| 2013 | 79.5 | 78.7 | 80.8 | 82.2 | 81.4 | 79.8 | 79.3 | 80.1 | 80.0 | 75.4 | 77.4 | 75.0 | 949.0 |
| 2014 | 78.6 | 84.9 | 81.9 | 80.2 | 80.6 | 80.3 | 76.8 | 79.1 | 79.8 | 78.9 | 78.0 | 77.8 | 954.0 |
| 2015 | 77.7 | 78.2 | 76.9 | 74.7 | 73.7 | 74.9 | 72.9 | 74.2 | 74.9 | 73.5 | 72.8 | 73.1 | 891.0 |
| 2016 | 73.4 | 73.9 | 74.2 | 73.3 | 73.7 | 71.2 | 72.7 | 73.8 | 73.5 | 75.1 | 72.8 | 72.1 | 879.7 |
| 2017 | 72.9 | 73.1 | 74.4 | 72.8 | 74.5 | 73.0 | 73.2 | 74.2 | 73.6 | 74.1 | 72.8 | 72.0 | 880.6 |
| 2018 | 73.5 | 73.4 | 74.0 | 73.6 | 74.0 | 73.8 | 73.7 | 74.2 | 73.3 | 73.9 | 73.4 | 73.0 | 883.8 |
| 2019 | 73.8 | 73.6 | 73.8 | 73.9 | 74.1 | 73.5 | 70.9 | 73.7 | 73.3 | 74.0 | 73.0 | 72.2 | 879.8 |
| 2020 | 74.2 | 73.6 | 74.1 | 73.5 | 73.4 | 73.6 | 73.3 | 73.6 | 73.7 | 74.0 | 73.8 | 74.5 | 885.3 |
| 2021 | 74.0 | 73.8 | 74.5 | 75.3 | 73.3 | 74.0 | 74.8 | 74.5 | 74.3 | 74.4 | 74.3 | 74.2 | 891.4 |
| 2022[1] | 74.3 | 75.8 | 77.0 | 76.1 | 74.3 | 74.9 | 74.8 | 75.2 | 79.4 | 75.1 | 74.8 | 74.3 | 906.0 |

[1] Preliminary.   Source: U.S. Geological Survey (USGS)

### Shipments of Copper at Wire-rod Mills in the United States   In Thousands of Metric Tons

| Year | Jan. | Feb. | Mar. | Apr. | May | June | July | Aug. | Sept. | Oct. | Nov. | Dec. | Total |
|---|---|---|---|---|---|---|---|---|---|---|---|---|---|
| 2013 | 115.0 | 108.0 | 112.0 | 115.0 | 114.0 | 105.0 | 110.0 | 115.0 | 115.0 | 116.0 | 103.0 | 89.6 | 1,320.0 |
| 2014 | 113.0 | 106.0 | 102.0 | 112.0 | 110.0 | 107.0 | 112.0 | 112.0 | 108.0 | 115.0 | 95.3 | 91.7 | 1,280.0 |
| 2015 | 109.0 | 109.0 | 120.0 | 113.0 | 114.0 | 113.0 | 110.0 | 111.0 | 106.0 | 114.0 | 100.0 | 92.2 | 1,310.0 |
| 2016 | 110.0 | 108.0 | 113.0 | 108.0 | 111.0 | 113.0 | 99.9 | 121.0 | 112.0 | 111.0 | 109.0 | 97.7 | 1,313.6 |
| 2017 | 117.0 | 98.0 | 120.0 | 104.0 | 117.0 | 117.0 | 97.4 | 125.0 | 109.0 | 118.0 | 108.0 | 89.8 | 1,320.2 |
| 2018 | 114.0 | 107.0 | 117.0 | 111.0 | 113.0 | 114.0 | 102.0 | 120.0 | 111.0 | 120.0 | 108.0 | 92.1 | 1,329.1 |
| 2019 | 116.0 | 110.0 | 112.0 | 111.0 | 112.0 | 116.0 | 113.0 | 116.0 | 110.0 | 114.0 | 100.0 | 94.1 | 1,324.1 |
| 2020 | 106.0 | 106.0 | 112.0 | 96.2 | 91.4 | 96.1 | 104.0 | 111.0 | 107.0 | 110.0 | 106.0 | 97.8 | 1,243.5 |
| 2021 | 106.0 | 103.0 | 123.0 | 117.0 | 117.0 | 119.0 | 114.0 | 113.0 | 120.0 | 110.0 | 110.0 | 95.1 | 1,347.1 |
| 2022[1] | 114.0 | 107.0 | 116.0 | 112.0 | 116.0 | 115.0 | 114.0 | 115.0 | 119.0 | 114.0 | 94.7 | 79.7 | 1,316.4 |

[1] Preliminary.   Source: U.S. Geological Survey (USGS)

### Consumption of Refined Copper at Brass Mills in the United States   In Thousands of Metric Tons

| Year | Jan. | Feb. | Mar. | Apr. | May | June | July | Aug. | Sept. | Oct. | Nov. | Dec. | Total |
|---|---|---|---|---|---|---|---|---|---|---|---|---|---|
| 2013 | 36.3 | 37.6 | 38.1 | 38.8 | 39.3 | 41.8 | 36.0 | 39.3 | 37.0 | 40.2 | 36.4 | 36.6 | 457.0 |
| 2014 | 39.0 | 36.5 | 38.8 | 38.6 | 35.4 | 37.4 | 35.4 | 35.2 | 35.2 | 34.4 | 35.9 | 35.1 | 424.0 |
| 2015 | 35.5 | 35.3 | 35.7 | 36.2 | 35.1 | 34.8 | 35.4 | 35.2 | 35.2 | 34.4 | 35.9 | 35.1 | 424.0 |
| 2016 | 34.8 | 35.7 | 35.4 | 34.9 | 34.4 | 35.5 | 35.5 | 35.2 | 35.5 | 34.9 | 35.3 | 35.0 | 422.0 |
| 2017 | 34.6 | 34.8 | 35.3 | 34.2 | 35.3 | 34.7 | 35.0 | 35.3 | 35.2 | 35.4 | 34.4 | 33.8 | 420.8 |
| 2018 | 34.6 | 35.1 | 34.9 | 35.1 | 34.9 | 34.9 | 34.8 | 35.1 | 35.1 | 34.9 | 34.7 | 34.9 | 419.4 |
| 2019 | 34.9 | 34.8 | 34.9 | 34.9 | 35.4 | 34.2 | 34.1 | 34.0 | 34.1 | 34.2 | 34.1 | 34.6 | 418.7 |
| 2020 | 34.5 | 33.6 | 33.6 | 34.5 | 34.1 | 34.7 | 34.3 | 34.7 | 34.6 | 34.6 | 34.6 | 34.8 | 412.7 |
| 2021 | 34.7 | 34.9 | 35.3 | 34.3 | 34.1 | 34.2 | 34.4 | 34.5 | 34.7 | 34.7 | 34.3 | 34.7 | 414.8 |
| 2022[1] | 34.9 | 34.8 | 36.6 | 34.6 | 34.9 | 34.8 | 34.9 | 35.0 | 34.9 | 35.0 | 35.0 | 35.2 | 420.6 |

[1] Preliminary.   Source: U.S. Geological Survey (USGS)

### Consumption of Refined Copper at Wire-rod Mills in the United States   In Thousands of Metric Tons

| Year | Jan. | Feb. | Mar. | Apr. | May | June | July | Aug. | Sept. | Oct. | Nov. | Dec. | Total |
|---|---|---|---|---|---|---|---|---|---|---|---|---|---|
| 2013 | 104.0 | 111.0 | 114.0 | 112.0 | 114.0 | 109.0 | 108.0 | 113.0 | 113.0 | 116.0 | 103.0 | 90.6 | 1,310.0 |
| 2014 | 115.0 | 104.0 | 102.0 | 111.0 | 107.0 | 111.0 | 115.0 | 113.0 | 103.0 | 114.0 | 98.8 | 78.5 | 1,270.0 |
| 2015 | 118.0 | 105.0 | 118.0 | 113.0 | 116.0 | 116.0 | 112.0 | 109.0 | 108.0 | 113.0 | 97.5 | 95.8 | 1,320.0 |
| 2016 | 110.0 | 107.0 | 116.0 | 107.0 | 108.0 | 115.0 | 98.3 | 119.0 | 107.0 | 116.0 | 116.0 | 93.2 | 1,312.5 |
| 2017 | 113.0 | 114.0 | 116.0 | 112.0 | 113.0 | 114.0 | 96.3 | 106.0 | 115.0 | 118.0 | 106.0 | 91.8 | 1,315.1 |
| 2018 | 114.0 | 107.0 | 115.0 | 105.0 | 115.0 | 106.0 | 104.0 | 121.0 | 122.0 | 112.0 | 113.0 | 98.0 | 1,332.0 |
| 2019 | 116.0 | 106.0 | 123.0 | 119.0 | 114.0 | 110.0 | 107.0 | 116.0 | 110.0 | 118.0 | 112.0 | 104.0 | 1,355.0 |
| 2020 | 120.0 | 117.0 | 104.0 | 107.0 | 102.0 | 95.3 | 107.0 | 103.0 | 105.0 | 106.0 | 105.0 | 99.9 | 1,271.2 |
| 2021 | 93.4 | 96.1 | 119.0 | 108.0 | 119.0 | 112.0 | 108.0 | 113.0 | 112.0 | 109.0 | 110.0 | 81.8 | 1,281.3 |
| 2022[1] | 111.0 | 101.0 | 114.0 | 113.0 | 109.0 | 107.0 | 112.0 | 106.0 | 101.0 | 105.0 | 83.7 | 79.9 | 1,242.6 |

[1] Preliminary.   Source: U.S. Geological Survey (USGS)

# COPPER

### Consumption of Refined Copper at Other Plants[2] in the United States    In Thousands of Metric Tons

| Year | Jan. | Feb. | Mar. | Apr. | May | June | July | Aug. | Sept. | Oct. | Nov. | Dec. | Total |
|---|---|---|---|---|---|---|---|---|---|---|---|---|---|
| 2013 | 4.9 | 4.9 | 4.9 | 4.9 | 4.9 | 4.9 | 4.9 | 4.9 | 4.9 | 4.9 | 4.9 | 4.9 | 59.0 |
| 2014 | 4.9 | 5.0 | 5.0 | 5.0 | 5.0 | 5.0 | 5.0 | 5.0 | 5.0 | 5.0 | 5.0 | 5.0 | 59.4 |
| 2015 | 4.7 | 4.7 | 4.7 | 4.7 | 4.7 | 4.7 | 4.7 | 4.7 | 4.7 | 4.7 | 4.7 | 4.7 | 56.2 |
| 2016 | 5.8 | 5.8 | 5.8 | 5.8 | 5.8 | 5.8 | 5.8 | 5.8 | 5.8 | 5.8 | 5.8 | 5.8 | 69.8 |
| 2017 | 5.6 | 5.6 | 5.6 | 5.6 | 5.6 | 5.6 | 5.6 | 5.1 | 5.1 | 5.1 | 5.1 | 5.1 | 64.7 |
| 2018 | 5.2 | 5.2 | 5.2 | 5.2 | 5.2 | 5.2 | 5.2 | 5.2 | 5.2 | 5.2 | 5.2 | 5.2 | 62.0 |
| 2019 | 5.5 | 5.5 | 5.5 | 5.5 | 5.5 | 5.5 | 5.5 | 5.5 | 5.5 | 5.5 | 5.5 | 5.5 | 65.4 |
| 2020 | 5.5 | 5.5 | 5.5 | 5.5 | 5.5 | 5.5 | 5.5 | 5.5 | 5.5 | 5.5 | 5.5 | 5.5 | 65.4 |
| 2021 | 5.2 | 5.2 | 5.2 | 5.2 | 5.2 | 5.2 | 5.2 | 5.2 | 5.2 | 5.2 | 5.2 | 5.2 | 62.2 |
| 2022[1] | 5.2 | 5.2 | 5.2 | 5.2 | 5.2 | 5.2 | 5.2 | 5.2 | 5.2 | 5.2 | 5.2 | 5.2 | 62.2 |

[1] Preliminary.    [2] Monthly estimates based on reported and annual data, comprising stocks at ingot makers, chemical plants, foundries, and miscellaneous manufacturers.    Source: U.S. Geological Survey (USGS)

### Consumption of Refined Copper in the United States    In Thousands of Metric Tons

| Year | Jan. | Feb. | Mar. | Apr. | May | June | July | Aug. | Sept. | Oct. | Nov. | Dec. | Total |
|---|---|---|---|---|---|---|---|---|---|---|---|---|---|
| 2013 | 146.0 | 154.0 | 157.0 | 156.0 | 159.0 | 156.0 | 149.0 | 157.0 | 155.0 | 161.0 | 144.0 | 132.0 | 1,820.0 |
| 2014 | 159.0 | 146.0 | 146.0 | 155.0 | 147.0 | 153.0 | 156.0 | 154.0 | 143.0 | 153.0 | 140.0 | 119.0 | 1,760.0 |
| 2015 | 158.0 | 145.0 | 146.0 | 155.0 | 155.0 | 155.0 | 150.0 | 149.0 | 148.0 | 152.0 | 137.0 | 135.0 | 1,800.0 |
| 2015 | 158.0 | 145.0 | 158.0 | 154.0 | 155.0 | 156.0 | 140.0 | 160.0 | 148.0 | 157.0 | 156.0 | 133.0 | 1,803.0 |
| 2016 | 150.0 | 149.0 | 157.0 | 148.0 | 149.0 | 156.0 | 137.0 | 147.0 | 156.0 | 159.0 | 145.0 | 132.0 | 1,801.0 |
| 2017 | 153.0 | 154.0 | 157.0 | 152.0 | 154.0 | 155.0 | 137.0 | 161.0 | 163.0 | 152.0 | 153.0 | 138.0 | 1,813.0 |
| 2018 | 154.0 | 147.0 | 155.0 | 145.0 | 155.0 | 146.0 | 144.0 | 161.0 | 150.0 | 158.0 | 151.0 | 142.0 | 1,831.0 |
| 2019 | 156.0 | 146.0 | 163.0 | 159.0 | 154.0 | 150.0 | 147.0 | 155.0 | 150.0 | 147.0 | 145.0 | 140.0 | 1,749.0 |
| 2020 | 160.0 | 156.0 | 143.0 | 146.0 | 142.0 | 135.0 | 147.0 | 143.0 | 145.0 | 147.0 | 145.0 | 140.0 | 1,749.0 |
| 2021 | 134.0 | 136.0 | 159.0 | 147.0 | 158.0 | 151.0 | 147.0 | 153.0 | 152.0 | 148.0 | 150.0 | 122.0 | 1,757.0 |
| 2022[1] | 151.0 | 141.0 | 155.0 | 153.0 | 149.0 | 147.0 | 152.0 | 146.0 | 141.0 | 145.0 | 124.0 | 120.0 | 1,724.0 |

[1] Preliminary.    Source: U.S. Geological Survey (USGS)

### Copper Stocks in the United States at Yearend    In Metric Tons

| Year | Crude Copper[2] | Refineries[3] | Wire-rod Mills[3] | Brass Mills[3] | Other[4] | Comex | LME[5] | Total Refined |
|---|---|---|---|---|---|---|---|---|
| 2013 | 12.7 | 15.0 | 32.6 | 6.7 | 4.2 | 15.0 | 185.0 | 258.0 |
| 2014 | 9.9 | 9.5 | 42.0 | 6.4 | 4.4 | 24.2 | 102.0 | 189.0 |
| 2015 | 13.9 | 12.0 | 36.2 | 7.6 | 7.6 | 63.3 | 83.8 | 210.0 |
| 2016 | 14.4 | 4.2 | 26.7 | 7.4 | 5.7 | 80.1 | 98.9 | 223.0 |
| 2017 | 12.6 | 5.8 | 27.8 | 7.9 | 5.5 | 192.0 | 27.1 | 265.0 |
| 2018 | 9.2 | 3.9 | 21.8 | 8.2 | 5.4 | 99.6 | 104.0 | 243.0 |
| 2019 | 16.4 | 7.0 | 20.0 | 7.5 | 7.1 | 34.1 | 35.0 | 111.0 |
| 2020 | 9.4 | 3.9 | 10.7 | 7.9 | 7.1 | 70.2 | 18.3 | 118.0 |
| 2021 | 16.1 | 5.4 | 11.5 | 9.1 | 6.9 | 63.8 | 20.2 | 117.0 |
| 2022[1] | 13.3 | 9.1 | 25.8 | 11.0 | 6.9 | 31.7 | 6.9 | 91.3 |

[1] Preliminary.    [2] Copper content of blister and anode.    [3] Stocks of refined copper as reported; no estimates are made for nonrespondents.    [4] Monthly estimates based on reported and 2011 annual data, comprising stocks at ingot makers, chemical plants, foundries, and miscellaneous manufacturers.
[5] London Metal Exchange Ltd., U.S. warehouses.    Source: U.S. Geological Survey (USGS)

### Stocks of Crude Copper[2] in the United States, at End of Month    In Thousands of Metric Tons

| Year | Jan. | Feb. | Mar. | Apr. | May | June | July | Aug. | Sept. | Oct. | Nov. | Dec. |
|---|---|---|---|---|---|---|---|---|---|---|---|---|
| 2013 | 8.6 | 20.1 | 17.9 | 21.8 | 28.7 | 11.5 | 12.8 | 10.7 | 11.2 | 14.2 | 15.3 | 12.7 |
| 2014 | 13.4 | 13.8 | 18.4 | 15.1 | 22.2 | 14.7 | 10.3 | 15.9 | 15.7 | 11.3 | 9.7 | 9.9 |
| 2015 | 14.2 | 11.3 | 11.3 | 11.3 | 16.6 | 15.4 | 13.2 | 14.3 | 21.2 | 17.9 | 13.5 | 13.9 |
| 2016 | 13.7 | 14.5 | 13.6 | 12.4 | 16.1 | 19.5 | 13.5 | 12.5 | 12.6 | 14.7 | 13.8 | 14.4 |
| 2017 | 11.7 | 13.2 | 13.5 | 26.1 | 11.0 | 11.0 | 11.0 | 7.4 | 12.1 | 13.6 | 16.7 | 12.6 |
| 2018 | 15.0 | 14.6 | 9.0 | 9.9 | 8.1 | 14.3 | 9.7 | 9.0 | 9.1 | 8.9 | 7.4 | 9.2 |
| 2019 | 9.6 | 10.2 | 15.0 | 8.9 | 9.2 | 13.6 | 15.5 | 14.5 | 8.3 | 25.4 | 10.2 | 16.4 |
| 2020 | 9.6 | 17.9 | 7.9 | 7.4 | 11.9 | 11.0 | 11.3 | 15.7 | 13.5 | 15.2 | 12.5 | 9.4 |
| 2021 | 17.5 | 23.8 | 15.3 | 12.4 | 13.1 | 10.3 | 12.3 | 12.0 | 10.2 | 15.7 | 15.9 | 16.1 |
| 2022[1] | 11.8 | 13.3 | 12.2 | 16.1 | 11.5 | 13.1 | 12.9 | 14.2 | 14.9 | 18.5 | 14.6 | 13.3 |

[1] Preliminary.    [2] Copper content of blister and anode.    Source: U.S. Geological Survey (USGS)

# COPPER

### Stocks of Refined Copper at Refineries[2] in the United States, at End of Month    In Thousands of Metric Tons

| Year | Jan. | Feb. | Mar. | Apr. | May | June | July | Aug. | Sept. | Oct. | Nov. | Dec. |
|---|---|---|---|---|---|---|---|---|---|---|---|---|
| 2013 | 12.5 | 12.4 | 9.4 | 6.5 | 5.9 | 7.2 | 7.9 | 8.0 | 8.8 | 7.0 | 8.5 | 15.0 |
| 2014 | 6.7 | 7.7 | 9.2 | 8.7 | 8.8 | 6.8 | 6.5 | 9.0 | 7.1 | 5.3 | 6.9 | 9.5 |
| 2015 | 6.7 | 8.3 | 6.6 | 6.7 | 5.7 | 5.5 | 6.3 | 8.7 | 6.6 | 9.3 | 8.1 | 12.0 |
| 2016 | 13.8 | 8.8 | 7.9 | 3.2 | 4.0 | 2.8 | 3.0 | 5.7 | 4.2 | 3.2 | 4.3 | 4.2 |
| 2017 | 9.3 | 8.0 | 3.9 | 6.0 | 5.3 | 4.7 | 5.8 | 5.6 | 8.7 | 5.6 | 4.7 | 5.8 |
| 2018 | 6.2 | 7.7 | 4.8 | 4.5 | 5.0 | 3.6 | 5.0 | 4.6 | 3.1 | 4.3 | 5.6 | 3.9 |
| 2019 | 2.7 | 2.8 | 3.0 | 6.6 | 3.6 | 5.0 | 4.4 | 5.1 | 7.2 | 10.6 | 6.7 | 7.0 |
| 2020 | 7.2 | 7.8 | 2.8 | 10.3 | 3.6 | 2.1 | 3.1 | 4.5 | 3.7 | 3.5 | 3.4 | 3.9 |
| 2021 | 3.8 | 5.3 | 3.4 | 3.3 | 2.9 | 3.2 | 4.4 | 3.6 | 5.4 | 6.4 | 5.3 | 5.4 |
| 2022[1] | 5.0 | 4.9 | 3.7 | 5.0 | 3.1 | 5.8 | 4.0 | 4.8 | 5.6 | 4.3 | 3.5 | 9.1 |

[1] Preliminary.    [2] As reported; no estimates are made for nonrespondents.    Source: U.S. Geological Survey (USGS)

### Stocks of Refined Copper at Wire Rod Mills[2] in the United States, at End of Month    In Thousands of Metric Tons

| Year | Jan. | Feb. | Mar. | Apr. | May | June | July | Aug. | Sept. | Oct. | Nov. | Dec. |
|---|---|---|---|---|---|---|---|---|---|---|---|---|
| 2013 | 31.3 | 26.3 | 23.7 | 26.2 | 25.9 | 21.8 | 15.0 | 19.1 | 17.9 | 16.3 | 16.0 | 32.6 |
| 2014 | 40.8 | 43.0 | 45.4 | 46.3 | 43.8 | 36.1 | 42.7 | 34.1 | 36.7 | 35.7 | 32.6 | 42.0 |
| 2015 | 41.2 | 40.6 | 38.9 | 44.7 | 35.6 | 36.0 | 40.5 | 41.8 | 43.3 | 35.6 | 34.0 | 36.2 |
| 2016 | 34.6 | 33.4 | 28.7 | 41.6 | 40.1 | 24.6 | 34.1 | 28.0 | 30.0 | 32.0 | 29.7 | 26.7 |
| 2017 | 30.3 | 27.7 | 34.4 | 27.9 | 24.4 | 22.7 | 21.5 | 25.7 | 24.6 | 27.4 | 32.9 | 27.8 |
| 2018 | 25.5 | 19.4 | 19.9 | 15.0 | 16.8 | 16.1 | 28.7 | 22.6 | 18.5 | 19.9 | 19.2 | 21.8 |
| 2019 | 19.7 | 32.3 | 24.8 | 28.1 | 23.2 | 20.7 | 25.0 | 15.4 | 16.2 | 17.5 | 18.2 | 20.0 |
| 2020 | 24.8 | 21.9 | 28.6 | 19.9 | 21.2 | 17.2 | 21.2 | 15.9 | 14.5 | 15.3 | 16.2 | 10.7 |
| 2021 | 9.2 | 11.9 | 13.2 | 12.8 | 12.4 | 19.3 | 14.0 | 14.2 | 13.7 | 17.2 | 16.3 | 11.5 |
| 2022[1] | 10.9 | 13.7 | 15.4 | 10.6 | 12.0 | 11.7 | 13.1 | 13.1 | 15.5 | 19.2 | 21.5 | 25.8 |

[1] Preliminary.    [2] As reported; no estimates are made for nonrespondents.    Source: U.S. Geological Survey (USGS)

### Stocks of Refined Copper at Brass Mills[2] in the United States, at End of Month    In Thousands of Metric Tons

| Year | Jan. | Feb. | Mar. | Apr. | May | June | July | Aug. | Sept. | Oct. | Nov. | Dec. |
|---|---|---|---|---|---|---|---|---|---|---|---|---|
| 2013 | 6.4 | 6.5 | 6.1 | 6.3 | 7.2 | 7.2 | 8.2 | 6.7 | 6.8 | 5.2 | 6.7 | 6.7 |
| 2014 | 6.3 | 5.9 | 6.1 | 6.5 | 8.3 | 6.7 | 6.0 | 6.3 | 6.2 | 6.7 | 6.0 | 6.4 |
| 2015 | 6.3 | 6.6 | 7.3 | 6.9 | 7.6 | 7.8 | 7.6 | 7.6 | 7.3 | 7.7 | 7.4 | 7.6 |
| 2016 | 8.3 | 7.8 | 7.5 | 8.0 | 8.7 | 7.7 | 7.9 | 7.9 | 7.7 | 7.3 | 7.1 | 7.4 |
| 2017 | 7.4 | 7.3 | 7.1 | 8.0 | 7.4 | 7.4 | 7.9 | 7.7 | 7.4 | 7.7 | 8.2 | 7.9 |
| 2018 | 8.0 | 7.9 | 8.0 | 7.9 | 8.2 | 8.0 | 8.2 | 7.9 | 7.7 | 7.5 | 7.7 | 8.2 |
| 2019 | 8.4 | 8.3 | 8.4 | 8.4 | 7.3 | 7.1 | 7.1 | 6.9 | 6.8 | 6.7 | 6.6 | 7.5 |
| 2020 | 7.3 | 7.3 | 7.3 | 7.2 | 7.7 | 7.9 | 7.8 | 8.2 | 8.2 | 8.2 | 8.1 | 7.9 |
| 2021 | 8.0 | 8.6 | 8.6 | 7.6 | 7.9 | 8.0 | 8.2 | 8.3 | 8.7 | 8.6 | 9.1 | 9.1 |
| 2022[1] | 9.5 | 9.9 | 8.2 | 8.6 | 8.3 | 8.3 | 8.6 | 9.0 | 9.8 | 10.4 | 10.8 | 11.0 |

[1] Preliminary.    [2] As reported; no estimates are made for nonrespondents.    Source: U.S. Geological Survey (USGS)

### Total Stocks of Refined Copper in the United States, at End of Month    In Thousands of Metric Tons

| Year | Jan. | Feb. | Mar. | Apr. | May | June | July | Aug. | Sept. | Oct. | Nov. | Dec. |
|---|---|---|---|---|---|---|---|---|---|---|---|---|
| 2013 | 261.0 | 275.0 | 308.0 | 325.0 | 318.0 | 314.0 | 306.0 | 292.0 | 273.0 | 260.0 | 250.0 | 258.0 |
| 2014 | 246.0 | 239.0 | 258.0 | 246.0 | 222.0 | 201.0 | 198.0 | 202.0 | 215.0 | 210.0 | 193.0 | 189.0 |
| 2015 | 182.0 | 186.0 | 195.0 | 197.0 | 178.0 | 171.0 | 166.0 | 185.0 | 187.0 | 190.0 | 198.0 | 210.0 |
| 2016 | 220.0 | 215.0 | 187.0 | 172.0 | 163.0 | 134.0 | 149.0 | 152.0 | 177.0 | 192.0 | 210.0 | 223.0 |
| 2017 | 241.0 | 242.0 | 248.0 | 243.0 | 218.0 | 219.0 | 222.0 | 246.0 | 256.0 | 268.0 | 266.0 | 265.0 |
| 2018 | 286.0 | 283.0 | 297.0 | 315.0 | 323.0 | 344.0 | 357.0 | 347.0 | 316.0 | 283.0 | 258.0 | 243.0 |
| 2019 | 229.0 | 191.0 | 135.0 | 128.0 | 117.0 | 107.0 | 117.0 | 118.0 | 120.0 | 117.0 | 121.0 | 111.0 |
| 2020 | 93.3 | 107.0 | 114.0 | 120.0 | 139.0 | 158.0 | 165.0 | 153.0 | 159.0 | 140.0 | 130.0 | 118.0 |
| 2021 | 111.0 | 109.0 | 109.0 | 101.0 | 86.6 | 83.5 | 76.2 | 79.5 | 86.0 | 91.5 | 105.0 | 117.0 |
| 2022[1] | 133.0 | 131.0 | 133.0 | 134.0 | 127.0 | 125.0 | 126.0 | 117.0 | 115.0 | 107.0 | 95.8 | 91.3 |

[1] Preliminary.    Source: U.S. Geological Survey (USGS)

# COPPER

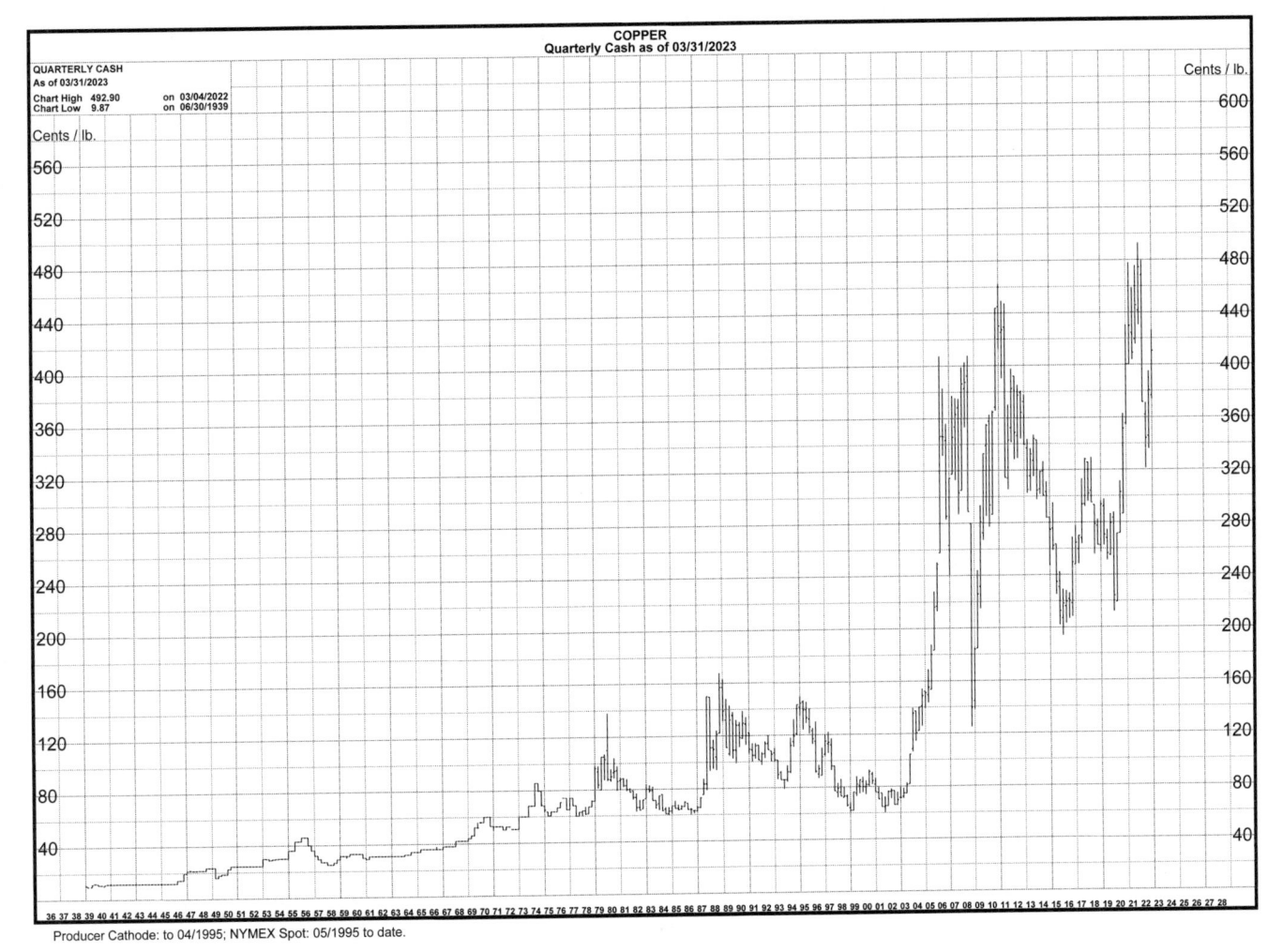

**COPPER**
Quarterly Cash as of 03/31/2023

QUARTERLY CASH
As of 03/31/2023
Chart High 492.90 on 03/04/2022
Chart Low 9.87 on 06/30/1939

Producer Cathode: to 04/1995; NYMEX Spot: 05/1995 to date.

## Producers' Price of Electrolytic (Wirebar) Copper, Delivered to U.S. Destinations — In Cents Per Pound

| Year | Jan. | Feb. | Mar. | Apr. | May | June | July | Aug. | Sept. | Oct. | Nov. | Dec. | Average |
|---|---|---|---|---|---|---|---|---|---|---|---|---|---|
| 2013 | 372.47 | 371.83 | 351.31 | 332.72 | 337.45 | 325.95 | 321.50 | 335.18 | 334.13 | 334.93 | 328.07 | 339.43 | 340.41 |
| 2014 | 342.10 | 334.93 | 315.05 | 313.99 | 320.45 | 317.04 | 329.34 | 322.01 | 315.28 | 309.62 | 308.64 | 296.45 | 318.74 |
| 2015 | 271.73 | 268.95 | 268.95 | 277.04 | 281.50 | 295.59 | 273.57 | 254.27 | 239.79 | 243.31 | 243.04 | 222.34 | 214.01 | 257.10 |
| 2015 | 271.73 | 268.95 | 277.04 | 281.50 | 295.59 | 273.57 | 254.27 | 239.79 | 243.31 | 243.04 | 222.34 | 214.01 | 257.10 |
| 2016 | 206.43 | 213.16 | 228.88 | 224.08 | 217.34 | 216.02 | 226.98 | 220.02 | 219.50 | 219.55 | 251.14 | 262.05 | 225.43 |
| 2017 | 267.08 | 274.55 | 269.56 | 264.04 | 260.33 | 265.44 | 278.13 | 301.13 | 303.66 | 314.81 | 314.38 | 315.32 | 285.70 |
| 2018 | 324.91 | 322.49 | 312.22 | 314.51 | 312.31 | 318.18 | 286.26 | 276.64 | 276.71 | 283.18 | 282.25 | 279.59 | 299.10 |
| 2019 | 275.49 | 292.82 | 297.25 | 299.38 | 281.88 | 275.57 | 276.24 | 264.69 | 267.12 | 268.29 | 272.78 | 284.49 | 279.67 |
| 2020 | 282.85 | 266.00 | 243.96 | 237.63 | 245.55 | 266.32 | 293.10 | 298.73 | 309.80 | 313.31 | 326.70 | 360.80 | 287.06 |
| 2021 | 369.82 | 393.69 | 416.35 | 432.58 | 47.62 | 448.00 | 443.73 | 437.72 | 435.04 | 453.61 | 445.52 | 441.72 | 397.12 |
| 2022 | 452.50 | 459.21 | 477.43 | 474.26 | 435.55 | 424.11 | 351.49 | 373.18 | 359.52 | 358.77 | 378.94 | 392.65 | 411.47 |

*Source: American Metal Market (AMM)*

## Dealers' Buying Price of No. 2 Heavy Copper Scrap in Chicago — In Cents Per Pound

| Year | Jan. | Feb. | Mar. | Apr. | May | June | July | Aug. | Sept. | Oct. | Nov. | Dec. | Average |
|---|---|---|---|---|---|---|---|---|---|---|---|---|---|
| 2011 | 285.00 | 292.50 | 299.13 | 295.00 | 290.72 | 295.23 | 315.00 | 311.41 | 293.69 | 241.55 | 261.50 | 256.97 | 286.48 |
| 2012 | 262.50 | 287.75 | 292.50 | 283.93 | 280.00 | 259.64 | 262.50 | 262.50 | 275.39 | 282.50 | 270.25 | 281.39 | 275.07 |
| 2013 | 287.74 | 292.24 | 287.02 | 272.50 | 263.18 | 269.00 | 255.23 | 260.55 | 265.00 | 274.63 | 272.76 | 277.76 | 273.13 |
| 2014 | 287.02 | 277.50 | 266.55 | 262.73 | 270.36 | 269.07 | 270.64 | 268.26 | 262.64 | 257.24 | 255.50 | 240.31 | 265.65 |
| 2015 | 220.60 | 205.08 | 215.50 | 218.86 | 232.50 | 219.77 | 212.86 | 195.79 | 195.12 | 193.91 | 184.97 | 165.64 | 205.05 |
| 2016 | 160.61 | 158.50 | 168.02 | 169.50 | 170.26 | 166.27 | 173.15 | 172.20 | 169.21 | 170.40 | 182.00 | 198.45 | 171.55 |
| 2017 | 194.80 | 202.97 | 199.67 | 195.50 | 193.23 | 191.95 | 195.50 | 205.93 | 213.85 | 218.95 | 222.00 | 220.00 | 204.53 |
| 2018 | 229.79 | 231.50 | 227.50 | 223.02 | 222.59 | 228.17 | 212.93 | 201.80 | 192.45 | 201.50 | 199.00 | 201.50 | 214.31 |
| 2019 | 196.50 | 205.87 | 214.50 | 218.50 | 210.32 | 195.00 | 193.32 | 188.68 | 177.50 | 177.50 | 179.50 | 179.12 | 194.69 |
| 2020 | ---- | ---- | ---- | ---- | ---- | ---- | ---- | ---- | ---- | ---- | ---- | ---- | ---- |

*Source: American Metal Market (AMM)*

# COPPER

**COPPER, HIGH GRADE - COMEX**
Weekly Selected Futures as of 03/31/2023

WEEKLY SELECTED FUTURES
As of 03/31/2023
Chart High 501.00 on 03/07/2022
Chart Low 193.55 on 01/19/2016

Nearby Futures through Last Trading Day using selected contract months: March, May, July, September and December.

## Volume of Trading of Copper Futures in Chicago    In Thousands of Contracts

| Year | Jan. | Feb. | Mar. | Apr. | May | June | July | Aug. | Sept. | Oct. | Nov. | Dec. | Total |
|------|------|------|------|------|------|------|------|------|------|------|------|------|-------|
| 2013 | 1,163.8 | 1,547.7 | 1,199.1 | 2,262.6 | 1,646.6 | 1,760.9 | 1,307.1 | 1,696.7 | 913.6 | 1,265.4 | 1,443.0 | 920.9 | 17,127.4 |
| 2014 | 1,049.9 | 1,236.2 | 1,401.8 | 1,422.9 | 933.0 | 1,434.3 | 1,081.3 | 1,276.8 | 1,089.7 | 1,269.0 | 1,459.4 | 927.7 | 14,582.2 |
| 2015 | 1,376.3 | 1,513.4 | 1,327.0 | 1,570.8 | 1,078.6 | 1,638.6 | 1,410.3 | 1,753.1 | 1,197.7 | 1,227.4 | 1,843.6 | 1,049.2 | 16,986.1 |
| 2016 | 1,324.0 | 1,754.8 | 1,611.4 | 2,018.8 | 1,522.9 | 2,148.7 | 1,510.2 | 1,876.0 | 1,294.0 | 1,498.6 | 3,531.3 | 1,433.8 | 21,524.5 |
| 2017 | 1,697.3 | 2,348.1 | 1,823.1 | 2,266.8 | 1,867.4 | 2,297.6 | 1,740.5 | 2,945.0 | 2,309.5 | 2,410.7 | 2,992.4 | 2,353.2 | 27,051.5 |
| 2018 | 2,761.2 | 3,000.6 | 2,510.6 | 3,091.0 | 2,562.9 | 3,619.8 | 2,833.2 | 3,402.4 | 2,349.7 | 2,625.9 | 2,546.7 | 1,406.1 | 32,710.1 |
| 2019 | 2,015.9 | 2,441.6 | 1,748.1 | 2,243.5 | 2,082.2 | 2,257.1 | 1,875.7 | 2,397.1 | 1,491.4 | 1,674.0 | 2,116.7 | 1,665.7 | 24,008.9 |
| 2020 | 2,072.0 | 2,823.8 | 2,324.8 | 1,761.1 | 1,252.2 | 2,228.5 | 1,944.9 | 2,322.5 | 1,984.5 | 1,837.2 | 2,214.5 | 1,551.7 | 24,317.8 |
| 2021 | 1,846.8 | 2,943.2 | 2,332.5 | 2,419.1 | 2,192.6 | 2,583.1 | 1,822.8 | 2,108.9 | 1,409.3 | 1,786.1 | 1,977.8 | 1,162.3 | 24,584.5 |
| 2022 | 1,678.1 | 2,021.7 | 1,610.7 | 1,731.5 | 1,354.8 | 2,021.0 | 1,658.9 | 2,117.6 | 1,735.8 | 1,820.5 | 2,498.1 | 1,285.3 | 21,534.1 |

*Source: CME Group; Commodity Exchange (COMEX)*

## Average Open Interest of Copper Futures in Chicago    In Contracts

| Year | Jan. | Feb. | Mar. | Apr. | May | June | July | Aug. | Sept. | Oct. | Nov. | Dec. |
|------|------|------|------|------|------|------|------|------|------|------|------|------|
| 2013 | 160,188 | 174,428 | 166,007 | 179,530 | 162,279 | 180,744 | 165,350 | 160,513 | 149,129 | 150,400 | 162,528 | 160,424 |
| 2014 | 160,638 | 155,280 | 153,880 | 153,104 | 148,544 | 148,751 | 171,388 | 153,255 | 146,669 | 170,902 | 167,274 | 155,661 |
| 2015 | 175,389 | 178,359 | 165,403 | 163,159 | 173,340 | 174,453 | 165,716 | 180,019 | 153,941 | 160,277 | 181,603 | 175,301 |
| 2016 | 192,827 | 185,631 | 174,735 | 192,037 | 197,457 | 211,980 | 174,617 | 187,041 | 193,526 | 198,811 | 230,065 | 233,247 |
| 2017 | 253,784 | 288,886 | 266,753 | 273,442 | 249,694 | 258,588 | 280,781 | 328,948 | 300,294 | 297,370 | 283,754 | 254,501 |
| 2018 | 287,421 | 266,506 | 275,877 | 253,876 | 256,236 | 273,982 | 294,730 | 270,229 | 234,947 | 241,389 | 235,321 | 214,508 |
| 2019 | 259,860 | 249,458 | 255,711 | 252,487 | 260,544 | 273,779 | 263,606 | 283,002 | 239,479 | 252,253 | 230,046 | 244,905 |
| 2020 | 269,401 | 265,190 | 211,541 | 182,166 | 169,597 | 186,131 | 220,836 | 229,403 | 240,197 | 238,695 | 231,769 | 245,818 |
| 2021 | 255,134 | 264,271 | 239,741 | 247,277 | 246,376 | 220,526 | 203,022 | 202,183 | 188,780 | 208,237 | 205,020 | 175,321 |
| 2022 | 198,849 | 205,541 | 197,709 | 203,487 | 186,330 | 188,062 | 178,699 | 178,405 | 164,430 | 173,241 | 165,627 | 158,649 |

*Source: CME Group; Commodity Exchange (COMEX)*

# Corn

Corn is a member of the grass family of plants and is a native grain of the American continents. Fossils of corn pollen that are over 80,000 years old have been found in lake sediment under Mexico City. Archaeological discoveries show that cultivated corn existed in the southwestern U.S. for at least 3,000 years, indicating that the indigenous people of the region cultivated corn as a food crop long before the Europeans reached the New World. Corn is a hardy plant that grows in many different areas of the world. It can grow at altitudes as low as sea level and as high as 12,000 feet in the South American Andes Mountains. Corn can also grow in tropical climates that receive up to 400 inches of rainfall per year, or in areas that receive only 12 inches of rainfall per year. Corn is used primarily as livestock feed in the United States and the rest of the world. Other uses for corn are alcohol additives for gasoline, adhesives, corn oil for cooking and margarine, sweeteners, and as food for humans. Corn is the largest crop in the U.S., both in terms of dollar value and the number of acres planted.

The largest futures market for corn is at the CME Group. Corn futures also trade at the B3 exchange, the Dalian Commodity Exchange, the Euronext Derivatives Market, the JSE Securities Exchange, the MATba ROFEX exchange, and the Osaka Exchange. The CME futures contract calls for the delivery of 5000 bushels of No. 2 yellow corn at par contract price, No. 1 yellow at 1-1/2 cents per bushel over the contract price, or No. 3 yellow at 1-1/2 cents per bushel below the contract price.

**Prices** – CME corn futures prices (Barchart.com symbol code ZC) trended higher into Q2 of 2022 and posted a 10-year high in April of $8.2700 per bushel. Russia's invasion of Ukraine roiled grain markets and sparked global supply concerns as the conflict snarled grain shipments out of the Black Sea region. Russia and Ukraine supply about a fifth of the world's corn sales. Also, sanctions by most countries against Russian exports sent fertilizer costs soaring to all-time highs, which prompted farmers to scale back on fertilizer use, which could undercut crop yields and further restrict global corn supplies. Russia is the world's second-biggest producer of potash, a key ingredient in fertilizer. The surge in fertilizer costs also prompted U.S. farmers to cut back on their 2022 corn plantings. The USDA's prospective planting report in late March projected U.S. corn seedings at an estimated 4-year low of 89.5 million acres, down -4.2% yr/yr. Also, a cold and wet spring in the U.S. left the corn planting pace in early June at its slowest start since 2013. In addition, removing Russian and Ukraine corn supplies from the world market boosted demand for U.S. corn, pushing prices even higher. However, corn prices plummeted to a 1-year low in July of $5.6150 per bushel after the USDA, in its July WASDE report, reported larger than expected U.S. and global corn stockpiles as livestock operators scaled back their cattle and hog herds due to soaring costs, reducing demand for corn for animal feed. Also, a deal brokered by Turkey and the United Nations in July to allow Ukrainian grain shipments from Black Sea ports eased supply concerns and weighed on corn prices after Russia blockaded the country's ports following its invasion. Corn prices then rallied into September as adverse weather curbed the prospects for the U.S. corn crop. The Pro Farmers crop tour in late August cut its U.S. corn harvest estimate to 13.759 billion bushels, 4.2% less than what the USDA had forecast in its August WASDE report. Corn prices slipped into December after the dollar index rallied to a 20-year high. Also, corn supply concerns eased after Ukraine said the deal to allow it to export grains from its Black Sea ports was extended into 2023. Corn prices recovered slightly into year-end and finished 2022 up +14.4% yr/yr at $6.7850 a bushel.

**Supply** – World production of corn in the 2022/23 marketing year is forecasted to fall by -4.9% yr/yr to 1.155 billion metric tons. The world's largest corn producers are expected to be the U.S. with 30.2% of world production, China with 24.0%, and Brazil with 10.8%. The world area harvested with corn in 2021/22 fell by -0.6% yr/yr to 342.0 million hectares. World ending stocks of corn and coarse grains in 2021/22 rose by +2.8% yr/yr to 330.2 million metric tons.

U.S. corn production for the 2022/23 marketing year (Sep-Aug) is forecasted to fall by -8.9% yr/yr to 13.729 billion bushels. U.S. farmers are forecasted to harvest 79.207 million acres of corn for grain usage in 2022/23, which is down by -7.2% yr/yr. The U.S. corn yield in 2022/23 is forecasted to fall -2.1% yr/yr to 173.3 bushels per acre. U.S. 2021/22 ending stocks increased +11.5% yr/yr to 1.241 billion bushels. The largest corn-producing states in the U.S. in 2022 were Iowa with 18.3% of U.S. production, Illinois with 16.5%, Nebraska with 11.4%, Minnesota with 10.5%, and Indiana with 7.0%.

**Demand** – World consumption of course grains in the 2021/22 crop year rose by +2.8% yr/yr to a record high of 1.492 billion metric tons. The largest category of usage in 2021/22, aside from animal feed, was for ethanol production (alcohol fuel) with 5.326 billion bushels, which is 78.7% of total non-feed usage. That was up by +5.9% yr/yr. After ethanol, the largest non-feed usage categories are high fructose corn syrup (HFCS) with 6.2% of U.S. usage, glucose and dextrose sugars with 5.5%, corn starch with 3.6%, cereal and other corn products with 3.2%, and alcoholic beverages with 2.4%.

**Trade** – U.S. exports of corn in 2022/23 are expected to fall by -22.1% yr/yr to 48.897 million metric tons. Brazil's corn exports in 2022/23 are expected to rise by +1.1% yr/yr to 47.000 million metric tons. Argentina's corn exports are expected to rise +7.0% yr/yr to 38.000 million metric tons.

# CORN

### World Production of Corn or Maize   In Thousands of Metric Tons

| Crop Year Beginning Oct. 1 | Argentina | Brazil | Canada | China | European Union | India | Indonesia | Mexico | Russia | South Africa | Ukraine | United States | World Total |
|---|---|---|---|---|---|---|---|---|---|---|---|---|---|
| 2013-14 | 26,000 | 80,000 | 14,191 | 248,453 | 64,931 | 24,259 | 9,100 | 22,880 | 11,635 | 14,925 | 30,900 | 351,316 | 1,027,319 |
| 2014-15 | 29,750 | 85,000 | 11,606 | 249,764 | 75,734 | 24,173 | 9,000 | 25,480 | 11,325 | 10,629 | 28,450 | 361,136 | 1,058,208 |
| 2015-16 | 29,500 | 67,000 | 13,680 | 264,992 | 58,748 | 22,567 | 10,500 | 25,971 | 13,168 | 8,214 | 23,333 | 345,506 | 1,014,663 |
| 2016-17 | 41,000 | 98,500 | 13,889 | 263,613 | 61,909 | 25,900 | 10,900 | 27,575 | 15,305 | 17,551 | 27,969 | 384,778 | 1,128,218 |
| 2017-18 | 32,000 | 82,000 | 14,096 | 259,071 | 62,021 | 28,753 | 11,900 | 27,569 | 13,201 | 13,104 | 24,115 | 371,096 | 1,081,503 |
| 2018-19 | 51,000 | 101,000 | 13,885 | 257,174 | 64,351 | 27,715 | 12,000 | 27,671 | 11,415 | 11,824 | 35,805 | 364,262 | 1,128,682 |
| 2019-20 | 51,000 | 102,000 | 13,404 | 260,779 | 66,742 | 28,766 | 12,000 | 26,658 | 14,275 | 15,844 | 35,887 | 345,962 | 1,123,144 |
| 2020-21[1] | 52,000 | 87,000 | 13,563 | 260,670 | 67,440 | 31,647 | 12,600 | 27,346 | 13,872 | 16,951 | 30,297 | 358,447 | 1,129,203 |
| 2021-22[2] | 49,500 | 116,000 | 13,984 | 272,552 | 70,979 | 33,600 | 12,700 | 26,762 | 15,225 | 16,100 | 42,126 | 382,893 | 1,214,875 |
| 2022-23[3] | 52,000 | 125,000 | 14,539 | 277,200 | 54,200 | 32,000 | 12,900 | 27,600 | 14,000 | 16,700 | 27,000 | 348,751 | 1,155,934 |

[1] Preliminary.   [2] Estimate.   [3] Forecast.   Source: Foreign Agricultural Service, U.S. Department of Agriculture (FAS-USDA)

### World Supply and Demand of Coarse Grains   In Millions of Metric Tons/Hectares

| Crop Year Beginning Oct. 1 | Area Harvested | Yield | Production | World Trade | Total Consumption | Ending Stocks | Stocks as % of Consumption[3] |
|---|---|---|---|---|---|---|---|
| 2013-14 | 331.0 | 4.00 | 1,314.1 | 165.3 | 1,238.6 | 251.1 | 20.3 |
| 2014-15 | 332.8 | 4.00 | 1,346.9 | 174.3 | 1,282.0 | 316.0 | 24.6 |
| 2015-16 | 325.7 | 4.00 | 1,303.4 | 185.8 | 1,270.9 | 348.5 | 27.4 |
| 2016-17 | 338.8 | 4.20 | 1,419.8 | 184.8 | 1,381.5 | 386.8 | 28.0 |
| 2017-18 | 329.8 | 4.10 | 1,362.3 | 191.7 | 1,376.2 | 372.9 | 27.1 |
| 2018-19 | 331.6 | 4.20 | 1,402.9 | 207.0 | 1,423.8 | 352.0 | 24.7 |
| 2019-20 | 335.4 | 4.20 | 1,420.0 | 214.8 | 1,434.7 | 337.3 | 23.5 |
| 2020-21[1] | 344.5 | 4.20 | 1,441.3 | 235.1 | 1,455.7 | 322.9 | 22.2 |
| 2021-22[2] | 346.0 | 4.30 | 1,502.4 | 237.3 | 1,492.4 | 332.9 | 22.3 |
| 2022-23[3] | 337.5 | 4.30 | 1,439.6 | 219.8 | 1,450.1 | 322.4 | 22.2 |

[1] Preliminary.   [2] Estimate.   [3] Represents the ratio of marketing year ending stocks to total consumption.   Source: Foreign Agricultural Service, U.S. Department of Agriculture (FAS-USDA)

### Acreage and Supply of Corn in the United States   In Millions of Bushels

| Crop Year Beginning Sept. 1 | Planted (Thousands of Acres) | Harvested For Grain (Thousands of Acres) | Harvested For Silage (Thousands of Acres) | Yield Per Harvested Acre Bushels | Carry-over Sept. 1 On Farms | Carry-over Sept. 1 Off Farms | Supply Beginning Stocks | Supply Production | Supply Imports | Total Supply |
|---|---|---|---|---|---|---|---|---|---|---|
| 2013-14 | 95,365 | 87,451 | 6,281 | 158.1 | 275 | 546 | 821 | 13,829 | 36 | 14,686 |
| 2014-15 | 90,597 | 83,136 | 6,371 | 171.0 | 462 | 770 | 1,232 | 14,216 | 32 | 15,479 |
| 2015-16 | 88,019 | 80,753 | 6,237 | 168.4 | 593 | 1,138 | 1,731 | 13,602 | 68 | 15,401 |
| 2016-17 | 94,004 | 86,748 | 6,186 | 174.6 | 627 | 1,110 | 1,737 | 15,148 | 57 | 16,942 |
| 2017-18 | 90,167 | 82,733 | 6,434 | 176.6 | 787 | 1,506 | 2,293 | 14,609 | 36 | 16,939 |
| 2018-19 | 88,871 | 81,276 | 5,061 | 176.4 | 620 | 1,520 | 2,140 | 14,340 | 28 | 16,509 |
| 2019-20 | 89,745 | 81,337 | 6,615 | 167.5 | 814 | 1,407 | 2,221 | 13,620 | 42 | 15,883 |
| 2020-21[1] | 90,652 | 82,313 | 6,711 | 171.4 | 751 | 1,169 | 1,919 | 14,111 | 24 | 16,055 |
| 2021-22[2] | 93,357 | 85,388 | 6,481 | 177.0 | 395 | 840 | 1,235 | 15,074 | 24 | 16,333 |
| 2022-23[3] | 88,579 | 79,207 | 6,860 | 173.3 | 510 | 867 | 1,377 | 13,730 | 50 | 15,157 |

[1] Preliminary.   [2] Estimate.   Source: Economic Research Service, U.S. Department of Agriculture (ERS-USDA)

### Production of Corn (For Grain) in the United States, by State   In Millions of Bushels

| Year | Illinois | Indiana | Iowa | Kansas | Michigan | Minnesota | Missouri | Nebraska | Ohio | South Dakota | Texas | Wisconsin | US Total |
|---|---|---|---|---|---|---|---|---|---|---|---|---|---|
| 2013 | 2,100.4 | 1,031.9 | 2,140.2 | 504.0 | 345.7 | 1,294.3 | 435.2 | 1,614.0 | 649.0 | 802.8 | 265.2 | 439.4 | 13,829.0 |
| 2014 | 2,350.0 | 1,084.8 | 2,367.4 | 566.2 | 355.8 | 1,177.8 | 628.7 | 1,602.1 | 610.7 | 787.4 | 294.5 | 485.2 | 14,215.5 |
| 2015 | 2,012.5 | 822.0 | 2,505.6 | 580.2 | 335.3 | 1,428.8 | 437.4 | 1,692.8 | 498.8 | 799.8 | 266.0 | 492.0 | 13,602.0 |
| 2016 | 2,255.7 | 946.3 | 2,740.5 | 698.6 | 320.3 | 1,544.0 | 570.5 | 1,699.9 | 524.7 | 825.9 | 323.9 | 573.2 | 15,148.0 |
| 2017 | 2,201.0 | 936.0 | 2,605.8 | 686.4 | 300.5 | 1,480.2 | 552.5 | 1,683.3 | 557.6 | 736.6 | 313.6 | 509.8 | 14,609.4 |
| 2018 | 2,268.0 | 967.7 | 2,499.0 | 642.4 | 289.2 | 1,357.7 | 466.2 | 1,785.6 | 617.1 | 777.6 | 189.0 | 545.2 | 14,340.4 |
| 2019 | 1,846.2 | 814.6 | 2,583.9 | 800.7 | 236.7 | 1,254.3 | 463.5 | 1,785.4 | 421.5 | 557.3 | 286.0 | 443.2 | 13,619.9 |
| 2020 | 2,120.1 | 981.8 | 2,283.3 | 766.5 | 304.5 | 1,434.4 | 560.9 | 1,780.2 | 564.3 | 720.9 | 231.7 | 506.9 | 14,111.4 |
| 2021 | 2,191.7 | 1,027.7 | 2,539.8 | 750.6 | 346.3 | 1,387.7 | 545.4 | 1,854.6 | 644.6 | 734.3 | 236.8 | 540.0 | 15,073.8 |
| 2022[1] | 2,268.3 | 964.6 | 2,514.9 | 592.3 | 323.1 | 1,442.1 | 492.8 | 1,562.4 | 580.3 | 656.3 | 167.3 | 536.9 | 13,729.7 |

[1] Preliminary.   Source: National Agricultural Statistics Service, U.S. Department of Agriculture (NASS-USDA)

# CORN

## Quarterly Supply and Disappearance of Corn in the United States    In Millions of Bushels

| Crop Year Beginning Sept. 1 | Beginning Stocks | Production | Imports | Total Supply | Food & Alcohol | Seed | Feed & Residual | Total | Exports | Total Disappearance | Total Ending Stocks |
|---|---|---|---|---|---|---|---|---|---|---|---|
| 2018-19 | 2,140 | 14,340 | 28.0 | 16,509 | 6,764 | 29.1 | 5,427 | 12,220 | 2,068 | 14,288 | 2,220.7 |
| Sept.-Nov. | 2,140 | 14,340 | 6.2 | 16,487 | 1,710 | ---- | 2,208 | 3,918 | 632 | 4,550 | 11,936.8 |
| Dec.-Feb. | 11,937 | ---- | 8.7 | 11,946 | 1,642 | ---- | 1,191 | 2,833 | 500 | 3,332 | 8,613.2 |
| Mar.-May | 8,613 | ---- | 6.4 | 8,620 | 1,694 | 18.6 | 1,118 | 2,831 | 586 | 3,417 | 5,202.2 |
| June-Aug. | 5,202 | ---- | 6.7 | 5,209 | 1,718 | 10.5 | 910 | 2,638 | 350 | 2,988 | 2,220.7 |
| 2019-20 | 2,221 | 13,620 | 41.9 | 15,883 | 6,256 | 29.8 | 5,900 | 12,186 | 1,777 | 13,963 | 1,919.5 |
| Sept.-Nov. | 2,221 | 13,620 | 17.9 | 15,859 | 1,628 | ---- | 2,632 | 4,260 | 271 | 4,531 | 11,327.3 |
| Dec.-Feb. | 11,327 | ---- | 8.9 | 11,336 | 1,713 | ---- | 1,318 | 3,031 | 353 | 3,385 | 7,951.6 |
| Mar.-May | 7,952 | ---- | 9.5 | 7,961 | 1,333 | 27.8 | 995 | 2,356 | 602 | 2,958 | 5,003.0 |
| June-Aug. | 5,003 | ---- | 5.6 | 5,009 | 1,582 | 2.1 | 955 | 2,539 | 550 | 3,089 | 1,919.5 |
| 2020-21 | 1,919 | 14,111 | 24.2 | 16,055 | 6,436 | 30.7 | 5,607 | 12,074 | 2,747 | 14,821 | 1,234.5 |
| Sept.-Nov. | 1,919 | 14,111 | 5.8 | 16,037 | 1,612 | | 2,682 | 4,294 | 449 | 4,743 | 11,293.8 |
| Dec.-Feb. | 11,294 | ---- | 5.4 | 11,299 | 1,509 | | 1,420 | 2,929 | 674 | 3,603 | 7,696.1 |
| Mar.-May | 7,696 | ---- | 7.1 | 7,703 | 1,645 | 29.5 | 889 | 2,563 | 1,029 | 3,592 | 4,111.2 |
| June-Aug. | 4,111 | ---- | 6.0 | 4,117 | 1,670 | 1.2 | 617 | 2,288 | 595 | 2,883 | 1,234.5 |
| 2021-22[1] | 1,235 | 15,074 | 24.2 | 16,333 | 6,737 | 29.3 | 5,718 | 12,484 | 2,471 | 14,956 | 1,376.9 |
| Sept.-Nov. | 1,235 | 15,074 | 6.7 | 16,315 | 1,689 | | 2,554 | 4,243 | 431 | 4,674 | 11,641.2 |
| Dec.-Feb. | 11,641 | ---- | 7.1 | 11,648 | 1,687 | | 1,540 | 3,228 | 662 | 3,890 | 7,758.0 |
| Mar.-May | 7,758 | ---- | 4.7 | 7,763 | 1,686 | 25.7 | 851 | 2,562 | 851 | 3,414 | 4,349.0 |
| June-Aug. | 4,349 | ---- | 5.8 | 4,355 | 1,674 | 3.5 | 773 | 2,451 | 527 | 2,978 | 1,376.9 |
| 2022-23[2] | 1,377 | 13,730 | 50.0 | 15,157 | 6,684 | 31.0 | 5,275 | 11,990 | 1,925 | 13,915 | 1,241.6 |
| Sept.-Nov. | 1,377 | 13,730 | 5.9 | 15,112 | 1,616 | | 2,405 | 4,021 | 282 | 4,303 | 10,809.4 |

[1] Preliminary.  [2] Estimate.  Source: Economic Research Service, U.S. Department of Agriculture (ERS-USDA)

## Corn Production Estimates and Cash Price in the United States

| Crop Year Beginning Sept. 1 | Aug. 1 | Sept. 1 | Oct. 1 | Nov. 1 | Final | St. Louis No. 2 Yellow | Omaha No. 2 Yellow | Gulf Ports No. 2 Yellow | Kansas City No. 2 White | Chicago No. 2 Yellow | Average Farm Price[2] | Value of Production (Mil. $) |
|---|---|---|---|---|---|---|---|---|---|---|---|---|
| | In Thousands of Bushels | | | | | Dollars Per Bushel | | | | | | |
| 2013-14 | 13,763,025 | 13,843,320 | NA | 13,988,720 | 13,828,964 | 4.91 | 4.35 | 5.16 | 4.63 | 4.47 | 4.48 | 61,928 |
| 2014-15 | 14,031,915 | 14,395,350 | 14,474,920 | 14,407,420 | 14,215,532 | 3.82 | 3.60 | 4.35 | 3.75 | 3.76 | 3.69 | 52,952 |
| 2015-16 | 13,686,063 | 13,584,945 | 13,554,923 | 13,653,507 | 13,601,964 | 3.80 | 3.49 | 4.18 | 3.75 | 3.75 | 3.61 | 49,339 |
| 2016-17 | 15,153,472 | 15,092,908 | 15,057,404 | 15,225,586 | 15,148,038 | 3.64 | 3.28 | 3.95 | 3.62 | 3.55 | 3.37 | 51,304 |
| 2017-18 | 14,152,966 | 14,184,466 | 14,280,112 | 14,577,502 | 14,609,407 | 3.63 | 3.46 | 4.07 | 3.71 | 3.55 | 3.40 | 49,568 |
| 2018-19 | 14,586,485 | 14,826,690 | 14,777,826 | 14,625,974 | 14,340,369 | 3.85 | 3.68 | 4.29 | 3.98 | 3.79 | 3.65 | 52,102 |
| 2019-20 | 13,900,651 | 13,799,151 | 13,779,335 | 13,661,005 | 13,619,928 | 3.74 | 3.26 | 3.93 | 3.65 | 3.65 | 3.52 | 48,941 |
| 2020-21 | 15,278,202 | 14,899,557 | 14,721,705 | 14,506,795 | 14,111,449 | 5.66 | 5.31 | 6.07 | 5.55 | 5.51 | 4.86 | 64,314 |
| 2021-22 | 14,750,368 | 14,996,417 | 15,018,542 | 15,062,002 | 15,073,820 | 6.84 | 6.74 | 7.62 | 7.48 | 6.78 | 6.30 | 90,616 |
| 2022-23[1] | 14,358,679 | 13,943,913 | 13,895,176 | 13,929,921 | 13,729,719 | 6.85 | 7.17 | 8.04 | 7.48 | 6.87 | 6.68 | 91,730 |

[1] Preliminary.  [2] Season-average price based on monthly prices weigthed by monthly marketings.
Source: Economic Research Service, U.S. Department of Agriculture (ERS-USDA)

## Distribution of Corn in the United States    In Millions of Bushels

| Crop Year Beginning Sept. 1 | HFCS | Glucose & Dextrose | Starch | Fuel | Beverage[3] | Seed | Cereal & Other Products | Total | Livestock Feed[4] | Exports (Including Grain Equiv. of Products) | Domestic Disappearance | Total Utilization |
|---|---|---|---|---|---|---|---|---|---|---|---|---|
| 2013-14 | 478 | 307 | 251 | 5,124 | 141 | 29.7 | 200 | 6,531 | 5,002 | 1,920.8 | 11,533 | 13,454 |
| 2014-15 | 478 | 298 | 246 | 5,200 | 142 | 29.3 | 201 | 6,595 | 5,287 | 1,866.9 | 11,883 | 13,750 |
| 2015-16 | 472 | 337 | 238 | 5,224 | 143 | 30.6 | 203 | 6,647 | 5,118 | 1,898.6 | 11,765 | 13,664 |
| 2016-17 | 467 | 371 | 235 | 5,432 | 146 | 29.3 | 204 | 6,885 | 5,470 | 2,294.0 | 12,355 | 14,649 |
| 2017-18 | 459 | 371 | 236 | 5,605 | 149 | 29.6 | 207 | 7,057 | 5,304 | 2,437.5 | 12,361 | 14,798 |
| 2018-19 | 441 | 355 | 231 | 5,378 | 150 | 29.1 | 209 | 6,793 | 5,275 | 2,060.0 | 12,080 | 14,140 |
| 2019-20 | 418 | 356 | 232 | 4,857 | 173 | 29.9 | 220 | 6,286 | 5,175 | 2,050.0 | 12,055 | 14,105 |
| 2020-21 | 421 | 365 | 252 | 5,028 | 157 | 30.7 | 214 | 6,467 | | | | |
| 2021-22[1] | 416 | 373 | 246 | 5,326 | 161 | 29.3 | 214 | 6,766 | | | | |
| 2022-23[2] | 415 | 370 | 245 | 5,275 | 162 | 31.0 | 217 | 6,715 | | | | |

[1] Preliminary.  [2] Estimate.  [3] Also includes nonfuel industrial alcohol.  [4] Feed and waste (residual, mostly feed).
Source: Economic Research Service, U.S. Department of Agriculture (ERS-USDA)

# CORN

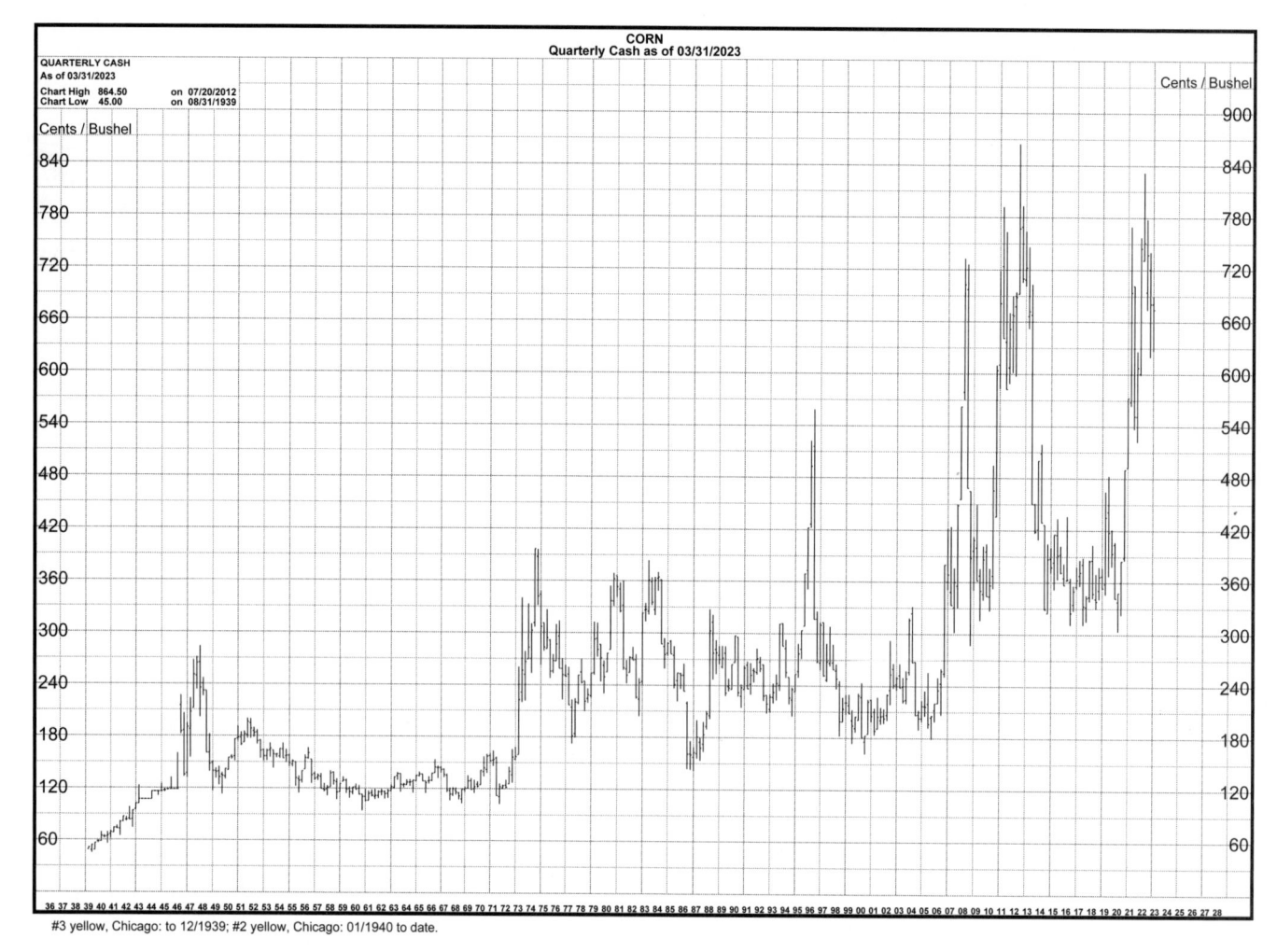

### Average Cash Price of Corn, No. 2 Yellow in Central Illinois    In Dollars Per Bushel

| Crop Year | Sept. | Oct. | Nov. | Dec. | Jan. | Feb. | Mar. | Apr. | May | June | July | Aug. | Average |
|---|---|---|---|---|---|---|---|---|---|---|---|---|---|
| 2013-14 | 4.78 | 4.20 | 4.10 | 4.13 | 4.13 | 4.33 | 4.64 | 4.98 | 4.72 | 4.37 | 3.74 | 3.59 | 4.31 |
| 2014-15 | 3.16 | 3.09 | 3.45 | 3.75 | 3.67 | 3.65 | 3.66 | 3.59 | 3.49 | 3.52 | 3.85 | 3.51 | 3.53 |
| 2015-16 | 3.55 | 3.67 | 3.62 | 3.62 | 3.55 | 3.56 | 3.54 | 3.61 | 3.74 | 3.91 | 3.28 | 3.09 | 3.56 |
| 2016-17 | 3.09 | 3.27 | 3.28 | 3.34 | 3.45 | 3.51 | 3.40 | 3.41 | 3.47 | 3.49 | 3.51 | 3.27 | 3.37 |
| 2017-18 | 3.15 | 3.15 | 3.14 | 3.21 | 3.29 | 3.45 | 3.52 | 3.54 | 3.73 | 3.38 | 3.22 | 3.24 | 3.34 |
| 2018-19 | 3.12 | 3.28 | 3.36 | 3.53 | 3.53 | 3.50 | 3.43 | 3.37 | 3.59 | 4.21 | 4.29 | 3.95 | 3.60 |
| 2019-20 | 3.55 | 3.79 | 3.66 | 3.73 | 3.82 | 3.75 | 3.51 | 3.06 | 2.99 | 3.13 | 3.21 | 3.84 | 3.50 |
| 2020-21 | 3.62 | 3.97 | 4.22 | 4.45 | 5.23 | 5.56 | 5.56 | 6.27 | 7.08 | 6.81 | 6.49 | 6.43 | 5.47 |
| 2021-22 | 5.35 | 5.37 | 5.80 | 6.03 | 6.16 | 6.54 | 7.46 | 7.93 | 8.04 | 7.95 | 7.09 | 6.87 | 6.72 |
| 2022-23[1] | 6.98 | 6.79 | 6.71 | 6.64 | 6.78 | | | | | | | | 6.78 |

[1] Preliminary.    Source: Economic Research Service, U.S. Department of Agriculture (ERS-USDA)

### Average Cash Price of Corn, No. 2 Yellow at Gulf Ports[2]    In Dollars Per Bushel

| Crop Year | Sept. | Oct. | Nov. | Dec. | Jan. | Feb. | Mar. | Apr. | May | June | July | Aug. | Average |
|---|---|---|---|---|---|---|---|---|---|---|---|---|---|
| 2013-14 | 5.27 | 5.13 | 5.06 | 5.06 | 5.03 | 5.32 | 5.65 | 5.65 | 5.51 | 5.14 | 4.64 | 4.48 | 5.16 |
| 2014-15 | 4.14 | 4.15 | 4.54 | 4.55 | 4.44 | 4.41 | 4.43 | 4.38 | 4.23 | 4.24 | 4.56 | 4.14 | 4.35 |
| 2015-16 | 4.22 | 4.36 | 4.22 | 4.17 | 4.09 | 4.06 | 4.05 | 4.17 | 4.30 | 4.62 | 4.11 | 3.82 | 4.18 |
| 2016-17 | 3.78 | 3.88 | 3.83 | 3.88 | 4.07 | 4.14 | 4.04 | 3.98 | 4.03 | 4.01 | 4.00 | 3.77 | 3.95 |
| 2017-18 | 3.74 | 3.77 | 3.78 | 3.79 | 3.96 | 4.15 | 4.36 | 4.46 | 4.55 | 4.19 | 3.98 | 4.13 | 4.07 |
| 2018-19 | 3.93 | 4.07 | 4.09 | 4.25 | 4.24 | 4.31 | 4.23 | 4.11 | 4.36 | 4.96 | 4.81 | 4.14 | 4.29 |
| 2019-20 | 4.00 | 4.25 | 4.23 | 4.24 | 4.36 | 4.29 | 4.12 | 3.73 | 2.66 | 3.76 | 3.88 | 3.65 | 3.93 |
| 2020-21 | 4.23 | 4.74 | 4.85 | 5.06 | 5.89 | 6.24 | 6.24 | 6.82 | 7.73 | 7.43 | 7.07 | 6.53 | 6.07 |
| 2021-22 | ---- | 6.09 | 6.32 | 6.72 | 7.04 | 7.44 | 8.54 | 8.85 | 8.76 | 8.53 | 8.20 | 7.36 | 7.62 |
| 2022-23[1] | 7.94 | 8.73 | 8.15 | 7.68 | 7.69 | | | | | | | | 8.04 |

[1] Preliminary.    [2] Barge delivered to Louisiana Gulf.    Source: Economic Research Service, U.S. Department of Agriculture (ERS-USDA)

# CORN

## Weekly Outstanding Export Sales and Cumulative Exports of U.S. Corn   In Thousands of Metric Tons

| Marketing Year 2021/2022 Week Ending | Weekly Exports | Accumulated Exports | Net Sales | Outstanding Sales | Marketing Year 2022/2023 Week Ending | Weekly Exports | Accumulated Exports | Net Sales | Outstanding Sales |
|---|---|---|---|---|---|---|---|---|---|
| Sep 02, 2021 | 167,908 | 167,908 | 3,883,880 | 24,158,207 | Sep 01, 2022 | 36,819 | 36,819 | 1,853,836 | 11,681,340 |
| Sep 09, 2021 | 192,003 | 359,911 | 246,583 | 24,212,787 | Sep 08, 2022 | 426,802 | 463,621 | 583,110 | 11,837,648 |
| Sep 16, 2021 | 485,813 | 845,724 | 373,007 | 24,099,981 | Sep 15, 2022 | 563,029 | 1,026,650 | 182,339 | 11,456,958 |
| Sep 23, 2021 | 676,247 | 1,521,971 | 370,388 | 23,794,122 | Sep 22, 2022 | 574,680 | 1,601,330 | 512,045 | 11,394,323 |
| Sep 30, 2021 | 974,642 | 2,496,613 | 1,265,083 | 24,084,563 | Sep 29, 2022 | 645,508 | 2,246,838 | 227,045 | 10,975,860 |
| Oct 07, 2021 | 918,143 | 3,414,756 | 1,039,883 | 24,206,303 | Oct 06, 2022 | 419,590 | 2,666,428 | 197,191 | 10,753,461 |
| Oct 14, 2021 | 1,041,681 | 4,456,437 | 1,273,146 | 24,437,768 | Oct 13, 2022 | 407,161 | 3,073,589 | 408,310 | 10,754,610 |
| Oct 21, 2021 | 688,505 | 5,144,942 | 890,448 | 24,639,711 | Oct 20, 2022 | 618,958 | 3,692,547 | 263,999 | 10,399,651 |
| Oct 28, 2021 | 748,531 | 5,893,473 | 1,223,772 | 25,114,952 | Oct 27, 2022 | 450,158 | 4,142,705 | 372,220 | 10,321,713 |
| Nov 04, 2021 | 718,018 | 6,611,491 | 1,067,299 | 25,464,233 | Nov 03, 2022 | 259,441 | 4,402,146 | 265,335 | 10,327,607 |
| Nov 11, 2021 | 1,167,734 | 7,779,225 | 904,565 | 25,201,064 | Nov 10, 2022 | 564,394 | 4,966,540 | 1,169,693 | 10,932,906 |
| Nov 18, 2021 | 929,019 | 8,708,244 | 1,429,161 | 25,701,206 | Nov 17, 2022 | 462,286 | 5,428,826 | 1,850,271 | 12,320,891 |
| Nov 25, 2021 | 938,435 | 9,646,679 | 1,020,816 | 25,783,587 | Nov 24, 2022 | 344,485 | 5,773,311 | 602,656 | 12,579,062 |
| Dec 02, 2021 | 904,632 | 10,551,311 | 1,132,460 | 26,011,415 | Dec 01, 2022 | 900,068 | 6,673,379 | 691,556 | 12,370,550 |
| Dec 09, 2021 | 1,093,543 | 11,644,854 | 1,948,742 | 26,866,614 | Dec 08, 2022 | 590,514 | 7,263,893 | 958,920 | 12,738,956 |
| Dec 16, 2021 | 1,101,432 | 12,746,286 | 982,870 | 26,748,052 | Dec 15, 2022 | 958,747 | 8,222,640 | 636,811 | 12,417,020 |
| Dec 23, 2021 | 921,417 | 13,667,703 | 1,246,453 | 27,073,088 | Dec 22, 2022 | 1,012,459 | 9,235,099 | 781,583 | 12,186,144 |
| Dec 30, 2021 | 985,066 | 14,652,769 | 256,084 | 26,344,106 | Dec 29, 2022 | 761,797 | 9,996,896 | 319,242 | 11,743,589 |
| Jan 06, 2022 | 1,011,806 | 15,664,575 | 457,675 | 25,789,975 | Jan 05, 2023 | 387,077 | 10,383,973 | 255,687 | 11,612,199 |
| Jan 13, 2022 | 1,297,657 | 16,962,232 | 1,091,257 | 25,583,575 | Jan 12, 2023 | 715,740 | 11,099,713 | 1,132,142 | 12,028,601 |
| Jan 20, 2022 | 1,436,867 | 18,399,099 | 1,402,309 | 25,549,017 | Jan 19, 2023 | 912,584 | 12,012,297 | 910,400 | 12,026,417 |
| Jan 27, 2022 | 1,166,611 | 19,565,710 | 1,175,186 | 25,557,592 | Jan 26, 2023 | 598,291 | 12,610,588 | 1,593,223 | 13,021,349 |
| Feb 03, 2022 | 1,149,390 | 20,715,100 | 589,080 | 24,997,282 | Feb 02, 2023 | 394,890 | 13,005,478 | 1,160,280 | 13,786,739 |
| Feb 10, 2022 | 1,617,553 | 22,332,653 | 820,041 | 24,199,770 | Feb 09, 2023 | 670,541 | 13,676,019 | 1,024,499 | 14,140,697 |
| Feb 17, 2022 | 1,886,226 | 24,218,879 | 1,040,946 | 23,354,490 | Feb 16, 2023 | 687,399 | 14,363,418 | 823,177 | 14,276,475 |
| Feb 24, 2022 | 1,550,805 | 25,769,684 | 485,118 | 22,288,803 | Feb 23, 2023 | 666,416 | 15,029,834 | 598,109 | 14,208,168 |
| Mar 03, 2022 | 1,763,327 | 27,533,011 | 2,143,700 | 22,669,176 | Mar 02, 2023 | | | | |
| Mar 10, 2022 | 1,273,476 | 28,806,487 | 1,836,357 | 23,232,057 | Mar 09, 2023 | | | | |
| Mar 17, 2022 | 1,491,438 | 30,297,925 | 978,775 | 22,719,394 | Mar 16, 2023 | | | | |
| Mar 24, 2022 | 1,882,409 | 32,180,334 | 636,852 | 21,473,837 | Mar 23, 2023 | | | | |
| Mar 31, 2022 | 1,632,992 | 33,813,326 | 782,434 | 20,623,279 | Mar 30, 2023 | | | | |
| Apr 07, 2022 | 1,560,206 | 35,373,532 | 1,332,871 | 20,395,944 | Apr 06, 2023 | | | | |
| Apr 14, 2022 | 1,196,423 | 36,569,955 | 879,212 | 20,078,733 | Apr 13, 2023 | | | | |
| Apr 21, 2022 | 1,562,052 | 38,132,007 | 866,755 | 19,383,436 | Apr 20, 2023 | | | | |
| Apr 28, 2022 | 1,904,846 | 40,036,853 | 782,543 | 18,261,133 | Apr 27, 2023 | | | | |
| May 05, 2022 | 1,504,276 | 41,541,129 | 192,739 | 16,949,596 | May 04, 2023 | | | | |
| May 12, 2022 | 1,358,392 | 42,899,521 | 413,633 | 16,004,837 | May 11, 2023 | | | | |
| May 19, 2022 | 1,821,104 | 44,720,625 | 151,646 | 14,335,379 | May 18, 2023 | | | | |
| May 26, 2022 | 1,579,723 | 46,300,348 | 185,760 | 12,941,416 | May 25, 2023 | | | | |
| Jun 02, 2022 | 1,381,597 | 47,681,945 | 280,416 | 11,840,235 | Jun 01, 2023 | | | | |
| Jun 09, 2022 | 1,387,083 | 49,069,028 | 140,935 | 10,594,087 | Jun 08, 2023 | | | | |
| Jun 16, 2022 | 1,147,258 | 50,216,286 | 671,919 | 10,118,748 | Jun 15, 2023 | | | | |
| Jun 23, 2022 | 1,254,725 | 51,471,011 | 88,795 | 8,952,818 | Jun 22, 2023 | | | | |
| Jun 30, 2022 | 1,027,365 | 52,498,376 | -66,577 | 7,858,876 | Jun 29, 2023 | | | | |
| Jul 07, 2022 | 916,123 | 53,414,499 | 59,027 | 7,001,780 | Jul 06, 2023 | | | | |
| Jul 14, 2022 | 1,109,081 | 54,523,580 | 33,899 | 5,926,598 | Jul 13, 2023 | | | | |
| Jul 21, 2022 | 867,932 | 55,391,512 | 150,302 | 5,208,968 | Jul 20, 2023 | | | | |
| Jul 28, 2022 | 1,021,051 | 56,412,563 | 57,914 | 4,245,831 | Jul 27, 2023 | | | | |
| Aug 04, 2022 | 705,390 | 57,117,953 | 191,813 | 3,732,254 | Aug 03, 2023 | | | | |
| Aug 11, 2022 | 622,991 | 57,740,944 | 99,321 | 3,208,584 | Aug 10, 2023 | | | | |
| Aug 18, 2022 | | 57,740,944 | | 3,208,584 | Aug 17, 2023 | | | | |
| Aug 25, 2022 | 1,007,988 | 58,748,932 | -16,380 | 2,184,216 | Aug 24, 2023 | | | | |
| Sep 01, 2022 | 1,014,782 | 59,763,714 | -131,562 | 1,037,872 | Aug 31, 2023 | | | | |

*Source: Foreign Agricultural Service, U.S. Department of Agriculture (FAS-USDA)*

# CORN

## Average Price Received by Farmers for Corn in the United States    In Dollars Per Bushel

| Crop Year | Sept. | Oct. | Nov. | Dec. | Jan. | Feb. | Mar. | Apr. | May | June | July | Aug. | Average |
|---|---|---|---|---|---|---|---|---|---|---|---|---|---|
| 2013-14 | 5.40 | 4.63 | 4.37 | 4.41 | 4.42 | 4.35 | 4.52 | 4.71 | 4.71 | 4.50 | 4.06 | 3.63 | 4.48 |
| 2014-15 | 3.49 | 3.57 | 3.60 | 3.79 | 3.82 | 3.79 | 3.81 | 3.75 | 3.64 | 3.59 | 3.80 | 3.68 | 3.69 |
| 2015-16 | 3.68 | 3.67 | 3.59 | 3.65 | 3.66 | 3.58 | 3.56 | 3.56 | 3.68 | 3.82 | 3.60 | 3.21 | 3.61 |
| 2016-17 | 3.22 | 3.29 | 3.24 | 3.32 | 3.40 | 3.44 | 3.49 | 3.43 | 3.45 | 3.43 | 3.49 | 3.27 | 3.37 |
| 2017-18 | 3.27 | 3.26 | 3.15 | 3.23 | 3.29 | 3.38 | 3.51 | 3.58 | 3.68 | 3.58 | 3.47 | 3.36 | 3.40 |
| 2018-19 | 3.40 | 3.42 | 3.41 | 3.54 | 3.56 | 3.60 | 3.61 | 3.53 | 3.63 | 3.98 | 4.16 | 3.93 | 3.65 |
| 2019-20 | 3.80 | 3.85 | 3.68 | 3.71 | 3.79 | 3.78 | 3.68 | 3.29 | 3.20 | 3.16 | 3.21 | 3.12 | 3.52 |
| 2020-21 | 3.41 | 3.61 | 3.79 | 3.97 | 4.24 | 4.75 | 4.89 | 5.31 | 5.91 | 6.00 | 6.12 | 6.32 | 4.86 |
| 2021-22 | 5.47 | 5.02 | 5.26 | 5.47 | 5.58 | 6.09 | 6.56 | 7.08 | 7.26 | 7.37 | 7.25 | 7.24 | 6.30 |
| 2022-23[1] | 7.09 | 6.50 | 6.49 | 6.58 | 6.64 | 6.80 | | | | | | | 6.68 |

[1] Preliminary.    Source: Economic Research Service, U.S. Department of Agriculture (ERS-USDA)

## Corn Price Support Data in the United States

| Crop Year Beginning Sept. 1 | National Average Loan Rate[3] | Target Price | Placed Under Loan | % of Production | Acquired by CCC | Owned by CCC Aug. 31 | CCC Inventory As of Dec. 31 CCC Owned | Under CCC Loan | Quantity Pledged (Thousands of Bushels) | Face Amount (Thousands of Dollars) |
|---|---|---|---|---|---|---|---|---|---|---|
| | --- Dollars Per Bushel ----- | | | | ---- Millions of Bushels ---- | | | | | |
| 2011-12 | 1.95 | 2.63 | 574 | 4.6 | 0 | 0 | 0 | ---- | 574,224 | 1,050,954 |
| 2012-13 | 1.95 | 2.63 | 368 | 3.4 | 0 | 0 | 0 | ---- | 367,998 | 675,046 |
| 2013-14 | 1.95 | 2.63 | 460 | 3.3 | 0 | 0 | 0 | ---- | 460,885 | 823,153 |
| 2014-15 | 1.95 | 3.70 | 574 | 4.0 | 0 | 0 | 0 | ---- | 7,822 | 16,432 |
| 2015-16 | 1.95 | 3.70 | 746 | 5.5 | 0 | 0 | 0 | ---- | 44,185 | 110,902 |
| 2016-17 | 1.95 | 3.70 | 880 | 5.8 | 0 | 0 | 0 | ---- | 59,619 | 116,982 |
| 2017-18 | 1.95 | 3.70 | 980 | 6.7 | 0 | 0 | 0 | ---- | 885,563 | 1,689,795 |
| 2018-19 | 1.95 | 3.70 | 919 | 6.4 | 0 | 0 | 0 | ---- | 78,890 | 152,614 |
| 2019-20[1] | 2.20 | 3.70 | 805 | 5.9 | 0 | 0 | 0 | ---- | 66,091 | 130,973 |
| 2020-21[2] | 2.20 | | | | | | | | | |

[1] Preliminary.   [2] Estimate.   [3] Findley or announced loan rate.   NA = Not available.
Source: National Agricultural Statistics Service, U.S. Department of Agriculture (NASS-USDA)

## U.S. Exports[1] of Corn (Including Seed), By Country of Destination    In Thousands of Metric Tons

| Crop Year Beginning Oct. 1 | Algeria | Canada | Egypt | Israel | Japan | Mexico | Korea, South | Russia | Saudi Arabia | Spain | Taiwan | Venezuela | Total |
|---|---|---|---|---|---|---|---|---|---|---|---|---|---|
| 2012-13 | ---- | 451 | ---- | 0 | 6,511 | 296 | 4,861 | ---- | 345 | 9 | 514 | 1,079 | 18,176 |
| 2013-14 | 76 | 604 | 2,940 | 469 | 12,379 | 5,312 | 10,895 | ---- | 1,030 | 693 | 1,772 | 1,058 | 50,599 |
| 2014-15 | 239 | 1,444 | 1,127 | 26 | 11,832 | 3,645 | 11,220 | 1 | 1,184 | 66 | 1,830 | 806 | 46,758 |
| 2015-16 | 663 | 926 | 792 | 388 | 11,187 | 3,881 | 13,535 | ---- | 1,522 | 66 | 2,302 | 1,078 | 50,989 |
| 2016-17 | 91 | 650 | 258 | 107 | 12,579 | 4,762 | 14,297 | ---- | 2,029 | 205 | 2,663 | 384 | 55,561 |
| 2017-18 | 48 | 1,724 | 1,640 | 757 | 13,811 | 6,047 | 15,498 | ---- | 1,577 | 1,167 | 2,766 | 440 | 63,569 |
| 2018-19 | ---- | 2,395 | 225 | 134 | 12,558 | 3,292 | 15,688 | ---- | 770 | 1 | 1,721 | 95 | 49,223 |
| 2019-20 | 43 | 1,712 | 49 | 497 | 10,086 | 2,894 | 14,506 | ---- | 850 | 0 | 779 | 469 | 46,970 |
| 2020-21 | 181 | 1,736 | 506 | 542 | 11,053 | 3,319 | 15,658 | 0 | 717 | 0 | 1,655 | 413 | 68,225 |
| 2021-22[2] | ---- | 5,997 | 22 | 225 | 10,106 | 1,370 | 16,758 | ---- | 766 | 498 | 799 | 480 | 62,901 |

[1] Excludes exports of corn by-products.   [2] Preliminary.   Source: Foreign Agricultural Service, U.S. Department of Agriculture (FAS-USDA)

## Stocks of Corn (Shelled and Ear) in the United States    In Millions of Bushels

| Year | On Farms Mar. 1 | June 1 | Sept. 1 | Dec. 1 | Off Farms Mar. 1 | June 1 | Sept. 1 | Dec. 1 | Total Stocks Mar. 1 | June 1 | Sept. 1 | Dec. 1 |
|---|---|---|---|---|---|---|---|---|---|---|---|---|
| 2013 | 2,669,200 | 1,260,100 | 275,000 | 6,380,000 | 2,730,726 | 1,506,144 | 546,185 | 4,072,532 | 5,399,926 | 2,766,244 | 821,185 | 10,452,532 |
| 2014 | 3,860,500 | 1,863,200 | 462,000 | 7,087,000 | 3,147,623 | 1,988,516 | 769,904 | 4,124,380 | 7,008,123 | 3,851,716 | 1,231,904 | 11,211,380 |
| 2015 | 4,380,000 | 2,275,000 | 593,000 | 6,829,000 | 3,369,806 | 2,177,988 | 1,138,164 | 4,406,178 | 7,749,806 | 4,452,988 | 1,731,164 | 11,234,178 |
| 2016 | 4,335,000 | 2,471,400 | 627,400 | 7,611,000 | 3,487,233 | 2,239,679 | 1,109,658 | 4,774,776 | 7,822,233 | 4,711,079 | 1,737,058 | 12,385,776 |
| 2017 | 4,908,000 | 2,841,400 | 787,000 | 7,739,000 | 3,713,992 | 2,387,682 | 1,506,303 | 4,827,501 | 8,621,992 | 5,229,082 | 2,293,303 | 12,566,501 |
| 2018 | 5,002,000 | 2,750,100 | 620,000 | 7,451,000 | 3,890,126 | 2,554,704 | 1,520,335 | 4,485,798 | 8,892,126 | 5,304,804 | 2,140,335 | 11,936,798 |
| 2019 | 5,131,000 | 2,949,600 | 814,100 | 7,103,000 | 3,482,206 | 2,252,636 | 1,406,649 | 4,224,338 | 8,613,206 | 5,202,236 | 2,220,749 | 11,327,338 |
| 2020 | 4,454,000 | 2,867,000 | 750,800 | 7,046,000 | 3,497,576 | 2,135,987 | 1,168,662 | 4,247,750 | 7,951,576 | 5,002,987 | 1,919,462 | 11,293,750 |
| 2021 | 4,036,500 | 1,743,600 | 394,900 | 7,234,000 | 3,659,648 | 2,367,581 | 839,612 | 4,407,181 | 7,696,148 | 4,111,181 | 1,234,512 | 11,641,181 |
| 2022[1] | 4,080,000 | 2,120,700 | 509,500 | 6,748,000 | 3,678,036 | 2,228,268 | 867,390 | 4,073,207 | 7,758,036 | 4,348,968 | 1,376,890 | 10,821,207 |

[1] Preliminary.   Source: National Agricultural Statistics Service, U.S. Department of Agriculture (NASS-USDA)

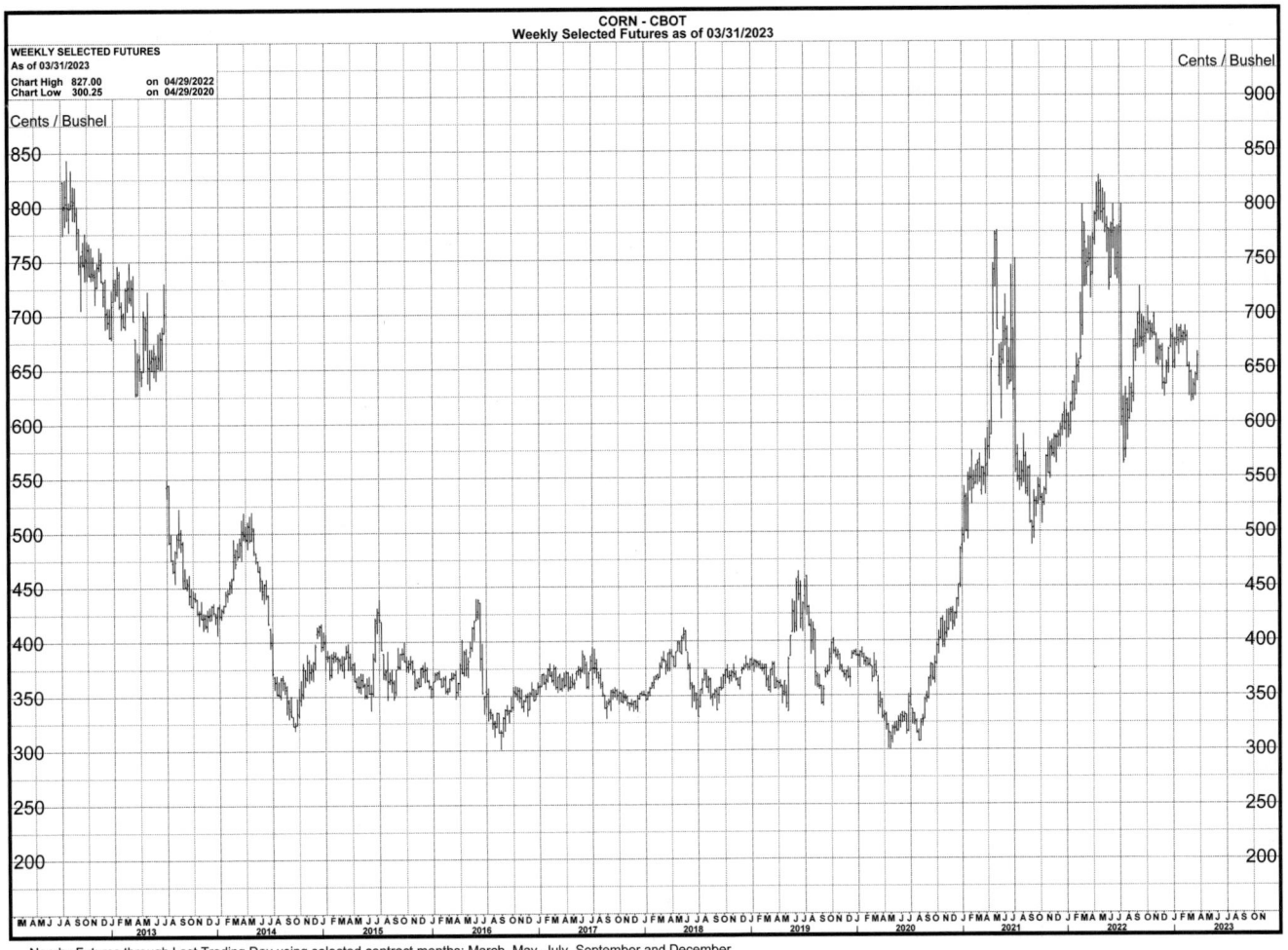

# CORN

**CORN - CBOT**
Weekly Selected Futures as of 03/31/2023

Chart High 827.00 on 04/29/2022
Chart Low 300.25 on 04/29/2020

## Volume of Trading of Corn Futures in Chicago   In Thousands of Contracts

| Year | Jan. | Feb. | Mar. | Apr. | May | June | July | Aug. | Sept. | Oct. | Nov. | Dec. | Total |
|---|---|---|---|---|---|---|---|---|---|---|---|---|---|
| 2013 | 5,151.4 | 6,347.6 | 4,929.5 | 7,089.9 | 4,937.7 | 5,823.6 | 4,824.9 | 6,128.2 | 3,436.3 | 4,919.5 | 7,695.2 | 3,039.0 | 64,322.6 |
| 2014 | 5,790.8 | 7,614.4 | 5,772.2 | 6,996.2 | 4,613.5 | 6,677.8 | 4,938.4 | 5,781.3 | 3,784.4 | 5,875.4 | 7,439.7 | 4,153.1 | 69,437.3 |
| 2015 | 5,468.9 | 6,810.9 | 6,111.2 | 7,860.2 | 5,957.5 | 10,795.4 | 8,553.2 | 7,835.9 | 4,880.3 | 5,708.6 | 8,736.5 | 4,375.5 | 83,094.3 |
| 2016 | 5,878.1 | 7,858.5 | 6,061.1 | 11,510.4 | 6,909.2 | 11,322.0 | 6,258.8 | 7,704.5 | 4,498.0 | 5,321.4 | 8,319.7 | 3,983.4 | 85,625.2 |
| 2017 | 5,911.2 | 8,379.3 | 6,001.8 | 8,751.1 | 6,167.8 | 11,804.7 | 8,516.1 | 9,294.9 | 4,606.4 | 5,878.6 | 10,685.8 | 3,879.2 | 89,876.8 |
| 2018 | 6,474.5 | 10,818.8 | 8,754.6 | 10,249.8 | 8,164.3 | 11,485.8 | 6,613.3 | 8,637.0 | 5,584.7 | 6,586.2 | 9,690.5 | 4,327.7 | 97,387.2 |
| 2019 | 6,008.6 | 10,270.7 | 7,945.3 | 10,348.0 | 13,559.8 | 13,195.1 | 8,041.4 | 10,317.4 | 5,322.1 | 6,103.5 | 8,302.7 | 3,774.4 | 103,189.1 |
| 2020 | 6,270.8 | 8,339.9 | 7,778.8 | 8,115.2 | 4,561.6 | 10,234.8 | 7,114.3 | 9,064.2 | 5,978.7 | 6,263.3 | 8,792.8 | 5,245.7 | 89,753.1 |
| 2021 | 8,734.3 | 8,568.1 | 6,261.9 | 10,045.0 | 7,913.4 | 10,020.6 | 5,491.8 | 7,366.9 | 4,903.3 | 4,961.3 | 8,162.8 | 4,472.6 | 86,902.0 |
| 2022 | 6,340.1 | 9,255.5 | 7,185.7 | 7,292.9 | 5,420.9 | 8,335.2 | 5,943.2 | 7,017.8 | 4,738.7 | 5,015.7 | 7,303.6 | 4,031.5 | 77,880.8 |

Contract size = 5,000 bu.   Source: CME Group; Chicago Board of Trade (CBT)

## Average Open Interest of Corn Futures in Chicago   In Thousands of Contracts

| Year | Jan. | Feb. | Mar. | Apr. | May | June | July | Aug. | Sept. | Oct. | Nov. | Dec. |
|---|---|---|---|---|---|---|---|---|---|---|---|---|
| 2013 | 1,187.9 | 1,275.3 | 1,264.8 | 1,270.8 | 1,160.8 | 1,196.6 | 1,135.7 | 1,166.2 | 1,114.6 | 1,252.2 | 1,335.0 | 1,193.8 |
| 2014 | 1,284.5 | 1,343.4 | 1,318.8 | 1,396.1 | 1,338.9 | 1,370.7 | 1,332.4 | 1,316.6 | 1,254.5 | 1,289.5 | 1,298.1 | 1,216.6 |
| 2015 | 1,291.3 | 1,332.4 | 1,296.8 | 1,360.9 | 1,370.6 | 1,428.7 | 1,350.7 | 1,346.0 | 1,253.1 | 1,309.6 | 1,365.9 | 1,291.4 |
| 2016 | 1,374.6 | 1,372.9 | 1,349.8 | 1,432.1 | 1,364.2 | 1,438.5 | 1,297.8 | 1,353.5 | 1,303.9 | 1,322.3 | 1,345.3 | 1,227.3 |
| 2017 | 1,306.7 | 1,431.1 | 1,403.8 | 1,443.3 | 1,364.3 | 1,406.1 | 1,377.3 | 1,412.7 | 1,378.6 | 1,496.8 | 1,641.6 | 1,522.8 |
| 2018 | 1,623.6 | 1,670.6 | 1,821.7 | 1,837.2 | 1,852.3 | 1,950.0 | 1,850.8 | 1,729.7 | 1,693.3 | 1,659.4 | 1,702.9 | 1,574.6 |
| 2019 | 1,646.1 | 1,720.2 | 1,769.3 | 1,774.3 | 1,688.8 | 1,789.0 | 1,781.6 | 1,732.2 | 1,612.6 | 1,597.3 | 1,589.0 | 1,471.0 |
| 2020 | 1,530.9 | 1,576.5 | 1,435.7 | 1,441.2 | 1,428.9 | 1,564.1 | 1,531.9 | 1,525.6 | 1,458.9 | 1,601.4 | 1,733.7 | 1,684.7 |
| 2021 | 1,884.2 | 1,940.5 | 1,774.0 | 1,769.6 | 1,706.6 | 1,671.3 | 1,486.5 | 1,436.3 | 1,383.0 | 1,416.8 | 1,550.9 | 1,469.5 |
| 2022 | 1,517.3 | 1,567.6 | 1,505.9 | 1,569.4 | 1,531.1 | 1,488.7 | 1,321.3 | 1,315.2 | 1,317.5 | 1,419.8 | 1,403.2 | 1,208.5 |

Contract size = 5,000 bu.   Source: CME Group; Chicago Board of Trade (CBT)

# Corn Oil

Corn oil is a bland, odorless oil produced by refining the crude corn oil that is mechanically extracted from the germ of the plant seed. High-oil corn, the most common type of corn used to make corn oil, typically has an oil content of 7% or higher compared to about 4% for normal corn. Corn oil is widely used as cooking oil, for making margarine and mayonnaise, and for making inedible products such as soap, paints, inks, varnishes, and cosmetics. For humans, studies have shown that no vegetable oil is more effective than corn oil in lowering blood cholesterol levels.

**Prices** – The average monthly price of corn oil (wet mill price in Chicago) in the 2021/22 marketing year (Oct-Sep) rose by +7.3% to 58.00 cents per pound.

**Supply** – U.S. corn oil production in 2022/23 marketing year rose by +0.2% yr/yr to 6.100 billion pounds. U.S. stocks in the 2022/23 marketing year (beginning Oct 1) fell by -4.9% to 148 million pounds.

**Demand** – U.S. usage (domestic disappearance) in 2022/23 remain unchanged yr/yr at 5.978 billion pounds.

**Exports** – U.S. corn oil exports in 2021/22 rose by +17.9% to 320 million pounds. U.S. corn oil imports in 2022/23 rose by +28.6% to 200 million pounds.

## Supply and Disappearance of Corn Oil in the United States    In Millions of Pounds

| Crop Year | Stocks Oct. 1 | Production | Imports | Total Supply | Baking and Frying Fats | Salad and Cooking Oil | Margarine | Total Edible Products | Domestic Disappearance | Exports | Total Disappearance |
|---|---|---|---|---|---|---|---|---|---|---|---|
| 2013-14 | 165 | 3,890 | 42.0 | 4,097 | ---- | ---- | ---- | ---- | 2,928 | 1,004 | 3,932 |
| 2014-15 | 165 | 4,740 | 39.0 | 4,944 | ---- | ---- | ---- | ---- | 3,870 | 909 | 4,779 |
| 2015-16 | 165 | 5,300 | 83.0 | 5,548 | ---- | ---- | ---- | ---- | 4,289 | 1,094 | 5,383 |
| 2016-17 | 165 | 5,850 | 74.0 | 6,089 | ---- | ---- | ---- | ---- | 4,841 | 1,120 | 5,961 |
| 2017-18 | 127 | 6,066 | 63.0 | 6,256 | ---- | ---- | ---- | ---- | 5,423 | 728 | 6,152 |
| 2018-19 | 104 | 5,765 | 65.0 | 5,934 | ---- | ---- | ---- | ---- | 5,279 | 573 | 5,852 |
| 2019-20 | 82 | 5,394 | 54.2 | 5,530 | ---- | ---- | ---- | ---- | 4,946 | 482 | 5,428 |
| 2020-21 | 102 | 5,724 | 51.3 | 5,877 | ---- | ---- | ---- | ---- | 5,297 | 424 | 5,721 |
| 2021-22[1] | 156 | 6,088 | 155.5 | 6,400 | ---- | ---- | ---- | ---- | 5,980 | 271 | 6,251 |
| 2022-23[2] | 148 | 6,100 | 200.0 | 6,448 | ---- | ---- | ---- | ---- | 5,978 | 320 | 6,298 |

[1] Preliminary.  [2] Estimate.  W = Withheld.  *Source: Economic Research Service, U.S. Department of Agriculture (ERS-USDA)*

## Production[2] of Crude Corn Oil in the United States    In Millions of Pounds

| Crop Year | Oct. | Nov. | Dec. | Jan. | Feb. | Mar. | Apr. | May | June | July | Aug. | Sept. | Total |
|---|---|---|---|---|---|---|---|---|---|---|---|---|---|
| 2004-05 | 208.8 | 187.1 | 191.0 | 205.2 | 182.5 | 206.6 | 217.2 | 188.2 | 211.5 | 206.7 | 198.5 | 189.0 | 2,392 |
| 2005-06 | 207.5 | 199.9 | 200.3 | 209.2 | 184.8 | 217.6 | 191.7 | 218.7 | 206.7 | 215.3 | 222.0 | 209.0 | 2,483 |
| 2006-07 | 228.7 | 216.0 | 226.1 | 224.7 | 187.9 | 216.4 | 194.1 | 214.4 | 212.7 | 219.8 | 209.5 | 209.4 | 2,560 |
| 2007-08 | 213.5 | 213.0 | 214.0 | 205.4 | 193.7 | 222.5 | 190.7 | 220.9 | 193.7 | 214.9 | 217.3 | 207.3 | 2,507 |
| 2008-09 | 206.3 | 210.6 | 198.7 | 200.3 | 199.8 | 218.8 | 189.4 | 202.5 | 189.0 | 186.0 | 201.4 | 215.8 | 2,419 |
| 2009-10 | 212.9 | 205.2 | 203.2 | 197.9 | 188.1 | 212.4 | 214.7 | 205.4 | 214.7 | 216.8 | 213.6 | 200.1 | 2,485 |
| 2010-11[1] | 205.1 | 211.2 | 198.9 | 220.9 | 199.4 | 218.1 | 203.1 | 215.0 | 216.3 | 205.7 | | | 2,512 |

[1] Preliminary.  [2] Not seasonally adjusted.  *Source: Bureau of the Census, U.S. Department of Commerce*

## Average Corn Oil Price, Wet Mill in Chicago    In Cents Per Pound

| Crop Year | Oct. | Nov. | Dec. | Jan. | Feb. | Mar. | Apr. | May | June | July | Aug. | Sept. | Average |
|---|---|---|---|---|---|---|---|---|---|---|---|---|---|
| 2013-14 | 37.85 | 38.79 | 38.31 | 38.79 | 41.07 | 43.19 | 41.94 | 41.02 | 40.01 | 39.02 | 38.00 | 35.17 | 39.43 |
| 2014-15 | 34.50 | 33.96 | 33.68 | 34.86 | 36.13 | 37.73 | 39.27 | 39.50 | 40.34 | 41.49 | 40.75 | 37.55 | 37.48 |
| 2015-16 | 36.60 | 36.43 | 38.25 | 39.93 | 40.29 | 41.05 | 42.12 | 40.33 | 39.94 | 38.86 | 39.06 | 38.11 | 39.25 |
| 2016-17 | 36.22 | 36.83 | 38.12 | 37.89 | 38.11 | 37.90 | 37.63 | 37.71 | 38.00 | 37.53 | 36.75 | 36.48 | 37.43 |
| 2017-18 | 34.96 | 34.46 | 33.96 | 30.68 | 29.72 | 29.66 | 29.50 | 29.65 | 29.54 | 28.76 | 26.80 | 26.46 | 30.35 |
| 2018-19 | 27.18 | 26.37 | 26.46 | 26.21 | 25.65 | 26.72 | 27.94 | 27.76 | 27.38 | 26.75 | 27.31 | 27.48 | 26.93 |
| 2019-20 | 28.30 | 30.36 | 31.25 | 33.30 | 36.00 | 36.94 | 44.88 | 47.64 | 51.34 | 45.45 | 44.75 | 43.38 | 39.47 |
| 2020-21 | 42.44 | 42.53 | 41.73 | 43.34 | 44.95 | 52.05 | 59.81 | 68.25 | 67.60 | 66.10 | 64.16 | 53.19 | 53.85 |
| 2021-22 | 57.07 | 57.92 | 56.09 | 54.09 | 59.29 | 67.19 | 71.55 | 77.80 | 76.38 | 62.25 | 65.44 | 66.26 | 64.28 |
| 2022-23[1] | 65.41 | 69.67 | 60.00 | 61.00 | | | | | | | | | 64.02 |

[1] Preliminary.  *Source: Economic Research Service, U.S. Department of Agriculture (ERS-USDA)*

# Cotton

Cotton is a natural vegetable fiber that comes from small trees and shrubs of a genus belonging to the mallow family, one of which is the common American Upland cotton plant. Cotton has been used in India for at least the last 5,000 years and probably much longer, and was also used by the ancient Chinese, Egyptians, and North and South Americans. Cotton was one of the earliest crops grown by European settlers in the U.S.

Cotton requires a long growing season, plenty of sunshine and water during the growing season, and then dry weather for harvesting. In the United States, the Cotton Belt stretches from northern Florida to North Carolina and westward to California. In the U.S., planting time varies from the beginning of February in Southern Texas to the beginning of June in the northern sections of the Cotton Belt. The flower bud of the plant blossoms and develops into an oval boll that splits open at maturity. At maturity, cotton is most vulnerable to damage from wind and rain. Approximately 95% of the cotton in the U.S. is now harvested mechanically with spindle-type pickers or strippers and then sent off to cotton gins for processing. There it is dried, cleaned, separated, and packed into bales.

Cotton is used in a wide range of products, from clothing to home furnishings to medical products. The value of cotton is determined by the staple, grade, and character of each bale. Staple refers to short, medium, long, or extra-long fiber length, with medium staple accounting for about 70% of all U.S. cotton. Grade refers to the color, brightness, and amount of foreign matter and is established by the U.S. Department of Agriculture. Character refers to the fiber's diameter, strength, body, maturity (ratio of mature to immature fibers), uniformity, and smoothness. Cotton is the fifth leading cash crop in the U.S. and is one of the nation's principal agricultural exports. The weight of cotton is typically measured in terms of a "bale," which equals 480 pounds.

Cotton futures and options are traded at the ICE Futures U.S exchange. Cotton futures are also traded on the B3 exchange and the Multi Commodity Exchange of India, and the Zhengzhou Commodity Exchange. Cotton yarn futures are traded on the Zhengzhou Commodity Exchange. The ICE Futures U.S. exchange's futures contract calls for the delivery of 50,000 pounds net weight (approximately 100 bales) of No. 2 cotton with a quality rating of Strict Low Middling and a staple length of 1-and-2/32 inch. Delivery points include Texas (Galveston and Houston), New Orleans, Memphis, and Greenville/Spartanburg in South Carolina.

**Prices** – ICE cotton futures prices (Barchart.com symbol CT) trended higher to begin 2022 and rallied into Q2 when they posted an 11-year high of 158.02 cents per pound in May 2022. The worst drought since 2011 in West Texas, the largest U.S. cotton-producing region, sparked cotton supply concerns in the U.S., which is the world's largest cotton exporter. Also, robust cotton demand from China, the world's biggest cotton importer, added fuel to the rally in cotton as the Chinese economy began to reopen from the pandemic. However, cotton prices fell sharply into July as the dollar index surged to a 20-year high, which curbed demand for U.S. cotton supplies. Also, surging inflation fueled commodity demand concerns after the U.S. June CPI jumped to a 41-year high. In addition, the USDA, in July's WASDE report, said, "global cotton consumption prospects have declined as negative macroeconomic forces dampen consumer demand." Due to flagging demand from high prices, Cotlook in July raised its 2022/23 global cotton ending stocks estimate to 1.11 MMT from a May estimate of 467,000 MT. Cotton prices in August then recovered about half of the May/July decline after the USDA, in its August WASDE report, cut its U.S. 2022/23 cotton crop estimate more than expected to 12.57 million bales, the smallest crop since 2009/10. The drought in Texas curbed its cotton production in 2022 to 2.9 million bales, down -62% yr/yr. Cotton prices then reversed and sold off into year-end, posting a 2-year low of 70.21 cents per pound in October. A resurgence of Covid in China prompted the government to implement its Covid-Zero policies that curbed economic activity. That reduced China's demand for cotton as Chinese cotton import from Jan-Sep dropped -21.2% y/y to 1.46 MMT. Cotton prices finished 2022 down -26% yr/yr at 83.37 cents a pound.

**Supply** – World cotton production in 2022/23 is forecasted to decrease by -0.3% yr/yr to 115.396 million bales (480 pounds per bale) and remain below the 2011/12 record high of 127.244 million bales. The world's largest cotton producers are forecasted to be China with 24.3% of world production in 2022/23, India with 23.0%, the U.S. with 12.7%, Brazil with 11.5%, and Australia with 4.3%. World ending stocks in 2022/23 are forecasted to rise by +5.4% yr/yr to 89.933 million bales, down from the 2014/15 record high of 108.002.

The U.S. cotton crop in 2022/23 is forecasted to decrease by -18.7% yr/yr to 14.242 million bales and remain below the 2005/06 record high of 23.890 million bales. U.S. farmers are forecasted to harvest 7.876 million acres of cotton in 2022/23, down by -23.3% yr/yr. The U.S. cotton yield in 2022/23 is forecasted to rise by +6.0% yr/yr to 868 pounds per acre, but still down from the 2017/18 record high of 905 pounds per acre. The leading U.S. producing states for cotton in 2022 were Texas with 23.5% of U.S. production, Georgia with 17.6%, Arkansas with 10.9%, Mississippi with 7.9%, North Carolina with 6.7%, Alabama with 5.7%, and Missouri with 5.2%.

**Demand** – World cotton consumption in 2022/23 is forecasted to fall by -5.4% yr/yr to 110.773 million bales. The largest consumers of cotton in 2022/23 are expected to be China with 32.0% of the world total, India with 20.3%, and Pakistan with 8.1%. U.S. consumption of cotton by mills in 2022/23 is expected to fall by -3.1% yr/yr to 2.235 million bales.

**Trade** – World exports of cotton in 2022/23 are expected to fall by -2.8% yr/yr to 41.656 million bales, falling back from the record high of 48.726 million bales in 2020/21. Major world cotton importers for 2022/23 are expected to be Bangladesh with 19.2% of total world imports, China with 18.6%, Vietnam with 15.4%, Pakistan with 12.0%, and Turkey with 10.3%.

# COTTON

## Supply and Distribution of All Cotton in the United States   In Thousands of 480-Pound Bales

| Crop Year Beginning Aug. 1 | Planted (1,000 Acres) | Harvested (1,000 Acres) | Yield Lbs./Acre | Beginning Stocks[3] | Production[4] | Imports | Total | Mill Use | Exports | Total | Unaccounted | Ending Stocks | Farm Price[5] | "A" Index Price[6] | Value of Production Million USD |
|---|---|---|---|---|---|---|---|---|---|---|---|---|---|---|---|
| 2013-14 | 10,407 | 7,544 | 821 | 3,800 | 12,909 | 13 | 16,722 | 3,550 | 10,530 | 14,080 | -292 | 2,350 | 83.8 | ---- | 5,191.5 |
| 2014-15 | 11,037 | 9,347 | 838 | 2,350 | 16,319 | 12 | 18,681 | 3,575 | 11,246 | 14,821 | -210 | 3,650 | 65.7 | ---- | 5,147.2 |
| 2015-16 | 8,581 | 8,075 | 766 | 3,650 | 12,888 | 33 | 16,571 | 3,450 | 9,153 | 12,603 | -168 | 3,800 | 64.5 | ---- | 3,989.0 |
| 2016-17 | 10,074 | 9,508 | 867 | 3,800 | 17,170 | 7 | 20,977 | 3,250 | 14,917 | 18,167 | -60 | 2,750 | 70.5 | ---- | 5,813.8 |
| 2017-18 | 12,718 | 11,100 | 905 | 2,750 | 20,923 | 3 | 23,676 | 3,225 | 16,281 | 19,506 | 30 | 4,200 | 71.9 | ---- | 7,222.5 |
| 2018-19 | 14,100 | 9,991 | 882 | 4,200 | 18,367 | 3 | 22,570 | 2,975 | 14,837 | 17,812 | 88 | 4,850 | 72.3 | ---- | 6,375.2 |
| 2019-20 | 13,736 | 11,613 | 810 | 4,850 | 19,913 | 3 | 24,766 | 2,150 | 15,527 | 17,677 | 146 | 7,250 | 61.4 | ---- | 5,865.1 |
| 2020-21 | 12,092 | 8,275 | 847 | 7,250 | 14,608 | 3 | 24,345 | 2,500 | 14,600 | 17,100 | 42 | 7,200 | 68.3 | ---- | 4,828.8 |
| 2021-22[1] | 11,216 | 10,272 | 819 | 2,988 | 17,523 | 5 | 20,180 | 2,538 | 14,160 | 16,698 | 244 | 3,726 | 94.3 | ---- | 7,963.0 |
| 2022-23[2] | 13,791 | 7,876 | 868 | 3,726 | 14,242 | 5 | 17,099 | 2,485 | 12,165 | 14,455 | 14 | 2,657 | 88.9 | ---- | 6,448.8 |

[1] Preliminary.  [2] Estimate.  [3] Excludes preseason ginnings (adjusted to 480-lb. bale net weight basis).  [4] Includes preseason ginnings.  [5] Marketing year average price.  [6] Average of 5 cheapest types of SLM 1 3/32" staple length cotton offered on the European market.
Source: Economic Research Service, U.S. Department of Agriculture (ERS-USDA)

## World Production of All Cotton   In Thousands of 480-Pound Bales

| Crop Year Beginning Aug. 1 | Australia | Brazil | Burkina | China | Greece | India | Mexico | Pakistan | Turkey | Turkmenistan | United States | Uzbekistan | World Total |
|---|---|---|---|---|---|---|---|---|---|---|---|---|---|
| 2013-14 | 4,100 | 7,960 | 1,250 | 32,750 | 1,369 | 31,000 | 933 | 9,500 | 2,300 | 1,550 | 12,909 | 4,100 | 120,309 |
| 2014-15 | 2,300 | 7,180 | 1,350 | 30,000 | 1,286 | 29,500 | 1,319 | 10,600 | 3,200 | 1,525 | 16,319 | 3,900 | 119,174 |
| 2015-16 | 2,850 | 5,920 | 1,100 | 22,000 | 1,010 | 25,900 | 943 | 7,000 | 2,650 | 1,450 | 12,888 | 3,800 | 96,146 |
| 2016-17 | 4,050 | 7,020 | 1,310 | 22,750 | 1,033 | 27,000 | 765 | 7,700 | 3,200 | 1,325 | 17,170 | 4,410 | 107,279 |
| 2017-18 | 4,800 | 9,220 | 1,200 | 27,500 | 1,222 | 29,000 | 1,560 | 8,200 | 4,000 | 1,340 | 20,923 | 4,360 | 124,381 |
| 2018-19 | 2,200 | 13,000 | 850 | 28,000 | 1,410 | 26,000 | 1,735 | 7,600 | 3,750 | 910 | 18,367 | 2,770 | 118,490 |
| 2019-20 | 625 | 13,780 | 880 | 27,450 | 1,675 | 28,500 | 1,570 | 6,200 | 3,450 | 920 | 19,913 | 2,440 | 120,163 |
| 2020-21 | 2,800 | 10,820 | 950 | 29,600 | 1,400 | 27,600 | 1,020 | 4,500 | 2,900 | 920 | 14,608 | 3,180 | 111,489 |
| 2021-22[1] | 5,750 | 11,720 | 960 | 26,800 | 1,400 | 24,400 | 1,220 | 6,000 | 3,800 | 900 | 17,523 | 2,700 | 115,715 |
| 2022-23[2] | 5,000 | 13,300 | 965 | 28,000 | 1,380 | 26,500 | 1,400 | 3,700 | 4,900 | 900 | 14,680 | 2,700 | 115,396 |

[1] Preliminary.  [2] Estimate.  Source: Foreign Agricultural Service, U.S. Department of Agriculture (FAS-USDA)

## World Consumption of Cotton   In Thousands of 480-Pound Bales

| Crop Year Beginning Aug. 1 | Bangladesh | Brazil | China | India | Indonesia | Mexico | Pakistan | Thailand | Turkey | United States | Uzbekistan | Vietnam | World Total |
|---|---|---|---|---|---|---|---|---|---|---|---|---|---|
| 2013-14 | 5,310 | 4,200 | 34,500 | 23,050 | 3,050 | 1,875 | 10,425 | 1,550 | 6,300 | 3,842 | 1,600 | 3,200 | 109,628 |
| 2014-15 | 5,810 | 3,400 | 34,500 | 24,500 | 3,250 | 1,875 | 10,625 | 1,500 | 6,500 | 3,785 | 1,750 | 4,100 | 112,525 |
| 2015-16 | 6,310 | 3,100 | 36,000 | 24,750 | 3,000 | 1,875 | 10,325 | 1,295 | 6,700 | 3,618 | 1,800 | 4,500 | 113,411 |
| 2016-17 | 6,810 | 3,200 | 38,500 | 24,350 | 3,300 | 1,775 | 10,325 | 1,225 | 6,650 | 3,310 | 2,100 | 5,400 | 116,622 |
| 2017-18 | 7,510 | 3,400 | 41,000 | 24,750 | 3,500 | 1,925 | 10,925 | 1,150 | 7,550 | 3,195 | 2,400 | 6,600 | 123,476 |
| 2018-19 | 7,210 | 3,400 | 39,500 | 24,300 | 3,150 | 2,020 | 10,725 | 1,075 | 6,900 | 2,887 | 1,950 | 7,000 | 119,710 |
| 2019-20 | 6,910 | 2,700 | 34,000 | 20,500 | 2,400 | 1,490 | 9,525 | 800 | 6,600 | 2,004 | 2,260 | 6,600 | 103,978 |
| 2020-21 | 8,510 | 3,103 | 41,000 | 26,000 | 2,450 | 1,715 | 10,825 | 620 | 7,700 | 2,358 | 3,120 | 7,300 | 123,129 |
| 2021-22[1] | 8,510 | 3,300 | 35,000 | 25,000 | 2,600 | 1,860 | 10,725 | 735 | 8,700 | 2,306 | 3,140 | 6,700 | 117,134 |
| 2022-23[2] | 8,210 | 3,200 | 35,500 | 22,500 | 2,200 | 1,810 | 9,025 | 710 | 8,000 | 2,235 | 2,750 | 6,400 | 110,773 |

[1] Preliminary.  [2] Estimate.  Source: Foreign Agricultural Service, U.S. Department of Agriculture (FAS-USDA)

## World Ending Stocks of Cotton   In Thousands of 480-Pound Bales

| Crop Year Beginning Aug. 1 | Argentina | Australia | Bangladesh | Brazil | China | India | Mexico | Pakistan | Turkey | Turkmenistan | United States | Uzbekistan | World Total |
|---|---|---|---|---|---|---|---|---|---|---|---|---|---|
| 2013-14 | 942 | 1,807 | 1,271 | 7,218 | 62,707 | 8,559 | 584 | 2,475 | 1,399 | 1,879 | 2,350 | 1,748 | 101,064 |
| 2014-15 | 727 | 1,748 | 1,331 | 7,112 | 66,420 | 10,586 | 693 | 2,890 | 1,671 | 1,279 | 3,650 | 1,298 | 108,002 |
| 2015-16 | 632 | 1,835 | 1,515 | 5,709 | 56,698 | 7,044 | 605 | 2,615 | 1,652 | 829 | 3,800 | 1,098 | 91,550 |
| 2016-17 | 472 | 2,259 | 1,630 | 6,929 | 45,927 | 7,880 | 445 | 2,315 | 1,594 | 654 | 2,750 | 1,658 | 81,993 |
| 2017-18 | 691 | 3,284 | 1,855 | 8,657 | 37,999 | 8,625 | 655 | 2,830 | 1,950 | 669 | 4,200 | 2,631 | 82,828 |
| 2018-19 | 696 | 1,922 | 1,783 | 12,256 | 35,914 | 8,604 | 699 | 2,495 | 1,694 | 629 | 4,850 | 2,745 | 82,575 |
| 2019-20 | 1,126 | 1,198 | 2,515 | 14,404 | 36,344 | 15,684 | 709 | 3,115 | 2,766 | 724 | 7,250 | 2,484 | 98,406 |
| 2020-21 | 1,388 | 2,507 | 2,452 | 11,119 | 37,794 | 11,939 | 454 | 2,165 | 2,708 | 744 | 3,150 | 2,119 | 86,733 |
| 2021-22[1] | 1,605 | 4,860 | 2,293 | 11,836 | 37,314 | 8,596 | 370 | 1,890 | 2,765 | 694 | 3,750 | 1,664 | 85,340 |
| 2022-23[2] | 1,680 | 4,140 | 2,238 | 13,651 | 37,439 | 11,196 | 460 | 1,540 | 3,265 | 669 | 4,200 | 1,589 | 89,933 |

[1] Preliminary.  [2] Estimate.  Source: Foreign Agricultural Service, U.S. Department of Agriculture (FAS-USDA)

# COTTON

**World Exports of Cotton**  In Thousands of 480-Pound Bales

| Crop Year Beginning Aug. 1 | Australia | Benin | Brazil | Burkina | Cote d'Ivoire | Greece | India | Malaysia | Mali | Turkmenistan | United States | Uzbekistan | World Total |
|---|---|---|---|---|---|---|---|---|---|---|---|---|---|
| 2013-14 | 4,852 | 600 | 2,230 | 1,391 | 830 | 1,288 | 9,261 | 210 | 900 | 1,625 | 10,530 | 2,300 | 41,293 |
| 2014-15 | 2,404 | 750 | 3,910 | 1,340 | 860 | 1,165 | 4,199 | 81 | 850 | 1,500 | 11,246 | 2,600 | 36,203 |
| 2015-16 | 2,828 | 650 | 4,314 | 1,077 | 780 | 959 | 5,764 | 142 | 1,000 | 1,250 | 9,153 | 2,200 | 34,908 |
| 2016-17 | 3,731 | 825 | 2,789 | 1,154 | 625 | 1,017 | 4,550 | 111 | 1,100 | 850 | 14,917 | 1,750 | 38,106 |
| 2017-18 | 3,915 | 1,070 | 4,174 | 1,218 | 620 | 1,076 | 5,182 | 152 | 1,300 | 625 | 16,281 | 987 | 41,602 |
| 2018-19 | 3,632 | 1,390 | 6,018 | 796 | 895 | 1,355 | 3,521 | 313 | 1,350 | 150 | 14,833 | 711 | 41,484 |
| 2019-20 | 1,359 | 970 | 8,937 | 950 | 643 | 1,467 | 3,200 | 220 | 1,175 | 100 | 15,512 | 456 | 41,057 |
| 2020-21 | 1,581 | 1,570 | 11,014 | 1,067 | 1,176 | 1,630 | 6,189 | 255 | 600 | 100 | 16,352 | 450 | 48,726 |
| 2021-22[1] | 3,577 | 1,400 | 7,727 | 900 | 1,350 | 1,428 | 3,743 | 10 | 1,300 | 150 | 14,622 | 75 | 42,863 |
| 2022-23[2] | 5,900 | 1,400 | 8,300 | 925 | 800 | 1,275 | 3,100 | 50 | 1,000 | 125 | 12,000 | 100 | 41,656 |

[1] Preliminary.  [2] Estimate.  *Source: Foreign Agricultural Service, U.S. Department of Agriculture (FAS-USDA)*

**World Imports of Cotton**  In Thousands of 480-Pound Bales

| Crop Year Beginning Aug. 1 | Bangladesh | China | India | Indonesia | Korea, South | Malaysia | Mexico | Pakistan | Taiwan | Thailand | Turkey | Vietnam | World Total |
|---|---|---|---|---|---|---|---|---|---|---|---|---|---|
| 2013-14 | 5,300 | 14,122 | 675 | 2,989 | 1,286 | 350 | 1,040 | 1,200 | 857 | 1,546 | 4,475 | 3,200 | 41,436 |
| 2014-15 | 5,750 | 8,284 | 1,226 | 3,345 | 1,321 | 280 | 830 | 950 | 873 | 1,475 | 4,074 | 4,275 | 36,492 |
| 2015-16 | 6,375 | 4,406 | 1,072 | 2,941 | 1,175 | 443 | 975 | 3,300 | 707 | 1,275 | 4,486 | 4,600 | 35,721 |
| 2016-17 | 6,800 | 5,040 | 2,736 | 3,391 | 1,025 | 392 | 1,000 | 2,450 | 644 | 1,226 | 3,851 | 5,508 | 37,892 |
| 2017-18 | 7,600 | 5,708 | 1,677 | 3,517 | 904 | 739 | 925 | 3,400 | 632 | 1,149 | 4,391 | 6,986 | 41,532 |
| 2018-19 | 7,000 | 9,628 | 1,800 | 3,051 | 781 | 744 | 850 | 2,850 | 592 | 1,075 | 3,607 | 6,931 | 42,451 |
| 2019-20 | 7,500 | 7,137 | 2,280 | 2,512 | 571 | 704 | 590 | 4,000 | 398 | 700 | 4,672 | 6,481 | 40,703 |
| 2020-21 | 8,300 | 12,860 | 844 | 2,307 | 556 | 629 | 928 | 5,400 | 260 | 598 | 5,327 | 7,288 | 48,693 |
| 2021-22[1] | 8,200 | 7,840 | 1,000 | 2,577 | 558 | 444 | 959 | 4,500 | 242 | 750 | 5,524 | 6,631 | 42,889 |
| 2022-23[2] | 8,000 | 7,750 | 1,700 | 2,200 | 560 | 500 | 1,000 | 5,000 | 225 | 700 | 4,300 | 6,400 | 41,626 |

[1] Preliminary.  [2] Estimate.  *Source: Foreign Agricultural Service, U.S. Department of Agriculture (FAS-USDA)*

**Average Spot Cotton, 1-3/32", Price (SLM) at Designated U.S. Markets[2]**  In Cents Per Pound (Net Weight)

| Crop Year | Aug. | Sept. | Oct. | Nov. | Dec. | Jan. | Feb. | Mar. | Apr. | May | June | July | Average |
|---|---|---|---|---|---|---|---|---|---|---|---|---|---|
| 2013-14 | 87.80 | 85.65 | 83.66 | 78.84 | 83.15 | 85.69 | 87.45 | 90.94 | 89.71 | 87.41 | 82.74 | 73.89 | 84.74 |
| 2014-15 | 68.94 | 68.70 | 67.32 | 63.40 | 63.13 | 62.12 | 66.02 | 64.89 | 67.33 | 67.30 | 67.09 | 66.60 | 66.07 |
| 2015-16 | 66.09 | 63.93 | 65.06 | 65.17 | 66.47 | 64.76 | 62.05 | 59.91 | 63.51 | 64.42 | 66.74 | 73.12 | 65.10 |
| 2016-17 | 72.48 | 71.58 | 71.93 | 73.41 | 73.31 | 75.24 | 75.92 | 77.10 | 76.91 | 78.55 | 72.72 | 69.05 | 74.02 |
| 2017-18 | 70.52 | 71.93 | 69.47 | 71.10 | 76.32 | 80.83 | 78.44 | 82.77 | 82.52 | 85.57 | 88.85 | 87.33 | 78.80 |
| 2018-19 | 84.10 | 80.10 | 77.12 | 77.06 | 76.07 | 72.23 | 70.61 | 73.25 | 75.65 | 67.58 | 64.71 | 61.60 | 73.34 |
| 2019-20 | 57.69 | 60.54 | 64.25 | 64.46 | 65.87 | 69.08 | 65.86 | 55.84 | 52.25 | 56.02 | 59.48 | 61.94 | 61.11 |
| 2020-21 | 62.08 | 62.94 | 67.40 | 69.92 | 74.03 | 80.38 | 86.37 | 84.08 | 83.41 | 84.38 | 85.40 | 88.54 | 77.41 |
| 2021-22 | 93.22 | 95.24 | 109.10 | 116.37 | 108.45 | 119.11 | 123.19 | 126.11 | 137.34 | 143.34 | 130.18 | 107.55 | 117.43 |
| 2022-23[1] | 119.51 | 103.61 | 85.12 | 86.28 | 85.49 | 86.36 | 85.09 | | | | | | 93.07 |

[1] Preliminary.  *Source: Agricultural Marketing Service, U.S. Department of Agriculture (AMS-USDA)*

**Average Producer Price Index of Gray Cotton Broadwovens**  Index 1982 = 100

| Year | Jan. | Feb. | Mar. | Apr. | May | June | July | Aug. | Sept. | Oct. | Nov. | Dec. | Average |
|---|---|---|---|---|---|---|---|---|---|---|---|---|---|
| 2009 | 111.0 | 111.0 | 111.0 | 107.2 | 107.2 | 107.2 | 107.2 | 107.5 | 107.5 | 107.5 | 108.9 | 108.9 | 108.5 |
| 2010 | 109.8 | 113.7 | 113.7 | 113.7 | 114.9 | 116.6 | 119.0 | 118.8 | 118.8 | 118.8 | 119.1 | 119.1 | 116.3 |
| 2011 | 144.8 | 145.4 | 147.0 | 153.5 | 154.3 | 154.3 | 162.1 | 162.0 | 161.3 | 148.5 | 148.5 | 141.1 | 151.9 |
| 2012 | 139.1 | 139.2 | 139.2 | 135.0 | 135.0 | 135.2 | 126.1 | 126.1 | 126.1 | 124.7 | 123.6 | 122.7 | 131.0 |
| 2013 | 122.6 | 122.3 | 123.3 | 126.9 | 126.4 | 126.4 | 126.4 | 126.4 | 126.4 | 127.7 | 127.7 | 127.7 | 125.9 |
| 2014 | 124.5 | 124.5 | 121.8 | 124.7 | 124.7 | 124.7 | 124.8 | 124.8 | 124.8 | 123.3 | 123.3 | 123.3 | 124.1 |
| 2015 | 118.2 | 121.2 | 121.2 | 121.5 | 121.5 | 121.5 | 123.7 | 123.7 | 123.7 | 123.5 | 123.5 | 123.5 | 122.2 |
| 2016 | 122.6 | 122.6 | 122.6 | 121.9 | 121.9 | 121.9 | 122.6 | 122.6 | 122.6 | 123.6 | 123.6 | 123.6 | 122.7 |
| 2017 | 125.2 | 125.3 | 125.3 | 129.2 | 129.2 | 129.2 | 128.5 | 128.5 | 128.5 | 126.4 | 126.4 | 126.4 | 127.3 |
| 2018[1] | 127.3 | 127.3 | 127.3 | 133.1 | 133.1 | 133.1 | 133.1 | ---- | ---- | ---- | ---- | ---- | 130.6 |

[1] Preliminary.  *Source: Bureau of Labor Statistics (0337-01), U.S. Department of Commerce*

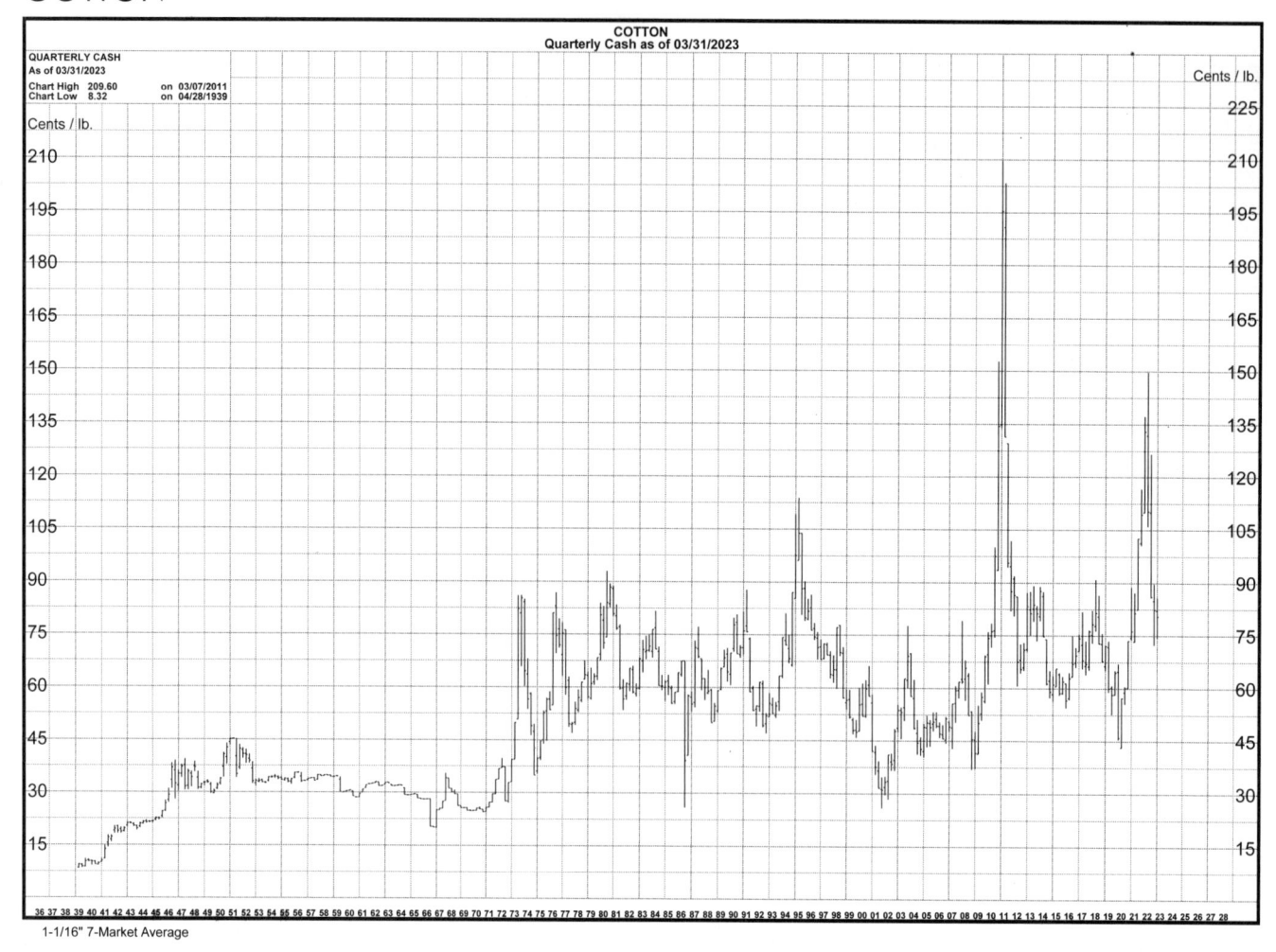

# COTTON

## Average Price of SLM 1-1/16", Cotton/5 at Designated U.S. Markets   In Cents Per Pound (Net Weight)

| Crop Year | Aug. | Sept. | Oct. | Nov. | Dec. | Jan. | Feb. | Mar. | Apr. | May | June | July | Average |
|---|---|---|---|---|---|---|---|---|---|---|---|---|---|
| 2013-14 | 83.36 | 81.25 | 77.37 | 74.43 | 78.75 | 81.43 | 83.21 | 86.70 | 85.48 | 83.20 | 78.54 | 69.63 | 80.28 |
| 2014-15 | 64.99 | 64.83 | 63.51 | 59.64 | 59.38 | 58.19 | 61.74 | 60.65 | 63.08 | 63.06 | 62.86 | 62.36 | 62.02 |
| 2015-16 | 61.85 | 59.70 | 60.83 | 60.99 | 62.32 | 60.69 | 58.06 | 55.96 | 59.65 | 60.36 | 62.78 | 69.25 | 61.04 |
| 2016-17 | 68.57 | 67.65 | 68.04 | 69.42 | 69.69 | 71.81 | 73.02 | 74.33 | 74.13 | 75.75 | 69.85 | 66.24 | 70.71 |
| 2017-18 | 67.71 | 69.12 | 66.67 | 68.09 | 73.13 | 77.58 | 75.24 | 79.57 | 79.34 | 82.40 | 85.54 | 83.95 | 75.70 |
| 2018-19 | 80.75 | 76.72 | 73.90 | 73.72 | 72.66 | 68.72 | 67.17 | 69.78 | 72.27 | 64.05 | 61.19 | 58.08 | 69.92 |
| 2019-20 | 54.17 | 57.01 | 60.63 | 60.89 | 62.39 | 65.60 | 62.38 | 52.35 | 48.73 | 52.40 | 56.00 | 58.46 | 57.58 |
| 2020-21 | 58.60 | 59.46 | 63.87 | 66.30 | 70.37 | 76.69 | 82.79 | 80.56 | 79.89 | 80.86 | 81.88 | 85.03 | 73.86 |
| 2021-22 | 89.70 | 91.67 | 105.50 | 112.87 | 105.14 | 115.90 | 120.09 | 123.02 | 134.25 | 140.06 | 127.09 | 104.26 | 114.13 |
| 2022-23[1] | 116.41 | 100.51 | 81.99 | 82.99 | 82.35 | 83.24 | 82.07 | | | | | | 92.85 |

[1] Preliminary.   [2] Grade 41, leaf 4, staple 34, mike 35-36 and 43-49, strength 23.5-26.4.   *Source: Agricultural Marketing Service, U.S. Department of Agriculture (AMS-USDA)*

## Average Price[1] Received by Farmers for Upland Cotton in the United States   In Cents Per Pound

| Crop Year | Aug. | Sept. | Oct. | Nov. | Dec. | Jan. | Feb. | Mar. | Apr. | May | June | July | Average |
|---|---|---|---|---|---|---|---|---|---|---|---|---|---|
| 2013-14 | 76.9 | 74.6 | 77.8 | 75.9 | 77.2 | 77.5 | 80.2 | 81.7 | 82.7 | 81.7 | 83.9 | 84.7 | 79.6 |
| 2014-15 | 70.5 | 68.9 | 64.5 | 62.7 | 60.8 | 59.1 | 57.8 | 61.3 | 62.6 | 65.9 | 66.8 | 69.3 | 64.2 |
| 2015-16 | 58.0 | 60.3 | 57.9 | 60.0 | 61.3 | 60.3 | 59.8 | 58.2 | 58.7 | 63.2 | 67.0 | 74.5 | 61.6 |
| 2016-17 | 67.1 | 67.0 | 66.0 | 67.2 | 67.9 | 67.0 | 68.8 | 69.2 | 69.3 | 69.9 | 70.4 | 73.0 | 68.6 |
| 2017-18 | 64.7 | 64.1 | 66.5 | 67.3 | 68.6 | 68.9 | 68.1 | 68.3 | 67.7 | 69.6 | 75.7 | 76.4 | 68.8 |
| 2018-19 | 69.7 | 70.8 | 72.1 | 72.9 | 72.6 | 65.4 | 67.6 | 68.9 | 70.5 | 69.6 | 68.2 | 74.7 | 70.3 |
| 2019-20 | 56.2 | 59.4 | 59.0 | 59.7 | 61.6 | 59.7 | 60.6 | 57.6 | 55.0 | 54.9 | 56.5 | 60.3 | 58.4 |
| 2020-21 | 57.1 | 59.3 | 60.1 | 63.4 | 65.2 | 69.3 | 72.8 | 70.0 | 71.1 | 71.2 | 72.9 | 74.5 | 67.3 |
| 2021-22 | 78.3 | 76.4 | 84.3 | 85.9 | 87.7 | 96.3 | 98.6 | 102.0 | 110.0 | 90.7 | 93.7 | 98.2 | 91.8 |
| 2022-23[2] | 93.0 | 85.9 | 86.4 | 80.0 | 84.4 | 80.2 | 79.8 | | | | | | 84.2 |

[1] Weighted average by sales.   [2] Preliminary.   *Source: Agricultural Marketing Service, U.S. Department of Agriculture (AMS-USDA)*

# COTTON

## Purchases Reported by Exchanges in Designated U.S. Spot Markets[1]   In Running Bales

| Crop Year Beginning Aug. 1 | Aug. | Sept. | Oct. | Nov. | Dec. | Jan. | Feb. | Mar. | Apr. | May | June | July | Market Total |
|---|---|---|---|---|---|---|---|---|---|---|---|---|---|
| 2012-13 | 38,533 | 55,227 | 81,437 | 408,050 | 417,927 | 382,992 | 112,442 | 62,556 | 65,991 | 27,923 | 25,573 | 12,135 | 1,690,786 |
| 2013-14 | 20,398 | 26,066 | 52,042 | 198,579 | 433,317 | 345,007 | 141,663 | 57,669 | 24,792 | 24,878 | 7,569 | 6,815 | 1,338,795 |
| 2014-15 | 21,486 | 35,934 | 141,203 | 200,756 | 593,113 | 425,345 | 404,710 | 121,097 | 117,746 | 26,509 | 19,259 | 20,128 | 2,127,286 |
| 2015-16 | 18,634 | 24,429 | 56,127 | 220,807 | 424,830 | 297,380 | 196,419 | 128,004 | 61,364 | 28,446 | 16,622 | 56,367 | 1,529,429 |
| 2016-17 | 9,555 | 26,482 | 54,441 | 251,092 | 253,534 | 549,344 | 214,644 | 159,483 | 38,442 | 8,097 | 2,411 | 3,121 | 1,570,646 |
| 2017-18 | 16,659 | 20,322 | 57,282 | 341,259 | 429,829 | 427,512 | 255,750 | 152,678 | 156,773 | 152,630 | 35,949 | 13,783 | 2,060,426 |
| 2018-19 | 11,511 | 5,796 | 18,533 | 79,339 | 122,132 | 226,334 | 204,858 | 331,767 | 115,807 | 74,715 | 64,716 | 27,775 | 1,283,283 |
| 2019-20 | 35,241 | 71,105 | 103,590 | 199,665 | 455,781 | 350,099 | 108,467 | 49,111 | 77,192 | 46,280 | 47,722 | ---- | 1,544,253 |
| 2020-21 | 111,277 | 70,474 | 120,167 | 192,423 | 419,707 | 229,316 | 109,048 | 64,204 | 36,866 | 13,682 | 15,765 | 13,755 | 1,396,684 |
| 2021-22 | 9,723 | 47,215 | 94,933 | 232,941 | 383,757 | 482,976 | 186,439 | | | | | | 1,437,984 |

[1] Seven markets.   Source: Agricultural Marketing Service, U.S. Department of Agriculture (AMS-USDA)

## Production of All Cotton in the United States   In Thousands of 480-Pound Bales

| Year | Alabama | Arizona | Arkansas | California | Georgia | Louisiana | Mississippi | Missouri | North Carolina | South Carolina | Tennessee | Texas | Total |
|---|---|---|---|---|---|---|---|---|---|---|---|---|---|
| 2013 | 590 | 483 | 720 | 943 | 2,320 | 326 | 719 | 496 | 766 | 360 | 414 | 4,185 | 12,909 |
| 2014 | 653 | 520 | 787 | 714 | 2,570 | 404 | 1,078 | 570 | 995 | 528 | 494 | 6,203 | 16,319 |
| 2015 | 554 | 308 | 471 | 526 | 2,255 | 189 | 672 | 400 | 527 | 155 | 305 | 5,748 | 12,888 |
| 2016 | 706 | 395 | 840 | 747 | 2,180 | 268 | 1,081 | 566 | 343 | 250 | 575 | 8,133 | 17,170 |
| 2017 | 808 | 515 | 1,074 | 865 | 2,225 | 404 | 1,351 | 750 | 741 | 471 | 732 | 9,296 | 20,923 |
| 2018 | 888 | 466 | 1,133 | 914 | 1,955 | 420 | 1,462 | 921 | 702 | 420 | 770 | 6,884 | 18,367 |
| 2019 | 1,028 | 393 | 1,506 | 821 | 2,740 | 582 | 1,621 | 915 | 1,040 | 497 | 960 | 6,337 | 19,913 |
| 2020 | 734 | 316 | 1,277 | 615 | 2,180 | 339 | 1,180 | 684 | 522 | 299 | 611 | 4,613 | 14,608 |
| 2021[1] | 690 | 334 | 1,235 | 374 | 2,210 | 219 | 893 | 814 | 773 | 425 | 583 | 7,726 | 17,523 |
| 2022[2] | 815 | 290 | 1,550 | 445 | 2,500 | 360 | 1,130 | 740 | 950 | 500 | 698 | 3,345 | 14,242 |

[1] Preliminary.   [2] Forecast.   Source: Agricultural Statistics Board, U.S. Department of Agriculture (ASB-USDA)

## Cotton Production and Yield Estimates in the United States

| | Forecasts of Production (1,000 Bales of 480 Lbs.[1]) | | | | | Actual | Forecasts of Yield (Lbs. Per Harvested Acre) | | | | | Actual |
|---|---|---|---|---|---|---|---|---|---|---|---|---|---|
| Year | Aug.1 | Sept.1 | Oct. 1 | Nov. 1 | Dec. 1 | Jan. 1 | Crop | Aug.1 | Sept.1 | Oct. 1 | Nov. 1 | Dec. 1 | Jan. 1 | Yield |
| 2013 | 13,053 | 12,899 | NA | 13,105 | 13,069 | ---- | 12,909 | 813 | 796 | NA | 808 | 806 | ---- | 821 |
| 2014 | 17,502 | 16,538 | 16,255 | 16,397 | 15,923 | ---- | 16,319 | 820 | 803 | 790 | 797 | 773 | ---- | 838 |
| 2015 | 13,082 | 13,428 | 13,338 | 13,281 | 13,031 | ---- | 12,888 | 795 | 789 | 784 | 782 | 768 | ---- | 766 |
| 2016 | 15,879 | 16,142 | 16,034 | 16,162 | 16,524 | ---- | 17,170 | 800 | 802 | 797 | 803 | 821 | ---- | 867 |
| 2017 | 20,545 | 21,758 | 21,115 | 21,377 | 21,440 | ---- | 20,923 | 892 | 908 | 889 | 900 | 902 | ---- | 905 |
| 2018 | 19,235 | 19,682 | 19,763 | 18,408 | 18,588 | ---- | 18,367 | 911 | 895 | 901 | 852 | 860 | ---- | 882 |
| 2019 | 22,516 | 21,862 | 21,705 | 20,817 | 20,206 | ---- | 19,913 | 855 | 839 | 833 | 799 | 775 | ---- | 810 |
| 2020 | 18,080 | 17,064 | 17,045 | 17,092 | 15,949 | ---- | 14,608 | 938 | 910 | 909 | 911 | 850 | ---- | 847 |
| 2021 | 17,264 | 18,509 | 18,004 | 18,198 | 18,284 | ---- | 17,523 | 800 | 895 | 871 | 880 | 885 | ---- | 819 |
| 2022 | 12,570 | 13,832 | 13,812 | 14,031 | 14,242 | ---- | 14,242 | 846 | 843 | 842 | 855 | 868 | ---- | 868 |

[1] Net weight bales.   Source: Agricultural Statistics Board, U.S. Department of Agriculture (ASB-USDA)

## Supply and Distribution of Upland Cotton in the United States   In Thousands of 480-Pound Bales

| Crop Year Beginning Aug. 1 | Area Planted 1,000 Acres | Area Harvested 1,000 Acres | Yield Lbs./Acre | Supply Beginning Stocks[3] | Supply Production | Supply Imports | Total Supply | Disappearance Mill Use | Disappearance Exports | Disappearance Total | Ending Stocks | Farm Price[5] Cents/Lb. |
|---|---|---|---|---|---|---|---|---|---|---|---|---|
| 2013-14 | 10,206 | 7,345 | 802 | 3,613 | 12,275 | 6 | 15,894 | 3,527 | 9,850 | 13,377 | 2,225 | 79.6 |
| 2014-15 | 10,845 | 9,157 | 826 | 2,225 | 15,753 | 9 | 17,987 | 3,550 | 10,836 | 14,386 | 3,391 | 64.2 |
| 2015-16 | 8,422 | 7,903 | 756 | 3,391 | 12,455 | 30 | 15,876 | 3,425 | 8,619 | 12,044 | 3,664 | 61.6 |
| 2016-17 | 9,878 | 9,320 | 855 | 3,664 | 16,601 | 5 | 20,270 | 3,221 | 14,303 | 17,524 | 2,686 | 68.6 |
| 2017-18 | 12,465 | 10,850 | 895 | 2,686 | 20,223 | 1 | 22,910 | 3,198 | 15,645 | 18,843 | 4,097 | 68.8 |
| 2018-19 | 13,850 | 9,742 | 865 | 4,097 | 17,566 | 5 | 21,663 | 2,953 | 14,162 | 17,115 | 4,636 | 70.3 |
| 2019-20 | 13,507 | 11,274 | 819 | 4,636 | 19,227 | 0 | 23,863 | 2,135 | 15,006 | 17,141 | 6,868 | 58.4 |
| 2020-21 | 11,890 | 8,081 | 835 | 6,868 | 14,061 | 0 | 20,929 | 2,385 | 15,586 | 17,971 | 3,020 | 67.3 |
| 2021-22[1] | 11,089 | 10,149 | 813 | 3,020 | 17,191 | 0 | 20,872 | 2,485 | 15,075 | 17,560 | 3,359 | 91.8 |
| 2022-23[2] | 13,622 | 7,712 | 832 | | 13,372 | | | | | | | |

[1] Preliminary.   [2] Estimate.   [3] Excludes preseason ginnings (adjusted to 480-lb. bale net weight basis).   [4] Includes preseason ginnings.
[5] Marketing year average price.   Source: Economic Research Service, U.S. Department of Agriculture (ERS-USDA)

# COTTON

**COTTON #2 - ICE-US**
Weekly Selected Futures as of 03/31/2023

Weekly Selected Futures
As of 03/31/2023
Chart High 158.02 on 05/04/2022
Chart Low 48.35 on 04/01/2020

Nearby Futures through Last Trading Day using selected contract months: March, May, July, October and December.

### Volume of Trading of Cotton #2 Futures in New York — In Contracts

| Year | Jan. | Feb. | Mar. | Apr. | May | June | July | Aug. | Sept. | Oct. | Nov. | Dec. | Total |
|---|---|---|---|---|---|---|---|---|---|---|---|---|---|
| 2013 | 599,171 | 738,954 | 474,475 | 725,015 | 494,848 | 729,167 | 282,565 | 464,074 | 273,354 | 487,233 | 588,624 | 297,544 | 6,155,024 |
| 2014 | 544,180 | 602,542 | 446,810 | 568,063 | 399,736 | 611,785 | 362,461 | 338,548 | 460,119 | 477,742 | 625,593 | 350,304 | 5,787,883 |
| 2015 | 474,061 | 764,365 | 532,511 | 774,667 | 504,552 | 748,679 | 391,137 | 541,234 | 378,522 | 492,136 | 718,549 | 405,429 | 6,725,842 |
| 2016 | 556,311 | 939,909 | 544,144 | 920,712 | 567,195 | 802,595 | 582,169 | 538,811 | 437,283 | 528,534 | 876,713 | 408,670 | 7,703,046 |
| 2017 | 621,642 | 919,593 | 648,217 | 805,263 | 728,004 | 731,750 | 367,996 | 499,490 | 527,357 | 539,450 | 954,722 | 564,023 | 7,907,507 |
| 2018 | 908,692 | 1,040,986 | 697,571 | 967,537 | 865,014 | 966,955 | 395,024 | 544,209 | 451,364 | 641,924 | 889,009 | 507,810 | 8,876,095 |
| 2019 | 607,201 | 901,354 | 685,982 | 877,964 | 771,698 | 778,893 | 467,666 | 555,618 | 498,553 | 771,503 | 953,641 | 591,376 | 8,461,449 |
| 2020 | 803,523 | 1,108,447 | 999,072 | 819,599 | 497,631 | 678,605 | 409,570 | 476,008 | 508,333 | 701,383 | 828,278 | 493,784 | 8,324,233 |
| 2021 | 678,039 | 1,073,253 | 765,629 | 821,506 | 529,388 | 726,755 | 464,057 | 549,246 | 699,970 | 837,650 | 889,742 | 466,475 | 8,501,710 |
| 2022 | 604,075 | 750,095 | 699,484 | 770,233 | 569,484 | 787,118 | 505,337 | 586,289 | 608,181 | 747,084 | 892,753 | 470,840 | 7,990,973 |

Contract size = 50,000 lbs.   *Source: ICE Futures U.S. (ICE)*

### Average Open Interest of Cotton #2 Futures in New York — In Contracts

| Year | Jan. | Feb. | Mar. | Apr. | May | June | July | Aug. | Sept. | Oct. | Nov. | Dec. |
|---|---|---|---|---|---|---|---|---|---|---|---|---|
| 2013 | 185,106 | 201,378 | 205,753 | 188,311 | 181,012 | 173,729 | 162,260 | 191,013 | 178,447 | 203,972 | 172,006 | 164,247 |
| 2014 | 180,149 | 171,213 | 178,245 | 178,514 | 190,808 | 169,165 | 152,321 | 167,437 | 181,359 | 190,436 | 181,192 | 175,349 |
| 2015 | 197,949 | 192,586 | 182,898 | 180,941 | 191,700 | 175,835 | 177,911 | 185,267 | 180,786 | 192,945 | 184,447 | 188,025 |
| 2016 | 188,149 | 196,230 | 211,958 | 203,691 | 191,903 | 197,043 | 216,925 | 236,332 | 238,644 | 251,736 | 250,363 | 248,786 |
| 2017 | 263,192 | 275,644 | 277,202 | 252,849 | 254,360 | 219,791 | 213,858 | 221,829 | 238,371 | 230,544 | 232,469 | 262,608 |
| 2018 | 301,515 | 271,212 | 272,354 | 270,033 | 290,493 | 289,963 | 257,708 | 260,562 | 253,033 | 259,661 | 241,659 | 217,465 |
| 2019 | 228,469 | 234,159 | 223,225 | 218,548 | 217,558 | 192,072 | 190,297 | 213,722 | 231,086 | 238,617 | 224,486 | 205,207 |
| 2020 | 251,311 | 219,080 | 204,701 | 183,388 | 179,296 | 172,208 | 173,848 | 194,284 | 218,706 | 237,465 | 229,699 | 220,397 |
| 2021 | 246,900 | 248,748 | 232,954 | 221,735 | 224,032 | 218,868 | 233,682 | 262,436 | 273,079 | 287,023 | 271,733 | 235,083 |
| 2022 | 248,960 | 251,289 | 229,142 | 215,618 | 205,319 | 196,138 | 178,838 | 197,036 | 214,220 | 237,548 | 214,383 | 195,515 |

Contract size = 50,000 lbs.   *Source: ICE Futures U.S. (ICE)*

# COTTON

## Average Spot Prices of U.S. Cotton,[2] Base Quality (SLM) at Designated Markets    In Cents Per Pound

| Crop Year Beginning Aug. 1 | Dallas (EastTex.-Okl.) | Fresno (San Joaquin Valley) | Greenville (Southeast) | Greenwood (South Delta) | Lubbock (West Texas) | Memphis (North Delta) | Phoenix Desert (Southwest) | Average |
|---|---|---|---|---|---|---|---|---|
| 2013-14 | 79.27 | 78.88 | 82.74 | 81.85 | 79.14 | 81.85 | 78.23 | 80.28 |
| 2014-15 | 60.75 | 62.32 | 63.55 | 62.64 | 60.71 | 62.64 | 61.57 | 62.02 |
| 2015-16 | 59.29 | 60.88 | 63.32 | 62.44 | 59.16 | 62.44 | 59.73 | 61.04 |
| 2016-17 | 70.25 | 69.62 | 72.91 | 71.81 | 70.06 | 71.81 | 68.51 | 70.71 |
| 2017-18 | 74.38 | 74.55 | 78.79 | 77.59 | 73.14 | 77.60 | 73.52 | 76.01 |
| 2018-19 | 68.59 | 69.92 | 71.52 | 68.67 | 68.04 | 71.52 | 68.54 | 72.55 |
| 2019-20 | 57.06 | 55.16 | 60.53 | 59.40 | 56.90 | 59.47 | 54.66 | 57.58 |
| 2020-21 | 66.91 | 72.67 | 76.20 | 74.47 | 72.20 | 75.62 | 71.34 | 75.11 |
| 2021-22 | 112.24 | 114.13 | 117.19 | 112.20 | 110.66 | 117.19 | 111.16 | 118.25 |
| 2022-23[1] | 88.39 | 89.94 | 92.20 | 88.46 | 87.37 | 92.20 | 87.77 | 93.18 |

[1] Preliminary    [2] Prices are for mixed lots, net weight, uncompressed in warehouse.
*Source: Agricultural Marketing Service, U.S. Department of Agriculture (AMS-USDA)*

## Cotton Ginnings[1] in the United States To:    In Thousands of Running Bales

| Crop Year | Aug. 1 | Sept. 1 | Sept. 15 | Oct. 1 | Oct. 15 | Nov. 1 | Nov. 15 | Dec. 1 | Dec. 15 | Jan. 1 | Jan. 15 | Feb. 1 | Mar. 1 | Total Crop |
|---|---|---|---|---|---|---|---|---|---|---|---|---|---|---|
| 2013-14 | W | 132 | 274 | 486 | 1,101 | 3,038 | 5,723 | 8,260 | 10,459 | 11,402 | 12,053 | 12,391 | ---- | 12,521 |
| 2014-15 | 1 | 367 | 696 | 1,154 | 2,108 | 4,807 | 7,530 | 10,246 | 12,601 | 14,214 | 15,030 | 15,538 | ---- | 15,876 |
| 2015-16 | ---- | 105 | 293 | 635 | 1,448 | 3,704 | 5,738 | 7,955 | 9,830 | 11,092 | 11,737 | 12,251 | 12,517 | 12,529 |
| 2016-17 | 35 | 438 | 701 | 1,167 | 2,308 | 5,016 | 7,584 | 10,296 | 12,261 | 13,858 | 14,840 | 15,881 | 16,559 | 16,710 |
| 2017-18 | 107 | 571 | 789 | 1,249 | 2,298 | 4,915 | 7,878 | 11,287 | 13,963 | 16,120 | 17,398 | 18,654 | 19,557 | 20,441 |
| 2018-19 | 20 | 489 | 745 | 1,287 | 2,421 | 4,878 | 7,083 | 10,265 | 12,275 | NA | NA | 16,651 | 17,473 | 17,909 |
| 2019-20 | 4 | 359 | 622 | 1,283 | 2,840 | 6,250 | 9,304 | 12,924 | 15,598 | 17,472 | 18,278 | 18,925 | 19,303 | 19,409 |
| 2020-21 | 4 | 288 | 587 | 915 | 1,661 | 3,987 | 6,535 | 9,570 | 11,538 | 12,966 | 13,417 | 13,955 | 14,153 | 14,255 |
| 2021-22 | W | 200 | W | 741 | 1,108 | 3,543 | 6,278 | 9,804 | 12,469 | 14,632 | 15,542 | 16,552 | 17,013 | 17,108 |
| 2022-23[2] | 31 | 507 | 695 | 1,110 | 2,008 | 4,384 | 6,733 | 9,439 | 11,414 | 12,981 | 13,707 | 14,100 | 14,313 | |

[1] Excluding linters.    [2] Preliminary.    W = Withheld.    *Source: National Agricultural Statistics Service, U.S. Department of Agriculture (NASS-USDA)*

## Exports of All Cotton[2] from the United States    In Thousands of Running Bales

| Crop Year | Aug. | Sept. | Oct. | Nov. | Dec. | Jan. | Feb. | Mar. | Apr. | May | June | July | Total |
|---|---|---|---|---|---|---|---|---|---|---|---|---|---|
| 2013-14 | 767 | 533 | 414 | 606 | 975 | 1,417 | 1,345 | 1,347 | 1,087 | 873 | 607 | 446 | 10,418 |
| 2014-15 | 499 | 380 | 354 | 572 | 1,024 | 1,126 | 1,430 | 1,596 | 1,418 | 1,369 | 945 | 769 | 11,482 |
| 2015-16 | 560 | 404 | 370 | 396 | 643 | 776 | 918 | 1,083 | 1,083 | 1,077 | 1,042 | 909 | 9,261 |
| 2016-17 | 966 | 799 | 569 | 828 | 1,291 | 1,580 | 1,734 | 1,936 | 1,634 | 1,592 | 1,209 | 1,175 | 15,313 |
| 2017-18 | 933 | 577 | 447 | 727 | 1,399 | 1,647 | 1,980 | 2,329 | 2,198 | 1,989 | 1,428 | 1,088 | 16,741 |
| 2018-19 | 815 | 715 | 609 | 681 | 976 | 1,225 | 1,484 | 2,110 | 1,758 | 1,831 | 1,687 | 1,430 | 15,320 |
| 2019-20 | 1,034 | 910 | 732 | 841 | 1,320 | 1,699 | 1,969 | 2,003 | 1,254 | 1,238 | 1,464 | 1,629 | 16,093 |
| 2020-21 | 1,424 | 924 | 1,195 | 1,329 | 1,425 | 1,614 | 1,571 | 1,637 | 1,585 | 1,637 | 1,208 | 1,102 | 16,650 |
| 2021-22 | 974 | 572 | 452 | 450 | 842 | 1,406 | 1,632 | 1,946 | 1,887 | 1,890 | 1,697 | 1,405 | 15,153 |
| 2022-23[1] | 1,231 | 704 | 547 | 760 | 675 | 981 | | | | | | | 9,794 |

[1] Preliminary.    *Source: Foreign Agricultural Service, U.S. Department of Agriculture (FAS-USDA)*

## U.S. Exports of American Cotton to Countries of Destination    In Thousands of 480-Pound Bales

| Crop Year Beginning Aug. 1 | Canada | China | Hong Kong | Indonesia | Italy | Japan | Korea, South | Mexico | Philippines | Taiwan | Thailand | United Kingdom | Total |
|---|---|---|---|---|---|---|---|---|---|---|---|---|---|
| 2012-13 | 2 | 5,615 | 105 | 533 | 8 | 120 | 355 | 979 | 31 | 419 | 353 | 0 | 13,330 |
| 2013-14 | 2 | 2,646 | 13 | 701 | 9 | 115 | 461 | 1,009 | 39 | 299 | 457 | 0 | 10,418 |
| 2014-15 | 2 | 2,709 | 16 | 978 | 22 | 114 | 670 | 950 | 42 | 349 | 466 | 7 | 11,460 |
| 2015-16 | 1 | 842 | 0 | 690 | 9 | 124 | 476 | 994 | 34 | 330 | 379 | 0 | 9,260 |
| 2016-17 | 1 | 2,310 | 1 | 1,476 | 9 | 121 | 598 | 1,007 | 65 | 422 | 577 | 1 | 15,314 |
| 2017-18 | 1 | 2,626 | 2 | 1,587 | 14 | 122 | 606 | 949 | 57 | 466 | 666 | 1 | 16,714 |
| 2018-19 | 1 | 1,637 | 7 | 1,037 | 9 | 101 | 450 | 794 | 46 | 431 | 563 | 1 | 15,449 |
| 2019-20 | 0 | 2,980 | 16 | 861 | 16 | 126 | 402 | 522 | 9 | 275 | 409 | 0 | 15,918 |
| 2020-21[1] | 1 | 5,233 | 33 | 686 | 9 | 104 | 340 | 820 | 16 | 171 | 311 | 0 | 16,612 |
| 2021-22[2] | 1 | 4,963 | 27 | 419 | 8 | 108 | 241 | 923 | 7 | 106 | 238 | 0 | 15,153 |

[1] Preliminary.    [2] Estimate.    *Source: Foreign Agricultural Service, U.S. Department of Agriculture (FAS-USDA)*

# COTTON

## Cotton[1] Government Loan Program in the United States

| Crop Year Beginning Aug. 1 | Support Price --- Cents Per Lb. --- | Target Price | Put Under Support Ths Bales | % of Production | Acquired ----- Ths. Bales ----- | Owned July 31 | Crop Year Beginning Aug. 1 | Support Price --- Cents Per Lb. --- | Target Price | Put Under Support Ths Bales | % of Production | Acquired ----- Ths. Bales ----- | Owned July 31 |
|---|---|---|---|---|---|---|---|---|---|---|---|---|---|
| 2011-12 | 52.00 | 71.3 | 7,268 | 49.3 | 1 | 0 | 2016-17 | 52.00 | NA | 9,373 | 56.4 | 0 | 0 |
| 2012-13 | 52.00 | 71.3 | 8,330 | 50.4 | 0 | 0 | 2017-18 | 49.49 | NA | 9,597 | 46.7 | 0 | 0 |
| 2013-14 | 52.00 | 71.3 | 3,981 | 32.4 | 0 | 0 | 2018-19 | 52.00 | 36.7 | 8,250 | 47.0 | 73 | 0 |
| 2014-15 | 52.00 | NA | 7,625 | 48.4 | 0 | 0 | 2019-20 | 52.00 | 36.7 | 11,787 | 61.3 | 0 | 0 |
| 2015-16 | 52.00 | NA | 6,758 | 54.3 | 0 | 0 | 2020-21[1] | 52.00 | 36.7 | 8,326 | 59.2 | 0 | 0 |

[1] Upland.  [2] Preliminary.  NA = Not applicable.  *Source: Economic Research Service, U.S. Department of Agriculture (ERS-USDA)*

## Weekly Outstanding Export Sales and Cumulative Exports of U.S. Cotton    In Running Bales

| Marketing Year 2021/2022 Week Ending | Weekly Exports | Accumulated Exports | Net Sales | Outstanding Sales | Marketing Year 2022/2023 Week Ending | Weekly Exports | Accumulated Exports | Net Sales | Outstanding Sales |
|---|---|---|---|---|---|---|---|---|---|
| Aug 05, 2021 | 190,648 | 190,648 | 1,653,650 | 4,785,765 | Aug 04, 2022 | 181,259 | 181,259 | 2,490,143 | 7,136,910 |
| Aug 12, 2021 | 221,063 | 411,711 | 242,381 | 4,807,083 | Aug 11, 2022 | 267,374 | 448,633 | 49,522 | 6,919,058 |
| Aug 19, 2021 | 201,731 | 613,442 | 245,134 | 4,850,486 | Aug 18, 2022 | | 448,633 | | 6,919,058 |
| Aug 26, 2021 | 168,636 | 782,078 | 105,225 | 4,787,075 | Aug 25, 2022 | 580,671 | 1,029,304 | 258,126 | 6,596,513 |
| Sep 02, 2021 | 155,270 | 937,348 | 453,042 | 5,084,847 | Sep 01, 2022 | 235,392 | 1,264,696 | 230,655 | 6,591,776 |
| Sep 09, 2021 | 237,495 | 1,174,843 | 284,813 | 5,132,165 | Sep 08, 2022 | 141,000 | 1,405,696 | 100,261 | 6,551,037 |
| Sep 16, 2021 | 176,779 | 1,351,622 | 345,383 | 5,300,769 | Sep 15, 2022 | 232,316 | 1,638,012 | 32,432 | 6,351,153 |
| Sep 23, 2021 | 163,879 | 1,515,501 | 571,393 | 5,708,283 | Sep 22, 2022 | 187,858 | 1,825,870 | 30,222 | 6,193,517 |
| Sep 30, 2021 | 125,100 | 1,640,601 | 246,697 | 5,829,880 | Sep 29, 2022 | 209,649 | 2,035,519 | 121,209 | 6,105,077 |
| Oct 07, 2021 | 95,164 | 1,735,765 | 146,653 | 5,881,369 | Oct 06, 2022 | 168,057 | 2,203,576 | 144,820 | 6,081,840 |
| Oct 14, 2021 | 117,442 | 1,853,207 | 391,796 | 6,155,723 | Oct 13, 2022 | 165,741 | 2,369,317 | 84,471 | 6,000,570 |
| Oct 21, 2021 | 63,424 | 1,916,631 | 360,753 | 6,453,052 | Oct 20, 2022 | 177,579 | 2,546,896 | 68,437 | 5,891,428 |
| Oct 28, 2021 | 141,853 | 2,058,484 | 139,110 | 6,450,309 | Oct 27, 2022 | 118,961 | 2,665,857 | 191,755 | 5,964,222 |
| Nov 04, 2021 | 87,875 | 2,146,359 | 127,968 | 6,490,402 | Nov 03, 2022 | 108,121 | 2,773,978 | 145,795 | 6,001,896 |
| Nov 11, 2021 | 77,867 | 2,224,226 | 136,702 | 6,549,237 | Nov 10, 2022 | 182,951 | 2,956,929 | 25,059 | 5,844,004 |
| Nov 18, 2021 | 97,097 | 2,321,323 | 196,934 | 6,649,074 | Nov 17, 2022 | 143,698 | 3,100,627 | -116,428 | 5,583,878 |
| Nov 25, 2021 | 71,388 | 2,392,711 | 374,896 | 6,952,582 | Nov 24, 2022 | 139,458 | 3,240,085 | 16,494 | 5,460,914 |
| Dec 02, 2021 | 114,784 | 2,507,495 | 382,586 | 7,220,384 | Dec 01, 2022 | 141,145 | 3,381,230 | 32,640 | 5,352,409 |
| Dec 09, 2021 | 131,460 | 2,638,955 | 286,437 | 7,375,361 | Dec 08, 2022 | 141,851 | 3,523,081 | 18,647 | 5,229,205 |
| Dec 16, 2021 | 130,762 | 2,769,717 | 243,561 | 7,488,160 | Dec 15, 2022 | 110,440 | 3,633,521 | -87,805 | 5,030,960 |
| Dec 23, 2021 | 162,183 | 2,931,900 | 192,204 | 7,518,181 | Dec 22, 2022 | 140,310 | 3,773,831 | 82,254 | 4,972,904 |
| Dec 30, 2021 | 104,869 | 3,036,769 | 143,152 | 7,556,464 | Dec 29, 2022 | 93,622 | 3,867,453 | 39,615 | 4,918,897 |
| Jan 06, 2022 | 167,613 | 3,204,382 | 400,985 | 7,789,836 | Jan 05, 2023 | 150,500 | 4,017,953 | 72,610 | 4,841,007 |
| Jan 13, 2022 | 198,682 | 3,403,064 | 273,045 | 7,864,199 | Jan 12, 2023 | 183,105 | 4,201,058 | 209,435 | 4,867,337 |
| Jan 20, 2022 | 197,912 | 3,600,976 | 391,338 | 8,057,625 | Jan 19, 2023 | 175,793 | 4,376,851 | 213,680 | 4,905,224 |
| Jan 27, 2022 | 302,135 | 3,903,111 | 332,098 | 8,087,588 | Jan 26, 2023 | 212,244 | 4,589,095 | 171,160 | 4,864,140 |
| Feb 03, 2022 | 299,656 | 4,202,767 | 185,218 | 7,973,150 | Feb 02, 2023 | 210,127 | 4,799,222 | 262,788 | 4,916,801 |
| Feb 10, 2022 | 270,022 | 4,472,789 | 158,493 | 7,861,621 | Feb 09, 2023 | 186,392 | 4,985,614 | 216,915 | 4,947,324 |
| Feb 17, 2022 | 376,107 | 4,848,896 | 247,234 | 7,732,748 | Feb 16, 2023 | 193,571 | 5,179,185 | 425,322 | 5,179,075 |
| Feb 24, 2022 | 354,123 | 5,203,019 | 348,589 | 7,727,214 | Feb 23, 2023 | 207,748 | 5,386,933 | 170,583 | 5,141,910 |
| Mar 03, 2022 | 321,258 | 5,524,277 | 354,174 | 7,760,130 | Mar 02, 2023 | | | | |
| Mar 10, 2022 | 325,467 | 5,849,744 | 371,353 | 7,806,016 | Mar 09, 2023 | | | | |
| Mar 17, 2022 | 442,672 | 6,292,416 | 307,539 | 7,670,883 | Mar 16, 2023 | | | | |
| Mar 24, 2022 | 331,060 | 6,623,476 | 233,951 | 7,573,774 | Mar 23, 2023 | | | | |
| Mar 31, 2022 | 455,470 | 7,078,946 | 62,883 | 7,181,187 | Mar 30, 2023 | | | | |
| Apr 07, 2022 | 333,848 | 7,412,794 | 59,282 | 6,906,621 | Apr 06, 2023 | | | | |
| Apr 14, 2022 | 367,148 | 7,779,942 | 50,470 | 6,589,943 | Apr 13, 2023 | | | | |
| Apr 21, 2022 | 385,975 | 8,165,917 | 121,142 | 6,325,110 | Apr 20, 2023 | | | | |
| Apr 28, 2022 | 426,631 | 8,592,548 | 232,356 | 6,130,835 | Apr 27, 2023 | | | | |
| May 05, 2022 | 364,519 | 8,957,067 | 27,505 | 5,793,821 | May 04, 2023 | | | | |
| May 12, 2022 | 343,189 | 9,300,256 | 110,914 | 5,561,546 | May 11, 2023 | | | | |
| May 19, 2022 | 318,472 | 9,618,728 | 37,009 | 5,280,083 | May 18, 2023 | | | | |
| May 26, 2022 | 484,199 | 10,102,927 | 354,196 | 5,150,080 | May 25, 2023 | | | | |
| Jun 02, 2022 | 335,890 | 10,438,817 | 259,188 | 5,073,378 | Jun 01, 2023 | | | | |
| Jun 09, 2022 | 335,819 | 10,774,636 | 26,547 | 4,764,106 | Jun 08, 2023 | | | | |
| Jun 16, 2022 | 371,867 | 11,146,503 | 16,207 | 4,408,446 | Jun 15, 2023 | | | | |
| Jun 23, 2022 | 364,415 | 11,510,918 | 48,123 | 4,092,154 | Jun 22, 2023 | | | | |
| Jun 30, 2022 | 377,831 | 11,888,749 | 37,350 | 3,751,673 | Jun 29, 2023 | | | | |
| Jul 07, 2022 | 312,703 | 12,201,452 | 10,167 | 3,449,137 | Jul 06, 2023 | | | | |
| Jul 14, 2022 | 330,795 | 12,532,247 | 54,071 | 3,172,413 | Jul 13, 2023 | | | | |
| Jul 21, 2022 | 252,866 | 12,785,113 | -3,959 | 2,915,588 | Jul 20, 2023 | | | | |
| Jul 28, 2022 | 279,734 | 13,064,847 | -112,406 | 2,523,448 | Jul 27, 2023 | | | | |
| Aug 04, 2022 | 114,211 | 13,179,058 | -21,466 | 2,387,771 | | | | | |

*Source: Foreign Agricultural Service, U.S. Department of Agriculture (FAS-USDA)*

# Cottonseed and Products

Cottonseed is crushed to produce both oil and meal. Cottonseed oil is typically used for cooking oil, and cottonseed meal is fed to livestock. Before the cottonseed is crushed for oil and meal, it is de-linted of its linters. Linters are used for padding in furniture, absorbent cotton swabs, and for the manufacture of many cellulose products. The sediment left by cottonseed oil refining, called "foots," provides fatty acids for industrial products. The value of cottonseeds represents a substantial 18% of a cotton producer's income.

**Prices** – The average monthly price of cottonseed oil in 2022 rose by +21.1% yr/yr to 110.77 cents per pound, a new record high. The average monthly price of cottonseed meal in 2022 rose by +6.5% yr/yr to $383.083 per short ton.

**Supply** – World production of cottonseed in the 2022/23 marketing year is forecasted to rise by +1.0% to 42.107 million metric tons, below the 2011/12 record high of 47.862. The world's largest cottonseed producers in 2022/23 are expected to be the European Union with 26.7% of world production, Burma with 26.1%, Brazil with 10.5%, and the U.S. with 9.6%. U.S. production of cottonseed in the 2022/23 marketing year is expected to fall by -16.3% yr/yr to 4.455 million tons. U.S. production of cottonseed oil in 2022/23 is expected to fall by -3.5% at 415 million pounds, far below the 20-year high of 957 million pounds posted in 2004-05.

**Demand** – U.S. cottonseed crushed (consumed) in the U.S. in the 2022/23 marketing year is expected to fall by -0.9% to 1.543 million tons, which is far below the levels of over 4 million tons seen in the 1970s.

**Trade** – U.S. exports of cottonseed in 2022/23 are expected to fall by -32.9% to 200 million tons. U.S. imports of cottonseed in 2022/23 are expected to rise by +120.0% to 55 short tons.

## World Production of Cottonseed    In Thousands of Metric Ton

| Crop Year Beginning Oct. 1 | Argentina | Australia | Brazil | Burkina | Burma | China | European Union | India | Mali | Pakistan | Turkey | United States | World Total |
|---|---|---|---|---|---|---|---|---|---|---|---|---|---|
| 2014-15 | 407 | 664 | 2,349 | 370 | 11,757 | 524 | 12,524 | 94 | 294 | 4,616 | 1,050 | 4,649 | 44,362 |
| 2015-16 | 180 | 881 | 1,937 | 295 | 8,600 | 409 | 10,996 | 78 | 276 | 3,032 | 870 | 3,668 | 35,619 |
| 2016-17 | 163 | 1,250 | 2,298 | 285 | 8,800 | 413 | 11,463 | 117 | 351 | 3,336 | 1,050 | 4,871 | 39,283 |
| 2017-18 | 218 | 1,442 | 3,019 | 310 | 10,800 | 489 | 12,312 | 117 | 396 | 3,552 | 1,300 | 5,826 | 45,255 |
| 2018-19 | 245 | 661 | 4,254 | 289 | 10,973 | 557 | 11,038 | 135 | 359 | 3,292 | 1,224 | 5,108 | 43,079 |
| 2019-20 | 283 | 187 | 4,575 | 299 | 10,758 | 642 | 12,100 | 141 | 382 | 2,686 | 1,126 | 5,393 | 43,629 |
| 2020-21 | 294 | 841 | 3,592 | 280 | 11,600 | 540 | 11,718 | 105 | 84 | 1,949 | 947 | 4,053 | 41,012 |
| 2021-22[1] | 326 | 1,727 | 3,891 | 290 | 10,503 | 536 | 10,359 | 103 | 404 | 2,599 | 1,241 | 4,829 | 41,701 |
| 2022-23[2] | 481 | 1,502 | 4,416 | 290 | 10,973 | 505 | 11,251 | 117 | 311 | 1,603 | 1,600 | 4,042 | 42,107 |

[1] Preliminary.   [2] Estimate.   Source: The Oil World

## Salient Statistics of Cottonseed in the United States    In Thousands of Short Tons

| Crop Year Beginning Aug. 1 | Stocks | Production | Imports | Total Supply | Crush | Exports | Other | Total | Farm Price USD/Ton | Value of Production Mil. USD | Oil (Million Pounds) | Meal (1,000 Short Tons) |
|---|---|---|---|---|---|---|---|---|---|---|---|---|
| 2014-15 | 425 | 5,125 | 60 | 5,610 | 1,900 | 228 | 3,045 | 5,173 | 437 | 194.0 | 1,016 | 610 |
| 2015-16 | 437 | 4,043 | 16 | 4,496 | 1,500 | 136 | 2,469 | 4,105 | 391 | 227.0 | 933 | 465 |
| 2016-17 | 391 | 5,369 | 51 | 5,811 | 1,769 | 342 | 3,300 | 5,411 | 400 | 195.0 | 1,056 | 542 |
| 2017-18 | 400 | 6,422 | 0 | 6,822 | 1,854 | 478 | 4,040 | 6,372 | 451 | 142.0 | 912 | 561 |
| 2018-19 | 451 | 5,631 | 1 | 6,083 | 1,760 | 387 | 3,458 | 5,606 | 477 | 155.0 | 878 | 456 |
| 2019-20 | 477 | 5,945 | 1 | 6,423 | 1,712 | 341 | 3,914 | 5,967 | 456 | 161.0 | 968 | 481 |
| 2020-21 | 456 | 4,468 | 1 | 4,925 | 1,563 | 280 | 2,687 | 4,529 | 396 | 194.0 | 875 | 400 |
| 2021-22[1] | 396 | 5,323 | 25 | 5,743 | 1,557 | 298 | 3,494 | 5,348 | 395 | 242.0 | 1,318 | 430 |
| 2022-23[2] | 395 | 4,455 | 55 | 4,905 | 1,500 | 200 | 2,782 | 4,482 | 423 | 253.0 | | |

[1] Preliminary.   [2] Estimate.   Source: Economic Research Service, U.S. Department of Agriculture (ERS-USDA)

## Average Wholesale Price of Cottonseed Meal (41% Solvent)[2] in Memphis    In Dollars Per Short Ton

| Year | Jan. | Feb. | Mar. | Apr. | May | June | July | Aug. | Sept. | Oct. | Nov. | Dec. | Average |
|---|---|---|---|---|---|---|---|---|---|---|---|---|---|
| 2014 | 378.34 | 388.75 | 401.25 | 405.50 | 416.88 | 412.50 | 359.50 | 310.00 | 360.63 | 346.88 | 313.13 | 334.38 | 368.98 |
| 2015 | 313.75 | 302.50 | 310.50 | 288.13 | 274.38 | 281.00 | 299.38 | 295.63 | 293.50 | 292.50 | 291.88 | 267.50 | 292.55 |
| 2016 | 248.75 | 238.13 | 216.50 | 207.50 | 242.50 | 284.00 | 280.00 | 280.00 | 285.00 | 241.88 | 221.00 | 217.50 | 246.90 |
| 2017 | 223.50 | 221.88 | 210.63 | 195.00 | 179.50 | 179.38 | 200.84 | 198.50 | 213.75 | 229.00 | 228.75 | 232.50 | 209.44 |
| 2018 | 259.00 | 303.13 | 323.13 | 263.13 | 262.50 | 257.50 | 253.13 | 260.00 | 258.75 | 249.00 | 240.00 | 243.75 | 264.42 |
| 2019 | 247.50 | 235.00 | 226.25 | 216.50 | 215.00 | 215.63 | 218.00 | 221.25 | 215.83 | 213.13 | 233.75 | 250.83 | 225.72 |
| 2020 | 239.38 | 250.63 | 259.00 | 281.88 | 251.88 | 245.50 | 245.00 | 245.00 | 248.50 | 301.88 | 365.63 | 435.83 | 280.84 |
| 2021 | 443.75 | 460.00 | 456.00 | 415.00 | 360.63 | 337.50 | 321.88 | 303.00 | 305.00 | 298.75 | 304.50 | 311.25 | 359.77 |
| 2022[1] | 318.13 | 333.75 | 345.63 | 355.00 | 388.75 | 383.75 | 369.50 | 405.00 | 450.00 | 451.88 | 405.00 | 390.63 | 383.08 |

[1] Preliminary.   Source: Economic Research Service, U.S. Department of Agriculture (ERS-USDA)

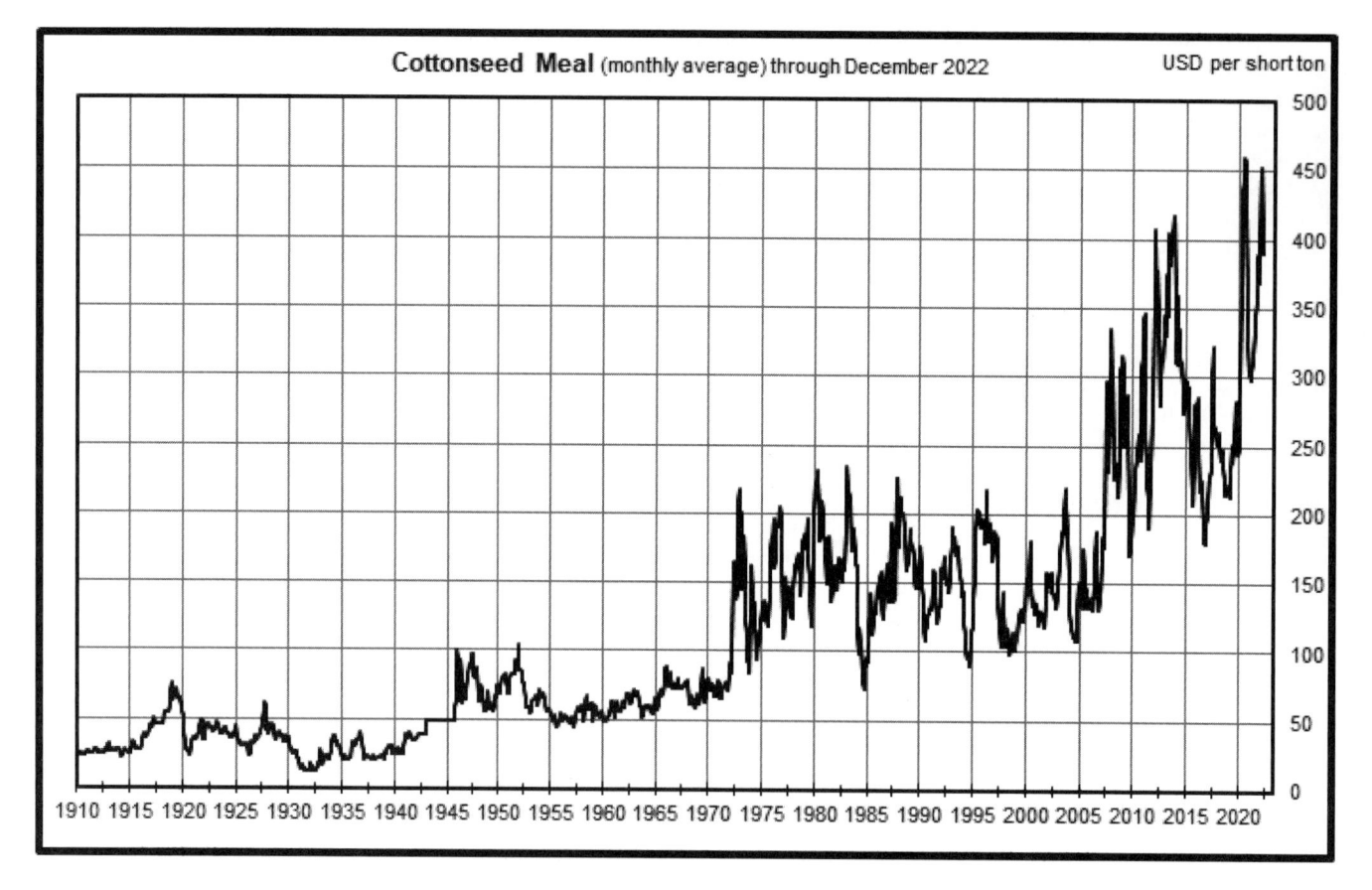

# COTTONSEED AND PRODUCTS

**Cottonseed Meal** (monthly average) through December 2022 — USD per short ton

## Supply and Distribution of Cottonseed Oil in the United States   In Millions of Pounds

| Crop Year Beginning Oct. 1 | Stocks | Production | Imports | Total Supply | Domestic | Exports | Total | Per Capita Consumption of Salad & Cooking Oils --- In Lbs. --- | Shortening | Salad & Cooking Oils | Total | U.S.[3] (Crude) $/Metric Ton | Rott[4] (Cif) |
|---|---|---|---|---|---|---|---|---|---|---|---|---|---|
| 2013-14 | 100 | 630 | 32.0 | 762 | 514 | 148 | 662 | 100 | ---- | ---- | ---- | 1,337 | ---- |
| 2014-15 | 90 | 610 | 17.0 | 717 | 541 | 119 | 659 | 58 | ---- | ---- | ---- | 1,008 | ---- |
| 2015-16 | 58 | 465 | 7.0 | 530 | 433 | 55 | 488 | 42 | ---- | ---- | ---- | 1,011 | ---- |
| 2016-17 | 42 | 542 | 0 | 583 | 435 | 104 | 539 | 44 | ---- | ---- | ---- | 902 | ---- |
| 2017-18 | 44 | 561 | 0 | 605 | 461 | 112 | 573 | 32 | ---- | ---- | ---- | 703 | ---- |
| 2018-19 | 32 | 456 | 0 | 488 | 370 | 83 | 453 | 35 | ---- | ---- | ---- | 775 | ---- |
| 2019-20 | 35 | 481 | 0 | 517 | 388 | 84 | 472 | 45 | ---- | ---- | ---- | 886 | ---- |
| 2020-21 | 45 | 400 | 21.0 | 466 | 355 | 63 | 418 | 48 | ---- | ---- | ---- | 1,784 | ---- |
| 2021-22[1] | 48 | 430 | 25.0 | 503 | 326 | 128 | 453 | 50 | ---- | ---- | ---- | 2,315 | ---- |
| 2022-23[2] | 50 | 400 | 20.0 | 470 | 355 | 65 | 420 | 50 | ---- | ---- | ---- | 1,874 | ---- |

[1] Preliminary.  [2] Estimate.  [3] Valley Points FOB; Tank Cars.  [4] Rotterdam; US, PBSY, fob gulf.  W = Withheld.
Source: Economic Research Service, U.S. Department of Agriculture (ERS-USDA)

## Exports of Cottonseed Oil (Crude and Refined) from the United States   In Thousands of Pounds

| Year | Jan. | Feb. | Mar. | Apr. | May | June | July | Aug. | Sept. | Oct. | Nov. | Dec. | Total |
|---|---|---|---|---|---|---|---|---|---|---|---|---|---|
| 2013 | 19,609 | 20,389 | 16,582 | 21,550 | 21,218 | 19,340 | 15,042 | 15,886 | 15,406 | 15,674 | 13,338 | 11,094 | 205,128 |
| 2014 | 13,667 | 19,061 | 18,084 | 20,029 | 8,709 | 7,165 | 2,999 | 5,895 | 12,687 | 12,384 | 11,780 | 14,205 | 146,664 |
| 2015 | 19,843 | 8,117 | 10,559 | 11,852 | 6,246 | 6,162 | 4,005 | 8,573 | 4,379 | 8,700 | 4,634 | 6,080 | 99,149 |
| 2016 | 5,390 | 1,338 | 3,211 | 5,406 | 4,703 | 3,031 | 2,271 | 5,894 | 4,168 | 6,622 | 15,929 | 10,107 | 68,070 |
| 2017 | 10,899 | 8,438 | 9,269 | 8,538 | 6,577 | 5,865 | 5,385 | 11,003 | 5,265 | 7,084 | 8,038 | 6,769 | 93,130 |
| 2018 | 16,387 | 9,282 | 10,793 | 6,797 | 7,626 | 6,980 | 18,567 | 8,421 | 4,152 | 13,262 | 13,725 | 4,527 | 120,518 |
| 2019 | 10,254 | 5,764 | 12,006 | 4,045 | 3,495 | 8,860 | 3,112 | 3,251 | 9,663 | 6,932 | 13,835 | 6,506 | 87,723 |
| 2020 | 7,387 | 4,120 | 6,094 | 14,813 | 4,922 | 5,424 | 4,624 | 3,120 | 5,917 | 6,340 | 5,883 | 4,765 | 73,409 |
| 2021 | 3,449 | 3,859 | 9,344 | 6,803 | 7,021 | 6,188 | 3,219 | 2,520 | 2,709 | 9,822 | 12,986 | 9,135 | 77,055 |
| 2022[1] | 12,105 | 11,748 | 7,332 | 10,476 | 6,901 | 18,294 | 10,869 | 8,983 | 9,146 | 7,125 | 5,920 | 4,634 | 113,533 |

[1] Preliminary.  Source: Economic Research Service, U.S. Department of Agriculture (ERS-USDA)

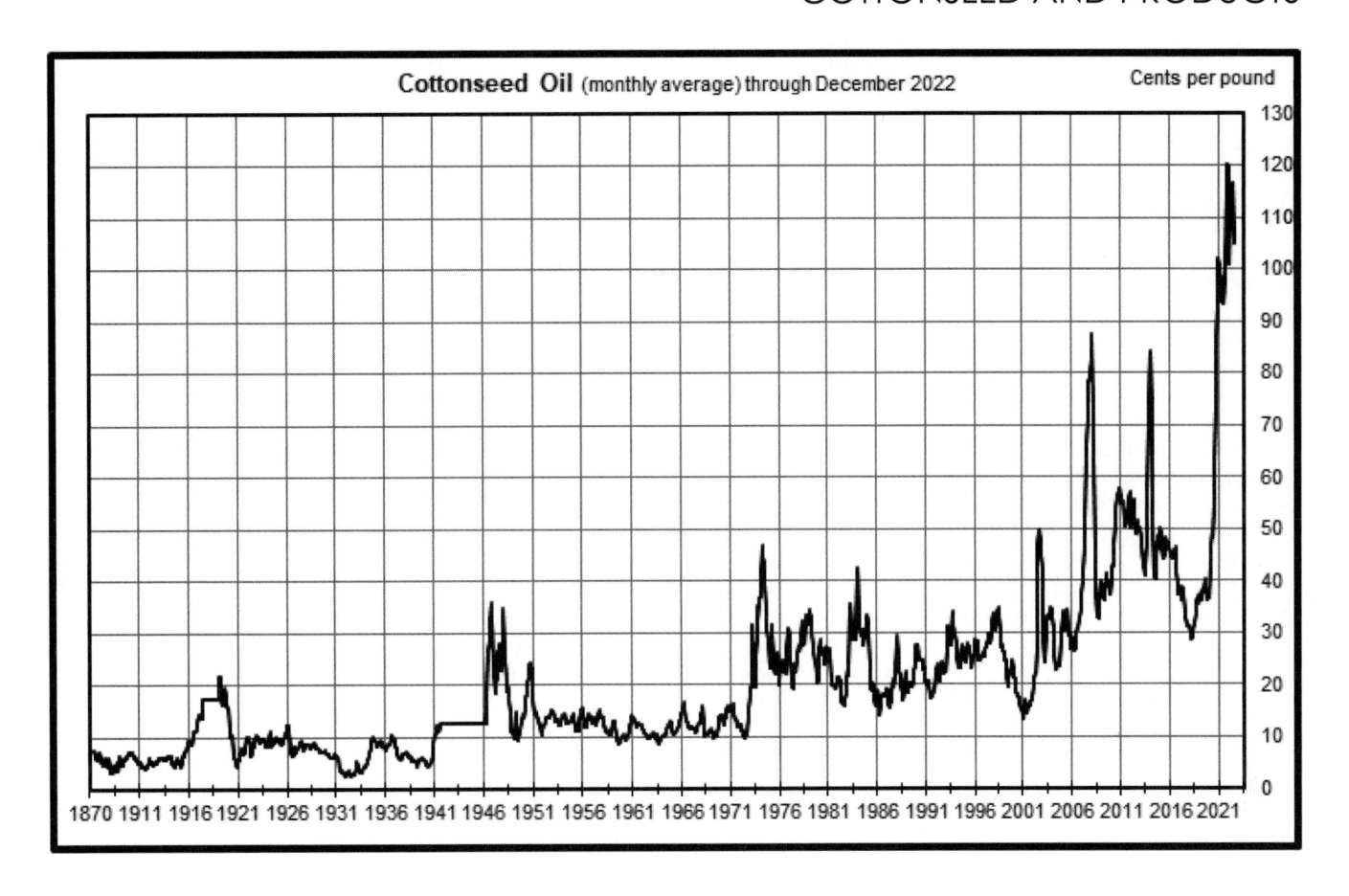

# COTTONSEED AND PRODUCTS

**Cottonseed Oil** (monthly average) through December 2022 — Cents per pound

### Average Price of Crude Cottonseed Oil, PBSY, Greenwood, MS.[1] in Tank Cars   In Cents Per Pound

| Year | Jan. | Feb. | Mar. | Apr. | May | June | July | Aug. | Sept. | Oct. | Nov. | Dec. | Average |
|---|---|---|---|---|---|---|---|---|---|---|---|---|---|
| 2013 | 50.94 | 51.56 | 50.20 | 49.94 | 49.75 | 48.25 | 46.19 | 43.10 | 42.81 | 41.19 | 42.05 | 43.19 | 46.60 |
| 2014 | 47.10 | 57.81 | 69.94 | 75.00 | 84.25 | 83.31 | 73.15 | 61.25 | 49.63 | 41.45 | 40.75 | 40.31 | 60.33 |
| 2015 | 44.95 | 48.81 | 46.06 | 48.19 | 48.90 | 49.94 | 49.15 | 46.25 | 44.13 | 44.25 | 45.19 | 48.35 | 47.01 |
| 2016 | 47.31 | 46.06 | 46.20 | 47.35 | 46.06 | 45.55 | 44.75 | 45.25 | 44.15 | 44.88 | 45.81 | 46.40 | 45.81 |
| 2017 | 44.56 | 41.50 | 39.45 | 37.56 | 38.63 | 38.60 | 38.88 | 36.38 | 38.45 | 37.06 | 37.00 | 34.25 | 38.53 |
| 2018 | 32.75 | 31.44 | 31.35 | 31.19 | 31.25 | 29.90 | 28.75 | 28.60 | 28.88 | 30.56 | 31.45 | 32.06 | 30.68 |
| 2019 | 33.94 | 36.44 | 35.70 | 37.13 | 35.65 | 36.69 | 37.50 | 36.45 | 38.07 | 37.94 | 38.40 | 40.25 | 37.01 |
| 2020 | 40.10 | 38.50 | 36.19 | 37.31 | 37.20 | 36.75 | 43.00 | 46.81 | 49.69 | 48.35 | 54.44 | 59.20 | 43.96 |
| 2021 | 63.19 | 73.63 | 86.94 | 92.65 | 102.19 | 100.69 | 99.90 | 96.50 | 93.63 | 98.50 | 96.75 | 93.30 | 91.49 |
| 2022[1] | 97.94 | 101.38 | 114.88 | 120.05 | 119.56 | 115.75 | 100.80 | 113.75 | 113.20 | 110.19 | 116.69 | 105.10 | 110.77 |

[1] Preliminary.   Source: Economic Research Service, U.S. Department of Agriculture (ERS-USDA)

### Exports of Cottonseed Oil to Important Countries from the United States   In Metric Tons

| Year | Canada | Dominican Republic | Egypt | Guatemala | Japan | Mexico | Netherlands | El Salvador | Korea, South | Turkey | Venezuela | Total |
|---|---|---|---|---|---|---|---|---|---|---|---|---|
| 2013 | 22,335.7 | ---- | ---- | ---- | 222.5 | 35.1 | 63,532.9 | 1,169.8 | ---- | 321.9 | ---- | 93,045.6 |
| 2014 | 11,934.5 | ---- | ---- | ---- | 2,118.0 | ---- | 36,433.4 | 925.6 | ---- | 315.9 | ---- | 66,688.9 |
| 2015 | 12,316.0 | ---- | ---- | 134.2 | 913.4 | 529.0 | 24,767.3 | 466.8 | ---- | 67.5 | ---- | 44,990.0 |
| 2016 | 3,473.7 | ---- | ---- | 311.2 | 473.6 | 512.3 | 19,599.3 | .8 | ---- | .6 | ---- | 30,837.0 |
| 2017 | 5,141.1 | ---- | ---- | 206.7 | 591.0 | ---- | 22,013.1 | 2.3 | ---- | 29.1 | ---- | 41,770.0 |
| 2018 | 6,303.6 | ---- | 3,149.7 | ---- | 1,100.6 | 42.7 | 17,088.9 | ---- | ---- | 20.3 | ---- | 47,319.2 |
| 2019 | 3,990.3 | ---- | ---- | ---- | 1,242.1 | 109.6 | 21,069.1 | ---- | ---- | 9.4 | ---- | 37,747.7 |
| 2020 | 5,096.9 | 2.4 | ---- | ---- | 1,800.4 | 68.6 | 18,882.9 | ---- | ---- | 9.4 | ---- | 33,348.1 |
| 2021 | 4,652.6 | 1.4 | ---- | ---- | 1,178.0 | 1,632.6 | 22,968.7 | ---- | ---- | 16.2 | ---- | 35,263.2 |
| 2022[1] | 8,028.3 | .2 | ---- | ---- | 199.1 | 8.3 | 20,411.0 | ---- | ---- | 19.1 | ---- | 49,396.3 |

[1] Preliminary.   Source: Foreign Agricultural Service, U.S. Department of Agriculture (FAS-USDA)

# Currencies

A "currency" rate involves the price of the base currency (e.g., the dollar) quoted in terms of another currency (e.g., the yen), or in terms of a basket of currencies (e.g., the dollar index). The world's major currencies have traded in a floating exchange rate regime ever since the Bretton-Woods international payments system broke down in 1971 when President Nixon broke the dollar's peg to gold. The two key factors affecting a currency's value are central bank monetary policy and the trade balance. An easy monetary policy (low interest rates) is bearish for a currency because the central bank is aggressively pumping new currency reserves into the marketplace and because foreign investors are not attracted to the low interest rate returns available in the country. By contrast, a tight monetary policy (high interest rates) is bullish for a currency because of the tight supply of new currency reserves and attractive interest rate returns for foreign investors.

The other key factor driving currency values is the nation's current account balance. A current account *surplus* is bullish for a currency due to the net inflow of the currency, while a current account *deficit* is bearish for a currency due to the net outflow of the currency. Currency values are also affected by economic growth and investment opportunities in the country. A country with a strong economy and lucrative investment opportunities will typically have a strong currency because global companies and investors want to buy into that country's investment opportunities. Futures on major currencies and on cross-currency rates are traded primarily at the CME Group.

**Dollar** – The dollar index (Barchart.com symbol DXY00) posted the low for 2022 of 94.629 in January. The dollar then rallied steadily into Q4 of 2022 as the Federal Reserve tightened monetary policy aggressively. The Fed raised the federal funds rate target by 75 basis points at its June 2022 policy meeting, the biggest rate hike since 1994, to combat soaring inflation. U.S. June consumer prices rose at a 9.1% yr/yr pace, the most in 41 years. Also, global geopolitical risks fueled demand for the dollar as a safe haven after Russia invaded Ukraine in February. The Fed continued to raise interest rates aggressively, hiking the federal funds target range by 75 basis points for four consecutive FOMC meetings up to 3.75%-4.00% at the November meeting. The dollar index continued higher and posted a 20-year high of 114.778 in late September. The surge in U.S. bond yields during 2022 to a 15-year high of 4.34% in October strengthened the dollar's interest rate differentials and supported the dollar. The dollar then fell back into year-end as the Fed began to slow its pace of rate hikes, raising the federal funds target range by only 50 basis points at the December FOMC meeting. Also, speculation increased that the Fed was close to ending its rake hike campaign as the U.S. CPI slowed to a 14-month low of +6.5% yr/yr in November. In addition, Fed Chair Powell at the December FOMC meeting said that policy was "getting close" to a sufficiently restrictive level. The dollar index finished 2022 up +8.2% yr/yr at 103.522.

**Euro** – EUR/USD (Barchart.com symbol ^EURUSD) posted the high for 2022 of 1.1495 in February. However, Russia's invasion of Ukraine in February 2022 sent EUR/USD tumbling through Q3. The war in Ukraine pushed energy prices sharply higher, causing concern about an energy crisis and the Eurozone economy. European natural gas prices surged to a record high in March after Russia threatened to cut off natural gas flows to Europe in retaliation for sanctions the European Union imposed on Russia for invading Ukraine. Roughly 40% of European gas imports were from Russia prior to the war. EUR/USD trended lower and posted a 20-year low of 0.9536 in September. However, surging consumer prices in the Eurozone forced the European Central Bank (ECB) to tighten monetary policy, sparking a recovery in EUR/USD. Eurozone consumer prices jumped to a record high of 10.6% yr/yr in October, prompting the ECB to raise its deposit rate during 2022 by a total of 250 basis points to 2.00% by December. That boosted European government bond yields and strengthened the euro's interest rate differentials. EUR/USD finished 2022 down -5.8% yr/yr at 1.0705.

**Yen** – USD/JPY (Barchart.com symbol ^USDJPY) posted its low for 2022 of 113.49 in January. The yen found support in Q1 2022 on safe-haven demand from global geopolitical risks after Russia invaded Ukraine in February. However, a surge in global inflation caused the Federal Reserve, the Bank of England, and the European Central Bank to end their quantitative easing (QE) programs and raise interest rates. The divergence in global central bank policies hammered the yen as the Bank of Japan (BOJ) boosted its QE program and maintained record-low interest rates. As a result, USD/JPY rallied sharply into Q4 and posted a 32-year high of 151.95 in October. USD/JPY reversed into year-end as the yen strengthened after the BOJ intervened in the currency market to support the yen. The yen also received a boost after the BOJ, at its December meeting, adjusted its yield-curve-control (YCC) program and raised the upper band of its 10-year yield target range to 0.50% from 0.25%. USD/JPY finished 2022 up +13.9% at 131.12.

# CURRENCIES

**BRITISH POUND - CME**
Weekly Selected Futures as of 03/31/2023
Chart High 1.7184 on 07/15/2014
Chart Low 1.0379 on 09/26/2022

Nearby Futures through Last Trading Day.

## U.S. Dollars per British Pound

| Year | Jan. | Feb. | Mar. | Apr. | May | June | July | Aug. | Sept. | Oct. | Nov. | Dec. | Average |
|------|------|------|------|------|-----|------|------|------|-------|------|------|------|---------|
| 2013 | 1.5961 | 1.5468 | 1.5083 | 1.5309 | 1.5287 | 1.5498 | 1.5184 | 1.5505 | 1.5875 | 1.6089 | 1.6112 | 1.6383 | 1.5646 |
| 2014 | 1.6468 | 1.6566 | 1.6617 | 1.6747 | 1.6841 | 1.6916 | 1.7075 | 1.6700 | 1.6303 | 1.6077 | 1.5773 | 1.5631 | 1.6476 |
| 2015 | 1.5139 | 1.5334 | 1.4969 | 1.4960 | 1.5454 | 1.5586 | 1.5558 | 1.5581 | 1.5334 | 1.5335 | 1.5193 | 1.4984 | 1.5286 |
| 2016 | 1.4387 | 1.4309 | 1.4256 | 1.4315 | 1.4523 | 1.4210 | 1.3145 | 1.3103 | 1.3148 | 1.2336 | 1.2441 | 1.2471 | 1.3554 |
| 2017 | 1.2351 | 1.2487 | 1.2348 | 1.2643 | 1.2923 | 1.2812 | 1.2999 | 1.2956 | 1.3317 | 1.3202 | 1.3232 | 1.3405 | 1.2890 |
| 2018 | 1.3828 | 1.3962 | 1.3976 | 1.4070 | 1.3462 | 1.3285 | 1.3169 | 1.2879 | 1.3057 | 1.3011 | 1.2896 | 1.2663 | 1.3355 |
| 2019 | 1.2907 | 1.3012 | 1.3174 | 1.3028 | 1.2839 | 1.2674 | 1.2462 | 1.2150 | 1.2353 | 1.2656 | 1.2881 | 1.3103 | 1.2770 |
| 2020 | 1.3074 | 1.2951 | 1.2355 | 1.2415 | 1.2291 | 1.2525 | 1.2684 | 1.3134 | 1.2953 | 1.2973 | 1.3214 | 1.3446 | 1.2835 |
| 2021 | 1.3640 | 1.3864 | 1.3856 | 1.3839 | 1.4085 | 1.4015 | 1.3808 | 1.3795 | 1.3721 | 1.3685 | 1.3446 | 1.3310 | 1.3755 |
| 2022 | 1.3551 | 1.3532 | 1.3162 | 1.2922 | 1.2450 | 1.2312 | 1.1997 | 1.1968 | 1.1320 | 1.1306 | 1.1753 | 1.2175 | 1.2371 |

Average. *Source: FOREX*

## Volume of Trading of British Pound Futures in Chicago   In Thousands of Contracts

| Year | Jan. | Feb. | Mar. | Apr. | May | June | July | Aug. | Sept. | Oct. | Nov. | Dec. | Total |
|------|------|------|------|------|-----|------|------|------|-------|------|------|------|-------|
| 2013 | 2,460.2 | 2,647.5 | 2,948.2 | 2,172.0 | 2,678.5 | 3,067.9 | 2,504.8 | 2,298.1 | 2,348.2 | 2,002.0 | 1,936.9 | 2,173.5 | 29,237.8 |
| 2014 | 2,123.0 | 2,139.8 | 2,315.4 | 1,415.6 | 1,592.2 | 2,547.6 | 1,728.8 | 1,781.2 | 3,181.2 | 2,283.2 | 1,740.6 | 1,988.2 | 24,837.0 |
| 2015 | 2,024.6 | 1,677.7 | 2,854.7 | 1,918.6 | 2,234.4 | 2,374.3 | 1,744.8 | 2,048.9 | 2,139.5 | 1,635.5 | 1,506.4 | 1,985.3 | 24,144.7 |
| 2016 | 1,919.1 | 2,025.0 | 2,574.4 | 1,967.0 | 1,953.3 | 4,034.0 | 2,337.1 | 1,855.1 | 2,559.9 | 2,714.9 | 2,678.6 | 2,507.8 | 29,126.0 |
| 2017 | 2,491.4 | 1,975.1 | 3,110.3 | 2,009.6 | 2,313.0 | 3,147.8 | 1,991.9 | 2,124.7 | 3,406.7 | 2,570.9 | 2,940.8 | 3,085.7 | 31,167.9 |
| 2018 | 2,930.4 | 2,739.3 | 3,020.1 | 2,256.6 | 2,838.9 | 3,023.7 | 2,501.4 | 2,318.6 | 2,974.4 | 2,407.6 | 2,873.0 | 2,555.1 | 32,439.0 |
| 2019 | 2,387.4 | 2,153.5 | 3,367.7 | 1,911.6 | 2,340.7 | 2,398.6 | 2,081.9 | 2,341.3 | 3,177.6 | 3,406.7 | 1,731.0 | 3,243.9 | 30,542.3 |
| 2020 | 1,979.5 | 2,268.4 | 3,581.3 | 1,329.0 | 1,635.6 | 2,592.6 | 2,052.1 | 1,964.1 | 2,959.7 | 2,410.4 | 1,893.8 | 3,325.5 | 27,991.8 |
| 2021 | 1,686.4 | 1,783.0 | 2,325.1 | 1,627.1 | 1,787.1 | 2,546.7 | 2,098.4 | 1,589.3 | 2,416.0 | 1,856.3 | 2,050.7 | 2,479.9 | 24,246.0 |
| 2022 | 1,941.3 | 2,139.9 | 2,951.2 | 1,995.0 | 2,190.9 | 2,949.1 | 2,279.8 | 2,427.1 | 4,450.5 | 3,109.1 | 2,388.5 | 2,410.4 | 31,232.7 |

Contract size = 62,500 GBP.   *Source: CME Group; Chicago Mercantile Exchange (CME)*

## Average Open Interest of British Pound Futures in Chicago   In Contracts

| Year | Jan. | Feb. | Mar. | Apr. | May | June | July | Aug. | Sept. | Oct. | Nov. | Dec. |
|------|------|------|------|------|-----|------|------|------|-------|------|------|------|
| 2013 | 165,256 | 184,350 | 248,526 | 201,357 | 202,681 | 172,212 | 145,625 | 145,596 | 167,475 | 181,110 | 186,634 | 226,964 |
| 2014 | 207,609 | 232,142 | 231,703 | 226,479 | 236,374 | 262,034 | 246,579 | 231,599 | 184,224 | 135,955 | 160,534 | 165,669 |
| 2015 | 178,585 | 173,893 | 187,709 | 180,094 | 179,361 | 174,693 | 167,418 | 168,889 | 163,232 | 155,414 | 169,080 | 191,263 |
| 2016 | 252,441 | 261,454 | 274,786 | 240,358 | 242,020 | 225,029 | 231,642 | 245,379 | 247,713 | 259,915 | 250,809 | 229,322 |
| 2017 | 223,750 | 212,997 | 257,227 | 252,578 | 258,691 | 226,183 | 199,970 | 215,422 | 220,244 | 182,430 | 180,126 | 203,247 |
| 2018 | 220,399 | 202,010 | 190,552 | 186,782 | 193,666 | 210,213 | 186,764 | 243,357 | 252,436 | 216,670 | 227,938 | 229,210 |
| 2019 | 210,633 | 197,522 | 170,408 | 150,947 | 179,450 | 216,885 | 249,765 | 278,217 | 256,642 | 234,991 | 214,554 | 228,383 |
| 2020 | 200,192 | 213,507 | 194,982 | 157,693 | 175,157 | 183,015 | 177,970 | 180,039 | 169,698 | 150,271 | 140,788 | 150,321 |
| 2021 | 149,906 | 170,763 | 156,694 | 153,697 | 167,714 | 171,653 | 179,481 | 185,703 | 171,516 | 166,856 | 200,514 | 222,783 |
| 2022 | 189,408 | 194,150 | 217,780 | 262,657 | 259,413 | 243,631 | 231,360 | 236,695 | 278,958 | 254,622 | 232,233 | 214,788 |

Contract size = 62,500 GBP.   *Source: CME Group; Chicago Mercantile Exchange (CME)*

# CURRENCIES

**Canadian Dollar - CME** Weekly Selected Futures as of 03/31/2023
Chart High 1.01580 on 01/14/2013
Chart Low .68090 on 01/20/2016

Nearby Futures through Last Trading Day.

## Canadian Dollars per U.S. Dollar

| Year | Jan. | Feb. | Mar. | Apr. | May | June | July | Aug. | Sept. | Oct. | Nov. | Dec. | Average |
|---|---|---|---|---|---|---|---|---|---|---|---|---|---|
| 2013 | 0.9919 | 1.0094 | 1.0240 | 1.0185 | 1.0206 | 1.0315 | 1.0404 | 1.0404 | 1.0354 | 1.0367 | 1.0488 | 1.0637 | 1.0301 |
| 2014 | 1.0947 | 1.1054 | 1.1106 | 1.0992 | 1.0890 | 1.0825 | 1.0734 | 1.0922 | 1.1007 | 1.1214 | 1.1332 | 1.1542 | 1.1047 |
| 2015 | 1.2128 | 1.2500 | 1.2610 | 1.2338 | 1.2183 | 1.2354 | 1.2851 | 1.3144 | 1.3270 | 1.3071 | 1.3275 | 1.3710 | 1.2786 |
| 2016 | 1.4229 | 1.3790 | 1.3212 | 1.2814 | 1.2949 | 1.2890 | 1.3037 | 1.3000 | 1.3091 | 1.3247 | 1.3446 | 1.3351 | 1.3255 |
| 2017 | 1.3206 | 1.3110 | 1.3382 | 1.3435 | 1.3597 | 1.3293 | 1.2698 | 1.2608 | 1.2295 | 1.2599 | 1.2766 | 1.2767 | 1.2980 |
| 2018 | 1.2432 | 1.2586 | 1.2930 | 1.2729 | 1.2867 | 1.3129 | 1.3133 | 1.3036 | 1.3033 | 1.3014 | 1.3205 | 1.3447 | 1.2962 |
| 2019 | 1.3296 | 1.3207 | 1.3370 | 1.3377 | 1.3459 | 1.3281 | 1.3100 | 1.3269 | 1.3242 | 1.3189 | 1.3236 | 1.3165 | 1.3266 |
| 2020 | 1.3084 | 1.3284 | 1.3943 | 1.4047 | 1.3969 | 1.3548 | 1.3501 | 1.3229 | 1.3221 | 1.3209 | 1.3064 | 1.2806 | 1.3409 |
| 2021 | 1.2716 | 1.2694 | 1.2570 | 1.2491 | 1.2119 | 1.2223 | 1.2512 | 1.2593 | 1.2668 | 1.2433 | 1.2562 | 1.2785 | 1.2530 |
| 2022 | 1.2623 | 1.2713 | 1.2649 | 1.2625 | 1.2838 | 1.2809 | 1.2920 | 1.2914 | 1.3325 | 1.3686 | 1.3433 | 1.3592 | 1.3011 |

Average. *Source: FOREX*

## Volume of Trading of Canadian Dollar Futures in Chicago   In Thousands of Contracts

| Year | Jan. | Feb. | Mar. | Apr. | May | June | July | Aug. | Sept. | Oct. | Nov. | Dec. | Total |
|---|---|---|---|---|---|---|---|---|---|---|---|---|---|
| 2013 | 1,472.2 | 1,439.5 | 1,815.4 | 1,502.0 | 1,770.9 | 1,891.0 | 1,434.3 | 1,327.6 | 1,256.7 | 1,077.0 | 986.0 | 1,455.2 | 17,427.8 |
| 2014 | 1,495.5 | 1,064.6 | 1,572.7 | 903.8 | 917.2 | 1,253.6 | 1,064.6 | 1,057.9 | 1,612.2 | 1,569.7 | 1,191.6 | 1,393.1 | 15,096.5 |
| 2015 | 1,371.7 | 1,298.8 | 1,881.8 | 1,394.8 | 1,170.1 | 1,595.7 | 1,447.1 | 1,477.1 | 1,710.6 | 1,283.7 | 1,040.4 | 1,630.2 | 17,301.9 |
| 2016 | 1,794.8 | 1,487.2 | 1,748.1 | 1,481.8 | 1,476.4 | 1,665.3 | 1,240.5 | 1,408.3 | 1,860.5 | 1,507.1 | 1,614.2 | 1,413.1 | 18,697.3 |
| 2017 | 1,405.8 | 1,093.9 | 1,726.1 | 1,277.3 | 1,559.2 | 2,136.4 | 1,641.9 | 1,517.9 | 2,143.3 | 1,559.1 | 1,420.4 | 1,741.3 | 19,222.5 |
| 2018 | 1,721.5 | 1,622.3 | 2,110.0 | 1,530.7 | 1,964.4 | 2,133.5 | 1,410.3 | 1,639.3 | 1,688.7 | 1,667.5 | 1,544.8 | 1,986.5 | 21,019.4 |
| 2019 | 1,526.4 | 1,255.7 | 1,866.9 | 1,538.3 | 1,735.1 | 1,939.3 | 1,391.6 | 1,651.6 | 1,931.9 | 1,886.1 | 1,347.5 | 1,936.1 | 20,006.5 |
| 2020 | 1,518.8 | 1,768.0 | 2,724.2 | 1,230.4 | 1,118.7 | 1,770.0 | 1,364.4 | 1,277.8 | 1,893.1 | 1,527.5 | 1,378.3 | 1,895.2 | 19,466.4 |
| 2021 | 1,389.7 | 1,451.9 | 2,136.3 | 1,502.6 | 1,427.4 | 1,991.3 | 1,686.4 | 1,503.3 | 2,055.5 | 1,495.8 | 1,566.5 | 1,895.8 | 20,102.5 |
| 2022 | 1,558.1 | 1,501.2 | 2,109.0 | 1,465.5 | 1,725.8 | 2,323.4 | 1,883.5 | 1,777.9 | 2,686.5 | 2,044.4 | 1,791.4 | 1,899.1 | 22,765.8 |

Contract size = 100,000 CAD.   *Source: CME Group; Chicago Mercantile Exchange (CME)*

## Average Open Interest of Canadian Dollar Futures in Chicago   In Contracts

| Year | Jan. | Feb. | Mar. | Apr. | May | June | July | Aug. | Sept. | Oct. | Nov. | Dec. |
|---|---|---|---|---|---|---|---|---|---|---|---|---|
| 2013 | 142,358 | 161,037 | 216,418 | 167,325 | 145,528 | 128,346 | 126,955 | 115,698 | 127,754 | 114,266 | 121,783 | 158,005 |
| 2014 | 159,815 | 152,844 | 144,262 | 119,310 | 123,899 | 117,918 | 125,230 | 111,259 | 91,900 | 100,526 | 106,812 | 106,069 |
| 2015 | 108,171 | 115,078 | 124,649 | 120,477 | 120,938 | 101,560 | 143,112 | 167,447 | 148,706 | 121,352 | 137,170 | 164,083 |
| 2016 | 165,688 | 157,798 | 129,610 | 111,929 | 124,671 | 127,872 | 117,139 | 122,876 | 115,488 | 105,483 | 122,002 | 102,506 |
| 2017 | 98,335 | 125,839 | 131,989 | 145,292 | 209,032 | 184,268 | 169,578 | 192,761 | 210,929 | 173,057 | 147,137 | 136,029 |
| 2018 | 158,422 | 156,598 | 142,004 | 125,633 | 132,447 | 160,264 | 154,993 | 145,448 | 136,094 | 119,192 | 130,139 | 163,042 |
| 2019 | 158,349 | 145,288 | 150,911 | 150,358 | 146,396 | 148,551 | 175,565 | 162,610 | 152,850 | 156,993 | 180,311 | 171,026 |
| 2020 | 189,278 | 169,358 | 149,473 | 118,708 | 124,870 | 115,870 | 135,503 | 135,224 | 126,834 | 119,361 | 135,770 | 159,984 |
| 2021 | 160,854 | 161,399 | 168,574 | 173,283 | 207,298 | 213,318 | 189,760 | 172,322 | 138,642 | 142,214 | 152,038 | 149,566 |
| 2022 | 142,071 | 143,762 | 136,806 | 155,457 | 146,940 | 149,879 | 141,970 | 148,925 | 148,272 | 143,086 | 141,720 | 152,318 |

Contract size = 100,000 CAD.   *Source: CME Group; Chicago Mercantile Exchange (CME)*

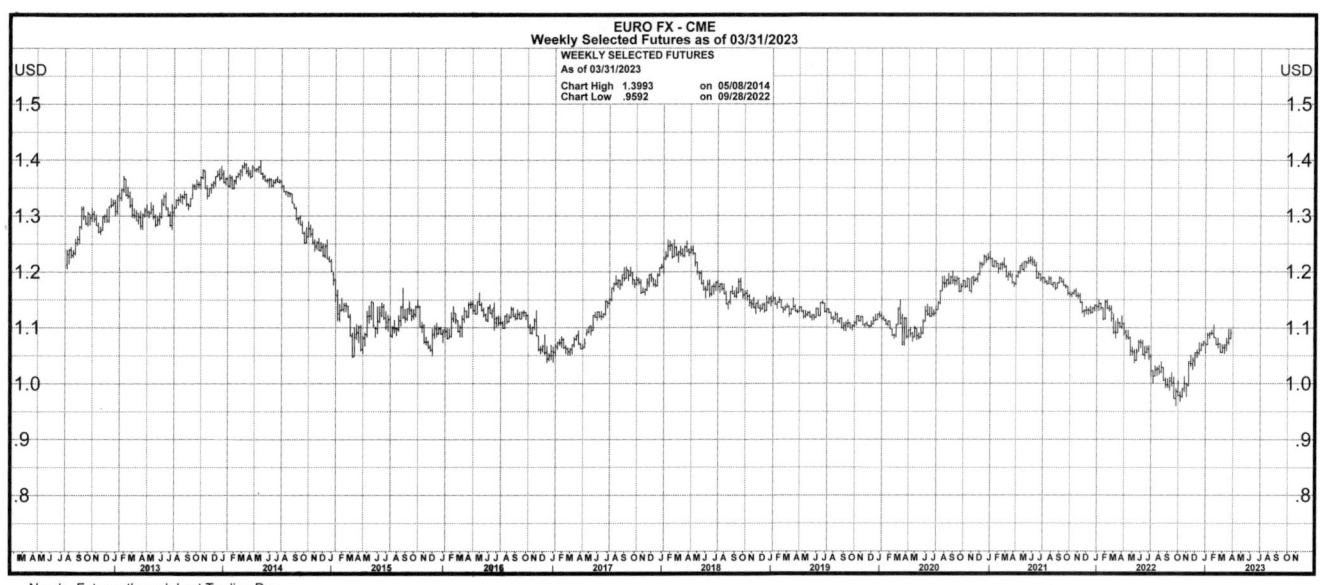

# CURRENCIES

## Euro per U.S. Dollar

| Year | Jan. | Feb. | Mar. | Apr. | May | June | July | Aug. | Sept. | Oct. | Nov. | Dec. | Average |
|---|---|---|---|---|---|---|---|---|---|---|---|---|---|
| 2013 | 1.3306 | 1.3340 | 1.2956 | 1.3025 | 1.2978 | 1.3202 | 1.3090 | 1.3320 | 1.3362 | 1.3638 | 1.3496 | 1.3704 | 1.3285 |
| 2014 | 1.3616 | 1.3669 | 1.3827 | 1.3811 | 1.3733 | 1.3600 | 1.3538 | 1.3315 | 1.2895 | 1.2680 | 1.2474 | 1.2307 | 1.3289 |
| 2015 | 1.1605 | 1.1352 | 1.0830 | 1.0817 | 1.1157 | 1.1237 | 1.0997 | 1.1144 | 1.1236 | 1.1218 | 1.0728 | 1.0896 | 1.1101 |
| 2016 | 1.0868 | 1.1106 | 1.1143 | 1.1339 | 1.1298 | 1.1241 | 1.1065 | 1.1205 | 1.1214 | 1.1023 | 1.0786 | 1.0538 | 1.1069 |
| 2017 | 1.0630 | 1.0640 | 1.0688 | 1.0718 | 1.1057 | 1.1238 | 1.1531 | 1.1820 | 1.1906 | 1.1757 | 1.1745 | 1.1835 | 1.1297 |
| 2018 | 1.2202 | 1.2345 | 1.2339 | 1.2274 | 1.1814 | 1.1675 | 1.1686 | 1.1548 | 1.1661 | 1.1483 | 1.1363 | 1.1377 | 1.1814 |
| 2019 | 1.1419 | 1.1346 | 1.1300 | 1.1232 | 1.1184 | 1.1295 | 1.1212 | 1.1122 | 1.1006 | 1.1056 | 1.1046 | 1.1113 | 1.1194 |
| 2020 | 1.1098 | 1.0904 | 1.1060 | 1.0869 | 1.0904 | 1.1257 | 1.1473 | 1.1829 | 1.1785 | 1.1765 | 1.1836 | 1.2170 | 1.1413 |
| 2021 | 1.2170 | 1.2094 | 1.1899 | 1.1970 | 1.2147 | 1.2039 | 1.1823 | 1.1766 | 1.1764 | 1.1598 | 1.1407 | 1.1305 | 1.1832 |
| 2022 | 1.1316 | 1.1342 | 1.1014 | 1.0796 | 1.0579 | 1.0559 | 1.0179 | 1.0120 | 0.9896 | 0.9841 | 1.0210 | 1.0588 | 1.0537 |

Average.  *Source: FOREX*

## Volume of Trading of Euro FX Futures in Chicago   In Thousands of Contracts

| Year | Jan. | Feb. | Mar. | Apr. | May | June | July | Aug. | Sept. | Oct. | Nov. | Dec. | Total |
|---|---|---|---|---|---|---|---|---|---|---|---|---|---|
| 2013 | 5,675.6 | 6,088.9 | 6,391.7 | 5,480.1 | 6,055.8 | 5,970.9 | 5,093.7 | 4,390.9 | 4,120.9 | 3,988.5 | 4,047.7 | 3,981.0 | 61,285.6 |
| 2014 | 4,422.1 | 3,733.1 | 4,781.4 | 3,046.6 | 3,338.3 | 4,261.9 | 3,048.4 | 3,507.4 | 6,106.3 | 5,900.3 | 4,564.9 | 5,497.7 | 52,208.3 |
| 2015 | 5,560.3 | 3,639.7 | 7,724.4 | 5,745.4 | 5,549.4 | 6,980.8 | 4,666.0 | 5,245.6 | 5,468.3 | 4,455.2 | 4,243.0 | 6,077.9 | 65,356.1 |
| 2016 | 4,077.1 | 4,559.6 | 5,453.9 | 3,688.1 | 3,192.6 | 4,996.0 | 2,734.2 | 2,994.6 | 4,677.7 | 3,357.0 | 4,596.8 | 5,128.3 | 49,455.9 |
| 2017 | 4,328.4 | 3,667.0 | 5,810.9 | 3,353.5 | 4,129.2 | 5,345.8 | 4,449.8 | 4,681.0 | 5,929.7 | 4,704.7 | 4,593.7 | 5,462.1 | 56,455.8 |
| 2018 | 6,129.6 | 4,985.2 | 6,336.2 | 4,410.2 | 7,312.1 | 7,459.5 | 4,527.2 | 6,009.6 | 6,216.1 | 5,419.0 | 4,626.7 | 5,353.7 | 68,785.1 |
| 2019 | 4,149.7 | 3,318.9 | 5,517.7 | 3,915.4 | 3,879.5 | 5,625.9 | 3,785.7 | 3,989.0 | 5,715.2 | 3,891.3 | 2,976.1 | 5,725.8 | 52,490.1 |
| 2020 | 3,592.5 | 4,460.3 | 7,943.4 | 2,910.0 | 3,047.6 | 5,615.9 | 4,709.7 | 4,291.7 | 5,891.3 | 3,726.3 | 3,359.6 | 5,870.9 | 55,419.2 |
| 2021 | 3,372.8 | 3,372.8 | 5,965.5 | 3,365.9 | 3,288.3 | 5,478.9 | 3,533.3 | 2,905.4 | 5,100.2 | 3,409.1 | 3,940.8 | 5,123.8 | 48,856.6 |
| 2022 | 3,431.2 | 3,985.7 | 6,936.4 | 3,582.5 | 4,072.3 | 6,099.8 | 4,798.2 | 5,018.3 | 8,107.4 | 4,652.7 | 4,687.2 | 6,132.8 | 61,504.4 |

Contract size = 125,000 EUR.   *Source: CME Group; Chicago Mercantile Exchange (CME)*

## Average Open Interest of Euro FX Futures in Chicago   In Contracts

| Year | Jan. | Feb. | Mar. | Apr. | May | June | July | Aug. | Sept. | Oct. | Nov. | Dec. |
|---|---|---|---|---|---|---|---|---|---|---|---|---|
| 2013 | 214,230 | 236,476 | 211,778 | 220,576 | 242,334 | 232,139 | 217,712 | 237,132 | 250,358 | 270,275 | 239,030 | 258,190 |
| 2014 | 251,507 | 285,722 | 289,786 | 266,980 | 270,902 | 302,019 | 322,167 | 390,128 | 429,750 | 434,763 | 467,267 | 427,194 |
| 2015 | 430,963 | 443,172 | 477,046 | 453,055 | 436,488 | 388,813 | 358,550 | 366,585 | 340,638 | 357,347 | 432,251 | 432,591 |
| 2016 | 402,675 | 425,594 | 367,707 | 340,746 | 352,037 | 344,370 | 380,293 | 367,126 | 350,287 | 403,624 | 430,112 | 425,424 |
| 2017 | 413,834 | 410,809 | 414,949 | 414,920 | 429,990 | 435,606 | 439,731 | 464,075 | 459,095 | 444,328 | 467,275 | 505,655 |
| 2018 | 587,907 | 576,878 | 540,887 | 501,746 | 521,277 | 539,601 | 491,694 | 522,487 | 503,058 | 486,553 | 526,379 | 541,129 |
| 2019 | 523,488 | 531,388 | 513,724 | 501,896 | 518,852 | 525,286 | 536,433 | 541,997 | 533,735 | 522,478 | 573,113 | 576,176 |
| 2020 | 575,652 | 614,696 | 620,821 | 546,543 | 550,837 | 592,110 | 630,078 | 705,319 | 684,320 | 643,667 | 637,589 | 676,072 |
| 2021 | 676,833 | 681,580 | 678,964 | 657,266 | 708,387 | 724,854 | 686,851 | 694,731 | 680,222 | 686,614 | 697,867 | 686,236 |
| 2022 | 686,407 | 698,994 | 694,818 | 678,280 | 703,595 | 696,563 | 683,016 | 702,536 | 702,466 | 649,608 | 680,220 | 742,950 |

Contract size = 125,000 EUR.   *Source: CME Group; Chicago Mercantile Exchange (CME)*

# CURRENCIES

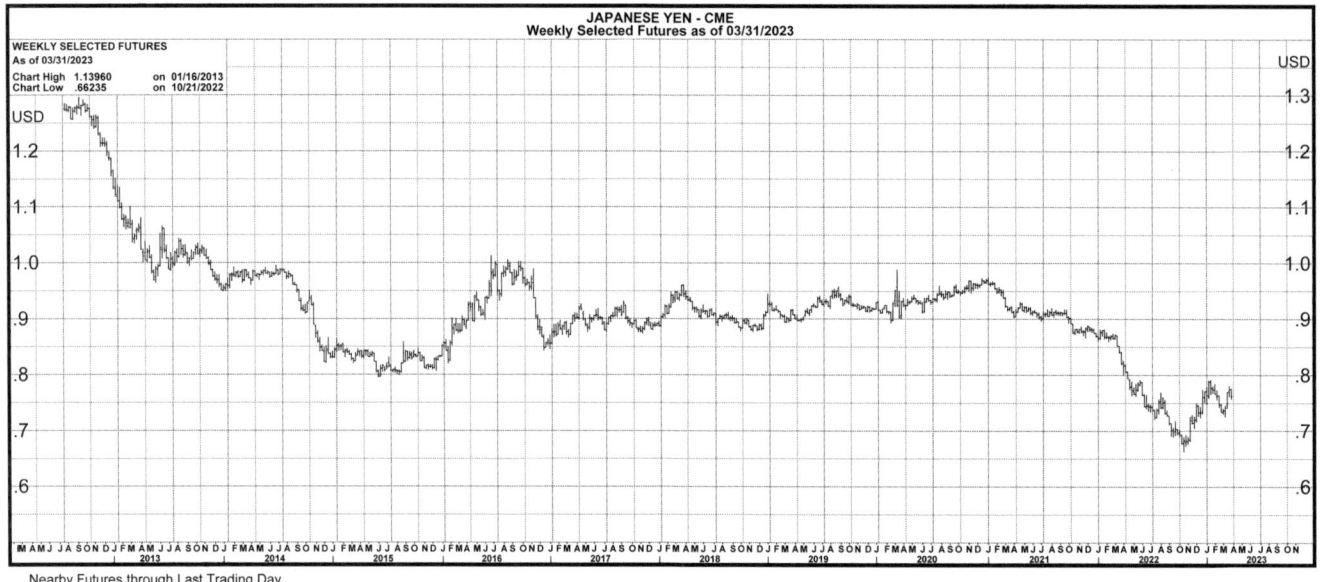

**JAPANESE YEN - CME**
Weekly Selected Futures as of 03/31/2023

Nearby Futures through Last Trading Day.

## Japanese Yen per U.S. Dollar

| Year | Jan. | Feb. | Mar. | Apr. | May | June | July | Aug. | Sept. | Oct. | Nov. | Dec. | Average |
|---|---|---|---|---|---|---|---|---|---|---|---|---|---|
| 2013 | 89.19 | 93.11 | 94.88 | 97.75 | 100.97 | 97.30 | 99.64 | 97.80 | 99.18 | 97.85 | 100.12 | 103.55 | 97.61 |
| 2014 | 103.80 | 102.12 | 102.34 | 102.51 | 101.83 | 102.07 | 101.75 | 102.97 | 107.37 | 108.03 | 116.37 | 119.42 | 105.88 |
| 2015 | 118.27 | 118.75 | 120.36 | 119.52 | 120.85 | 123.67 | 123.31 | 123.04 | 120.08 | 120.15 | 122.63 | 121.63 | 121.02 |
| 2016 | 118.20 | 114.63 | 112.94 | 109.58 | 109.00 | 105.46 | 104.08 | 101.31 | 101.84 | 103.85 | 108.63 | 116.12 | 108.80 |
| 2017 | 114.94 | 112.98 | 112.90 | 110.05 | 112.23 | 110.96 | 112.37 | 109.85 | 110.81 | 112.93 | 112.82 | 112.92 | 112.14 |
| 2018 | 110.89 | 107.87 | 106.09 | 107.62 | 109.69 | 110.13 | 111.48 | 111.04 | 112.04 | 112.77 | 113.35 | 112.25 | 110.43 |
| 2019 | 108.95 | 110.46 | 111.14 | 111.69 | 109.98 | 108.06 | 108.24 | 106.21 | 107.50 | 108.16 | 108.90 | 109.09 | 109.03 |
| 2020 | 109.30 | 110.03 | 107.67 | 107.77 | 107.19 | 107.60 | 106.72 | 106.04 | 105.60 | 105.20 | 104.40 | 103.75 | 106.77 |
| 2021 | 103.74 | 105.34 | 108.71 | 109.02 | 109.13 | 110.14 | 110.21 | 109.82 | 110.15 | 113.16 | 114.04 | 113.89 | 109.78 |
| 2022 | 114.84 | 115.18 | 118.66 | 126.37 | 128.74 | 134.09 | 136.59 | 135.36 | 143.18 | 147.09 | 142.04 | 134.90 | 131.42 |

Average. *Source: FOREX*

## Volume of Trading of Japanese Yen Futures in Chicago   In Thousands of Contracts

| Year | Jan. | Feb. | Mar. | Apr. | May | June | July | Aug. | Sept. | Oct. | Nov. | Dec. | Total |
|---|---|---|---|---|---|---|---|---|---|---|---|---|---|
| 2013 | 3,831.3 | 4,175.7 | 3,820.2 | 4,510.5 | 4,431.7 | 5,387.8 | 2,849.1 | 2,885.5 | 3,045.1 | 2,564.9 | 2,379.8 | 2,880.5 | 42,762.3 |
| 2014 | 3,335.1 | 2,865.2 | 3,324.4 | 2,335.1 | 2,285.1 | 2,615.9 | 2,143.3 | 2,335.6 | 3,904.6 | 4,728.3 | 3,791.3 | 4,655.9 | 38,319.8 |
| 2015 | 4,041.9 | 2,593.2 | 3,160.9 | 2,462.5 | 2,548.1 | 3,539.0 | 2,236.0 | 3,410.2 | 3,926.7 | 2,985.0 | 2,201.2 | 3,075.8 | 36,180.5 |
| 2016 | 3,637.8 | 3,997.1 | 3,022.3 | 2,736.8 | 2,141.9 | 3,547.6 | 2,632.9 | 2,225.8 | 3,262.3 | 2,343.2 | 3,889.4 | 3,151.8 | 36,588.8 |
| 2017 | 3,844.0 | 2,739.9 | 4,044.3 | 2,989.3 | 3,355.7 | 3,767.5 | 2,819.8 | 3,398.4 | 4,610.2 | 3,425.4 | 3,496.3 | 3,132.6 | 41,623.4 |
| 2018 | 3,479.6 | 3,457.9 | 3,574.2 | 2,600.7 | 3,248.2 | 3,097.7 | 2,775.9 | 2,522.3 | 2,585.9 | 3,624.0 | 2,707.5 | 3,305.4 | 36,979.3 |
| 2019 | 2,676.8 | 2,013.3 | 2,896.6 | 2,126.6 | 3,223.0 | 3,162.4 | 2,168.4 | 3,377.7 | 2,995.4 | 2,562.4 | 2,303.3 | 3,067.8 | 32,573.8 |
| 2020 | 2,894.9 | 3,621.5 | 4,886.9 | 1,517.2 | 1,465.3 | 2,354.0 | 1,858.3 | 1,849.7 | 2,070.0 | 1,762.1 | 2,067.2 | 2,597.3 | 28,944.4 |
| 2021 | 1,721.2 | 1,889.3 | 2,806.3 | 2,207.4 | 1,961.2 | 2,507.8 | 2,028.8 | 1,958.9 | 2,825.5 | 2,332.1 | 2,485.0 | 2,377.6 | 27,101.0 |
| 2022 | 2,172.2 | 2,145.8 | 3,417.4 | 2,869.2 | 2,959.4 | 3,975.5 | 3,080.9 | 3,671.9 | 5,025.5 | 3,665.6 | 3,038.4 | 3,543.0 | 39,564.9 |

Contract size = 12,500,000 JPY.   *Source: CME Group; Chicago Mercantile Exchange (CME)*

## Average Open Interest of Japanese Yen Futures in Chicago   In Contracts

| Year | Jan. | Feb. | Mar. | Apr. | May | June | July | Aug. | Sept. | Oct. | Nov. | Dec. |
|---|---|---|---|---|---|---|---|---|---|---|---|---|
| 2013 | 203,930 | 217,961 | 246,456 | 211,493 | 222,136 | 199,960 | 182,942 | 168,128 | 184,355 | 160,423 | 204,490 | 251,937 |
| 2014 | 217,565 | 201,386 | 190,296 | 174,544 | 163,960 | 170,679 | 163,460 | 202,088 | 234,084 | 205,740 | 233,431 | 252,694 |
| 2015 | 218,141 | 204,791 | 206,382 | 190,770 | 217,291 | 275,725 | 249,546 | 259,312 | 213,125 | 181,162 | 237,763 | 217,541 |
| 2016 | 243,541 | 246,520 | 196,787 | 171,510 | 161,320 | 155,959 | 156,403 | 163,674 | 156,868 | 157,987 | 177,739 | 247,079 |
| 2017 | 206,164 | 203,979 | 208,760 | 199,364 | 209,490 | 199,979 | 238,520 | 221,773 | 210,652 | 262,262 | 270,180 | 240,954 |
| 2018 | 242,152 | 261,583 | 232,642 | 151,792 | 163,587 | 159,871 | 195,077 | 189,113 | 204,846 | 225,418 | 222,065 | 225,312 |
| 2019 | 218,956 | 188,471 | 182,210 | 186,856 | 183,500 | 150,681 | 136,179 | 154,403 | 149,503 | 155,896 | 185,665 | 189,780 |
| 2020 | 185,583 | 207,128 | 148,638 | 127,937 | 154,095 | 145,299 | 146,576 | 150,267 | 155,711 | 170,881 | 179,877 | 203,787 |
| 2021 | 195,954 | 186,577 | 177,791 | 160,902 | 155,987 | 176,021 | 200,529 | 195,981 | 204,572 | 247,775 | 243,804 | 196,904 |
| 2022 | 212,141 | 198,166 | 226,901 | 245,026 | 243,487 | 235,455 | 227,188 | 234,905 | 266,006 | 260,853 | 239,717 | 201,962 |

Contract size = 12,500,000 JPY.   *Source: CME Group; Chicago Mercantile Exchange (CME)*

# CURRENCIES

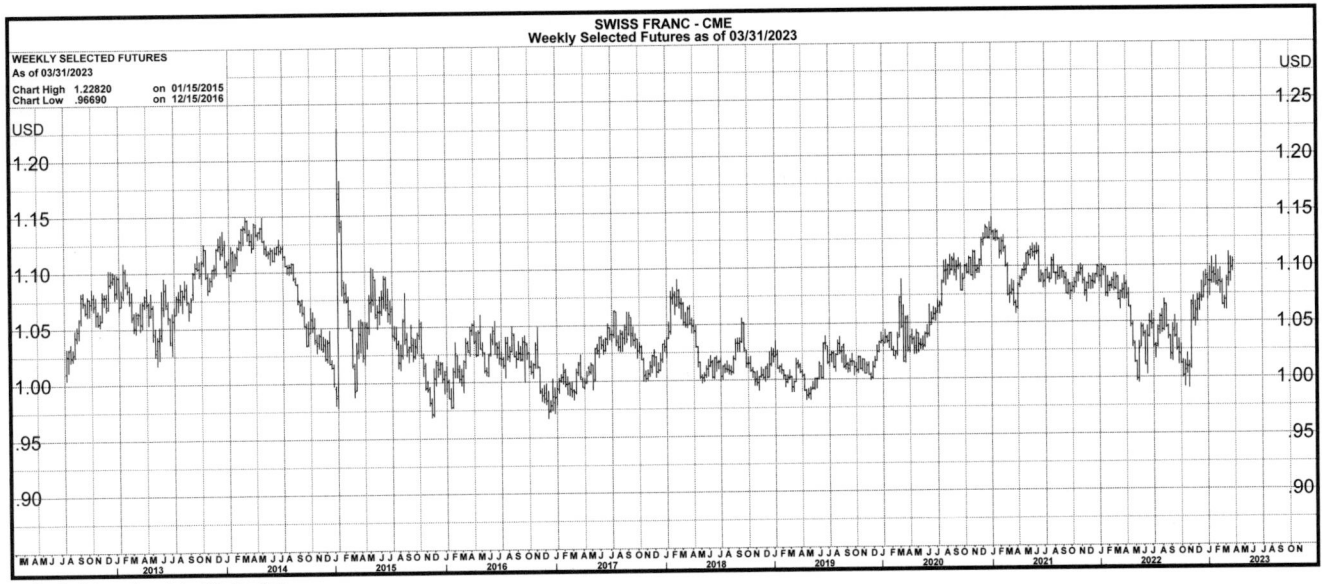

**SWISS FRANC - CME**
Weekly Selected Futures as of 03/31/2023

Nearby Futures through Last Trading Day.

## Swiss Francs per U.S. Dollar

| Year | Jan. | Feb. | Mar. | Apr. | May | June | July | Aug. | Sept. | Oct. | Nov. | Dec. | Average |
|---|---|---|---|---|---|---|---|---|---|---|---|---|---|
| 2013 | 0.9243 | 0.9215 | 0.9465 | 0.9368 | 0.9564 | 0.9330 | 0.9446 | 0.9255 | 0.9232 | 0.9032 | 0.9126 | 0.8937 | 0.9268 |
| 2014 | 0.9039 | 0.8934 | 0.8805 | 0.8830 | 0.8888 | 0.8955 | 0.8977 | 0.9100 | 0.9367 | 0.9526 | 0.9641 | 0.9769 | 0.9152 |
| 2015 | 0.9412 | 0.9361 | 0.9796 | 0.9602 | 0.9325 | 0.9309 | 0.9544 | 0.9685 | 0.9723 | 0.9697 | 1.0099 | 0.9938 | 0.9624 |
| 2016 | 1.0070 | 0.9916 | 0.9809 | 0.9642 | 0.9792 | 0.9691 | 0.9820 | 0.9716 | 0.9737 | 0.9872 | 0.9969 | 1.0201 | 0.9853 |
| 2017 | 1.0079 | 1.0017 | 1.0022 | 1.0007 | 0.9863 | 0.9678 | 0.9602 | 0.9653 | 0.9626 | 0.9820 | 0.9913 | 0.9869 | 0.9846 |
| 2018 | 0.9605 | 0.9346 | 0.9478 | 0.9686 | 0.9972 | 0.9901 | 0.9945 | 0.9879 | 0.9682 | 0.9940 | 1.0009 | 0.9922 | 0.9780 |
| 2019 | 0.9895 | 1.0018 | 1.0003 | 1.0087 | 1.0105 | 0.9878 | 0.9878 | 0.9788 | 0.9906 | 0.9929 | 0.9931 | 0.9819 | 0.9936 |
| 2020 | 0.9693 | 0.9763 | 0.9578 | 0.9700 | 0.9692 | 0.9517 | 0.9334 | 0.9101 | 0.9150 | 0.9123 | 0.9107 | 0.8880 | 0.9387 |
| 2021 | 0.8865 | 0.8976 | 0.9296 | 0.9214 | 0.9023 | 0.9080 | 0.9170 | 0.9144 | 0.9227 | 0.9227 | 0.9216 | 0.9200 | 0.9136 |
| 2022 | 0.9189 | 0.9220 | 0.9291 | 0.9456 | 0.9789 | 0.9697 | 0.9687 | 0.9570 | 0.9728 | 0.9951 | 0.9636 | 0.9321 | 0.9545 |

Average. *Source: FOREX*

## Volume of Trading of Swiss Franc Futures in Chicago    In Thousands of Contracts

| Year | Jan. | Feb. | Mar. | Apr. | May | June | July | Aug. | Sept. | Oct. | Nov. | Dec. | Total |
|---|---|---|---|---|---|---|---|---|---|---|---|---|---|
| 2013 | 767.5 | 643.9 | 850.4 | 696.4 | 1,085.0 | 938.7 | 665.1 | 677.3 | 688.4 | 711.0 | 632.6 | 705.7 | 9,061.8 |
| 2014 | 714.1 | 552.0 | 819.7 | 535.8 | 607.3 | 792.8 | 721.4 | 758.5 | 1,121.3 | 1,026.6 | 834.4 | 1,154.9 | 9,638.9 |
| 2015 | 752.0 | 244.8 | 537.2 | 472.1 | 421.0 | 513.2 | 379.8 | 433.0 | 433.6 | 381.7 | 458.4 | 607.8 | 5,634.4 |
| 2016 | 406.6 | 559.6 | 531.2 | 399.3 | 393.9 | 650.6 | 328.1 | 418.4 | 596.9 | 454.4 | 604.0 | 625.8 | 5,968.8 |
| 2017 | 474.3 | 372.0 | 598.5 | 391.8 | 645.0 | 638.1 | 603.4 | 687.9 | 772.9 | 551.5 | 527.2 | 715.5 | 6,978.1 |
| 2018 | 712.9 | 521.6 | 651.2 | 504.3 | 626.3 | 699.4 | 502.7 | 633.4 | 709.1 | 564.5 | 483.6 | 653.0 | 7,262.1 |
| 2019 | 470.9 | 340.4 | 688.3 | 514.3 | 526.3 | 809.6 | 463.6 | 623.8 | 725.4 | 645.6 | 532.9 | 805.3 | 7,146.4 |
| 2020 | 574.8 | 644.6 | 1,190.5 | 379.1 | 399.9 | 578.0 | 517.6 | 510.5 | 646.6 | 408.3 | 436.8 | 619.2 | 6,906.0 |
| 2021 | 384.6 | 475.1 | 645.8 | 397.5 | 410.5 | 600.0 | 473.1 | 437.5 | 634.7 | 466.6 | 543.4 | 516.1 | 5,984.8 |
| 2022 | 432.9 | 409.2 | 647.0 | 381.5 | 529.1 | 743.0 | 550.1 | 545.0 | 783.5 | 458.6 | 452.5 | 460.0 | 6,392.4 |

Contract size = 125,000 CHF.   *Source: CME Group; Chicago Mercantile Exchange (CME)*

## Average Open Interest of Swiss Franc Futures in Chicago    In Contracts

| Year | Jan. | Feb. | Mar. | Apr. | May | June | July | Aug. | Sept. | Oct. | Nov. | Dec. |
|---|---|---|---|---|---|---|---|---|---|---|---|---|
| 2013 | 42,982 | 44,119 | 58,519 | 49,385 | 59,413 | 47,741 | 36,890 | 38,631 | 39,298 | 51,347 | 45,586 | 53,657 |
| 2014 | 42,329 | 48,122 | 56,682 | 47,081 | 49,564 | 42,368 | 38,273 | 52,798 | 61,701 | 58,348 | 60,929 | 63,108 |
| 2015 | 54,230 | 35,769 | 42,525 | 32,785 | 32,615 | 26,518 | 26,717 | 40,075 | 40,143 | 37,866 | 64,828 | 62,677 |
| 2016 | 50,939 | 51,074 | 43,286 | 40,453 | 46,929 | 48,028 | 42,074 | 42,193 | 43,527 | 58,626 | 57,887 | 63,292 |
| 2017 | 48,235 | 47,924 | 48,104 | 45,251 | 49,672 | 45,409 | 40,566 | 40,367 | 41,027 | 56,027 | 80,732 | 88,812 |
| 2018 | 72,099 | 71,614 | 56,365 | 60,123 | 100,513 | 102,678 | 91,755 | 89,149 | 66,738 | 65,735 | 78,129 | 79,614 |
| 2019 | 64,926 | 72,668 | 80,612 | 83,816 | 92,633 | 66,089 | 52,993 | 55,459 | 60,491 | 64,391 | 70,885 | 68,183 |
| 2020 | 50,882 | 53,178 | 41,286 | 33,135 | 39,248 | 41,089 | 49,709 | 55,420 | 53,401 | 48,887 | 51,484 | 53,062 |
| 2021 | 49,008 | 50,264 | 46,672 | 41,958 | 42,158 | 43,685 | 44,316 | 44,076 | 51,682 | 55,297 | 50,744 | 43,939 |
| 2022 | 42,130 | 44,359 | 46,913 | 43,812 | 51,052 | 44,171 | 41,654 | 43,057 | 45,804 | 45,032 | 45,045 | 38,765 |

Contract size = 125,000 CHF.   *Source: CME Group; Chicago Mercantile Exchange (CME)*

# CURRENCIES

## United States Merchandise Trade Balance[2]  In Millions of Dollars

| Year | Jan. | Feb. | Mar. | Apr. | May | June | July | Aug. | Sept. | Oct. | Nov. | Dec. | Total |
|---|---|---|---|---|---|---|---|---|---|---|---|---|---|
| 2013 | -40,127 | -40,991 | -34,300 | -38,476 | -41,693 | -34,420 | -36,353 | -36,616 | -39,920 | -36,292 | -33,993 | -33,649 | -446,830 |
| 2014 | -37,448 | -40,137 | -42,958 | -43,754 | -39,594 | -38,914 | -38,953 | -36,952 | -41,688 | -41,081 | -39,819 | -42,845 | -484,143 |
| 2015 | -38,871 | -33,883 | -48,691 | -39,844 | -38,562 | -42,500 | -40,379 | -44,251 | -41,691 | -40,934 | -40,555 | -41,099 | -491,260 |
| 2016 | -40,026 | -43,215 | -36,551 | -37,566 | -39,342 | -41,658 | -40,537 | -40,563 | -36,545 | -39,232 | -44,465 | -41,469 | -481,169 |
| 2017 | -42,918 | -39,520 | -40,889 | -43,807 | -43,588 | -42,223 | -42,853 | -41,517 | -41,165 | -42,644 | -45,558 | -47,109 | -513,791 |
| 2018 | -46,809 | -48,929 | -43,735 | -45,435 | -41,672 | -45,138 | -49,658 | -49,233 | -50,891 | -52,475 | -49,550 | -55,070 | -578,595 |
| 2019 | -48,874 | -47,196 | -49,138 | -48,979 | -50,544 | -48,902 | -48,351 | -48,233 | -44,958 | -41,926 | -38,684 | -43,891 | -559,676 |
| 2020 | -44,357 | -40,501 | -44,847 | -52,246 | -54,367 | -48,972 | -58,818 | -61,115 | -59,105 | -62,107 | -64,985 | -62,570 | -653,990 |
| 2021 | -63,828 | -65,294 | -68,069 | -65,724 | -66,633 | -71,357 | -69,382 | -71,426 | -78,334 | -68,156 | -77,977 | -78,867 | -845,047 |
| 2022[1] | -87,447 | -87,251 | -106,445 | -85,975 | -85,446 | -80,773 | -69,770 | -64,557 | -72,638 | -77,161 | -60,646 | -67,210 | -945,319 |

[1] Preliminary.  [2] Not seasonally adjusted.  Source: Bureau of Economic Analysis, U.S. Department of Commerce (BEA)

## Index of Real Trade-Weighted Dollar Exchange Rates for Total Agriculture[3] (U.S. Markets)  (2000 = 100)

| Year | Jan. | Feb. | Mar. | Apr. | May | June | July | Aug. | Sept. | Oct. | Nov. | Dec. |
|---|---|---|---|---|---|---|---|---|---|---|---|---|
| 2014 | 99.3 | 99.6 | 99.7 | 99.0 | 98.7 | 98.8 | 98.5 | 99.0 | 100.1 | 100.9 | 101.9 | 103.4 |
| 2015 | 104.8 | 106.3 | 108.2 | 107.4 | 107.2 | 108.6 | 110.2 | 112.4 | 113.0 | 111.6 | 112.5 | 113.5 |
| 2016 | 115.8 | 114.8 | 112.6 | 111.0 | 112.3 | 112.9 | 113.0 | 112.1 | 113.0 | 113.8 | 116.4 | 118.3 |
| 2017 | 118.4 | 116.7 | 116.3 | 115.4 | 115.5 | 114.1 | 112.4 | 111.4 | 110.8 | 112.5 | 112.6 | 112.1 |
| 2018 | 110.2 | 109.7 | 110.2 | 110.1 | 113.0 | 114.8 | 114.9 | 115.2 | 115.7 | 116.0 | 116.9 | 116.5 |
| 2019 | 114.9 | 114.8 | 115.5 | 115.9 | 117.0 | 116.5 | 115.7 | 117.4 | 117.7 | 117.1 | 116.5 | 115.9 |
| 2020 | 115.2 | 116.3 | 120.5 | 122.7 | 121.8 | 119.4 | 119.3 | 118.3 | 117.6 | 116.6 | 114.7 | 112.9 |
| 2021 | 112.2 | 113.0 | 114.7 | 114.7 | 114.2 | 115.4 | 116.9 | 117.2 | 117.3 | 118.1 | 119.0 | 120.1 |
| 2022[1] | 119.7 | 120.0 | 121.5 | 122.2 | 125.5 | 126.8 | 128.7 | 128.0 | 131.0 | 133.2 | 130.6 | 127.6 |
| 2023[2] | 125.9 | 130.9 | 131.1 | 130.7 | 131.1 | 130.9 | 130.3 | 129.3 | 129.7 | 130.1 | 130.5 | 130.8 |

[1] Preliminary.  [2] Forecast.  [3] Real indexes adjust nominal exchange rates for differences in rates of inflation, to avoid the distortion caused by high-inflation countries. A higher value means the dollar has appreciated. Federal Reserve Board Index of trade-weighted value of the U.S. dollar against 10 major currencies. Weights are based on relative importance in world financial markets.
Source: Bureau of Economic Analysis, U.S. Department of Commerce (BEA)

## Index of Real Trade-Weighted Dollar Exchange Rates for Total Agriculture[3] (U.S. Competitors)  (2000 = 100)

| Year | Jan. | Feb. | Mar. | Apr. | May | June | July | Aug. | Sept. | Oct. | Nov. | Dec. |
|---|---|---|---|---|---|---|---|---|---|---|---|---|
| 2014 | 101.3 | 101.6 | 100.7 | 100.1 | 100.3 | 100.9 | 100.7 | 101.8 | 104.1 | 105.6 | 106.6 | 108.0 |
| 2015 | 111.4 | 113.7 | 117.6 | 117.0 | 115.4 | 116.5 | 118.4 | 119.9 | 121.4 | 120.3 | 122.5 | 122.7 |
| 2016 | 125.5 | 123.8 | 121.8 | 119.3 | 119.9 | 120.2 | 120.2 | 119.1 | 119.7 | 120.6 | 123.1 | 124.8 |
| 2017 | 124.3 | 122.8 | 122.5 | 121.7 | 120.4 | 119.3 | 117.3 | 115.7 | 115.1 | 116.4 | 116.8 | 115.8 |
| 2018 | 113.6 | 113.3 | 113.9 | 114.4 | 119.0 | 120.9 | 121.2 | 122.8 | 124.2 | 123.9 | 123.9 | 123.7 |
| 2019 | 122.9 | 122.9 | 124.0 | 124.7 | 126.0 | 124.5 | 123.9 | 126.7 | 127.9 | 127.3 | 127.1 | 125.7 |
| 2020 | 125.8 | 128.0 | 131.3 | 133.7 | 133.3 | 129.2 | 128.5 | 127.1 | 127.1 | 127.3 | 125.6 | 122.3 |
| 2021 | 122.4 | 122.9 | 125.2 | 125.1 | 123.9 | 124.8 | 127.0 | 127.3 | 127.1 | 128.5 | 129.8 | 131.2 |
| 2022[1] | 130.6 | 130.0 | 131.9 | 132.0 | 135.5 | 136.7 | 140.3 | 139.3 | 141.9 | 143.5 | 140.2 | 136.1 |
| 2023[2] | 134.7 | 140.7 | 141.5 | 141.0 | 141.2 | 140.5 | 139.2 | 137.7 | 138.3 | 138.8 | 139.5 | 140.1 |

[1] Preliminary.  [2] Forecast.  [3] Real indexes adjust nominal exchange rates for differences in rates of inflation, to avoid the distortion caused by high-inflation countries. A higher value means the dollar has appreciated. Federal Reserve Board Index of trade-weighted value of the U.S. dollar against 10 major currencies. Weights are based on relative importance in world financial markets.
Source: Bureau of Economic Analysis, U.S. Department of Commerce (BEA)

## Merchandise Trade and Current Account Balances[3]  In Billions of Dollars

| | Merchandise Trade Balance | | | | | Current Account Balance | | | | |
|---|---|---|---|---|---|---|---|---|---|---|
| Year | Canada | Germany | Japan | Switzerland | United Kingdom | Canada | Germany | Japan | Switzerland | United Kingdom |
| 2011 | -49.7 | 229.4 | 128.3 | 54.5 | -51.5 | -40.7 | 195.3 | 146.5 | 40.7 | -84.4 |
| 2012 | -65.7 | 252.1 | 62.5 | 71.2 | -101.3 | -58.2 | 185.7 | 221.3 | 86.1 | -83.0 |
| 2013 | -59.4 | 245.9 | 46.4 | 79.7 | -142.3 | -49.7 | 226.3 | 128.1 | 54.5 | -51.5 |
| 2014 | -43.1 | 282.4 | 36.8 | 60.2 | -149.3 | -65.7 | 250.5 | 62.5 | 71.3 | -101.3 |
| 2015 | -55.3 | 289.1 | 136.9 | 76.5 | -142.1 | -59.4 | 254.7 | 46.3 | 79.7 | -142.3 |
| 2016 | -49.0 | 292.0 | 193.6 | 63.2 | -139.7 | -43.1 | 292.9 | 36.6 | 60.2 | -149.3 |
| 2017 | -46.5 | 297.7 | 204.4 | 45.2 | -88.1 | -56.1 | 302.5 | 136.4 | 75.6 | -142.1 |
| 2018 | -45.4 | 297.7 | 175.6 | 72.5 | -108.5 | -49.4 | 296.2 | 189.2 | 66.1 | -139.7 |
| 2019[1] | -48.9 | 286.2 | 150.5 | 65.9 | -157.7 | -48.9 | 297.1 | 196.6 | 64.4 | -98.6 |
| 2020[2] | -47.1 | 281.2 | 162.6 | 65.9 | -145.7 | -52.8 | 311.0 | 163.6 | 78.6 | -94.4 |

[1] Estimate.  [2] Projection.  [3] Not seasonally adjusted.  Source: Organization for Economic Cooperation and Development (OECD)

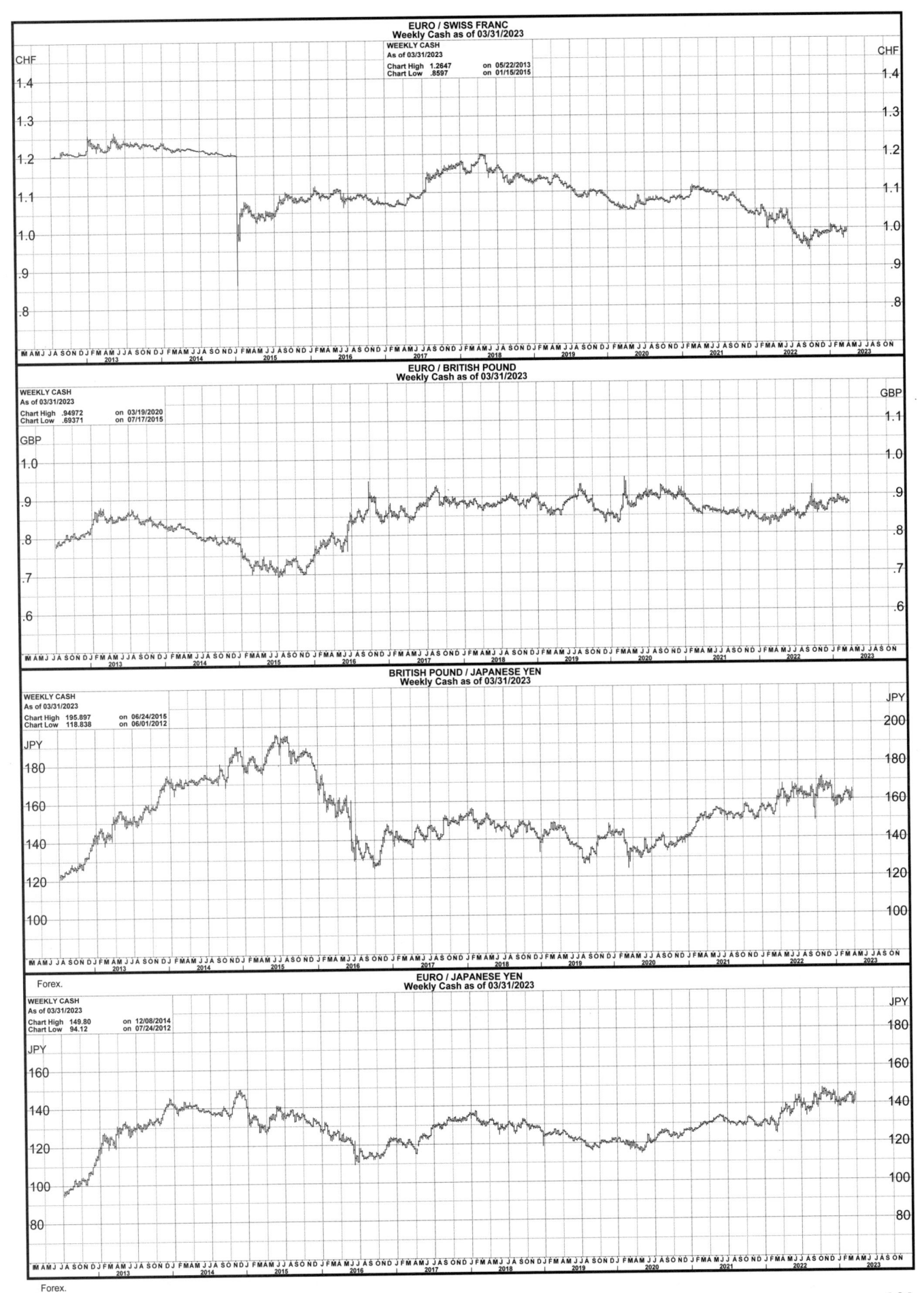

# CURRENCIES

## EURO / SWISS FRANC
Weekly Cash as of 03/31/2023

WEEKLY CASH
As of 03/31/2023
Chart High 1.2647 on 05/22/2013
Chart Low .8597 on 01/15/2015

## EURO / BRITISH POUND
Weekly Cash as of 03/31/2023

WEEKLY CASH
As of 03/31/2023
Chart High .94972 on 03/19/2020
Chart Low .69371 on 07/17/2015

## BRITISH POUND / JAPANESE YEN
Weekly Cash as of 03/31/2023

WEEKLY CASH
As of 03/31/2023
Chart High 195.897 on 06/24/2015
Chart Low 118.838 on 06/01/2012

## EURO / JAPANESE YEN
Weekly Cash as of 03/31/2023

WEEKLY CASH
As of 03/31/2023
Chart High 149.80 on 12/08/2014
Chart Low 94.12 on 07/24/2012

Forex.

# Diamonds

The diamond, which is the mineral form of carbon, is the hardest, strongest natural material known on earth. The name *diamond* is derived from *adamas*, the ancient Greek term meaning "invincible." Diamonds form deep within the Earth's crust and are typically billions of years old. Diamonds have also have been found in and near meteorites and their craters. Diamonds are considered precious gemstones but lower grade diamonds are used for industrial applications such as drilling, cutting, grinding and polishing.

**Supply** – World production of natural gem diamonds in 2022 rose by +2.8% yr/yr to 76.0 million carats, well below the 2008 record high of 114.0 million carats (one carat equals 1/5 gram or 200 milligrams). The world's largest producers of natural gem diamonds are Russia with 27.6% of world production in 2022, Botswana with 23.7%, Angola with 13.2%, and South Africa with 5.1%. World production of natural industrial diamonds in 2022 rose by +2.2% yr/yr at 46.000 million carats. The main producers of natural industrial diamonds in 2022 were Russia with 37.0% of world production, Congo with 23.9%, Botswana with 15.2%, and South Africa with 13.0%.

**Trade** – The U.S. in 2022 imported 640,000 carats of natural diamonds and relied on imports for 62% of its consumption.

### World Production of Natural Gem Diamonds    In Thousands of Carats

| Year | Angola | Australia | Botswana | Brazil, unspecified | Central African Republic | China, unspecified | Congo (Kinshasa) | Ghana, unspecified | Namibia | Russia | Sierra Leone | South Africa | World Total |
|---|---|---|---|---|---|---|---|---|---|---|---|---|---|
| 2017 | 8,490 | 343 | 16,000 | 255 | 38 | 230 | 3,800 | 82 | 1,948 | 23,900 | 231 | 3,880 | 84,400 |
| 2018 | 7,570 | 281 | 17,200 | 251 | 11 | 99 | 3,030 | 54 | 2,397 | 24,200 | 593 | 3,960 | 85,200 |
| 2019 | 8,230 | 260 | 16,600 | 166 | 21 | 51 | 2,670 | 38 | 2,018 | 25,400 | 649 | 2,870 | 79,500 |
| 2020 | 6,960 | 219 | 11,900 | 125 | | | 2,550 | | 1,550 | 17,500 | 513 | 6,780 | 62,300 |
| 2021[1] | 7,850 | 220 | 16,000 | 143 | 73 | | 2,820 | | 1,760 | 21,900 | 671 | 3,890 | 73,900 |
| 2022[2] | 10,000 | | 18,000 | 150 | 73 | | 2,500 | | 2,300 | 21,000 | 680 | 3,900 | 76,000 |

[1] Preliminary.   [2] Estimate.   [3] Less than 1/2 unit.   Source: U.S. Geological Survey (USGS)

### World Production of Natural Industrial Diamonds[4]    In Thousands of Carats

| Year | Angola | Australia | Botswana | Brazil | Central African Republic | China | Congo (Kinshasa) | Ghana | Russia | Sierra Leone | South Africa | Venezuela | World Total |
|---|---|---|---|---|---|---|---|---|---|---|---|---|---|
| 2017 | 944 | 16,800 | 6,900 | ---- | 10 | ---- | 15,300 | ---- | 18,800 | 58 | 5,820 | ---- | 67,000 |
| 2018 | 841 | 13,800 | 7,300 | ---- | 3 | ---- | 12,100 | ---- | 19,000 | 148 | 5,950 | ---- | 62,200 |
| 2019 | 915 | 12,700 | 7,110 | ---- | 6 | ---- | 10,800 | ---- | 19,900 | 162 | 4,310 | ---- | 58,000 |
| 2020 | | 11,000 | 5,000 | ---- | | | 10,000 | ---- | 19,900 | | 2,000 | ---- | 45,000 |
| 2021[1] | | 8,000 | 7,000 | ---- | | | 10,000 | ---- | 14,000 | | 6,000 | ---- | 45,000 |
| 2022[2] | | | 7,000 | ---- | | | 11,000 | ---- | 17,000 | | 6,000 | ---- | 46,000 |

[1] Preliminary.   [2] Estimate.   [3] Formerly Zaire.   Source: U.S. Geological Survey (USGS)

### U.S. Exports of Industrial Diamonds    In Thousands of Carats

| Year | Belgium | France | Hong Kong | India | Israel | Mexico | Singapore | Switzerland | Thailand | United Arab Emirates | United Kingdom | Other | World Total |
|---|---|---|---|---|---|---|---|---|---|---|---|---|---|
| 2014 | 55.6 | 3.3 | 1,980.0 | 381.0 | 78.5 | 416.0 | 3.9 | 2.2 | 153.0 | 88.7 | 26.3 | 5.6 | 3,470.0 |
| 2015 | 187.0 | 67.1 | 1,660.0 | 672.0 | 243.0 | 316.0 | 6.8 | 12.3 | 146.0 | 391.0 | 6.7 | 6.2 | 4,020.0 |
| 2016 | 564.0 | 9.4 | 1,170.0 | 669.0 | 184.0 | 331.0 | 5.1 | 44.2 | 148.0 | 408.0 | 49.7 | 6.3 | 3,790.0 |
| 2017 | 85.7 | 0.9 | 1,420.0 | 561.0 | 61.0 | 609.0 | 1.1 | 22.8 | 96.4 | 97.3 | 6.4 | 9.0 | 3,130.0 |
| 2018[1] | 14.1 | 22.4 | 761.0 | 620.0 | 54.8 | 253.0 | 6.7 | 5.9 | 56.5 | 183.0 | 21.9 | 12.9 | 2,220.0 |
| 2019[2] | 25.4 | 1.4 | 593.0 | 291.0 | 34.9 | 286.0 | 2.4 | 4.8 | 536.0 | 80.7 | 4.8 | 22.4 | 2,000.0 |

[1] Preliminary.   [2] Estimate.   Source: U.S. Geological Survey (USGS)

### Salient Statistics of Industrial Diamonds in the United States    In Millions of Carats

| | Bort, Grit & Powder & Dust — Natural and Synthetic | | | | | | | Stones (Natural) | | | | | Net Import Reliance % of Consumption |
|---|---|---|---|---|---|---|---|---|---|---|---|---|---|
| Year | Production Manufactured Diamond | Secondary | Imports for Consumption | Exports & Reexports | In Manufactured Products | Gov't Sales | Apparent Consumption | Price Value of Imports $/Carat | Secondary Production | Imports for Consumption | Exports & Reexports | Gov't Sales | Apparent Consumption | Price Value of Imports $/Carat | |
| 2017 | ---- | 11.0 | 399.0 | 161.0 | ---- | ---- | 253.0 | .16 | ---- | 1.2 | ---- | ---- | ---- | 12.90 | 79 |
| 2018 | ---- | 32.0 | 574.0 | 39.0 | ---- | ---- | 652.0 | .12 | ---- | 2.5 | ---- | ---- | ---- | 2.96 | 67 |
| 2019 | ---- | 36.0 | 310.0 | 114.0 | ---- | ---- | 347.0 | .14 | ---- | 1.1 | ---- | ---- | ---- | 5.82 | 57 |
| 2020 | ---- | 35.0 | 190.0 | 90.0 | ---- | ---- | 265.0 | .19 | ---- | .5 | ---- | ---- | ---- | 8.41 | 38 |
| 2021[1] | ---- | 1.2 | 261.0 | 99.0 | ---- | ---- | 295.0 | .18 | ---- | .3 | ---- | ---- | ---- | 13.00 | 55 |
| 2022[2] | ---- | 1.2 | 340.0 | 100.0 | ---- | ---- | 390.0 | .19 | ---- | .6 | ---- | ---- | ---- | 10.00 | 62 |

[1] Preliminary.   [2] Estimate.   [3] Less than 1/2 unit.   Source: U.S. Geological Survey (USGS)

# Eggs

Eggs provide a low-priced protein source worldwide. Each commercial chicken lays between 265-280 eggs per year. In the United States, the grade and size of eggs are regulated under the federal Egg Products Inspection Act (1970). The grades of eggs are AA, A, and B, and must have sound, whole shells and must be clean. The difference among the grades of eggs is internal and mostly reflects the freshness of the egg. Table eggs vary in color and can be determined by the color of the chicken's earlobe. For example, chickens with white earlobes lay white eggs and chickens with reddish-brown earlobes lay brown eggs. In the U.S., egg size is determined by the weight of a dozen eggs, not individual eggs, and range from Peewee to Jumbo. Store-bought eggs in the shell stay fresh for 3 to 5 weeks in a home refrigerator, according to the USDA.

Eggs are primarily used as a source of food, although eggs are also widely used for medical purposes. Fertile eggs, as a source of purified proteins, are used to produce many vaccines. Flu vaccines are produced by growing single strains of the flu virus in eggs, which are then extracted to make the vaccine. Eggs are also used in biotechnology to create new drugs. The hen's genetic make-up can be altered so that the whites of the eggs are rich in tailored proteins that form the basis of medicines to fight cancer and other diseases. The U.S. biotech company Viragen and the Roslin Institute in Edinburgh have produced eggs with 100 mg or more of the easily extracted proteins used in new drugs to treat various illnesses, including ovarian and breast cancers.

Futures on eggs are traded on the Dalian Commodity Exchange.

**Prices** – The average monthly price of all eggs received by farmers in the U.S. in 2022 rose by +141.0% yr/yr to 239.3 cents per dozen, a new record.

**Supply** – World egg production in 2021 fell by -0.9% at 1.633 billion eggs. The world's largest egg producers were China with 36.4% of world production, the U.S. with 6.8%, Mexico with 3.5%, Russia with 2.7%, Japan with 2.6%, Germany with 1.0%, Ukraine with 0.9%, and United Kingdom with 0.8%. U.S. egg production in 2022 fell by -2.5% to 108.107 billion eggs, below the 2019 record high of 113.370. The average number of hens and pullets on U.S. farms in 2020 fell by -2.3% yr/yr to 390.351 million, below the 2019 record of high 399.500.

**Demand** – U.S. consumption of eggs in 2020 rose by +1.0% yr/yr to 8.085 billion dozen eggs, a new record high. U.S. consumption of eggs is up sharply by about 25% from ten years earlier, reflecting the increased popularity of eggs in American diets. U.S. per capita egg consumption in 2022 is forecasted to rise by +3.2% yr/yr to 286.7 eggs per year per person. Per capita egg consumption reached a high of 277.2 eggs in 1970, fell sharply in the 1990s to a low of 174.9 in 1995, and then began rebounding in 1997 to current levels.

**Trade** – U.S. imports of eggs in 2020 fell by -0.6% yr/yr to 18.0 million dozen eggs. U.S. exports of eggs in 2020 fell by -0.6% yr/yr to 280.0 million dozen eggs, down from the 2014 record high of 393.844 million dozen.

## World Production of Eggs    In Millions of Eggs

| Year | Brazil | China | France | Germany | Italy | Japan | Mexico | Russia | Spain | Ukraine | United Kingdom | United States | World Total |
|---|---|---|---|---|---|---|---|---|---|---|---|---|---|
| 2013 | 43,431 | 495,741 | 15,766 | 12,593 | 12,679 | 42,033 | 50,317 | 40,779 | 11,787 | 19,419 | 11,517 | 97,555 | 1,284,506 |
| 2014 | 44,811 | 459,063 | 15,935 | 12,685 | 12,749 | 41,699 | 48,438 | 41,313 | 12,498 | 19,391 | 11,653 | 100,879 | 1,274,944 |
| 2015 | 45,219 | 465,424 | 16,319 | 11,807 | 13,093 | 42,015 | 50,048 | 42,093 | 12,780 | 16,615 | 11,966 | 97,208 | 1,296,459 |
| 2016 | 46,115 | 465,802 | 13,605 | 11,979 | 13,300 | 42,704 | 51,324 | 43,043 | 13,183 | 14,799 | 12,370 | 102,112 | 1,316,769 |
| 2017 | 50,574 | 538,822 | 14,631 | 12,087 | 12,994 | 43,353 | 52,287 | 44,290 | 13,503 | 15,351 | 12,886 | 107,242 | 1,494,299 |
| 2018 | 53,163 | 544,305 | 16,567 | 12,325 | 13,150 | 43,796 | 54,187 | 44,398 | 14,018 | 15,971 | 13,303 | 110,074 | 1,524,440 |
| 2019 | 55,265 | 576,786 | 15,441 | 12,511 | 12,810 | 43,996 | 55,656 | 44,492 | 13,717 | 16,511 | 13,541 | 113,206 | 1,584,784 |
| 2020[1] | 57,208 | 604,681 | 16,411 | 13,765 | 12,372 | 43,881 | 56,905 | 44,503 | 14,485 | 16,006 | 13,266 | 111,734 | 1,647,935 |
| 2021[2] | 58,196 | 594,655 |  | 16,020 |  | 42,904 | 57,489 | 44,578 |  | 13,931 | 13,806 | 110,729 | 1,633,018 |

[1] Preliminary.   [2] Forecast.   [3] Selected countries.   Source: Food and Agricultural Organization of the United Nations (FAO)

## Salient Statistics of Eggs in the United States

| | Hens & Pullets On Farm Dec. 1[3] | Average Number During Year | Rate of Lay Per Layer During Year[4] | Eggs Total Produced | Price in cents Per Dozen | Value of Production[5] | Total Egg Production | Imports[6] | Exports[6] | Used for Hatching | Total | Per Capita Eggs[6] |
|---|---|---|---|---|---|---|---|---|---|---|---|---|
| Year | ----- Thousands ----- | | (Number) | ----- Millions ----- | | Million USD | ------------------- Million Dozen ------------------- | | | | | Number |
| 2014 | 370,637 | 364,707 | 277 | 101,186 | 125.8 | 10,258 | 8,404 | 34.7 | 393.8 | 980.6 | 7,106 | 267.5 |
| 2015 | 346,343 | 352,411 | 276 | 97,208 | 164.6 | 13,608 | 8,101 | 123.3 | 313.6 | 995.6 | 6,781 | 256.3 |
| 2016 | 377,371 | 365,997 | 279 | 102,112 | 76.6 | 6,514 | 8,579 | 129.5 | 302.8 | 1,009.6 | 7,327 | 272.0 |
| 2017 | 382,266 | 378,787 | 281 | 105,841 | 86.3 | 7,597 | 8,879 | 34.2 | 354.9 | 1,035.2 | 7,589 | 280.3 |
| 2018 | 396,870 | 394,361 | 279 | 109,633 | 115.2 | 10,586 | 9,173 | 17.8 | 333.1 | 1,057.5 | 7,751 | 287.5 |
| 2019 | 403,273 | 399,500 | 283 | 113,370 | 79.9 | | 9,434 | 18.1 | 281.8 | 1,179.3 | 8,009 | 291.6 |
| 2020 | 391,010 | 391,772 | 285 | 111,337 | 91.4 | | 9,298 | 18.0 | 280.0 | 1,221.3 | 8,085 | 292.8 |
| 2021[1] | 393,078 | 391,242 | 285 | 110,953 | 99.3 | | | | | | | |
| 2022[2] | 375,354 | 379,304 | 289 | 108,885 | 239.3 | | | | | | | |

[1] Preliminary.   [2] Forecast.   [3] All layers of laying age.   [4] Number of eggs produced during the year divided by the average number of all layers of laying age on hand during the year.   [5] Value of sales plus value of eggs consumed in households of producers. 6/ Shell-egg equivalent of eggs and egg products.
Source: National Agricultural Statistics Service, U.S. Department of Agriculture (NASS-USDA)

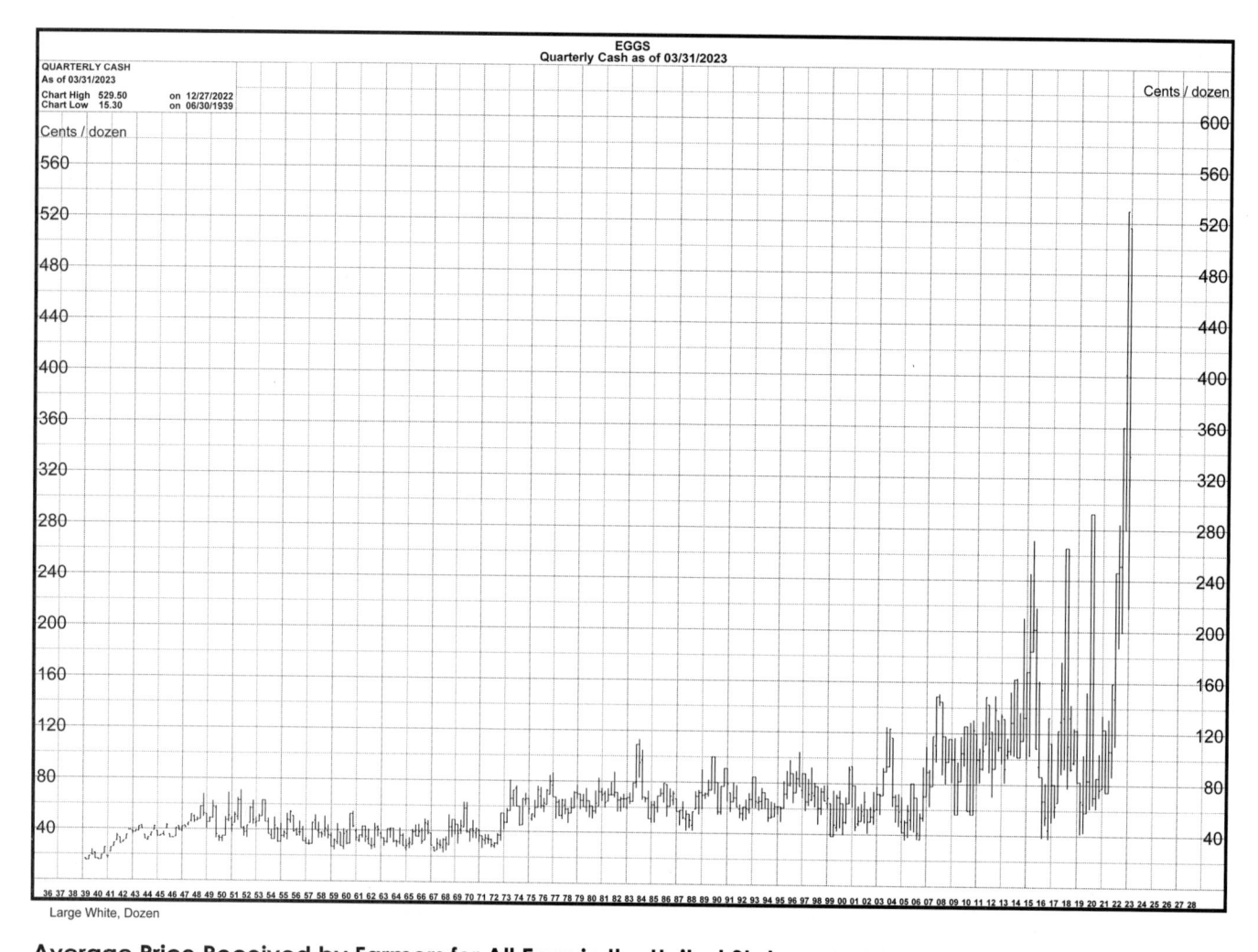

# EGGS

## Average Price Received by Farmers for All Eggs in the United States — In Cents Per Dozen

| Year | Jan. | Feb. | Mar. | Apr. | May | June | July | Aug. | Sept. | Oct. | Nov. | Dec. | Average |
|------|------|------|------|------|------|------|------|------|------|------|------|------|---------|
| 2013 | 106.0 | 99.3 | 115.0 | 88.5 | 117.0 | 93.0 | 104.0 | 108.0 | 103.0 | 104.0 | 132.0 | 136.0 | 108.8 |
| 2014 | 112.0 | 140.0 | 124.0 | 127.0 | 117.0 | 109.0 | 124.0 | 108.0 | 105.0 | 114.0 | 152.0 | 177.0 | 125.8 |
| 2015 | 125.0 | 129.0 | 154.0 | 108.0 | 173.0 | 200.0 | 190.0 | 239.0 | 190.0 | 143.0 | 200.0 | 124.0 | 164.6 |
| 2016 | 118.0 | 108.0 | 96.7 | 67.6 | 54.7 | 53.7 | 64.8 | 65.1 | 60.1 | 51.0 | 58.8 | 121.0 | 76.6 |
| 2017 | 79.5 | 62.3 | 78.3 | 63.3 | 61.9 | 63.5 | 82.3 | 74.9 | 109.0 | 90.1 | 138.0 | 133.0 | 86.3 |
| 2018 | 115.0 | 126.0 | 201.0 | 120.0 | 85.1 | 103.0 | 109.0 | 109.0 | 93.1 | 91.2 | 113.0 | 117.0 | 115.2 |
| 2019 | 101.0 | 92.3 | 86.6 | 63.3 | 47.5 | 71.4 | 51.1 | 89.1 | 68.0 | 66.3 | 129.0 | 93.1 | 79.9 |
| 2020 | 75.3 | 89.3 | 172.0 | 104.0 | 77.4 | 71.9 | 76.2 | 77.6 | 83.2 | 99.4 | 96.8 | 73.4 | 91.4 |
| 2021 | 93.5 | 99.4 | 115.0 | 85.9 | 83.1 | 81.1 | 86.9 | 108.0 | 103.0 | 90.3 | 109.0 | 136.0 | 99.3 |
| 2022[1] | 147.0 | 143.0 | 160.0 | 230.0 | 201.0 | 203.0 | 264.0 | 194.0 | 265.0 | 281.0 | 334.0 | 449.0 | 239.3 |

[1] Preliminary. Source: Economic Research Service, U.S. Department of Agriculture (ERS-USDA)

## Average Wholesale Price of Shell Eggs (Large) Delivered, Chicago — In Cents Per Dozen

| Year | Jan. | Feb. | Mar. | Apr. | May | June | July | Aug. | Sept. | Oct. | Nov. | Dec. | Average |
|------|------|------|------|------|------|------|------|------|------|------|------|------|---------|
| 2013 | 112.93 | 112.92 | 114.30 | 97.86 | 105.45 | 89.75 | 104.77 | 106.82 | 106.50 | 106.41 | 133.60 | 150.21 | 111.79 |
| 2014 | 113.10 | 135.97 | 133.93 | 145.98 | 116.21 | 115.83 | 122.16 | 116.02 | 111.93 | 117.11 | 143.18 | 194.45 | 130.49 |
| 2015 | 111.10 | 133.50 | 149.18 | 113.10 | 136.20 | 223.82 | 206.55 | 260.40 | 217.02 | 161.95 | 192.55 | 157.14 | 171.88 |
| 2016 | 106.71 | 131.80 | 93.05 | 62.93 | 55.45 | 46.18 | 69.70 | 57.24 | 64.74 | 44.07 | 58.07 | 94.31 | 73.69 |
| 2017 | 78.47 | 65.84 | 63.76 | 68.39 | 55.77 | 60.32 | 74.45 | 80.85 | 104.85 | 110.00 | 130.74 | 169.80 | 88.60 |
| 2018 | 116.40 | 150.24 | 205.07 | 177.93 | 90.95 | 88.93 | 129.55 | 105.22 | 93.45 | 99.54 | 115.26 | 120.80 | 124.45 |
| 2019 | 104.98 | 103.45 | 83.98 | 67.73 | 45.27 | 56.25 | 51.68 | 67.50 | 84.25 | 59.91 | 120.10 | 119.50 | 80.38 |
| 2020 | 70.29 | 96.50 | 151.59 | 200.77 | 83.70 | 69.14 | 73.00 | 66.93 | 81.21 | 100.41 | 101.10 | 78.73 | 97.78 |
| 2021 | 85.39 | 119.55 | 125.67 | 92.86 | 76.75 | 75.32 | 89.60 | 106.50 | 120.55 | 96.45 | 102.55 | 147.68 | 103.24 |
| 2022[1] | 128.95 | 164.13 | 155.85 | 260.31 | 238.74 | 205.98 | 306.00 | 236.28 | 266.93 | 332.40 | 368.52 | 474.21 | 261.53 |

[1] Preliminary. Source: National Agricultural Statistics Service, U.S. Department of Agriculture (NASS-USDA)

# EGGS

## Total Egg Production in the United States    In Millions of Eggs

| Year | Jan. | Feb. | Mar. | Apr. | May | June | July | Aug. | Sept. | Oct. | Nov. | Dec. | Total |
|---|---|---|---|---|---|---|---|---|---|---|---|---|---|
| 2013 | 8,125 | 7,321 | 8,195 | 7,929 | 8,139 | 7,857 | 8,082 | 8,178 | 7,969 | 8,267 | 8,098 | 8,538 | 96,698 |
| 2014 | 8,490 | 7,636 | 8,522 | 8,298 | 8,523 | 8,242 | 8,597 | 8,591 | 8,289 | 8,632 | 8,521 | 8,845 | 101,186 |
| 2015 | 8,656 | 7,730 | 8,688 | 8,352 | 8,141 | 7,577 | 7,850 | 7,878 | 7,647 | 7,970 | 7,875 | 8,261 | 97,208 |
| 2016 | 8,308 | 7,948 | 8,622 | 8,333 | 8,643 | 8,349 | 8,672 | 8,751 | 8,507 | 8,851 | 8,707 | 9,100 | 102,112 |
| 2017 | 9,053 | 8,124 | 9,007 | 8,687 | 8,918 | 8,636 | 8,953 | 8,922 | 8,578 | 8,920 | 8,791 | 9,252 | 105,841 |
| 2018 | 9,132 | 8,278 | 9,243 | 8,932 | 9,252 | 8,966 | 9,239 | 9,305 | 9,052 | 9,370 | 9,171 | 9,693 | 109,633 |
| 2019 | 9,658 | 8,689 | 9,675 | 9,378 | 9,618 | 9,215 | 9,454 | 9,491 | 9,223 | 9,664 | 9,497 | 9,809 | 113,370 |
| 2020 | 9,690 | 8,946 | 9,539 | 9,096 | 9,121 | 8,832 | 9,317 | 9,353 | 9,057 | 9,505 | 9,327 | 9,554 | 111,337 |
| 2021 | 9,482 | 8,542 | 9,461 | 9,121 | 9,284 | 8,922 | 9,242 | 9,285 | 9,066 | 9,469 | 9,301 | 9,778 | 110,953 |
| 2022[1] | 9,677 | 8,684 | 9,471 | 8,895 | 9,028 | 8,697 | 9,056 | 9,158 | 8,899 | 9,225 | 8,947 | 9,149 | 108,885 |

[1] Preliminary.    Source: National Agricultural Statistics Service, U.S. Department of Agriculture (NASS-USDA)

## Per Capita Disappearance of Eggs[4] in the United States    In Number of Eggs

| Year | First Quarter | Second Quarter | Third Quarter | Fourth Quarter | Total | Year | First Quarter | Second Quarter | Third Quarter | Fourth Quarter | Total |
|---|---|---|---|---|---|---|---|---|---|---|---|
| 2012 | 63.3 | 62.3 | 63.3 | 65.6 | 254.6 | 2018 | 69.6 | 70.9 | 72.7 | 74.3 | 287.5 |
| 2013 | 64.2 | 63.3 | 64.5 | 66.0 | 258.0 | 2019 | 72.7 | 72.6 | 72.3 | 74.0 | 291.6 |
| 2014 | 65.6 | 66.2 | 67.2 | 68.5 | 267.5 | 2020 | 72.1 | 69.3 | 71.1 | 72.8 | 285.5 |
| 2015 | 65.7 | 62.9 | 61.9 | 65.7 | 256.3 | 2021[1] | 69.8 | 68.7 | 69.3 | 72.6 | 280.4 |
| 2016 | 67.4 | 66.4 | 67.4 | 70.8 | 272.0 | 2022[2] | 70.4 | 67.8 | 68.9 | 69.6 | 276.6 |
| 2017 | 69.0 | 69.3 | 70.3 | 71.2 | 280.3 | 2023[3] | 69.1 | 71.3 | 72.5 | 74.5 | 287.4 |

[1] Preliminary.    [2] Estimate.    [3] Forecast.    Source: Economic Research Service, U.S. Department of Agriculture (ERS-USDA)

## Egg-Feed Ratio[1] in the United States

| Year | Jan. | Feb. | Mar. | Apr. | May | June | July | Aug. | Sept. | Oct. | Nov. | Dec. | Average |
|---|---|---|---|---|---|---|---|---|---|---|---|---|---|
| 2013 | 5.6 | 5.0 | 6.1 | 4.2 | 6.3 | 4.4 | 5.3 | 6.1 | 6.4 | 7.3 | 10.4 | 10.7 | 6.5 |
| 2014 | 8.0 | 10.9 | 8.9 | 8.9 | 7.9 | 7.3 | 9.6 | 8.6 | 9.0 | 10.5 | 15.1 | 17.7 | 10.2 |
| 2015 | 11.4 | 12.2 | 15.3 | 9.6 | 18.2 | 21.8 | 19.5 | 26.5 | 20.7 | 14.7 | 22.9 | 12.2 | 17.1 |
| 2016 | 11.4 | 10.2 | 8.8 | 4.6 | 2.7 | 2.5 | 4.0 | 4.4 | 3.9 | 2.6 | 3.7 | 12.1 | 5.9 |
| 2017 | 6.7 | 4.3 | 6.4 | 4.4 | 4.2 | 4.5 | 6.9 | 6.1 | 10.9 | 8.3 | 15.3 | 14.4 | 7.7 |
| 2018 | 11.6 | 12.8 | 22.2 | 11.3 | 6.8 | 9.3 | 10.5 | 11.0 | 8.7 | 8.5 | 11.7 | 11.8 | 11.4 |
| 2019 | 9.5 | 8.4 | 7.6 | 4.6 | 2.3 | 5.1 | 2.5 | 7.6 | 5.0 | 4.7 | 13.0 | 8.3 | 6.6 |
| 2020 | 5.6 | 7.4 | 18.7 | 10.1 | 6.3 | 5.5 | 6.1 | 6.3 | 6.6 | 8.5 | 7.7 | 4.6 | 7.8 |
| 2021 | 6.6 | 6.3 | 7.5 | 4.4 | 3.7 | 3.6 | 4.1 | 5.8 | 6.2 | 5.4 | 7.0 | 9.3 | 5.8 |
| 2022[1] | 9.8 | 8.5 | 9.2 | 13.8 | 11.4 | 11.4 | 16.1 | 11.2 | 17.0 | 19.7 | 23.6 | 32.2 | 15.3 |

[1] Pounds of laying feed equivalent in value to one dozen eggs.    [2] Preliminary.    Source: Economic Research Service, U.S. Department of Agriculture (ERS-USDA)

## Hens and Pullets of Laying Age (Layers) in the United States, on First of Month    In Thousands

| Year | Jan. 1 | Feb. 1 | Mar. 1 | Apr. 1 | May 1 | June 1 | July 1 | Aug. 1 | Sept. 1 | Oct. 1 | Nov. 1 | Dec. 1 |
|---|---|---|---|---|---|---|---|---|---|---|---|---|
| 2013 | 344,920 | 344,916 | 347,025 | 348,468 | 344,363 | 345,740 | 343,944 | 349,862 | 351,870 | 349,950 | 352,971 | 356,923 |
| 2014 | 363,828 | 362,628 | 363,000 | 364,610 | 364,840 | 363,604 | 363,572 | 365,799 | 365,748 | 366,306 | 366,329 | 370,637 |
| 2015 | 368,380 | 364,996 | 365,857 | 366,022 | 357,858 | 332,788 | 332,422 | 334,040 | 334,912 | 338,273 | 340,554 | 346,343 |
| 2016 | 356,109 | 359,429 | 366,253 | 366,749 | 366,217 | 365,830 | 364,432 | 364,935 | 368,128 | 370,254 | 371,438 | 377,371 |
| 2017 | 377,198 | 376,955 | 375,688 | 376,790 | 374,671 | 372,584 | 372,241 | 372,995 | 374,769 | 376,694 | 379,323 | 382,266 |
| 2018 | 382,305 | 388,227 | 392,297 | 392,843 | 391,760 | 371,749 | 391,377 | 389,840 | 391,569 | 391,885 | 393,060 | 396,870 |
| 2019 | 403,274 | 402,220 | 404,853 | 406,457 | 402,890 | 397,289 | 392,406 | 392,182 | 394,418 | 396,565 | 400,204 | 403,273 |
| 2020 | 403,751 | 399,049 | 394,752 | 396,432 | 389,069 | 384,983 | 381,290 | 380,700 | 383,643 | 385,628 | 387,664 | 391,010 |
| 2021 | 392,205 | 394,810 | 394,342 | 392,330 | 387,478 | 382,924 | 383,120 | 384,082 | 385,268 | 388,051 | 391,369 | 393,078 |
| 2022[1] | 397,208 | 392,677 | 392,528 | 372,344 | 366,991 | 365,999 | 365,627 | 370,737 | 373,448 | 373,659 | 375,058 | 375,354 |

[1] Preliminary.    Source: National Agricultural Statistics Service, U.S. Department of Agriculture (NASS-USDA)

# EGGS

### Eggs Laid Per Hundred Layers in the United States    In Number of Eggs

| Year | Jan. | Feb. | Mar. | Apr. | May | June | July | Aug. | Sept. | Oct. | Nov. | Dec. | Average |
|---|---|---|---|---|---|---|---|---|---|---|---|---|---|
| 2013 | 2,327 | 2,090 | 2,326 | 2,259 | 2,329 | 2,249 | 2,315 | 2,331 | 2,271 | 2,352 | 2,281 | 2,354 | 2,290 |
| 2014 | 2,337 | 2,105 | 2,342 | 2,275 | 2,340 | 2,267 | 2,357 | 2,349 | 2,265 | 2,356 | 2,312 | 2,388 | 2,308 |
| 2015 | 2,349 | 2,103 | 2,360 | 2,292 | 2,339 | 2,258 | 2,334 | 2,332 | 2,247 | 2,319 | 2,261 | 2,335 | 2,294 |
| 2016 | 2,322 | 2,190 | 2,352 | 2,274 | 2,361 | 2,287 | 2,378 | 2,387 | 2,304 | 2,386 | 2,328 | 2,411 | 2,332 |
| 2017 | 2,400 | 2,159 | 2,394 | 2,312 | 2,387 | 2,319 | 2,403 | 2,386 | 2,283 | 2,360 | 2,308 | 2,381 | 2,341 |
| 2018 | 2,351 | 2,121 | 2,354 | 2,277 | 2,362 | 2,290 | 2,365 | 2,381 | 2,311 | 2,387 | 2,322 | 2,406 | 2,327 |
| 2019 | 2,398 | 2,153 | 2,385 | 2,317 | 2,404 | 2,334 | 2,410 | 2,413 | 2,332 | 2,426 | 2,364 | 2,427 | 2,364 |
| 2020 | 2,414 | 2,254 | 2,411 | 2,316 | 2,357 | 2,305 | 2,445 | 2,447 | 2,355 | 2,458 | 2,396 | 2,438 | 2,383 |
| 2021 | 2,410 | 2,165 | 2,405 | 2,339 | 2,410 | 2,329 | 2,409 | 2,413 | 2,345 | 2,430 | 2,371 | 2,465 | 2,374 |
| 2022[1] | 2,450 | 2,212 | 2,464 | 2,389 | 2,453 | 2,366 | 2,447 | 2,448 | 2,365 | 2,442 | 2,366 | 2,434 | 2,403 |

[1] Preliminary.    Source: National Agricultural Statistics Service, U.S. Department of Agriculture (NASS-USDA)

### Egg-Type Chicks Hatched by Commercial Hatcheries in the United States    In Thousands

| Year | Jan. | Feb. | Mar. | Apr. | May | June | July | Aug. | Sept. | Oct. | Nov. | Dec. | Total |
|---|---|---|---|---|---|---|---|---|---|---|---|---|---|
| 2013 | 43,831 | 42,236 | 43,584 | 46,031 | 50,154 | 42,252 | 39,936 | 38,794 | 42,166 | 42,506 | 41,845 | 41,144 | 514,479 |
| 2014 | 44,345 | 41,269 | 44,801 | 46,384 | 49,684 | 44,271 | 42,489 | 39,731 | 43,671 | 44,665 | 36,544 | 42,991 | 520,845 |
| 2015 | 43,868 | 43,774 | 50,187 | 50,193 | 48,315 | 47,212 | 42,790 | 47,131 | 49,391 | 50,194 | 45,848 | 46,679 | 565,582 |
| 2016 | 47,775 | 54,289 | 57,055 | 51,266 | 57,306 | 57,562 | 41,609 | 43,258 | 44,892 | 43,344 | 41,648 | 45,731 | 585,735 |
| 2017 | 45,367 | 48,127 | 55,919 | 52,762 | 53,506 | 49,722 | 41,862 | 45,861 | 42,725 | 51,495 | 48,363 | 46,697 | 582,406 |
| 2018 | 51,900 | 50,148 | 58,147 | 58,986 | 59,756 | 53,019 | 50,806 | 53,207 | 49,610 | 54,960 | 47,043 | 46,370 | 633,952 |
| 2019 | 56,219 | 52,182 | 55,658 | 60,668 | 60,816 | 51,858 | 50,919 | 46,246 | 50,386 | 50,266 | 48,113 | 46,114 | 629,445 |
| 2020 | 52,727 | 48,148 | 56,212 | 61,015 | 52,790 | 55,537 | 46,140 | 50,007 | 49,989 | 50,597 | 48,042 | 51,765 | 622,969 |
| 2021 | 50,982 | 52,273 | 62,319 | 59,877 | 57,332 | 53,799 | 50,284 | 49,005 | 49,236 | 45,629 | 45,718 | 48,209 | 624,663 |
| 2022[1] | 49,048 | 51,796 | 60,099 | 50,636 | 57,802 | 56,816 | 49,915 | 55,991 | 53,242 | 50,330 | 46,679 | 48,438 | 630,792 |

[1] Preliminary.    Source: National Agricultural Statistics Service, U.S. Department of Agriculture (NASS-USDA)

### Cold Storage Holdings of Frozen Eggs in the United States, on First of Month    In Thousands of Pounds[2]

| Year | Jan. | Feb. | Mar. | Apr. | May | June | July | Aug. | Sept. | Oct. | Nov. | Dec. |
|---|---|---|---|---|---|---|---|---|---|---|---|---|
| 2013 | 27,376 | 29,659 | 28,620 | 27,138 | 29,339 | 28,856 | 30,591 | 26,118 | 30,144 | 33,577 | 33,832 | 29,754 |
| 2014 | 30,350 | 34,687 | 34,631 | 29,044 | 27,430 | 28,300 | 30,142 | 31,453 | 29,820 | 31,126 | 31,960 | 30,349 |
| 2015 | 30,718 | 34,670 | 35,648 | 31,978 | 31,260 | 28,216 | 26,890 | 27,408 | 30,572 | 32,324 | 37,486 | 36,013 |
| 2016 | 40,896 | 42,158 | 37,400 | 31,741 | 33,670 | 35,961 | 37,960 | 37,209 | 31,725 | 33,084 | 34,344 | 36,490 |
| 2017 | 35,652 | 36,913 | 41,071 | 41,911 | 41,176 | 39,033 | 41,712 | 40,193 | 35,166 | 33,934 | 32,928 | 27,911 |
| 2018 | 30,162 | 31,041 | 32,308 | 28,175 | 27,763 | 30,236 | 30,705 | 29,791 | 31,990 | 28,935 | 30,267 | 29,603 |
| 2019 | 29,376 | 32,257 | 34,492 | 37,561 | 36,093 | 35,413 | 37,369 | 36,266 | 36,362 | 36,299 | 33,680 | 35,236 |
| 2020 | 40,771 | 38,272 | 38,423 | 39,586 | 44,175 | 37,985 | 39,293 | 39,036 | 39,254 | 37,878 | 34,887 | 32,436 |
| 2021 | 31,696 | 32,006 | 29,581 | 26,739 | 24,164 | 26,172 | 25,342 | 26,859 | 26,769 | 25,183 | 26,391 | 23,067 |
| 2022[1] | 24,726 | 26,085 | 27,978 | 24,328 | 22,433 | 21,937 | 23,686 | 22,989 | 25,685 | 26,645 | 24,195 | 23,798 |

[1] Preliminary.    [2] Converted on basis 39.5 pounds frozen eggs equals 1 case.    Source: National Agricultural Statistics Service, U.S. Department of Agriculture (NASS-USDA)

### Electric Power Production by Electric Utilities in the United States    In Millions of Kilowatt Hours

| Year | Jan. | Feb. | Mar. | Apr. | May | June | July | Aug. | Sept. | Oct. | Nov. | Dec. | Total |
|---|---|---|---|---|---|---|---|---|---|---|---|---|---|
| 2013 | 207,123 | 180,975 | 189,129 | 173,761 | 190,354 | 213,033 | 232,867 | 229,557 | 198,719 | 182,713 | 181,991 | 207,837 | 2,388,059 |
| 2014 | 222,165 | 191,345 | 193,194 | 170,329 | 191,866 | 212,311 | 227,343 | 225,392 | 194,390 | 176,990 | 180,869 | 196,279 | 2,382,473 |
| 2015 | 208,073 | 194,871 | 184,609 | 165,379 | 184,165 | 208,270 | 229,212 | 223,696 | 196,273 | 172,561 | 165,247 | 182,965 | 2,315,323 |
| 2016 | 203,384 | 179,182 | 171,452 | 162,936 | 179,569 | 213,557 | 234,890 | 232,277 | 195,105 | 171,134 | 164,301 | 197,136 | 2,304,923 |
| 2017 | 199,391 | 164,437 | 179,245 | 164,153 | 183,781 | 205,299 | 233,807 | 220,364 | 185,458 | 174,251 | 168,569 | 195,521 | 2,274,276 |
| 2018 | 214,525 | 171,847 | 175,132 | 165,093 | 189,538 | 212,232 | 235,229 | 228,767 | 198,116 | 177,541 | 178,265 | 190,963 | 2,337,248 |
| 2019 | 202,052 | 174,633 | 177,458 | 159,490 | 185,133 | 198,468 | 229,082 | 224,601 | 197,147 | 168,516 | 168,594 | 180,830 | 2,266,004 |
| 2020 | 185,460 | 172,751 | 166,102 | 147,107 | 164,989 | 192,144 | 227,824 | 222,608 | 181,674 | 165,437 | 157,891 | 186,330 | 2,170,317 |
| 2021 | 191,445 | 180,728 | 163,643 | 151,506 | 170,419 | 207,176 | 226,361 | 227,827 | 185,991 | 164,951 | 162,702 | 177,439 | 2,210,188 |
| 2022[1] | 204,586 | 171,564 | 165,261 | 150,268 | 176,959 | 206,913 | 232,027 | 224,779 | 184,762 | 159,634 | 164,868 | 195,010 | 2,236,631 |

[1] Preliminary.    Source: Energy Information Administration, U.S. Department of Energy (EIA-DOE)

# Electric Power

The modern electric utility industry began in the 1800s. In 1807, Humphry Davy constructed a practical battery and demonstrated both incandescent and arc light. In 1831, Michael Faraday built the first electric generator proving that rotary mechanical power could be converted into electric power. In 1879, Thomas Edison perfected a practical incandescent light bulb. The electric utility industry evolved from gas and electric carbon-arc commercial and street lighting systems. In 1882, in New York City, Thomas Edison's Pearl Street electricity generating station established the industry by displaying the four key elements of a modern electric utility system: reliable central generation, efficient distribution, successful end-use, and a competitive price.

Electricity is measured in units called watts and watt-hours. Electricity must be used when it is generated and cannot be stored to any significant degree. That means the power utilities must match the level of electricity generation to the level of demand to avoid wasteful over-production. The power industry has been deregulated to some degree in the past decade, and now major utility companies sell power back and forth across major national grids to meet supply and demand needs. The rapid changes in the supply-demand situation mean that the cost of electricity can be very volatile.

Electricity futures and options are traded on the ASX 24 exchange. Electricity futures are traded on Borsa Istanbul, Borsa Italiana (IDEM), ICE Futures Europe, Nasdaq Commodities, New York Mercantile Exchange, Singapore Exchange, and Tokyo Commodity Exchange.

**Supply** – U.S. electricity production in 2022 rose by +1.2% yr/yr to 2.236 trillion kilowatt-hours. That was still well below the record high of 3.212 trillion kilowatt-hours in 1998 and indicates how electricity production has been reduced mainly by more efficient production and distribution systems, and to some extent by conservation of electricity by both business and residential consumers. U.S. electricity generation in 2022 required the use of 12.411 billion cubic feet of natural gas (up +7.9% yr/yr), 466 million tons of coal (down -6.8% yr/yr), and 39 million barrels of petroleum (up +4.5% yr/yr).

In terms of kilowatt-hours, natural gas is the most widely used source of electricity production in the U.S., accounting for 37.3% of electricity production in 2021, followed by coal (22.6%), followed by nuclear (19.7%), followed by hydro (6.3%), and followed by fuel oil (0.5%). Alternative sources of fuel for electricity generation that are gaining favor include geothermal, biomass, solar, wind, etc. but so far, they only account for about 10.0% of total electricity production in the United States.

**Demand** – Residential use of electricity accounts for the largest single category of electricity demand with usage of 1.470 trillion kilowatt-hours in 2021, accounting for 38.6% of overall usage. Business users in total use more electricity than residential users, with commercial businesses accounting for 34.9% of usage and industrial businesses accounting for 26.3% of usage.

## World Net Generation of Electricity   In Billions of Kilowatt Hours

| Year | Brazil | Canada | China | France | Germany | India | Japan | Korea, South | Russia | Spain | United Kingdom | United States | World Total |
|---|---|---|---|---|---|---|---|---|---|---|---|---|---|
| 2012 | 547.2 | 612.2 | 4,740.3 | 543.1 | 591.4 | 1,099.3 | 1,043.6 | 510.2 | 1,014.0 | 282.4 | 344.7 | 4,054.3 | 21,745.3 |
| 2013 | 563.5 | 637.7 | 5,171.5 | 552.4 | 601.5 | 1,164.9 | 1,027.4 | 515.9 | 1,003.6 | 270.5 | 339.3 | 4,074.1 | 22,439.7 |
| 2014 | 581.9 | 636.0 | 5,400.1 | 542.4 | 592.1 | 1,269.7 | 1,027.2 | 523.0 | 1,007.4 | 264.3 | 321.3 | 4,104.8 | 22,848.8 |
| 2015 | 571.6 | 638.9 | 5,584.8 | 550.2 | 611.5 | 1,334.3 | 1,003.0 | 523.5 | 1,010.0 | 266.1 | 328.1 | 4,092.9 | 23,292.9 |
| 2016 | 571.4 | 644.8 | 5,904.6 | 536.0 | 616.1 | 1,411.8 | 1,002.3 | 535.1 | 1,033.2 | 260.5 | 326.0 | 4,096.4 | 23,971.0 |
| 2017 | 581.1 | 644.6 | 6,389.8 | 533.0 | 620.1 | 1,490.1 | 1,005.9 | 539.8 | 1,036.3 | 262.3 | 324.6 | 4,059.4 | 24,690.7 |
| 2018 | 594.2 | 635.8 | 6,800.8 | 552.9 | 607.6 | 1,586.9 | 1,008.9 | 561.1 | 1,046.8 | 261.9 | 320.1 | 4,210.5 | 25,517.6 |
| 2019 | 618.7 | 627.8 | 7,152.5 | 543.8 | 577.6 | 1,615.9 | 989.0 | 553.3 | 1,062.9 | 261.9 | 313.5 | 4,165.5 | 25,887.4 |
| 2020[1] | 614.4 | 624.0 | 7,455.5 | 506.0 | 545.4 | 1,581.3 | 960.8 | 550.3 | 1,044.3 | 251.2 | 303.5 | 4,051.3 | 25,884.2 |
| 2021[2] | 662.6 | 625.9 | 8,151.5 | 530.4 | 557.1 | 1,702.1 | 954.9 | 587.3 | 1,109.7 | 259.4 | 288.6 | 4,164.6 | 27,295.2 |

[1] Preliminary.   [2] Estimate.   NA = Not avaliable.   Source: Energy Information Administration, U.S. Department of Energy (EIA-DOE)

## World Consumption of Electricity   In Billions of Kilowatt Hours

| Year | Brazil | Canada | China | France | Germany | India | Italy | Japan | Korea, South | Russia | United Kingdom | United States | World Total |
|---|---|---|---|---|---|---|---|---|---|---|---|---|---|
| 2012 | 493.1 | 539.2 | 4,439.9 | 460.7 | 546.3 | 891.7 | 309.5 | 1,000.3 | 492.9 | 890.8 | 328.3 | 3,838.8 | 19,923.5 |
| 2013 | 508.8 | 560.7 | 4,846.2 | 465.2 | 544.8 | 946.3 | 299.8 | 979.9 | 497.6 | 882.9 | 327.2 | 3,876.5 | 20,578.4 |
| 2014 | 522.5 | 559.3 | 5,078.7 | 440.7 | 534.1 | 1,041.9 | 294.0 | 983.9 | 504.7 | 892.8 | 314.4 | 3,914.5 | 20,986.5 |
| 2015 | 512.9 | 543.4 | 5,273.5 | 450.0 | 537.6 | 1,093.5 | 300.1 | 962.4 | 505.5 | 891.8 | 320.6 | 3,914.3 | 21,405.4 |
| 2016 | 513.9 | 548.5 | 5,585.6 | 457.0 | 539.8 | 1,161.5 | 298.3 | 956.7 | 516.6 | 911.4 | 317.5 | 3,921.1 | 22,027.5 |
| 2017 | 519.9 | 547.0 | 6,057.2 | 454.2 | 540.6 | 1,228.6 | 304.7 | 965.2 | 521.0 | 920.4 | 312.5 | 3,888.3 | 22,721.7 |
| 2018 | 531.2 | 554.1 | 6,450.4 | 451.3 | 532.2 | 1,312.6 | 306.3 | 963.9 | 542.9 | 931.1 | 313.6 | 4,032.6 | 23,536.4 |
| 2019 | 538.0 | 547.3 | 6,802.7 | 448.0 | 517.5 | 1,342.1 | 284.0 | 944.9 | 534.3 | 945.4 | 309.3 | 3,989.4 | 23,921.4 |
| 2020[1] | 533.4 | 533.5 | 7,115.1 | 425.1 | 499.2 | 1,328.7 | 287.3 | 914.5 | 531.7 | 940.0 | 295.1 | 3,897.9 | 23,965.6 |
| 2021[2] | 577.3 | 554.7 | 7,805.7 | 447.4 | 511.7 | 1,442.8 | 299.9 | 913.1 | 567.7 | 996.4 | 287.3 | 3,979.3 | 25,342.8 |

[1] Preliminary.   [2] Estimate.   NA = Not avaliable.   Source: Energy Information Administration, U.S. Department of Energy (EIA-DOE)

# ELECTRIC POWER

## World Installed Capacity of Electricity    In Billions of Kilowatt Hours

| Year | Brazil | Canada | China | France | Germany | India | Italy | Japan | Russia | Spain | United Kingdom | United States | World Total |
|---|---|---|---|---|---|---|---|---|---|---|---|---|---|
| 2012 | 130.8 | 135.4 | 1,155.0 | 131.7 | 185.5 | 263.5 | 127.5 | 296.4 | 231.3 | 106.1 | 98.7 | 1,063.0 | 5,585.2 |
| 2013 | 138.2 | 135.3 | 1,267.2 | 131.2 | 192.9 | 285.3 | 127.5 | 304.1 | 238.9 | 107.0 | 96.6 | 1,060.1 | 5,820.3 |
| 2014 | 146.2 | 138.5 | 1,379.7 | 131.3 | 205.3 | 314.4 | 124.8 | 274.7 | 259.5 | 107.0 | 100.2 | 1,075.7 | 6,051.4 |
| 2015 | 154.1 | 146.0 | 1,518.6 | 133.5 | 211.3 | 346.9 | 120.0 | 285.0 | 257.5 | 107.5 | 100.5 | 1,073.8 | 6,313.6 |
| 2016 | 164.5 | 148.6 | 1,660.1 | 134.6 | 216.5 | 370.6 | 117.3 | 298.2 | 265.0 | 106.7 | 102.3 | 1,087.1 | 6,622.8 |
| 2017 | 172.2 | 149.5 | 1,790.8 | 134.6 | 222.7 | 393.5 | 117.4 | 308.9 | 267.2 | 104.9 | 108.3 | 1,100.5 | 6,888.7 |
| 2018 | 178.7 | 150.5 | 1,912.0 | 136.9 | 236.2 | 428.3 | 118.4 | 318.6 | 268.0 | 104.7 | 113.0 | 1,114.3 | 7,174.7 |
| 2019 | 187.6 | 151.6 | 2,023.6 | 138.1 | 239.3 | 442.6 | 120.0 | 323.3 | 273.0 | 110.7 | 109.6 | 1,122.3 | 7,406.9 |
| 2020[1] | 195.0 | 152.4 | 2,224.8 | 138.3 | 243.8 | 453.5 | 119.4 | 328.3 | 276.5 | 109.9 | 109.2 | 1,143.3 | 7,735.2 |
| 2021[2] | 205.0 | 153.6 | 2,355.6 | 142.2 | 250.4 | 469.5 | 120.9 | 334.6 | 282.6 | 114.0 | 108.7 | 1,176.7 | 8,013.0 |

[1] Preliminary.  [2] Estimate.  NA = Not avaliable.  Source: Energy Information Administration, U.S. Department of Energy (EIA-DOE)

## Electricity in the United States    In Billions of Kilowatt Hours

| | Net Generation | | | | Trade | | | T&D Losses[6] and Unaccounted for[7] | End Use | | |
|---|---|---|---|---|---|---|---|---|---|---|---|
| Year | Electric Power Sector[2] | Commercial Sector[3] | Industrial Sector[4] | Total | Imports[5] | Exports[5] | Net Imports[5] | | Retail Sales[8] | Direct Use[9] | Total |
| 2013 | 3,903.7 | 12.2 | 150.0 | 4,066.0 | 70.4 | 11.4 | 59.0 | 256.6 | 3,724.9 | 143.5 | 3,868.3 |
| 2014 | 3,937.0 | 12.5 | 144.1 | 4,093.6 | 66.5 | 13.3 | 53.2 | 243.5 | 3,764.7 | 138.6 | 3,903.3 |
| 2015 | 3,919.3 | 12.6 | 145.7 | 4,077.6 | 75.8 | 9.1 | 66.7 | 244.1 | 3,759.0 | 141.2 | 3,900.2 |
| 2016 | 3,918.1 | 12.7 | 145.9 | 4,076.7 | 72.7 | 6.2 | 66.5 | 240.9 | 3,762.5 | 139.8 | 3,902.3 |
| 2017 | 3,877.5 | 13.1 | 143.8 | 4,034.3 | 65.7 | 9.4 | 56.3 | 226.1 | 3,723.4 | 141.1 | 3,864.5 |
| 2018 | 4,018.2 | 13.3 | 146.8 | 4,178.3 | 58.3 | 13.8 | 44.5 | 219.6 | 3,860.1 | 143.9 | 4,003.1 |
| 2019 | 3,965.6 | 13.7 | 148.5 | 4,127.9 | 59.1 | 20.0 | 39.0 | 212.5 | 3,811.2 | 143.3 | 3,954.4 |
| 2020 | 3,853.7 | 13.0 | 143.1 | 4,009.8 | 61.4 | 14.1 | 47.3 | 200.7 | 3,717.7 | 138.7 | 3,856.4 |
| 2021 | 3,955.8 | 12.8 | 139.8 | 4,108.3 | 53.2 | 13.9 | 39.3 | 202.8 | 3,805.9 | 138.9 | 3,944.8 |
| 2022[1] | 4,080.3 | 12.8 | 139.7 | 4,232.9 | 58.4 | 16.0 | 42.4 | 228.7 | 3,907.6 | 138.9 | 4,046.5 |

[1] Preliminary.  [2] Electricity-only and combined-heat-and-power (CHP) plants within the NAICS 22 category whose primary business is to sell electricity, or electricity and heat, to the public.  [3] Commercial combined-heat-and-power (CHP) and commercial electricity-only plants.  [4] Industrial combined-heat-and-power (CHP) and industrial electricity-only plants.  [5] Electricity transmitted across U.S. borders. Net imports equal imports minus exports.  [6] Transmission and distribution losses.  [7] Data collection frame differences and nonsampling error.  [8] Electricity retail sales to ultimate customers by electric utilities and other energy service providers.  [9] Use of electricity that is 1) self-generated, 2) produced by either the same entity that consumes the power or an affiliate, and 3) used in direct support of a service or industrial process located within the same facility or group of facilities that house the generating equipment. Direct use is exclusive of station use.  Source: U.S. Geological Survey (USGS)

## Electricity Net Generation in the United States by Sector    In Millions of Kilowatt Hours

| | Fossil Fuels | | | | Nuclear electric power | Hydro-electric Pumped Storage[6] | Renewable Energy | | | | | | |
|---|---|---|---|---|---|---|---|---|---|---|---|---|---|
| | Coal[2] | Petroleum[3] | Natural Gas[4] | Other Gases[5] | | | Conventional Hydroelectric Power | Biomass: Wood[7] | Biomass: Waste[8] | Geothermal | Solar/PV[9] | Wind | Total |
| 2010 | 1,847,290 | 37,061 | 987,697 | 11,313 | 806,968 | -5,501 | 260,203 | 37,172 | 18,917 | 15,219 | 1,212 | 94,652 | 4,125,060 |
| 2011 | 1,733,430 | 30,182 | 1,013,689 | 11,566 | 790,204 | -6,421 | 319,355 | 37,449 | 19,222 | 15,316 | 1,818 | 120,177 | 4,100,141 |
| 2012 | 1,514,043 | 23,190 | 1,225,894 | 11,898 | 769,331 | -4,950 | 276,240 | 37,799 | 19,823 | 15,562 | 4,327 | 140,822 | 4,047,765 |
| 2013 | 1,581,115 | 27,164 | 1,124,836 | 12,853 | 789,016 | -4,681 | 268,565 | 40,028 | 20,830 | 15,775 | 9,036 | 167,840 | 4,065,964 |
| 2014 | 1,581,710 | 30,232 | 1,126,609 | 12,022 | 797,166 | -6,174 | 259,367 | 42,340 | 21,650 | 15,877 | 17,691 | 181,655 | 4,093,606 |
| 2015 | 1,352,398 | 28,249 | 1,333,482 | 13,117 | 797,178 | -5,091 | 249,080 | 41,929 | 21,703 | 15,918 | 24,893 | 190,719 | 4,077,601 |
| 2016 | 1,239,149 | 24,205 | 1,378,307 | 12,807 | 805,694 | -6,686 | 267,812 | 40,947 | 21,813 | 15,826 | 36,054 | 226,993 | 4,076,827 |
| 2017 | 1,205,835 | 21,390 | 1,296,415 | 12,469 | 804,950 | -6,495 | 300,333 | 41,152 | 21,610 | 15,927 | 53,286 | 254,303 | 4,034,268 |
| 2018 | 1,145,962 | 25,226 | 1,468,727 | 13,463 | 807,084 | -5,905 | 292,524 | 41,005 | 17,410 | 15,967 | 63,825 | 272,650 | 4,170,912 |
| 2019[1] | 966,148 | 18,567 | 1,581,815 | 13,634 | 809,409 | -5,261 | 273,707 | 39,851 | 18,561 | 16,011 | 72,234 | 300,071 | 4,118,051 |

[1] Preliminary.  [2] Anthracite, bituminous coal, subbituminous coal, lignite, waste coal, and coal synfuel.  [3] Distillate fuel oil, residual fuel oil, petroleum coke, jet fuel, kerosene, other petroleum, waste oil, and propane.  [4] Natural gas, plus a small amount of supplemental gaseous fuels.  [5] Blast furnace gas, and other manufactured and waste gases derived from fossil fuels.  [6] Pumped storage facility production minus energy used for pumping.  [7] Wood and wood-derived fuels.  [8] Municipal solid waste from biogenic sources, landfill gas, sludge waste, agricultural byproducts, and other biomass.  [9] Solar thermal and photovoltaic (PV) energy.  Source: U.S. Geological Survey (USGS)

# ELECTRIC POWER

## Total Electricity Net Generation in the United States    In Billions of Kilowatt Hours

| Year | Jan. | Feb. | Mar. | Apr. | May | June | July | Aug. | Sept. | Oct. | Nov. | Dec. | Total |
|---|---|---|---|---|---|---|---|---|---|---|---|---|---|
| 2013 | 349.0 | 309.7 | 325.4 | 299.3 | 322.2 | 356.8 | 394.8 | 385.3 | 340.9 | 314.9 | 314.5 | 353.0 | 4,066.0 |
| 2014 | 377.3 | 324.3 | 331.8 | 297.6 | 324.7 | 357.8 | 385.8 | 384.3 | 339.9 | 314.5 | 317.5 | 338.0 | 4,093.6 |
| 2015 | 360.5 | 334.5 | 324.2 | 294.1 | 322.1 | 362.4 | 400.4 | 392.1 | 350.1 | 312.1 | 300.7 | 324.4 | 4,077.6 |
| 2016 | 352.7 | 313.7 | 304.4 | 292.9 | 316.8 | 367.8 | 411.9 | 409.7 | 351.5 | 313.0 | 297.1 | 345.4 | 4,076.8 |
| 2017 | 343.2 | 289.7 | 317.9 | 294.3 | 322.5 | 357.9 | 404.4 | 384.3 | 335.9 | 320.4 | 310.3 | 353.5 | 4,034.3 |
| 2018 | 373.2 | 306.9 | 321.5 | 300.7 | 338.0 | 371.0 | 410.3 | 407.3 | 356.2 | 324.9 | 322.3 | 338.5 | 4,170.9 |
| 2019 | 359.5 | 315.0 | 326.7 | 296.7 | 330.4 | 353.0 | 410.0 | 401.4 | 360.5 | 320.4 | 315.8 | 338.4 | 4,127.9 |
| 2020 | 342.0 | 319.7 | 309.9 | 279.8 | 304.8 | 352.0 | 409.9 | 398.5 | 333.5 | 313.7 | 301.4 | 344.5 | 4,009.8 |
| 2021 | 349.2 | 323.9 | 311.4 | 293.3 | 320.2 | 373.9 | 405.6 | 412.9 | 347.7 | 318.8 | 314.3 | 337.2 | 4,108.3 |
| 2022[1] | 377.5 | 327.0 | 325.1 | 303.4 | 342.2 | 380.6 | 423.7 | 412.5 | 350.9 | 314.0 | 323.2 | | 4,232.9 |

[1] Preliminary.    Source: Energy Information Administration, U.S. Department of Energy (EIA-DOE)


## Imports[2] of Electricity in the United States    In Billions of Kilowatt Hours

| Year | Jan. | Feb. | Mar. | Apr. | May | June | July | Aug. | Sept. | Oct. | Nov. | Dec. | Total |
|---|---|---|---|---|---|---|---|---|---|---|---|---|---|
| 2013 | 5.8 | 5.3 | 5.8 | 5.0 | 5.9 | 6.0 | 6.7 | 6.9 | 5.6 | 5.6 | 6.0 | 5.9 | 70.4 |
| 2014 | 5.5 | 4.4 | 5.6 | 4.8 | 5.4 | 5.5 | 6.3 | 6.7 | 6.0 | 5.4 | 5.6 | 5.4 | 66.5 |
| 2015 | 6.0 | 5.6 | 6.6 | 6.5 | 6.6 | 6.7 | 6.9 | 7.2 | 6.6 | 5.3 | 5.8 | 5.9 | 75.8 |
| 2016 | 6.5 | 5.4 | 5.8 | 4.7 | 5.6 | 6.7 | 7.7 | 7.3 | 5.3 | 5.8 | 6.4 | 5.4 | 72.7 |
| 2017 | 7.0 | 5.7 | 6.0 | 5.6 | 5.1 | 6.0 | 5.9 | 6.5 | 5.2 | 4.0 | 3.9 | 4.8 | 65.7 |
| 2018 | 5.2 | 4.8 | 5.6 | 4.5 | 5.2 | 5.5 | 5.4 | 6.1 | 4.3 | 3.7 | 3.8 | 4.1 | 58.3 |
| 2019 | 4.8 | 4.6 | 5.0 | 4.4 | 4.7 | 5.2 | 5.6 | 5.9 | 5.3 | 3.7 | 4.8 | 5.2 | 59.1 |
| 2020 | 4.6 | 4.5 | 5.1 | 4.7 | 5.2 | 5.2 | 6.6 | 6.8 | 4.7 | 4.7 | 4.2 | 5.1 | 61.4 |
| 2021 | 5.1 | 4.0 | 4.6 | 4.4 | 4.7 | 5.2 | 5.5 | 4.6 | 3.9 | 4.2 | 3.0 | 4.0 | 53.2 |
| 2022[1] | 4.5 | 3.4 | 3.7 | 3.9 | 4.4 | 5.5 | 6.7 | 7.2 | 5.2 | 4.3 | 4.8 | | 58.4 |

[1] Preliminary.    [2] Electricity transmitted across U.S. borders. Net imports equal imports minus exports.    Source: Energy Information Administration, U.S. Department of Energy (EIA-DOE)


## Exports[2] of Electricity in the United States    In Billions of Kilowatt Hours

| Year | Jan. | Feb. | Mar. | Apr. | May | June | July | Aug. | Sept. | Oct. | Nov. | Dec. | Total |
|---|---|---|---|---|---|---|---|---|---|---|---|---|---|
| 2013 | 1.0 | 0.8 | 0.9 | 1.2 | 1.0 | 0.8 | 1.0 | 0.9 | 0.7 | 1.0 | 0.9 | 1.1 | 11.4 |
| 2014 | 1.3 | 1.3 | 1.9 | 1.3 | 0.8 | 1.0 | 1.0 | 0.9 | 0.8 | 1.0 | 0.9 | 1.1 | 13.3 |
| 2015 | 0.8 | 1.4 | 0.9 | 0.6 | 0.6 | 0.6 | 0.6 | 0.7 | 0.7 | 0.7 | 0.7 | 0.8 | 9.1 |
| 2016 | 0.4 | 0.6 | 0.7 | 0.5 | 0.4 | 0.6 | 0.6 | 0.6 | 0.6 | 0.4 | 0.4 | 0.6 | 6.2 |
| 2017 | 0.5 | 0.7 | 1.0 | 1.1 | 0.8 | 0.8 | 0.7 | 0.8 | 0.7 | 0.7 | 0.8 | 0.7 | 9.4 |
| 2018 | 1.1 | 1.3 | 1.2 | 1.6 | 1.1 | 1.2 | 0.9 | 1.1 | 1.1 | 0.9 | 1.3 | 0.9 | 13.8 |
| 2019 | 1.5 | 1.4 | 2.5 | 2.0 | 1.7 | 1.5 | 2.0 | 1.8 | 1.8 | 1.5 | 1.2 | 1.2 | 20.0 |
| 2020 | 1.4 | 1.7 | 1.3 | 1.5 | 1.5 | 1.3 | 1.2 | 0.9 | 1.0 | 0.8 | 0.8 | 0.8 | 14.1 |
| 2021 | 0.9 | 1.1 | 0.7 | 1.1 | 1.0 | 0.8 | 1.1 | 1.3 | 1.2 | 1.3 | 1.8 | 1.6 | 13.9 |
| 2022[1] | 1.5 | 1.5 | 1.7 | 1.4 | 1.6 | 1.1 | 1.3 | 1.3 | 1.4 | 0.9 | 1.1 | | 16.0 |

[1] Preliminary.    [2] Electricity transmitted across U.S. borders. Net imports equal imports minus exports.    Source: Energy Information Administration, U.S. Department of Energy (EIA-DOE)


## Total End Use of Electricity in the United States    In Billions of Kilowatt Hours

| Year | Jan. | Feb. | Mar. | Apr. | May | June | July | Aug. | Sept. | Oct. | Nov. | Dec. | Total |
|---|---|---|---|---|---|---|---|---|---|---|---|---|---|
| 2013 | 333.0 | 302.6 | 309.2 | 288.9 | 301.0 | 332.2 | 371.7 | 366.3 | 335.2 | 306.0 | 293.2 | 329.1 | 3,868.3 |
| 2014 | 353.3 | 319.6 | 313.8 | 286.7 | 302.6 | 334.2 | 363.9 | 364.3 | 338.5 | 307.9 | 296.7 | 321.8 | 3,903.3 |
| 2015 | 341.9 | 317.5 | 316.5 | 286.1 | 299.3 | 338.3 | 375.9 | 374.7 | 345.0 | 307.6 | 287.6 | 309.8 | 3,900.2 |
| 2016 | 332.8 | 307.9 | 297.4 | 280.4 | 296.1 | 341.6 | 384.7 | 393.9 | 348.4 | 308.0 | 288.6 | 322.4 | 3,902.3 |
| 2017 | 330.3 | 286.7 | 303.1 | 284.0 | 303.3 | 340.6 | 380.4 | 372.8 | 332.9 | 310.9 | 294.8 | 324.7 | 3,864.5 |
| 2018 | 356.9 | 303.8 | 308.5 | 289.5 | 315.0 | 350.1 | 388.0 | 394.2 | 349.3 | 321.0 | 302.5 | 324.6 | 4,003.1 |
| 2019 | 341.1 | 306.7 | 313.6 | 284.8 | 308.2 | 333.2 | 388.9 | 385.4 | 352.5 | 320.0 | 297.5 | 322.4 | 3,954.4 |
| 2020 | 328.2 | 306.4 | 301.8 | 273.1 | 285.6 | 331.4 | 391.6 | 381.0 | 333.7 | 307.9 | 288.2 | 327.5 | 3,856.4 |
| 2021 | 334.0 | 309.8 | 306.3 | 283.3 | 301.1 | 350.2 | 386.6 | 393.6 | 347.8 | 313.6 | 298.8 | 319.5 | 3,944.8 |
| 2022[1] | 349.8 | 315.5 | 315.5 | 294.6 | 319.2 | 357.7 | 400.1 | 400.1 | 349.5 | 306.4 | 300.9 | | 4,046.5 |

[1] Preliminary.    Source: Energy Information Administration, U.S. Department of Energy (EIA-DOE)

# Ethanol

## World Production of Fuel Ethanol    In Thousands of Barrels per Day

| Year | Australia | Brazil | Canada | China | Colombia | France | Germany | India | Jamaica | Spain | Thailand | United States | World Total |
|---|---|---|---|---|---|---|---|---|---|---|---|---|---|
| 2012 | 95.8 | 5,723.8 | 467.8 | 788.8 | 102.1 | 315.8 | 192.7 | 84.2 | ---- | 95.5 | 130.0 | 13,218.0 | 22,790.6 |
| 2013 | 84.5 | 6,727.9 | 473.3 | 809.8 | 107.1 | 298.3 | 198.6 | 105.4 | ---- | 114.2 | 262.2 | 13,292.7 | 24,418.7 |
| 2014 | 71.8 | 7,061.3 | 484.4 | 814.5 | 112.1 | 314.3 | 220.0 | 96.6 | ---- | 121.1 | 292.0 | 14,312.8 | 25,868.0 |
| 2015 | 69.0 | 7,525.8 | 474.7 | 804.2 | 125.9 | 313.9 | 213.4 | 189.1 | ---- | 123.5 | 324.0 | 14,807.2 | 26,991.0 |
| 2016 | 62.5 | 7,059.9 | 470.7 | 699.4 | 119.8 | 314.5 | 245.0 | 306.4 | 26.1 | 91.3 | 352.2 | 15,413.2 | 27,275.7 |
| 2017 | 52.7 | 6,977.7 | 479.2 | 839.3 | 108.5 | 293.8 | 198.6 | 186.3 |  | 104.5 | 403.2 | 15,936.3 | 27,721.2 |
| 2018 | 65.3 | 8,060.0 | 460.0 | 810.0 | 129.7 | 329.1 | 195.8 | 430.0 | ---- | 130.4 | 390.0 | 16,060.8 | 29,631.4 |
| 2019 | 74.5 | 8,860.0 | 497.0 | 1,010.0 | 135.2 | 313.2 | 168.5 | 460.0 | ---- | 135.5 | 430.0 | 15,776.4 | 29,330.0 |
| 2020[1] |  | 8,100.0 | 429.0 | 930.0 |  |  |  | 540.0 | ---- |  | 390.0 | 13,941.0 | 26,470.0 |
| 2021[2] |  | 7,320.0 | 434.0 | 870.0 |  |  |  | 850.0 | ---- |  | 360.0 | 15,015.7 | 27,290.0 |

[1] Preliminary.  [2] Estimate.  Source: Renewable Fuels Association

## Salient Statistics of Ethanol in the United States

| Year | Ethanol Plants | Ethanol Production Capacity (mgy) | Plants Under Construction | Capacity Under Construction (mgy) | Farmer Owned Plants | Farmer Owned Capacity (mgy) | Percent of Total Capacity Farmer | Farmer Owned UC Plants | Farmers Owned UC Capacity | Percent of Total UC Capacity | States with Ethanol Plants |
|---|---|---|---|---|---|---|---|---|---|---|---|
| 2013 | 211 | 14,837.4 | 2 | 50.0 | ---- | ---- | ---- | ---- | ---- | ---- | 28 |
| 2014 | 210 | 14,879.5 | 7 | 167.0 | ---- | ---- | ---- | ---- | ---- | ---- | 28 |
| 2015 | 213 | 15,077.0 | 3 | 100.0 | ---- | ---- | ---- | ---- | ---- | ---- | 29 |
| 2016 | 214 | 15,594.0 | 3 | 162.0 | ---- | ---- | ---- | ---- | ---- | ---- | 28 |
| 2017 | 213 | 15,998.0 | 3 | 91.0 | ---- | ---- | ---- | ---- | ---- | ---- | 28 |
| 2018 | 211 | 16,241.0 | 7 | 465.0 | ---- | ---- | ---- | ---- | ---- | ---- | 28 |
| 2019 | 205 | 16,924.0 | 4 | 183.0 | ---- | ---- | ---- | ---- | ---- | ---- | 26 |
| 2020 | 210 | 16,501.0 | 9 | 350.0 | ---- | ---- | ---- | ---- | ---- | ---- | 27 |
| 2021[1] | 208 | 17,436.0 | 1 | 16.0 | ---- | ---- | ---- | ---- | ---- | ---- |  |
| 2022[2] | 208 | 17,655.0 | 5 | 160.0 | ---- | ---- | ---- | ---- | ---- | ---- |  |

[1] Preliminary.  [2] Estimate.  Source: Renewable Fuels Association

## Production of Fuel Ethanol in the United States    In Thousands of Barrels

| Year | Jan. | Feb. | Mar. | Apr. | May | June | July | Aug. | Sept. | Oct. | Nov. | Dec. | Total |
|---|---|---|---|---|---|---|---|---|---|---|---|---|---|
| 2013 | 24,778 | 22,494 | 25,620 | 25,601 | 27,197 | 26,722 | 26,923 | 26,279 | 25,564 | 27,995 | 27,915 | 29,405 | 316,493 |
| 2014 | 28,194 | 25,269 | 28,120 | 27,733 | 28,888 | 28,629 | 29,413 | 28,665 | 27,807 | 28,644 | 28,588 | 30,831 | 340,781 |
| 2015 | 29,770 | 26,814 | 29,485 | 27,910 | 29,666 | 29,684 | 30,249 | 29,762 | 28,571 | 29,886 | 29,675 | 31,081 | 352,553 |
| 2016 | 30,452 | 28,810 | 30,957 | 28,208 | 30,346 | 30,443 | 31,469 | 31,856 | 30,048 | 31,006 | 30,706 | 32,680 | 366,981 |
| 2017 | 32,887 | 29,307 | 32,393 | 29,639 | 31,863 | 30,794 | 31,384 | 32,672 | 30,701 | 32,212 | 32,631 | 32,952 | 379,435 |
| 2018 | 32,428 | 29,519 | 32,216 | 30,532 | 32,215 | 31,924 | 33,496 | 33,773 | 30,667 | 32,380 | 31,514 | 31,736 | 382,400 |
| 2019 | 31,601 | 28,576 | 30,895 | 30,951 | 32,443 | 31,895 | 32,541 | 31,921 | 29,232 | 30,941 | 31,358 | 33,275 | 375,629 |
| 2020 | 33,346 | 30,511 | 29,409 | 17,003 | 21,157 | 25,959 | 28,708 | 28,420 | 27,779 | 29,614 | 29,915 | 30,108 | 331,928 |
| 2021 | 28,809 | 22,895 | 29,327 | 28,213 | 31,224 | 30,641 | 31,449 | 29,087 | 28,080 | 32,276 | 32,383 | 33,132 | 357,517 |
| 2022[1] | 32,207 | 28,321 | 31,585 | 28,971 | 31,313 | 31,276 | 31,480 | 30,473 | 27,130 | 31,455 | 31,545 |  | 366,279 |

[1] Preliminary.  Source: Energy Information Administration, U.S. Department of Energy (EIA-DOE)

## Stocks of Fuel Ethanol in the United States    In Thousands of Barrels

| Year | Jan. | Feb. | Mar. | Apr. | May | June | July | Aug. | Sept. | Oct. | Nov. | Dec. |
|---|---|---|---|---|---|---|---|---|---|---|---|---|
| 2013 | 19,894 | 19,009 | 18,410 | 17,370 | 16,804 | 16,428 | 17,072 | 16,945 | 15,986 | 15,750 | 15,569 | 16,424 |
| 2014 | 17,153 | 16,865 | 17,310 | 17,610 | 18,330 | 18,785 | 18,696 | 18,218 | 18,724 | 17,341 | 17,035 | 18,739 |
| 2015 | 20,647 | 21,057 | 20,878 | 20,854 | 20,154 | 20,128 | 19,701 | 19,390 | 18,944 | 18,984 | 20,099 | 21,596 |
| 2016 | 23,347 | 23,171 | 22,730 | 21,336 | 20,962 | 21,284 | 21,381 | 21,198 | 20,713 | 20,113 | 19,463 | 19,758 |
| 2017 | 22,679 | 23,195 | 23,981 | 23,671 | 22,855 | 21,770 | 21,167 | 21,186 | 21,507 | 21,663 | 23,203 | 23,043 |
| 2018 | 24,342 | 24,722 | 23,084 | 23,379 | 22,654 | 21,877 | 22,668 | 22,824 | 24,412 | 23,698 | 23,618 | 23,418 |
| 2019 | 25,115 | 24,506 | 23,396 | 23,331 | 22,843 | 22,583 | 22,892 | 22,727 | 23,012 | 21,784 | 21,646 | 22,352 |
| 2020 | 23,884 | 24,582 | 27,505 | 26,124 | 22,190 | 19,472 | 19,784 | 20,142 | 20,008 | 21,738 | 23,502 | 24,663 |
| 2021 | 26,117 | 24,712 | 22,869 | 22,368 | 22,057 | 21,980 | 22,656 | 21,135 | 20,235 | 20,067 | 20,503 | 22,036 |
| 2022[1] | 25,759 | 26,476 | 26,615 | 24,255 | 23,417 | 23,248 | 24,126 | 23,340 | 21,529 | 21,632 | 23,556 |  |

[1] Preliminary.  Source: Energy Information Administration, U.S. Department of Energy (EIA-DOE)

# ETHANOL

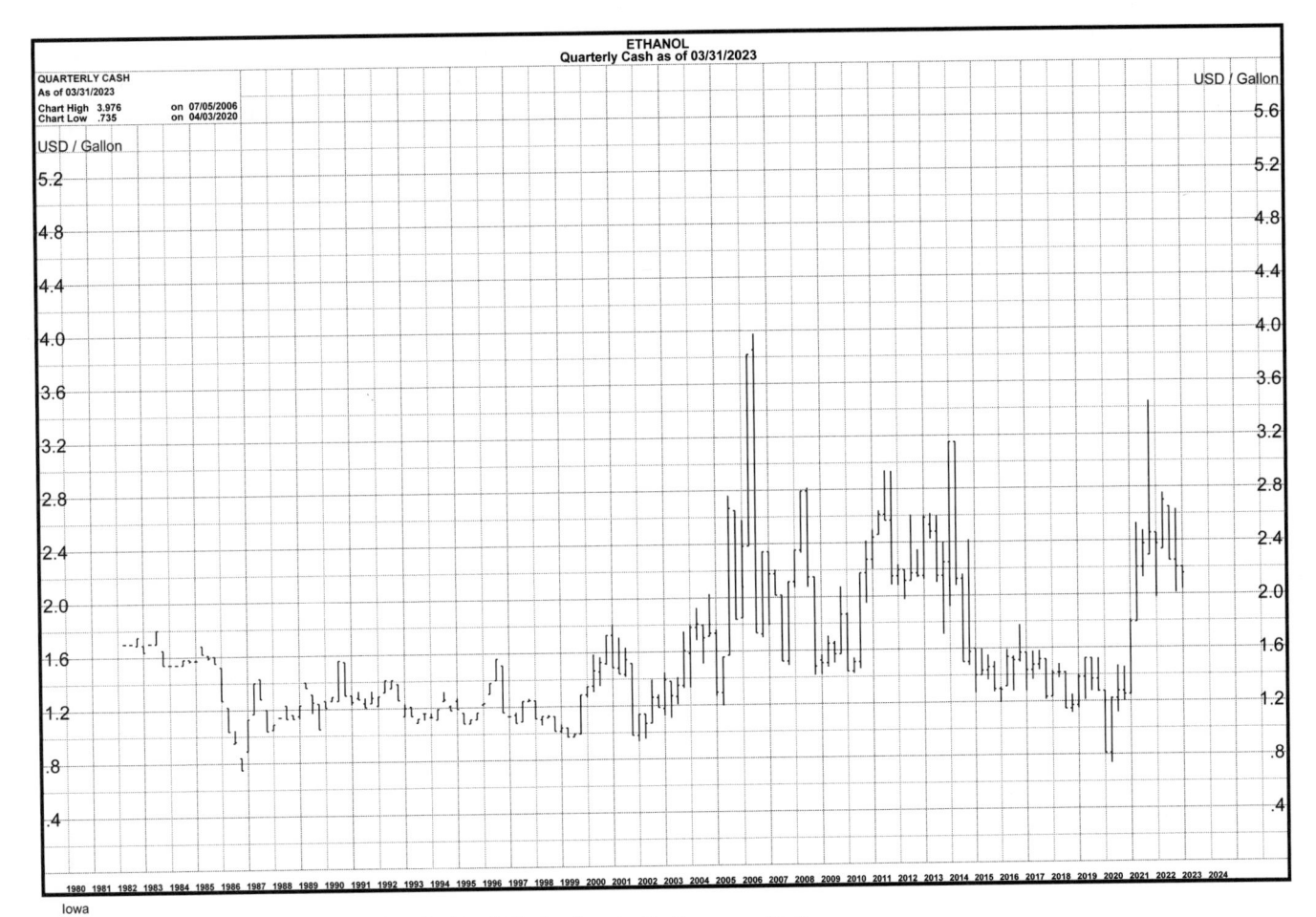

**ETHANOL Quarterly Cash as of 03/31/2023**

QUARTERLY CASH
As of 03/31/2023
Chart High 3.976 on 07/05/2006
Chart Low .735 on 04/03/2020
USD / Gallon

Iowa

## Average Price of Ethanol in the United States[1]   In Dollars per Gallon

| Year | Jan. | Feb. | Mar. | Apr. | May | June | July | Aug. | Sept. | Oct. | Nov. | Dec. | Average |
|---|---|---|---|---|---|---|---|---|---|---|---|---|---|
| 2015 | 1.382 | 1.313 | 1.386 | 1.479 | 1.568 | 1.440 | 1.493 | 1.418 | 1.408 | 1.472 | 1.425 | 1.347 | 1.428 |
| 2017 | 1.400 | 1.381 | 1.378 | 1.541 | 1.446 | 1.505 | 1.472 | 1.487 | 1.510 | 1.407 | 1.357 | 1.267 | 1.429 |
| 2018 | 1.270 | 1.338 | 1.408 | 1.430 | 1.397 | 1.403 | 1.406 | 1.341 | 1.223 | 1.196 | 1.230 | 1.156 | 1.317 |
| 2019 | 1.172 | 1.209 | 1.309 | 1.305 | 1.253 | 1.449 | 1.477 | 1.360 | 1.302 | 1.482 | 1.434 | 1.360 | 1.343 |
| 2020 | 1.245 | 1.238 | 1.079 | 0.774 | 0.997 | 1.188 | 1.284 | 1.182 | 1.303 | 1.370 | 1.387 | 1.211 | 1.188 |
| 2021 | 1.392 | 1.542 | 1.729 | 1.977 | 2.439 | 2.315 | 2.183 | 2.152 | 2.290 | 2.397 | 3.112 | 3.067 | 2.216 |
| 2022 | 2.225 | 2.027 | 2.351 | 2.500 | 2.711 | 2.700 | 2.504 | 2.483 | 2.456 | 2.336 | 2.468 | 2.119 | 2.407 |

[1] Northeast and Northwest Iowa.   Source: Agricultural Marketing Service, U.S. Department of Agriculture (AMS-USDA)

## Average Price of Corn Gluten Feed, 21% protein, Midwest   In Dollars per Ton

| Crop Year | Oct. | Nov. | Dec. | Jan. | Feb. | Mar. | Apr. | May | June | July | Aug. | Sept. | Average |
|---|---|---|---|---|---|---|---|---|---|---|---|---|---|
| 2016-17 | 77.00 | 83.50 | 92.83 | 97.50 | 88.13 | 87.13 | 75.00 | 71.00 | 68.38 | 71.35 | 73.10 | 75.00 | 79.99 |
| 2017-18 | 80.70 | 93.00 | 96.25 | 98.80 | 106.25 | 105.15 | 113.38 | 138.20 | 117.63 | 111.30 | 106.75 | 110.13 | 106.46 |
| 2018-19 | 108.70 | 114.25 | 114.67 | 109.00 | 103.25 | 95.50 | 90.80 | 89.40 | 104.38 | 102.00 | 100.38 | 91.25 | 101.97 |
| 2019-20 | 96.10 | 110.00 | 125.13 | 141.80 | 112.11 | 104.80 | 111.63 | 104.38 | 102.80 | 100.00 | 96.25 | 100.00 | 108.75 |
| 2020-21 | 120.63 | 137.50 | 147.50 | 160.00 | 174.38 | 178.70 | 173.75 | 195.63 | 172.50 | 135.25 | 139.60 | 148.38 | 156.99 |
| 2021-22 | 156.88 | 174.00 | 183.34 | 191.25 | 195.75 | 217.79 | 226.35 | 224.37 | 216.25 | 189.38 | 198.54 | 226.15 | 200.00 |
| 2022-23[1] | 208.88 | 205.94 | 206.25 | 210.89 | | | | | | | | | 207.99 |

[1] Preliminary.   Source: Agricultural Marketing Service, U.S. Department of Agriculture (AMS-USDA)

## Average Price of Corn Gluten Meal, 60% protein, Midwest   In Dollars per Ton

| Crop Year | Oct. | Nov. | Dec. | Jan. | Feb. | Mar. | Apr. | May | June | July | Aug. | Sept. | Average |
|---|---|---|---|---|---|---|---|---|---|---|---|---|---|
| 2016-17 | 466.13 | 477.50 | 501.67 | 502.50 | 516.50 | 505.63 | 501.13 | 485.30 | 475.75 | 467.88 | 475.50 | 469.25 | 487.06 |
| 2017-18 | 469.30 | 487.24 | 482.88 | 477.60 | 483.13 | 524.75 | 515.00 | 500.00 | 455.00 | 430.00 | 435.00 | 444.00 | 475.32 |
| 2018-19 | 435.00 | 470.00 | 478.00 | 450.00 | 426.00 | 406.00 | 384.00 | 359.00 | 356.00 | 357.00 | 366.00 | 360.00 | 403.92 |
| 2019-20 | 373.00 | 385.50 | 395.00 | 423.13 | 456.25 | 464.50 | 493.75 | 453.75 | 383.40 | 397.50 | 405.63 | 405.50 | 419.74 |
| 2020-21 | 435.00 | 516.88 | 550.50 | 594.38 | 631.63 | 633.00 | 611.25 | 588.75 | 539.00 | 495.00 | 504.00 | 518.13 | 551.46 |
| 2021-22 | 530.00 | 562.50 | 591.67 | 610.00 | 614.07 | 659.84 | 681.64 | 642.70 | 627.29 | 642.03 | 658.08 | 652.08 | 622.66 |
| 2022-23[1] | 653.13 | 652.98 | 674.53 | 666.75 | | | | | | | | | 661.85 |

[1] Preliminary.   Source: Agricultural Marketing Service, U.S. Department of Agriculture (AMS-USDA)

# ETHANOL

## World Production of Biodiesel   In Thousands of Barrels per Day

| Year | Argentina | Austria | Belgium | Brazil | China | France | Germany | Indo-nesia | Italy | Spain | Thailand | United States | World Total |
|---|---|---|---|---|---|---|---|---|---|---|---|---|---|
| 2010 | 35.7 | 6.1 | 7.5 | 41.1 | 9.8 | 39.9 | 58.5 | 13.4 | 15.8 | 16.8 | 11.4 | 22.4 | 357.2 |
| 2011 | 47.6 | 5.4 | 7.5 | 46.1 | 12.7 | 35.6 | 58.3 | 31.2 | 11.7 | 13.3 | 10.9 | 63.1 | 430.2 |
| 2012 | 48.3 | 3.4 | 6.1 | 46.8 | 16.0 | 39.8 | 52.0 | 39.1 | 6.4 | 9.1 | 15.7 | 64.6 | 456.8 |
| 2013 | 39.1 | 3.3 | 5.9 | 50.9 | 18.6 | 39.1 | 54.9 | 50.8 | 10.1 | 13.3 | 18.6 | 88.4 | 522.1 |
| 2014 | 50.6 | 4.8 | 8.2 | 59.6 | 19.5 | 42.9 | 62.8 | 60.3 | 12.4 | 22.3 | 20.2 | 83.4 | 591.2 |
| 2015 | 35.5 | 6.2 | 4.7 | 69.1 | 13.6 | 44.2 | 57.0 | 20.7 | 13.7 | 20.5 | 21.5 | 82.4 | 532.7 |
| 2016 | 52.0 | 5.9 | 4.4 | 65.5 | 15.7 | 44.5 | 61.4 | 60.3 | 14.9 | 25.1 | 21.4 | 102.3 | 620.8 |
| 2017 | 56.2 | 4.9 | 5.7 | 73.9 | 18.0 | 47.9 | 59.3 | 48.3 | 13.6 | 32.5 | 24.6 | 103.8 | 661.8 |
| 2018[1] | 47.6 | 4.6 | 5.0 | 92.2 | 14.4 | 53.1 | 65.8 | 96.5 | 14.8 | 31.7 | 27.0 | 121.2 | 762.0 |
| 2019[2] | 43.1 | 5.2 | 4.7 | 99.9 | 20.7 | 40.0 | 62.3 | 137.9 | 22.9 | 36.6 | 30.2 | 112.5 | 804.6 |

[1] Preliminary.  [2] Estimate.  *Source: Renewable Fuels Association*

## Production of Biodiesel in the United States   In Thousands of Barrels (mbbl)

| Year | Jan. | Feb. | Mar. | Apr. | May | June | July | Aug. | Sept. | Oct. | Nov. | Dec. | Average |
|---|---|---|---|---|---|---|---|---|---|---|---|---|---|
| 2014 | 1,727 | 1,801 | 2,361 | 2,223 | 2,531 | 2,645 | 2,926 | 2,987 | 2,754 | 2,928 | 2,610 | 2,958 | 30,452 |
| 2015 | 1,727 | 1,851 | 2,326 | 2,568 | 2,784 | 2,901 | 2,883 | 2,933 | 2,479 | 2,535 | 2,521 | 2,573 | 30,080 |
| 2016 | 2,490 | 2,504 | 2,861 | 2,856 | 3,222 | 3,205 | 3,331 | 3,385 | 3,206 | 3,433 | 3,408 | 3,425 | 37,327 |
| 2017 | 2,208 | 2,238 | 2,761 | 3,020 | 3,242 | 3,344 | 3,560 | 3,559 | 3,507 | 3,515 | 3,523 | 3,515 | 37,993 |
| 2018 | 2,945 | 2,996 | 3,493 | 3,344 | 3,538 | 3,718 | 3,892 | 4,028 | 3,850 | 4,039 | 3,783 | 3,991 | 43,616 |
| 2019 | 3,427 | 3,108 | 3,353 | 3,623 | 3,675 | 3,370 | 3,776 | 3,712 | 3,377 | 3,436 | 3,034 | 3,163 | 41,054 |
| 2020 | 3,196 | 3,139 | 3,594 | 3,422 | 3,630 | 3,590 | 3,849 | 3,872 | 3,790 | 3,743 | 3,621 | 3,761 | 43,207 |
| 2021 | 3,352 | 2,578 | 3,585 | 3,430 | 3,537 | 3,415 | 3,552 | 3,560 | 3,185 | 3,473 | 3,360 | 3,661 | 40,686 |
| 2022[1] | 2,858 | 2,710 | 3,163 | 3,024 | 3,238 | 3,268 | 3,492 | 3,521 | 3,354 | 3,396 | 3,384 |  | 38,626 |

[1] Preliminary.  *Source: Energy Information Administration, U.S. Department of Energy (EIA-DOE)*

## Stocks of Biodiesel in the United States   In Thousands of Barrels (Mbbl)

| Year | Jan. | Feb. | Mar. | Apr. | May | June | July | Aug. | Sept. | Oct. | Nov. | Dec. |
|---|---|---|---|---|---|---|---|---|---|---|---|---|
| 2015 | 4,032 | 4,245 | 4,244 | 4,071 | 3,599 | 3,063 | 3,404 | 3,333 | 3,021 | 3,070 | 3,600 | 3,943 |
| 2016 | 4,222 | 4,133 | 4,167 | 4,358 | 4,091 | 4,726 | 4,443 | 4,265 | 4,227 | 4,690 | 5,314 | 6,398 |
| 2017 | 6,397 | 6,475 | 6,189 | 5,706 | 4,909 | 5,052 | 5,405 | 5,356 | 4,849 | 4,485 | 4,233 | 4,268 |
| 2018 | 4,565 | 4,934 | 4,925 | 4,716 | 4,275 | 3,850 | 3,742 | 3,425 | 3,371 | 3,647 | 4,039 | 4,662 |
| 2019 | 5,354 | 5,502 | 5,389 | 5,330 | 4,815 | 4,408 | 4,088 | 3,860 | 3,706 | 3,738 | 3,887 | 3,907 |
| 2020 | 4,273 | 4,220 | 4,429 | 4,411 | 4,513 | 4,318 | 3,879 | 3,563 | 3,221 | 3,418 | 3,741 | 3,665 |
| 2021 | 4,580 | 4,189 | 4,284 | 4,183 | 3,805 | 3,748 | 3,697 | 3,369 | 3,230 | 3,340 | 3,747 | 4,187 |
| 2022[1] | 4,337 | 4,395 | 4,526 | 4,029 | 3,659 | 3,240 | 3,045 | 2,712 | 2,849 | 2,930 | 3,251 |  |

[1] Preliminary.  *Source: Energy Information Administration, U.S. Department of Energy (EIA-DOE)*

## Imports of Biodiesel in the United States   In Thousands of Barrels (mbbl)

| Year | Jan. | Feb. | Mar. | Apr. | May | June | July | Aug. | Sept. | Oct. | Nov. | Dec. | Total |
|---|---|---|---|---|---|---|---|---|---|---|---|---|---|
| 2015 | 372 | 526 | 340 | 330 | 336 | 673 | 1,157 | 961 | 1,062 | 863 | 701 | 1,078 | 8,399 |
| 2016 | 248 | 287 | 565 | 969 | 1,117 | 1,630 | 1,681 | 1,873 | 1,835 | 1,822 | 2,184 | 2,668 | 16,879 |
| 2017 | 241 | 549 | 650 | 681 | 948 | 1,736 | 1,670 | 1,582 | 205 | 386 | 222 | 504 | 9,374 |
| 2018 | 246 | 146 | 457 | 308 | 325 | 296 | 157 | 281 | 277 | 468 | 416 | 536 | 3,913 |
| 2019 | 308 | 267 | 509 | 410 | 281 | 310 | 333 | 140 | 280 | 314 | 417 | 433 | 4,002 |
| 2020 | 336 | 302 | 333 | 611 | 475 | 446 | 346 | 234 | 360 | 420 | 448 | 373 | 4,684 |
| 2021 | 228 | 263 | 361 | 500 | 316 | 446 | 357 | 287 | 418 | 473 | 660 | 696 | 5,005 |
| 2022[1] | 388 | 121 | 636 | 672 | 315 | 346 | 284 | 371 | 405 | 658 | 903 |  | 5,563 |

[1] Preliminary.  *Source: Energy Information Administration, U.S. Department of Energy (EIA-DOE)*

## Exports of Biodiesel in the United States   In Thousands of Barrels (mbbl)

| Year | Jan. | Feb. | Mar. | Apr. | May | June | July | Aug. | Sept. | Oct. | Nov. | Dec. | Total |
|---|---|---|---|---|---|---|---|---|---|---|---|---|---|
| 2015 | 22 | 23 | 191 | 240 | 255 | 260 | 255 | 275 | 200 | 161 | 76 | 133 | 2,091 |
| 2016 | 42 | 49 | 234 | 246 | 335 | 220 | 250 | 235 | 150 | 114 | 143 | 80 | 2,098 |
| 2017 | 42 | 59 | 136 | 283 | 239 | 226 | 453 | 387 | 100 | 217 | 49 | 35 | 2,228 |
| 2018 | 102 | 103 | 255 | 217 | 382 | 275 | 259 | 263 | 190 | 188 | 156 | 61 | 2,453 |
| 2019 | 72 | 92 | 240 | 370 | 419 | 300 | 392 | 290 | 238 | 158 | 56 | 83 | 2,710 |
| 2020 | 31 | 89 | 228 | 526 | 496 | 523 | 376 | 512 | 426 | 113 | 73 | 64 | 3,458 |
| 2021 | 166 | 122 | 267 | 494 | 564 | 658 | 489 | 549 | 474 | 213 | 166 | 291 | 4,452 |
| 2022[1] | 1,124 | 111 | 405 | 584 | 812 | 770 | 607 | 823 | 765 | 468 | 221 |  | 7,299 |

[1] Preliminary.  *Source: Energy Information Administration, U.S. Department of Energy (EIA-DOE)*

# Fertilizer

A fertilizer is a natural or a synthetic chemical substance, or a mixture of both, that enriches the soil to promote plant growth. The three primary nutrients that fertilizers provide are nitrogen, potassium, and phosphorus. In ancient times, and still today, many commonly used fertilizers contain one or more of the three primary ingredients: manure (containing nitrogen), bones (containing small amounts of nitrogen and large quantities of phosphorus), and potash (containing potassium).

At least fourteen different nutrients have been found essential for crops. These include three organic nutrients (carbon, hydrogen, and oxygen, which are taken directly from air and water), three primary chemical nutrients (nitrogen, phosphorus, and potassium), and three secondary chemical nutrients (magnesium, calcium, and sulfur). The others are micronutrients or trace elements and include iron, manganese, copper, zinc, boron, and molybdenum.

**Prices** – The average price of ammonia (Gulf Coast delivery), a key source of ingredients for fertilizers, rose by +171.4% yr/yr in 2021 to $578 per metric ton, remaining below the 2008 record high of $590 per metric ton. The average price of potash in the U.S. in 2021 rose by +27.5% yr/yr to $650.00 per metric ton, remaining below the 2009 record high of $800.00 per metric ton.

**Supply** – World production of ammonia (as contained in nitrogen) in 2022 remained unchanged at 150.000 million metric tons, remaining the record high. The world's largest producers of ammonia in 2022 were China with 28.0% of world production, Russia with 10.7%, the U.S. with 8.7%, and India with 8.0%.

World production of phosphate rock, basic slag, and guano in 2022 fell by -2.7% yr/yr to 220.000 million metric tons. The world's largest producers of phosphate rock in 202 were China with 38.6% of world production, Morocco with 18.2%, the U.S. with 9.5%, and Russia with 5.9%. U.S. production in 2022 fell by -2.8% yr/yr to 21.000 million metric tons.

World production of marketable potash in 2022 fell by -13.6% yr/yr to 40.000 million metric tons. The world's largest producers of potash in 2022 were Canada with 40.0% of world production, China with 15.0%, Russia with 12.5%, and Belarus with 7.5%. U.S. production of potash in fell by -8.3% to 440,000 metric tons.

**Demand** – U.S. consumption of phosphate rock in 2022 fell by -1.6% to 24.000 million metric tons. U.S. consumption of potash in 2022 rose by +2.9% yr/yr to 7.1 million metric tons. U.S. consumption of nitrogen in 2021 fell by -1.5% to 9.680 million metric tons.

**Trade** – U.S. imports of nitrogen in 2022 rose by +1.0% yr/yr to 2.100 million metric tons, and the U.S. relied on imports for 9% of its consumption. U.S. imports of phosphate rock in 2022 fell by -2.4% yr/yr to 2.400 million metric tons. U.S. imports of potash in 2022 rose by +8.0% to 7.000 million metric tons, much higher than the low of 2.220 million metric tons in 2009. Imports accounted for 94% of U.S. consumption.

### World Production of Ammonia — In Thousands of Metric Tons of Contained Nitrogen

| Year | Canada | China | France | Germany | India | Indonesia | Japan | Mexico | Netherlands | Poland | Russia | United States | Total |
|---|---|---|---|---|---|---|---|---|---|---|---|---|---|
| 2013 | 3,830 | 47,175 | 810 | 2,757 | 10,840 | 5,000 | 828 | 758 | 2,300 | 2,119 | 11,879 | 9,170 | 140,000 |
| 2014 | 3,716 | 46,850 | 760 | 2,540 | 10,780 | 5,000 | 787 | 714 | 2,200 | 2,200 | 12,030 | 9,330 | 140,000 |
| 2015 | 4,004 | 47,603 | 1,040 | 2,370 | 11,309 | 5,000 | 790 | 473 | 2,300 | 2,200 | 12,455 | 9,590 | 142,000 |
| 2016 | 4,133 | 46,922 | 1,010 | 2,500 | 11,574 | 4,700 | 725 | 438 | 2,300 | 2,237 | 13,300 | 10,200 | 144,000 |
| 2017 | 3,745 | 40,656 | 750 | 2,580 | 11,405 | 4,900 | 717 | 411 | 2,300 | 2,367 | 14,056 | 11,600 | 141,000 |
| 2018 | 3,832 | 37,907 | 914 | 2,580 | 11,900 | 5,400 | 673 | 124 | 2,200 | 2,172 | 14,859 | 13,100 | 142,000 |
| 2019 | 3,909 | 38,922 | 884 | 2,415 | 12,200 | 6,100 | 694 | ---- | 2,200 | 2,101 | 15,802 | 13,500 | 145,000 |
| 2020 | 3,895 | 42,063 | 822 | 2,333 | 12,200 | 5,900 | 643 | 112 | 2,100 | 2,262 | 16,126 | 14,000 | 150,000 |
| 2021[1] | 3,760 | 42,000 | 880 | 2,290 | 12,100 | 6,000 | 691 | 201 | 2,000 | 2,100 | 16,300 | 12,700 | 150,000 |
| 2022[2] | 3,800 | 42,000 | | 2,000 | 12,000 | 6,000 | | | 2,000 | 2,100 | 16,000 | 13,000 | 150,000 |

[1] Preliminary.  [2] Estimate.  Source: U.S. Geological Survey (USGS)

### Salient Statistics of Nitrogen[3] (Ammonia) in the United States — In Thousands of Metric Tons

| Year | Net Import Reliance As a % of Apparent Consumption | Production[3] (Fixed) Fertilizer | Non-fertilizer | Total | Imprts[4] (Fixed) | Exports | Nitrogen[5] Compounds Produced | Consumption | Stocks, Dec. 31 Ammonia | Fixed Nitrogen Compounds | Ammonia Consumption (Apparent) | Urea FOB Gulf[6] Coast | Urea FOB Corn Belt | Ammonium Nitrate: FOB Corn Belt | Ammonia FOB Gulf Coast |
|---|---|---|---|---|---|---|---|---|---|---|---|---|---|---|---|
| 2013 | 34 | 8,070 | 1,100 | 9,170 | 4,960 | 196 | 8,759 | 11,900 | 240 | 240 | 13,900 | 325-342 | 370-380 | 510-550 | 541 |
| 2014 | 30 | 8,210 | 1,120 | 9,330 | 4,150 | 111 | 8,391 | 11,400 | 280 | 280 | 13,300 | 322-333 | 360-385 | 570-640 | 531 |
| 2015 | 30 | 8,440 | 1,150 | 9,590 | 4,320 | 93 | 8,266 | 12,000 | 420 | 420 | 13,700 | 225-230 | 265-295 | 445-470 | 481 |
| 2016 | 26 | 8,930 | 1,220 | 10,200 | 3,840 | 183 | 8,918 | 11,700 | 400 | 400 | 13,800 | 225-230 | 265-295 | 445-470 | 481 |
| 2017 | 18 | 10,200 | 1,390 | 11,600 | 3,090 | 612 | 9,666 | 11,900 | 320 | 480 | 14,100 | 232-242 | 255-275 | 290-405 | 245 |
| 2018 | 14 | 11,600 | 1,540 | 13,100 | 2,530 | 224 | 10,087 | 10,600 | 490 | 450 | 15,300 | 243-260 | 270-280 | 260-270 | 280-300 |
| 2019 | 11 | 11,900 | 1,570 | 13,500 | 2,020 | 338 | 10,260 | 10,600 | 420 | 570 | 15,200 | 261 | 310 | 265 | 295 |
| 2020 | 11 | 12,300 | 1,630 | 14,000 | 1,990 | 369 | 10,522 | 9,830 | 310 | 420 | 15,700 | 217 | 255 | 245 | 220 |
| 2021[1] | 13 | 11,200 | 1,480 | 12,700 | 2,080 | 231 | 9,597 | 9,680 | 270 | 570 | 14,600 | | | | |
| 2022[2] | 9 | | | 13,000 | 2,100 | 700 | | | 390 | | 14,000 | | | | |

[1] Preliminary.  [2] Estimate.  [3] Anhydrous ammonia, synthetic.  [4] For consumption.  [5] Major downstream nitrogen compounds.  [6] Granular.
Source: U.S. Geological Survey (USGS)

# FERTILIZER

## World Production of Phosphate Rock, Basic Slag & Guano   In Thousands of Metric Tons (Gross Weight)

| Year | Brazil | China | Egypt | Israel | Jordan | Morocco | Russia | Senegal | Syria | Togo | Tunisia | United States | World Total |
|---|---|---|---|---|---|---|---|---|---|---|---|---|---|
| 2013 | 6,715 | 111,700 | 5,922 | 3,578 | 5,399 | 26,400 | 10,700 | 909 | 1,000 | 1,214 | 3,283 | 31,200 | 232,000 |
| 2014 | 6,513 | 120,000 | 5,378 | 3,357 | 7,144 | 27,390 | 10,800 | 1,285 | 1,234 | 1,098 | 3,784 | 25,300 | 237,000 |
| 2015 | 5,800 | 142,000 | 5,303 | 3,849 | 8,336 | 26,264 | 11,600 | 2,100 | 538 | 1,150 | 3,240 | 27,400 | 263,000 |
| 2016 | 5,850 | 144,400 | 4,300 | 3,946 | 7,991 | 26,900 | 12,300 | 1,610 | 30 | 850 | 3,664 | 27,100 | 265,000 |
| 2017 | 5,200 | 123,100 | 4,800 | 3,332 | 8,688 | 32,800 | 13,200 | 1,385 | 30 | 733 | 4,422 | 27,900 | 252,000 |
| 2018 | 5,740 | 96,310 | 5,000 | 3,550 | 8,022 | 34,400 | 13,600 | 1,649 | 100 | 800 | 3,341 | 25,800 | 225,000 |
| 2019 | 3,049 | 93,320 | 5,000 | 2,807 | 9,223 | 35,200 | 13,800 | 3,421 | 100 | 681 | 4,108 | 23,300 | 224,000 |
| 2020 | 5,223 | 90,900 | 4,800 | 3,090 | 8,938 | 37,400 | 13,800 | 2,013 | 130 | 942 | 3,194 | 23,500 | 223,000 |
| 2021[1] | 6,000 | 90,000 | 5,000 | 2,431 | 10,015 | 38,100 | 14,000 | 2,100 | 350 | 1,000 | 3,726 | 21,600 | 226,000 |
| 2022[2] | 5,500 | 85,000 | 5,000 | 3,000 | 10,000 | 40,000 | 13,000 | 2,600 |  | 1,500 | 4,000 | 21,000 | 220,000 |

[1] Preliminary.   [2] Estimate.   Source: U.S. Geological Survey (USGS)

## Salient Statistics of Phosphate Rock in the United States   In Thousands of Metric Tons

| Year | Mine Production | Marketable Production | Value Million Dollars | Imports for Consumption | Exports | Apparent Consumption | Producer Stocks, Dec. 31 | Avg. Price FOB Mine $/Metric Ton | Avg. Price of Florida & N. Carolina - $/Met. Ton - FOB Mine (-60% to +74%) - Domestic | Export | Average |
|---|---|---|---|---|---|---|---|---|---|---|---|
| 2013 | 139,000 | 31,200 | 2,850 | 3,170 | ---- | 31,900 | 9,000 | 91.11 | ---- | ---- | ---- |
| 2014 | 112,000 | 25,300 | 1,990 | 2,380 | ---- | 29,100 | 5,880 | 78.59 | ---- | ---- | ---- |
| 2015 | 127,000 | 27,400 | 1,980 | 1,960 | ---- | 28,100 | 6,730 | 72.41 | ---- | ---- | ---- |
| 2016 | 130,000 | 27,100 | 2,090 | 1,590 | ---- | 28,200 | 7,450 | 76.90 | ---- | ---- | ---- |
| 2017 | 123,000 | 27,900 | 2,060 | 2,470 | ---- | 28,800 | 8,440 | 73.67 | ---- | ---- | ---- |
| 2018 | 115,000 | 25,800 | 1,830 | 2,770 | ---- | 26,000 | 10,600 | 70.77 | ---- | ---- | ---- |
| 2019 | 105,000 | 23,300 | 1,580 | 2,140 | ---- | 25,500 | 9,830 | 67.98 | ---- | ---- | ---- |
| 2020 | 102,000 | 23,500 | 1,780 | 2,520 | ---- | 25,100 | 11,000 | 75.86 | ---- | ---- | ---- |
| 2021[1] | 91,000 | 21,600 | 1,800 | 2,460 | ---- | 24,400 | 10,700 | 83.10 | ---- | ---- | ---- |
| 2022[2] |  | 21,000 |  | 2,400 | ---- | 24,000 | 10,000 | 90.00 | ---- | ---- | ---- |

[1] Preliminary.   [2] Estimate.   Source: U.S. Geological Survey (USGS)

## World Production of Marketable Potash   In Thousands of Metric Tons ($K_2O$ Equivalent)

| Year | Belarus | Brazil | Canada | Chile | China | Germany | Israel | Jordan | Russia | Spain | United Kingdom | United States | World Total |
|---|---|---|---|---|---|---|---|---|---|---|---|---|---|
| 2013 | 4,243 | 311 | 10,196 | 1,130 | 5,300 | 3,075 | 2,268 | 1,046 | 6,100 | 711 | 549 | 960 | 36,100 |
| 2014 | 6,340 | 311 | 10,818 | 1,200 | 6,110 | 3,130 | 2,213 | 1,255 | 7,439 | 685 | 610 | 850 | 41,300 |
| 2015 | 6,468 | 304 | 11,462 | 1,200 | 5,710 | 3,110 | 1,540 | 1,413 | 6,954 | 668 | 384 | 740 | 40,400 |
| 2016 | 6,180 | 316 | 10,790 | 1,200 | 5,780 | 2,751 | 2,068 | 1,202 | 6,588 | 667 | 287 | 510 | 38,700 |
| 2017 | 7,102 | 306 | 12,563 | 1,100 | 5,510 | 2,964 | 1,900 | 1,392 | 7,320 | 789 | 200 | 480 | 42,100 |
| 2018 | 7,346 | 201 | 14,024 | 950 | 5,450 | 2,754 | 2,200 | 1,486 | 7,168 | 604 | 175 | 520 | 43,400 |
| 2019 | 7,348 | 250 | 12,770 | 660 | 5,900 | 2,615 | 2,034 | 1,516 | 7,340 | 520 | 89 | 510 | 42,100 |
| 2020 | 7,562 | 255 | 13,784 | 921 | 5,570 | 2,874 | 2,416 | 1,598 | 8,114 | 340 | 99 | 460 | 44,700 |
| 2021[1] | 7,630 | 270 | 14,239 | 858 | 6,000 | 2,800 | 2,379 | 1,563 | 9,101 | 365 | 110 | 480 | 46,300 |
| 2022[2] | 3,000 | 270 | 16,000 | 850 | 6,000 | 2,800 | 2,500 | 1,700 | 5,000 | 450 |  | 440 | 40,000 |

[1] Preliminary.   [2] Estimate.   Source: U.S. Geological Survey (USGS)

## Salient Statistics of Potash in the United States   In Thousands of Metric Tons ($K_2O$ Equivalent)

| Year | Net Import Reliance As a % of Apparent Consump | Production | Sales by Producers | Value Million Dollars | Imports for Consumption | Exports | Apparent Consumption | Producer Stocks Dec. 31 | Avg Value of Product | Avg Value of $K_2O$ Equiv | Avg. Price[3] (Metric Ton) |
|---|---|---|---|---|---|---|---|---|---|---|---|
| 2013 | 82 | 960 | 880 | 630.0 | 4,650 | 255 | 5,300 | ---- | 315.00 | 715.00 | 590.00 |
| 2014 | 85 | 850 | 930 | 680.0 | 4,970 | 100 | 5,800 | ---- | 345.00 | 735.00 | 555.00 |
| 2015 | 89 | 740 | 620 | 550.0 | 5,190 | 106 | 5,700 | ---- | 360.00 | 880.00 | 570.00 |
| 2016 | 88 | 510 | 600 | 410.0 | 4,550 | 96 | 5,100 | ---- | 290.00 | 680.00 | 460.00 |
| 2017 | 92 | 480 | 490 | 380.0 | 5,860 | 128 | 6,200 | ---- | 285.00 | 775.00 | 440.00 |
| 2018 | 92 | 520 | 520 | 390.0 | 5,710 | 105 | 6,100 | ---- | 280.00 | 755.00 | 490.00 |
| 2019 | 91 | 510 | 480 | 390.0 | 5,150 | 145 | 5,500 | ---- | 290.00 | 820.00 | 530.00 |
| 2020 | 92 | 460 | 500 | 420.0 | 5,370 | 147 | 5,700 | ---- | 310.00 | 850.00 | 510.00 |
| 2021[1] | 93 | 480 | 490 | 550.0 | 6,480 | 112 | 6,900 | ---- | 425.00 | 1,120.00 | 650.00 |
| 2022[2] | 94 | 440 | 440 |  | 7,000 | 300 | 7,100 | ---- |  |  |  |

[1] Preliminary.   [2] Estimate.   [3] Unit of $K_2O$, standard 60% muriate F.O.B. mine.   Source: U.S. Geological Survey (USGS)

# Fish

Fish are the primary source of protein for a large portion of the world's population. The worldwide yearly harvest of all sea fish (including aquaculture) is between 85 and 130 million metric tons. There are approximately 20,000 species of fish, of which 9,000 are regularly caught. Only 22 fish species are harvested in large amounts. Ground-fish, which are fish that live near or on the ocean floor, account for about 10% of the world's fishery harvest and include cod, haddock, pollock, flounder, halibut, and sole. Large pelagic fish such as tuna, swordfish, marlin, and mahi-mahi, account for about 5% of world harvest. The fish eaten most often in the United States is canned tuna.

Rising global demand for fish has increased the pressure to harvest more fish to the point where all 17 of the world's major fishing areas have either reached or exceeded their limits. Atlantic stocks of cod, haddock, and bluefin tuna are all depleted, while in the Pacific, anchovies, salmon, and halibut are all over-fished. Aquaculture, or fish farming, reduces pressure on wild stocks and now accounts for nearly 20% of world harvest.

**Supply** – The U.S. total of fishery products in 2020 (latest data) fell by -2.1% to 21.342 billion pounds, which is down from the 2017 record high of 22.266. The U.S. total domestic catch in 2020 fell by -10.5% to 8.378 billion pounds, and that comprised 39.3% of total U.S. supply. Of the U.S. total domestic catch in 2020, 69.0% of the catch was finfish for human consumption, 19.6% of the catch was a variety of fish for industrial use, and 11.0% was shellfish for human consumption.

The principal species of U.S. fishery landings in 2019 were Pollock with 3.359 billion pounds, Menhaden with 1.507 billion pounds, Pacific Salmon with 838.0 million pounds, Flounder with 551.7 million pounds, and Sea Herring with 82.8 million pounds.

About 30% of the fish harvested in the world are processed directly into fishmeal and fish oil. Fishmeal is used primarily in animal feed. Fish oil is used in both animal feed and human food products. World fishmeal production in the 2021/22 marketing year fell by -0/2% to 5.354 million metric tons. Peru, the European Union, and Thailand are the world's largest producers of fish meal. World production of fish oil in the 2021/22 marketing year fell by -6.6% to 1.024 million metric tons. Chile, Peru, and Japan are the world's largest producers of fish oil.

## Fisheries -- Landings of Principal Species in the United States      In Millions of Pounds

| Year | Grand Total | For Human Food Finfish | Shellfish[3] | For Industrial Use[4] | Domestic Catch Total | Percent of Grand Total | For Human Food Finfish | Shellfish[3] | For Industrial Use[4] | Imports Total | Percent of Grand Total | For Human Food Finfish | Shellfish[3] | For Industrial Use[4] |
|---|---|---|---|---|---|---|---|---|---|---|---|---|---|---|
| 2014 | 21,431 | 14,060 | 5,054 | 2,317 | 9,486 | 44.3 | 6,588 | 1,240 | 1,658 | 11,945 | 55.7 | 7,473 | 3,814 | 659 |
| 2015 | 21,426 | 13,862 | 4,986 | 2,579 | 9,718 | 45.4 | 6,621 | 1,129 | 1,968 | 11,709 | 54.6 | 7,241 | 3,857 | 611 |
| 2016 | 21,542 | 13,746 | 5,034 | 2,762 | 9,572 | 44.4 | 6,393 | 1,092 | 2,088 | 11,970 | 55.6 | 7,353 | 3,942 | 675 |
| 2017 | 22,266 | 14,421 | 5,384 | 2,461 | 9,916 | 44.5 | 7,121 | 1,107 | 1,688 | 12,350 | 55.5 | 7,301 | 4,276 | 773 |
| 2018 | 22,355 | 13,976 | 5,754 | 2,625 | 9,385 | 42.0 | 6,409 | 1,091 | 1,886 | 12,969 | 58.0 | 7,568 | 4,663 | 739 |
| 2019 | 21,794 | 13,822 | 5,552 | 2,392 | 9,362 | 43.0 | 6,619 | 964 | 1,751 | 12,432 | 57.0 | 7,203 | 4,588 | 641 |
| 2020[1] | 21,342 | 13,247 | 5,669 | 2,393 | 8,378 | 39.3 | 5,781 | 922 | 1,642 | 12,964 | 60.7 | 7,466 | 4,747 | 751 |

[1] Preliminary.  [2] Live weight, except percent.  [3] For univalue and bivalues mollusks (conchs, clams, oysters, scallops, etc.) the weight of meats, excluding the shell is reported.  [4] Fish meal and sea herring.  Source: Fisheries Statistics Division, U.S. Department of Commerce

## Fisheries -- Landings of Principal Species in the United States      In Millions of Pounds

| Year | Cod, Atlantic | Flounder | Halibut | Herring, Sea | Menhaden | Pollock | Salmon, Pacific | Tuna | Whiting | Clams (Meats) | Lobsters Crabs American | Oysters (Meats) | Scallops | Shrimp |
|---|---|---|---|---|---|---|---|---|---|---|---|---|---|---|
| 2013 | 5 | 717 | 30 | 298 | 1,467 | 3,014 | 1,069 | 56 | 14 | 91 | 332  149 | 35 | 41 | 283 |
| 2014 | 5 | 714 | 23 | 309 | 1,256 | 3,156 | 720 | 59 | 16 | 91 | 295  148 | 34 | 34 | 295 |
| 2015 | 3 | 555 | 25 | 247 | 1,618 | 3,269 | 1,066 | 57 | 14 | 86 | 326  146 | 28 | 36 | 327 |
| 2016 | 3 | 565 | 25 | 192 | 1,728 | 3,361 | 561 | 56 | 14 | 89 | 317  159 | 33 | 41 | 271 |
| 2017 | 2 | 545 | 26 | 180 | 1,413 | 3,396 | 1,008 | 55 | 12 | 85 | 275  133 | 32 | 52 | 283 |
| 2018 | 2 | 525 | 22 | 146 | 1,582 | 3,371 | 576 | 52 | 11 | 86 | 289  146 | 30 | 58 | 289 |
| 2019[1] | 1 | 552 | 10 | 83 | 1,508 | 3,360 | 838 | 49 | 12 | 76 | 272  126 | 28 | 61 | 248 |

[1] Preliminary.  Source: National Marine Fisheries Service, U.S. Department of Commerce

## U.S. Fisheries: Quantity & Value of Domestic Catch & Consumption & World Fish Oil Production

| Year | Fresh & Frozen | Canned | Cured | For Meal, Oil, etc. | Total | For Human Food | For Industrial Products | Ex-vessel Value[3] - Million $ - | Average Price - Cents /Lb. - | Per Capita Consumption - Pounds - | World[2] Fish Oil Production - 1,000 Tons - |
|---|---|---|---|---|---|---|---|---|---|---|---|
| 2013 | 8,009 | 365 | 45 | 1,451 | 9,870 | 8,043 | 1,827 | 5,466 | ---- | 17.9 | 941 |
| 2014 | 7,916 | 196 | 63 | 1,311 | 9,486 | 7,828 | 1,658 | 5,448 | ---- | 17.3 | 917 |
| 2015 | 7,622 | 364 | 65 | 1,667 | 9,718 | 7,750 | 1,968 | 5,203 | ---- | 18.8 | 909 |
| 2016 | 7,509 | 186 | 57 | 1,820 | 9,572 | 7,484 | 2,088 | 5,312 | ---- | 18.3 | 894 |
| 2017 | 8,091 | 289 | 136 | 1,400 | 9,916 | 8,228 | 1,688 | 5,421 | ---- | 19.1 | 919 |
| 2018 | 7,443 | 180 | 139 | 1,623 | 9,385 | 7,500 | 1,885 | 5,571 | ---- | 19.0 | 1,130 |
| 2019[1] | 7,405 | 172 | 145 | 1,587 | 9,309 | 7,542 | 1,766 | 5,458 | ---- | 19.2 | 1,001 |

[1] Preliminary.  [2] Crop years on a marketing year basis.  [3] At the Dock Prices.  Source: Fisheries Statistics Division, U.S. Department of Commerce

# FISH

## Imports of Seafood Products into the United States — In Thousands of Pounds

| Year | Trout, fresh and frozen | Atlantic salmon, fresh | Pacific salmon, fresh[2] | Atlantic salmon, frozen | Pacific salmon, frozen[2] | Atlantic salmon, fillets | Salmon, canned and prepared[3] | Tilapia[4] | Shrimp, frozen | Shrimp, fresh and prepared[5] | Oysters[6] | Mussels[6] | Clams[6] | Scallops[6] |
|---|---|---|---|---|---|---|---|---|---|---|---|---|---|---|
| 2012 | 19,616 | 222,313 | 9,770 | 4,828 | 65,491 | 276,703 | 27,539 | 503,644 | 922,877 | 253,456 | 18,566 | 75,384 | 45,518 | 34,021 |
| 2013 | 18,713 | 190,427 | 12,153 | 5,604 | 71,480 | 317,981 | 37,106 | 504,698 | 865,142 | 248,812 | 19,830 | 70,916 | 48,705 | 60,429 |
| 2014 | 19,312 | 172,283 | 11,070 | 6,853 | 76,248 | 360,274 | 32,381 | 508,484 | 989,966 | 265,538 | 21,356 | 74,665 | 50,989 | 60,041 |
| 2015 | 26,708 | 236,674 | 10,051 | 6,112 | 78,790 | 371,476 | 32,387 | 496,083 | 996,935 | 292,139 | 24,498 | 71,002 | 52,969 | 48,365 |
| 2016 | 31,366 | 239,288 | 14,670 | 8,223 | 89,165 | 371,643 | 30,619 | 434,606 | 1,039,634 | 290,126 | 25,096 | 78,855 | 54,918 | 50,178 |
| 2017 | 27,929 | 262,441 | 9,658 | 6,367 | 96,676 | 390,807 | 33,582 | 402,947 | 1,139,829 | 325,782 | 25,775 | 78,107 | 51,859 | 40,077 |
| 2018 | 34,712 | 273,251 | 9,068 | 6,172 | 105,803 | 439,352 | 35,074 | 415,889 | 1,182,010 | 353,579 | 29,577 | 67,374 | 56,242 | 45,498 |
| 2019[1] | 31,806 | 245,435 | 7,254 | 5,110 | 86,012 | 385,755 | 37,635 | 307,305 | 994,596 | 262,634 | 19,454 | 66,964 | 40,251 | 28,475 |

[1] Preliminary.  [2] Includes salmon with no specific species noted.  [3] Includes smoked and cured salmon.  [4] Frozen whole fish plus fresh and frozen fillets.  [5] Canned, breaded or otherwise prepared.  [6] Fresh or prepared.  Source: Bureau of the Census, U.S. Department of Commerce

## Exports of Seafood Products From the United States — In Thousands of Pounds

| Year | Trout, fresh and frozen | Atlantic salmon, fresh[2] | Pacific salmon, fresh[2] | Atlantic salmon, frozen | Pacific salmon, frozen[2] | Salmon, canned and prepared[3] | Shrimp, frozen | Shrimp, fresh and prepared[4] | Oysters[5] | Mussels[5] | Clams[5] | Scallops[5] |
|---|---|---|---|---|---|---|---|---|---|---|---|---|
| 2012 | 1,779 | 17,234 | 20,934 | 380 | 222,933 | 92,838 | 14,951 | 9,260 | 7,781 | 931 | 14,056 | 28,756 |
| 2013 | 2,148 | 15,574 | 24,129 | 223 | 359,834 | 101,469 | 14,760 | 7,897 | 7,624 | 1,043 | 18,114 | 21,206 |
| 2014 | 2,232 | 11,868 | 17,704 | 295 | 310,551 | 94,793 | 15,251 | 12,972 | 8,229 | 1,275 | 17,483 | 20,064 |
| 2015 | 1,317 | 9,590 | 23,825 | 335 | 413,075 | 87,624 | 25,699 | 11,931 | 8,370 | 1,217 | 18,491 | 16,824 |
| 2016 | 2,188 | 23,094 | 33,543 | 1,342 | 272,348 | 82,959 | 11,441 | 13,367 | 7,765 | 1,262 | 19,494 | 18,236 |
| 2017 | 3,836 | 12,655 | 26,168 | 1,516 | 427,477 | 64,462 | 8,020 | 9,535 | 7,533 | 1,944 | 16,612 | 16,437 |
| 2018 | 3,460 | 18,181 | 14,641 | 642 | 280,138 | 56,269 | 8,347 | 11,988 | 7,674 | 1,321 | 15,383 | 14,173 |
| 2019[1] | 3,468 | 15,596 | 14,784 | 643 | 296,899 | 37,286 | 4,224 | 10,136 | 6,279 | 1,690 | 11,584 | 11,108 |

[1] Preliminary.  [2] Includes salmon with no specific species noted.  [3] Includes smoked and cured salmon.  [4] Canned, breaded, or prepared.  [5] Fresh or prepared.  Source: Bureau of the Census, U.S. Department of Commerce

## World Production of Fish Meal — In Thousands of Metric Tons

| Year | Chile | Denmark | European Union | Iceland | Japan | Norway | Peru | Russia | South Africa | Spain | Thailand | United States | World Total |
|---|---|---|---|---|---|---|---|---|---|---|---|---|---|
| 2012-13 | 336.6 | 140.4 | 368.2 | 123.0 | 207.0 | 101.0 | 775.0 | 81.9 | 28.4 | 30.5 | 462.5 | 236.7 | 4,334.2 |
| 2013-14 | 395.9 | 161.8 | 392.3 | 82.0 | 201.0 | 132.7 | 1,070.9 | 75.3 | 74.8 | 30.1 | 460.0 | 227.0 | 4,738.5 |
| 2014-15 | 338.8 | 192.0 | 427.1 | 152.0 | 198.0 | 174.1 | 671.2 | 87.8 | 72.2 | 30.4 | 430.0 | 279.1 | 4,482.3 |
| 2015-16 | 236.9 | 175.0 | 377.4 | 90.0 | 194.8 | 139.0 | 558.7 | 93.4 | 85.1 | 30.0 | 400.0 | 252.5 | 4,265.3 |
| 2016-17 | 313.2 | 222.1 | 428.4 | 117.0 | 192.0 | 156.8 | 1,087.0 | 98.8 | 80.3 | 31.0 | 366.0 | 251.3 | 5,001.3 |
| 2017-18 | 335.0 | 192.6 | 410.2 | 133.2 | 189.9 | 145.2 | 1,008.0 | 104.6 | 71.8 | 35.0 | 375.0 | 280.2 | 5,049.1 |
| 2018-19 | 364.2 | 174.6 | 397.8 | 93.0 | 185.0 | 142.1 | 1,006.5 | 126.9 | 59.1 | 33.0 | 387.0 | 252.7 | 5,176.2 |
| 2019-20[1] | 340.9 | 172.2 | 407.4 | 78.1 | 183.0 | 173.1 | 807.9 | 123.3 | 80.0 | 34.0 | 398.0 | 221.7 | 4,880.5 |
| 2020-21[2] | 362.1 | 162.9 | 402.1 | 75.9 | 188.2 | 131.2 | 1,267.4 | 135.0 | 67.0 | 35.0 | 380.0 | 195.1 | 5,366.2 |
| 2021-22[3] | 360.0 | 172.0 | 400.9 | 176.0 | 189.0 | 138.0 | 1,110.0 | 138.0 | 76.0 | 31.7 | 388.0 | 215.0 | 5,354.6 |

[1] Preliminary.  [2] Estimate.  [3] Forecast.  Source: The Oil World

## World Production of Fish Oil — In Thousands of Metric Tons

| Year | Canada | Chile | China | Denmark | Iceland | Japan | Norway | Peru | Africa | Russia | United States | World Total | Fish Oil CIF[4] $ Per Tonne |
|---|---|---|---|---|---|---|---|---|---|---|---|---|---|
| 2012-13 | 6.2 | 91.1 | 18.7 | 46.8 | 50.5 | 58.4 | 36.0 | 137.6 | 2.2 | 7.3 | 78.1 | 892.9 | 2,190 |
| 2013-14 | 6.0 | 137.9 | 20.0 | 50.1 | 44.3 | 60.0 | 53.2 | 174.4 | 4.8 | 8.6 | 60.8 | 969.4 | 1,791 |
| 2014-15 | 6.1 | 110.3 | 24.0 | 50.1 | 48.2 | 62.6 | 58.8 | 85.7 | 7.3 | 8.6 | 64.8 | 871.2 | 1,909 |
| 2015-16 | 6.1 | 87.9 | 44.3 | 53.7 | 29.2 | 61.8 | 56.8 | 77.0 | 7.6 | 21.0 | 80.7 | 858.1 | 1,713 |
| 2016-17 | 6.0 | 111.9 | 43.5 | 55.7 | 36.3 | 62.1 | 56.0 | 165.7 | 7.3 | 7.5 | 52.0 | 954.0 | 1,445 |
| 2017-18 | 6.0 | 136.2 | 55.8 | 49.7 | 44.3 | 71.0 | 46.8 | 178.4 | 6.4 | 14.1 | 76.8 | 1,041.5 | 1,683 |
| 2018-19 | 6.0 | 135.7 | 68.5 | 51.1 | 27.4 | 71.2 | 41.1 | 168.9 | 3.9 | 16.0 | 67.9 | 1,053.2 | 1,645 |
| 2019-20[1] | 5.8 | 125.8 | 66.2 | 48.0 | 27.2 | 66.3 | 52.2 | 110.1 | 7.6 | 21.3 | 63.1 | 973.6 | 1,969 |
| 2020-21[2] | 6.0 | 156.8 | 61.0 | 49.8 | 24.4 | 66.0 | 39.2 | 218.0 | 5.6 | 14.8 | 64.6 | 1,097.0 | 1,905 |
| 2021-22[3] | 5.0 | 142.0 | 62.0 | 51.0 | 57.6 | 67.2 | 42.0 | 119.0 | 6.6 | 17.3 | 64.6 | 1,024.9 | 2,571 |

[1] Preliminary.  [2] Estimate.  [3] Forecast.  [4] Any origin, N.W. Europe.  Source: The Oil World

# FISH

### Catfish Sales of Foodsize Fish in the United States — In Thousands of Fish

| Year | Alabama | Arkansas | California | Mississippi | North Carolina | Texas | Other[2] | Total |
|---|---|---|---|---|---|---|---|---|
| 2013 | 62,400 | 15,500 | 1,510 | 106,000 | 2,750 | 10,200 | 2,400 | 201,810 |
| 2014 | 63,400 | 9,980 | 1,340 | 97,900 | 1,990 | 7,050 | 2,940 | 184,600 |
| 2015 | 63,000 | 9,560 | 1,050 | 110,000 | 2,120 | 7,880 | 1,900 | 195,510 |
| 2016 | 62,300 | 10,300 | 1,150 | 105,000 | 1,930 | 8,020 | 1,880 | 190,580 |
| 2017 | 66,300 | 11,100 | 910 | 112,000 | 1,380 | 6,740 | 1,400 | 199,830 |
| 2018 | 63,600 | 10,900 | 1,600 | 121,000 | 1,400 | 8,520 | 1,780 | 208,800 |
| 2019 | 60,300 | 10,700 | 1,210 | 113,000 | W | W | 11,235 | 196,445 |
| 2020 | 55,300 | 9,960 | W | 128,000 | W | 8,100 | 3,025 | 204,385 |
| 2021 | 47,700 | 10,400 | W | 121,000 | W | 8,950 | 3,250 | 191,300 |
| 2022[1] | 46,600 | 10,400 | W | 137,000 | W | 9,440 | 2,555 | 205,995 |

[1] Preliminary.  [2] Other States include State estimates not shown and States suppressed due to disclosure.
Source: National Agricultural Statistics Service, U.S. Department of Agriculture (NASS-USDA)

### Catfish Sales of Foodsize Fish in the United States — In Thousands of Pounds (Live Weight)

| Year | Alabama | Arkansas | California | Mississippi | North Carolina | Texas | Other[2] | Total |
|---|---|---|---|---|---|---|---|---|
| 2013 | 109,300 | 25,300 | 2,800 | 175,300 | 4,000 | 15,800 | 3,500 | 337,130 |
| 2014 | 105,300 | 17,200 | 2,550 | 161,500 | 3,400 | 14,300 | 3,248 | 307,498 |
| 2015 | 107,500 | 14,500 | 2,200 | 171,700 | 3,250 | 15,600 | 2,694 | 317,444 |
| 2016 | 109,000 | 16,300 | 1,640 | 172,000 | 3,500 | 15,400 | 2,334 | 320,174 |
| 2017 | 112,900 | 16,800 | 1,580 | 180,500 | 2,600 | 14,000 | 2,048 | 330,428 |
| 2018 | 104,600 | 18,300 | 2,850 | 192,000 | 2,500 | 20,200 | 3,151 | 343,601 |
| 2019 | 102,500 | 18,600 | 2,400 | 203,500 | W | W | 20,990 | 347,990 |
| 2020 | 94,000 | 15,700 | W | 192,100 | W | 17,000 | 5,328 | 324,128 |
| 2021 | 90,600 | 17,300 | W | 194,300 | W | 17,400 | 5,823 | 325,423 |
| 2022[1] | 83,900 | 18,000 | W | 203,400 | W | 18,500 | 5,096 | 328,896 |

[1] Preliminary.  [2] Other States include State estimates not shown and States suppressed due to disclosure.
Source: National Agricultural Statistics Service, U.S. Department of Agriculture (NASS-USDA)

### Trout Sales of Fish 12" or longer (Foodsize) in the United States — In Thousands of Fish

| Year | California | Colorado | Georgia | Idaho | Michigan | North Carolina | Pennsylvania | Virginia | Washington | West Virginia | Wisconsin | Other[2] | Total |
|---|---|---|---|---|---|---|---|---|---|---|---|---|---|
| 2013 | W | 250 | 145 | 30,100 | 145 | 3,310 | 870 | 430 | W | 440 | 480 | 4,380 | 41,170 |
| 2014 | 1,310 | 210 | W | 36,100 | 105 | 3,310 | 880 | 480 | W | 420 | 410 | 4,150 | 48,285 |
| 2015 | 1,350 | 310 | W | 32,700 | W | 3,220 | 910 | 590 | W | 550 | 440 | 4,460 | 45,350 |
| 2016 | W | 380 | W | 33,000 | W | 3,960 | 980 | 460 | W | 630 | W | 6,035 | 46,305 |
| 2017 | W | 640 | W | 27,700 | W | 3,500 | 970 | 500 | W | 590 | 390 | 5,965 | 40,965 |
| 2018 | W | 430 | W | 22,200 | W | 3,640 | 1,210 | 460 | W | 450 | 370 | 6,975 | 35,935 |
| 2019 | W | W | W | 19,900 | W | W | 1,090 | 440 | W | 400 | 340 | 9,960 | 32,390 |
| 2020 | W | 680 | W | W | W | W | 990 | 450 | W | 350 | 310 | 22,975 | 25,855 |
| 2021 | W | 610 | W | 15,400 | W | 3,100 | 1,280 | 510 | W | W | 270 | 5,145 | 26,480 |
| 2022[1] | W | 570 | W | 17,100 | W | 2,910 | 1,090 | 550 | W | W | 250 | 4,515 | 27,205 |

[1] Preliminary.  [2] Other States include State estimates not shown and States suppressed due to disclosure.  W = Withheld.
Source: National Agricultural Statistics Service, U.S. Department of Agriculture (NASS-USDA)

### Trout Sales of Fish 12" or longer (Foodsize) in the United States — In Thousands of Pounds (Live Weight)

| Year | California | Colorado | Georgia | Idaho | Michigan | North Carolina | Pennsylvania | Virginia | Washington | West Virginia | Wisconsin | Other[2] | Total |
|---|---|---|---|---|---|---|---|---|---|---|---|---|---|
| 2013 | W | 441 | 163 | 35,700 | 167 | 3,700 | 1,050 | 498 | W | 551 | 447 | 13,178 | 56,666 |
| 2014 | 1,550 | 404 | W | 42,200 | 119 | 4,050 | 1,030 | 489 | W | 518 | 403 | 9,121 | 60,733 |
| 2015 | 1,600 | 405 | W | 39,100 | W | 3,700 | 1,050 | 567 | W | 464 | 414 | 9,767 | 57,947 |
| 2016 | W | 441 | W | 39,700 | W | 4,400 | 1,090 | 427 | W | 569 | W | 11,598 | 59,087 |
| 2017 | W | 634 | W | 33,600 | W | 4,150 | 1,070 | 524 | W | 515 | 378 | 12,168 | 53,887 |
| 2018 | W | 591 | W | 27,000 | W | 4,000 | 1,200 | 512 | W | 435 | 357 | 13,261 | 47,548 |
| 2019 | W | W | W | 25,000 | W | W | 1,200 | 540 | W | 410 | 314 | 16,006 | 43,758 |
| 2020 | W | 814 | W | W | W | W | 1,160 | 683 | W | 343 | 291 | 41,222 | 44,513 |
| 2021 | W | 712 | W | 21,700 | W | 3,450 | 1,370 | 653 | W | W | 272 | 16,598 | 44,931 |
| 2022[1] | W | 664 | W | 24,300 | W | 3,250 | 1,350 | 637 | W | W | 257 | 12,553 | 43,255 |

[1] Preliminary.  [2] Other States include State estimates not shown and States suppressed due to disclosure.  W = Withheld.
Source: National Agricultural Statistics Service, U.S. Department of Agriculture (NASS-USDA)

# Flaxseed and Linseed Oil

Flaxseed, also called linseed, is an ancient crop that was cultivated by the Babylonians around 3,000 BC. Flaxseed is used for fiber in textiles and to produce oil. Flaxseeds contain approximately 35% oil, of which 60% is omega-3 fatty acid. Flaxseed or linseed oil is obtained through either the expeller extraction or solvent extraction method. Manufacturers filter the processed oil to remove some impurities and then sell it as unrefined. Unrefined oil retains its full flavor, aroma, color, and naturally occurring nutrients. Flaxseed oil is used for cooking and as a dietary supplement as well as for animal feed. Industrial linseed oil is not for internal consumption due to possible poisonous additives and is used for making putty, sealants, linoleum, wood preservation, varnishes, and oil paints.

**Prices** – The average monthly price received by U.S. farmers for flaxseed in the 2021/22 marketing year rose by +103.8% yr/yr to $26.57 per bushel.

**Supply** – World production of flaxseed in the 2021/22 marketing year fell by -7.7% yr/yr to 2.989 million metric tons, falling below the record high of 3.329 million metric tons in 2020/21. The world's largest producer of flaxseed in 2021/22 was Russia at 59.3% of total world production, Canada with 11.6%, China with 11.4%, and India with 4.5%. U.S. production of flaxseed in 2022 rose by +58.9% to 4.304 million bushels, far below the record level of 10.095 million bushels in 2015. North Dakota is by far the largest producing state for flaxseed and accounted for 79.0% of flaxseed production in 2022, followed by Montana with 21.0%.

World production of linseed oil in 2021/22 fell by -1.5% yr/yr to 795,000 metric tons. The world's largest producers of linseed oil were China with 28.0% of world production in 2021/22, Russia with 20.7%, Belgium with 15.0%, and the U.S. with 8.8%. U.S. production of linseed oil in 2021/22 remained unchanged yr/yr at 70.3 million pounds.

**Demand** – U.S. distribution of flaxseed in 2022/23 rose by +11.9% yr/yr to 7.371 million bushels. The breakdown of usage was 85.8% for crushing into meal and oil, 8.2% for residual, 3.5% for exports, and 2.5% for seed.

**Trade** – U.S. exports of flaxseed in 2022/23 fell by -16.3% yr/yr to 400,000 thousand bushels. U.S. imports of flaxseed in 2022/23 rose by +0.1% yr/yr to 6.687 million bushels.

## World Production of Flaxseed   In Thousands of Metric Tons

| Crop Year | Argentina | Australia | Bangladesh | Canada | China | Egypt | France | Hungary | India | Romania | United States | Former USSR | World Total |
|---|---|---|---|---|---|---|---|---|---|---|---|---|---|
| 2012-13 | 17 | 7 | 6 | 489 | 391 | 5 | 26 | ---- | 149 | 4 | 147 | 571 | 2,053 |
| 2013-14 | 20 | 6 | 6 | 731 | 399 | 2 | 16 | 1 | 140 | 4 | 85 | 618 | 2,255 |
| 2014-15 | 17 | 6 | 9 | 840 | 350 | 5 | 23 | 1 | 155 | 3 | 162 | 688 | 2,457 |
| 2015-16 | 20 | 6 | 5 | 943 | 330 | 5 | 48 | 1 | 125 | 4 | 256 | 873 | 2,835 |
| 2016-17 | 17 | 6 | 5 | 591 | 365 | 8 | 42 | 1 | 184 | 3 | 221 | 1,139 | 2,815 |
| 2017-18 | 14 | 6 | 4 | 555 | 362 | 8 | 55 | 2 | 174 | 4 | 98 | 1,350 | 2,848 |
| 2018-19 | 20 | 6 | 5 | 492 | 366 | 9 | 46 | 1 | 99 | 3 | 113 | 1,518 | 2,889 |
| 2019-20[1] | 10 | 6 | 4 | 486 | 360 | 8 | 46 | 2 | 16 | 6 | 162 | 1,689 | 3,113 |
| 2020-21[2] | 20 | 6 | 3 | 578 | 340 | 8 | 59 | 2 | 140 | 3 | 145 | 1,727 | 3,238 |
| 2021-22[3] | 12 | 6 | 4 | 346 | 340 | 9 | 71 | 2 | 135 | 2 | 69 | 1,772 | 2,989 |

[1] Preliminary.  [2] Estimate.  [3] Forecast.   Source: The Oil World

## Supply and Distribution of Flaxseed in the United States   In Thousands of Bushels

| Crop Year Beginning June 1 | Planted (1,000 Acres) | Harvested (1,000 Acres) | Yield Per Acre (Bushels) | Beginning Stocks | Production | Imports | Total Supply | Seed | Crush | Exports | Residual | Total |
|---|---|---|---|---|---|---|---|---|---|---|---|---|
| 2013-14 | 181 | 172 | 19.5 | 924 | 3,356 | 6,759 | 11,039 | 252 | 8,700 | 599 | 725 | 10,276 |
| 2014-15 | 311 | 302 | 21.1 | 763 | 6,368 | 7,464 | 14,595 | 375 | 11,850 | 528 | 1,034 | 13,787 |
| 2015-16 | 463 | 456 | 22.1 | 808 | 10,095 | 4,436 | 15,339 | 303 | 10,700 | 870 | 553 | 12,425 |
| 2016-17 | 374 | 366 | 23.7 | 2,914 | 8,656 | 3,086 | 14,656 | 245 | 10,500 | 1,332 | 410 | 12,486 |
| 2017-18 | 303 | 272 | 14.1 | 2,170 | 3,842 | 5,451 | 11,463 | 168 | 9,000 | 480 | 186 | 9,834 |
| 2018-19 | 208 | 198 | 22.6 | 1,629 | 4,466 | 5,503 | 11,598 | 303 | 9,150 | 262 | 321 | 10,036 |
| 2019-20 | 374 | 284 | 19.8 | 1,562 | 5,625 | 4,382 | 11,569 | 247 | 8,950 | 875 | 234 | 10,306 |
| 2020-21[1] | 305 | 296 | 19.3 | 1,263 | 5,706 | 4,068 | 11,037 | 263 | 8,000 | 1,188 | 243 | 9,694 |
| 2021-22[2] | 325 | 268 | 10.1 | 1,343 | 2,708 | 6,684 | 10,745 | 213 | 9,300 | 478 | 266 | 10,257 |
| 2022-23[3] | 263 | 244 | 17.3 | 488 | 4,304 | 6,687 | 11,479 | 284 | 9,850 | 400 | 946 | 11,479 |

[1] Preliminary.  [2] Estimate.  [3] Forecast.  NA = not avaliable.  Source: Economic Research Service, U.S. Department of Agriculture (ERS-USDA)

# FLAXSEED AND LINSEED OIL

## Supply and Distribution of Linseed Meal in the United States    In Millions of Pounds

| Crop Year Beginning June 1 | Stocks June 1 | Production | Imports | Total Supply | Domestic Disappearance | Exports | Total Disappearance | Ending Stocks | Average Price at Minneapolis (34% Protein) Cents/Lb. |
|---|---|---|---|---|---|---|---|---|---|
| 2013-14 | 5 | 157 | 1 | 163 | 153 | 6 | 158 | 5 | 359.42 |
| 2014-15 | 5 | 213 | 3 | 221 | 212 | 4 | 216 | 5 | 263.90 |
| 2015-16 | 5 | 193 | 7 | 205 | 196 | 4 | 200 | 5 | 234.78 |
| 2016-17 | 5 | 189 | 6 | 200 | 190 | 5 | 195 | 5 | 313.17 |
| 2017-18 | 5 | 162 | 7 | 174 | 166 | 3 | 169 | 5 | 236.92 |
| 2018-19 | 5 | 165 | 8 | 177 | 170 | 2 | 172 | 5 | 236.37 |
| 2019-20 | 5 | 161 | 4 | 170 | 164 | 1 | 165 | 5 | 241.57 |
| 2020-21 | 5 | 144 | 4 | 153 | 152 | 2 | 148 | 5 | 277.36 |
| 2021-22[1] | 5 | 167 | 4 | 177 | 116 | 2 | 172 | 5 | 311.36 |
| 2022-23[2] | 5 | 177 | 10 | 192 | 116 | 2 | 187 | 5 | 390.00 |

[1] Preliminary.   [2] Forecast.   Source: Economic Research Service, U.S. Department of Agriculture (ERS-USDA)

## Supply and Distribution of Linseed Oil in the United States    In Millions of Pounds

| Crop Year Beginning June 1 | Stocks June 1 | Production | Total Supply | Exports | Domestic Disappearance | Total Disappearance | Average Price at Minneapolis Cents/Lb. |
|---|---|---|---|---|---|---|---|
| 2013-14 | 35 | 170 | 210 | 117 | 58 | 175 | NA |
| 2014-15 | 35 | 231 | 270 | 183 | 52 | 235 | NA |
| 2015-16 | 35 | 209 | 248 | 196 | 17 | 213 | NA |
| 2016-17 | 35 | 205 | 244 | 194 | 15 | 209 | NA |
| 2017-18 | 35 | 176 | 215 | 166 | 14 | 180 | NA |
| 2018-19 | 35 | 178 | 219 | 173 | 11 | 184 | NA |
| 2019-20 | 35 | 175 | 213 | 173 | 5 | 178 | NA |
| 2020-21 | 35 | 156 | 195 | 142 | 18 | 160 | NA |
| 2021-22[1] | 35 | 181 | 224 | 178 | 11 | 189 | NA |
| 2022-23[2] | 35 | 192 | 235 | 187 | 13 | 200 | NA |

[1] Preliminary.   [2] Forecast.   Source: Economic Research Service, U.S. Department of Agriculture (ERS-USDA)

## World Production and Price of Linseed Oil    In Thousands of Metric Tons

| Crop Year | Argentina | Bangladesh | Belgium | China | Egypt | Germany | India | Japan | United Kingdom | United States | Former USSR | World Total | Rotterdam Ex-Tank USD $/Tonne |
|---|---|---|---|---|---|---|---|---|---|---|---|---|---|
| 2012-13 | 1.6 | 2.0 | 107.2 | 152.0 | 2.9 | 44.8 | 38.6 | 2.0 | 4.9 | 94.3 | 21.4 | 592.5 | 1,217 |
| 2013-14 | ---- | ---- | 112.0 | 186.6 | 2.9 | 48.7 | 35.3 | 1.5 | 6.7 | 81.6 | 19.4 | 601.1 | 1,191 |
| 2014-15 | ---- | ---- | 123.2 | 216.7 | 3.3 | 49.4 | 38.6 | 2.6 | 6.1 | 108.7 | 40.2 | 696.7 | 1,162 |
| 2015-16 | ---- | ---- | 131.8 | 225.7 | 4.5 | 49.4 | 34.3 | ---- | 6.9 | 97.8 | 73.3 | 764.9 | 825 |
| 2016-17 | ---- | ---- | 125.4 | 210.7 | 5.2 | 52.6 | 46.8 | ---- | 8.5 | 89.0 | 91.5 | 821.2 | 828 |
| 2017-18 | ---- | ---- | 127.6 | 207.7 | 6.6 | 51.9 | 47.0 | ---- | 8.9 | 78.4 | 109.5 | 781.5 | 837 |
| 2018-19 | ---- | ---- | 127.6 | 216.7 | 6.6 | 57.6 | 39.6 | ---- | 10.2 | 82.3 | 144.4 | 808.8 | 835 |
| 2019-20 | ---- | ---- | 120.0 | 219.7 | 5.2 | 49.1 | 40.6 | ---- | 7.1 | 81.6 | 151.1 | 794.9 | 977 |
| 2020-21[1] | ---- | ---- | 122.5 | 231.8 | 5.3 | 47.6 | 36.2 | ---- | 8.8 | 70.3 | 161.3 | 807.4 | 1,738 |
| 2021-22[2] | ---- | ---- | 119.3 | 222.7 | 5.1 | 44.1 | 34.7 | ---- | 9.5 | 70.3 | 164.3 | 795.0 | 2,129 |

[1] Preliminary.   [2] Forecast.   Source: The Oil World

## Production of Flaxseed in the United States, by States    In Thousands of Bushels

| Year | Minnesota | Montana | North Dakota | South Dakota | Total |
|---|---|---|---|---|---|
| 2013 | 76 | 240 | 2,920 | 120 | 3,356 |
| 2014 | 48 | 425 | 5,805 | 90 | 6,368 |
| 2015 | 42 | 450 | 9,315 | 288 | 10,095 |
| 2016 | ---- | 616 | 7,896 | 144 | 8,656 |
| 2017 | ---- | 342 | 3,435 | 65 | 3,842 |
| 2018 | ---- | 629 | 3,792 | 45 | 4,466 |
| 2019 | ---- | 1,335 | 4,290 | ---- | 5,625 |
| 2020 | ---- | 1,632 | 4,074 | ---- | 5,706 |
| 2021 | ---- | 485 | 2,223 | ---- | 2,708 |
| 2022[1] | ---- | 902 | 3,402 | ---- | 4,304 |

[1] Preliminary.   Source: National Agricultural Statistics Service, U.S. Department of Agriculture (NASS-USDA)

# FLAXSEED AND LINSEED OIL

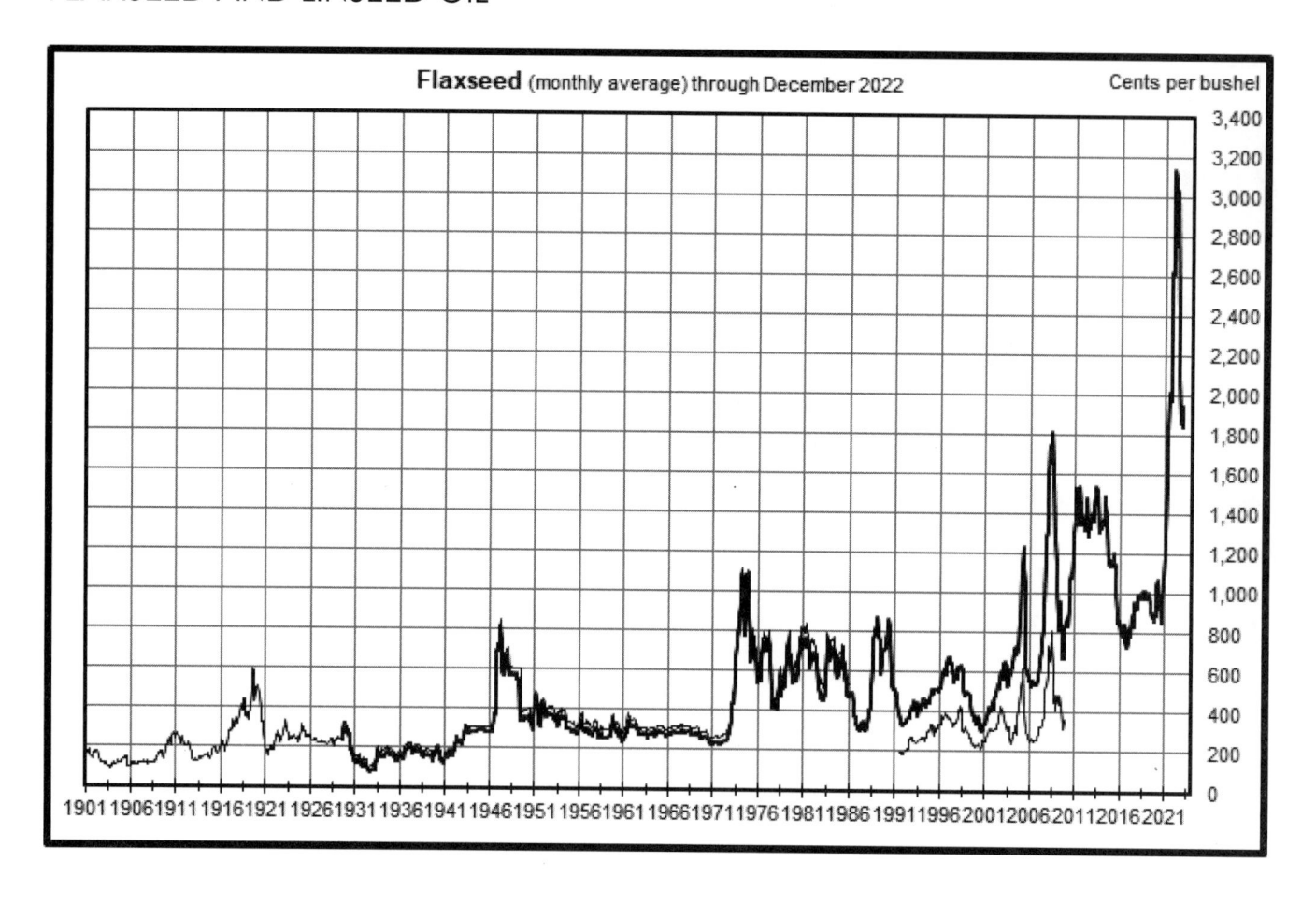

**Flaxseed** (monthly average) through December 2022 — Cents per bushel

### Average Price Received by Farmers for Flaxseed in the United States — In Dollars Per Bushel

| Crop Year | July | Aug. | Sept. | Oct. | Nov. | Dec. | Jan. | Feb. | Mar. | Apr. | May | June | Average |
|---|---|---|---|---|---|---|---|---|---|---|---|---|---|
| 2013-14 | 15.10 | 14.90 | 13.10 | 13.50 | 13.40 | 13.40 | 13.30 | 13.80 | 13.50 | 13.90 | 14.90 | 14.40 | 13.93 |
| 2014-15 | 14.00 | 13.30 | 11.70 | 11.50 | 11.60 | 11.40 | 11.70 | 11.50 | 11.50 | 12.00 | 12.10 | 11.40 | 11.98 |
| 2015-16 | 11.50 | 10.00 | 9.07 | 8.57 | 8.71 | 8.62 | 8.46 | 8.10 | 8.37 | 8.10 | 7.93 | 8.44 | 8.82 |
| 2016-17 | 8.48 | 8.25 | 7.61 | 7.37 | 7.36 | 7.59 | 8.26 | 7.86 | 8.34 | 8.03 | 8.96 | 8.52 | 8.05 |
| 2017-18 | 8.40 | 9.30 | 9.55 | 9.23 | 9.21 | 9.36 | 9.40 | 10.00 | 9.76 | 9.92 | 10.10 | 10.00 | 9.52 |
| 2018-19 | 9.96 | 10.20 | 9.79 | 9.79 | 10.20 | 9.87 | 9.85 | 9.79 | 10.10 | 9.93 | 9.54 | 9.08 | 9.84 |
| 2019-20 | 9.10 | 8.84 | 8.84 | 9.01 | 8.70 | 8.91 | 8.97 | 10.40 | 10.70 | 9.31 | 9.57 | 10.00 | 9.36 |
| 2020-21 | 9.64 | 8.56 | 9.64 | 9.76 | 10.70 | 10.90 | 12.00 | 13.20 | 15.70 | 18.10 | 18.30 | 19.90 | 13.03 |
| 2021-22 | 20.10 | 20.20 | 19.80 | 26.20 | 26.10 | 31.30 | 31.00 | 27.50 | 29.10 | 30.30 | 29.70 | 23.90 | 26.27 |
| 2022-23[1] | 24.20 | 20.80 | 18.90 | 18.60 | 19.50 | 18.40 | 17.70 | 16.20 | | | | | 19.29 |

[1] Preliminary.  Source: National Agricultural Statistics Service, U.S. Department of Agriculture (NASS-USDA)

### Average Price of Linseed Meal (34% protein) at Minneapolis — In Dollars Per Ton

| Crop Year | July | Aug. | Sept. | Oct. | Nov. | Dec. | Jan. | Feb. | Mar. | Apr. | May | June | Average |
|---|---|---|---|---|---|---|---|---|---|---|---|---|---|
| 2013-14 | 382.50 | 317.50 | 400.00 | 363.75 | 316.25 | 328.75 | 330.00 | 377.50 | 413.75 | 388.00 | 355.00 | 323.75 | 358.06 |
| 2014-15 | 295.00 | 252.50 | 302.50 | 214.38 | 283.75 | 287.50 | 250.00 | 230.63 | 230.50 | 239.38 | 256.88 | 258.00 | 258.42 |
| 2015-16 | 284.38 | 287.50 | 256.00 | 215.00 | 209.80 | 200.00 | 195.00 | 197.50 | 195.00 | 218.13 | 301.50 | 375.63 | 244.62 |
| 2016-17 | 364.38 | 335.00 | 316.25 | 305.63 | 296.00 | 290.00 | 297.00 | 299.38 | 297.50 | 291.25 | 290.00 | 282.63 | 305.42 |
| 2017-18 | 250.63 | 253.00 | 236.88 | 214.00 | 205.00 | 209.17 | 215.50 | 233.13 | 237.50 | 238.13 | 267.50 | 271.25 | 235.97 |
| 2018-19 | 278.00 | 265.63 | 235.00 | 196.50 | 209.38 | 225.83 | 219.00 | 225.00 | 235.63 | 241.50 | 233.75 | 228.88 | 232.84 |
| 2019-20 | 232.50 | 235.00 | 226.25 | 226.50 | 226.88 | 231.67 | 248.13 | 262.50 | 263.00 | 260.00 | 257.50 | 245.63 | 242.96 |
| 2020-21 | 250.00 | 251.75 | 227.00 | 239.38 | 253.75 | 275.00 | 313.13 | 296.25 | 322.00 | 318.75 | 335.63 | 293.50 | 281.35 |
| 2021-22 | 262.50 | 287.50 | 260.00 | 265.63 | 252.00 | 309.17 | 326.25 | 350.00 | 392.50 | 386.00 | 351.25 | 322.50 | 313.77 |
| 2022-23[1] | 351.50 | 347.50 | NA | NA | 357.50 | 368.50 | 397.50 | 412.50 | | | | | 372.50 |

[1] Preliminary.  Source: Economic Research Service, U.S. Department of Agriculture (ERS-USDA)

# Fruits

A fruit is any seed-bearing structure produced from a flowering plant. A widely used classification system divides fruit into fleshy or dry types. Fleshy fruits are juicy and include peaches, mangos, apples, and blueberries. Dry fruits include tree nuts such as almonds, walnuts, and pecans. Some foods that are commonly called vegetables, such as tomatoes, squash, peppers, and eggplant, are technically fruits because they develop from the ovary of a flower.

Worldwide, over 430 million tons of fruit are produced each year and are grown everywhere except the Arctic and the Antarctic. The tropics, because of their abundant moisture and warm temperatures, produce the most diverse and abundant fruits. Mexico and Chile produce more than half of all the fresh and frozen fruit imported into the U.S. In the U.S., the top three fruits produced are oranges, grapes, and apples. Virtually all U.S. production of almonds, pistachios, and walnuts occurs in California, which leads the U.S. in tree nut production.

**Prices** – The fresh fruit component of the U.S. Consumer Price Index (CPI) rose by +5.4% yr/yr to 376.5, and the processed fruit component rose by +2.2% to 166.4. In 2021, banana prices rose by +3.8% to $0.600 per pound, Thompson seedless grapes rose by +7.8% to $2.460 per pound, lemons rose by +3.3% to $1.999 per pound, and navel oranges rose by +1.8% to $1.36 per pound.

**Supply** – U.S. commercial production of selected fruits in 2021 fell by -4.6% to 22.144 million short tons. By weight, grapes accounted for 27.3% of that U.S. fruit production figure, followed by apples at 22.2%, and oranges at 19.8%. The value of U.S. fruit production in 2021 rose by +8.1% yr/yr to $30.163 billion.

**Demand** – U.S. per capita fresh fruit consumption in 2021 fell by -0.3% to 116.860 pounds per year, down from the 2020 record high of 117.250. The highest per capita consumption categories for non-citrus fruits in 2021 were bananas (26.870 pounds) and apples (17.750 pounds). Per capita consumption of citrus fruits were oranges (8.170 pounds), tangerines and tangelos (6.990 pounds), lemons (4.920 pounds), limes (4.660 pounds), and grapefruit (1.470 pounds). The utilization breakdown for 2017 shows that total U.S. non-citrus fruit was used for fresh fruit (43.2%), wine (25.5%), dried fruit (9.7%), juice (8.2%), canned fruit (6.5%), and frozen fruit (4.1%). The value of utilized non-citrus fruit production in 2021 rose by +13.3% to $17.065 billion.

## Commercial Production for Selected Fruits in the United States    In Thousands of Short Tons

| Year | Apples | Cherries[2] | Cran-berries | Grapes | Grape-fruit | Lemons | Nect-arines | Oranges | Peach-es | Pears | Pine-apple[3] | Prunes & Plums | Straw-berries | Tang-elos | Tang-erines | Total All Fruits |
|---|---|---|---|---|---|---|---|---|---|---|---|---|---|---|---|---|
| 2015 | 5,051 | 461 | 428 | 7,621 | 910 | 904 | 160 | 6,353 | 845 | 817 | ---- | 441 | 1,533 | 30 | 863 | 26,801 |
| 2016 | 5,748 | 515 | 481 | 7,697 | 803 | 904 | 151 | 6,088 | 792 | 739 | ---- | 265 | 1,480 | 18 | 935 | 26,930 |
| 2017 | 5,777 | 568 | 420 | 7,384 | 698 | 882 | 142 | 5,088 | 701 | 737 | ---- | 443 | 1,360 | 7 | 1,029 | 25,586 |
| 2018 | 5,120 | 493 | 446 | 7,596 | 509 | 888 | 121 | 3,875 | 652 | 806 | ---- | 380 | 1,305 | 7 | 804 | 23,304 |
| 2019 | 5,543 | 483 | 396 | 6,961 | 604 | 1,002 | 126 | 5,427 | 681 | 715 | ---- | 362 | 1,141 | 7 | 1,107 | 24,835 |
| 2020 | 5,143 | 395 | 390 | 6,040 | 570 | 1,084 | 123 | 5,254 | 653 | 656 | ---- | 270 | 1,334 | 7 | 944 | 23,200 |
| 2021[1] | 4,924 | 464 | 354 | 6,050 | 438 | 886 | 117 | 4,388 | 689 | 702 | ---- | 306 | 1,335 | 7 | 1,194 | 22,144 |

[1] Preliminary.   [2] Sweet and tart.   [3] Utilized production.   Source: Economic Research Service, U.S. Department of Agriculture (ERS-USDA)

## Utilized Production for Selected Fruits in the United States    In Thousands of Short Tons

| | ---------- Utilized Production ---------- | | | | ---------- Value of Production ---------- | | | |
|---|---|---|---|---|---|---|---|---|
| Year | Citrus[2] | Noncitrus | Tree nuts[3] | Total | Citrus[2] | Noncitrus | Tree nuts[3] | Total |
| | In Thousands of Short Tons | | | | In Thousands of Dollars | | | |
| 2015 | 9,060 | 18,334 | 2,552 | 29,946 | 3,353,750 | 16,602,493 | 8,461,676 | 28,417,919 |
| 2016 | 8,748 | 18,598 | 3,110 | 30,456 | 3,435,675 | 17,571,574 | 8,690,836 | 29,698,085 |
| 2017 | 7,697 | 18,313 | 2,985 | 28,995 | 3,532,125 | 18,032,949 | 9,023,875 | 30,588,949 |
| 2018 | 6,076 | 17,487 | 3,226 | 26,789 | 3,330,152 | 16,184,328 | 9,690,038 | 29,204,518 |
| 2019 | 8,140 | 17,020 | 3,328 | 28,487 | 3,399,879 | 15,531,610 | 10,095,499 | 29,026,988 |
| 2020 | 7,852 | 15,666 | 4,131 | 27,649 | 3,396,467 | 15,060,995 | 9,434,960 | 27,892,422 |
| 2021[1] | 6,906 | 15,619 | 3,946 | 26,472 | 3,355,041 | 17,065,720 | 9,742,288 | 30,163,049 |

[1] Preliminary.   [2] Year harvest was completed.   [3] Tree nuts on an in-shell equivalent.
Source: Economic Research Service, U.S. Department of Agriculture (ERS-USDA)

## Annual Average Retail Prices for Selected Fruits in the United States    In Dollars Per Pound

| | Red Delicious | | Anjou | Thompson Seedless | | | ---------- Oranges ---------- | |
|---|---|---|---|---|---|---|---|---|
| Year | Apples | Bananas | Pears | Grapes | Lemons | Grapefruit | Navel | Valencias |
| 2015 | 1.358 | .586 | NA | 2.591 | 1.981 | 1.091 | 1.304 | NA |
| 2016 | 1.442 | .573 | 1.674 | 2.758 | 2.037 | .970 | 1.246 | NA |
| 2017 | 1.294 | .563 | 1.603 | 2.641 | 2.007 | 1.279 | 1.341 | NA |
| 2018 | NA | .574 | 1.579 | 2.584 | 2.249 | 1.346 | 1.413 | NA |
| 2019 | NA | .574 | 1.603 | 2.445 | 2.129 | 1.345 | 1.367 | NA |
| 2020 | NA | .578 | NA | 2.283 | 1.935 | 1.208 | 1.336 | NA |
| 2021[1] | NA | .600 | NA | 2.460 | 1.999 | NA | 1.360 | NA |

[1] Estimate.   Source: Economic Research Service, U.S. Department of Agriculture (ERS-USDA)

# FRUITS

## Utilization of Noncitrus Fruit Production, and Value in the United States    1,000 Short Tons (Fresh Equivalent)

| Year | Utilized Production | Fresh | Canned | Dried | Juice | Frozen | Wine | Other Processed | Value of Utilized Production $1,000 |
|---|---|---|---|---|---|---|---|---|---|
| 2012 | 17,635 | 7,443 | 1,100 | 2,091 | 1,213 | 707 | 4,707 | 374 | 15,611,441 |
| 2013 | 19,433 | 7,824 | 1,396 | 2,321 | 1,636 | 896 | 5,068 | 406 | 16,220,440 |
| 2014 | 19,151 | 8,291 | 1,221 | 2,194 | 1,638 | 897 | 4,526 | 459 | 16,410,049 |
| 2015 | 18,334 | 7,695 | 1,258 | 2,323 | 1,397 | 877 | 4,255 | 530 | 16,602,493 |
| 2016 | 18,598 | 7,916 | 1,232 | 1,858 | 1,547 | 898 | 4,668 | 479 | 17,571,574 |
| 2017 | 18,313 | 7,909 | 1,186 | 1,778 | 1,498 | 746 | 4,663 | 534 | 18,032,949 |
| 2018 | 17,487 | 5 | 5 | 5 | 5 | 5 | 5 | 5 | 16,184,328 |
| 2019 | 17,020 | 5 | 5 | 5 | 5 | 5 | 5 | 5 | 15,531,610 |
| 2020 | 15,666 | 5 | 5 | 5 | 5 | 5 | 5 | 5 | 15,060,995 |
| 2021[1] | 15,619 | 5 | 5 | 5 | 5 | 5 | 5 | 5 | 17,065,720 |

[1] Preliminary.    Source: Economic Research Service, U.S. Department of Agriculture (ERS-USDA)

## Average Price Indexes for Fruits in the United States

| | Index of all Fruit & Nut Prices Received by Growers | Producer Price Index | | | | Consumer Price Index | |
|---|---|---|---|---|---|---|---|
| Year | (1990-92=100) | Fresh Fruit | Dried Fruit | Canned Fruits and Juices | Frozen Fruits and Juices | Fresh Fruit | Processed Fruit |
| | | 1982 = 100 | | | | 1982-84 = 100 | |
| 2012 | 112.4 | 119.0 | ---- | 203.8 | 168.9 | 336.6 | 150.4 |
| 2013 | 119.1 | 121.2 | ---- | 206.4 | 170.3 | 343.2 | 154.5 |
| 2014 | 136.3 | 124.5 | ---- | 208.7 | 172.7 | 359.7 | 154.0 |
| 2015 | 138.6 | 124.2 | ---- | 217.1 | 176.8 | 352.0 | 157.5 |
| 2016 | 137.8 | 138.7 | ---- | 223.2 | 177.0 | 359.8 | 158.2 |
| 2017 | 129.6 | 147.9 | ---- | 229.4 | 180.4 | 361.4 | 156.5 |
| 2018 | 128.1 | 145.1 | ---- | 227.3 | 180.8 | 365.2 | 154.9 |
| 2019 | 118.1 | 136.3 | ---- | 223.0 | 179.5 | 360.1 | 158.2 |
| 2020 | 138.6 | 139.1 | ---- | 225.8 | 178.6 | 357.1 | 162.8 |
| 2021[1] | 135.6 | 146.4 | ---- | 232.7 | 180.2 | 376.5 | 166.4 |

[1] Estimate.   NA = Not availvle.   Source: Economic Research Service, U.S. Department of Agriculture (ERS-USDA)

## Fresh Fruit: Per Capita Consumption[1] in the United States    In Pounds

| | Cıtrus Fruit | | | | | | Noncitrus Fruit | | | | | | |
|---|---|---|---|---|---|---|---|---|---|---|---|---|---|
| Year | Oranges | Tangerines & Tangelos | Lemons | Limes | Grape-fruit | U.S. Total | Apples | Apricots | Avoc-ados | Bananas | Blue-berries | Cherries | Cran-berries |
| 2012 | 10.47 | 4.18 | 3.95 | 2.57 | 2.37 | 23.54 | 16.05 | .10 | 5.62 | 26.90 | 1.33 | 1.50 | .07 |
| 2013 | 10.39 | 4.49 | 3.48 | 2.96 | 2.64 | 23.97 | 17.43 | .11 | 6.11 | 27.99 | 1.41 | .99 | .08 |
| 2014 | 9.38 | 5.00 | 3.43 | 3.07 | 2.40 | 23.28 | 18.71 | .12 | 6.98 | 27.86 | 1.51 | 1.17 | .07 |
| 2015 | 8.67 | 5.22 | 3.60 | 3.02 | 2.24 | 22.75 | 17.48 | .08 | 7.19 | 27.92 | 1.60 | 1.15 | .12 |
| 2016 | 9.18 | 5.29 | 4.13 | 3.48 | 1.97 | 24.05 | 19.15 | .13 | 6.86 | 27.43 | 1.78 | 1.17 | .12 |
| 2017 | 8.03 | 5.86 | 4.25 | 3.75 | 1.92 | 23.81 | 18.06 | .09 | 8.02 | 28.59 | 1.74 | 1.47 | .09 |
| 2018 | 8.19 | 5.92 | 4.21 | 4.06 | 1.56 | 23.96 | 16.80 | .12 | 8.47 | 28.22 | 2.00 | 1.28 | .07 |
| 2019 | 8.46 | 6.80 | 4.66 | 4.10 | 1.43 | 25.46 | 17.59 | .13 | 8.17 | 27.38 | 2.33 | 1.24 | .07 |
| 2020 | 9.42 | 6.73 | 4.90 | 4.27 | 1.68 | 26.90 | 16.17 | .08 | 9.22 | 27.22 | 2.34 | 1.23 | .07 |
| 2021[1] | 8.17 | 6.99 | 4.92 | 4.66 | 1.47 | 26.21 | 15.75 | .10 | 8.43 | 26.87 | 2.54 | 1.44 | .05 |

[1] Preliminary.   [2] All data on calendar-year basis except for citrus fruits; apples, August; grapes and pears, July; grapefruit, September; lemons, August of prior year; all other citrus, November.   Source: Economic Research Service, U.S. Department of Agriculture (ERS-USDA)

## Fresh Fruit: Per Capita Consumption[1] in the United States    In Pounds

| | Noncitrus Fruit Continued | | | | | | | | | | |
|---|---|---|---|---|---|---|---|---|---|---|---|
| Year | Grapes | Kiwifruit | Mangos | & Peaches | Pears | Pineapples | Papaya | Prunes | Straw-berries | Total Noncitrus | Total Fruit |
| 2012 | 7.59 | .55 | 2.49 | 3.86 | 2.76 | 6.42 | .97 | .63 | 5.62 | 85.12 | 108.66 |
| 2013 | 7.76 | .46 | 2.87 | 3.02 | 2.84 | 6.74 | 1.12 | .54 | 5.63 | 87.85 | 111.82 |
| 2014 | 7.67 | .56 | 2.52 | 3.15 | 2.85 | 7.19 | 1.14 | .53 | 5.69 | 90.73 | 114.01 |
| 2015 | 7.87 | .63 | 2.60 | 2.91 | 2.67 | 6.98 | 1.33 | .56 | 5.46 | 89.71 | 112.46 |
| 2016 | 8.09 | .58 | 2.96 | 2.73 | 2.76 | 7.28 | 1.43 | .66 | 5.75 | 91.31 | 115.36 |
| 2017 | 8.23 | .61 | 3.22 | 2.66 | 2.69 | 7.75 | 1.36 | .68 | 5.94 | 91.19 | 115.00 |
| 2018 | 8.07 | .62 | 3.17 | 2.20 | 2.92 | 7.81 | 1.26 | .60 | 6.32 | 89.95 | 113.91 |
| 2019 | 8.38 | .64 | 3.25 | 2.08 | 2.72 | 7.64 | 1.26 | .56 | 6.00 | 89.45 | 114.91 |
| 2020 | 8.20 | .73 | 3.63 | 2.36 | 2.83 | 7.30 | 1.25 | .58 | 7.13 | 90.35 | 117.25 |
| 2021[1] | 8.50 | .80 | 3.66 | 2.38 | 3.12 | 7.88 | 1.34 | .50 | 7.30 | 90.65 | 116.86 |

[1] Preliminary.   [2] All data on calendar-year basis except for citrus fruits; apples, August; grapes and pears, July; grapefruit, September; lemons, August of prior year; all other citrus, November.   Source: Economic Research Service, U.S. Department of Agriculture (ERS-USDA)

# FRUITS

## Average Price Received by Growers for Grapefruit in the United States — In Dollars Per Box

| Year | Jan. | Feb. | Mar. | Apr. | May | June | July | Aug. | Sept. | Oct. | Nov. | Dec. | Average |
|---|---|---|---|---|---|---|---|---|---|---|---|---|---|
| 2013 | 7.19 | 5.71 | 4.29 | 4.33 | 8.26 | 8.76 | 6.66 | 6.36 | 8.76 | 7.96 | 8.54 | 7.51 | 7.03 |
| 2014 | 7.30 | 5.78 | 5.60 | 5.34 | 7.89 | 7.69 | 7.19 | 8.05 | 13.40 | 12.33 | 9.82 | 8.92 | 8.28 |
| 2015 | 7.03 | 4.83 | 5.34 | 5.33 | 5.47 | 12.21 | 9.33 | 5.63 | 7.79 | 13.21 | 13.36 | 11.43 | 8.41 |
| 2016 | 10.70 | 9.13 | 8.86 | 12.77 | 14.81 | 13.82 | 15.26 | 14.08 | W | 19.08 | 13.14 | 12.14 | 13.07 |
| 2017 | 11.25 | 11.57 | 11.95 | 13.62 | 16.44 | 15.18 | 14.10 | W | 14.66 | 20.91 | 19.88 | 16.13 | 15.06 |
| 2018 | 15.88 | 15.80 | 16.04 | 18.21 | 17.02 | 14.71 | 13.34 | 9.57 | 15.16 | 20.61 | 20.89 | 18.68 | 16.33 |
| 2019 | 15.99 | 14.61 | 11.44 | 13.51 | 13.94 | 11.95 | 11.34 | 5.81 | 8.08 | 11.09 | 15.86 | 12.81 | 12.20 |
| 2020 | 10.23 | 8.95 | 9.56 | 11.03 | 12.00 | 13.80 | 16.13 | 16.56 | 14.55 | 24.09 | 21.30 | 15.95 | 14.51 |
| 2021 | 17.88 | 11.06 | 13.64 | 23.74 | 26.86 | 24.85 | 22.98 | 23.21 | 26.59 | 25.64 | 21.03 | 17.41 | 21.24 |
| 2022[1] | 15.71 | 13.12 | 10.95 | 16.62 | 7.17 | 19.50 | 12.91 | 11.78 | 13.24 | 25.60 | 27.48 | 24.11 | 16.52 |

On-tree equivalent.  [1]Preliminary.  Source: National Agricultural Statistics Service, U.S. Department of Agriculture (NASS-USDA)

## Average Price Received by Growers for Lemons in the United States — In Dollars Per Box

| Year | Jan. | Feb. | Mar. | Apr. | May | June | July | Aug. | Sept. | Oct. | Nov. | Dec. | Average |
|---|---|---|---|---|---|---|---|---|---|---|---|---|---|
| 2013 | 10.65 | 7.28 | 7.08 | 9.18 | 14.77 | 16.35 | 18.98 | 28.45 | 27.85 | 32.77 | 26.65 | 23.52 | 18.63 |
| 2014 | 21.17 | 21.69 | 21.31 | 22.39 | 24.54 | 29.91 | 40.05 | 33.68 | 37.40 | 38.47 | 29.54 | 21.15 | 28.44 |
| 2015 | 18.53 | 13.44 | 16.14 | 21.65 | 31.76 | 38.51 | 37.34 | 29.40 | 31.71 | 36.54 | 30.18 | 24.42 | 27.47 |
| 2016 | 23.05 | 22.04 | 24.29 | 25.09 | 31.67 | 29.95 | 26.47 | 29.54 | 31.84 | 31.49 | 27.88 | 23.13 | 27.20 |
| 2017 | 23.44 | 25.12 | 24.65 | 27.10 | 31.30 | 40.90 | 41.85 | 29.79 | 29.58 | 25.49 | 28.32 | 30.84 | 29.87 |
| 2018 | 30.17 | 23.65 | 20.72 | 18.20 | 21.73 | 29.14 | 40.34 | 53.01 | 49.63 | 41.29 | 31.76 | 26.23 | 32.16 |
| 2019 | 22.58 | 15.76 | 15.54 | 13.38 | 16.25 | 19.43 | 22.12 | 27.97 | 29.34 | 30.34 | 29.70 | 22.43 | 22.07 |
| 2020 | 16.14 | 14.35 | 10.25 | 10.72 | 14.38 | 19.50 | 21.01 | 21.50 | 21.85 | 24.41 | 25.52 | 23.23 | 18.57 |
| 2021 | 21.99 | 18.96 | 20.46 | 20.10 | 25.82 | 29.83 | 31.28 | 27.67 | 24.90 | 25.79 | 22.24 | 19.95 | 24.08 |
| 2022[1] | 18.29 | 13.00 | 13.93 | 12.88 | 11.77 | 11.24 | 9.06 | 15.90 | 20.62 | 24.35 | 20.24 | 14.19 | 15.46 |

On-tree equivalent.  [1]Preliminary.  Source: National Agricultural Statistics Service, U.S. Department of Agriculture (NASS-USDA)

## Average Price Received by Growers for Grapes in the United States — In Dollars Per Box

| Year | Jan. | Feb. | Mar. | Apr. | May | June | July | Aug. | Sept. | Oct. | Nov. | Dec. | Average |
|---|---|---|---|---|---|---|---|---|---|---|---|---|---|
| 2013 | NQ | NQ | NQ | NQ | NQ | NQ | NQ | NQ | NQ | NQ | NQ | NQ | NQ |
| 2014 | NQ | NQ | NQ | NQ | NQ | 1,870 | 1,550 | 1,360 | 1,350 | 1,530 | 1,660 | 1,680 | 1,571 |
| 2015 | NQ | NQ | NQ | NQ | 2,330 | 1,690 | 1,340 | 1,470 | 1,490 | 1,590 | 1,810 | 2,070 | 1,724 |
| 2016 | NQ | NQ | NQ | NQ | NQ | 1,480 | 1,330 | 1,360 | 1,460 | 1,520 | 2,310 | 1,577 | |
| 2017 | NQ | NQ | NQ | NQ | NQ | NQ | 1,590 | 1,500 | 1,500 | 1,460 | 1,540 | 1,660 | 1,542 |
| 2018 | NQ | NQ | NQ | NQ | NQ | 2,550 | 1,600 | 1,310 | 1,210 | 1,080 | 1,030 | 1,140 | 1,417 |
| 2019 | NQ | NQ | NQ | NQ | NQ | 1,620 | 1,400 | 1,260 | 1,310 | 1,300 | 1,500 | 2,090 | 1,497 |
| 2020 | NQ | NQ | NQ | NQ | NQ | 2,630 | 2,280 | 2,150 | 2,040 | 2,010 | 2,020 | 2,100 | 2,176 |
| 2021 | 2,280 | NQ | NQ | NQ | NQ | 3,010 | 2,410 | 2,180 | 2,060 | 2,030 | 2,100 | 2,440 | 2,314 |
| 2022[1] | 3,290 | NQ | NQ | NQ | NQ | 3,110 | 2,470 | 2,240 | 2,280 | 2,270 | 2,270 | 2,310 | 2,530 |

Fresh.  [1]Preliminary.  NQ = No quote.  Source: National Agricultural Statistics Service, U.S. Department of Agriculture (NASS-USDA)

## Average Price Received by Growers for Peaches in the United States — In Dollars Per Box

| Year | Jan. | Feb. | Mar. | Apr. | May | June | July | Aug. | Sept. | Oct. | Nov. | Dec. | Average |
|---|---|---|---|---|---|---|---|---|---|---|---|---|---|
| 2013 | NQ | NQ | NQ | NQ | NQ | NQ | NQ | NQ | NQ | NQ | NQ | NQ | NQ |
| 2014 | NQ | NQ | NQ | NQ | NQ | 1,270 | 1,180 | 1,070 | 954 | NQ | NQ | NQ | 1,119 |
| 2015 | NQ | NQ | NQ | NQ | 1,480 | 1,110 | 937 | 1,030 | 835 | NQ | NQ | NQ | 1,078 |
| 2016 | NQ | NQ | NQ | NQ | 1,220 | 993 | 1,230 | 1,320 | 1,080 | NQ | NQ | NQ | 1,169 |
| 2017 | NQ | NQ | NQ | NQ | NQ | 1,530 | 1,710 | 1,400 | 1,310 | NQ | NQ | NQ | 1,488 |
| 2018 | NQ | NQ | NQ | NQ | NQ | 1,130 | 1,140 | 1,110 | 918 | NQ | NQ | NQ | 1,075 |
| 2019 | NQ | NQ | NQ | NQ | 1,720 | 1,180 | 1,090 | 1,150 | 941 | NQ | NQ | NQ | 1,216 |
| 2020 | NQ | NQ | NQ | NQ | 1,500 | 1,190 | 1,310 | 1,680 | 1,810 | NQ | NQ | NQ | 1,498 |
| 2021 | NQ | NQ | NQ | NQ | 1,560 | 1,270 | 1,210 | 1,220 | 1,310 | NQ | NQ | NQ | 1,314 |
| 2022[1] | NQ | NQ | NQ | NQ | 2,260 | 1,800 | 1,880 | 1,820 | 2,050 | NQ | NQ | NQ | 1,962 |

Fresh.  [1]Preliminary.  NQ = No quote.  Source: National Agricultural Statistics Service, U.S. Department of Agriculture (NASS-USDA)

# FRUITS

### Average Price Received by Growers for Pears in the United States — In Dollars Per Box

| Year | Jan. | Feb. | Mar. | Apr. | May | June | July | Aug. | Sept. | Oct. | Nov. | Dec. | Average |
|---|---|---|---|---|---|---|---|---|---|---|---|---|---|
| 2013 | 774 | 778 | 753 | NQ | NQ | NQ | NQ | NQ | NQ | NQ | NQ | NQ | 768 |
| 2014 | NQ | NQ | NQ | 592 | 686 | 893 | 695 | 531 | 631 | 696 | 692 | 702 | 680 |
| 2015 | 725 | 729 | 652 | 610 | 619 | 633 | 635 | 706 | 690 | 747 | 778 | 813 | 695 |
| 2016 | 844 | 785 | 749 | 793 | 914 | 1,050 | 810 | 810 | 816 | 829 | 787 | 756 | 829 |
| 2017 | 782 | 806 | 722 | 668 | 694 | 734 | 631 | 764 | 829 | 848 | 832 | 888 | 767 |
| 2018 | 879 | 857 | 779 | 678 | 680 | 798 | 788 | 688 | 660 | 663 | 616 | 614 | 725 |
| 2019 | 574 | 561 | 539 | 545 | 620 | 731 | 781 | 696 | 722 | 693 | 678 | 721 | 655 |
| 2020 | 733 | 1,200 | 1,170 | 1,050 | 1,040 | 1,050 | 1,340 | 1,590 | 1,390 | 1,400 | 1,340 | 1,310 | 1,218 |
| 2021 | 1,290 | 1,290 | 1,280 | 1,300 | 1,310 | 1,330 | 1,430 | 1,420 | 1,340 | 1,300 | 1,230 | 1,220 | 1,312 |
| 2022[1] | 1,230 | 1,240 | 1,230 | 1,200 | 1,200 | 1,210 | 1,450 | 1,830 | 1,700 | 1,220 | 1,260 | 1,380 | 1,346 |

Fresh. [1] Preliminary. NA = Not available. *Source: National Agricultural Statistics Service, U.S. Department of Agriculture (NASS-USDA)*

### Average Price Received by Growers for Strawberries in the United States — In Dollars Per Box

| Year | Jan. | Feb. | Mar. | Apr. | May | June | July | Aug. | Sept. | Oct. | Nov. | Dec. | Average |
|---|---|---|---|---|---|---|---|---|---|---|---|---|---|
| 2013 | 109.00 | 123.00 | 117.00 | NA | NA | NA | NA | NA | NA | NA | NA | NA | 116.33 |
| 2014 | NA | NA | NA | 87.60 | 96.10 | 91.80 | 89.30 | 92.70 | 133.00 | 112.00 | 152.00 | 209.00 | 118.17 |
| 2015 | 135.00 | 101.00 | 63.60 | 76.80 | 72.60 | 61.50 | 60.20 | 86.70 | 71.30 | 100.00 | 190.00 | 193.00 | 100.98 |
| 2016 | 195.00 | 167.00 | 81.00 | 84.30 | 68.60 | 60.50 | 59.40 | 69.40 | 50.90 | 71.00 | 167.00 | 154.00 | 102.34 |
| 2017 | 147.00 | 128.00 | 94.90 | 66.60 | 53.20 | 59.20 | 74.10 | 84.70 | 109.00 | 98.00 | 164.00 | 182.00 | 105.06 |
| 2018 | 169.00 | 125.00 | 118.00 | 105.00 | 55.30 | 52.70 | 66.60 | 50.50 | 84.00 | 67.30 | 99.00 | W | 90.22 |
| 2019 | 222.00 | 126.00 | 114.00 | 79.20 | 61.80 | 80.30 | 79.20 | 83.30 | 104.00 | 100.00 | 115.00 | W | 105.89 |
| 2020 | 264.00 | 257.00 | 189.00 | 123.00 | 107.00 | 108.00 | 199.00 | 145.00 | 171.00 | 208.00 | 231.00 | 186.00 | 182.33 |
| 2021 | 245.00 | 207.00 | 143.00 | 216.00 | 145.00 | 131.00 | 130.00 | 175.00 | 142.00 | 151.00 | 301.00 | 247.00 | 186.08 |
| 2022[1] | 231.00 | 192.00 | 125.00 | 145.00 | 129.00 | 90.60 | 124.00 | 204.00 | 149.00 | 258.00 | 349.00 | 296.00 | 191.05 |

Fresh. [1] Preliminary. NA = Not available.. *Source: National Agricultural Statistics Service, U.S. Department of Agriculture (NASS-USDA)*

### Cold Storage Stocks of Frozen Apples in the United States, on First of Month — In Thousands of Pounds

| Year | Jan. | Feb. | Mar. | Apr. | May | June | July | Aug. | Sept. | Oct. | Nov. | Dec. |
|---|---|---|---|---|---|---|---|---|---|---|---|---|
| 2013 | 56,202 | 51,297 | 48,411 | 46,119 | 42,047 | 39,547 | 34,354 | 34,202 | 31,733 | 32,414 | 37,339 | 50,486 |
| 2014 | 49,831 | 56,312 | 60,384 | 61,220 | 60,693 | 58,666 | 56,046 | 55,517 | 52,050 | 49,676 | 53,072 | 52,828 |
| 2015 | 55,400 | 55,350 | 53,314 | 52,079 | 50,761 | 49,547 | 46,985 | 42,987 | 36,586 | 31,854 | 35,761 | 38,917 |
| 2016 | 37,596 | 38,707 | 37,994 | 37,761 | 39,147 | 38,682 | 39,040 | 36,171 | 32,361 | 29,104 | 28,198 | 32,407 |
| 2017 | 34,929 | 37,963 | 36,919 | 38,679 | 44,495 | 40,049 | 37,418 | 34,995 | 34,475 | 29,471 | 26,836 | 29,408 |
| 2018 | 32,007 | 34,420 | 35,915 | 36,968 | 35,087 | 32,441 | 33,715 | 30,609 | 24,822 | 22,366 | 21,602 | 23,141 |
| 2019 | 28,276 | 31,782 | 35,345 | 35,219 | 35,149 | 28,196 | 28,122 | 26,479 | 22,539 | 20,286 | 20,326 | 21,713 |
| 2020 | 27,323 | 28,963 | 29,614 | 28,680 | 29,494 | 30,574 | 29,982 | 29,829 | 28,310 | 27,780 | 26,264 | 29,653 |
| 2021 | 33,235 | 32,850 | 30,537 | 29,992 | 25,603 | 23,500 | 26,084 | 25,158 | 21,353 | 17,710 | 19,046 | 20,453 |
| 2022[1] | 20,665 | 23,963 | 22,821 | 26,350 | 30,272 | 31,508 | 29,414 | 23,681 | 19,781 | 21,064 | 40,670 | 41,875 |

[1] Preliminary. *Source: Economic Research Service, U.S. Department of Agriculture (ERS-USDA)*

### Cold Storage Stocks of Frozen Apricots in the United States, on First of Month — In Thousands of Pounds

| Year | Jan. | Feb. | Mar. | Apr. | May | June | July | Aug. | Sept. | Oct. | Nov. | Dec. |
|---|---|---|---|---|---|---|---|---|---|---|---|---|
| 2013 | 4,018 | 3,395 | 2,340 | 1,907 | 1,452 | 1,668 | 11,874 | 7,871 | 7,204 | 6,276 | 4,639 | 4,501 |
| 2014 | 3,895 | 3,532 | 3,406 | 3,380 | 2,384 | 1,974 | 12,488 | 9,847 | 7,852 | 7,533 | 6,471 | 6,191 |
| 2015 | 5,941 | 5,246 | 4,720 | 4,162 | 4,051 | 3,390 | 11,760 | 11,058 | 10,059 | 7,931 | 6,128 | 5,640 |
| 2016 | 4,921 | 4,319 | 3,804 | 3,434 | 2,968 | 3,301 | 11,086 | 16,226 | 13,454 | 11,690 | 9,998 | 8,958 |
| 2017 | 8,456 | 6,506 | 4,103 | 3,163 | 2,848 | 2,279 | 11,696 | 11,048 | 8,512 | 7,335 | 6,098 | 5,506 |
| 2018 | 4,873 | 4,295 | 3,616 | 2,974 | 2,275 | 1,664 | 8,301 | 9,538 | 8,843 | 8,148 | 7,549 | 6,640 |
| 2019 | 6,458 | 4,762 | 4,248 | 3,432 | 2,770 | 2,082 | 3,760 | 3,819 | 3,528 | 3,237 | 6,689 | 6,054 |
| 2020 | 5,294 | 4,224 | 3,436 | 3,101 | 2,340 | 2,461 | 8,706 | 6,774 | 6,871 | 4,703 | 3,751 | 3,156 |
| 2021 | 2,602 | 2,073 | 2,278 | 1,841 | 1,830 | 1,443 | 6,381 | 10,289 | 10,314 | 9,807 | 8,991 | 7,777 |
| 2022[1] | 6,244 | 6,133 | 4,982 | 2,943 | 2,603 | 3,151 | 9,042 | 9,014 | 8,292 | 7,249 | 6,412 | 6,768 |

[1] Preliminary. *Source: Economic Research Service, U.S. Department of Agriculture (ERS-USDA)*

# FRUITS

### Cold Storage Stocks of Frozen Blackberries[2] in the United States, on First of Month    In Thousands of Pounds

| Year | Jan. | Feb. | Mar. | Apr. | May | June | July | Aug. | Sept. | Oct. | Nov. | Dec. |
|---|---|---|---|---|---|---|---|---|---|---|---|---|
| 2013 | 35,272 | 33,021 | 25,975 | 24,247 | 21,792 | 17,887 | 18,727 | 40,606 | 39,237 | 37,880 | 33,468 | 32,048 |
| 2014 | 30,066 | 28,823 | 27,183 | 22,994 | 21,110 | 21,107 | 22,053 | 42,581 | 40,339 | 37,494 | 34,756 | 32,368 |
| 2015 | 30,925 | 28,843 | 25,499 | 23,071 | 20,892 | 19,931 | 25,158 | 34,001 | 35,240 | 33,078 | 30,553 | 28,366 |
| 2016 | 26,594 | 24,457 | 23,752 | 23,008 | 20,296 | 19,131 | 36,373 | 43,885 | 43,330 | 38,711 | 36,110 | 33,134 |
| 2017 | 31,753 | 29,540 | 26,983 | 24,151 | 23,147 | 20,956 | 22,085 | 36,913 | 34,707 | 31,603 | 28,024 | 26,682 |
| 2018 | 24,449 | 21,402 | 18,205 | 16,182 | 14,751 | 12,534 | 14,481 | 38,714 | 33,447 | 32,294 | 30,098 | 27,069 |
| 2019 | 24,639 | 22,803 | 20,594 | 19,569 | 17,377 | 14,258 | 12,664 | 32,157 | 31,509 | 29,664 | 27,854 | 23,989 |
| 2020 | 21,741 | 18,410 | 16,608 | 13,943 | 14,291 | 12,998 | 14,030 | 34,685 | 33,928 | 28,560 | 23,801 | 23,249 |
| 2021 | 18,802 | 15,385 | 12,277 | 12,942 | 12,042 | 10,396 | 11,473 | 22,348 | 22,785 | 18,133 | 16,886 | 14,743 |
| 2022[1] | 14,265 | 13,502 | 11,730 | 10,976 | 10,444 | 10,772 | 11,038 | 28,752 | 31,034 | 30,863 | 28,106 | 26,116 |

[1] Preliminary.    [2] Includes IQF, Pails and Tubs, Barrels (400lbs net), and Concentrate.    Source: Economic Research Service, U.S. Department of Agriculture (ERS-USDA)

### Cold Storage Stocks of Frozen Blueberries in the United States, on First of Month    In Thousands of Pounds

| Year | Jan. | Feb. | Mar. | Apr. | May | June | July | Aug. | Sept. | Oct. | Nov. | Dec. |
|---|---|---|---|---|---|---|---|---|---|---|---|---|
| 2013 | 171,296 | 165,932 | 152,187 | 137,358 | 119,814 | 100,876 | 103,559 | 166,382 | 260,094 | 251,279 | 235,007 | 217,393 |
| 2014 | 201,834 | 172,718 | 150,626 | 130,825 | 117,065 | 98,716 | 102,012 | 171,661 | 269,537 | 265,303 | 240,830 | 229,225 |
| 2015 | 208,324 | 187,523 | 166,469 | 152,745 | 133,836 | 119,276 | 132,732 | 236,349 | 273,614 | 280,085 | 259,198 | 245,754 |
| 2016 | 224,696 | 211,459 | 191,351 | 164,927 | 154,142 | 145,414 | 157,928 | 260,675 | 315,436 | 332,379 | 308,554 | 294,135 |
| 2017 | 268,895 | 241,947 | 223,211 | 195,417 | 184,367 | 157,140 | 147,915 | 197,723 | 276,632 | 266,423 | 256,727 | 230,843 |
| 2018 | 222,060 | 192,354 | 162,564 | 134,469 | 116,387 | 96,891 | 99,912 | 175,163 | 244,902 | 247,396 | 228,308 | 199,883 |
| 2019 | 182,857 | 178,750 | 148,696 | 129,739 | 112,147 | 92,992 | 93,422 | 174,711 | 280,464 | 290,020 | 278,570 | 262,652 |
| 2020 | 246,625 | 240,304 | 215,903 | 196,198 | 175,610 | 166,842 | 176,415 | 233,701 | 319,296 | 316,717 | 291,261 | 261,142 |
| 2021 | 237,064 | 209,994 | 188,111 | 148,965 | 119,167 | 102,080 | 104,582 | 208,514 | 285,462 | 276,908 | 259,259 | 233,268 |
| 2022[1] | 218,041 | 192,947 | 173,490 | 153,110 | 130,925 | 116,790 | 117,312 | 154,556 | 271,598 | 280,833 | 258,650 | 243,187 |

[1] Preliminary.    Source: Economic Research Service, U.S. Department of Agriculture (ERS-USDA)

### Cold Storage Stocks of Frozen Cherries[2] in the United States, on First of Month    In Thousands of Pounds

| Year | Jan. | Feb. | Mar. | Apr. | May | June | July | Aug. | Sept. | Oct. | Nov. | Dec. |
|---|---|---|---|---|---|---|---|---|---|---|---|---|
| 2013 | 51,161 | 44,651 | 38,315 | 33,746 | 26,644 | 19,127 | 14,227 | 114,938 | 150,224 | 139,064 | 128,171 | 114,676 |
| 2014 | 112,101 | 99,639 | 91,631 | 82,926 | 71,746 | 58,869 | 50,181 | 103,362 | 178,542 | 164,429 | 153,521 | 144,280 |
| 2015 | 134,908 | 129,319 | 120,870 | 105,707 | 98,519 | 85,866 | 79,028 | 146,251 | 158,170 | 159,154 | 141,734 | 132,880 |
| 2016 | 123,378 | 113,844 | 102,584 | 91,204 | 81,431 | 72,293 | 63,925 | 173,739 | 196,001 | 184,839 | 174,878 | 156,973 |
| 2017 | 142,913 | 131,911 | 121,549 | 111,923 | 102,192 | 93,736 | 83,809 | 155,363 | 166,554 | 158,660 | 154,858 | 142,281 |
| 2018 | 134,946 | 125,530 | 115,381 | 108,226 | 98,931 | 88,879 | 74,151 | 167,724 | 184,463 | 169,664 | 156,443 | 145,503 |
| 2019 | 141,203 | 126,955 | 120,147 | 114,474 | 111,041 | 94,508 | 84,115 | 117,089 | 162,132 | 152,361 | 145,276 | 139,349 |
| 2020 | 128,711 | 118,983 | 105,679 | 102,965 | 93,006 | 85,708 | 77,292 | 108,801 | 112,451 | 107,092 | 100,699 | 93,002 |
| 2021 | 82,348 | 77,159 | 68,157 | 62,644 | 50,294 | 40,469 | 34,438 | 97,760 | 92,257 | 85,863 | 77,715 | 76,808 |
| 2022[1] | 66,106 | 58,781 | 51,912 | 46,866 | 41,922 | 36,972 | 29,130 | 96,930 | 107,985 | 99,267 | 88,179 | 82,424 |

[1] Preliminary.    [2] Tart (ripe tart pitted).    Source: Economic Research Service, U.S. Department of Agriculture (ERS-USDA)

### Cold Storage Stocks of Frozen Peaches in the United States, on First of Month    In Thousands of Pounds

| Year | Jan. | Feb. | Mar. | Apr. | May | June | July | Aug. | Sept. | Oct. | Nov. | Dec. |
|---|---|---|---|---|---|---|---|---|---|---|---|---|
| 2013 | 50,717 | 45,535 | 40,062 | 33,489 | 28,880 | 22,290 | 19,137 | 36,193 | 59,642 | 72,610 | 73,147 | 65,548 |
| 2014 | 61,092 | 53,367 | 47,862 | 39,621 | 32,936 | 25,714 | 19,497 | 34,001 | 54,810 | 63,033 | 57,543 | 52,384 |
| 2015 | 47,465 | 44,353 | 38,646 | 35,803 | 30,722 | 27,566 | 26,877 | 41,488 | 63,360 | 78,572 | 75,817 | 75,253 |
| 2016 | 74,308 | 68,463 | 62,266 | 54,489 | 52,746 | 49,601 | 48,346 | 62,290 | 83,003 | 93,794 | 91,530 | 88,731 |
| 2017 | 81,881 | 74,285 | 69,924 | 64,477 | 58,878 | 53,696 | 53,066 | 62,003 | 83,564 | 87,901 | 85,238 | 84,813 |
| 2018 | 76,686 | 68,986 | 60,036 | 54,899 | 46,756 | 40,717 | 35,517 | 37,622 | 47,951 | 69,188 | 69,577 | 64,956 |
| 2019 | 62,532 | 58,556 | 54,491 | 52,611 | 43,830 | 41,729 | 38,043 | 39,840 | 47,955 | 65,860 | 66,485 | 57,342 |
| 2020 | 52,109 | 45,926 | 43,092 | 38,683 | 33,640 | 32,659 | 28,069 | 35,796 | 48,826 | 52,050 | 47,520 | 43,389 |
| 2021 | 39,210 | 29,907 | 28,627 | 23,547 | 19,724 | 17,035 | 16,723 | 24,463 | 38,672 | 56,519 | 57,220 | 52,804 |
| 2022[1] | 49,403 | 44,159 | 38,984 | 35,308 | 32,763 | 28,322 | 24,391 | 28,957 | 37,567 | 43,200 | 46,194 | 43,028 |

[1] Preliminary.    Source: Economic Research Service, U.S. Department of Agriculture (ERS-USDA)

# FRUITS

### Cold Storage Stocks of Frozen Raspberries[2] in the United States, on First of Month  In Thousands of Pounds

| Year | Jan. | Feb. | Mar. | Apr. | May | June | July | Aug. | Sept. | Oct. | Nov. | Dec. |
|---|---|---|---|---|---|---|---|---|---|---|---|---|
| 2013 | 716 | 619 | 543 | 421 | 320 | 354 | 763 | 1,518 | 1,395 | 1,121 | 1,050 | 985 |
| 2014 | 852 | 710 | 677 | 620 | 592 | 462 | 1,442 | 2,027 | 1,401 | 1,381 | 1,353 | 1,245 |
| 2015 | 1,145 | 1,089 | 969 | 944 | 924 | 867 | 2,152 | 2,555 | 1,828 | 1,655 | 1,625 | 1,444 |
| 2016 | 1,356 | 1,303 | 1,227 | 1,131 | 1,122 | 1,065 | 3,149 | 2,381 | 1,625 | 1,633 | 1,455 | 1,340 |
| 2017 | 1,281 | 1,047 | 960 | 1,012 | 1,021 | 870 | 911 | 2,015 | 1,995 | 1,905 | 1,584 | 1,590 |
| 2018 | 1,498 | 1,756 | 1,677 | 1,703 | 1,423 | 1,306 | 2,081 | 2,718 | 1,992 | 1,796 | 1,625 | 1,513 |
| 2019 | 1,467 | 1,170 | 1,088 | 904 | 793 | 822 | 998 | 1,694 | 1,430 | 1,437 | 1,362 | 1,164 |
| 2020 | 890 | 707 | 637 | 828 | 843 | 721 | 991 | 1,245 | 1,507 | 1,449 | 1,482 | 1,541 |
| 2021 | 1,018 | 977 | 1,076 | 863 | 712 | 595 | 997 | 1,488 | 1,181 | 1,062 | 845 | 774 |
| 2022[1] | 634 | 670 | 653 | 422 | 367 | 332 | 263 | 1,173 | 855 | 756 | 903 | 695 |

[1] Preliminary.  [2] Red: Includes IQF, Pails and Tubs, Barrels (400 lbs net), and Concentrate.  Source: Economic Research Service, U.S. Department of Agriculture (ERS-USDA)

### Cold Storage Stocks of Frozen Strawberries[2] in the United States, on First of Month  In Thousands of Pounds

| Year | Jan. | Feb. | Mar. | Apr. | May | June | July | Aug. | Sept. | Oct. | Nov. | Dec. |
|---|---|---|---|---|---|---|---|---|---|---|---|---|
| 2013 | 302,987 | 265,250 | 240,083 | 218,149 | 334,359 | 397,352 | 421,128 | 463,698 | 428,160 | 392,032 | 345,152 | 320,036 |
| 2014 | 279,977 | 240,382 | 215,168 | 211,064 | 233,147 | 257,783 | 357,526 | 362,127 | 330,666 | 294,969 | 270,553 | 236,828 |
| 2015 | 206,841 | 175,520 | 163,599 | 186,817 | 199,290 | 238,106 | 341,295 | 360,045 | 328,775 | 314,350 | 278,860 | 253,146 |
| 2016 | 235,852 | 208,274 | 190,132 | 203,784 | 225,525 | 264,440 | 390,681 | 396,716 | 377,156 | 376,035 | 367,939 | 331,389 |
| 2017 | 304,827 | 289,622 | 274,147 | 255,978 | 266,206 | 312,244 | 357,628 | 411,241 | 402,915 | 363,542 | 333,050 | 309,351 |
| 2018 | 281,076 | 253,019 | 216,083 | 195,880 | 186,979 | 249,528 | 377,233 | 373,196 | 350,619 | 328,177 | 286,210 | 253,178 |
| 2019 | 227,433 | 193,851 | 172,444 | 157,833 | 182,594 | 228,838 | 269,490 | 277,960 | 275,315 | 250,277 | 211,085 | 188,847 |
| 2020 | 157,388 | 129,425 | 115,173 | 127,571 | 159,405 | 231,699 | 265,090 | 268,538 | 263,164 | 216,688 | 186,749 | 157,224 |
| 2021 | 150,715 | 136,961 | 132,102 | 125,174 | 125,115 | 193,297 | 261,584 | 305,177 | 283,250 | 249,126 | 231,367 | 205,936 |
| 2022[1] | 195,102 | 175,389 | 161,781 | 154,239 | 181,596 | 236,226 | 316,675 | 321,727 | 292,450 | 269,496 | 249,652 | 230,173 |

[1] Preliminary.  [2] Includes IQF and Poly, Pails and Tubs, Barrels and Drums, and Juice Stock.  Source: Economic Research Service, U.S. Department of Agriculture (ERS-USDA)

### Cold Storage Stocks of Other Frozen Fruit in the United States, on First of Month  In Thousands of Pounds

| Year | Jan. | Feb. | Mar. | Apr. | May | June | July | Aug. | Sept. | Oct. | Nov. | Dec. |
|---|---|---|---|---|---|---|---|---|---|---|---|---|
| 2013 | 493,200 | 444,506 | 417,678 | 382,611 | 355,428 | 316,247 | 284,810 | 277,685 | 238,619 | 224,171 | 470,098 | 589,226 |
| 2014 | 575,025 | 528,790 | 475,527 | 440,532 | 389,071 | 341,283 | 305,249 | 286,727 | 264,490 | 293,231 | 542,534 | 576,843 |
| 2015 | 535,775 | 482,436 | 434,463 | 385,477 | 348,811 | 321,532 | 297,358 | 309,251 | 309,356 | 377,612 | 659,912 | 665,020 |
| 2016 | 587,967 | 603,399 | 557,741 | 521,065 | 525,633 | 489,438 | 473,450 | 483,812 | 464,629 | 514,081 | 853,189 | 872,413 |
| 2017 | 808,397 | 764,821 | 738,926 | 665,196 | 604,047 | 543,809 | 491,595 | 502,270 | 493,106 | 515,569 | 700,422 | 709,259 |
| 2018 | 666,624 | 595,561 | 554,544 | 487,759 | 462,212 | 399,596 | 404,649 | 395,232 | 361,493 | 398,684 | 741,609 | 710,973 |
| 2019 | 654,518 | 598,220 | 547,960 | 501,052 | 457,599 | 399,196 | 357,543 | 335,751 | 318,388 | 332,966 | 668,223 | 645,653 |
| 2020 | 592,537 | 514,997 | 447,440 | 401,446 | 371,327 | 324,116 | 284,967 | 250,533 | 259,942 | 326,544 | 538,236 | 506,235 |
| 2021 | 445,109 | 399,775 | 372,138 | 345,953 | 316,800 | 281,912 | 267,014 | 263,298 | 260,666 | 311,788 | 418,656 | 378,251 |
| 2022[1] | 368,941 | 358,995 | 330,581 | 294,262 | 303,704 | 293,366 | 264,477 | 260,490 | 247,895 | 331,564 | 434,112 | 522,739 |

[1] Preliminary.  Source: Economic Research Service, U.S. Department of Agriculture (ERS-USDA)

### Cold Storage Stocks of Total Frozen Fruit in the United States, on First of Month  In Millions of Pounds

| Year | Jan. | Feb. | Mar. | Apr. | May | June | July | Aug. | Sept. | Oct. | Nov. | Dec. |
|---|---|---|---|---|---|---|---|---|---|---|---|---|
| 2013 | 1,246.6 | 1,123.5 | 1,030.1 | 934.9 | 985.0 | 962.6 | 954.1 | 1,251.3 | 1,335.0 | 1,270.0 | 1,431.1 | 1,489.0 |
| 2014 | 1,405.6 | 1,261.1 | 1,140.4 | 1,052.0 | 981.1 | 912.1 | 972.2 | 1,176.0 | 1,317.9 | 1,286.1 | 1,461.4 | 1,426.8 |
| 2015 | 1,315.4 | 1,191.8 | 1,084.2 | 1,016.4 | 949.2 | 921.6 | 1,028.1 | 1,294.3 | 1,322.6 | 1,385.6 | 1,580.9 | 1,535.4 |
| 2016 | 1,398.6 | 1,349.4 | 1,240.4 | 1,165.4 | 1,163.7 | 1,141.0 | 1,309.2 | 1,611.2 | 1,658.5 | 1,707.9 | 1,993.9 | 1,934.0 |
| 2017 | 1,788.9 | 1,673.4 | 1,585.8 | 1,439.9 | 1,360.5 | 1,291.0 | 1,262.8 | 1,530.3 | 1,633.1 | 1,585.8 | 1,707.8 | 1,650.3 |
| 2018 | 1,547.8 | 1,390.3 | 1,256.2 | 1,119.0 | 1,041.0 | 992.9 | 1,117.5 | 1,379.1 | 1,417.4 | 1,425.1 | 1,677.2 | 1,556.3 |
| 2019 | 1,449.4 | 1,320.6 | 1,195.1 | 1,095.5 | 1,039.6 | 974.6 | 953.7 | 1,128.3 | 1,267.9 | 1,266.4 | 1,535.3 | 1,446.4 |
| 2020 | 1,325.1 | 1,183.9 | 1,046.0 | 973.1 | 935.1 | 938.6 | 933.0 | 1,079.0 | 1,194.9 | 1,189.5 | 1,315.0 | 1,216.9 |
| 2021 | 1,091.8 | 976.3 | 900.6 | 809.0 | 726.5 | 719.6 | 777.8 | 1,059.5 | 1,118.6 | 1,117.9 | 1,176.5 | 1,072.3 |
| 2022[1] | 1,017.8 | 945.0 | 862.4 | 784.6 | 789.8 | 805.2 | 848.2 | 1,039.7 | 1,139.9 | 1,209.4 | 1,267.2 | 1,302.1 |

[1] Preliminary.  Source: Economic Research Service, U.S. Department of Agriculture (ERS-USDA)

# Gas

Natural gas is a fossil fuel that is colorless, shapeless, and odorless in its pure form. It is a mixture of hydrocarbon gases formed primarily of methane, but it can also include ethane, propane, butane, and pentane. Natural gas is combustible, clean-burning, and gives off a great deal of energy. Around 500 BC, the Chinese discovered that the energy in natural gas could be harnessed. They passed it through crude bamboo-shoot pipes and then burned it to boil sea water to create potable fresh water. Around 1785, Britain became the first country to commercially use natural gas produced from coal for streetlights and indoor lights. In 1821, William Hart dug the first well specifically intended to obtain natural gas, and he is generally regarded as the "father of natural gas" in America. There is a vast amount of natural gas estimated to still be in the ground in the U.S. Natural gas as a source of energy is significantly less expensive than electricity per Btu.

Natural gas futures and options are traded at the CME Group. The CME natural gas futures contract calls for the delivery of natural gas representing 10,000 million British thermal units (mmBtu) at the Henry Hub in Louisiana, which is the nexus of 16 intra-state and inter-state pipelines. The contract is priced in terms of U.S. Dollars per mmBtu. CME also has basic swap futures contracts available for 30 different natural gas pricing locations versus the benchmark Henry Hub location. Natural gas futures are also traded at ICE Futures Europe.

**Prices** – CME natural gas futures (Barchart.com symbol code NG) on the nearest-futures chart closed 2022 up by +20.0% at 4.475 per mmBtu.

**Supply** – U.S. recovery of natural gas in 2020 fell by -0.4% to 40.613 trillion cubic feet. The top U.S. producing states for natural gas in 2020 were Texas with 25.8% of U.S. production, Pennsylvania with 19.7%, Louisiana with 8.9%, Oklahoma with 7.7%, Colorado with 5.5%, New Mexico with 5.4, and Wyoming with 3.6%. In 2019 the world's largest natural gas producers were the U.S. with 3,003,354 Terajoules and Russia with 2,051,081 Terajoules of production.

**Demand** – U.S. total delivered consumption of natural gas in 2020 fell by -2.2% yr/yr to 27.660 trillion cubic feet, of which about 42.0% was delivered to electrical utility plants, 29.5% to industrial establishments, 16.9% to residences, and 11.5% to commercial establishments.

**Trade** – U.S. imports of natural gas (consumed) in 2017 rose by +1.2% yr/yr to 3,042 billion cubic feet, down from the 2007 record high of 4,608 billion cubic feet. U.S. exports of natural gas in 2017 rose by +35.6% yr/yr to 3,168 billion cubic feet for a new record high.

### World Dry Natural Gas Production   In Billion Cubic Feet

| Year | Algeria | Canada | China | Indonesia | Iran | Nether-lands | Norway | Qatar | Russia | Saudi Arabia | United States | Uzbek-istan | World Total |
|---|---|---|---|---|---|---|---|---|---|---|---|---|---|
| 2006 | 3,079 | 6,548 | 2,067 | 2,199 | 3,836 | 2,732 | 3,094 | 1,790 | 21,736 | 2,594 | 18,504 | 2,216 | 101,621 |
| 2007 | 2,996 | 6,416 | 2,446 | 2,422 | 3,952 | 2,687 | 3,168 | 2,232 | 21,595 | 2,628 | 19,266 | 2,302 | 104,141 |
| 2008 | 3,055 | 6,046 | 2,685 | 2,472 | 4,107 | 2,957 | 3,503 | 2,719 | 21,515 | 2,841 | 20,159 | 2,387 | 107,858 |
| 2009 | 2,876 | 5,634 | 2,975 | 2,557 | 4,986 | 2,786 | 3,664 | 3,154 | 18,890 | 2,770 | 20,624 | 2,169 | 105,418 |
| 2010 | 2,988 | 5,390 | 3,334 | 2,917 | 5,161 | 3,131 | 3,756 | 4,121 | 20,915 | 2,969 | 21,316 | 2,123 | 112,438 |
| 2011 | 2,923 | 5,218 | 3,629 | 2,693 | 5,361 | 2,851 | 3,576 | 5,130 | 22,202 | 3,127 | 22,902 | 2,226 | 116,690 |
| 2012 | 3,053 | 5,070 | 3,666 | 2,619 | 5,640 | 2,843 | 4,052 | 5,546 | 21,764 | 3,439 | 24,033 | 2,222 | 119,302 |
| 2013 | 2,813 | 5,129 | 3,986 | 2,606 | 5,696 | 3,053 | 3,841 | 5,800 | 22,139 | 3,462 | 24,334 | 2,106 | 120,879 |
| 2014[1] | 2,942 | 5,349 | 4,360 | 2,594 | 6,162 | 2,482 | 3,843 | 5,650 | 21,225 | 3,547 | 25,890 | 2,180 | 122,305 |
| 2015[2] | 2,933 | 5,295 | 4,487 | 2,571 | 6,526 | 1,935 | 4,139 | 5,794 | 21,141 | 3,614 | 27,059 | 1,967 | 124,090 |

[1] Preliminary.   [2] Estimate.   Source: Energy Information Administration, U.S. Department of Energy (EIA-DOE)

### Marketed Production of Natural Gas in the United States, by States   In Million Cubic Feet

| Year | Alaska | Arkansas | California | Colorado | Kansas | Louisiana | New Mexico | Oklahoma | Pennsyl-vania | Texas | Wyoming | Total |
|---|---|---|---|---|---|---|---|---|---|---|---|---|
| 2013 | 338,182 | 1,139,654 | 252,310 | 1,604,860 | 292,467 | 2,360,202 | 1,171,640 | 1,993,754 | 3,259,042 | 7,633,618 | 1,858,207 | 25,562,232 |
| 2014 | 345,310 | 1,122,733 | 238,988 | 1,643,487 | 286,480 | 1,960,813 | 1,229,519 | 2,331,086 | 4,257,693 | 7,985,019 | 1,794,413 | 27,497,754 |
| 2015 | 343,625 | 1,010,382 | 236,648 | 1,688,733 | 284,184 | 1,805,197 | 1,245,145 | 2,499,599 | 4,812,983 | 7,890,459 | 1,808,519 | 28,772,044 |
| 2016 | 332,749 | 823,196 | 205,025 | 1,685,755 | 244,795 | 1,784,396 | 1,229,647 | 2,468,312 | 5,210,209 | 7,225,472 | 1,662,909 | 28,400,049 |
| 2017 | 344,385 | 694,676 | 212,458 | 1,706,364 | 219,639 | 2,139,830 | 1,299,732 | 2,513,897 | 5,453,638 | 7,223,841 | 1,590,059 | 29,237,825 |
| 2018 | 341,315 | 589,985 | 202,617 | 1,847,402 | 201,391 | 2,832,404 | 1,493,082 | 2,875,787 | 6,264,832 | 8,041,010 | 1,637,517 | 33,008,867 |
| 2019 | 329,361 | 524,757 | 196,823 | 1,986,916 | 183,087 | 3,212,318 | 1,769,086 | 3,036,052 | 6,896,792 | 9,378,489 | 1,488,854 | 36,446,918 |
| 2020 | 338,329 | 480,982 | 170,579 | 1,990,462 | 163,356 | 3,206,163 | 1,948,168 | 2,786,366 | 7,148,295 | 9,336,110 | 1,306,368 | 36,202,446 |
| 2021 | 354,660 | 448,187 | 140,604 | 1,879,457 | 152,986 | 3,431,429 | 2,237,706 | 2,571,834 | 7,626,504 | 9,875,390 | 1,109,232 | 37,328,378 |
| 2022[1] | 373,141 | 426,976 | 133,826 | 1,819,437 | 144,899 | 4,019,440 | 2,679,427 | 2,744,688 | 7,483,256 | 10,475,873 | 991,853 | 38,930,383 |

[1] Preliminary.   Source: Energy Information Administration, U.S. Department of Energy (EIA-DOE)

# GAS

## World Production of Natural Gas Plant Liquids    Thousand Barrels per Day

| Year | Algeria | Canada | Mexico | Saudi Arabia | Russia | United States | Persian Gulf[2] | OAPEC[3] | OPEC-12[4] | OPEC-11[4] | World |
|---|---|---|---|---|---|---|---|---|---|---|---|
| 2006 | 270 | 685 | 338 | 472 | 1,860 | 1,739 | 2,722 | 2,554 | 3,292 | 3,270 | 8,178 |
| 2007 | 260 | 726 | 328 | 486 | 1,940 | 1,783 | 2,813 | 2,582 | 3,407 | 3,383 | 8,394 |
| 2008 | 250 | 677 | 318 | 500 | 2,080 | 1,784 | 2,985 | 2,592 | 3,550 | 3,540 | 8,514 |
| 2009 | 325 | 640 | 326 | 539 | 1,980 | 1,910 | 2,922 | 2,744 | 3,562 | 3,552 | 8,641 |
| 2010 | 340 | 597 | 332 | 574 | 1,920 | 2,074 | 2,935 | 2,972 | 3,592 | 3,582 | 8,901 |
| 2011 | 322 | 591 | 334 | 611 | 1,920 | 2,216 | 3,102 | 2,958 | 3,637 | 3,627 | 9,130 |
| 2012 | 342 | 611 | 318 | 647 | 1,920 | 2,408 | 3,152 | 3,164 | 3,786 | 3,776 | 9,502 |
| 2013 | 300 | 639 | 320 | 684 | 1,920 | 2,606 | 3,141 |  | 3,685 | 3,673 | 9,636 |
| 2014[1] | 300 | 665 | 320 | 720 | 1,800 | 2,964 | 3,117 |  | 3,644 | 3,629 | 10,013 |

Average.   [1] Preliminary.   [2] Bahrain, Iran, Iraq, Kuwait, Qatar, Saudi Arabia, and the United Arab Emirates.   [3] Organization of Arab Petroleum Exporting Countries: Algeria, Iraq, Kuwait, Libya, Qatar, Saudi Arabia, and the United Arab Emirates.   [4] OPEC-12: Organization of the Petroleum Exporting Countries: Algeria, Angola, Indonesia, Iran, Iraq, Kuwait, Libya, Nigeria, Qatar, Saudi Arabia, the United Arab Emirates, and Venezuela. OPEC-11 does not include Angola.   Source: Energy Information Administration, U.S. Department of Energy (EIA-DOE)

## Recoverable Reserves and Deliveries of Natural Gas in the United States    In Billions of Cubic Feet

| Year | Gross Withdrawals | Recoverable Reserves of Natural Gas Dec. 31[2] | Residential | Commercial | Electric Utility Plants[3] | Industrial | Total | Lease & Plant Fuel | Used as Pipline Fuel | Heating Value BTU per Cubic Foot |
|---|---|---|---|---|---|---|---|---|---|---|
| 2014 | 31,405 | 368,704 | 5,087 | 3,466 | 8,146 | 7,646 | 24,381 | 1,512 | 700 | 1,032 |
| 2015 | 32,915 | 307,730 | 4,613 | 3,202 | 9,613 | 7,522 | 24,989 | 1,576 | 678 | 1,037 |
| 2016 | 32,592 | 322,234 | 4,347 | 3,110 | 9,985 | 7,729 | 25,212 | 1,545 | 687 | 1,037 |
| 2017 | 33,292 | 438,460 | 4,413 | 3,165 | 9,266 | 7,943 | 24,835 | 1,583 | 722 | 1,036 |
| 2018 | 37,326 | 474,821 | 4,998 | 3,514 | 10,589 | 8,417 | 27,568 | 1,694 | 877 | 1,036 |
| 2019 | 40,780 | 465,405 | 5,019 | 3,515 | 11,288 | 8,417 | 28,291 | 1,823 | 1,018 | 1,038 |
| 2020 | 40,614 | 445,299 | 4,674 | 3,170 | 11,616 | 8,151 | 27,660 | 1,805 | 1,007 | 1,037 |
| 2021 | 41,666 | 589,236 | 4,716 | 3,298 | 11,271 | 8,295 | 27,634 | 1,901 | 1,130 | 1,037 |
| 2022[1] | 43,370 |  | 4,990 | 3,525 | 12,118 | 8,455 | 29,140 | 1,983 | 1,190 | 1,036 |

[1] Preliminary.   [2] Estimated proved recoverable reserves of dry natural gas.   [3] Figures include gas other than natural (impossible to segregate); therefore, shown separately from other consumption.   Source: Energy Information Administration, U.S. Department of Energy (EIA-DOE)

## Salient Statistics of Natural Gas in the United States

| Year | Marketed Production | Extraction Loss | Dry Production | Storage Withdrawals | Imports (Consumed) | Total Supply | Consumption | Exports | Added to Storage | Total Disposition | Wellhead Price | Imports | Exports | Residential | Commercial | Industrial | Electric Utilities |
|---|---|---|---|---|---|---|---|---|---|---|---|---|---|---|---|---|---|
| | In Billions of Cubic Feet | | | | | | | | | | Dollars Per Thousand Cubic Feet | | | | | | |
| 2014 | 27,498 | 1,608 | 25,890 | 3,586 | 2,695 | 33,779 | 26,593 | 1,514 | 3,839 | 31,946 | ---- | 5.30 | 5.51 | 10.97 | 8.90 | 5.62 | 5.19 |
| 2015 | 28,772 | 1,707 | 27,065 | 3,100 | 2,718 | 34,590 | 27,244 | 1,784 | 3,638 | 32,666 | ---- | 2.99 | 3.07 | 10.38 | 7.91 | 3.93 | 3.38 |
| 2016 | 28,400 | 1,808 | 26,592 | 3,325 | 3,006 | 34,731 | 27,444 | 2,335 | 2,977 | 32,756 | ---- | 2.24 | 2.79 | 10.05 | 7.28 | 3.51 | 2.99 |
| 2017 | 29,204 | 1,897 | 27,306 | 3,590 | 3,033 | 35,827 | 27,146 | 3,154 | 3,337 | 33,636 | ---- | 2.60 | 3.54 | 10.91 | 7.88 | 4.08 | 3.51 |
| 2018 | 33,009 | 2,235 | 30,774 | 3,999 | 2,889 | 39,897 | 30,149 | 3,608 | 3,676 | 37,433 | ---- | 2.69 | 3.89 | 10.50 | 7.79 | 4.19 | 3.68 |
| 2019 | 36,447 | 2,548 | 33,899 | 3,653 | 2,742 | 42,841 | 31,143 | 4,658 | 4,153 | 39,953 | ---- | 2.55 | 3.64 | 10.51 | 7.61 | 3.90 | 2.99 |
| 2020 | 36,202 | 2,710 | 33,493 | 3,412 | 2,551 | 42,166 | 30,513 | 5,285 | 3,590 | 39,388 | ---- | 2.07 | 3.70 | 10.78 | 7.49 | 3.32 | 2.49 |
| 2021[1] | 37,328 | 2,811 | 34,518 | 3,761 | 2,808 | 43,897 | 30,625 | 6,653 | 3,678 | 40,955 | ---- | | | 12.18 | 8.79 | 5.50 | 5.17 |
| 2022[2] | 38,924 | 3,120 | 35,804 | 4,172 | 3,023 | 46,119 | 32,318 | 6,892 | 3,897 | 43,108 | ---- | | | 14.80 | 11.34 | 7.90 | 7.52 |

[1] Preliminary.   [2] Estimate.   Source: Energy Information Administration, U.S. Department of Energy (EIA-DOE)

## Average Price of Natural Gas at Henry Hub    In Dollars Per MMBtu

| Year | Jan. | Feb. | Mar. | Apr. | May | June | July | Aug. | Sept. | Oct. | Nov. | Dec. | Average |
|---|---|---|---|---|---|---|---|---|---|---|---|---|---|
| 2013 | 3.33 | 3.33 | 3.81 | 4.17 | 4.04 | 3.83 | 3.62 | 3.43 | 3.62 | 3.68 | 3.64 | 4.24 | 3.73 |
| 2014 | 4.71 | 6.00 | 4.90 | 4.66 | 4.58 | 4.59 | 4.05 | 3.91 | 3.92 | 3.78 | 4.12 | 3.48 | 4.39 |
| 2015 | 3.00 | 2.88 | 2.83 | 2.61 | 2.85 | 2.78 | 2.84 | 2.77 | 2.66 | 2.34 | 2.09 | 1.94 | 2.63 |
| 2016 | 2.29 | 1.98 | 1.73 | 1.92 | 1.93 | 2.59 | 2.82 | 2.82 | 3.00 | 2.98 | 2.54 | 3.59 | 2.52 |
| 2017 | 3.28 | 2.86 | 2.88 | 3.11 | 3.15 | 2.98 | 2.98 | 2.90 | 2.98 | 2.88 | 3.01 | 2.82 | 2.99 |
| 2018 | 3.91 | 2.67 | 2.69 | 2.80 | 2.80 | 2.96 | 2.83 | 2.96 | 3.00 | 3.26 | 4.12 | 3.97 | 3.16 |
| 2019 | 3.11 | 2.69 | 2.89 | 2.65 | 2.64 | 2.40 | 2.36 | 2.22 | 2.56 | 2.33 | 2.65 | 2.22 | 2.56 |
| 2020 | 2.02 | 1.90 | 1.79 | 1.77 | 1.75 | 1.65 | 1.76 | 2.30 | 1.92 | 2.39 | 2.61 | 2.58 | 2.04 |
| 2021 | 2.71 | 5.35 | 2.62 | 2.66 | 2.91 | 3.26 | 3.84 | 4.07 | 5.16 | 5.51 | 5.05 | 3.79 | 3.91 |
| 2022 | 4.38 | 4.69 | 4.90 | 6.60 | 8.15 | 7.70 | 7.29 | 8.81 | 7.88 | 5.69 | 5.45 | 5.53 | 6.42 |

Source: Energy Information Administration, U.S. Department of Energy (EIA-DOE)

# GAS

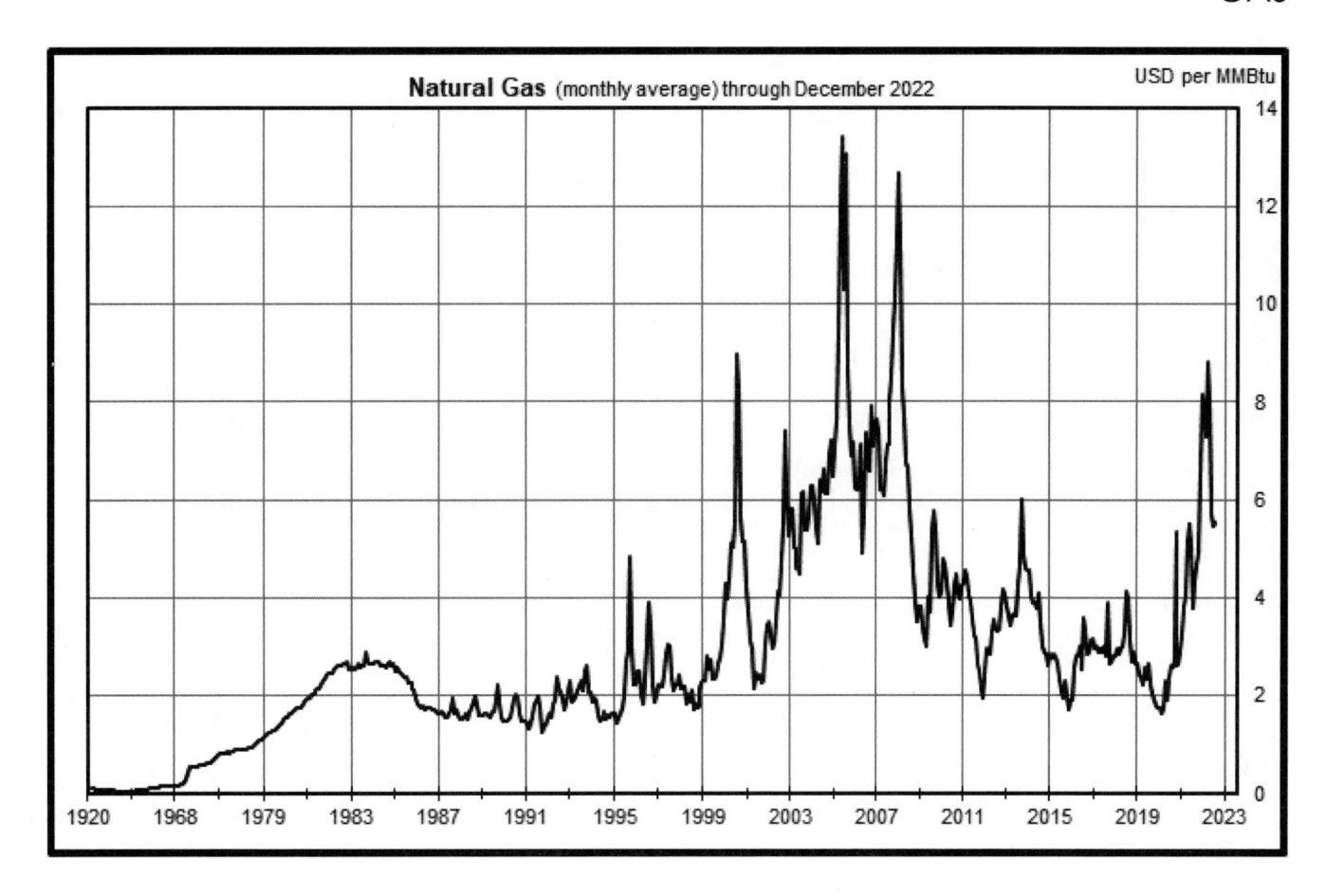

**Natural Gas** (monthly average) through December 2022 — USD per MMBtu

**Volume of Trading of Natural Gas Futures in New York**   In Thousands of Contracts

| Year | Jan. | Feb. | Mar. | Apr. | May | June | July | Aug. | Sept. | Oct. | Nov. | Dec. | Total |
|---|---|---|---|---|---|---|---|---|---|---|---|---|---|
| 2013 | 7,329.4 | 6,910.3 | 8,343.9 | 9,484.9 | 6,796.2 | 6,271.5 | 5,626.2 | 6,944.2 | 5,741.2 | 6,991.3 | 5,618.2 | 8,225.0 | 84,282.5 |
| 2014 | 8,872.0 | 8,301.5 | 4,804.4 | 5,114.8 | 5,031.3 | 5,425.1 | 5,022.7 | 5,374.9 | 5,623.7 | 6,087.8 | 7,980.1 | 6,568.4 | 74,206.6 |
| 2015 | 7,617.0 | 7,014.7 | 6,255.0 | 6,141.5 | 6,663.2 | 7,705.9 | 6,403.9 | 6,458.0 | 5,714.9 | 7,578.3 | 6,236.2 | 7,984.0 | 81,772.5 |
| 2016 | 6,472.9 | 7,003.9 | 7,649.5 | 8,350.1 | 7,090.1 | 8,875.2 | 6,769.1 | 8,506.9 | 7,646.7 | 10,240.1 | 9,073.3 | 9,802.9 | 97,480.6 |
| 2017 | 8,858.6 | 8,635.1 | 9,138.2 | 7,911.2 | 9,389.8 | 9,195.0 | 7,515.3 | 8,159.4 | 8,498.8 | 10,583.3 | 10,006.5 | 10,500.6 | 108,391.8 |
| 2018 | 14,188.6 | 8,454.1 | 7,287.5 | 8,409.2 | 8,241.5 | 8,010.4 | 7,091.6 | 8,462.0 | 9,776.6 | 12,263.9 | 14,219.3 | 7,851.3 | 114,256.1 |
| 2019 | 9,169.8 | 7,329.3 | 6,074.7 | 6,944.0 | 7,049.8 | 8,344.2 | 9,037.2 | 9,283.3 | 9,893.5 | 10,971.2 | 9,960.5 | 9,337.3 | 103,394.5 |
| 2020 | 11,404.6 | 12,025.5 | 12,118.2 | 11,076.8 | 9,852.9 | 9,631.0 | 8,484.7 | 9,607.2 | 9,345.8 | 9,313.3 | 8,484.7 | 9,454.9 | 120,799.5 |
| 2021 | 7,930.8 | 10,928.2 | 6,723.9 | 6,860.4 | 6,018.5 | 9,016.1 | 7,187.7 | 8,269.1 | 10,407.5 | 9,021.2 | 7,555.3 | 7,670.1 | 97,588.8 |
| 2022 | 8,112.7 | 8,646.7 | 7,002.2 | 8,928.4 | 6,647.4 | 8,045.0 | 5,825.1 | 5,827.7 | 6,109.8 | 6,409.6 | 6,955.9 | 7,340.9 | 85,851.4 |

Contract size = 10,000 MMBtu.   Source: CME Group; New York Mercantile Exchange (NYMEX)

**Average Open Interest of Natural Gas Futures in New York**   In Thousands of Contracts

| Year | Jan. | Feb. | Mar. | Apr. | May | June | July | Aug. | Sept. | Oct. | Nov. | Dec. |
|---|---|---|---|---|---|---|---|---|---|---|---|---|
| 2013 | 1,172.0 | 1,196.1 | 1,315.3 | 1,539.1 | 1,511.7 | 1,434.8 | 1,389.5 | 1,356.6 | 1,306.4 | 1,263.8 | 1,271.2 | 1,302.4 |
| 2014 | 1,278.0 | 1,246.6 | 1,160.8 | 1,104.7 | 1,021.9 | 1,032.9 | 1,017.1 | 962.3 | 970.3 | 914.8 | 952.5 | 939.1 |
| 2015 | 991.0 | 1,004.6 | 979.6 | 1,016.3 | 1,015.3 | 1,038.6 | 1,001.3 | 957.0 | 918.7 | 977.8 | 1,011.8 | 1,007.1 |
| 2016 | 912.6 | 995.9 | 1,076.7 | 1,117.9 | 1,081.1 | 1,061.2 | 1,014.6 | 1,057.1 | 1,059.3 | 1,142.7 | 1,169.7 | 1,220.4 |
| 2017 | 1,195.9 | 1,247.4 | 1,364.8 | 1,432.0 | 1,537.9 | 1,421.3 | 1,337.6 | 1,324.8 | 1,317.7 | 1,374.0 | 1,377.5 | 1,505.8 |
| 2018 | 1,426.6 | 1,365.8 | 1,392.4 | 1,463.5 | 1,484.9 | 1,512.8 | 1,507.3 | 1,583.4 | 1,642.3 | 1,621.5 | 1,409.2 | 1,258.8 |
| 2019 | 1,313.6 | 1,253.7 | 1,180.5 | 1,226.5 | 1,290.5 | 1,317.6 | 1,314.3 | 1,337.1 | 1,214.9 | 1,235.8 | 1,185.8 | 1,297.0 |
| 2020 | 1,442.7 | 1,460.9 | 1,332.2 | 1,227.5 | 1,246.1 | 1,303.0 | 1,295.0 | 1,255.1 | 1,254.9 | 1,221.3 | 1,220.2 | 1,191.7 |
| 2021 | 1,138.8 | 1,180.2 | 1,206.4 | 1,187.5 | 1,201.0 | 1,304.0 | 1,449.0 | 1,423.5 | 1,413.8 | 1,321.4 | 1,294.4 | 1,164.5 |
| 2022 | 1,146.1 | 1,122.8 | 1,094.4 | 1,154.1 | 1,116.2 | 1,054.3 | 971.2 | 978.9 | 964.9 | 971.5 | 984.1 | 1,004.2 |

Contract size = 10,000 MMBtu.   Source: CME Group; New York Mercantile Exchange (NYMEX)

# Gasoline

Gasoline is a complex mixture of hundreds of lighter liquid hydrocarbons and is used chiefly as a fuel for internal-combustion engines. Petroleum crude, or crude oil, is still the most economical source of gasoline with refineries turning more than half of every barrel of crude oil into gasoline. The three main steps to all refining operations are the separation process (separating crude oil into various chemical components), conversion process (breaking the chemicals down into molecules called hydrocarbons), and treatment process (transforming and combining hydrocarbon molecules and other additives). Another process, called *hydro treating*, removes a significant amount of sulfur from finished gasoline, as is currently required by the state of California.

Octane is a measure of a gasoline's ability to resist pinging or knocking noise from an engine. Most gasoline stations offer three octane grades of unleaded fuel—regular at 87 (R+M)/2, mid-grade at 89 (R+M)/2, and premium at 93 (R+M)/2. Additional refining steps are needed to increase the octane, which increases the retail price. This does not make the gasoline any cleaner or better but yields a different blend of hydrocarbons that burn more slowly.

In an attempt to improve air quality and reduce harmful emissions from internal combustion engines, Congress in 1990 amended the Clean Air Act to mandate the addition of ethanol to gasoline. Some 2 billion gallons of ethanol are now added to gasoline each year in the U.S. The most common blend is E10, which contains 10% ethanol and 90% gasoline. Auto manufacturers have approved that mixture for use in all U.S. vehicles. Ethanol is an alcohol-based fuel produced by fermenting and distilling crops such as corn, barley, wheat, and sugar.

RBOB gasoline futures and options trade at the CME Group. The CME's gasoline futures contract calls for the delivery of 1,000 barrels (42,000 gallons) of RBOB gasoline in the New York harbor and is priced in terms of U.S. Dollars and cents per gallon.

**Price** – CME gasoline futures prices (Barchart.com symbol code RB) rallied early in 2022 but then fell back and closed the year up +10.4% at $2.4595 per gallon. The average monthly retail price of regular unleaded gasoline in 2022 rose by +34.2% yr/yr to $4.09 per gallon. The average monthly retail price of unleaded premium motor gasoline in the U.S. in 2022 rose by +31.7% to $4.86 per gallon.

**Supply** – U.S. production of finished motor gasoline in 2022 rose by +0.3% yr/yr to 9.551 million barrels per day. Gasoline stocks in December of 2021 were down by -30.1% to 17.743 million barrels.

**Demand** – U.S. consumption of finished motor gasoline in 2022 fell by -0.9% yr/yr to 8.732 million barrels per day, but still down from the 2018 record high of 9.325 million barrels per day.

**World Production of Motor Gasoline**     In Thousands of Barrels Per Day

| Year | Brazil | Canada | China | France | Germany | India | Italy | Japan | Mexico | Russia | United Kingdom | United States | World Total |
|---|---|---|---|---|---|---|---|---|---|---|---|---|---|
| 2008 | 364.0 | 703.8 | 1,483.0 | 386.8 | 584.7 | 374.0 | 460.4 | 974.1 | 430.0 | 832.0 | 471.0 | 8,548.0 | 21,425.0 |
| 2009 | 374.0 | 717.8 | 1,711.0 | 365.8 | 559.9 | 527.0 | 434.0 | 980.0 | 454.5 | 837.0 | 472.3 | 8,786.0 | 22,247.9 |
| 2010 | 399.0 | 719.0 | 1,720.0 | 317.0 | 499.0 | 605.0 | 438.0 | 1,012.0 | 408.0 | 840.0 | 460.0 | 9,059.0 | 22,306.5 |
| 2011 | 425.0 | 670.4 | 1,850.0 | 303.5 | 499.3 | 627.0 | 405.3 | 943.4 | 387.2 | 857.0 | 453.3 | 9,058.0 | 22,288.5 |
| 2012 | 462.0 | 687.4 | 2,098.0 | 276.0 | 478.7 | 704.0 | 395.7 | 919.9 | 404.5 | 893.0 | 396.5 | 8,926.0 | 22,451.4 |
| 2013 | 491.0 | 675.3 | 2,298.0 | 250.7 | 473.4 | 708.0 | 357.8 | 934.0 | 422.8 | 920.0 | 406.8 | 9,234.0 | 22,882.9 |
| 2014 | 533.7 | 672.0 | 2,577.5 | 265.4 | 465.1 | 755.4 | 343.5 | 920.5 | 407.2 | 909.9 | 363.7 | 9,571.0 | 23,605.1 |
| 2015[1] | | | 810.9 | | 164.2 | 421.9 | | 183.9 | 893.4 | 766.9 | | 294.3 | 9,178.4 | |
| 2016[2] | | | 847.5 | | 169.3 | 420.9 | | 181.2 | 896.8 | 795.9 | | 289.8 | | |
| 2017[2] | | | 778.4 | | 166.9 | 396.4 | | 159.3 | 803.1 | 700.9 | | 262.6 | | |

[1] Preliminary.    [2] Estimate.    *Source: Energy Information Administration, U.S. Department of Energy (EIA-DOE)*

**World Imports of Motor Gasoline**     In Thousands of Barrels Per Day

| Year | Australia | Canada | Indonesia | Iran | Malaysia | Mexico | Netherlands | Nigeria | Saudi Arabia | Singapore | United Kingdom | United States | World Total |
|---|---|---|---|---|---|---|---|---|---|---|---|---|---|
| 2004 | 59.6 | 65.0 | 99.7 | 142.6 | 54.7 | 161.7 | 181.3 | 136.9 | ---- | 161.6 | 50.2 | 496.4 | 2,891.4 |
| 2005 | 57.5 | 81.7 | 125.2 | 156.0 | 66.3 | 214.2 | 212.2 | 128.1 | 41.1 | 166.6 | 55.1 | 602.7 | 3,242.9 |
| 2006 | 56.1 | 98.8 | 128.9 | 172.9 | 76.3 | 245.5 | 242.4 | 126.4 | 79.2 | 172.4 | 87.8 | 475.2 | 3,212.4 |
| 2007 | 46.8 | 75.3 | 145.3 | 119.8 | 73.3 | 284.7 | 170.7 | 135.4 | 75.2 | 200.0 | 75.6 | 412.6 | 3,040.0 |
| 2008 | 70.7 | 94.2 | 94.8 | 130.0 | 78.1 | 307.1 | 225.2 | 107.4 | 108.0 | 230.3 | 53.7 | 301.6 | 3,030.0 |
| 2009 | 77.1 | 89.1 | 199.3 | 132.5 | 74.0 | 307.6 | 234.1 | 140.0 | 102.9 | 20.2 | 77.8 | 223.4 | 2,943.9 |
| 2010 | 47.3 | 79.9 | 219.0 | 93.9 | 97.1 | 354.4 | 217.2 | 162.7 | 86.2 | 324.9 | 85.3 | 134.3 | 3,366.9 |
| 2011 | 57.2 | 90.4 | 268.8 | 31.1 | 104.6 | 386.8 | 240.5 | 142.0 | 51.9 | 323.3 | 88.0 | 104.8 | 3,508.0 |
| 2012[1] | 57.3 | 62.2 | 307.9 | 9.6 | 134.9 | 374.9 | 276.2 | 137.3 | 92.2 | 305.7 | 111.5 | 44.1 | 3,628.2 |
| 2013[2] | 63.6 | 54.7 | | | | 319.4 | 225.1 | | | | 108.7 | 45.0 | |

[1] Preliminary.    [2] Estimate.    *Source: Energy Information Administration, U.S. Department of Energy (EIA-DOE)*

# GASOLINE

**World Exports of Motor Gasoline**   In Thousands of Barrels Per Day

| Year | Canada | France | Germany | India | Italy | Nether-lands | Russia | Singa-pore | United Kingdom | United States | Vene-zuela | Virgin Islands | World Total |
|---|---|---|---|---|---|---|---|---|---|---|---|---|---|
| 2004 | 156.2 | 161.7 | 121.5 | 67.5 | 127.6 | 340.4 | 98.3 | 240.4 | 169.3 | 124.3 | 178.0 | 158.9 | 3,358.6 |
| 2005 | 161.4 | 179.1 | 132.1 | 53.1 | 161.3 | 376.4 | 138.4 | 332.0 | 152.5 | 135.5 | 172.0 | 159.3 | 3,655.9 |
| 2006 | 138.8 | 160.0 | 128.6 | 86.4 | 161.3 | 400.4 | 147.4 | 330.2 | 161.5 | 141.8 | 132.0 | 131.6 | 3,669.6 |
| 2007 | 147.4 | 147.0 | 125.4 | 105.3 | 208.7 | 297.6 | 140.4 | 376.5 | 169.7 | 127.0 | 115.1 | 140.1 | 3,562.2 |
| 2008 | 129.3 | 182.6 | 132.2 | 126.8 | 196.6 | 357.1 | 104.3 | 428.7 | 162.6 | 171.7 | 117.0 | 131.9 | 3,635.9 |
| 2009 | 136.5 | 148.4 | 125.5 | 228.1 | 166.8 | 376.0 | 105.2 | 216.8 | 177.2 | 195.4 | 127.5 | 115.8 | 3,564.1 |
| 2010 | 149.7 | 133.2 | 112.1 | 318.9 | 192.7 | 382.9 | 69.2 | 525.4 | 208.4 | 295.8 | 9.5 | 107.9 | 3,887.4 |
| 2011 | 130.7 | 118.5 | 109.6 | 329.1 | 187.2 | 348.7 | 90.3 | 535.7 | 214.3 | 478.8 | 27.9 | 102.3 | 4,052.4 |
| 2012[1] | 138.4 | 107.9 | 114.9 | 336.8 | 201.8 | 448.9 | 74.9 | 530.9 | 196.5 | 408.9 | 8.7 | 18.0 | 4,020.3 |
| 2013[2] | 143.2 | 85.8 | 115.4 | | 180.4 | 409.3 | | | 238.5 | 373.0 | | | |

[1] Preliminary.  [2] Estimate.  *Source: Energy Information Administration, U.S. Department of Energy (EIA-DOE)*

**Production of Finished Motor Gasoline in the United States**   In Thousands of Barrels Per Day

| Year | Jan. | Feb. | Mar. | Apr. | May | June | July | Aug. | Sept. | Oct. | Nov. | Dec. | Average |
|---|---|---|---|---|---|---|---|---|---|---|---|---|---|
| 2013 | 8,718 | 8,926 | 8,971 | 9,042 | 9,299 | 9,472 | 9,374 | 9,340 | 9,190 | 9,484 | 9,476 | 9,495 | 9,232 |
| 2014 | 8,849 | 9,111 | 9,368 | 9,652 | 9,834 | 9,809 | 9,983 | 9,741 | 9,404 | 9,552 | 9,607 | 9,898 | 9,567 |
| 2015 | 9,260 | 9,504 | 9,524 | 9,720 | 9,771 | 9,846 | 9,989 | 9,998 | 9,878 | 9,935 | 9,799 | 9,806 | 9,752 |
| 2016 | 9,378 | 9,834 | 9,932 | 9,876 | 10,058 | 10,280 | 10,224 | 10,293 | 10,020 | 10,059 | 9,969 | 10,013 | 9,995 |
| 2017 | 9,281 | 9,507 | 9,802 | 9,855 | 10,126 | 10,270 | 10,164 | 10,176 | 9,778 | 10,129 | 10,220 | 10,104 | 9,951 |
| 2018 | 9,529 | 9,797 | 10,053 | 9,974 | 10,138 | 10,314 | 10,174 | 10,243 | 9,927 | 10,301 | 10,240 | 10,020 | 10,059 |
| 2019 | 9,747 | 9,744 | 10,060 | 10,020 | 10,229 | 10,236 | 10,240 | 10,437 | 9,916 | 10,259 | 10,229 | 9,992 | 10,092 |
| 2020 | 9,626 | 9,742 | 8,576 | 6,365 | 7,476 | 8,748 | 9,026 | 9,312 | 9,090 | 9,252 | 8,883 | 8,809 | 8,742 |
| 2021 | 8,523 | 8,395 | 9,286 | 9,644 | 9,874 | 9,961 | 9,934 | 9,866 | 9,686 | 9,698 | 9,731 | 9,666 | 9,522 |
| 2022[1] | 8,756 | 9,386 | 9,524 | 9,548 | 9,838 | 9,835 | 9,572 | 9,873 | 9,754 | 9,654 | 9,589 | 9,290 | 9,552 |

[1] Preliminary.  *Source: Energy Information Administration, U.S. Department of Energy (EIA-DOE)*

**Disposition of Finished Motor Gasoline, Total Product Supplied in the United States**   In Thousand Barrels per Day

| Year | Jan. | Feb. | Mar. | Apr. | May | June | July | Aug. | Sept. | Oct. | Nov. | Dec. | Average |
|---|---|---|---|---|---|---|---|---|---|---|---|---|---|
| 2013 | 8,331 | 8,395 | 8,641 | 8,855 | 9,033 | 9,078 | 9,146 | 9,124 | 8,946 | 8,944 | 8,923 | 8,670 | 8,841 |
| 2014 | 8,273 | 8,647 | 8,697 | 8,955 | 9,023 | 9,039 | 9,249 | 9,311 | 8,822 | 9,148 | 8,921 | 8,941 | 8,919 |
| 2015 | 8,639 | 8,829 | 9,057 | 9,189 | 9,262 | 9,417 | 9,470 | 9,460 | 9,289 | 9,245 | 9,112 | 9,148 | 9,176 |
| 2016 | 8,653 | 9,221 | 9,373 | 9,176 | 9,417 | 9,608 | 9,578 | 9,687 | 9,484 | 9,093 | 9,233 | 9,283 | 9,317 |
| 2017 | 8,507 | 9,008 | 9,325 | 9,295 | 9,550 | 9,772 | 9,595 | 9,752 | 9,378 | 9,357 | 9,110 | 9,247 | 9,325 |
| 2018 | 8,788 | 8,796 | 9,465 | 9,206 | 9,515 | 9,797 | 9,640 | 9,778 | 9,153 | 9,294 | 9,290 | 9,179 | 9,325 |
| 2019 | 8,778 | 9,072 | 9,184 | 9,411 | 9,497 | 9,703 | 9,533 | 9,834 | 9,198 | 9,308 | 9,209 | 8,971 | 9,308 |
| 2020 | 8,724 | 9,050 | 7,779 | 5,866 | 7,198 | 8,292 | 8,460 | 8,524 | 8,541 | 8,316 | 8,001 | 7,855 | 8,051 |
| 2021 | 7,723 | 7,824 | 8,553 | 8,839 | 9,081 | 9,362 | 9,297 | 9,182 | 8,932 | 9,027 | 9,021 | 8,879 | 8,810 |
| 2022[1] | 7,982 | 8,598 | 8,856 | 8,754 | 9,107 | 9,127 | 8,750 | 9,080 | 8,815 | 8,828 | 8,496 | 8,392 | 8,732 |

[1] Preliminary.  *Source: Energy Information Administration, U.S. Department of Energy (EIA-DOE)*

**Stocks of Finished Gasoline[2] on Hand in the United States, at End of Month**   In Thousands of Barrels

| Year | Jan. | Feb. | Mar. | Apr. | May | June | July | Aug. | Sept. | Oct. | Nov. | Dec. |
|---|---|---|---|---|---|---|---|---|---|---|---|---|
| 2013 | 55,228 | 53,143 | 47,327 | 45,108 | 46,376 | 48,634 | 49,726 | 47,655 | 39,780 | 37,595 | 37,548 | 38,976 |
| 2014 | 39,790 | 37,687 | 34,274 | 30,710 | 31,057 | 28,854 | 28,320 | 27,514 | 28,773 | 27,432 | 29,532 | 30,615 |
| 2015 | 29,923 | 30,558 | 26,891 | 25,898 | 26,580 | 25,678 | 24,418 | 26,048 | 29,028 | 27,638 | 27,805 | 28,453 |
| 2016 | 26,800 | 27,218 | 26,468 | 25,039 | 23,708 | 24,874 | 24,773 | 25,641 | 25,088 | 25,892 | 26,525 | 28,610 |
| 2017 | 28,496 | 25,727 | 21,728 | 21,828 | 21,983 | 22,480 | 23,157 | 24,584 | 21,765 | 23,154 | 23,595 | 24,641 |
| 2018 | 24,969 | 24,769 | 22,863 | 22,583 | 23,776 | 24,550 | 24,229 | 23,227 | 24,748 | 24,888 | 24,107 | 25,769 |
| 2019 | 28,705 | 23,864 | 20,865 | 20,866 | 22,169 | 21,491 | 21,916 | 23,084 | 23,007 | 23,330 | 24,834 | 26,129 |
| 2020 | 28,537 | 26,397 | 22,585 | 22,889 | 24,069 | 23,495 | 24,293 | 25,151 | 22,543 | 25,205 | 25,039 | 25,398 |
| 2021 | 22,939 | 20,896 | 20,259 | 21,280 | 20,361 | 18,600 | 17,887 | 18,165 | 18,506 | 18,286 | 18,045 | 17,743 |
| 2022[1] | 18,089 | 18,624 | 17,260 | 17,832 | 17,163 | 17,132 | 16,960 | 17,035 | 17,623 | 17,101 | 16,685 | |

[1] Preliminary.  [2] Includes oxygenated and other finished.  *Source: Energy Information Administration, U.S. Department of Energy (EIA-DOE)*

# GASOLINE

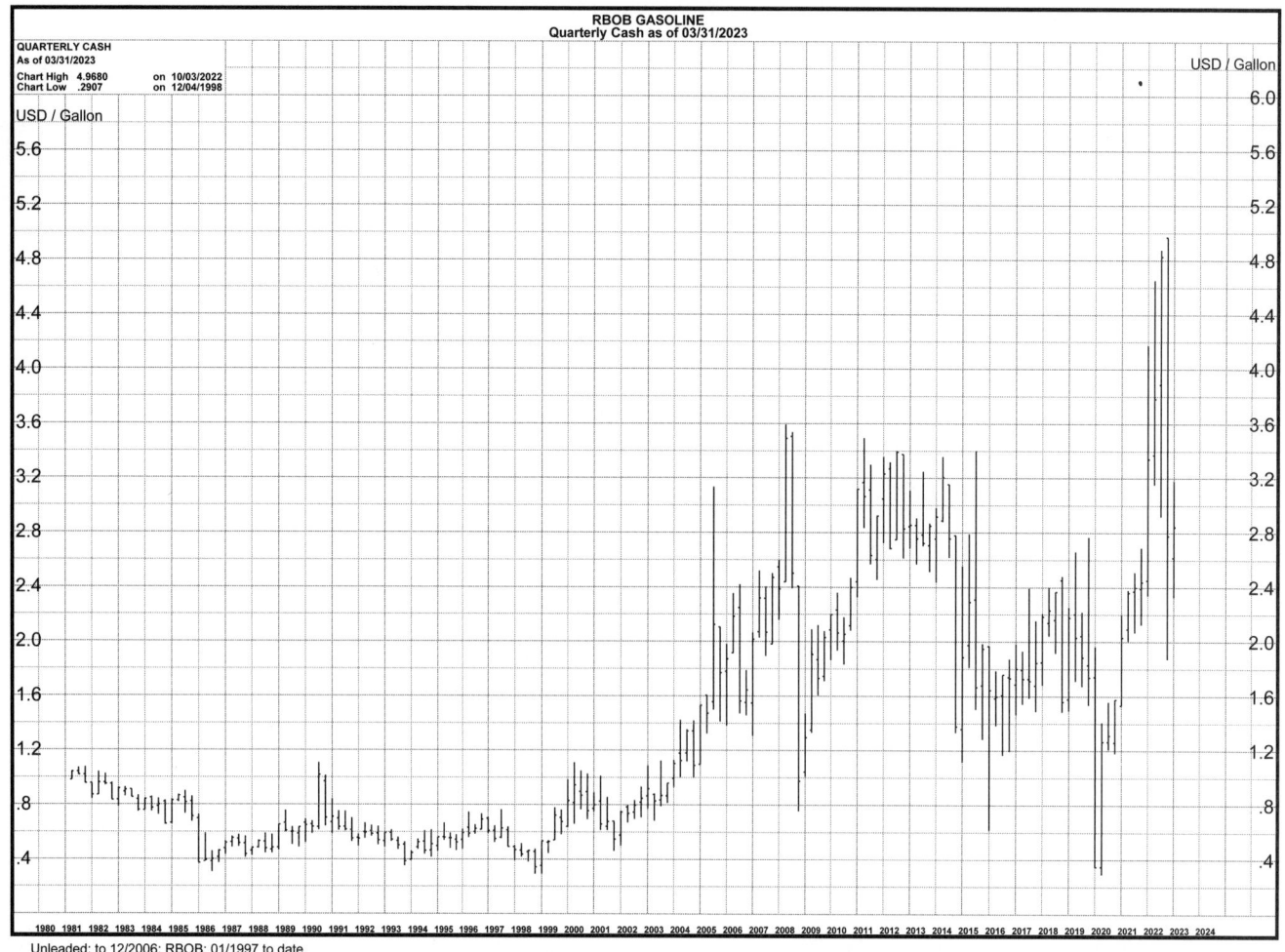

**RBOB GASOLINE**
Quarterly Cash as of 03/31/2023

QUARTERLY CASH
As of 03/31/2023
Chart High 4.9680 on 10/03/2022
Chart Low .2907 on 12/04/1998

Unleaded: to 12/2006; RBOB: 01/1997 to date.

### Average Spot Price of Unleaded Gasoline in New York    In Dollars Per Gallon

| Year | Jan. | Feb. | Mar. | Apr. | May | June | July | Aug. | Sept. | Oct. | Nov. | Dec. | Average |
|---|---|---|---|---|---|---|---|---|---|---|---|---|---|
| 2013 | 2.8520 | 3.0530 | 2.9140 | 2.7060 | 2.7420 | 2.7400 | 2.9240 | 2.9330 | 2.7970 | 2.6850 | 2.6730 | 2.7360 | 2.8110 |
| 2014 | 2.6720 | 2.7950 | 2.7530 | 2.8960 | 2.8620 | 2.8960 | 2.8020 | 2.7050 | 2.7210 | 2.3980 | 2.1650 | 1.6830 | 2.6100 |
| 2015 | 1.3640 | 1.6070 | 1.6440 | 1.7930 | 1.9380 | 2.0050 | 1.8600 | 1.6200 | 1.4600 | 1.3970 | 1.3770 | 1.2760 | 1.6120 |
| 2016 | 1.1210 | 1.0580 | 1.2010 | 1.4480 | 1.5660 | 1.5060 | 1.3540 | 1.3790 | 1.4380 | 1.5220 | 1.4620 | 1.6340 | 1.3908 |
| 2017 | 1.6200 | 1.5470 | 1.4920 | 1.6110 | 1.5400 | 1.4450 | 1.5620 | 1.6880 | 1.8670 | 1.7150 | 1.8300 | 1.7570 | 1.6395 |
| 2018 | 1.8990 | 1.8170 | 1.8340 | 1.9950 | 2.1290 | 2.0300 | 2.0740 | 2.0770 | 2.0930 | 2.0280 | 1.6250 | 1.4490 | 1.9208 |
| 2019 | 1.4250 | 1.5680 | 1.8120 | 2.0420 | 1.9160 | 1.7400 | 1.8900 | 1.6940 | 1.7260 | 1.7280 | 1.7240 | 1.7130 | 1.7482 |
| 2020 | 1.6580 | 1.5800 | 0.8910 | 0.5930 | 0.8760 | 1.1210 | 1.2200 | 1.2480 | 1.2270 | 1.2010 | 1.1900 | 1.3590 | 1.1803 |
| 2021 | 1.5630 | 1.7610 | 1.9860 | 1.9880 | 2.1160 | 2.1670 | 2.2570 | 2.2350 | 2.2840 | 2.5000 | 2.3900 | 2.2030 | 2.1208 |
| 2022 | 2.4490 | 2.7390 | 3.1840 | 3.1930 | 3.8280 | 4.0820 | 3.4840 | 3.0270 | 2.6420 | 3.0130 | 2.8520 | 2.3660 | 3.0716 |

*Source: Energy Information Administration, U.S. Department of Energy (EIA-DOE)*

### Average Refiner Price of Finished Motor Gasoline to End Users[2] in the United States    In Dollars Per Gallon

| Year | Jan. | Feb. | Mar. | Apr. | May | June | July | Aug. | Sept. | Oct. | Nov. | Dec. | Average |
|---|---|---|---|---|---|---|---|---|---|---|---|---|---|
| 2013 | 2.850 | 3.221 | 3.233 | 3.102 | 3.188 | 3.184 | 3.146 | 3.097 | 3.059 | 2.893 | 2.759 | 2.759 | 3.041 |
| 2014 | 2.816 | 2.913 | 3.104 | 3.214 | 3.245 | 3.265 | 3.128 | 3.016 | 2.936 | 2.670 | 2.406 | 2.013 | 2.894 |
| 2015 | 1.673 | 1.858 | 2.054 | 2.058 | 2.322 | 2.374 | 2.338 | 2.218 | 1.920 | 1.849 | 1.711 | 1.604 | 1.998 |
| 2016 | 1.505 | 1.332 | 1.552 | 1.725 | 1.869 | 1.961 | 1.804 | 1.754 | 1.788 | 1.819 | 1.759 | 1.849 | 1.726 |
| 2017 | 1.900 | 1.862 | 1.904 | 1.997 | 1.963 | 1.906 | 1.871 | 1.952 | 2.154 | 2.042 | 2.122 | 2.034 | 1.976 |
| 2018 | 2.108 | 2.127 | 2.160 | 2.315 | 2.494 | 2.469 | 2.442 | 2.421 | 2.428 | 2.441 | 2.205 | 1.973 | 2.299 |
| 2019 | 1.854 | 1.949 | 2.137 | 2.487 | 2.520 | 2.366 | 2.375 | 2.252 | 2.242 | 2.289 | 2.229 | 2.182 | 2.240 |
| 2020 | 2.150 | 2.060 | 1.862 | 1.490 | 1.598 | 1.768 | 1.806 | 1.814 | 1.804 | 1.773 | 1.736 | 1.828 | 1.807 |
| 2021 | 1.986 | 2.201 | 2.442 | 2.493 | 2.683 | 3.000 | 3.105 | 3.146 | 3.143 | 3.201 | 3.318 | 3.283 | 2.833 |
| 2022[1] | 3.145 | 3.313 | 3.991 | | | | | | | | | | 3.483 |

[1] Preliminary.   [2] Excludes aviation and taxes.   *Source: Energy Information Administration, U.S. Department of Energy (EIA-DOE)*

# GASOLINE

**BLENDSTOCK GASOLINE (RBOB) - NYMEX**
Weekly Nearest Futures as of 03/31/2023

Chart High 4.3260 on 06/06/2022
Chart Low .3760 on 03/23/2020

Nearby Futures through Last Trading Day.

## Volume of Trading of Gasoline, RBOB[1] Futures in New York   In Thousands of Contracts

| Year | Jan. | Feb. | Mar. | Apr. | May | June | July | Aug. | Sept. | Oct. | Nov. | Dec. | Total |
|------|------|------|------|------|-----|------|------|------|-------|------|------|------|-------|
| 2013 | 2,981.2 | 3,000.0 | 3,079.8 | 3,578.7 | 3,090.8 | 2,566.9 | 3,105.3 | 2,810.5 | 2,516.6 | 2,664.8 | 2,777.1 | 2,298.6 | 34,470.3 |
| 2014 | 2,470.9 | 2,417.0 | 2,562.7 | 3,316.9 | 3,240.6 | 2,679.3 | 3,001.7 | 2,894.1 | 3,173.3 | 3,170.5 | 2,713.5 | 2,781.4 | 34,421.9 |
| 2015 | 3,070.7 | 3,387.9 | 3,396.1 | 3,449.5 | 3,113.9 | 3,869.0 | 3,621.4 | 3,736.9 | 2,961.2 | 3,158.0 | 3,171.9 | 3,365.6 | 40,302.1 |
| 2016 | 3,362.4 | 3,841.7 | 3,723.6 | 3,546.6 | 3,874.1 | 4,362.3 | 3,427.0 | 4,134.4 | 4,677.2 | 3,413.1 | 3,844.7 | 3,221.5 | 45,428.7 |
| 2017 | 3,748.5 | 4,433.7 | 4,380.3 | 3,721.6 | 4,343.5 | 4,454.4 | 4,065.8 | 5,803.7 | 4,139.1 | 3,734.5 | 3,717.3 | 3,368.5 | 49,910.9 |
| 2018 | 4,290.5 | 3,815.0 | 3,992.9 | 4,067.4 | 4,569.1 | 4,175.0 | 3,959.4 | 4,858.9 | 3,901.0 | 4,626.3 | 3,953.8 | 3,404.7 | 49,613.9 |
| 2019 | 3,927.9 | 3,660.4 | 5,049.3 | 5,243.9 | 4,833.5 | 4,270.2 | 4,235.3 | 3,663.8 | 4,111.6 | 3,832.5 | 3,585.7 | 3,437.8 | 49,851.8 |
| 2020 | 4,556.7 | 4,861.5 | 5,625.8 | 3,936.0 | 3,244.3 | 3,495.7 | 3,338.0 | 3,613.2 | 3,361.7 | 3,635.1 | 3,386.0 | 3,438.6 | 46,492.5 |
| 2021 | 3,772.1 | 4,165.3 | 4,517.7 | 3,733.2 | 3,951.0 | 3,883.5 | 3,567.4 | 4,801.2 | 4,001.5 | 3,996.1 | 4,136.0 | 3,312.9 | 47,838.0 |
| 2022 | 3,747.8 | 4,413.8 | 4,222.9 | 3,152.3 | 3,992.0 | 3,718.9 | 2,960.3 | 3,246.7 | 2,801.7 | 3,049.6 | 2,890.2 | 2,796.1 | 40,992.4 |

Contract size = 42,000 US gallons.   Source: CME Group; New York Mercantile Exchange (NYMEX)

## Average Open Interest of Gasoline, RBOB[1] Futures in New York   In Contracts

| Year | Jan. | Feb. | Mar. | Apr. | May | June | July | Aug. | Sept. | Oct. | Nov. | Dec. |
|------|------|------|------|------|-----|------|------|------|-------|------|------|------|
| 2013 | 312,415 | 328,903 | 318,974 | 301,346 | 283,215 | 277,107 | 270,359 | 271,797 | 264,119 | 232,420 | 240,735 | 246,590 |
| 2014 | 252,519 | 274,087 | 283,756 | 310,549 | 332,460 | 314,754 | 307,808 | 274,978 | 283,206 | 310,119 | 334,015 | 349,589 |
| 2015 | 366,741 | 362,191 | 372,013 | 383,705 | 383,960 | 372,487 | 367,208 | 378,562 | 371,326 | 345,971 | 360,109 | 365,200 |
| 2016 | 379,473 | 406,615 | 420,305 | 392,100 | 405,314 | 401,323 | 389,932 | 406,922 | 395,691 | 408,750 | 380,734 | 390,804 |
| 2017 | 425,330 | 421,979 | 398,661 | 406,054 | 403,723 | 402,039 | 392,477 | 408,427 | 415,138 | 403,480 | 429,908 | 400,346 |
| 2018 | 437,285 | 434,342 | 424,422 | 450,029 | 479,806 | 461,515 | 441,321 | 459,928 | 438,527 | 406,263 | 406,427 | 406,667 |
| 2019 | 419,362 | 415,527 | 410,706 | 432,882 | 408,391 | 373,707 | 393,550 | 403,171 | 378,190 | 366,086 | 398,540 | 378,433 |
| 2020 | 408,399 | 391,038 | 368,635 | 378,558 | 373,104 | 361,741 | 346,636 | 355,345 | 362,771 | 366,985 | 397,811 | 417,834 |
| 2021 | 418,253 | 416,260 | 402,728 | 376,515 | 390,452 | 419,925 | 362,481 | 352,072 | 333,672 | 325,172 | 315,505 | 297,385 |
| 2022 | 347,487 | 385,832 | 302,944 | 299,953 | 308,214 | 302,167 | 267,906 | 257,653 | 246,989 | 248,498 | 251,950 | 255,689 |

Contract size = 42,000 US gallons.   Source: CME Group; New York Mercantile Exchange (NYMEX)

# GASOLINE

### Average Retail Price of Unleaded Premium Motor Gasoline[2] in the United States — In Dollars per Gallon

| Year | Jan. | Feb. | Mar. | Apr. | May | June | July | Aug. | Sept. | Oct. | Nov. | Dec. | Average |
|---|---|---|---|---|---|---|---|---|---|---|---|---|---|
| 2013 | 3.646 | 3.990 | 4.038 | 3.901 | 3.936 | 3.957 | 3.951 | 3.919 | 3.881 | 3.702 | 3.585 | 3.604 | 3.843 |
| 2014 | 3.651 | 3.694 | 3.858 | 3.986 | 4.020 | 4.027 | 3.976 | 3.835 | 3.758 | 3.547 | 3.262 | 2.940 | 3.713 |
| 2015 | 2.497 | 2.621 | 2.867 | 2.868 | 3.166 | 3.218 | 3.252 | 3.120 | 2.860 | 2.749 | 2.640 | 2.532 | 2.866 |
| 2016 | 2.455 | 2.248 | 2.411 | 2.585 | 2.710 | 2.807 | 2.702 | 2.629 | 2.682 | 2.719 | 2.675 | 2.698 | 2.610 |
| 2017 | 2.815 | 2.793 | 2.827 | 2.909 | 2.894 | 2.859 | 2.800 | 2.883 | 3.120 | 2.996 | 3.056 | 2.985 | 2.911 |
| 2018 | 3.042 | 3.091 | 3.101 | 3.258 | 3.423 | 3.440 | 3.399 | 3.384 | 3.400 | 3.431 | 3.251 | 3.015 | 3.270 |
| 2019 | 2.874 | 2.901 | 3.079 | 3.382 | 3.471 | 3.328 | 3.327 | 3.222 | 3.214 | 3.297 | 3.254 | 3.190 | 3.212 |
| 2020 | 3.157 | 3.071 | 2.893 | 2.527 | 2.490 | 2.673 | 2.783 | 2.795 | 2.810 | 2.782 | 2.727 | 2.778 | 2.791 |
| 2021 | 2.921 | 3.073 | 3.386 | 3.455 | 3.596 | 3.802 | 3.897 | 3.938 | 3.945 | 4.040 | 4.148 | 4.100 | 3.692 |
| 2022[1] | 4.102 | 4.244 | 5.015 | 5.037 | 5.318 | 5.774 | 5.459 | 4.916 | 4.732 | 4.914 | 4.679 | 4.167 | 4.863 |

[1] Preliminary.  [2] Including taxes.  Source: Energy Information Administration, U.S. Department of Energy (EIA-DOE)

### Average Retail Price of Unleaded Regular Motor Gasoline[2] in the United States — In Dollars per Gallon

| Year | Jan. | Feb. | Mar. | Apr. | May | June | July | Aug. | Sept. | Oct. | Nov. | Dec. | Average |
|---|---|---|---|---|---|---|---|---|---|---|---|---|---|
| 2013 | 3.351 | 3.693 | 3.735 | 3.590 | 3.623 | 3.633 | 3.628 | 3.600 | 3.556 | 3.375 | 3.251 | 3.277 | 3.526 |
| 2014 | 3.320 | 3.364 | 3.532 | 3.659 | 3.691 | 3.695 | 3.633 | 3.481 | 3.403 | 3.182 | 2.887 | 2.560 | 3.367 |
| 2015 | 2.110 | 2.249 | 2.483 | 2.485 | 2.775 | 2.832 | 2.832 | 2.679 | 2.394 | 2.289 | 2.185 | 2.060 | 2.448 |
| 2016 | 1.967 | 1.767 | 1.958 | 2.134 | 2.264 | 2.363 | 2.225 | 2.155 | 2.208 | 2.243 | 2.187 | 2.230 | 2.142 |
| 2017 | 2.351 | 2.299 | 2.323 | 2.418 | 2.386 | 2.337 | 2.281 | 2.374 | 2.630 | 2.484 | 2.548 | 2.459 | 2.408 |
| 2018 | 2.539 | 2.575 | 2.572 | 2.737 | 2.907 | 2.914 | 2.873 | 2.862 | 2.873 | 2.887 | 2.671 | 2.414 | 2.735 |
| 2019 | 2.289 | 2.353 | 2.564 | 2.835 | 2.901 | 2.752 | 2.776 | 2.655 | 2.630 | 2.673 | 2.620 | 2.587 | 2.636 |
| 2020 | 2.567 | 2.465 | 2.267 | 1.876 | 1.879 | 2.076 | 2.176 | 2.177 | 2.193 | 2.159 | 2.090 | 2.168 | 2.174 |
| 2021 | 2.326 | 2.496 | 2.791 | 2.839 | 2.972 | 3.154 | 3.233 | 3.255 | 3.265 | 3.385 | 3.482 | 3.408 | 3.051 |
| 2022[1] | 3.413 | 3.592 | 4.312 | 4.271 | 4.604 | 5.058 | 4.667 | 4.101 | 3.881 | 4.016 | 3.853 | 3.356 | 4.094 |

[1] Preliminary.  [2] Including taxes.  Source: Energy Information Administration, U.S. Department of Energy (EIA-DOE)

### Average Retail Price of All-Types[2] Motor Gasoline[3] in the United States — In Dollars per Gallon

| Year | Jan. | Feb. | Mar. | Apr. | May | June | July | Aug. | Sept. | Oct. | Nov. | Dec. | Average |
|---|---|---|---|---|---|---|---|---|---|---|---|---|---|
| 2013 | 3.407 | 3.748 | 3.792 | 3.647 | 3.682 | 3.693 | 3.687 | 3.658 | 3.616 | 3.434 | 3.310 | 3.333 | 3.584 |
| 2014 | 3.378 | 3.422 | 3.590 | 3.717 | 3.745 | 3.750 | 3.690 | 3.540 | 3.463 | 3.241 | 2.945 | 2.618 | 3.425 |
| 2015 | 2.170 | 2.308 | 2.544 | 2.545 | 2.832 | 2.889 | 2.893 | 2.745 | 2.463 | 2.357 | 2.249 | 2.125 | 2.510 |
| 2016 | 2.034 | 1.833 | 2.021 | 2.196 | 2.324 | 2.422 | 2.287 | 2.218 | 2.269 | 2.304 | 2.246 | 2.289 | 2.204 |
| 2017 | 2.409 | 2.360 | 2.386 | 2.479 | 2.448 | 2.400 | 2.344 | 2.436 | 2.688 | 2.545 | 2.608 | 2.521 | 2.469 |
| 2018 | 2.596 | 2.632 | 2.631 | 2.795 | 2.963 | 2.970 | 2.930 | 2.919 | 2.930 | 2.945 | 2.733 | 2.479 | 2.794 |
| 2019 | 2.352 | 2.412 | 2.620 | 2.894 | 2.963 | 2.814 | 2.836 | 2.716 | 2.694 | 2.741 | 2.687 | 2.652 | 2.698 |
| 2020 | 2.631 | 2.530 | 2.334 | 1.946 | 1.946 | 2.141 | 2.243 | 2.245 | 2.260 | 2.228 | 2.159 | 2.235 | 2.242 |
| 2021 | 2.391 | 2.559 | 2.856 | 2.907 | 3.041 | 3.245 | 3.326 | 3.351 | 3.361 | 3.477 | 3.576 | 3.505 | 3.133 |
| 2022[1] | 3.500 | 3.675 | 4.401 | 4.369 |  | 5.149 | 4.768 | 4.205 | 3.990 | 4.130 | 3.958 | 3.459 | 4.146 |

[1] Preliminary.  [2] Also includes types of motor oil not shown separately.  [3] Including taxes.  Source: Energy Information Administration, U.S. Department of Energy (EIA-DOE)

### Average Refiner Price of Finished Aviation Gasoline to End Users[2] in the United States — In Dollars per Gallon

| Year | Jan. | Feb. | Mar. | Apr. | May | June | July | Aug. | Sept. | Oct. | Nov. | Dec. | Average |
|---|---|---|---|---|---|---|---|---|---|---|---|---|---|
| 2013 | W | 4.060 | 4.022 | 3.860 | 3.900 | 4.191 | 4.224 | 4.298 | 3.982 | 3.653 | 3.673 | 3.678 | 3.932 |
| 2014 | W | 4.142 | W | W | W | W | W | W | W | W | W | W | 3.986 |
| 2015 | W | W | W | W | W | W | W | W | W | W | W | W | W |
| 2016 | W | W | W | W | W | W | W | W | W | W | W | W | W |
| 2017 | W | W | W | W | W | W | W | W | W | W | W | W | W |
| 2018 | W | W | W | W | W | W | W | W | W | W | W | W | W |
| 2019 | W | W | W | W | W | W | W | W | W | W | W | W | W |
| 2020 | W | W | W | W | W | W | 2.761 | 2.805 | 2.613 | 2.495 | 2.485 | 2.674 | 2.639 |
| 2021 | 2.829 | 3.148 | 3.364 | 3.363 | 3.447 | 3.492 | W | W | W | 3.783 | 3.778 | W | 3.401 |
| 2022[1] | 3.689 | W | 4.581 |  |  |  |  |  |  |  |  |  | 4.135 |

[1] Preliminary.  [2] Excluding taxes.  NA = Not available.  W = Withheld proprietary data.  Source: Energy Information Administration, U.S. Department Energy (EIA-DOE)

# Gold

Gold is a dense, bright yellow metallic element with a high luster. Gold is an inactive substance and is unaffected by air, heat, moisture, and most solvents. Gold has been coveted for centuries for its unique blend of rarity, beauty, and near indestructibility. The Egyptians mined gold before 2,000 BC. King Croesus of Lydia created the first known, pure gold coin in the sixth century BC.

Gold is found in nature in quartz veins and secondary alluvial deposits as a free metal. Gold is produced from mines on every continent apart from Antarctica, where mining is forbidden. Because gold is virtually indestructible, much of the gold that has ever been mined still exists in one form or another. The largest producer of gold in the U.S. by far is the state of Nevada, with Alaska and California running a distant second and third.

Gold is a vital industrial commodity. Pure gold is one of the most malleable and ductile of all the metals. It is a good conductor of heat and electricity. The prime industrial use of gold is in electronics. Another important sector is dental gold, where it has been used for almost 3,000 years. Other applications for gold include decorative gold leaf, reflective glass, and jewelry.

In 1792, the United States first assigned a formal monetary role for gold when Congress put the nation's currency on a bimetallic standard, backing it with gold and silver. Under the gold standard, the U.S. government was willing to exchange its paper currency for a set amount of gold, meaning its currency was backed by gold. However, President Nixon in 1971 severed the convertibility between the U.S. dollar and gold, which led to the breakdown of the Bretton Woods international payments system. Since then, the prices of gold and paper currencies have floated freely. U.S. and other central banks now hold physical gold reserves primarily as a store of wealth.

Gold futures and options are traded at the CME Group. Gold futures are traded at the Bolsa de Mercadorias and Futuros (BM&F) and at the Tokyo Commodity Exchange (TOCOM), and the Korea Futures Exchange (KOFEX). The CME gold futures contract calls for the delivery of 100 troy ounces of gold (0.995 fineness), and the contract trades in terms of dollars and cents per troy ounce.

**Prices** – CME gold futures prices (Barchart.com symbol GC) raced higher in Q1 of 2022 and posted an all-time nearest-futures high of $2,072 per ounce in March. Russia's invasion of Ukraine stoked safe-haven demand for gold, and a surge in global inflation to a four-decade high boosted demand for gold as a hedge against inflation. Gold prices then ratcheted lower into Q3 and fell to a 2-1/2 year low of $1,613 per ounce in September. Gold prices sank as the aggressive interest rate-hike campaign by the Federal Reserve to combat inflation boosted T-note yields and sent the dollar soaring. The dollar index surged to a 20-year high in September, which sparked an exodus of investors from gold as holdings in gold ETFs fell to a 2-1/2 year low. Gold prices then stabilized and rose into year-end as an easing of U.S. inflation pressures prompted the Fed to slow the pace of its aggressive rate-hike regime. The Fed raised the fed funds target range by only 50 bp at the December FOMC meeting, a slower pace than the 75 bp rate hikes seen at the previous four FOMC meetings. Gold prices finished 2022 little changed, down -0.4% yr/yr at $1,819.70 per troy ounce.

**Supply** – World mine production of gold in 2022 rose by +0.3% yr/yr to 3.100 million kilograms, down from the 2018 record high of 3.310 million kilograms (1 kilogram equals 32.1507 troy ounces). The world's largest producers of gold in 2022 were China with 10.6% of world production, followed by Australia and Russia with 10.3%, Canada with 7.1%, the U.S with 5.5%, South Africa with 3.5%, and Peru as well as Uzbekistan with 3.2%.

U.S. gold mine production in 2022 fell by -9.1% yr/yr to 170,000 kilograms. Canada's gold mine production in 2022 fell by -1.3% yr/yr at 220,000 kilograms, down from the 2021 record high of 223,000 kilograms.

U.S. refinery production of gold from domestic and foreign ore sources in 2022 fell by -5.9% yr/yr to 160,000 kilograms. In addition, U.S. refinery production of gold from secondary scrap sources in 2022 fell by -2.2% yr/yr to 90,000 kilograms.

**Demand** – U.S. consumption of gold in 2022 fell by -6.0% yr/yr to 250,000 kilograms. U.S. usage of gold is mostly for jewelry.

**Trade** – U.S. exports of gold (excluding coinage) in 2022 rose by +11.4% yr/yr to 430,000 kilograms, well below the 2012 record high of 699,000 kilograms. U.S. imports of gold for consumption in 2022 fell by -27.1% yr/yr to 140,000 kilograms.

**World Mine Production of Gold**  In Kilograms (1 Kilogram = 32.1507 Troy Ounces)

| Year | Australia | Brazil | Canada | China | Ghana | Indonesia | Papua New Guinea | Peru | Russia | South Africa | United States | Uzbekistan | World Total |
|---|---|---|---|---|---|---|---|---|---|---|---|---|---|
| 2014 | 269,138 | 81,038 | 151,742 | 451,000 | 137,090 | 69,023 | 57,939 | 140,088 | 246,904 | 151,622 | 210,000 | 100,000 | 3,040,000 |
| 2015 | 275,160 | 84,814 | 160,751 | 450,000 | 125,325 | 92,171 | 60,046 | 146,822 | 248,945 | 144,504 | 214,000 | 100,000 | 3,110,000 |
| 2016 | 290,800 | 77,845 | 161,497 | 453,500 | 124,196 | 80,868 | 62,293 | 152,990 | 253,579 | 142,202 | 232,000 | 102,000 | 3,190,000 |
| 2017 | 294,171 | 85,000 | 168,072 | 426,142 | 127,573 | 101,000 | 64,000 | 151,964 | 270,300 | 137,133 | 237,000 | 104,000 | 3,270,000 |
| 2018 | 315,100 | 85,000 | 183,047 | 401,119 | 127,000 | 135,000 | 67,000 | 142,642 | 311,000 | 117,200 | 226,000 | 104,000 | 3,310,000 |
| 2019 | 325,000 | 90,000 | 175,000 | 380,000 | 142,000 | 139,000 | 74,000 | 128,000 | 305,000 | 105,000 | 200,000 | 93,000 | 3,300,000 |
| 2020 | 328,000 | 78,000 | 170,000 | 365,000 | 125,000 | 86,000 | 54,000 | 87,000 | 305,000 | 96,000 | 193,000 | 101,000 | 3,030,000 |
| 2021[1] | 315,000 | 61,000 | 223,000 | 329,000 | 88,000 | 66,000 | 54,000 | 97,000 | 320,000 | 107,000 | 187,000 | 100,000 | 3,090,000 |
| 2022[2] | 320,000 | 60,000 | 220,000 | 330,000 | 90,000 | 70,000 | 50,000 | 100,000 | 320,000 | 110,000 | 170,000 | 100,000 | 3,100,000 |

[1] Preliminary.  [2] Estimate.  Source: *U.S. Geological Survey (USGS)*

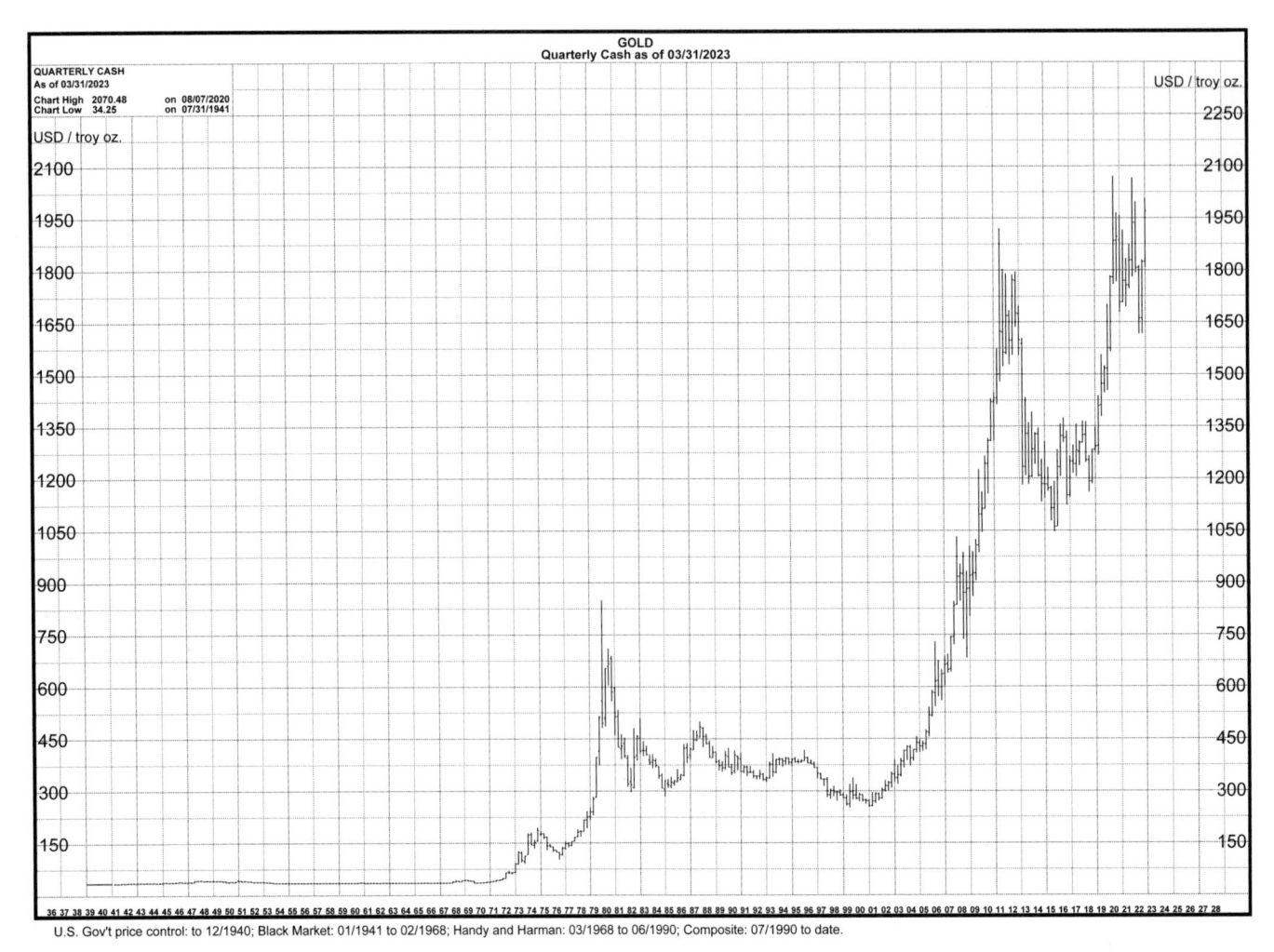

# GOLD

## Salient Statistics of Gold in the United States   In Kilograms (1 Kilogram = 32.1507 Troy Ounces)

|  | | - Refinery Production - | | | | | -------- Stocks, Dec. 31 -------- | | | ---------- Consumption ---------- | | | | |
|---|---|---|---|---|---|---|---|---|---|---|---|---|---|---|
| Year | Mine Pro- duction | Value Million $ | Domestic & Foreign Ores | Secondary (Old Scrap) | Exports, Excluding Coinage | Imports for Con- sumption | Treasury Depart- ment[3] | Futures Exchange | Industry | Official World Reserves[4] | Dental | Indus- trial[5] | Jewelry & Arts | Total |
| 2013 | 230,000 | 10,400.0 | 223,000 | 210,000 | 686,000 | 315,000 | 8,140,000 | 243,000 | 5,940 | 31,900 | ---- | ---- | ---- | 160,000 |
| 2014 | 210,000 | 8,570.0 | 253,000 | 135,000 | 492,000 | 308,000 | 8,140,000 | 325,000 | 7,540 | 32,000 | ---- | ---- | ---- | 152,000 |
| 2015 | 214,000 | 8,000.0 | 244,000 | 238,000 | 478,000 | 265,000 | 8,140,000 | 198,000 | 7,250 | 32,700 | ---- | ---- | ---- | 165,000 |
| 2016 | 222,000 | 9,350.0 | 242,000 | 220,000 | 393,000 | 374,000 | 8,140,000 | 285,000 | 4,030 | 33,300 | ---- | ---- | ---- | 210,000 |
| 2017 | 237,000 | 9,600.0 | 207,000 | 119,000 | 461,000 | 255,000 | 8,130,000 | 284,000 | 1,680 | 34,000 | ---- | ---- | ---- | 159,000 |
| 2018 | 225,600 | 9,220.0 | 205,000 | 117,000 | 474,000 | 213,000 | 8,130,000 | 262,000 | 3,380 | 34,200 | ---- | ---- | ---- | 154,000 |
| 2019 | 200,400 | 9,010.0 | 205,000 | 116,000 | 360,000 | 199,000 | 8,130,000 | 271,000 | 3,380 | 34,800 | ---- | ---- | ---- | 151,000 |
| 2020 | 192,400 | 11,000.0 | 181,000 | 91,700 | 297,000 | 545,000 | 8,130,000 | 1,190,000 | 3,670 | 35,300 | ---- | ---- | ---- | 187,000 |
| 2021[1] | 187,500 | | 170,000 | 92,000 | 386,000 | 192,000 | 8,130,000 | | | | ---- | ---- | ---- | 266,000 |
| 2022[2] | 169,600 | | 160,000 | 90,000 | 430,000 | 140,000 | 8,130,000 | | | | ---- | ---- | ---- | 250,000 |

[1] Preliminary.   [2] Estimate.   [3] Includes gold in Exchange Stabilization Fund.   [4] Held by market economy country central banks and governments and international monetary orgainzations.   [5] Including space and defense.   NA = Not available.   Source: U.S. Geological Survey (USGS)

## Monthly Average Gold Price (Handy & Harman) in New York   In Dollars Per Troy Ounce

| Year | Jan. | Feb. | Mar. | Apr. | May | June | July | Aug. | Sept. | Oct. | Nov. | Dec. | Average |
|---|---|---|---|---|---|---|---|---|---|---|---|---|---|
| 2013 | 1,670.17 | 1,628.47 | 1,592.85 | 1,490.22 | 1,415.91 | 1,342.36 | 1,288.31 | 1,349.30 | 1,346.63 | 1,316.19 | 1,276.94 | 1,220.65 | 1,411.50 |
| 2014 | 1,244.53 | 1,300.60 | 1,336.08 | 1,298.45 | 1,288.74 | 1,279.10 | 1,310.59 | 1,295.13 | 1,236.14 | 1,222.49 | 1,175.33 | 1,200.62 | 1,265.65 |
| 2015 | 1,250.75 | 1,227.08 | 1,178.63 | 1,198.93 | 1,198.63 | 1,181.50 | 1,128.31 | 1,117.93 | 1,124.88 | 1,159.25 | 1,086.44 | 1,068.25 | 1,160.05 |
| 2016 | 1,097.81 | 1,199.50 | 1,245.14 | 1,242.26 | 1,260.95 | 1,276.40 | 1,336.66 | 1,340.17 | 1,326.01 | 1,266.57 | 1,238.35 | 1,150.13 | 1,248.33 |
| 2017 | 1,192.10 | 1,234.20 | 1,231.09 | 1,266.88 | 1,246.04 | 1,260.26 | 1,236.84 | 1,283.04 | 1,314.07 | 1,279.51 | 1,281.90 | 1,264.44 | 1,257.53 |
| 2018 | 1,331.30 | 1,330.73 | 1,324.66 | 1,334.76 | 1,303.45 | 1,281.57 | 1,237.71 | 1,201.71 | 1,198.39 | 1,215.37 | 1,220.65 | 1,250.94 | 1,269.27 |
| 2019 | 1,291.75 | 1,320.06 | 1,300.90 | 1,285.91 | 1,283.70 | 1,359.04 | 1,412.89 | 1,500.41 | 1,510.58 | 1,494.81 | 1,470.50 | 1,481.23 | 1,392.65 |
| 2020 | 1,561.07 | 1,600.37 | 1,593.48 | 1,682.71 | 1,717.63 | 1,734.11 | 1,855.45 | 1,972.67 | 1,926.24 | 1,903.27 | 1,875.95 | ---- | 1,765.72 |
| 2021 | 1,868.77 | 1,807.69 | 1,718.23 | 1,760.04 | 1,850.26 | 1,834.57 | 1,807.84 | 1,785.74 | 1,775.14 | 1,776.85 | 1,822.81 | 1,790.43 | 1,799.86 |
| 2022 | 1,816.15 | 1,859.15 | 1,951.27 | 1,935.05 | 1,848.28 | 1,837.05 | 1,736.74 | 1,763.25 | 1,681.16 | 1,666.04 | | | 1,809.41 |

Source: U.S. Geological Survey (USGS)

# GOLD

**GOLD - COMEX**
Weekly Selected Futures as of 03/31/2023

Chart High 2078.80 on 03/08/2022
Chart Low 1046.20 on 12/03/2015

Nearby Futures through Last Trading Day using selected contract months: February, April, June, August, October and December.

## Volume of Trading of Gold Futures in Chicago    In Thousands of Contracts

| Year | Jan. | Feb. | Mar. | Apr. | May | June | July | Aug. | Sept. | Oct. | Nov. | Dec. | Total |
|---|---|---|---|---|---|---|---|---|---|---|---|---|---|
| 2013 | 4,221.1 | 3,632.3 | 3,906.6 | 5,218.8 | 5,312.3 | 3,744.7 | 4,647.2 | 3,466.7 | 3,331.9 | 3,458.2 | 3,577.1 | 2,777.7 | 47,294.6 |
| 2014 | 3,754.8 | 2,607.5 | 4,200.3 | 2,692.9 | 3,631.1 | 2,508.1 | 3,848.3 | 2,381.8 | 3,205.8 | 3,703.7 | 4,676.7 | 3,307.7 | 40,518.8 |
| 2015 | 4,507.9 | 2,558.8 | 4,403.4 | 3,057.0 | 3,721.5 | 2,856.0 | 4,554.8 | 3,431.6 | 2,917.1 | 3,070.1 | 4,034.0 | 2,735.2 | 41,847.3 |
| 2016 | 4,102.0 | 4,369.5 | 5,720.2 | 3,902.5 | 5,880.1 | 4,936.3 | 5,798.5 | 4,387.9 | 4,022.6 | 3,815.0 | 7,108.7 | 3,521.6 | 57,564.8 |
| 2017 | 5,978.9 | 4,392.4 | 6,119.4 | 4,612.2 | 6,367.4 | 4,906.6 | 5,957.0 | 6,808.8 | 7,184.1 | 6,665.5 | 8,623.3 | 5,186.6 | 72,802.2 |
| 2018 | 9,161.9 | 6,078.6 | 8,036.1 | 6,655.1 | 8,676.6 | 5,739.0 | 7,231.2 | 6,274.2 | 5,495.6 | 6,470.2 | 6,351.2 | 4,132.0 | 80,301.6 |
| 2019 | 6,245.8 | 4,010.5 | 6,711.5 | 5,096.3 | 7,142.7 | 7,308.6 | 9,490.3 | 9,582.3 | 8,582.9 | 8,016.2 | 8,927.4 | 5,394.2 | 86,508.7 |
| 2020 | 9,827.2 | 7,936.4 | 10,356.4 | 4,285.5 | 5,155.4 | 4,427.6 | 7,278.5 | 7,735.9 | 6,265.9 | 4,645.3 | 6,177.1 | 4,035.4 | 78,126.5 |
| 2021 | 6,164.8 | 4,569.4 | 6,266.2 | 3,590.4 | 6,310.8 | 4,800.1 | 5,603.2 | 3,910.7 | 3,926.2 | 4,119.0 | 6,130.6 | 3,073.6 | 58,465.0 |
| 2022 | 5,860.3 | 4,161.2 | 6,310.9 | 3,375.2 | 4,936.5 | 3,574.9 | 5,400.9 | 3,437.7 | 4,530.2 | 3,997.9 | 5,419.1 | 3,254.8 | 54,259.7 |

Contract size = 100 oz.    *Source: CME Group; Commodity Exchange (COMEX)*

## Average Open Interest of Gold Futures in Chicago    In Contracts

| Year | Jan. | Feb. | Mar. | Apr. | May | June | July | Aug. | Sept. | Oct. | Nov. | Dec. |
|---|---|---|---|---|---|---|---|---|---|---|---|---|
| 2013 | 442,707 | 435,425 | 437,300 | 416,489 | 431,460 | 383,314 | 424,302 | 388,278 | 380,768 | 382,216 | 395,583 | 383,980 |
| 2014 | 397,700 | 381,045 | 404,828 | 369,755 | 395,313 | 385,660 | 400,977 | 365,066 | 381,961 | 400,455 | 433,102 | 372,432 |
| 2015 | 415,408 | 399,097 | 415,894 | 397,632 | 411,656 | 417,416 | 451,224 | 430,894 | 416,389 | 448,795 | 425,138 | 398,843 |
| 2016 | 403,929 | 421,355 | 491,060 | 496,873 | 561,027 | 553,721 | 616,676 | 571,588 | 576,954 | 508,303 | 484,383 | 401,266 |
| 2017 | 444,716 | 423,037 | 436,599 | 458,759 | 447,814 | 462,182 | 468,238 | 490,304 | 562,694 | 524,694 | 530,233 | 460,378 |
| 2018 | 563,606 | 528,812 | 525,719 | 505,825 | 496,142 | 461,716 | 499,723 | 471,934 | 468,159 | 472,864 | 490,986 | 416,930 |
| 2019 | 489,807 | 488,012 | 503,968 | 439,367 | 485,122 | 530,157 | 602,830 | 604,243 | 628,729 | 626,969 | 697,262 | 720,262 |
| 2020 | 770,857 | 690,974 | 592,184 | 492,108 | 509,613 | 501,447 | 583,285 | 549,531 | 565,752 | 555,588 | 553,266 | 551,544 |
| 2021 | 549,566 | 500,908 | 472,695 | 466,965 | 505,511 | 474,172 | 489,673 | 490,011 | 500,431 | 494,196 | 567,607 | 504,782 |
| 2022 | 536,208 | 557,923 | 612,579 | 566,980 | 550,695 | 498,898 | 511,093 | 457,632 | 462,882 | 442,675 | 470,246 | 432,849 |

Contract size = 100 oz.    *Source: CME Group; Commodity Exchange (COMEX)*

# GOLD

## Commodity Exchange Warehouse Stocks of Gold, on First of Month   In Thousands of Troy Ounces

| Year | Jan. 1 | Feb. 1 | Mar. 1 | Apr. 1 | May 1 | June 1 | July 1 | Aug. 1 | Sept. 1 | Oct. 1 | Nov. 1 | Dec. 1 |
|---|---|---|---|---|---|---|---|---|---|---|---|---|
| 2013 | 11,058.7 | 11,009.3 | 10,289.3 | 9,279.4 | 8,129.2 | 8,054.9 | 7,534.5 | 6,991.4 | 7,013.2 | 6,862.8 | 7,153.7 | 7,247.9 |
| 2014 | 7,828.1 | 7,081.3 | 7,177.1 | 7,740.8 | 7,935.6 | 8,262.7 | 8,298.5 | 8,684.3 | 9,927.3 | 9,127.3 | 8,056.0 | 7,928.7 |
| 2015 | 7,932.1 | 7,983.9 | 8,321.5 | 8,010.7 | 7,718.4 | 7,871.5 | 8,043.6 | 7,572.3 | 7,221.1 | 6,852.5 | 6,700.8 | 6,377.6 |
| 2016 | 6,352.5 | 6,427.0 | 6,785.0 | 6,851.2 | 7,250.3 | 8,452.7 | 9,286.6 | 10,718.8 | 10,932.9 | 10,702.4 | 10,600.9 | 10,002.9 |
| 2017 | 9,158.9 | 8,986.3 | 8,942.2 | 8,956.9 | 8,931.0 | 8,750.3 | 8,616.7 | 8,660.6 | 8,693.6 | 8,761.4 | 8,707.2 | 8,914.8 |
| 2018 | 9,142.7 | 9,257.9 | 9,132.9 | 9,060.6 | 9,049.6 | 9,017.2 | 8,564.6 | 8,641.4 | 8,388.7 | 8,330.7 | 8,066.5 | 8,020.7 |
| 2019 | 8,434.3 | 8,439.1 | 8,162.5 | 8,034.0 | 7,782.0 | 7,677.3 | 7,696.7 | 7,783.6 | 8,057.1 | 8,188.4 | 8,284.4 | 8,828.0 |
| 2020 | 8,699.0 | 8,712.8 | 8,647.4 | 9,245.5 | 10,362.6 | 10,423.1 | 12,758.9 | 14,820.9 | 16,093.3 | 16,718.8 | 17,356.2 | 17,326.8 |
| 2021 | 18,911.1 | 19,181.4 | 19,326.8 | 17,968.1 | 17,570.5 | 18,343.0 | 18,460.2 | 19,129.3 | 18,429.8 | 18,031.2 | 17,574.3 | 18,131.4 |
| 2022 | 17,679.6 | 17,570.8 | 17,360.7 | 18,087.3 | 18,358.7 | 18,026.7 | 17,179.4 | 15,264.1 | 13,684.7 | 13,093.0 | 11,331.3 | 11,296.9 |

*Source: CME Group; Commodity Exchange (COMEX)*

## Central Gold Bank Reserves   In Millions of Troy Ounces

| Year | Belgium | Canada | France | Ger-many | Italy | Japan | Nether-lands | Switzer-land | United Kingdom | United States | World Total |
|---|---|---|---|---|---|---|---|---|---|---|---|
| 2012 | 7.3 | 0.1 | 78.3 | 109.0 | 78.8 | 24.6 | 19.7 | 33.4 | 10.0 | 261.5 | 1,017.5 |
| 2013 | 7.3 | 0.1 | 78.3 | 108.9 | 78.8 | 24.6 | 19.7 | 33.4 | 10.0 | 261.5 | 1,023.0 |
| 2014 | 7.3 | 0.1 | 78.3 | 108.8 | 78.8 | 24.6 | 19.7 | 33.4 | 10.0 | 261.5 | 1,028.7 |
| 2015 | 7.3 | 0.1 | 78.3 | 108.7 | 78.8 | 24.6 | 19.7 | 33.4 | 10.0 | 261.5 | 1,051.5 |
| 2016 | 7.3 | ---- | 78.3 | 108.6 | 78.8 | 24.6 | 19.7 | 33.4 | 10.0 | 261.5 | 1,080.1 |
| 2017 | 7.3 | ---- | 78.3 | 108.5 | 78.8 | 24.6 | 19.7 | 33.4 | 10.0 | 261.5 | 1,093.1 |
| 2018 | 7.3 | ---- | 78.3 | 108.3 | 78.8 | 24.6 | 19.7 | 33.4 | 10.0 | 261.5 | 1,100.6 |
| 2019 | 7.3 | ---- | 78.3 | 108.2 | 78.8 | 24.6 | 19.7 | 33.4 | 10.0 | 261.5 | 1,118.3 |
| 2020 | 7.3 | ---- | 78.3 | 108.1 | 78.8 | 24.6 | 19.7 | 33.4 | 10.0 | 261.5 | 1,134.0 |
| 2021[1] | 7.3 | ---- | 78.3 | 108.0 | 78.8 | 27.2 | 19.7 | 33.4 | 10.0 | 261.5 | 1,142.5 |

[1] Preliminary.   [2] International Monetary Fund.   *Source: American Metal Market (AMM)*

## Mine Production of Recoverable Gold in the United States   In Kilograms

| Year | Alaska | California | Nevada | Washington | Other States[2] | Total |
|---|---|---|---|---|---|---|
| 2013 | 32,200 | W | 170,000 | W | 27,800 | 230,000 |
| 2014 | 31,400 | W | 151,000 | W | 27,800 | 210,000 |
| 2015 | 28,000 | W | 162,000 | W | 24,200 | 214,000 |
| 2016 | 27,600 | W | 165,000 | W | 30,000 | 222,000 |
| 2017 | 26,200 | W | 173,000 | W | 37,400 | 237,000 |
| 2018 | 20,640 | W | 173,100 | W | 31,640 | 225,600 |
| 2019 | 16,930 | W | 151,600 | W | 55,250 | 200,400 |
| 2020 | 20,240 | W | 144,200 | W | 28,810 | 192,400 |
| 2021 | 19,950 | W | 139,500 | W | 28,020 | 187,500 |
| 2022[1] | 21,320 | W | 122,800 | W | 25,380 | 169,600 |

[1] Preliminary.   W = Withheld proprietary data, included in "Other States."   [2] Includes Arizona, California, Colorado, Idaho, Montana, New Mexico, South Dakota, Utah, and Washington.   *Source: U.S. Geological Survey (USGS)*

## U.S. Exports of Gold, Total   In Kilograms

| Year | Australia | Canada | China | Germany | Hong Kong | India | Mexico | South Africa | Switzer-land | Thailand | United Arab Emirates | United Kingdom | Total |
|---|---|---|---|---|---|---|---|---|---|---|---|---|---|
| 2011 | 18,200 | 1,460 | 5,150 | 1,440 | 111,000 | 15,500 | 5,160 | 11,900 | 105,000 | 21,200 | 10,300 | 161,000 | 474,000 |
| 2012 | 5,140 | 18,400 | 1,200 | 2,230 | 133,000 | 66,900 | 7,040 | 8,260 | 280,000 | 9,280 | 64,200 | 137,000 | 692,000 |
| 2013 | 5,200 | 18,900 | 14,400 | 941 | 217,000 | 32,500 | 947 | 19,600 | 284,000 | 27,000 | 34,300 | 29,000 | 691,000 |
| 2014 | 6,430 | 3,300 | 12,600 | 232 | 147,000 | 27,300 | 434 | ---- | 173,000 | 13,800 | 20,300 | 80,000 | 500,000 |
| 2015 | 336 | 2,650 | 5,730 | 694 | 120,000 | 60,500 | 2,910 | ---- | 167,000 | 6,490 | 17,900 | 96,200 | 478,000 |
| 2016 | 952 | 5,390 | 4,500 | 1,430 | 69,900 | 41,400 | 1,880 | ---- | 150,000 | 2,030 | 17,000 | 94,900 | 393,000 |
| 2017 | 2,550 | 2,030 | 17,700 | 2,040 | 99,600 | 53,100 | 898 | 7 | 148,000 | 13 | 14,700 | 116,000 | 461,000 |
| 2018 | 6 | 16,000 | 24,200 | 721 | 51,500 | 46,100 | 1,680 | 29 | 161,000 | 3,010 | 8,780 | 149,000 | 474,000 |
| 2019 | 5,170 | 9,110 | 32 | 1,300 | 309 | 33,800 | 1,050 | 5 | 47,900 | 29 | 5,720 | 237,000 | 360,000 |
| 2020 | 9,090 | 5,010 | 31 | 641 | 3,860 | 5,390 | 305 | ---- | 76,600 | 1,060 | 1,800 | 185,000 | 297,000 |

*Source: U.S. Geological Survey (USGS)*

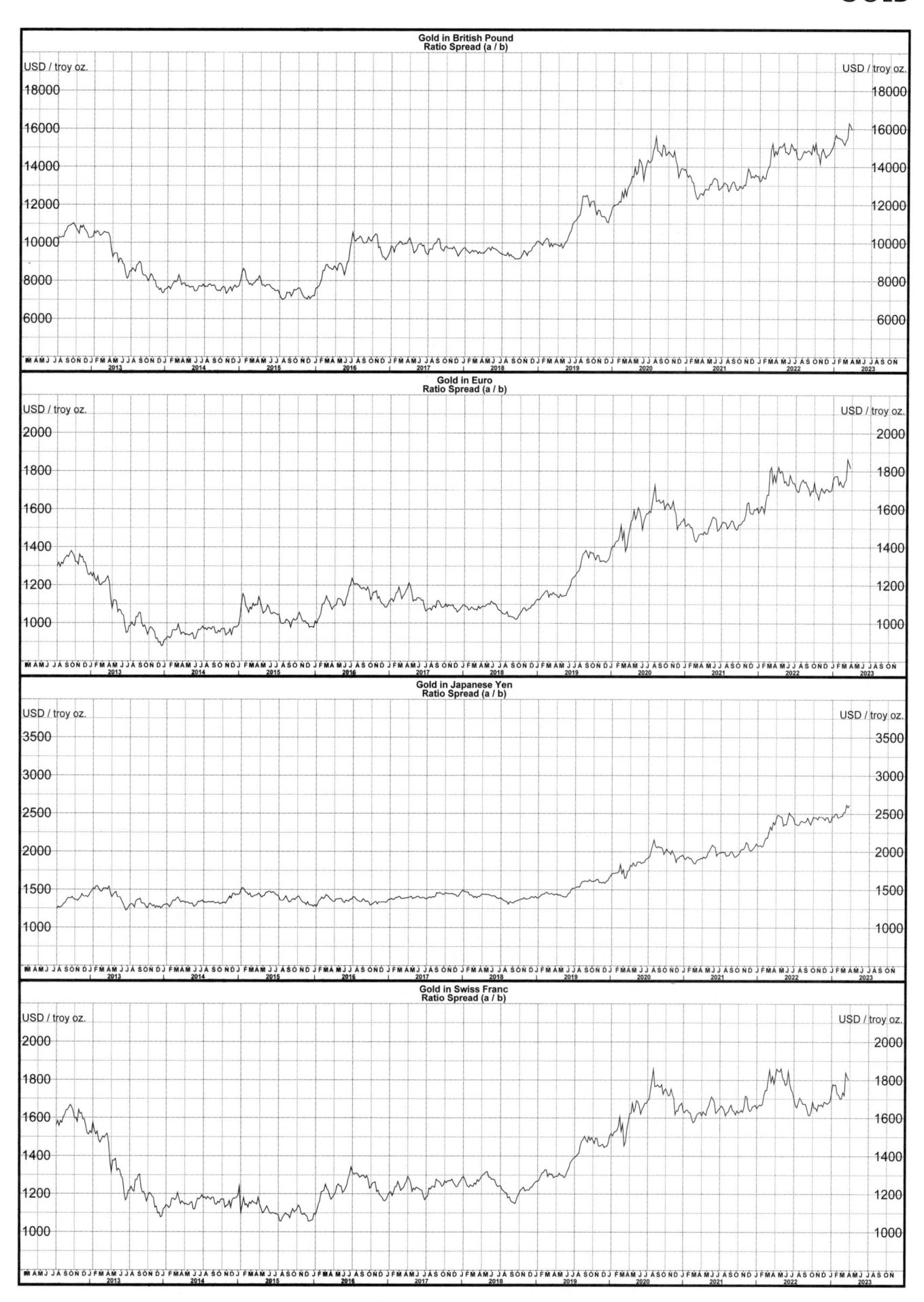

# GOLD

**Gold in British Pound**
Ratio Spread (a / b)

**Gold in Euro**
Ratio Spread (a / b)

**Gold in Japanese Yen**
Ratio Spread (a / b)

**Gold in Swiss Franc**
Ratio Spread (a / b)

# Grain Sorghum

Grain sorghums include milo, kafir, durra, feterita, and kaoliang. Grain sorghums are tolerant of drought by going into dormancy during dry and hot conditions and then resuming growth as conditions improve. Grain sorghums are a staple food in China, India, and Africa, but in the U.S., they are mainly used as livestock feed. The two key U.S. producing states are Texas and Kansas, each with about one-third of total U.S. production. U.S. sorghum production has become more popular with the breeding of dwarf grain sorghum hybrids, which are only about 3 feet tall (versus up to 10 feet tall for wild sorghum) and are easier to harvest with a combine. The U.S. sorghum crop year begins September 1.

**Prices** – The monthly average price for sorghum grain received by U.S. farmers in the 2021/22 marketing year rose by +10.6% yr/yr to $11.15 per hundred pounds. The value of U.S. grain sorghum production in the 2021/22 marketing year rose by +41.0% to $2.492 billion.

**Supply** – World production of sorghum in the 2022/23 marketing year is expected to fall by -5.4% to 58.842 million metric tons, below the record high of 66.683 million metric tons posted in 2007/08. U.S. grain sorghum production in 2022/23 is expected to fall by -58.1% yr/yr to 187.785 million bushels. Sorghum acreage harvested in 2022/23 is forecasted to fall by -29.6% to 4.570 million acres. The harvested yield in 2022/23 is expected to fall by -40.4% to 40.1 bushels per acre.

**Demand** – World utilization (consumption) of grain sorghum in the 2022/23 marketing year is expected to fall by -6.2% to 58.522 million metric tons. The biggest consumers will be China, utilizing 14.7% of the world supply, and Nigeria, utilizing 11.6%.

**Trade** – World exports of sorghum in the 2022/23 marketing year are expected to fall by -35.0% to 7.762 million metric tons, falling below the 2014/15 record high of 12.162 million metric tons. U.S. exports in 2022/23 are expected to fall by -66.0% yr/yr to 2.540 million metric tons, accounting for 32.7% of total world exports. The other major exporters are Argentina with 2.500 million metric tons and Australia, with 2.400 million metric tons of exports expected. World imports of sorghum in 2022/23 are expected to fall by -45.4% yr/yr to 6.866 million metric tons. The world's largest importer is China.

## World Production of Grain Sorghum   In Thousands of Metric Tons

| Crop Year | Argentina | Australia | Brazil | Burkina | China | Ethiopia | India | Mexico | Niger | Nigeria | Sudan | United States | World Total |
|---|---|---|---|---|---|---|---|---|---|---|---|---|---|
| 2013-14 | 2,700 | 905 | 2,000 | 1,900 | 6,500 | 3,900 | 5,200 | 8,300 | 1,300 | 5,258 | 4,550 | 4,130 | 59,466 |
| 2014-15 | 2,800 | 505 | 2,000 | 1,700 | 12,700 | 4,100 | 5,100 | 6,600 | 1,450 | 6,833 | 6,000 | 2,459 | 65,887 |
| 2015-16 | 2,900 | 905 | 1,150 | 1,465 | 10,500 | 4,700 | 4,600 | 6,300 | 2,000 | 6,905 | 3,100 | 6,130 | 63,456 |
| 2016-17 | 2,900 | 675 | 1,700 | 1,640 | 7,400 | 4,700 | 4,500 | 5,300 | 2,000 | 7,350 | 5,950 | 6,283 | 62,366 |
| 2017-18 | 3,100 | 800 | 2,100 | 1,400 | 6,900 | 5,000 | 4,600 | 4,700 | 1,850 | 6,950 | 4,400 | 4,119 | 58,752 |
| 2018-19 | 2,150 | 1,050 | 2,200 | 1,800 | 3,600 | 5,000 | 3,550 | 5,100 | 2,100 | 6,650 | 5,300 | 6,212 | 58,480 |
| 2019-20 | 2,050 | 280 | 2,400 | 1,870 | 6,800 | 5,300 | 4,500 | 5,000 | 2,000 | 6,650 | 4,350 | 4,365 | 58,446 |
| 2020-21[1] | 1,150 | 95 | 2,100 | 1,900 | 11,400 | 5,200 | 4,550 | 4,500 | 2,050 | 6,550 | 5,100 | 2,638 | 60,959 |
| 2021-22[2] | 1,450 | 110 | 3,000 | 1,650 | 14,000 | 4,650 | 4,450 | 5,000 | 1,400 | 6,650 | 3,700 | 3,214 | 62,399 |
| 2022-23[3] | 1,350 | 510 | 2,900 | 1,850 | 8,600 | 4,600 | 4,450 | 5,100 | 1,850 | 6,800 | 4,950 | 2,794 | 58,522 |

[1] Preliminary.   [2] Estimate.   [3] Forecast.   Source: Foreign Agricultural Service, U.S. Department of Agriculture (FAS-USDA)

## Salient Statistics of Grain Sorghum in the United States

| | Acreage Planted[4] | ----- For Grain ----- | | | | ----- For Silage ----- | | | ----- Sorghum Grain Stocks ----- | | | |
|---|---|---|---|---|---|---|---|---|---|---|---|---|
| | | | | | | | | | Dec. 1 | | June 1 | |
| Crop Year Beginning Sept. 1 | for All Purposes -- 1,000 Acres -- | Acreage Harvested | Production (1,000 Bushels) | Yield Per Acre Harvested (Bushels) | Price in Cents Per Bushel | Value of Production (Million $) | Acreage Harvested (1,000 Acres) | Production (1,000 Tons) | Yield Per Acre Harvested (Tons) | On Farms | Off Farms | On Farms | Off Farms |
| 2017-18 | 5,626 | 5,044 | 361,871 | 71.7 | 322 | 1,168.5 | 284 | 3,772 | 13.4 | 33,800 | 193,692 | 5,220 | 60,113 |
| 2018-19 | 5,690 | 5,061 | 364,986 | 72.1 | 326 | 1,180.8 | 264 | 3,326 | 12.6 | 44,200 | 214,580 | 9,470 | 107,962 |
| 2019-20 | 5,265 | 4,675 | 341,460 | 73.0 | 325 | 1,125.8 | 339 | 4,019 | 11.9 | 30,200 | 220,161 | 8,360 | 64,227 |
| 2020-21[1] | 5,880 | 5,095 | 372,960 | 73.2 | 310 | 1,767.8 | 239 | 3,125 | 13.1 | 21,300 | 198,386 | 2,050 | 38,929 |
| 2021-22[2] | 7,305 | 6,490 | 447,810 | 69.0 | | 2,666.2 | 331 | 5,083 | 15.4 | 29,450 | 260,226 | | |
| 2022-23[3] | 6,325 | 4,570 | 187,785 | 41.1 | | 1,253.0 | 525 | 5,662 | 10.8 | | | | |

[1] Preliminary.   [2] Estimate.   [3] Forecast.   Source: Foreign Agricultural Service, U.S. Department of Agriculture (FAS-USDA)

## Production of All Sorghum for Grain in the United States, by States   In Thousands of Bushels

| Year | Arkansas | Colorado | Illinois | Kansas | Louisiana | Mississippi | Missouri | Nebraska | New Mexico | Oklahoma | South Dakota | Texas | Total |
|---|---|---|---|---|---|---|---|---|---|---|---|---|---|
| 2017 | 546 | 18,720 | 1,245 | 200,900 | 1,183 | 288 | 2,461 | 11,570 | 1,680 | 15,635 | 11,560 | 94,500 | 361,871 |
| 2018 | 770 | 17,225 | 1,776 | 233,200 | 504 | 270 | 2,100 | 15,980 | 1,786 | 12,000 | 16,000 | 62,100 | 364,986 |
| 2019 | ---- | 12,710 | ---- | 204,000 | ---- | ---- | ---- | 12,090 | ---- | 13,260 | 14,000 | 85,400 | 341,460 |
| 2020 | ---- | 5,100 | ---- | 238,000 | ---- | ---- | ---- | 13,650 | ---- | 13,050 | 11,360 | 94,500 | 372,960 |
| 2021 | ---- | 14,800 | ---- | 265,200 | ---- | ---- | ---- | 19,780 | ---- | 20,520 | 13,440 | 114,070 | 447,810 |
| 2022[1] | ---- | 13,500 | ---- | 139,500 | ---- | ---- | ---- | 15,900 | ---- | 10,080 | 13,735 | 59,400 | 187,785 |

[1] Preliminary.   Source: National Agricultural Statistics Service, U.S. Department of Agriculture (NASS-USDA)

# GRAIN SORGHUM

## Quarterly Supply and Disappearance of Grain Sorghum in the United States    In Millions of Bushels

| Crop Year Beginning Sept. 1 | Beginning Stocks | Pro-duction | Imports[3] | Total Supply | Food & Alcohol | Seed | Feed & Residual | Total | Exports[3] | Total Disap-pearance | Ending Stocks |
|---|---|---|---|---|---|---|---|---|---|---|---|
| 2019-20 | 63.7 | 341.5 | .1 | 405.2 | 74.4 | .7 | 96.7 | 171.9 | 203.2 | 375.1 | 30.1 |
| Sept.-Nov. | 63.7 | 341.5 | .0 | 405.1 | 23.8 | 0 | 106.5 | 130.3 | 24.4 | 154.8 | 250.4 |
| Dec.-Feb. | 250.4 | ---- | .0 | 250.4 | 29.0 | 0 | 17.4 | 46.3 | 39.1 | 85.4 | 164.9 |
| Mar.-May | 164.9 | ---- | .0 | 165.0 | 16.9 | .4 | -8.6 | 8.6 | 83.8 | 92.4 | 72.6 |
| June-Aug. | 72.6 | ---- | .0 | 72.6 | 4.7 | .4 | -18.5 | -13.5 | 56.0 | 42.5 | 30.1 |
| 2020-21 | 30.1 | 373.0 | .0 | 403.1 | 5.9 | .9 | 97.1 | 103.8 | 278.9 | 382.8 | 20.3 |
| Sept.-Nov. | 30.1 | 373.0 | .0 | 403.1 | 2.3 |  | 118.8 | 121.1 | 62.3 | 183.4 | 219.7 |
| Dec.-Feb. | 219.7 | ---- | .0 | 219.7 | 1.3 |  | -7.6 | -6.3 | 89.1 | 82.8 | 136.9 |
| Mar.-May | 136.9 | ---- | .0 | 136.9 | .6 | .4 | .5 | 1.5 | 94.4 | 95.9 | 41.0 |
| June-Aug. | 41.0 | ---- | .0 | 41.0 | 1.8 | .5 | -14.7 | -12.4 | 33.1 | 20.7 | 20.3 |
| 2021-22[1] | 20.3 | 447.8 | .0 | 468.1 | 44.3 | .9 | 81.3 | 126.6 | 294.3 | 420.9 | 47.3 |
| Sept.-Nov. | 20.3 | 447.8 | .0 | 468.1 | 4.7 |  | 129.0 | 133.7 | 44.8 | 178.5 | 289.7 |
| Dec.-Feb. | 289.7 | ---- | .0 | 289.7 | 7.8 |  | -6.9 | .9 | 81.7 | 82.6 | 207.1 |
| Mar.-May | 207.1 | ---- | .0 | 207.1 | 9.0 | .4 | -27.2 | -17.8 | 117.1 | 99.3 | 107.8 |
| June-Aug. | 107.8 | ---- | .0 | 107.8 | 22.9 | .5 | -13.6 | 9.8 | 50.7 | 60.5 | 47.3 |
| 2022-23[2] | 47.3 | 187.8 | .1 | 235.1 | 39.1 | .9 | 70.0 | 110.0 | 100.0 | 210.0 | 25.1 |
| Sept.-Nov. | 47.3 | 187.8 | .0 | 235.1 | 19.0 |  | 39.6 | 58.6 | 16.2 | 74.8 | 160.2 |

[1] Preliminary.   [2] Estimate.   [3] Uncommitted inventory.   [4] Includes quantity under loan and farmer-owned reserve.   Source: Economic Research Service, U.S. Department of Agriculture (ERS-USDA)

## Average Price of Sorghum Grain, No. 2, Yellow in Kansas City    In Dollars Per Hundred Pounds (Cwt.)

| Crop Year | Sept. | Oct. | Nov. | Dec. | Jan. | Feb. | Mar. | Apr. | May | June | July | Aug. | Average |
|---|---|---|---|---|---|---|---|---|---|---|---|---|---|
| 2015-16 | 6.09 | 6.31 | 6.22 | 6.53 | ---- | ---- | 5.91 | 5.92 | 6.00 | 6.34 | 5.05 | 4.90 | 5.93 |
| 2016-17 | 4.94 | 5.18 | 5.09 | 5.28 | 5.48 | 5.67 | 5.50 | 5.61 | 5.94 | 5.88 | 5.66 | 5.32 | 5.46 |
| 2017-18 | 5.39 | 5.49 | 5.51 | 5.85 | 6.12 | 5.81 | 6.13 | 6.17 | 6.22 | 6.07 | 5.62 | 5.73 | 5.84 |
| 2018-19 | 5.41 | 5.50 | 5.64 | 5.98 | 5.92 | 5.97 | 6.00 | 5.81 | 6.32 | 7.29 | 7.10 | 6.18 | 6.09 |
| 2019-20 | 5.90 | 6.39 | 6.14 | 6.22 | 6.36 | 6.25 | 6.24 | 6.00 | 5.90 | 6.30 | 6.37 | 6.00 | 6.17 |
| 2020-21 | 7.82 | 8.97 | 9.75 | 10.24 | 11.78 | 12.39 | 11.76 | 10.68 | 11.81 | 11.46 | 10.54 | 10.31 | 10.63 |
| 2021-22 | 9.50 | 9.72 | 10.65 | 11.30 | 11.59 | 12.40 | 12.82 | 13.49 | 13.44 | 12.71 | 10.39 | 11.08 | 11.59 |
| 2022-23[1] | 12.61 | 13.19 | 13.11 | 12.51 | 12.52 |  |  |  |  |  |  |  | 12.79 |

[1] Preliminary.   Source: Economic Research Service, U.S. Department of Agriculture (ERS-USDA)

## Exports of Grain Sorghum, by Country of Destination from the United States    In Metric Tons

| Crop Year | Canada | Ecuador | Eritrea (Ethiopia) | Israel | Japan | Jordan | Mexico | South Africa | Spain | Sudan | Turkey | World Total |
|---|---|---|---|---|---|---|---|---|---|---|---|---|
| 2015-16 | 5,505 | ---- | ---- | ---- | 71,971 | ---- | 640,676 | 99,264 | 8,540 | 188,490 | ---- | 7,888,245 |
| 2016-17 | 4,937 | ---- | ---- | ---- | 220,243 | ---- | 530,086 | 68,936 | ---- | 121,825 | ---- | 5,982,920 |
| 2017-18 | 5,306 | ---- | 30,047 | ---- | 300,353 | ---- | 72,470 | 42,266 | 168,572 | 135,904 | ---- | 4,806,201 |
| 2018-19 | 4,469 | ---- | 60,300 | ---- | 244,358 | ---- | 516,439 | 73,835 | 512,968 | 117,330 | ---- | 2,372,692 |
| 2019-20 | 6,069 | ---- | 33,000 | ---- | 224,737 | ---- | 555,619 | 26,699 | ---- | 254,140 | ---- | 5,385,597 |
| 2020-21[1] | 6,704 | ---- | 60,686 | ---- | 30,450 | ---- | 120,933 | 15,000 | ---- | 143,100 | ---- | 6,905,773 |
| 2021-22[2] | 6,992 | ---- | 95,211 | ---- | 11,804 | ---- | 347,614 | 14,590 | ---- | 114,868 | ---- | 7,328,468 |

[1] Preliminary.   [2] Estimate.   Source: Economic Research Service, U.S. Department of Agriculture (ERS-USDA)

## Grain Sorghum Price Support Program and Market Prices in the United States

| Crop Year | Price Support Quantity (Million Cwt.) | % of Pro-duction | Aquired by CCC (Million Cwt.) | Owned by CCC at Year End | Basic Loan Rate | Target Price | Findley Loan Rate | Effective Base[3] (Million Acres) | Partici-pation Rate[4] % of Base | Kansas City | Texas High Plains | Los Angeles | Gulf Ports |
|---|---|---|---|---|---|---|---|---|---|---|---|---|---|
| 2014-15 | .4 | .2 | 0 | 0 | 3.48 | 7.05 | 1.95 | ---- | ---- | 6.94 | ---- | ---- | 9.10 |
| 2015-16 | 1.4 | .4 | 0 | 0 | 3.48 | 7.05 | 1.95 | ---- | ---- | 5.93 | ---- | ---- | 8.07 |
| 2016-17 | 1.9 | .7 | 0 | 0 | 3.48 | 7.05 | 1.95 | ---- | ---- | 5.46 | ---- | ---- | 7.56 |
| 2017-18 | 1.3 | .6 | 0 | 0 | 3.48 | 7.05 | 1.95 | ---- | ---- | 5.84 | ---- | ---- | ---- |
| 2018-19 | 1.2 | .6 | 0 | 0 | 3.48 | 7.05 | 1.95 | ---- | ---- | 6.09 | ---- | ---- | ---- |
| 2019-20[1] | 1.6 | .8 | 0 | 0 | 3.93 | 7.05 | 2.20 | ---- | ---- | 6.17 | ---- | ---- | ---- |
| 2020-21[2] | 1.7 | .8 | 0 | 0 | 3.93 | 7.05 | 2.20 | ---- | ---- | 10.63 | ---- | ---- | ---- |

[1] Preliminary.   [2] Estimate.   [3] National effective crop acreage base as determined by ASCS.   [4] Percentage of effective base acres enrolled in acreage reduction programs.   5/ Beginning with the 1996-7 marketing year, target prices are no longer applicable.   Source: Economic Research Service, U.S. Department of Agriculture (ERS-USDA)

# Hay

Hay is a catchall term for forage plants, typically grasses such as timothy and Sudan-grass, and legumes such as alfalfa and clover. Alfalfa and alfalfa mixtures account for nearly half of all hay production. Hay is generally used to make cured feed for livestock. Curing, which is the proper drying of hay, is necessary to prevent spoilage. Hay, when properly cured, contains about 20% moisture. If hay is dried excessively, however, there is a loss of protein, which makes it less effective as livestock feed. Hay is harvested in almost all the lower 48 states.

**Prices** – The average monthly price of hay received by U.S. farmers in the 2021/22 marketing year (May through April) rose by +20.5% yr/yr to $189.83 per ton. The farm production value of hay produced in 2021/22 rose by +9.8% to $19.277 million.

**Supply** – U.S. hay production in 2022/23 is expected to fall by -6.8% yr/yr to 112.061 million tons. U.S. farmers are expected to harvest 49.546 million acres of hay in 2022/23, down -2.3%. The yield in 2022/23 is expected to fall by -4.2% at 2.27 tons per acre, below the 2004/05 record high of 2.55. U.S. ending stocks (May 1) in 2022/23 are expected to fall by -6.9% to 16.767 million tons. The largest hay-producing states in the U.S. for 2021 were Texas with 8.9% of U.S. hay production, Missouri with 5.4%, Nebraska with 5.2%, California with 4.3%, and Oklahoma with 4.2%.

## Salient Statistics of All Hay in the United States

| Crop Year Beginning May 1 | Acres Harvested (1,000 Acres) | Yield Per Acre (Tons) | Production (Millions of Tons) | Carry-over May 1 (Millions of Tons) | Disap-pearance (Millions of Tons) | Supply Per Animal Unit (In Tons) | Disap-pearance Per Animal Unit (In Tons) | Animal Units Fed[3] (Millions) | Farm Price ($ Per Ton) | Farm Production Value Million $ | Retail Alfalfa (Certified) | Retail Timothy | Retail Red Clover | Retail Sudan-grass |
|---|---|---|---|---|---|---|---|---|---|---|---|---|---|---|
| 2017-18 | 52,777 | 2.43 | 128.2 | 24.4 | | 1.13 | 1.01 | | 142.9 | 16,109 | | | | |
| 2018-19 | 52,839 | 2.34 | 123.6 | 15.3 | | 1.02 | 0.91 | | 166.7 | 17,288 | | | | |
| 2019-20 | 52,425 | 2.46 | 128.9 | 14.9 | | 1.07 | 0.92 | | 163.1 | 18,040 | | | | |
| 2020-21 | 52,238 | 2.43 | 126.8 | 20.4 | | 2.09 | 1.83 | | 157.5 | 17,552 | | | | |
| 2021-22[1] | 50,736 | 2.37 | 120.2 | 18.0 | | 0.99 | 0.87 | | 191.0 | 19,662 | | | | |
| 2022-23[2] | 49,546 | 2.27 | 112.1 | 16.8 | | 0.95 | | | 232.8 | 21,252 | | | | |

[1] Preliminary.  [2] Estimate.  [3] Roughage-consuming animal units fed annually.  NA = Not available.
Source: Economic Research Service, U.S. Department of Agriculture (ERS-USDA)

## Production of All Hay in the United States, by States    In Thousands of Tons

| Year | California | Idaho | Iowa | Minnesota | Missouri | New York | North Dakota | Ohio | Oklahoma | South Dakota | Texas | Wisconsin | Total |
|---|---|---|---|---|---|---|---|---|---|---|---|---|---|
| 2017 | 6,388 | 5,128 | 3,268 | 3,797 | 5,985 | 5,955 | 3,423 | 2,371 | 5,638 | 4,603 | 9,548 | 3,522 | 128,207 |
| 2018 | 5,682 | 5,019 | 2,998 | 3,077 | 5,408 | 6,985 | 4,419 | 2,356 | 5,121 | 5,788 | 8,374 | 2,953 | 123,600 |
| 2019 | 5,795 | 5,111 | 3,116 | 2,966 | 7,367 | 6,085 | 4,116 | 2,137 | 5,935 | 7,003 | 9,216 | 2,784 | 128,864 |
| 2020 | 4,610 | 5,270 | 3,697 | 3,546 | 6,437 | 6,370 | 3,596 | 2,102 | 5,364 | 5,365 | 9,604 | 3,483 | 126,812 |
| 2021 | 5,152 | 4,552 | 4,130 | 2,330 | 6,532 | 6,289 | 2,093 | 2,355 | 4,990 | 3,105 | 10,715 | 3,520 | 120,196 |
| 2022[1] | 4,418 | 5,328 | 3,641 | 3,202 | 5,828 | 4,339 | 3,825 | 2,243 | 3,940 | 4,560 | 6,528 | 2,990 | 112,061 |

[1] Preliminary.  Source: Agricultural Statistics Board, U.S. Department of Agriculture (ASB-USDA)

## Hay Production and Farm Stocks in the United States    In Thousands of Short Tons

| Year | Alfalfa & Mixtures | All Others | All Hay | Corn for Silage[1] | Sorghum Silage[1] | Farm Stocks May 1 | Farm Stocks Dec. 1 |
|---|---|---|---|---|---|---|---|
| 2017 | 55,812 | 72,395 | 128,207 | 127,434 | 3,772 | 24,400 | 84,422 |
| 2018 | 52,634 | 70,966 | 123,600 | 121,564 | 3,326 | 15,348 | 79,055 |
| 2019 | 54,875 | 73,989 | 128,864 | 132,807 | 4,019 | 14,906 | 84,488 |
| 2020 | 53,067 | 73,745 | 126,812 | 137,675 | 3,125 | 20,426 | 84,020 |
| 2021 | 49,245 | 70,951 | 120,196 | 130,317 | 5,083 | 18,006 | 79,016 |
| 2022[2] | 48,820 | 63,241 | 112,061 | 128,567 | 5,662 | 16,767 | 71,911 |

[1] Not included in all tame hay.  [2] Preliminary.  Source: Agricultural Statistics Board, U.S. Department of Agriculture (ASB-USDA)

## Average Price Received by Farmers for All Hay (Baled) in the United States    In Dollars Per Ton

| Crop Year | May | June | July | Aug. | Sept. | Oct. | Nov. | Dec. | Jan. | Feb. | Mar. | Apr. | Average |
|---|---|---|---|---|---|---|---|---|---|---|---|---|---|
| 2017-18 | 147.0 | 145.0 | 141.0 | 137.0 | 137.0 | 141.0 | 138.0 | 137.0 | 140.0 | 142.0 | 148.0 | 162.0 | 142.9 |
| 2018-19 | 167.0 | 160.0 | 161.0 | 163.0 | 164.0 | 163.0 | 162.0 | 166.0 | 167.0 | 170.0 | 173.0 | 184.0 | 166.7 |
| 2019-20 | 187.0 | 177.0 | 164.0 | 162.0 | 160.0 | 161.0 | 159.0 | 158.0 | 155.0 | 157.0 | 156.0 | 161.0 | 163.1 |
| 2020-21 | 164.0 | 162.0 | 156.0 | 157.0 | 151.0 | 155.0 | 153.0 | 152.0 | 152.0 | 158.0 | 163.0 | 167.0 | 157.5 |
| 2021-22 | 176.0 | 179.0 | 186.0 | 193.0 | 193.0 | 196.0 | 192.0 | 193.0 | 188.0 | 195.0 | 192.0 | 209.0 | 191.0 |
| 2022-23[1] | 210.0 | 212.0 | 235.0 | 246.0 | 242.0 | 250.0 | 239.0 | 235.0 | 228.0 | 231.0 | | | 232.8 |

[1] Preliminary.  [2] Marketing year average.  Source: Economic Research Service, U.S. Department of Agriculture (ERS-USDA)

# Heating Oil

Heating oil is a heavy fuel oil that is refined from crude oil. Heating oil is also known as No. 2 fuel oil and accounts for about 25% of the yield from a barrel of crude oil. That is the second-largest "cut" after gasoline. The price to consumers of home heating oil is generally comprised of 42% for crude oil, 12% for refining costs, and 46% for marketing and distribution costs (Source: EIA's Petroleum Marketing Monthly). Generally, a $1 increase in the price of crude oil translates into a 2.5-cent per gallon rise in heating oil. Because of this, heating oil prices are highly correlated with crude oil prices, although heating oil prices are also subject to swift supply and demand shifts due to weather changes or refinery shutdowns.

The primary use of heating oil is for residential heating. In the U.S., approximately 8.1 million households use heating oil as their main heating fuel. Most of the demand for heating oil occurs from October through March. The Northeast region, which includes the New England and the Central Atlantic States, is most reliant on heating oil. This region consumes approximately 70% of U.S. heating oil. However, demand for heating oil has been dropping as households switch to a more convenient heating source like natural gas. In fact, demand for heating oil is down by about 10 billion gallons/year from its peak use in 1976 (Source: American Petroleum Institute).

Refineries produce approximately 85% of U.S. heating oil as part of the "distillate fuel oil" product family, which includes heating oil and diesel fuel. The remainder of U.S. heating oil is imported from Canada, the Virgin Islands, and Venezuela.

Recently, a team of Purdue University researchers developed a way to make home heating oil from a mixture of soybean oil and conventional fuel oil. The oil blend is made by replacing 20% of the fuel oil with soybean oil, potentially saving 1.3 billion gallons of fuel oil per year. This soybean heating oil can be used in conventional furnaces without altering existing equipment. The soybean heating oil is relatively easy to produce and creates no sulfur emissions.

The "crack-spread" is the processing margin earned when refiners buy crude oil and refine it into heating oil and gasoline. The crack-spread ratio commonly used in the industry is the 3-2-1, which involves buying one heating oil contract and two gasoline futures contracts, and then selling three crude oil contracts. If the crack spread is positive, it is profitable for refiners to buy crude oil and refine it into products. The NYMEX has a crack-spread calculator on their web site at www.NYMEX.com.

Heating oil futures and options are traded at the CME Group. The CME's heating oil futures contract calls for the delivery of 1,000 barrels of fungible No. 2 heating oil in the New York harbor. Futures are also traded on ICE Futures Europe and the Multi Commodity Exchange of Index (MCX).

**Prices** – CME heating oil futures prices (Barchart.com symbol code HO) on the nearest-futures chart rallied sharply in early 2022 but then settled back somewhat, closing the year +41.7% at $3.2950 per gallon.

**Supply** – U.S. production of distillate fuel oil in 2022 rose by +7.1% yr/yr to 4.991 million barrels per day, below the 2018 record high of 5.164. Stocks of distillate fuel oil in December 2021 were down by -19.4% yr/yr at 129.928 million barrels. U.S. production of residual fuel in 2022 rose by +16.7% yr/yr to an average of 248,521 barrels per day, which is about a fifth of the production level of over 1 million barrels per day produced in the 1970s. U.S. stocks of residual fuel oil as of December 2021 were down by -14.6% to 25.770 million barrels, below the 2015 record high of 42.189 million barrels.

**Demand** – U.S. usage of distillate fuel oil in 2022 fell by -1.0% yr/yr to 3.933 million barrels per day, below the 2007 record high of 4.198 million barrels a day.

**Trade** – U.S. imports of distillate fuel oil in 2022 fell by -35.8% to an average of 185,103 barrels per day, below the 2006 record high of 365,000 barrels per day. U.S. imports of residual fuel oil in 2021 rose by +11.9% yr/yr to 186,307 barrels per day, far less than the levels of over 1 million barrels per day seen back in the 1970s.

**World Production of Distillate Fuel Oil**   In Thousands of Barrels Per Day

| Year | Brazil | Canada | China | France | Germany | India | Italy | Japan | Korea, South | Russia | Saudi Arabia | United States | World Total |
|---|---|---|---|---|---|---|---|---|---|---|---|---|---|
| 2008 | 793.0 | 557.0 | 2,767.5 | 991.2 | 1,104.4 | 1,054.0 | 642.0 | 908.7 | 388.3 | 640.0 | 577.8 | 3,945.4 | 25,428.5 |
| 2009 | 758.0 | 516.7 | 2,777.0 | 985.1 | 1,062.7 | 1,182.0 | 617.1 | 820.8 | 385.9 | 570.0 | 605.0 | 3,631.1 | 24,914.9 |
| 2010 | 855.0 | 569.6 | 3,011.3 | 983.7 | 1,096.5 | 1,226.0 | 614.5 | 825.8 | 399.4 | 583.0 | 618.9 | 3,800.3 | 25,366.6 |
| 2011 | 927.0 | 601.8 | 3,195.3 | 962.2 | 1,049.0 | 1,298.0 | 608.9 | 807.6 | 393.3 | 641.0 | 651.0 | 3,898.9 | 25,981.4 |
| 2012 | 992.0 | 582.7 | 3,461.4 | 962.9 | 1,076.1 | 1,420.0 | 569.5 | 811.3 | 405.2 | 582.0 | 704.8 | 3,741.4 | 26,602.0 |
| 2013 | 996.0 | 592.3 | 3,503.2 | 970.8 | 1,125.3 | 1,385.0 | 550.6 | 796.4 | 423.7 | 596.0 | 729.6 | 3,827.5 | 26,848.6 |
| 2014 | 1,023.0 | 580.8 | 3,513.6 | 949.2 | 1,079.8 | 1,417.7 | 568.2 | 772.8 | 432.2 | 577.1 | 753.3 | 4,037.2 | 27,209.9 |
| 2015[1] |  | 571.5 |  | 965.1 | 1,100.8 |  | 558.0 | 770.1 | 472.6 |  |  | 3,995.2 |  |
| 2016[2] |  | 541.1 |  | 953.5 | 1,114.9 |  | 548.9 | 774.8 | 501.0 |  |  |  |  |
| 2017[2] |  | 533.1 |  | 890.3 | 1,046.5 |  | 505.0 | 696.4 | 462.5 |  |  |  |  |

[1] Preliminary.   [2] Estimate.   *Source: Energy Information Administration, U.S. Department of Energy (EIA-DOE)*

# HEATING OIL

## World Imports of Distillate Fuel Oil   In Thousands of Barrels Per Day

| Year | Australia | Belgium | France | Germany | Indonesia | Nether-lands | Singa-pore | Spain | Turkey | United Kingdom | United States | Vietnam | World Total |
|---|---|---|---|---|---|---|---|---|---|---|---|---|---|
| 2004 | 63.0 | 164.7 | 322.3 | 265.8 | 130.1 | 203.0 | 112.5 | 230.1 | 77.8 | 81.8 | 325.5 | 111.6 | 4,268.5 |
| 2005 | 81.7 | 198.1 | 380.7 | 277.6 | 170.2 | 196.2 | 78.9 | 263.4 | 84.7 | 98.6 | 328.8 | 120.4 | 4,499.6 |
| 2006 | 105.7 | 166.1 | 317.3 | 332.0 | 176.1 | 278.0 | 125.2 | 264.9 | 130.9 | 158.3 | 364.7 | 110.8 | 4,906.3 |
| 2007 | 105.2 | 148.9 | 271.6 | 187.8 | 229.7 | 188.4 | 127.0 | 286.6 | 162.3 | 159.0 | 304.1 | 132.5 | 5,090.9 |
| 2008 | 147.8 | 156.4 | 292.1 | 317.2 | 211.6 | 250.9 | 178.6 | 246.3 | 169.8 | 152.6 | 212.9 | 132.6 | 5,466.6 |
| 2009 | 144.0 | 124.6 | 380.2 | 297.0 | 146.7 | 333.5 | 155.0 | 234.1 | 186.2 | 127.5 | 225.1 | 132.9 | 5,485.7 |
| 2010 | 141.7 | 111.8 | 414.0 | 318.9 | 259.0 | 385.2 | 393.5 | 220.7 | 197.9 | 193.0 | 228.4 | 100.5 | 6,318.7 |
| 2011 | 176.6 | 161.7 | 408.0 | 278.9 | 244.3 | 375.1 | 383.0 | 174.1 | 207.5 | 191.4 | 178.7 | 108.5 | 6,444.8 |
| 2012[1] | 202.0 | 128.3 | 469.9 | 276.1 | 290.2 | 384.2 | 279.2 | 136.4 | 226.1 | 218.6 | 126.2 | 113.6 | 6,523.9 |
| 2013[2] | 226.8 | 246.5 | 478.1 | 322.7 |  | 378.6 |  | 95.2 | 245.5 | 217.2 | 154.7 |  |  |

[1] Preliminary.   [2] Estimate.   Source: Energy Information Administration, U.S. Department of Energy (EIA-DOE)

## World Exports of Distillate Fuel Oil   In Thousands of Barrels Per Day

| Year | Belgium | Germany | India | Italy | Japan | Korea, South | Kuwait | Nether-lands | Russia | Singa-pore | Taiwan | United States | World Total |
|---|---|---|---|---|---|---|---|---|---|---|---|---|---|
| 2004 | 167.0 | 166.1 | 148.5 | 187.3 | 29.4 | 185.8 | 225.3 | 411.2 | 614.3 | 294.0 | 119.9 | 109.6 | 4,692.3 |
| 2005 | 182.3 | 204.4 | 173.0 | 179.8 | 64.1 | 234.3 | 221.2 | 430.4 | 649.2 | 300.0 | 149.2 | 138.4 | 5,038.9 |
| 2006 | 162.1 | 223.0 | 238.0 | 160.2 | 70.5 | 250.6 | 185.5 | 495.9 | 752.6 | 341.3 | 150.0 | 215.1 | 5,394.9 |
| 2007 | 177.9 | 250.6 | 292.4 | 183.5 | 137.2 | 281.9 | 194.0 | 420.4 | 751.9 | 359.3 | 176.5 | 267.7 | 5,268.0 |
| 2008 | 171.7 | 203.2 | 300.2 | 170.2 | 220.5 | 357.6 | 190.2 | 464.7 | 767.8 | 406.8 | 181.1 | 528.3 | 5,830.8 |
| 2009 | 140.2 | 181.8 | 377.3 | 168.2 | 215.7 | 343.6 | 152.8 | 562.3 | 812.9 | 346.3 | 206.6 | 587.4 | 6,153.4 |
| 2010 | 142.4 | 138.8 | 376.5 | 189.1 | 197.4 | 358.0 | 143.8 | 636.1 | 851.0 | 540.0 | 177.2 | 656.0 | 6,209.9 |
| 2011 | 156.2 | 132.2 | 430.5 | 153.6 | 160.0 | 436.8 | 143.8 | 631.1 | 807.8 | 553.7 | 157.5 | 854.1 | 6,404.8 |
| 2012[1] | 160.7 | 128.9 | 459.1 | 178.8 | 120.2 | 481.8 | 153.0 | 608.5 | 840.9 | 469.8 | 191.7 | 1,007.2 | 6,781.3 |
| 2013[2] | 226.4 | 135.0 |  | 142.8 | 167.6 | 446.6 |  | 604.1 |  |  |  | 1,133.9 |  |

[1] Preliminary.   [2] Estimate.   Source: Energy Information Administration, U.S. Department of Energy (EIA-DOE)

## Production of Distillate Fuel Oil in the United States   In Thousands of Barrels Per Day

| Year | Jan. | Feb. | Mar. | Apr. | May | June | July | Aug. | Sept. | Oct. | Nov. | Dec. | Average |
|---|---|---|---|---|---|---|---|---|---|---|---|---|---|
| 2013 | 4,479.8 | 4,280.5 | 4,283.8 | 4,416.4 | 4,767.1 | 4,791.5 | 4,933.8 | 4,930.0 | 4,888.4 | 4,814.8 | 5,049.7 | 5,121.6 | 4,729.8 |
| 2014 | 4,685.3 | 4,594.5 | 4,779.7 | 4,987.9 | 5,026.1 | 4,896.0 | 5,021.2 | 5,042.5 | 4,939.8 | 4,662.0 | 5,011.6 | 5,322.9 | 4,914.1 |
| 2015 | 4,835.2 | 4,752.4 | 4,893.7 | 4,991.4 | 4,982.8 | 5,031.8 | 5,101.2 | 5,106.6 | 5,060.8 | 4,816.5 | 5,169.0 | 5,042.1 | 4,982.0 |
| 2016 | 4,530.3 | 4,667.8 | 4,848.3 | 4,658.8 | 4,760.4 | 4,953.6 | 4,933.4 | 4,939.2 | 4,888.1 | 4,614.1 | 5,066.0 | 5,147.6 | 4,834.0 |
| 2017 | 4,785.5 | 4,656.6 | 4,792.5 | 5,018.9 | 5,215.5 | 5,283.8 | 5,161.9 | 5,044.1 | 4,559.7 | 4,972.0 | 5,362.1 | 5,407.9 | 5,021.7 |
| 2018 | 5,005.9 | 4,584.1 | 4,822.5 | 5,119.5 | 5,214.1 | 5,410.4 | 5,257.1 | 5,369.5 | 5,230.0 | 5,035.4 | 5,350.1 | 5,575.6 | 5,164.5 |
| 2019 | 5,249.5 | 4,904.7 | 4,968.4 | 5,059.2 | 5,211.7 | 5,350.7 | 5,245.8 | 5,266.5 | 5,035.0 | 4,793.9 | 5,231.1 | 5,309.4 | 5,135.5 |
| 2020 | 5,086.5 | 4,812.9 | 4,952.9 | 5,078.8 | 4,818.2 | 4,579.7 | 4,842.7 | 4,822.7 | 4,493.5 | 4,204.2 | 4,522.0 | 4,632.9 | 4,737.3 |
| 2021 | 4,560.2 | 3,782.0 | 4,519.3 | 4,595.9 | 4,745.0 | 4,980.5 | 4,855.9 | 4,741.6 | 4,555.2 | 4,727.3 | 4,950.2 | 4,926.2 | 4,661.6 |
| 2022[1] | 4,644.0 | 4,665.8 | 5,000.7 | 4,836.6 | 4,982.8 | 5,193.0 | 5,118.9 | 5,142.3 | 5,183.9 | 5,077.3 | 5,207.7 | 4,843.5 | 4,991.4 |

[1] Preliminary.   Source: Energy Information Administration; U.S. Department of Energy (EIA-DOE)

## Stocks of Distillate Fuel in the United States, on First of Month   In Thousands of Barrels

| Year | Jan. | Feb. | Mar. | Apr. | May | June | July | Aug. | Sept. | Oct. | Nov. | Dec. |
|---|---|---|---|---|---|---|---|---|---|---|---|---|
| 2013 | 131,268 | 121,963 | 118,737 | 118,791 | 122,132 | 122,463 | 126,020 | 129,060 | 129,326 | 118,035 | 121,118 | 127,543 |
| 2014 | 114,534 | 112,897 | 115,337 | 116,827 | 121,757 | 121,674 | 125,559 | 128,132 | 131,289 | 120,093 | 126,085 | 136,065 |
| 2015 | 131,992 | 123,137 | 128,294 | 129,022 | 134,028 | 139,437 | 142,144 | 152,145 | 148,846 | 143,317 | 156,666 | 160,741 |
| 2016 | 160,583 | 162,696 | 160,620 | 154,692 | 154,389 | 149,239 | 155,969 | 159,534 | 160,378 | 153,884 | 160,173 | 165,456 |
| 2017 | 168,937 | 162,241 | 151,080 | 154,640 | 153,793 | 151,608 | 151,068 | 147,820 | 137,461 | 129,885 | 132,700 | 145,574 |
| 2018 | 141,340 | 138,888 | 130,478 | 120,928 | 115,580 | 120,549 | 127,215 | 132,266 | 137,249 | 124,773 | 126,543 | 140,162 |
| 2019 | 140,129 | 136,323 | 132,172 | 128,274 | 129,865 | 131,094 | 137,674 | 135,636 | 131,838 | 120,073 | 126,221 | 140,083 |
| 2020 | 143,190 | 132,918 | 126,782 | 150,922 | 176,627 | 176,947 | 178,800 | 179,763 | 172,502 | 156,235 | 157,205 | 161,188 |
| 2021 | 162,810 | 143,404 | 145,477 | 136,014 | 139,961 | 140,060 | 142,049 | 137,850 | 131,656 | 132,559 | 131,609 | 129,928 |
| 2022[1] | 124,989 | 120,848 | 114,647 | 106,448 | 109,489 | 111,356 | 112,525 | 113,261 | 110,511 | 110,528 | 120,527 |  |

[1] Preliminary.   Source: Energy Information Administration; U.S. Department of Energy (EIA-DOE)

# HEATING OIL

## Imports of Distillate Fuel Oil in the United States    In Thousands of Barrels Per Day

| Year | Jan. | Feb. | Mar. | Apr. | May | June | July | Aug. | Sept. | Oct. | Nov. | Dec. | Average |
|---|---|---|---|---|---|---|---|---|---|---|---|---|---|
| 2013 | 213 | 174 | 146 | 238 | 168 | 121 | 107 | 123 | 132 | 128 | 145 | 164 | 155 |
| 2014 | 283 | 337 | 324 | 181 | 198 | 121 | 129 | 143 | 126 | 120 | 136 | 245 | 195 |
| 2015 | 349 | 388 | 324 | 243 | 191 | 132 | 143 | 140 | 103 | 101 | 150 | 155 | 202 |
| 2016 | 172 | 231 | 150 | 177 | 123 | 88 | 123 | 164 | 150 | 75 | 145 | 167 | 147 |
| 2017 | 204 | 199 | 108 | 116 | 124 | 102 | 111 | 112 | 112 | 134 | 180 | 282 | 149 |
| 2018 | 290 | 284 | 157 | 91 | 122 | 90 | 144 | 175 | 172 | 161 | 227 | 190 | 175 |
| 2019 | 307 | 361 | 180 | 121 | 160 | 126 | 174 | 154 | 118 | 186 | 258 | 295 | 203 |
| 2020 | 220 | 157 | 171 | 231 | 190 | 154 | 116 | 145 | 180 | 280 | 305 | 464 | 218 |
| 2021 | 371 | 353 | 470 | 198 | 272 | 240 | 165 | 257 | 224 | 291 | 330 | 292 | 288 |
| 2022[1] | 242 | 399 | 189 | 129 | 180 | 117 | 169 | 176 | 127 | 106 | 197 | 192 | 185 |

[1] Preliminary.    Source: Energy Information Administration, U.S. Department of Energy (EIA-DOE)

## Disposition of Distillate Fuel Oil, Total Product Supplied in the United States    In Thousands of Barrels Per Day

| Year | Jan. | Feb. | Mar. | Apr. | May | June | July | Aug. | Sept. | Oct. | Nov. | Dec. | Average |
|---|---|---|---|---|---|---|---|---|---|---|---|---|---|
| 2013 | 4,061.8 | 3,984.4 | 3,769.1 | 3,854.4 | 3,749.0 | 3,662.9 | 3,621.0 | 3,693.2 | 3,724.6 | 4,038.8 | 3,893.2 | 3,886.8 | 3,828.3 |
| 2014 | 4,340.0 | 4,160.3 | 4,066.2 | 3,989.8 | 3,951.6 | 3,901.6 | 3,866.5 | 3,874.8 | 3,933.4 | 4,266.3 | 3,917.2 | 4,178.2 | 4,037.1 |
| 2015 | 4,185.7 | 4,559.2 | 4,078.1 | 4,027.4 | 3,777.5 | 3,896.8 | 3,901.2 | 3,914.7 | 4,063.0 | 4,014.1 | 3,740.2 | 3,831.1 | 3,999.1 |
| 2016 | 3,850.3 | 3,996.1 | 3,947.0 | 3,798.9 | 3,732.0 | 3,852.7 | 3,597.4 | 3,880.4 | 3,912.0 | 3,986.3 | 3,938.4 | 4,043.1 | 3,877.9 |
| 2017 | 3,735.6 | 3,934.8 | 4,126.6 | 3,762.8 | 3,955.0 | 3,963.6 | 3,641.8 | 4,003.5 | 3,921.2 | 4,011.2 | 4,157.4 | 3,975.3 | 3,932.4 |
| 2018 | 4,491.0 | 3,979.3 | 4,196.5 | 4,139.0 | 4,208.8 | 3,959.4 | 3,962.6 | 4,195.7 | 4,022.2 | 4,347.8 | 4,203.8 | 4,019.4 | 4,143.8 |
| 2019 | 4,327.5 | 4,307.3 | 4,184.1 | 4,119.6 | 4,109.7 | 3,993.2 | 3,911.2 | 4,029.5 | 3,920.6 | 4,224.2 | 4,201.5 | 3,927.1 | 4,104.6 |
| 2020 | 4,024.4 | 4,079.6 | 3,960.9 | 3,528.1 | 3,446.2 | 3,494.6 | 3,614.6 | 3,667.8 | 3,814.0 | 4,036.5 | 3,879.5 | 3,888.2 | 3,786.2 |
| 2021 | 3,936.5 | 3,968.4 | 4,077.1 | 4,048.4 | 3,900.2 | 3,945.7 | 3,674.6 | 3,984.4 | 4,032.0 | 3,967.4 | 4,190.4 | 3,950.1 | 3,972.9 |
| 2022[1] | 4,080.5 | 4,176.6 | 4,160.7 | 3,808.2 | 3,874.0 | 3,994.3 | 3,719.0 | 3,870.9 | 4,009.8 | 4,097.9 | 3,777.7 | 3,626.4 | 3,933.0 |

[1] Preliminary.    Source: Energy Information Administration, U.S. Department of Energy (EIA-DOE)

## World Production of Residual Fuel Oil    In Thousands of Barrels Per Day

| Year | Brazil | China | India | Iran | Italy | Japan | Korea, South | Mexico | Russia | Saudi Arabia | United States | Venezuela | World Total |
|---|---|---|---|---|---|---|---|---|---|---|---|---|---|
| 2008 | 213.0 | 738.9 | 241.0 | 328.2 | 212.7 | 546.7 | 331.7 | 265.1 | 264.0 | 363.7 | 622.2 | 100.5 | 10,326.9 |
| 2009 | 160.0 | 684.5 | 295.0 | 359.9 | 180.1 | 411.4 | 320.5 | 246.0 | 324.0 | 275.5 | 511.1 | 105.0 | 10,106.0 |
| 2010 | 184.0 | 878.4 | 179.0 | 318.6 | 144.0 | 395.6 | 321.3 | 224.0 | 303.0 | 272.0 | 535.1 | 117.0 | 9,856.0 |
| 2011 | 161.0 | 609.1 | 185.0 | 379.2 | 115.9 | 446.6 | 277.7 | 242.6 | 423.0 | 316.9 | 461.1 | 123.1 | 9,534.6 |
| 2012 | 167.0 | 583.7 | 184.0 | 420.3 | 107.2 | 565.4 | 268.8 | 244.9 | 407.0 | 330.9 | 368.8 | 115.0 | 9,371.2 |
| 2013 | 114.0 | 580.3 | 155.0 | 357.6 | 82.6 | 475.1 | 256.8 | 226.9 | 350.0 | 370.2 | 318.6 | 109.1 | 9,044.0 |
| 2014 | 139.3 | 552.9 | 148.4 | 335.3 | 72.7 | 413.3 | 218.8 | 164.7 | 243.5 | 438.3 | 257.2 | 71.3 | 8,836.6 |
| 2015[1] | | | | | 77.7 | 368.1 | 237.3 | 144.6 | | | 259.3 | | |
| 2016[2] | | | | | 64.4 | 340.2 | 277.0 | 133.0 | | | | | |
| 2017[2] | | | | | 62.3 | 260.9 | 210.3 | 139.6 | | | | | |

[1] Preliminary.    [2] Estimate.    Source: Energy Information Administration, U.S. Department of Energy (EIA-DOE)

## Supply and Disposition of Residual Fuel Oil in the United States

| | Supply | | Disposition | | | Ending Stocks (Million Barrels) | Average Sales to End Users[3] (USD per Gallon) |
|---|---|---|---|---|---|---|---|
| Year | Total Production | Imports | Stock Change | Exports | Product Supplied | | |
| | In Thousands of Barrels Per Day | | | | | | |
| 2012 | 501 | 256 | ---- | ---- | 369 | 34 | 2.59 |
| 2013 | 467 | 225 | ---- | ---- | 319 | 38 | 2.48 |
| 2014 | 435 | 173 | ---- | ---- | 257 | 34 | 2.33 |
| 2015 | 417 | 192 | ---- | ---- | 259 | 42 | 1.29 |
| 2016 | 418 | 205 | ---- | ---- | 326 | 41 | 0.95 |
| 2017 | 427 | 189 | ---- | ---- | 342 | 29 | 1.29 |
| 2018 | 425 | 211 | ---- | ---- | 318 | 28 | 1.66 |
| 2019 | 361 | 149 | ---- | ---- | 275 | 31 | 1.58 |
| 2020 | 188 | 166 | ---- | ---- | 208 | 30 | 1.25 |
| 2021[1] | 213 | 186 | ---- | ---- | 314 | 26 | 1.86 |

[1] Preliminary.    [2] Less than +500 barrels per day and greater than -500 barrels per day.    [3] Refiner price excluding taxes.
Source: Energy Information Administration, U.S. Department of Energy (EIA-DOE)

# HEATING OIL

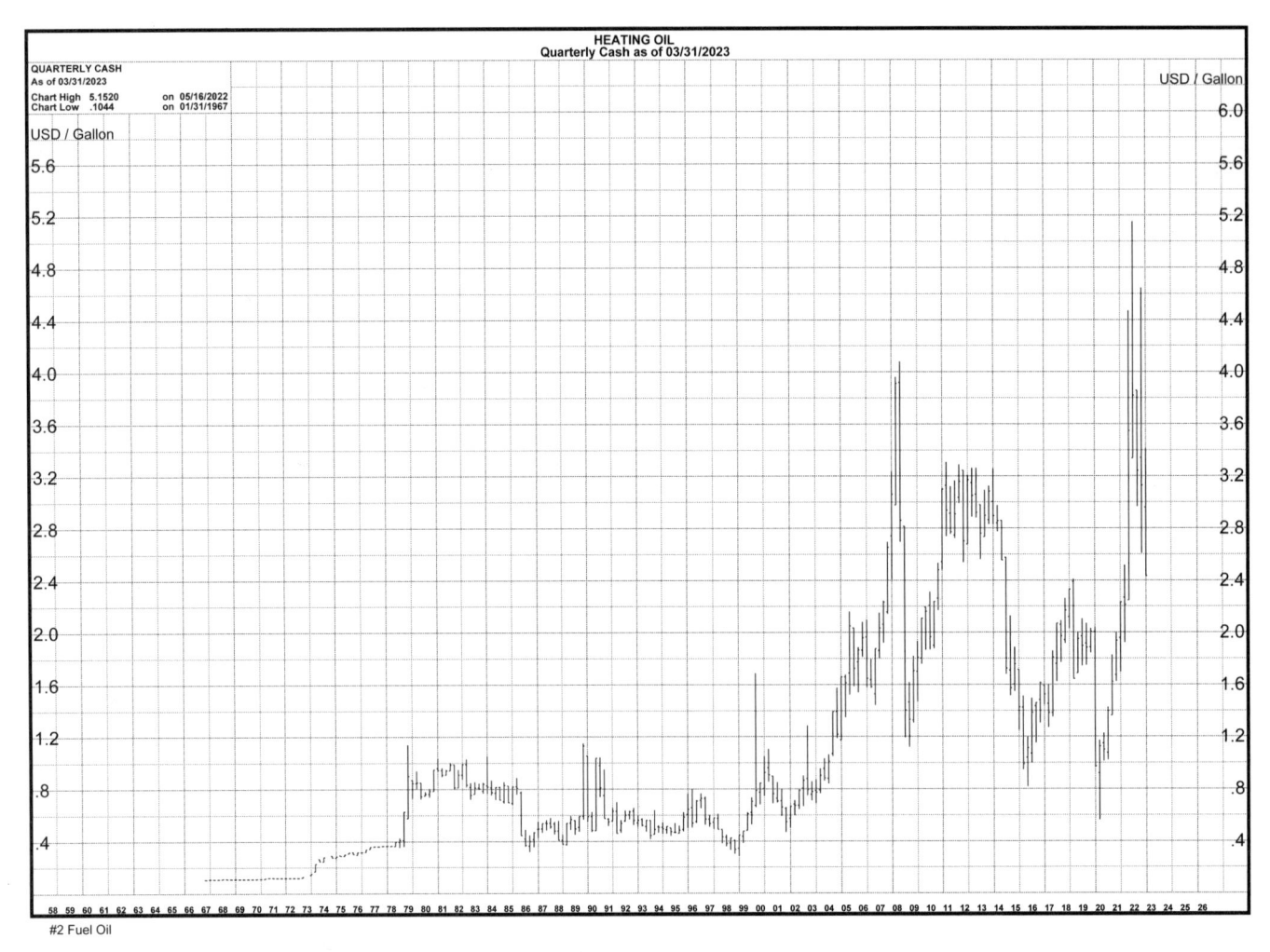

**HEATING OIL**
Quarterly Cash as of 03/31/2023

QUARTERLY CASH
As of 03/31/2023
Chart High 5.1520 on 05/16/2022
Chart Low .1044 on 01/31/1967

#2 Fuel Oil

## Production of Residual Fuel Oil in the United States     In Thousands of Barrels Per Day

| Year | Jan. | Feb. | Mar. | Apr. | May | June | July | Aug. | Sept. | Oct. | Nov. | Dec. | Average |
|---|---|---|---|---|---|---|---|---|---|---|---|---|---|
| 2013 | 395.4 | 504.1 | 569.4 | 508.2 | 488.1 | 469.0 | 481.4 | 416.9 | 433.8 | 420.3 | 466.2 | 454.8 | 467.3 |
| 2014 | 476.3 | 427.5 | 460.8 | 420.4 | 454.3 | 454.7 | 402.1 | 438.7 | 409.8 | 415.6 | 462.0 | 401.2 | 435.3 |
| 2015 | 376.7 | 419.5 | 478.3 | 466.8 | 435.5 | 413.3 | 426.1 | 403.7 | 414.1 | 419.3 | 376.5 | 376.4 | 417.2 |
| 2016 | 395.0 | 403.4 | 399.9 | 435.0 | 427.0 | 389.4 | 400.6 | 419.8 | 436.0 | 454.8 | 450.1 | 400.9 | 417.7 |
| 2017 | 485.2 | 482.5 | 405.7 | 416.6 | 407.7 | 406.3 | 390.5 | 452.5 | 459.2 | 442.2 | 407.8 | 372.5 | 427.4 |
| 2018 | 467.4 | 461.5 | 403.2 | 450.4 | 414.8 | 347.6 | 444.2 | 391.3 | 429.4 | 397.2 | 449.8 | 440.3 | 424.8 |
| 2019 | 397.8 | 309.0 | 357.4 | 389.0 | 363.5 | 429.9 | 389.9 | 409.5 | 382.8 | 340.0 | 313.6 | 249.1 | 361.0 |
| 2020 | 225.7 | 251.0 | 240.9 | 138.6 | 142.7 | 238.4 | 218.7 | 192.7 | 167.3 | 147.5 | 153.2 | 145.7 | 188.5 |
| 2021 | 178.9 | 187.7 | 223.8 | 187.1 | 209.5 | 229.3 | 245.2 | 231.1 | 184.9 | 222.3 | 246.4 | 210.4 | 213.0 |
| 2022[1] | 262.7 | 218.3 | 300.6 | 226.7 | 242.2 | 204.0 | 217.7 | 274.2 | 295.7 | 253.2 | 228.4 | 258.5 | 248.5 |

[1] Preliminary.    Source: Energy Information Administration, U.S. Department of Energy (EIA-DOE)

## Average Price of Heating Oil #2     In Dollars Per Gallon

| Year | Jan. | Feb. | Mar. | Apr. | May | June | July | Aug. | Sept. | Oct. | Nov. | Dec. | Average |
|---|---|---|---|---|---|---|---|---|---|---|---|---|---|
| 2013 | 3.0720 | 3.1669 | 2.9468 | 2.7278 | 2.6882 | 2.7424 | 2.8863 | 2.9581 | 2.9613 | 2.9422 | 2.9228 | 3.0325 | 2.9206 |
| 2014 | 3.0633 | 3.0656 | 2.9124 | 2.8878 | 2.8603 | 2.8822 | 2.7758 | 2.7535 | 2.6332 | 2.4237 | 2.2493 | 1.8555 | 2.6969 |
| 2015 | 1.6163 | 1.8727 | 1.6315 | 1.7404 | 1.8317 | 1.7680 | 1.5505 | 1.3875 | 1.4311 | 1.4042 | 1.3198 | 1.0392 | 1.5494 |
| 2016 | 0.9396 | 0.9721 | 1.1289 | 1.1877 | 1.3527 | 1.4162 | 1.2850 | 1.3251 | 1.3521 | 1.4877 | 1.3872 | 1.5521 | 1.2822 |
| 2017 | 1.5474 | 1.5622 | 1.4925 | 1.5202 | 1.4521 | 1.3320 | 1.4248 | 1.5412 | 1.7915 | 1.7111 | 1.8216 | 1.8619 | 1.5882 |
| 2018 | 2.0315 | 1.8541 | 1.8698 | 2.0372 | 2.1880 | 2.1132 | 2.1067 | 2.1246 | 2.2260 | 2.3158 | 2.0360 | 1.7877 | 2.0576 |
| 2019 | 1.8310 | 1.9278 | 1.9668 | 2.0359 | 2.0086 | 1.8197 | 1.8894 | 1.7950 | 1.9247 | 1.9204 | 1.9146 | 1.9638 | 1.9165 |
| 2020 | 1.8290 | 1.5891 | 1.1564 | 0.8580 | 0.8425 | 1.0732 | 1.1874 | 1.1799 | 1.0694 | 1.0992 | 1.1673 | 1.3366 | 1.1990 |
| 2021 | 1.4766 | 1.6696 | 1.7051 | 1.7044 | 1.8341 | 1.9064 | 1.9470 | 1.8852 | 2.0531 | 2.3966 | 2.2518 | 2.1183 | 1.9124 |
| 2022 | 2.4809 | 2.7368 | 3.6350 | 3.9523 | 4.4974 | 4.2464 | 3.5523 | 3.4370 | 3.2574 | 4.1585 | 3.8732 | 2.9370 | 3.5637 |

Source: Energy Information Administration, U.S. Department of Energy (EIA-DOE)

# HEATING OIL

**ULSD NY Harbor - NYMEX**
Weekly Nearest Futures as of 03/31/2023

WEEKLY NEAREST FUTURES
As of 03/31/2023
Chart High 5.8595 on 04/29/2022
Chart Low .5800 on 04/28/2020

Nearby Futures through Last Trading Day.

## Volume of Trading of Heating Oil #2 Futures in New York    In Thousands of Contracts

| Year | Jan. | Feb. | Mar. | Apr. | May | June | July | Aug. | Sept. | Oct. | Nov. | Dec. | Total |
|---|---|---|---|---|---|---|---|---|---|---|---|---|---|
| 2013 | 3,122.0 | 2,801.6 | 2,900.0 | 3,057.7 | 2,852.8 | 2,540.0 | 2,700.0 | 2,490.4 | 2,384.5 | 2,932.3 | 2,608.5 | 2,359.7 | 32,749.6 |
| 2014 | 3,400.6 | 2,893.3 | 2,533.8 | 2,209.6 | 2,253.3 | 2,483.3 | 2,857.3 | 2,719.9 | 2,875.9 | 3,409.5 | 3,126.2 | 3,183.6 | 33,946.4 |
| 2015 | 3,247.1 | 3,451.1 | 3,022.4 | 2,733.6 | 2,616.5 | 2,981.7 | 3,024.6 | 3,254.2 | 2,906.7 | 3,473.0 | 2,765.9 | 3,470.1 | 36,947.0 |
| 2016 | 3,341.1 | 3,201.8 | 2,861.8 | 3,286.1 | 3,452.2 | 3,431.1 | 3,052.5 | 3,455.0 | 3,288.4 | 3,183.1 | 3,518.7 | 3,317.7 | 39,389.3 |
| 2017 | 3,322.5 | 3,332.7 | 3,497.4 | 3,091.7 | 3,867.4 | 3,642.3 | 3,601.1 | 4,759.9 | 3,577.9 | 3,849.6 | 3,549.3 | 3,504.4 | 43,596.2 |
| 2018 | 4,542.6 | 3,826.2 | 3,715.8 | 4,066.3 | 4,334.6 | 3,738.0 | 3,326.2 | 3,566.0 | 3,440.1 | 3,966.1 | 4,516.8 | 3,239.0 | 46,277.9 |
| 2019 | 3,428.3 | 3,043.1 | 3,382.3 | 2,999.0 | 4,011.8 | 3,370.8 | 3,082.3 | 3,379.1 | 3,916.7 | 5,096.9 | 3,973.8 | 3,716.7 | 43,400.8 |
| 2020 | 5,655.2 | 4,206.4 | 5,101.5 | 3,880.6 | 3,347.1 | 2,772.6 | 2,454.6 | 2,927.0 | 3,547.1 | 3,714.6 | 3,420.4 | 2,975.9 | 44,003.2 |
| 2021 | 2,945.6 | 3,644.0 | 3,758.3 | 2,510.6 | 2,828.3 | 2,724.3 | 2,668.8 | 3,564.8 | 3,558.3 | 3,886.4 | 3,817.3 | 2,804.9 | 38,711.5 |
| 2022 | 4,437.3 | 4,231.2 | 3,562.7 | 2,470.0 | 2,949.7 | 3,135.6 | 2,894.3 | 3,300.6 | 3,517.0 | 3,543.6 | 2,672.8 | 2,922.2 | 39,637.1 |

Contract size = 42,000 US gallons.    *Source: CME Group; New York Mercantile Exchange (NYMEX)*

## Average Open Interest of Heating Oil #2 Futures in New York    In Contracts

| Year | Jan. | Feb. | Mar. | Apr. | May | June | July | Aug. | Sept. | Oct. | Nov. | Dec. |
|---|---|---|---|---|---|---|---|---|---|---|---|---|
| 2013 | 297,517 | 316,763 | 297,280 | 304,306 | 307,574 | 291,583 | 287,422 | 290,885 | 284,372 | 280,863 | 298,480 | 292,422 |
| 2014 | 281,102 | 294,144 | 280,719 | 263,461 | 269,766 | 285,931 | 313,266 | 353,133 | 373,004 | 390,505 | 391,923 | 355,367 |
| 2015 | 375,870 | 384,974 | 375,278 | 361,933 | 360,017 | 362,447 | 388,442 | 425,342 | 399,488 | 382,414 | 367,273 | 348,763 |
| 2016 | 349,641 | 365,010 | 367,707 | 389,364 | 399,419 | 404,855 | 370,778 | 396,411 | 391,168 | 408,496 | 395,976 | 431,825 |
| 2017 | 422,678 | 424,439 | 413,555 | 428,260 | 418,050 | 405,141 | 411,503 | 404,442 | 444,276 | 442,998 | 445,430 | 443,590 |
| 2018 | 469,402 | 433,230 | 401,046 | 436,876 | 438,501 | 403,757 | 403,666 | 390,752 | 420,964 | 422,927 | 376,499 | 369,267 |
| 2019 | 367,498 | 415,805 | 401,238 | 397,296 | 399,818 | 407,129 | 412,377 | 439,510 | 415,640 | 443,137 | 436,588 | 427,092 |
| 2020 | 415,494 | 408,798 | 378,779 | 365,527 | 382,637 | 378,457 | 358,653 | 376,359 | 424,716 | 425,509 | 398,259 | 374,290 |
| 2021 | 376,292 | 417,912 | 43,047 | 400,920 | 417,322 | 435,112 | 409,357 | 395,072 | 427,718 | 429,260 | 382,227 | 301,670 |
| 2022 | 350,798 | 344,310 | 236,804 | 225,758 | 248,510 | 264,245 | 266,402 | 288,448 | 289,423 | 277,553 | 272,789 | 263,472 |

Contract size = 42,000 US gallons.    *Source: CME Group; New York Mercantile Exchange (NYMEX)*

# Hides and Leather

Hides and leather have been used since ancient times for boots, clothing, shields, armor, tents, bottles, buckets, and cups. Leather is produced through the tanning of hides, pelts, and skins of animals. The remains of leather have been found in the Middle East dating back at least 7,000 years.

Today, most leather is made of cowhide, but it is also made from the hides of lamb, deer, ostrich, snakes, crocodiles, and even stingray. Cattle hides are the most valuable byproduct of the meat-packing industry. U.S. exports of cowhides bring more than $1 billion in foreign trade, and U.S. finished leather production is worth about $4 billion.

**Prices** – The average monthly price of wholesale cattle hides (packer heavy native steers FOB Chicago) in 2022 fell by -14.9 yr/yr to 41.34 cents per pound.

**Supply** – World production of cattle and buffalo hides in 2021 rose by +1.5% yr/yr to 10.209 million metric tons. The world's largest producers of cattle and buffalo hides in 2021 were the U.S. with 11.4% of world production, Brazil with 9.6%, and Argentina with 4.7%.

**Trade** – U.S. net exports of cattle hides in 2021 rose by +29.5% to 25.898 million hides. The largest destinations for U.S. exports in 2021 were China (which took 68.9% of U.S. exports), Mexico (13.9%), and South Korea (9.0%).

### World Production of Cattle and Buffalo Hides — In Metric Tons

| Year | Argentina | Australia | Brazil | Canada | Colombia | France | Germany | Italy | Mexico | Russia | United Kingdom | United States | World Total |
|---|---|---|---|---|---|---|---|---|---|---|---|---|---|
| 2012 | 419,749 | 249,636 | 930,700 | 86,186 | 102,856 | 143,641 | 136,253 | 127,686 | 225,883 | 195,830 | 81,944 | 1,087,080 | 9,077,610 |
| 2013 | 456,260 | 273,651 | 967,500 | 86,016 | 103,097 | 134,647 | 132,717 | 110,719 | 224,172 | 194,845 | 78,426 | 1,075,452 | 9,269,402 |
| 2014 | 432,391 | 301,037 | 972,300 | 89,762 | 100,828 | 135,659 | 135,819 | 92,177 | 226,702 | 197,335 | 81,204 | 1,067,197 | 9,343,377 |
| 2015 | 440,962 | 308,750 | 942,500 | 85,474 | 102,866 | 139,222 | 134,599 | 102,425 | 228,946 | 196,767 | 81,944 | 986,842 | 9,342,104 |
| 2016 | 427,540 | 268,655 | 928,400 | 93,407 | 95,910 | 140,971 | 137,350 | 105,260 | 233,099 | 189,537 | 84,722 | 1,049,782 | 9,351,479 |
| 2017 | 459,963 | 239,959 | 955,000 | 101,054 | 91,676 | 137,767 | 135,154 | 98,315 | 239,078 | 187,211 | 83,796 | 1,089,581 | 9,574,581 |
| 2018 | 495,794 | 259,570 | 990,000 | 106,339 | 92,874 | 138,111 | 133,542 | 105,362 | 245,772 | 191,848 | 85,370 | 1,118,080 | 9,799,947 |
| 2019 | 507,083 | 272,808 | 1,020,000 | 112,728 | 92,709 | ---- | ---- | ---- | 251,577 | 193,879 | 84,630 | 1,129,828 | 10,149,620 |
| 2020[1] | 512,349 | 275,106 | 997,500 | 111,744 | 89,572 | ---- | ---- | ---- | 258,231 | 194,903 | 86,296 | 1,130,179 | 10,056,255 |
| 2021[2] | 482,146 | 224,181 | 975,000 | 116,386 | 91,358 | ---- | ---- | ---- | 264,351 | 199,651 | 82,222 | 1,161,666 | 10,209,258 |

[1] Preliminary. [2] Forecast. Source: Food and Agricultural Organization of the United Nations (FAO-UN)

### Exports of Bovine Hides and Skins from the United States — In Thousands of Hides

| Year | Canada | China | Hong Kong | Italy | Japan | Korea, South | Mexico | Netherlands | Taiwan | Thailand | Turkey | Vietnam | World Total |
|---|---|---|---|---|---|---|---|---|---|---|---|---|---|
| 2013 | 62 | 9,319 | 348 | 228 | 97 | 2,426 | 1,075 | 15 | 865 | 173 | 53 | 257 | 15,173 |
| 2014 | 33 | 10,881 | 227 | 174 | 180 | 2,282 | 1,277 | 127 | 1,232 | 221 | 37 | 53 | 16,882 |
| 2015 | 57 | 9,835 | 36 | 172 | 153 | 2,307 | 1,275 | 163 | 620 | 281 | 65 | 147 | 15,260 |
| 2016 | 79 | 9,856 | 39 | 292 | 164 | 2,538 | 1,906 | 69 | 481 | 292 | 65 | 115 | 16,180 |
| 2017 | ---- | 10,540 | 29 | 192 | 152 | 2,540 | 1,541 | 33 | 557 | 881 | 101 | 51 | 17,095 |
| 2018 | ---- | 8,882 | 12 | 183 | 175 | 2,474 | 1,670 | 64 | 374 | 1,497 | 114 | 30 | 16,047 |
| 2019 | ---- | 8,809 | 14 | 60 | 182 | 2,685 | 2,023 | 72 | 385 | 923 | 42 | 63 | 15,664 |
| 2020 | ---- | 12,940 | 31 | 45 | 42 | 1,434 | 1,857 | 10 | 249 | 369 | 98 | 86 | 17,587 |
| 2021 | ---- | 17,670 | 6 | 68 | 128 | 2,328 | 3,579 | 19 | 418 | 639 | 35 | 61 | 25,731 |
| 2022[1] | ---- | 13,158 | 2 | 281 | 131 | 2,448 | 3,093 | 12 | 263 | 1,357 | 452 | 93 | 22,458 |

[1] Preliminary. Source: Foreign Agricultural Service, U.S. Department of Agriculture (FAS-USDA)

### Imports of Bovine Hides and Skins in the United States — In Thousands of Hides

| Year | Australia | Belgium-Luxembourg | Brazil | Canada | China | Colombia | Italy | Mexico | New Zealand | Pakistan | Thailand | Turkey | World Total |
|---|---|---|---|---|---|---|---|---|---|---|---|---|---|
| 2013 | 2.6 | 11.4 | 15.2 | 1,007.6 | 80.6 | 0.9 | 12.2 | 432.9 | 4.4 | 2.5 | 5.3 | 22.0 | 1,623.0 |
| 2014 | 72.2 | 24.4 | 7.1 | 1,181.0 | 92.9 | 0.6 | 5.0 | 638.2 | 6.8 | 0.5 | 6.9 | 0.8 | 2,077.4 |
| 2015 | 97.2 | 43.8 | 1.0 | 1,218.8 | 5.2 | 33.7 | 5.9 | 375.8 | 1.0 | 0.1 | 8.8 | 0.8 | 2,193.2 |
| 2016 | 0.0 | 139.4 | 8.2 | 794.2 | 8.5 | 107.1 | 11.9 | 69.4 | 1.9 | 1.1 | 20.3 | 0.7 | 2,336.2 |
| 2017 | 5.2 | 203.7 | 18.5 | 625.1 | 0.2 | 27.1 | 10.2 | 16.6 | 4.1 | 0.8 | 5.7 | 0.0 | 1,449.7 |
| 2018 | 3.4 | 196.5 | 19.6 | 653.7 | 4.9 | 13.7 | 10.6 | 9.2 | 16.5 | 1.2 | 4.7 | 0.0 | 1,404.5 |
| 2019 | 8.1 | 118.8 | 14.6 | 347.1 | 0.2 | 2.0 | 6.9 | 31.8 | 3.9 | ---- | 7.9 | 5.8 | 912.4 |
| 2020 | 1.4 | 30.2 | 45.3 | 267.2 | 1.2 | 6.8 | 21.1 | 333.4 | 4.6 | ---- | 15.9 | 0.9 | 785.8 |
| 2021 | 3.7 | 18.0 | 47.6 | 365.5 | 0.0 | 9.3 | 1.9 | 489.9 | 5.8 | ---- | 14.9 | 0.9 | 1,081.8 |
| 2022[1] | ---- | 11.8 | 33.4 | 149.7 | 15.9 | 3.6 | 4.9 | 21.7 | 1.3 | ---- | 14.4 | 0.3 | 302.2 |

[1] Preliminary. Source: Foreign Agricultural Service, U.S. Department of Agriculture (FAS-USDA)

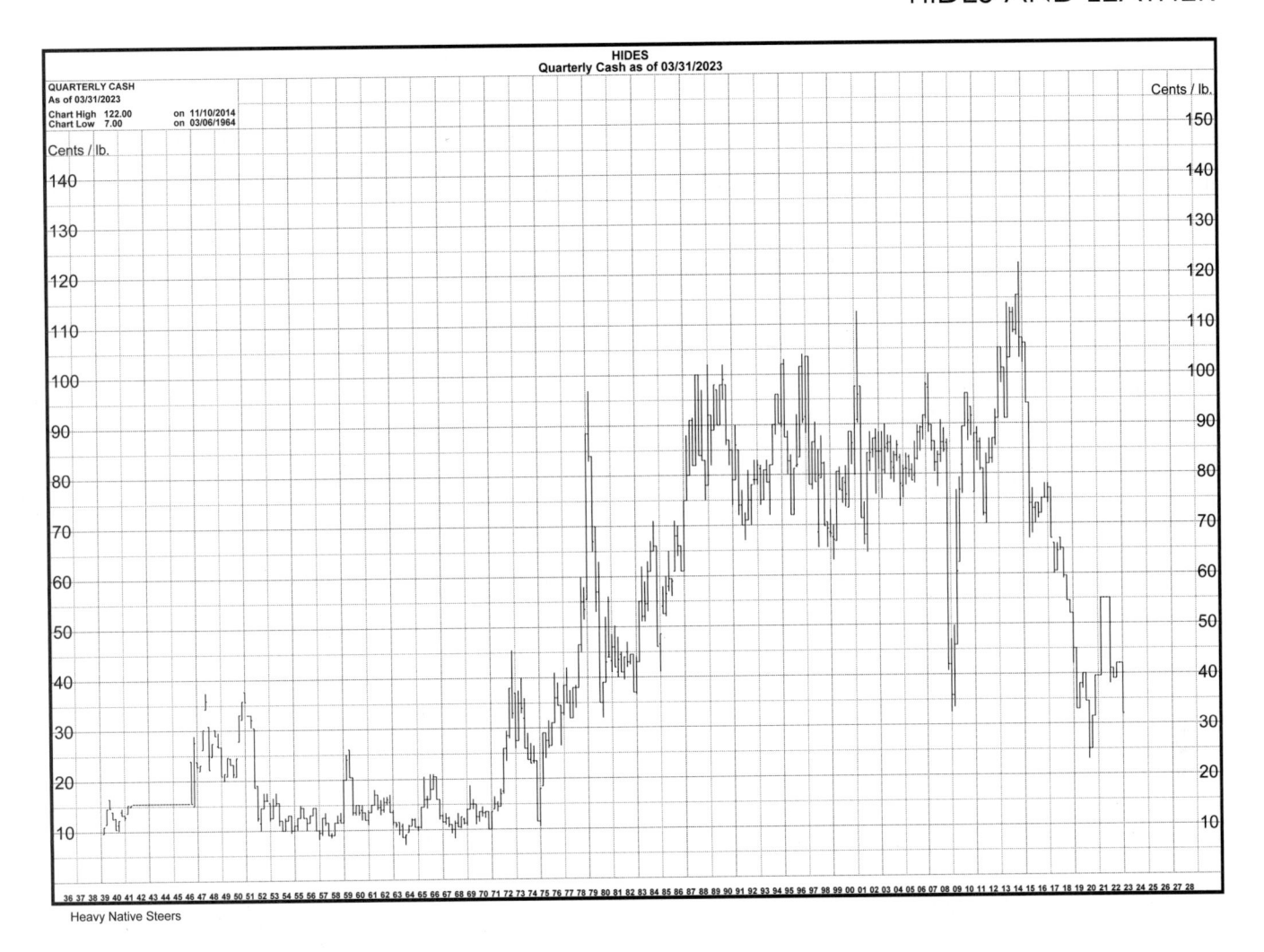

# HIDES AND LEATHER

**HIDES** — Quarterly Cash as of 03/31/2023

QUARTERLY CASH
As of 03/31/2023
Chart High 122.00 on 11/10/2014
Chart Low 7.00 on 03/06/1964

Heavy Native Steers

## Wholesale Price of Hides (Packer Heavy Native Steers) F.O.B. Chicago   In Cents Per Pound

| Year | Jan. | Feb. | Mar. | Apr. | May | June | July | Aug. | Sept. | Oct. | Nov. | Dec. | Average |
|---|---|---|---|---|---|---|---|---|---|---|---|---|---|
| 2013 | 91.45 | 97.00 | 96.81 | 103.14 | 99.66 | 98.93 | 99.32 | 95.39 | 91.50 | 94.39 | 106.00 | 105.38 | 98.25 |
| 2014 | 104.76 | 107.00 | 110.62 | 112.00 | 108.90 | 108.14 | 108.59 | 112.00 | 114.43 | 114.37 | 114.29 | 107.16 | 110.19 |
| 2015 | 104.20 | 103.24 | 103.68 | 98.57 | 95.90 | 94.00 | 73.86 | 71.86 | 75.90 | 73.64 | 68.95 | 71.64 | 86.29 |
| 2016 | 72.37 | 70.85 | 73.18 | 72.93 | 71.86 | 72.77 | 73.80 | 73.70 | 73.81 | 75.43 | 77.33 | 75.45 | 73.62 |
| 2017 | 75.15 | 75.61 | 77.04 | 74.79 | 68.50 | 67.64 | 63.90 | 61.74 | 61.17 | 60.80 | 61.19 | 64.15 | 67.64 |
| 2018 | 66.17 | 66.24 | 65.89 | 63.86 | 61.36 | 59.98 | 57.52 | 55.63 | 54.92 | 54.17 | 52.10 | 52.00 | 59.15 |
| 2019 | 47.71 | 43.42 | 45.00 | 45.00 | 38.86 | 34.00 | 33.00 | 36.86 | 38.00 | 38.74 | 38.90 | 37.95 | 39.79 |
| 2020 | 40.00 | 40.00 | 36.75 | 29.50 | 24.62 | 24.50 | 25.05 | 27.14 | 30.07 | 34.64 | 36.10 | 39.25 | 32.30 |
| 2021 | 39.50 | 39.50 | 39.50 | 39.50 | 40.95 | 54.36 | 55.00 | 55.00 | 55.00 | 55.00 | 55.00 | 55.00 | 48.61 |
| 2022 | 45.65 | 39.37 | 41.00 | 41.00 | 40.71 | 39.00 | 40.05 | 42.00 | 42.00 | 42.00 | 42.00 | 42.00 | 41.40 |

*Source: National Agricultural Statistics Service, U.S. Department of Agriculture (NASS-USDA)*

# Hogs

Hogs are generally bred twice a year in a continuous cycle designed to provide a steady flow of production. The gestation period for hogs is 3-1/2 months, and the average litter size is nine pigs. The pigs are weaned at 3-4 weeks of age. The pigs are then fed to maximize weight gain. The feed consists primarily of grains such as corn, barley, milo, oats, and wheat. Protein is added from oilseed meals. Hogs typically gain 3.1 pounds per pound of feed. The time from birth to slaughter is typically six months. Hogs are ready for slaughter at about 254 pounds, producing a dressed carcass weight of around 190 pounds and an average 88.6 pounds of lean meat. The lean meat consists of 21% ham, 20% loin, 14% belly, 3% spareribs, 7% Boston butt roast and blade steaks, and 10% picnic, with the remaining 25% going into jowl, lean trim, fat, miscellaneous cuts, and trimmings. Futures on lean hogs are traded at the CME Group. The futures contract is settled in cash based on the CME Lean Hog Index price, meaning that no physical delivery of hogs occurs. The CME Lean Hog Index is based on the 2-day average net price of slaughtered hogs at the average lean percentage level.

**Prices** – CME lean hog futures prices (Barchart.com electronic symbol HE) posted the low for 2022 of 77.050 cents per pound in January. Hog prices were well-supported by tight U.S. pork supplies in the first half of 2022. The USDA's Jan cold storage report showed stocks of pork in U.S. cold storage as of December 1, 2021, fell -4.1% yr/yr to 399 million pounds, the lowest since 2010. Also, the spread of the omicron variant of the Covid virus prompted slaughterhouses to curb output as workers called in sick, further limiting pork production. The Q2 USDA Hogs & Pigs Inventory report showed the U.S. hog herd on June 1 fell -1.1% yr/yr to a 4-year low of 72.314 million hogs. Hog prices climbed to a 1-1/2 year high of 122.525 cents per pound in August. Tight hog supplies pushed the price of cash hogs to a record high of 132.48 USD/cwt (data from 2004) in August. Also, ham prices soared to an 8-year high in August. Hog prices then tumbled into October on signs of shrinking pork demand in China, the world's largest pork importer, as it ramped up its domestic pork production after African swine fever in 2021 decimated its hog herds. Chinese pork demand also suffered as a resurgence of the pandemic in 2022 prompted lockdowns that closed restaurants. The subsequent decline in U.S. pork exports boosted domestic pork supplies as stocks of pork in U.S. cold storage as of August 1 jumped +17.1% yr/yr to 532 million pounds. Hog prices then stabilized and moved sideways into year-end. Hog prices ended 2022 up +7.6% yr/yr at 87.700 cents per pound.

**Supply** – The number of hogs on world farms as of January 1, 2023, fell by -1.8% yr/yr to 769.706 million head. The number of hogs in the U.S. as of January 1, 2023, fell by -1.8% yr/yr to 73.119 million head. The countries with the largest number of hogs as of January 1, 2023, were China with 57.2% of the world's hogs, the European Union with 18.2%, the U.S. with 9.5%, and Brazil with 4.4%.

**Demand** – The federally-inspected hog slaughter in the U.S. in 2022 fell by -2.8% yr/yr to 124.673 million head.

## Salient Statistics of Pigs and Hogs in the United States

| Year | Spring[3] Sows Farrowed (1,000 Head) | Spring[3] Pig Crop (1,000 Head) | Spring[3] Pigs Per Litter | Fall[4] Sows Farrowed (1,000 Head) | Fall[4] Pig Crop (1,000 Head) | Fall[4] Pigs Per Litter | Value of Hogs on Farms, Dec. 1 $ Per Head | Value of Hogs on Farms, Dec. 1 Total Million $ | Hog Marketings (1,000 Head) | Quantity Produced (Live Wt.) (Mil. Lbs.) | Value of Production (Million$) | Hogs Slaughtered Federally Inspected | Hogs Slaughtered Other | Commercial U.S. Total | Farm | U.S. Total |
|---|---|---|---|---|---|---|---|---|---|---|---|---|---|---|---|---|
| 2013 | 5,595 | 57,020 | 10.19 | 5,670 | 58,115 | 10.25 | 138.0 | 8,920 | 154,923 | 32,620 | 21,666 | 111,248 | 829 | 112,077 | 84 | 112,161 |
| 2014 | 5,573 | 53,821 | 9.66 | 5,985 | 61,035 | 10.20 | 144.0 | 9,732 | 149,097 | 32,126 | 24,184 | 106,123 | 753 | 106,876 | 82 | 106,958 |
| 2015 | 5,749 | 59,219 | 10.30 | 5,946 | 62,191 | 10.46 | 96.0 | 6,636 | 159,725 | 34,739 | 18,814 | 114,616 | 811 | 115,427 | 87 | 115,514 |
| 2016 | 5,896 | 61,236 | 10.39 | 6,103 | 64,703 | 10.60 | 92.0 | 6,578 | 165,539 | 35,899 | 17,363 | 117,388 | 831 | 118,219 | 84 | 118,303 |
| 2017 | 6,007 | 63,025 | 10.49 | 6,209 | 66,402 | 10.69 | 99.0 | 7,207 | 171,320 | 36,963 | 19,159 | 120,517 | 801 | 121,317 | 73 | 121,390 |
| 2018 | 6,041 | 64,053 | 10.60 | 6,377 | 68,515 | 10.74 | 98.0 | 7,299 | 180,251 | 38,498 | 18,770 | 123,696 | 738 | 124,435 | 76 | 124,511 |
| 2019 | 6,231 | 67,619 | 10.85 | 6,471 | 71,829 | 11.10 | | | 187,661 | 43,103 | 21,243 | 129,211 | 702 | 129,913 | 77 | 129,990 |
| 2020 | 6,329 | 69,637 | 11.00 | 6,425 | 71,044 | 11.06 | | | 180,247 | 41,920 | 19,196 | 130,782 | 780 | 131,562 | 76 | 131,638 |
| 2021[1] | 5,964 | 65,292 | 10.95 | 6,098 | 68,067 | 11.16 | | | 180,247 | 39,973 | 28,057 | 128,288 | 696 | 128,984 | 77 | 129,060 |
| 2022[2] | 5,886 | 64,582 | 10.97 | 6,114 | 68,326 | 11.18 | | | | | | 124,674 | 641 | 125,315 | | 125,315 |

[1] Preliminary.  [2] Estimate.  [3] December-May.  [4] June-November.  Source: Economic Research Service, U.S. Department of Agriculture (ERS-USDA)

## World Hog Numbers in Specified Countries as of January 1    In Thousands of Head

| Year | Australia | Belarus | Brazil | Canada | China | European Union | Japan | Korea, South | Mexico | Russia | Ukraine | United States | World Total |
|---|---|---|---|---|---|---|---|---|---|---|---|---|---|
| 2014 | 2,098 | 3,267 | 38,844 | 12,835 | 478,931 | 146,172 | 9,537 | 9,912 | 9,775 | 19,010 | 7,922 | 64,775 | 803,078 |
| 2015 | 2,308 | 2,925 | 39,395 | 13,180 | 471,602 | 148,341 | 9,440 | 10,090 | 9,788 | 19,308 | 7,492 | 67,626 | 801,495 |
| 2016 | 2,272 | ---- | 39,422 | 13,630 | 458,029 | 144,294 | 9,313 | 10,187 | 10,043 | 21,239 | 7,240 | 69,019 | 789,110 |
| 2017 | ---- | ---- | 39,215 | 13,935 | 442,092 | 142,650 | 9,346 | 11,487 | 10,229 | 21,782 | 6,816 | 71,345 | 773,435 |
| 2018 | ---- | ---- | 38,829 | 14,245 | 441,589 | 145,544 | 9,280 | 11,273 | 10,410 | 22,945 | 6,236 | 73,145 | 778,209 |
| 2019 | ---- | ---- | 38,427 | 14,070 | 428,070 | 143,519 | 9,156 | 11,333 | 10,700 | 23,600 | 6,150 | 75,070 | 764,743 |
| 2020 | ---- | ---- | 37,850 | 14,065 | 310,410 | 143,146 | 9,090 | 11,280 | 11,050 | 25,048 | 5,842 | 76,833 | 649,355 |
| 2021 | ---- | ---- | 37,350 | 14,120 | 406,500 | 145,843 | 9,290 | 11,078 | 11,500 | 25,744 | 5,986 | 77,312 | 749,551 |
| 2022[1] | ---- | ---- | 35,688 | 14,175 | 449,220 | 141,656 | 8,949 | 11,217 | 11,775 | 26,200 | 5,718 | 74,446 | 784,194 |
| 2023[2] | ---- | ---- | 34,250 | 13,850 | 440,000 | 140,200 | 8,895 | 11,832 | 12,250 | 25,660 | 5,000 | 73,119 | 769,706 |

[1] Preliminary.  [2] Forecast.  Source: Foreign Agricultural Service, U.S. Department of Agriculture (FAS-USDA)

# HOGS

## Hogs and Pigs on Farms in the United States on December 1 — In Thousands of Head

| Year | Georgia | Illinois | Indiana | Iowa | Kansas | Minnesota | Missouri | Nebraska | North Carolina | Ohio | South Dakota | Wisconsin | Total |
|---|---|---|---|---|---|---|---|---|---|---|---|---|---|
| 2013 | 141 | 4,550 | 3,650 | 20,200 | 1,750 | 7,800 | 2,750 | 3,050 | 8,500 | 2,200 | 1,200 | 295 | 64,775 |
| 2014 | 155 | 4,700 | 3,700 | 21,300 | 1,840 | 8,100 | 2,850 | 3,200 | 8,800 | 2,230 | 1,270 | 310 | 67,776 |
| 2015 | 160 | 5,100 | 3,850 | 20,900 | 1,940 | 8,100 | 3,050 | 3,300 | 8,900 | 2,500 | 1,360 | 320 | 68,919 |
| 2016 | 65 | 5,100 | 4,100 | 22,200 | 1,910 | 8,500 | 3,100 | 3,400 | 9,300 | 2,700 | 1,450 | 335 | 71,545 |
| 2017 | 80 | 5,400 | 4,000 | 22,800 | 2,110 | 8,500 | 3,400 | 3,600 | 9,000 | 2,700 | 1,560 | 305 | 73,145 |
| 2018 | 72 | 5,400 | 4,250 | 23,600 | 2,050 | 9,100 | 3,650 | 3,550 | 9,200 | 2,550 | 1,750 | 320 | 75,070 |
| 2019 | 62 | 5,450 | 4,400 | 24,900 | 2,160 | 9,400 | 3,350 | 3,800 | 9,400 | 2,750 | 2,000 | 365 | 78,228 |
| 2020 | 38 | 5,450 | 4,450 | 24,600 | 2,060 | 9,400 | 3,750 | 3,800 | 9,800 | 2,700 | 2,030 | 370 | 77,312 |
| 2021 | 45 | 5,400 | 4,350 | 23,900 | 1,990 | 8,900 | 3,450 | 3,650 | 8,000 | 2,750 | 2,010 | 370 | 74,446 |
| 2022[1] | | 5,450 | 4,450 | 24,000 | 1,910 | 8,800 | 3,300 | 3,600 | 8,200 | 2,800 | 2,750 | | 74,399 |

[1] Preliminary.  Source: National Agricultural Statistics Service, U.S. Department of Agriculture (NASS-USDA)

## Cold Storage Holdings of Frozen Pork[2] in the United States, on First of Month — In Thousands of Pounds

| Year | Jan. | Feb. | Mar. | Apr. | May | June | July | Aug. | Sept. | Oct. | Nov. | Dec. |
|---|---|---|---|---|---|---|---|---|---|---|---|---|
| 2013 | 551,510 | 606,425 | 633,399 | 647,784 | 700,977 | 658,947 | 565,063 | 543,668 | 548,975 | 567,827 | 565,020 | 546,238 |
| 2014 | 554,328 | 618,746 | 654,712 | 575,539 | 583,891 | 575,818 | 537,447 | 533,259 | 543,666 | 550,622 | 533,076 | 492,752 |
| 2015 | 503,792 | 595,673 | 686,063 | 672,431 | 701,083 | 655,301 | 634,525 | 633,214 | 653,760 | 655,930 | 603,454 | 560,915 |
| 2016 | 545,696 | 625,246 | 628,948 | 613,803 | 637,320 | 616,124 | 586,479 | 598,592 | 608,955 | 642,303 | 599,010 | 518,813 |
| 2017 | 475,387 | 524,215 | 567,855 | 545,463 | 590,324 | 588,216 | 559,010 | 554,854 | 575,698 | 618,563 | 598,374 | 502,324 |
| 2018 | 490,047 | 580,714 | 609,813 | 611,013 | 634,722 | 623,725 | 561,879 | 552,029 | 581,513 | 589,403 | 570,917 | 507,688 |
| 2019 | 505,287 | 562,733 | 615,674 | 608,379 | 621,456 | 628,956 | 619,454 | 611,692 | 606,784 | 598,750 | 611,916 | 574,840 |
| 2020 | 580,464 | 625,588 | 648,975 | 616,946 | 611,222 | 467,927 | 460,173 | 460,635 | 465,465 | 465,619 | 447,115 | 419,772 |
| 2021 | 415,935 | 457,508 | 483,374 | 451,042 | 456,921 | 462,446 | 441,916 | 441,664 | 454,203 | 469,917 | 442,370 | 402,189 |
| 2022[1] | 396,461 | 434,415 | 478,315 | 485,929 | 533,396 | 546,061 | 538,720 | 526,478 | 538,596 | 536,980 | 509,669 | 451,555 |

[1] Preliminary.  [2] Excludes lard.  Source: Economic Research Service, U.S. Department of Agriculture (ERS-USDA)

## Cold Storage Holdings of Frozen Pork Belly in the United States, on First of Month — In Thousands of Pounds

| Year | Jan. | Feb. | Mar. | Apr. | May | June | July | Aug. | Sept. | Oct. | Nov. | Dec. |
|---|---|---|---|---|---|---|---|---|---|---|---|---|
| 2013 | 36,037 | 36,425 | 42,976 | 51,473 | 56,352 | 54,829 | 42,033 | 28,177 | 19,335 | 23,491 | 26,674 | 48,298 |
| 2014 | 80,367 | 87,171 | 87,675 | 79,721 | 83,579 | 85,888 | 83,936 | 64,644 | 45,562 | 34,311 | 29,006 | 35,894 |
| 2015 | 47,455 | 53,507 | 67,794 | 68,297 | 70,412 | 64,805 | 44,432 | 23,634 | 13,738 | 10,872 | 17,853 | 41,160 |
| 2016 | 53,392 | 60,698 | 61,433 | 65,028 | 72,592 | 77,683 | 62,921 | 50,733 | 32,053 | 25,084 | 20,386 | 18,526 |
| 2017 | 17,986 | 13,995 | 16,153 | 20,570 | 33,536 | 31,589 | 22,291 | 17,602 | 19,213 | 20,897 | 32,268 | 35,164 |
| 2018 | 39,620 | 43,810 | 49,012 | 59,202 | 64,563 | 61,234 | 53,279 | 38,556 | 34,805 | 30,354 | 26,690 | 36,859 |
| 2019 | 42,251 | 53,736 | 53,771 | 58,783 | 61,110 | 64,124 | 56,468 | 52,647 | 45,723 | 40,543 | 45,414 | 54,416 |
| 2020 | 66,647 | 70,872 | 74,270 | 78,157 | 80,728 | 60,322 | 53,840 | 42,374 | 31,053 | 24,846 | 19,025 | 23,292 |
| 2021 | 30,715 | 31,232 | 37,556 | 35,398 | 35,204 | 36,391 | 36,385 | 27,778 | 17,562 | 12,928 | 11,614 | 25,224 |
| 2022[1] | 38,069 | 44,707 | 50,115 | 56,779 | 58,331 | 56,728 | 53,183 | 42,842 | 35,684 | 36,513 | 40,247 | 54,429 |

[1] Preliminary.  Source: National Agricultural Statistics Service, U.S. Department of Agriculture (NASS-USDA)

## Cold Storage Holdings of Pork Hams in the United States, on First of Month — In Thousands of Pounds

| Year | Jan. | Feb. | Mar. | Apr. | May | June | July | Aug. | Sept. | Oct. | Nov. | Dec. |
|---|---|---|---|---|---|---|---|---|---|---|---|---|
| 2013 | 79,266 | 108,450 | 110,763 | 94,487 | 126,931 | 153,979 | 161,648 | 180,677 | 207,006 | 221,633 | 192,947 | 116,076 |
| 2014 | 76,773 | 106,183 | 117,464 | 89,452 | 81,785 | 109,999 | 126,493 | 148,905 | 179,483 | 194,077 | 162,035 | 96,397 |
| 2015 | 66,349 | 110,404 | 127,712 | 98,031 | 136,222 | 158,882 | 180,473 | 205,549 | 236,531 | 247,145 | 196,460 | 109,042 |
| 2016 | 67,813 | 111,142 | 115,780 | 96,511 | 130,217 | 144,060 | 166,451 | 188,441 | 226,070 | 248,972 | 191,430 | 106,101 |
| 2017 | 68,821 | 95,365 | 125,167 | 90,193 | 112,815 | 143,641 | 178,311 | 194,968 | 203,887 | 232,034 | 195,327 | 98,224 |
| 2018 | 81,082 | 118,407 | 122,743 | 96,339 | 112,145 | 139,295 | 148,657 | 167,563 | 204,763 | 214,628 | 176,109 | 96,375 |
| 2019 | 73,118 | 112,660 | 127,740 | 103,486 | 121,331 | 150,109 | 168,599 | 182,555 | 202,454 | 201,258 | 173,804 | 110,635 |
| 2020 | 85,995 | 114,618 | 114,534 | 88,308 | 113,328 | 107,550 | 122,993 | 136,621 | 143,909 | 145,994 | 123,324 | 74,862 |
| 2021 | 53,675 | 84,208 | 92,122 | 60,776 | 80,389 | 109,337 | 130,550 | 152,598 | 185,640 | 194,549 | 150,043 | 76,788 |
| 2022[1] | 61,354 | 74,775 | 84,212 | 74,105 | 98,038 | 126,491 | 139,283 | 151,634 | 163,716 | 159,488 | 121,624 | 55,284 |

[1] Preliminary.  Source: National Agricultural Statistics Service, U.S. Department of Agriculture (NASS-USDA)

# HOGS

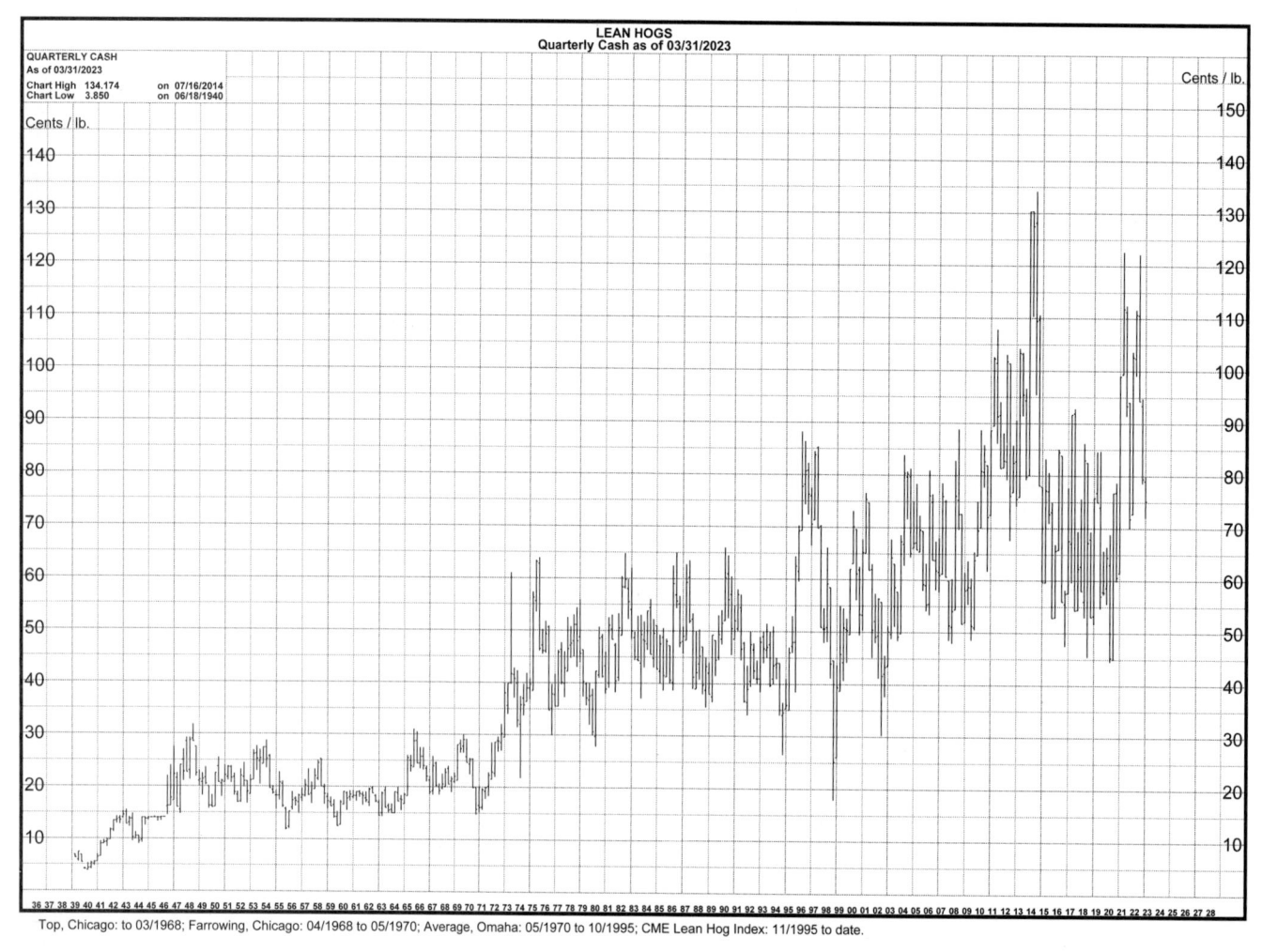

**LEAN HOGS**
Quarterly Cash as of 03/31/2023

QUARTERLY CASH
As of 03/31/2023
Chart High 134.174 on 07/16/2014
Chart Low 3.850 on 06/18/1940

Top, Chicago: to 03/1968; Farrowing, Chicago: 04/1968 to 05/1970; Average, Omaha: 05/1970 to 10/1995; CME Lean Hog Index: 11/1995 to date.

### Average Price of Hogs, National Base 51-52% lean — In Dollars Per Hundred Pounds (Cwt.)

| Year | Jan. | Feb. | Mar. | Apr. | May | June | July | Aug. | Sept. | Oct. | Nov. | Dec. | Average |
|---|---|---|---|---|---|---|---|---|---|---|---|---|---|
| 2013 | 61.22 | 61.59 | 54.28 | 57.71 | 66.03 | 72.65 | 72.88 | 71.03 | 67.84 | 64.95 | 60.21 | 58.16 | 64.05 |
| 2014 | 58.36 | 63.88 | 83.82 | 89.09 | 81.76 | 85.35 | 95.17 | 80.39 | 74.36 | 75.24 | 63.76 | 61.24 | 76.03 |
| 2015 | 54.05 | 45.75 | 45.61 | 45.13 | 57.23 | 57.25 | 56.21 | 55.91 | 51.64 | 52.68 | 42.01 | 39.30 | 50.23 |
| 2016 | 40.34 | 46.61 | 46.95 | 47.96 | 54.75 | 58.42 | 56.28 | 48.12 | 43.36 | 37.07 | 34.45 | 39.45 | 46.15 |
| 2017 | 45.60 | 53.02 | 50.56 | 44.04 | 50.46 | 60.61 | 65.15 | 57.99 | 43.64 | 43.75 | 46.46 | 44.23 | 50.46 |
| 2018 | 50.40 | 51.49 | 45.46 | 39.88 | 46.86 | 56.99 | 55.38 | 37.88 | 38.43 | 47.54 | 42.19 | 38.58 | 45.92 |
| 2019 | 40.50 | 39.03 | 42.46 | 57.69 | 59.61 | 56.58 | 53.05 | 55.45 | 41.74 | 44.74 | 42.33 | 42.27 | 47.95 |
| 2020 | 43.43 | 40.56 | 43.56 | 36.09 | 46.53 | 34.25 | 34.20 | 38.87 | 48.41 | 55.92 | 50.34 | 46.00 | 43.18 |
| 2021 | 47.44 | 53.93 | 65.75 | 75.59 | 81.01 | 86.15 | 81.00 | 78.59 | 68.84 | 62.80 | 54.53 | 51.75 | 67.28 |
| 2022[1] | 56.02 | 67.01 | 73.61 | 73.47 | 74.08 | 79.19 | 83.99 | 85.62 | 71.00 | 67.78 | 63.72 | 58.96 | 71.20 |

[1] Preliminary. Source: Economic Research Service, U.S. Department of Agriculture (ERS-USDA)

### Average Price Received by Farmers for Hogs in the United States — In Cents Per Pound

| Year | Jan. | Feb. | Mar. | Apr. | May | June | July | Aug. | Sept. | Oct. | Nov. | Dec. | Average |
|---|---|---|---|---|---|---|---|---|---|---|---|---|---|
| 2013 | 63.8 | 64.5 | 59.2 | 61.8 | 68.6 | 74.4 | 75.8 | 74.2 | 70.7 | 68.5 | 63.6 | 61.5 | 67.2 |
| 2014 | 61.2 | 65.5 | 81.9 | 88.8 | 82.8 | 84.8 | 93.3 | 83.2 | 75.7 | 77.0 | 66.7 | 64.3 | 77.1 |
| 2015 | 57.4 | 50.4 | 50.3 | 49.0 | 58.9 | 59.9 | 58.7 | 59.0 | 54.5 | 55.5 | 45.9 | 42.8 | 53.5 |
| 2016 | 43.6 | 49.6 | 50.0 | 51.0 | 57.2 | 60.6 | 59.4 | 52.6 | 47.8 | 41.7 | 39.0 | 43.1 | 49.6 |
| 2017 | 48.1 | 54.4 | 53.0 | 48.4 | 53.6 | 62.1 | 67.3 | 61.5 | 48.9 | 47.3 | 50.0 | 48.6 | 53.6 |
| 2018 | 52.5 | 54.6 | 50.0 | 45.3 | 51.5 | 59.1 | 58.6 | 44.3 | 43.2 | 50.3 | 46.2 | 43.4 | 49.9 |
| 2019 | 44.6 | 43.4 | 46.5 | 59.4 | 62.3 | 59.5 | 56.6 | 58.5 | 47.7 | 49.1 | 48.0 | 47.3 | 51.9 |
| 2020 | 47.8 | 45.5 | 47.7 | 42.3 | 51.0 | 41.3 | 39.9 | 42.9 | 49.7 | 56.3 | 51.9 | 49.1 | 47.1 |
| 2021 | 50.2 | 56.4 | 67.2 | 75.6 | 79.3 | 82.7 | 80.0 | 79.0 | 70.8 | 65.5 | 58.6 | 56.5 | 68.5 |
| 2022[1] | 58.8 | 68.6 | 75.1 | 76.2 | 75.9 | 78.7 | 83.0 | 85.8 | 73.8 | 70.5 | 66.7 | 62.5 | 73.0 |

[1] Preliminary. Source: Economic Research Service, U.S. Department of Agriculture (ERS-USDA)

# HOGS

## Quarterly Hogs and Pigs Report in the United States, 10 States   In Thousands of Head

| Year[2] | Inventory[3] | Breeding[3] | Market[3] | Farrowings | Pig Crop | Year[2] | Inventory[3] | Breeding[3] | Market[3] | Farrowings | Pig Crop |
|---|---|---|---|---|---|---|---|---|---|---|---|
| 2013 | 66,374 | 5,819 | 60,555 | 11,264 | 115,135 | 2018 | 73,145 | 6,179 | 66,966 | 12,418 | 132,568 |
| I | 66,374 | 5,819 | 60,555 | 2,788 | 28,099 | I | 73,145 | 6,179 | 66,966 | 2,977 | 31,497 |
| II | 65,071 | 5,834 | 59,237 | 2,806 | 28,921 | II | 72,055 | 6,210 | 65,845 | 3,064 | 32,556 |
| III | 65,188 | 5,884 | 59,304 | 2,890 | 29,862 | III | 72,231 | 6,320 | 65,911 | 3,172 | 34,019 |
| IV | 66,906 | 5,816 | 61,090 | 2,780 | 28,253 | IV | 74,556 | 6,330 | 68,226 | 3,205 | 34,496 |
| 2014 | 64,775 | 5,757 | 59,018 | 11,558 | 114,856 | 2019 | 75,070 | 6,326 | 68,745 | 12,701 | 139,448 |
| I | 64,775 | 5,757 | 59,018 | 2,763 | 26,326 | I | 75,070 | 6,326 | 68,745 | 3,098 | 33,164 |
| II | 61,494 | 5,851 | 55,643 | 2,810 | 27,495 | II | 74,661 | 6,349 | 68,313 | 3,132 | 34,455 |
| III | 61,568 | 5,855 | 55,713 | 2,991 | 30,402 | III | 75,725 | 6,410 | 69,316 | 3,274 | 36,370 |
| IV | 65,979 | 5,920 | 60,059 | 2,994 | 30,633 | IV | 78,583 | 6,431 | 72,153 | 3,197 | 35,459 |
| 2015 | 67,776 | 5,939 | 61,838 | 11,695 | 121,411 | 2020 | 78,228 | 6,471 | 72,577 | 12,754 | 140,680 |
| I | 67,776 | 5,939 | 61,838 | 2,895 | 29,627 | I | 78,228 | 6,471 | 72,577 | 3,182 | 35,016 |
| II | 67,399 | 5,982 | 61,418 | 2,854 | 29,593 | II | 75,164 | 6,425 | 68,739 | 3,147 | 34,621 |
| III | 67,165 | 5,926 | 61,240 | 3,017 | 31,343 | III | 77,664 | 6,426 | 71,238 | 3,260 | 36,056 |
| IV | 69,185 | 5,986 | 63,200 | 2,929 | 30,848 | IV | 78,104 | 6,333 | 71,771 | 3,165 | 34,987 |
| 2016 | 68,919 | 6,002 | 62,917 | 11,998 | 125,939 | 2021 | 77,312 | 6,176 | 71,136 | 12,062 | 133,359 |
| I | 68,919 | 6,002 | 62,917 | 2,927 | 30,139 | I | 77,312 | 6,176 | 71,136 | 2,929 | 32,059 |
| II | 68,124 | 5,980 | 62,144 | 2,968 | 31,097 | II | 73,933 | 6,215 | 67,718 | 3,034 | 33,233 |
| III | 69,281 | 5,979 | 63,302 | 3,057 | 32,331 | III | 73,153 | 6,220 | 66,933 | 3,050 | 33,944 |
| IV | 71,786 | 6,016 | 65,770 | 3,046 | 32,372 | IV | 74,867 | 6,190 | 68,677 | 3,049 | 34,123 |
| 2017 | 71,545 | 6,110 | 65,435 | 12,217 | 129,429 | 2022[1] | 74,446 | 6,125 | 68,321 | 12,000 | 132,909 |
| I | 71,545 | 6,110 | 65,435 | 2,990 | 31,187 | I | 74,446 | 6,125 | 68,321 | 2,919 | 31,947 |
| II | 70,916 | 6,098 | 64,818 | 3,018 | 31,839 | II | 72,689 | 6,098 | 66,591 | 2,967 | 32,635 |
| III | 71,210 | 6,109 | 65,101 | 3,106 | 33,075 | III | 72,314 | 6,168 | 66,146 | 3,062 | 34,096 |
| IV | 73,309 | 6,117 | 67,192 | 3,103 | 33,328 | IV | 74,125 | 6,152 | 67,973 | 3,052 | 34,231 |

[1] Preliminary.  [2] Quarters are Dec. preceding year-Feb.(I), Mar.-May(II), June-Aug.(III) and Sept.-Nov.(IV).
[3] Beginning of period.   Source: National Agricultural Statistics Service, U.S. Department of Agriculture (NASS-USDA)

## Federally Inspected Hog Slaughter in the United States   In Thousands of Head

| Year | Jan. | Feb. | Mar. | Apr. | May | June | July | Aug. | Sept. | Oct. | Nov. | Dec. | Total |
|---|---|---|---|---|---|---|---|---|---|---|---|---|---|
| 2013 | 9,885 | 8,526 | 9,252 | 9,292 | 9,147 | 8,132 | 9,003 | 9,474 | 8,952 | 10,341 | 9,579 | 9,665 | 111,248 |
| 2014 | 9,726 | 8,609 | 8,614 | 8,794 | 8,561 | 8,040 | 8,394 | 8,199 | 8,762 | 9,880 | 8,754 | 9,788 | 106,123 |
| 2015 | 9,698 | 9,018 | 9,818 | 9,612 | 8,686 | 9,364 | 9,332 | 9,272 | 9,652 | 10,173 | 9,700 | 10,292 | 114,616 |
| 2016 | 9,682 | 9,364 | 10,015 | 9,303 | 9,114 | 9,505 | 8,696 | 10,308 | 10,096 | 10,369 | 10,539 | 10,398 | 117,388 |
| 2017 | 10,059 | 9,310 | 10,611 | 9,282 | 9,886 | 9,809 | 8,953 | 10,583 | 10,213 | 10,922 | 10,487 | 10,400 | 120,517 |
| 2018 | 10,653 | 9,578 | 10,661 | 9,939 | 10,163 | 9,553 | 9,532 | 11,081 | 9,583 | 11,571 | 10,982 | 10,403 | 123,696 |
| 2019 | 10,984 | 10,051 | 10,667 | 10,526 | 10,301 | 9,939 | 10,516 | 10,798 | 10,581 | 12,233 | 11,279 | 11,336 | 129,211 |
| 2020 | 11,760 | 10,670 | 11,883 | 9,353 | 8,524 | 11,104 | 11,155 | 11,047 | 10,957 | 11,949 | 10,961 | 11,419 | 130,782 |
| 2021 | 11,192 | 10,376 | 11,678 | 10,767 | 9,596 | 10,594 | 9,737 | 10,546 | 10,697 | 11,020 | 11,081 | 11,005 | 128,288 |
| 2022[1] | 10,362 | 9,897 | 11,197 | 10,032 | 9,986 | 10,451 | 9,264 | 10,922 | 10,597 | 10,857 | 10,863 | 10,247 | 124,674 |

[1] Preliminary.  Source: National Agricultural Statistics Service, U.S. Department of Agriculture (NASS-USDA)

## Average Live Weight of all Hogs Slaughtered Under Federal Inspection   In Pounds Per Head

| Year | Jan. | Feb. | Mar. | Apr. | May | June | July | Aug. | Sept. | Oct. | Nov. | Dec. | Average |
|---|---|---|---|---|---|---|---|---|---|---|---|---|---|
| 2013 | 277 | 277 | 277 | 277 | 276 | 274 | 271 | 271 | 273 | 279 | 283 | 283 | 277 |
| 2014 | 284 | 283 | 285 | 287 | 287 | 285 | 284 | 283 | 283 | 286 | 287 | 287 | 285 |
| 2015 | 287 | 285 | 285 | 285 | 284 | 282 | 280 | 278 | 280 | 284 | 286 | 285 | 283 |
| 2016 | 286 | 284 | 284 | 285 | 283 | 281 | 278 | 276 | 280 | 282 | 283 | 283 | 282 |
| 2017 | 285 | 284 | 284 | 285 | 282 | 279 | 277 | 278 | 282 | 283 | 286 | 286 | 283 |
| 2018 | 286 | 286 | 287 | 287 | 285 | 280 | 277 | 278 | 280 | 283 | 286 | 286 | 283 |
| 2019 | 288 | 287 | 287 | 287 | 287 | 285 | 280 | 279 | 282 | 285 | 288 | 288 | 285 |
| 2020 | 290 | 288 | 288 | 290 | 294 | 288 | 283 | 283 | 285 | 291 | 294 | 294 | 289 |
| 2021 | 295 | 291 | 291 | 290 | 288 | 284 | 281 | 280 | 283 | 288 | 291 | 292 | 288 |
| 2022[1] | 294 | 293 | 293 | 293 | 291 | 288 | 284 | 282 | 285 | 289 | 290 | 292 | 290 |

[1] Preliminary.  Source: National Agricultural Statistics Service, U.S. Department of Agriculture (NASS-USDA)

# HOGS

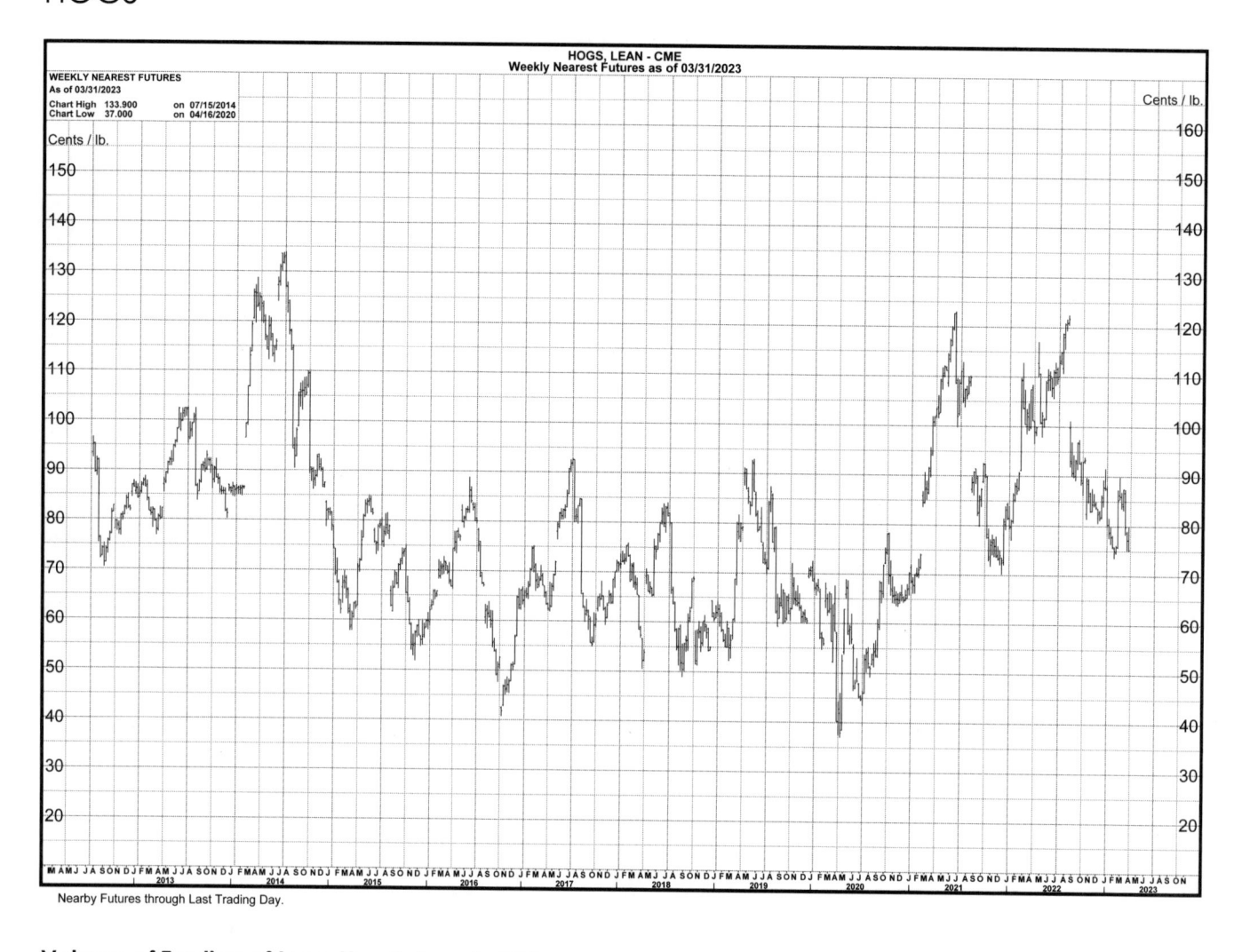

HOGS, LEAN - CME
Weekly Nearest Futures as of 03/31/2023

WEEKLY NEAREST FUTURES
As of 03/31/2023
Chart High 133.900 on 07/15/2014
Chart Low 37.000 on 04/16/2020

Nearby Futures through Last Trading Day.

## Volume of Trading of Lean Hog Futures in Chicago   In Thousands of Contracts

| Year | Jan. | Feb. | Mar. | Apr. | May | June | July | Aug. | Sept. | Oct. | Nov. | Dec. | Total |
|---|---|---|---|---|---|---|---|---|---|---|---|---|---|
| 2013 | 999.0 | 808.0 | 1,017.5 | 832.9 | 1,100.6 | 1,151.0 | 1,076.2 | 778.1 | 1,155.6 | 861.5 | 833.8 | 662.8 | 11,277.0 |
| 2014 | 940.1 | 880.1 | 1,402.3 | 760.6 | 893.0 | 937.5 | 1,046.6 | 818.8 | 1,000.4 | 674.1 | 708.0 | 595.5 | 10,656.9 |
| 2015 | 883.0 | 743.3 | 961.8 | 716.4 | 830.1 | 962.1 | 971.2 | 640.8 | 745.3 | 717.5 | 836.7 | 567.7 | 9,575.9 |
| 2016 | 665.2 | 645.4 | 797.0 | 589.4 | 726.5 | 937.8 | 826.5 | 645.5 | 849.8 | 762.7 | 915.4 | 833.8 | 9,195.0 |
| 2017 | 847.3 | 742.4 | 963.2 | 690.5 | 1,012.1 | 1,120.1 | 981.2 | 976.0 | 1,124.1 | 955.6 | 1,098.2 | 731.3 | 11,242.0 |
| 2018 | 992.4 | 936.4 | 1,149.9 | 962.6 | 1,236.1 | 1,312.5 | 1,250.9 | 1,308.4 | 1,241.2 | 1,140.7 | 1,267.2 | 753.3 | 13,551.7 |
| 2019 | 1,112.4 | 982.8 | 1,716.1 | 1,353.3 | 1,435.2 | 1,417.1 | 1,570.5 | 1,216.7 | 1,456.4 | 1,240.1 | 1,235.0 | 886.4 | 15,621.8 |
| 2020 | 1,351.2 | 977.4 | 1,381.6 | 1,197.2 | 995.6 | 1,046.9 | 1,050.0 | 750.5 | 1,236.2 | 873.0 | 854.0 | 682.8 | 12,396.4 |
| 2021 | 916.6 | 827.4 | 1,080.1 | 868.6 | 1,044.2 | 1,301.1 | 1,017.5 | 786.1 | 1,099.7 | 748.7 | 969.0 | 752.7 | 11,411.7 |
| 2022 | 1,115.2 | 926.7 | 1,062.2 | 734.8 | 1,034.8 | 979.8 | 970.8 | 875.3 | 1,051.7 | 897.4 | 948.7 | 800.9 | 11,398.3 |

Contract size = 40,000 lbs.    Source: Chicago Mercantile Exchange (CME)

## Average Open Interest of Lean Hog Futures in Chicago   In Contracts

| Year | Jan. | Feb. | Mar. | Apr. | May | June | July | Aug. | Sept. | Oct. | Nov. | Dec. |
|---|---|---|---|---|---|---|---|---|---|---|---|---|
| 2013 | 244,228 | 226,691 | 235,834 | 229,097 | 247,125 | 279,932 | 297,930 | 306,652 | 326,192 | 302,314 | 282,782 | 263,509 |
| 2014 | 266,366 | 282,321 | 288,484 | 265,981 | 256,474 | 248,869 | 248,878 | 234,967 | 237,877 | 236,417 | 230,578 | 216,735 |
| 2015 | 208,643 | 192,716 | 208,128 | 216,998 | 219,669 | 221,626 | 210,767 | 196,682 | 196,033 | 198,965 | 204,049 | 173,053 |
| 2016 | 168,096 | 191,458 | 218,393 | 224,392 | 233,337 | 255,818 | 234,949 | 212,182 | 215,947 | 227,447 | 225,542 | 199,554 |
| 2017 | 210,582 | 227,286 | 214,122 | 207,945 | 223,068 | 251,117 | 272,856 | 258,984 | 256,269 | 253,357 | 260,573 | 239,469 |
| 2018 | 246,345 | 232,492 | 230,504 | 241,846 | 244,654 | 231,674 | 233,594 | 230,352 | 222,734 | 225,483 | 227,359 | 207,286 |
| 2019 | 211,589 | 236,596 | 270,420 | 296,832 | 311,184 | 303,772 | 284,851 | 265,214 | 264,332 | 277,164 | 293,006 | 287,240 |
| 2020 | 294,780 | 291,757 | 257,704 | 222,412 | 208,909 | 218,716 | 225,379 | 219,996 | 223,259 | 223,208 | 206,542 | 189,728 |
| 2021 | 209,599 | 245,463 | 271,935 | 289,151 | 289,477 | 289,656 | 266,321 | 269,392 | 249,579 | 243,855 | 231,422 | 215,756 |
| 2022 | 230,763 | 273,066 | 242,790 | 226,703 | 207,407 | 189,158 | 200,317 | 227,873 | 207,701 | 192,337 | 194,307 | 184,800 |

Contract size = 40,000 lbs.    Source: Chicago Mercantile Exchange (CME)

# HOGS

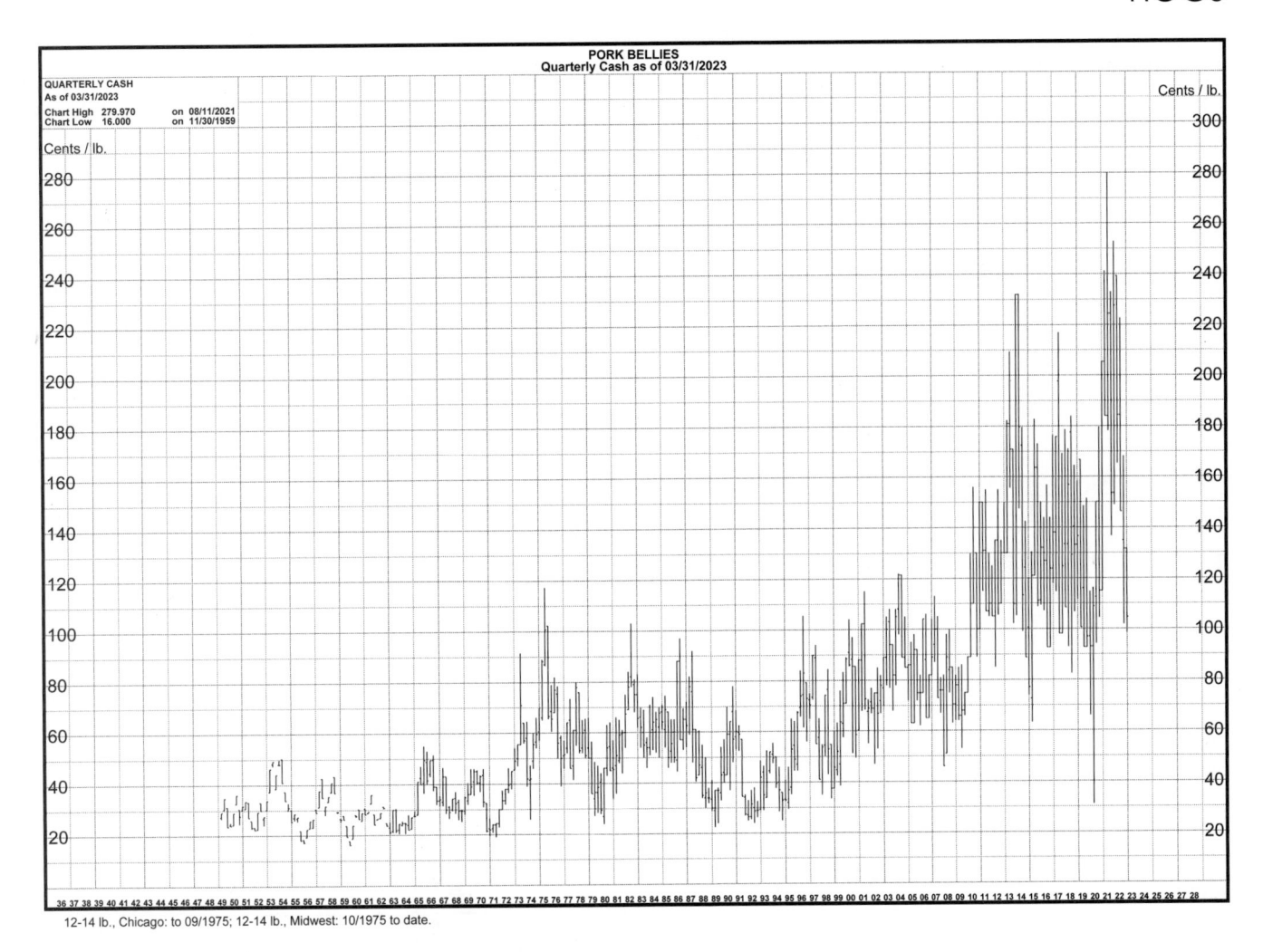

**PORK BELLIES**
Quarterly Cash as of 03/31/2023

### Average Price of Pork Bellies (12-14 lbs.), Central, U.S.  In Cents Per Pound

| Year | Jan. | Feb. | Mar. | Apr. | May | June | July | Aug. | Sept. | Oct. | Nov. | Dec. | Average |
|---|---|---|---|---|---|---|---|---|---|---|---|---|---|
| 2013 | NA | NA | NA | 151.44 | 161.60 | 175.55 | 163.12 | 177.24 | 149.62 | 134.99 | 128.41 | 127.35 | 152.15 |
| 2014 | 124.07 | 137.58 | 176.77 | 191.73 | 156.63 | 173.03 | 174.29 | 139.46 | 120.57 | 127.81 | 111.33 | 105.57 | 144.90 |
| 2015 | 122.30 | 102.97 | 81.14 | 75.33 | 82.51 | 108.15 | NA | 184.67 | 166.82 | 165.54 | 127.35 | 114.96 | 121.07 |
| 2016 | 128.18 | NA | NA | 134.91 | 119.13 | 130.09 | 146.67 | 115.14 | 96.21 | 127.29 | 120.69 | 121.10 | 123.94 |
| 2017 | 136.39 | NA | 158.66 | 136.79 | 139.18 | 176.76 | 216.28 | 170.18 | 116.74 | 107.75 | 135.04 | 142.64 | 148.76 |
| 2018 | 137.69 | 157.64 | 133.63 | 111.96 | 110.14 | 157.22 | NA | 106.71 | 109.96 | NA | 181.14 | 131.26 | 133.73 |
| 2019 | 146.10 | 121.61 | 142.66 | 160.07 | 138.55 | 123.36 | 122.41 | NA | 113.37 | 140.82 | 131.25 | 110.06 | 131.84 |
| 2020 | 108.16 | 88.40 | 91.46 | 51.13 | 101.79 | 104.92 | 107.72 | 113.28 | NA | NA | NA | NA | 95.86 |
| 2021 | 144.35 | 154.48 | NA | NA | 185.04 | 212.84 | 206.00 | 247.07 | 196.04 | 217.17 | 154.49 | NA | 190.83 |
| 2022[1] | NA | 204.40 | 214.90 | 222.72 | NA | NA | NA | NA | 160.24 | 148.98 | 142.43 | 115.99 | 172.81 |

[1] Preliminary.  Source: Economic Research Service, U.S. Department of Agriculture (ERS-USDA)

### Average Price of Pork Loins (12-14 lbs.)[2], Central, U.S.  In Cents Per Pound

| Year | Jan. | Feb. | Mar. | Apr. | May | June | July | Aug. | Sept. | Oct. | Nov. | Dec. | Average |
|---|---|---|---|---|---|---|---|---|---|---|---|---|---|
| 2013 | 107.12 | 111.73 | 108.86 | 106.77 | 120.28 | 138.64 | 129.84 | 128.96 | 116.92 | 115.78 | 107.25 | 106.24 | 116.53 |
| 2014 | 115.27 | 128.19 | 165.28 | 147.55 | 135.39 | 153.75 | 167.79 | 150.01 | 153.69 | 152.92 | 117.50 | 115.82 | 141.93 |
| 2015 | 108.25 | 99.88 | 100.25 | 101.55 | 124.08 | 112.35 | 111.13 | 107.61 | 102.46 | 103.50 | 88.44 | 85.76 | 103.77 |
| 2016 | 100.14 | 93.52 | 90.52 | 89.61 | 111.77 | 112.56 | 104.71 | 98.27 | 110.10 | 89.52 | 76.73 | 85.90 | 96.95 |
| 2017 | 91.73 | 90.66 | 99.36 | 88.58 | 106.12 | 118.21 | 118.69 | 100.58 | 94.97 | 89.85 | 85.62 | 82.96 | 97.28 |
| 2018 | 83.63 | 89.53 | 88.98 | 84.45 | 96.25 | 101.34 | 98.72 | 98.35 | 107.17 | 92.36 | 98.72 | 75.40 | 92.91 |
| 2019 | 79.70 | 75.19 | 82.42 | 88.03 | 101.05 | 103.19 | 98.04 | 92.14 | 85.29 | 88.61 | 86.24 | 86.68 | 88.88 |
| 2020 | 85.62 | 85.04 | 112.98 | 129.14 | 192.07 | 88.83 | 74.05 | 82.25 | 81.48 | 100.89 | 80.43 | 77.82 | 99.22 |
| 2021 | 88.61 | 90.84 | 103.36 | 108.46 | 126.13 | 124.34 | 112.00 | 114.47 | 110.03 | 103.68 | 82.19 | 72.22 | 103.03 |
| 2022[1] | 93.34 | 124.53 | 109.32 | 115.91 | 122.56 | 126.86 | 132.61 | 127.18 | 121.11 | 111.50 | 105.80 | 102.29 | 116.08 |

[1] Preliminary.  Source: Economic Research Service, U.S. Department of Agriculture (ERS-USDA)

# HOGS

## Average Retail Price of Bacon, Sliced   In U.S. Dollars per Pound

| Year | Jan. | Feb. | Mar. | Apr. | May | June | July | Aug. | Sept. | Oct. | Nov. | Dec. | Average |
|---|---|---|---|---|---|---|---|---|---|---|---|---|---|
| 2013 | 4.72 | 4.83 | 4.91 | 4.89 | 5.09 | 5.33 | 5.49 | 5.62 | 5.68 | 5.71 | 5.62 | 5.54 | 5.29 |
| 2014 | 5.56 | 5.46 | 5.55 | 5.69 | 6.05 | 6.11 | 6.01 | 6.07 | 5.95 | 5.76 | 5.57 | 5.53 | 5.78 |
| 2015 | 5.59 | 5.47 | 5.37 | 5.21 | 4.94 | 5.06 | 5.18 | 5.41 | 5.73 | 5.90 | 5.85 | 5.73 | 5.45 |
| 2016 | 5.66 | 5.39 | 5.49 | 5.61 | 5.55 | 5.37 | 5.45 | 5.45 | 5.48 | 5.38 | 5.11 | 5.10 | 5.42 |
| 2017 | 5.18 | 5.33 | 5.75 | 5.78 | 5.70 | 5.67 | 5.82 | 6.24 | 6.37 | 6.07 | 5.71 | 5.63 | 5.77 |
| 2018 | 5.65 | 5.53 | 5.53 | 5.42 | 5.45 | 5.25 | 5.42 | 5.58 | 5.50 | 5.37 | 5.39 | 5.50 | 5.47 |
| 2019 | 5.52 | 5.50 | 5.61 | 5.55 | 5.81 | 5.88 | 5.70 | 5.58 | 5.58 | 5.65 | 5.51 | 5.47 | 5.61 |
| 2020 | 5.51 | 5.50 | 5.26 | 5.35 | 5.35 | 5.77 | 5.78 | 5.56 | 5.62 | 5.72 | 5.75 | 5.83 | 5.58 |
| 2021 | 5.83 | 5.78 | 5.85 | 6.22 | 6.35 | 6.67 | 6.86 | 7.10 | 7.22 | 7.32 | 7.27 | 7.21 | 6.64 |
| 2022[1] | 7.22 | 7.10 | 7.20 | 7.42 | 7.36 | 7.40 | 7.42 | 7.37 | 7.38 | 7.61 | 7.24 | 6.96 | 7.31 |

[1] Preliminary.   Source: Economic Research Service, U.S. Department of Agriculture (ERS-USDA)


## Average Wholesale Price of Pork Hams (20-23 lb) Bl trmd. TS1   In U.S. Cents per Pound

| Year | Jan. | Feb. | Mar. | Apr. | May | June | July | Aug. | Sept. | Oct. | Nov. | Dec. | Average |
|---|---|---|---|---|---|---|---|---|---|---|---|---|---|
| 2013 | 71.87 | NA | 60.48 | 69.77 | 68.47 | 77.90 | 87.46 | 87.69 | 87.46 | 90.92 | 87.00 | 81.27 | 79.12 |
| 2014 | 75.35 | 83.70 | 99.82 | 103.06 | 105.67 | 123.85 | 143.57 | 118.74 | 119.35 | 121.85 | 103.13 | 85.94 | 107.00 |
| 2015 | 73.24 | 64.53 | 53.89 | 53.37 | 69.21 | 64.04 | 58.78 | 72.53 | 67.42 | 71.54 | 66.91 | 65.83 | 65.11 |
| 2016 | 58.79 | 60.71 | 55.25 | 64.45 | 67.08 | 75.28 | 79.41 | 70.85 | 71.60 | 55.07 | 67.25 | 75.05 | 66.73 |
| 2017 | 55.74 | 58.15 | 60.54 | 60.25 | 67.75 | 69.53 | 78.14 | 67.81 | 63.87 | 67.00 | 66.81 | 59.97 | 64.63 |
| 2018 | 64.21 | 60.28 | 55.33 | 54.87 | 53.34 | 61.67 | 55.57 | 57.35 | 57.37 | 53.69 | 55.57 | 52.32 | 56.80 |
| 2019 | 48.42 | 43.76 | 63.16 | 66.82 | 77.59 | 73.51 | 72.68 | 71.31 | 60.75 | 64.86 | 90.53 | 78.54 | 67.66 |
| 2020 | 71.83 | 60.93 | 53.37 | 38.41 | 41.42 | 34.77 | 46.11 | 44.96 | 62.63 | 66.68 | 71.22 | 63.62 | 54.66 |
| 2021 | 62.07 | 70.62 | 73.25 | 86.90 | 82.07 | 79.41 | 88.00 | 70.80 | 62.06 | 55.17 | 58.28 | 53.52 | 70.18 |
| 2022[1] | 47.86 | 51.73 | 62.73 | 72.56 | 83.99 | 94.77 | 111.68 | 103.44 | 103.65 | 108.85 | 100.42 | 84.82 | 85.54 |

[1] Preliminary.   Source: Economic Research Service, U.S. Department of Agriculture (ERS-USDA)


## Average Wholesale Price of Pork Cutout Composite   In U.S. Dollars per Pound

| Year | Jan. | Feb. | Mar. | Apr. | May | June | July | Aug. | Sept. | Oct. | Nov. | Dec. | Average |
|---|---|---|---|---|---|---|---|---|---|---|---|---|---|
| 2013 | 84.13 | 81.85 | 78.36 | 84.81 | 92.25 | 103.26 | 102.19 | 101.71 | 98.12 | 94.29 | 91.84 | 87.42 | 91.69 |
| 2014 | 86.84 | 95.80 | 122.60 | 122.73 | 113.87 | 125.07 | 133.58 | 113.66 | 110.82 | 111.71 | 94.59 | 89.90 | 110.10 |
| 2015 | 83.28 | 72.57 | 67.96 | 67.58 | 82.56 | 84.84 | 83.33 | 88.37 | 84.41 | 86.43 | 74.24 | 72.00 | 78.96 |
| 2016 | 73.26 | 76.03 | 76.16 | 79.52 | 85.62 | 87.96 | 87.77 | 76.29 | 72.79 | 73.06 | 73.80 | 78.07 | 78.36 |
| 2017 | 80.67 | 83.75 | 79.86 | 74.83 | 84.79 | 97.12 | 102.97 | 91.02 | 77.36 | 75.11 | 81.55 | 79.19 | 84.02 |
| 2018 | 80.90 | 78.22 | 72.89 | 68.01 | 73.87 | 83.34 | 81.13 | 68.35 | 74.98 | 78.60 | 81.13 | 71.62 | 76.09 |
| 2019 | 69.36 | 62.80 | 72.36 | 84.69 | 85.08 | 80.27 | 77.37 | 83.65 | 71.01 | 76.42 | 83.41 | 79.20 | 77.14 |
| 2020 | 74.72 | 64.92 | 72.75 | 65.80 | 105.78 | 68.47 | 67.87 | 72.14 | 84.82 | 94.09 | 81.18 | 75.21 | 77.31 |
| 2021 | 80.31 | 88.34 | 101.25 | 111.17 | 117.46 | 123.27 | 120.00 | 119.40 | 107.99 | 102.62 | 90.95 | 86.60 | 104.11 |
| 2022[1] | 90.56 | 105.56 | 105.73 | 106.56 | 104.43 | 109.49 | 120.60 | 116.99 | 102.86 | 101.15 | 93.43 | 87.24 | 103.72 |

[1] Preliminary.   Source: Economic Research Service, U.S. Department of Agriculture (ERS-USDA)


## Hog-Corn Price Ratio[2] in the United States   In Bushels

| Year | Jan. | Feb. | Mar. | Apr. | May | June | July | Aug. | Sept. | Oct. | Nov. | Dec. | Average |
|---|---|---|---|---|---|---|---|---|---|---|---|---|---|
| 2013 | 9.2 | 9.2 | 8.3 | 8.9 | 9.8 | 10.7 | 11.2 | 11.9 | 13.1 | 14.8 | 14.6 | 13.9 | 11.3 |
| 2014 | 13.8 | 15.1 | 18.1 | 18.9 | 17.6 | 18.8 | 23.0 | 22.9 | 21.7 | 21.6 | 18.5 | 17.0 | 18.9 |
| 2015 | 15.0 | 13.3 | 13.2 | 13.1 | 16.2 | 16.7 | 15.4 | 16.0 | 14.8 | 15.1 | 12.8 | 11.7 | 14.4 |
| 2016 | 11.9 | 13.9 | 14.0 | 14.3 | 15.5 | 15.9 | 16.5 | 16.4 | 14.8 | 12.7 | 12.0 | 13.0 | 14.2 |
| 2017 | 14.1 | 15.8 | 15.2 | 14.1 | 15.5 | 18.1 | 19.3 | 18.8 | 15.0 | 14.5 | 15.9 | 15.0 | 15.9 |
| 2018 | 16.0 | 16.2 | 14.2 | 12.7 | 14.0 | 16.5 | 16.9 | 13.2 | 12.7 | 14.7 | 13.5 | 12.3 | 14.4 |
| 2019 | 12.5 | 12.1 | 12.9 | 16.8 | 17.2 | 14.9 | 13.6 | 14.9 | 12.6 | 12.8 | 13.0 | 12.7 | 13.8 |
| 2020 | 12.6 | 12.0 | 13.0 | 12.9 | 15.9 | 13.1 | 12.4 | 13.8 | 14.6 | 15.6 | 13.7 | 12.4 | 13.5 |
| 2021 | 11.8 | 11.9 | 13.7 | 14.2 | 13.4 | 13.8 | 13.1 | 12.5 | 12.9 | 13.0 | 11.1 | 10.3 | 12.6 |
| 2022[1] | 10.5 | 11.3 | 11.4 | 10.8 | 10.5 | 10.7 | 11.4 | 11.9 | 10.4 | 10.8 | 10.3 | 9.5 | 10.8 |

[1] Preliminary.   [2] Bushels of corn equal in value to 100 pounds of hog, live weight.   Source: Economic Research Service, U.S. Department of Agriculture (ERS-USDA)

# Honey

Honey is the thick, supersaturated sugar solution produced by bees to feed their larvae. It is composed of fructose, glucose, and water in varying proportions and also contains several enzymes and oils. The color of honey varies due to the source of nectar and the age of the honey. Light-colored honeys are usually of higher quality than darker honeys. The average honeybee colony can produce more than 700 pounds of honey per year, but only 10 percent is usually harvested by the beekeeper. The rest of the honey is consumed by the colony during the year. American per capita honey consumption is 1 pound per person per year. Honey is said to be humanity's oldest sweet and beeswax the first plastic.

Honey is used in many ways, including direct human consumption, baking, and medicine. Honey has several healing properties. Its high sugar content nourishes injured tissues, thus enhancing faster healing time. Honey's phytochemicals create a form of hydrogen peroxide that cleans out the wound, and the thick consistency protects the wound from contact with air. Honey has also proven superior to antibiotic ointments for reducing rates of infection in people with burns.

**Prices** – U.S. average domestic honey prices in 2021 rose by +21.0% to a new record high of 254.0 cents per pound. The value of U.S. honey production in 2021 rose by +3.6% to $321.224 million, below the 2018 record high of $340.358 million.

**Supply** – World production of honey in 2021 fell by -0.1% to 1.771 million metric tons, below the 2017 record high of 1.878 million metric tons. The major producers of honey in 2021 were China with 27.4% of the world's total, Argentina with 4.0%, and Russia with 3.6%. U.S. production of honey in 2021 fell by -14.3% to 126.466 million pounds, remaining well below the 20-year high of 220.339 million pounds posted in 2000. Honey yield per colony in 2021 fell by -13.9% to 46.9 pounds per colony. The number of colonies in 2021 fell by -0.4% to 2.696 million.

**Trade** – U.S. imports of honey in 2018 rose by +2.4% to 442.390 million pounds, a new record high U.S. exports of honey in 2018 fell by -1.9% to 9.716 million pounds.

## Salient Statistics of Honey in the United States    In Millions of Pounds

| Year | Number of Colonies (1,000) | Yield Per Colony (Pounds) | Stocks Jan. 1 | Total U.S. Production | Imports for Consumption | Domestic Disappearance | Exports | Total Supply | Domestic Avg. Price All Honey (cents/lb.) | Value of Production ($1,000) | U.S. Production: Beeswax | Domestic Avg. Price: Beeswax (cents/lb.) |
|---|---|---|---|---|---|---|---|---|---|---|---|---|
| 2013 | 2,640 | 56.6 | 38.2 | 149.5 | 337.5 | ---- | 12.0 | 525.2 | 214.1 | 320.1 | ---- | ---- |
| 2014 | 2,740 | 65.1 | 41.2 | 178.3 | 365.5 | ---- | 10.9 | 584.9 | 217.3 | 387.4 | ---- | ---- |
| 2015 | 2,660 | 58.9 | 42.2 | 156.5 | 386.3 | ---- | 11.3 | 585.1 | 208.3 | 326.1 | ---- | ---- |
| 2016 | 2,775 | 58.3 | 41.3 | 161.9 | 367.0 | ---- | 11.1 | 570.2 | 211.9 | 343.0 | ---- | ---- |
| 2017 | 2,683 | 55.5 | 30.7 | 149.0 | 432.1 | ---- | 9.9 | 611.7 | 219.9 | 334.2 | ---- | ---- |
| 2018 | 2,828 | 54.5 | 29.3 | 154.0 | 442.4 | ---- | 9.7 | 625.7 | 221.0 | 340.4 | ---- | ---- |
| 2019 | 2,812 | 55.8 | 40.9 | 156.9 | | ---- | | | 199.0 | 312.3 | ---- | ---- |
| 2020 | 2,706 | 54.5 | 39.7 | 147.6 | | ---- | | | 210.0 | 309.9 | ---- | ---- |
| 2021 | 2,697 | 47.0 | 23.5 | 126.7 | | ---- | | | 265.0 | 335.9 | ---- | ---- |
| 2022[1] | 2,667 | 47.0 | 23.3 | 125.3 | | ---- | | | 296.0 | 371.0 | ---- | ---- |

[1] Preliminary.  Source: Economic Research Service, U.S. Department of Agriculture (ERS-USDA)

## Average Price of Honey, by Color Class in the United States    In U.S. Dollars per Pound

| | Co-op and Private | | | | | Retail | | | | | All | | | | |
|---|---|---|---|---|---|---|---|---|---|---|---|---|---|---|---|
| Year | Water White, Extra White, White | Extra Light Amber | Light Amber, Amber, Dark Amber | All Other Honey, Area Specialties | All Honey | Water White, Extra White, White | Extra Light Amber | Light Amber, Amber, Dark Amber | All Other Honey, Area Specialties | All Honey | Water White, Extra White, White | Extra Light Amber | Light Amber, Amber, Dark Amber | All Other Honey, Area Specialties | All Honey |
| 2013 | 2.109 | 2.040 | 1.973 | 2.224 | 2.058 | 3.409 | 3.306 | 4.051 | 4.925 | 3.824 | 2.129 | 2.090 | 2.192 | 2.489 | 2.141 |
| 2014 | 2.046 | 2.096 | 2.088 | 2.554 | 2.071 | 3.285 | 3.922 | 4.171 | 5.352 | 4.054 | 2.062 | 2.183 | 2.342 | 3.182 | 2.173 |
| 2015 | 1.886 | 2.025 | 2.004 | 2.849 | 1.950 | 3.054 | 4.118 | 4.121 | 6.566 | 4.099 | 1.906 | 2.132 | 2.347 | 3.515 | 2.083 |
| 2016 | 1.891 | 1.908 | 1.948 | 2.457 | 1.920 | 4.638 | 4.337 | 4.529 | 7.816 | 4.745 | 1.955 | 2.008 | 2.330 | 3.852 | 2.119 |
| 2017 | 2.047 | 2.060 | 2.028 | 2.872 | 2.051 | 3.143 | 4.873 | 4.970 | 6.279 | 4.450 | 2.063 | 2.173 | 2.411 | 3.834 | 2.199 |
| 2018 | 1.980 | 2.010 | 2.100 | 2.640 | 2.030 | 3.630 | 3.440 | 4.890 | 7.170 | 7.380 | 2.010 | 2.120 | 2.510 | 3.620 | 2.210 |
| 2019 | 1.630 | 1.700 | 1.950 | 3.160 | 1.730 | 4.700 | 3.630 | 5.300 | 6.620 | 4.820 | 1.700 | 1.900 | 2.570 | 3.990 | 1.990 |
| 2020 | 1.730 | 1.810 | 2.000 | 2.390 | 1.840 | 4.180 | 4.670 | 5.510 | 7.230 | 5.230 | 1.810 | 1.930 | 2.530 | 3.000 | 2.100 |
| 2021 | 2.330 | 2.340 | 2.520 | 2.640 | 2.400 | 5.360 | 4.150 | 5.550 | 6.480 | 5.270 | 2.430 | 2.470 | 2.980 | 3.760 | 2.650 |
| 2022[1] | 2.690 | 2.650 | 2.810 | 3.410 | 2.740 | 5.620 | 5.620 | 6.140 | 7.860 | 6.040 | 2.810 | 2.750 | 3.150 | 4.020 | 2.960 |

[1] Preliminary.  Source: National Agricultural Statistics Service, U.S. Department of Agriculture (NASS-USDA)

# HONEY

## World Production of Honey   In Metric Tons

| Year | Argentina | Australia | Brazil | Canada | China | Germany | Japan | Mexico | Russia | United States | World Total |
|---|---|---|---|---|---|---|---|---|---|---|---|
| 2012 | 76,000 | 12,006 | 33,932 | 41,168 | 462,203 | 17,869 | 2,763 | 58,602 | 64,898 | 64,544 | 1,640,272 |
| 2013 | 67,500 | 13,864 | 35,365 | 34,685 | 461,431 | 18,953 | 2,766 | 56,907 | 68,446 | 67,812 | 1,688,386 |
| 2014 | 76,000 | 13,094 | 38,481 | 38,847 | 474,786 | 20,195 | 2,839 | 60,624 | 74,868 | 80,862 | 1,760,925 |
| 2015 | 52,600 | 12,281 | 37,859 | 41,735 | 484,726 | 23,398 | 2,865 | 61,881 | 67,736 | 71,008 | 1,821,403 |
| 2016 | 68,123 | 13,080 | 39,677 | 42,900 | 562,875 | 21,600 | 2,754 | 55,358 | 69,764 | 73,429 | 1,862,678 |
| 2017 | 76,379 | 12,180 | 41,696 | 43,550 | 548,857 | 21,600 | 2,827 | 51,066 | 65,167 | 67,596 | 1,878,308 |
| 2018 | 79,468 | 12,466 | 42,268 | 43,089 | 457,182 | ---- | 2,826 | 64,253 | 65,006 | 69,857 | 1,838,509 |
| 2019 | 78,909 | 12,121 | 45,801 | 39,295 | 446,961 | 24,100 | 2,911 | 61,986 | 63,526 | 71,179 | 1,757,124 |
| 2020 | 72,441 | 11,874 | 51,508 | 37,723 | 466,487 | 29,200 | 2,954 | 54,165 | 66,368 | 66,948 | 1,774,477 |
| 2021[1] | 71,318 | 11,403 | 55,828 | 40,720 | 485,960 | 19,600 | 2,729 | 62,080 | 64,533 | 57,364 | 1,771,944 |

[1] Preliminary.   Source: Food and Agricultural Organization of the United Nations (FAO)

## United States Imports of Honey   In Metric Tons

| Year | Argentina | Brazil | Canada | India | Mexico | New Zealand | Taiwan | Thailand | Turkey | Ukraine | Uruguay | Vietnam | World Total |
|---|---|---|---|---|---|---|---|---|---|---|---|---|---|
| 2012 | 42,482 | 11,303 | 15,971 | 21,454 | 6,179 | 966 | 1,324 | 258 | 1,073 | 1,302 | 10,877 | 20,700 | 141,016 |
| 2013 | 44,221 | 11,677 | 9,385 | 25,867 | 5,648 | 1,234 | 1,827 | 846 | 1,897 | 3,308 | 8,710 | 33,586 | 153,102 |
| 2014 | 36,888 | 19,249 | 5,612 | 20,290 | 7,254 | 1,625 | 2,523 | 3,458 | 2,581 | 8,876 | 5,362 | 47,107 | 165,777 |
| 2015 | 27,081 | 15,440 | 8,234 | 36,123 | 5,364 | 1,992 | 4,442 | 10,753 | 5,195 | 11,411 | 7,243 | 36,973 | 175,243 |
| 2016 | 34,708 | 19,062 | 13,510 | 29,364 | 4,557 | 1,840 | 1,580 | 4,238 | 1,852 | 11,086 | 1,767 | 38,494 | 166,442 |
| 2017 | 35,378 | 24,031 | 15,762 | 45,143 | 4,783 | 4,200 | 1,649 | 4,490 | 2,393 | 19,362 | 4,025 | 36,288 | 202,415 |
| 2018 | 36,219 | 23,604 | 15,221 | 44,200 | 3,303 | 1,671 | 1,680 | 4,639 | 2,248 | 8,324 | 1,326 | 39,156 | 186,935 |
| 2019 | 36,468 | 23,913 | 7,872 | 49,657 | 3,239 | 1,660 | 1,651 | 1,579 | 826 | 8,738 | 1,362 | 36,980 | 178,964 |
| 2020 | 39,805 | 34,198 | 4,143 | 37,578 | 3,465 | 1,898 | 831 | 1,039 | 1,062 | 11,084 | 4,063 | 50,669 | 196,507 |
| 2021[1] | 42,858 | 34,581 | 2,992 | 56,572 | 4,125 | 2,810 | 1,100 | 720 | 2,268 | 5,953 | 4,229 | 55,933 | 219,991 |

[1] Preliminary.   Source: Foreign Agricultural Service, U.S. Department of Agriculture (FAS-USDA)

## Production of Honey in the United States   In Thousands of Pounds

| Year | California | Florida | Georgia | Idaho | Louisiana | Michigan | Minnesota | Montana | North Dakota | South Dakota | Texas | Wisconsin | Total |
|---|---|---|---|---|---|---|---|---|---|---|---|---|---|
| 2013 | 10,890 | 13,420 | 3,350 | 2,656 | 4,900 | 4,675 | 7,540 | 14,946 | 33,120 | 14,840 | 6,254 | 3,540 | 149,499 |
| 2014 | 12,480 | 14,700 | 4,526 | 3,400 | 4,032 | 5,733 | 7,920 | 14,256 | 42,140 | 24,360 | 9,048 | 2,862 | 178,270 |
| 2015 | 8,250 | 11,880 | 2,760 | 2,848 | 4,356 | 5,220 | 8,296 | 12,118 | 36,260 | 19,140 | 8,316 | 3,484 | 156,544 |
| 2016 | 11,160 | 10,750 | 3,744 | 3,298 | 4,300 | 5,340 | 7,316 | 12,243 | 37,830 | 19,880 | 9,310 | 3,348 | 161,882 |
| 2017 | 13,735 | 8,815 | 3,168 | 4,180 | 3,483 | 3,915 | 7,812 | 10,440 | 33,670 | 14,535 | 7,920 | 2,968 | 148,980 |
| 2018 | 13,735 | 10,535 | 3,332 | 2,976 | 3,735 | 4,048 | 7,259 | 14,720 | 38,160 | 11,985 | 7,392 | 2,295 | 154,008 |
| 2019 | 16,080 | 9,225 | 3,366 | 2,944 | 3,888 | 4,700 | 6,962 | 14,878 | 33,800 | 19,440 | 7,560 | 2,162 | 156,922 |
| 2020 | 13,760 | 8,832 | 3,434 | 3,745 | 2,277 | 4,465 | 5,940 | 8,910 | 38,610 | 14,945 | 8,949 | 2,250 | 147,594 |
| 2021 | 9,570 | 8,492 | 3,264 | 3,000 | 2,146 | 5,100 | 7,125 | 6,669 | 28,325 | 12,250 | 7,672 | 1,974 | 126,744 |
| 2022[1] | 11,590 | 7,350 | 3,296 | 2,726 | 2,562 | 3,362 | 5,202 | 7,503 | 31,200 | 7,215 | 8,321 | 2,915 | 125,331 |

[1] Preliminary.   Source: National Agricultural Statistics Service, U.S. Department of Agriculture (NASS-USDA)

## Honey Producing Colonies in the United States   In Thousands

| Year | California | Florida | Georgia | Idaho | Louisiana | Michigan | Minnesota | Montana | North Dakota | South Dakota | Texas | Wisconsin | Total |
|---|---|---|---|---|---|---|---|---|---|---|---|---|---|
| 2013 | 330 | 220 | 67 | 83 | 50 | 85 | 130 | 159 | 480 | 265 | 106 | 59 | 2,640 |
| 2014 | 320 | 245 | 73 | 100 | 48 | 91 | 122 | 162 | 490 | 280 | 116 | 53 | 2,740 |
| 2015 | 275 | 220 | 69 | 89 | 44 | 90 | 122 | 146 | 490 | 290 | 126 | 52 | 2,660 |
| 2016 | 310 | 215 | 96 | 97 | 50 | 89 | 124 | 159 | 485 | 280 | 133 | 54 | 2,775 |
| 2017 | 335 | 205 | 99 | 95 | 43 | 87 | 126 | 145 | 455 | 255 | 120 | 53 | 2,683 |
| 2018 | 335 | 215 | 98 | 96 | 45 | 97 | 119 | 160 | 550 | 255 | 132 | 51 | 2,828 |
| 2019 | 335 | 205 | 102 | 92 | 54 | 94 | 118 | 173 | 520 | 270 | 126 | 46 | 2,812 |
| 2020 | 320 | 192 | 101 | 107 | 33 | 95 | 108 | 110 | 495 | 245 | 157 | 45 | 2,706 |
| 2021 | 290 | 193 | 96 | 100 | 37 | 101 | 125 | 117 | 515 | 250 | 137 | 42 | 2,697 |
| 2022[1] | 305 | 210 | 103 | 94 | 42 | 82 | 102 | 123 | 520 | 185 | 157 | 53 | 2,667 |

[1] Preliminary.   Source: National Agricultural Statistics Service, U.S. Department of Agriculture (NASS-USDA)

# Hops

## Hop Stocks[2] in the United States     In Thousands of Pounds

| Year | March 1: Growers | March 1: Dealers/ Growers | March 1: Brewers | March 1: Total Stocks | September 1: Growers | September 1: Dealers/ Growers | September 1: Brewers | September 1: Total Stocks |
|---|---|---|---|---|---|---|---|---|
| 2014 | ---- | 72,000 | 49,000 | 121,000 | ---- | 47,000 | 43,000 | 90,000 |
| 2015 | ---- | 76,000 | 43,000 | 119,000 | ---- | 46,000 | 37,000 | 83,000 |
| 2016 | ---- | 88,000 | 40,000 | 128,000 | ---- | 49,000 | 36,000 | 85,000 |
| 2017 | ---- | 105,000 | 35,000 | 140,000 | ---- | 64,000 | 34,000 | 98,000 |
| 2018 | ---- | 132,000 | 37,000 | 169,000 | ---- | 74,000 | 39,000 | 113,000 |
| 2019 | ---- | 130,000 | 35,000 | 165,000 | ---- | 78,000 | 37,000 | 115,000 |
| 2020 | ---- | 145,000 | 35,000 | 180,000 | ---- | 94,000 | 36,000 | 130,000 |
| 2021 | ---- | 150,000 | 35,000 | 185,000 | ---- | 97,000 | 31,000 | 128,000 |
| 2022 | ---- | 160,000 | 33,000 | 193,000 | ---- | 109,000 | 28,000 | 137,000 |
| 2023[1] | ---- | 159,000 | 27,000 | 186,000 | ---- | | | |

[1] Preliminary.   [2] Includes equivalent pounds of dry hops held in form of extract or pellets.   Source: National Agricultural Statistics Service (NASS), Agricultural Statistics Board, United States Department of Agriculture (USDA)

## Salient Statistics of Hops in the United States

| Year | Area Harvested (Acres) | Yield (Pounds) | Production (1,000 Pounds) | Price per Unit (US Dollars per Pound) | Value of Production (1,000 US Dollars) |
|---|---|---|---|---|---|
| 2013 | 35,288 | 1,969 | 69,246 | $3.35 | $232,308 |
| 2014 | 38,011 | 1,868 | 70,996 | $3.67 | $260,627 |
| 2015 | 43,633 | 1,807 | 78,846 | $4.38 | $345,388 |
| 2016 | 50,857 | 1,713 | 87,140 | $5.72 | $498,420 |
| 2017 | 53,989 | 1,956 | 105,622 | $5.60 | $591,375 |
| 2018 | 55,035 | 1,943 | 106,907 | $5.46 | $583,444 |
| 2019 | 56,544 | 1,981 | 112,041 | $5.68 | $636,580 |
| 2020 | 58,641 | 1,770 | 103,810 | $5.97 | $619,424 |
| 2021[1] | 60,872 | 1,900 | 115,631 | $5.72 | $661,618 |
| 2022[2] | 59,785 | 1,694 | 101,286 | $6.10 | $617,607 |

[1] Preliminary.   [2] Forecast.   Source: National Agricultural Statistics Service (NASS), Agricultural Statistics Board, United States Department of Agriculture (USDA)

## Production of Hops in the United States, by States     In Thousands of Pounds

| Year | California | Idaho | Oregon | Washington | Total |
|---|---|---|---|---|---|
| 2013 | ---- | 5,837.9 | 8,530.5 | 54,877.7 | 69,246.1 |
| 2014 | ---- | 6,913.8 | 8,221.0 | 55,861.1 | 70,995.9 |
| 2015 | ---- | 8,724.9 | 10,667.8 | 59,453.3 | 78,846.0 |
| 2016 | ---- | 9,297.7 | 12,395.3 | 65,446.6 | 87,139.6 |
| 2017 | ---- | 14,067.3 | 12,470.4 | 79,083.8 | 105,621.5 |
| 2018 | ---- | 16,242.8 | 12,936.2 | 77,727.7 | 106,906.7 |
| 2019 | ---- | 17,003.1 | 13,023.2 | 82,014.9 | 112,041.2 |
| 2020 | ---- | 17,190.1 | 12,468.7 | 74,151.5 | 103,810.3 |
| 2021[1] | ---- | 18,414.8 | 12,607.9 | 84,608.2 | 115,630.9 |
| 2022[2] | ---- | 16,072.5 | 13,402.3 | 71,811.5 | 101,286.3 |

[1] Preliminary.   [2] Forecast.   Source: National Agricultural Statistics Service (NASS), Agricultural Statistics Board, United States Department of Agriculture (USDA)

## Production of Hops in Washington, by Variety     In Thousands of Pounds

| Year | Amarillo, VGXP01 | Cascade | Centennial | Citra, HBC 394 | Columbus/ Tomahawk | Mosaic, HBC 369 | Pahto, HBC 682 | Simcoe, YCR 14 | Summit | Zeus | Total |
|---|---|---|---|---|---|---|---|---|---|---|---|
| 2013 | ---- | 7,300.0 | 2,905.2 | 1,820.3 | 6,006.0 | 652.8 | ---- | 2,183.4 | 5,326.6 | 9,635.7 | 54,877.7 |
| 2014 | ---- | 8,821.0 | 3,818.8 | 2,622.5 | 4,569.2 | 1,493.2 | ---- | 2,805.8 | 5,308.3 | 9,488.4 | 55,861.1 |
| 2015 | W | 9,553.3 | 4,317.3 | 3,597.2 | 4,223.4 | 3,111.6 | ---- | 4,489.5 | 3,189.6 | 8,426.3 | 59,453.3 |
| 2016 | W | 9,638.8 | 5,908.6 | 5,035.0 | 2,787.9 | 4,720.4 | W | 6,305.1 | 2,914.5 | 6,178.5 | 65,446.6 |
| 2017 | 3,347.0 | 10,547.8 | 7,450.6 | 6,493.8 | 4,389.7 | 4,578.0 | W | 6,725.4 | 3,342.3 | 6,836.8 | 79,083.8 |
| 2018 | 3,539.9 | 8,428.3 | 5,285.5 | 7,792.4 | 5,048.4 | 4,542.1 | 3,591.7 | 5,095.1 | 2,874.1 | 6,788.4 | 77,727.7 |
| 2019 | 3,107.8 | 7,138.6 | 5,516.4 | 9,569.3 | 6,002.6 | 5,810.8 | 5,057.4 | 6,020.2 | 1,946.8 | 6,843.4 | 82,014.9 |
| 2020 | 2,300.4 | 4,462.2 | 4,008.2 | 12,426.2 | 10,507.9 | 7,422.6 | 4,458.0 | 5,280.6 | 701.4 | ---- | 74,151.5 |
| 2021 | 2,213.1 | 5,045.1 | 3,135.1 | 13,850.3 | 12,013.1 | 8,926.9 | 5,206.8 | 5,221.1 | 590.4 | ---- | 84,608.2 |
| 2022[1] | 1,967.5 | 5,323.1 | 2,992.4 | 11,719.9 | 9,019.5 | 8,166.1 | 3,643.6 | 4,821.7 | W | ---- | 71,811.5 |

[1] Preliminary.   [2] Includes data withheld to avoid disclosure of individual operations and varieties not listed.   W = Withheld to avoid disclosing data for individual operations.   Source: National Agricultural Statistics Service (NASS), Agricultural Statistics Board, United States Department of Agriculture (USDA)

# Interest Rates - U.S.

U.S. interest rates can be characterized in two main ways, by credit quality and by maturity. Credit quality refers to the level of risk associated with a particular borrower. U.S. Treasury securities, for example, carry the lowest risk. Maturity refers to the time at which the security matures and must be repaid. Treasury securities carry a full spectrum of maturities, from short-term cash management bills, to T-bills (4-weeks, 3-months, 6-months), T-notes (2-year, 3-year, 5-year, 7-year, and 10-year), and 30-year T-bonds. The most active futures markets are the 10-year T-note futures, 30-year T-bond futures, and Eurodollar futures, all of which are traded at the CME Group.

**Prices** – CME 10-year T-note futures prices (Barchart.com symbol ZN) posted their high for 2022 in January as they fell further from the all-time high posted in March 2020.

T-note prices were under pressure throughout 2022 as soaring inflation prompted the Federal Reserve (Fed) to aggressively raise interest rates. U.S. consumer prices in March rose +8.5% y/y, the fastest pace in 40 years. At the March 2022 FOMC meeting, the Fed raised the federal funds target range by 25 basis points to 0.25%-0.50%, and the Fed's dot-plot signaled six more 25 basis point rate increases for 2022. Fed Chair Powell said, "if appropriate to move more quickly, we'll do so."

The Fed ramped up its pace of interest rate increases at the May 2022 FOMC meeting, lifting the federal funds target range by 50 basis points to 0.75%-1.00%. The sell-off in T-note prices paused briefly in Q2 after Fed Chair Powell said at the May FOMC meeting that a "75 basis point rate hike isn't being actively considered, but more 50 basis point rate hikes were on the table." Also, inflation eased as consumer prices in April fell to +8.3% y/y from March's 40-year high of +8.5% y/y.

At the June FOMC meeting, the Fed raised the federal funds target range by 75 basis points to 1.50%-1.75%, the largest increase since 1994, as strength in the U.S. labor market and rising inflation kept the Fed hawkish. The U.S. unemployment rate continued to fall throughout 2022 and dropped to a 2-year low of 3.5% in July. The Fed also raised its interest rate hike estimates at the June FOMC meeting, projecting another 175 basis points of rate hikes for the year.

After moving sideways to slightly higher into August, T-note prices continued their sell-off into Q4 of 2022, falling to a 15-year low in October. U.S. consumer price pressures peaked in June at +9.1% y/y, the most in four decades, which kept the Fed hawkish and prompted four consecutive 75 basis point interest rate hikes from June through November. At the September FOMC meeting, policymakers said ongoing rate hikes were "appropriate," and Fed Chair Powell said the Fed intended to return to "sufficiently restrictive" rates.

T-note prices staged a modest recovery into the year-end of 2022 as inflation eased and allowed the Fed to slow its pace of interest rate hikes. After posting a 40-year high of 9.1% y/y in June, U.S. consumer prices fell to a 14-month low of 6.5% y/y by December. At the December FOMC meeting, the Fed slowed its pace of interest rate hikes to 50 basis points to 4.25%-4.50% after raising rates by 75 basis points at the previous four consecutive meetings. The FOMC also projected a peak interest rate of 5.1% for 2023, and Fed Chair Powell said the size of future rate hikes would depend on incoming data. The 10-year T-note yield finished 2022 up +2.37 percentage points at 3.88%.

### U.S. Producer Price Index[2] for All Commodities     1982 = 100

| Year | Jan. | Feb. | Mar. | Apr. | May | June | July | Aug. | Sept. | Oct. | Nov. | Dec. | Average |
|---|---|---|---|---|---|---|---|---|---|---|---|---|---|
| 2013 | 202.5 | 204.3 | 204.0 | 203.5 | 204.1 | 204.3 | 204.4 | 204.2 | 203.9 | 202.5 | 201.2 | 202.0 | 203.4 |
| 2014 | 203.8 | 205.7 | 207.0 | 208.3 | 208.0 | 208.3 | 208.0 | 207.0 | 206.4 | 203.4 | 200.9 | 197.0 | 205.3 |
| 2015 | 192.0 | 191.1 | 191.5 | 190.9 | 193.4 | 194.8 | 193.9 | 191.9 | 189.1 | 187.5 | 185.7 | 183.5 | 190.4 |
| 2016 | 182.6 | 181.3 | 182.1 | 183.2 | 185.3 | 187.6 | 187.7 | 186.6 | 186.9 | 186.7 | 186.3 | 188.2 | 185.4 |
| 2017 | 190.7 | 191.6 | 191.5 | 193.0 | 192.8 | 193.6 | 193.5 | 193.8 | 194.8 | 194.9 | 195.9 | 196.3 | 193.5 |
| 2018 | 197.9 | 199.3 | 199.3 | 200.3 | 203.2 | 204.2 | 204.3 | 203.4 | 203.6 | 204.6 | 202.3 | 201.0 | 202.0 |
| 2019 | 199.1 | 199.2 | 200.8 | 202.1 | 201.7 | 200.3 | 200.7 | 199.2 | 198.4 | 198.6 | 199.0 | 199.0 | 199.8 |
| 2020 | 199.3 | 196.7 | 193.1 | 185.5 | 188.6 | 191.2 | 193.0 | 194.3 | 195.5 | 196.5 | 198.3 | 200.5 | 194.4 |
| 2021 | 204.8 | 210.6 | 215.0 | 217.9 | 224.9 | 228.9 | 231.9 | 233.4 | 235.7 | 240.5 | 243.3 | 241.3 | 227.3 |
| 2022[1] | 246.5 | 252.7 | 260.0 | 265.3 | 273.3 | 280.3 | 272.3 | 269.5 | 267.9 | 265.0 | 263.2 | 257.9 | 264.5 |

[1] Preliminary.   [2] Not seasonally adjusted.   Source: Bureau of Labor Statistics, U.S. Department of Commerce (BLS)

### U.S. Consumer Price Index[2] for All Urban Consumers     1982-84 = 100

| Year | Jan. | Feb. | Mar. | Apr. | May | June | July | Aug. | Sept. | Oct. | Nov. | Dec. | Average |
|---|---|---|---|---|---|---|---|---|---|---|---|---|---|
| 2013 | 230.3 | 232.2 | 232.8 | 232.5 | 232.9 | 233.5 | 233.6 | 233.9 | 234.1 | 233.5 | 233.1 | 233.0 | 233.0 |
| 2014 | 233.9 | 234.8 | 236.3 | 237.1 | 237.9 | 238.3 | 238.3 | 237.9 | 238.0 | 237.4 | 236.2 | 234.8 | 236.7 |
| 2015 | 233.7 | 234.7 | 236.1 | 236.6 | 237.8 | 238.6 | 238.7 | 238.3 | 237.9 | 237.8 | 237.3 | 236.5 | 237.0 |
| 2016 | 236.9 | 237.1 | 238.1 | 239.3 | 240.2 | 241.0 | 240.6 | 240.8 | 241.4 | 241.7 | 241.4 | 241.4 | 240.0 |
| 2017 | 242.8 | 243.6 | 243.8 | 244.5 | 244.7 | 245.0 | 244.8 | 245.5 | 246.8 | 246.7 | 246.7 | 246.5 | 245.1 |
| 2018 | 247.9 | 249.0 | 249.6 | 250.5 | 251.6 | 252.0 | 252.0 | 252.1 | 252.4 | 252.9 | 252.0 | 251.2 | 251.1 |
| 2019 | 251.7 | 252.8 | 254.2 | 255.5 | 256.1 | 256.1 | 256.6 | 256.6 | 256.8 | 257.3 | 257.2 | 257.0 | 255.7 |
| 2020 | 258.0 | 258.7 | 258.1 | 256.4 | 256.4 | 257.8 | 259.1 | 259.9 | 260.3 | 260.4 | 260.2 | 260.5 | 258.8 |
| 2021 | 261.6 | 263.0 | 264.9 | 267.1 | 269.2 | 271.7 | 273.0 | 273.6 | 274.3 | 276.6 | 277.9 | 278.8 | 271.0 |
| 2022[1] | 281.1 | 283.7 | 287.5 | 289.1 | 292.3 | 296.3 | 296.3 | 296.2 | 296.8 | 298.0 | 297.7 | 296.8 | 292.7 |

[1] Preliminary.   [2] Not seasonally adjusted.   Source: Bureau of Labor Statistics, U.S. Department of Commerce (BLS)

# INTEREST RATES - U.S.

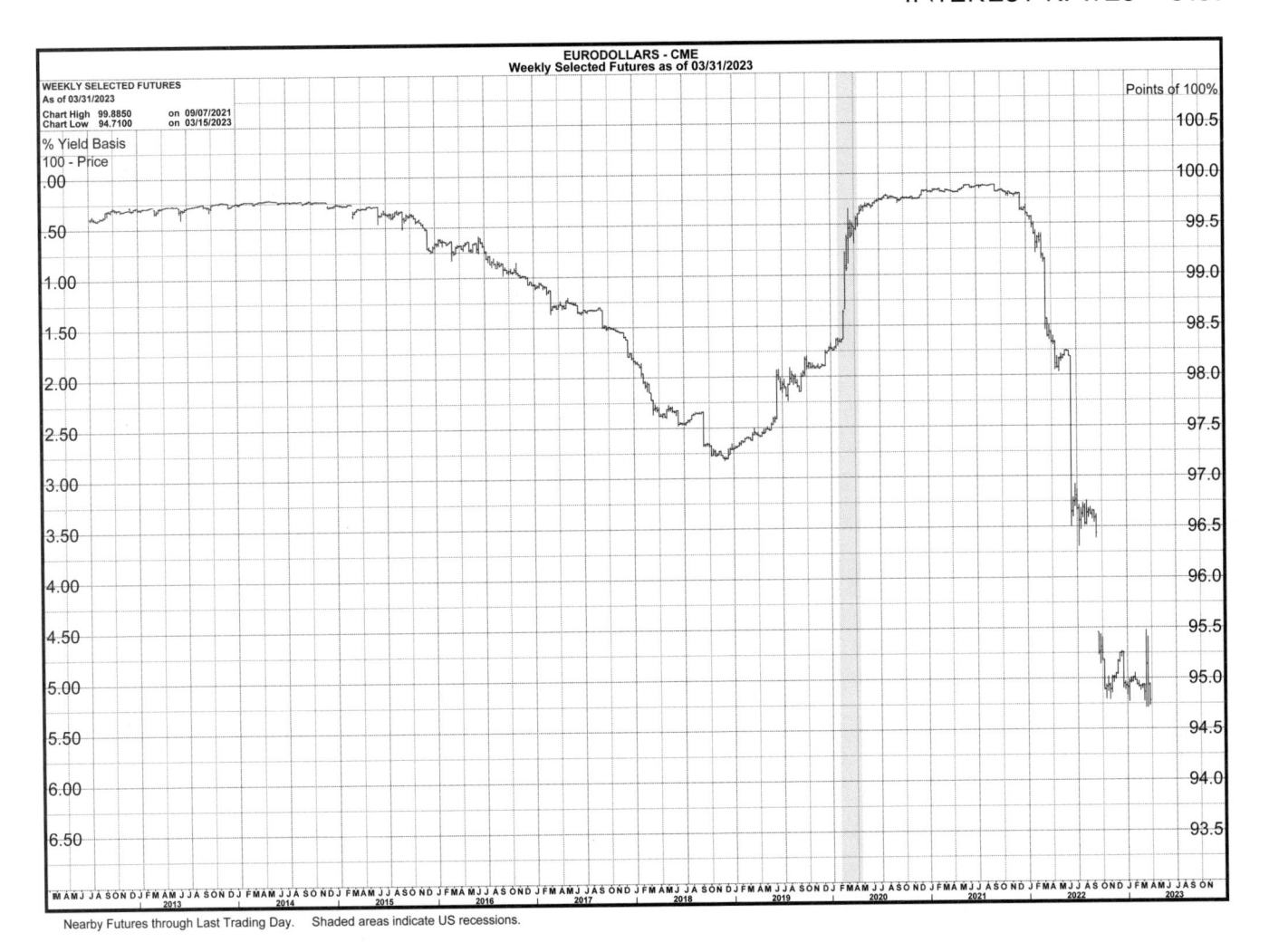

**EURODOLLARS - CME**
Weekly Selected Futures as of 03/31/2023

Chart High 99.8850 on 09/07/2021
Chart Low 94.7100 on 03/15/2023

Nearby Futures through Last Trading Day. Shaded areas indicate US recessions.

### Volume of Trading of 3-month Eurodollar Futures in Chicago   In Thousands of Contracts

| Year | Jan. | Feb. | Mar. | Apr. | May | June | July | Aug. | Sept. | Oct. | Nov. | Dec. | Total |
|---|---|---|---|---|---|---|---|---|---|---|---|---|---|
| 2013 | 40,800.6 | 32,152.3 | 37,526.2 | 30,235.7 | 51,371.9 | 69,283.3 | 41,177.9 | 38,851.4 | 51,413.1 | 43,321.9 | 39,422.5 | 41,693.4 | 517,250 |
| 2014 | 54,761.3 | 38,750.1 | 57,945.4 | 46,118.3 | 54,063.9 | 55,196.8 | 57,448.5 | 47,862.5 | 67,835.8 | 86,823.2 | 34,561.1 | 63,066.5 | 664,433 |
| 2015 | 60,557.7 | 53,474.6 | 56,886.5 | 39,486.9 | 46,358.9 | 55,022.2 | 45,717.3 | 51,075.2 | 47,750.9 | 44,983.2 | 39,937.9 | 45,661.9 | 586,913 |
| 2016 | 60,730.2 | 58,698.8 | 53,857.5 | 41,209.6 | 46,085.8 | 56,564.7 | 49,539.9 | 49,707.1 | 49,586.2 | 42,365.9 | 84,793.1 | 61,808.7 | 654,947 |
| 2017 | 62,542.9 | 57,145.8 | 72,934.8 | 51,369.1 | 53,434.7 | 54,122.6 | 40,527.4 | 44,393.5 | 54,731.0 | 52,213.9 | 49,599.8 | 46,831.7 | 639,847 |
| 2018 | 69,710.4 | 90,635.0 | 87,329.3 | 54,086.4 | 68,834.0 | 53,227.4 | 38,782.1 | 43,758.4 | 55,084.0 | 72,841.9 | 58,947.3 | 71,972.4 | 765,209 |
| 2019 | 61,232.1 | 46,129.1 | 69,360.8 | 50,245.2 | 73,665.3 | 78,392.8 | 56,286.0 | 73,101.1 | 52,788.6 | 53,025.6 | 36,353.1 | 36,492.9 | 687,073 |
| 2020 | 43,767.3 | 70,530.7 | 109,077.1 | 40,101.1 | 34,866.2 | 34,777.6 | 22,937.0 | 28,911.5 | 27,773.7 | 26,825.1 | 39,452.2 | 30,893.0 | 509,913 |
| 2021 | 42,111.1 | 57,854.3 | 65,666.3 | 38,424.2 | 41,200.7 | 60,571.6 | 48,300.5 | 40,873.1 | 43,998.8 | 67,575.3 | 60,504.9 | 43,350.3 | 610,431 |
| 2022 | 53,318.5 | 56,591.2 | 59,306.5 | 34,998.7 | 31,282.7 | 35,267.2 | 25,660.9 | 27,238.2 | 27,324.1 | 17,791.1 | 15,161.9 | 10,087.1 | 394,028 |

Contract size = $1,000,000.   Source: CME Group; International Monetary Market (IOM), division of the Chicago Mercantile Exchange (CME)

### Average Open Interest of 3-month Eurodollar Futures in Chicago   In Thousands of Contracts

| Year | Jan. | Feb. | Mar. | Apr. | May | June | July | Aug. | Sept. | Oct. | Nov. | Dec. |
|---|---|---|---|---|---|---|---|---|---|---|---|---|
| 2013 | 8,320.7 | 8,898.0 | 9,261.8 | 9,350.3 | 9,681.0 | 9,020.2 | 8,685.1 | 9,291.6 | 9,141.1 | 9,420.5 | 10,163.4 | 10,422.3 |
| 2014 | 10,142.7 | 10,022.8 | 10,453.9 | 10,875.2 | 11,635.9 | 11,593.8 | 12,101.1 | 12,734.0 | 13,139.9 | 11,819.9 | 11,685.4 | 10,902.1 |
| 2015 | 10,860.6 | 11,099.2 | 10,806.9 | 10,972.8 | 11,415.8 | 11,292.4 | 11,483.9 | 12,050.4 | 11,528.6 | 11,072.0 | 11,202.6 | 10,704.9 |
| 2016 | 10,869.1 | 10,865.4 | 10,132.9 | 10,143.2 | 10,621.0 | 10,281.7 | 10,434.1 | 10,977.1 | 11,138.0 | 11,410.5 | 12,131.6 | 12,064.2 |
| 2017 | 11,865.7 | 12,254.8 | 12,710.3 | 13,160.6 | 13,531.5 | 13,596.4 | 12,979.5 | 13,523.7 | 13,474.4 | 12,863.1 | 13,241.6 | 13,513.2 |
| 2018 | 14,034.4 | 15,871.7 | 17,114.1 | 16,815.8 | 16,141.1 | 14,660.5 | 14,124.0 | 14,084.0 | 14,114.7 | 14,373.2 | 14,151.3 | 13,543.0 |
| 2019 | 12,512.6 | 12,419.9 | 12,454.4 | 12,738.4 | 12,954.5 | 12,974.4 | 13,014.0 | 13,194.8 | 12,634.5 | 12,047.7 | 12,116.6 | 11,583.0 |
| 2020 | 11,060.8 | 11,742.0 | 11,096.0 | 10,613.3 | 10,799.8 | 10,252.2 | 9,703.1 | 9,768.4 | 9,420.7 | 9,336.8 | 9,801.5 | 9,439.9 |
| 2021 | 10,017.5 | 11,304.1 | 11,209.8 | 11,618.0 | 12,636.6 | 12,706.4 | 12,202.5 | 12,338.7 | 12,367.6 | 12,711.8 | 12,342.1 | 11,576.3 |
| 2022 | 11,231.7 | 11,141.0 | 10,948.3 | 10,778.6 | 10,444.7 | 9,791.9 | 9,503.1 | 9,617.2 | 8,891.8 | 8,116.1 | 7,675.2 | 6,691.9 |

Contract size = $1,000,000.   Source: CME Group; International Monetary Market (IOM), division of the Chicago Mercantile Exchange (CME)

# INTEREST RATES - U.S.

**T-NOTE, 2-YEAR - CBOT**
Weekly Nearest Futures as of 03/31/2023

Chart High 110-66 on 02/18/2021
Chart Low 101-25 on 03/08/2023

Nearby Futures through Last Trading Day. Shaded areas indicate US recessions.

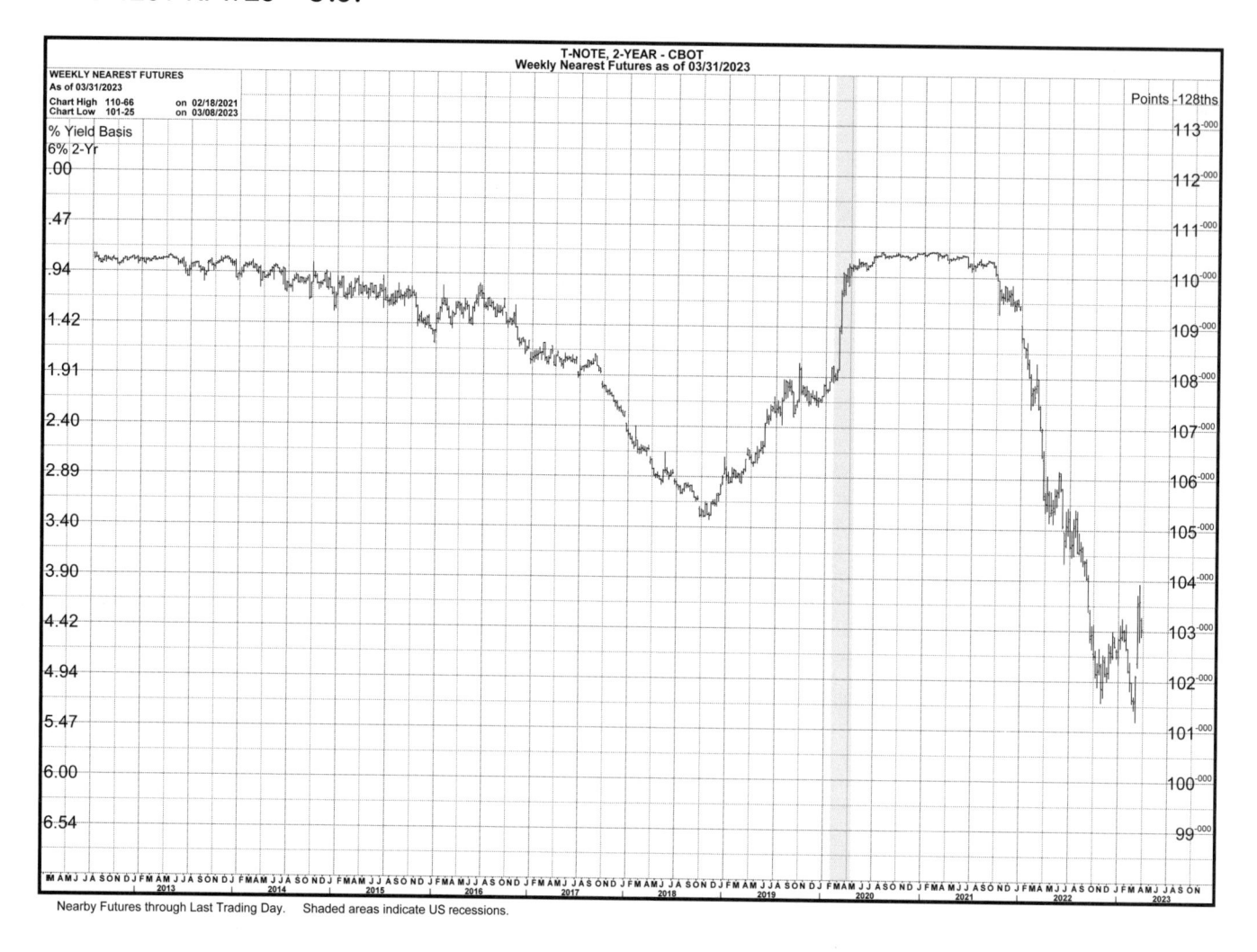

## Volume of Trading of 2-Year U.S. Treasury Note Futures in Chicago  In Thousands of Contracts

| Year | Jan. | Feb. | Mar. | Apr. | May | June | July | Aug. | Sept. | Oct. | Nov. | Dec. | Total |
|---|---|---|---|---|---|---|---|---|---|---|---|---|---|
| 2013 | 4,249.9 | 7,408.8 | 3,786.5 | 3,169.7 | 8,812.1 | 4,703.0 | 3,008.5 | 6,380.5 | 4,134.8 | 3,133.0 | 5,982.2 | 3,046.9 | 57,815.9 |
| 2014 | 4,004.9 | 4,637.1 | 4,670.2 | 4,402.3 | 8,206.8 | 4,404.6 | 3,913.5 | 9,120.7 | 6,155.0 | 6,801.9 | 8,643.1 | 5,054.2 | 70,014.3 |
| 2015 | 5,113.2 | 11,269.7 | 6,108.6 | 4,349.9 | 10,776.5 | 6,555.7 | 4,983.7 | 10,933.2 | 5,556.6 | 4,681.9 | 7,946.4 | 4,765.3 | 83,040.7 |
| 2016 | 5,229.6 | 9,923.0 | 5,521.3 | 4,421.2 | 8,907.1 | 6,095.0 | 5,000.2 | 8,969.9 | 5,775.0 | 5,733.4 | 11,524.6 | 4,773.8 | 81,874.2 |
| 2017 | 5,753.0 | 10,850.4 | 6,893.6 | 5,031.7 | 11,816.4 | 6,878.7 | 4,794.3 | 11,174.2 | 6,379.3 | 6,749.4 | 14,716.4 | 6,212.1 | 97,249.5 |
| 2018 | 8,227.0 | 19,349.2 | 9,652.2 | 7,441.3 | 17,938.9 | 6,815.9 | 5,398.5 | 14,407.6 | 6,704.9 | 10,226.4 | 20,088.5 | 9,248.8 | 135,499.2 |
| 2019 | 10,151.3 | 20,428.2 | 10,462.9 | 9,357.5 | 25,719.8 | 12,310.8 | 11,126.1 | 25,807.0 | 11,851.2 | 13,137.1 | 22,728.1 | 9,543.9 | 182,624.0 |
| 2020 | 11,002.4 | 26,537.8 | 19,825.0 | 7,580.4 | 14,444.6 | 6,637.1 | 4,419.0 | 12,570.6 | 5,110.8 | 4,401.1 | 11,777.0 | 4,544.2 | 128,850.1 |
| 2021 | 5,906.0 | 15,733.1 | 8,958.7 | 5,667.9 | 13,870.4 | 7,288.9 | 6,380.9 | 12,767.6 | 5,826.1 | 10,052.8 | 16,059.2 | 6,986.2 | 115,497.8 |
| 2022 | 9,990.1 | 20,210.9 | 13,750.9 | 12,885.0 | 20,621.1 | 12,879.6 | 9,994.5 | 19,609.0 | 12,297.1 | 10,599.6 | 18,542.8 | 8,282.9 | 169,663.5 |

Contract size = $200,000.  Source: CME Group; Chicago Board of Trade (CBT)

## Average Open Interest of 2-Year U.S. Treasury Note Futures in Chicago  In Thousands of Contracts

| Year | Jan. | Feb. | Mar. | Apr. | May | June | July | Aug. | Sept. | Oct. | Nov. | Dec. |
|---|---|---|---|---|---|---|---|---|---|---|---|---|
| 2013 | 998.1 | 1,046.5 | 989.2 | 916.5 | 945.3 | 816.8 | 791.7 | 864.5 | 863.5 | 925.2 | 978.2 | 866.6 |
| 2014 | 858.0 | 934.8 | 942.0 | 1,077.5 | 1,153.4 | 1,051.2 | 1,164.8 | 1,400.5 | 1,546.2 | 1,425.6 | 1,432.8 | 1,292.8 |
| 2015 | 1,269.4 | 1,462.5 | 1,346.2 | 1,378.7 | 1,363.1 | 1,183.6 | 1,274.7 | 1,356.3 | 1,143.8 | 1,117.1 | 1,091.9 | 989.4 |
| 2016 | 1,048.4 | 1,164.5 | 961.0 | 1,021.2 | 1,117.2 | 1,004.6 | 1,053.3 | 1,124.5 | 1,008.8 | 1,225.0 | 1,202.6 | 1,140.2 |
| 2017 | 1,215.9 | 1,444.9 | 1,412.6 | 1,378.3 | 1,392.5 | 1,350.8 | 1,354.0 | 1,488.8 | 1,527.0 | 1,667.8 | 1,837.2 | 1,765.6 |
| 2018 | 1,900.4 | 2,030.6 | 1,896.1 | 1,973.5 | 2,138.0 | 1,828.2 | 1,930.1 | 4,255.5 | 2,164.6 | 2,268.6 | 2,682.1 | 2,636.3 |
| 2019 | 2,681.8 | 3,159.8 | 3,027.8 | 3,614.3 | 4,089.5 | 3,615.8 | 3,634.0 | 3,849.5 | 3,557.2 | 3,872.6 | 3,972.1 | 3,581.8 |
| 2020 | 3,643.6 | 3,813.2 | 3,203.0 | 2,607.4 | 2,389.1 | 2,130.8 | 2,110.2 | 2,129.6 | 2,006.4 | 1,982.9 | 2,001.6 | 1,883.6 |
| 2021 | 2,018.0 | 2,297.2 | 2,344.3 | 2,291.7 | 2,310.7 | 2,107.0 | 2,011.4 | 1,986.9 | 1,899.5 | 1,935.1 | 2,024.3 | 1,927.3 |
| 2022 | 2,084.2 | 2,219.9 | 2,169.2 | 2,229.5 | 2,333.7 | 2,081.2 | 2,060.9 | 2,095.5 | 1,993.5 | 2,068.5 | 2,231.4 | 2,188.3 |

Contract size = $200,000.  Source: CME Group; Chicago Board of Trade (CBT)

# INTEREST RATES - U.S.

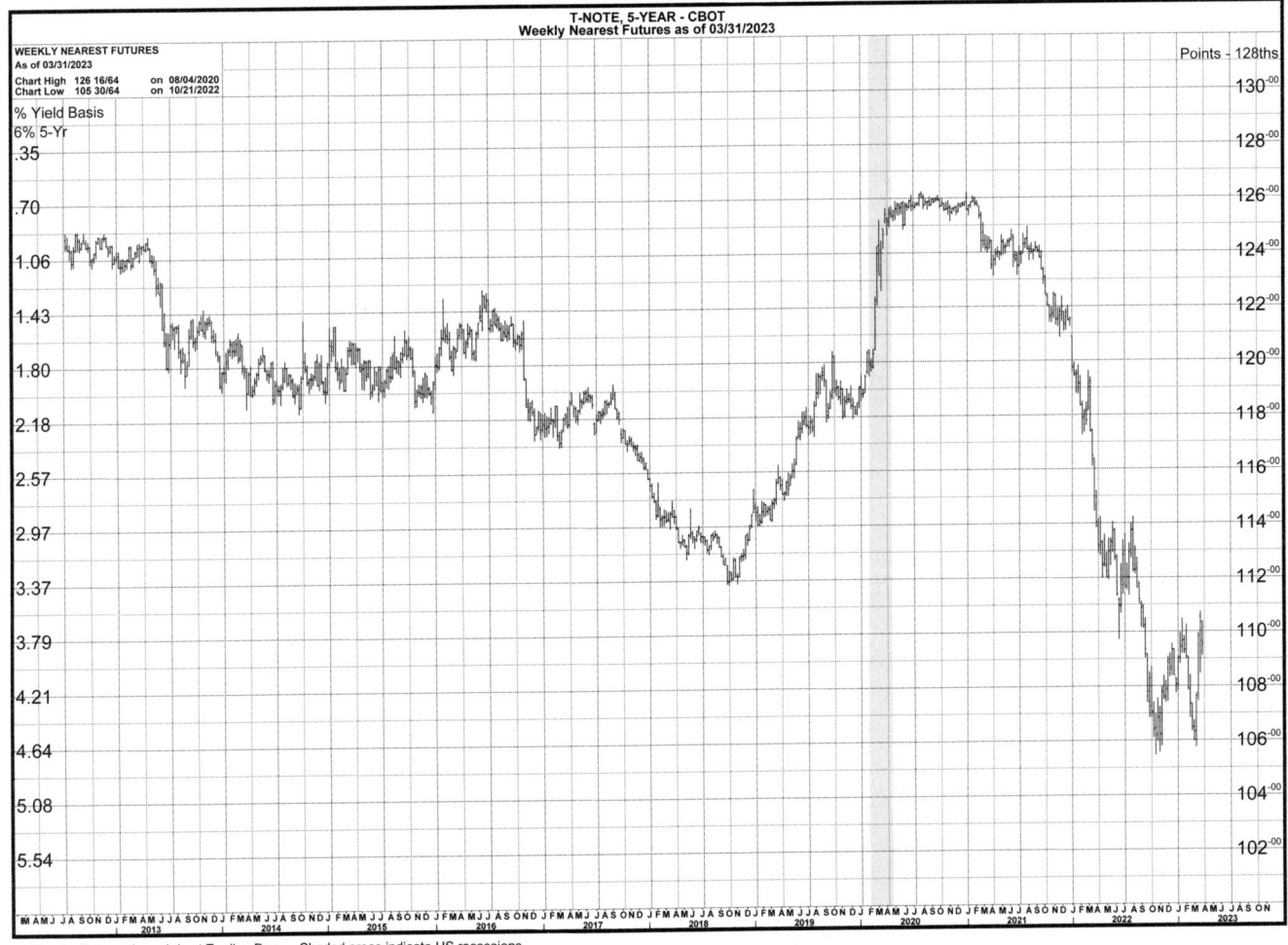

**T-NOTE, 5-YEAR - CBOT**
Weekly Nearest Futures as of 03/31/2023

Nearby Futures through Last Trading Day.   Shaded areas indicate US recessions.

## Volume of Trading of 5-Year U.S. Treasury Note Futures in Chicago    In Thousands of Contracts

| Year | Jan. | Feb. | Mar. | Apr. | May | June | July | Aug. | Sept. | Oct. | Nov. | Dec. | Total |
|------|------|------|------|------|-----|------|------|------|-------|------|------|------|-------|
| 2013 | 12,206.3 | 18,750.5 | 11,971.1 | 11,023.9 | 23,914.4 | 17,072.7 | 11,763.4 | 18,021.9 | 13,464.8 | 10,198.2 | 16,397.4 | 10,543.6 | 175,328 |
| 2014 | 13,081.6 | 18,022.0 | 16,060.6 | 14,088.2 | 20,473.5 | 13,605.3 | 14,182.4 | 20,546.3 | 16,596.0 | 20,858.3 | 15,933.0 | 12,982.0 | 196,429 |
| 2015 | 14,739.3 | 20,925.8 | 14,020.7 | 11,619.5 | 20,929.9 | 15,289.6 | 12,668.2 | 22,856.6 | 12,974.5 | 12,321.4 | 20,512.7 | 11,849.6 | 190,708 |
| 2016 | 13,618.7 | 24,294.8 | 13,229.2 | 11,144.4 | 22,079.7 | 15,245.5 | 11,120.9 | 23,442.5 | 12,453.2 | 11,484.3 | 30,046.2 | 13,745.4 | 201,905 |
| 2017 | 15,623.7 | 26,990.8 | 17,509.9 | 13,761.0 | 26,563.2 | 16,462.0 | 12,784.2 | 24,543.1 | 14,990.7 | 14,944.5 | 27,741.3 | 14,526.8 | 226,441 |
| 2018 | 18,302.4 | 35,388.6 | 19,974.6 | 16,208.0 | 36,454.5 | 17,379.4 | 14,187.0 | 30,353.9 | 15,664.4 | 25,561.2 | 36,989.9 | 20,757.0 | 287,221 |
| 2019 | 21,297.1 | 31,298.5 | 20,637.9 | 16,018.8 | 39,172.1 | 21,319.0 | 18,801.4 | 40,355.5 | 19,616.5 | 18,960.9 | 31,401.5 | 15,520.5 | 294,400 |
| 2020 | 17,703.1 | 39,907.6 | 33,449.4 | 13,308.2 | 26,063.5 | 14,361.0 | 9,499.5 | 25,390.4 | 11,492.4 | 13,501.2 | 26,265.6 | 13,900.9 | 244,843 |
| 2021 | 17,300.4 | 37,059.2 | 25,189.4 | 15,676.2 | 30,367.2 | 19,107.2 | 17,387.0 | 28,580.7 | 18,279.8 | 21,639.7 | 35,103.7 | 16,170.3 | 281,861 |
| 2022 | 22,603.0 | 39,905.0 | 27,667.2 | 22,967.4 | 37,472.0 | 23,186.2 | 20,411.4 | 34,940.9 | 23,725.9 | 22,351.7 | 34,850.5 | 16,721.0 | 326,802 |

Contract size = $100,000.   *Source: CME Group; Chicago Board of Trade (CBT)*

## Average Open Interest of 5-Year U.S. Treasury Note Futures in Chicago    In Thousands of Contracts

| Year | Jan. | Feb. | Mar. | Apr. | May | June | July | Aug. | Sept. | Oct. | Nov. | Dec. |
|------|------|------|------|------|-----|------|------|------|-------|------|------|------|
| 2013 | 1,532.5 | 1,653.7 | 1,733.6 | 1,847.6 | 1,842.2 | 1,535.0 | 1,584.4 | 1,641.0 | 1,668.5 | 1,745.1 | 1,968.7 | 1,865.1 |
| 2014 | 1,939.7 | 2,002.5 | 1,959.1 | 2,036.7 | 2,126.3 | 2,070.6 | 2,130.6 | 2,190.1 | 2,130.5 | 1,992.7 | 1,993.5 | 1,844.4 |
| 2015 | 1,837.5 | 1,983.8 | 1,992.9 | 2,016.3 | 2,038.9 | 2,096.2 | 2,200.8 | 2,398.5 | 2,352.1 | 2,422.1 | 2,469.2 | 2,371.4 |
| 2016 | 2,497.2 | 2,734.3 | 2,476.6 | 2,477.3 | 2,575.0 | 2,632.8 | 2,676.0 | 2,866.4 | 2,799.2 | 2,756.9 | 2,961.3 | 2,924.3 |
| 2017 | 3,019.1 | 3,313.3 | 3,035.8 | 3,103.9 | 3,261.9 | 3,144.0 | 1,350.8 | 3,000.0 | 3,144.0 | 2,998.1 | 3,293.4 | 3,051.2 |
| 2018 | 3,236.9 | 3,538.2 | 3,376.7 | 3,519.0 | 3,813.1 | 3,742.6 | 3,892.1 | 4,255.5 | 4,380.4 | 4,536.9 | 4,922.3 | 4,702.5 |
| 2019 | 4,539.9 | 4,511.1 | 4,256.0 | 4,485.2 | 4,870.6 | 4,535.7 | 4,475.3 | 4,567.4 | 4,129.1 | 4,360.5 | 4,613.6 | 4,248.8 |
| 2020 | 4,334.7 | 4,699.7 | 4,280.2 | 3,683.9 | 3,658.0 | 3,471.2 | 3,481.9 | 3,455.3 | 3,261.6 | 3,126.7 | 3,204.8 | 3,184.9 |
| 2021 | 3,274.8 | 3,582.7 | 3,520.7 | 3,426.9 | 3,539.8 | 3,506.4 | 3,473.4 | 3,506.7 | 3,540.8 | 3,604.1 | 3,673.3 | 3,625.6 |
| 2022 | 3,861.1 | 4,065.8 | 3,798.7 | 3,812.4 | 3,836.6 | 3,868.5 | 3,971.2 | 4,040.0 | 3,993.0 | 4,045.0 | 4,295.5 | 4,144.8 |

Contract size = $100,000.   *Source: CME Group; Chicago Board of Trade (CBT)*

# INTEREST RATES - U.S.

**T-NOTE, 10-YEAR - CBOT**
Weekly Nearest Futures as of 03/31/2023

Weekly Nearest Futures As of 03/31/2023
Chart High 140 47/64 on 03/09/2020
Chart Low 108 53/64 on 10/21/2022

Nearby Futures through Last Trading Day.  Shaded areas indicate US recessions.

## Volume of Trading of 10-year U.S. Treasury Note Futures in Chicago   In Thousands of Contracts

| Year | Jan. | Feb. | Mar. | Apr. | May | June | July | Aug. | Sept. | Oct. | Nov. | Dec. | Total |
|---|---|---|---|---|---|---|---|---|---|---|---|---|---|
| 2013 | 24,720.9 | 33,572.4 | 24,606.7 | 23,859.0 | 43,005.7 | 32,912.7 | 21,673.6 | 31,715.3 | 23,332.5 | 21,265.7 | 27,463.8 | 17,800.2 | 325,928 |
| 2014 | 23,218.1 | 29,772.2 | 27,675.3 | 25,202.1 | 34,569.3 | 24,098.5 | 23,402.1 | 34,087.3 | 28,122.5 | 39,126.2 | 28,205.8 | 23,005.8 | 340,485 |
| 2015 | 27,499.2 | 33,705.2 | 24,770.7 | 22,343.8 | 38,005.7 | 29,805.4 | 23,574.7 | 34,287.1 | 22,586.7 | 23,505.9 | 28,612.5 | 19,644.2 | 328,341 |
| 2016 | 27,310.1 | 41,327.8 | 24,480.8 | 22,290.2 | 32,571.1 | 28,364.5 | 23,198.0 | 34,699.7 | 24,140.8 | 22,878.3 | 46,296.5 | 23,204.4 | 350,762 |
| 2017 | 28,552.5 | 38,619.2 | 29,608.9 | 25,570.4 | 39,797.5 | 28,177.2 | 24,476.4 | 39,078.3 | 27,756.7 | 28,826.3 | 41,497.4 | 23,377.8 | 375,338 |
| 2018 | 32,939.1 | 51,555.5 | 33,837.1 | 27,450.9 | 53,075.1 | 31,980.5 | 25,504.3 | 44,233.8 | 27,721.0 | 48,099.0 | 49,321.5 | 32,001.5 | 457,719 |
| 2019 | 31,722.5 | 41,654.0 | 34,503.4 | 27,261.9 | 56,919.4 | 33,426.3 | 29,998.8 | 56,558.9 | 34,095.1 | 32,378.8 | 42,883.4 | 28,427.2 | 449,830 |
| 2020 | 37,977.1 | 64,744.5 | 49,588.5 | 22,902.6 | 35,352.9 | 25,639.6 | 17,848.0 | 36,685.9 | 21,867.6 | 27,856.3 | 41,447.0 | 24,080.3 | 405,990 |
| 2021 | 32,660.6 | 56,374.6 | 45,442.0 | 31,239.9 | 47,982.2 | 33,519.7 | 32,475.6 | 44,239.3 | 33,123.8 | 37,373.5 | 49,554.6 | 25,760.8 | 469,747 |
| 2022 | 36,353.2 | 53,719.1 | 41,450.8 | 33,977.3 | 47,749.8 | 33,701.4 | 29,789.4 | 43,518.4 | 35,985.6 | 34,806.2 | 45,668.7 | 25,482.9 | 462,203 |

Contract size = $100,000.   Source: CME Group; Chicago Board of Trade (CBT)

## Average Open Interest of 10-year U.S. Treasury Note Futures in Chicago   In Thousands of Contracts

| Year | Jan. | Feb. | Mar. | Apr. | May | June | July | Aug. | Sept. | Oct. | Nov. | Dec. |
|---|---|---|---|---|---|---|---|---|---|---|---|---|
| 2013 | 1,815.9 | 2,089.8 | 2,125.6 | 2,230.3 | 2,331.8 | 2,132.2 | 2,199.4 | 2,308.6 | 2,031.6 | 2,079.2 | 2,341.3 | 2,261.2 |
| 2014 | 2,260.5 | 2,426.0 | 2,433.4 | 2,526.5 | 2,720.3 | 2,591.6 | 2,679.0 | 2,853.2 | 2,705.4 | 2,776.0 | 2,855.5 | 2,652.6 |
| 2015 | 2,684.1 | 2,610.3 | 2,690.8 | 2,822.7 | 2,884.8 | 2,730.7 | 2,751.9 | 2,941.1 | 2,729.8 | 2,776.5 | 2,680.6 | 2,594.4 |
| 2016 | 2,747.8 | 3,065.1 | 2,714.8 | 2,726.7 | 2,732.6 | 2,750.5 | 2,815.6 | 2,849.5 | 2,818.1 | 2,890.3 | 3,017.2 | 3,026.9 |
| 2017 | 3,130.7 | 3,343.9 | 3,139.4 | 3,137.3 | 3,365.2 | 3,179.9 | 3,162.4 | 3,384.4 | 3,277.1 | 3,132.4 | 3,399.8 | 3,271.5 |
| 2018 | 3,420.6 | 3,740.6 | 3,480.6 | 3,590.4 | 3,854.8 | 3,462.9 | 3,696.0 | 3,990.4 | 3,963.9 | 4,153.7 | 4,281.3 | 4,136.0 |
| 2019 | 4,067.1 | 4,130.2 | 3,880.5 | 3,966.4 | 4,183.5 | 3,887.9 | 3,816.5 | 3,989.9 | 3,589.1 | 3,683.7 | 3,935.0 | 3,663.1 |
| 2020 | 3,779.7 | 4,161.3 | 3,629.1 | 3,243.8 | 3,449.8 | 3,318.0 | 3,442.3 | 3,491.5 | 3,287.1 | 3,214.7 | 3,271.9 | 3,188.9 |
| 2021 | 3,378.4 | 3,672.0 | 3,780.1 | 3,939.2 | 4,309.2 | 4,336.3 | 4,153.2 | 4,094.4 | 3,964.1 | 4,051.7 | 3,960.1 | 3,809.5 |
| 2022 | 3,830.0 | 4,005.7 | 3,678.5 | 3,688.4 | 3,669.6 | 3,452.9 | 3,484.2 | 3,565.5 | 3,681.2 | 3,873.2 | 4,008.5 | 3,785.5 |

Contract size = $100,000.   Source: CME Group; Chicago Board of Trade (CBT)

# INTEREST RATES - U.S.

**T-BOND - CBOT**
Weekly Nearest Futures as of 03/31/2023

Nearby Futures through Last Trading Day.   Shaded areas indicate US recessions.

## Volume of Trading of 30-year U.S. Treasury Bond Futures in Chicago    In Thousands of Contracts

| Year | Jan. | Feb. | Mar. | Apr. | May | June | July | Aug. | Sept. | Oct. | Nov. | Dec. | Total |
|---|---|---|---|---|---|---|---|---|---|---|---|---|---|
| 2013 | 7,892.2 | 10,758.6 | 7,691.9 | 8,269.7 | 13,337.5 | 9,601.6 | 5,788.0 | 8,792.7 | 6,759.6 | 6,193.9 | 7,712.2 | 5,165.3 | 97,963 |
| 2014 | 5,871.1 | 8,211.2 | 6,867.7 | 6,259.9 | 9,648.8 | 7,044.9 | 6,719.0 | 9,948.4 | 7,678.1 | 10,370.2 | 7,827.0 | 6,742.1 | 93,188 |
| 2015 | 7,956.2 | 8,611.4 | 5,183.2 | 4,747.5 | 6,832.7 | 5,708.3 | 5,453.9 | 7,438.7 | 4,884.1 | 4,927.9 | 5,625.7 | 4,531.9 | 71,902 |
| 2016 | 5,569.8 | 8,184.8 | 5,000.5 | 4,428.4 | 6,276.8 | 5,736.6 | 4,734.9 | 6,655.2 | 5,245.9 | 5,042.9 | 8,707.2 | 4,620.4 | 70,203 |
| 2017 | 5,165.8 | 7,149.6 | 5,818.2 | 4,614.0 | 7,713.7 | 6,144.7 | 4,672.2 | 7,620.6 | 5,442.3 | 5,668.0 | 8,212.6 | 5,115.4 | 73,337 |
| 2018 | 6,648.4 | 10,573.9 | 6,380.0 | 5,517.2 | 10,025.2 | 6,048.6 | 5,244.4 | 8,677.5 | 5,961.9 | 10,301.0 | 10,299.4 | 6,984.4 | 92,662 |
| 2019 | 6,441.9 | 8,404.9 | 6,758.6 | 4,783.9 | 9,727.9 | 6,005.7 | 5,736.2 | 12,286.6 | 6,763.9 | 6,752.0 | 8,383.3 | 5,750.6 | 87,796 |
| 2020 | 7,429.5 | 12,839.9 | 10,085.2 | 4,285.4 | 7,990.3 | 5,747.3 | 5,080.8 | 10,012.5 | 6,187.7 | 7,678.1 | 11,469.9 | 6,877.9 | 95,685 |
| 2021 | 8,031.6 | 13,439.3 | 11,047.3 | 7,472.6 | 11,631.7 | 7,779.6 | 7,393.7 | 10,433.7 | 8,496.7 | 9,022.5 | 12,060.4 | 6,637.8 | 113,447 |
| 2022 | 7,760.3 | 11,073.9 | 8,272.6 | 6,804.5 | 11,066.6 | 7,396.9 | 6,272.4 | 9,453.5 | 7,202.5 | 6,959.0 | 9,508.4 | 5,574.4 | 97,345 |

Contract size = $100,000.   Source: CME Group; Chicago Board of Trade (CBT)

## Average Open Interest of 30-year U.S. Treasury Bond Futures in Chicago    In Contracts

| Year | Jan. | Feb. | Mar. | Apr. | May | June | July | Aug. | Sept. | Oct. | Nov. | Dec. |
|---|---|---|---|---|---|---|---|---|---|---|---|---|
| 2013 | 551,333 | 632,060 | 630,148 | 681,045 | 667,210 | 568,046 | 574,724 | 626,392 | 630,549 | 644,843 | 696,333 | 656,867 |
| 2014 | 666,663 | 716,926 | 712,174 | 722,390 | 780,781 | 738,607 | 758,214 | 870,115 | 860,417 | 870,759 | 850,561 | 889,272 |
| 2015 | 829,094 | 640,877 | 414,934 | 437,101 | 478,017 | 484,216 | 500,019 | 533,913 | 505,812 | 501,845 | 491,806 | 519,574 |
| 2016 | 517,291 | 562,305 | 510,970 | 525,831 | 528,077 | 570,427 | 575,832 | 583,950 | 562,062 | 562,046 | 574,628 | 586,673 |
| 2017 | 616,403 | 637,810 | 646,801 | 644,707 | 706,590 | 737,002 | 729,176 | 873,263 | 730,878 | 740,311 | 798,709 | 772,841 |
| 2018 | 790,518 | 834,751 | 806,285 | 798,849 | 878,533 | 804,968 | 826,864 | 878,497 | 859,024 | 917,822 | 964,126 | 966,317 |
| 2019 | 954,146 | 1,007,000 | 967,026 | 947,620 | 1,001,286 | 958,051 | 929,612 | 994,150 | 974,482 | 987,321 | 1,022,854 | 1,010,372 |
| 2020 | 1,052,137 | 1,294,602 | 1,154,433 | 997,024 | 1,048,643 | 1,003,052 | 1,048,720 | 1,152,639 | 1,168,654 | 1,212,653 | 1,248,831 | 1,155,056 |
| 2021 | 1,163,969 | 1,209,695 | 1,204,552 | 1,179,879 | 1,220,707 | 1,190,103 | 1,194,247 | 1,229,063 | 1,221,810 | 1,199,351 | 1,217,755 | 1,213,951 |
| 2022 | 1,206,255 | 1,195,809 | 1,117,441 | 1,129,546 | 1,226,123 | 1,188,242 | 1,181,664 | 1,192,749 | 1,217,481 | 1,215,548 | 1,206,085 | 1,184,506 |

Contract size = $100,000.   Source: CME Group; Chicago Board of Trade (CBT)

# INTEREST RATES - U.S.

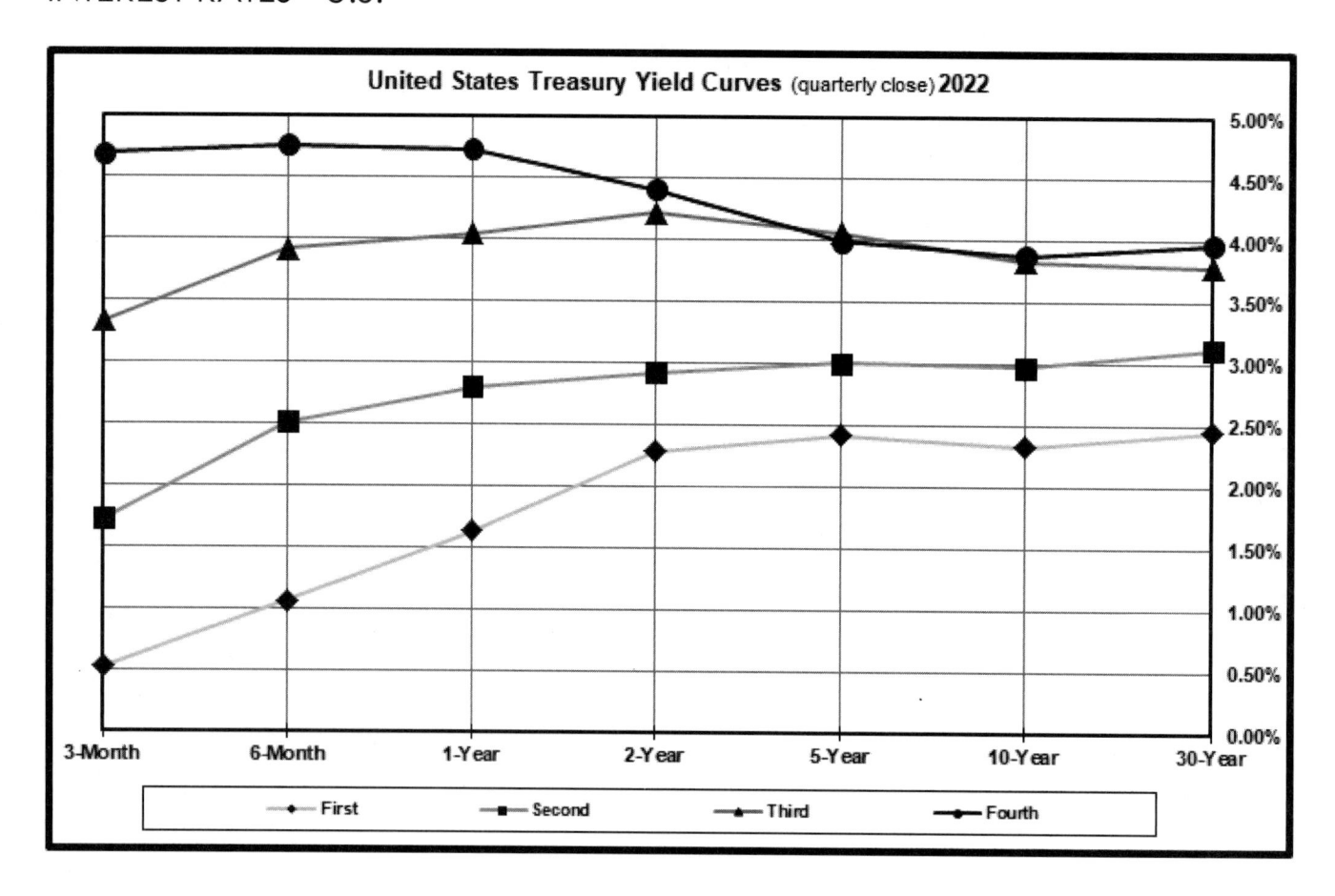

**United States Treasury Yield Curves** (quarterly close) **2022**

Maturities: 3-Month, 6-Month, 1-Year, 2-Year, 5-Year, 10-Year, 30-Year
Series: First, Second, Third, Fourth

## U.S. Federal Funds Rate   In Percent

| Year | Jan. | Feb. | Mar. | Apr. | May | June | July | Aug. | Sept. | Oct. | Nov. | Dec. | Average |
|---|---|---|---|---|---|---|---|---|---|---|---|---|---|
| 2013 | 0.14 | 0.15 | 0.14 | 0.15 | 0.11 | 0.09 | 0.09 | 0.08 | 0.08 | 0.09 | 0.08 | 0.09 | 0.11 |
| 2014 | 0.07 | 0.07 | 0.08 | 0.09 | 0.09 | 0.10 | 0.09 | 0.09 | 0.09 | 0.09 | 0.09 | 0.12 | 0.09 |
| 2015 | 0.11 | 0.11 | 0.11 | 0.12 | 0.12 | 0.13 | 0.13 | 0.14 | 0.14 | 0.12 | 0.12 | 0.24 | 0.13 |
| 2016 | 0.34 | 0.38 | 0.36 | 0.37 | 0.37 | 0.38 | 0.39 | 0.40 | 0.40 | 0.40 | 0.41 | 0.54 | 0.40 |
| 2017 | 0.65 | 0.66 | 0.79 | 0.90 | 0.91 | 1.04 | 1.15 | 1.16 | 1.15 | 1.15 | 1.16 | 1.30 | 1.00 |
| 2018 | 1.41 | 1.42 | 1.51 | 1.69 | 1.70 | 1.82 | 1.91 | 1.91 | 1.95 | 2.19 | 2.20 | 2.27 | 1.83 |
| 2019 | 2.40 | 2.40 | 2.41 | 2.42 | 2.39 | 2.38 | 2.40 | 2.13 | 2.04 | 1.83 | 1.55 | 1.55 | 2.16 |
| 2020 | 1.55 | 1.58 | 0.65 | 0.05 | 0.05 | 0.08 | 0.09 | 0.10 | 0.09 | 0.09 | 0.09 | 0.09 | 0.38 |
| 2021 | 0.09 | 0.08 | 0.07 | 0.07 | 0.06 | 0.08 | 0.10 | 0.09 | 0.08 | 0.08 | 0.08 | 0.08 | 0.08 |
| 2022 | 0.08 | 0.08 | 0.20 | 0.33 | 0.77 | 1.21 | 1.68 | 2.33 | 2.56 | 3.08 | 3.78 | 4.10 | 1.68 |

*Source: Bureau of Economic Analysis, U.S. Department of Commerce (BEA)*

## U.S. Municipal Bond Yield[1]   In Percent

| Year | Jan. | Feb. | Mar. | Apr. | May | June | July | Aug. | Sept. | Oct. | Nov. | Dec. | Average |
|---|---|---|---|---|---|---|---|---|---|---|---|---|---|
| 2007 | 4.23 | 4.22 | 4.15 | 4.26 | 4.31 | 4.60 | 4.56 | 4.64 | 4.51 | 4.39 | 4.46 | 4.42 | 4.40 |
| 2008 | 4.27 | 4.64 | 4.93 | 4.70 | 4.58 | 4.69 | 4.68 | 4.69 | 4.86 | 5.50 | 5.23 | 5.56 | 4.86 |
| 2009 | 5.07 | 4.90 | 4.99 | 4.78 | 4.56 | 4.81 | 4.72 | 4.60 | 4.24 | 4.20 | 4.37 | 4.21 | 4.62 |
| 2010 | 4.33 | 4.36 | 4.36 | 4.41 | 4.29 | 4.36 | 4.32 | 4.03 | 3.87 | 3.87 | 4.40 | 4.92 | 4.29 |
| 2011 | 5.28 | 5.15 | 4.92 | 4.99 | 4.59 | 4.51 | 4.52 | 4.02 | 4.01 | 4.13 | 4.05 | 3.95 | 4.51 |
| 2012 | 3.68 | 3.66 | 3.91 | 3.95 | 3.77 | 3.94 | 3.78 | 3.74 | 3.73 | 3.65 | 3.46 | 3.48 | 3.73 |
| 2013 | 3.60 | 3.72 | 3.96 | 3.92 | 3.72 | 4.27 | 4.56 | 4.82 | 4.79 | 4.56 | 4.60 | 4.73 | 4.27 |
| 2014 | 4.59 | 4.44 | 4.46 | 4.35 | 4.29 | 4.35 | 4.33 | 4.23 | 4.13 | 3.96 | 3.96 | 3.70 | 4.23 |
| 2015 | 3.40 | 3.58 | 3.59 | 3.51 | 3.76 | 3.82 | 3.79 | 3.74 | 3.78 | 3.67 | 3.68 | 3.57 | 3.66 |
| 2016 | 3.41 | 3.30 | 3.38 | 3.30 | 3.29 | 3.13 | 2.83 | 2.85 | 2.93 | 3.20 | Discontinued | | 3.16 |

[1] 20-bond average.   *Source: Bureau of Economic Analysis, U.S. Department of Commerce (BEA)*

# INTEREST RATES - U.S.

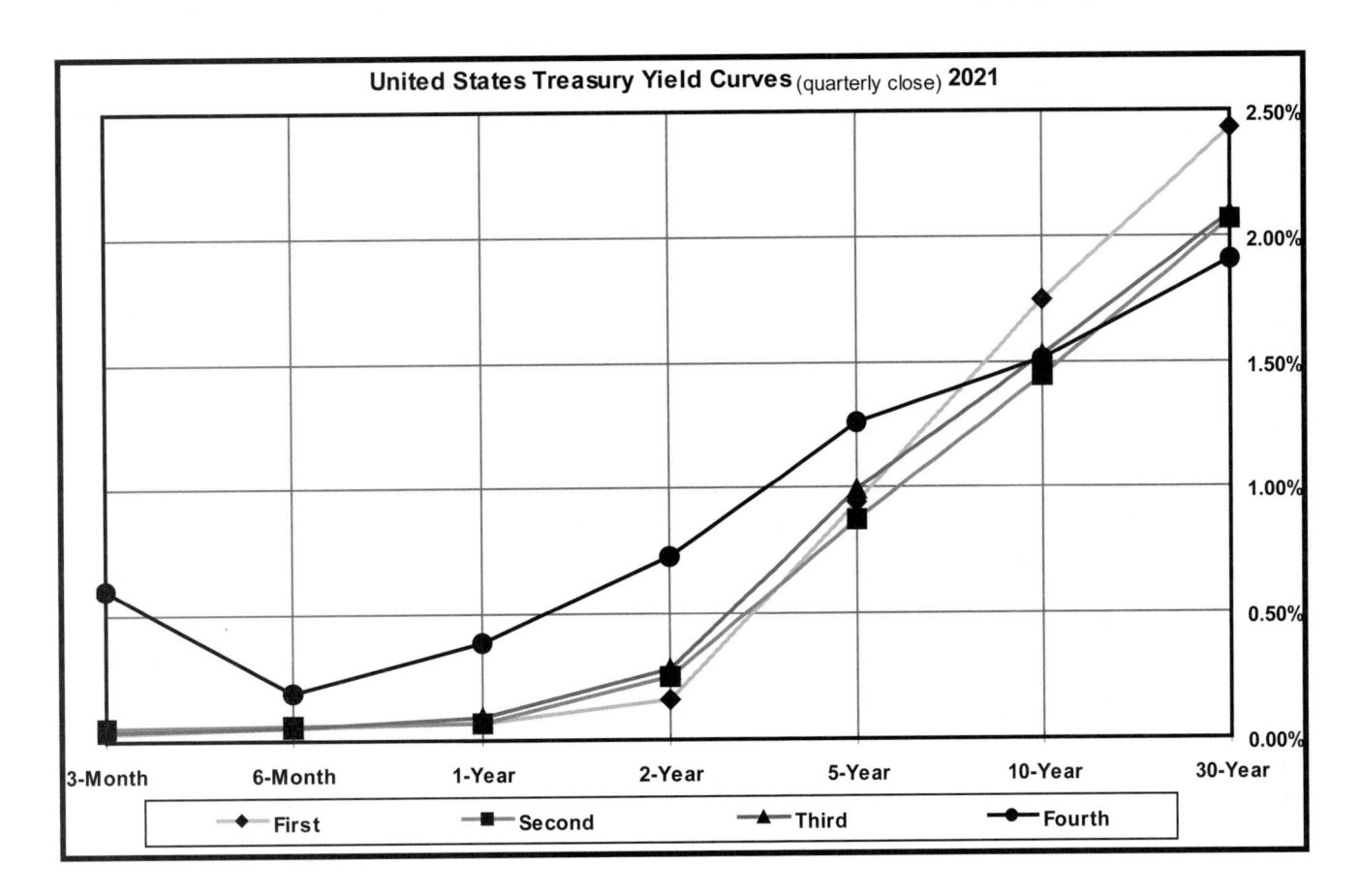

**United States Treasury Yield Curves** (quarterly close) **2021**

## U.S. Industrial Production Index[1]    1997 = 100

| Year | Jan. | Feb. | Mar. | Apr. | May | June | July | Aug. | Sept. | Oct. | Nov. | Dec. | Average |
|---|---|---|---|---|---|---|---|---|---|---|---|---|---|
| 2013 | 100.8 | 101.4 | 101.8 | 101.6 | 101.7 | 102.0 | 101.5 | 102.2 | 102.7 | 102.5 | 102.8 | 103.2 | 102.0 |
| 2014 | 102.7 | 103.6 | 104.6 | 104.6 | 105.0 | 105.4 | 105.6 | 105.5 | 105.8 | 105.8 | 106.7 | 106.5 | 105.2 |
| 2015 | 106.0 | 105.4 | 105.1 | 104.5 | 104.1 | 103.7 | 104.3 | 104.2 | 103.8 | 103.4 | 102.7 | 102.1 | 104.1 |
| 2016 | 103.0 | 102.2 | 101.4 | 101.5 | 101.4 | 101.9 | 102.1 | 102.0 | 102.0 | 102.2 | 102.1 | 102.9 | 102.1 |
| 2017 | 103.0 | 102.6 | 103.3 | 104.3 | 104.4 | 104.6 | 104.5 | 104.0 | 104.1 | 105.6 | 106.2 | 106.5 | 104.4 |
| 2018 | 101.3 | 101.7 | 102.3 | 103.4 | 102.5 | 103.3 | 103.5 | 104.2 | 104.2 | 104.0 | 104.0 | 103.9 | 103.2 |
| 2019 | 103.3 | 102.8 | 102.9 | 102.4 | 102.6 | 102.6 | 102.2 | 102.9 | 102.6 | 101.8 | 102.1 | 101.8 | 102.5 |
| 2020 | 101.3 | 101.7 | 97.9 | 85.0 | 86.3 | 91.8 | 95.2 | 96.1 | 96.1 | 96.8 | 97.1 | 98.1 | 95.3 |
| 2021 | 99.3 | 96.2 | 98.9 | 99.0 | 99.8 | 100.2 | 100.9 | 100.8 | 99.8 | 101.4 | 102.0 | 101.8 | 100.0 |
| 2022[1] | 102.1 | 102.9 | 103.6 | 104.3 | 104.2 | 103.9 | 104.5 | 104.4 | 104.6 | 104.6 | 104.0 | 102.9 | 103.8 |

[1] Total Index of the Federal Reserve Index of Quantity Output, seasonally adjusted.    [2] Preliminary.    *Source: Bureau of Economic Analysis, U.S. Department of Commerce (BEA)*

## U.S. Gross National Product, National Income, and Personal Income    In Billions of Constant Dollars[1]

| | Gross Domestic Product | | | | | National Income | | | | | Personal Income | | | | |
|---|---|---|---|---|---|---|---|---|---|---|---|---|---|---|---|
| Year | First Quarter | Second Quarter | Third Quarter | Fourth Quarter | Total | First Quarter | Second Quarter | Third Quarter | Fourth Quarter | Total | First Quarter | Second Quarter | Third Quarter | Fourth Quarter | Total |
| 2013 | 16,629 | 16,700 | 16,911 | 17,133 | 16,843 | 14,324 | 14,465 | 14,536 | 14,704 | 14,507 | 14,020 | 14,153 | 14,244 | 14,358 | 14,194 |
| 2014 | 17,144 | 17,463 | 17,743 | 17,853 | 17,551 | 14,826 | 15,141 | 15,412 | 15,533 | 15,228 | 14,625 | 14,875 | 15,100 | 15,307 | 14,977 |
| 2015 | 17,991 | 18,194 | 18,307 | 18,332 | 18,206 | 15,605 | 15,747 | 15,808 | 15,839 | 15,750 | 15,498 | 15,640 | 15,757 | 15,846 | 15,685 |
| 2016 | 18,425 | 18,612 | 18,776 | 18,968 | 18,695 | 15,905 | 15,911 | 16,056 | 16,261 | 16,033 | 15,919 | 16,002 | 16,152 | 16,315 | 16,097 |
| 2017 | 19,148 | 19,305 | 19,562 | 19,895 | 19,477 | 16,474 | 16,633 | 16,838 | 17,122 | 16,767 | 16,552 | 16,741 | 16,921 | 17,145 | 16,840 |
| 2018 | 20,156 | 20,470 | 20,687 | 20,819 | 20,533 | 17,364 | 17,530 | 17,793 | 17,960 | 17,662 | 17,355 | 17,551 | 17,801 | 18,029 | 17,684 |
| 2019 | 21,013 | 21,272 | 21,532 | 21,707 | 21,381 | 18,110 | 18,256 | 18,365 | 18,580 | 18,328 | 18,345 | 18,505 | 18,656 | 18,842 | 18,587 |
| 2020 | 21,538 | 19,637 | 21,362 | 21,705 | 21,060 | 18,611 | 16,507 | 17,773 | 18,688 | 17,895 | 19,034 | 20,479 | 20,019 | 19,797 | 19,832 |
| 2021 | 22,314 | 23,047 | 23,550 | 24,349 | 23,315 | 19,055 | 19,442 | 19,976 | 20,670 | 19,786 | 22,096 | 20,916 | 21,005 | 21,162 | 21,295 |
| 2022[1] | 24,741 | 25,249 | 25,724 | 26,145 | 25,464 | 21,093 | 21,484 | 21,771 | | 21,449 | 21,320 | 21,578 | 21,970 | 22,358 | 21,806 |

[1] Seasonally adjusted at annual rates.    [2] Preliminary.    *Source: Bureau of Economic Analysis, U.S. Department of Commerce (BEA)*

# INTEREST RATES - U.S.

## U.S. Money Supply M1[2]   In Billions of Dollars

| Year | Jan. | Feb. | Mar. | Apr. | May | June | July | Aug. | Sept. | Oct. | Nov. | Dec. | Average |
|---|---|---|---|---|---|---|---|---|---|---|---|---|---|
| 2013 | 2,473.3 | 2,472.4 | 2,480.4 | 2,515.8 | 2,530.7 | 2,531.4 | 2,545.8 | 2,552.1 | 2,584.5 | 2,623.0 | 2,623.1 | 2,664.4 | 2,549.7 |
| 2014 | 2,696.4 | 2,726.4 | 2,754.8 | 2,778.6 | 2,795.2 | 2,829.5 | 2,841.6 | 2,802.9 | 2,862.2 | 2,868.8 | 2,884.9 | 2,940.7 | 2,815.2 |
| 2015 | 2,941.0 | 3,007.1 | 2,999.6 | 3,000.9 | 2,986.6 | 3,020.0 | 3,039.7 | 3,028.5 | 3,044.2 | 3,018.6 | 3,081.7 | 3,094.9 | 3,021.9 |
| 2016 | 3,099.0 | 3,130.4 | 3,151.1 | 3,200.3 | 3,238.7 | 3,245.7 | 3,247.9 | 3,315.1 | 3,326.5 | 3,335.7 | 3,354.1 | 3,342.4 | 3,248.9 |
| 2017 | 3,390.9 | 3,404.7 | 3,445.5 | 3,454.2 | 3,517.3 | 3,525.9 | 3,550.9 | 3,580.7 | 3,574.2 | 3,606.7 | 3,630.6 | 3,612.0 | 3,524.5 |
| 2018 | 3,668.4 | 3,633.9 | 3,672.5 | 3,653.6 | 3,646.2 | 3,644.7 | 3,669.2 | 3,682.7 | 3,692.3 | 3,721.5 | 3,708.4 | 3,771.2 | 3,680.4 |
| 2019 | 3,772.9 | 3,783.4 | 3,746.4 | 3,770.6 | 3,775.4 | 3,813.4 | 3,844.8 | 3,844.0 | 3,887.7 | 3,926.1 | 3,955.6 | 4,011.2 | 3,844.3 |
| 2020 | 3,993.6 | 4,002.4 | 4,257.6 | 4,775.5 | 16,228.5 | 16,558.9 | 16,759.2 | 16,892.6 | 17,157.1 | 17,361.0 | 17,621.5 | 17,828.7 | 12,786.4 |
| 2021 | 18,101.8 | 18,362.8 | 18,636.5 | 18,921.6 | 19,252.1 | 19,311.3 | 19,481.8 | 19,717.7 | 19,862.8 | 20,053.6 | 20,269.4 | 20,419.0 | 19,365.8 |
| 2022[1] | 20,576.8 | 20,652.4 | 20,699.6 | 20,618.2 | 20,626.6 | 20,552.3 | 20,527.1 | 20,466.2 | 20,279.8 | 20,107.4 | 19,987.3 | 19,734.3 | 20,402.3 |

[1] Preliminary.  [2] *M1* -- The sum of currency held outside the vaults of depository institutions, Federal Reserve Banks, and the U.S. Treasury; travelers checks; and demand and other checkable deposits issued by financial institutions (except demand deposits due to the Treasury and depository institutions), minus cash items in process of collection and Federal Reserve float. Seasonally adjusted.   *Source: Board of Governors of the Federal Reserve System*

## U.S. Money Supply M2[2]   In Billions of Dollars

| Year | Jan. | Feb. | Mar. | Apr. | May | June | July | Aug. | Sept. | Oct. | Nov. | Dec. | Average |
|---|---|---|---|---|---|---|---|---|---|---|---|---|---|
| 2013 | 10,471.7 | 10,468.5 | 10,540.0 | 10,575.3 | 10,611.5 | 10,666.0 | 10,721.9 | 10,780.3 | 10,832.7 | 10,945.6 | 10,953.3 | 11,015.9 | 10,715.2 |
| 2014 | 11,066.4 | 11,148.9 | 11,190.5 | 11,246.9 | 11,314.6 | 11,366.8 | 11,428.0 | 11,457.3 | 11,492.2 | 11,552.6 | 11,591.7 | 11,670.3 | 11,377.2 |
| 2015 | 11,733.4 | 11,852.6 | 11,869.0 | 11,916.4 | 11,947.8 | 11,993.3 | 12,045.5 | 12,097.0 | 12,154.0 | 12,187.9 | 12,277.7 | 12,336.1 | 12,034.2 |
| 2016 | 12,461.5 | 12,533.7 | 12,595.4 | 12,685.0 | 12,751.2 | 12,819.6 | 12,880.8 | 12,968.2 | 13,031.5 | 13,105.4 | 13,178.6 | 13,209.8 | 12,851.7 |
| 2017 | 13,282.5 | 13,340.2 | 13,405.5 | 13,470.3 | 13,520.9 | 13,550.8 | 13,616.1 | 13,671.0 | 13,716.9 | 13,779.0 | 13,809.5 | 13,852.0 | 13,584.6 |
| 2018 | 13,872.0 | 13,914.6 | 13,971.2 | 14,001.3 | 14,066.0 | 14,125.8 | 14,155.2 | 14,197.7 | 14,228.4 | 14,235.8 | 14,254.9 | 14,373.9 | 14,116.4 |
| 2019 | 14,443.3 | 14,486.2 | 14,533.5 | 14,568.9 | 14,668.4 | 14,787.0 | 14,857.9 | 14,935.2 | 15,026.6 | 15,153.1 | 15,251.3 | 15,325.8 | 14,836.4 |
| 2020 | 15,401.8 | 15,457.9 | 15,984.1 | 16,997.9 | 17,830.8 | 18,124.6 | 18,273.2 | 18,353.3 | 18,570.8 | 18,731.3 | 18,964.5 | 19,118.9 | 17,650.8 |
| 2021 | 19,367.2 | 19,610.6 | 19,848.9 | 20,104.5 | 20,411.0 | 20,451.7 | 20,605.0 | 20,824.2 | 20,955.9 | 21,133.8 | 21,338.4 | 21,478.1 | 20,510.8 |
| 2022/1 | 21,640.7 | 21,699.2 | 21,739.0 | 21,643.6 | 21,646.8 | 21,602.0 | 21,635.0 | 21,636.8 | 21,516.7 | 21,432.3 | 21,400.6 | 21,236.2 | 21,569.1 |

[1] Preliminary.  [2] *M2* -- M1 plus savings deposits (including money market deposit accounts) and small-denomination (less than $100,000) time deposits issued by financial institutions; and shares in retail money market mutual funds (funds with initial investments of less than $50,000), net of retirement accounts. Seasonally adjusted.   *Source: Board of Governors of the Federal Reserve System*

## U.S. Money Supply MZM[2]   In Billions of Dollars

| Year | Jan. | Feb. | Mar. | Apr. | May | June | July | Aug. | Sept. | Oct. | Nov. | Dec. | Average |
|---|---|---|---|---|---|---|---|---|---|---|---|---|---|
| 2012 | 10,708.1 | 10,752.8 | 10,818.0 | 10,878.0 | 10,918.3 | 10,989.7 | 11,073.0 | 11,164.1 | 11,258.3 | 11,319.5 | 11,383.2 | 11,530.3 | 11,066.1 |
| 2013 | 11,591.3 | 11,599.4 | 11,659.7 | 11,714.3 | 11,753.8 | 11,825.0 | 11,893.8 | 11,952.7 | 12,037.8 | 12,145.5 | 12,159.9 | 12,210.3 | 11,878.6 |
| 2014 | 12,274.0 | 12,359.2 | 12,395.3 | 12,439.2 | 12,509.1 | 12,557.7 | 12,623.4 | 12,641.8 | 12,695.2 | 12,779.8 | 12,838.9 | 12,940.7 | 12,587.9 |
| 2015 | 13,012.5 | 13,131.5 | 13,166.5 | 13,212.8 | 13,259.4 | 13,325.0 | 13,414.1 | 13,493.6 | 13,542.7 | 13,611.1 | 13,707.3 | 13,745.8 | 13,385.2 |
| 2016 | 13,795.8 | 13,886.7 | 13,988.5 | 14,084.8 | 14,162.4 | 14,245.4 | 14,314.8 | 14,415.7 | 14,457.0 | 14,489.1 | 14,568.4 | 14,599.0 | 14,250.6 |
| 2017 | 14,643.3 | 14,699.4 | 14,757.5 | 14,828.4 | 14,894.3 | 14,915.7 | 14,966.2 | 15,050.3 | 15,118.0 | 15,185.8 | 15,201.7 | 15,267.7 | 14,960.7 |
| 2018 | 15,277.6 | 15,311.7 | 15,374.6 | 15,417.1 | 15,466.5 | 15,528.3 | 15,542.1 | 15,562.0 | 15,586.7 | 15,571.9 | 15,574.1 | 15,680.7 | 15,491.1 |
| 2019 | 15,768.9 | 15,800.1 | 15,854.0 | 15,902.5 | 16,028.7 | 16,199.2 | 16,339.7 | 16,453.3 | 16,580.4 | 16,756.9 | 16,901.3 | 16,976.1 | 16,296.8 |
| 2020 | 17,118.8 | 17,183.9 | 17,984.2 | 19,649.8 | 20,744.3 | 20,995.0 | 21,089.2 | 21,113.5 | 21,271.5 | 21,365.5 | 21,576.9 | 21,649.5 | 20,145.2 |
| 2021[1] | 21,970.5 | Discontinued | | | | | | | | | | | 21,970.5 |

[1] Preliminary.  [2] *MZM* (money, zero maturity): M2 minus small-denomination time deposits, plus institutional money market mutual funds (that is, those included in M3 but excluded from M2). The label MZM was coined by William Poole (1991); the aggregate itself was proposed earlier by Motley (1988). Seasonally adjusted.   *Source: Board of Governors of the Federal Reserve System*

## U.S. Money Supply M3[2]   In Billions of Dollars

| Year | Jan. | Feb. | Mar. | Apr. | May | June | July | Aug. | Sept. | Oct. | Nov. | Dec. | Average |
|---|---|---|---|---|---|---|---|---|---|---|---|---|---|
| 1997 | 5,013.2 | 5,041.7 | 5,080.2 | 5,119.8 | 5,147.1 | 5,177.4 | 5,235.8 | 5,291.4 | 5,332.3 | 5,376.3 | 5,417.1 | 5,460.5 | 5,224.4 |
| 1998 | 5,508.8 | 5,541.3 | 5,611.5 | 5,647.3 | 5,686.9 | 5,728.4 | 5,750.0 | 5,815.0 | 5,882.0 | 5,953.7 | 6,010.1 | 6,051.9 | 5,765.6 |
| 1999 | 6,080.7 | 6,129.5 | 6,133.6 | 6,172.3 | 6,201.0 | 6,237.7 | 6,269.0 | 6,299.1 | 6,323.0 | 6,378.4 | 6,464.1 | 6,551.8 | 6,270.0 |
| 2000 | 6,605.5 | 6,642.2 | 6,704.0 | 6,767.3 | 6,776.9 | 6,823.6 | 6,875.2 | 6,945.0 | 7,003.5 | 7,027.0 | 7,038.3 | 7,117.6 | 6,860.5 |
| 2001 | 7,237.2 | 7,308.5 | 7,372.0 | 7,507.8 | 7,564.1 | 7,644.7 | 7,691.9 | 7,696.3 | 7,853.2 | 7,897.8 | 7,973.0 | 8,035.4 | 7,648.5 |
| 2002 | 8,063.9 | 8,109.3 | 8,117.3 | 8,142.6 | 8,175.1 | 8,190.8 | 8,244.2 | 8,298.1 | 8,331.5 | 8,368.9 | 8,498.8 | 8,568.0 | 8,259.0 |
| 2003 | 8,588.1 | 8,628.7 | 8,648.8 | 8,686.0 | 8,741.9 | 8,791.6 | 8,888.7 | 8,918.2 | 8,906.5 | 8,896.8 | 8,880.3 | 8,872.3 | 8,787.3 |
| 2004 | 8,930.2 | 9,000.3 | 9,080.7 | 9,149.6 | 9,243.8 | 9,275.7 | 9,282.7 | 9,314.4 | 9,351.8 | 9,359.4 | 9,395.1 | 9,433.0 | 9,234.7 |
| 2005 | 9,487.2 | 9,531.6 | 9,565.3 | 9,620.9 | 9,665.0 | 9,725.3 | 9,762.4 | 9,864.6 | 9,950.8 | 10,032.0 | 10,078.5 | 10,154.0 | 9,786.5 |
| 2006[1] | 10,242.8 | 10,298.7 | Discontinued | | | | | | | | | | 10,270.8 |

[1] Preliminary.  [2] *M3* -- M2 plus large-denomination ($100,000 or more) time deposits; repurchase agreements issued by depository institutions; Eurodollar deposits, specifically, dollar-denominated deposits due to nonbank U.S. addresses held at foreign offices of U.S. banks worldwide and all banking offices in Canada and the United Kingdom; and institutional money market mutual funds (funds with initial investments of $50,000 or more). Seasonally adjusted.
*Source: Board of Governors of the Federal Reserve System*

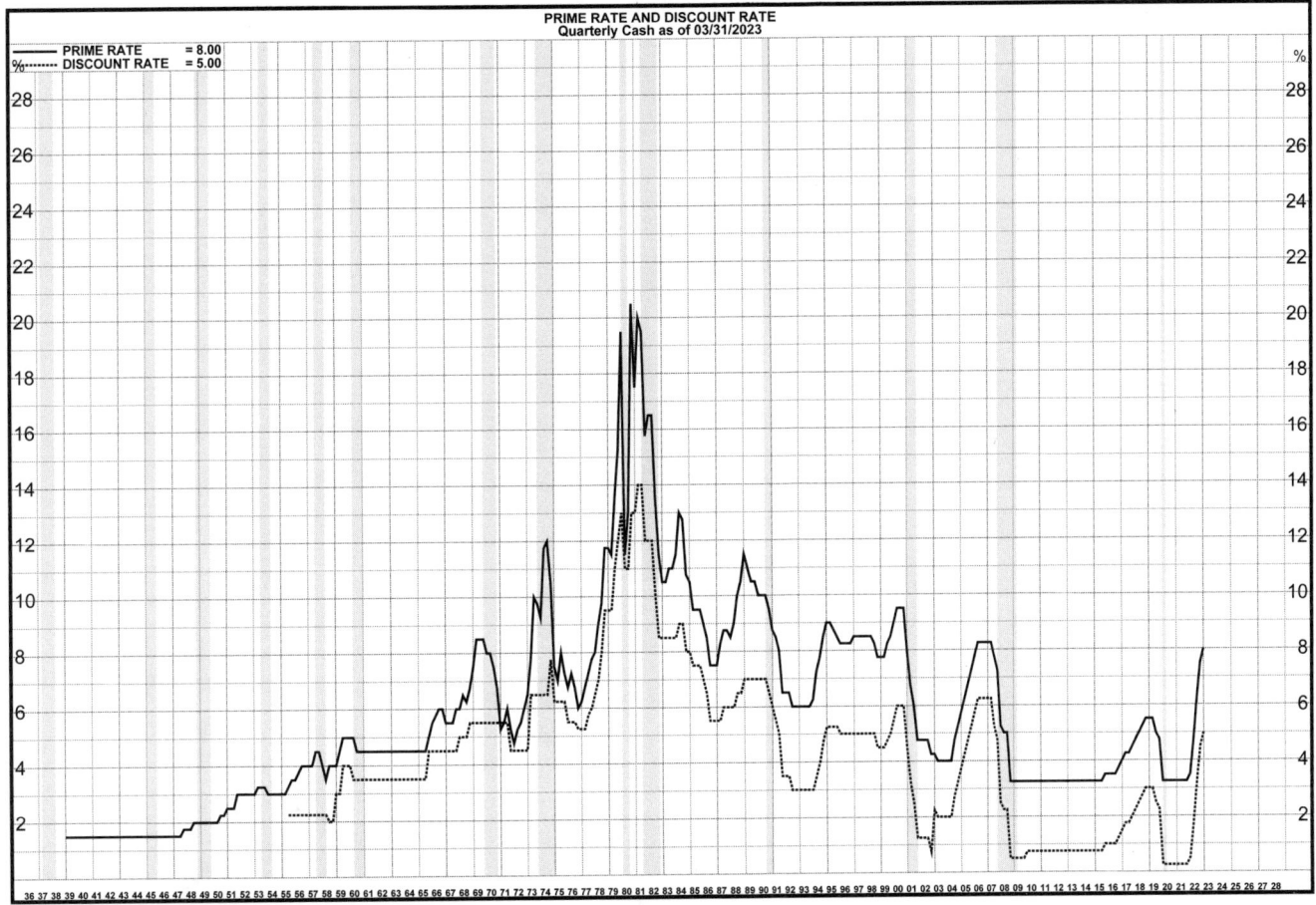

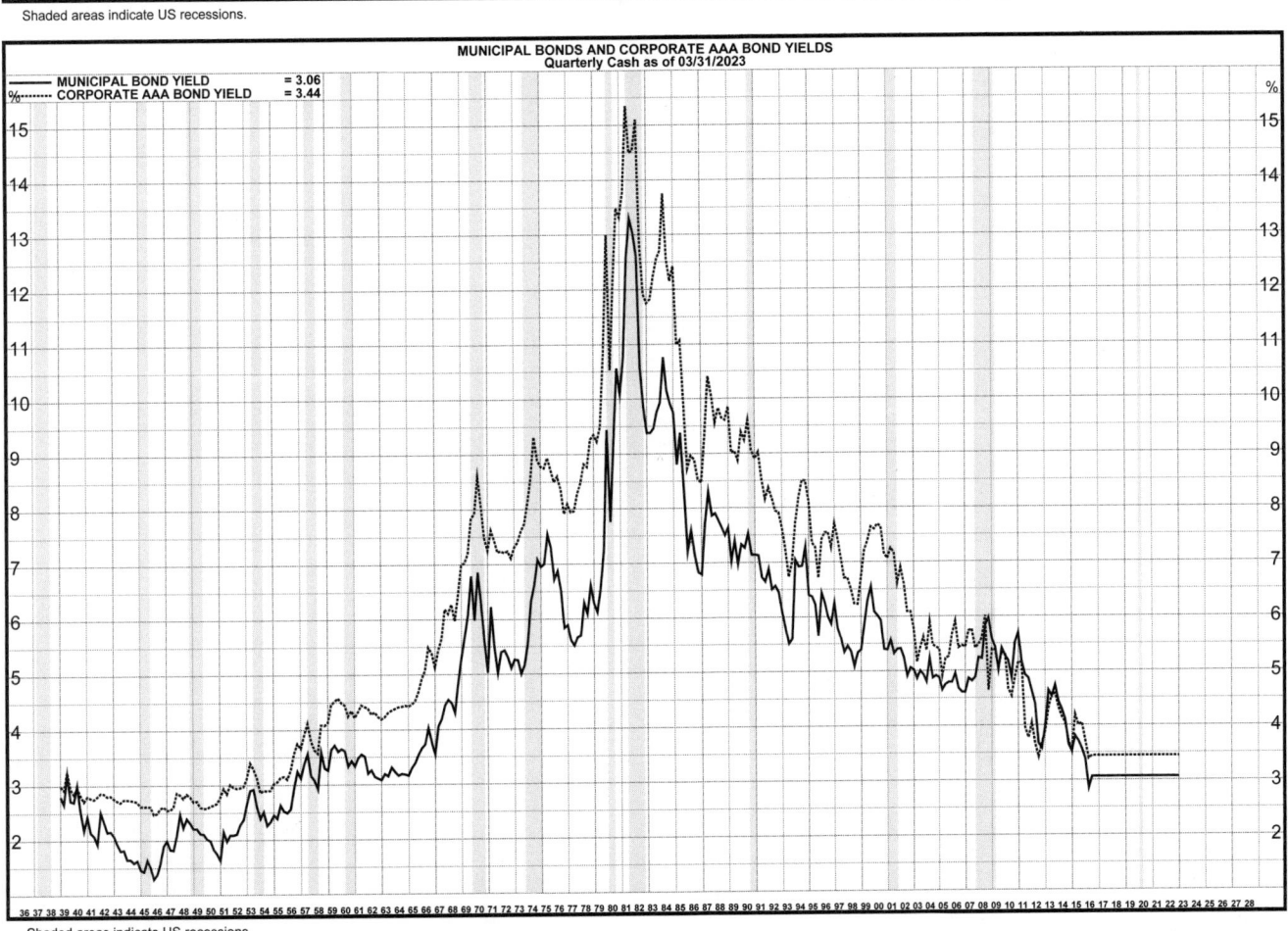

# INTEREST RATES - U.S.

**PRIME RATE AND DISCOUNT RATE**
Quarterly Cash as of 03/31/2023

- PRIME RATE = 8.00
- DISCOUNT RATE = 5.00

Shaded areas indicate US recessions.

**MUNICIPAL BONDS AND CORPORATE AAA BOND YIELDS**
Quarterly Cash as of 03/31/2023

- MUNICIPAL BOND YIELD = 3.06
- CORPORATE AAA BOND YIELD = 3.44

Shaded areas indicate US recessions.

# INTEREST RATES - U.S.

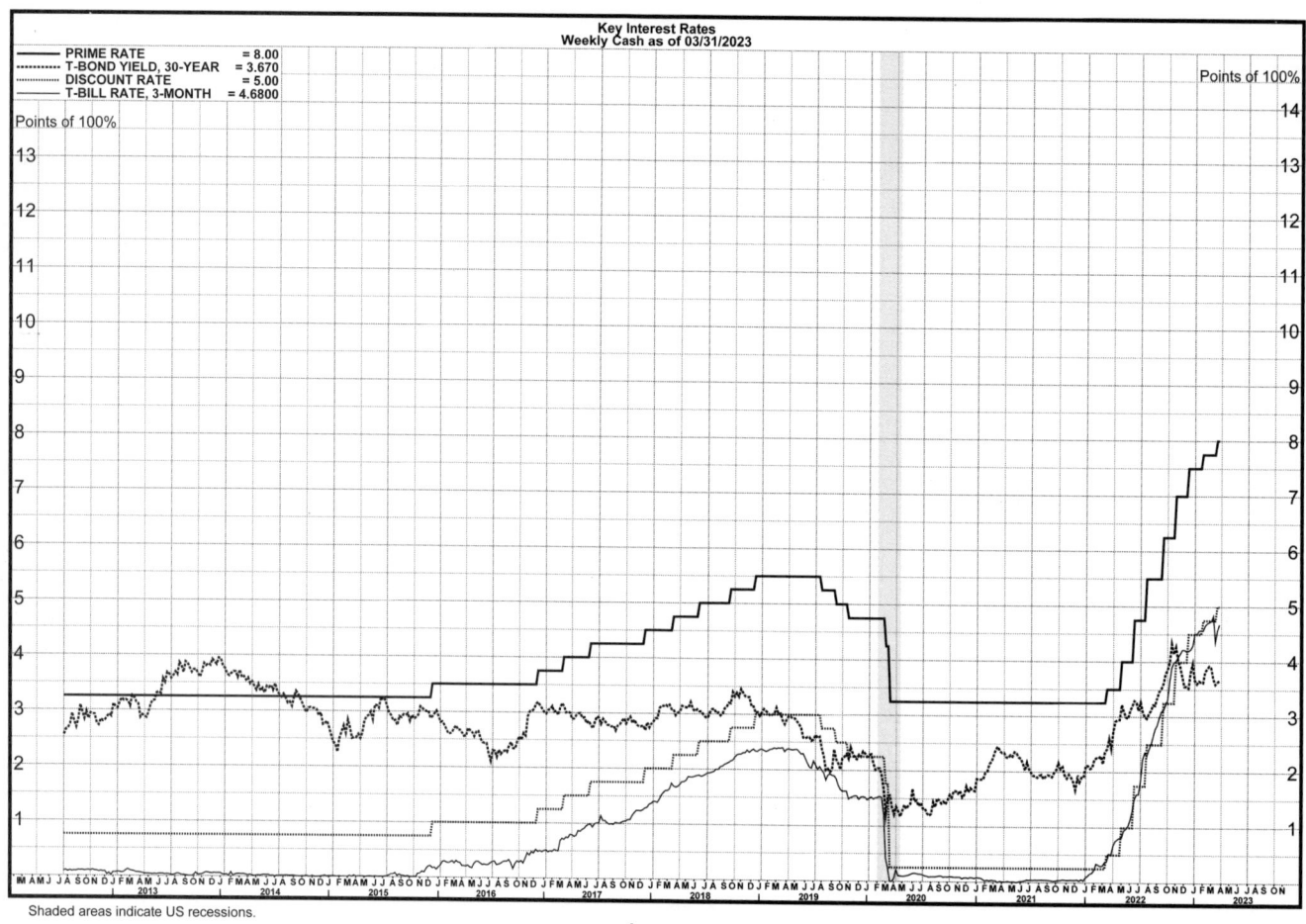

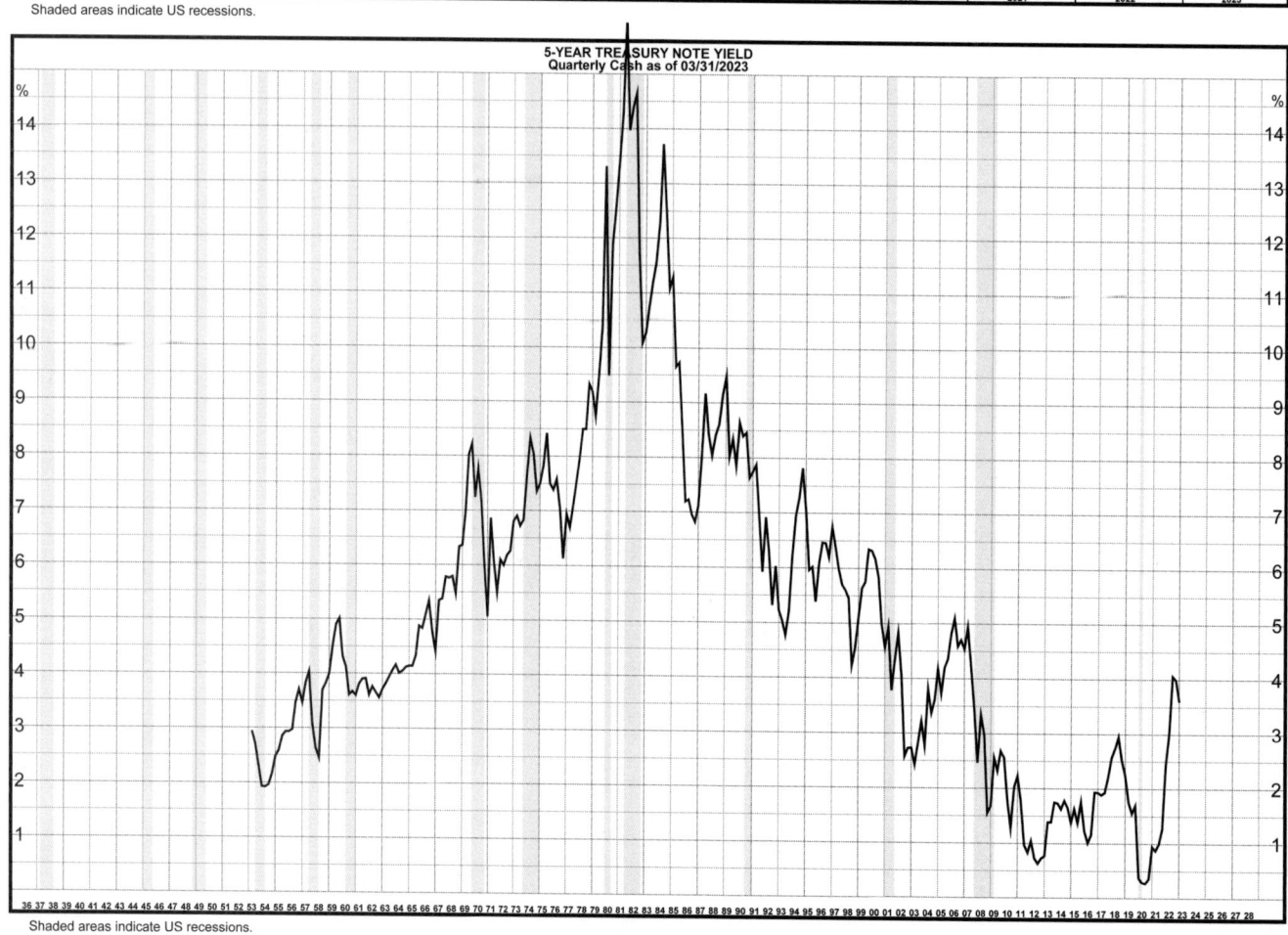

**Key Interest Rates**
Weekly Cash as of 03/31/2023

- PRIME RATE = 8.00
- T-BOND YIELD, 30-YEAR = 3.670
- DISCOUNT RATE = 5.00
- T-BILL RATE, 3-MONTH = 4.6800

Shaded areas indicate US recessions.

**5-YEAR TREASURY NOTE YIELD**
Quarterly Cash as of 03/31/2023

Shaded areas indicate US recessions.

# Interest Rates - Worldwide

Interest rate futures contracts are widely traded throughout the world. The most popular futures contracts are generally 10-year government bonds and 3-month interest rate contracts. In Europe, futures on German interest rates are traded at the Eurex Exchange. Futures on UK interest rates are traded at the EuroNext-Liffe Exchange in London. Futures on Canadian interest rates are traded at the Montreal Exchange. Futures on Japanese interest rates are traded at the Singapore Exchange (SGX) and at the Tokyo Stock Exchange. A variety of other interest rate futures contracts are traded throughout the rest of the world (please see the front of this Yearbook for a complete list).

**Eurozone** – The Eurex German 10-year Euro Bund futures contract (Barchart.com symbol GG) fell sharply during 2022 and closed the year down -38.44 points at 132.93. The Eurex French 10-year OAT bond futures contract (Barchart.com symbol FN) also fell sharply during 2022 and closed the year down -35.85 points at 127.30. The Eurex Italy Euro BTP 10-year bond futures contract (Barchart.com symbol II) fell sharply during 2022 and closed the year down -38.09 points at 108.92.

European 10-year bond prices posted their highs for the year in early March 2022 after Russia invaded Ukraine, which prompted a surge of safe-haven buying of government debt. That prompted the ECB at the March policy meeting to cut its 2022 Eurozone GDP forecast to 3.7% from a December forecast of 4.2% and raise its 2022 inflation forecast to 5.1% from 3.2%.

European bond prices sold off into June as inflation surged and the ECB policymakers began discussing ending quantitative easing (QE) and raising interest rates. At the May ECB meeting, ECB President Lagarde said the ECB's first rate hike in over a decade would begin "weeks" after policymakers concluded net bond-buying, likely in Q3.

After sinking to a 9-year low in mid-June, European bond prices began a countertrend rally into early August. Bond prices rallied after the ECB, at its July policy meeting, raised its key deposit interest rate by 50 basis points to 0%, its first increase in 11 years, and a larger hike than expectations of 25 basis points. Soaring inflation prompted a more hawkish response from the ECB after Eurozone June CPI rose to a then-record high of 8.6% yr/yr.

After briefly climbing to a 4-month high in early August, European bond prices continued to decline the rest of the year as inflation accelerated, and the ECB maintained its aggressive rate-hike regime. The ECB raised its deposit rate by 75 basis points to 1.50% at its September and October meetings, and at the October meeting, the ECB said it "expects to raise interest rates further as inflation remains too high." The Eurozone CPI in October climbed to its record high of +10.7% yr/yr.

European bond prices sank to an 11-year low in late December after the ECB raised its deposit rate by 50 basis points to 2.00% at its December meeting and remained hawkish after ECB President Lagarde said, "we should expect to raise interest rates at a 50 basis point pace for a period of time."

**UK** – The ICE UK 10-year gilt government bond futures contract (Barchart.com symbol G) sold off throughout 2022 and finished the year down sharply by -25.00 points. Gilt prices posted their high for 2022 in late-February after Russia's invasion of Ukraine sparked safe-haven demand for gilts. However, gilts sold off throughout the rest of 2022 as inflation surged and the Bank of England (BOE) ended its quantitative easing (QE) program and began raising interest rates. At its May policy meeting, the BOE raised its main benchmark rate by 25 basis points for the fourth consecutive meeting to 1.00% and warned of double-digit inflation. Gilts extended their declines after the BOE, at its September meeting, raised interest rates by 50 basis points for the second consecutive meeting. The BOE then raised its benchmark rate by 75 basis points to 3.00% at the November meeting as inflation continued to soar. The UK CPI in October climbed +11.1% yr/yr, the fastest pace of increase in 41 years. Nearest-futures (GZ22) 10-year gilt prices sank to a 14-year low of 90.38 in October. Gilt prices recovered modestly into year-end after the BOE slowed its rate hike pace to 50 basis points as it raised rates to 3.50% at its December meeting and said the UK was in recession and "inflation may have already peaked."

**Canada** – The Montreal Exchange's Canadian 10-year government note futures contract (Barchart.com symbol CG) sold off in 2022 and closed the year down -20.07 points. Canadian bond prices sold off into October as soaring inflation prompted the Bank of Canada (BOC) to raise interest rates aggressively. Canada's June CPI accelerated at a +8.1% yr/yr pace, the most in 40 years. The surge in inflation prompted the BOC at its July meeting to raise its benchmark rate by a more-than-expected 100 basis points to 2.50%, the first full-point increase since 1998. Canadian 10-year bond prices posted a 12-year nearest-futures low of 118.11 (CGZ22) in October. Bond prices rebounded modestly into year-end as the pace of inflation slowed, and the BOC signaled a potential pause in its rate-hike campaign. The BOC, at its December meeting, raised its benchmark rate by 50 basis points to 4.25% and said it was "considering" the need for further rate hikes to curb inflation.

**Japan** – The SGX Japan 10-year Japanese government bond (JGB) futures contract (Barchart.com symbol JX) posted its high for 2022 in January at 151.78. Japanese bond prices then tumbled into Q2 and posted an 8-1/2 year low in June. The Bank of Japan (BOJ), at its April meeting, expanded its quantitative easing (QE) program by announcing that it would purchase an unlimited amount of JGBs, on an as-needed basis, to prevent the 10-year JGB yield from going above the BOJ's 0.25% ceiling for its yield-curve control (YCC) target. Despite the bullish implications of the BOJ's asset-buying program, bond prices retreated as a plunge in the yen to a 20-year low boosted inflation expectations. However, JGB bond prices rebounded into early August after the BOJ, at its June meeting, left its YCC policy unchanged and maintained its negative-rate policy. Japanese government bond prices fell back into Q4 and remained under pressure into year-end. The yen sank to a 32-year low in October, boosting inflation expectations. Japan's CPI in December climbed at a +4.0% yr/yr pace, the most in 32 years. At its December meeting, the BOJ unexpectedly widened its YCC target band, raising the upper limit of its 10-year JGB bond yield target range to 0.50% from the previous upper limit of 0.25%. That action pushed the 10-year JGB bond yield up to a 7-1/2 year high of 0.487% in December. The BOJ's move to widen its YCC target also sparked speculation the BOJ may end QE and begin raising interest rates in 2023.

# INTEREST RATES - WORLDWIDE

## GILT, LONG - ICE-LIFF
Weekly Nearest Futures as of 03/31/2023

WEEKLY NEAREST FUTURES
As of 03/31/2023
Chart High 140.32 on 03/09/2020
Chart Low 90.38 on 10/12/2022
% Yield Basis
6% 10-Yr

Points- 100ths

Nearby Futures through Last Trading Day.

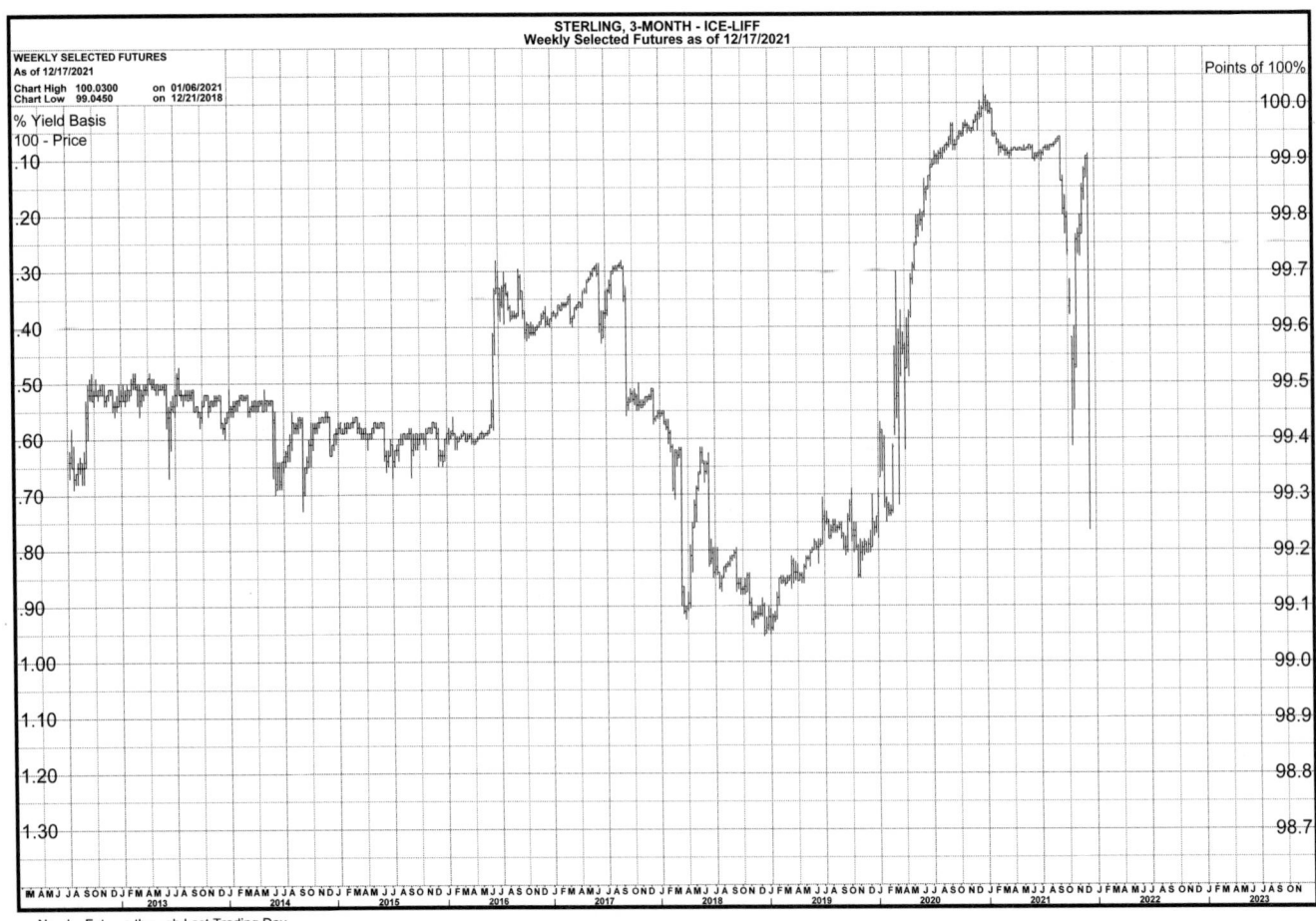

## STERLING, 3-MONTH - ICE-LIFF
Weekly Selected Futures as of 12/17/2021

WEEKLY SELECTED FUTURES
As of 12/17/2021
Chart High 100.0300 on 01/06/2021
Chart Low 99.0450 on 12/21/2018
% Yield Basis
100 - Price

Points of 100%

Nearby Futures through Last Trading Day.

# INTEREST RATES - WORLDWIDE

**JAPANESE GOVT BOND, 10-YEAR - JPX**
Weekly Nearest Futures as of 03/31/2023

WEEKLY NEAREST FUTURES
As of 03/31/2023
Chart High 155.89 on 03/10/2020
Chart Low 140.70 on 05/23/2013

% Yield Basis
6% 10-Yr

Points- 100ths

Nearby Futures through Last Trading Day.

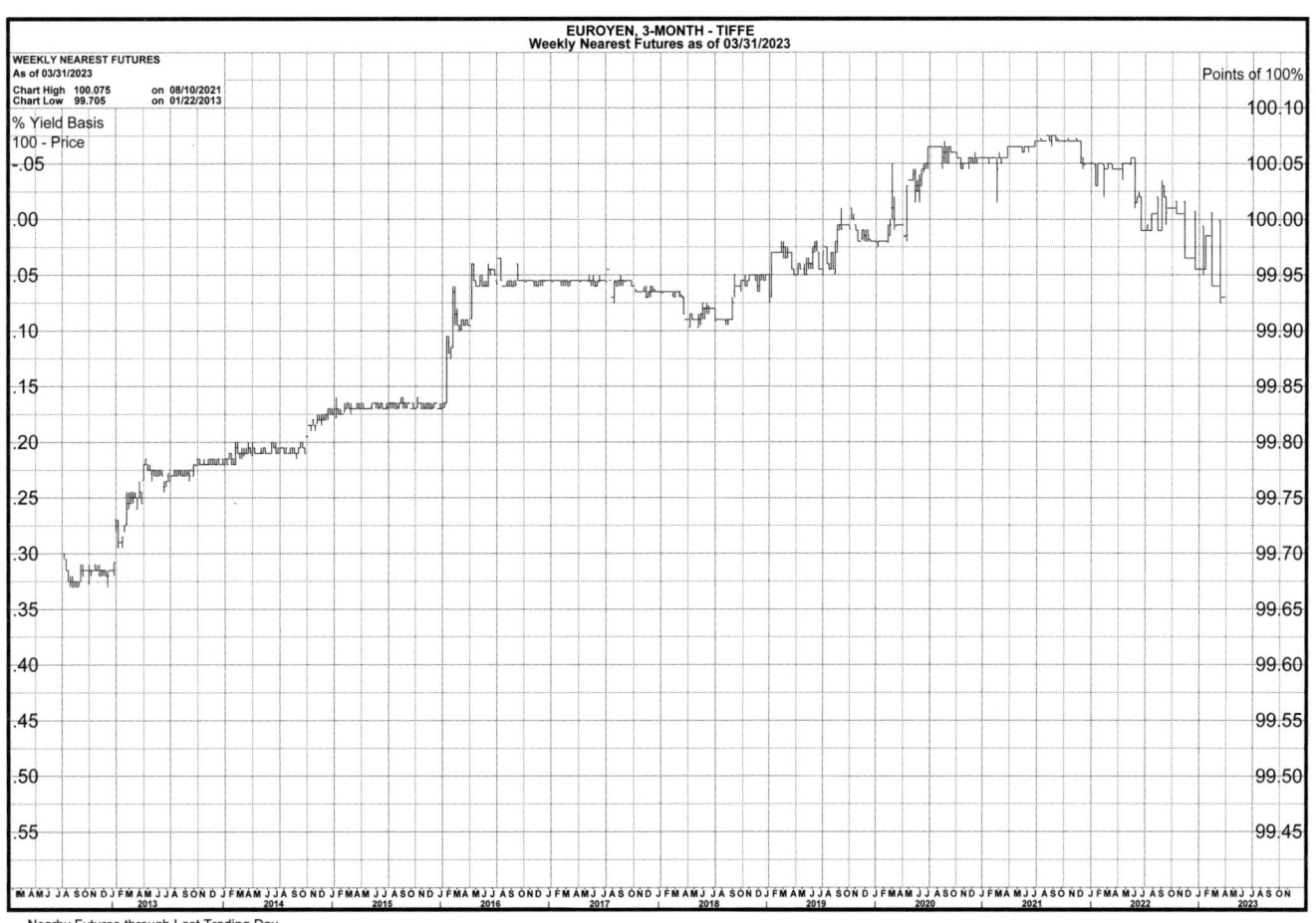

**EUROYEN, 3-MONTH - TIFFE**
Weekly Nearest Futures as of 03/31/2023

WEEKLY NEAREST FUTURES
As of 03/31/2023
Chart High 100.075 on 08/10/2021
Chart Low 99.705 on 01/22/2013

% Yield Basis
100 - Price

Points of 100%

Nearby Futures through Last Trading Day.

173

# INTEREST RATES - WORLDWIDE

**CANADIAN GOVT BOND, 10-YR - MNTRL**
Weekly Nearest Futures as of 03/31/2023

WEEKLY NEAREST FUTURES
As of 03/31/2023
Chart High 155.220 on 07/31/2020
Chart Low 118.110 on 10/21/2022
% Yield Basis
6% 10-Yr

Points- 100ths of pt

Nearby Futures through Last Trading Day.

**CAN. BANKERS' ACCEPTANCE, 3-MO - MNTRL**
Weekly Selected Futures as of 03/31/2023

WEEKLY SELECTED FUTURES
As of 03/31/2023
Chart High 99.600 on 01/18/2021
Chart Low 94.855 on 01/06/2023
% Yield Basis
100 - Price

Points of 100%

Nearby Futures through Last Trading Day.

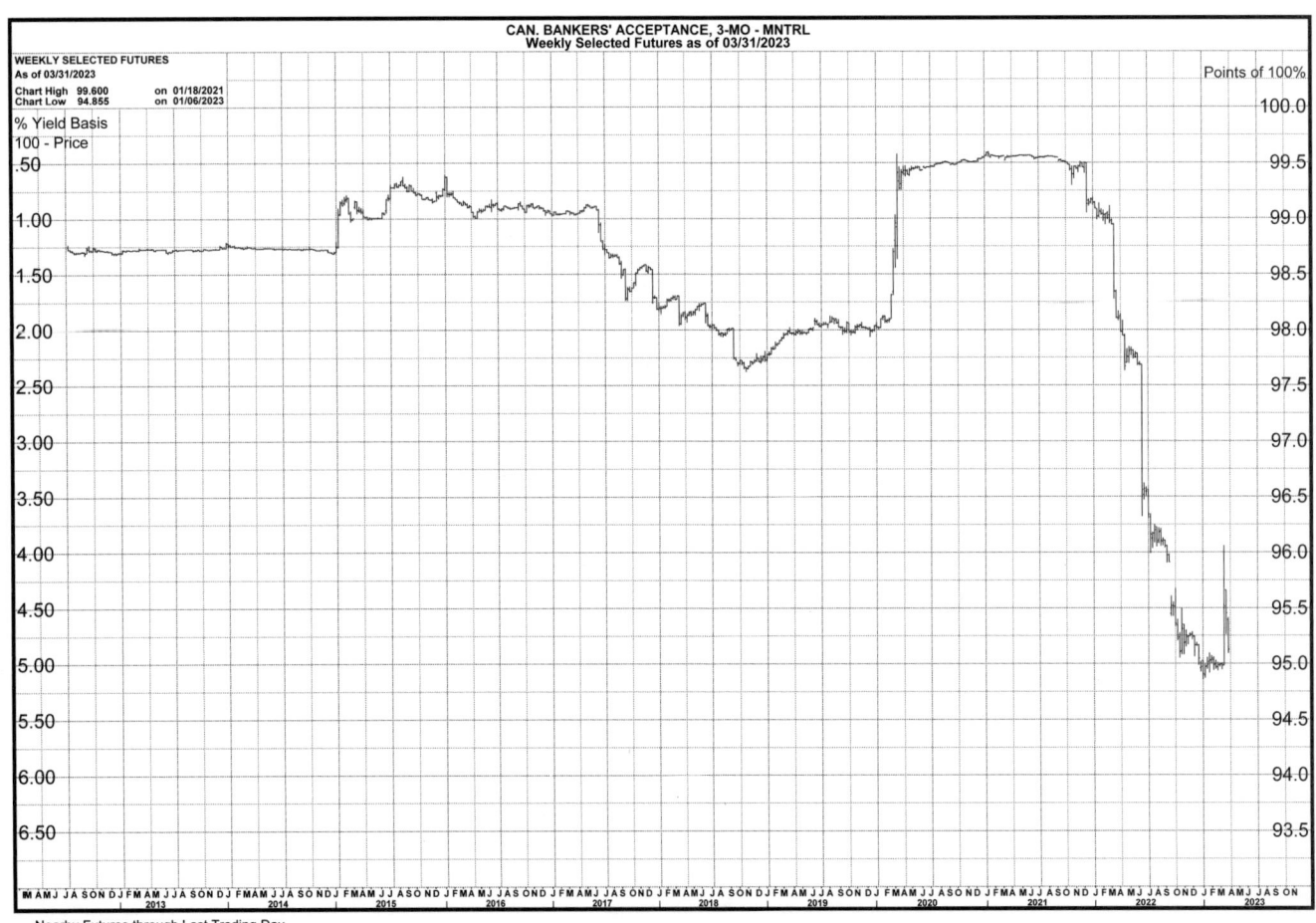

174

# INTEREST RATES - WORLDWIDE

**Australia -- Economic Statistics**  Percentage Change from Previous Period

| Year | Real GDP | Nominal GDP | Real Private Consump-tion | Real Public Consump-tion | Grossed Fixed Invest-ment | Real Total Domestic Demand | Real Exports of Goods & Services | Real Imports of Goods & Services | Consumer Prices[3] | Unem-ployment Rate |
|---|---|---|---|---|---|---|---|---|---|---|
| 2015 | 2.3 | 1.6 | 2.4 | 4.1 | -4.0 | 1.3 | 6.1 | 2.0 | 1.5 | 6.1 |
| 2016 | 2.7 | 3.8 | 2.6 | 5.4 | -2.3 | 1.9 | 6.7 | .4 | 1.3 | 5.7 |
| 2017 | 2.4 | 6.1 | 2.4 | 3.9 | 3.4 | 2.8 | 3.7 | 7.8 | 2.0 | 5.6 |
| 2018 | 2.8 | 5.1 | 2.4 | 4.1 | 2.5 | 3.0 | 5.1 | 4.5 | 1.9 | 5.3 |
| 2019 | 2.0 | 5.3 | .8 | 6.4 | -2.6 | 2.6 | 3.1 | -1.8 | 1.6 | 5.2 |
| 2020 | -2.2 | -1.3 | -5.8 | 7.3 | -2.9 | 2.9 | -9.5 | -12.9 | .9 | 6.5 |
| 2021 | 4.9 | 10.6 | 5.0 | 5.4 | 9.8 |  | -2.1 | 6.5 | 2.8 | 5.1 |
| 2022[1] | 4.0 | 11.1 | 7.0 | 5.4 | 8.3 |  | 2.7 | 12.2 | 6.5 | 3.7 |
| 2023[2] | 1.9 | 4.8 | 2.0 | 1.2 | 2.4 |  | 5.0 | 3.7 | 4.5 | 3.5 |

[1] Estimate.  [2] Projection.  [3] National accounts implicit private consumption deflator.  *Source: Organization for Economic Co-operation and Development (OECD)*

**Canada -- Economic Statistics**  Percentage Change from Previous Period

| Year | Real GDP | Nominal GDP | Real Private Consump-tion | Real Public Consump-tion | Grossed Fixed Invest-ment | Real Total Domestic Demand | Real Exports of Goods & Services | Real Imports of Goods & Services | Consumer Prices[3] | Unem-ployment Rate |
|---|---|---|---|---|---|---|---|---|---|---|
| 2015 | .7 | -.2 | 2.3 | 1.4 | -5.2 | -.1 | 3.4 | .8 | 1.1 | 6.9 |
| 2016 | 1.0 | 1.8 | 2.1 | 1.8 | -4.7 | .7 | 1.4 | .1 | 1.4 | 7.0 |
| 2017 | 3.0 | 5.7 | 3.7 | 2.1 | 3.3 | 3.9 | 1.4 | 4.6 | 1.6 | 6.4 |
| 2018 | 2.8 | 4.4 | 2.6 | 3.2 | 2.5 | 1.7 | 3.8 | 3.3 | 2.2 | 5.9 |
| 2019 | 1.9 | 3.4 | 1.4 | 1.7 | .0 | .6 | 2.3 | .4 | 2.0 | 5.7 |
| 2020 | -5.2 | -4.5 | -6.1 | .0 | -2.8 | 1.7 | -9.7 | -10.8 | .7 | 9.5 |
| 2021 | 4.5 | 13.0 | 4.9 | 5.8 | 7.1 |  | 1.4 | 7.7 | 3.4 | 7.4 |
| 2022[1] | 3.2 | 11.8 | 5.4 | 1.6 | .0 |  | 2.3 | 8.7 | 6.8 | 5.4 |
| 2023[2] | 1.0 | 3.7 | 2.0 | .7 | .3 |  | 2.4 | 3.8 | 4.1 | 5.7 |

[1] Estimate.  [2] Projection.  [3] National accounts implicit private consumption deflator.  *Source: Organization for Economic Co-operation and Development (OECD)*

**France -- Economic Statistics**  Percentage Change from Previous Period

| Year | Real GDP | Nominal GDP | Real Private Consump-tion | Real Public Consump-tion | Grossed Fixed Invest-ment | Real Total Domestic Demand | Real Exports of Goods & Services | Real Imports of Goods & Services | Consumer Prices[3] | Unem-ployment Rate |
|---|---|---|---|---|---|---|---|---|---|---|
| 2015 | 1.1 | 2.2 | 1.4 | 1.0 | .9 | 1.5 | 4.5 | 5.6 | .1 | 10.4 |
| 2016 | 1.0 | 1.5 | 1.6 | 1.4 | 2.5 | 1.6 | 1.6 | 2.8 | .3 | 10.1 |
| 2017 | 2.4 | 3.0 | 1.6 | 1.4 | 5.0 | 2.2 | 4.6 | 4.7 | 1.2 | 9.5 |
| 2018 | 1.8 | 2.8 | 1.0 | .8 | 3.2 | .9 | 4.5 | 3.1 | 2.1 | 9.1 |
| 2019 | 1.9 | 3.2 | 1.8 | 1.0 | 4.1 | 1.3 | 1.6 | 2.4 | 1.3 | 8.5 |
| 2020 | -7.9 | -5.3 | -6.8 | -4.0 | -8.4 | 1.3 | -17.0 | -13.0 | .5 | 8.1 |
| 2021 | 6.8 | 8.2 | 5.3 | 6.4 | 11.4 |  | 8.6 | 7.8 | 2.1 | 7.9 |
| 2022[1] | 2.6 | 5.0 | 2.5 | 2.4 | 2.0 |  | 7.5 | 8.5 | 5.9 | 7.4 |
| 2023[2] | .6 | 4.0 | .4 | .5 | 1.1 |  | 2.8 | 3.0 | 5.7 | 7.7 |

[1] Estimate.  [2] Projection.  [3] National accounts implicit private consumption deflator.  *Source: Organization for Economic Co-operation and Development (OECD)*

**Germany -- Economic Statistics**  Percentage Change from Previous Period

| Year | Real GDP | Nominal GDP | Real Private Consump-tion | Real Public Consump-tion | Grossed Fixed Invest-ment | Real Total Domestic Demand | Real Exports of Goods & Services | Real Imports of Goods & Services | Consumer Prices[3] | Unem-ployment Rate |
|---|---|---|---|---|---|---|---|---|---|---|
| 2015 | 1.2 | 3.1 | 1.8 | 2.9 | 1.2 | 1.4 | 4.9 | 5.3 | .7 | 4.4 |
| 2016 | 2.1 | 3.5 | 2.2 | 4.0 | 3.6 | 2.9 | 2.3 | 4.4 | .4 | 3.9 |
| 2017 | 3.0 | 4.5 | 1.7 | 1.7 | 3.3 | 2.2 | 5.6 | 5.7 | 1.7 | 3.5 |
| 2018 | 1.0 | 3.0 | 1.5 | .8 | 3.4 | 1.9 | 2.4 | 4.1 | 1.9 | 3.2 |
| 2019 | 1.1 | 3.2 | 1.7 | 2.6 | 2.0 | 1.6 | 1.3 | 2.9 | 1.4 | 3.0 |
| 2020 | -4.1 | -2.3 | -5.9 | 4.0 | -3.0 | 1.5 | -10.1 | -9.1 | .4 | 3.7 |
| 2021 | 2.6 | 5.7 | .4 | 3.8 | 1.0 |  | 9.5 | 8.9 | 3.2 | 3.6 |
| 2022[1] | 1.8 | 7.6 | 4.5 | 3.8 | .3 |  | 1.8 | 5.8 | 8.5 | 3.1 |
| 2023[2] | -.3 | 6.8 | -.2 | -.7 | .4 |  | 1.7 | 2.1 | 8.0 | 3.5 |

[1] Estimate.  [2] Projection.  [3] National accounts implicit private consumption deflator.  *Source: Organization for Economic Co-operation and Development (OECD)*

# INTEREST RATES - WORLDWIDE

**Italy -- Economic Statistics**   Percentage Change from Previous Period

| Year | Real GDP | Nominal GDP | Real Private Consumption | Real Public Consumption | Grossed Fixed Investment | Real Total Domestic Demand | Real Exports of Goods & Services | Real Imports of Goods & Services | Consumer Prices[3] | Unemployment Rate |
|---|---|---|---|---|---|---|---|---|---|---|
| 2015 | .6 | 1.6 | 1.9 | -.6 | 1.5 | 1.4 | 4.1 | 6.3 | .1 | 12.0 |
| 2016 | 1.4 | 2.6 | 1.2 | .7 | 4.2 | 1.6 | 2.0 | 4.2 | -.1 | 11.7 |
| 2017 | 1.7 | 2.5 | 1.5 | -.1 | 3.4 | 1.4 | 6.0 | 6.6 | 1.3 | 11.3 |
| 2018 | .8 | 1.9 | 1.0 | .1 | 2.8 | .9 | 1.6 | 2.8 | 1.2 | 10.6 |
| 2019 | .5 | 1.4 | .2 | -.6 | 1.2 | -.2 | 1.8 | -.5 | .6 | 9.9 |
| 2020 | -9.1 | -7.6 | -10.4 | .0 | -8.2 | .6 | -14.2 | -12.7 | -.1 | 9.3 |
| 2021 | 6.7 | 7.3 | 5.1 | 1.5 | 16.5 | | 13.5 | 14.8 | 1.9 | 9.5 |
| 2022[1] | 3.7 | 7.0 | 3.4 | .0 | 8.7 | | 10.4 | 12.9 | 8.1 | 8.1 |
| 2023[2] | .2 | 5.1 | .2 | -.7 | .9 | | 1.8 | 1.7 | 6.5 | 8.3 |

[1] Estimate.   [2] Projection.   [3] National accounts implicit private consumption deflator.   *Source: Organization for Economic Co-operation and Development (OECD)*

**Japan -- Economic Statistics**   Percentage Change from Previous Period

| Year | Real GDP | Nominal GDP | Real Private Consumption | Real Public Consumption | Grossed Fixed Investment | Real Total Domestic Demand | Real Exports of Goods & Services | Real Imports of Goods & Services | Consumer Prices[3] | Unemployment Rate |
|---|---|---|---|---|---|---|---|---|---|---|
| 2015 | 1.6 | 3.7 | -.2 | 1.9 | 2.3 | .8 | 3.2 | .4 | .8 | 3.4 |
| 2016 | .8 | 1.2 | -.4 | 1.6 | 1.2 | .0 | 1.6 | -1.2 | -.1 | 3.1 |
| 2017 | 1.7 | 1.6 | 1.1 | .1 | 1.6 | 1.4 | 6.6 | 3.3 | .5 | 2.8 |
| 2018 | .6 | .6 | .2 | 1.0 | .6 | .8 | 3.8 | 3.8 | 1.0 | 2.4 |
| 2019 | -.4 | .3 | -.5 | 1.9 | .5 | 1.0 | -1.5 | 1.0 | .5 | 2.4 |
| 2020 | -4.6 | -3.7 | -5.2 | 2.3 | -4.9 | .2 | -11.6 | -6.7 | | 2.8 |
| 2021 | 1.6 | .8 | 1.3 | 2.1 | -1.5 | | 11.8 | 5.1 | -.2 | 2.8 |
| 2022[1] | 1.6 | 1.3 | 2.9 | 1.8 | -1.0 | | 4.6 | 7.4 | 2.3 | 2.6 |
| 2023[2] | 1.8 | 3.0 | 1.4 | .1 | 3.7 | | 2.9 | 2.4 | 2.0 | 2.5 |

[1] Estimate.   [2] Projection.   [3] National accounts implicit private consumption deflator.   *Source: Organization for Economic Co-operation and Development (OECD)*

**Switzerland -- Economic Statistics**   Percentage Change from Previous Period

| Year | Real GDP | Nominal GDP | Real Private Consumption | Real Public Consumption | Grossed Fixed Investment | Real Total Domestic Demand | Real Exports of Goods & Services | Real Imports of Goods & Services | Consumer Prices[3] | Unemployment Rate |
|---|---|---|---|---|---|---|---|---|---|---|
| 2015 | 1.6 | .3 | 2.5 | .7 | 2.1 | 2.2 | 3.8 | 4.8 | -1.1 | 4.8 |
| 2016 | 2.1 | 1.5 | 1.6 | .3 | 2.6 | .3 | 6.0 | 5.2 | -.4 | 4.9 |
| 2017 | 1.4 | 1.1 | 1.2 | 1.0 | 3.5 | 1.5 | -.2 | -.3 | .5 | 4.8 |
| 2018 | 2.9 | 3.7 | .6 | .8 | .8 | .2 | 3.3 | .7 | .9 | 4.7 |
| 2019 | 1.2 | 1.1 | 1.2 | .8 | .9 | .9 | -.6 | .3 | .4 | 4.4 |
| 2020 | -2.5 | -3.3 | -4.2 | 3.5 | -3.1 | 1.7 | -5.5 | -3.0 | -.7 | 4.8 |
| 2021 | 4.2 | 5.3 | 1.7 | 3.5 | 4.1 | | 12.2 | 4.9 | .6 | 5.1 |
| 2022[1] | 2.1 | 5.1 | 3.7 | .9 | .1 | | .4 | 2.1 | 2.9 | 4.4 |
| 2023[2] | .6 | 2.8 | .7 | -.2 | .6 | | .7 | 2.0 | 2.5 | 4.6 |

[1] Estimate.   [2] Projection.   [3] National accounts implicit private consumption deflator.   *Source: Organization for Economic Co-operation and Development (OECD)*

**United Kingdom -- Economic Statistics**   Percentage Change from Previous Period

| Year | Real GDP | Nominal GDP | Real Private Consumption | Real Public Consumption | Grossed Fixed Investment | Real Total Domestic Demand | Real Exports of Goods & Services | Real Imports of Goods & Services | Consumer Prices[3] | Unemployment Rate |
|---|---|---|---|---|---|---|---|---|---|---|
| 2015 | 2.4 | 3.1 | 3.1 | 1.2 | 6.5 | 2.7 | 4.0 | 5.0 | .1 | 5.4 |
| 2016 | 2.2 | 4.1 | 3.6 | .8 | 4.9 | 2.4 | 3.2 | 4.0 | .6 | 4.9 |
| 2017 | 2.4 | 4.3 | 1.9 | .4 | 3.5 | 1.4 | 6.8 | 3.3 | 2.7 | 4.4 |
| 2018 | 1.7 | 3.5 | 2.5 | .3 | -.2 | 1.6 | 3.1 | 3.3 | 2.5 | 4.1 |
| 2019 | 1.6 | 3.8 | 1.1 | 4.1 | 1.9 | 3.6 | 1.7 | 2.6 | 1.8 | 3.8 |
| 2020 | -11.0 | -5.8 | -13.2 | -7.3 | -10.5 | .9 | -12.1 | -16.0 | .9 | 4.6 |
| 2021 | 7.5 | 7.9 | 6.2 | 12.6 | 5.6 | | -.3 | 2.8 | 2.6 | 4.5 |
| 2022[1] | 4.4 | 9.5 | 4.7 | 1.6 | 5.6 | | 9.7 | 12.4 | 8.9 | 3.7 |
| 2023[2] | -.4 | 4.3 | -1.1 | 2.3 | 1.0 | | 5.5 | -.5 | 6.6 | 4.3 |

[1] Estimate.   [2] Projection.   [3] National accounts implicit private consumption deflator.   *Source: Organization for Economic Co-operation and Development (OECD)*

# Iron and Steel

Iron (atomic symbol Fe) is a soft, malleable, and ductile metallic element. Next to aluminum, iron is the most abundant of all metals. Pure iron melts at about 1535 degrees Celsius and boils at 2750 degrees Celsius. Archaeologists in Egypt discovered the earliest iron implements dating back to about 3000 BC, and iron ornaments were used even earlier.

Steel is an alloy of iron and carbon, often with an admixture of other elements. The physical properties of various types of steel and steel alloys depend primarily on the amount of carbon present and how it is distributed in the iron. Steel is marketed in a variety of sizes and shapes, such as rods, pipes, railroad rails, tees, channels, and I-beams. Steel mills roll and form heated ingots into the required shapes. The working of steel improves the quality of the steel by refining its crystalline structure and making the metal tougher. There are five classifications of steel: carbon steels, alloy steels, high-strength low-alloy steels, stainless steel, and tool steels.

**Prices** – In 2022, the average wholesale price for No. 1 heavy-melting steel scrap in Chicago fell by -13.6% yr/yr to $380.00 per metric ton.

**Supply** – World production of iron ore in 2022 fell by -3.0% yr/yr to 2.600 billion metric tons, falling below the record high in 2021. The world's largest producers of iron ore are Australia with 33.8% of world production, Brazil with 15.8%, and China with 14.6%. The U.S. accounted for only 1.8% of world iron ore production.

World production of raw steel (ingots and castings) in 2022 fell by -2.6 % yr/yr to 1.900 billion metric tons, falling below the record high in 2021. The largest producers were China with 52.1% of world production, Japan with 5.1%, and the U.S. with 4.3%. U.S. production of steel ingots in 2022 fell by -4.7% yr/yr at 82.0 million metric tons, well above the 2009 record low of 59.400 million metric tons.

U.S. production of pig iron (excluding ferro-alloys) in 2022 fell by -11.9% yr/yr to 20.618 million short tons.

**Demand** – U.S. consumption of ferrous scrap and pig iron in 2020 fell by -10.6% yr/yr to 61.850 million metric tons, which was a record low. The largest consumers of ferrous scrap and pig iron were the manufacturers of steel ingots and castings, with 92.8% of consumption. Iron foundries and miscellaneous users accounted for 5.1% of consumption, and manufacturers of steel castings (scrap) accounted for 1.3% of consumption.

## World Production of Raw Steel (Ingots and Castings)    In Thousands of Metric Tons

| Year | Brazil | Canada | China | France | Germany | Italy | Japan | Korea, South | Russia | Ukraine | United Kindom | United States | World Total |
|---|---|---|---|---|---|---|---|---|---|---|---|---|---|
| 2013 | 34,163 | 12,417 | 779,040 | 15,685 | 42,645 | 23,093 | 110,595 | 66,061 | 68,861 | 32,771 | 11,858 | 86,900 | 1,610,000 |
| 2014 | 33,912 | 12,730 | 822,300 | 16,143 | 42,943 | 23,714 | 110,666 | 71,542 | 70,548 | 27,373 | 12,120 | 88,200 | 1,670,000 |
| 2015 | 33,258 | 12,473 | 803,820 | 14,984 | 42,674 | 22,018 | 103,134 | 69,670 | 69,422 | 22,935 | 10,907 | 78,800 | 1,610,000 |
| 2016 | 31,642 | 12,646 | 807,610 | 14,413 | 42,081 | 23,373 | 104,775 | 68,575 | 70,808 | 24,197 | 7,635 | 78,500 | 1,630,000 |
| 2017 | 34,778 | 13,208 | 870,740 | 15,505 | 43,297 | 24,068 | 104,661 | 71,030 | 71,300 | 21,334 | 7,491 | 81,600 | 1,730,000 |
| 2018 | 35,407 | 13,443 | 920,027 | 15,387 | 42,435 | 24,532 | 104,319 | 72,463 | 71,682 | 21,101 | 7,268 | 86,600 | 1,820,000 |
| 2019 | 32,236 | 12,790 | 996,342 | 14,451 | 39,675 | 23,245 | 99,284 | 71,411 | 71,570 | 20,848 | 7,225 | 87,800 | 1,880,000 |
| 2020 | 31,415 | 10,986 | 1,056,970 | 11,596 | 35,658 | 20,379 | 83,195 | 67,098 | 71,621 | 20,626 | 7,086 | 73,000 | 1,860,000 |
| 2021[1] | 36,000 | | 1,030,000 | | 40,000 | 24,000 | 96,000 | 71,000 | 76,000 | 21,000 | | 86,000 | 1,950,000 |
| 2022[2] | 33,000 | | 990,000 | | 38,000 | 24,000 | 97,000 | 69,000 | 71,000 | 23,000 | | 82,000 | 1,900,000 |

[1] Preliminary.  [2] Estimate.  Source: U.S. Geological Survey (USGS)

## Average Wholesale Prices of Iron and Steel in the United States

| | No. 1 Heavy Melting Steel Scrap | | | | Sheet Bars | | Pittsburg Prices | | | | | |
| | Pittsburg | Chicago | Hot Rolled | Hot Rolled | Cold Finished | Hot Rolled Strip | Carbon Steel Plates | Cold Rolled Strip | Galvanized Sheets | Rail Road Steel Scrap[2] | Used Steel Cans[3] |
| Year | $ Per Gross Ton | | Cents Per Pound | | | | | | | $ Per Gross Ton | |
|---|---|---|---|---|---|---|---|---|---|---|---|
| 2002 | 101.06 | 89.92 | 16.46 | ---- | 23.26 | ---- | ---- | ---- | 22.00 | NA | 66.71 |
| 2003 | 128.32 | 113.82 | 14.80 | ---- | 25.15 | ---- | ---- | ---- | 20.08 | ---- | 116.21 |
| 2004 | 221.05 | 220.13 | 30.84 | ---- | 38.67 | ---- | ---- | ---- | 36.69 | ---- | 192.80 |
| 2005 | 199.10 | 196.75 | 27.83 | ---- | 44.96 | ---- | ---- | ---- | 33.77 | ---- | 172.00 |
| 2006 | 222.39 | 225.21 | 29.78 | ---- | 44.02 | ---- | ---- | ---- | 38.09 | ---- | 212.63 |
| 2007 | 250.98 | 262.80 | 26.89 | ---- | 45.26 | ---- | ---- | ---- | 38.25 | ---- | 244.65 |
| 2008 | 365.62 | 357.88 | 44.56 | ---- | 61.67 | ---- | ---- | ---- | 54.91 | ---- | 314.63 |
| 2009 | 204.21 | 206.14 | 24.60 | ---- | 42.10 | ---- | ---- | ---- | 34.23 | ---- | 121.84 |
| 2010 | 339.54 | 334.48 | 31.65 | ---- | 50.82 | ---- | ---- | ---- | 41.72 | ---- | 296.91 |
| 2011[1] | 408.64 | 417.00 | 38.02 | ---- | 63.63 | ---- | ---- | ---- | 48.45 | ---- | 391.50 |

[1] Preliminary.  [2] Specialties scrap.  [3] Consumer buying prices.  NA = Not available.  Source: American Metal Market (AMM)

# IRON AND STEEL

## Salient Statistics of Steel in the United States     In Thousands of Short Tons

| Year | Pig Iron Production | Producer Price Index for Steel Mill Products (1982=100) | Basic Oxygen | Open Hearth | Electric[2] | Stainless | Carbon | Alloy | Total | Net Shipments Steel Mill Products | Exports | Imports |
|---|---|---|---|---|---|---|---|---|---|---|---|---|
| 2013 | 30,300 | 195.0 | | ---- | | 2,238 | 88,956 | 4,530 | 95,790 | 86,600 | 11,500 | 29,200 |
| 2014 | 29,400 | 200.2 | | ---- | | 2,634 | 89,727 | 4,872 | 97,223 | 89,100 | 10,900 | 40,200 |
| 2015 | 25,400 | 177.1 | | ---- | | 2,590 | 81,129 | 3,230 | 86,861 | 78,500 | 9,050 | 35,200 |
| 2016 | 22,300 | 167.8 | | ---- | | 2,734 | 80,688 | 3,108 | 86,531 | 78,500 | 8,450 | 30,000 |
| 2017 | 22,400 | 187.4 | | ---- | | | | | | | | |
| 2018 | 24,100 | 211.1 | | ---- | | | | | | | | |
| 2019 | 22,300 | 204.0 | | ---- | | | | | | | | |
| 2020 | 18,300 | 184.4 | | ---- | | | | | | | | |
| 2021 | 22,200 | 350.9 | | ---- | | | | | | | | |
| 2022[1] | 21,000 | 382.5 | | ---- | | | | | | | | |

[1] Preliminary.  [2] Includes crucible steels.  Sources: American Iron & Steel Institute (AISI); U.S. Geological Survey (USGS)

## Production of Steel Ingots, Rate of Capability Utilization[1] in the United States     In Percent

| Year | Jan. | Feb. | Mar. | Apr. | May | June | July | Aug. | Sept. | Oct. | Nov. | Dec. | Average |
|---|---|---|---|---|---|---|---|---|---|---|---|---|---|
| 2013 | 76.5 | 78.3 | 76.2 | 76.7 | 76.5 | 76.1 | 77.3 | 77.6 | 78.3 | 76.5 | 76.2 | 74.0 | 76.7 |
| 2014 | 75.8 | 77.9 | 77.7 | 76.6 | 77.3 | 78.5 | 79.6 | 80.2 | 78.1 | 76.5 | 77.2 | 74.6 | 77.5 |
| 2015 | 76.4 | 72.1 | 67.7 | 69.8 | 72.1 | 74.4 | 73.2 | 72.2 | 70.5 | 68.1 | 62.7 | 62.1 | 70.1 |
| 2016 | 68.7 | 73.1 | 72.1 | 72.6 | 74.3 | 75.1 | 71.3 | 70.8 | 68.0 | 65.4 | 67.1 | 67.8 | 70.5 |
| 2017 | 73.3 | 75.9 | 73.6 | 73.6 | 73.7 | 74.9 | 74.3 | 75.8 | 73.4 | 73.2 | 73.3 | 71.9 | 73.9 |
| 2018 | 73.6 | 77.9 | 78.3 | 76.0 | 77.1 | 77.4 | 78.4 | 79.4 | 79.6 | 80.2 | 81.2 | 79.4 | 78.2 |
| 2019 | 80.4 | 82.4 | 82.2 | 81.3 | 80.8 | 80.1 | 79.4 | 79.1 | 77.4 | 78.0 | 78.8 | 78.5 | 79.9 |
| 2020 | 81.7 | 81.3 | 75.3 | 55.4 | 54.6 | 56.8 | 60.3 | 65.9 | 68.6 | 70.1 | 73.3 | 72.9 | 68.0 |
| 2021 | 76.6 | 76.8 | 78.0 | 80.8 | 81.0 | 83.0 | 84.4 | 84.8 | 83.3 | 83.2 | 82.7 | 80.1 | 81.2 |
| 2022[1] | 79.8 | 80.8 | 78.7 | 81.9 | 81.1 | 79.6 | 78.1 | 78.0 | 76.4 | | | | 79.4 |

[1] Based on tonnage capability to produce raw steel for a full order book.  [2] Preliminary.  Sources: American Iron and Steel Institute (AISI); U.S. Geological Survey (USGS)

## World Production of Pig Iron (Excludes Ferro-Alloys)     In Thousands of Metric Tons

| Year | Belgium | Brazil | China | France | Germany | India | Italy | Japan | Russia | Ukraine | United Kingdom | United States | World Total |
|---|---|---|---|---|---|---|---|---|---|---|---|---|---|
| 2013 | 4,343 | 26,200 | 708,970 | 10,276 | 26,678 | 51,359 | 6,933 | 83,849 | 49,945 | 29,089 | 9,471 | 30,300 | 1,240,000 |
| 2014 | 4,388 | 27,016 | 713,740 | 10,866 | 27,379 | 55,166 | 6,371 | 83,872 | 51,460 | 24,801 | 9,705 | 29,400 | 1,260,000 |
| 2015 | 4,248 | 27,803 | 691,410 | 10,097 | 27,844 | 58,393 | 5,051 | 81,011 | 52,411 | 21,878 | 8,774 | 25,400 | 1,240,000 |
| 2016 | 4,869 | 26,129 | 702,270 | 9,724 | 27,269 | 63,714 | 6,048 | 80,186 | 51,874 | 23,560 | 6,142 | 22,300 | 1,250,000 |
| 2017 | 4,895 | 28,331 | 713,620 | 10,678 | 27,816 | 66,808 | 5,052 | 78,330 | 52,127 | 20,123 | 5,996 | 22,400 | 1,280,000 |
| 2018 | 4,754 | 28,655 | 779,880 | 10,530 | 27,271 | 72,641 | 4,836 | 77,328 | 51,797 | 20,531 | 5,590 | 24,100 | 1,370,000 |
| 2019 | 4,690 | 26,166 | 809,365 | 9,878 | 25,490 | 74,099 | 4,607 | 74,907 | 51,184 | 20,056 | 5,643 | 22,300 | 1,390,000 |
| 2020 | 3,600 | 24,628 | 887,719 | 7,700 | 25,459 | 67,783 | 3,405 | 61,600 | 51,908 | 20,423 | 5,235 | 18,200 | 1,420,000 |
| 2021[1] | | 28,000 | 869,000 | | 26,000 | 78,000 | 4,000 | 70,000 | 54,000 | 21,000 | | 22,000 | 1,350,000 |
| 2022[2] | | 26,000 | 830,000 | | 24,000 | 83,000 | 4,000 | 71,000 | 50,000 | 19,000 | | 21,000 | 1,300,000 |

[1] Preliminary.  [2] Estimate.  Source: U.S. Geological Survey (USGS)

## Production of Pig Iron (Excludes Ferro-Alloys) in the United States     In Thousands of Short Tons

| Year | Jan. | Feb. | Mar. | Apr. | May | June | July | Aug. | Sept. | Oct. | Nov. | Dec. | Total |
|---|---|---|---|---|---|---|---|---|---|---|---|---|---|
| 2013 | 3,060 | 2,760 | 3,040 | 2,800 | 2,880 | 2,760 | 2,760 | 2,890 | 2,880 | 2,870 | 2,760 | 2,780 | 34,240 |
| 2014 | 2,430 | 2,450 | 2,820 | 2,580 | 2,710 | 2,760 | 2,930 | 2,920 | 2,740 | 2,690 | 2,740 | 2,860 | 32,630 |
| 2015 | 2,760 | 2,310 | 2,390 | 2,330 | 2,530 | 2,670 | 2,830 | 2,690 | 2,390 | 2,270 | 2,120 | 2,110 | 29,400 |
| 2016 | 2,200 | 2,260 | 2,380 | 2,150 | 1,910 | 2,280 | 2,220 | 1,860 | 1,770 | 1,610 | 1,660 | 1,810 | 24,110 |
| 2017 | 1,940 | 1,930 | 1,960 | 1,870 | 1,940 | 1,830 | 1,860 | 1,930 | 1,850 | 1,690 | 1,770 | 1,840 | 22,410 |
| 2018 | 1,920 | 1,790 | 1,970 | 1,930 | 2,070 | 2,060 | 2,100 | 2,030 | 2,010 | 2,060 | 2,030 | 2,100 | 24,070 |
| 2019 | 1,880 | 1,840 | 2,080 | 1,860 | 1,930 | 1,900 | 1,830 | 1,840 | 1,870 | 1,700 | 1,720 | 1,850 | 22,300 |
| 2020 | 1,680 | 1,920 | 1,910 | 1,110 | 949 | 1,170 | 1,310 | 1,520 | 1,610 | 1,700 | 1,700 | 1,660 | 18,239 |
| 2021 | 1,870 | 1,760 | 1,950 | 1,920 | 2,020 | 1,970 | 2,040 | 2,050 | 1,950 | 2,010 | 1,930 | 1,940 | 23,410 |
| 2022[1] | 1,740 | 1,640 | 1,820 | 1,840 | 1,850 | 1,750 | 1,710 | 1,720 | 1,630 | 1,650 | 1,550 | | 20,618 |

[1] Preliminary.  Source: American Iron and Steel Institute

# IRON AND STEEL

## Salient Statistics of Ferrous Scrap and Pig Iron in the United States    In Thousands of Metric Tons

| | Mfg. of Pig Iron & Steel Ingots & Castings | | | Iron Foundries & Misc. Users | | | Mfg. of Steel Castings | All Uses | | | Imports of | Exports of | Stocks, Dec. 31 Ferrous Scrap & Pig Iron at Consumers | | |
|---|---|---|---|---|---|---|---|---|---|---|---|---|---|---|---|
| Year | Scrap | Pig Iron | Total | Scrap | Pig Iron | Total | (Scrap) | Ferrous Scrap | Pig Iron | Grand Total | Scrap[2] | Scrap[3] | | | Total |
| 2011 | 56,400 | 34,900 | 92,920 | 5,960 | 1,970 | 7,933 | 756 | 63,100 | 36,900 | 101,620 | 4,010 | 24,300 | 3,980 | 423 | 4,529 |
| 2012 | 55,800 | 35,400 | 94,780 | 6,710 | 1,980 | 8,693 | 639 | 63,100 | 37,400 | 104,080 | 3,720 | 21,400 | 4,170 | 405 | 4,722 |
| 2013 | 52,100 | 31,800 | 88,390 | 5,660 | 2,260 | 7,923 | 1,180 | 59,000 | 34,100 | 97,590 | 3,930 | 18,500 | 3,970 | 427 | 4,504 |
| 2014 | 51,900 | 25,900 | 82,590 | 5,560 | 2,100 | 7,663 | 1,190 | 58,600 | 28,100 | 91,490 | 4,220 | 15,300 | 4,070 | 442 | 4,729 |
| 2015 | 46,100 | 22,200 | 72,430 | 4,420 | 632 | 5,055 | 1,970 | 52,500 | 22,900 | 79,530 | 3,510 | 12,800 | 4,200 | 672 | 5,088 |
| 2016 | 44,900 | 20,700 | 70,380 | 5,020 | 1,620 | 6,643 | 3,100 | 53,000 | 22,400 | 80,180 | 3,860 | 12,600 | 4,340 | 440 | 5,017 |
| 2017 | 45,600 | 19,800 | 67,290 | 4,130 | 634 | 4,767 | 409 | 50,200 | 20,500 | 72,590 | 4,630 | 15,000 | 4,530 | 453 | 5,248 |
| 2018 | 47,200 | 16,700 | 66,270 | 3,890 | 654 | 4,547 | 682 | 51,800 | 17,400 | 71,570 | 5,030 | 17,100 | 5,120 | 577 | 6,031 |
| 2019 | 46,700 | 16,100 | 65,290 | 2,490 | 482 | 2,975 | 436 | 50,100 | 16,600 | 69,200 | 4,270 | 17,600 | 3,960 | 496 | 4,680 |
| 2020[1] | 41,700 | 13,300 | 57,420 | 2,720 | 454 | 3,177 | 794 | 45,200 | 14,100 | 61,850 | 4,510 | 16,900 | 3,960 | 345 | 4,517 |

[1] Preliminary.  [2] Includes tinplate and terneplate.  [3] Excludes used rails for rerolling and other uses and ships, boats, and other vessels for scrapping.
Source: U.S. Geological Survey (USGS)

## Consumption of Pig Iron in the United States, by Type of Furance or Equipment    In Thousands of Metric Tons

| Year | Open Hearth | Electric | Cupola | Basic Oxygen Process | Air & Other Furnace | Direct Casting | Total |
|---|---|---|---|---|---|---|---|
| 2011 | ---- | 5,410 | 76 | 31,300 | 12 | 36 | 36,900 |
| 2012 | ---- | 5,790 | 57 | 31,500 | 10 | 36 | 37,400 |
| 2013 | ---- | 4,150 | 345 | 29,600 | ---- | ---- | 34,100 |
| 2014 | ---- | 4,230 | 148 | 23,800 | ---- | ---- | 28,100 |
| 2015 | ---- | 2,350 | 152 | 20,300 | ---- | ---- | 22,900 |
| 2016 | ---- | 3,620 | 155 | 18,600 | ---- | ---- | 22,400 |
| 2017 | ---- | 3,310 | 160 | 17,000 | ---- | ---- | 20,500 |
| 2018 | ---- | 2,790 | 182 | 14,400 | ---- | ---- | 17,400 |
| 2019 | ---- | W | W | 13,900 | ---- | ---- | 16,600 |
| 2020[1] | ---- | 2,290 | 137 | 11,700 | ---- | ---- | 14,100 |

[1] Preliminary.  W = Withheld.  Source: U.S. Geological Survey (USGS)

## Volume of Trading of Hot Rolled Steel Futures in New York    In Contracts

| Year | Jan. | Feb. | Mar. | Apr. | May | June | July | Aug. | Sept. | Oct. | Nov. | Dec. | Total |
|---|---|---|---|---|---|---|---|---|---|---|---|---|---|
| 2013 | 4,567 | 6,619 | 6,814 | 6,972 | 3,415 | 3,700 | 2,874 | 2,572 | 1,728 | 8,033 | 3,869 | 2,630 | 53,793 |
| 2014 | 3,953 | 2,376 | 6,002 | 4,292 | 4,220 | 1,082 | 3,543 | 905 | 4,863 | 5,777 | 7,661 | 3,556 | 48,230 |
| 2015 | 3,096 | 2,344 | 4,705 | 6,489 | 4,084 | 3,083 | 6,478 | 6,156 | 7,222 | 6,559 | 5,405 | 3,196 | 58,817 |
| 2016 | 3,058 | 7,225 | 4,165 | 8,576 | 2,303 | 4,454 | 3,415 | 5,006 | 4,506 | 5,836 | 2,623 | 2,717 | 53,884 |
| 2017 | 5,501 | 2,870 | 2,897 | 1,182 | 7,188 | 4,905 | 6,639 | 7,316 | 7,495 | 7,107 | 4,598 | 5,531 | 63,229 |
| 2018 | 10,435 | 9,072 | 9,655 | 12,074 | 9,487 | 5,226 | 10,861 | 17,235 | 6,668 | 9,665 | 11,986 | 7,205 | 119,569 |
| 2019 | 21,700 | 15,281 | 13,165 | 19,031 | 28,415 | 14,031 | 13,715 | 5,113 | 9,200 | 14,616 | 10,396 | 9,093 | 173,756 |
| 2020 | 15,359 | 11,979 | 30,709 | 14,865 | 17,503 | 18,463 | 10,608 | 21,175 | 20,827 | 22,823 | 19,194 | 16,901 | 220,406 |
| 2021 | 24,250 | 21,666 | 20,714 | 21,954 | 20,976 | 18,215 | 19,341 | 14,950 | 24,003 | 23,211 | 17,776 | 19,761 | 246,817 |
| 2022 | 28,166 | 20,424 | 38,809 | 20,984 | 17,278 | 21,505 | 16,521 | 22,324 | 21,551 | 22,649 | 21,823 | 21,531 | 273,565 |

Contract size = 20 short tons.  Source: CME Group; New York Mercantile Exchange (CME-NYMEX)

## Average Open Interest of Hot Rolled Steel Futures in New York    In Contracts

| Year | Jan. | Feb. | Mar. | Apr. | May | June | July | Aug. | Sept. | Oct. | Nov. | Dec. |
|---|---|---|---|---|---|---|---|---|---|---|---|---|
| 2013 | 9,679 | 10,033 | 12,210 | 14,098 | 14,810 | 14,668 | 14,328 | 14,565 | 14,114 | 13,517 | 13,613 | 11,741 |
| 2014 | 10,308 | 10,308 | 9,720 | 9,537 | 10,242 | 10,769 | 11,092 | 11,507 | 12,037 | 15,739 | 19,703 | 22,501 |
| 2015 | 21,609 | 20,954 | 18,637 | 18,859 | 19,351 | 19,356 | 20,474 | 20,783 | 21,273 | 22,758 | 23,472 | 24,299 |
| 2016 | 23,157 | 24,528 | 24,610 | 22,721 | 21,525 | 20,796 | 19,304 | 18,927 | 17,829 | 18,390 | 16,825 | 14,694 |
| 2017 | 13,068 | 12,862 | 13,145 | 12,646 | 12,815 | 13,952 | 13,369 | 14,007 | 14,493 | 14,065 | 13,384 | 13,600 |
| 2018 | 12,892 | 12,056 | 13,044 | 14,466 | 14,375 | 13,879 | 13,800 | 16,712 | 15,926 | 16,338 | 17,185 | 16,261 |
| 2019 | 17,430 | 20,320 | 19,221 | 17,425 | 18,040 | 18,600 | 17,519 | 16,597 | 15,791 | 14,393 | 15,249 | 15,535 |
| 2020 | 17,062 | 18,409 | 22,053 | 23,953 | 23,226 | 22,892 | 23,499 | 24,443 | 23,059 | 21,712 | 21,311 | 22,280 |
| 2021 | 23,040 | 25,836 | 29,109 | 31,690 | 32,270 | 32,562 | 31,293 | 31,891 | 35,619 | 38,615 | 38,812 | 39,800 |
| 2022 | 40,401 | 37,781 | 31,833 | 28,285 | 26,844 | 26,565 | 24,287 | 23,518 | 21,424 | 22,290 | 23,740 | 23,486 |

Contract size = 20 short tons.  Source: CME Group; New York Mercantile Exchange (CME-NYMEX)

# IRON AND STEEL

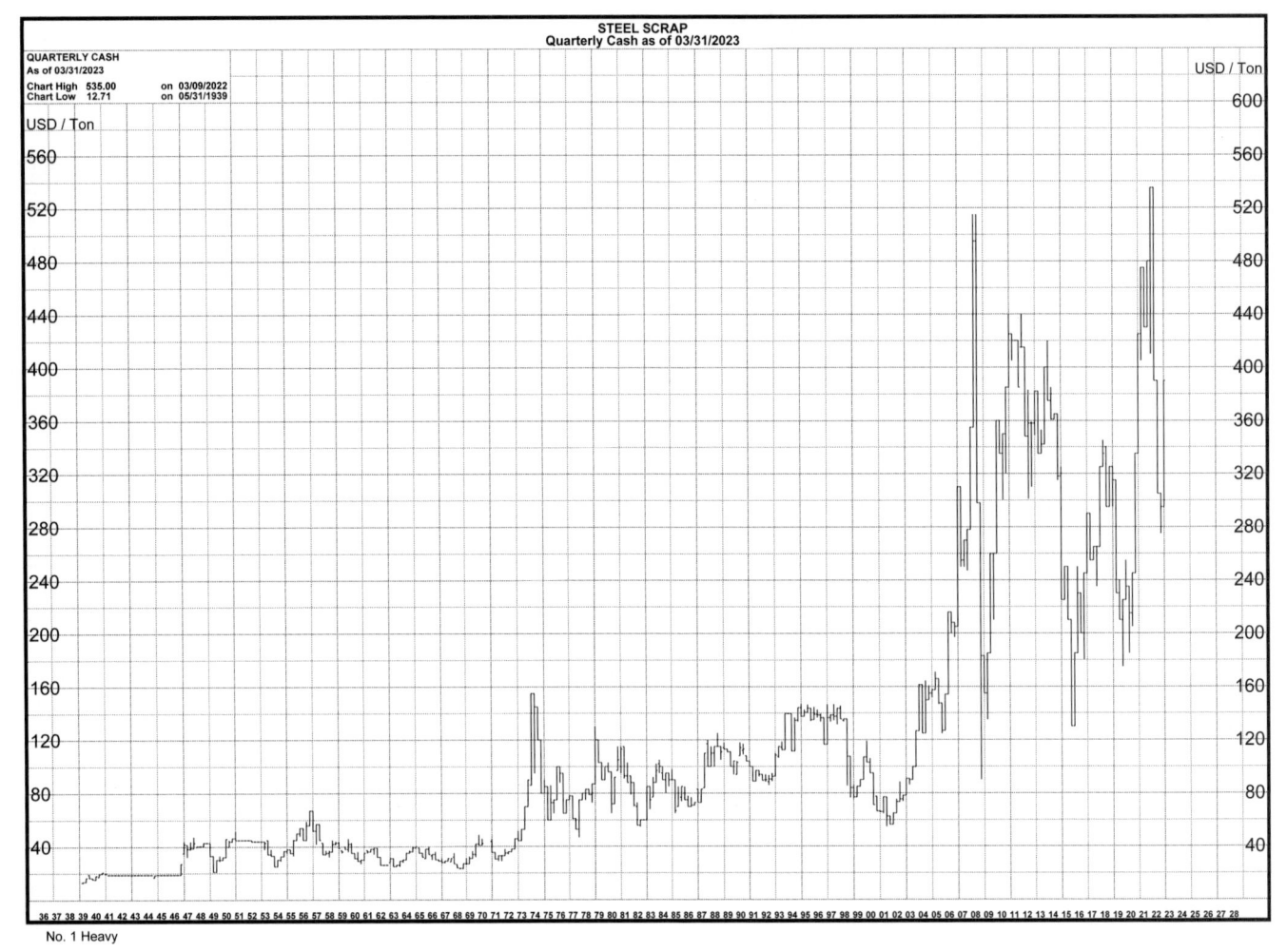

**STEEL SCRAP**
Quarterly Cash as of 03/31/2023

QUARTERLY CASH
As of 03/31/2023
Chart High 535.00 on 03/09/2022
Chart Low 12.71 on 05/31/1939

## Wholesale Price of No. 1 Heavy Melting Steel Scrap in Chicago   In Dollars Per Metric Ton

| Year | Jan. | Feb. | Mar. | Apr. | May | June | July | Aug. | Sept. | Oct. | Nov. | Dec. | Average |
|---|---|---|---|---|---|---|---|---|---|---|---|---|---|
| 2013 | 358.00 | 350.89 | 375.71 | 363.86 | 342.82 | 336.20 | 351.36 | 351.18 | 343.35 | 344.61 | 370.26 | 395.16 | 356.95 |
| 2014 | 414.29 | 396.00 | 378.10 | 383.64 | 373.67 | 362.90 | 362.55 | 363.00 | 364.71 | 350.13 | 322.11 | 317.43 | 365.71 |
| 2015 | 323.60 | 250.00 | 225.91 | 225.00 | 229.00 | 246.36 | 242.27 | 222.86 | 211.43 | 171.36 | 136.32 | 130.00 | 217.84 |
| 2016 | 146.84 | 150.00 | 180.43 | 221.43 | 246.19 | 233.64 | 222.00 | 220.00 | 204.76 | 183.81 | 198.75 | 235.48 | 203.61 |
| 2017 | 274.75 | 261.58 | 283.91 | 266.00 | 260.00 | 255.91 | 255.00 | 263.26 | 265.00 | 240.45 | 235.00 | 259.00 | 259.99 |
| 2018 | 289.29 | 295.00 | 319.55 | 341.19 | 336.82 | 335.00 | 340.00 | 321.74 | 300.26 | 303.26 | 324.00 | 325.00 | 319.26 |
| 2019 | 302.14 | 295.00 | 311.19 | 294.76 | 266.82 | 236.00 | 222.27 | 236.36 | 216.00 | 181.09 | 190.79 | 219.29 | 247.64 |
| 2020 | 249.29 | 239.21 | 235.00 | 201.67 | 210.50 | 215.00 | 207.27 | 205.00 | 239.29 | 245.00 | 252.89 | 320.45 | 235.05 |
| 2021 | 425.00 | 375.00 | 425.00 | 405.00 | 425.00 | 475.00 | 475.00 | 455.00 | 430.00 | 430.00 | 480.00 | 480.00 | 440.00 |
| 2022 | 410.00 | 410.00 | 535.00 | 515.00 | 440.00 | 390.00 | 360.00 | 330.00 | 305.00 | 295.00 | 275.00 | 295.00 | 380.00 |

*Source: American Metal Market (AMM)*

# IRON AND STEEL

**World Production of Iron Ore[3]**  In Thousands of Metric Tons (Gross Weight)

| Year | Australia | Brazil | Canada | China | India | Mauritania | Russia | South Africa | Sweden | Ukraine | United States | Venezuela | World Total |
|---|---|---|---|---|---|---|---|---|---|---|---|---|---|
| 2013 | 609,730 | 386,270 | 42,063 | 417,287 | 140,416 | 11,975 | 102,157 | 71,645 | 25,300 | 70,400 | 52,800 | 11,198 | 2,190,000 |
| 2014 | 739,682 | 411,183 | 43,173 | 438,860 | 138,000 | 13,306 | 102,019 | 80,759 | 25,700 | 68,300 | 56,100 | 11,256 | 2,370,000 |
| 2015 | 809,882 | 430,838 | 46,220 | 396,899 | 142,399 | 11,607 | 101,049 | 72,806 | 24,500 | 66,900 | 46,100 | 11,716 | 2,370,000 |
| 2016 | 858,026 | 421,358 | 46,731 | 365,573 | 184,501 | 13,268 | 101,097 | 66,456 | 26,900 | 62,876 | 41,800 | 12,000 | 2,370,000 |
| 2017 | 885,357 | 453,704 | 50,300 | 345,472 | 201,815 | 11,714 | 95,042 | 74,857 | 31,764 | 60,574 | 47,900 | 4,005 | 2,440,000 |
| 2018 | 907,819 | 460,000 | 52,387 | 334,790 | 204,091 | 10,711 | 96,063 | 74,264 | 35,774 | 60,549 | 49,500 | 2,474 | 2,470,000 |
| 2019 | 918,731 | 404,900 | 58,472 | 351,000 | 238,144 | 12,200 | 97,531 | 72,430 | 35,700 | 63,205 | 46,900 | 1,096 | 2,450,000 |
| 2020 | 912,000 | 388,000 | 60,100 | 360,000 | 204,000 | 12,200 | 100,000 | 55,600 | 35,800 | 78,800 | 38,100 | ---- | 2,470,000 |
| 2021[1] | 912,000 | 431,000 | 57,500 | 394,000 | 273,000 | 12,800 | 96,000 | 73,100 | 40,200 | 83,800 | 47,500 | ---- | 2,680,000 |
| 2022[2] | 880,000 | 410,000 | 58,000 | 380,000 | 290,000 | 13,000 | 90,000 | 76,000 | 39,000 | 76,000 | 46,000 | ---- | 2,600,000 |

[1] Preliminary.  [2] Estimate.  [3] Iron ore, iron ore concentrates and iron ore agglomerates.  Source: U.S. Geological Survey (USGS)

**Salient Statistics of Iron Ore[3] in the United States**  In Thousands of Metric Tons

| Year | Net Import Reliance As a % of Apparent Consump | Production Total | Production Lake Superior | Production Other Regions | Shipments | Value Million $ (at Mine) | Average Value $ at Mine Per Ton | Stock, Dec. 31 Mines | Stock, Dec. 31 Consuming Plants | Stock, Dec. 31 Lake Erie Docks | Imports | Exports | Consumption | Total |
|---|---|---|---|---|---|---|---|---|---|---|---|---|---|---|
| 2013 | E | 52,800 | ---- | ---- | 53,400 | 4,610.0 | 87.42 | 2,350 | ---- | ---- | 3,200 | 11,000 | 47,100 | 426.0 |
| 2014 | E | 56,100 | ---- | ---- | 55,000 | 4,730.0 | 84.43 | 4,460 | ---- | ---- | 5,140 | 12,400 | 46,700 | 676.0 |
| 2015 | E | 46,100 | ---- | ---- | 43,500 | 3,750.0 | 81.19 | 4,760 | ---- | ---- | 4,550 | 7,500 | 42,100 | 455.0 |
| 2016 | E | 41,800 | ---- | ---- | 46,600 | 3,050.0 | 73.11 | 2,990 | ---- | ---- | 3,010 | 8,710 | 37,900 | 241.0 |
| 2017 | E | 47,900 | ---- | ---- | 46,900 | 3,760.0 | 78.54 | 3,930 | ---- | ---- | 3,720 | 10,600 | 40,100 | 357.0 |
| 2018 | E | 49,500 | ---- | ---- | 50,400 | 4,600.0 | 93.00 | 3,100 | ---- | ---- | 3,790 | 12,700 | 41,400 | 388.0 |
| 2019 | E | 46,900 | ---- | ---- | 47,000 | 4,370.0 | 92.94 | 3,470 | ---- | ---- | 3,980 | 11,400 | 39,100 | 499.0 |
| 2020 | E | 38,100 | ---- | ---- | 38,000 | 3,480.0 | 91.27 | 3,290 | ---- | ---- | 3,240 | 10,400 | 31,100 | 389.0 |
| 2021[1] | E | 47,500 | ---- | ---- | 43,400 | | 141.75 | 3,170 | ---- | ---- | 3,740 | 14,300 | 36,800 | |
| 2022[2] | E | 46,000 | ---- | ---- | 46,000 | | 114.00 | 2,800 | ---- | ---- | 3,200 | 9,400 | 40,000 | |

[1] Preliminary.  [2] Estimate.  [3] Usable iron ore exclusive of ore containing 5% or more manganese and includes byproduct ore.
NA = Not available.  Source: U.S. Geological Survey (USGS)

**U.S. Imports (for Consumption) of Iron Ore[2]**  In Thousands of Metric Tons

| Year | Australia | Brazil | Canada | Chile | Mauritania | Peru | Sweden | Venezuela | Total |
|---|---|---|---|---|---|---|---|---|---|
| 2011 | ---- | 562 | 3,910 | 165 | ---- | 14 | 81 | 279 | 5,270 |
| 2012 | ---- | 739 | 3,820 | 104 | ---- | 44 | 72 | 75 | 5,160 |
| 2013 | ---- | 630 | 2,090 | 152 | ---- | 12 | 49 | ---- | 3,250 |
| 2014 | ---- | 1,730 | 2,860 | ---- | ---- | 35 | 154 | ---- | 5,100 |
| 2015 | ---- | 2,050 | 2,040 | 1 | ---- | 22 | 85 | 25 | 4,550 |
| 2016 | [3] | 1,760 | 557 | 62 | ---- | 66 | 350 | 28 | 3,010 |
| 2017 | 24 | 2,040 | 793 | 283 | ---- | 31 | 363 | ---- | 3,710 |
| 2018 | 42 | 2,370 | 853 | 96 | 6 | 31 | 163 | 16 | 3,810 |
| 2019 | 42 | 2,190 | 838 | 117 | ---- | ---- | 122 | ---- | 5,100 |
| 2020[1] | 24 | 1,510 | 775 | 81 | ---- | ---- | 463 | ---- | |

[1] Preliminary.  [2] Including agglomerates.  [3] Less than 1/2 unit.  Source: U.S. Geological Survey (USGS)

**Iron Ore Stocks in the United States, at End of Month**  In Thousands of Metric Tons

| Year | Jan. | Feb. | Mar. | Apr. | May | June | July | Aug. | Sept. | Oct. | Nov. | Dec. |
|---|---|---|---|---|---|---|---|---|---|---|---|---|
| 2013 | 3,290 | 6,580 | 8,960 | 7,830 | 6,350 | 5,390 | 4,130 | 3,320 | 2,770 | 2,110 | 2,470 | 3,690 |
| 2014 | 6,530 | 9,240 | 12,400 | 13,600 | 12,500 | 11,300 | 9,770 | 8,190 | 7,320 | 6,600 | 6,290 | 5,430 |
| 2015 | 6,640 | 10,600 | 14,500 | 14,800 | 13,100 | 11,500 | 9,740 | 8,040 | 7,460 | 7,070 | 7,550 | 7,490 |
| 2016 | 8,940 | 11,800 | 13,600 | 12,100 | 11,000 | 10,200 | 9,470 | 8,300 | 7,630 | 7,170 | 6,500 | 6,050 |
| 2017 | 6,730 | 9,970 | 12,400 | 12,200 | 11,200 | 10,100 | 9,080 | 7,670 | 6,470 | 6,210 | 6,300 | 6,120 |
| 2018 | 8,290 | 12,000 | 14,700 | 14,300 | 13,000 | 12,200 | 10,900 | 9,520 | 8,270 | 7,480 | 4,120 | 3,100 |
| 2019 | 4,390 | 7,490 | 9,910 | 9,330 | 9,150 | 8,020 | 6,850 | 5,550 | 4,460 | 3,800 | 3,230 | 2,720 |
| 2020 | 4,790 | 8,100 | 10,700 | 9,430 | 6,900 | 4,980 | 3,760 | 4,410 | 4,470 | 4,150 | 3,770 | 3,530 |
| 2021 | 5,110 | 9,110 | 12,000 | 11,300 | 9,980 | 8,470 | 6,910 | 5,120 | 3,520 | 2,740 | 2,170 | 1,340 |
| 2022[1] | 3,170 | 6,100 | 7,860 | 7,330 | 6,300 | 5,040 | 3,540 | 3,150 | 2,430 | 2,440 | 2,980 | |

[1] Preliminary.  Source: U.S. Geological Survey (USGS)

# Lard

Lard is the layer of fat found along the back and underneath the skin of a hog. The hog's fat is purified by washing it with water, melting it under constant heat, and straining it several times. Lard is an important byproduct of the meatpacking industry. It is valued highly as cooking oil because there is very little smoke when it is heated. However, demand for lard in cooking is declining because of the trend toward healthier eating. Lard is also used for medicinal purposes such as ointments, plasters, liniments, and occasionally as a laxative for children. Lard production is directly proportional to commercial hog production, meaning the largest producers of hogs are the largest producers of lard.

**Supply** – World production of lard in the 2021/22 marketing year rose by +2.5% yr/yr to 8.759 million metric tons, a new record high. The world's largest lard producers were China with 41.7% of world production, the U.S with 8.1%, Brazil with 6.6%, Germany with 5.7%, Spain with 5.2%, Russia with 4.9%, and Poland with 2.7%. U.S. production of lard in 2021/22 fell by -2.2% yr/yr to 1.561 billion pounds.

**Trade** – U.S. exports of lard in 2021/22 fell by -67.1% to 58.9 million pounds and accounted for only 3.8% of U.S. production.

## World Production of Lard    In Thousands of Metric Tons

| Year | Brazil | Canada | China | France | Germany | Italy | Japan | Poland | Romania | Spain | United States | Ex-USSR | World Total |
|---|---|---|---|---|---|---|---|---|---|---|---|---|---|
| 2012-13 | 439.6 | 131.9 | 3,670.5 | 132.1 | 562.3 | 213.0 | 51.3 | 213.9 | 73.7 | 301.3 | 598.7 | 499.2 | 8,356.7 |
| 2013-14 | 443.5 | 131.3 | 3,745.1 | 132.1 | 558.0 | 186.3 | 51.0 | 231.5 | 70.5 | 310.7 | 594.3 | 514.5 | 8,434.5 |
| 2014-15 | 444.3 | 132.5 | 3,623.4 | 133.5 | 570.4 | 190.9 | 49.0 | 243.7 | 72.1 | 334.4 | 625.1 | 528.3 | 8,435.7 |
| 2015-16 | 470.8 | 136.9 | 3,599.9 | 135.6 | 566.1 | 198.4 | 51.0 | 252.6 | 68.7 | 356.0 | 639.9 | 557.1 | 8,567.3 |
| 2016-17 | 488.1 | 165.7 | 3,584.4 | 143.2 | 565.6 | 193.7 | 50.5 | 236.2 | 53.1 | 366.0 | 657.6 | 366.9 | 8,389.9 |
| 2017-18 | 504.4 | 164.7 | 3,678.6 | 148.9 | 547.1 | 193.4 | 51.2 | 248.6 | 52.0 | 393.5 | 674.3 | 380.6 | 8,594.0 |
| 2018-19 | 518.0 | 165.5 | 3,170.3 | 149.3 | 534.6 | 188.4 | 51.6 | 242.3 | 49.0 | 403.0 | 703.0 | 394.3 | 8,136.0 |
| 2019-20[1] | 536.1 | 171.2 | 2,601.5 | 150.1 | 526.6 | 167.9 | 52.0 | 233.9 | 46.5 | 426.7 | 730.8 | 419.4 | 7,634.1 |
| 2020-21[2] | 561.4 | 170.8 | 3,432.4 | 150.0 | 511.5 | 173.7 | 53.0 | 240.0 | 46.9 | 450.0 | 724.0 | 423.8 | 8,547.1 |
| 2021-22[3] | 577.3 | 168.8 | 3,649.8 | 148.7 | 495.1 | 170.2 | 52.0 | 235.9 | 44.5 | 454.3 | 708.1 | 428.6 | 8,759.9 |

[1] Preliminary.  [2] Estimate.  [3] Forecast.    Source: The Oil World

## Supply and Distribution of Lard in the United States    In Millions of Pounds

| | ------- Supply ------- | | | ------- Disappearance ------- | | | | | | |
|---|---|---|---|---|---|---|---|---|---|---|
| Year | Production | Stocks Oct. 1 | Total Supply | Domestic | Baking or Frying Fats | Margarine[3] | Exports | Total Disappearance | Direct Use | Per Capita (Lbs.) |
| 2012-13 | 1,319.9 | 20.0 | 1,339.9 | 816.4 | W | W | 64.8 | 881.2 | NA | NA |
| 2013-14 | 1,310.2 | 20.0 | 1,330.2 | 821.1 | W | W | 47.2 | 868.3 | NA | NA |
| 2014-15 | 1,378.1 | 20.0 | 1,398.1 | 896.9 | W | W | 43.6 | 940.5 | NA | NA |
| 2015-16 | 1,410.7 | 9.0 | 1,419.7 | 901.4 | W | W | 42.1 | 943.5 | NA | NA |
| 2016-17 | 1,449.7 | 8.0 | 1,457.7 | 934.9 | W | W | 37.9 | 972.8 | NA | NA |
| 2017-18 | 1,486.6 | 7.0 | 1,493.6 | 960.5 | W | W | 37.1 | 997.6 | NA | NA |
| 2018-19 | 1,549.8 | 11.0 | 1,560.8 | 1,005.6 | W | W | 49.6 | 1,055.3 | NA | NA |
| 2019-20 | 1,611.1 | 5.9 | 1,617.1 | 1,031.9 | W | W | 39.9 | 1,071.8 | NA | NA |
| 2020-21[1] | 1,596.1 | 8.6 | 1,604.7 | 880.5 | W | W | 179.3 | 1,059.8 | NA | NA |
| 2021-22[2] | 1,561.1 | 5.0 | 1,566.0 | 987.3 | W | W | 58.9 | 1,046.2 | NA | NA |

[1] Preliminary.  [2] Forecast.  [3] Includes edible tallow.    W = Withheld.
Source: Economic Research Service, U.S. Department of Agriculture (ERS-USDA)

## Average Wholesale Price of Lard--Loose, Tank Cars, in Chicago    In Cents Per Pound

| Year | Jan. | Feb. | Mar. | Apr. | May | June | July | Aug. | Sept. | Oct. | Nov. | Dec. | Average |
|---|---|---|---|---|---|---|---|---|---|---|---|---|---|
| 2013 | 52.45 | 45.56 | NA | 43.50 | 44.50 | 48.50 | 53.25 | 56.89 | 64.78 | 43.00 | 48.00 | 41.50 | 49.27 |
| 2014 | 33.00 | 38.00 | 40.67 | 53.00 | NA | 45.00 | NA | 46.50 | 50.67 | 48.00 | 42.81 | 35.91 | 43.36 |
| 2015 | 29.50 | 28.00 | NA | 26.64 | 28.00 | NA | 31.00 | 31.00 | NA | 34.23 | 35.50 | 28.80 | 30.30 |
| 2016 | 24.00 | NA | 29.00 | 33.00 | NA | NA | NA | 36.53 | 36.75 | 34.00 | NA | 31.00 | 32.04 |
| 2017 | 30.10 | NA | NA | NA | NA | 34.50 | NA | NA | 35.75 | 36.00 | 38.17 | 37.00 | 35.25 |
| 2018 | 32.08 | 32.20 | NA | NA | NA | 32.50 | NA | 32.38 | 32.93 | 33.00 | 34.33 | 31.00 | 32.55 |
| 2019 | NA | NA | NA | NA | NA | NA | NA | NA | NA | NA | NA | NA | NA |
| 2020 | NA | NA | NA | 32.00 | 35.50 | 36.50 | NA | 39.00 | NA | NA | 41.00 | NA | 36.80 |
| 2021 | NA | NA | 55.00 | NA | 58.00 | 68.00 | NA | 72.33 | NA | NA | NA | NA | 63.33 |
| 2022 | NA | 82.00 | NA | NA | NA | NA | NA | NA | NA | 88.00 | NA | NA | 85.00 |

Source: Economic Research Service, U.S. Department of Agriculture (ERS-USDA)

# Lead

Lead (atomic symbol Pb) is a dense, toxic, bluish-gray metallic element, and is the heaviest stable element. Lead was one of the first known metals. The ancients used lead in face powders, rouges, mascaras, paints, condiments, wine preservatives, and water supply plumbing. The Romans were slowly poisoned by lead because of its diverse daily usage.

Lead is usually found in ore with zinc, silver, and most often copper. The most common lead ore is galena, containing 86.6% lead. Cerussite and angleside are other common varieties of lead. More than half of the lead currently used comes from recycling.

Lead is used in building construction, bullets and shot, tank and pipe lining, storage batteries, and electric cable sheathing. Lead is used extensively as a protective shielding for radioactive material (e.g., X-ray apparatus) because of its high density and nuclear properties. Lead is also part of solder, pewter, and fusible alloys.

Lead futures and options trade at the London Metal Exchange (LME). The LME lead futures contract calls for the delivery of 25 metric tons of at least 99.970% purity lead ingots (pigs). The contract is priced in U.S. dollars per metric ton. Lead first started trading on the LME in 1903.

**Prices** – The average price of pig lead among U.S. producers in 2022 rose +2.6% yr/yr to $1.1508 per pound, below the record high of $1.2474 per pound in 2007.

**Supply** – World smelter production of lead (both primary and secondary) in 2019 remained unchanged yr/yr to 11.600 million metric tons, for a new record high.

The world's largest smelter producers of lead (both primary and secondary) in 2019 were China with 42.8% of world production, followed by the U.S. with 10.2%, India with 7.9%, South Korea with 6.8%, Mexico with 3.9%, the UK and Germany with 2.7%.

U.S. mine production of recoverable lead in 2022 fell by -8.3% yr/yr to 263,000 metric tons. Missouri was responsible for 94% of U.S. production in 2009, with the remainder produced mainly by Idaho and Montana. Lead recovered from scrap in the U.S. (secondary production) fell by -13.0% yr/yr in 2021 to 1.002 million metric tons, below the 2008 record high of 1.220 million metric tons. The value of U.S. secondary lead production in 2019 fell by -9.1% yr/yr to $2.590 billion, well below the 2007 record high of $3.220 billion.

**Demand** – U.S. lead consumption in 2021 rose by +5.0% yr/yr to 1.519 million metric tons, below the 2017 record high of 1.760 million metric tons.

**Trade** – U.S. imports of lead pigs and bars in 2019 fell by -9.4% yr/yr to 406,000 metric tons. U.S. lead exports in 2019 were comprised of ore concentrate (259,000 metric tons), unwrought lead (25,500 metric tons), scrap (14,600 metric tons), and wrought lead (6,600 metric tons).

## World Smelter (Primary and Secondary) Production of Lead   In Thousands of Metric Tons

| Year | Australia[3] | Belgium[4] | Canada[3] | China[2] | France | Germany | Italy | Japan | Mexico[3] | Spain | United Kingdom[3] | United States | World Total |
|---|---|---|---|---|---|---|---|---|---|---|---|---|---|
| 2011 | 213.0 | 282.6 | 4,600.0 | 429.0 | 419.0 | 149.5 | 218.0 | 416.9 | 317.7 | 177.0 | 269.0 | 1,248 | 10,300 |
| 2012 | 210.0 | 299.2 | 4,590.0 | 424.0 | 460.0 | 138.4 | 209.0 | 460.0 | 384.0 | 160.0 | 311.9 | 1,261 | 10,600 |
| 2013 | 232.5 | 281.8 | 4,940.0 | 400.0 | 463.0 | 180.0 | 208.1 | 427.7 | 371.0 | 157.0 | 329.2 | 1,274 | 10,800 |
| 2014 | 192.4 | 281.5 | 4,740.0 | 408.0 | 477.0 | 209.6 | 202.7 | 639.0 | 363.5 | 166.0 | 267.0 | 1,060 | 10,600 |
| 2015 | 227.3 | 268.9 | 4,422.0 | 378.0 | 501.0 | 209.9 | 194.7 | 641.0 | 493.8 | 165.0 | 307.0 | 1,050 | 10,500 |
| 2016 | 223.8 | 274.2 | 4,680.0 | 339.0 | 689.0 | 187.2 | 198.7 | 831.0 | 324.7 | 169.0 | 328.0 | 1,110 | 11,100 |
| 2017 | 211.3 | 149.5 | 4,698.0 | 354.0 | 812.1 | 173.7 | 199.4 | 803.0 | 322.5 | 188.0 | 325.0 | 1,140 | 11,300 |
| 2018[1] | 188.5 | 129.5 | 4,943.0 | 315.0 | 883.1 | 167.5 | 196.2 | 800.0 | 434.0 | 190.0 | 318.0 | 1,170 | 11,600 |
| 2019[2] | 125.0 | 147.4 | 4,959.0 | 315.0 | 922.0 | 158.9 | 198.1 | 794.0 | 447.0 | 188.0 | 318.0 | 1,180 | 11,600 |

[1] Preliminary.   [2] Estimate.   [3] Refinded & bullion.   [4] Includes scrap.   Source: U.S. Geological Survey (USGS)

## Consumption of Lead in the United States, by Products   In Metric Tons

| Year | Ammunition: Shot and Bullets | Bearing Metals | Brass and Bronze | Cable Covering | Calking Lead | Casting Metals | Pipes, Traps & Bends[2] | Sheet Lead | Solder | Storage Batteries: Total | Other Metal Products[3] | Other Oxides[4] | Total U.S. Consumption |
|---|---|---|---|---|---|---|---|---|---|---|---|---|---|
| 2011 | 75,100 | 1,150 | 1,620 | W | W | 16,000 | 6,110 | 7,170 | 6,170 | 1,250,000 | 23,100 | 9,760 | 1,410,000 |
| 2012 | 73,900 | 1,090 | 1,120 | W | W | 16,700 | 6,240 | 7,390 | 6,280 | 1,190,000 | 18,500 | 9,740 | 1,350,000 |
| 2013 | 84,800 | 1,110 | 1,420 | W | W | 20,400 | 7,030 | 4,870 | 8,200 | 1,200,000 | 177 | 9,740 | 1,390,000 |
| 2014 | 85,300 | 1,150 | 2,990 | W | W | 19,100 | 6,900 | 6,090 | 7,380 | 1,320,000 | 33,000 | 9,740 | 1,510,000 |
| 2015 | 78,400 | 1,090 | 1,580 | W | W | 14,200 | 7,060 | 9,020 | 6,490 | 1,770,000 | 31,100 | 11,500 | 1,960,000 |
| 2016 | 69,800 | 1,060 | 1,580 | W | W | 15,000 | 7,160 | 6,510 | 6,460 | 1,810,000 | 149 | 11,700 | 1,980,000 |
| 2017 | 67,000 | 1,010 | 1,600 | W | W | 12,700 | 6,560 | 5,110 | 6,590 | 1,940,000 | W | 11,100 | 2,110,000 |
| 2018 | 68,700 | 1,010 | 1,710 | 1,170 | W | 14,000 | 6,590 | 7,070 | 6,720 | 1,900,000 | 109 | 10,900 | 2,040,000 |
| 2019[1] | 71,900 | 3,220 | 1,630 | 1,920 | W | 13,300 | 6,580 | 6,520 | 7,030 | 2,010,000 | 60 | 10,100 | 2,150,000 |

[1] Preliminary.   [2] Including building.   [3] Including terne metal, type metal, and lead consumed in foil, collapsible tubes, annealing, plating, galvanizing and fishing weights.   [4] Includes paints, glass and ceramic products, and other pigments and chemicals.   W = Withheld.
Source: U.S. Geological Survey (USGS)

# LEAD

## Salient Statistics of Lead in the United States    In Thousands of Metric Tons

| Year | Net Import Reliance as a % of Apparent Consump | Production of Refined Lead From Domestic Ores[3] | Production of Refined Lead From Foreign Ores[3] | Total Primary | Total Value of Refined Million $ | Secondary Lead Recovered As Soft Lead | Secondary Lead Recovered In Antimonial Lead | Secondary Lead Recovered In Other Alloys | Total | Total Value of Secondary Million USD | Stocks, Dec. 31 Primary | Stocks, Dec. 31 Consumer[4] | Average Price Cents Per Pound New York | Average Price Cents Per Pound London |
|---|---|---|---|---|---|---|---|---|---|---|---|---|---|---|
| 2013 | 26 | 114 | W | 114 | ---- | 860 | 282 | ---- | 1,160 | 2,910 | W | 61.1 | ---- | 97.15 |
| 2014 | 35 | ---- | W | ---- | ---- | 786 | 224 | 8.8 | 1,060 | 2,640 | W | 56.4 | ---- | 95.04 |
| 2015 | 31 | ---- | W | ---- | ---- | 827 | 214 | 4.8 | 1,050 | 2,110 | W | 60.1 | ---- | 81.02 |
| 2016 | 33 | ---- | W | ---- | ---- | 882 | 225 | 5.7 | 1,110 | 2,320 | W | 60.3 | ---- | 84.84 |
| 2017 | 36 | ---- | W | ---- | ---- | 920 | W | W | 1,140 | 2,870 | W | 64.4 | ---- | 105.10 |
| 2018 | 30 | ---- | W | ---- | ---- | 957 | W | W | 1,170 | 2,850 | W | 66.8 | ---- | 101.80 |
| 2019 | 31 | ---- | W | ---- | ---- | 967 | W | W | 1,180 | 2,590 | W | 69.5 | ---- | 90.60 |
| 2020 | 26 | ---- | W | ---- | ---- | | | | 1,030 | | W | | ---- | 82.70 |
| 2021[1] | 38 | ---- | W | ---- | ---- | | | | 975 | | W | | ---- | 100.00 |
| 2022[2] | 42 | ---- | W | ---- | ---- | | | | 950 | | W | | ---- | |

[1] Preliminary.   [2] Estimate.   [3] And base bullion.   [4] Also at secondary smelters.   W = Withheld.   E = Net exporter.
*Source: U.S. Geological Survey (USGS)*

## U.S. Foreign Trade of Lead    In Thousands of Metric Tons

| Year | Exports Ore Concentrate | Exports Unwrought Lead[3] | Exports Wrought Lead[4] | Exports Ash & Residues[5] | Imports for Consumption Ores, Flue Dust or Fume & Mattes | Imports for Consumption Base Bullion | Imports for Consumption Pigs & Bars | Imports for Consumption Reclaimed Scrap, Etc. | Value Million $ | General Import From: Ore, Flue, Dust & Matte Australia | General Import From: Canada | General Import From: Peru | General Import From: Pigs & Bars Canada | General Import From: Mexico | General Import From: Peru |
|---|---|---|---|---|---|---|---|---|---|---|---|---|---|---|---|
| 2010 | 299.0 | 77.7 | 5.6 | 43.5 | ---- | ---- | 0.6 | 271.0 | 3.7 | 575.9 | ---- | ---- | ---- | 237.0 | 29.4 | ---- |
| 2011 | 223.0 | 40.1 | 7.0 | 31.1 | ---- | ---- | 0.4 | 313.0 | 2.4 | 718.4 | ---- | ---- | ---- | 250.0 | 56.0 | 0.1 |
| 2012 | 214.0 | 47.0 | 6.3 | 25.9 | ---- | 1.5 | 1.0 | 349.0 | 16.8 | 730.4 | ---- | ---- | ---- | 240.0 | 56.1 | 0.0 |
| 2013 | 215.0 | 41.6 | 6.6 | 34.9 | ---- | 0.0 | 1.9 | 500.0 | 15.6 | 1,060.4 | ---- | ---- | ---- | 257.0 | 111.0 | 39.6 |
| 2014 | 356.0 | 55.3 | 5.0 | 36.4 | ---- | | 1.1 | 593.0 | 11.4 | 1,243.8 | ---- | ---- | ---- | 264.0 | 120.0 | 49.7 |
| 2015 | 350.0 | 50.1 | 2.9 | 29.1 | ---- | | 0.3 | 417.0 | 3.5 | 771.2 | ---- | ---- | ---- | 162.0 | 105.0 | ---- |
| 2016 | 341.0 | 42.7 | 5.9 | 16.7 | ---- | | 0.2 | 416.0 | 1.5 | 841.6 | ---- | ---- | ---- | 176.0 | 71.8 | 1.4 |
| 2017 | 269.0 | 23.9 | 7.6 | 22.7 | ---- | | ---- | 538.0 | 4.2 | 1,239.9 | ---- | ---- | ---- | 160.0 | 103.0 | 3.9 |
| 2018[1] | 251.0 | 66.9 | 6.0 | 12.0 | ---- | | 0.9 | 448.0 | 1.7 | 1,034.5 | ---- | ---- | ---- | 148.0 | 107.0 | 3.4 |
| 2019[2] | 259.0 | 25.5 | 6.6 | 14.6 | ---- | | 1.9 | 406.0 | 2.3 | 840.4 | ---- | ---- | ---- | 159.0 | 96.7 | 3.0 |

[1] Preliminary.   [2] Estimate.   [3] And lead alloys.   [4] Blocks, pigs, etc.   [5] Less than 1/2 unit.   *Source: U.S. Geological Survey (USGS)*

## Annual Mine Production of Recoverable Lead in the United States    In Metric Tons

| Year | Idaho | Missouri | Montana | Total |
|---|---|---|---|---|
| 2013 | ---- | ---- | ---- | 331,000 |
| 2014 | ---- | ---- | ---- | 367,000 |
| 2015 | ---- | ---- | ---- | 360,000 |
| 2016 | ---- | ---- | ---- | 336,000 |
| 2017 | ---- | ---- | ---- | 311,000 |
| 2018 | ---- | ---- | ---- | 271,000 |
| 2019 | ---- | ---- | ---- | 266,800 |
| 2020 | ---- | ---- | ---- | 291,200 |
| 2021[1] | ---- | ---- | ---- | 287,200 |
| 2022[2] | ---- | ---- | ---- | 264,000 |

[1] Preliminary.   [2] Estimate.   W = Withheld, included in Total.   *Source: U.S. Geological Survey (USGS)*

## Mine Production of Recoverable Lead in the United States    In Metric Tons

| Year | Jan. | Feb. | Mar. | Apr. | May | June | July | Aug. | Sept. | Oct. | Nov. | Dec. | Total |
|---|---|---|---|---|---|---|---|---|---|---|---|---|---|
| 2013 | 27,000 | 25,717 | 26,000 | 28,600 | 28,900 | 28,000 | 28,500 | 28,700 | 29,600 | 27,200 | 25,700 | 28,600 | 331,000 |
| 2014 | 30,300 | 26,600 | 28,800 | 31,300 | 32,800 | 29,600 | 30,500 | 30,389 | 31,200 | 32,000 | 32,700 | 34,500 | 367,000 |
| 2015 | 28,200 | 30,100 | 35,700 | 32,100 | 31,300 | 28,900 | 31,200 | 31,500 | 26,100 | 27,100 | 27,200 | 27,400 | 360,000 |
| 2016 | 29,100 | 26,000 | 27,900 | 30,100 | 27,000 | 28,400 | 24,800 | 30,400 | 28,400 | 28,000 | 22,000 | 20,000 | 336,000 |
| 2017 | 25,400 | 25,500 | 31,300 | 27,900 | 24,400 | 25,300 | 23,100 | 25,400 | 21,000 | 24,900 | 27,500 | 21,900 | 311,000 |
| 2018 | 21,700 | 17,400 | 20,700 | 22,200 | 23,000 | 23,400 | 24,000 | W | W | W | W | W | 271,000 |
| 2019 | 22,800 | 19,800 | 18,100 | 24,600 | 26,700 | 23,800 | 22,100 | 24,700 | 24,000 | 17,200 | 21,300 | 21,700 | 266,800 |
| 2020 | 22,800 | 22,900 | 23,100 | 19,900 | 23,500 | 24,600 | 26,100 | 28,700 | 23,700 | 24,000 | 22,700 | 29,200 | 291,200 |
| 2021 | 25,600 | 22,000 | 25,000 | 24,000 | 23,800 | 25,800 | 23,500 | 25,700 | 23,700 | 26,400 | 18,000 | 23,700 | 287,200 |
| 2022[1] | 20,800 | 22,000 | 25,700 | 26,400 | 24,100 | 19,800 | 22,600 | 20,800 | 20,000 | 21,200 | 18,400 | 22,200 | 264,000 |

[1] Preliminary.   W = Withheld to avoid disclosing company proprietary data.   *Source: U.S. Geological Survey (USGS)*

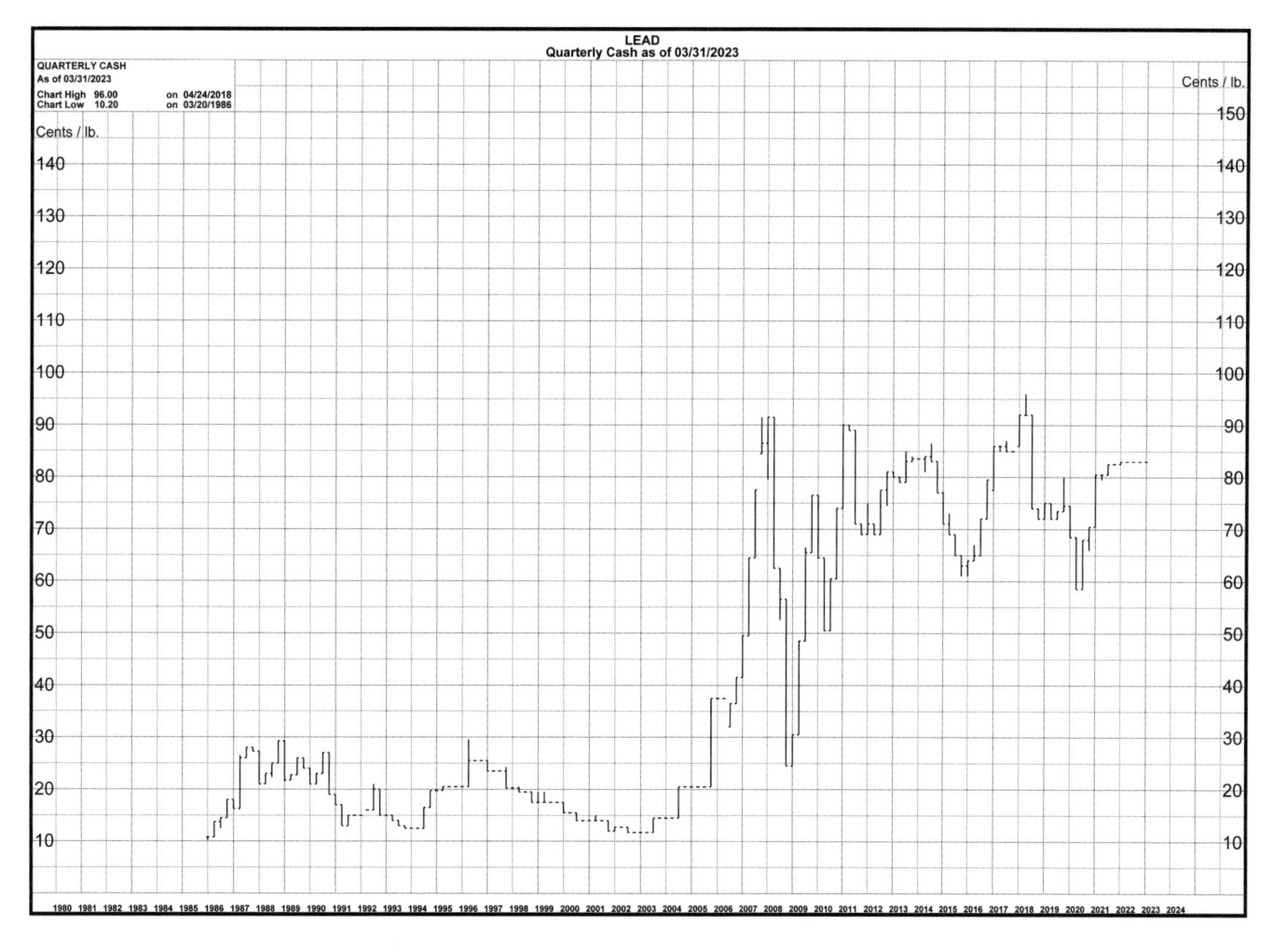

# LEAD

## Average Price of Pig Lead, U.S. Primary Producers (Common Corroding)[1]   In Cents Per Pound

| Year | Jan. | Feb. | Mar. | Apr. | May | June | July | Aug. | Sept. | Oct. | Nov. | Dec. | Average |
|---|---|---|---|---|---|---|---|---|---|---|---|---|---|
| 2013 | 120.19 | 121.68 | 112.79 | 106.17 | 105.82 | 109.38 | 106.18 | 111.56 | 107.53 | 108.72 | 107.97 | 109.40 | 110.62 |
| 2014 | 110.40 | 108.69 | 106.23 | 107.71 | 107.99 | 108.35 | 112.31 | 114.44 | 108.97 | 105.16 | 104.11 | 100.29 | 107.89 |
| 2015 | 95.45 | 94.25 | 93.41 | 102.60 | 103.12 | 94.25 | 92.01 | 93.72 | 91.66 | 88.54 | 84.72 | 89.21 | 93.58 |
| 2016 | 86.75 | 92.12 | 93.74 | 90.37 | 89.89 | 89.70 | 95.09 | 95.44 | 100.00 | 103.71 | 109.36 | 111.81 | 96.50 |
| 2017 | 111.53 | 114.71 | 112.58 | 110.76 | 106.56 | 106.67 | 112.97 | 116.68 | 117.90 | 123.74 | 121.73 | 123.64 | 114.96 |
| 2018 | 127.40 | 126.93 | 118.69 | 116.99 | 116.98 | 120.64 | 109.97 | 103.62 | 101.77 | 99.98 | 97.87 | 99.13 | 111.66 |
| 2019 | 100.38 | 103.54 | 103.14 | 98.27 | 92.49 | 95.74 | 99.68 | 102.70 | 103.98 | 108.61 | 102.06 | 95.79 | 100.53 |
| 2020 | 96.89 | 94.35 | 88.10 | 83.78 | 81.89 | 87.40 | 91.00 | 96.85 | 94.32 | 90.19 | 96.04 | 101.42 | 91.85 |
| 2021 | 102.42 | 106.75 | 102.53 | 105.85 | 113.98 | 114.74 | 122.16 | 126.70 | 118.58 | 122.54 | 123.06 | 121.60 | 115.08 |
| 2022 | 124.99 | 123.13 | 126.01 | 128.25 | 116.93 | 113.87 | 109.63 | 115.93 | 106.92 | 112.09 | 117.00 | 121.44 | 118.02 |

[1] New York Delivery.   Source: American Metal Market

## Salient Statistics of Recycling Lead in the United States

| Year | New Scrap[1] | Old Scrap[2] | Recycled Metal[3] | Apparent Supply | Percent Recycled | New Scrap[1] | Old Scrap[2] | Recycled Metal[3] | Apparent Supply |
|---|---|---|---|---|---|---|---|---|---|
| | ------------------------- In Metric Tons ------------------------- | | | | | ---------------- Value in Thousands of Dollars ---------------- | | | |
| 2011 | 21,600 | 1,110,000 | 1,130,000 | 1,520,000 | 73.0 | 58,000 | 2,980,000 | 3,040,000 | 4,080,000 |
| 2012 | 19,200 | 1,090,000 | 1,110,000 | 1,490,000 | 74.0 | 48,200 | 2,740,000 | 2,790,000 | 3,760,000 |
| 2013 | 19,200 | 1,140,000 | 1,160,000 | 1,440,000 | 80.0 | 46,600 | 3,760,000 | 3,800,000 | 3,870,000 |
| 2014 | 16,900 | 1,010,000 | 1,020,000 | 1,470,000 | 69.0 | 39,500 | 2,350,000 | 2,390,000 | 3,650,000 |
| 2015 | 16,900 | 989,000 | 1,010,000 | 1,410,000 | 71.0 | 34,000 | 1,990,000 | 2,020,000 | 2,830,000 |
| 2016 | 19,200 | 1,090,000 | 1,110,000 | 1,480,000 | 75.0 | 39,900 | 2,280,000 | 2,320,000 | 3,080,000 |
| 2017 | 20,000 | 1,120,000 | 1,140,000 | 1,650,000 | 69.0 | 50,600 | 2,820,000 | 2,870,000 | 4,170,000 |
| 2018 | 20,900 | 1,150,000 | 1,170,000 | 1,550,000 | 75.0 | 51,100 | 2,800,000 | 2,850,000 | 3,780,000 |
| 2019 | 20,100 | 1,160,000 | 1,180,000 | 1,560,000 | 76.0 | 44,300 | 2,550,000 | 2,590,000 | 3,430,000 |
| 2020 | 15,000 | 1,020,000 | 1,030,000 | 1,330,000 | 78.0 | 30,200 | 2,050,000 | 2,080,000 | 2,680,000 |

[1] Scrap that results from the manufacturing process.   [2] Scrap that results from consumer products.   [3] Metal recovered from new plus old scrap.
Source: U.S. Geological Survey (USGS)

# LEAD

## Total[2] Lead Consumption in the United States   In Metric Tons

| Year | Jan. | Feb. | Mar. | Apr. | May | June | July | Aug. | Sept. | Oct. | Nov. | Dec. | Total |
|---|---|---|---|---|---|---|---|---|---|---|---|---|---|
| 2013 | 146,000 | 123,000 | 118,000 | 117,000 | 117,000 | 117,000 | 116,000 | 118,000 | 117,000 | 119,000 | 115,000 | 134,000 | 1,750,000 |
| 2014 | 159,000 | 159,000 | 148,000 | 153,000 | 148,000 | 146,000 | 131,000 | 155,309 | 128,000 | 134,000 | 131,000 | 138,000 | 1,670,000 |
| 2015 | 132,000 | 121,000 | 135,000 | 151,000 | 130,000 | 135,000 | 128,000 | 125,000 | 121,000 | 145,000 | 134,000 | 129,000 | 1,590,000 |
| 2016 | 97,300 | 120,000 | 136,000 | 133,000 | 128,000 | 133,000 | 134,000 | 125,000 | 119,000 | 129,000 | 149,000 | 153,000 | 1,490,000 |
| 2017 | 146,000 | 157,000 | 167,000 | 156,000 | 171,000 | 125,000 | 147,000 | 128,000 | 147,000 | 130,000 | 129,000 | 120,000 | 1,760,000 |
| 2018 | 131,000 | 154,000 | 161,000 | 139,000 | 129,000 | 144,000 | 127,000 | 128,000 | 144,000 | 121,000 | 126,000 | 128,000 | 1,630,000 |
| 2019 | 139,000 | 130,000 | 133,000 | 149,000 | 124,000 | 133,000 | 127,000 | 154,000 | 142,000 | 134,000 | 125,000 | 140,000 | 1,630,000 |
| 2020 | 141,000 | 125,000 | 128,000 | 126,000 | 109,000 | 132,000 | 125,000 | 121,000 | 119,000 | 146,000 | 126,000 | 121,000 | 1,519,000 |
| 2021 | 132,000 | 129,000 | 135,000 | 151,000 | 132,000 | 142,000 | 116,000 | 142,000 | 135,000 | 131,000 | 114,000 | 136,000 | 1,595,000 |
| 2022[1] | 146,000 | 128,000 | 135,000 | 119,000 | 136,000 | 151,000 | 113,000 | 154,000 | 122,000 | 123,000 | 107,000 | 143,000 | 1,577,000 |

[1] Preliminary.   [2] Represents total consumption of primary & secondary lead as metal, in chemicals, or in alloys.   Source: U.S. Geological Survey (USGS)

## Lead Recovered from Scrap in the United States   In Metric Tons (Lead Content)

| Year | Jan. | Feb. | Mar. | Apr. | May | June | July | Aug. | Sept. | Oct. | Nov. | Dec. | Total |
|---|---|---|---|---|---|---|---|---|---|---|---|---|---|
| 2013 | 104,000 | 96,700 | 100,000 | 97,300 | 100,000 | 98,100 | 97,200 | 100,000 | 99,500 | 104,000 | 102,000 | 95,000 | 1,200,000 |
| 2014 | 92,700 | 91,100 | 97,300 | 96,300 | 94,500 | 94,500 | 96,900 | 93,796 | 94,800 | 94,400 | 88,600 | 94,800 | 1,130,000 |
| 2015 | 88,600 | 88,900 | 92,200 | 94,600 | 93,600 | 92,900 | 92,500 | 95,400 | 96,300 | 97,500 | 96,100 | 89,700 | 1,120,000 |
| 2016 | 94,300 | 90,800 | 92,300 | 93,500 | 91,900 | 86,500 | 83,900 | 92,600 | 86,700 | 106,000 | 102,000 | 102,000 | 1,000,000 |
| 2017 | 82,900 | 105,000 | 108,000 | 107,000 | 101,000 | 83,700 | 85,000 | 85,300 | 83,300 | 84,600 | 81,400 | 84,300 | 1,130,000 |
| 2018 | 95,100 | 90,300 | 96,300 | 97,300 | 91,400 | 92,400 | 97,000 | 96,600 | 92,900 | 94,600 | 93,600 | 96,000 | 1,140,000 |
| 2019 | 94,100 | 94,500 | 96,700 | 94,600 | 90,600 | 93,800 | 97,000 | 97,200 | 98,200 | 101,000 | 97,800 | 100,000 | 1,155,500 |
| 2020 | 101,000 | 99,500 | 95,900 | 86,100 | 82,600 | 98,100 | 99,700 | 98,100 | 95,800 | 97,800 | 98,700 | 98,400 | 1,151,700 |
| 2021 | 89,100 | 94,500 | 89,600 | 83,700 | 85,100 | 84,200 | 83,600 | 77,300 | 78,700 | 78,200 | 78,200 | 79,400 | 1,001,600 |
| 2022[1] | 75,500 | 76,100 | 81,200 | 82,700 | 80,900 | 78,600 | 79,500 | 79,800 | 79,600 | 80,100 | 78,600 | 78,400 | 951,000 |

[1] Preliminary.   Source: U.S. Geological Survey (USGS)

## Total Stocks of Lead[1] in the United States at Refiners, at End of Month   In Metric Tons

| Year | Jan. | Feb. | Mar. | Apr. | May | June | July | Aug. | Sept. | Oct. | Nov. | Dec. |
|---|---|---|---|---|---|---|---|---|---|---|---|---|
| 2010 | 60,200 | 60,200 | 55,700 | 50,700 | 55,500 | 57,200 | 57,600 | 59,100 | 59,800 | 58,700 | 67,700 | 67,400 |
| 2011 | 67,100 | 53,000 | 53,200 | 61,100 | 62,600 | 61,500 | 62,800 | 60,500 | 58,800 | 56,300 | 53,500 | 54,800 |
| 2012 | 58,700 | 63,300 | 54,800 | 54,000 | 51,800 | 56,600 | 62,600 | 65,700 | 63,400 | 63,800 | 56,000 | 57,500 |
| 2013 | 69,900 | 76,200 | 83,100 | 94,300 | 98,000 | 93,400 | 83,600 | 81,400 | 77,400 | 69,300 | 65,100 | 69,400 |
| 2014 | 68,100 | 63,600 | 65,400 | 65,700 | 64,000 | 66,600 | 62,500 | 62,080 | 63,300 | 63,100 | 66,300 | 66,300 |
| 2015 | 64,900 | 63,800 | 63,600 | 64,100 | 62,700 | 62,400 | 60,800 | 66,900 | 69,500 | 68,600 | 67,900 | 64,500 |
| 2016 | 97,300 | 63,800 | 63,200 | 65,500 | 70,000 | 67,100 | 66,900 | 85,300 | 84,600 | 74,800 | 79,800 | 101,000 |
| 2017[1] | 111,000 | 103,000 | 113,000 | 106,000 | 126,000 | 128,000 | 131,000 | 132,000 | 115,000 | 116,000 | 139,000 | 161,000 |
| 2018[1] | ---- | ---- | ---- | ---- | ---- | ---- | ---- | ---- | ---- | ---- | ---- | ---- |
| 2019[1] | ---- | ---- | ---- | ---- | ---- | ---- | ---- | ---- | ---- | ---- | ---- | ---- |

[1] Preliminary.   [2] Secondary smelters and consumers.   Source: U.S. Geological Survey (USGS)

## Refiners Production[1] of Lead in the United States   In Metric Tons

| Year | Jan. | Feb. | Mar. | Apr. | May | June | July | Aug. | Sept. | Oct. | Nov. | Dec. | Total |
|---|---|---|---|---|---|---|---|---|---|---|---|---|---|
| 2001 | NA | NA | NA | NA | NA | NA | NA | NA | NA | NA | NA | NA | 290,000 |
| 2002 | NA | NA | NA | NA | NA | NA | NA | NA | NA | NA | NA | NA | 262,000 |
| 2003 | NA | NA | NA | NA | NA | NA | NA | NA | NA | NA | NA | NA | 245,000 |
| 2004 | NA | NA | NA | NA | NA | NA | NA | NA | NA | NA | NA | NA | NA |
| 2005 | NA | NA | NA | NA | NA | NA | NA | NA | NA | NA | NA | NA | 143,000 |
| 2006 | NA | NA | NA | NA | NA | NA | NA | NA | NA | NA | NA | NA | 143,000 |
| 2007 | NA | NA | NA | NA | NA | NA | NA | NA | NA | NA | NA | NA | NA |
| 2008 | NA | NA | NA | NA | NA | NA | NA | NA | NA | NA | NA | NA | NA |
| 2009 | NA | NA | NA | NA | NA | NA | NA | NA | NA | NA | NA | NA | NA |
| 2010[2] | NA | NA | NA | NA | NA | NA | NA | NA | NA | NA | NA | NA | NA |

[1] Represents refined lead produced from domestic ores by primary smelters plus small amounts of secondary material passing through these smelters. Includes GSA metal purchased for remelt.   [2] Preliminary.   NA = Not available.   Source: U.S. Geological Survey (USGS)

# Lithium

## World Production of Lithium Minerals and Brine    In Metric Tons (gross weight)

| | Argentina | | Australia | Brazil | Chile | | | China | Portugal | United States | Zimbabwe |
|---|---|---|---|---|---|---|---|---|---|---|---|
| Year | Subsurface Brine: Lithium Carbonate | Subsurface Brine: Lithium Chloride | Spodumene | Concentrates (Spodumene) | Subsurface Brine: Lithium Carbonate | Subsurface Brine: Lithium Chloride | Subsurface Brine: Lithium Hydroxide | Lithium Carbonate equivalent[3] | Lepidolite | Lithium Carbonate | Amblygonite, Eucryptite, Lepidolite, and Petalite |
| 2012 | 10,535 | 4,297 | 456,921 | 7,084 | 62,002 | 4,145 | 5,447 | 10,000 | 20,698 | W | 53,000 |
| 2013 | 9,248 | 5,156 | 405,119 | 7,982 | 52,358 | 4,091 | 4,197 | 19,068 | 19,940 | 4,600 | 50,000 |
| 2014 | 11,698 | 7,370 | 444,546 | 8,519 | 55,074 | 2,985 | 4,194 | 18,810 | 17,459 | W | 50,000 |
| 2015 | 21,111 | 5,848 | 439,514 | 5,781 | 50,418 | 2,069 | 3,888 | 20,470 | 17,120 | W | 50,000 |
| 2016 | 24,409 | 6,468 | 522,181 | 8,804 | 70,831 | 1,775 | 5,576 | 25,400 | 25,758 | W | 50,000 |
| 2017 | 26,559 | 4,501 | 1,706,618 | 10,547 | 73,563 | 2,535 | 5,280 | 37,300 | 52,741 | W | 40,000 |
| 2018 | 29,385 | 5,005 | 1,965,944 | 41,000 | 87,029 | 3,826 | 6,468 | 37,800 | 76,818 | W | 80,000 |
| 2019[1] | 29,994 | 4,284 | 1,587,980 | 38,500 | 100,787 | 1,886 | 9,934 | 57,500 | 59,912 | W | 60,400 |
| 2020[2] | 26,911 | 4,836 | 1,427,380 | 51,000 | 114,260 | ---- | 9,030 | 70,600 | 23,185 | W | 20,859 |

[1] Preliminary.    [2] Estimate.    [3] Produced from subsurface brine and concentrates.    W = Withheld to avoid disclosing proprietary data.
*Source: U.S. Geological Survey (USGS)*

## Salient U.S. Lithium Statistics    In Metric Tons (contained Lithium)

| Year | Production[2] | Imports[3] | Exports[4] | Consumption: Estimated | Rest of World: Production[2] | Battery-grade Lithium Carbonate (USD per Metric ton) | Net Import Reliance as a % of Apparent Consumption | Employment, Mine and Mill (Number) |
|---|---|---|---|---|---|---|---|---|
| 2014 | W | 2,120 | 1,420 | 2,000 | 31,300 | $6,690 | >25 | 70 |
| 2015 | W | 2,750 | 1,789 | 2,000 | 32,200 | $6,500 | >25 | 70 |
| 2016 | W | 3,140 | 1,520 | 3,000 | 40,200 | $8,650 | >50 | 70 |
| 2017 | W | 3,330 | 1,960 | 3,000 | 76,400 | $15,000 | >50 | 70 |
| 2018 | W | 3,420 | 1,660 | 3,000 | 91,800 | $16,000 | >50 | 70 |
| 2019 | W | 2,620 | 1,660 | 2,000 | 84,000 | $11,700 | >25 | 70 |
| 2020 | W | 2,460 | 1,170 | 2,000 | 82,500 | $8,400 | >50 | 70 |
| 2021 | W | 2,640 | 1,870 | 2,000 | | $12,600 | >25 | 70 |
| 2022[1] | W | 3,400 | 2,700 | 3,000 | | $37,000 | >25 | 70 |

[1] Preliminary.    [2] Mineral concentrate and carbonate.    [3] Compounds, concentrate, ores, and metal.    [4] Compounds.    W = Withheld to avoid disclosing proprietary data.    *Source: U.S. Geological Survey (USGS)*

## U.S. Exports of Lithium Chemicals    In Metric Tons (gross weight)

| Year | Lithium Carbonate | Lithium Carbonate (Li content) | Lithium Carbonate, U.S.P. | Lithium Carbonate, U.S.P. (Li content) | Lithium Hydroxide | Lithium Hydroxide (Li content) |
|---|---|---|---|---|---|---|
| 2012 | 1,060 | 200 | 201 | 38 | 6,440 | 1,060 |
| 2013 | 1,010 | 190 | 391 | 73 | 5,850 | 966 |
| 2014 | 904 | 170 | 77 | 14 | 7,590 | 1,240 |
| 2015 | 1,350 | 255 | 85 | 16 | 9,200 | 1,520 |
| 2016 | 1,040 | 195 | 108 | 20 | 7,910 | 1,300 |
| 2017 | 1,310 | 246 | 94 | 18 | 10,300 | 1,700 |
| 2018 | 1,320 | 249 | 141 | 27 | 8,400 | 1,390 |
| 2019[1] | 819 | 154 | 95 | 18 | 9,040 | 1,490 |
| 2020[2] | 1,000 | 188 | 213 | 40 | 5,690 | 939 |

[1] Preliminary.    [2] Estimate.    [3] Less than 1/2 unit.    *Source: U.S. Geological Survey (USGS)*

## U.S. Imports for Consumption of Lithium Chemicals    In Metric Tons (gross weight)

| Year | Lithium Carbonate | Lithium Carbonate (Li content) | Lithium Carbonate, U.S.P. | Lithium Carbonate, U.S.P. (Li content) | Lithium Hydroxide | Lithium Hydroxide (Li content) |
|---|---|---|---|---|---|---|
| 2012 | 13,200 | 2,480 | 34 | 6 | 1,640 | 271 |
| 2013 | 10,500 | 1,980 | 45 | 8 | 1,340 | 221 |
| 2014 | 9,580 | 1,800 | 48 | 9 | 1,920 | 316 |
| 2015 | 12,900 | 2,420 | 31 | 6 | 1,960 | 324 |
| 2016 | 15,600 | 2,920 | 16 | 3 | 1,280 | 211 |
| 2017 | 16,100 | 3,030 | ---- | ---- | 1,830 | 302 |
| 2018 | 17,200 | 3,240 | [3] | [3] | 1,060 | 176 |
| 2019[1] | 12,800 | 2,410 | [3] | [3] | 1,240 | 206 |
| 2020[2] | 11,700 | 2,190 | [3] | [3] | 1,600 | 265 |

[1] Preliminary.    [2] Estimate.    [3] Less than 1/2 unit.    *Source: U.S. Geological Survey (USGS)*

# Lumber and Plywood

Humans have utilized lumber for construction for thousands of years, but due to the heaviness of timber and the manual methods of harvesting, large-scale lumbering didn't occur until the mechanical advances of the Industrial Revolution. Lumber is produced from both hardwood and softwood. Hardwood lumber comes from deciduous trees that have broad leaves. Most hardwood lumber is used for miscellaneous industrial applications, primarily wood pallets, and includes oak, gum, maple, and ash. Hardwood species with beautiful colors and patterns are used for such high-grade products as furniture, flooring, paneling, and cabinets and include black walnut, black cherry, and red oak. Wood from cone-bearing trees is called softwood, regardless of its actual hardness. Most lumber from the U.S. is softwood. Softwoods, such as southern yellow pine, Douglas fir, ponderosa pine, and true firs, are primarily used as structural lumber, such as 2x4s and 2x6s, poles, paper, and cardboard.

Plywood consists of several thin layers of veneer bonded together with adhesives. The veneer sheets are layered so that the grain of one sheet is perpendicular to that of the next, which makes plywood exceptionally strong for its weight. Most plywood has from three to nine layers of wood. Plywood manufacturers use both hard and softwoods, although hardwoods serve primarily for appearance and are not as strong as those made from softwoods. Plywood is used in construction, particularly for floors, roofs, walls, and doors. Homebuilding and remodeling account for two-thirds of U.S. lumber consumption. The price of lumber and plywood is highly correlated with the strength of the U.S. homebuilding market.

The forest and wood products industry is dominated by Weyerhaeuser Company (ticker symbol WY). Weyerhaeuser is a forest products conglomerate that engages not only in growing and harvesting timber but also in the production and distribution of forest products, real estate development, and construction of single-family homes. To maximize its long-term yield from its acreage, Weyerhaeuser engages in a number of forest management activities such as extensive planting, suppression of non-merchantable species, thinning, fertilization, and operational pruning.

Lumber futures and options are traded at the CME Group. The CME Group's lumber futures contract calls for the delivery of 111,000 board feet (one 73-foot rail car) of random length 8 to 12-foot 2 x 4s, the type used in construction. The contract is priced in terms of dollars per thousand board feet.

**Prices** – CME lumber futures prices (Barchart.com electronic symbol code LS) on the nearest-futures chart in 2022 rallied early in the year, but then fell back and closed the year down -56.2% at $373.70 per thousand feet.

**Supply** – The U.S. leads the world in the production of industrial round wood. In 2021, U.S. production was 382.956 million cubic meters (+3.7% yr/yr), Russian production was 201.891 million cubic meters (unchanged yr/yr), and Canadian production was 141.068 cubic meters (unchanged yr/yr).

The U.S. also led the world in the production of plywood in 2021 with 9.705 million cubic meters of production (+2.2% yr/yr), followed by Russia with 3.999 million cubic meters (unchanged yr/yr), and Japan with 3.172 million cubic meters (+5.8% yr/yr).

**Trade** – World exports of plywood in 2021 rose by +11.7% yr/yr to 31.716 million cubic meters. The world's largest exporter of plywood is Russia, with a 9.2% share of world plywood exports in 2021, followed by Finland with 3.0%, and Canada with 2.0%. In 2021 U.S. exports rose by +2.4% yr/yr to 759,000 cubic meters.

World exports of industrial roundwood in 2021 rose by +3.3% yr/yr to 143.152 million cubic meters. The Czech Republic was the world's largest exporter of roundwood in 2021 with a 12.7% share of world exports, followed by Russia with an 11.4% share, and Germany with a 7.9% share. Czech exports of industrial roundwood in 2021 were unchanged yr/yr at 18.163 million cubic meters. U.S. exports of industrial roundwood in 2021 rose by +6.6% yr/yr to 9.415 million cubic meters.

# LUMBER AND PLYWOOD

**World Production of Industrial Roundwood by Selected Countries**  In Thousands of Cubic Meters

| Year | Austria | Canada | Czech Republic | Finland | France | Germany | Poland | Romania | Russia | Spain | Sweden | Turkey | United States |
|---|---|---|---|---|---|---|---|---|---|---|---|---|---|
| 2012 | 12,831 | 146,741 | 13,041 | 44,614 | 24,945 | 45,851 | 32,972 | 11,050 | 177,455 | 11,627 | 63,599 | 17,701 | 347,076 |
| 2013 | 12,433 | 147,751 | 13,149 | 49,331 | 24,451 | 44,700 | 33,795 | 10,091 | 180,378 | 12,124 | 63,700 | 16,762 | 354,937 |
| 2014 | 12,030 | 148,825 | 13,365 | 49,202 | 25,750 | 45,386 | 35,677 | 10,471 | 188,300 | 12,686 | 67,400 | 18,535 | 356,812 |
| 2015 | 12,570 | 151,358 | 13,827 | 51,446 | 24,998 | 45,654 | 35,878 | 10,235 | 190,507 | 12,905 | 67,300 | 20,008 | 354,678 |
| 2016 | 12,173 | 154,694 | 15,273 | 54,327 | 25,086 | 44,016 | 37,106 | 9,953 | 198,194 | 13,325 | 67,900 | 20,389 | 374,476 |
| 2017 | 12,738 | 155,183 | 17,011 | 55,330 | 25,361 | 43,328 | 40,064 | 9,578 | 197,612 | 14,642 | 67,580 | 19,462 | 376,415 |
| 2018 | 13,949 | 155,629 | 21,443 | 60,530 | 25,721 | 52,874 | 41,353 | 10,436 | 219,569 | 15,457 | 67,712 | 22,466 | 392,510 |
| 2019 | 13,325 | 139,817 | 26,664 | 55,654 | 25,445 | 54,124 | 38,199 | 10,186 | 203,194 | 15,405 | 69,000 | 22,700 | 387,702 |
| 2020[1] | 11,462 | 141,068 | 26,621 | 51,191 | 24,064 | 58,436 | 35,859 | 11,629 | 201,891 | 13,881 | 69,000 | 23,306 | 369,175 |
| 2021[2] | 13,521 | 141,068 | 26,621 | 57,803 | 26,189 | 59,187 | 38,498 | 12,247 | 201,891 | 13,786 | 69,000 | 24,790 | 382,956 |

[1] Preliminary.  [2] Estimate.  *Source: Food and Agriculture Organization of the United Nations (FAO)*

**Imports of Industrial Roundwood by Selected Countries**  In Thousands of Cubic Meters

| Year | Austria | Belgium | Canada | Finland | France | Germany | Italy | Norway | Poland | Portugal | Spain | Sweden | United States |
|---|---|---|---|---|---|---|---|---|---|---|---|---|---|
| 2012 | 7,319 | 4,338 | 4,495 | 5,457 | 1,368 | 6,567 | 2,802 | 940 | 2,469 | 1,644 | 1,727 | 6,855 | 1,167 |
| 2013 | 8,214 | 4,507 | 4,872 | 6,694 | 1,244 | 8,442 | 2,691 | 661 | 2,270 | 2,320 | 2,047 | 7,532 | 926 |
| 2014 | 7,239 | 4,472 | 4,262 | 6,257 | 1,512 | 8,417 | 2,913 | 447 | 2,633 | 2,600 | 1,750 | 8,127 | 909 |
| 2015 | 7,849 | 4,021 | 4,616 | 5,709 | 1,349 | 8,745 | 2,665 | 378 | 2,535 | 2,014 | 751 | 6,941 | 1,191 |
| 2016 | 9,188 | 3,899 | 6,185 | 5,911 | 1,444 | 8,697 | 2,763 | 417 | 2,482 | 2,131 | 599 | 6,807 | 1,248 |
| 2017 | 8,825 | 3,373 | 4,293 | 4,830 | 1,222 | 8,783 | 2,846 | 513 | 1,682 | 2,042 | 584 | 6,673 | 1,154 |
| 2018 | 10,113 | 4,133 | 5,133 | 6,935 | 1,143 | 8,910 | 3,860 | 455 | 1,071 | 2,010 | 638 | 9,479 | 1,778 |
| 2019 | 10,586 | 4,253 | 4,744 | 6,234 | 1,263 | 7,318 | 3,374 | 402 | 1,607 | 2,051 | 667 | 8,804 | 942 |
| 2020[1] | 12,298 | 5,387 | 4,364 | 6,274 | 943 | 6,081 | 2,694 | 337 | 2,953 | 2,538 | 764 | 7,240 | 1,319 |
| 2021[2] | 10,864 | 5,745 | 4,373 | 6,298 | 985 | 6,084 | 3,090 | 349 | 2,266 | 2,615 | 892 | 6,343 | 772 |

[1] Preliminary.  [2] Estimate.  *Source: Food and Agricultural Organization of the United Nations (FAO)*

**Exports of Industrial Roundwood by Selected Countries**  In Thousands of Cubic Meters

| Year | Canada | Czech Republic | Estonia | France | Germany | Hungary | Latvia | Lithuania | Russia | Slovakia | Sweden | Switzerland | United States |
|---|---|---|---|---|---|---|---|---|---|---|---|---|---|
| 2012 | 6,094 | 3,912 | 2,392 | 4,571 | 3,398 | 858 | 4,107 | 1,464 | 17,652 | 2,085 | 794 | 801 | 12,227 |
| 2013 | 7,023 | 4,292 | 2,747 | 4,740 | 3,316 | 975 | 3,737 | 1,809 | 19,045 | 2,662 | 756 | 740 | 14,700 |
| 2014 | 6,696 | 4,931 | 2,758 | 4,398 | 3,387 | 871 | 3,836 | 1,716 | 20,909 | 2,932 | 630 | 764 | 13,962 |
| 2015 | 6,060 | 4,530 | 2,431 | 4,311 | 3,747 | 680 | 3,002 | 1,406 | 19,437 | 2,358 | 570 | 641 | 11,561 |
| 2016 | 8,172 | 5,225 | 2,548 | 4,000 | 3,947 | 683 | 2,871 | 1,473 | 20,046 | 2,157 | 573 | 559 | 12,047 |
| 2017 | 7,402 | 6,583 | 2,557 | 4,092 | 4,259 | 634 | 2,652 | 1,559 | 19,430 | 1,955 | 963 | 570 | 12,200 |
| 2018 | 8,494 | 8,309 | 2,927 | 4,066 | 5,364 | 547 | 2,652 | 2,028 | 19,197 | 2,042 | 755 | 753 | 12,270 |
| 2019 | 7,546 | 14,146 | 2,396 | 3,877 | 8,916 | 624 | 3,579 | 1,890 | 15,857 | 1,711 | 870 | 642 | 7,922 |
| 2020[1] | 5,994 | 18,163 | 1,583 | 3,583 | 13,051 | 728 | 2,930 | 1,774 | 16,276 | 2,219 | 1,071 | 642 | 7,355 |
| 2021[2] | 7,265 | 18,163 | 1,734 | 4,112 | 11,333 | 728 | 3,065 | 1,517 | 16,276 | 2,015 | 1,318 | 476 | 9,415 |

[1] Preliminary.  [2] Estimate.  *Source: Food and Agriculture Organization of the United Nations (FAO)*

**U.S. Housing Starts: Seasonally Adjusted Annual Rate**  In Thousands

| Year | Jan. | Feb. | Mar. | Apr. | May | June | July | Aug. | Sept. | Oct. | Nov. | Dec. | Average |
|---|---|---|---|---|---|---|---|---|---|---|---|---|---|
| 2013 | 888 | 962 | 1,010 | 835 | 930 | 839 | 880 | 917 | 850 | 925 | 1,100 | 1,002 | 928 |
| 2014 | 888 | 944 | 970 | 1,043 | 1,007 | 911 | 1,085 | 984 | 1,023 | 1,074 | 1,001 | 1,073 | 1,000 |
| 2015 | 1,085 | 886 | 960 | 1,190 | 1,079 | 1,205 | 1,146 | 1,130 | 1,224 | 1,058 | 1,172 | 1,146 | 1,107 |
| 2016 | 1,092 | 1,225 | 1,111 | 1,163 | 1,148 | 1,203 | 1,239 | 1,171 | 1,068 | 1,313 | 1,140 | 1,252 | 1,177 |
| 2017 | 1,193 | 1,281 | 1,190 | 1,145 | 1,160 | 1,247 | 1,202 | 1,159 | 1,175 | 1,248 | 1,278 | 1,182 | 1,205 |
| 2018 | 1,301 | 1,279 | 1,324 | 1,286 | 1,358 | 1,199 | 1,199 | 1,289 | 1,247 | 1,220 | 1,177 | 1,089 | 1,247 |
| 2019 | 1,232 | 1,129 | 1,200 | 1,280 | 1,308 | 1,235 | 1,232 | 1,370 | 1,297 | 1,328 | 1,343 | 1,538 | 1,291 |
| 2020 | 1,569 | 1,571 | 1,270 | 938 | 1,055 | 1,269 | 1,510 | 1,376 | 1,461 | 1,530 | 1,541 | 1,651 | 1,395 |
| 2021 | 1,602 | 1,430 | 1,711 | 1,505 | 1,605 | 1,664 | 1,573 | 1,576 | 1,559 | 1,563 | 1,706 | 1,768 | 1,605 |
| 2022[1] | 1,666 | 1,777 | 1,716 | 1,805 | 1,562 | 1,575 | 1,377 | 1,508 | 1,465 | 1,426 | 1,419 | 1,371 | 1,556 |

[1] Preliminary.  Total Privately owned.  *Source: Bureau of the Census, U.S. Department of Commerce*

# LUMBER AND PLYWOOD

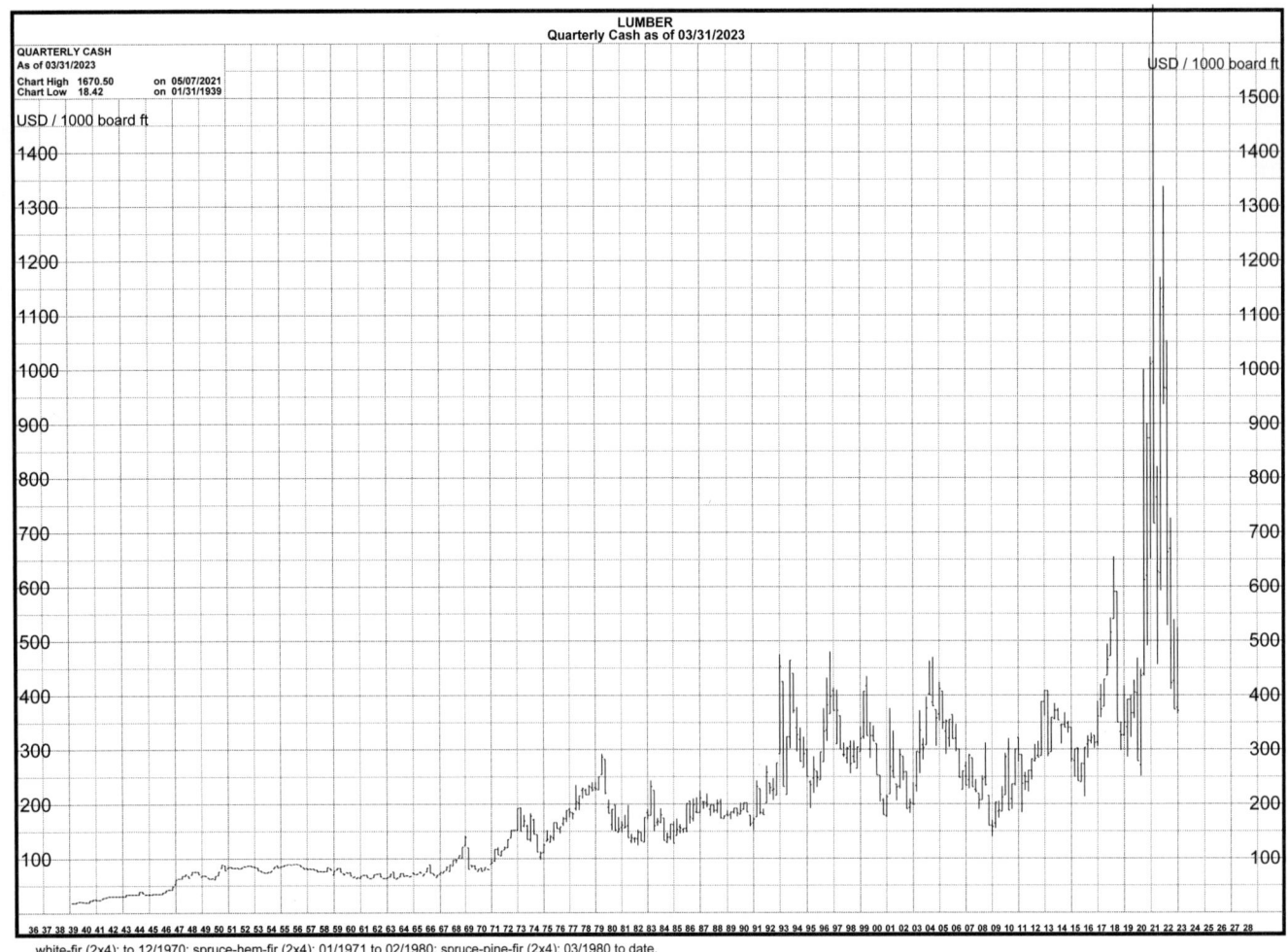

**LUMBER**
Quarterly Cash as of 03/31/2023

QUARTERLY CASH
As of 03/31/2023
Chart High 1670.50 on 05/07/2021
Chart Low 18.42 on 01/31/1939

USD / 1000 board ft

white-fir (2x4): to 12/1970; spruce-hem-fir (2x4): 01/1971 to 02/1980; spruce-pine-fir (2x4): 03/1980 to date.

### Average Price of Lumber in the United States — In Dollars per Thousand Board Feet

| Year | Jan. | Feb. | Mar. | Apr. | May | June | July | Aug. | Sept. | Oct. | Nov. | Dec. | Average |
|---|---|---|---|---|---|---|---|---|---|---|---|---|---|
| 2010 | 238.50 | 287.00 | 281.50 | 312.00 | 272.50 | 207.50 | 203.40 | 219.75 | 231.75 | 245.80 | 275.33 | 283.80 | 254.90 |
| 2011 | 307.25 | 286.25 | 294.25 | 269.50 | 227.25 | 222.75 | 254.50 | 231.75 | 250.80 | 236.50 | 230.25 | 248.00 | 254.92 |
| 2012 | 253.50 | 262.67 | 280.75 | 281.25 | 305.50 | 300.00 | 294.25 | 310.20 | 292.33 | 298.00 | 339.50 | 370.00 | 299.00 |
| 2013 | 382.25 | 377.33 | 401.50 | 386.60 | 325.50 | 298.40 | 312.25 | 326.00 | 346.75 | 360.25 | 381.80 | 364.25 | 355.24 |
| 2014 | 373.20 | 364.00 | 362.75 | 339.00 | 342.00 | 323.75 | 351.50 | 361.00 | 355.25 | 347.00 | 333.75 | 337.75 | 349.25 |
| 2015 | 326.00 | 313.50 | 283.75 | 261.50 | 256.40 | 292.25 | 294.25 | 267.75 | 246.00 | 259.20 | 259.75 | 267.25 | 277.30 |
| 2016 | 258.75 | 251.50 | 292.00 | 298.60 | 317.50 | 319.50 | 323.40 | 326.00 | 313.60 | 318.75 | 306.25 | 319.60 | 303.79 |
| 2017 | 309.50 | 374.75 | 359.20 | 405.33 | 387.75 | 368.40 | 403.25 | 394.50 | 413.80 | 446.25 | 485.00 | 461.40 | 400.76 |
| 2018 | 492.50 | 523.25 | 524.20 | 551.75 | 621.33 | 617.80 | 564.25 | 468.20 | 413.75 | 316.33 | 338.00 | 320.25 | 479.30 |
| 2019 | 334.50 | 405.75 | 370.80 | 326.00 | 312.00 | 359.75 | 356.00 | 330.00 | ---- | ---- | ---- | ---- | 349.35 |

*Source: National Agricultural Statistics Service, U.S. Department of Agriculture (NASS-USDA)*

### Average Price of Plywood in the United States — In Dollars per Thousand Board Feet

| Year | Jan. | Feb. | Mar. | Apr. | May | June | July | Aug. | Sept. | Oct. | Nov. | Dec. | Average |
|---|---|---|---|---|---|---|---|---|---|---|---|---|---|
| 2010 | 191.50 | 220.00 | 233.00 | 353.75 | 330.00 | 206.25 | 217.20 | 171.25 | 164.50 | 183.00 | 189.33 | 196.40 | 221.35 |
| 2011 | 210.75 | 196.75 | 189.25 | 178.25 | 167.25 | 180.25 | 171.25 | 192.25 | 188.60 | 190.75 | 185.00 | 192.00 | 186.86 |
| 2012 | 201.00 | 194.67 | 213.25 | 212.50 | 233.75 | 252.00 | 257.50 | 331.00 | 343.33 | 300.00 | 343.75 | 354.50 | 269.77 |
| 2013 | 401.50 | 412.67 | 430.00 | 410.00 | 354.33 | 279.25 | 256.25 | 254.40 | 244.75 | 263.00 | 244.00 | 227.75 | 314.83 |
| 2014 | 226.60 | 215.00 | 214.50 | 210.33 | 233.00 | 210.25 | 212.25 | 215.40 | 222.00 | 222.00 | 219.00 | 204.00 | 217.03 |
| 2015 | 200.80 | 194.25 | 183.50 | 177.50 | 194.00 | 207.25 | 194.00 | 200.50 | 218.33 | 239.20 | 257.00 | 233.50 | 208.32 |
| 2016 | 232.50 | 230.75 | 224.25 | 244.20 | 275.75 | 278.00 | 295.40 | 306.25 | 300.00 | 287.00 | 285.75 | 282.00 | 270.15 |
| 2017 | 278.50 | 291.25 | 307.00 | 327.00 | 329.75 | 330.40 | 378.00 | 412.00 | 432.20 | 454.25 | 396.25 | 304.00 | 353.38 |
| 2018 | 318.75 | 377.50 | 405.00 | 405.00 | 418.33 | 445.00 | 403.75 | 347.00 | 342.50 | 268.33 | 242.00 | 208.25 | 348.45 |
| 2019 | 209.50 | 214.50 | 212.00 | 188.75 | 189.00 | 184.25 | 211.75 | 218.00 | ---- | ---- | ---- | ---- | 203.47 |

*Source: National Agricultural Statistics Service, U.S. Department of Agriculture (NASS-USDA)*

# LUMBER AND PLYWOOD

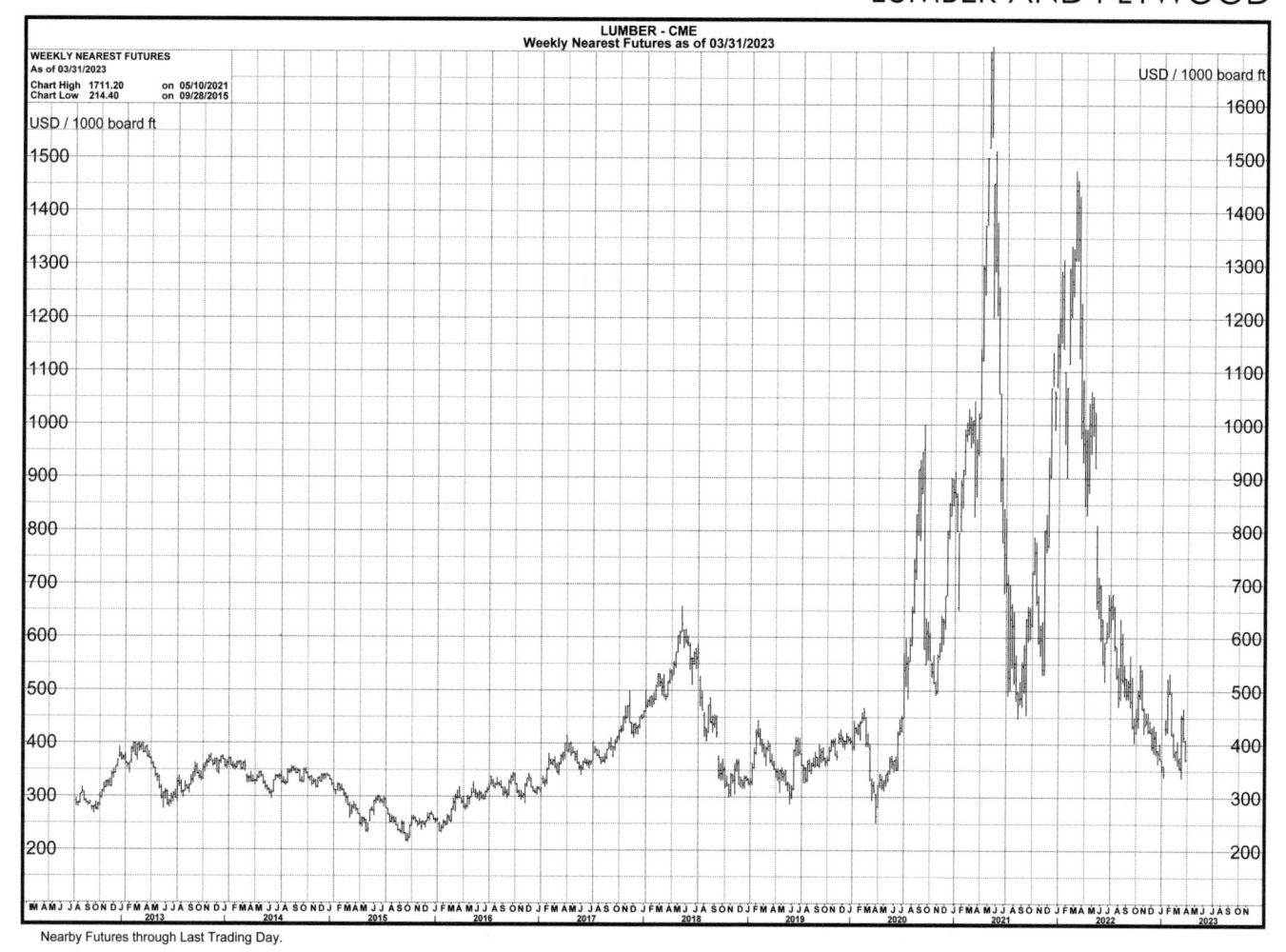

**LUMBER - CME**
Weekly Nearest Futures as of 03/31/2023

WEEKLY NEAREST FUTURES
As of 03/31/2023
Chart High 1711.20 on 05/10/2021
Chart Low 214.40 on 09/28/2015

USD / 1000 board ft

Nearby Futures through Last Trading Day.

## Volume of Trading of Random Lumber Futures in Chicago   In Contracts

| Year | Jan. | Feb. | Mar. | Apr. | May | June | July | Aug. | Sept. | Oct. | Nov. | Dec. | Total |
|---|---|---|---|---|---|---|---|---|---|---|---|---|---|
| 2013 | 26,219 | 29,842 | 18,671 | 26,472 | 23,349 | 19,914 | 18,572 | 18,118 | 19,271 | 17,021 | 11,100 | 15,073 | 243,622 |
| 2014 | 13,001 | 14,025 | 12,632 | 14,563 | 13,365 | 17,276 | 10,119 | 14,977 | 11,766 | 16,481 | 8,959 | 13,333 | 160,497 |
| 2015 | 13,744 | 16,696 | 14,710 | 21,116 | 16,757 | 19,374 | 14,253 | 20,509 | 15,592 | 21,061 | 11,475 | 16,065 | 201,352 |
| 2016 | 13,340 | 14,415 | 16,933 | 15,931 | 12,953 | 16,806 | 10,911 | 19,397 | 13,373 | 16,510 | 13,574 | 12,839 | 176,982 |
| 2017 | 11,400 | 20,115 | 14,942 | 21,705 | 16,706 | 15,346 | 14,333 | 15,684 | 16,030 | 21,713 | 18,739 | 18,386 | 205,099 |
| 2018 | 15,690 | 21,225 | 15,354 | 22,545 | 22,211 | 23,128 | 15,731 | 19,983 | 14,424 | 20,532 | 14,222 | 11,541 | 216,586 |
| 2019 | 14,464 | 14,588 | 11,140 | 17,457 | 13,524 | 16,484 | 12,478 | 13,524 | 10,085 | 14,511 | 12,554 | 11,873 | 162,682 |
| 2020 | 11,487 | 20,021 | 14,549 | 9,142 | 7,448 | 11,808 | 15,612 | 24,128 | 10,932 | 9,071 | 7,691 | 14,136 | 156,025 |
| 2021 | 8,548 | 9,838 | 8,078 | 12,051 | 12,761 | 14,019 | 11,012 | 8,470 | 6,196 | 7,935 | 7,368 | 9,801 | 116,077 |
| 2022 | 8,334 | 10,138 | 7,808 | 7,007 | 6,534 | 9,110 | 6,392 | 11,658 | 9,976 | 12,168 | 7,919 | 12,445 | 109,489 |

Contract size = 110,000 board feet.   *Source: CME Group; Chicago Mercantile Exchange (CME)*

## Average Open Interest of Random Lumber Futures in Chicago   In Contracts

| Year | Jan. | Feb. | Mar. | Apr. | May | June | July | Aug. | Sept. | Oct. | Nov. | Dec. |
|---|---|---|---|---|---|---|---|---|---|---|---|---|
| 2013 | 9,354 | 8,222 | 8,609 | 7,345 | 5,872 | 6,726 | 5,816 | 5,539 | 5,699 | 4,816 | 4,672 | 4,086 |
| 2014 | 3,945 | 4,602 | 4,618 | 5,020 | 4,422 | 5,013 | 4,080 | 4,419 | 3,751 | 3,698 | 4,610 | 4,289 |
| 2015 | 4,831 | 5,256 | 6,336 | 6,860 | 6,379 | 4,660 | 4,389 | 6,151 | 6,104 | 5,553 | 3,974 | 4,158 |
| 2016 | 4,619 | 5,292 | 4,478 | 4,561 | 5,050 | 4,782 | 4,692 | 5,167 | 3,479 | 4,323 | 3,818 | 4,005 |
| 2017 | 3,786 | 4,992 | 5,353 | 6,044 | 5,180 | 4,378 | 4,158 | 4,510 | 5,489 | 6,494 | 6,800 | 6,278 |
| 2018 | 6,775 | 7,290 | 6,406 | 6,964 | 6,827 | 6,550 | 5,649 | 4,714 | 3,986 | 4,078 | 4,120 | 3,984 |
| 2019 | 3,657 | 3,334 | 2,510 | 3,357 | 3,913 | 3,497 | 2,541 | 2,593 | 2,052 | 2,554 | 3,108 | 3,240 |
| 2020 | 3,302 | 4,078 | 2,990 | 2,761 | 2,602 | 2,509 | 3,672 | 4,520 | 3,642 | 3,300 | 2,829 | 3,026 |
| 2021 | 2,745 | 3,042 | 3,088 | 2,830 | 2,264 | 2,228 | 2,190 | 2,463 | 1,818 | 1,910 | 1,661 | 2,266 |
| 2022 | 2,446 | 2,595 | 2,548 | 2,760 | 2,381 | 2,351 | 1,991 | 2,425 | 2,417 | 2,559 | 2,267 | 2,962 |

Contract size = 110,000 board feet.   *Source: CME Group; Chicago Mercantile Exchange (CME)*

# LUMBER AND PLYWOOD

## Production of Plywood by Selected Countries — In Thousands of Cubic Meters

| Year | Austria | Canada | Finland | France | Germany | Italy | Japan | Poland | Romania | Russia | Spain | Sweden | United States |
|---|---|---|---|---|---|---|---|---|---|---|---|---|---|
| 2012 | 241 | 1,824 | 1,020 | 324 | 178 | 280 | 2,549 | 388 | 472 | 3,150 | 255 | 54 | 9,493 |
| 2013 | 311 | 1,792 | 1,090 | 255 | 135 | 225 | 2,761 | 430 | 665 | 3,303 | 275 | 87 | 9,680 |
| 2014 | 306 | 1,810 | 1,160 | 245 | 148 | 266 | 2,813 | 406 | 623 | 3,540 | 284 | 82 | 11,151 |
| 2015 | 241 | 1,929 | 1,150 | 246 | 108 | 244 | 2,756 | 390 | 316 | 3,607 | 371 | 60 | 10,972 |
| 2016 | 291 | 2,205 | 1,140 | 250 | 114 | 280 | 3,063 | 462 | 285 | 3,759 | 379 | 60 | 11,239 |
| 2017 | 291 | 2,253 | 1,240 | 254 | 100 | 236 | 3,287 | 546 | 277 | 3,729 | 509 | 85 | 11,600 |
| 2018 | 290 | 1,742 | 1,230 | 258 | 118 | 320 | 3,298 | 583 | 73 | 4,013 | 541 | 85 | 10,104 |
| 2019 | 157 | 1,922 | 1,090 | 253 | 111 | 320 | 3,337 | 519 | 260 | 4,061 | 565 | 85 | 9,925 |
| 2020[1] | 167 | 1,672 | 990 | 234 | 100 | 265 | 2,999 | 483 | 239 | 3,999 | 508 | 90 | 9,500 |
| 2021[2] | 183 | 1,698 | 1,130 | 270 | 103 | 265 | 3,172 | 490 | 258 | 3,999 | 582 | 101 | 9,705 |

[1] Preliminary.  [2] Estimate.  Source: Food and Agricultural Organization of the United Nations (FAO)

## Imports of Plywood by Selected Countries — In Thousands of Cubic Meters

| Year | Austria | Belgium | Canada | Denmark | France | Germany | Italy | Japan | Netherlands | Sweden | Switzerland | United Kingdom | United States |
|---|---|---|---|---|---|---|---|---|---|---|---|---|---|
| 2012 | 209 | 533 | 1,621 | 270 | 374 | 1,336 | 420 | 3,645 | 476 | 173 | 86 | 1,285 | 3,113 |
| 2013 | 145 | 537 | 1,469 | 266 | 368 | 1,338 | 428 | 3,765 | 399 | 155 | 99 | 1,370 | 2,829 |
| 2014 | 160 | 554 | 1,587 | 266 | 429 | 1,369 | 453 | 3,597 | 468 | 163 | 184 | 1,399 | 2,872 |
| 2015 | 190 | 525 | 1,492 | 211 | 420 | 1,412 | 448 | 2,886 | 552 | 150 | 182 | 1,466 | 4,253 |
| 2016 | 181 | 575 | 1,228 | 242 | 478 | 1,458 | 458 | 2,770 | 536 | 175 | 192 | 1,479 | 4,877 |
| 2017 | 231 | 589 | 1,744 | 242 | 529 | 1,528 | 539 | 3,017 | 632 | 206 | 203 | 1,215 | 4,934 |
| 2018 | 242 | 589 | 1,562 | 281 | 539 | 1,620 | 527 | 2,934 | 640 | 222 | 200 | 1,598 | 5,466 |
| 2019 | 217 | 501 | 1,406 | 276 | 533 | 1,486 | 602 | 2,558 | 605 | 248 | 197 | 1,453 | 4,664 |
| 2020[1] | 234 | 423 | 1,174 | 276 | 649 | 1,437 | 413 | 2,227 | 635 | 235 | 197 | 1,362 | 6,461 |
| 2021[2] | 267 | 574 | 1,452 | 276 | 859 | 1,464 | 530 | 2,648 | 695 | 206 | 198 | 1,541 | 8,086 |

[1] Preliminary.  [2] Estimate.  Source: Food and Agricultural Organization of the United Nations (FAO)

## Exports of Plywood by Selected Countries — In Thousands of Cubic Meters

| Year | Austria | Baltic States | Belgium | Canada | Finland | France | Germany | Italy | Netherlands | Poland | Russia | Spain | United States |
|---|---|---|---|---|---|---|---|---|---|---|---|---|---|
| 2012 | 334 | 310 | 368 | 287 | 855 | 143 | 298 | 201 | 89 | 169 | 1,717 | 152 | 914 |
| 2013 | 339 | 312 | 369 | 426 | 920 | 141 | 297 | 192 | 71 | 181 | 1,758 | 166 | 888 |
| 2014 | 346 | 302 | 403 | 482 | 998 | 145 | 310 | 210 | 75 | 203 | 1,969 | 189 | 828 |
| 2015 | 298 | 345 | 381 | 647 | 981 | 156 | 334 | 215 | 68 | 250 | 2,206 | 224 | 643 |
| 2016 | 340 | 439 | 437 | 625 | 940 | 153 | 349 | 240 | 73 | 257 | 2,458 | 252 | 697 |
| 2017 | 348 | 454 | 404 | 670 | 1,039 | 171 | 381 | 279 | 83 | 307 | 2,483 | 274 | 936 |
| 2018 | 307 | 474 | 395 | 733 | 1,012 | 174 | 393 | 211 | 102 | 336 | 2,696 | 291 | 700 |
| 2019 | 309 | 493 | 352 | 655 | 918 | 160 | 376 | 217 | 84 | 286 | 2,748 | 326 | 556 |
| 2020[1] | 299 | 544 | 214 | 543 | 828 | 225 | 373 | 204 | 89 | 309 | 2,904 | 249 | 528 |
| 2021[2] | 357 | 560 | 334 | 634 | 955 | 206 | 382 | 223 | 95 | 350 | 2,904 | 327 | 759 |

[1] Preliminary.  [2] Estimate.  Source: Food and Agricultural Organization of the United Nations (FAO)

# Magnesium

Magnesium (atomic symbol Mg) is a silvery-white, light, and fairly tough, metallic element and is relatively stable. Magnesium is one of the alkaline earth metals. Magnesium is the eighth-most abundant element in the earth's crust and the third most plentiful element found in seawater. Magnesium is ductile and malleable when heated, and except for beryllium, is the lightest metal that remains stable under ordinary conditions. First isolated by the British chemist Sir Humphrey Davy in 1808, magnesium today is obtained mainly by electrolysis of fused magnesium chloride.

Magnesium compounds, primarily magnesium oxide, are used in the refractory material that line the furnaces used to produce iron and steel, nonferrous metals, glass, and cement. Magnesium oxide and other compounds are also used in the chemical, agricultural, and construction industries. Magnesium's principal use is as an alloying addition for aluminum. These aluminum-magnesium alloys are used primarily in beverage cans. Due to their lightness and considerable tensile strength, the alloys are also used in structural components in airplanes and automobiles.

**Prices** – The average monthly price of ferromanganese (high carbon, FOB plant) in 2021 surged +69.1% yr/yr to $2,038.93 per gross ton, below the 2008 record high of $2,953.84 per gross ton.

**Supply** – World primary production of magnesium in 2022 fell by -6.5% yr/yr to 1.0 million metric tons. The world's largest primary producer of magnesium in 2022 was China, with 800,000 metric tons, which is 90.0% of the world's total production. Russia produced 50,000 metric tons, and Israel produced 20,000 metric tons

**Demand** – Total U.S. consumption of magnesium for all structural products in 2020 fell by -4.1% yr/yr to 24,156 metric tons. In 2020, for structural products, 99.1% of magnesium was used for castings, and the remaining 0.9% was used for wrought product. U.S. consumption of magnesium for aluminum alloys in 2020 fell by -7.3% yr/yr to 15.200 metric tons. The consumption of magnesium for other uses in 2020 fell by -4.4% yr/yr to 38.8 metric tons. Total U.S. consumption of primary magnesium in 2021 fell by -5.6% at 51,000 metric tons.

**Trade** – U.S. exports of magnesium in 2022 fell by -37.5% yr/yr to a record low of 5,000 metric tons. U.S. imports of magnesium in 2022 rose by +94.0% yr/yr to 97,000 metric tons.

## World Production of Magnesium (Primary)   In Metric Tons

| Year | Brazil | Canada | China | Israel | Kazakhstan | Russia | Serbia | Ukraine | United States | Total |
|---|---|---|---|---|---|---|---|---|---|---|
| 2013 | 16,000 | 770,000 | 27,399 | 13,000 | 7,500 | 66,000 | ---- | 10,300 | W | 910,000 |
| 2014 | 16,000 | 874,000 | 25,993 | 9,500 | ---- | 62,000 | ---- | 7,200 | W | 995,000 |
| 2015 | 15,000 | 859,000 | 19,307 | 8,100 | ---- | 60,000 | 200 | 7,700 | W | 970,000 |
| 2016 | 16,000 | 872,800 | 22,548 | 10,000 | ---- | 58,900 | 3,750 | 6,770 | W | 993,000 |
| 2017 | 20,000 | 904,600 | 23,000 | 12,000 | ---- | 65,000 | 14,000 | 7,300 | W | 1,050,000 |
| 2018 | 21,000 | 863,000 | 21,000 | 17,000 | ---- | 67,000 | 4,000 | 7,000 | W | 1,000,000 |
| 2019 | 22,000 | 970,000 | 21,000 | 25,000 | ---- | 67,000 | 7,000 | 8,000 | W | 1,120,000 |
| 2020 | 18,000 | 886,000 | 19,000 | 16,000 | ---- | 48,000 | 12,000 | 6,000 | W | 1,000,000 |
| 2021[1] | 20,000 | 930,000 | 18,000 | 16,000 | ---- | 58,000 | 13,000 | 10,000 | W | 1,070,000 |
| 2022[2] | 20,000 | 900,000 | 20,000 | 15,000 | ---- | 50,000 | 13,000 | 2,000 | W | 1,000,000 |

[1] Preliminary.   [2] Estimate.   W = Withheld.   *Source: U.S. Geological Survey (USGS)*

## Salient Statistics of Magnesium in the United States   In Metric Tons

| Year | Primary (Ingot) | New Scrap | Old Scrap | Total | Total Exports[3] | Imports for Consumption | Stocks Dec. 31[4] | Price $ Per Pound[5] | Castings | Wrought | Total Structural Products | Aluminum Alloys | Other Uses | Total |
|---|---|---|---|---|---|---|---|---|---|---|---|---|---|---|
| 2013 | W | 54,200 | 25,000 | 79,200 | 16,100 | 45,900 | W | 2.13 | 10,829 | 2,240 | 13,069 | 24,400 | 42,000 | 66,400 |
| 2014 | W | 55,200 | 25,000 | 81,100 | 17,000 | 51,900 | W | 2.15 | 9,638 | 2,340 | 11,978 | 22,600 | 41,100 | 63,700 |
| 2015 | W | 65,600 | 22,900 | 88,500 | 15,200 | 49,200 | W | 2.15 | 9,361 | 1,040 | 10,401 | 21,400 | 42,400 | 63,800 |
| 2016 | W | 72,700 | 29,400 | 102,000 | 19,300 | 45,500 | W | 2.15 | 29,739 | 1,870 | 31,609 | 13,000 | 56,000 | 69,000 |
| 2017 | W | 85,400 | 29,000 | 114,000 | 13,700 | 41,900 | W | 2.15 | 28,372 | 892 | 29,264 | 15,300 | 49,700 | 65,000 |
| 2018 | W | 80,400 | 28,700 | 109,000 | 12,000 | 47,000 | W | 2.17 | 25,093 | 206 | 25,299 | 15,100 | 40,900 | 56,000 |
| 2019 | W | 74,500 | 26,100 | 103,000 | 10,000 | 59,000 | W | 2.45 | 24,990 | 206 | 25,196 | 16,400 | 40,600 | 57,000 |
| 2020 | W | 70,300 | 24,500 | 95,000 | 15,000 | 61,000 | W | 2.49 | 23,950 | 206 | 24,156 | 15,200 | 38,800 | 54,000 |
| 2021[1] | W | | | 103,000 | 8,000 | 50,000 | W | 3.55 | | | | | | 51,000 |
| 2022[2] | W | | | 120,000 | 5,000 | 97,000 | W | 7.60 | | | | | | 50,000 |

[1] Preliminary.   [2] Estimate.   [3] Metal & alloys in crude form & scrap.   [4] Estimate of Industry Stocks, metal.   [5] Magnesium ingots (99.8%), f.o.b. Valasco, Texas.   [6] Distributive or sacrificial purposes.   W = Withheld proprietary data.   *Source: U.S. Geological Survey (USGS)*

# Manganese

Manganese (atomic symbol Mn) is a silvery-white, very brittle, metallic element used primarily in making alloys. Manganese was first distinguished as an element and isolated in 1774 by Johan Gottlieb Gahn. Manganese dissolves in acid and corrodes in moist air.

Manganese is found in the earth's crust in the form of ores such as rhodochrosite, franklinite, psilomelane, and manganite. Pyrolusite is the principal ore of manganese. Pure manganese is produced by igniting pyrolusite with aluminum powder or by electrolyzing manganese sulfate.

Manganese is used primarily in the steel industry for creating alloys, such as ferromanganese and spiegeleisen. In steel, manganese improves forging and rolling qualities, strength, toughness, stiffness, wear resistance, and hardness. Manganese is also used in plant fertilizers, animal feed, pigments, and dry cell batteries.

**Prices** – The average monthly price of ferromanganese (high carbon, FOB plant) in 2022 rose by +24.4% yr/yr to $2,537.21 per gross ton, below the 2008 record high of $2,953.84 per gross ton.

**Supply** – World production of manganese ore in 2021 rose by +1.1% yr/yr to 56,900 million metric tons. The world's largest producers of manganese ore in 2021 were South Africa with 33.2% of world production, Gabon with 16.9%, Australia with 13.9%, and China with 13.7%.

**Demand** – U.S. consumption of manganese ore in 2022 fell by -7.3% yr/yr to 370,000 metric tons. U.S. consumption of ferromanganese in 2022 rose by +1.5% yr/yr to 340,000 metric tons, below the 2012 record high of 382,000 metric tons.

**Trade** – The U.S. still relies on imports for 100% of its manganese consumption, as it has since 1985. U.S. imports of manganese ore for consumption in 2022 rose by +30.8% yr/yr to 650,000 metric tons, the most since 2007. U.S. imports of ferromanganese for consumption in 2022 rose by +0.3% yr/yr to 330,000 metric tons. U.S. imports of silico-manganese in 2022 rose by +34.2% yr/yr to 420,000 metric tons.

## World Production of Manganese Ore — In Thousands of Metric Tons (Gross Weight)

| Year | Australia[2] (37%-53%) | Brazil (37%) | China (20%-30%) | Gabon (45%-53%) | Ghana (32%-34%) | India (10%-54%) | Kazakh-stan (29%-30%) | Malaysia (32%-45%) | Mexico (27%-50%) | South Africa (30%-48%+) | Ukraine (30%-35%) | Other | World Total |
|---|---|---|---|---|---|---|---|---|---|---|---|---|---|
| 2012 | 7,208 | 2,796 | 21,930 | 3,337 | 1,467 | 1,196 | 1,071 | 1,100 | 511 | 8,931 | 1,234 | 1,340 | 52,900 |
| 2013 | 7,447 | 2,883 | 17,478 | 3,997 | 1,812 | 3,112 | 1,121 | 1,125 | 580 | 10,958 | 1,525 | 1,670 | 54,500 |
| 2014 | 7,505 | 2,723 | 19,590 | 3,781 | 1,497 | 2,200 | 1,092 | 835 | 652 | 14,051 | 1,526 | ---- | 57,600 |
| 2015 | 7,400 | 2,868 | 10,566 | 4,112 | 1,478 | 2,300 | 616 | 502 | 600 | 11,033 | 1,203 | ---- | 44,500 |
| 2016 | 5,164 | 2,811 | 14,117 | 3,379 | 1,967 | 3,365 | 510 | 701 | 600 | 10,806 | 1,250 | ---- | 46,200 |
| 2017 | 6,473 | 3,334 | 19,032 | 4,717 | 3,004 | 1,957 | 464 | 1,226 | 590 | 14,653 | 1,425 | ---- | 59,100 |
| 2018 | 8,193 | 3,189 | 10,403 | 5,071 | 4,552 | 3,924 | 434 | 1,263 | 560 | 14,920 | 1,521 | ---- | 57,000 |
| 2019 | 7,545 | 3,726 | 10,325 | 6,169 | 5,383 | 3,134 | 460 | 1,131 | 576 | 17,000 | 1,687 | ---- | 60,900 |
| 2020 | 7,976 | 2,469 | 10,394 | 7,916 | 2,358 | 2,146 | 276 | 870 | 575 | 16,021 | 1,888 | ---- | 56,300 |
| 2021[1] | 7,911 | 1,426 | 7,799 | 9,643 | 3,336 | 1,609 | 280 | 913 | 594 | 18,880 | 1,760 | ---- | 56,900 |

[1] Preliminary.  [2] Metallurgical Ore.  [3] Concentrate.  [4] Ranges of percentage of manganese.  Source: U.S. Geological Survey (USGS)

## Salient Statistics of Manganese in the United States — In Thousands of Metric Tons (Gross Weight)

| Year | Net Import Reliance As a % of Apparent Consump | Manganese Ore (35% or More Manganese) Imports for Consumption | Exports | Consumption | Stocks Dec. 31[3] | Ferromanganese Imports for Consumption | Exports | Consumption | Avg Price Mn. Metallurgical Ore $/Metric Ton Unit[4] | Silicomanganese Exports | Imports |
|---|---|---|---|---|---|---|---|---|---|---|---|
| 2013 | 100 | 558 | 1 | 523 | 217 | 335 | 2 | 368 | 4.61 | 6.0 | 329.0 |
| 2014 | 100 | 387 | 1 | 508 | 189 | 365 | 6 | 360 | 4.49 | 3.0 | 448.0 |
| 2015 | 100 | 441 | 1 | 451 | 187 | 292 | 5 | 344 | 3.53 | 1.0 | 301.0 |
| 2016 | 100 | 282 | 1 | 410 | 207 | 229 | 7 | 342 | 3.41 | 2.0 | 264.0 |
| 2017 | 100 | 297 | 1 | 378 | 141 | 331 | 9 | 345 | 6.43 | 8.0 | 351.0 |
| 2018 | 100 | 440 | 3 | 369 | 139 | 427 | 10 | 348 | 7.17 | 4.0 | 412.0 |
| 2019 | 100 | 434 | 1 | 442 | 143 | 332 | 5 | 336 | 6.60 | 2.0 | 351.0 |
| 2020 | 100 | 367 | 1 | 378 | 229 | 223 | 5 | 325 | ---- | 2.0 | 269.0 |
| 2021[1] | 100 | 497 | 1 | 399 | 237 | 329 | 9 | 335 | ---- | 5.0 | 313.0 |
| 2022[2] | 100 | 650 | 1 | 370 | 240 | 330 | 2 | 340 | ---- | 4.0 | 420.0 |

[1] Preliminary.  [2] Estimate.  [3] Including bonded warehouses; excludes Gov't stocks; also excludes small tonnages of dealers' stocks.
[4] 46-48% Mn, C.I.F. U.S. Ports.  Source: U.S. Geological Survey (USGS)

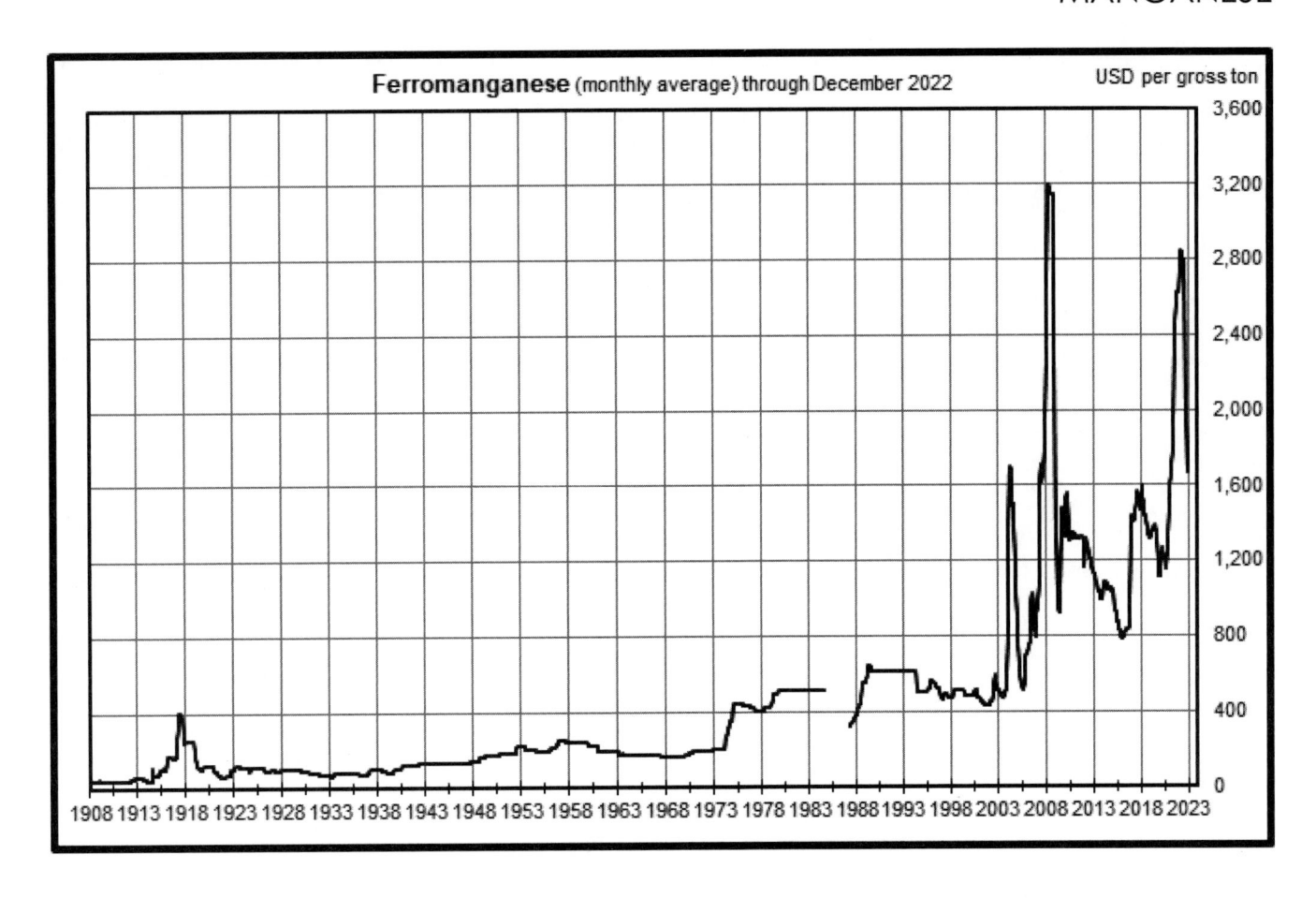

# MANGANESE

**Ferromanganese** (monthly average) through December 2022 — USD per gross ton

## Imports[3] of Manganese Ore (20% or More Mn) in the United States     In Metric Tons (Mn Content)

| Year | Australia | Brazil | Gabon | Mexico | Morocco | South Africa | Total | Customs Value ($1,000) |
|---|---|---|---|---|---|---|---|---|
| 2012 | 15,000 | 3,970 | 152,000 | 2,200 | 2,670 | 46,400 | 226,000 | 101,000 |
| 2013 | 29,200 | 3,850 | 192,000 | 4,810 | 3,800 | 12,900 | 263,000 | 126,000 |
| 2014 | 17,500 | 1,690 | 143,000 | 3,440 | 954 | 17,200 | 186,000 | 88,300 |
| 2015 | 16,700 | 2,210 | 171,000 | 2,100 | 128 | 23,800 | 232,000 | 92,500 |
| 2016 | 3,510 | 290 | 106,530 | 8,820 | 87 | 14,968 | 135,200 | 40,700 |
| 2017 | 9,770 | 340 | 134,640 | 10,690 | 135 | 14,400 | 170,100 | 73,300 |
| 2018 | 13,500 | 3,890 | 141,130 | 15,290 | 66 | 38,170 | 204,800 | 122,000 |
| 2019 | ---- | 9,070 | 187,000 | 21,400 | 165 | 22,540 | 241,000 | 126,000 |
| 2020[1] | ---- | 273 | 123,000 | 30,000 | 762 | 31,500 | 186,000 | 86,700 |
| 2021[2] | ---- | 97 | 202,000 | 21,300 | 1,210 | 36,600 | 261,000 | 99,800 |

[1] Preliminary.   [2] Estimate.   [3] Imports for consumption.   Source: U.S. Geological Survey (USGS)

## Average Price of Ferromanganese[1]     In Dollars Per Gross Ton -- Carloads

| Year | Jan. | Feb. | Mar. | Apr. | May | June | July | Aug. | Sept. | Oct. | Nov. | Dec. | Average |
|---|---|---|---|---|---|---|---|---|---|---|---|---|---|
| 2013 | 1,140.00 | 1,128.16 | 1,128.81 | 1,121.14 | 1,076.94 | 1,071.25 | 1,037.50 | 1,037.50 | 1,031.88 | 1,000.00 | 1,000.00 | 1,000.00 | 1,064.43 |
| 2014 | 1,006.19 | 1,066.50 | 1,088.58 | 1,090.00 | 1,080.00 | 1,078.22 | 1,041.25 | 1,060.00 | 1,053.34 | 1,055.22 | 1,060.00 | 1,039.53 | 1,059.90 |
| 2015 | 1,042.00 | 1,036.06 | 1,029.09 | 944.66 | 939.75 | 929.77 | 876.82 | 875.00 | 841.67 | 836.36 | 825.00 | 797.73 | 914.49 |
| 2016 | 779.34 | 792.00 | 797.50 | 805.00 | 813.57 | 821.59 | 836.25 | 835.00 | 836.67 | 845.00 | 1,012.12 | 1,320.24 | 874.52 |
| 2017 | 1,410.00 | 1,438.42 | 1,430.87 | 1,406.50 | 1,418.64 | 1,470.68 | 1,509.00 | 1,547.39 | 1,568.50 | 1,552.84 | 1,540.00 | 1,473.12 | 1,480.50 |
| 2018 | 1,500.60 | 1,564.21 | 1,595.45 | 1,527.62 | 1,509.32 | 1,438.57 | 1,433.57 | 1,404.57 | 1,375.00 | 1,345.65 | 1,337.50 | 1,327.12 | 1,446.60 |
| 2019 | 1,321.90 | 1,324.34 | 1,346.67 | 1,379.76 | 1,374.55 | 1,374.00 | 1,358.18 | 1,386.36 | 1,344.50 | 1,296.09 | 1,193.42 | 1,115.63 | 1,317.95 |
| 2020 | 1,112.50 | 1,125.63 | 1,167.50 | 1,265.00 | 1,247.50 | 1,220.00 | 1,220.00 | 1,191.25 | 1,155.00 | 1,172.50 | 1,247.50 | 1,343.00 | 1,205.62 |
| 2021 | 1,464.00 | 1,605.00 | 1,644.38 | 1,665.00 | 1,717.50 | 1,783.75 | 1,975.00 | 2,325.00 | 2,475.00 | 2,562.50 | 2,625.00 | 2,625.00 | 2,038.93 |
| 2022 | 2,625.00 | 2,625.00 | 2,750.00 | 2,850.00 | 2,837.50 | 2,800.00 | 2,800.00 | 2,800.00 | 2,790.00 | 1,950.00 | 1,950.00 | 1,669.00 | 2,537.21 |

[1] Domestic standard, high carbon, FOB plant, carloads.   Source: American Metal Market (AMM)

# Meats

U.S. commercial red meat includes beef, veal, lamb, and pork. Red meat is a good source of iron, vitamin B12, and protein, and eliminating it from the diet can lead to iron and zinc deficiencies. Today, red meat is far leaner than it was 30 years ago due to newer breeds of livestock that carry less fat. The leanest cuts of beef include tenderloin, sirloin, and flank. The leanest cuts of pork include pork tenderloin, loin chops, and rib chops.

The USDA (United States Department of Agriculture) grades various cuts of meat. "Prime" is the highest USDA grade for beef, veal, and lamb. "Choice" is the grade designation below Prime for beef, veal, and lamb. "Commercial" and "Cutter" grades are two of the lower designations for beef, usually sold as ground meat, sausage, and canned meat. "Canner" is the lowest USDA grade designation for beef and is used primarily in canned meats not sold at retail.

**Supply** – World total meat production in 2021 rose by +4.4% to 164.917 million metric tons, moderately below the record high of 173.611 million metric tons in 2018. China was the world's largest meat producer in 2021, with 50.185 million metric tons of production (up +12.6% yr/yr), accounting for 30.4% of world production. U.S. production of red meats in 2021 rose by +0.2% yr/yr to 55.896 billion pounds, a new record high. U.S. production of beef in 2021 rose by +2.8% yr/yr to 28.007 billion pounds, a new record high. Beef accounted for 50.1% of all U.S. meat production in 2021. U.S. production of pork in 2021 fell by -2.2% yr/yr to 27.688 billion pounds, below the record high of 28.318 in 2020. Pork accounted for 50.5% of U.S. meat production. Based on 2021 data, veal accounted for only 0.1% of U.S. meat production, and lamb and mutton account for only 0.3% of U.S. meat production.

**Demand** – U.S. per-capita meat consumption in 2021 rose by +0.2% yr/yr to 111.5 pounds per person per year, above the 2014 record low of 101.7 pounds per person. Meat consumption has fallen sharply from 192 pounds per person back in 1970, reflecting the trend towards eating more chicken and fish and the availability of meat substitutes. Per-capita beef consumption in 2021 rose by +1.4% from 2020's 58.1 pounds, half the record high of 127.5 pounds seen in 1976. Per capita pork consumption in 2021 fell by -1.2% yr/yr to 51.1 pounds per person per year and remains above the 2011 record low of 45.7 pounds. Based on 2015 data, per-capita consumption of veal is negligible at 0.2 pounds per person. Based on 2020 data, per-capita in 2021 lamb/mutton consumption rose by +16.7% to 1.4 pounds per person.

**Trade** – World red meat exports in 2021 rose by +0.1% to 21.869 million metric tons, a new record high. The world's largest red meat exporters in 2021 were the U.S. with 21.3% of world exports, the European Union with 20.4%, Brazil with 17.8%, Canada with 9.1%, Australia with 6.4%, and India with 5.5%.

## World Total Meat Production[4]    In Thousands of Metric Tons

| Year | Argentina | Australia | Brazil | Canada | China[4] | European Union | India | Mexico | New Zealand | Russia | South Africa | United States | World Total |
|---|---|---|---|---|---|---|---|---|---|---|---|---|---|
| 2013 | 3,266 | 2,719 | 13,335 | 2,879 | 62,314 | 29,747 | 3,800 | 2,937 | 667 | 3,761 | 1,119 | 22,276 | 167,181 |
| 2014 | 3,142 | 2,957 | 13,123 | 2,906 | 64,365 | 29,983 | 4,000 | 2,962 | 705 | 3,846 | 1,207 | 21,443 | 169,073 |
| 2015 | 3,204 | 2,921 | 12,944 | 2,946 | 62,623 | 30,933 | 4,080 | 3,014 | 734 | 3,953 | 1,271 | 21,938 | 169,361 |
| 2016 | 3,152 | 2,511 | 13,100 | 3,044 | 60,424 | 29,886 | 4,170 | 3,090 | 693 | 4,159 | 1,334 | 22,827 | 165,619 |
| 2017 | 3,394 | 2,557 | 13,475 | 3,159 | 60,864 | 29,709 | 4,230 | 3,192 | 700 | 4,284 | 1,278 | 23,554 | 167,579 |
| 2018 | 3,638 | 2,733 | 13,738 | 3,220 | 60,480 | 30,223 | 4,240 | 3,301 | 718 | 4,512 | 1,275 | 24,199 | 169,731 |
| 2019 | 3,735 | 2,830 | 14,025 | 3,342 | 49,220 | 29,960 | 4,270 | 3,435 | 757 | 4,698 | 1,281 | 24,928 | 159,557 |
| 2020 | 3,825 | 2,544 | 14,100 | 3,429 | 43,060 | 30,101 | 3,760 | 3,530 | 772 | 4,989 | 1,280 | 25,234 | 153,417 |
| 2021[1] | 3,695 | 2,332 | 14,115 | 3,486 | 54,480 | 30,480 | 4,195 | 3,613 | 799 | 5,080 | 1,290 | 25,294 | 165,973 |
| 2022[2] | 3,810 | 2,305 | 14,700 | 3,480 | 62,125 | 29,460 | 4,350 | 3,710 | 770 | 5,180 | 1,297 | 25,147 | 173,188 |

[1] Preliminary.  [2] Forecast.  [4] Predominately pork production.  Source: Foreign Agricultural Service, U.S. Department of Agriculture (FAS-USDA)

## Production and Consumption of Red Meats in The United States

|  | Beef | | | Veal | | | Lamb & Mutton | | | Pork (Excluding Lard) | | | All Meats | | |
|---|---|---|---|---|---|---|---|---|---|---|---|---|---|---|---|
| | Commercial Production | Consumption Total | Per Capita | Commercial Production | Consumption Total | Per Capita | Commercial Production | Consumption Total | Per Capita | Commercial Production | Consumption Total | Per Capita | Commercial Production | Consumption Total | Per Capita |
| Year | Million Pounds | Million Pounds | Lbs. | Million Pounds | Million Pounds | Lbs. | Million Pounds | Million Pounds | Lbs. | Million Pounds | Million Pounds | Lbs. | Million Pounds | Million Pounds | Lbs. |
| 2013 | 25,720 | 25,476 | 56.3 | 117 | 119 | 0.3 | 161 | 324 | 0.9 | 23,203 | 19,104 | 46.9 | 49,271 | 45,022 | 104.4 |
| 2014 | 24,250 | 24,687 | 54.2 | 100 | 98 | 0.3 | 161 | 340 | 0.9 | 22,858 | 18,836 | 45.9 | 47,435 | 43,955 | 101.3 |
| 2015 | 23,698 | 24,773 | 54.0 | 88 | 88 | 0.2 | 155 | 357 | 1.0 | 24,517 | 20,592 | 49.8 | 48,520 | 45,806 | 105.0 |
| 2016 | 25,288 | 25,673 | 55.6 | 81 | 73 | 0.2 | 155 | 381 | 1.0 | 24,957 | 20,892 | 50.2 | 50,481 | 47,015 | 107.0 |
| 2017 | 26,250 | 26,492 | 57.0 | 80 | 78 | 0.2 | 150 | 396 | 1.1 | 25,598 | 21,034 | 50.2 | 52,078 | 48,000 | 108.5 |
| 2018 | 26,938 | 26,763 | 57.3 | 81 | 89 | 0.2 | 158 | 415 | 1.1 | 26,329 | 21,490 | 51.0 | 53,507 | 48,758 | 109.7 |
| 2019 | 27,224 | 27,276 | 57.8 | 79 | 81 | 0.2 | 153 | 422 | 1.1 | 27,652 | 22,189 | 52.1 | 55,108 | 49,968 | 111.9 |
| 2020[1] | 27,244 | 27,559 | 58.1 | 69 | 66 | 0.2 | 143 | 451 | 1.2 | 28,318 | 22,122 | 51.7 | 55,774 | 50,198 | 111.3 |
| 2021[2] | 28,016 | 27,962 | 58.9 | 58 | 64 | 0.2 | 143 | 506 | 1.4 | 27,690 | 21,865 | 51.1 | 55,906 | 50,397 | 111.5 |
| 2022[3] | 28,358 | 28,165 | 59.1 | 59 | 61 | 0.2 | 135 | 483 | 1.3 | 27,009 | 21,957 | 51.1 | 55,561 | 50,666 | 111.6 |

[1] Preliminary.  [2] Estimate.  [3] Forecast.  Source: Economic Research Service, U.S. Department of Agriculture (ERS-USDA)

# MEATS

## Total Red Meat Imports (Carcass Weight Equivalent) of Principal Countries    In Thousands of Metric Tons

| Year | Brazil | Canada | Egypt | European Union | Hong Kong | Japan | Korea, South | Mexico | Philippines | Russia | Taiwan | United States | World Total |
|---|---|---|---|---|---|---|---|---|---|---|---|---|---|
| 2013 | 57 | 499 | 195 | 382 | 869 | 1,960 | 716 | 877 | 310 | 1,757 | 165 | 1,419 | 12,875 |
| 2014 | 80 | 485 | 270 | 377 | 989 | 2,049 | 823 | 879 | 357 | 1,375 | 196 | 1,796 | 13,173 |
| 2015 | 59 | 482 | 360 | 365 | 727 | 1,955 | 963 | 982 | 313 | 954 | 237 | 2,034 | 13,441 |
| 2016 | 65 | 456 | 340 | 560 | 851 | 2,058 | 1,065 | 1,024 | 350 | 809 | 226 | 1,861 | 15,921 |
| 2017 | 56 | 447 | 250 | 548 | 971 | 2,266 | 1,113 | 1,073 | 401 | 836 | 264 | 1,864 | 16,039 |
| 2018 | 48 | 464 | 300 | 591 | 932 | 2,320 | 1,268 | 1,166 | 470 | 533 | 279 | 1,833 | 16,860 |
| 2019 | 45 | 446 | 340 | 599 | 687 | 2,346 | 1,244 | 1,174 | 407 | 516 | 291 | 1,816 | 18,394 |
| 2020 | 52 | 523 | 230 | 510 | 891 | 2,244 | 1,103 | 1,107 | 358 | 376 | 269 | 1,925 | 21,378 |
| 2021[1] | 65 | 475 | 300 | 419 | 735 | 2,227 | 1,158 | 1,327 | 682 | 314 | 266 | 2,053 | 21,480 |
| 2022[2] | 74 | 445 | 315 | 520 | 395 | 2,310 | 1,325 | 1,440 | 810 | 210 | 330 | 2,142 | 19,940 |

[1] Preliminary.    [2] Forecast.    Source: Foreign Agricultural Service, U.S. Department of Agriculture (FAS-USDA)

## Total Red Meat Exports (Carcass Weight Equivalent) of Principal Countries    In Thousands of Metric Tons

| Year | Argentina | Australia | Brazil | Canada | China | European Union | India | New Zealand | Russia | Ukraine | United States | Uruguay | World Total |
|---|---|---|---|---|---|---|---|---|---|---|---|---|---|
| 2013 | 183 | 1,552 | 2,367 | 1,508 | 279 | 2,387 | 1,713 | 507 | 13 | 32 | 3,436 | 323 | 15,617 |
| 2014 | 193 | 1,795 | 2,398 | 1,528 | 312 | 2,375 | 2,022 | 552 | 14 | 35 | 3,477 | 331 | 16,423 |
| 2015 | 181 | 1,802 | 2,277 | 1,561 | 257 | 2,585 | 1,754 | 609 | 18 | 65 | 3,300 | 352 | 16,200 |
| 2016 | 211 | 1,445 | 2,472 | 1,684 | 217 | 4,577 | 1,709 | 560 | 33 | 44 | 3,536 | 396 | 18,744 |
| 2017 | 286 | 1,454 | 2,579 | 1,734 | 228 | 4,378 | 1,786 | 565 | 44 | 56 | 3,852 | 409 | 19,283 |
| 2018 | 509 | 1,623 | 2,743 | 1,754 | 223 | 4,407 | 1,511 | 603 | 53 | 53 | 4,099 | 436 | 19,997 |
| 2019 | 772 | 1,772 | 3,175 | 1,811 | 156 | 4,967 | 1,494 | 624 | 85 | 51 | 4,240 | 436 | 21,743 |
| 2020 | 846 | 1,507 | 3,717 | 2,059 | 116 | 5,889 | 1,284 | 639 | 189 | 35 | 4,640 | 411 | 23,797 |
| 2021[1] | 755 | 1,329 | 3,641 | 2,078 | 121 | 5,665 | 1,397 | 684 | 208 | 41 | 4,748 | 557 | 23,661 |
| 2022[2] | 825 | 1,292 | 4,217 | 2,010 | 122 | 4,825 | 1,475 | 648 | 210 | 15 | 4,480 | 570 | 23,072 |

[1] Preliminary.    [2] Forecast.    Source: Foreign Agricultural Service, U.S. Department of Agriculture (FAS-USDA)

## Exports and Imports of Meats in the United States (Carcass Weight Equivalent)[3]

| | Exports | | | | Imports | | | |
|---|---|---|---|---|---|---|---|---|
| Year | Beef and Veal | Lamb and Mutton | Pork[3] | All Meat | Beef and Veal | Lamb and Mutton | Pork[3] | All Meat |
| 2013 | 2,588 | 7 | 4,986 | 7,581 | 2,250 | 173 | 880 | 3,303 |
| 2014 | 2,574 | 7 | 5,092 | 7,673 | 2,947 | 195 | 1,011 | 4,153 |
| 2015 | 2,267 | 4 | 5,010 | 7,281 | 3,368 | 214 | 1,116 | 4,698 |
| 2016 | 2,557 | 5 | 5,239 | 7,801 | 3,012 | 216 | 1,091 | 4,319 |
| 2017 | 2,859 | 6 | 5,632 | 8,497 | 2,993 | 252 | 1,116 | 4,361 |
| 2018 | 3,160 | 6 | 5,877 | 9,043 | 2,998 | 273 | 1,042 | 4,313 |
| 2019 | 3,026 | 6 | 6,321 | 9,353 | 3,058 | 272 | 945 | 4,275 |
| 2020 | 2,951 | 3 | 7,279 | 10,233 | 3,339 | 302 | 904 | 4,545 |
| 2021[1] | 3,441 | 3 | 7,026 | 10,470 | 3,346 | 364 | 1,180 | 4,890 |
| 2022[2] | 3,536 | 6 | 6,338 | 9,880 | 3,391 | 358 | 1,344 | 5,093 |

[1] Preliminary.    [2] Estimate.    [3] Includes meat content of minor meats and of mixed products.
Source: Economic Research Service, U.S. Department of Agriculture (FAS-USDA)

## Average Wholesale Prices of Meats in the United States    In Cent Per Pound

| Year | Composite Retail Price of Beef, Choice, Grade 3 | Composite Retail Price of Pork[3] | Wholesale Value[4] Beef | Wholesale Value[4] Pork | Net Farm Value[5] of Pork | Cow Beef Canner & Cutter, Central US | Boxed Beef Cut-out, Choice 1-3, Central US 550-700 Lb. | Pork Carcass Cut-out, U.S., No. 2 | Lamb Carcass, Choice-Prime, E. Coast, 55-65 lbs. | Pork[6] Loins, Central US 14-18 lbs. | Skinned Ham, Central US 17-20 lbs. | Pork Bellies, Central US 12-14 lbs. |
|---|---|---|---|---|---|---|---|---|---|---|---|---|
| 2013 | 528.93 | 364.39 | 298.48 | 157.58 | 110.07 | ---- | 195.64 | 91.69 | 281.52 | 116.53 | 79.12 | 152.15 |
| 2014 | 597.03 | 401.88 | 364.71 | 187.66 | 131.80 | ---- | 238.94 | 110.10 | 339.65 | 141.93 | 107.00 | 144.90 |
| 2015 | 628.89 | 385.25 | 362.78 | 145.72 | 87.39 | ---- | 237.48 | 78.96 | 343.07 | 103.77 | 65.11 | 121.07 |
| 2016 | 596.38 | 374.67 | 316.78 | 150.12 | 80.05 | ---- | 207.00 | 78.36 | 332.90 | 96.95 | 66.73 | 123.94 |
| 2017 | 590.86 | 378.42 | 321.47 | 155.37 | 87.41 | ---- | 209.74 | 84.02 | 339.16 | 97.28 | 64.63 | 148.76 |
| 2018 | 592.33 | 374.45 | 328.55 | 140.14 | 79.16 | ---- | 214.06 | 76.09 | ---- | 92.91 | 56.80 | 133.73 |
| 2019 | 604.37 | 384.33 | 341.48 | 145.38 | 82.95 | ---- | 222.86 | 77.14 | ---- | 88.88 | 67.66 | 131.84 |
| 2020 | 653.55 | 402.93 | 365.51 | 148.09 | 74.51 | ---- | 236.36 | 77.31 | ---- | 99.22 | 54.66 | 95.86 |
| 2021[1] | 724.52 | 450.31 | 423.19 | 200.96 | 116.03 | ---- | 280.30 | 104.11 | ---- | 103.03 | 70.18 | 190.83 |
| 2022[2] | 758.59 | 489.71 | 397.88 | 199.53 | 121.52 | ---- | 263.94 | 103.72 | ---- | 116.08 | 85.54 | 172.81 |

[1] Preliminary.    [2] Estimate.    [3] Sold as retail cuts (ham, bacon, loin, etc.).    [4] Quantity equivalent to 1 pound of retail cuts.
[5] Portion of gross farm value minus farm by-product allowance.    Source: Economic Research Service, U.S. Department of Agriculture (ERS-USDA)

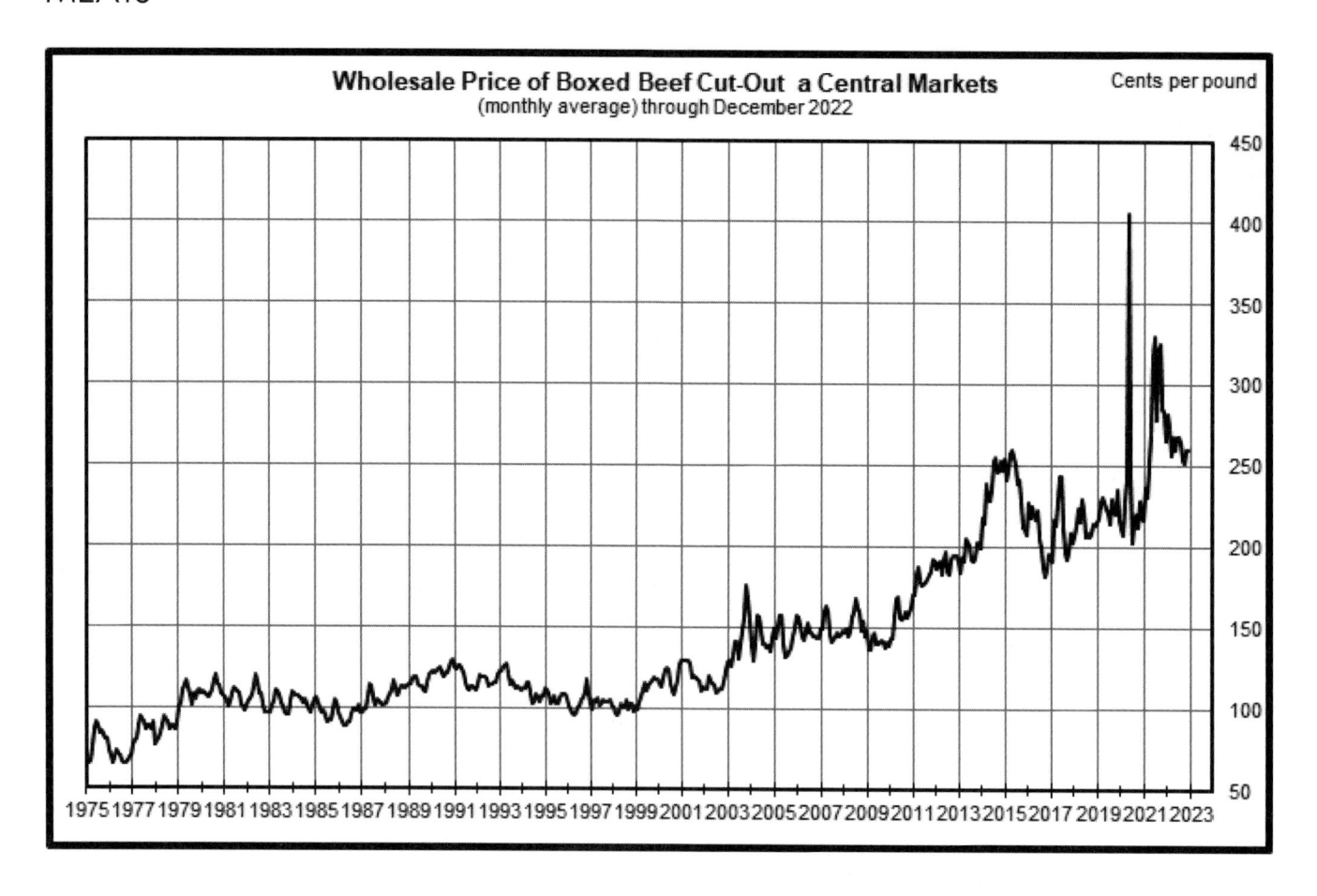

# MEATS

**Wholesale Price of Boxed Beef Cut-Out a Central Markets**
(monthly average) through December 2022 — Cents per pound

## Average Wholesale Price of Boxed Beef Cut-Out[2], Choice 1-3, at Central US     In Cents Per Pound

| Year | Jan. | Feb. | Mar. | Apr. | May | June | July | Aug. | Sept. | Oct. | Nov. | Dec. | Average |
|---|---|---|---|---|---|---|---|---|---|---|---|---|---|
| 2013 | 191.12 | 183.60 | 193.79 | 191.01 | 205.64 | 200.83 | 191.87 | 191.66 | 194.01 | 202.33 | 202.01 | 199.77 | 195.64 |
| 2014 | 218.00 | 214.43 | 239.03 | 229.14 | 228.96 | 236.60 | 252.87 | 254.83 | 246.14 | 246.80 | 253.18 | 247.35 | 238.94 |
| 2015 | 254.45 | 241.30 | 247.62 | 257.44 | 260.25 | 250.06 | 238.91 | 241.81 | 227.68 | 212.10 | 210.63 | 207.46 | 237.48 |
| 2016 | 227.76 | 217.46 | 224.61 | 218.88 | 216.91 | 222.59 | 204.88 | 199.30 | 187.77 | 182.29 | 186.27 | 195.23 | 207.00 |
| 2017 | 194.40 | 191.42 | 216.36 | 213.78 | 243.43 | 244.16 | 212.22 | 197.48 | 192.79 | 198.65 | 209.08 | 203.09 | 209.74 |
| 2018 | 207.94 | 213.66 | 223.50 | 215.29 | 229.34 | 221.03 | 206.32 | 209.15 | 206.07 | 208.18 | 214.59 | 213.60 | 214.06 |
| 2019 | 215.03 | 217.81 | 227.45 | 230.30 | 223.61 | 221.28 | 214.81 | 230.17 | 221.35 | 219.70 | 235.53 | 217.24 | 222.86 |
| 2020 | 211.87 | 207.60 | 228.05 | 241.94 | 405.80 | 242.31 | 203.24 | 216.71 | 220.56 | 212.41 | 228.00 | 217.82 | 236.36 |
| 2021 | 216.73 | 236.49 | 231.23 | 271.67 | 317.59 | 329.70 | 278.00 | 321.67 | 325.24 | 285.97 | 283.46 | 265.82 | 280.30 |
| 2022[1] | 282.54 | 272.77 | 256.95 | 268.39 | 260.08 | 268.16 | 267.86 | 264.90 | 254.11 | 251.58 | 259.56 | 260.37 | 263.94 |

[1] Preliminary.   [2] 600-900 pounds.   Source: Economic Research Service, U.S. Department of Agriculture (ERS-USDA)

## Production (Commercial) of All Red Meats in the United States     In Millions of Pounds (Carcass Weight)

| Year | Jan. | Feb. | Mar. | Apr. | May | June | July | Aug. | Sept. | Oct. | Nov. | Dec. | Total |
|---|---|---|---|---|---|---|---|---|---|---|---|---|---|
| 2013 | 4,348.4 | 3,673.2 | 3,994.3 | 4,091.6 | 4,151.4 | 3,859.7 | 4,158.0 | 4,203.2 | 3,937.9 | 4,509.5 | 4,119.5 | 4,136.0 | 49,183 |
| 2014 | 4,248.9 | 3,653.1 | 3,814.8 | 3,976.9 | 3,952.8 | 3,824.0 | 3,906.9 | 3,795.3 | 3,958.8 | 4,319.3 | 3,759.3 | 4,136.2 | 47,346 |
| 2015 | 4,087.0 | 3,731.8 | 4,064.3 | 4,015.5 | 3,805.3 | 4,017.4 | 4,038.5 | 3,901.4 | 4,140.2 | 4,313.4 | 4,033.2 | 4,274.0 | 48,422 |
| 2016 | 4,055.6 | 3,904.2 | 4,261.8 | 3,982.9 | 3,997.1 | 4,225.9 | 3,866.0 | 4,432.2 | 4,323.1 | 4,426.5 | 4,498.4 | 4,402.2 | 50,376 |
| 2017 | 4,291.4 | 3,937.9 | 4,535.1 | 3,968.1 | 4,276.0 | 4,350.8 | 3,988.9 | 4,630.5 | 4,403.8 | 4,635.3 | 4,553.2 | 4,402.4 | 51,973 |
| 2018 | 4,588.4 | 4,059.5 | 4,520.5 | 4,278.2 | 4,501.5 | 4,327.7 | 4,235.3 | 4,765.9 | 4,187.8 | 4,901.4 | 4,682.7 | 4,367.8 | 53,417 |
| 2019 | 4,701.6 | 4,172.4 | 4,433.7 | 4,551.5 | 4,566.2 | 4,369.3 | 4,588.8 | 4,650.2 | 4,443.5 | 5,064.0 | 4,743.1 | 4,726.6 | 55,011 |
| 2020 | 4,959.2 | 4,452.7 | 4,995.3 | 3,862.1 | 3,762.5 | 4,792.1 | 4,810.8 | 4,691.6 | 4,706.2 | 5,085.9 | 4,683.8 | 4,852.6 | 55,655 |
| 2021 | 4,801.4 | 4,386.3 | 5,047.9 | 4,707.8 | 4,295.6 | 4,669.0 | 4,383.1 | 4,588.2 | 4,580.1 | 4,755.0 | 4,804.8 | 4,782.9 | 55,802 |
| 2022[1] | 4,561.0 | 4,431.8 | 4,978.9 | 4,545.5 | 4,484.9 | 4,724.6 | 4,233.5 | 4,826.2 | 4,665.4 | 4,757.1 | 4,790.6 | 4,470.9 | 55,470 |

[1] Preliminary.   Source: Economic Research Service, U.S. Department of Agriculture (ERS-USDA)

# MEATS

### Production (Commercial) of Beef in the United States    In Millions of Pounds (Carcass Weight)

| Year | Jan. | Feb. | Mar. | Apr. | May | June | July | Aug. | Sept. | Oct. | Nov. | Dec. | Total |
|---|---|---|---|---|---|---|---|---|---|---|---|---|---|
| 2013 | 2,260.0 | 1,873.7 | 2,038.6 | 2,127.3 | 2,228.0 | 2,161.4 | 2,293.5 | 2,241.6 | 2,073.6 | 2,316.5 | 2,057.3 | 2,046.5 | 25,718 |
| 2014 | 2,141.1 | 1,788.9 | 1,938.4 | 2,042.8 | 2,071.6 | 2,068.7 | 2,085.9 | 2,024.4 | 2,067.4 | 2,171.5 | 1,850.6 | 2,000.7 | 24,252 |
| 2015 | 1,963.8 | 1,768.7 | 1,931.6 | 1,928.5 | 1,924.9 | 2,001.2 | 2,046.1 | 1,934.1 | 2,085.7 | 2,125.3 | 1,934.1 | 2,045.9 | 23,690 |
| 2016 | 1,953.5 | 1,885.0 | 2,096.0 | 1,964.0 | 2,029.5 | 2,193.0 | 2,024.4 | 2,264.4 | 2,179.2 | 2,210.1 | 2,239.3 | 2,173.3 | 25,212 |
| 2017 | 2,118.3 | 1,933.7 | 2,247.7 | 1,962.7 | 2,162.1 | 2,279.1 | 2,107.5 | 2,401.2 | 2,222.3 | 2,300.7 | 2,289.6 | 2,148.0 | 26,173 |
| 2018 | 2,279.0 | 1,983.9 | 2,203.5 | 2,117.7 | 2,307.0 | 2,300.9 | 2,231.6 | 2,429.6 | 2,157.5 | 2,430.6 | 2,315.1 | 2,116.0 | 26,872 |
| 2019 | 2,308.9 | 1,987.6 | 2,117.7 | 2,261.5 | 2,327.9 | 2,224.6 | 2,359.9 | 2,373.5 | 2,189.3 | 2,438.1 | 2,297.0 | 2,265.0 | 27,151 |
| 2020 | 2,387.6 | 2,130.7 | 2,410.8 | 1,815.4 | 1,865.1 | 2,373.6 | 2,421.2 | 2,334.6 | 2,354.5 | 2,471.5 | 2,262.9 | 2,324.8 | 27,153 |
| 2021 | 2,309.0 | 2,105.5 | 2,480.6 | 2,346.3 | 2,210.9 | 2,399.3 | 2,318.8 | 2,360.0 | 2,299.2 | 2,366.4 | 2,379.4 | 2,362.0 | 27,937 |
| 2022[1] | 2,266.2 | 2,250.4 | 2,505.8 | 2,327.1 | 2,287.7 | 2,453.7 | 2,249.0 | 2,506.5 | 2,391.0 | 2,404.0 | 2,424.3 | 2,225.6 | 28,291 |

[1] Preliminary.    Source: Economic Research Service, U.S. Department of Agriculture (ERS-USDA)

### Production (Commercial) of Pork in the United States    In Millions of Pounds (Carcass Weight)

| Year | Jan. | Feb. | Mar. | Apr. | May | June | July | Aug. | Sept. | Oct. | Nov. | Dec. | Total |
|---|---|---|---|---|---|---|---|---|---|---|---|---|---|
| 2013 | 2,065.5 | 1,779.0 | 1,932.7 | 1,941.8 | 1,900.0 | 1,677.1 | 1,840.8 | 1,938.7 | 1,844.1 | 2,169.9 | 2,041.3 | 2,066.5 | 23,197 |
| 2014 | 2,086.1 | 1,844.4 | 1,854.5 | 1,910.5 | 1,859.5 | 1,734.3 | 1,799.3 | 1,752.1 | 1,871.9 | 2,126.7 | 1,890.7 | 2,114.5 | 22,845 |
| 2015 | 2,104.7 | 1,945.2 | 2,111.5 | 2,066.8 | 1,861.9 | 1,995.8 | 1,972.6 | 1,949.1 | 2,035.5 | 2,168.9 | 2,080.2 | 2,207.1 | 24,499 |
| 2016 | 2,084.2 | 2,000.6 | 2,145.1 | 2,000.1 | 1,948.6 | 2,013.3 | 1,824.6 | 2,149.1 | 2,125.7 | 2,198.1 | 2,240.3 | 2,209.0 | 24,939 |
| 2017 | 2,154.5 | 1,987.4 | 2,267.3 | 1,988.1 | 2,095.8 | 2,053.0 | 1,864.7 | 2,210.1 | 2,164.2 | 2,316.3 | 2,244.8 | 2,235.0 | 25,581 |
| 2018 | 2,290.1 | 2,058.1 | 2,296.8 | 2,141.9 | 2,174.4 | 2,008.6 | 1,985.5 | 2,316.3 | 2,012.9 | 2,450.5 | 2,348.0 | 2,232.1 | 26,315 |
| 2019 | 2,373.6 | 2,167.5 | 2,297.2 | 2,268.8 | 2,218.6 | 2,127.6 | 2,210.7 | 2,258.1 | 2,237.2 | 2,606.2 | 2,428.8 | 2,443.0 | 27,637 |
| 2020 | 2,553.3 | 2,306.2 | 2,566.5 | 2,030.8 | 1,879.6 | 2,400.4 | 2,371.7 | 2,341.2 | 2,335.9 | 2,598.5 | 2,405.5 | 2,510.2 | 28,300 |
| 2021 | 2,477.4 | 2,265.3 | 2,548.5 | 2,343.6 | 2,070.0 | 2,254.3 | 2,049.7 | 2,213.6 | 2,265.8 | 2,372.6 | 2,408.8 | 2,404.0 | 27,674 |
| 2022[1] | 2,280.3 | 2,168.0 | 2,455.9 | 2,201.6 | 2,182.0 | 2,254.9 | 1,970.1 | 2,303.3 | 2,259.4 | 2,338.2 | 2,350.8 | 2,229.9 | 26,994 |

[1] Preliminary.    Source: Economic Research Service, U.S. Department of Agriculture (ERS-USDA)

### Cold Storage Holdings of All[2] Meats in the United States, on First of Month    In Millions of Pounds

| Year | Jan. | Feb. | Mar. | Apr. | May | June | July | Aug. | Sept. | Oct. | Nov. | Dec. |
|---|---|---|---|---|---|---|---|---|---|---|---|---|
| 2013 | 1,043.8 | 1,114.8 | 1,148.1 | 1,182.4 | 1,238.0 | 1,166.3 | 1,071.3 | 1,035.5 | 1,005.0 | 1,041.0 | 1,033.0 | 1,021.9 |
| 2014 | 1,022.2 | 1,077.0 | 1,093.6 | 1,012.3 | 1,015.9 | 981.4 | 930.1 | 939.1 | 934.0 | 970.8 | 956.5 | 930.3 |
| 2015 | 988.5 | 1,131.2 | 1,224.3 | 1,196.3 | 1,229.0 | 1,172.9 | 1,147.6 | 1,136.2 | 1,170.0 | 1,202.1 | 1,159.5 | 1,122.8 |
| 2016 | 1,105.9 | 1,213.4 | 1,182.7 | 1,142.9 | 1,151.1 | 1,129.1 | 1,099.2 | 1,118.1 | 1,130.5 | 1,205.1 | 1,173.3 | 1,079.2 |
| 2017 | 1,083.8 | 1,101.3 | 1,112.9 | 1,051.4 | 1,092.7 | 1,042.4 | 1,012.8 | 1,029.8 | 1,100.0 | 1,159.7 | 1,149.4 | 1,032.3 |
| 2018 | 1,021.2 | 1,129.2 | 1,118.6 | 1,124.4 | 1,159.9 | 1,142.2 | 1,064.1 | 1,096.5 | 1,136.4 | 1,150.8 | 1,135.7 | 1,069.3 |
| 2019 | 1,045.6 | 1,119.9 | 1,134.5 | 1,095.9 | 1,098.1 | 1,077.8 | 1,069.4 | 1,113.9 | 1,128.7 | 1,115.1 | 1,121.6 | 1,092.6 |
| 2020 | 1,101.5 | 1,157.3 | 1,185.8 | 1,162.0 | 1,136.9 | 936.2 | 939.5 | 950.9 | 960.7 | 968.6 | 981.7 | 966.2 |
| 2021 | 986.1 | 1,010.5 | 1,031.7 | 967.9 | 937.6 | 907.5 | 870.7 | 868.9 | 897.2 | 940.3 | 947.8 | 920.4 |
| 2022[1] | 929.3 | 986.4 | 1,035.1 | 1,048.5 | 1,092.8 | 1,097.2 | 1,081.0 | 1,066.8 | 1,084.5 | 1,098.4 | 1,051.2 | 1,006.7 |

[1] Preliminary.    [2] Includes beef and veal, mutton and lamb, pork and products, rendered pork fat, and miscellaneous meats. Excludes lard.
Source: Economic Research Service, U.S. Department of Agriculture (ERS-USDA)

### Cold Storage Holdings of Frozen Beef in the United States, on First of Month    In Millions of Pounds

| Year | Jan. | Feb. | Mar. | Apr. | May | June | July | Aug. | Sept. | Oct. | Nov. | Dec. |
|---|---|---|---|---|---|---|---|---|---|---|---|---|
| 2013 | 465.7 | 484.6 | 490.0 | 511.2 | 510.1 | 482.6 | 481.2 | 462.6 | 430.2 | 445.2 | 440.1 | 450.8 |
| 2014 | 439.4 | 429.3 | 409.5 | 405.8 | 402.3 | 377.6 | 358.2 | 367.9 | 346.6 | 378.2 | 380.9 | 400.8 |
| 2015 | 444.4 | 492.0 | 491.9 | 481.5 | 484.3 | 474.6 | 474.3 | 460.1 | 470.3 | 498.3 | 509.1 | 510.6 |
| 2016 | 512.5 | 534.1 | 506.4 | 481.8 | 467.8 | 461.7 | 464.5 | 469.7 | 476.6 | 519.0 | 533.1 | 531.0 |
| 2017 | 567.9 | 538.2 | 502.4 | 464.0 | 458.4 | 411.5 | 415.3 | 431.8 | 476.6 | 496.0 | 507.0 | 485.2 |
| 2018 | 488.1 | 501.7 | 459.3 | 464.0 | 471.2 | 464.7 | 448.6 | 484.2 | 501.3 | 507.2 | 515.6 | 514.7 |
| 2019 | 495.6 | 510.2 | 474.0 | 451.9 | 430.2 | 405.2 | 405.6 | 454.5 | 469.9 | 469.0 | 466.3 | 478.3 |
| 2020 | 480.1 | 488.2 | 494.6 | 502.3 | 479.5 | 417.4 | 429.3 | 440.2 | 449.3 | 463.0 | 500.2 | 511.4 |
| 2021 | 535.9 | 519.4 | 512.5 | 483.0 | 448.9 | 416.7 | 401.5 | 400.8 | 414.9 | 439.6 | 473.8 | 490.4 |
| 2022[1] | 507.1 | 525.7 | 531.6 | 535.8 | 532.2 | 526.1 | 516.8 | 511.9 | 513.8 | 526.2 | 510.3 | 523.3 |

[1] Preliminary.    Source: Economic Research Service, U.S. Department of Agriculture (ERS-USDA)

# Mercury

Mercury (atomic symbol Hg) was known to the ancient Hindus and Chinese and was also found in Egyptian tombs dating back to 1500 BC. The ancient Greeks used mercury in ointments, and the Romans used it in cosmetics. Alchemists thought mercury turned into gold when it hardened.

Mercury, also called quicksilver, is a heavy, silvery, toxic, transitional metal. Mercury is the only common metal that is liquid at room temperatures. When subjected to a pressure of 7,640 atmospheres (7.7 million millibars), mercury becomes a solid. Mercury dissolves in nitric or concentrated sulfuric acid but is resistant to alkalis. It is a poor conductor of heat. Mercury has superconductivity when cooled to sufficiently low temperatures. It has a freezing point of about −39 degrees Celsius and a boiling point of about 357 degrees Celsius.

Mercury is found in its pure form or combined in small amounts with silvers, but is found most often in the ore cinnabar, a mineral consisting of mercuric sulfide. Pure mercury is produced by heating the cinnabar ore in the air until the mercuric sulfide breaks down. Mercury forms alloys called amalgams with all common metals except iron and platinum. Most mercury is used for the manufacture of industrial chemicals and electrical and electronic applications. Other uses for mercury include its use in gold recovery from ores, barometers, diffusion pumps, laboratory instruments, mercury-vapor lamps, pesticides, batteries, and catalysts. A decline in mercury production and usage since the 1970s reflects a trend for using mercury substitutes due to its toxicity.

**Supply** – World mine production of mercury in 2022 remained unchanged yr/yr at 2,200 metric tons. The world's largest miners of mercury in 2022 were China, with 90.9% of world production, and Tajikistan with 5.5%.

**Trade** – U.S. imports of mercury in 2022 rose by +100.0% yr/yr to 2.0 metric tons. U.S. imports were mostly from Chile and Peru.

## World Mine Production of Mercury    In Metric Tons (1 tonne = 29.008216 flasks)

| Year | Chile (byproduct) | China | Finland | Kyrgyzstan | Mexico (Exports) | Morocco | Peru (Exports) | Russia | Tajikistan | United States | World Total |
|---|---|---|---|---|---|---|---|---|---|---|---|
| 2013 | 19 | 1,820 | ---- | 71 | 266 | 8 | 45 | NA | 30 | NA | 2,320 |
| 2014 | 18 | 2,260 | ---- | 48 | 301 | 8 | 40 | NA | 35 | NA | 2,770 |
| 2015 | 14 | 2,801 | ---- | 46 | 306 | 5 | 35 | NA | 30 | NA | 3,300 |
| 2016 | 2 | 3,482 | ---- | 20 | 262 | 5 | 40 | ---- | 30 | ---- | 4,000 |
| 2017 | 11 | 3,573 | ---- | 20 | 225 | 14 | 40 | ---- | 100 | ---- | 4,060 |
| 2018 | 10 | 3,600 | ---- | 20 | 234 | 32 | 40 | ---- | 100 | ---- | 4,080 |
| 2019 | 10 | 3,600 | ---- | 15 | 63 | 2 | 40 | ---- | 100 | ---- | 3,900 |
| 2020 |   | 2,200 | ---- | 15 | 40 | 2 | 30 | ---- | 178 | ---- | 2,490 |
| 2021[1] |   | 2,000 | ---- | 20 | 39 | 2 | 30 | ---- | 120 | ---- | 2,200 |
| 2022[2] |   | 2,000 | ---- | 6 | 40 | 2 | 30 | ---- | 120 | ---- | 2,200 |

[1] Preliminary.  [2] Estimate.  NA = Not available.  W = Withheld.  Source: U.S. Geological Survey (USGS)

## Salient Statistics of Mercury in the United States    In Metric Tons

| Year | Producing Mines | Secondary Production Industrial | Secondary Production Government[3] | NDS[4] Shipments | Consumer & Dealer Stocks, Dec. 31 | Industrial Demand | Exports | Imports |
|---|---|---|---|---|---|---|---|---|
| 2013 | NA | NA | ---- | ---- | NA | NA | 0 | 38 |
| 2014 | NA | NA | ---- | ---- | NA | NA | ---- | 50 |
| 2015 | NA | NA | ---- | ---- | NA | NA | 0 | 26 |
| 2016 | NA | NA | ---- | ---- | NA | NA | ---- | 24 |
| 2017 | NA | NA | ---- | ---- | NA | NA | ---- | 20 |
| 2018 | NA | NA | ---- | ---- | NA | NA | ---- | 6 |
| 2019 | NA | NA | ---- | ---- | NA | NA | ---- | 9 |
| 2020 | NA | NA | ---- | ---- | NA | NA | ---- | 3 |
| 2021[1] | NA | NA | ---- | ---- | NA | NA | ---- | 1 |
| 2022[2] | NA | NA | ---- | ---- | NA | NA | ---- | 2 |

[1] Preliminary.  [2] Estimate.  [3] Secondary mercury shipped from the Department of Energy.  [4] National Defense Stockpile.  [5] Less than 1/2 unit.  NA = Not available.  Source: U.S. Geological Survey (USGS)

# Milk

Evidence of human consumption of animal milk was discovered in a temple in the Euphrates Valley near Babylon, dating back to 3,000 BC. Humans drink the milk produced from a variety of domesticated mammals, including cows, goats, sheep, camels, reindeer, buffaloes, and llama. In India, half of all milk consumed is from water buffalo. Camels' milk spoils slower than other types of milk in the hot desert, but virtually all milk used for commercial production and consumption comes from cows.

Milk directly from a cow in its natural form is called raw milk. Raw milk is processed by spinning it in a centrifuge, homogenizing it to create a consistent texture (i.e., by forcing hot milk under high pressure through small nozzles), and then sterilizing it through pasteurization (i.e., heating to a high temperature for a specified length of time to destroy pathogenic bacteria). Condensed, powdered, and evaporated milk are produced by evaporating some or all of the water content. Whole milk contains 3.5% milk fat. Lower-fat milks include 2% low-fat milk, 1% low-fat milk, and skim milk, which has only 1/2 gram of milk fat per serving.

The CME Group has three different milk futures contracts: Milk Class III which is milk used in the manufacturing of cheese, Milk Class IV which is milk used in the production of butter and all dried milk products, and Nonfat Dry Milk which is used in commercial or consumer cooking or to reconstitute nonfat milk by the consumer. The Milk Class III contract has the largest volume and open interest.

**Prices** – The average monthly price received by farmers for all milk sold to plants in 2022 rose by +37.3% yr/yr to $25.56 per hundred pounds.

**Supply** – World milk production in 2023 is expected to rise by +1.2% to 666.263 million metric tons, a new record high. The biggest producers are expected to be India with 31.1% of world production, the European Union with 22.1%, and the U.S. with 15.6%. U.S. 2021 milk production rose by +0.2% yr/yr to 226.620 billion pounds, setting a record high.

The number of dairy cows on U.S. farms has fallen sharply in the past three decades from the 12 million level seen in 1970. In 2022, there were 9.404 million dairy cows on U.S. farms, down by -0.5% yr/yr. Dairy farmers have been able to increase milk production even with fewer cows because of a dramatic increase in milk yield per cow. In 2022, the average cow produced a record 24,097 pounds of milk per year, a +0.6% yr/yr increase, more than double the 9,751 pounds seen in 1970.

**Trade** – U.S. imports of milk in 2021 were down by -3.6% yr/yr at 6.532 billion pounds, still well below the record high of 7.500 billion pounds posted in 2005-06.

### World Fluid Milk Production (Cow's Milk)   In Thousands of Metric Tons

| Year | Argentina | Australia | Brazil | Canada | China | European Union | India | Mexico | New Zealand | Russia | Ukraine | United States | World Total |
|---|---|---|---|---|---|---|---|---|---|---|---|---|---|
| 2014 | 11,326 | 9,798 | 25,489 | 8,437 | 33,149 | 150,850 | 146,313 | 11,624 | 21,893 | 29,795 | 11,426 | 93,462 | 570,245 |
| 2015 | 11,552 | 10,091 | 25,650 | 8,773 | 33,298 | 154,550 | 155,481 | 11,900 | 21,587 | 29,688 | 10,864 | 94,579 | 585,047 |
| 2016 | 10,191 | 9,486 | 25,857 | 9,081 | 32,240 | 142,507 | 165,118 | 12,122 | 21,224 | 29,587 | 10,625 | 96,367 | 595,997 |
| 2017 | 10,090 | 9,462 | 26,766 | 9,675 | 31,886 | 144,794 | 176,061 | 12,288 | 21,530 | 29,972 | 10,520 | 97,762 | 613,081 |
| 2018 | 10,837 | 9,451 | 26,745 | 9,944 | 32,250 | 146,305 | 187,700 | 12,537 | 22,017 | 30,398 | 10,300 | 98,688 | 629,489 |
| 2019 | 10,640 | 8,832 | 27,292 | 9,903 | 32,976 | 147,106 | 191,000 | 12,820 | 21,896 | 31,154 | 9,866 | 99,084 | 635,219 |
| 2020 | 11,445 | 9,099 | 28,015 | 10,035 | 35,500 | 149,732 | 194,800 | 12,921 | 21,980 | 32,010 | 9,466 | 101,292 | 649,540 |
| 2021 | 11,900 | 9,067 | 27,825 | 10,157 | 37,950 | 148,978 | 199,000 | 13,022 | 21,995 | 32,020 | 9,000 | 102,630 | 656,865 |
| 2022[1] | 11,900 | 8,550 | 26,630 | 10,230 | 40,350 | 148,050 | 202,500 | 13,152 | 21,100 | 32,150 | 7,480 | 102,967 | 658,322 |
| 2023[2] | 12,000 | 8,475 | 27,480 | 10,330 | 42,100 | 147,200 | 207,500 | 13,420 | 21,000 | 32,300 | 7,160 | 104,101 | 666,263 |

[1] Preliminary.  [2] Forecast.  Source: Foreign Agricultural Service, U.S. Department of Agriculture (FAS-USDA)

### Salient Statistics of Milk in the United States   In Millions of Pounds

| Year | Number of Milk Cows on Farms[3] (Thousands) | Production Per Cow[4] (Pounds) | Production Total[4] | Beginning Stocks[5] | Imports | Total Supply | Exports[5] | Fed to Calves | Humans | Total Use | All Milk, Wholesale | Milk, Eligible for Fluid Market | Milk, Manufacturing Grade | Per Capita Consumption[6] (Fluid Milk in Lbs) |
|---|---|---|---|---|---|---|---|---|---|---|---|---|---|---|
| 2013 | 9,215 | 21,413 | 201,218 | 11,403 | 3,772 | 216,393 | 12,065 | 877 | 192,137 | 205,079 | 20.04 | ---- | ---- | ---- |
| 2014 | 9,257 | 22,259 | 206,046 | 10,344 | 4,372 | 220,762 | 12,159 | 872 | 196,308 | 209,340 | 23.98 | ---- | ---- | ---- |
| 2015 | 9,314 | 22,396 | 208,633 | 10,487 | 5,759 | 224,879 | 8,500 | 879 | 202,260 | 211,639 | 17.11 | ---- | ---- | ---- |
| 2016 | 9,328 | 22,775 | 212,436 | 12,335 | 6,937 | 231,708 | 8,395 | 898 | 211,412 | 220,705 | 16.30 | ---- | ---- | ---- |
| 2017 | 9,392 | 22,941 | 215,466 | 12,722 | 5,977 | 234,165 | 9,223 | 901 | 214,535 | 224,659 | 17.66 | ---- | ---- | ---- |
| 2018 | 9,399 | 23,149 | 217,575 | 13,397 | 6,347 | 237,319 | 10,458 | 928 | 216,551 | 227,937 | 16.26 | ---- | ---- | ---- |
| 2019 | 9,336 | 23,391 | 218,382 | 13,790 | 6,500 | 238,672 | 10,700 | 932 | 217,362 | 228,994 | 18.63 | ---- | ---- | ---- |
| 2020 | 9,388 | 23,778 | 223,220 | 13,623 | 6,775 | 243,618 | 10,200 | 993 | 222,230 | 233,423 | 18.25 | ---- | ---- | ---- |
| 2021[1] | 9,447 | 23,947 | 226,258 | 14,339 | 6,535 | 247,132 | 11,541 | 958 | 225,216 | 237,715 | 18.61 | ---- | ---- | ---- |
| 2022[2] | 9,402 | 24,087 | 226,462 | 14,409 | 7,063 | 247,934 | 13,366 | | | | 25.56 | ---- | ---- | ---- |

[1] Preliminary.  [2] Estimate.  [3] Average number on farms during year including dry cows, excluding heifers not yet fresh.  [4] Excludes milk sucked by calves.  [5] Government and commercial.  [6] Product pounds of commercial sales and on farm consumption.
Source: Economic Research Service, U.S. Department of Agriculture (ERS-USDA)

# MILK

## Milk-Feed Price Ratio[1] in the United States     In Pounds

| Year | Jan. | Feb. | Mar. | Apr. | May | June | July | Aug. | Sept. | Oct. | Nov. | Dec. | Average |
|---|---|---|---|---|---|---|---|---|---|---|---|---|---|
| 2013 | 1.57 | 1.52 | 1.48 | 1.54 | 1.53 | 1.52 | 1.53 | 1.68 | 1.88 | 2.10 | 2.27 | 2.30 | 1.74 |
| 2014 | 2.46 | 2.59 | 2.54 | 2.42 | 2.24 | 2.20 | 2.36 | 2.63 | 2.96 | 2.92 | 2.75 | 2.40 | 2.54 |
| 2015 | 2.11 | 2.05 | 2.01 | 1.95 | 1.97 | 2.07 | 2.01 | 2.10 | 2.23 | 2.30 | 2.45 | 2.29 | 2.13 |
| 2016 | 2.18 | 2.18 | 2.12 | 1.99 | 1.89 | 1.91 | 2.16 | 2.44 | 2.49 | 2.38 | 2.59 | 2.73 | 2.26 |
| 2017 | 2.71 | 2.62 | 2.40 | 2.22 | 2.20 | 2.31 | 2.27 | 2.51 | 2.46 | 2.47 | 2.54 | 2.38 | 2.42 |
| 2018 | 2.18 | 2.03 | 1.99 | 1.89 | 1.90 | 1.98 | 1.93 | 2.06 | 2.13 | 2.22 | 2.21 | 2.07 | 2.05 |
| 2019 | 2.06 | 2.07 | 2.14 | 2.11 | 2.10 | 2.08 | 2.16 | 2.26 | 2.34 | 2.42 | 2.65 | 2.57 | 2.25 |
| 2020 | 2.42 | 2.35 | 2.24 | 1.85 | 1.78 | 2.38 | 2.72 | 2.48 | 2.27 | 2.49 | 2.58 | 2.17 | 2.31 |
| 2021 | 2.00 | 1.80 | 1.76 | 1.75 | 1.69 | 1.59 | 1.52 | 1.48 | 1.66 | 1.84 | 1.92 | 1.96 | 1.75 |
| 2022[1] | 2.16 | 2.06 | 2.06 | 2.00 | 1.98 | 1.93 | 1.79 | 1.70 | 1.74 | 1.92 | 1.93 | 1.84 | 1.93 |

[1] Pounds of 16% protein mixed dairy feed equal in value to one pound of whole milk.   [2] Preliminary.   Source: Economic Research Service, U.S. Department of Agriculture (ERS-USDA)

## Milk Production[2] in the United States     In Millions of Pounds

| Year | Jan. | Feb. | Mar. | Apr. | May | June | July | Aug. | Sept. | Oct. | Nov. | Dec. | Total |
|---|---|---|---|---|---|---|---|---|---|---|---|---|---|
| 2013 | 17,109 | 15,759 | 17,677 | 17,249 | 17,813 | 16,935 | 16,788 | 16,789 | 15,831 | 16,475 | 16,003 | 16,790 | 201,218 |
| 2014 | 17,284 | 15,907 | 17,829 | 17,480 | 18,094 | 17,323 | 17,435 | 17,224 | 16,514 | 17,071 | 16,551 | 17,334 | 206,046 |
| 2015 | 17,685 | 16,166 | 18,085 | 17,788 | 18,428 | 17,504 | 17,665 | 17,403 | 16,617 | 17,130 | 16,689 | 17,473 | 208,633 |
| 2016 | 17,693 | 16,904 | 18,401 | 17,947 | 18,613 | 17,771 | 17,908 | 17,692 | 16,990 | 17,565 | 17,100 | 17,852 | 212,436 |
| 2017 | 18,128 | 16,694 | 18,740 | 18,332 | 18,952 | 18,060 | 18,268 | 18,049 | 17,156 | 17,769 | 17,260 | 18,058 | 215,466 |
| 2018 | 18,437 | 16,973 | 18,989 | 18,412 | 19,131 | 18,288 | 18,329 | 18,245 | 17,395 | 17,873 | 17,348 | 18,155 | 217,575 |
| 2019 | 18,612 | 16,966 | 18,845 | 18,433 | 19,058 | 18,225 | 18,375 | 18,267 | 17,595 | 18,135 | 17,506 | 18,365 | 218,382 |
| 2020 | 18,877 | 17,895 | 19,402 | 18,684 | 18,972 | 18,414 | 18,756 | 18,632 | 18,031 | 18,603 | 18,103 | 18,851 | 223,220 |
| 2021 | 19,365 | 17,685 | 19,797 | 19,350 | 19,855 | 18,942 | 19,097 | 18,721 | 18,018 | 18,623 | 18,015 | 18,790 | 226,258 |
| 2022[1] | 19,050 | 17,540 | 19,715 | 19,147 | 19,755 | 18,920 | 19,180 | 19,016 | 18,242 | 18,809 | 18,184 | 18,904 | 226,462 |

[1] Preliminary.   [2] Excludes milk sucked by calves.   Source: Economic Research Service, U.S. Department of Agriculture (ERS-USDA)

## Milk Cows[2] in the United States     In Thousands of Head

| Year | Jan. | Feb. | Mar. | Apr. | May | June | July | Aug. | Sept. | Oct. | Nov. | Dec. | Total |
|---|---|---|---|---|---|---|---|---|---|---|---|---|---|
| 2013 | 9,222 | 9,223 | NA | NA | NA | NA | 9,235 | 9,229 | 9,208 | 9,203 | 9,198 | 9,202 | 9,215 |
| 2014 | 9,212 | 9,212 | 9,223 | 9,240 | 9,252 | 9,267 | 9,268 | 9,268 | 9,274 | 9,277 | 9,284 | 9,299 | 9,257 |
| 2015 | 9,308 | 9,308 | 9,311 | 9,316 | 9,324 | 9,323 | 9,314 | 9,315 | 9,317 | 9,320 | 9,322 | 9,320 | 9,314 |
| 2016 | 9,304 | 9,311 | 9,321 | 9,321 | 9,322 | 9,326 | 9,329 | 9,334 | 9,331 | 9,335 | 9,344 | 9,354 | 9,328 |
| 2017 | 9,359 | 9,365 | 9,383 | 9,392 | 9,401 | 9,404 | 9,404 | 9,404 | 9,399 | 9,395 | 9,398 | 9,400 | 9,392 |
| 2018 | 9,438 | 9,436 | 9,430 | 9,418 | 9,422 | 9,414 | 9,392 | 9,389 | 9,368 | 9,367 | 9,358 | 9,353 | 9,399 |
| 2019 | 9,354 | 9,352 | 9,333 | 9,332 | 9,333 | 9,327 | 9,315 | 9,318 | 9,333 | 9,347 | 9,345 | 9,343 | 9,336 |
| 2020 | 9,365 | 9,377 | 9,391 | 9,377 | 9,360 | 9,355 | 9,372 | 9,374 | 9,395 | 9,414 | 9,432 | 9,442 | 9,388 |
| 2021 | 9,450 | 9,456 | 9,482 | 9,500 | 9,507 | 9,501 | 9,483 | 9,438 | 9,405 | 9,387 | 9,382 | 9,373 | 9,447 |
| 2022[1] | 9,367 | 9,380 | 9,404 | 9,404 | 9,417 | 9,413 | 9,413 | 9,406 | 9,406 | 9,412 | 9,404 | 9,396 | 9,402 |

[1] Preliminary.   [2] Includes dry cows, excludes heifers not yet fresh.   Source: Economic Research Service, U.S. Department of Agriculture (ERS-USDA)

## Milk Per Cow[2] in the United States     In Pounds

| Year | Jan. | Feb. | Mar. | Apr. | May | June | July | Aug. | Sept. | Oct. | Nov. | Dec. | Total |
|---|---|---|---|---|---|---|---|---|---|---|---|---|---|
| 2013 | 1,855 | 1,709 | NA | NA | NA | NA | 1,818 | 1,819 | 1,719 | 1,790 | 1,740 | 1,825 | 21,413 |
| 2014 | 1,876 | 1,727 | 1,933 | 1,892 | 1,956 | 1,869 | 1,881 | 1,858 | 1,781 | 1,840 | 1,783 | 1,864 | 22,259 |
| 2015 | 1,900 | 1,737 | 1,942 | 1,909 | 1,976 | 1,878 | 1,897 | 1,868 | 1,784 | 1,838 | 1,790 | 1,875 | 22,396 |
| 2016 | 1,902 | 1,815 | 1,974 | 1,925 | 1,997 | 1,906 | 1,920 | 1,895 | 1,821 | 1,882 | 1,830 | 1,908 | 22,775 |
| 2017 | 1,937 | 1,783 | 1,997 | 1,952 | 2,016 | 1,920 | 1,943 | 1,919 | 1,825 | 1,891 | 1,837 | 1,921 | 22,941 |
| 2018 | 1,953 | 1,799 | 2,014 | 1,955 | 2,030 | 1,943 | 1,952 | 1,943 | 1,857 | 1,908 | 1,854 | 1,941 | 23,149 |
| 2019 | 1,990 | 1,814 | 2,019 | 1,975 | 2,042 | 1,954 | 1,973 | 1,960 | 1,885 | 1,940 | 1,873 | 1,966 | 23,391 |
| 2020 | 2,016 | 1,908 | 2,066 | 1,993 | 2,027 | 1,968 | 2,001 | 1,988 | 1,919 | 1,976 | 1,919 | 1,997 | 23,778 |
| 2021 | 2,049 | 1,868 | 2,088 | 2,037 | 2,088 | 1,994 | 2,014 | 1,984 | 1,916 | 1,984 | 1,920 | 2,005 | 23,947 |
| 2022[1] | 2,034 | 1,870 | 2,096 | 2,036 | 2,098 | 2,010 | 2,038 | 2,022 | 1,939 | 1,998 | 1,934 | 2,012 | 24,087 |

[1] Preliminary.   [2] Excludes milk sucked by calves.   Source: Economic Research Service, U.S. Department of Agriculture (ERS-USDA)

# MILK

## Average Price Received by Farmers for All Milk (Sold to Plants)   In Dollars Per Hundred Pounds (Cwt.)

| Year | Jan. | Feb. | Mar. | Apr. | May | June | July | Aug. | Sept. | Oct. | Nov. | Dec. | Average |
|---|---|---|---|---|---|---|---|---|---|---|---|---|---|
| 2013 | 19.90 | 19.50 | 19.10 | 19.50 | 19.70 | 19.50 | 19.10 | 19.60 | 20.10 | 20.90 | 21.60 | 22.00 | 20.04 |
| 2014 | 23.50 | 24.90 | 25.10 | 25.30 | 24.20 | 23.20 | 23.30 | 24.20 | 25.70 | 24.90 | 23.00 | 20.40 | 23.98 |
| 2015 | 17.60 | 16.80 | 16.60 | 16.50 | 16.80 | 17.00 | 16.70 | 16.70 | 17.50 | 17.70 | 18.20 | 17.20 | 17.11 |
| 2016 | 16.10 | 15.70 | 15.30 | 15.10 | 14.50 | 14.80 | 16.10 | 17.20 | 17.40 | 16.70 | 17.80 | 18.90 | 16.30 |
| 2017 | 18.90 | 18.50 | 17.30 | 16.50 | 16.70 | 17.30 | 17.20 | 18.10 | 17.90 | 18.10 | 18.20 | 17.20 | 17.66 |
| 2018 | 16.10 | 15.30 | 15.70 | 15.70 | 16.20 | 16.30 | 15.50 | 16.10 | 16.90 | 17.50 | 17.20 | 16.60 | 16.26 |
| 2019 | 16.60 | 16.80 | 17.60 | 17.70 | 18.00 | 18.10 | 18.70 | 18.90 | 19.30 | 20.00 | 21.10 | 20.70 | 18.63 |
| 2020 | 19.60 | 18.90 | 17.90 | 14.40 | 13.70 | 18.20 | 20.60 | 18.60 | 17.70 | 20.00 | 21.10 | 18.30 | 18.25 |
| 2021 | 17.50 | 17.10 | 17.30 | 18.30 | 19.10 | 18.20 | 17.90 | 17.60 | 18.30 | 19.60 | 20.70 | 21.70 | 18.61 |
| 2022[1] | 24.20 | 24.70 | 25.90 | 27.10 | 27.30 | 26.90 | 25.70 | 24.30 | 24.40 | 25.90 | 25.60 | 24.70 | 25.56 |

[1] Preliminary.   Source: Economic Research Service, U.S. Department of Agriculture (ERS-USDA)

## Production of Nonfat Dry Milk in the United States   In Thousands of Pounds

| Year | Jan. | Feb. | Mar. | Apr. | May | June | July | Aug. | Sept. | Oct. | Nov. | Dec. | Total |
|---|---|---|---|---|---|---|---|---|---|---|---|---|---|
| 2013 | 142,799 | 137,674 | 146,576 | 160,117 | 150,531 | 130,901 | 116,616 | 106,039 | 74,026 | 85,830 | 101,185 | 125,570 | 1,477,864 |
| 2014 | 138,661 | 141,187 | 167,853 | 160,342 | 162,139 | 148,648 | 166,602 | 116,134 | 112,467 | 134,973 | 151,402 | 164,224 | 1,764,632 |
| 2015 | 167,705 | 150,960 | 180,878 | 180,771 | 180,013 | 165,441 | 155,265 | 123,892 | 119,974 | 118,360 | 127,939 | 151,150 | 1,822,348 |
| 2016 | 137,463 | 142,978 | 172,003 | 170,796 | 165,837 | 146,643 | 150,787 | 117,550 | 125,486 | 140,051 | 128,105 | 154,935 | 1,752,634 |
| 2017 | 153,868 | 143,252 | 160,931 | 172,840 | 167,912 | 162,827 | 151,831 | 136,767 | 134,587 | 145,008 | 141,440 | 164,014 | 1,835,277 |
| 2018 | 159,272 | 157,105 | 177,980 | 169,428 | 165,670 | 152,244 | 150,193 | 129,077 | 114,030 | 121,595 | 134,424 | 142,522 | 1,773,540 |
| 2019 | 172,690 | 153,806 | 161,829 | 167,758 | 173,666 | 157,948 | 172,329 | 132,525 | 117,806 | 132,716 | 138,880 | 164,869 | 1,846,822 |
| 2020 | 176,259 | 159,128 | 173,665 | 202,632 | 127,236 | 154,033 | 166,138 | 147,194 | 126,249 | 141,255 | 155,435 | 208,252 | 1,937,476 |
| 2021 | 198,025 | 183,614 | 198,254 | 193,792 | 205,470 | 185,604 | 137,789 | 121,559 | 139,384 | 120,721 | 161,011 | 167,804 | 2,013,027 |
| 2022[1] | 170,306 | 170,815 | 191,349 | 195,709 | 192,965 | 169,272 | 165,624 | 134,138 | 123,476 | 123,977 | 158,223 | 167,586 | 1,963,440 |

[1] Preliminary.   Source: Economic Research Service, U.S. Department of Agriculture (ERS-USDA)

## Production of Dry Whey in the United States   In Thousands of Pounds

| Year | Jan. | Feb. | Mar. | Apr. | May | June | July | Aug. | Sept. | Oct. | Nov. | Dec. | Total |
|---|---|---|---|---|---|---|---|---|---|---|---|---|---|
| 2013 | 86,558 | 77,097 | 83,248 | 81,653 | 75,535 | 75,425 | 76,416 | 73,122 | 68,692 | 71,883 | 74,718 | 108,633 | 952,980 |
| 2014 | 70,011 | 65,603 | 71,504 | 71,629 | 82,480 | 79,309 | 73,475 | 71,192 | 69,537 | 68,684 | 70,994 | 75,283 | 869,701 |
| 2015 | 75,342 | 76,630 | 86,409 | 76,512 | 80,778 | 85,506 | 81,225 | 83,585 | 78,823 | 75,576 | 82,959 | 94,223 | 977,568 |
| 2016 | 83,459 | 74,891 | 82,762 | 82,075 | 81,836 | 80,002 | 82,354 | 76,505 | 75,864 | 83,966 | 72,893 | 78,534 | 955,141 |
| 2017 | 82,255 | 77,548 | 87,602 | 85,218 | 83,545 | 87,886 | 99,652 | 94,248 | 90,561 | 79,749 | 81,237 | 85,913 | 1,035,414 |
| 2018 | 90,569 | 89,431 | 91,368 | 85,731 | 85,904 | 86,603 | 90,171 | 78,814 | 69,951 | 84,003 | 72,306 | 74,505 | 999,356 |
| 2019 | 81,202 | 74,948 | 77,378 | 74,998 | 79,090 | 82,976 | 82,906 | 84,897 | 90,627 | 90,843 | 75,111 | 79,821 | 974,797 |
| 2020 | 84,272 | 76,490 | 83,482 | 75,824 | 84,109 | 81,713 | 82,616 | 78,720 | 76,954 | 75,148 | 68,652 | 81,301 | 949,281 |
| 2021 | 83,988 | 75,323 | 76,909 | 77,435 | 77,277 | 76,350 | 81,016 | 82,302 | 75,185 | 74,882 | 75,856 | 76,044 | 932,567 |
| 2022[1] | 80,406 | 70,288 | 83,060 | 82,819 | 84,244 | 80,229 | 85,745 | 78,268 | 78,075 | 77,347 | 71,902 | 74,815 | 947,198 |

[1] Preliminary.   Excludes all modified dry whey products.   Source: Economic Research Service, U.S. Department of Agriculture (ERS-USDA)

## Production of Whey Protein Concentrate in the United States   In Thousands of Pounds

| Year | Jan. | Feb. | Mar. | Apr. | May | June | July | Aug. | Sept. | Oct. | Nov. | Dec. | Total |
|---|---|---|---|---|---|---|---|---|---|---|---|---|---|
| 2013 | 39,262 | 36,941 | 41,742 | 40,396 | 43,391 | 41,501 | 40,265 | 39,461 | 39,386 | 45,542 | 43,194 | 46,567 | 497,648 |
| 2014 | 44,325 | 42,165 | 45,076 | 46,127 | 46,630 | 43,871 | 44,876 | 44,945 | 41,621 | 46,971 | 46,066 | 47,428 | 540,101 |
| 2015 | 44,061 | 38,365 | 42,234 | 42,375 | 43,812 | 39,307 | 41,736 | 39,380 | 37,474 | 41,302 | 40,137 | 42,766 | 492,949 |
| 2016 | 42,602 | 39,780 | 41,851 | 39,027 | 39,349 | 38,037 | 38,437 | 35,665 | 36,745 | 38,060 | 39,419 | 39,457 | 468,429 |
| 2017 | 40,714 | 36,457 | 42,736 | 42,469 | 41,993 | 40,669 | 41,587 | 38,737 | 39,109 | 41,203 | 40,935 | 42,313 | 488,922 |
| 2018 | 44,257 | 41,182 | 50,463 | 41,887 | 42,424 | 41,001 | 40,877 | 42,856 | 41,991 | 42,392 | 40,919 | 43,722 | 513,971 |
| 2019 | 43,170 | 39,295 | 42,026 | 40,639 | 41,911 | 38,840 | 39,802 | 39,903 | 40,068 | 40,672 | 40,696 | 43,106 | 490,128 |
| 2020 | 41,935 | 35,600 | 40,094 | 37,341 | 39,074 | 40,189 | 39,655 | 40,061 | 40,988 | 40,971 | 39,311 | 43,137 | 478,356 |
| 2021 | 43,800 | 37,512 | 40,832 | 49,956 | 40,450 | 38,515 | 68,689 | 41,587 | 44,812 | 46,622 | 43,440 | 46,935 | 543,150 |
| 2022[1] | 47,226 | 40,718 | 40,768 | 45,511 | 42,988 | 42,650 | 44,588 | 42,938 | 45,985 | 46,411 | 40,072 | 42,625 | 522,480 |

[1] Preliminary.   Source: Economic Research Service, U.S. Department of Agriculture (ERS-USDA)

# MILK

### Production of Cottage Cheese, Creamed[2] in the United States — In Thousands of Pounds

| Year | Jan. | Feb. | Mar. | Apr. | May | June | July | Aug. | Sept. | Oct. | Nov. | Dec. | Total |
|---|---|---|---|---|---|---|---|---|---|---|---|---|---|
| 2013 | 27,129 | 24,811 | 26,455 | 25,636 | 27,039 | 24,157 | 27,252 | 27,680 | 25,122 | 25,770 | 23,307 | 23,033 | 307,391 |
| 2014 | 25,477 | 22,723 | 25,455 | 26,364 | 26,281 | 26,174 | 26,226 | 25,656 | 26,631 | 25,318 | 21,499 | 25,309 | 303,113 |
| 2015 | 24,103 | 25,188 | 26,991 | 25,811 | 26,284 | 27,179 | 28,791 | 27,810 | 27,369 | 27,130 | 24,212 | 26,663 | 317,531 |
| 2016 | 25,636 | 26,945 | 29,154 | 27,052 | 28,946 | 28,335 | 27,163 | 29,684 | 27,782 | 26,901 | 26,041 | 25,805 | 329,444 |
| 2017 | 26,122 | 25,698 | 29,010 | 25,942 | 29,538 | 27,626 | 28,007 | 30,434 | 27,146 | 28,829 | 26,066 | 26,066 | 330,484 |
| 2018 | 27,933 | 27,261 | 32,655 | 29,410 | 32,320 | 31,006 | 30,114 | 31,920 | 27,141 | 29,828 | 27,051 | 26,146 | 352,785 |
| 2019 | 28,322 | 26,094 | 29,846 | 30,945 | 29,312 | 28,265 | 32,350 | 31,495 | 29,488 | 31,956 | 27,025 | 28,427 | 353,525 |
| 2020 | 27,622 | 26,172 | 31,391 | 31,530 | 31,032 | 29,649 | 31,016 | 30,517 | 33,831 | 32,294 | 27,508 | 29,258 | 361,820 |
| 2021 | 26,622 | 27,470 | 31,597 | 27,116 | 28,165 | 28,624 | 39,474 | 29,527 | 28,604 | 27,437 | 26,136 | 27,472 | 348,244 |
| 2022[1] | 27,422 | 28,452 | 29,744 | 26,671 | 27,576 | 29,313 | 28,808 | 31,541 | 29,587 | 27,357 | 28,426 | 29,175 | 344,072 |

[1] Preliminary.  [2] Fat content 4 percent or more.  Source: Economic Research Service, U.S. Department of Agriculture (ERS-USDA)

### Production of Cottage Cheese, Lowfat[2] in the United States — In Thousands of Pounds

| Year | Jan. | Feb. | Mar. | Apr. | May | June | July | Aug. | Sept. | Oct. | Nov. | Dec. | Total |
|---|---|---|---|---|---|---|---|---|---|---|---|---|---|
| 2013 | 33,742 | 29,688 | 31,470 | 32,012 | 32,711 | 30,224 | 32,492 | 32,229 | 30,522 | 30,816 | 27,014 | 27,403 | 370,323 |
| 2014 | 29,755 | 28,227 | 31,134 | 32,698 | 31,304 | 32,664 | 31,289 | 30,662 | 31,799 | 31,225 | 25,088 | 28,769 | 364,614 |
| 2015 | 28,993 | 28,913 | 32,157 | 29,848 | 29,919 | 32,113 | 31,483 | 31,377 | 31,918 | 29,543 | 26,652 | 30,088 | 363,004 |
| 2016 | 30,270 | 30,311 | 34,486 | 30,326 | 32,490 | 30,751 | 30,359 | 32,260 | 30,566 | 29,954 | 28,456 | 27,586 | 367,815 |
| 2017 | 28,655 | 28,142 | 30,711 | 29,610 | 31,746 | 27,924 | 28,450 | 31,370 | 27,396 | 29,205 | 26,060 | 25,152 | 344,421 |
| 2018 | 29,299 | 27,577 | 31,340 | 29,982 | 31,476 | 28,321 | 29,296 | 29,342 | 26,943 | 28,706 | 25,181 | 24,621 | 342,084 |
| 2019 | 28,134 | 25,374 | 27,765 | 29,039 | 27,512 | 25,433 | 29,611 | 29,747 | 26,427 | 27,922 | 24,008 | 23,879 | 324,851 |
| 2020 | 26,333 | 24,434 | 27,979 | 26,753 | 24,688 | 24,951 | 27,393 | 25,885 | 26,719 | 27,540 | 22,228 | 23,495 | 308,398 |
| 2021 | 24,428 | 24,271 | 29,719 | 25,862 | 24,753 | 25,730 | 26,481 | 26,252 | 25,745 | 24,129 | 22,085 | 23,028 | 302,483 |
| 2022[1] | 24,313 | 24,832 | 26,934 | 25,403 | 24,355 | 24,490 | 25,305 | 27,516 | 25,933 | 23,982 | 22,066 | 21,937 | 297,066 |

[1] Preliminary.  [2] Fat content less than 4 percent.  Source: Economic Research Service, U.S. Department of Agriculture (ERS-USDA)

### Production of Cottage Cheese, Curd in the United States — In Thousands of Pounds

| Year | Jan. | Feb. | Mar. | Apr. | May | June | July | Aug. | Sept. | Oct. | Nov. | Dec. | Total |
|---|---|---|---|---|---|---|---|---|---|---|---|---|---|
| 2013 | 36,003 | 31,456 | 33,537 | 31,908 | 33,947 | 30,964 | 34,594 | 35,201 | 31,386 | 31,845 | 29,777 | 28,778 | 389,396 |
| 2014 | 32,401 | 27,764 | 32,362 | 33,612 | 32,119 | 32,656 | 33,684 | 32,565 | 33,149 | 32,647 | 26,851 | 31,336 | 381,146 |
| 2015 | 31,334 | 31,903 | 34,171 | 33,099 | 33,498 | 34,206 | 35,767 | 35,753 | 34,670 | 33,065 | 30,026 | 33,142 | 400,634 |
| 2016 | 32,489 | 33,018 | 36,339 | 33,039 | 35,043 | 33,896 | 33,004 | 35,510 | 39,670 | 32,558 | 30,965 | 30,897 | 406,428 |
| 2017 | 32,063 | 31,222 | 34,803 | 32,599 | 35,558 | 32,374 | 33,267 | 35,563 | 30,998 | 33,444 | 29,668 | 28,850 | 390,409 |
| 2018 | 32,660 | 31,545 | 36,016 | 33,353 | 36,368 | 34,349 | 34,706 | 36,300 | 33,010 | 33,463 | 31,073 | 29,519 | 402,362 |
| 2019 | 32,575 | 30,242 | 33,388 | 34,505 | 32,004 | 31,947 | 36,978 | 34,227 | 31,108 | 33,497 | 28,701 | 28,837 | 388,009 |
| 2020 | 30,838 | 28,990 | 33,225 | 33,349 | 30,987 | 30,864 | 32,906 | 31,733 | 34,376 | 33,867 | 27,989 | 29,688 | 378,812 |
| 2021 | 29,551 | 29,790 | 34,363 | 28,853 | 28,192 | 30,328 | 31,629 | 30,533 | 30,042 | 29,015 | 26,924 | 29,212 | 358,432 |
| 2022[1] | 29,080 | 29,912 | 31,927 | 29,410 | 29,404 | 30,137 | 31,319 | 33,538 | 31,999 | 28,974 | 28,311 | 29,059 | 363,070 |

[1] Preliminary.  [2] Fat content less than 4 percent.  Source: Economic Research Service, U.S. Department of Agriculture (ERS-USDA)

### Production of Sour Cream in the United States — In Thousands of Pounds

| Year | Jan. | Feb. | Mar. | Apr. | May | June | July | Aug. | Sept. | Oct. | Nov. | Dec. | Total |
|---|---|---|---|---|---|---|---|---|---|---|---|---|---|
| 2013 | 108,303 | 94,266 | 105,130 | 98,057 | 110,185 | 100,505 | 104,464 | 107,790 | 100,162 | 116,530 | 118,715 | 117,259 | 1,281,366 |
| 2014 | 107,452 | 94,174 | 107,114 | 107,177 | 105,491 | 106,167 | 106,911 | 105,603 | 103,548 | 117,465 | 120,244 | 121,564 | 1,302,900 |
| 2015 | 109,701 | 96,386 | 110,972 | 103,654 | 104,424 | 110,833 | 105,239 | 107,407 | 108,576 | 121,581 | 126,165 | 120,691 | 1,325,629 |
| 2016 | 106,584 | 106,240 | 115,534 | 100,532 | 113,834 | 118,015 | 103,622 | 114,645 | 108,701 | 123,534 | 133,364 | 129,454 | 1,374,059 |
| 2017 | 113,967 | 99,700 | 115,648 | 109,615 | 118,884 | 117,764 | 107,401 | 118,709 | 108,314 | 126,023 | 129,312 | 121,812 | 1,387,149 |
| 2018 | 120,265 | 98,965 | 116,365 | 111,335 | 119,221 | 114,106 | 109,820 | 119,327 | 107,914 | 128,883 | 130,767 | 126,443 | 1,403,411 |
| 2019 | 120,975 | 100,923 | 108,617 | 117,973 | 120,332 | 111,416 | 118,403 | 119,252 | 111,282 | 133,320 | 129,785 | 130,139 | 1,422,417 |
| 2020 | 121,591 | 101,869 | 115,545 | 110,956 | 135,931 | 121,733 | 112,681 | 117,149 | 120,885 | 138,408 | 130,353 | 132,789 | 1,459,890 |
| 2021 | 115,248 | 113,749 | 133,781 | 119,051 | 120,142 | 126,500 | 121,174 | 122,915 | 118,932 | 132,583 | 133,456 | 136,439 | 1,493,970 |
| 2022[1] | 121,358 | 117,010 | 129,936 | 117,676 | 125,224 | 123,948 | 115,682 | 127,408 | 121,755 | 130,720 | 135,801 | 133,664 | 1,500,182 |

[1] Preliminary.  Source: Economic Research Service, U.S. Department of Agriculture (ERS-USDA)

# MILK

**Production of Ice Cream, Regular, Hard in the United States**  In Thousands of Gallons

| Year | Jan. | Feb. | Mar. | Apr. | May | June | July | Aug. | Sept. | Oct. | Nov. | Dec. | Total |
|---|---|---|---|---|---|---|---|---|---|---|---|---|---|
| 2013 | 56,773 | 63,046 | 71,632 | 72,119 | 76,380 | 77,470 | 77,233 | 72,503 | 62,761 | 65,254 | 52,814 | 43,377 | 791,362 |
| 2014 | 56,393 | 56,987 | 68,176 | 70,217 | 70,554 | 74,048 | 73,797 | 67,794 | 62,494 | 60,880 | 53,604 | 52,138 | 767,082 |
| 2015 | 57,146 | 59,915 | 71,944 | 68,966 | 65,730 | 72,674 | 72,497 | 69,632 | 65,485 | 63,399 | 54,998 | 52,826 | 775,212 |
| 2016 | 58,997 | 61,075 | 72,610 | 72,627 | 72,194 | 76,456 | 71,210 | 72,745 | 63,055 | 59,325 | 51,477 | 49,392 | 781,163 |
| 2017 | 53,262 | 55,868 | 70,879 | 66,450 | 69,130 | 70,987 | 66,406 | 70,143 | 57,909 | 55,392 | 48,794 | 45,942 | 731,162 |
| 2018 | 53,684 | 55,447 | 63,553 | 62,821 | 64,551 | 70,263 | 68,966 | 70,111 | 56,601 | 60,610 | 48,070 | 43,855 | 718,532 |
| 2019 | 53,551 | 52,120 | 65,957 | 64,681 | 67,414 | 64,920 | 64,846 | 64,242 | 58,155 | 58,581 | 46,927 | 47,039 | 708,433 |
| 2020 | 52,157 | 52,484 | 64,287 | 63,439 | 64,598 | 72,777 | 73,592 | 70,473 | 38,194 | 63,264 | 54,826 | 53,441 | 723,532 |
| 2021 | 56,990 | 55,630 | 68,982 | 68,856 | 61,168 | 66,028 | 64,257 | 63,201 | 55,511 | 54,598 | 52,137 | 52,283 | 719,641 |
| 2022[1] | 51,240 | 54,872 | 65,973 | 64,748 | 61,516 | 66,887 | 59,078 | 66,434 | 60,890 | 57,121 | 54,080 | 52,400 | 715,239 |

[1] Preliminary.  Source: Economic Research Service, U.S. Department of Agriculture (ERS-USDA)


**Production of Ice Cream, Lowfat Total in the United States**  In Thousands of Gallons

| Year | Jan. | Feb. | Mar. | Apr. | May | June | July | Aug. | Sept. | Oct. | Nov. | Dec. | Total |
|---|---|---|---|---|---|---|---|---|---|---|---|---|---|
| 2013 | 27,874 | 29,920 | 36,743 | 37,401 | 40,204 | 42,767 | 40,220 | 36,475 | 32,059 | 29,381 | 25,249 | 22,632 | 400,925 |
| 2014 | 29,551 | 30,222 | 35,523 | 40,702 | 39,490 | 42,314 | 39,978 | 35,453 | 33,149 | 31,617 | 26,229 | 27,473 | 411,701 |
| 2015 | 30,422 | 32,283 | 38,429 | 40,473 | 40,067 | 46,059 | 43,039 | 43,451 | 36,576 | 32,920 | 27,531 | 27,741 | 438,991 |
| 2016 | 30,247 | 31,851 | 40,659 | 40,323 | 39,399 | 44,492 | 40,516 | 43,295 | 35,503 | 32,383 | 28,692 | 28,508 | 435,868 |
| 2017 | 31,700 | 38,803 | 45,145 | 41,629 | 46,354 | 46,392 | 42,695 | 43,891 | 34,944 | 34,414 | 27,499 | 27,948 | 461,414 |
| 2018 | 32,568 | 34,823 | 41,108 | 40,800 | 42,471 | 45,471 | 42,333 | 41,742 | 34,907 | 36,607 | 30,121 | 28,152 | 451,103 |
| 2019 | 31,559 | 32,235 | 42,538 | 44,505 | 47,873 | 44,364 | 43,582 | 42,021 | 37,206 | 36,315 | 29,068 | 28,110 | 459,376 |
| 2020 | 30,886 | 33,278 | 42,867 | 39,368 | 45,133 | 47,269 | 45,547 | 45,371 | 41,756 | 38,173 | 33,279 | 32,167 | 475,094 |
| 2021 | 30,737 | 33,507 | 47,296 | 42,986 | 43,855 | 43,004 | 42,723 | 40,724 | 36,106 | 35,214 | 29,451 | 28,727 | 454,330 |
| 2022[1] | 27,545 | 30,891 | 40,461 | 38,157 | 40,244 | 42,926 | 40,321 | 41,624 | 35,080 | 31,129 | 28,295 | 25,264 | 421,937 |

[1] Preliminary.  Source: Economic Research Service, U.S. Department of Agriculture (ERS-USDA)


**Production of Sherbet, Hard in the United States**  In Thousands of Gallons

| Year | Jan. | Feb. | Mar. | Apr. | May | June | July | Aug. | Sept. | Oct. | Nov. | Dec. | Total |
|---|---|---|---|---|---|---|---|---|---|---|---|---|---|
| 2013 | 3,094 | 3,460 | 4,453 | 4,514 | 4,553 | 4,684 | 4,209 | 3,651 | 3,097 | 3,255 | 2,493 | 2,052 | 43,515 |
| 2014 | 3,181 | 3,339 | 3,988 | 3,986 | 3,791 | 4,109 | 3,923 | 3,201 | 3,438 | 2,752 | 2,688 | 2,528 | 40,924 |
| 2015 | 2,982 | 3,224 | 3,873 | 3,527 | 3,743 | 3,876 | 3,769 | 3,554 | 3,407 | 2,927 | 2,535 | 2,080 | 39,497 |
| 2016 | 2,731 | 3,369 | 4,014 | 3,953 | 3,768 | 3,892 | 3,376 | 3,351 | 3,585 | 2,848 | 2,166 | 2,360 | 39,413 |
| 2017 | 3,291 | 3,005 | 3,764 | 3,779 | 3,574 | 3,815 | 3,308 | 3,681 | 3,274 | 2,542 | 2,346 | 2,182 | 38,561 |
| 2018 | 2,858 | 3,112 | 3,368 | 3,578 | 3,513 | 3,563 | 3,151 | 3,255 | 3,084 | 2,978 | 2,341 | 2,100 | 36,901 |
| 2019 | 2,551 | 2,653 | 3,225 | 3,067 | 3,191 | 3,166 | 2,795 | 2,382 | 2,703 | 2,445 | 2,053 | 2,056 | 32,287 |
| 2020 | 2,577 | 3,021 | 2,721 | 2,425 | 2,328 | 3,246 | 3,210 | 3,416 | 2,962 | 2,882 | 2,300 | 2,816 | 33,904 |
| 2021 | 2,666 | 2,605 | 2,497 | 2,823 | 2,364 | 2,617 | 2,793 | 2,336 | 2,148 | 1,957 | 1,773 | 1,833 | 28,412 |
| 2022[1] | 2,303 | 2,519 | 2,826 | 2,208 | 2,228 | 2,186 | 2,431 | 2,192 | 2,155 | 2,356 | 1,805 | 1,864 | 27,073 |

[1] Preliminary.  Source: Economic Research Service, U.S. Department of Agriculture (ERS-USDA)


**Production of Yogurt, Plain and Flavored in the United States**  In Thousands of Pounds

| Year | Jan. | Feb. | Mar. | Apr. | May | June | July | Aug. | Sept. | Oct. | Nov. | Dec. | Total |
|---|---|---|---|---|---|---|---|---|---|---|---|---|---|
| 2013 | 389,241 | 367,570 | 426,853 | 387,970 | 403,676 | 396,993 | 394,537 | 420,999 | 434,131 | 377,752 | 330,856 | 384,498 | 4,715,076 |
| 2014 | 392,831 | 403,679 | 436,674 | 392,677 | 389,082 | 400,769 | 388,147 | 405,926 | 463,704 | 381,177 | 319,921 | 381,975 | 4,756,562 |
| 2015 | 372,687 | 420,942 | 435,314 | 385,454 | 397,051 | 390,556 | 382,686 | 385,322 | 421,638 | 371,200 | 334,443 | 348,301 | 4,645,594 |
| 2016 | 379,455 | 377,179 | 400,818 | 373,280 | 364,390 | 378,786 | 341,896 | 399,633 | 411,235 | 361,347 | 311,210 | 359,170 | 4,458,399 |
| 2017 | 381,760 | 369,737 | 411,605 | 375,287 | 385,257 | 376,339 | 349,476 | 396,288 | 393,702 | 368,553 | 317,597 | 352,603 | 4,478,204 |
| 2018 | 372,015 | 376,710 | 389,848 | 358,160 | 373,431 | 373,079 | 360,886 | 396,296 | 369,989 | 363,128 | 310,848 | 343,698 | 4,388,088 |
| 2019 | 360,050 | 365,389 | 399,699 | 379,341 | 354,516 | 364,013 | 348,614 | 377,322 | 381,495 | 357,443 | 319,612 | 348,979 | 4,356,473 |
| 2020 | 347,758 | 375,155 | 438,213 | 361,848 | 373,099 | 398,683 | 365,149 | 382,228 | 391,449 | 386,630 | 326,611 | 358,291 | 4,505,114 |
| 2021 | 385,594 | 381,121 | 443,374 | 414,884 | 393,724 | 389,530 | 401,106 | 411,210 | 409,977 | 386,014 | 355,335 | 370,532 | 4,742,401 |
| 2022[1] | 372,943 | 373,445 | 431,500 | 378,182 | 399,052 | 389,218 | 377,622 | 401,770 | 391,913 | 390,982 | 346,852 | 371,853 | 4,625,332 |

[1] Preliminary.  Source: Economic Research Service, U.S. Department of Agriculture (ERS-USDA)

# MILK

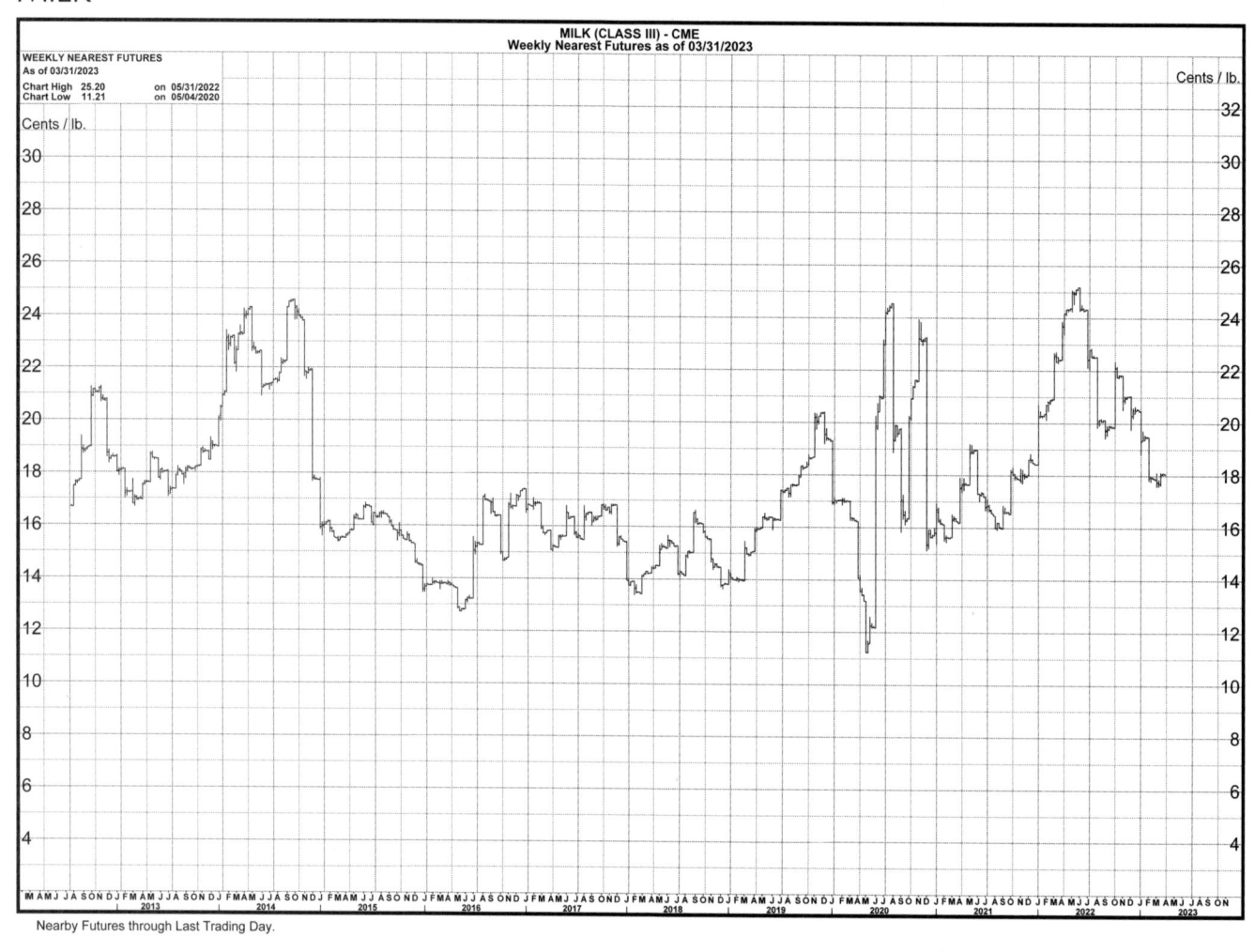

**MILK (CLASS III) - CME**
Weekly Nearest Futures as of 03/31/2023

WEEKLY NEAREST FUTURES
As of 03/31/2023
Chart High 25.20 on 05/31/2022
Chart Low 11.21 on 05/04/2020

Nearby Futures through Last Trading Day.

## Volume of Trading of Class III Milk Futures in Chicago    In Contracts

| Year | Jan. | Feb. | Mar. | Apr. | May | June | July | Aug. | Sept. | Oct. | Nov. | Dec. | Total |
|---|---|---|---|---|---|---|---|---|---|---|---|---|---|
| 2013 | 22,182 | 20,654 | 25,964 | 29,668 | 24,403 | 22,482 | 23,762 | 28,680 | 19,519 | 24,806 | 21,210 | 30,611 | 293,941 |
| 2014 | 37,317 | 27,468 | 31,390 | 23,084 | 22,764 | 21,118 | 26,702 | 28,532 | 38,651 | 33,233 | 25,464 | 42,936 | 358,659 |
| 2015 | 30,448 | 29,457 | 23,844 | 22,999 | 21,087 | 21,649 | 23,920 | 16,422 | 19,958 | 18,049 | 22,488 | 25,218 | 275,539 |
| 2016 | 20,769 | 20,574 | 19,533 | 22,613 | 27,322 | 44,457 | 18,030 | 30,654 | 28,089 | 24,141 | 28,134 | 37,643 | 321,959 |
| 2017 | 27,439 | 28,001 | 33,774 | 20,263 | 30,371 | 25,574 | 25,564 | 31,494 | 22,438 | 22,205 | 27,303 | 25,402 | 319,828 |
| 2018 | 23,610 | 18,682 | 17,419 | 19,020 | 21,425 | 33,116 | 23,538 | 27,829 | 22,004 | 35,993 | 30,999 | 28,617 | 302,252 |
| 2019 | 27,638 | 25,049 | 23,083 | 26,149 | 24,669 | 22,034 | 26,154 | 24,635 | 35,003 | 36,380 | 31,377 | 33,676 | 335,847 |
| 2020 | 29,402 | 29,816 | 35,523 | 41,515 | 38,908 | 40,852 | 38,242 | 37,938 | 27,094 | 36,808 | 33,363 | 39,179 | 428,640 |
| 2021 | 31,111 | 20,329 | 21,789 | 24,751 | 22,622 | 21,903 | 24,560 | 25,672 | 22,299 | 30,414 | 32,169 | 31,501 | 309,120 |
| 2022 | 34,866 | 26,791 | 36,614 | 27,800 | 27,238 | 29,126 | 28,648 | 27,857 | 25,869 | 21,666 | 25,144 | 27,903 | 339,522 |

Contract size = 200,000 lbs.    Source: CME Group; Chicago Mercantile Exchange (CME)

## Average Open Interest of Class III Milk Futures in Chicago    In Contracts

| Year | Jan. | Feb. | Mar. | Apr. | May | June | July | Aug. | Sept. | Oct. | Nov. | Dec. |
|---|---|---|---|---|---|---|---|---|---|---|---|---|
| 2013 | 19,320 | 20,206 | 21,408 | 23,180 | 22,062 | 21,456 | 21,802 | 23,267 | 23,463 | 22,153 | 22,480 | 24,287 |
| 2014 | 26,264 | 28,094 | 29,393 | 28,695 | 27,114 | 26,298 | 26,128 | 29,218 | 32,844 | 36,731 | 39,197 | 43,959 |
| 2015 | 46,134 | 44,918 | 42,292 | 37,710 | 34,509 | 31,725 | 28,890 | 28,792 | 26,554 | 25,839 | 27,821 | 29,784 |
| 2016 | 32,267 | 33,051 | 31,996 | 31,881 | 32,970 | 30,976 | 30,323 | 29,969 | 31,548 | 31,845 | 31,605 | 33,695 |
| 2017 | 31,058 | 31,194 | 34,015 | 34,006 | 31,200 | 28,498 | 28,226 | 25,863 | 25,933 | 23,510 | 24,940 | 25,949 |
| 2018 | 24,834 | 23,883 | 23,021 | 22,280 | 22,375 | 22,572 | 23,397 | 22,391 | 22,843 | 25,498 | 29,760 | 28,206 |
| 2019 | 26,355 | 25,593 | 23,301 | 21,497 | 22,591 | 22,221 | 20,718 | 19,169 | 20,918 | 21,182 | 22,763 | 20,166 |
| 2020 | 17,223 | 17,888 | 18,801 | 23,000 | 23,875 | 24,576 | 26,035 | 23,371 | 19,973 | 21,649 | 22,465 | 20,318 |
| 2021 | 21,022 | 21,665 | 22,925 | 25,416 | 25,925 | 24,870 | 26,145 | 25,126 | 23,727 | 23,445 | 25,508 | 27,655 |
| 2022 | 30,313 | 30,813 | 31,801 | 32,978 | 32,901 | 30,806 | 30,725 | 30,274 | 28,593 | 26,196 | 23,555 | 23,337 |

Contract size = 200,000 lbs.    Source: CME Group; Chicago Mercantile Exchange (CME)

# Molybdenum

Molybdenum (atomic symbol Mo) is a silvery-white, hard, malleable, metallic element. Molybdenum melts at about 2610 degrees Celsius and boils at about 4640 degrees Celsius. Swedish chemist Carl Wilhelm Scheele discovered molybdenum in 1778.

Molybdenum occurs in nature in the form of molybdenite and wulfenite. Contributing to the growth of plants, it is an important trace element in soils. Approximately 70% of the world supply of molybdenum is obtained as a by-product of copper mining. Molybdenum is chiefly used as an alloy to strengthen steel and resist corrosion. It is used for structural work, aircraft parts, and forged automobile parts because it withstands high temperatures and pressures and adds strength. Other uses include lubricants, a refractory metal in chemical applications, electron tubing, and as a catalyst.

**Prices** – The average monthly U.S. merchant price of molybdic oxide in 2022 rose by +19.9% yr/yr to $19.23 per pound, the highest since 2008.

**Supply** – World mine production of molybdenum in 2022 fell by -2.0% yr/yr to 250,000 metric tons. The major producers in 2022 were China with 40.0% of world production, Chile with 17.6% and the U.S. with 16.8%. U.S. mine production of molybdenum in 2022 rose by +2.2% yr/yr to 42,000 metric tons.

**Demand** – U.S. consumption of molybdenum products in 2022 rose by +0.6% yr/yr to 16,000 metric tons.

**Trade** – U.S. imports of molybdenum concentrate for consumption in 2022 rose by +9.3% yr/yr to 33,000 metric tons.

## World Mine Production of Molybdenum  In Metric Tons (Contained Molybdenum)

| Year | Armenia | Canada[3] | Chile | China | Iran | Kazakhstan | Mexico | Mongolia | Peru | Russia | United States | Uzbekistan | World Total |
|---|---|---|---|---|---|---|---|---|---|---|---|---|---|
| 2013 | 6,900 | 7,956 | 38,715 | 122,000 | 3,471 | ---- | 12,562 | 1,819 | 18,140 | 4,753 | 61,000 | 490 | 281,000 |
| 2014 | 7,162 | 9,358 | 48,770 | 129,000 | 3,494 | ---- | 14,370 | 1,999 | 17,018 | 3,114 | 68,200 | 450 | 306,000 |
| 2015 | 6,300 | 2,505 | 52,579 | 135,000 | 3,500 | ---- | 12,279 | 2,557 | 20,153 | 3,000 | 47,400 | 450 | 288,000 |
| 2016 | 6,300 | 2,708 | 55,647 | 129,000 | 3,500 | ---- | 11,896 | 2,444 | 25,757 | 3,000 | 36,200 | 450 | 278,000 |
| 2017 | 5,800 | 5,290 | 62,500 | 130,000 | 3,500 | ---- | 14,000 | 1,800 | 28,100 | 3,100 | 40,700 | 450 | 297,000 |
| 2018 | 5,000 | 4,680 | 60,200 | 133,000 | 3,500 | ---- | 15,100 | 1,800 | 28,000 | 2,800 | 41,400 | 200 | 297,000 |
| 2019 | 5,000 | 3,900 | 56,000 | 130,000 | 3,500 | ---- | 16,600 | 1,800 | 30,400 | 2,800 | 43,600 | 200 | 294,000 |
| 2020 | 8,700 | 2,530 | 59,400 | 120,000 | 1,400 | ---- | 16,600 | 2,890 | 32,200 | 2,700 | 51,100 | 200 | 298,000 |
| 2021[1] | 7,760 | 1,390 | 49,400 | 95,300 | 3,100 | ---- | 16,300 | 2,970 | 34,100 | 1,700 | 41,100 | 1,600 | 255,000 |
| 2022[2] | 7,800 | 970 | 44,000 | 100,000 | 3,500 | ---- | 16,000 | 2,300 | 32,000 | 1,700 | 42,000 | 1,600 | 250,000 |

[1] Preliminary.  [2] Estimate.  [3] Shipments.  Source: U.S. Geological Survey (USGS)

## Salient Statistics of Molybdenum in the United States  In Metric Tons (Contained Molybdenum)

| | | Concentrate | | | | | | | Primary Products[4] | | | | | |
| | | Shipments | | | | | | | Net Production | | Shipments | | | |
| Year | Total Production | Pro- (Including Exports) | Value Million $ | For Exports | Con- sumption | Imports For Con- sumption | Stocks Dec. 31[3] | Grand Total | Molybolic Oxide[5] | Molyb- denum Metal Powder | Avg Price Value $ / Kg.[6] | Domestic Dest- inations | To Oxide for Exports, Gross Weight | Con- sumption | Producer Stocks, Dec. 31 |
|---|---|---|---|---|---|---|---|---|---|---|---|---|---|---|---|
| 2013 | 61,000 | 68,100 | ---- | ---- | W | 13,100 | W | ---- | ---- | ---- | 22.85 | W | 1,320 | 18,600 | W |
| 2014 | 68,200 | 71,900 | ---- | ---- | W | 15,800 | W | ---- | ---- | ---- | 25.84 | W | 1,740 | 19,500 | W |
| 2015 | 47,400 | 50,500 | ---- | ---- | W | 12,900 | W | ---- | ---- | ---- | 15.01 | W | 1,300 | 17,600 | W |
| 2016 | 36,200 | 38,600 | ---- | ---- | W | 14,900 | W | ---- | ---- | ---- | 14.40 | W | 853 | 15,800 | W |
| 2017 | 40,700 | 43,200 | ---- | ---- | W | 36,000 | W | ---- | ---- | ---- | 18.06 | W | 534 | 17,400 | W |
| 2018 | 41,400 | 48,400 | ---- | ---- | W | 37,500 | W | ---- | ---- | ---- | 27.04 | W | 874 | 16,700 | W |
| 2019 | 43,600 | 67,200 | ---- | ---- | W | 34,200 | W | ---- | ---- | ---- | 26.50 | W | 524 | 16,400 | W |
| 2020 | 51,100 | 62,500 | ---- | ---- | W | 24,700 | W | ---- | ---- | ---- | 19.90 | W | 1,110 | 15,800 | W |
| 2021[1] | 41,100 | 60,000 | ---- | ---- | W | 30,200 | W | ---- | ---- | ---- | 35.30 | W | | 15,900 | W |
| 2022[2] | 42,000 | 53,000 | ---- | ---- | W | 33,000 | W | ---- | ---- | ---- | 39.25 | W | | 16,000 | W |

[1] Preliminary.  [2] Estimate.  [3] At mines & at plants making molybdenum products.  [4] Comprises ferromolybdenum, molybdic oxide, & molybdenum salts & metal.  [5] Includes molybdic oxide briquets, molybdic acid, molybdenum trioxide, all other.  [6] U.S. producer price per kilogram of molybdenum oxide contained in technical-grade molybdic oxide.  W = Withheld proprietary data.  E = Net exporter.  Source: U.S. Geological Survey (USGS)

## US Merchant Price of Molybdic Oxide  In Dollars Per Pound

| Year | Jan. | Feb. | Mar. | Apr. | May | June | July | Aug. | Sept. | Oct. | Nov. | Dec. | Average |
|---|---|---|---|---|---|---|---|---|---|---|---|---|---|
| 2015 | 9.41 | 8.58 | 8.17 | 8.02 | 7.63 | 7.32 | 6.04 | 6.11 | 5.88 | 5.01 | 4.73 | 5.02 | 6.83 |
| 2016 | 5.32 | 5.45 | 5.45 | 5.55 | 6.87 | 7.95 | 6.91 | 7.11 | 7.13 | 6.88 | 6.82 | 6.71 | 6.51 |
| 2017 | 7.22 | 7.75 | 8.38 | 9.03 | 8.56 | 7.49 | 7.41 | 8.22 | 8.76 | 8.53 | 8.53 | 9.33 | 8.27 |
| 2018 | 11.42 | 12.33 | 12.96 | 12.48 | 11.95 | 11.43 | 11.28 | 12.15 | 12.16 | 12.06 | 12.01 | 12.22 | 12.04 |
| 2019 | 11.59 | 11.64 | 12.50 | 12.14 | 12.33 | 12.32 | 12.10 | 11.99 | 11.91 | 11.28 | 9.41 | 9.53 | 11.56 |
| 2020 | 9.89 | 10.34 | 9.14 | 8.31 | 8.66 | 8.18 | 7.27 | 7.73 | 8.35 | 8.55 | 9.20 | 9.31 | 8.74 |
| 2021 | 10.29 | 11.85 | 12.19 | 11.25 | 13.04 | 17.63 | 18.90 | 19.83 | 19.69 | 19.31 | 19.31 | 19.16 | 16.04 |
| 2022 | 19.24 | 19.18 | 19.68 | 19.80 | 19.23 | 18.48 | 17.37 | 16.41 | 17.44 | 19.43 | 19.65 | 24.79 | 19.23 |

Source: American Metal Market (AMM)

# Nickel

Nickel (atomic symbol Ni) is a hard, malleable, ductile metal that has a silvery tinge that can take on a high polish. Nickel is somewhat ferromagnetic and is a fair conductor of heat and electricity. Nickel is primarily used in the production of stainless steel and other corrosion-resistant alloys. Nickel is used in coins to replace silver, in rechargeable batteries, and in electronic circuitry. Nickel plating techniques, like electro-less coating or single-slurry coating, are employed in such applications as turbine blades, helicopter rotors, extrusion dies, and rolled steel strip.

Nickel futures and options trade at the London Metal Exchange (LME). The nickel futures contract calls for the delivery of 6 metric tons of primary nickel with at least 99.80% purity in the form of full plate, cut cathodes, pellets or briquettes. The contract is priced in terms of U.S. dollars per metric ton.

**Supply** – World mine production of nickel in 2022 rose by +20.9% yr/yr to a record 3.300 million metric tons.

The world's largest mine producers of nickel in 2022 were Indonesia with 48.5% of world production, the Philippines with 10.0%, Russia with 6.7%, and New Caledonia with 5.8%.

**Demand** – U.S. consumption of nickel in 2022 rose by +10.0% yr/yr to 220,000 metric tons. In 2019, the primary U.S. nickel consumption use was for stainless and heat-resisting steels, which accounted for 67.7% of U.S. consumption. Other consumption uses in 2019 were superalloys at 14.6%, nickel alloys at 9.0% electroplating anodes at 3.5%, alloy steels at 3.4% and chemicals at 1.1%.

**Trade** – The U.S. relied on imports for 56% of its nickel consumption in 2022. U.S. imports of primary and secondary nickel in 2022 rose by +15.2% yr/yr to 164,000 metric tons, still well above the 2009 record low of 117,600 metric tons. U.S. exports of primary and secondary nickel in 2022 rose by +32.7% yr/yr to 54,000 metric tons.

### World Mine Production of Nickel   In Metric Tons (Contained Nickel)

| Year | Australia[3] | Botswana | Brazil | Canada | China | Dominican Republic | Greece | Indonesia | New Caledonia | Philippines | Russia | South Africa | World Total |
|---|---|---|---|---|---|---|---|---|---|---|---|---|---|
| 2014 | 266,181 | 14,958 | 102,000 | 218,233 | 101,100 | ---- | 21,405 | 177,100 | 175,174 | 393,262 | 283,200 | 54,956 | 2,130,000 |
| 2015 | 225,227 | 16,789 | 94,800 | 225,351 | 101,400 | 4,000 | 19,610 | 129,600 | 193,199 | 415,021 | 276,710 | 56,689 | 2,110,000 |
| 2016 | 203,135 | 16,878 | 86,400 | 230,210 | 100,200 | 19,900 | 19,431 | 204,000 | 204,207 | 300,506 | 258,840 | 48,994 | 2,010,000 |
| 2017 | 185,466 | ---- | 76,800 | 206,354 | 102,300 | 28,300 | 19,073 | 355,000 | 215,382 | 339,377 | 267,300 | 48,383 | 2,200,000 |
| 2018 | 160,022 | ---- | 74,400 | 177,867 | 110,000 | 34,700 | 17,925 | 606,000 | 216,225 | 344,966 | 272,300 | 43,236 | 2,400,000 |
| 2019 | 158,751 | ---- | 60,600 | 181,410 | 120,000 | 56,900 | 13,655 | 853,000 | 208,185 | 323,325 | 278,700 | 42,936 | 2,610,000 |
| 2020 | 169,000 | ---- | 77,100 | 167,000 | 120,000 | 47,000 | | 771,000 | 200,000 | 334,000 | 283,000 | | 2,510,000 |
| 2021[1] | 151,000 | ---- | 76,000 | 134,000 | 109,000 | | | 1,040,000 | 18,600 | 387,000 | 205,000 | | 2,730,000 |
| 2022[2] | 160,000 | ---- | 83,000 | 130,000 | 110,000 | | | 1,600,000 | 190,000 | 330,000 | 220,000 | | 3,300,000 |

[1] Preliminary.   [2] Estimate.   [3] Content of nickel sulfate and concentrates.   Source: U.S. Geological Survey (USGS)

### Salient Statistics of Nickel in the United States   In Metric Tons (Contained Nickel)

| Year | Net Import Reliance As a % of Apparent Consumption | Production Plant[4] | Secondary[5] | Alloy Sheets | Cast Iron | Copper Base Alloys | Electroplating Anodes | Nickel Alloys | Stainless & Heat Resisting Steels | Super Alloys | Chemicals | Apparent Consumption | Stocks Dec. 31 At Consumer Plants | At Producer Plants | Primary & Secondary Exports | Imports | Avg. Price LME $/Lb. |
|---|---|---|---|---|---|---|---|---|---|---|---|---|---|---|---|---|---|
| 2014 | 58 | ---- | 91,510 | 4,960 | 272 | 2,300 | 8,100 | 15,000 | 133,000 | 25,700 | 2,120 | 264,000 | 23,300 | 9,030 | 66,700 | 195,000 | 7.65 |
| 2015 | 50 | ---- | 115,590 | 3,330 | 205 | 2,240 | 7,490 | W | 127,000 | 26,900 | 252 | 234,000 | 8,570 | 10,600 | 61,510 | 157,100 | 5.37 |
| 2016 | 44 | ---- | 130,790 | 5,380 | 160 | 2,780 | 7,370 | 14,700 | 153,000 | 24,400 | 1,750 | 235,000 | 8,690 | 6,370 | 74,000 | 143,300 | 4.35 |
| 2017 | 51 | ---- | 132,740 | 6,810 | ---- | ---- | 7,350 | 16,500 | 169,000 | 27,300 | 1,550 | 273,000 | 8,040 | 6,550 | 62,500 | 188,100 | 4.72 |
| 2018 | 52 | ---- | 122,690 | 8,510 | ---- | ---- | 7,240 | 20,600 | 159,000 | 27,300 | 2,830 | 259,000 | 9,570 | 6,780 | 69,180 | 189,100 | 5.95 |
| 2019 | 49 | ---- | 110,820 | 7,340 | ---- | ---- | 7,590 | 19,600 | 147,000 | 31,600 | 2,460 | 217,000 | 6,500 | 6,860 | 60,600 | 156,700 | 6.31 |
| 2020 | 48 | ---- | | | | | | | | | | 200,000 | | | 57,600 | 136,800 | 6.25 |
| 2021[1] | 49 | ---- | | | | | | | | | | 200,000 | | | 40,700 | 142,400 | 8.38 |
| 2022[2] | 56 | ---- | | | | | | | | | | 220,000 | | | 54,000 | 164,000 | 11.00 |

[1] Exclusive of scrap.   [2] Preliminary.   [3] Estimate.   [4] Smelter & refinery.   [5] From purchased scrap (ferrous & nonferrous).
W = Withheld proprietary data.   NA = Not available.   Source: U.S. Geological Survey (USGS)

### Average Price of Nickel (Cash) in London   In U.S. Dollars per Metric Ton

| Year | Jan. | Feb. | Mar. | Apr. | May | June | July | Aug. | Sept. | Oct. | Nov. | Dec. | Average |
|---|---|---|---|---|---|---|---|---|---|---|---|---|---|
| 2016 | 8,507.3 | 8,298.5 | 8,717.3 | 8,878.9 | 8,660.4 | 8,928.4 | 10,262.9 | 10,336.0 | 10,191.8 | 10,259.7 | 11,128.9 | 10,972.3 | 9,595.2 |
| 2017 | 9,971.5 | 10,643.3 | 10,204.7 | 9,609.3 | 9,155.1 | 8,931.8 | 9,491.4 | 10,890.0 | 11,215.8 | 11,335.8 | 11,972.1 | 11,499.4 | 10,410.0 |
| 2018 | 12,840.1 | 13,566.4 | 13,416.6 | 13,938.1 | 14,366.5 | 15,105.7 | 13,793.9 | 13,411.4 | 12,510.4 | 12,314.9 | 11,239.7 | 10,835.1 | 13,111.5 |
| 2019 | 11,523.1 | 12,685.2 | 13,026.3 | 12,772.8 | 12,016.3 | 11,943.9 | 13,546.3 | 15,748.6 | 17,656.9 | 17,046.2 | 15,171.8 | 13,829.4 | 13,913.9 |
| 2020 | 13,506.9 | 12,715.6 | 11,846.2 | 11,804.0 | 12,179.6 | 12,727.2 | 13,402.3 | 14,537.8 | 14,857.5 | 15,239.4 | 15,807.7 | 16,283.0 | 13,742.3 |
| 2021 | 17,863.2 | 18,584.4 | 16,406.7 | 16,521.3 | 17,577.1 | 17,979.6 | 18,818.5 | 19,141.3 | 19,376.9 | 19,362.4 | 19,932.9 | 20,015.6 | 18,465.0 |
| 2022 | 22,355.4 | 24,015.6 | 37,652.0 | 33,132.7 | 28,102.2 | 25,658.6 | 21,481.9 | 22,057.4 | 22,689.1 | 22,032.9 | 25,562.7 | 28,946.8 | 26,140.6 |

Contract Size = 6 Metric Tons   Source: London Metal Exchange (LME)

# Oats

Oats are seeds or grains of a genus of plants that thrive in cool, moist climates. There are about 25 species of oats that grow worldwide in the cooler temperate regions. The oldest known cultivated oats were found inside caves in Switzerland and are believed to be from the Bronze Age. Oats are usually sown in early spring and harvested in mid to late summer, but in southern regions of the northern hemisphere, they may be sown in the fall. Oats are used in many processed foods such as flour, livestock feed, and furfural, a chemical used as a solvent in various refining industries. The oat crop year begins in June and ends in May. Oat futures and options are traded at the CME Group.

**Prices** – CME oat futures prices (Barchart.com electronic symbol ZO) on the nearest-futures chart showed strength in early 2022 but then fell back and closed the year down -46.2% at $3.6725 per bushel.

**Supply** – World oat production in 2022/23 is expected to rise by +10.3% yr/yr to 24.853 million metric tons, above the record low of 19.625 million metric tons posted in 2010/11. World annual oat production in the past three decades has dropped very sharply from levels above 50 million metric tons in the early 1970s. The world's largest oat producers in 2022/23 are expected to be the European Union with 30.6% of world production, Canada with 21.0%, Russia with 15.3%, and Australia with 5.6%.

U.S. oat production in the 2022/23 marketing year is expected to rise by +44.7% yr/yr to 57.655 million bushels. U.S. oat production has fallen sharply from levels mostly above 1 billion bushels seen from the early 1900s into the early 1960s. U.S. farmers are expected to harvest 890,000 acres of oats in 2022/23, up +36.9% yr/yr. That is far below the almost 40 million acres harvested back in the 1950s. The oat yield in 2022/23 is expected to rise by +5.7% yr/yr to 64.8 bushels per acre. Oat stocks in the U.S. as of December 2022 were down by -3.3% yr/yr to 53.584 million bushels. The largest U.S. oat-producing states in 2022 were the states of North Dakota with 23.4% of U.S. production, Minnesota with 14.3%, South Dakota with 8.3%, Wisconsin with 8.3%, Pennsylvania with 6.2%, and Iowa with 5.6%.

**Demand** – U.S. usage of oats in 2022/23 is expected to rise by +12.4% yr/yr to 141.000 million bushels. U.S. usage of oats in 2022/23 is expected to be 52.6% for food, alcohol, and industrial, 42.6% for feed and residual, 4.8% for seed, and the rest for export.

**Trade** – U.S. exports of oats in 2022/23 are expected to fall by -20.5% yr/yr to 2.000 million bushels. U.S. imports of oats in 2022/23 are expected to rise by +5.1% yr/yr to 85.000 million bushels.

**World Production of Oats** In Thousands of Metric Tons

| Crop Year | Argentina | Australia | Belarus | Brazil | Canada | Chile | China | European Union | Kazakhstan | Russia | Ukraine | United States | World Total |
|---|---|---|---|---|---|---|---|---|---|---|---|---|---|
| 2013-14 | 445 | 1,255 | 352 | 380 | 3,928 | 610 | 235 | 8,380 | 305 | 4,932 | 467 | 938 | 23,190 |
| 2014-15 | 525 | 1,198 | 522 | 307 | 2,977 | 421 | 310 | 7,821 | 226 | 5,267 | 610 | 1,019 | 22,123 |
| 2015-16 | 553 | 1,300 | 492 | 351 | 3,425 | 533 | 340 | 7,524 | 244 | 4,527 | 498 | 1,298 | 22,082 |
| 2016-17 | 785 | 2,266 | 390 | 828 | 3,231 | 713 | 500 | 7,228 | 335 | 4,750 | 510 | 938 | 24,346 |
| 2017-18 | 492 | 1,227 | 460 | 634 | 3,733 | 571 | 550 | 7,183 | 285 | 5,448 | 481 | 720 | 23,628 |
| 2018-19 | 572 | 1,135 | 342 | 795 | 3,436 | 385 | 560 | 6,940 | 336 | 4,715 | 423 | 815 | 22,205 |
| 2019-20 | 600 | 1,143 | 368 | 879 | 4,227 | 477 | 600 | 6,965 | 267 | 4,420 | 427 | 773 | 23,214 |
| 2020-21[1] | 510 | 1,898 | 445 | 853 | 4,576 | 525 | 600 | 8,473 | 240 | 4,127 | 515 | 954 | 25,723 |
| 2021-22[2] | 725 | 1,619 | 350 | 1,143 | 2,808 | 578 | 600 | 7,528 | 182 | 3,733 | 478 | 578 | 22,528 |
| 2022-23[3] | 645 | 1,400 | 375 | 1,155 | 5,226 | 550 | 600 | 7,608 | 225 | 3,800 | 400 | 837 | 24,853 |

[1] Preliminary.  [2] Estimate.  [3] Forecast.  Source: Foreign Agricultural Service, U.S. Department of Agriculture (FAS-USDA)

**World Consumption of Oats** In Thousands of Metric Tons

| Crop Year | Argentina | Australia | Belarus | Brazil | Canada | Chile | China | European Union | Norway | Russia | Ukraine | United States | World Total |
|---|---|---|---|---|---|---|---|---|---|---|---|---|---|
| 2013-14 | 425 | 950 | 375 | 375 | 1,666 | 570 | 350 | 8,075 | 245 | 4,900 | 475 | 2,757 | 22,511 |
| 2014-15 | 525 | 950 | 500 | 305 | 1,682 | 355 | 400 | 7,730 | 295 | 5,200 | 600 | 2,447 | 22,227 |
| 2015-16 | 550 | 1,025 | 500 | 345 | 1,600 | 495 | 500 | 7,400 | 296 | 4,600 | 450 | 2,700 | 21,806 |
| 2016-17 | 760 | 1,500 | 400 | 775 | 1,874 | 655 | 730 | 7,150 | 315 | 4,800 | 450 | 2,537 | 24,143 |
| 2017-18 | 525 | 900 | 460 | 675 | 2,041 | 570 | 850 | 7,050 | 320 | 5,400 | 480 | 2,358 | 23,869 |
| 2018-19 | 550 | 900 | 375 | 775 | 2,083 | 390 | 870 | 7,000 | 250 | 4,700 | 450 | 2,326 | 23,021 |
| 2019-20 | 600 | 970 | 370 | 845 | 2,419 | 520 | 870 | 6,900 | 345 | 4,200 | 420 | 2,344 | 23,153 |
| 2020-21[1] | 525 | 1,200 | 440 | 845 | 2,340 | 615 | 900 | 8,175 | 320 | 4,050 | 475 | 2,362 | 24,619 |
| 2021-22[2] | 710 | 1,100 | 350 | 1,125 | 1,861 | 570 | 925 | 7,650 | 322 | 3,650 | 465 | 2,013 | 23,166 |
| 2022-23[3] | 650 | 1,000 | 375 | 1,125 | 2,900 | 675 | 950 | 7,650 | 335 | 3,700 | 425 | 2,364 | 24,540 |

[1] Preliminary.  [2] Estimate.  [3] Forecast.  Source: Foreign Agricultural Service, U.S. Department of Agriculture (FAS-USDA)

# OATS

## Oat Stocks in the United States    In Thousands of Bushels

| | On Farms | | | | Off Farms | | | | Total Stocks | | | |
|---|---|---|---|---|---|---|---|---|---|---|---|---|
| Year | Mar. 1 | June 1 | Sept. 1 | Dec. 1 | Mar. 1 | June 1 | Sept. 1 | Dec. 1 | Mar. 1 | June 1 | Sept. 1 | Dec. 1 |
| 2013 | 18,900 | 11,380 | 37,150 | 25,650 | 33,726 | 24,957 | 26,339 | 22,394 | 52,626 | 36,337 | 63,489 | 48,044 |
| 2014 | 19,800 | 9,710 | 41,400 | 31,300 | 15,323 | 15,029 | 32,910 | 35,670 | 35,123 | 24,739 | 74,310 | 66,970 |
| 2015 | 20,810 | 15,120 | 47,800 | 36,750 | 38,609 | 38,625 | 46,066 | 45,981 | 59,419 | 53,745 | 93,866 | 82,731 |
| 2016 | 26,800 | 18,350 | 37,400 | 30,430 | 48,429 | 38,452 | 41,190 | 45,003 | 75,229 | 56,802 | 78,590 | 75,433 |
| 2017 | 22,320 | 13,540 | 33,950 | 23,300 | 40,885 | 36,790 | 38,039 | 43,166 | 63,205 | 50,330 | 71,989 | 66,466 |
| 2018 | 17,240 | 11,410 | 39,200 | 25,410 | 37,699 | 29,606 | 35,573 | 41,864 | 54,939 | 41,016 | 74,773 | 67,274 |
| 2019 | 18,050 | 10,500 | 37,900 | 24,770 | 32,232 | 27,314 | 22,153 | 29,139 | 50,282 | 37,814 | 60,053 | 53,909 |
| 2020 | 16,970 | 10,070 | 39,850 | 28,830 | 30,722 | 26,693 | 27,017 | 33,712 | 47,692 | 36,763 | 66,867 | 62,542 |
| 2021 | 16,880 | 12,540 | 32,150 | 18,530 | 34,585 | 25,513 | 29,912 | 36,871 | 51,465 | 38,053 | 62,062 | 55,401 |
| 2022[1] | 13,560 | 9,890 | 41,650 | 24,180 | 29,444 | 22,763 | 20,897 | 29,515 | 43,004 | 32,653 | 62,547 | 53,695 |

[1] Preliminary.    Source: National Agricultural Statistics Service, U.S. Department of Agriculture (NASS-USDA)

## Supply and Utilization of Oats in the United States    In Millions of Bushels

| Crop Year Beginning June 1 | Acreage Planted | Harvested | Yield Per Acre (Bushels) | Production | Imports | Total Supply | Feed & Residual | Food, Alcohol & Industrial | Seed | Exports | Total Use | Ending Stocks | Farm Price | Findley Loan Rate | Target Price |
|---|---|---|---|---|---|---|---|---|---|---|---|---|---|---|---|
| 2013-14 | 2,980 | 1,009 | 64.1 | 64.6 | 97.1 | 198.1 | 98.4 | 66.2 | 7.2 | 173.4 | 1.6 | 24.7 | 3.75 | 1.39 | 1.79 |
| 2014-15 | 2,753 | 1,035 | 67.9 | 70.2 | 108.9 | 203.8 | 71.2 | 69.0 | 8.0 | 148.2 | 1.8 | 53.7 | 3.21 | 1.39 | 2.40 |
| 2015-16 | 3,088 | 1,276 | 70.2 | 89.5 | 85.6 | 228.8 | 93.5 | 69.4 | 7.1 | 170.1 | 2.0 | 56.8 | 2.12 | 1.39 | 2.40 |
| 2016-17 | 2,829 | 981 | 66.0 | 64.8 | 90.2 | 211.7 | 81.6 | 69.9 | 6.4 | 157.9 | 3.4 | 50.3 | 2.06 | 1.39 | 2.40 |
| 2017-18 | 2,589 | 804 | 61.7 | 49.6 | 89.2 | 189.1 | 68.3 | 70.6 | 6.8 | 145.7 | 2.4 | 41.0 | 2.59 | 1.39 | 2.40 |
| 2018-19 | 2,746 | 865 | 64.9 | 56.1 | 86.5 | 183.6 | 66.2 | 70.9 | 7.0 | 144.1 | 1.7 | 37.8 | 2.66 | 1.39 | 2.40 |
| 2019-20 | 2,830 | 828 | 64.3 | 53.3 | 92.0 | 183.1 | 62.7 | 74.0 | 7.5 | 144.2 | 2.1 | 36.8 | 2.82 | 2.00 | 2.40 |
| 2020-21 | 3,009 | 1,009 | 65.1 | 65.4 | 85.4 | 187.9 | 68.3 | 72.2 | 6.1 | 146.6 | 3.2 | 38.1 | 2.77 | 2.00 | |
| 2021-22[1] | 2,550 | 650 | 61.3 | 39.8 | 80.9 | 158.7 | 46.0 | 73.0 | 6.4 | 125.4 | 2.5 | 30.8 | 4.55 | 2.00 | |
| 2022-23[2] | 2,581 | 890 | 64.8 | 57.7 | 85.0 | 173.5 | 60.0 | 74.2 | 6.8 | 141.0 | 2.0 | 30.5 | 4.75 | 2.00 | |

[1] Preliminary.    [2] Forecast.    [3] Less than 500,000 bushels.    NA = Not available.
Source: Economic Research Service, U.S. Department of Agiculture (ERS-USDA)

## Production of Oats in the United States, by States    In Thousands of Bushels

| Year | Illinois | Iowa | Michigan | Minnesota | Nebraska | New York | North Dakota | Ohio | Pennsylvania | South Dakota | Texas | Wisconsin | Total |
|---|---|---|---|---|---|---|---|---|---|---|---|---|---|
| 2013 | 1,725 | 3,960 | 1,860 | 5,985 | 1,625 | 3,082 | 8,370 | 1,575 | 3,100 | 9,240 | 1,840 | 6,825 | 64,642 |
| 2014 | 2,000 | 3,520 | 2,760 | 7,875 | 2,400 | 2,520 | 7,665 | 2,205 | 3,480 | 9,300 | 1,710 | 8,680 | 70,232 |
| 2015 | 1,925 | 4,161 | 3,350 | 12,480 | 2,680 | 2,320 | 10,360 | 2,520 | 3,575 | 12,615 | 2,640 | 14,040 | 89,535 |
| 2016 | 1,620 | 3,268 | 1,740 | 8,160 | 1,500 | 3,300 | 7,260 | 1,850 | 3,350 | 9,020 | 3,000 | 6,600 | 64,770 |
| 2017 | 1,580 | 3,234 | 2,160 | 7,125 | 1,715 | 1,925 | 4,640 | 1,400 | 2,320 | 4,200 | 2,700 | 5,015 | 49,585 |
| 2018 | 2,075 | 2,079 | 3,150 | 6,195 | 1,518 | 2,322 | 8,610 | 1,950 | 1,610 | 7,790 | 2,500 | 5,490 | 56,130 |
| 2019 | 650 | 4,002 | 1,425 | 6,200 | 1,134 | 2,340 | 9,890 | 1,150 | 2,650 | 6,150 | 2,000 | 6,480 | 53,258 |
| 2020 | 870 | 5,694 | 1,650 | 10,560 | 1,827 | 1,696 | 8,190 | 900 | 2,750 | 10,780 | 2,700 | 8,253 | 65,355 |
| 2021 | 1,245 | 4,004 | 1,260 | 4,389 | 1,456 | 1,972 | 3,984 | 1,340 | 2,340 | 3,752 | 1,575 | 3,782 | 39,836 |
| 2022[1] | 830 | 3,200 | 1,830 | 8,260 | 918 | 2,754 | 13,490 | 1,050 | 3,599 | 6,000 | 1,925 | 4,810 | 57,655 |

[1] Preliminary.    Source: National Agricultural Statistics Service, U.S. Department of Agriculture (NASS-USDA)

## Official Oats Crop Production Reports in the United States    In Thousands of Bushels

| Year | July 1 | Aug. 1 | Sept. 1 | Oct. 1 | Dec. 1 | Final | Year | July 1 | Aug. 1 | Sept. 1 | Oct. 1 | Dec. 1 | Final |
|---|---|---|---|---|---|---|---|---|---|---|---|---|---|
| 2011 | 56,551 | 57,489 | ---- | ---- | ---- | 53,649 | 2017 | 53,674 | 53,719 | ---- | ---- | ---- | 49,585 |
| 2012 | 65,276 | 66,519 | ---- | ---- | ---- | 61,486 | 2018 | 66,384 | 65,668 | ---- | ---- | ---- | 56,130 |
| 2013 | 74,459 | 75,210 | ---- | ---- | ---- | 64,642 | 2019 | 61,628 | 60,385 | ---- | ---- | ---- | 53,258 |
| 2014 | 75,507 | 77,267 | ---- | ---- | ---- | 70,232 | 2020 | 65,024 | 64,907 | ---- | ---- | ---- | 65,355 |
| 2015 | 83,640 | 85,456 | ---- | ---- | ---- | 89,535 | 2021 | 41,309 | 41,431 | ---- | ---- | ---- | 39,836 |
| 2016 | 76,609 | 76,854 | ---- | ---- | ---- | 64,770 | 2022[1] | 52,613 | 52,576 | ---- | ---- | ---- | 57,655 |

[1] Preliminary.    Source: National Agricultural Statistics Service, U.S. Department of Agriculture (NASS-USDA)

# OATS

## OATS - CBOT
### Weekly Nearest Futures as of 03/31/2023

## Volume of Trading in Oats Futures in Chicago    In Contracts

| Year | Jan. | Feb. | Mar. | Apr. | May | June | July | Aug. | Sept. | Oct. | Nov. | Dec. | Total |
|---|---|---|---|---|---|---|---|---|---|---|---|---|---|
| 2013 | 21,246 | 34,411 | 16,949 | 31,035 | 16,891 | 28,267 | 18,156 | 16,459 | 17,388 | 21,863 | 22,977 | 9,316 | 254,958 |
| 2014 | 18,860 | 30,902 | 18,786 | 18,113 | 11,938 | 19,491 | 11,446 | 13,556 | 11,300 | 16,754 | 21,903 | 7,482 | 200,531 |
| 2015 | 14,618 | 19,923 | 12,461 | 25,243 | 15,152 | 21,734 | 11,399 | 13,953 | 9,614 | 13,216 | 24,979 | 12,283 | 194,575 |
| 2016 | 15,634 | 25,543 | 14,663 | 26,235 | 14,762 | 34,447 | 11,971 | 19,094 | 9,399 | 21,957 | 21,435 | 10,090 | 225,230 |
| 2017 | 15,129 | 16,691 | 13,180 | 17,122 | 10,845 | 24,381 | 10,292 | 11,920 | 8,370 | 11,522 | 19,561 | 10,239 | 169,252 |
| 2018 | 15,633 | 14,913 | 14,719 | 21,901 | 10,995 | 16,616 | 7,060 | 16,254 | 9,029 | 17,965 | 20,659 | 7,195 | 172,939 |
| 2019 | 10,494 | 16,765 | 10,206 | 19,410 | 14,000 | 22,122 | 9,460 | 9,034 | 9,145 | 12,466 | 19,901 | 9,548 | 162,551 |
| 2020 | 10,088 | 17,749 | 13,193 | 9,646 | 10,702 | 18,060 | 6,579 | 9,703 | 10,037 | 10,124 | 15,829 | 8,962 | 140,672 |
| 2021 | 7,568 | 11,486 | 7,479 | 12,665 | 9,657 | 15,397 | 11,563 | 9,872 | 11,009 | 14,010 | 20,154 | 10,043 | 140,903 |
| 2022 | 10,480 | 13,898 | 7,366 | 8,564 | 6,991 | 9,820 | 5,102 | 7,648 | 7,471 | 9,780 | 12,155 | 8,303 | 107,578 |

Contract size = 5,000 bu.    Source: CME Group; Chicago Board of Trade (CBT)

## Average Open Interest of Oats in Chicago    In Contracts

| Year | Jan. | Feb. | Mar. | Apr. | May | June | July | Aug. | Sept. | Oct. | Nov. | Dec. |
|---|---|---|---|---|---|---|---|---|---|---|---|---|
| 2013 | 10,568 | 11,022 | 10,619 | 9,356 | 8,634 | 10,207 | 8,659 | 9,000 | 9,941 | 10,805 | 9,767 | 8,937 |
| 2014 | 10,414 | 11,168 | 9,529 | 8,350 | 7,356 | 7,793 | 7,292 | 8,382 | 8,987 | 9,787 | 9,813 | 8,151 |
| 2015 | 7,684 | 8,794 | 8,965 | 8,729 | 8,375 | 8,570 | 7,926 | 8,408 | 8,902 | 10,129 | 10,793 | 8,789 |
| 2016 | 9,457 | 10,452 | 10,883 | 10,418 | 9,947 | 10,282 | 9,969 | 10,511 | 10,755 | 9,261 | 8,304 | 6,946 |
| 2017 | 7,314 | 7,952 | 6,597 | 6,656 | 6,104 | 6,764 | 6,687 | 6,369 | 5,902 | 6,674 | 7,795 | 6,561 |
| 2018 | 6,491 | 5,995 | 5,740 | 6,470 | 5,468 | 5,232 | 4,898 | 4,723 | 3,990 | 6,113 | 6,608 | 5,712 |
| 2019 | 5,686 | 5,322 | 4,562 | 5,973 | 6,623 | 6,305 | 4,809 | 4,560 | 5,178 | 6,016 | 6,991 | 5,585 |
| 2020 | 5,004 | 5,405 | 4,391 | 3,450 | 4,211 | 4,809 | 4,420 | 4,677 | 5,238 | 5,491 | 5,783 | 4,519 |
| 2021 | 4,754 | 4,509 | 4,347 | 4,501 | 4,602 | 3,907 | 4,135 | 4,651 | 4,676 | 5,184 | 5,456 | 4,625 |
| 2022 | 3,944 | 3,745 | 3,005 | 3,210 | 3,024 | 2,992 | 2,530 | 2,919 | 3,718 | 4,113 | 4,171 | 3,968 |

Contract size = 5,000 bu.    Source: CME Group; Chicago Board of Trade (CBT)

# OATS

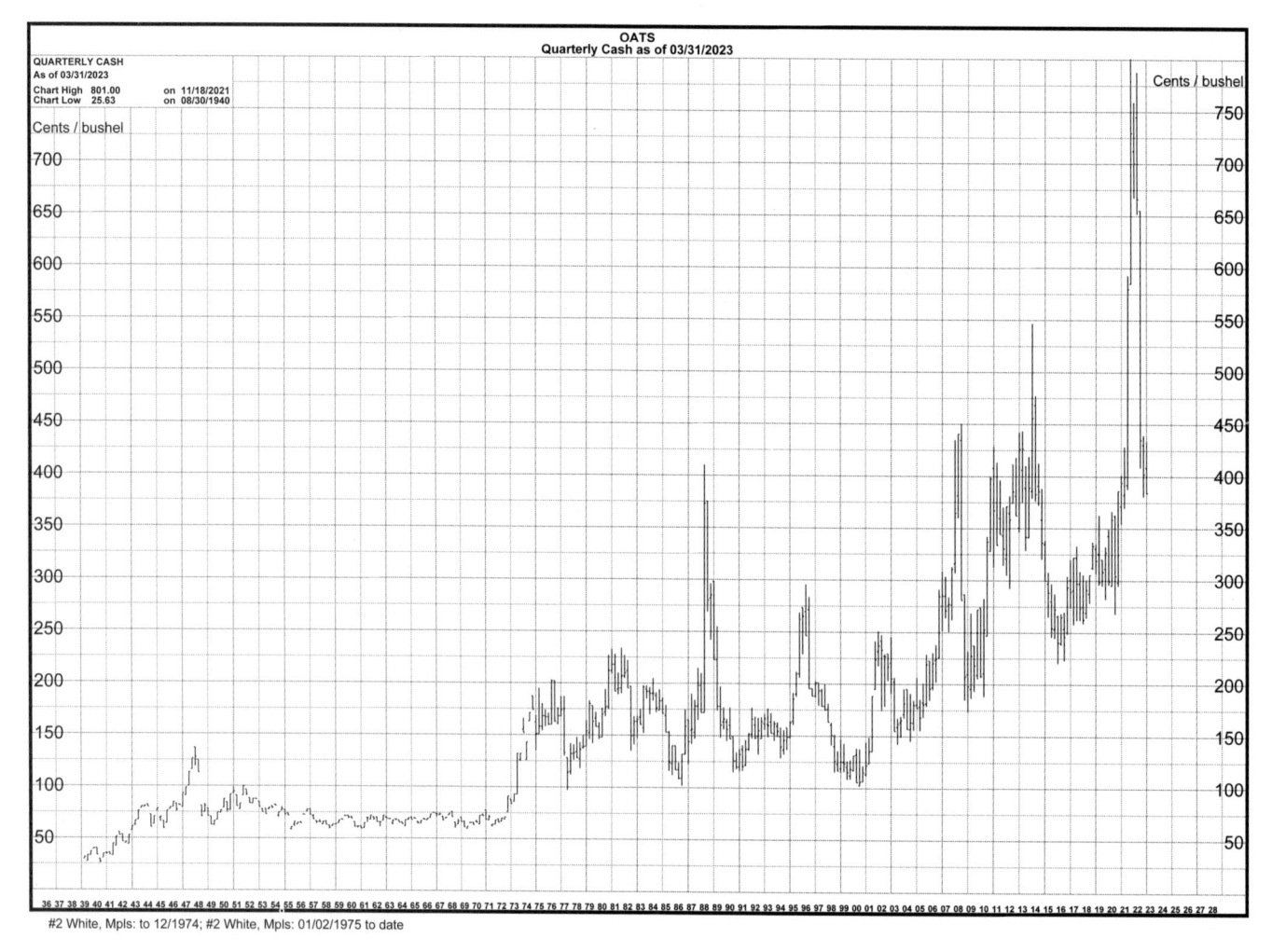

## Average Cash Price of No. 2 Heavy White Oats in Minneapolis   In U.S. Dollars Per Bushel

| Crop Year | June | July | Aug. | Sept. | Oct. | Nov. | Dec. | Jan. | Feb. | Mar. | Apr. | May | Average |
|---|---|---|---|---|---|---|---|---|---|---|---|---|---|
| 2013-14 | 4.21 | 3.84 | 3.78 | 3.40 | 3.57 | 3.79 | 3.80 | 4.30 | 4.64 | 4.66 | 4.58 | 4.03 | 4.05 |
| 2014-15 | 3.88 | 3.85 | 3.83 | 3.86 | 3.68 | 3.53 | 3.49 | 3.26 | 3.11 | 3.14 | 2.94 | 2.75 | 3.44 |
| 2015-16 | 2.89 | 2.82 | 2.63 | 2.70 | 2.58 | 2.67 | 2.60 | 2.64 | 2.60 | 2.43 | 2.49 | 2.49 | 2.63 |
| 2016-17 | 2.58 | 2.61 | 2.34 | 2.29 | 2.67 | 2.84 | 2.97 | 2.92 | 3.07 | 2.90 | 2.86 | 2.88 | 2.74 |
| 2017-18 | 2.95 | 3.17 | 2.98 | 2.87 | 2.97 | 2.94 | 2.90 | 2.73 | 2.96 | 2.79 | 2.72 | 2.89 | 2.90 |
| 2018-19 | 2.88 | 2.84 | 2.91 | 2.91 | 3.18 | 3.22 | 3.28 | 3.31 | 3.23 | 3.18 | 3.25 | 3.25 | 3.12 |
| 2019-20 | 3.15 | 3.10 | 3.01 | 3.03 | 3.15 | 3.22 | 3.21 | 3.43 | 3.37 | 3.21 | 3.21 | 3.40 | 3.21 |
| 2020-21 | 3.43 | 3.35 | 2.94 | 2.97 | 3.07 | 3.17 | 3.59 | 3.71 | 3.68 | 3.85 | 3.92 | 3.88 | 3.46 |
| 2021-22 | 3.89 | 4.17 | 4.68 | 5.47 | 6.26 | 7.47 | 7.66 | 7.02 | 7.38 | 7.06 | 7.33 | 7.10 | 6.29 |
| 2022-23[1] | 7.01 | 5.54 | 4.57 | 4.34 | 4.23 | 4.29 | 4.17 | 4.12 | | | | | 4.78 |

[1] Preliminary.   Source: Economic Research Service, U.S. Department of Agriculture (ERS-USDA)

## Average Price Received by Farmers for Oats in the United States   In U.S. Dollars Per Bushel

| Crop Year | June | July | Aug. | Sept. | Oct. | Nov. | Dec. | Jan. | Feb. | Mar. | Apr. | May | Average |
|---|---|---|---|---|---|---|---|---|---|---|---|---|---|
| 2013-14 | 3.93 | 3.88 | 3.67 | 3.57 | 3.49 | 3.63 | 3.59 | 3.70 | 3.75 | 4.13 | 3.96 | 3.98 | 3.77 |
| 2014-15 | 3.73 | 3.49 | 3.24 | 3.20 | 3.16 | 2.95 | 3.21 | 3.02 | 3.08 | 2.96 | 2.82 | 2.90 | 3.15 |
| 2015-16 | 2.83 | 2.33 | 2.07 | 2.04 | 2.20 | 2.11 | 2.12 | 1.93 | 2.21 | 2.20 | 1.97 | 2.26 | 2.19 |
| 2016-17 | 1.98 | 1.89 | 1.84 | 1.97 | 2.03 | 2.23 | 2.35 | 2.31 | 2.39 | 2.39 | 2.32 | 2.63 | 2.19 |
| 2017-18 | 2.74 | 2.33 | 2.32 | 2.56 | 2.55 | 2.68 | 2.94 | 3.29 | 2.63 | 2.80 | 2.93 | 3.14 | 2.74 |
| 2018-19 | 3.04 | 2.61 | 2.47 | 2.62 | 2.71 | 2.55 | 2.67 | 2.67 | 2.84 | 2.67 | 3.01 | 3.11 | 2.75 |
| 2019-20 | 3.31 | 3.09 | 2.72 | 2.67 | 2.83 | 2.95 | 3.02 | 2.84 | 2.73 | 2.79 | 2.97 | 3.10 | 2.92 |
| 2020-21 | 3.16 | 2.97 | 2.54 | 2.47 | 2.72 | 2.97 | 2.69 | 3.00 | 3.11 | 3.07 | 3.41 | 3.42 | 2.96 |
| 2021-22 | 3.42 | 3.60 | 3.63 | 3.73 | 4.30 | 4.81 | 5.65 | 5.68 | 6.05 | 5.89 | 6.48 | 6.35 | 4.97 |
| 2022-23[1] | 6.61 | 5.68 | 4.64 | 4.43 | 4.38 | 4.36 | 4.66 | 4.33 | 4.02 | | | | 4.79 |

[1] Preliminary.   Source: National Agricultural Statistics Service, U.S. Department of Agriculture (NASS-USDA)

# Olive Oil

Olive oil is derived from the fruit of the olive tree and originated in the Mediterranean area. Olives designated for oil are picked before ripening in the fall. Olive picking is usually done by hand. The olives are then weighed and washed in cold water. The olives, along with their oil-rich pits, are then crushed and kneaded until a homogeneous paste is formed. The paste is spread by hand onto metal plates, which are then stacked and pressed hydraulically to yield a liquid. The liquid is then centrifuged to separate the oil. It takes 1,300 to 2,000 olives to produce 1 quart of olive oil. The best olive oil is still produced from the first pressing, which is usually performed within 24 to 72 hours after harvest and is called *extra virgin* olive oil.

**Supply** – World production of olive oil (pressed oil) in the marketing year 2021/22 rose +9.0% to 3.537 million metric tons, below the 2011/12 record high of 3.629 million metric tons. The world's largest producers of olive oil in 2021/22 were Spain with 45.8% of world production, Italy with 9.2%, Greece with 7.5%, Tunisia with 7.2%, Turkey with 6.9%, Morocco with 5.8%, and Portugal with 3.7%.

**Demand** – World consumption of olive oil in the 2021/22 marketing year rose by +0.7% yr/yr to 3.532 million metric tons, a new record from the 2020/21 record high of 3.508 million metric tons. The U.S. consumption of olive oil in the 2021/22 period remained the record high yr/yr to 393,000 metric tons. That was 11.1% of world consumption.

**Trade** – World olive oil imports in 2021/22 fell by -0.8% to 1.372 million metric tons. The U.S. was the world's largest importer in 2021/22, with 380,000 metric tons, representing 27.7% of world imports. World olive oil exports in 2021/22 rose by +0.7% to 1.380 million metric tons. The world's largest exporters were Spain with 37.2 of world exports, Italy with 17.7%, and Tunisia with 16.7%.

## World Production of Olive Oil (Pressed Oil)   In Thousands of Metric Tons

| Crop Year | Algeria | Argentina | Greece | Italy | Jordan | Libya | Morocco | Portugal | Spain | Syria | Tunisia | Turkey | World Total |
|---|---|---|---|---|---|---|---|---|---|---|---|---|---|
| 2013-14 | 44.0 | 30.0 | 146.6 | 491.5 | 19.0 | 18.0 | 140.0 | 102.9 | 1,913.0 | 147.0 | 84.0 | 149.0 | 3,440.3 |
| 2014-15 | 69.5 | 15.0 | 333.0 | 235.3 | 23.0 | 15.5 | 132.0 | 69.0 | 959.3 | 113.0 | 374.0 | 174.0 | 2,685.0 |
| 2015-16 | 82.0 | 24.0 | 354.0 | 498.3 | 29.5 | 18.0 | 142.0 | 123.0 | 1,518.0 | 127.0 | 154.0 | 164.0 | 3,419.8 |
| 2016-17 | 63.0 | 24.0 | 219.0 | 193.3 | 20.0 | 16.0 | 122.0 | 78.0 | 1,398.0 | 121.0 | 114.0 | 192.0 | 2,768.8 |
| 2017-18 | 82.5 | 45.0 | 388.0 | 446.1 | 21.0 | 18.0 | 156.0 | 149.7 | 1,340.7 | 106.0 | 340.0 | 278.0 | 3,584.8 |
| 2018-19 | 97.0 | 28.0 | 207.0 | 180.6 | 21.0 | 16.0 | 225.0 | 105.7 | 1,935.1 | 121.0 | 153.0 | 207.0 | 3,509.6 |
| 2019-20[1] | 125.5 | 30.0 | 313.5 | 381.2 | 34.5 | 17.0 | 157.0 | 150.5 | 1,247.1 | 132.0 | 455.0 | 245.0 | 3,507.5 |
| 2020-21[2] | 70.5 | 30.0 | 311.0 | 285.1 | 24.5 | 16.5 | 180.0 | 105.0 | 1,501.7 | 133.5 | 155.0 | 225.0 | 3,244.5 |
| 2021-22[3] | 98.0 | 30.0 | 266.0 | 326.6 | 22.0 | 16.5 | 205.0 | 130.0 | 1,620.0 | 123.5 | 255.0 | 242.5 | 3,537.6 |

[1] Preliminary.   [2] Estimate.   [3] Forecast.   *Source: The Oil World*

## World Imports and Exports of Olive Oil (Pressed Oil)   In Thousands of Metric Tons

| Crop Year | Australia | Brazil | Italy | Japan | Spain | United States | World Total (Imports) | Greece | Italy | Spain | Tunisia | Turkey | World Total (Exports) |
|---|---|---|---|---|---|---|---|---|---|---|---|---|---|
| 2013-14 | 28.9 | 73.6 | 29.1 | 56.2 | 20.4 | 312.4 | 895.1 | 17.9 | 255.6 | 333.8 | 84.0 | 34.9 | 919.6 |
| 2014-15 | 22.8 | 67.8 | 98.2 | 61.9 | 119.8 | 312.1 | 1,049.7 | 18.8 | 220.5 | 282.5 | 313.1 | 16.9 | 1,056.1 |
| 2015-16 | 26.9 | 50.6 | 42.6 | 56.7 | 58.7 | 331.5 | 1,023.6 | 23.0 | 244.5 | 395.7 | 114.3 | 12.8 | 994.3 |
| 2016-17 | 29.6 | 58.5 | 37.1 | 56.9 | 60.7 | 316.6 | 1,027.5 | 22.0 | 231.3 | 389.0 | 99.3 | 34.7 | 1,008.2 |
| 2017-18 | 31.7 | 78.6 | 64.5 | 57.0 | 124.1 | 322.2 | 1,163.6 | 22.1 | 216.9 | 389.1 | 217.5 | 70.0 | 1,171.8 |
| 2018-19 | 32.3 | 86.4 | 49.2 | 71.0 | 117.4 | 356.5 | 1,244.1 | 24.1 | 228.7 | 452.4 | 184.6 | 59.8 | 1,225.6 |
| 2019-20[1] | 36.6 | 104.2 | 81.8 | 72.0 | 170.6 | 398.0 | 1,453.9 | 25.2 | 247.3 | 531.3 | 351.9 | 49.3 | 1,490.6 |
| 2020-21[2] | 36.6 | 106.8 | 51.2 | 61.1 | 125.9 | 390.5 | 1,384.1 | 26.7 | 244.4 | 535.0 | 226.8 | 45.3 | 1,370.8 |
| 2021-22[3] | 28.0 | 100.0 | 51.0 | 62.0 | 140.0 | 380.0 | 1,372.5 | 30.0 | 245.0 | 513.0 | 230.0 | 62.0 | 1,380.6 |

[1] Preliminary.   [2] Estimate.   [3] Forecast.   *Source: The Oil World*

## World Consumption and Ending Stocks of Olive Oil (Pressed Oil)   In Thousands of Metric Tons

| Crop Year | Brazil | Morocco | Syria | Tunisia | Turkey | United States | World Total (Consumption) | European Union | Morocco | Syria | Tunisia | Turkey | World Total (Ending Stocks) |
|---|---|---|---|---|---|---|---|---|---|---|---|---|---|
| 2013-14 | 73.6 | 120.1 | 144.7 | 43.5 | 149.2 | 309.3 | 3,237.5 | 690.7 | 90.0 | 20.0 | 26.0 | 30.0 | 1,002.9 |
| 2014-15 | 67.8 | 130.7 | 119.8 | 45.5 | 149.7 | 310.0 | 3,070.6 | 330.0 | 60.0 | 10.0 | 43.0 | 40.0 | 601.9 |
| 2015-16 | 50.6 | 132.5 | 111.2 | 44.0 | 157.7 | 321.0 | 3,145.8 | 590.0 | 55.0 | 15.0 | 69.0 | 35.0 | 918.2 |
| 2016-17 | 58.5 | 134.9 | 99.9 | 40.2 | 162.3 | 323.9 | 3,071.5 | 387.2 | 26.0 | ---- | 52.0 | 30.0 | 639.8 |
| 2017-18 | 78.6 | 140.3 | 89.7 | 40.4 | 183.1 | 326.3 | 3,203.9 | 655.4 | 26.0 | ---- | 137.0 | 55.0 | 1,012.5 |
| 2018-19 | 86.4 | 148.2 | 87.0 | 39.4 | 189.9 | 347.3 | 3,350.0 | 862.8 | 61.0 | ---- | 68.0 | 34.0 | 1,190.6 |
| 2019-20[1] | 104.2 | 150.2 | 88.0 | 38.7 | 199.0 | 380.8 | 3,474.2 | 702.0 | 58.0 | ---- | 134.0 | 65.2 | 1,187.2 |
| 2020-21[2] | 106.8 | 152.9 | 93.0 | 36.2 | 205.0 | 392.9 | 3,508.6 | 571.0 | 66.0 | ---- | 28.0 | 67.0 | 936.4 |
| 2021-22[3] | 100.0 | 156.0 | 95.0 | 35.0 | 205.0 | 393.0 | 3,532.7 | 577.0 | 80.0 | ---- | 20.0 | 65.0 | 933.3 |

[1] Preliminary.   [2] Estimate.   [3] Forecast.   *Source: The Oil World*

# Onions

Onions are the bulbs of plants in the lily family. Onions can be eaten raw, cooked, pickled, used as a flavoring or seasoning, or dehydrated. Onions rank in the top 10 vegetables produced in the U.S. in terms of dollar value. Since 1629, onions have been cultivated in the U.S., but are believed to be indigenous to Asia.

The two main types of onions produced in the U.S. are yellow and white onions. Yellow varieties comprise approximately 75% of all onions grown for bulb production in the U.S. Onions that are planted as a winter crop in warm areas are milder in taste and odor than onions planted during the summer in cooler regions.

**Prices** – Onion prices in 2022 averaged $42.98 per hundred pounds, up +57.6% yr/yr.

**Supply** –The farm value of the U.S. production crop in 2021 rose by +8.2% to $1.037 billion. In 2021 U.S. farmers harvested 136,800 acres, up +4.2% yr/yr . The yield in 2021 was down by -11.2% at 500.0 pounds per acre still below the record high of 566.5 pounds per acre in 2016.

### Salient Statistics of Onions in the United States

| Crop Year | Harvested Acres | Yield Per Acre | Production 1,000 Cwt. | Price Per Cwt. | Farm Value $1,000 | Jan. 1 Pack Frozen | Anual Pack Frozen | Imports Canned | Exports (Fresh) | Imports (Fresh) | Per Capita[3] Utilization Lbs., Farm Weight All | Fresh |
|---|---|---|---|---|---|---|---|---|---|---|---|---|
| 2013 | 143,340 | 486 | 69,654 | 15.00 | 969,183 | 58.0 | ---- | | 702.4 | 994.4 | 19.4 | 18.5 |
| 2014 | 139,150 | 523 | 72,806 | 13.60 | 933,630 | 49.8 | ---- | | 656.2 | 1,134.7 | 19.8 | 18.4 |
| 2015 | 132,900 | 507 | 67,380 | 17.60 | 993,360 | 45.0 | ---- | | 605.5 | 1,109.7 | 20.3 | 18.3 |
| 2016 | 147,900 | 567 | 83,791 | 13.70 | 1,059,318 | 45.0 | ---- | | 671.6 | 1,191.4 | 20.8 | 22.8 |
| 2017 | 151,500 | 544 | 82,389 | 12.90 | 1,042,090 | 62.1 | ---- | | 682.2 | 1,257.9 | 22.4 | 25.0 |
| 2018 | 129,600 | 559 | 72,438 | 12.50 | 886,941 | 69.8 | ---- | | 713.5 | 1,300.9 | | 20.6 |
| 2019 | 129,400 | 540 | 69,893 | 14.60 | 1,001,986 | 68.8 | ---- | | 823.7 | 1,253.4 | | 19.9 |
| 2020 | 131,300 | 563 | 73,932 | 13.30 | 958,393 | 65.9 | ---- | | 760.5 | 1,304.3 | | 21.3 |
| 2021[1] | 135,800 | 500 | 67,910 | 18.60 | 1,246,994 | 74.7 | ---- | | 702.5 | 1,555.3 | | 19.7 |
| 2022[2] | 127,200 | 506 | 64,352 | 25.70 | 1,633,206 | 50.9 | ---- | | | | | |

[1] Preliminary. [2] Forecast. [3] Includes fresh and processing. Source: Economic Research Service, U.S. Department of Agiculture (ERS-USDA)

### Cold Storage Stocks of Frozen Onions in the United States, on First of Month    In Thousands of Pounds

| Year | Jan. | Feb. | Mar. | Apr. | May | June | July | Aug. | Sept. | Oct. | Nov. | Dec. |
|---|---|---|---|---|---|---|---|---|---|---|---|---|
| 2013 | 58,030 | 53,882 | 55,947 | 52,566 | 52,835 | 51,059 | 50,557 | 53,048 | 50,048 | 50,252 | 49,506 | 52,770 |
| 2014 | 49,806 | 50,425 | 47,054 | 46,423 | 46,175 | 50,046 | 55,773 | 64,252 | 60,862 | 52,736 | 50,282 | 45,791 |
| 2015 | 45,001 | 43,865 | 48,055 | 48,960 | 52,702 | 56,379 | 56,673 | 53,467 | 53,428 | 48,106 | 48,935 | 46,921 |
| 2016 | 45,024 | 46,533 | 48,136 | 50,950 | 58,093 | 57,549 | 57,806 | 54,588 | 61,991 | 58,574 | 59,158 | 59,871 |
| 2017 | 62,106 | 61,514 | 63,908 | 66,174 | 72,770 | 76,063 | 71,368 | 68,219 | 73,667 | 70,900 | 64,044 | 67,319 |
| 2018 | 69,847 | 68,858 | 73,548 | 77,794 | 80,907 | 78,747 | 78,136 | 74,810 | 76,314 | 72,265 | 64,402 | 65,232 |
| 2019 | 68,823 | 69,721 | 71,636 | 75,066 | 82,588 | 89,921 | 87,458 | 77,280 | 78,543 | 76,481 | 67,368 | 68,541 |
| 2020 | 65,942 | 67,871 | 74,223 | 84,038 | 92,375 | 87,078 | 87,703 | 77,129 | 80,875 | 78,285 | 73,373 | 73,626 |
| 2021 | 74,651 | 75,867 | 74,888 | 70,476 | 74,722 | 74,524 | 71,915 | 66,844 | 64,683 | 58,904 | 54,307 | 52,979 |
| 2022[1] | 50,945 | 50,246 | 49,500 | 50,177 | 57,639 | 58,660 | 53,081 | 52,341 | 56,660 | 62,271 | 55,661 | 60,494 |

[1] Preliminary. Source: National Agricultural Statistics Service, U.S. Department of Agiculture (NASS-USDA)

### Average Price Received by Growers for Onions in the United States    In Dollars Per Hundred Pounds (Cwt.)

| Year | Jan. | Feb. | Mar. | Apr. | May | June | July | Aug. | Sept. | Oct. | Nov. | Dec. | Season Average |
|---|---|---|---|---|---|---|---|---|---|---|---|---|---|
| 2013 | 32.30 | 28.80 | 21.10 | NQ | NQ | NQ | NQ | NQ | NQ | NQ | NQ | NQ | 15.00 |
| 2014 | NQ | NQ | NQ | 25.10 | 27.20 | 17.30 | 23.50 | 14.50 | 11.90 | 10.30 | 9.12 | 9.56 | 13.60 |
| 2015 | 8.39 | 7.67 | 7.89 | 18.90 | 19.30 | 30.20 | 31.90 | 15.60 | 11.80 | 12.50 | 12.00 | 12.20 | 17.60 |
| 2016 | 14.40 | 15.30 | 14.90 | 21.10 | 25.80 | 27.70 | 26.70 | 12.70 | 9.78 | 7.58 | 6.76 | 6.43 | 13.70 |
| 2017 | 11.10 | 8.82 | 7.77 | 14.00 | 14.00 | 20.90 | 22.30 | 13.60 | 16.40 | 16.30 | 15.60 | 17.00 | 12.90 |
| 2018 | 15.00 | 13.20 | 11.60 | 14.80 | 17.10 | 18.20 | 21.40 | 15.20 | 11.20 | 11.20 | 11.30 | 10.90 | 12.50 |
| 2019 | 14.20 | 12.30 | 17.90 | 23.60 | 24.30 | 32.40 | 39.80 | 30.30 | 11.90 | 13.70 | 10.90 | 11.20 | 14.60 |
| 2020 | 14.10 | 19.30 | 20.60 | 24.80 | 27.90 | 30.40 | 30.80 | 23.30 | 19.40 | 20.00 | 20.50 | 19.50 | 13.30 |
| 2021 | 19.50 | 19.20 | 20.40 | 22.20 | 25.70 | 28.20 | 31.30 | 27.90 | 29.30 | 33.80 | 34.70 | 35.10 | 27.28 |
| 2022[1] | 39.80 | 46.50 | 51.50 | 48.30 | 50.50 | 46.80 | 47.90 | 43.40 | 42.10 | 34.00 | 32.70 | 32.30 | 42.98 |

[1] Preliminary. NQ = Not quoted. Source: Economic Research Service, U.S. Department of Agiculture (ERS-USDA)

# Oranges and Orange Juice

The orange tree is a semi-tropical, non-deciduous tree, and the fruit is technically a hesperidium, a kind of berry. The three major varieties of oranges include the sweet orange, the sour orange, and the mandarin orange (or tangerine). In the U.S., only sweet oranges are grown commercially. These include Hamlin, Jaffa, navel, Pineapple, blood orange, and Valencia. Sour oranges are mainly used in marmalade and in liqueurs such as triple sec and curacao.

Frozen Concentrated Orange Juice (FCOJ) was developed in 1945, which led to oranges becoming the main fruit crop in the U.S. Two to four medium-sized oranges will produce about 1 cup of juice, and modern mechanical extractors can remove the juice from 400 to 700 oranges per minute. Before juice extraction, orange oil is recovered from the peel. Approximately 50% of the orange weight is juice, with the remainder being peel, pulp, and seeds, which are dried to produce nutritious cattle feed.

The U.S. marketing year for oranges begins December 1 of the first year shown (e.g., the 2020-21 marketing year extends from December 1, 2020, to November 30, 2021). Orange juice futures prices are subject to upward spikes during the U.S. hurricane season (officially June 1 to November 30), and the Florida freeze season (late-November through March).

Frozen concentrate orange juice futures and options are traded at the Intercontinental Exchange (ICE). The ICE orange juice futures contract calls for the delivery of 15,000 pounds of orange solids and is priced in terms of cents per pound.

**Prices** – ICE frozen concentrate orange juice (FCOJ) futures prices (Barchart.com symbol OJ) posted their low for 2022 of 132.35 cents in February. FCOJ prices pushed higher into Q2 when they posted a 6-year high of 194.95 cents in April. Citrus greening disease decimated Florida's 2021/22 orange crop, which fell to 41.05 million boxes, the smallest since 1943. Also, drought in Brazil, the world's largest orange juice exporter, ravaged its crop and sent Brazil's orange juice inventory to a 5-year low. FCOJ prices fell back slightly into July as the drought in Brazil eased, which prompted the USDA to project a global 2021/22 orange crop of 49.014 MMT, up +4% y/y. FCOJ prices then resumed their rally to a new 6-year high in November of 231.00 cents. Hurricane Ian blew fruit from trees and flooded Florida's orange groves in October, prompting the USDA to cut the Florida 2022/23 orange crop to 16 million boxes, down 61% yr//y and the smallest crop since 1936. Also, U.S. FCOJ supplies tightened further as U.S. stockpiles of orange juice in cold storage sank to a 51-year low in December. FCOJ prices finished 2022 up +41% yr/yr at 206.40 cents.

**Supply** – World production of oranges in the 2021/22 marketing year rose by +3.8% yr/yr to 49.014 million metric tons. The world's largest producers of oranges in the 2021/22 marketing year were Brazil with 34.5% of world production, followed by China with 15.4%, the European Union with 12.4%, Mexico with 8.7%, and the U.S. with 7.1%.

U.S. production of oranges in 2021/22 fell by -20.7% yr/yr to 81.650 million boxes (1 box equals 90 lbs). Florida's production in 2021/22 fell by -22.5% yr/yr to 41.050 million boxes, and California's production fell by -17.6% yr/yr to 40.400 million boxes.

## World Production of Oranges    In Thousands of Metric Tons

| Crop Year | Argentina | Australia | Brazil | China | Egypt | European Union | Mexico | Morocco | South Africa | Turkey | United States | Vietnam | World Total |
|---|---|---|---|---|---|---|---|---|---|---|---|---|---|
| 2013-14 | 800 | 467 | 17,870 | 7,600 | 2,570 | 6,550 | 4,533 | 1,001 | 1,723 | 1,700 | 6,140 | 590 | 52,436 |
| 2014-15 | 800 | 504 | 16,714 | 6,600 | 2,635 | 5,954 | 4,515 | 868 | 1,645 | 1,650 | 5,763 | 566 | 48,971 |
| 2015-16 | 800 | 506 | 14,414 | 6,900 | 2,930 | 6,038 | 4,603 | 925 | 1,275 | 1,800 | 5,523 | 637 | 47,242 |
| 2016-17 | 700 | 526 | 20,890 | 7,000 | 3,000 | 6,739 | 4,630 | 1,037 | 1,363 | 1,850 | 4,616 | 768 | 53,995 |
| 2017-18 | 750 | 528 | 15,953 | 7,300 | 3,120 | 6,270 | 4,737 | 1,021 | 1,586 | 1,905 | 3,515 | 855 | 48,412 |
| 2018-19 | 800 | 515 | 19,298 | 7,200 | 3,600 | 6,800 | 4,716 | 1,183 | 1,590 | 1,900 | 4,923 | 855 | 54,302 |
| 2019-20 | 700 | 485 | 14,870 | 7,400 | 3,200 | 6,268 | 2,530 | 806 | 1,414 | 1,700 | 4,766 | 1,017 | 46,112 |
| 2020-21[1] | 750 | 505 | 14,676 | 7,500 | 3,570 | 6,540 | 4,649 | 1,039 | 1,511 | 1,300 | 3,981 | 1,150 | 48,197 |
| 2021-22[2] | 830 | 535 | 16,932 | 7,550 | 3,000 | 6,720 | 4,595 | 1,150 | 1,600 | 1,750 | 3,149 | 1,150 | 50,002 |
| 2022-23[3] | 800 | 505 | 16,524 | 7,600 | 3,600 | 5,854 | 4,200 | 750 | 1,650 | 1,400 | 2,452 | 1,150 | 47,528 |

[1] Preliminary.  [2] Estimate.  [3] Forecast.  NA = Not available.  Source: Foreign Agricultural Service, U.S. Department of Agriculture (FAS-USDA)

## Salient Statistics of Oranges & Orange Juice in the United States

| | Production[4] | | | | | Florida Crop Processed | | | | Frozen Concentrated Orange Juice - Florida | | | |
|---|---|---|---|---|---|---|---|---|---|---|---|---|---|
| Crop Year | California | Florida | Total U.S. | Farm Price $ Per Box | Farm Value Million $ | Frozen Concentrates | Chilled Products | Total Processed | Yield Per Box Gallons[5] | Carry-in | Pack | Total Supply | Total Season Movement |
| | --------- Million Boxes --------- | | | | | --------- Million Boxes --------- | | | | ---- In Millions of Gallons (42 Deg. Brix) ---- | | | |
| 2012-13 | 54.5 | 133.6 | 189.9 | 10.85 | 2,073.6 | 48.0 | 79.2 | 127.6 | 1.6 | 61.1 | 127.9 | 189.0 | 108.4 |
| 2013-14 | 49.5 | 104.7 | 156.0 | 14.29 | 2,254.3 | 22.7 | 76.0 | 99.2 | 1.6 | 76.9 | 85.4 | 162.3 | 97.3 |
| 2014-15 | 48.2 | 97.0 | 146.6 | 13.29 | 1,963.4 | 19.2 | 71.9 | 92.0 | 1.5 | 66.0 | 72.6 | 138.5 | 86.2 |
| 2015-16 | 58.5 | 81.7 | 141.9 | 13.55 | 1,927.3 | 15.8 | 61.8 | 77.8 | 1.4 | 70.8 | 63.7 | 134.5 | 88.2 |
| 2016-17 | 48.3 | 68.9 | 118.5 | 16.30 | 1,943.7 | 12.6 | 53.2 | 66.0 | 1.4 | 52.7 | 55.9 | 108.6 | 87.5 |
| 2017-18 | 44.2 | 45.1 | 91.1 | 19.82 | 1,830.4 | 7.7 | 34.4 | 42.3 | | 46.2 | 38.4 | 84.7 | 73.1 |
| 2018-19 | 52.2 | 71.9 | 126.6 | 14.43 | 1,765.3 | 15.2 | 53.8 | 69.1 | | 58.5 | 51.1 | 109.6 | 76.3 |
| 2019-20[1] | 54.1 | 67.4 | 122.8 | 13.93 | 1,711.6 | 14.1 | 49.8 | 64.2 | | 76.5 | 47.9 | 124.3 | 75.9 |
| 2020-21[2] | 49.0 | 53.0 | 103.0 | 15.65 | 1,611.8 | 5.8 | 43.6 | 49.7 | | 62.5 | 32.4 | 94.8 | 68.4 |
| 2021-22[3] | 40.4 | 41.1 | 81.7 | 17.97 | 1,467.5 | 4.2 | 34.4 | 38.6 | | 56.0 | 35.8 | 91.8 | 78.6 |

[1] Preliminary.  [2] Estimate.  [3] Forecast.  [4] Fruit ripened on trees, but destroyed prior to picking not included.  [5] 42 deg. Brix equivalent.
Source: Economic Research Service, U.S. Department of Agriculture (ERS-USDA); Florida Department of Citrus

# ORANGES AND ORANGE JUICE

**Orange Juice FCOJ-1 - ICE-US Weekly Nearest Futures as of 03/31/2023**

Chart High 282.50 on 02/28/2023
Chart Low 90.30 on 05/01/2019

Nearby Futures through Last Trading Day.

## Volume of Trading of Frozen Concentrated Orange Juice Futures in New York    In Contracts

| Year | Jan. | Feb. | Mar. | Apr. | May | June | July | Aug. | Sept. | Oct. | Nov. | Dec. | Total |
|---|---|---|---|---|---|---|---|---|---|---|---|---|---|
| 2013 | 46,432 | 54,711 | 37,532 | 67,361 | 31,399 | 63,622 | 26,724 | 43,047 | 29,937 | 40,275 | 24,295 | 39,684 | 505,019 |
| 2014 | 27,695 | 39,560 | 29,605 | 51,337 | 24,033 | 51,811 | 21,141 | 36,438 | 18,068 | 35,974 | 27,182 | 35,685 | 398,529 |
| 2015 | 21,377 | 37,435 | 34,855 | 39,065 | 23,789 | 42,032 | 18,914 | 42,607 | 18,068 | 35,974 | 27,182 | 35,685 | 398,529 |
| 2016 | 28,008 | 34,218 | 25,553 | 40,101 | 20,743 | 50,207 | 24,414 | 47,704 | 24,848 | 49,991 | 22,202 | 45,915 | 413,904 |
| 2017 | 30,883 | 37,187 | 35,311 | 33,218 | 25,193 | 34,836 | 18,627 | 36,316 | 34,697 | 25,936 | 16,504 | 34,791 | 363,499 |
| 2018 | 23,671 | 29,581 | 16,795 | 36,685 | 27,571 | 36,726 | 16,771 | 40,982 | 18,075 | 46,573 | 25,131 | 38,293 | 356,854 |
| 2019 | 23,436 | 50,269 | 30,857 | 55,326 | 27,698 | 43,007 | 17,848 | 51,082 | 18,589 | 47,780 | 14,462 | 53,282 | 433,636 |
| 2020 | 21,096 | 55,057 | 43,596 | 23,691 | 18,093 | 29,550 | 16,520 | 27,567 | 21,867 | 28,658 | 20,472 | 28,289 | 334,456 |
| 2021 | 19,272 | 36,891 | 20,474 | 33,674 | 22,776 | 38,150 | 22,018 | 35,756 | 16,070 | 36,477 | 23,241 | 38,503 | 343,302 |
| 2022 | 26,044 | 37,281 | 23,007 | 37,893 | 18,926 | 33,453 | 19,857 | 31,241 | 19,688 | 32,612 | 15,834 | 32,405 | 328,241 |

Contract size = 15,000 lbs.    *Source: ICE Futures U.S. (ICE)*

## Average Open Interest of Frozen Concentrated Orange Juice Futures in New York    In Contracts

| Year | Jan. | Feb. | Mar. | Apr. | May | June | July | Aug. | Sept. | Oct. | Nov. | Dec. |
|---|---|---|---|---|---|---|---|---|---|---|---|---|
| 2013 | 20,672 | 20,900 | 18,819 | 20,972 | 20,719 | 22,432 | 19,760 | 19,241 | 16,646 | 15,809 | 14,609 | 14,636 |
| 2014 | 15,542 | 15,905 | 16,793 | 18,372 | 18,487 | 17,605 | 13,552 | 13,068 | 12,175 | 13,385 | 13,798 | 12,089 |
| 2015 | 10,973 | 12,605 | 15,506 | 15,799 | 14,630 | 14,192 | 12,421 | 13,196 | 13,358 | 15,172 | 14,651 | 14,759 |
| 2016 | 12,887 | 12,224 | 12,408 | 13,452 | 13,239 | 17,154 | 18,182 | 16,433 | 16,312 | 15,940 | 16,285 | 14,857 |
| 2017 | 12,528 | 11,357 | 10,887 | 11,104 | 11,212 | 11,929 | 11,277 | 11,441 | 8,972 | 8,741 | 9,378 | 9,882 |
| 2018 | 10,670 | 10,703 | 12,349 | 13,460 | 14,934 | 15,644 | 15,041 | 14,133 | 13,370 | 16,227 | 17,994 | 16,807 |
| 2019 | 19,118 | 21,665 | 20,689 | 20,601 | 21,261 | 19,818 | 19,459 | 19,413 | 17,375 | 17,719 | 17,325 | 18,687 |
| 2020 | 18,961 | 19,374 | 15,961 | 11,510 | 10,593 | 11,095 | 10,244 | 9,590 | 9,214 | 10,873 | 10,713 | 10,877 |
| 2021 | 10,181 | 12,474 | 11,929 | 12,737 | 13,472 | 12,030 | 11,580 | 12,052 | 11,612 | 11,895 | 11,730 | 11,152 |
| 2022 | 12,017 | 12,645 | 12,348 | 13,270 | 12,223 | 12,811 | 10,847 | 10,627 | 10,094 | 11,145 | 11,180 | 11,278 |

Contract size = 15,000 lbs.    *Source: ICE Futures U.S. (ICE)*

# ORANGES AND ORANGE JUICE

## Cold Storage Stocks of Orange Juice Concentrate[2] in the U.S., on First of Month    In Millions of Pounds

| Year | Jan. | Feb. | Mar. | Apr. | May | June | July | Aug. | Sept. | Oct. | Nov. | Dec. |
|---|---|---|---|---|---|---|---|---|---|---|---|---|
| 2013 | 695.4 | 781.6 | 875.4 | 946.8 | 1,021.3 | 1,042.3 | 996.2 | 915.0 | 864.6 | 795.8 | 785.9 | 732.6 |
| 2014 | 739.5 | 750.5 | 799.3 | 813.0 | 877.8 | 872.9 | 853.7 | 815.9 | 773.0 | 712.0 | 721.9 | 676.8 |
| 2015 | 734.8 | 720.7 | 728.4 | 832.3 | 857.5 | 947.9 | 943.8 | 868.1 | 807.8 | 757.1 | 695.9 | 641.7 |
| 2016 | 639.3 | 623.0 | 633.4 | 702.0 | 751.4 | 772.5 | 766.5 | 711.0 | 653.1 | 603.1 | 579.9 | 519.6 |
| 2017 | 516.6 | 503.4 | 506.3 | 517.1 | 542.2 | 575.4 | 544.4 | 505.5 | 471.5 | 495.6 | 493.5 | 468.1 |
| 2018 | 505.1 | 517.1 | 501.0 | 563.1 | 632.6 | 730.9 | 733.8 | 691.1 | 633.4 | 609.0 | 566.4 | 528.9 |
| 2019 | 547.9 | 604.7 | 633.5 | 704.4 | 795.4 | 884.2 | 859.8 | 822.3 | 808.0 | 809.6 | 757.8 | 725.6 |
| 2020 | 766.2 | 772.9 | 784.9 | 802.4 | 838.5 | 852.7 | 830.4 | 777.8 | 723.9 | 677.1 | 653.1 | 620.3 |
| 2021 | 626.9 | 635.7 | 662.6 | 664.5 | 754.9 | 737.1 | 698.6 | 695.1 | 630.9 | 614.5 | 551.0 | 527.7 |
| 2022[1] | 496.6 | 447.0 | 457.7 | 479.6 | 488.6 | 530.5 | 520.6 | 493.8 | 396.2 | 353.2 | 307.7 | 309.3 |

[1] Preliminary.   [2] Adjusted to 42.0 degrees Brix equivalent (9.896 pounds per gallon).   Source: Agricultural Statistics Board, U.S. Department of Agriculture (ASB-USDA)

## Producer Price Index of Frozen Orange Juice Concentrate    1982 = 100

| Year | Jan. | Feb. | Mar. | Apr. | May | June | July | Aug. | Sept. | Oct. | Nov. | Dec. | Average |
|---|---|---|---|---|---|---|---|---|---|---|---|---|---|
| 2013 | 2.511 | 2.487 | 2.484 | 2.555 | 2.606 | 2.512 | 2.540 | 2.539 | 2.518 | 2.540 | 2.443 | 2.431 | 2.514 |
| 2014 | 2.414 | 2.430 | 2.457 | 2.426 | 2.571 | 2.510 | 2.547 | 2.547 | 2.566 | 2.605 | 2.646 | 2.651 | 2.531 |
| 2015 | 2.732 | 2.734 | 2.678 | 2.662 | 2.709 | 2.680 | 2.658 | 2.739 | 2.732 | 2.753 | 2.715 | 2.733 | 2.710 |
| 2016 | 2.731 | 2.752 | 2.758 | 2.747 | 2.796 | 2.772 | 2.768 | 2.774 | 2.810 | 2.550 | 2.530 | 2.571 | 2.713 |
| 2017 | 2.608 | 2.653 | 2.661 | 2.645 | 2.579 | 2.582 | 2.827 | 2.868 | 2.619 | 2.619 | 2.573 | 2.615 | 2.654 |
| 2018 | 2.521 | 2.538 | 2.513 | 2.481 | 2.481 | 2.469 | 2.504 | 2.440 | 2.493 | 2.478 | 2.475 | 2.434 | 2.486 |
| 2019 | 2.407 | 2.427 | 2.450 | 2.448 | 2.454 | 2.486 | 2.404 | 2.416 | 2.414 | 2.369 | 2.264 | 2.336 | 2.406 |
| 2020 | 2.321 | 2.319 | 2.277 | 2.398 | 2.375 | 2.360 | 2.339 | 2.339 | 2.257 | 2.307 | 2.285 | 2.333 | 2.326 |
| 2021 | 2.341 | 2.359 | 2.285 | 2.364 | 2.387 | 2.594 | 2.612 | 2.580 | 2.544 | 2.631 | 2.651 | 2.654 | 2.500 |
| 2022[1] | 2.621 | 2.754 | 2.696 | 2.770 | 2.856 | 2.887 | 2.889 | 2.751 | 2.777 | 2.744 | 2.672 | 2.718 | 2.761 |

[1] Preliminary.   Source: Bureau of Labor Statistics, U.S. Department of Labor (BLS)

## Average Price Received by Farmers for Oranges (Equivalent On-Tree) in the U.S.    In Dollars Per Box

| Year | Jan. | Feb. | Mar. | Apr. | May | June | July | Aug. | Sept. | Oct. | Nov. | Dec. | Average |
|---|---|---|---|---|---|---|---|---|---|---|---|---|---|
| 2013 | 6.85 | 7.05 | 7.84 | 8.46 | 9.27 | 12.85 | 10.64 | 10.00 | 12.24 | 12.94 | 13.07 | 6.93 | 9.85 |
| 2014 | 8.24 | 10.71 | 10.90 | 9.68 | 10.27 | 11.12 | 14.60 | 14.78 | 15.84 | 13.82 | 16.26 | 9.43 | 12.14 |
| 2015 | 9.35 | 9.85 | 11.32 | 10.78 | 10.74 | 10.53 | 10.79 | 12.01 | 15.25 | 17.73 | 17.35 | 9.59 | 12.11 |
| 2016 | 8.96 | 9.78 | 9.30 | 9.08 | 9.47 | 8.21 | 8.19 | 8.62 | 8.66 | 10.11 | 16.57 | 9.64 | 9.72 |
| 2017 | 9.63 | 11.62 | 12.35 | 11.81 | 12.46 | 18.53 | 20.33 | 18.18 | 20.52 | 25.61 | 16.47 | 12.55 | 15.84 |
| 2018 | 15.06 | 21.28 | 15.05 | 13.93 | 16.32 | 23.08 | 20.29 | 17.73 | 20.17 | 19.60 | 15.61 | 10.46 | 17.38 |
| 2019 | 10.10 | 9.95 | 11.70 | 11.23 | 11.06 | 7.56 | 7.26 | 7.31 | 7.70 | 11.95 | 15.18 | 10.20 | 10.10 |
| 2020 | 9.40 | 9.68 | 10.06 | 11.03 | 12.82 | 16.15 | 15.53 | 15.56 | 15.62 | 23.96 | 19.03 | 11.30 | 14.18 |
| 2021 | 10.95 | 12.88 | 11.58 | 11.36 | 12.83 | 11.05 | 13.79 | 12.14 | 12.49 | 18.00 | 18.21 | 11.95 | 13.10 |
| 2022[1] | 12.51 | 15.37 | 15.10 | 14.53 | 17.48 | 23.58 | 19.32 | 22.97 | 31.31 | 27.23 | 17.71 | 12.63 | 19.15 |

[1] Preliminary.   Source: Economic Research Service, U.S. Department of Agriculture (ERS-USDA)

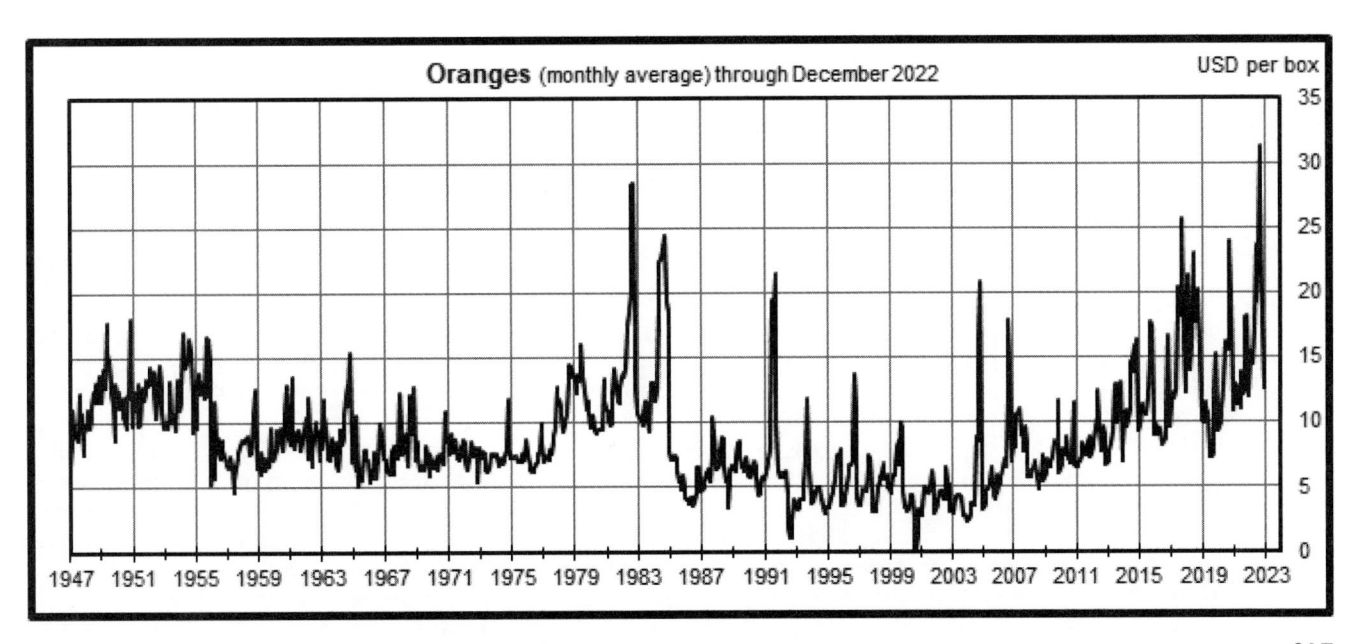

Oranges (monthly average) through December 2022 — USD per box

# Palm Oil

Palm oil is an edible vegetable oil produced from the flesh of the fruit of the oil palm tree. The oil palm tree is a tropical palm tree native to Africa's west coast and is different from the coconut palm tree. The fruit of the oil palm tree is reddish, about the size of a large plum, and grows in large bunches. A single seed, the palm kernel, is contained in each fruit. Oil is extracted from the fruit's pulp (becoming palm oil) and the kernel (palm kernel oil). About one metric ton of palm kernel oil is obtained for every ten metric tons of palm oil.

Palm oil is commercially used in soap, ointments, cosmetics, detergents, and machinery lubricants. It is also used worldwide as cooking oil, shortening, and margarine. Palm kernel oil is a lighter oil and is used exclusively for food use. Crude palm oil and crude palm kernel oil are traded on the Kuala Lumpur Commodity Exchange.

**Prices** – The monthly average wholesale price of palm oil (CIF, bulk, U.S. ports) in 2022 rose by +11.7% yr/yr to 63.14 cents per pound, which was a new record high.

**Supply** – World production of palm oil in the 2022/23 marketing year rose by +5.1% to 77.559 million metric tons, a new record high. World palm oil production has grown sharply from the production level of 1.922 million metric tons seen back in 1970. Indonesia and Malaysia are the world's two major global producers of palm oil. Indonesian production in 2022/23 rose by +5.3% yr/yr to a record high of 45.500 million metric tons, and Indonesian production accounted for 58.7% of world production. Malaysian production in 2022/23 rose by +5.8% to 19.200 million metric tons, and Malaysian production accounted for 24.8% of world production. Other smaller global producers include Thailand with 4.2% of world production, Columbia with 2.3%, and Nigeria with 1.8%.

**Trade** – World palm oil exports in 2022/23 rose by +16.9% yr/yr to 51.218 million metric tons. The world's largest exporters of palm oil in 2022/23 were Indonesia, with a 55.5% share of world exports, and Malaysia, with a share of 33.0%. World palm oil imports in 2022/23 rose by +16.7% to 49.863 million metric tons. The world's largest importers were India with an 18.1% share of world imports and China with a 14.4% share.

## World Production of Palm Oil    In Thousands of Metric Tons

| Crop Year | Brazil | Colombia | Costa Rica | Cote d'Ivoire | Ecuador | Guatemala | Honduras | Indonesia | Malaysia | Nigeria | Papua New Guinea | Thailand | World Total |
|---|---|---|---|---|---|---|---|---|---|---|---|---|---|
| 2013-14 | 370 | 1,041 | 203 | 415 | 499 | 434 | 460 | 30,500 | 20,161 | 880 | 500 | 2,000 | 59,125 |
| 2014-15 | 400 | 1,110 | 188 | 415 | 694 | 510 | 470 | 33,000 | 19,879 | 940 | 537 | 2,068 | 61,998 |
| 2015-16 | 415 | 1,275 | 251 | 415 | 535 | 625 | 490 | 32,000 | 17,700 | 955 | 560 | 1,804 | 58,852 |
| 2016-17 | 485 | 1,146 | 247 | 486 | 587 | 740 | 620 | 36,000 | 18,858 | 990 | 650 | 2,500 | 65,173 |
| 2017-18 | 500 | 1,627 | 245 | 483 | 604 | 852 | 580 | 39,500 | 19,683 | 1,025 | 680 | 2,778 | 70,559 |
| 2018-19 | 525 | 1,632 | 243 | 514 | 584 | 862 | 580 | 41,500 | 20,800 | 1,130 | 705 | 3,034 | 74,171 |
| 2019-20 | 540 | 1,529 | 260 | 525 | 509 | 862 | 580 | 42,500 | 19,255 | 1,140 | 575 | 2,652 | 73,043 |
| 2020-21[1] | 545 | 1,558 | 266 | 550 | 465 | 865 | 450 | 43,500 | 17,854 | 1,275 | 600 | 2,963 | 73,081 |
| 2021-22[2] | 550 | 1,747 | 265 | 575 | 380 | 880 | 600 | 43,200 | 18,152 | 1,400 | 625 | 3,150 | 73,826 |
| 2022-23[3] | 570 | 1,768 | 270 | 600 | 470 | 910 | 600 | 45,500 | 19,200 | 1,400 | 650 | 3,260 | 77,559 |

[1] Preliminary.  [2] Estimate.  [3] Forecast.  Source: Foreign Agricultural Service, U.S. Department of Agriculture (FAS-USDA)

## World Trade of Palm Oil    In Thousands of Metric Tons

| | Imports | | | | | | Exports | | | | | |
|---|---|---|---|---|---|---|---|---|---|---|---|---|
| Crop Year | China | European Union | India | Pakistan | Other | World Total | Benin | European Union | Indonesia | Malaysia | Papua/New Guinea | United Arab Emirates | World Total |
| 2013-14 | 5,573 | 6,969 | 7,820 | 2,725 | 18,631 | 41,718 | 600 | 162 | 21,719 | 17,344 | 556 | 250 | 43,190 |
| 2014-15 | 5,696 | 6,935 | 9,139 | 2,826 | 19,888 | 44,484 | 500 | 116 | 25,964 | 17,403 | 607 | 250 | 47,397 |
| 2015-16 | 4,689 | 6,717 | 8,857 | 2,720 | 19,397 | 42,380 | 450 | 148 | 22,906 | 16,667 | 580 | 210 | 43,895 |
| 2016-17 | 4,881 | 6,964 | 9,341 | 3,285 | 21,913 | 46,384 | 500 | 259 | 27,633 | 16,313 | 622 | 270 | 49,030 |
| 2017-18 | 5,320 | 6,834 | 8,608 | 3,285 | 22,746 | 46,793 | 476 | 261 | 26,967 | 16,472 | 615 | 180 | 48,759 |
| 2018-19 | 6,795 | 7,070 | 9,710 | 3,482 | 23,484 | 50,541 | 275 | 214 | 28,279 | 18,362 | 571 | 170 | 51,746 |
| 2019-20 | 6,719 | 7,112 | 7,398 | 3,416 | 22,832 | 47,477 | 200 | 152 | 26,249 | 17,212 | 598 | 170 | 48,491 |
| 2020-21[1] | 6,818 | 5,970 | 8,411 | 3,500 | 22,827 | 47,526 | 190 | 159 | 26,874 | 15,878 | 645 | 200 | 48,188 |
| 2021-22[2] | 4,387 | 4,970 | 8,004 | 2,824 | 22,554 | 42,739 | 170 | 185 | 22,321 | 15,527 | 634 | 225 | 43,821 |
| 2022-23[3] | 7,200 | 5,300 | 9,030 | 3,600 | 24,733 | 49,863 | 150 | 150 | 28,450 | 16,900 | 664 | 190 | 51,218 |

[1] Preliminary.  [2] Estimate.  [3] Forecast.  Source: Foreign Agricultural Service, U.S. Department of Agriculture (FAS-USDA)

# PALM OIL

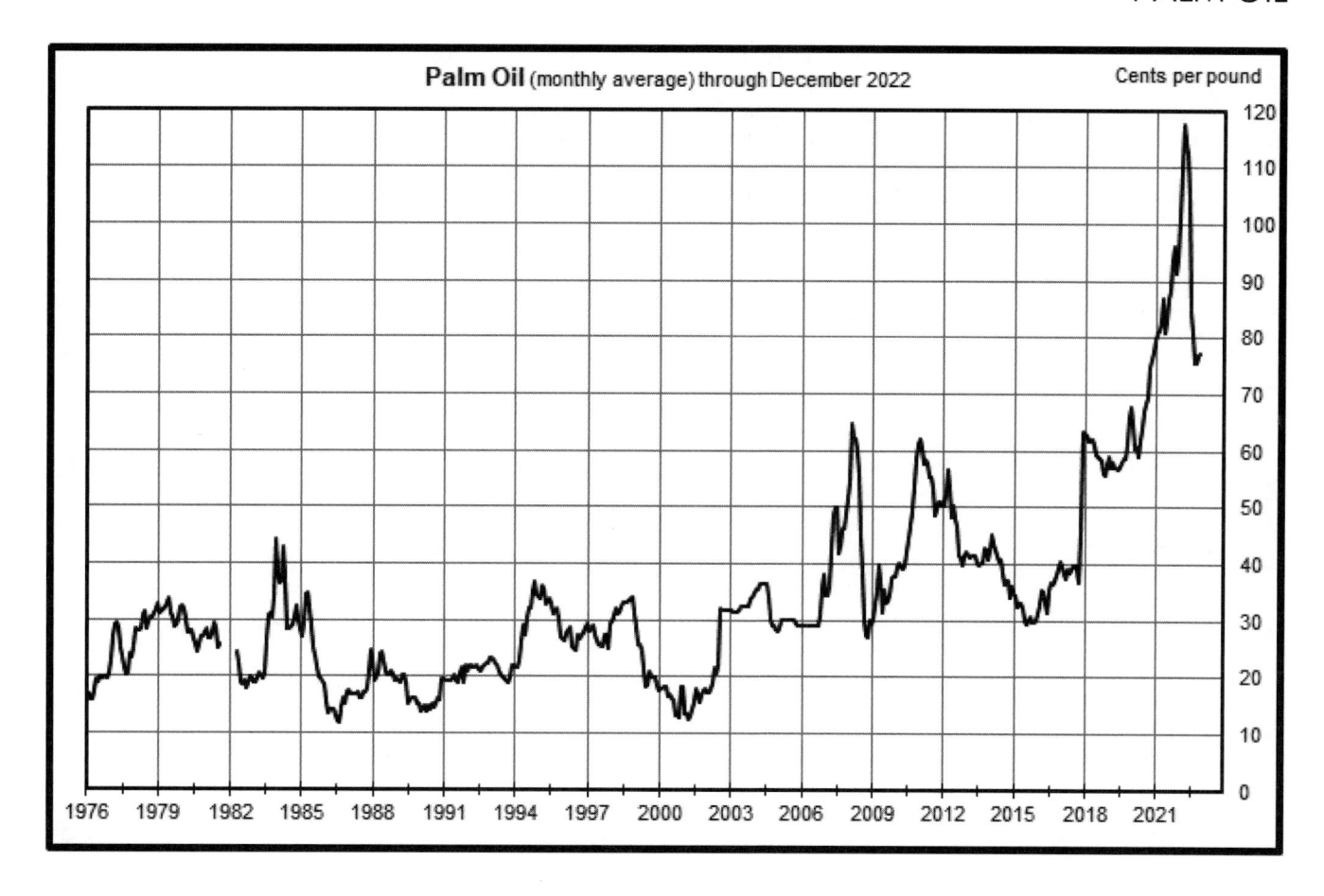

**Palm Oil** (monthly average) through December 2022 — Cents per pound

## Supply and Distribution of Palm Oil in the United States   In Thousands of Metric Tons

| Crop Year Beginning Oct. 1 | Stocks Oct. 1 | Imports | Total Supply | Edible Products | Inedible Products | Total End Products | Total Disappearance | Exports | U.S. Import Value[4] | Malaysia, F.O.B., RBD | Palm Kernel Oil, Malaysia, C.I.F Rotterdam |
|---|---|---|---|---|---|---|---|---|---|---|---|
| | | | | --- In Millions of Pounds --- | | | | | --- U.S. $ Per Metric Ton --- | | |
| 2013-14 | 136.0 | 1,220.0 | 1,356.0 | ---- | ---- | ---- | 1,356.0 | 13.0 | ---- | 867 | 1,146 |
| 2014-15 | 136.0 | 1,143.0 | 1,279.0 | ---- | ---- | ---- | 1,279.0 | 22.0 | ---- | 659 | 941 |
| 2015-16 | 165.0 | 1,307.0 | 1,472.0 | ---- | ---- | ---- | 1,472.0 | 14.0 | ---- | 655 | 1,126 |
| 2016-17 | 189.0 | 1,367.0 | 1,556.0 | ---- | ---- | ---- | 1,556.0 | 17.0 | ---- | 727 | 1,307 |
| 2017-18 | 184.0 | 1,527.0 | 1,711.0 | ---- | ---- | ---- | 1,711.0 | 16.0 | ---- | 649 | 1,082 |
| 2018-19 | 132.0 | 1,526.0 | 1,658.0 | ---- | ---- | ---- | 1,658.0 | 6.0 | ---- | 522 | 662 |
| 2019-20 | 156.0 | 1,503.0 | 1,659.0 | ---- | ---- | ---- | 1,659.0 | 5.0 | ---- | 669 | 756 |
| 2020-21[1] | 171.0 | 1,576.0 | 1,747.0 | ---- | ---- | ---- | 1,747.0 | 7.0 | ---- | 1,073 | 1,305 |
| 2021-22[2] | 142.0 | 1,593.0 | 1,735.0 | ---- | ---- | ---- | 1,735.0 | 9.0 | ---- | 1,494 | 2,101 |
| 2022-23[3] | 160.0 | 1,725.0 | 1,885.0 | ---- | ---- | ---- | 1,885.0 | 10.0 | ---- | | |

[1] Preliminary.  [2] Estimate.  [3] Forecast.  [4] Market value in the foreign country, excluding import duties, ocean freight and marine insurance.
W = Withheld.   *Sources: The Oil World; Economic Research Service, U.S. Department of Agriculture (ERS-USDA)*

## Average Wholesale Palm Oil Prices, CIF, Bulk, U.S. Ports   In Cents Per Pound

| Year | Jan. | Feb. | Mar. | Apr. | May | June | July | Aug. | Sept. | Oct. | Nov. | Dec. | Average |
|---|---|---|---|---|---|---|---|---|---|---|---|---|---|
| 2013 | 41.38 | 42.06 | 41.00 | 41.38 | 41.35 | 41.31 | 40.19 | 39.70 | 40.00 | 40.19 | 42.65 | 42.38 | 41.13 |
| 2014 | 40.90 | 42.50 | 45.00 | 43.44 | 42.40 | 40.38 | 40.63 | 38.35 | 36.56 | 37.00 | 36.94 | 34.19 | 39.86 |
| 2015 | 36.05 | 34.88 | 34.50 | 32.38 | 33.05 | 33.19 | 32.15 | 29.88 | 29.25 | 30.75 | 29.50 | 29.60 | 32.10 |
| 2016 | 30.06 | 31.44 | 32.80 | 35.35 | 34.94 | 33.00 | 31.45 | 35.25 | 36.85 | 36.44 | 37.13 | 37.95 | 34.39 |
| 2017 | 37.75 | 37.38 | 35.90 | 34.06 | 36.31 | 35.05 | 35.19 | 35.06 | 36.44 | 36.19 | 35.44 | 33.25 | 35.67 |
| 2018 | 34.13 | 33.69 | 34.10 | 33.81 | 32.88 | 32.35 | 30.38 | 30.10 | 29.94 | 29.63 | 27.00 | 27.13 | 31.26 |
| 2019 | 28.94 | 30.00 | 28.40 | 28.63 | 28.00 | 27.75 | 27.19 | 28.90 | 28.63 | 28.94 | 32.95 | 37.25 | 29.63 |
| 2020 | 39.40 | 35.31 | 31.38 | 30.81 | 29.20 | 32.38 | 34.00 | 37.00 | 38.56 | 39.35 | 44.44 | 47.45 | 36.61 |
| 2021 | 49.81 | 52.13 | 52.13 | 54.25 | 57.75 | 50.63 | 53.30 | 56.69 | 58.31 | 64.35 | 66.31 | 62.55 | 56.52 |
| 2022 | 65.75 | 73.44 | 85.06 | 82.80 | 82.31 | 74.59 | 55.10 | 51.44 | 46.33 | 45.75 | 47.50 | 47.60 | 63.14 |

*Source: Economic Research Service, U.S. Department of Agriculture (ERS-USDA)*

# Paper

The earliest known paper that is still in existence was made from cotton rags around 150 AD. Around 800 AD, paper made its appearance in Egypt but was not manufactured there until 900 AD. The Moors introduced the use of paper to Europe, and around 1150, the first papermaking mill was established in Spain, followed by England in 1495, and the U.S. in 1690.

During the 17th and 18th centuries, the increased usage of paper created a shortage of cotton rags, which were then the only source for papermaking. The solution to this problem led to the introduction of the ground-wood process of pulp-making in 1840 and the first chemical pulp process ten years later.

Today, the paper and paperboard industries, including newsprint, are sensitive to the economic cycle. As the economy strengthens, paper use increases, and vice versa.

**Prices** – The average monthly index price (1982 = 100) for paperboard in 2022 rose by +17.1% yr/yr to 347.5, a new record high. The average monthly producer price index of standard newsprint paper in 2022 rose by +29.5% to 164.5, a new record high.

**Supply** – U.S. production of paper and paperboard in 2021 rose by +1.9% yr/yr to 67.476 million metric tons. The U.S. is the world's largest producer of paper and paperboard by far with 16.2% of the world's supply, followed by Germany with 5.5%, Italy with 2.4%, and Russia with 2.3%.

### Production of Paper and Paperboard by Selected Countries    In Thousands of Metric Tons

| Year | Austria | Canada | Finland | France | Germany | Italy | Nether-lands | Norway | Russia/3 | Spain | Sweden | United Kingdom | United States |
|---|---|---|---|---|---|---|---|---|---|---|---|---|---|
| 2012 | 5,004 | 10,756 | 10,847 | 8,354 | 22,603 | 8,588 | 2,761 | 1,209 | 7,670 | 6,177 | 11,417 | 4,292 | 74,492 |
| 2013 | 4,837 | 11,174 | 10,592 | 8,043 | 22,401 | 8,652 | 2,792 | 1,079 | 7,747 | 6,685 | 10,792 | 4,561 | 71,732 |
| 2014 | 4,865 | 10,775 | 10,408 | 8,096 | 22,540 | 8,648 | 2,767 | 1,023 | 8,023 | 6,036 | 10,419 | 4,397 | 73,093 |
| 2015 | 4,965 | 10,300 | 10,320 | 7,984 | 22,601 | 8,840 | 2,643 | 979 | 8,068 | 6,195 | 10,255 | 3,970 | 72,397 |
| 2016 | 4,995 | 9,911 | 10,140 | 7,984 | 22,629 | 8,888 | 2,671 | 1,099 | 8,547 | 6,219 | 10,102 | 3,677 | 71,902 |
| 2017 | 4,860 | 9,958 | 10,276 | 8,021 | 22,925 | 9,071 | 2,983 | 1,097 | 8,717 | 6,218 | 10,261 | 3,857 | 72,045 |
| 2018 | 5,055 | 10,142 | 10,540 | 7,864 | 22,682 | 9,081 | 2,980 | 1,134 | 9,048 | 6,157 | 10,141 | 3,895 | 70,891 |
| 2019 | 4,985 | 9,473 | 9,720 | 7,325 | 22,080 | 8,909 | 2,895 | 1,155 | 9,150 | 6,437 | 9,616 | 3,851 | 68,157 |
| 2020 | 4,719 | 8,665 | 8,190 | 6,873 | 21,348 | 8,514 | 2,869 | 933 | 9,527 | 6,341 | 9,280 | 3,634 | 66,239 |
| 2021[1] | 5,065 | 9,180 | 8,660 | 7,359 | 23,125 | 9,889 | 2,942 | 1,010 | 9,527 | 6,587 | 8,924 | 3,537 | 67,476 |

[1] Preliminary.    Source: Food and Agriculture Organization of the United Nations (FAO)

### Index Price of Paperboard    (1982 = 100)

| Year | Jan. | Feb. | Mar. | Apr. | May | June | July | Aug. | Sept. | Oct. | Nov. | Dec. | Average |
|---|---|---|---|---|---|---|---|---|---|---|---|---|---|
| 2013 | 235.7 | 235.8 | 236.8 | 236.8 | 241.1 | 246.4 | 247.7 | 249.3 | 249.0 | 249.0 | 248.8 | 248.3 | 243.7 |
| 2014 | 249.0 | 249.6 | 249.7 | 249.2 | 249.3 | 249.3 | 249.2 | 248.8 | 247.7 | 247.3 | 247.0 | 246.9 | 248.6 |
| 2015 | 246.9 | 245.2 | 244.5 | 242.6 | 243.6 | 242.6 | 241.9 | 241.4 | 242.2 | 242.1 | 242.2 | 242.0 | 243.1 |
| 2016 | 241.2 | 236.0 | 232.2 | 230.6 | 230.9 | 230.5 | 230.6 | 230.0 | 230.0 | 232.3 | 236.2 | 240.7 | 233.4 |
| 2017 | 244.7 | 244.1 | 244.2 | 249.3 | 252.5 | 262.7 | 264.0 | 264.5 | 265.5 | 266.3 | 266.1 | 266.6 | 257.5 |
| 2018 | 265.5 | 265.9 | 264.8 | 266.6 | 275.6 | 276.8 | 278.3 | 278.1 | 277.9 | 278.0 | 276.9 | 277.3 | 273.5 |
| 2019 | 276.9 | 274.6 | 273.9 | 273.1 | 272.9 | 270.4 | 264.8 | 262.3 | 262.2 | 262.4 | 261.9 | 260.9 | 268.0 |
| 2020 | 259.0 | 256.5 | 256.0 | 255.0 | 255.7 | 254.7 | 256.1 | 256.3 | 255.3 | 256.3 | 256.3 | 261.7 | 256.6 |
| 2021 | 270.6 | 274.6 | 275.4 | 280.5 | 289.3 | 293.6 | 298.8 | 304.7 | 308.4 | 320.4 | 321.0 | 323.4 | 296.7 |
| 2022[1] | 325.2 | 329.6 | 333.9 | 340.3 | 343.9 | 354.0 | 356.4 | 356.4 | 356.7 | 357.5 | 358.5 | 357.3 | 347.5 |

[1] Preliminary.    Source: Bureau of Labor Statistics, U.S. Department of Commerce (BLS) (0914)

### Producer Price Index of Standard Newsprint    (1982 = 100)

| Year | Jan. | Feb. | Mar. | Apr. | May | June | July | Aug. | Sept. | Oct. | Nov. | Dec. | Average |
|---|---|---|---|---|---|---|---|---|---|---|---|---|---|
| 2013 | 136.3 | 132.6 | 130.1 | 129.7 | 129.1 | 127.8 | 130.8 | 129.6 | 129.4 | 129.9 | 131.3 | 130.3 | 130.6 |
| 2014 | 130.7 | 130.5 | 130.2 | 129.2 | 128.3 | 129.2 | 129.1 | 129.0 | 128.7 | 128.4 | 128.1 | 127.2 | 129.1 |
| 2015 | 126.3 | 123.3 | 121.4 | 119.1 | 116.1 | 114.4 | 112.9 | 106.5 | 106.3 | 105.6 | 105.4 | 105.4 | 113.6 |
| 2016 | 106.7 | 109.6 | 111.9 | 112.3 | 113.3 | 114.9 | 116.4 | 117.8 | 118.3 | 118.4 | 118.1 | 118.3 | 114.7 |
| 2017 | 118.8 | 118.3 | 117.4 | 117.0 | 117.3 | 118.1 | 118.0 | 117.5 | 118.0 | 118.1 | 120.8 | 122.9 | 118.5 |
| 2018 | 124.8 | 127.0 | 128.1 | 130.4 | 136.0 | 141.2 | 143.5 | 146.0 | 146.3 | 146.2 | 146.0 | 146.2 | 138.5 |
| 2019 | 146.2 | 146.0 | 147.5 | 145.9 | 137.9 | 137.4 | 136.4 | 136.8 | 136.0 | 134.3 | 130.8 | 129.9 | 138.8 |
| 2020 | 125.8 | 123.0 | 119.8 | 118.8 | 116.6 | 116.6 | 115.3 | 111.6 | 110.4 | 110.7 | 109.7 | 109.4 | 115.6 |
| 2021 | 110.3 | 114.3 | 115.8 | 117.9 | 123.1 | 125.7 | 128.2 | 134.7 | 136.6 | 138.1 | 140.0 | 140.0 | 127.1 |
| 2022[1] | 144.6 | 147.5 | 152.0 | 156.9 | 160.4 | 168.3 | 169.5 | 171.1 | 176.0 | 176.0 | 176.0 | 176.0 | 164.5 |

[1] Preliminary.    Source: Bureau of Labor Statistics, U.S. Department of Commerce (BLS) (0913-02)

# Peanuts and Peanut Oil

Peanuts are the edible seeds of a plant from the pea family. Although called a nut, the peanut is actually a legume. Ancient South American Inca Indians were the first to grind peanuts to make peanut butter. Peanuts originated in Brazil and were later brought to the U.S. via Africa. The first major use of peanuts was as feed for pigs. It wasn't until the Civil War that peanuts were used as human food when both Northern and Southern troops used the peanut as a food source during hard times. In 1903, Dr. George Washington Carver, a talented botanist who is considered the "father of commercial peanuts," introduced peanuts as a rotation crop in cotton-growing areas. Carver discovered over 300 uses for the peanut, including shaving cream, leather dye, coffee, ink, cheese, and shampoo.

Peanuts come in many varieties, but there are four basic types grown in the U.S.: Runner, Spanish, Valencia, and Virginia. Over half of Runner peanuts are used to make peanut butter. Spanish peanuts are primarily used to make candies and peanut oil. Valencia peanuts are the sweetest of the four types. Virginia peanuts are mainly roasted and sold in and out of the shell.

Peanut oil is extracted from shelled and crushed peanuts through hydraulic pressing, expelled pressing, or solvent extraction. Crude peanut oil is used as a flavoring agent, salad oil, and cooking oil. Refined, bleached and deodorized peanut oil is used for cooking and in margarines and shortenings. The by-product called press cake is used for cattle feed along with the tops of the plants after the pods are removed. The dry shells can be burned as fuel.

**Prices** – The average monthly price received by farmers for peanuts (in the shell) in the first five months of the 2022/23 marketing year (Aug/July) rose by +7.5% to 26.3 cents per pound. The record high is 34.7 cents posted in 1990/91. The average monthly price of peanut oil in the first three months of the 2022/23 marketing year fell by -0.6% yr/yr to 106.58 cents per pound, falling back from the 2021/22 record high of 107.22 cents per pound.

**Supply** – World peanut production in 2022/23 is forecasted to fall by -0.4% to 50.229 million metric tons. The world's largest peanut producers are expected to be China with 36.4% of world production, India with 13.2%, Nigeria with 9.0%, and both the U. S. and Sudan with 5.0%.

U.S. peanut production in the 2022/23 marketing year is expected to fall by -12.9% yr/yr to 5.568 billion pounds, below the 2017/18 record high of 7.115. U.S. farmers are expected to harvest 1.385 million acres of peanuts in 2022/23, down -10.3% yr/yr, well below the 30-year high harvest of 2.015 million acres in 1992-93. U.S. peanut yield in 2022/23 is expected to fall by -2.8% yr/yr to 4,019 pounds per acre, remaining below the 2012/13 record high of 4,211 pounds per acre. The largest peanut-producing states in the U.S. in 2022 were Georgia with 53.7% of U.S. production, Alabama with 11.4%, Florida with 10.3%, North Carolina with 8.5%, Texas with 6.8%, and South Carolina with 5.1%. U.S. shelled peanut oil production in 2021/22 fell by -6.7% yr/yr to 353.341 million pounds.

**Demand** – U.S. disposition of peanuts in 2022/23 is expected to rise by +4.7% yr/yr to 6.359 billion pounds. Of that disposition, 54.2% of the peanuts will go for food, 19.7% for exports, 13.6% for crushing into peanut oil, and 12.5% for seed, loss, and residual. The most popular type of peanut grown in the U.S. is the Runner peanut, with 89.1% of U.S. production in 2021/22. The next most popular peanut is the Virginia peanut, with 9.6% of a production market share. Peanut butter is a primary use for Runner and Virginia peanuts. Peanut butter accounts for 57.7% of Runner peanut usage. Snack peanuts are also a key usage category and account for 28.5% of Virginia peanut usage.

**Trade** – U.S. exports of peanuts in 2022/23 are expected to rise by +4.2% yr/yr to 1.250 billion pounds. U.S. imports of peanuts are expected to fall by -1.8% yr/yr to 110 million pounds.

**World Production of Peanuts (in the Shell)**   In Thousands of Metric Tons

| Crop Year | Argentina | Burma | Cameroon | China | India | Indonesia | Nigeria | Senegal | Sudan | Tanzania | United States | Vietnam | World Total |
|---|---|---|---|---|---|---|---|---|---|---|---|---|---|
| 2013-14 | 997 | 1,428 | 636 | 16,082 | 6,482 | 1,160 | 2,475 | 677 | 1,767 | 1,425 | 1,893 | 455 | 41,769 |
| 2014-15 | 1,188 | 1,465 | 579 | 15,901 | 4,855 | 1,150 | 3,399 | 669 | 1,871 | 1,635 | 2,354 | 452 | 41,790 |
| 2015-16 | 930 | 1,502 | 609 | 15,961 | 4,470 | 1,130 | 3,467 | 1,050 | 1,042 | 1,836 | 2,722 | 441 | 41,273 |
| 2016-17 | 1,288 | 1,518 | 748 | 16,361 | 6,924 | 1,120 | 4,361 | 991 | 1,826 | 1,100 | 2,532 | 462 | 45,930 |
| 2017-18 | 867 | 1,572 | 600 | 17,092 | 6,665 | 1,075 | 4,521 | 1,405 | 1,648 | 1,100 | 3,228 | 450 | 47,100 |
| 2018-19 | 1,419 | 1,583 | 600 | 17,333 | 4,685 | 1,025 | 4,422 | 1,502 | 2,884 | 1,100 | 2,493 | 439 | 46,621 |
| 2019-20 | 1,285 | 1,375 | 600 | 17,520 | 6,255 | 990 | 4,441 | 1,421 | 2,828 | 1,100 | 2,480 | 425 | 48,173 |
| 2020-21 | 1,270 | 1,562 | 600 | 17,993 | 6,700 | 970 | 4,231 | 1,797 | 2,773 | 1,100 | 2,793 | 413 | 50,257 |
| 2021-22[1] | 1,340 | 1,600 | 600 | 18,308 | 6,800 | 960 | 4,228 | 1,678 | 2,355 | 1,100 | 2,885 | 400 | 50,434 |
| 2022-23[2] | 1,250 | 1,650 | 600 | 18,300 | 6,650 | 950 | 4,500 | 1,700 | 2,500 | 1,100 | 2,526 | 388 | 50,229 |

[1] Preliminary.   [2] Estimate.   *Source: Foreign Agricultural Service, U.S. Department of Agriculture (FAS-USDA)*

# PEANUTS AND PEANUT OIL

## World Exports of Peanuts (in the Shell)   In Thousands of Metric Tons

| Crop Year | Argentina | Brazil | China | Egypt | European Union | Gambia, The | India | Malawi | Nicaragua | Senegal | South Africa | United States | World Total |
|---|---|---|---|---|---|---|---|---|---|---|---|---|---|
| 2013-14 | 578 | 93 | 565 | 52 | 26 | 18 | 785 | 27 | 133 | 1 | 25 | 497 | 3,000 |
| 2014-15 | 848 | 141 | 501 | 28 | 31 | 18 | 875 | 10 | 130 | 113 | 37 | 490 | 3,423 |
| 2015-16 | 883 | 163 | 483 | 28 | 32 | 15 | 773 | 7 | 102 | 193 | 12 | 700 | 3,629 |
| 2016-17 | 734 | 221 | 644 | 82 | 62 | 8 | 940 | 2 | 115 | 135 | 18 | 602 | 3,904 |
| 2017-18 | 586 | 297 | 651 | 49 | 61 | 8 | 752 | 2 | 131 | 97 | 22 | 577 | 3,504 |
| 2018-19 | 800 | 272 | 646 | 45 | 57 | 3 | 623 | 2 | 125 | 312 | 21 | 544 | 3,830 |
| 2019-20 | 985 | 352 | 554 | 39 | 53 | 1 | 929 | 2 | 100 | 430 | 29 | 730 | 4,928 |
| 2020-21 | 937 | 352 | 459 | 44 | 48 | 1 | 881 | 2 | 132 | 497 | 22 | 648 | 4,916 |
| 2021-22[1] | 925 | 375 | 454 | 66 | 55 | 1 | 732 | 2 | 151 | 241 | 15 | 536 | 4,284 |
| 2022-23[2] | 900 | 375 | 450 | 45 | 50 | 1 | 750 | 2 | 145 | 475 | 20 | 499 | 4,540 |

[1] Preliminary.  [2] Estimate.  Source: Foreign Agricultural Service, U.S. Department of Agriculture (FAS-USDA)

## Salient Statistics of Peanuts in the United States

| Crop Year Beginning Aug. 1 | Acreage Planted (1,000 Acres) | Acreage Harvested for Nuts (1,000 Acres) | Average Yield Per Acre In Lbs. | Production (1,000 Lbs) | Season Farm Price (Cents Lb.) | Farm Value (Million Dollars) | Exports Unshelled (1,000 Lbs) | Exports Shelled (1,000 Lbs) | Imports Unshelled (1,000 Lbs) | Imports Shelled (1,000 Lbs) |
|---|---|---|---|---|---|---|---|---|---|---|
| 2013-14 | 1,067.0 | 1,043.0 | 4,001 | 4,173,170 | 24.9 | 1,055.1 | 1,096,000 | 708,141 | 88,000 | 60,738 |
| 2014-15 | 1,353.5 | 1,322.5 | 3,923 | 5,188,665 | 22.0 | 1,158.3 | 1,080,000 | 676,509 | 90,000 | 64,345 |
| 2015-16 | 1,625.0 | 1,560.9 | 3,845 | 6,001,357 | 19.3 | 1,160.6 | 1,544,000 |  | 94,000 |  |
| 2016-17 | 1,671.0 | 1,536.0 | 3,634 | 5,581,570 | 19.7 | 1,088.2 | 1,328,000 |  | 162,000 |  |
| 2017-18 | 1,871.6 | 1,775.6 | 4,007 | 7,115,410 | 22.9 | 1,634.0 | 1,271,000 |  | 171,000 |  |
| 2018-19 | 1,425.5 | 1,373.5 | 4,001 | 5,461,600 | 21.5 | 1,170.0 | 1,200,000 |  | 117,000 |  |
| 2019-20 | 1,432.7 | 1,389.7 | 3,934 | 5,466,487 | 20.5 | 1,131.4 | 1,610,000 |  | 114,000 |  |
| 2020-21 | 1,662.5 | 1,615.2 | 3,813 | 6,158,350 | 21.0 | 1,294.5 | 1,429,000 |  | 121,000 |  |
| 2021-22[1] | 1,585.2 | 1,545.0 | 4,135 | 6,389,300 | 24.3 | 1,508.7 | 1,182,000 |  | 107,000 |  |
| 2022-23[2] | 1,450.3 | 1,385.4 | 4,019 | 5,568,150 | 24.5 |  | 1,100,000 |  | 110,000 |  |

[1] Preliminary.  [2] Estimate.  Source: Economic Research Service, U.S. Department of Agriculture (ERS-USDA)

## Supply and Disposition of Peanuts (Farmer's Stock Basis) in the United States

| Crop Year Beginning Aug. 1 | Production | Imports | Stocks Aug. 1 | Total | Exports | Crushed for Oil | Seed, Loss & Residual | Food | Total Disappearance |
|---|---|---|---|---|---|---|---|---|---|
| 2013-14 | 2,771 | 4,173 | 88 | 7,032 | 2,886 | 663 | 530 | 1,096 | 5,174 |
| 2014-15 | 1,858 | 5,189 | 90 | 7,136 | 2,982 | 675 | 298 | 1,080 | 5,035 |
| 2015-16 | 2,101 | 6,001 | 94 | 8,197 | 3,053 | 709 | 1,100 | 1,544 | 6,406 |
| 2016-17 | 1,791 | 5,582 | 162 | 7,534 | 3,086 | 880 | 799 | 1,328 | 6,093 |
| 2017-18 | 1,442 | 7,115 | 171 | 8,728 | 3,149 | 705 | 887 | 1,271 | 6,011 |
| 2018-19 | 2,717 | 5,462 | 117 | 8,330 | 3,099 | 648 | 962 | 1,200 | 5,909 |
| 2019-20 | 2,421 | 5,466 | 114 | 8,001 | 3,221 | 774 | 287 | 1,610 | 5,883 |
| 2020-21 | 2,118 | 6,158 | 121 | 8,398 | 3,357 | 873 | 771 | 1,429 | 6,429 |
| 2021-22[1] | 1,968 | 6,389 | 107 | 8,437 | 3,313 | 842 | 738 | 1,182 | 6,076 |
| 2022-23[2] | 2,360 | 5,568 | 110 | 8,038 | 3,288 | 800 | 651 | 1,100 | 5,838 |

In Millions of Pounds

[1] Preliminary.  [2] Estimate.  Source: Economic Research Service, U.S. Department of Agriculture (ERS-USDA)

## Production of Peanuts (Harvested for Nuts) in the United States, by States   In Thousands of Pounds

| Crop Year | Alabama | Florida | Georgia | Mississippi | New Mexico | North Carolina | Oklahoma | South Carolina | Texas | Virginia | Total |
|---|---|---|---|---|---|---|---|---|---|---|---|
| 2013 | 489,900 | 517,450 | 1,887,180 | 122,100 | 21,700 | 315,900 | 59,200 | 273,000 | 423,540 | 63,200 | 4,173,170 |
| 2014 | 544,950 | 668,000 | 2,435,515 | 124,000 | 15,750 | 401,760 | 44,000 | 410,400 | 459,740 | 84,550 | 5,188,665 |
| 2015 | 637,000 | 648,000 | 3,364,410 | 143,500 | 15,337 | 302,760 | 30,600 | 262,400 | 528,000 | 69,350 | 6,001,357 |
| 2016 | 619,200 | 554,800 | 2,753,400 | 152,000 | 22,400 | 349,470 | 44,400 | 339,200 | 559,650 | 76,650 | 5,581,570 |
| 2017 | 704,450 | 638,250 | 3,572,250 | 172,000 | 26,600 | 479,700 | 79,380 | 472,000 | 697,200 | 119,880 | 7,115,410 |
| 2018 | 571,550 | 564,850 | 2,875,450 | 93,600 | 15,675 | 379,260 | 46,050 | 272,000 | 464,000 | 100,800 | 5,461,600 |
| 2019 | 522,600 | 589,000 | 2,752,200 | 76,000 | 15,087 | 448,800 | 56,000 | 235,600 | 488,000 | 111,600 | 5,466,487 |
| 2020 | 622,200 | 564,400 | 3,316,600 | 96,800 | 14,820 | 409,500 | 59,080 | 296,000 | 484,500 | 112,050 | 6,158,350 |
| 2021 | 609,700 | 584,600 | 3,337,500 | 69,700 | 25,641 | 495,900 | 66,750 | 277,200 | 578,340 | 141,000 | 6,389,300 |
| 2022[1] | 635,700 | 573,300 | 2,992,000 | 53,300 | 21,300 | 475,600 | 64,600 | 285,600 | 378,000 | 131,600 | 5,568,150 |

[1] Preliminary.  Source: Agricultural Statistics Board, U.S. Department of Agriculture (ASB-USDA)

# PEANUTS AND PEANUT OIL

## Supply and Reported Uses of Shelled Peanuts and Products in the United States    In Thousands of Pounds

| Crop Year Beginning Aug. 1 | Shelled Peanuts -- Stocks, Aug. 1 -- Edible | Oil Stock[2] | Shelled Peanuts ----- Production ----- Edible | Oil Stock[2] | Candy[3] | Snack[4] | Butter[5] | Other Products | Total | Shelled Peanuts Crushed[6] | Crude Oil Production | Cake & Meal Production |
|---|---|---|---|---|---|---|---|---|---|---|---|---|
| 2012-13 | 547,965 | 33,883 | 3,125,786 | 351,284 | 381,914 | 400,429 | 1,227,859 | 20,664 | 2,030,866 | 493,205 | 210,702 | 270,328 |
| 2013-14 | 519,824 | 25,364 | 3,098,392 | 373,008 | 395,726 | 429,796 | 1,218,170 | 29,103 | 2,072,795 | 497,272 | 209,808 | 268,554 |
| 2014-15 | 431,674 | 31,012 | 2,997,078 | 391,728 | 375,856 | 428,477 | 1,303,755 | 53,179 | 2,161,267 | 506,677 | 214,041 | 278,380 |
| 2015-16 | 467,139 | 65,350 | 3,141,099 | 442,650 | 377,505 | 505,692 | 1,299,634 | 61,388 | 2,244,219 | 531,770 | 226,219 | 291,193 |
| 2016-17 | 482,010 | 26,372 | 2,944,760 | 448,377 | 407,701 | 470,292 | 1,338,195 | 56,769 | 2,272,957 | 659,966 | 283,689 | 357,751 |
| 2017-18 | 535,730 | 24,232 | 2,853,147 | 358,282 | 379,504 | 524,845 | 1,314,567 | 95,943 | 2,314,859 | 528,750 | 231,748 | 282,346 |
| 2018-19 | 540,802 | 23,498 | 2,932,229 | 368,168 | 380,936 | 467,676 | 1,342,437 | 112,651 | 2,303,700 | 486,398 | 219,334 | 255,683 |
| 2019-20 | 510,369 | 29,092 | 2,908,778 | 405,622 | 395,647 | 481,430 | 1,410,264 | 91,567 | 2,378,908 | 580,628 | 254,109 | 304,718 |
| 2020-21 | 466,158 | 27,227 | 2,975,072 | 378,693 | 433,206 | 505,548 | 1,448,852 | 72,676 | 2,460,282 | 654,699 | 282,503 | 337,127 |
| 2021-22[1] | 521,131 | 25,843 | 3,292,875 | 353,341 | 490,132 | 485,359 | 1,409,120 | 60,173 | 2,444,784 | 631,840 | 283,736 | 330,684 |

[1] Preliminary.  [2] Includes straight run oil stock peanuts.  [3] Includes peanut butter made by manufacturers for own use in candy.  [4] Formerly titled "Salted Peanuts."  [5] Includes peanut butter made by manufacturers for own use in cookies and sandwiches, but excludes peanut butter used in candy.  [6] All crushings regardless of grade.    Source: National Agricultural Statistics Service, U.S. Department of Agriculture (NASS-USDA)

## Shelled Peanuts (Raw Basis) Used in Primary Products, by Type    In Thousands of Pounds

| Crop Year Beginning Aug. 1 | Virginia Candy[2] | Peanuts | Butter[3] | Total | Runner Candy[2] | Peanuts | Butter[3] | Total | Spanish Candy[2] | Peanuts | Butter[3] | Total |
|---|---|---|---|---|---|---|---|---|---|---|---|---|
| 2012-13 | 17,731 | 83,722 | 82,981 | 192,888 | 347,428 | 309,860 | 1,143,108 | 1,812,591 | 16,755 | 6,847 | W | 25,389 |
| 2013-14 | 17,109 | 85,298 | 86,759 | 202,536 | W | 337,934 | 1,128,206 | 1,844,490 | 15,996 | 6,564 | W | W |
| 2014-15 | 12,079 | 91,909 | 102,340 | 232,768 | 348,367 | 329,930 | 1,196,277 | 1,901,311 | 15,410 | 6,638 | W | 27,188 |
| 2015-16 | 14,319 | 89,766 | 108,156 | 238,494 | 346,831 | 408,726 | 1,186,810 | 1,977,495 | 16,355 | 7,200 | W | 28,225 |
| 2016-17 | 13,427 | 92,331 | 118,109 | 247,473 | 379,549 | 370,766 | 1,215,212 | 1,998,683 | 14,725 | 7,195 | W | 26,801 |
| 2017-18 | 15,455 | 84,479 | 129,823 | 258,754 | 346,985 | 434,139 | 1,179,186 | 2,027,253 | 17,064 | 6,227 | W | 28,851 |
| 2018-19 | 15,589 | 81,418 | 120,939 | 236,696 | 349,081 | 380,165 | 1,213,018 | 2,036,161 | 16,266 | 6,093 | W | 30,840 |
| 2019-20 | 9,145 | 94,614 | 140,527 | 264,121 | 372,153 | W | 1,259,768 | 2,084,164 | 14,349 | W | W | 30,622 |
| 2020-21 | W | 68,725 | W | 249,240 | 408,607 | W | 1,285,959 | 2,166,988 | W | W | W | 44,058 |
| 2021-22[1] | W | 66,873 | W | 234,844 | 463,268 | W | 1,256,040 | 2,177,468 | W | W | W | 32,474 |

[1] Preliminary.  [2] Includes peanut butter made by manufacturers for own use in candy.  [3] Includes peanut butter made by manufacturers for own use in cookies and sandwiches, but excludes peanut butter used in candy.
Source: National Agricultural Statistics Service, U.S. Department of Agriculture (NASS-USDA)

## Farmer Stock Equivalent Total[2/3] Stocks of Peanuts in the United States at End of Month    In Million Pounds

| Crop Year | Aug. | Sept. | Oct. | Nov. | Dec. | Jan. | Feb. | Mar. | Apr. | May. | June | July |
|---|---|---|---|---|---|---|---|---|---|---|---|---|
| 2013-14 | 2,427.0 | 2,172.4 | 3,776.3 | 4,641.5 | 4,710.1 | 4,299.6 | 3,919.4 | 3,505.5 | 3,092.3 | 2,741.2 | 2,304.4 | 1,857.8 |
| 2014-15 | 1,426.7 | 1,330.5 | 4,246.1 | 4,717.3 | 4,573.2 | 4,297.1 | 3,893.3 | 3,487.2 | 3,105.8 | 2,717.9 | 2,401.4 | 2,101.0 |
| 2015-16 | 1,455.3 | 1,846.4 | 4,496.2 | 5,317.9 | 5,360.6 | 4,863.2 | 4,347.8 | 3,798.7 | 3,279.7 | 2,656.4 | 2,108.6 | 1,790.9 |
| 2016-17 | 1,239.1 | 1,509.3 | 4,156.1 | 4,701.6 | 4,389.9 | 3,992.8 | 3,550.0 | 3,087.8 | 2,668.3 | 2,241.0 | 1,806.7 | 1,441.6 |
| 2017-18 | 1,013.5 | 1,806.4 | 4,739.2 | 5,587.7 | 5,379.1 | 5,032.3 | 4,585.7 | 4,225.5 | 3,787.6 | 3,357.5 | 2,982.1 | 2,717.1 |
| 2018-19 | 2,309.8 | 2,594.7 | 4,195.3 | 5,002.8 | 5,056.8 | 4,727.8 | 4,326.0 | 3,976.9 | 3,490.6 | 3,075.9 | 2,765.4 | 27,421.1 |
| 2019-20 | 2,045.2 | 2,442.1 | 4,106.7 | 4,637.5 | 4,610.5 | 4,322.4 | 4,001.2 | 3,636.6 | 3,214.2 | 2,744.7 | 2,379.4 | 2,118.2 |
| 2020-21 | 1,557.9 | 1,465.0 | 3,493.8 | 4,496.8 | 4,386.8 | 4,142.3 | 4,337.6 | 3,834.8 | 3,323.8 | 2,900.3 | 2,377.9 | 1,968.2 |
| 2021-22 | 1,596.1 | 1,451.8 | 4,493.1 | 5,484.6 | 5,301.1 | 4,960.7 | 4,554.6 | 4,086.9 | 3,643.4 | 3,219.2 | 2,774.7 | 2,360.3 |
| 2022-23[1] | 1,913.1 | 2,599.2 | 4,870.5 | 5,457.2 | 5,050.7 | 4,632.9 | 4,243.3 | | | | | |

[1] Preliminary.  [2] Excludes stocks on farms. Includes stocks owned by or held for account of peanut producers and CCC in commercial storage facilities. Farmer stock on net weight basis.  [3] Actual farmer stock, plus roasting stock, plus shelled peanuts.  W = Withheld.    Source: Agricultural Marketing Service, U.S. Department of Agriculture (AMS-USDA)

## Farmer Stock Peanuts[2], Total All Types, in the United States at End of Month    In Millions of Pounds

| Crop Year | Aug. | Sept. | Oct. | Nov. | Dec. | Jan. | Feb. | Mar. | Apr. | May. | June | July |
|---|---|---|---|---|---|---|---|---|---|---|---|---|
| 2013-14 | 1,527.6 | 1,296.5 | 2,909.0 | 3,790.8 | 3,876.1 | 3,472.0 | 3,045.7 | 2,615.1 | 2,195.8 | 1,819.1 | 1,423.3 | 1,059.5 |
| 2014-15 | 661.8 | 573.0 | 3,517.7 | 4,046.4 | 3,947.9 | 3,622.6 | 3,224.0 | 2,789.6 | 2,394.6 | 2,056.4 | 1,697.5 | 1,445.3 |
| 2015-16 | 874.6 | 1,305.6 | 3,883.8 | 4,690.3 | 4,733.5 | 4,207.8 | 3,621.4 | 3,058.7 | 2,584.2 | 1,948.7 | 1,413.6 | 1,051.1 |
| 2016-17 | 648.2 | 960.2 | 3,594.2 | 4,093.3 | 3,747.5 | 3,317.9 | 2,828.0 | 2,342.8 | 1,919.8 | 1,465.8 | 1,050.4 | 733.0 |
| 2017-18 | 393.9 | 1,252.0 | 4,131.7 | 4,977.2 | 4,679.2 | 4,283.4 | 3,831.6 | 3,351.3 | 2,906.0 | 2,508.7 | 2,192.0 | 1,916.8 |
| 2018-19 | 1,568.9 | 1,811.5 | 3,426.7 | 4,286.5 | 4,301.9 | 3,976.5 | 3,576.0 | 3,144.1 | 2,703.0 | 2,334.7 | 1,964.9 | 1,627.9 |
| 2019-20 | 1,312.9 | 1,703.2 | 3,350.0 | 3,905.2 | 3,865.2 | 3,577.5 | 3,247.9 | 2,851.6 | 2,442.2 | 2,048.5 | 1,685.8 | 1,363.4 |
| 2020-21 | 839.0 | 792.9 | 2,878.8 | 3,858.8 | 3,713.5 | 3,418.6 | 3,578.2 | 3,006.2 | 2,514.8 | 2,063.9 | 1,641.6 | 1,280.3 |
| 2021-22 | 914.4 | 798.1 | 3,842.2 | 4,839.1 | 4,644.5 | 4,249.1 | 3,786.9 | 3,253.4 | 2,805.9 | 2,419.0 | 1,957.7 | 1,589.1 |
| 2022-23[1] | 1,185.9 | 1,885.3 | 4,176.0 | 4,782.8 | 4,394.6 | 3,959.3 | 3,497.4 | | | | | |

[1] Preliminary.  [2] Excludes stocks on farms. Includes stocks owned by or held for account of peanut producers and CCC in commercial storage facilities. Farmer stock on net weight basis.    Source: Agricultural Marketing Service, U.S. Department of Agriculture (AMS-USDA)

# PEANUTS AND PEANUT OIL

### Peanuts (monthly average) through December 2022 — Cents per pound

### Average Price[2] Received by Farmers for Peanuts (in the Shell) in the United States — In Cents Per Pound

| Crop Year | Aug. | Sept. | Oct. | Nov. | Dec. | Jan. | Feb. | Mar. | Apr. | May. | June | July | Average[1] |
|---|---|---|---|---|---|---|---|---|---|---|---|---|---|
| 2013-14 | 25.1 | 25.3 | 26.0 | 26.6 | 24.6 | 25.4 | 24.3 | 25.0 | 24.2 | 23.7 | 20.0 | 21.7 | 24.3 |
| 2014-15 | 22.1 | 21.5 | 21.0 | 21.4 | 20.9 | 22.5 | 22.2 | 22.5 | 22.1 | 22.5 | 21.8 | 23.0 | 22.0 |
| 2015-16 | 20.7 | 19.6 | 18.8 | 18.5 | 17.8 | 19.3 | 19.8 | 19.5 | 19.8 | 19.6 | 19.5 | 19.0 | 19.3 |
| 2016-17 | 19.0 | 19.1 | 19.5 | 19.0 | 18.6 | 19.8 | 20.1 | 20.6 | 19.8 | 19.4 | 19.7 | 20.5 | 19.6 |
| 2017-18 | 19.7 | 23.0 | 23.2 | 22.7 | 23.0 | 22.9 | 22.7 | 24.4 | 23.3 | 22.7 | 22.7 | 22.4 | 22.7 |
| 2018-19 | 22.0 | 22.3 | 21.8 | 21.6 | 20.5 | 22.7 | 22.3 | 19.8 | 20.3 | 20.5 | 21.5 | 20.6 | 21.3 |
| 2019-20 | 20.5 | 19.8 | 20.4 | 19.2 | 19.6 | 20.9 | 20.5 | 20.6 | 20.6 | 21.1 | 20.7 | 20.7 | 20.4 |
| 2020-21 | 20.6 | 20.5 | 20.9 | 21.2 | 20.4 | 20.5 | 20.5 | 21.2 | 21.4 | 21.3 | 21.3 | 21.6 | 21.0 |
| 2021-22 | 21.3 | 22.2 | 23.9 | 25.4 | 24.1 | 25.9 | 24.8 | 25.0 | 24.7 | 25.3 | 25.2 | 25.3 | 24.4 |
| 2022-23[1] | 25.0 | 25.7 | 26.6 | 29.9 | 24.1 | 27.9 | 27.2 | | | | | | 26.6 |

[1] Preliminarly.  [2] Weighted average by sales.  Source: National Agricultural Statistics Service, U.S. Department of Agriculture (NASS-USDA)

### Average Price of Domestic Crude Peanut Oil (in Tanks) F.O.B. Southeast Mills — In Cents Per Pound

| Crop Year | Oct. | Nov. | Dec. | Jan. | Feb. | Mar. | Apr. | May | June | July | Aug. | Sept. | Average |
|---|---|---|---|---|---|---|---|---|---|---|---|---|---|
| 2013-14 | 81.00 | 78.70 | 75.38 | 65.70 | 62.06 | 59.06 | 57.75 | 57.20 | 58.25 | 58.63 | 62.80 | 61.75 | 64.86 |
| 2014-15 | 59.95 | 60.63 | 60.13 | 56.15 | 55.56 | 54.69 | 54.81 | 54.65 | 56.31 | 58.15 | 58.63 | 58.69 | 57.36 |
| 2015-16 | 57.70 | 58.06 | 58.50 | 56.19 | 55.00 | 55.55 | 56.20 | 61.38 | 61.10 | 62.10 | 61.00 | 61.60 | 58.70 |
| 2016-17 | 64.88 | 66.00 | 63.10 | 62.88 | 63.13 | 65.80 | 69.69 | 70.75 | 76.20 | 75.75 | 69.63 | 66.60 | 67.87 |
| 2017-18 | 65.44 | 65.00 | 65.20 | 66.13 | 66.63 | 67.00 | 66.88 | 66.50 | 67.70 | 68.00 | 68.00 | 67.63 | 66.68 |
| 2018-19 | 66.63 | 64.80 | 62.25 | 61.88 | 61.13 | 61.00 | 65.25 | 66.00 | 66.00 | 66.13 | 66.00 | 67.00 | 64.51 |
| 2019-20 | 61.50 | 63.10 | 60.13 | 59.00 | 59.00 | 59.75 | 59.50 | 62.10 | 84.75 | 85.00 | 90.00 | 90.00 | 69.49 |
| 2020-21 | 93.00 | 98.75 | 100.00 | 90.00 | 93.00 | 105.25 | 109.20 | 110.00 | 108.19 | 106.00 | 108.75 | 105.00 | 102.26 |
| 2021-22 | 101.50 | 100.00 | 100.00 | 103.13 | 105.00 | 107.50 | 115.00 | 116.25 | 116.25 | 103.20 | 107.25 | 111.60 | 107.22 |
| 2022-23[1] | 107.75 | 111.00 | 101.00 | 95.38 | 88.00 | | | | | | | | 100.63 |

[1] Preliminary.  Source: Agricultural Marketing Service, U.S. Department of Agriculture (AMS-USDA)

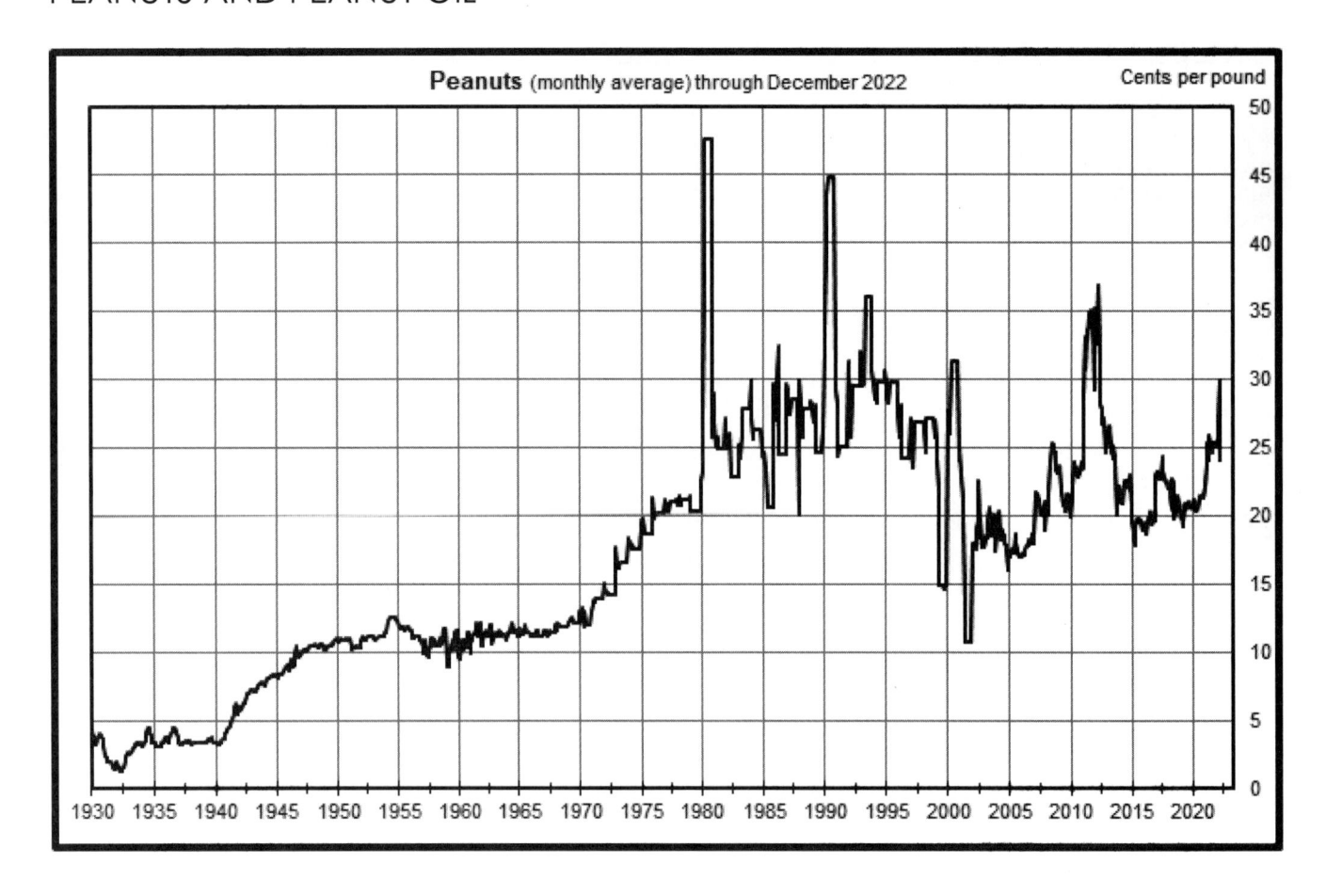

# Pepper

The pepper plant is a perennial climbing shrub that originated in India and Sri Lanka. Pepper is considered the world's most important spice and has been used to flavor foods for over 3,000 years. Pepper was once considered so valuable that it was used to ransom Rome from Attila the Hun. Black pepper alone accounts for nearly 35% of the world's spice trade. Unlike many other popular herbs and spices, pepper can only be cultivated in tropical climates. The pepper plant produces a berry called a peppercorn. Both black and white pepper are obtained from the same plant. The colors of pepper are determined by the maturity of the berry at harvest and by different processing methods.

Black pepper is picked when the berries are still green and immature. The peppercorns are then dried in the sun until they turn black. White pepper is picked when the berries are fully ripe and bright red. The red peppercorns are then soaked, washed to remove the skin of the berry, and dried to produce a white to yellowish-white peppercorn. Black pepper has a slightly hotter flavor and stronger aroma than white pepper. Piperine, an alkaloid of pyridine, is the active ingredient in pepper that makes it hot.

Black pepper oil is obtained from crushed berries using solvent extraction. Black pepper oil is used in the treatment of pain, chills, flu, muscular aches, and in some perfumes. It is also helpful in promoting digestion in the colon.

The world's key pepper varieties are known by their place of origin. Popular types of pepper include Lampong Black and Muntok White from Indonesia, Brazilian Black, and Malabar Black and Tellicherry from India.

**Production** – World production of pepper in 2021 rose by +.6% yr/yr to 793,818 metric tons. The world's largest pepper producer in 2021 was Vietnam with a 36.3% share of world production, followed by Brazil with a 14.9% share, Indonesia with a 10.2% share, and India with a 8.2% share. Pepper production in 2021 in Vietnam rose by +6.7% yr/yr to 288,167 metric tons. Also, in 2021 Brazil production rose by +2.9% yr/yr to 118,057 metric tons.

**Trade** – The world's largest exporters of pepper in 2021 were Vietnam with a 41.7% share of 217,182 metric tons of exports, Brazil with a 17.7% share of 92,065 metric tons, the European Union with a 8.9% share of 46,319 metric tons, Indonesia with a 7.2% share of 37,738 metric tons, India with a 4.2% share of 21,971 metric tons, and Sri Lanka with a 3.4% share of 17,959 metric tons.

## World Production of Pepper   In Metric Tons

| Year | Brazil | Cambodia | China | India | Indonesia | Madagascar | Malaysia | Mexico | Philippines | Sri Lanka | Thailand | Vietnam | World Total |
|---|---|---|---|---|---|---|---|---|---|---|---|---|---|
| 2014 | 42,339 | 2,505 | 32,940 | 51,000 | 87,400 | 4,465 | 27,500 | 3,309 | 2,563 | 27,847 | 1,174 | 151,761 | 491,394 |
| 2015 | 51,739 | 2,503 | 34,224 | 65,000 | 81,501 | 6,881 | 28,300 | 3,567 | 1,847 | 31,226 | 1,405 | 176,789 | 547,124 |
| 2016 | 54,430 | 2,500 | 32,859 | 55,000 | 86,334 | 6,183 | 29,245 | 5,206 | 1,436 | 32,145 | 1,409 | 216,432 | 592,321 |
| 2017 | 79,106 | 2,499 | 33,340 | 72,000 | 87,991 | 5,559 | 30,433 | 7,951 | 1,369 | 35,142 | 2,536 | 252,576 | 668,724 |
| 2018 | 101,624 | 2,515 | 33,481 | 66,000 | 88,949 | 5,000 | 32,292 | 9,141 | 1,308 | 48,253 | 2,005 | 262,658 | 785,839 |
| 2019 | 109,401 | 2,508 | 33,232 | 66,000 | 87,619 | 4,500 | 33,940 | 9,384 | 1,132 | 41,429 | 2,219 | 264,854 | 784,041 |
| 2020[1] | 114,749 | 2,512 | 33,356 | 66,000 | 86,083 | 4,498 | 30,804 | 10,399 | 1,028 | 43,557 | 1,031 | 270,192 | 781,638 |
| 2021[2] | 118,057 | 2,516 | 33,356 | 64,816 | 81,219 | 5,283 | 31,636 | 9,841 | 965 | 42,485 | 516 | 288,167 | 793,818 |

[1] Preliminary.   [2] Estimate.   Source: Food and Agricultural Organization of the United Nations (FAO-UN)

## World Imports of Pepper   In Metric Tons

| Year | European Union | France | Germany | India | Japan | Netherlands | Pakistan | Russia | Singapore | United Arab Em. | United Kingdom | United States | World Total |
|---|---|---|---|---|---|---|---|---|---|---|---|---|---|
| 2014 | 85,779 | 9,564 | 25,978 | 23,068 | 8,833 | 15,862 | 8,105 | 7,996 | 27,005 | 19,967 | 10,936 | 68,987 | 378,064 |
| 2015 | 89,428 | 10,203 | 29,239 | 21,460 | 9,068 | 13,630 | 7,119 | 6,922 | 20,177 | 18,363 | 12,038 | 80,357 | 392,340 |
| 2016 | 89,449 | 11,505 | 29,452 | 23,484 | 8,741 | 12,450 | 10,160 | 7,699 | 6,452 | 14,969 | 14,270 | 75,178 | 386,250 |
| 2017 | 93,228 | 10,814 | 32,630 | 30,431 | 8,193 | 13,063 | 8,932 | 8,204 | 5,583 | 19,361 | 12,963 | 78,287 | 422,994 |
| 2018 | 94,971 | 11,372 | 30,765 | 26,009 | 9,485 | 14,219 | 8,240 | 8,047 | 5,784 | 17,257 | 11,771 | 74,923 | 419,783 |
| 2019 | 100,378 | 11,264 | 33,955 | 29,357 | 9,714 | 15,215 | 11,187 | 10,306 | 2,753 | 27,003 | 12,722 | 84,312 | 475,889 |
| 2020[1] | 98,380 | 12,044 | 32,862 | 27,441 | 9,428 | 12,388 | 13,302 | 9,867 | 3,569 | 35,359 | 13,609 | 86,550 | 493,110 |
| 2021[2] | 105,597 | 13,311 | 32,812 | 38,059 | 9,079 | 15,809 | 18,272 | 9,270 | 2,864 | 46,664 | 13,454 | 94,174 | 519,743 |

[1] Preliminary.   [2] Estimate.   Source: Food and Agricultural Organization of the United Nations (FAO-UN)

## World Exports of Pepper   In Metric Tons

| Year | Brazil | European Union | Germany | India | Indonesia | Malaysia | Mexico | Netherlands | Singapore | Sri Lanka | United States | Vietnam | World Total |
|---|---|---|---|---|---|---|---|---|---|---|---|---|---|
| 2014 | 34,269 | 40,494 | 11,709 | 27,415 | 34,733 | 13,634 | 7,176 | 12,858 | 25,405 | 7,930 | 11,790 | 155,036 | 403,970 |
| 2015 | 38,034 | 40,526 | 14,067 | 34,801 | 58,075 | 13,910 | 8,216 | 10,115 | 19,088 | 16,657 | 15,933 | 131,544 | 421,058 |
| 2016 | 31,085 | 42,286 | 14,841 | 23,863 | 53,100 | 12,549 | 8,556 | 9,283 | 5,485 | 7,876 | 14,129 | 178,134 | 419,093 |
| 2017 | 59,501 | 44,357 | 15,482 | 18,269 | 45,780 | 12,184 | 6,478 | 9,916 | 3,859 | 13,312 | 12,947 | 215,049 | 484,369 |
| 2018 | 72,580 | 42,410 | 15,304 | 16,726 | 47,614 | 11,777 | 8,415 | 8,582 | 4,807 | 12,706 | 9,292 | 186,202 | 462,610 |
| 2019 | 84,676 | 41,585 | 13,964 | 19,642 | 66,218 | 9,860 | 3,525 | 8,500 | 2,023 | 7,813 | 7,891 | 262,917 | 563,295 |
| 2020[1] | 89,756 | 41,140 | 13,724 | 17,489 | 58,378 | 8,518 | 3,104 | 8,005 | 1,713 | 9,761 | 7,959 | 259,290 | 555,012 |
| 2021[2] | 92,065 | 46,319 | 15,726 | 21,971 | 37,738 | 7,451 | 2,367 | 10,482 | 1,529 | 17,959 | 8,620 | 217,182 | 520,817 |

[1] Preliminary.   [2] Estimate.   Source: Food and Agricultural Organization of the United Nations (FAO-UN)

# Petroleum

Crude oil is petroleum that is acquired directly from the ground. Crude oil was formed millions of years ago from the remains of tiny aquatic plants and animals that lived in ancient seas. Ancient societies such as the Persians, 10th century Sumatrans, and pre-Columbian Indians believed that crude oil had medicinal benefits. Around 4,000 BC in Mesopotamia, bitumen, a tarry crude, was used as caulking for ships, as a setting for jewels and mosaics, and as an adhesive to secure weapon handles. The walls of Babylon and the famed pyramids were held together with bitumen, and Egyptians used it for embalming. During the 19th century in America, an oil find was often met with dismay. Pioneers, who dug wells to find water or brine, were disappointed when they struck oil. It wasn't until 1854, with the invention of the kerosene lamp, that the first large-scale demand for petroleum emerged. Crude oil is a relatively abundant commodity. The world has produced approximately 650 billion barrels of oil, but another trillion barrels of proved reserves have yet to be extracted. Crude oil was the world's first trillion-dollar industry and accounts for the single largest product in world trade.

Futures and options on crude oil trade at the CME Group and at the ICE Futures Europe exchange in London. The CME trades two main types of crude oil: light sweet crude oil and Brent crude oil. The light sweet futures contract calls for the delivery of 1,000 barrels of crude oil in Cushing, Oklahoma. Light sweet crude is preferred by refiners because of its low sulfur content and relatively high yield of high-value products such as gasoline, diesel fuel, heating oil, and jet fuel. The Brent blend crude is based on a light, sweet North Sea crude oil. Brent blend crude production is approximately 500,000 barrels per day and is shipped from Sullom Voe in the Shetland Islands.

**Prices** – CME West-Texas Intermediate (WTI) crude oil prices (Barchart.com symbol CL) raced higher in Q1 of 2022 and posted a 14-year high in March at $130.50 a barrel. Crude prices surged after Russia invaded Ukraine in February and sparked global supply concerns after the U.S. and its European allies announced a ban on Russian crude oil. U.S. crude supplies had tightened even before the war began, with EIA U.S. crude oil inventories falling to a 4-year low in March. Crude prices mainly remained above $100 a barrel into Q2 on strength in Chinese energy demand as the country emerged from strict pandemic lockdowns. China's fuel demand in June rose to 90% of 2019 levels. Crude prices fell below $100 a barrel in July as the dollar rallied and energy demand concerns emerged. The Federal Reserve in 2022 began an aggressive interest-rate-hike campaign due to surging inflationary pressures, which boosted the dollar index to a 20-year high and raised concerns about a weaker U.S. economy and energy demand. The dollar index continued to post new 20-year highs into Q4, which weighed on most commodity prices. Crude prices remained under pressure in Q4 and posted a 1-year low in December at $70.08 a barrel. The Bank of England and European Central bank joined the Federal Reserve in raising interest rates, which darkened the global growth outlook and weighed on crude prices. Also, new Covid variants in China prompted the Chinese government to impose travel restrictions and lockdowns that sharply reduced the country's energy demand. In addition, U.S. crude supplies rebounded as EIA crude inventories climbed to a 1-1/2 year high in November. Crude oil finished 2022 up by +6.7% yr/yr at $80.26 a barrel.

**Supply** – World crude oil supply in 2021 rose by +1.8% yr/yr to 93.440 million bpd. U.S. crude oil production in 2021 fell by -0.6% yr/yr to 11.253 million barrels per day. Alaskan oil production in 2021 fell by -2.3% yr/yr to 437,323 barrels per day and was far below the peak level of 2.017 million barrels per day seen in 1988.

**Demand** – U.S. demand for crude oil in 2021 rose by +6.6% yr/yr to 15.146 million barrels per day. Most of that demand was for U.S. refinery production of petroleum products such as gasoline fuel, diesel fuel, aviation fuel, heating oil, kerosene, asphalt, and lubricants.

**Trade** – The U.S. is still dependent on imports of crude oil to meet its energy needs, but imports in 2021 rose by +4.1% yr/yr to 6.113 million barrels per day, down sharply from the 2005 record high of 10.126 million barrels. U.S. exports of crude oil in 2021 fell by -7.6% yr/yr to 2.962 million barrels per day.

### World Production of Crude Petroleum   In Thousands of Barrels Per Day

| Year | Canada | China | Iran | Iraq | Kuwait | Mexico | Nigeria | Russia | Saudi Arabia | United Arab Em | United States | Venezuela | World Total |
|---|---|---|---|---|---|---|---|---|---|---|---|---|---|
| 2012 | 3,783 | 4,477 | 3,597 | 3,027 | 2,835 | 2,911 | 2,507 | 10,580 | 11,484 | 3,389 | 10,083 | 2,675 | 88,595 |
| 2013 | 4,001 | 4,609 | 3,354 | 3,095 | 2,900 | 2,882 | 2,357 | 10,748 | 11,267 | 3,429 | 11,309 | 2,675 | 89,114 |
| 2014 | 4,322 | 4,737 | 3,482 | 3,420 | 2,892 | 2,789 | 2,402 | 10,836 | 11,324 | 3,531 | 13,077 | 2,675 | 91,672 |
| 2015 | 4,434 | 4,838 | 3,549 | 4,105 | 3,064 | 2,592 | 2,231 | 11,010 | 11,745 | 3,660 | 14,093 | 2,569 | 94,353 |
| 2016 | 4,516 | 4,569 | 4,432 | 4,512 | 3,184 | 2,459 | 1,934 | 11,220 | 12,152 | 3,753 | 13,732 | 2,322 | 94,834 |
| 2017 | 4,881 | 4,457 | 4,773 | 4,531 | 3,028 | 2,229 | 2,016 | 11,205 | 11,814 | 3,708 | 14,562 | 2,057 | 95,464 |
| 2018 | 5,286 | 4,469 | 4,552 | 4,693 | 3,062 | 2,064 | 1,984 | 11,359 | 12,095 | 3,770 | 16,772 | 1,531 | 98,127 |
| 2019 | 5,409 | 4,574 | 3,275 | 4,795 | 3,021 | 1,899 | 2,016 | 11,447 | 11,448 | 4,114 | 18,402 | 919 | 97,889 |
| 2020[1] | 5,170 | 4,611 | 2,984 | 4,163 | 2,738 | 1,917 | 1,867 | 10,471 | 10,828 | 3,765 | 17,687 | 545 | 91,760 |
| 2021[2] | 5,467 | 4,712 | 3,450 | 4,162 | 2,720 | 1,906 | 1,647 | 10,749 | 10,816 | 3,769 | 18,026 | 605 | 93,441 |

Includes lease condensate.   [1] Preliminary.   [2] Estimate.   *Source: Energy Information Administration, U.S. Department of Energy (EIA-DOE)*

# PETROLEUM

## World Imports of Crude Petroleum    In Thousands of Barrels Per Day

| Year | China | France | Germany | India | Italy | Japan | Korea, South | Nether-lands | Singa-pore | Spain | United Kingdom | United States | World Total |
|---|---|---|---|---|---|---|---|---|---|---|---|---|---|
| 2011 | 5,096 | 1,296 | 1,828 | 3,366 | 1,449 | 3,398 | 2,528 | 996 | 980 | 1,053 | 1,003 | 8,935 | 42,909 |
| 2012 | 5,428 | 1,139 | 1,881 | 3,746 | 1,377 | 3,429 | 2,583 | 1,008 | 974 | 1,184 | 1,083 | 8,527 | 43,509 |
| 2013 | 5,658 | 1,120 | 1,829 | 3,857 | 1,154 | 3,393 | 2,475 | 953 | 948 | 1,169 | 1,016 | 7,730 | 42,344 |
| 2014 | 6,193 | 1,082 | 1,805 | 3,785 | 1,059 | 3,205 | 2,525 | 959 | 954 | 1,192 | 940 | 7,344 | 42,072 |
| 2015 | 6,737 | 1,160 | 1,843 | 3,927 | 1,261 | 3,187 | 2,802 | 1,055 | 993 | 1,307 | 864 | 7,363 | 44,034 |
| 2016 | 7,599 | 1,105 | 1,837 | 4,267 | 1,226 | 3,138 | 2,931 | 1,094 | 956 | 1,292 | 794 | 7,850 | 45,275 |
| 2017 | 8,389 | 1,152 | 1,832 | 4,409 | 1,340 | 3,145 | 3,041 | 1,067 | 1,136 | 1,332 | 888 | 7,969 | 47,140 |
| 2018[1] | 9,238 | 1,065 | 1,721 | 4,530 | 1,253 | 3,013 | 3,034 | 1,097 | 1,121 | 1,365 | 892 | 7,768 | 47,536 |
| 2019[2] |  | 986 | 1,742 |  | 1,284 | 3,007 | 2,934 | 1,157 |  | 1,336 | 920 | 6,801 |  |
| 2020[2] |  | 663 | 1,663 |  | 1,009 | 2,419 | 2,646 | 994 |  | 1,099 | 705 | 5,877 |  |

Includes lease condensate.    [1] Preliminary.    [2] Estimate.    Source: Energy Information Administration, U.S. Department of Energy (EIA-DOE)

## World Exports of Crude Petroleum    In Thousands of Barrels Per Day

| Year | Angola | Canada | Iran | Iraq | Kuwait | Mexico | Nigeria | Norway | Russia | Saudi Arabia | United Arab Em | Vene-zuela | World Total |
|---|---|---|---|---|---|---|---|---|---|---|---|---|---|
| 2011 | 1,585 | 1,808 | 2,328 | 2,163 | 1,816 | 1,421 | 2,222 | 1,455 | 4,943 | 7,077 | 2,487 | 1,785 | 41,822 |
| 2012 | 1,663 | 1,933 | 1,455 | 2,414 | 2,070 | 1,333 | 2,288 | 1,314 | 4,759 | 7,397 | 2,571 | 1,741 | 41,930 |
| 2013 | 1,677 | 2,218 | 1,086 | 2,363 | 2,058 | 1,270 | 2,028 | 1,226 | 4,700 | 7,553 | 2,654 | 1,857 | 41,168 |
| 2014 | 1,632 | 2,382 | 1,084 | 2,518 | 1,995 | 1,208 | 2,120 | 1,294 | 4,500 | 7,120 | 2,651 | 1,729 | 40,640 |
| 2015 | 1,746 | 2,487 | 1,113 | 2,990 | 1,964 | 1,210 | 2,114 | 1,311 | 4,937 | 7,242 | 2,593 | 1,872 | 42,275 |
| 2016 | 1,658 | 2,907 | 2,313 | 3,916 | 1,859 | 1,277 | 1,847 | 1,398 | 5,080 | 7,599 | 2,457 | 1,645 | 45,376 |
| 2017 | 1,518 | 2,922 | 2,531 | 3,914 | 1,734 | 1,264 | 1,906 | 1,354 | 5,040 | 7,120 | 2,428 | 1,510 | 45,691 |
| 2018[1] | 1,367 | 3,177 | 2,231 | 3,976 | 1,838 | 1,283 | 1,889 | 1,243 | 5,196 | 7,341 | 2,427 | 1,003 | 46,656 |
| 2019[2] |  | 3,195 |  |  |  | 1,151 |  | 1,254 |  |  |  |  |  |
| 2020[2] |  | 3,017 |  |  |  | 1,192 |  | 1,494 |  |  |  |  |  |

Includes lease condensate.    [1] Preliminary.    [2] Estimate.    Source: Energy Information Administration, U.S. Department of Energy (EIA-DOE)

## World Production of Petroleum Products    In Thousands of Barrels Per Day

| Year | Brazil | Canada | China | Germany | India | Italy | Japan | Korea, South | Russia | Saudi Arabia | United Kingdom | United States | World Total |
|---|---|---|---|---|---|---|---|---|---|---|---|---|---|
| 2005 | 2,180 | 2,102 | 6,354 | 2,617 | 2,745 | 2,116 | 4,360 | 2,502 | 4,361 | 2,088 | 1,823 | 17,800 | 82,535 |
| 2006 | 2,167 | 2,069 | 6,495 | 2,580 | 2,896 | 2,050 | 4,262 | 2,559 | 4,548 | 2,289 | 1,757 | 17,975 | 82,611 |
| 2007 | 2,184 | 2,117 | 7,018 | 2,539 | 3,122 | 2,112 | 4,215 | 2,552 | 4,568 | 2,146 | 1,719 | 17,994 | 81,606 |
| 2008 | 2,007 | 2,029 | 7,069 | 2,484 | 3,226 | 1,971 | 4,136 | 2,535 | 4,803 | 2,103 | 1,678 | 18,146 | 81,772 |
| 2009 | 2,237 | 1,962 | 8,209 | 2,333 | 3,836 | 1,823 | 3,863 | 2,476 | 4,935 | 1,935 | 1,570 | 17,882 | 82,410 |
| 2010 | 2,467 | 2,015 | 8,737 | 2,197 | 4,220 | 1,886 | 3,857 | 2,537 | 5,299 | 1,935 | 1,532 | 18,453 | 84,163 |
| 2011 | 2,472 | 1,905 | 9,298 | 2,183 | 4,356 | 1,791 | 3,658 | 2,686 | 5,390 | 1,901 | 1,578 | 18,673 | 84,687 |
| 2012 | 2,555 | 1,926 | 9,880 | 2,207 | 4,506 | 1,693 | 3,645 | 2,789 | 5,516 | 1,971 | 1,436 | 18,564 | 85,182 |
| 2013[1] | 2,810 | 1,893 | 10,345 | 2,151 | 4,776 | 1,506 | 3,689 | 2,697 | 5,770 | 1,884 | 1,380 | 19,106 | 86,426 |
| 2014[2] | 2,899 | 1,877 | 10,852 | 2,126 | 4,793 | 1,418 | 3,536 | 2,772 | 6,174 | 2,221 | 1,301 | 19,654 | 87,766 |

Includes lease condensate.    [1] Preliminary.    [2] Estimate.    Source: Energy Information Administration, U.S. Department of Energy (EIA-DOE)

## Supply and Disposition of Crude Oil in the United States    In Thousands of Barrels Per Day

| | Supply | | | | | | Stock | | Disposition | | Ending Stocks | | |
|---|---|---|---|---|---|---|---|---|---|---|---|---|---|
| | Field Production | | Imports | | | Unaccounted for Crude Oil | Withdrawal[3] | | Refinery | | | | Other |
| Year | Total Domestic | Alaskan | Total | SPR[2] | Other | | SPR[2] | Other | Inputs | Exports | Total | SPR[2] | Primary |
| | In Thousands of Barrels Per Day | | | | | | | | | | In Millions of Barrels | | |
| 2014 | 8,793 | 496 | 7,344 | ---- | ---- | ---- | ---- | ---- | 15,848 | 351 | 1,052 | 691 | 361 |
| 2015 | 9,442 | 483 | 7,363 | ---- | ---- | ---- | ---- | ---- | 16,188 | 465 | 1,144 | 695 | 449 |
| 2016 | 8,848 | 490 | 7,850 | ---- | ---- | ---- | ---- | ---- | 16,187 | 591 | 1,180 | 695 | 485 |
| 2017 | 9,359 | 495 | 7,969 | ---- | ---- | ---- | ---- | ---- | 16,590 | 1,158 | 1,084 | 663 | 422 |
| 2018 | 10,953 | 479 | 7,768 | ---- | ---- | ---- | ---- | ---- | 16,969 | 2,048 | 1,092 | 649 | 443 |
| 2019 | 12,315 | 466 | 6,801 | ---- | ---- | ---- | ---- | ---- | 16,563 | 2,982 | 1,068 | 635 | 433 |
| 2020 | 11,318 | 448 | 5,875 | ---- | ---- | ---- | ---- | ---- | 14,212 | 3,206 | 1,124 | 638 | 485 |
| 2021[1] | 11,254 | 437 | 6,114 | ---- | ---- | ---- | ---- | ---- | 15,147 | 2,963 | 1,015 | 594 | 421 |

[1] Preliminary.    [2] Strategic Petroleum Reserve.    [3] A negative number indicates a decrease in stocks and a positive number indicates an increase.
Source: Energy Information Administration, U.S. Department of Energy (EIA-DOE)

# PETROLEUM

## Crude Petroleum Refinery Operations Ratio[2] in the United States — In Percent of Capacity

| Year | Jan. | Feb. | Mar. | Apr. | May | June | July | Aug. | Sept. | Oct. | Nov. | Dec. | Average |
|---|---|---|---|---|---|---|---|---|---|---|---|---|---|
| 2013 | 83.8 | 81.7 | 84.0 | 85.8 | 88.2 | 91.7 | 92.6 | 91.5 | 90.7 | 86.9 | 90.6 | 92.0 | 88.3 |
| 2014 | 87.2 | 86.6 | 85.8 | 90.7 | 90.2 | 90.3 | 94.6 | 93.7 | 91.8 | 87.7 | 92.0 | 94.2 | 90.4 |
| 2015 | 88.4 | 87.6 | 88.7 | 92.0 | 92.5 | 94.0 | 95.1 | 93.9 | 90.5 | 86.6 | 91.8 | 92.6 | 91.1 |
| 2016 | 89.4 | 88.3 | 88.8 | 88.6 | 89.9 | 91.1 | 92.2 | 92.1 | 90.4 | 85.4 | 89.6 | 91.3 | 89.8 |
| 2017 | 88.4 | 85.0 | 88.0 | 92.7 | 94.3 | 94.3 | 95.0 | 92.8 | 85.3 | 88.3 | 92.5 | 94.7 | 90.9 |
| 2018 | 91.1 | 88.1 | 91.3 | 92.0 | 93.3 | 97.0 | 95.1 | 96.6 | 93.5 | 90.0 | 94.1 | 95.4 | 93.1 |
| 2019 | 91.1 | 85.8 | 86.1 | 88.8 | 90.6 | 94.2 | 94.1 | 94.9 | 89.0 | 85.8 | 90.7 | 92.5 | 90.3 |
| 2020 | 88.8 | 86.7 | 83.1 | 70.2 | 72.0 | 76.3 | 79.6 | 78.8 | 76.9 | 75.3 | 79.3 | 79.1 | 78.8 |
| 2021 | 82.6 | 70.6 | 81.9 | 86.3 | 89.0 | 92.4 | 90.9 | 90.4 | 87.2 | 86.1 | 89.1 | 91.2 | 86.5 |
| 2022[1] | 88.7 | 88.5 | 91.3 | 89.6 | 92.9 | 95.2 | 94.0 | 94.1 | 92.5 | 90.3 | 94.1 | 88.0 | 91.6 |

[1] Preliminary. [2] Based on the ration of the daily average crude runs to stills to the rated capacity of refineries per day. *Source: Energy Information Administration, U.S. Department of Energy (EIA-DOE)*

## Crude Oil Refinery Inputs in the United States — In Thousands of Barrels Per Day

| Year | Jan. | Feb. | Mar. | Apr. | May | June | July | Aug. | Sept. | Oct. | Nov. | Dec. | Average |
|---|---|---|---|---|---|---|---|---|---|---|---|---|---|
| 2013 | 14,567 | 14,230 | 14,703 | 14,864 | 15,305 | 15,833 | 16,042 | 15,793 | 15,636 | 14,991 | 15,633 | 16,069 | 15,306 |
| 2014 | 15,311 | 15,128 | 15,116 | 15,864 | 15,946 | 15,817 | 16,534 | 16,460 | 16,074 | 15,361 | 16,043 | 16,469 | 15,844 |
| 2015 | 15,456 | 15,342 | 15,640 | 16,273 | 16,402 | 16,701 | 16,879 | 16,700 | 16,168 | 15,440 | 16,458 | 16,742 | 16,183 |
| 2016 | 15,951 | 15,843 | 16,082 | 15,920 | 16,237 | 16,433 | 16,621 | 16,593 | 16,340 | 15,454 | 16,235 | 16,516 | 16,186 |
| 2017 | 16,118 | 15,493 | 16,048 | 16,954 | 17,222 | 17,204 | 17,317 | 16,981 | 15,460 | 16,061 | 16,840 | 17,274 | 16,581 |
| 2018 | 16,599 | 15,936 | 16,665 | 16,766 | 16,969 | 17,666 | 17,357 | 17,623 | 16,991 | 16,412 | 17,162 | 17,409 | 16,963 |
| 2019 | 16,783 | 15,846 | 15,935 | 16,341 | 16,719 | 17,236 | 17,175 | 17,297 | 16,403 | 15,681 | 16,482 | 16,793 | 16,558 |
| 2020 | 16,229 | 15,865 | 15,230 | 12,772 | 12,968 | 13,734 | 14,334 | 14,152 | 13,573 | 13,445 | 14,124 | 14,140 | 14,214 |
| 2021 | 14,542 | 12,371 | 14,387 | 15,162 | 15,596 | 16,190 | 15,852 | 15,726 | 15,232 | 15,045 | 15,684 | 15,757 | 15,129 |
| 2022[1] | 15,451 | 15,376 | 15,823 | 15,612 | 16,131 | 16,514 | 16,318 | 16,381 | 16,075 | 15,719 | 16,384 | 15,496 | 15,940 |

[1] Preliminary. *Source: Energy Information Administration, U.S. Department of Energy (EIA-DOE)*

## Production of Major Refined Petroleum Products in Continental United States — In Millions of Barrels

| Year | Asphalt | Aviation Gasoline | Fuel Oil Distillate | Fuel Oil Residual | Gasoline | Jet Fuel | Kerosene | Natural Gas Plant Liquids | Lubricants | Liquified Gasses Total | at L.P.G.[2] | AT L.P.G.[3] |
|---|---|---|---|---|---|---|---|---|---|---|---|---|
| 2013 | 117.0 | 4.2 | 1,727.0 | 170.4 | 3,347 | 547.8 | 4.0 | 809.0 | 59.8 | 1,162.2 | 933.1 | 229.1 |
| 2014 | 118.7 | 4.3 | 1,463.7 | 93.9 | 3,257 | 536.6 | 3.2 | 940.7 | 45.2 | 1,322.3 | 1,081.9 | 240.3 |
| 2015 | 125.4 | 4.2 | 1,451.1 | 94.7 | 3,344 | 561.6 | 2.4 | 1,038.1 | 49.4 | 1,418.1 | 1,194.6 | 223.4 |
| 2016 | 128.8 | 4.1 | 1,419.1 | 130.6 | 3,414 | 587.9 | 2.6 | 1,114.4 | 47.4 | 1,501.5 | 1,272.9 | 228.6 |
| 2017 | 128.7 | 4.1 | 1,437.3 | 130.9 | 3,401 | 613.8 | 1.6 | 1,363.7 | 39.7 | 1,593.1 | 1,363.7 | 229.4 |
| 2018 | 120.1 | 4.4 | 1,508.8 | 117.4 | 3,402 | 624.5 | 1.9 | 1,090.2 | 41.0 | 1,818.8 | 1,587.4 | 231.4 |
| 2019 | 116.7 | 4.5 | 1,875.0 | 131.8 | 3,685 | 655.7 | 3.7 | 1,145.7 | 60.9 | 1,982.1 | 1,760.9 | 221.1 |
| 2020 | 117.5 | 3.7 | 1,734.9 | 69.8 | 3,199 | 372.6 | 4.4 | 1,170.0 | 55.6 | 2,088.8 | 1,889.0 | 199.8 |
| 2021 | 135.2 | 4.3 | 1,439.2 | 114.1 | 3,210 | 500.5 | 1.9 | 1,134.1 | 37.8 | 2,090.8 | 1,970.0 | 120.8 |
| 2022[1] | 136.0 | 4.4 | 1,446.3 | 125.3 | 3,204 | 568.8 | 1.4 | 1,209.1 | 40.8 | 2,275.5 | 2,147.2 | 128.3 |

[1] Preliminary. [2] Gas processing plants. [3] Refineries. *Source: Energy Information Administration, U.S. Department of Energy (EIA-DOE)*

## Stocks of Petroleum and Products in the United States on January 1 — In Millions of Barrels

| Year | Crude Petroleum | Strategic Reserve | Total | Asphalt | Aviation Gasoline | Fuel Oil Distillate | Fuel Oil Residual | Finished Gasoline | Jet Fuel | Kerosene | Gases[2] | Lubricants | Motor Gasoline Total | Motor Gasoline Finished[3] |
|---|---|---|---|---|---|---|---|---|---|---|---|---|---|---|
| 2014 | 1,023.2 | 696.0 | 291.3 | 21.4 | 0.9 | 127.5 | 38.1 | 39.7 | 37.2 | 1.9 | 112.7 | 10.1 | 228 | 40 |
| 2015 | 1,051.8 | 691.0 | 286.9 | 21.2 | 1.1 | 136.3 | 33.7 | 30.6 | 38.3 | 2.1 | 154.8 | 11.2 | 240 | 31 |
| 2016 | 1,144.3 | 695.1 | 325.1 | 24.6 | 0.9 | 161.3 | 42.1 | 28.5 | 40.4 | 2.6 | 176.7 | 13.5 | 235 | 28 |
| 2017 | 1,179.7 | 695.1 | 329.7 | 22.9 | 1.0 | 166.1 | 41.5 | 28.6 | 43.0 | 2.3 | 178.4 | 12.4 | 239 | 29 |
| 2018 | 1,084.5 | 662.8 | 291.6 | 21.5 | 1.0 | 145.6 | 29.4 | 24.6 | 41.3 | 2.1 | 184.8 | 12.0 | 237 | 25 |
| 2019 | 1,091.6 | 649.1 | 294.3 | 27.0 | 1.0 | 140.0 | 28.3 | 25.7 | 41.6 | 2.6 | 188.5 | 14.0 | 221 | 26 |
| 2020 | 1,067.9 | 635.0 | 291.9 | 23.1 | 1.1 | 140.0 | 30.9 | 26.0 | 40.5 | 2.9 | 208.8 | 12.7 | 228 | 26 |
| 2021 | 1,123.3 | 638.1 | 303.9 | 23.0 | 1.1 | 160.4 | 30.2 | 25.3 | 38.6 | 2.7 | 226.9 | 9.7 | 218 | 25 |
| 2022 | 1,015.1 | 593.7 | 260.6 | 23.9 | 1.3 | 129.9 | 25.4 | 17.7 | 35.8 | 2.2 | 186.3 | 12.8 | 214 | 18 |
| 2023[1] | 801.6 | 372.2 | 256.2 | 25.7 | 1.3 | 118.8 | 30.7 | 17.4 | 35.0 | 2.1 | 209.2 | 13.3 | 207 | 17 |

[1] Preliminary. [2] Includes ethane & ethylene at plants and refineries. [3] Includes oxygenated. *Source: Energy Information Administration, U.S. Department of Energy (EIA-DOE)*

# PETROLEUM

## Stocks of Crude Petroleum in the United States, on First of Month      In Millions of Barrels

| Year | Jan. | Feb. | Mar. | Apr. | May | June | July | Aug. | Sept. | Oct. | Nov. | Dec. |
|---|---|---|---|---|---|---|---|---|---|---|---|---|
| 2013 | 1,073.5 | 1,080.9 | 1,088.1 | 1,091.8 | 1,088.2 | 1,071.7 | 1,062.5 | 1,059.5 | 1,067.1 | 1,079.8 | 1,072.5 | 1,053.6 |
| 2014 | 1,059.7 | 1,069.3 | 1,079.7 | 1,086.5 | 1,085.0 | 1,074.9 | 1,059.7 | 1,051.6 | 1,051.9 | 1,073.0 | 1,078.5 | 1,084.7 |
| 2015 | 1,112.4 | 1,139.0 | 1,165.8 | 1,174.3 | 1,171.7 | 1,163.4 | 1,150.6 | 1,152.9 | 1,155.9 | 1,181.8 | 1,182.5 | 1,176.5 |
| 2016 | 1,166.9 | 1,187.3 | 1,199.9 | 1,204.4 | 1,207.0 | 1,196.0 | 1,188.6 | 1,181.8 | 1,166.6 | 1,186.3 | 1,185.8 | 1,179.7 |
| 2017 | 1,201.9 | 1,220.2 | 1,230.1 | 1,213.1 | 1,201.3 | 1,180.7 | 1,162.3 | 1,138.8 | 1,143.2 | 1,128.7 | 1,114.3 | 1,084.5 |
| 2018 | 1,085.0 | 1,089.3 | 1,090.4 | 1,100.5 | 1,094.4 | 1,075.2 | 1,069.7 | 1,067.6 | 1,076.7 | 1,088.6 | 1,098.9 | 1,091.6 |
| 2019 | 1,098.1 | 1,100.8 | 1,108.0 | 1,118.4 | 1,125.9 | 1,108.3 | 1,086.4 | 1,074.9 | 1,070.4 | 1,084.5 | 1,080.9 | 1,067.7 |
| 2020 | 1,075.2 | 1,087.5 | 1,118.3 | 1,166.9 | 1,169.9 | 1,188.7 | 1,176.3 | 1,151.9 | 1,139.9 | 1,132.5 | 1,138.8 | 1,123.6 |
| 2021 | 1,114.4 | 1,131.6 | 1,140.2 | 1,122.6 | 1,104.6 | 1,069.4 | 1,060.0 | 1,042.8 | 1,038.1 | 1,047.2 | 1,034.9 | 1,014.9 |
| 2022[1] | 1,002.6 | 988.0 | 980.5 | 967.0 | 937.4 | 910.8 | 892.2 | 864.8 | 845.2 | 838.0 | 804.8 | 798.2 |

[1] Preliminary.   Source: Energy Information Administration; U.S. Department of Energy

## Production of Crude Petroleum in the United States      In Thousands of Barrels Per Day

| Year | Jan. | Feb. | Mar. | Apr. | May | June | July | Aug. | Sept. | Oct. | Nov. | Dec. | Average |
|---|---|---|---|---|---|---|---|---|---|---|---|---|---|
| 2013 | 7,025 | 7,144 | 7,208 | 7,355 | 7,316 | 7,268 | 7,483 | 7,531 | 7,784 | 7,699 | 7,873 | 7,899 | 7,465 |
| 2014 | 8,051 | 8,136 | 8,274 | 8,573 | 8,612 | 8,718 | 8,782 | 8,886 | 9,041 | 9,221 | 9,303 | 9,467 | 8,755 |
| 2015 | 9,385 | 9,511 | 9,578 | 9,650 | 9,464 | 9,344 | 9,430 | 9,400 | 9,460 | 9,388 | 9,318 | 9,251 | 9,431 |
| 2016 | 9,197 | 9,055 | 9,081 | 8,866 | 8,824 | 8,671 | 8,635 | 8,670 | 8,519 | 8,787 | 8,888 | 8,778 | 8,831 |
| 2017 | 8,861 | 9,101 | 9,162 | 9,100 | 9,183 | 9,108 | 9,235 | 9,248 | 9,512 | 9,653 | 10,071 | 9,973 | 9,351 |
| 2018 | 10,018 | 10,281 | 10,504 | 10,510 | 10,460 | 10,649 | 10,891 | 11,361 | 11,498 | 11,631 | 11,999 | 12,038 | 10,987 |
| 2019 | 11,848 | 11,653 | 11,899 | 12,125 | 12,141 | 12,179 | 11,896 | 12,475 | 12,572 | 12,771 | 12,966 | 12,910 | 12,286 |
| 2020 | 12,852 | 12,842 | 12,797 | 11,914 | 9,713 | 10,442 | 11,006 | 10,577 | 10,921 | 10,457 | 11,196 | 11,169 | 11,324 |
| 2021 | 11,124 | 9,925 | 11,326 | 11,305 | 11,356 | 11,356 | 11,347 | 11,277 | 10,918 | 11,569 | 11,790 | 11,634 | 11,244 |
| 2022[1] | 11,369 | 11,316 | 11,701 | 11,668 | 11,629 | 11,797 | 11,844 | 12,002 | 12,337 | 12,410 | 12,375 | 12,087 | 11,878 |

[1] Preliminary.   Source: Energy Information Administration, U.S. Department of Energy (EIA-DOE)

## U.S. Foreign Trade of Petroleum and Products      In Thousands of Barrels Per Day

| | Exports | | Imports | | | | |
|---|---|---|---|---|---|---|---|
| Year | Total[2] | Petroleum Products | Crude | Petroleum Products | Distillate Fuel Oil | Residual Fuel Oil | Net Imports[3] |
| 2012 | 3,205 | 3,308 | 8,527 | 1,689 | 126 | 256 | 7,393 |
| 2013 | 3,621 | 3,789 | 7,730 | 1,749 | 155 | 225 | 6,237 |
| 2014 | 4,176 | 4,247 | 7,344 | 1,529 | 195 | 173 | 5,065 |
| 2015 | 4,738 | 4,888 | 7,363 | 1,694 | 200 | 192 | 4,711 |
| 2016 | 5,261 | 5,469 | 7,850 | 1,854 | 147 | 205 | 4,795 |
| 2017 | 6,376 | 6,132 | 7,969 | 1,836 | 151 | 189 | 3,768 |
| 2018 | 7,601 | 6,502 | 7,768 | 1,788 | 175 | 211 | 2,341 |
| 2019 | 8,471 | 6,587 | 6,801 | 1,989 | 202 | 149 | 670 |
| 2020 | 8,498 | 6,554 | 5,875 | 1,604 | 218 | 166 | -635 |
| 2021[1] | 8,536 | 6,900 | 6,114 | 1,885 | 288 | 186 | -62 |

[1] Preliminary.   [2] Includes crude oil.   [3] Equals imports minus exports.
Source: Energy Information Administration, U.S. Department of Energy (EIA-DOE)

## Domestic First Purchase Price of Crude Petroleum at Wells[2]      In U.S. Dollars Per Barrel

| Year | Jan. | Feb. | Mar. | Apr. | May | June | July | Aug. | Sept. | Oct. | Nov. | Dec. | Average |
|---|---|---|---|---|---|---|---|---|---|---|---|---|---|
| 2013 | 95.00 | 95.01 | 95.54 | 94.41 | 94.75 | 93.82 | 101.41 | 102.96 | 102.32 | 96.18 | 88.70 | 91.85 | 96.00 |
| 2014 | 89.57 | 96.86 | 96.17 | 96.49 | 95.74 | 98.68 | 96.70 | 90.72 | 86.87 | 78.84 | 71.07 | 54.86 | 87.71 |
| 2015 | 43.06 | 44.35 | 42.66 | 49.30 | 54.38 | 55.88 | 47.70 | 39.98 | 41.60 | 42.33 | 38.19 | 32.26 | 44.31 |
| 2016 | 27.02 | 25.51 | 31.87 | 35.59 | 41.02 | 43.96 | 40.70 | 40.46 | 40.54 | 45.00 | 41.65 | 47.12 | 38.37 |
| 2017 | 48.19 | 49.41 | 46.39 | 47.23 | 45.19 | 42.19 | 43.42 | 44.96 | 47.17 | 49.13 | 55.19 | 56.98 | 47.95 |
| 2018 | 62.25 | 61.20 | 60.68 | 63.50 | 66.16 | 62.80 | 67.00 | 62.64 | 63.55 | 65.18 | 55.65 | 47.72 | 61.53 |
| 2019 | 47.85 | 52.51 | 57.47 | 63.01 | 59.68 | 54.22 | 56.47 | 53.63 | 55.07 | 53.14 | 54.96 | 58.41 | 55.54 |
| 2020 | 56.55 | 49.66 | 31.01 | 15.18 | 18.02 | 33.81 | 37.44 | 39.37 | 36.82 | 36.39 | 38.25 | 43.92 | 36.37 |
| 2021 | 49.47 | 56.44 | 60.43 | 59.87 | 62.80 | 68.58 | 70.12 | 65.68 | 69.09 | 78.51 | 76.45 | 70.56 | 65.67 |
| 2022[1] | 80.33 | 89.41 | 107.07 | 103.32 | 108.29 | 113.77 | 100.84 | 93.76 | 84.62 | 86.61 | 84.43 | | 95.68 |

[1] Preliminary.   [2] Buyers posted prices.   Source: Energy Information Administration, U.S. Department of Energy (EIA-DOE)

# PETROLEUM

### Refiner Sales Prices of Residual Fuel Oil  In U.S. Dollars Per Gallon

| Year | Jan. | Feb. | Mar. | Apr. | May | June | July | Aug. | Sept. | Oct. | Nov. | Dec. | Average |
|---|---|---|---|---|---|---|---|---|---|---|---|---|---|
| 2015 | 0.936 | 1.150 | 1.093 | 1.124 | 1.198 | 1.175 | 1.080 | 0.797 | 0.819 | 0.812 | 0.766 | 0.552 | 0.959 |
| 2016 | 0.477 | 0.475 | 0.582 | 0.633 | 0.729 | 0.850 | 0.876 | 0.842 | 0.846 | 0.961 | 0.920 | 1.024 | 0.768 |
| 2017 | 1.099 | 1.174 | 1.103 | 1.038 | 0.986 | 0.937 | 1.026 | 1.042 | 1.150 | 1.153 | 1.302 | 1.254 | 1.105 |
| 2018 | 1.301 | 1.221 | 1.227 | 1.311 | 1.462 | 1.487 | 1.543 | 1.499 | 1.520 | 1.620 | 1.360 | 1.252 | 1.400 |
| 2019 | 1.626 | 1.808 | W | W | W | W | 1.455 | 1.331 | W | 1.535 | 1.681 | 1.758 | 1.599 |
| 2020 | 1.788 | 1.673 | 1.188 | 0.796 | 0.792 | 1.018 | 1.153 | 1.189 | 1.098 | 1.078 | 1.164 | 1.351 | 1.191 |
| 2021 | 1.491 | 1.583 | 1.780 | 1.780 | 1.828 | 1.909 | 1.852 | 1.842 | 1.913 | 2.124 | 2.065 | 1.940 | 1.842 |
| 2022[1] | 2.210 | 2.415 | 2.932 | | | | | | | | | | 2.519 |

Sulfur 1% or less, excluding taxes.  [1] Preliminary.  *Source: Energy Information Administration, U.S. Department of Energy (EIA-DOE)*

### Refiner Sales Prices of No. 2 Fuel Oil  In U.S. Dollars Per Gallon

| Year | Jan. | Feb. | Mar. | Apr. | May | June | July | Aug. | Sept. | Oct. | Nov. | Dec. | Average |
|---|---|---|---|---|---|---|---|---|---|---|---|---|---|
| 2015 | 1.669 | 1.850 | 1.847 | 1.740 | 1.852 | 1.813 | 1.654 | 1.461 | 1.438 | 1.411 | 1.356 | 1.126 | 1.601 |
| 2016 | 0.976 | 0.948 | 1.070 | 1.113 | 1.291 | 1.404 | 1.305 | 1.307 | 1.341 | 1.443 | 1.386 | 1.507 | 1.258 |
| 2017 | 1.560 | 1.553 | 1.495 | 1.499 | 1.447 | 1.375 | 1.392 | 1.522 | 1.668 | 1.695 | 1.781 | 1.841 | 1.569 |
| 2018 | 1.990 | 1.889 | 1.848 | 1.982 | 2.143 | 2.089 | 2.079 | 2.114 | 2.214 | 2.281 | 2.098 | 1.796 | 2.044 |
| 2019 | 1.813 | 1.907 | 1.958 | 1.993 | 1.989 | 1.824 | 1.847 | 1.795 | 1.901 | 1.926 | 1.884 | 1.919 | 1.896 |
| 2020 | 1.863 | 1.627 | 1.238 | 0.872 | 0.795 | 1.002 | 1.152 | 1.179 | 1.091 | 1.089 | 1.156 | 1.341 | 1.200 |
| 2021 | 1.481 | 1.667 | 1.726 | 1.700 | 1.806 | 1.927 | 1.931 | 1.885 | 2.041 | 2.356 | 2.267 | 2.111 | 1.908 |
| 2022[1] | 2.438 | 2.742 | 3.479 | | | | | | | | | | 2.886 |

Excluding taxes.  [1] Preliminary.  *Source: Energy Information Administration, U.S. Department of Energy (EIA-DOE)*

### Refiner Sales Prices of No. 2 Diesel Fuel  In U.S. Dollars Per Gallon

| Year | Jan. | Feb. | Mar. | Apr. | May | June | July | Aug. | Sept. | Oct. | Nov. | Dec. | Average |
|---|---|---|---|---|---|---|---|---|---|---|---|---|---|
| 2015 | 1.616 | 1.861 | 1.815 | 1.805 | 1.973 | 1.881 | 1.729 | 1.562 | 1.551 | 1.572 | 1.456 | 1.176 | 1.666 |
| 2016 | 1.015 | 1.043 | 1.189 | 1.251 | 1.432 | 1.531 | 1.426 | 1.440 | 1.471 | 1.592 | 1.469 | 1.606 | 1.372 |
| 2017 | 1.636 | 1.641 | 1.581 | 1.627 | 1.552 | 1.465 | 1.533 | 1.681 | 1.847 | 1.852 | 1.936 | 1.918 | 1.689 |
| 2018 | 2.042 | 1.972 | 1.952 | 2.099 | 2.258 | 2.203 | 2.192 | 2.203 | 2.282 | 2.379 | 2.130 | 1.794 | 2.126 |
| 2019 | 1.789 | 1.950 | 2.020 | 2.100 | 2.106 | 1.874 | 1.938 | 1.865 | 1.955 | 1.984 | 1.974 | 1.943 | 1.958 |
| 2020 | 1.858 | 1.671 | 1.278 | 0.908 | 0.878 | 1.135 | 1.254 | 1.275 | 1.195 | 1.215 | 1.315 | 1.475 | 1.288 |
| 2021 | 1.580 | 1.806 | 1.956 | 1.911 | 2.072 | 2.147 | 2.182 | 2.146 | 2.240 | 2.504 | 2.454 | 2.273 | 2.106 |
| 2022[1] | 2.550 | 2.830 | 3.582 | | | | | | | | | | 2.987 |

Excluding taxes.  [1] Preliminary.  *Source: Energy Information Administration, U.S. Department of Energy (EIA-DOE)*

### Refiner Sales Prices of Kerosine-Type Jet Fuel  In U.S. Dollars Per Gallon

| Year | Jan. | Feb. | Mar. | Apr. | May | June | July | Aug. | Sept. | Oct. | Nov. | Dec. | Average |
|---|---|---|---|---|---|---|---|---|---|---|---|---|---|
| 2015 | 1.612 | 1.722 | 1.731 | 1.709 | 1.933 | 1.813 | 1.655 | 1.479 | 1.443 | 1.451 | 1.400 | 1.207 | 1.596 |
| 2016 | 1.022 | 1.017 | 1.100 | 1.155 | 1.311 | 1.428 | 1.354 | 1.313 | 1.366 | 1.471 | 1.406 | 1.511 | 1.288 |
| 2017 | 1.561 | 1.592 | 1.520 | 1.545 | 1.459 | 1.378 | 1.436 | 1.587 | 1.771 | 1.704 | 1.795 | 1.846 | 1.600 |
| 2018 | 1.969 | 1.911 | 1.893 | 2.032 | 2.175 | 2.152 | 2.140 | 2.148 | 2.214 | 2.296 | 2.100 | 1.811 | 2.070 |
| 2019 | 1.822 | 1.925 | 1.960 | 2.022 | 2.061 | 1.879 | 1.938 | 1.864 | 1.898 | 1.931 | 1.922 | 1.932 | 1.930 |
| 2020 | 1.891 | 1.613 | 1.189 | 0.703 | 0.690 | 1.002 | 1.144 | 1.162 | 1.076 | 1.107 | 1.180 | 1.353 | 1.176 |
| 2021 | 1.456 | 1.599 | 1.720 | 1.688 | 1.790 | 1.871 | 1.946 | 1.922 | 2.008 | 2.281 | 2.283 | 2.145 | 1.892 |
| 2022[1] | 2.422 | 2.655 | 3.285 | | | | | | | | | | 2.787 |

Excluding taxes.  [1] Preliminary.  *Source: Energy Information Administration, U.S. Department of Energy (EIA-DOE)*

### Refiner Sales Prices of Propane[2]  In U.S. Dollars Per Gallon

| Year | Jan. | Feb. | Mar. | Apr. | May | June | July | Aug. | Sept. | Oct. | Nov. | Dec. | Average |
|---|---|---|---|---|---|---|---|---|---|---|---|---|---|
| 2015 | 0.713 | 0.748 | 0.689 | 0.566 | 0.475 | 0.404 | 0.405 | 0.402 | 0.469 | 0.524 | 0.505 | 0.499 | 0.533 |
| 2016 | 0.460 | 0.470 | 0.497 | 0.458 | 0.511 | 0.497 | 0.476 | 0.453 | 0.494 | 0.608 | 0.588 | 0.703 | 0.518 |
| 2017 | 0.788 | 0.792 | 0.671 | 0.641 | 0.631 | 0.585 | 0.634 | 0.742 | 0.864 | 0.942 | 0.997 | 0.991 | 0.773 |
| 2018 | 0.990 | 0.889 | 0.827 | 0.792 | 0.867 | 0.807 | 0.854 | 0.907 | 0.951 | 0.948 | 0.826 | 0.798 | 0.871 |
| 2019 | 0.775 | 0.772 | 0.754 | 0.660 | 0.595 | 0.493 | 0.478 | 0.458 | 0.477 | 0.544 | 0.655 | 0.632 | 0.608 |
| 2020 | 0.557 | 0.530 | 0.410 | 0.378 | 0.454 | 0.514 | 0.507 | 0.536 | 0.516 | 0.597 | 0.630 | 0.725 | 0.530 |
| 2021 | 0.922 | 1.032 | 0.985 | 0.849 | 0.824 | 0.950 | 1.075 | 1.110 | 1.280 | 1.460 | 1.329 | 1.140 | 1.080 |
| 2022[1] | 1.249 | 1.376 | 1.483 | | | | | | | | | | 1.369 |

[1] Preliminary.  [2] Consumer Grade, Excluding taxes.  *Source: Energy Information Administration, U.S. Department of Energy (EIA-DOE)*

# PETROLEUM

**WTI CRUDE OIL - NYMEX**
Weekly Nearest Futures as of 03/31/2023

WEEKLY NEAREST FUTURES
As of 03/31/2023
Chart High 130.50 on 03/07/2022
Chart Low -40.32 on 04/20/2020

Nearby Futures through Last Trading Day.

## Volume of Trading of Crude Oil Futures in New York    In Thousands of Contracts

| Year | Jan. | Feb. | Mar. | Apr. | May | June | July | Aug. | Sept. | Oct. | Nov. | Dec. | Total |
|---|---|---|---|---|---|---|---|---|---|---|---|---|---|
| 2013 | 12,028 | 11,540 | 10,515 | 13,354 | 13,825 | 13,111 | 15,384 | 12,849 | 11,139 | 13,792 | 10,569 | 9,586 | 147,691 |
| 2014 | 11,162 | 9,862 | 11,700 | 11,467 | 10,283 | 11,398 | 13,174 | 11,016 | 12,824 | 15,939 | 12,204 | 14,119 | 145,147 |
| 2015 | 16,514 | 20,263 | 17,884 | 17,638 | 13,553 | 13,995 | 14,863 | 19,197 | 16,605 | 17,484 | 16,145 | 18,064 | 202,202 |
| 2016 | 21,710 | 25,607 | 22,954 | 23,614 | 21,494 | 20,790 | 18,841 | 23,051 | 24,332 | 23,019 | 27,375 | 23,981 | 276,768 |
| 2017 | 22,430 | 20,528 | 26,417 | 21,225 | 27,527 | 29,141 | 27,618 | 34,725 | 27,571 | 25,031 | 27,636 | 20,205 | 310,053 |
| 2018 | 28,504 | 26,784 | 25,003 | 27,977 | 30,951 | 28,578 | 23,056 | 19,661 | 21,113 | 24,507 | 27,571 | 22,909 | 306,613 |
| 2019 | 25,965 | 22,698 | 23,824 | 27,629 | 28,524 | 23,436 | 22,825 | 27,902 | 26,970 | 23,298 | 19,066 | 19,327 | 291,465 |
| 2020 | 26,079 | 28,131 | 40,910 | 39,351 | 21,325 | 19,172 | 16,204 | 15,728 | 17,103 | 17,063 | 17,680 | 15,434 | 274,180 |
| 2021 | 18,924 | 22,104 | 26,039 | 18,813 | 19,084 | 20,264 | 20,471 | 18,842 | 18,938 | 24,524 | 22,982 | 17,330 | 248,314 |
| 2022 | 20,272 | 23,349 | 23,658 | 14,055 | 13,854 | 16,135 | 16,082 | 17,553 | 15,268 | 14,319 | 16,388 | 14,786 | 205,718 |

Contract size = 1,000 bbl.  *Source: CME Group; New York Mercantile Exchange (NYMEX)*

## Average Open Interest of Crude Oil Futures in New York    In Thousands of Contracts

| Year | Jan. | Feb. | Mar. | Apr. | May | June | July | Aug. | Sept. | Oct. | Nov. | Dec. |
|---|---|---|---|---|---|---|---|---|---|---|---|---|
| 2013 | 1,504.5 | 1,636.4 | 1,690.3 | 1,751.8 | 1,753.7 | 1,813.5 | 1,835.7 | 1,872.0 | 1,896.1 | 1,821.8 | 1,682.1 | 1,631.0 |
| 2014 | 1,607.4 | 1,628.5 | 1,653.4 | 1,654.8 | 1,633.4 | 1,703.8 | 1,687.6 | 1,572.7 | 1,518.4 | 1,495.4 | 1,464.1 | 1,450.3 |
| 2015 | 1,699.2 | 1,713.6 | 1,725.0 | 1,734.5 | 1,683.7 | 1,648.2 | 1,693.9 | 1,702.7 | 1,661.4 | 1,652.0 | 1,666.0 | 1,674.5 |
| 2016 | 1,741.4 | 1,821.0 | 1,774.8 | 1,751.3 | 1,708.3 | 1,737.3 | 1,727.7 | 1,810.2 | 1,842.7 | 1,851.9 | 1,982.7 | 2,063.4 |
| 2017 | 2,143.1 | 2,148.1 | 2,181.9 | 2,190.6 | 2,241.2 | 2,168.4 | 2,158.7 | 2,259.7 | 2,379.9 | 2,446.4 | 2,550.6 | 2,513.1 |
| 2018 | 2,589.4 | 2,509.2 | 2,444.7 | 2,567.8 | 2,662.5 | 2,501.2 | 2,425.1 | 2,292.2 | 2,246.9 | 2,182.7 | 2,044.7 | 2,065.2 |
| 2019 | 2,082.0 | 2,044.0 | 2,000.5 | 2,077.4 | 2,121.6 | 2,039.0 | 2,049.8 | 2,033.4 | 2,071.4 | 2,094.0 | 2,141.0 | 2,170.0 |
| 2020 | 2,193.9 | 2,195.2 | 2,199.0 | 2,321.5 | 2,200.6 | 2,073.0 | 1,984.7 | 2,049.4 | 2,065.0 | 2,047.8 | 2,070.4 | 2,135.4 |
| 2021 | 2,253.1 | 2,464.2 | 2,436.5 | 2,341.3 | 2,446.7 | 2,444.5 | 2,341.2 | 2,154.2 | 2,138.5 | 2,199.9 | 2,065.3 | 1,926.7 |
| 2022 | 2,013.9 | 2,117.7 | 1,851.8 | 1,769.5 | 1,742.6 | 1,714.4 | 1,607.3 | 1,539.9 | 1,492.9 | 1,467.5 | 1,442.1 | 1,424.2 |

Contract size = 1,000 bbl.  *Source: CME Group; New York Mercantile Exchange (NYMEX)*

# Platinum-Group Metals

Platinum (atomic symbol Pt) is a relatively rare, chemically inert metallic element that is more valuable than gold. Platinum is a grayish-white metal that has a high fusing point, is malleable and ductile, and has a high electrical resistance. Chemically, platinum is relatively inert and resists attack by air, water, single acids, and ordinary reagents. Platinum is the most important of the six-metal group, which also includes ruthenium, rhodium, palladium, osmium, and iridium. The word "platinum" is derived from the Spanish word *platina* meaning silver.

Platinum is one of the world's rarest metals with new mine production totaling only about 5 million troy ounces a year. All the platinum mined to date would fit in the average-size living room. Platinum is mined all over the world with supplies concentrated in South Africa. South Africa accounts for nearly 80% of world supply, followed by Russia, and North America.

Because platinum will never tarnish, lose its rich white luster, or even wear down after many years, it is prized by the jewelry industry. The international jewelry industry is the largest consumer sector for platinum, accounting for 51% of total platinum demand. In Europe and the U.S., the normal purity of platinum is 95%. Ten tons of ore must be mined, and a five-month process is needed, to produce one ounce of pure platinum.

The second major consumer sector for platinum is for auto catalysts, with 21% of total platinum demand. Catalysts in autos are used to convert most of vehicle emissions into less harmful carbon dioxide, nitrogen, and water vapor. Platinum is also used in the production of hard disk drive coatings, fiber optic cables, infra-red detectors, fertilizers, explosives, petrol additives, platinum-tipped spark plugs, glassmaking equipment, biodegradable elements for household detergents, dental restorations, and in anti-cancer drugs.

Palladium (atomic symbol Pd) is very similar to platinum and is part of the same general metals group. Palladium is mined with platinum, but it is somewhat more common because it is also a by-product of nickel mining. The primary use for palladium is in the use of automotive catalysts, with that sector accounting for about 63% of total palladium demand. Other uses for palladium include electronic equipment (21%), dental alloys (12%), and jewelry (4%).

Rhodium (atomic symbol Rh), another member of the platinum group, is also used in the automotive industry in pollution control devices. To some extent, palladium has replaced rhodium. Iridium (atomic symbol Ir) is used to process catalysts, and it has also found use in some auto catalysts. Iridium and ruthenium (atomic symbol Ru) are used in the production of polyvinyl chloride. As the prices of these metals change, there is some substitution. Therefore, strength of platinum prices relative to palladium should lead to the substitution of palladium for platinum in catalytic converters.

Platinum futures and options and palladium futures are traded at the CME Group. Platinum and palladium futures are traded on the Tokyo Commodity Exchange (TOCOM). The CME platinum futures contract calls for the delivery of 50 troy ounces of platinum (0.9995 fineness) and the contract trades in terms of dollars and cents per troy ounce. The CME palladium futures contract calls for the delivery of 50 troy ounces of palladium (0.9995 fineness), and the contract is priced in terms of dollars and cents per troy ounce.

**Prices** – CME platinum futures prices (Barchart.com symbol PL) on the nearest-futures chart in 2022 closed the year up +11.3% at $1073.7 per troy ounce. CME palladium futures prices (Barchart.com symbol PA) on the nearest-futures chart in 2022 closed the year down by -6.2% at $1,789.3 per troy ounce.

**Supply** – World mine production of platinum in 2021 rose by +17.1% yr/yr to 190,000 kilograms and remained well below the 2006 record high of 218,000 kilograms. South Africa is the world's largest producer of platinum by far, with 73.8% of world production in 2021, followed by Russia with 10.9%, Zimbabwe with 7.7%, and Canada with 3.1%. World mine production of palladium in 2021 was up +5.4% at 214,000 kilograms. The world's largest palladium producers were Russia with 40.2% of world production in 2021, South Africa with 39.4%, Canada with 7.0%, and the U.S. with 6.4%. World production of platinum group metals other than platinum and palladium in 2021 rose by +19.6% yr/yr to 65,980 kilograms, below the 2005 record high of 77,700 kilograms.

U.S. mine production of platinum in 2021 fell by -4.3% yr/yr at 4,020 kilograms, below the record high of 4,390 kilograms posted in 2002. U.S. mine production of palladium in 2021 fell by -6.2% yr/yr to 13,700 kilograms, below the record high of 14,800 kilograms posted in 2002.

**Trade** – U.S. imports of refined platinum and palladium in 2021 remained unchanged yr/yr to 362,310 kilograms. U.S. exports of refined platinum and palladium in 2021 rose by +0.2% yr/yr to 112,450 kilograms. The U.S. relied on imports for 72% of its platinum and palladium consumption in 2021.

# PLATINUM-GROUP METALS

**World Mine Production of Platinum**  In Kilograms

| Year | Australia | Canada | Colombia[3] | Finland | Japan | Russia | Serbia/Montenegro | South Africa | United States | Zimbabwe | World Total |
|---|---|---|---|---|---|---|---|---|---|---|---|
| 2013 | 170 | 8,900 | 1,520 | 946 | 1,273 | 23,000 | 2 | 137,024 | 3,720 | 13,066 | 192,000 |
| 2014 | 170 | 7,200 | 1,142 | 1,060 | 1,124 | 23,000 | 3 | 93,991 | 3,660 | 12,483 | 145,000 |
| 2015 | 120 | 8,600 | 861 | 992 | 1,379 | 23,000 | 4 | 139,125 | 3,670 | 12,564 | 191,000 |
| 2016 | 170 | 8,400 | 917 | 1,178 | 1,485 | 22,000 | 4 | 133,241 | 3,890 | 15,110 | 188,000 |
| 2017 | 170 | 7,600 | 567 | 1,418 | 1,747 | 22,000 | 2 | 132,500 | 4,000 | 14,257 | 185,000 |
| 2018 | 120 | 7,600 | 270 | 1,576 | ---- | 22,000 | 5 | 137,053 | 4,160 | 14,703 | 190,000 |
| 2019 | 110 | 8,500 | 178 | 953 | ---- | 24,000 | 10 | 132,989 | 4,150 | 13,857 | 187,000 |
| 2020 | 110 | 5,300 | 414 | 1,277 | ---- | 23,000 | 20 | 111,993 | 4,200 | 15,005 | 164,000 |
| 2021[1] | 100 | 6,000 | 400 | 1,447 | ---- | 21,000 | 20 | 141,626 | 4,020 | 14,732 | 192,000 |
| 2022[2] |  | 6,000 |  |  | ---- | 20,000 |  | 140,000 | 3,300 | 15,000 | 190,000 |

[1] Preliminary.  [2] Estimate.  [3] Placer platinum.  W = Withheld.  *Source: U.S. Geological Survey (USGS)*

**World Mine Production of Palladium and Other Group Metals**  In Kilograms

| | | | | Palladium | | | | | | | Other Group Metals | | |
|---|---|---|---|---|---|---|---|---|---|---|---|---|---|
| Year | Australia | Canada | Finland | Japan | Russia | Serbia/Montenegro | South Africa | United States | Zimbabwe | Total | Russia | South Africa | World Total |
| 2013 | 610 | 16,000 | 766 | 6,239 | 80,247 | 25 | 76,008 | 12,600 | 10,153 | 205,000 | 7,400 | 51,156 | 62,100 |
| 2014 | 600 | 23,000 | 808 | 6,969 | 86,000 | 23 | 58,410 | 12,400 | 10,138 | 193,000 | 8,200 | 36,043 | 48,000 |
| 2015 | 420 | 24,000 | 784 | 7,073 | 85,000 | 31 | 82,691 | 12,500 | 10,055 | 218,000 | 7,600 | 53,699 | 65,100 |
| 2016 | 590 | 22,000 | 901 | 7,172 | 83,000 | 31 | 76,273 | 13,100 | 12,222 | 209,000 | 7,700 | 54,139 | 66,000 |
| 2017 | 600 | 19,000 | 1,021 | 7,715 | 88,000 | 38 | 80,713 | 14,000 | 11,822 | 217,000 | 3,415 | 49,543 | 56,680 |
| 2018 | 420 | 21,000 | 1,157 | ---- | 90,000 | 55 | 80,629 | 14,300 | 12,094 | 221,000 | 3,428 | 52,964 | 60,940 |
| 2019 | 380 | 23,000 | 699 | ---- | 98,000 | 100 | 80,684 | 14,300 | 11,640 | 230,000 | 4,026 | 54,395 | 63,010 |
| 2020 | 410 | 14,000 | 858 | ---- | 93,000 | 100 | 66,264 | 14,600 | 12,890 | 203,000 | 3,054 | 48,216 | 55,170 |
| 2021[1] | 350 | 15,000 | 1,036 | ---- | 86,000 | 150 | 84,336 | 13,700 | 12,398 | 214,000 | 2,878 | 59,344 | 65,980 |
| 2022[2] |  | 15,000 |  | ---- | 88,000 |  | 80,000 | 11,000 | 12,000 | 210,000 |  |  |  |

[1] Preliminary.  [2] Estimate.  *Source: U.S. Geological Survey (USGS)*

**Salient Statistics of Platinum and Allied Metals[3] in the United States**  In Kilograms

| Year | Net Import Reliance as a % of Apparent Consump | Mine Production Platinum | Palladium | Refinery Production (Secondary) | Total Refined | Refiner, Importer & Dealer Stocks as of Dec. 31 Platinum | Palladium | Other[4] | Total | Imports Refined | Total | Exports Refined | Total | Apparent Consumptio |
|---|---|---|---|---|---|---|---|---|---|---|---|---|---|---|
| 2013 | 67 | 3,720 | 12,600 | 74,500 | 74,500 | 261 | ---- | 18 | 279 | 227,217 | ---- | 403,540 | ---- | ---- |
| 2014 | 69 | 3,660 | 12,400 | 69,400 | 69,400 | 261 | ---- | 15 | 276 | 274,682 | ---- | 292,234 | ---- | ---- |
| 2015 | 66 | 3,670 | 12,500 | 65,100 | 65,100 | 261 | ---- | 15 | 276 | 270,848 | ---- | 284,940 | ---- | ---- |
| 2016 | 66 | 3,890 | 13,100 | 69,900 | 69,900 | 261 | ---- | 15 | 276 | 297,137 | ---- | 81,130 | ---- | ---- |
| 2017 | 71 | 4,000 | 14,000 | 80,900 | 80,900 | 261 | ---- | 15 | 276 | 521,676 | ---- | 107,544 | ---- | ---- |
| 2018 | 74 | 4,160 | 14,300 | 103,100 | 103,100 | 261 | ---- | 15 | 276 | 225,545 | ---- | 105,510 | ---- | ---- |
| 2019 | 67 | 4,150 | 14,300 | 100,000 | 100,000 | 261 | ---- | 15 | 276 | 188,875 | ---- | 94,910 | ---- | ---- |
| 2020 | 75 | 4,200 | 14,600 | 111,800 | 111,800 | 261 | ---- | 15 | 276 | 362,420 | ---- | 112,180 | ---- | ---- |
| 2021[1] | 72 | 4,020 | 13,700 | 139,400 | 139,400 | 261 | ---- | 15 | 276 | 362,310 | ---- | 112,450 | ---- | ---- |
| 2022[2] | 66 | 3,300 | 11,000 |  |  |  | ---- |  |  | 197,700 | ---- | 111,720 | ---- | ---- |

[1] Preliminary.  [2] Estimate.  [3] Includes platinum, palladium, iridium, osmium, rhodium, and ruthenium.  [4] Includes iridium, osmium, rhodium, and ruthenium.  W = Withheld.  *Source: U.S. Geological Survey (USGS)*

**Average Producer Price of Rhodium in the United States**  In Dollars Per Troy Ounce

| Year | Jan. | Feb. | Mar. | Apr. | May | June | July | Aug. | Sept. | Oct. | Nov. | Dec. | Average |
|---|---|---|---|---|---|---|---|---|---|---|---|---|---|
| 2013 | 1,123.6 | 1,226.0 | 1,254.0 | 1,184.3 | 1,128.0 | 1,037.0 | 988.6 | 1,000.2 | 1,000.0 | 987.8 | 958.5 | 916.4 | 1,067.0 |
| 2014 | 1,047.7 | 1,068.0 | 1,092.1 | 1,134.5 | 1,071.7 | 1,118.8 | 1,187.3 | 1,375.2 | 1,310.5 | 1,228.7 | 1,224.4 | 1,206.4 | 1,172.1 |
| 2015 | 1,196.0 | 1,184.5 | 1,166.6 | 1,146.9 | 1,105.8 | 976.1 | 857.1 | 847.9 | 772.4 | 768.0 | 741.9 | 678.7 | 953.5 |
| 2016 | 650.0 | 654.3 | 711.5 | 740.0 | 690.9 | 657.3 | 647.4 | 640.2 | 675.0 | 692.1 | 786.1 | 783.0 | 694.0 |
| 2017 | 833.4 | 874.1 | 959.6 | 1,023.5 | 955.7 | 982.1 | 1,023.8 | 1,052.8 | 1,160.2 | 1,401.1 | 1,443.9 | 1,607.6 | 1,109.8 |
| 2018 | 1,709.6 | 1,848.8 | 1,932.3 | 2,070.7 | 2,137.2 | 2,255.2 | 2,296.4 | 2,360.2 | 2,468.3 | 2,511.5 | 2,515.7 | 2,533.3 | 2,219.9 |
| 2019 | 2,473.3 | 2,624.8 | 3,152.6 | 2,992.3 | 2,896.1 | 3,173.8 | 3,493.5 | 3,960.7 | 5,008.6 | 5,364.1 | 5,744.1 | 6,048.0 | 3,911.0 |
| 2020 | 8,863.6 | 11,851.3 | 10,511.4 | 8,266.7 | 7,682.5 | 8,406.8 | 8,645.5 | 11,348.8 | 13,790.5 | 14,004.6 | 15,138.2 | 16,485.7 | 11,249.6 |
| 2021 | 19,744.7 | 22,755.3 | 27,452.2 | 28,742.9 | 27,267.5 | 21,588.6 | 18,723.8 | 18,377.3 | 14,459.5 | 13,947.6 | 14,195.0 | 14,034.1 | 20,107.4 |
| 2022 | 16,737.5 | 18,265.8 | 19,567.4 | 18,810.0 | 16,133.3 | 14,154.6 | 14,452.2 | 14,361.0 | 14,361.9 | 13,990.5 | 13,507.5 | 12,582.5 | 15,577.0 |

*Source: American Metal Market (AMM)*

# PLATINUM-GROUP METALS

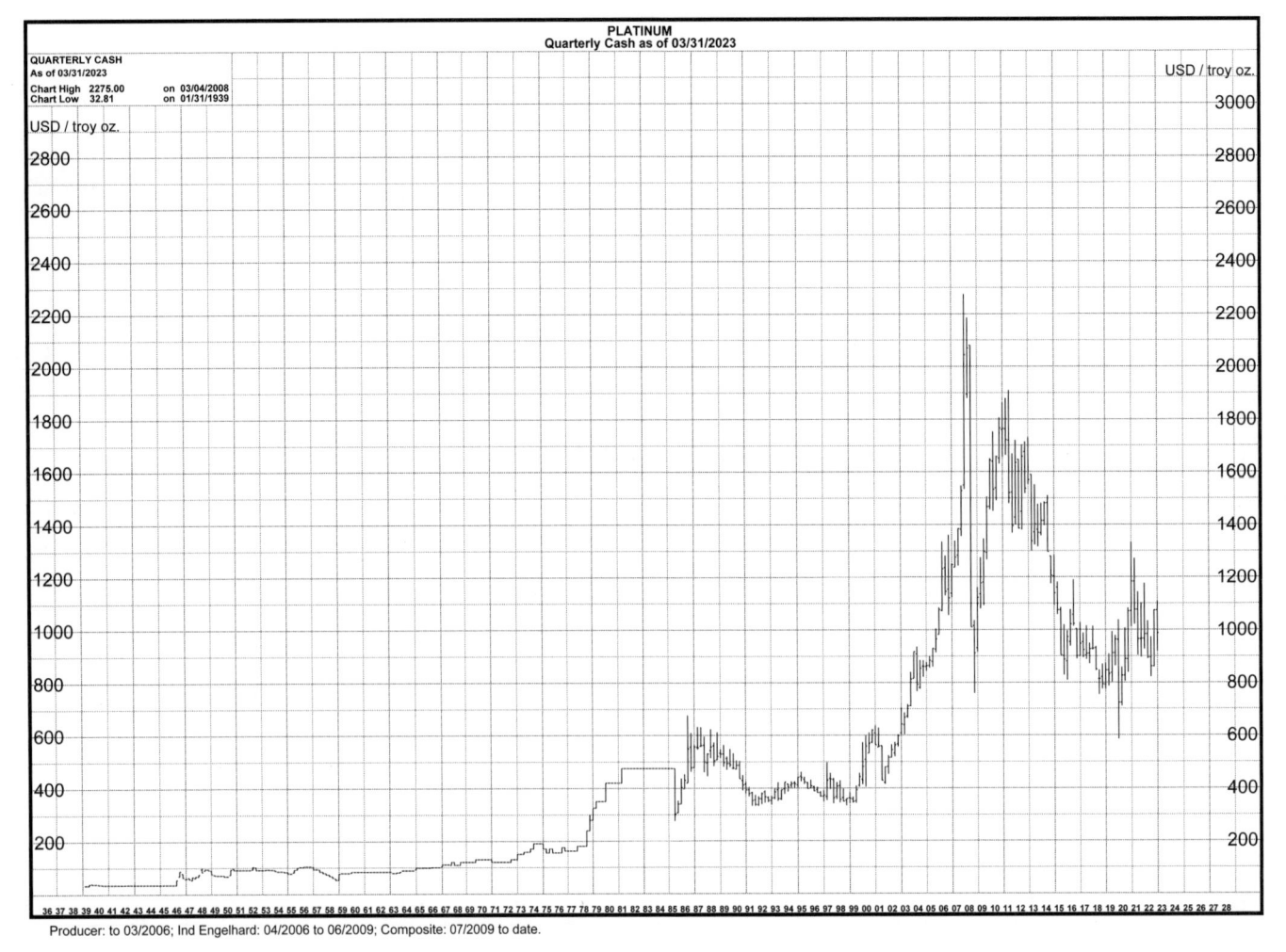

**PLATINUM**
Quarterly Cash as of 03/31/2023

QUARTERLY CASH
As of 03/31/2023
Chart High 2275.00 on 03/04/2008
Chart Low 32.81 on 01/31/1939

Producer: to 03/2006; Ind Engelhard: 04/2006 to 06/2009; Composite: 07/2009 to date.

## Average Merchant's Price of Platinum in the United States — In Dollars Per Troy Ounce

| Year | Jan. | Feb. | Mar. | Apr. | May | June | July | Aug. | Sept. | Oct. | Nov. | Dec. | Average |
|---|---|---|---|---|---|---|---|---|---|---|---|---|---|
| 2013 | 1,646.43 | 1,676.95 | 1,586.30 | 1,497.23 | 1,478.95 | 1,431.20 | 1,405.14 | 1,496.50 | 1,454.05 | 1,415.52 | 1,423.85 | 1,355.25 | 1,488.95 |
| 2014 | 1,423.73 | 1,411.30 | 1,457.52 | 1,435.38 | 1,461.07 | 1,457.81 | 1,497.05 | 1,449.90 | 1,362.10 | 1,263.61 | 1,213.00 | 1,222.48 | 1,387.91 |
| 2015 | 1,247.38 | 1,200.79 | 1,140.00 | 1,154.33 | 1,143.25 | 1,091.77 | 1,011.23 | 985.86 | 966.38 | 978.95 | 885.10 | 863.30 | 1,055.70 |
| 2016 | 857.19 | 924.14 | 971.78 | 997.19 | 1,036.73 | 986.50 | 1,087.29 | 1,123.91 | 1,047.36 | 961.10 | 955.91 | 919.27 | 989.03 |
| 2017 | 970.55 | 1,009.75 | 965.22 | 963.35 | 934.35 | 933.64 | 921.52 | 975.65 | 968.76 | 924.00 | 937.73 | 912.52 | 951.42 |
| 2018 | 991.35 | 991.20 | 956.82 | 927.05 | 907.78 | 887.90 | 835.27 | 807.91 | 807.20 | 833.57 | 849.45 | 793.62 | 882.43 |
| 2019 | 808.91 | 820.45 | 847.05 | 890.32 | 834.96 | 811.20 | 846.48 | 861.86 | 947.70 | 900.78 | 905.10 | 929.00 | 866.98 |
| 2020 | 990.41 | 963.79 | 764.18 | 756.86 | 795.35 | 823.77 | 867.64 | 943.57 | 911.95 | 879.95 | 912.58 | 1,032.81 | 886.91 |
| 2021 | 1,095.58 | 1,206.79 | 1,187.48 | 1,212.19 | 1,219.30 | 1,128.00 | 1,090.43 | 1,012.55 | 977.05 | 1,020.86 | 1,046.30 | 947.90 | 1,095.37 |
| 2022 | 993.21 | 1,046.41 | 1,041.63 | 962.98 | 957.70 | 952.36 | 871.81 | 906.38 | 877.12 | 915.12 | 1,000.50 | 1,021.10 | 962.19 |

*Source: American Metal Market (AMM)*

## Average Dealer Price[1] of Palladium in the United States — In Dollars Per Troy Ounce

| Year | Jan. | Feb. | Mar. | Apr. | May | June | July | Aug. | Sept. | Oct. | Nov. | Dec. | Average |
|---|---|---|---|---|---|---|---|---|---|---|---|---|---|
| 2013 | 716.62 | 755.68 | 761.20 | 710.27 | 723.91 | 716.70 | 725.18 | 746.23 | 711.75 | 727.61 | 737.20 | 721.45 | 729.48 |
| 2014 | 738.59 | 733.90 | 783.19 | 804.62 | 829.67 | 841.19 | 880.95 | 884.10 | 844.57 | 784.30 | 783.78 | 810.71 | 809.96 |
| 2015 | 788.29 | 789.95 | 789.55 | 771.86 | 787.00 | 729.77 | 643.64 | 598.24 | 612.76 | 693.82 | 575.57 | 555.96 | 694.70 |
| 2016 | 505.67 | 510.48 | 572.78 | 578.81 | 582.64 | 557.27 | 649.19 | 703.57 | 686.32 | 652.62 | 700.68 | 706.20 | 617.19 |
| 2017 | 749.09 | 780.35 | 780.65 | 803.90 | 797.04 | 867.68 | 859.29 | 917.26 | 937.52 | 963.91 | 1,005.45 | 1,028.48 | 874.22 |
| 2018 | 1,097.74 | 1,027.60 | 990.91 | 974.81 | 984.70 | 990.00 | 936.41 | 924.17 | 1,017.90 | 1,089.52 | 1,147.50 | 1,254.14 | 1,036.28 |
| 2019 | 1,333.96 | 1,448.70 | 1,541.14 | 1,396.95 | 1,336.96 | 1,449.65 | 1,551.39 | 1,460.73 | 1,611.00 | 1,735.22 | 1,771.14 | 1,910.85 | 1,545.64 |
| 2020 | 2,247.77 | 2,535.42 | 2,136.64 | 2,097.05 | 1,910.40 | 1,930.77 | 2,056.55 | 2,181.90 | 2,313.71 | 2,363.41 | 2,367.21 | 2,369.10 | 2,209.16 |
| 2021 | 2,397.11 | 2,368.26 | 2,508.83 | 2,796.76 | 2,896.10 | 2,741.27 | 2,749.86 | 2,561.09 | 2,114.76 | 2,018.33 | 2,033.90 | 1,811.14 | 2,416.45 |
| 2022 | 2,021.38 | 2,328.56 | 2,574.08 | 2,302.22 | 2,045.86 | 1,898.42 | 1,973.95 | 2,121.40 | 2,112.97 | 2,060.83 | 1,948.30 | 1,839.50 | 2,102.29 |

[1] Based on wholesale quantities, prompt delivery. *Source: American Metal Market (AMM)*

# PLATINUM-GROUP METALS

**PLATINUM - NYMEX**
Weekly Selected Futures as of 03/31/2023

WEEKLY SELECTED FUTURES
As of 03/31/2023
Chart High 1744.50 on 02/06/2013
Chart Low 562.00 on 03/16/2020

Nearby Futures through Last Trading Day.

## Volume of Trading of Platinum Futures in Chicago    In Contracts

| Year | Jan. | Feb. | Mar. | Apr. | May | June | July | Aug. | Sept. | Oct. | Nov. | Dec. | Total |
|---|---|---|---|---|---|---|---|---|---|---|---|---|---|
| 2013 | 280,979 | 275,013 | 335,276 | 277,634 | 243,442 | 388,436 | 188,942 | 216,194 | 341,340 | 222,190 | 185,380 | 307,949 | 3,262,775 |
| 2014 | 217,465 | 194,296 | 389,315 | 182,628 | 239,397 | 379,860 | 210,163 | 179,938 | 399,265 | 271,921 | 211,151 | 360,542 | 3,235,941 |
| 2015 | 243,017 | 200,204 | 408,528 | 217,744 | 211,710 | 434,374 | 262,007 | 268,391 | 443,850 | 281,094 | 261,514 | 408,711 | 3,641,144 |
| 2016 | 284,203 | 262,873 | 413,082 | 248,758 | 249,861 | 435,018 | 279,689 | 278,246 | 456,092 | 302,621 | 360,457 | 423,172 | 3,994,072 |
| 2017 | 345,619 | 286,893 | 515,593 | 280,575 | 354,263 | 529,562 | 321,062 | 394,884 | 528,953 | 344,217 | 381,004 | 569,535 | 4,852,160 |
| 2018 | 444,074 | 346,507 | 562,720 | 423,705 | 392,326 | 652,863 | 393,517 | 412,710 | 580,643 | 383,720 | 372,849 | 498,165 | 5,463,799 |
| 2019 | 362,449 | 384,444 | 633,174 | 398,312 | 414,824 | 593,552 | 444,188 | 496,003 | 739,168 | 408,309 | 399,670 | 588,197 | 5,862,290 |
| 2020 | 468,298 | 473,531 | 738,101 | 218,691 | 242,913 | 350,424 | 316,024 | 301,382 | 453,351 | 271,140 | 277,596 | 466,080 | 4,577,531 |
| 2021 | 287,469 | 375,176 | 512,365 | 275,683 | 300,637 | 493,395 | 294,112 | 302,530 | 500,154 | 299,521 | 364,392 | 445,429 | 4,450,863 |
| 2022 | 359,631 | 402,774 | 592,236 | 325,352 | 335,096 | 527,835 | 312,283 | 373,986 | 556,416 | 415,982 | 433,587 | 541,880 | 5,177,058 |

Contract size = 50 oz.   *Source: CME Group; New York Mercantile Exchange (NYMEX)*

## Average Open Interest of Platinum Futures in Chicago    In Contracts

| Year | Jan. | Feb. | Mar. | Apr. | May | June | July | Aug. | Sept. | Oct. | Nov. | Dec. |
|---|---|---|---|---|---|---|---|---|---|---|---|---|
| 2013 | 64,184 | 70,544 | 64,608 | 63,193 | 63,406 | 62,590 | 61,937 | 65,515 | 61,739 | 59,391 | 59,092 | 63,028 |
| 2014 | 59,980 | 63,324 | 69,278 | 65,308 | 68,150 | 68,004 | 71,271 | 64,416 | 64,103 | 59,701 | 61,768 | 65,647 |
| 2015 | 66,436 | 66,642 | 70,775 | 69,165 | 71,645 | 79,378 | 79,326 | 76,953 | 73,817 | 72,160 | 72,938 | 73,105 |
| 2016 | 68,301 | 65,306 | 62,884 | 59,152 | 64,862 | 63,825 | 72,441 | 80,327 | 74,296 | 70,022 | 66,480 | 65,869 |
| 2017 | 62,849 | 66,421 | 66,618 | 65,191 | 72,742 | 73,137 | 72,273 | 72,013 | 76,162 | 75,280 | 78,273 | 85,097 |
| 2018 | 86,391 | 87,064 | 78,963 | 76,759 | 80,900 | 86,235 | 81,652 | 83,049 | 86,436 | 74,712 | 72,385 | 81,227 |
| 2019 | 84,646 | 82,418 | 74,956 | 73,945 | 78,080 | 87,406 | 77,906 | 77,789 | 93,443 | 86,189 | 90,358 | 96,111 |
| 2020 | 104,485 | 99,383 | 69,178 | 62,027 | 50,911 | 49,719 | 50,513 | 57,638 | 59,353 | 52,240 | 53,169 | 62,949 |
| 2021 | 61,411 | 71,241 | 71,866 | 65,309 | 66,412 | 64,205 | 57,303 | 63,857 | 70,049 | 59,490 | 60,009 | 53,793 |
| 2022 | 56,525 | 59,917 | 65,982 | 63,707 | 66,397 | 66,333 | 73,668 | 63,748 | 66,521 | 54,622 | 62,157 | 69,331 |

Contract size = 50 oz.   *Source: CME Group; New York Mercantile Exchange (NYMEX)*

# PLATINUM-GROUP METALS

### Volume of Trading of Palladium Futures in Chicago    In Contracts

| Year | Jan. | Feb. | Mar. | Apr. | May | June | July | Aug. | Sept. | Oct. | Nov. | Dec. | Total |
|---|---|---|---|---|---|---|---|---|---|---|---|---|---|
| 2013 | 126,987 | 198,821 | 87,681 | 122,520 | 181,016 | 93,497 | 77,175 | 163,892 | 82,470 | 99,944 | 182,133 | 69,880 | 1,486,016 |
| 2014 | 87,502 | 158,760 | 136,126 | 111,648 | 195,880 | 101,610 | 97,809 | 208,474 | 126,132 | 115,708 | 161,947 | 72,376 | 1,573,972 |
| 2015 | 99,787 | 146,928 | 100,748 | 78,232 | 131,105 | 91,044 | 102,665 | 185,094 | 87,201 | 92,284 | 162,382 | 66,956 | 1,344,426 |
| 2016 | 90,129 | 151,159 | 96,917 | 93,887 | 142,585 | 94,937 | 104,219 | 169,852 | 88,440 | 113,977 | 198,537 | 91,224 | 1,435,863 |
| 2017 | 111,959 | 141,648 | 98,308 | 97,861 | 191,603 | 120,488 | 82,725 | 164,153 | 80,618 | 87,270 | 153,217 | 72,890 | 1,402,740 |
| 2018 | 98,800 | 164,476 | 101,277 | 145,138 | 127,272 | 93,661 | 98,611 | 176,108 | 89,368 | 116,003 | 148,110 | 74,888 | 1,433,712 |
| 2019 | 107,039 | 147,433 | 113,193 | 96,677 | 129,839 | 74,368 | 79,652 | 133,300 | 80,152 | 90,724 | 131,275 | 83,049 | 1,266,701 |
| 2020 | 148,896 | 127,560 | 76,650 | 23,544 | 39,796 | 23,542 | 41,067 | 51,521 | 29,227 | 34,644 | 59,389 | 34,951 | 690,787 |
| 2021 | 38,520 | 68,969 | 45,404 | 33,356 | 65,204 | 31,687 | 35,785 | 71,896 | 48,616 | 42,972 | 84,800 | 37,373 | 604,582 |
| 2022 | 44,742 | 82,539 | 51,573 | 27,933 | 53,027 | 29,050 | 32,801 | 55,490 | 33,013 | 40,121 | 77,831 | 42,915 | 571,035 |

Contract size = 100 oz.    Source: CME Group; New York Mercantile Exchange (NYMEX)

### Average Open Interest of Palladium Futures in Chicago    In Contracts

| Year | Jan. | Feb. | Mar. | Apr. | May | June | July | Aug. | Sept. | Oct. | Nov. | Dec. |
|---|---|---|---|---|---|---|---|---|---|---|---|---|
| 2013 | 31,036 | 37,519 | 37,181 | 37,118 | 36,554 | 36,219 | 35,682 | 38,564 | 34,971 | 37,152 | 39,264 | 36,781 |
| 2014 | 39,059 | 40,226 | 41,494 | 42,071 | 43,466 | 39,964 | 43,791 | 44,286 | 38,776 | 33,587 | 34,170 | 32,060 |
| 2015 | 33,813 | 33,807 | 31,897 | 32,138 | 31,396 | 33,426 | 36,629 | 34,717 | 27,329 | 25,978 | 27,440 | 25,030 |
| 2016 | 26,200 | 27,339 | 22,964 | 23,573 | 23,912 | 23,048 | 24,043 | 28,475 | 25,272 | 23,968 | 24,431 | 26,124 |
| 2017 | 27,919 | 29,500 | 29,601 | 34,312 | 35,204 | 35,544 | 33,508 | 35,549 | 32,465 | 32,910 | 35,411 | 35,320 |
| 2018 | 38,468 | 29,987 | 24,894 | 23,645 | 23,008 | 23,045 | 21,676 | 22,511 | 19,056 | 26,129 | 27,046 | 26,158 |
| 2019 | 27,723 | 28,365 | 26,618 | 22,825 | 20,757 | 20,861 | 25,138 | 22,436 | 22,028 | 26,569 | 25,844 | 25,338 |
| 2020 | 25,122 | 19,937 | 10,294 | 7,754 | 7,209 | 6,698 | 8,719 | 9,970 | 9,523 | 10,030 | 10,608 | 9,322 |
| 2021 | 9,604 | 9,811 | 9,788 | 11,167 | 11,544 | 10,086 | 10,130 | 10,011 | 8,827 | 9,619 | 11,024 | 9,569 |
| 2022 | 9,002 | 7,831 | 7,102 | 6,663 | 8,255 | 7,396 | 6,982 | 7,349 | 6,091 | 7,090 | 8,520 | 8,012 |

Contract size = 100 oz.    Source: CME Group; New York Mercantile Exchange (NYMEX)

# Potatoes

The potato is a member of the nightshade family. The leaves of the potato plant are poisonous, and a potato will begin to turn green if left too long in the light. This green skin contains solanine, a substance that can cause the potato to taste bitter and even cause illness in humans.

In Peru, the Inca Indians were the first to cultivate potatoes around 200 BC. The Indians developed potato crops because their staple diet of corn would not grow above an altitude of 3,350 meters. In 1536, after conquering the Incas, the Spanish Conquistadors brought potatoes back to Europe. At first, Europeans did not accept the potato because it was not mentioned in the Bible and was therefore considered an "evil" food. But after Marie Antoinette wore a crown of potato flowers, it finally became a popular food. In 1897, during the Alaskan Klondike gold rush, potatoes were so valued for their vitamin C content that miners traded gold for potatoes. The potato became the first vegetable to be grown in outer space in October 1995.

The potato is a highly nutritious, fat-free, cholesterol-free, and sodium-free food. The potato is an important dietary staple in over 130 countries. A medium-sized potato contains only 100 calories. Potatoes are an excellent source of vitamin C and provide B vitamins as well as potassium, copper, magnesium, and iron. According to the U.S. Department of Agriculture, "a diet of whole milk and potatoes would supply almost all of the food elements necessary for the maintenance of the human body."

Potatoes are one of the largest vegetable crops grown in the U.S. and are grown in all fifty states. The U.S. ranks about 4th in world potato production. The top three types of potatoes grown extensively in the U.S. are white, red, and Russets (Russets account for about two-thirds the U.S. crop). Potatoes in the U.S. are harvested in all four seasons, but the vast majority of the crop is harvested in fall. Potatoes harvested in the winter, spring, and summer are used mainly to supplement fresh supplies of fall-harvested potatoes and are also important to the processing industries. The four principal categories for U.S. potato exports are frozen, potato chips, fresh, and dehydrated. Fries account for approximately 95% of U.S. frozen potato exports.

**Prices** – The average monthly price received for potatoes by U.S. farmers in 2022 rose by +56.8% yr/yr to $19.08 per hundred pounds.

**Supply** –The total U.S. potato crop in 2022 fell by -3.9% yr/yr to 39.688 billion pounds, well below the record high of 50.936 billion pounds posted in 2000. The fall crop in 2018 rose by +1.9% yr/yr to 41.450 billion pounds, and it accounted for 81.4% of the total crop. Stocks of the fall crop (as of Dec 1, 2018) were 28.360 billion pounds. In 2018, the spring crop fell by -18.4% yr/yr to 1.757 billion pounds, and the summer crop fell by -20.6% yr/yr to 1.776 billion pounds.

The largest producing states for the 2022 fall crop were Idaho with 30.4% of the crop, Washington with 23.9%, Wisconsin with 7.0%, Oregon with 6.4%, North Dakota with 5.6%, and Colorado with 5.3%. Farmers harvested 895.6 acres in 2022, down -4.3% yr/yr. The yield per harvested acre in 2022 remained unchanged to 438 pounds per acre.

**Demand** – Total utilization of potatoes in 2021 was down by -2.4% yr/yr at 40.982 billion pounds, but still above the 2010 record low of 40.427 billion pounds. The breakdown shows that the largest consumption category for potatoes is frozen French fries with 39.0% of total consumption, followed closely by table stock with 23.0%, chips, shoestrings with 14.7%, and dehydration with 9.9%. U.S. per capita consumption of potatoes in 2019 rose by +2.4% to 118.83 pounds, below the record high of 145.0 pounds per capita seen in 1996.

## Salient Statistics of Potatoes in the United States

| Crop Year | Acreage Planted (1,000 Acres) | Acreage Harvested (1,000 Acres) | Yield Per Harvested Acre Cwt. | Total Production | Seed & Feed | Shrinkage & Loss | Sold[2] | Farm Price ($ Cwt.) | Value of Production[3] (Million $) | Sales (Million $) | Stocks Jan. 1 (1,000 Cwt) | Exports (Fresh) (Millions of Lbs.) | Imports (Millions of Lbs.) | Consumption[4] Per Capita Fresh (Pounds) | Consumption[4] Per Capita Total (Pounds) |
|---|---|---|---|---|---|---|---|---|---|---|---|---|---|---|---|
| 2013 | 1,064 | 1,051 | 414 | 434,652 | 4,323 | 26,211 | 404,118 | 9.75 | 4,237 | 3,943 | NA | 1,055,601 | | 34.5 | 113.3 |
| 2014 | 1,063 | 1,051 | 421 | 442,170 | 4,192 | 26,762 | 411,216 | 8.88 | 3,928 | 3,658 | NA | 922,366 | | 33.5 | 112.1 |
| 2015 | 1,066 | 1,054 | 418 | 441,205 | 4,631 | 26,509 | 410,065 | 8.76 | 3,866 | 3,597 | NA | 904,958 | | 34.1 | 113.7 |
| 2016 | 1,057 | 1,038 | 434 | 450,324 | 4,437 | 26,883 | 419,004 | 9.08 | 4,091 | 3,812 | NA | 1,073,734 | | 33.2 | |
| 2017 | 1,053 | 1,045 | 432 | 450,921 | 4,410 | 25,139 | 421,372 | 9.17 | 4,133 | 3,875 | | | | | |
| 2018 | 1,027 | 1,015 | 443 | 450,020 | 4,047 | 25,526 | 420,447 | 8.48 | 4,006 | 3,747 | | | | | |
| 2019 | 963 | 937 | 453 | 424,419 | 4,608 | 25,016 | 394,795 | 12.36 | 4,217 | 3,935 | | | | | |
| 2020 | 919 | 912 | 761 | 420,020 | 4,550 | 23,453 | 392,017 | 13.23 | 3,907 | 3,654 | | | | | |
| 2021 | 943 | 936 | 438 | 409,671 | 3,579 | 23,367 | 382,883 | 12.17 | 4,174 | 3,912 | | | | | |
| 2022[1] | 901 | 896 | 438 | 392,243 | | | | 19.08 | | | | | | | |

[1] Preliminary. [2] For all purposes, including food, seed processing & livestock feed. [3] Farm weight basis, excluding canned and frozen potatoes. [4] Calendar year. Source: Economic Research Service, U.S. Department of Agriculture (ERS-USDA)

# POTATOES

## Potato Crop Production Estimates, Stocks and Disappearance in the United States   In Millions of Cwt.

| Year | Crop Production Estimates Total Crop Oct. 1 | Nov. 1 | Dec. 1 | Fall Crop Oct. 1 | Nov. 1 | Dec. 1 | Total Storage Stocks² Following Year Jan. 1 | Feb. 1 | Mar. 1 | Apr. 1 | May 1 | Fall Crop 1,000 Cwt. Production | Disappearance (Sold) | Stocks Dec. 1 | Average Price ($/Cwt.) | Value of Sales ($1,000) |
|---|---|---|---|---|---|---|---|---|---|---|---|---|---|---|---|---|
| 2013 | ---- | 439.7 | ---- | ---- | 401.5 | NA | NA | NA | NA | 119.5 | NA | 396,655 | 404,118 | NA | 9.05 | 3,320,712 |
| 2014 | ---- | 442.8 | ---- | ---- | 406.2 | 267.5 | ---- | 206.6 | ---- | 139.2 | ---- | 406,080 | 411,216 | 265,700 | 8.35 | 3,113,990 |
| 2015 | ---- | 441.2 | ---- | ---- | 404.7 | 267.9 | ---- | 205.9 | ---- | 137.2 | ---- | 409,281 | 410,667 | 262,700 | 8.27 | 3,094,832 |
| 2016 | ---- | 439.6 | ---- | ---- | 405.2 | 275.8 | ---- | 213.0 | ---- | 142.6 | ---- | 412,688 | 382,471 | 272,900 | 8.46 | 3,231,305 |
| 2017 | ---- | 439.0 | ---- | ---- | 398.9 | 277.9 | ---- | 210.6 | ---- | 138.8 | ---- | 406,800 | 377,994 | 274,900 | 8.28 | 3,135,521 |
| 2018 | ---- | 452.6 | ---- | ---- | 417.5 | 279.3 | ---- | 212.8 | ---- | 144.7 | ---- | 414,499 | 385,794 | 283,600 | 8.48 | 3,269,884 |
| 2019 | ---- | 424.4 | ---- | ---- | ---- | 269.2 | ---- | 203.0 | ---- | 127.0 | ---- | ---- | ---- | ---- | ---- | ---- |
| 2020 | ---- | 415.5 | ---- | ---- | ---- | 270.3 | ---- | 205.1 | ---- | 124.8 | ---- | ---- | ---- | ---- | ---- | ---- |
| 2021 | ---- | 413.2 | ---- | ---- | ---- | 265.5 | ---- | 198.6 | ---- | 127.3 | ---- | ---- | ---- | ---- | ---- | ---- |
| 2022¹ | ---- | 396.9 | ---- | ---- | ---- | 254.4 | ---- | 192.4 | ---- | ---- | ---- | ---- | ---- | ---- | ---- | ---- |

¹ Preliminary.   ² Held by growers and local dealers in the fall producing areas.
*Source: Agricultural Statistics Board, U.S. Department of Agriculture (ASB-USDA)*

## Production of Potatoes in the United States   In Thousands of Cwt.

| Year | California | Colorado | Idaho | Maine | Michigan | Minnesota | Nebraska | New York | North Dakota | Oregon | Washington | Wisconsin | U.S. Total |
|---|---|---|---|---|---|---|---|---|---|---|---|---|---|
| 2013 | 3,504 | 20,304 | 131,131 | 15,660 | 15,840 | 17,325 | 8,418 | 4,959 | 22,620 | 21,582 | 96,000 | 26,040 | 396,655 |
| 2014 | 3,901 | 23,196 | 132,880 | 14,645 | 15,725 | 16,400 | 7,943 | 4,345 | 23,870 | 22,562 | 101,475 | 26,240 | 406,080 |
| 2015 | 3,528 | 22,575 | 130,400 | 16,160 | 17,550 | 16,200 | 6,885 | 4,144 | 27,600 | 21,784 | 100,300 | 27,813 | 409,281 |
| 2016 | 3,516 | 22,236 | 139,320 | 15,113 | 17,390 | 17,200 | 7,380 | 3,552 | 21,600 | 22,951 | 105,625 | 27,840 | 412,688 |
| 2017 | 3,321 | 21,220 | 134,850 | 15,200 | 18,315 | 18,428 | 9,025 | 4,032 | 24,420 | 25,245 | 99,220 | 29,750 | 406,800 |
| 2018 | 3,212 | 21,722 | 141,750 | 15,035 | 18,240 | 18,705 | 9,264 | 3,886 | 23,725 | 27,000 | 100,800 | 27,135 | 414,499 |
| 2019 | 16,842 | 19,666 | 130,900 | 16,738 | 20,370 | 17,845 | 9,595 | ---- | 19,430 | 25,311 | 104,960 | 28,700 | 424,419 |
| 2020 | 12,861 | 22,596 | 134,775 | 13,462 | 17,550 | 17,922 | 9,212 | ---- | 23,800 | 27,000 | 99,653 | 28,770 | 420,020 |
| 2021 | 11,049 | 21,484 | 132,090 | 18,389 | 19,350 | 17,553 | 9,261 | ---- | 22,500 | 26,280 | 91,928 | 29,025 | 409,829 |
| 2022¹ | 9,160 | 21,080 | 120,745 | 18,113 | 16,720 | 19,298 | 9,552 | ---- | 22,265 | 25,311 | 94,903 | 27,598 | 396,889 |

¹ Preliminary.   *Source: Agricultural Statistics Board, U.S. Department of Agriculture (ASB-USDA)*

## Utilization of Potatoes in the United States   In Thousands of Cwt.

| Crop Year | Table Stock | Chips, Shoestrings | Dehydration | Frozen French Fries | Other Frozen Products | Canned Potatoes | Other Canned Products² | Starch & Flour | Livestock Feed | Seed | Total Sales | Used on Farms Where Grown | Shrinkage & Loss | Total Non-Sales | Total |
|---|---|---|---|---|---|---|---|---|---|---|---|---|---|---|---|
| 2012 | 118,535 | 59,304 | 49,894 | 142,993 | 20,635 | 1,741 | 734 | 7,919 | 4,080 | 23,706 | 429,541 | 3,286 | 28,356 | 33,225 | 462,766 |
| 2013 | 106,930 | 60,485 | 47,411 | 134,966 | 18,451 | 188 | 1,089 | 8,579 | 1,251 | 22,431 | 404,118 | 3,215 | 26,211 | 30,534 | 434,652 |
| 2014 | 107,344 | 73,960 | 48,707 | 152,832 | 9,208 | 435 | 886 | 6,907 | 768 | 22,774 | 411,216 | 3,343 | 26,762 | 30,954 | 442,170 |
| 2015 | 110,960 | 56,807 | 48,016 | 152,329 | 13,573 | 985 | 730 | 6,420 | 919 | 25,648 | 410,065 | 3,765 | 26,509 | 31,140 | 441,205 |
| 2016 | 114,227 | 60,266 | 48,015 | 156,985 | 12,695 | 1,234 | 698 | 6,000 | 1,150 | 26,811 | 419,004 | 3,758 | 26,883 | 31,320 | 450,324 |
| 2017 | 109,824 | 58,751 | 45,761 | 155,798 | 13,803 | 1,152 | 703 | 6,160 | 1,913 | 25,224 | 421,372 | 3,526 | 25,139 | 29,549 | 450,921 |
| 2018 | 106,462 | 62,700 | 49,066 | 163,140 | 15,956 | 1,113 | 758 | 5,550 | 697 | 24,079 | 420,447 | 3,491 | 25,526 | 29,573 | 450,020 |
| 2019 | 97,865 | 59,639 | 41,621 | 162,394 | 11,848 | 898 | 836 | 6,031 | 1,528 | 19,677 | 394,795 | 3,995 | 25,016 | 29,624 | 424,419 |
| 2020 | 101,195 | 59,217 | 44,893 | 155,623 | 10,968 | 1,429 | 1,172 | 6,490 | 1,173 | 19,399 | 392,017 | 3,949 | 23,453 | 28,003 | 420,020 |
| 2021¹ | 94,399 | 60,289 | 40,553 | 159,637 | 11,118 | 1,314 | 862 | 7,200 | 1,236 | 19,149 | 382,883 | 3,027 | 23,367 | 26,946 | 409,829 |

¹ Preliminary.   ² Hash, stews and soups.   *Source: Agricultural Statistics Board, U.S. Department of Agriculture (ASB-USDA)*

## Cold Storage Stocks of All Frozen Potatoes in the United States, on First of Month   In Millions of Pounds

| Year | Jan. | Feb. | Mar. | Apr. | May | June | July | Aug. | Sept. | Oct. | Nov. | Dec. |
|---|---|---|---|---|---|---|---|---|---|---|---|---|
| 2013 | 1,110.4 | 1,175.1 | 1,232.7 | 1,226.8 | 1,222.4 | 1,181.3 | 1,270.3 | 1,138.4 | 1,091.3 | 1,137.6 | 1,175.3 | 1,150.8 |
| 2014 | 1,095.3 | 1,104.8 | 1,124.1 | 1,044.3 | 1,009.2 | 983.4 | 1,012.8 | 924.2 | 936.6 | 1,039.7 | 1,099.5 | 1,105.6 |
| 2015 | 1,030.4 | 1,091.7 | 1,132.9 | 1,146.4 | 1,127.2 | 1,135.6 | 1,151.7 | 1,065.4 | 1,047.0 | 1,058.0 | 1,093.0 | 1,055.6 |
| 2016 | 1,006.9 | 1,021.7 | 1,046.0 | 1,072.2 | 1,095.0 | 1,122.2 | 1,175.8 | 1,149.0 | 1,160.5 | 1,217.2 | 1,253.5 | 1,180.5 |
| 2017 | 1,124.6 | 1,195.7 | 1,210.6 | 1,212.3 | 1,219.7 | 1,209.3 | 1,230.6 | 1,201.7 | 1,190.2 | 1,237.0 | 1,273.5 | 1,274.1 |
| 2018 | 1,183.0 | 1,258.3 | 1,265.2 | 1,225.8 | 1,192.8 | 1,156.7 | 1,212.0 | 1,096.7 | 1,140.8 | 1,185.0 | 1,250.2 | 1,198.4 |
| 2019 | 1,174.6 | 1,265.2 | 1,299.0 | 1,291.8 | 1,211.8 | 1,172.9 | 1,184.5 | 1,134.3 | 1,162.3 | 1,160.7 | 1,170.7 | 1,180.9 |
| 2020 | 1,155.9 | 1,201.2 | 1,249.5 | 1,309.5 | 1,192.8 | 1,099.4 | 1,085.1 | 1,087.7 | 1,139.7 | 1,175.4 | 1,241.4 | 1,176.5 |
| 2021 | 1,122.1 | 1,162.4 | 1,159.5 | 1,146.6 | 1,117.5 | 1,132.8 | 1,114.3 | 1,080.5 | 1,079.8 | 1,090.9 | 1,163.0 | 1,113.2 |
| 2022¹ | 1,064.0 | 1,150.1 | 1,211.9 | 1,178.0 | 1,173.6 | 1,189.9 | 1,238.3 | 1,218.2 | 1,214.2 | 1,199.5 | 1,257.7 | 1,180.8 |

¹ Preliminary.   *Source: Agricultural Statistics Board, U.S. Department of Agriculture (ASB-USDA)*

# POTATOES

**Potatoes** (monthly average) through December 2022 — USD per Cwt

## Average Price Received by Farmers for Potatoes in the U.S.   In Dollars Per Hundred Pounds (Cwt.)

| Year | Jan. | Feb. | Mar. | Apr. | May | June | July | Aug. | Sept. | Oct. | Nov. | Dec. | Season Average |
|---|---|---|---|---|---|---|---|---|---|---|---|---|---|
| 2013 | 7.87 | 8.12 | 8.72 | 9.63 | 12.89 | 12.57 | 13.56 | 11.15 | 8.48 | 7.96 | 8.87 | 9.02 | 9.75 |
| 2014 | 9.02 | 9.22 | 9.47 | 9.92 | 9.53 | 10.28 | 9.72 | 8.88 | 7.76 | 7.30 | 8.19 | 8.63 | 8.88 |
| 2015 | 9.12 | 9.14 | 9.38 | 9.69 | 9.26 | 9.27 | 8.62 | 8.45 | 7.58 | 7.24 | 8.23 | 8.38 | 8.76 |
| 2016 | 8.63 | 8.64 | 9.41 | 9.61 | 9.98 | 10.52 | 9.58 | 12.80 | 10.48 | 9.59 | 9.91 | 9.59 | 9.08 |
| 2017 | 8.27 | 8.42 | 8.65 | 8.40 | 9.40 | 10.25 | 10.79 | 14.61 | 13.86 | 11.33 | 11.22 | 11.39 | 9.17 |
| 2018 | 11.30 | 11.20 | 11.10 | 11.20 | 11.40 | 11.80 | 11.50 | 11.20 | 9.44 | 8.65 | 9.22 | 9.37 | 8.48 |
| 2019 | 9.88 | 10.70 | 11.30 | 11.50 | 11.10 | 12.10 | 13.30 | 14.50 | 13.30 | 12.80 | 13.90 | 13.90 | 12.36 |
| 2020 | 14.30 | 14.50 | 15.90 | 14.60 | 12.80 | 12.20 | 14.80 | 15.20 | 12.00 | 11.20 | 10.90 | 10.30 | 13.23 |
| 2021 | 9.70 | 9.70 | 10.40 | 10.80 | 11.40 | 12.00 | 13.20 | 14.70 | 14.00 | 13.10 | 13.50 | 13.50 | 12.17 |
| 2022[1] | 13.50 | 13.90 | 14.30 | 14.80 | 16.30 | 18.10 | 23.70 | 28.20 | 25.90 | 18.50 | 20.40 | 21.30 | 19.08 |

[1] Preliminary.   Source: Agricultural Statistics Board, U.S. Department of Agriculture (ASB-USDA)

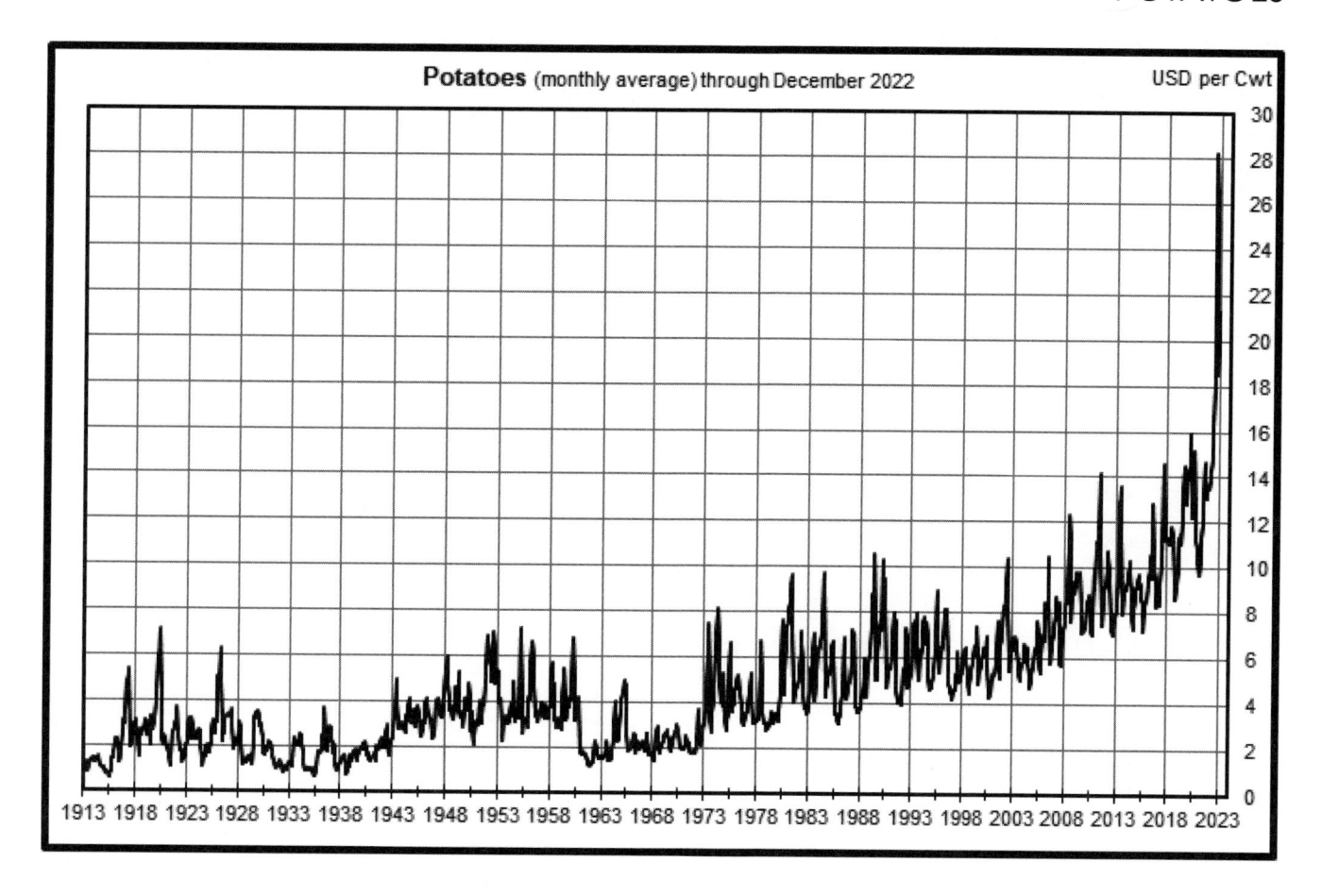

## Per Capita Utilization of Potatoes in the United States   In Pounds (Farm Weight)

|  |  |  | Processing | | | | |
|---|---|---|---|---|---|---|---|
| Year | Total | Fresh | Freezing | Chips & Shoestring | Dehydrating | Canning | Total Processing |
| 2012 | 114.9 | 34.6 | 48.1 | 17.6 | 13.9 | 0.8 | 80.3 |
| 2013 | 113.6 | 34.6 | 47.7 | 17.8 | 12.9 | 0.6 | 79.0 |
| 2014 | 113.1 | 33.6 | 47.1 | 20.0 | 12.1 | 0.3 | 79.5 |
| 2015 | 113.4 | 34.2 | 47.7 | 19.6 | 11.6 | 0.4 | 79.2 |
| 2016 | 110.2 | 33.7 | 47.4 | 16.6 | 12.0 | 0.4 | 76.5 |
| 2017 | 117.8 | 34.9 | 51.8 | 17.8 | 12.9 | 0.5 | 82.9 |
| 2018 | 117.6 | 33.1 | 53.4 | 17.8 | 12.9 | 0.5 | 84.5 |
| 2019 | 112.6 | 30.1 | 52.4 | 17.9 | 11.9 | 0.4 | 82.5 |
| 2020[1] | 115.0 | 30.3 | 54.6 | 17.6 | 12.1 | 0.5 | 84.8 |
| 2021[2] | 112.1 | 29.3 | 52.5 | 17.0 | 12.8 | 0.6 | 82.8 |

[1] Preliminary.   [2] Forecast.   Source: Agricultural Statistics Board, U.S. Department of Agriculture (ASB-USDA)

# POTATOES

## Potatoes Processed[1] in the United States, Eight States    In Thousands of Cwt.

| States | Storage Season | to Dec. 1 | to Jan. 1 | to Feb. 1 | to Mar. 1 | to Apr. 1 | to May 1 | to June 1 | Entire Season |
|---|---|---|---|---|---|---|---|---|---|
| Idaho and Oregon- Malheur Co. | 2014-15 | 27,685 | 33,995 | 40,850 | 47,985 | 54,665 | 63,025 | 70,600 | 86,870 |
| | 2015-16 | 26,850 | 33,115 | 39,655 | 46,455 | 53,710 | 61,050 | 68,435 | 86,250 |
| | 2016-17 | 25,720 | 32,650 | 39,475 | 46,880 | 54,625 | 61,950 | 70,110 | 92,760 |
| | 2017-18 | 24,840 | 31,920 | 38,950 | 46,610 | 54,060 | 61,285 | 69,840 | 87,379 |
| | 2018-19 | 25,325 | 32,020 | 39,495 | 47,395 | 55,250 | 63,225 | 71,340 | 95,974 |
| | 2019-20 | 26,655 | 33,170 | 39,840 | 47,980 | 55,775 | 61,640 | 69,395 | 86,863 |
| | 2020-21 | 27,195 | 34,360 | 41,695 | 49,565 | 57,390 | 64,815 | 73,065 | 90,755 |
| | 2021-22 | 27,070 | 34,300 | 41,530 | 48,715 | 56,370 | 63,875 | 71,680 | 83,070 |
| | 2022-23 | 25,800 | 33,145 | 40,455 | | | | | |
| Maine[2] | 2014-15 | 1,410 | 1,845 | 2,415 | 2,930 | 3,475 | 3,980 | 4,445 | 5,622 |
| | 2015-16 | 1,170 | 1,590 | 2,050 | 2,490 | 2,980 | 3,495 | 4,065 | 5,724 |
| | 2016-17 | 1,260 | 1,665 | 2,175 | 2,660 | 3,080 | 3,470 | 3,825 | 5,059 |
| | 2017-18 | 1,510 | 1,880 | 2,370 | 2,880 | 3,460 | 4,010 | 4,560 | 4,829 |
| | 2018-19 | 1,470 | 1,890 | 2,400 | 2,870 | 3,450 | 3,870 | 4,290 | 5,050 |
| | 2019-20 | 1,585 | 2,050 | 2,610 | 2,875 | 3,285 | 3,590 | 4,040 | 5,050 |
| | 2020-21 | 1,475 | 1,750 | 2,095 | 2,400 | 2,720 | 3,055 | 3,375 | 4,307 |
| | 2021-22 | 1,735 | 2,250 | 2,890 | 3,475 | 4,065 | 4,590 | 5,050 | 5,399 |
| | 2022-23 | W | W | W | | | | | |
| Washington & Oregon- Other | 2014-15 | 31,870 | 37,190 | 42,715 | 50,380 | 57,340 | 64,525 | 72,365 | 88,615 |
| | 2015-16 | 33,955 | 39,970 | 46,320 | 54,455 | 60,985 | 67,560 | 74,285 | 91,720 |
| | 2016-17 | 36,700 | 42,180 | 47,835 | 55,365 | 62,125 | 68,705 | 76,635 | 90,785 |
| | 2017-18 | 32,885 | 39,925 | 46,515 | 54,355 | 61,780 | 68,555 | 76,495 | 91,160 |
| | 2018-19 | 36,405 | 43,420 | 50,400 | 57,720 | 65,095 | 71,405 | 79,130 | 97,176 |
| | 2019-20 | 34,755 | 42,045 | 49,685 | 59,535 | 67,325 | 71,280 | 78,895 | 94,700 |
| | 2020-21 | 31,930 | 38,235 | 45,085 | 53,300 | 60,990 | 68,955 | 78,055 | 89,406 |
| | 2021-22 | 34,920 | 42,380 | 49,870 | 59,620 | 67,870 | 76,105 | 84,965 | 94,882 |
| | 2022-23 | 36,630 | 43,550 | 50,160 | | | | | |
| Other States[3] | 2014-15 | 13,705 | 17,295 | 20,865 | 24,685 | 28,550 | 32,080 | 35,415 | 40,456 |
| | 2015-16 | 8,995 | 12,515 | 16,380 | 20,720 | 24,550 | 28,665 | 33,020 | 38,742 |
| | 2016-17 | 10,035 | 13,570 | 17,140 | 21,005 | 25,085 | 28,505 | 32,385 | 38,631 |
| | 2017-18 | 10,030 | 14,181 | 18,075 | 22,740 | 26,535 | 30,425 | 34,740 | 42,856 |
| | 2018-19 | 10,643 | 15,048 | 18,836 | 23,479 | 27,079 | 30,423 | 34,392 | 40,470 |
| | 2019-20 | 13,315 | 17,485 | 21,170 | 24,940 | 28,430 | 31,263 | 34,565 | 39,346 |
| | 2020-21 | 11,380 | 14,854 | 18,134 | 21,545 | 25,200 | 28,587 | 32,302 | 38,101 |
| | 2021-22 | 11,882 | 16,011 | 19,773 | 22,981 | 26,364 | 29,486 | 33,035 | 39,642 |
| | 2022-23 | 12,208 | 16,894 | 23,825 | | | | | |
| Total | 2014-15 | 74,670 | 90,325 | 106,845 | 125,980 | 144,030 | 163,610 | 182,825 | 221,563 |
| | 2015-16 | 70,970 | 87,190 | 104,405 | 124,120 | 142,225 | 160,770 | 179,805 | 222,436 |
| | 2016-17 | 73,715 | 90,065 | 106,625 | 125,910 | 144,915 | 162,630 | 182,955 | 227,235 |
| | 2017-18 | 69,265 | 87,906 | 105,910 | 126,585 | 145,835 | 164,275 | 185,635 | 226,224 |
| | 2018-19 | 73,843 | 92,378 | 111,131 | 131,464 | 150,874 | 168,923 | 189,152 | 238,670 |
| | 2019-20 | 76,310 | 94,750 | 113,305 | 135,330 | 154,815 | 167,773 | 186,895 | 225,959 |
| | 2020-21 | 71,980 | 89,199 | 107,009 | 124,810 | 146,300 | 165,412 | 186,797 | 222,569 |
| | 2021-22 | 75,607 | 94,941 | 114,063 | 134,791 | 154,669 | 174,056 | 194,730 | 222,993 |
| | 2022-23 | 75,378 | 93,589 | 111,685 | | | | | |
| Dehydrated[4] | 2014-15 | 13,045 | 16,325 | 19,965 | 23,645 | 26,345 | 31,515 | 35,490 | 46,340 |
| | 2015-16 | 12,155 | 15,885 | 19,620 | 23,560 | 27,605 | 31,585 | 35,645 | 45,735 |
| | 2016-17 | 11,560 | 15,305 | 19,085 | 22,675 | 26,565 | 30,545 | 34,890 | 46,317 |
| | 2017-18 | 10,595 | 14,304 | 18,085 | 21,680 | 25,775 | 29,800 | 34,410 | 44,263 |
| | 2018-19 | 13,810 | 17,065 | 20,775 | 24,420 | 28,315 | 32,620 | 36,660 | 47,648 |
| | 2019-20 | 11,850 | 15,075 | 18,620 | 21,865 | 25,510 | 28,780 | 32,080 | 40,285 |
| | 2020-21 | 13,140 | 16,435 | 19,715 | 23,245 | 27,090 | 30,780 | 34,430 | 43,735 |
| | 2021-22 | 11,855 | 15,715 | 19,495 | 22,335 | 26,080 | 29,360 | 32,415 | 40,406 |
| | 2022-23 | 11,095 | 14,560 | 17,750 | | | | | |

[1] Total quantity received and used for processing regardless of the State in which the potatoes were produced. Amount excludes quantities used for potato chips in Maine, Michigan and Wisconsin.    [2] Includes Maine grown potatoes only.    [3] Colorado, Minnesota, , Nevada, North Dakota and Wisconsin.
[4] Dehydrated products except starch and flour. Included in above totals. Includes CO, ID, NV, ND, OR, WA, and WI.
*Source: National Agricultural Statistics Service, U.S. Department of Agriculture (NASS-USDA)*

# Rice

Rice is a grain that is cultivated on every continent except Antarctica and is the primary food for half the people in the world. Rice cultivation probably originated as early as 10,000 BC in Asia. Rice is grown at varying altitudes (sea level to about 3,000 meters), in varying climates (tropical to temperate), and on dry to flooded land. The growth duration of rice plants is 3-6 months, depending on variety and growing conditions. Rice is harvested by hand in developing countries or by combines in industrialized countries. Asian countries produce about 90% of rice grown worldwide. Rough rice futures and options are traded at the CME Group.

**Prices** – CME rough rice futures price (Barchart.com electronic symbol ZR) on the monthly nearest-futures chart rallied during 2022 and closed the year up +23.4% yr/yr at $18.050 per hundredweight (cwt).

**Supply** – World rice production in the 2022/23 marketing year is expected to fall by -2.3% to 751.319 million metric tons. The world's largest rice producers are expected to be China with 27.8% of world production in 2022/23, India with 25.0%, Indonesia with 7.3%, Bangladesh with 7.1%, Vietnam with 5.8%, and Thailand with 4.1%. U.S. production of rice in 2022/23 is expected to fall by -16.3% yr/yr to 7.274 million metric tons.

**Demand** – World consumption of rice in 2022/23 is expected to fall by -0.6% yr/yr to 515.052 million metric tons. U.S. rice consumption in 2022/23 is expected to fall by -2.8% yr/yr to 4.667 million metric tons.

**Trade** – World exports of rice in 2022/23 is expected to fall by -4.4% yr/yr to 54.336 million metric tons. The world's largest rice exporters will be India with 37.7% of world exports, Thailand with 15.6%, Vietnam with 13.6%, Pakistan with 7.4%, Burma with 4.4%, and the U.S. with 3.9%. U.S. rice imports in 2022/23 are expected to rise by +19.2% yr/yr to a new record high of 1.429 million metric tons. U.S. rice exports in 2022/23 are expected to fall by -19.7% yr/yr to 2.096 million metric tons.

### World Production of Rough Rice   In Thousands of Metric Tons

| Crop Year | Bangladesh | Brazil | Burma | China | India | Indonesia | Japan | Pakistan | Philippines | Thailand | United States | Vietnam | World Total |
|---|---|---|---|---|---|---|---|---|---|---|---|---|---|
| 2013-14 | 4,000 | 800 | 1,530 | 1,225 | 1,500 | 1,024 | 989 | 2,800 | 1,200 | 1,459 | 1,100 | 975 | 39,088 |
| 2014-15 | 4,700 | 1,300 | 1,706 | 1,350 | 1,350 | 1,205 | 1,051 | 2,600 | 1,800 | 1,601 | 1,200 | 980 | 41,710 |
| 2015-16 | 4,800 | 1,250 | 1,804 | 1,050 | 1,100 | 912 | 823 | 2,100 | 1,600 | 1,260 | 1,020 | 950 | 38,690 |
| 2016-17 | 5,300 | 1,300 | 1,505 | 350 | 1,250 | 1,191 | 900 | 2,500 | 1,100 | 1,195 | 1,100 | 1,006 | 41,664 |
| 2017-18 | 5,500 | 1,370 | 1,652 | 2,350 | 1,000 | 1,170 | 800 | 2,000 | 1,300 | 1,290 | 1,100 | 1,074 | 47,333 |
| 2018-19 | 3,200 | 1,350 | 1,803 | 600 | 1,300 | 1,209 | 1,000 | 1,900 | 3,600 | 1,425 | 1,100 | 1,010 | 44,230 |
| 2019-20 | 2,600 | 980 | 2,009 | 550 | 1,200 | 1,154 | 1,220 | 1,400 | 2,450 | 1,613 | 1,050 | 934 | 42,433 |
| 2020-21[1] | 4,215 | 1,350 | 1,784 | 650 | 850 | 1,227 | 1,150 | 2,200 | 2,200 | 1,200 | 1,100 | 990 | 46,434 |
| 2021-22[2] | 5,949 | 1,665 | 2,429 | 750 | 1,270 | 1,721 | 1,200 | 2,450 | 3,600 | 1,300 | 1,500 | 1,054 | 54,664 |
| 2022-23[3] | 5,200 | 1,550 | 2,650 | 750 | 1,200 | 1,650 | 1,200 | 2,200 | 3,600 | 1,300 | 1,100 | 1,100 | 53,291 |

[1] Preliminary.   [2] Estimate.   [3] Forecast.   Source: Foreign Agricultural Service, U.S. Department of Agriculture (FAS-USDA)

### World Imports of Rice (Milled Basis)   In Thousands of Metric Tons

| Crop Year | China | Cote d'Ivoire | European Union | Indonesia | Iran | Iraq | Malaysia | Nigeria | Philippines | Saudi Arabia | Senegal | South Africa | World Total |
|---|---|---|---|---|---|---|---|---|---|---|---|---|---|
| 2013-14 | 51,590 | 12,206 | 18,683 | 206,286 | 159,985 | 57,165 | 11,154 | 10,198 | 18,822 | 31,000 | 8,615 | 45,058 | 718,262 |
| 2014-15 | 51,755 | 12,449 | 19,688 | 209,609 | 158,239 | 56,000 | 11,098 | 10,506 | 18,911 | 28,409 | 10,079 | 45,066 | 720,611 |
| 2015-16 | 51,755 | 10,603 | 19,000 | 212,141 | 156,628 | 57,008 | 10,819 | 10,204 | 17,473 | 23,939 | 8,759 | 44,134 | 711,102 |
| 2016-17 | 51,872 | 12,328 | 19,766 | 211,094 | 164,563 | 58,505 | 10,891 | 10,275 | 18,549 | 29,091 | 10,167 | 43,840 | 734,460 |
| 2017-18 | 48,980 | 12,065 | 20,625 | 212,676 | 169,157 | 58,268 | 10,696 | 11,176 | 19,421 | 31,177 | 8,084 | 44,251 | 738,805 |
| 2018-19 | 52,369 | 10,500 | 20,625 | 212,129 | 174,737 | 53,858 | 10,518 | 10,804 | 18,622 | 30,818 | 10,153 | 43,750 | 743,834 |
| 2019-20 | 53,780 | 11,179 | 19,766 | 209,614 | 178,323 | 54,646 | 10,455 | 10,810 | 18,932 | 26,750 | 8,396 | 43,360 | 745,046 |
| 2020-21[1] | 51,905 | 11,766 | 19,688 | 211,857 | 186,574 | 54,331 | 10,398 | 12,631 | 19,708 | 28,580 | 10,320 | 43,810 | 760,476 |
| 2021-22[2] | 53,780 | 10,790 | 19,300 | 212,843 | 195,455 | 54,173 | 10,529 | 13,986 | 19,905 | 30,118 | 8,690 | 43,110 | 768,892 |
| 2022-23[3] | 53,480 | 10,640 | 19,531 | 208,494 | 187,519 | 54,488 | 10,234 | 9,901 | 19,700 | 30,455 | 7,274 | 43,560 | 751,319 |

[1] Preliminary.   [2] Estimate.   [3] Forecast.   Source: Foreign Agricultural Service, U.S. Department of Agriculture (FAS-USDA)

### World Exports of Rice (Milled Basis)   In Thousands of Metric Tons

| Crop Year | Argentina | Brazil | Burma | Cambodia | Guyana | India | Pakistan | Paraguay | Thailand | United States | Uruguay | Vietnam | World Total |
|---|---|---|---|---|---|---|---|---|---|---|---|---|---|
| 2013-14 | 467 | 819 | 1,688 | 1,000 | 346 | 10,619 | 3,950 | 380 | 10,969 | 3,004 | 890 | 6,325 | 43,342 |
| 2014-15 | 312 | 930 | 1,735 | 1,150 | 446 | 12,238 | 3,800 | 371 | 9,779 | 3,078 | 766 | 6,606 | 43,867 |
| 2015-16 | 526 | 546 | 1,300 | 1,050 | 513 | 10,357 | 4,200 | 556 | 9,891 | 3,384 | 972 | 5,088 | 40,735 |
| 2016-17 | 343 | 830 | 3,350 | 1,150 | 478 | 11,710 | 3,548 | 538 | 11,658 | 3,645 | 947 | 6,488 | 47,892 |
| 2017-18 | 426 | 1,122 | 2,750 | 1,300 | 516 | 12,041 | 4,011 | 653 | 11,213 | 2,763 | 773 | 6,590 | 47,885 |
| 2018-19 | 350 | 878 | 2,700 | 1,350 | 448 | 10,420 | 4,493 | 689 | 7,565 | 2,959 | 846 | 6,581 | 44,184 |
| 2019-20 | 361 | 1,219 | 2,300 | 1,350 | 511 | 12,520 | 3,820 | 803 | 5,715 | 2,991 | 865 | 6,167 | 43,448 |
| 2020-21[1] | 385 | 950 | 1,900 | 1,850 | 552 | 20,216 | 3,877 | 640 | 6,283 | 2,969 | 785 | 6,272 | 51,153 |
| 2021-22[2] | 400 | 1,300 | 2,300 | 1,700 | 406 | 22,025 | 4,800 | 720 | 7,900 | 2,609 | 950 | 7,200 | 56,844 |
| 2022-23[3] | 350 | 1,100 | 2,400 | 1,600 | 380 | 20,500 | 4,000 | 700 | 8,500 | 2,096 | 900 | 7,400 | 54,336 |

[1] Preliminary.   [2] Estimate.   [3] Forecast.   Source: Foreign Agricultural Service, U.S. Department of Agriculture (FAS-USDA)

# RICE

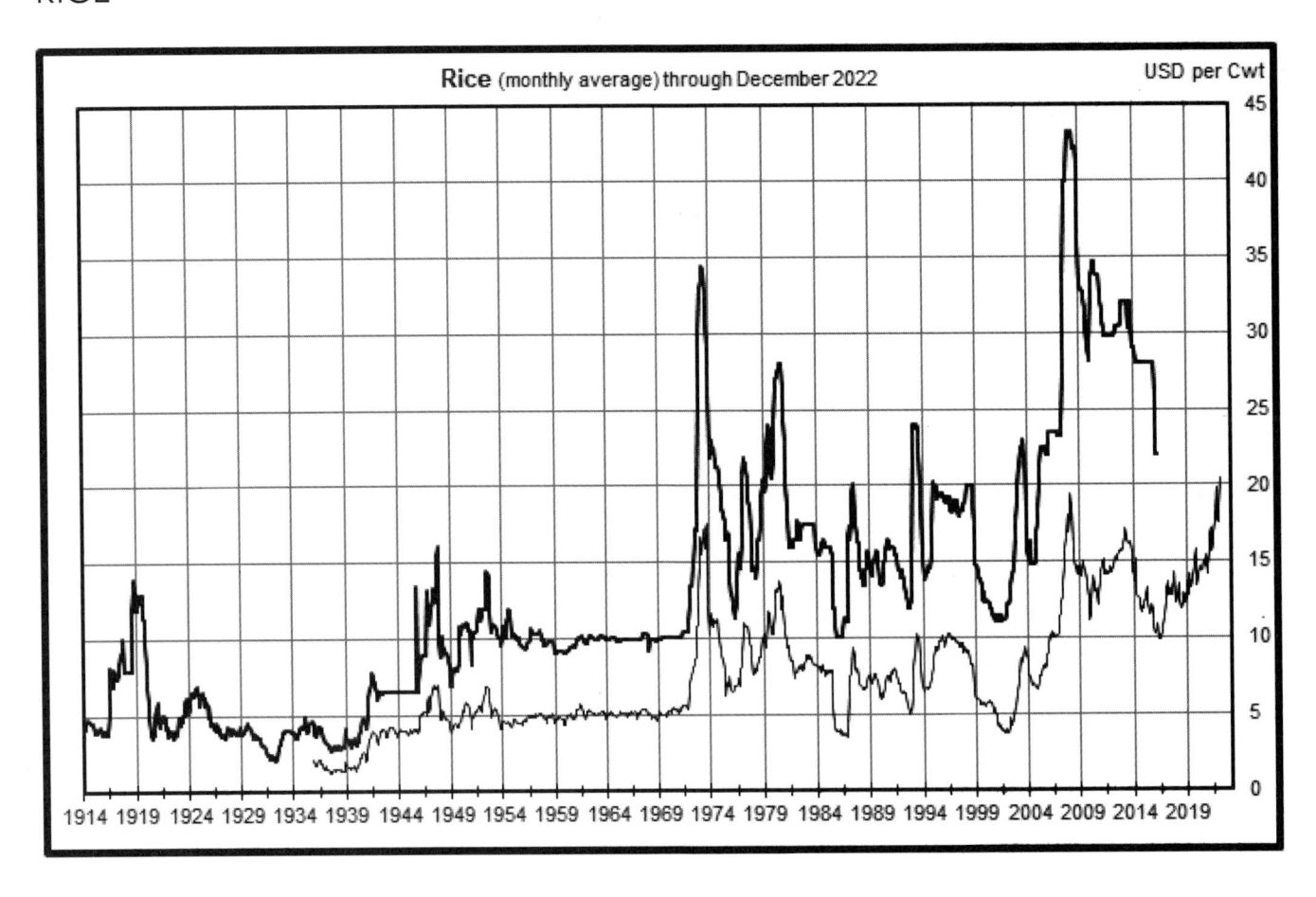

Rice (monthly average) through December 2022 — USD per Cwt

### Average Wholesale Price of Rice No. 2 (Medium)[2] Southwest Louisiana   In Dollars Per Cwt. Bagged

| Crop Year | Aug. | Sept. | Oct. | Nov. | Dec. | Jan. | Feb. | Mar. | Apr. | May | June | July | Average |
|---|---|---|---|---|---|---|---|---|---|---|---|---|---|
| 2013-14 | 30.44 | 30.50 | 32.00 | 32.00 | 32.00 | 32.00 | 32.00 | 32.00 | 32.00 | 30.25 | 32.00 | 32.00 | 31.60 |
| 2014-15 | 30.50 | 29.00 | 29.00 | 29.00 | 29.00 | 28.75 | 28.00 | 28.00 | 28.00 | 28.00 | 28.00 | 28.00 | 28.60 |
| 2015-16 | 28.00 | 28.00 | 28.00 | 28.00 | 28.00 | 28.00 | 28.00 | 28.00 | 28.00 | 28.00 | 28.00 | 28.00 | 28.00 |
| 2016-17 | 28.00 | 28.00 | 28.00 | 26.00 | 22.00 | 22.00 | 22.00 | 22.00 | 22.00 | 22.00 | 22.00 | 22.20 | 23.85 |
| 2017-18 | 23.00 | 23.60 | 24.50 | 24.50 | 24.50 | 25.63 | 28.00 | 28.00 | 28.00 | 29.50 | 30.00 | 30.00 | 26.60 |
| 2018-19 | 30.00 | 30.00 | 31.13 | 31.50 | 31.50 | 31.50 | 31.50 | 31.50 | 31.50 | 31.50 | 31.50 | 31.50 | 31.22 |
| 2019-20 | 31.50 | 31.50 | 31.50 | 31.50 | 31.50 | 31.50 | 31.50 | 31.50 | 31.50 | 31.50 | 31.50 | 31.50 | 31.50 |
| 2020-21 | 31.50 | 31.50 | 31.50 | 31.50 | 31.50 | 31.50 | 31.50 | 31.50 | 31.50 | 31.50 | 31.50 | 31.50 | 31.50 |
| 2021-22 | 31.50 | 31.50 | 31.83 | 32.50 | 32.50 | 32.50 | 32.50 | 34.50 | 35.00 | 35.00 | 35.00 | 35.00 | 33.28 |
| 2022-23[1] | 40.00 | 40.00 | 40.00 | 42.50 | 45.00 | 45.00 | 45.00 | | | | | | 42.50 |

[1] Preliminary.  [2] U.S. No. 2 -- broken not to exceed 4%.   Source: Economic Research Service, U.S. Department of Agriculture (ERS-USDA)

### Average Price Received by Farmers for Rice (Rough) in the United States   In Dollars Per Hundred Pounds (Cwt.)

| Crop Year | Aug. | Sept. | Oct. | Nov. | Dec. | Jan. | Feb. | Mar. | Apr. | May | June | July | Average[2] |
|---|---|---|---|---|---|---|---|---|---|---|---|---|---|
| 2013-14 | 15.80 | 15.60 | 15.80 | 16.20 | 16.50 | 17.10 | 16.70 | 16.40 | 16.20 | 16.20 | 16.30 | 16.10 | 16.24 |
| 2014-15 | 15.60 | 14.40 | 14.00 | 14.30 | 13.60 | 15.10 | 12.80 | 12.60 | 12.60 | 12.50 | 12.00 | 11.60 | 13.43 |
| 2015-16 | 12.00 | 11.90 | 12.20 | 12.50 | 12.80 | 13.30 | 12.10 | 11.80 | 11.50 | 11.70 | 11.70 | 12.10 | 12.13 |
| 2016-17 | 11.80 | 10.60 | 10.30 | 10.40 | 10.50 | 10.90 | 10.10 | 10.10 | 10.10 | 10.20 | 10.20 | 10.70 | 10.49 |
| 2017-18 | 11.30 | 11.50 | 12.20 | 13.30 | 12.90 | 13.70 | 12.70 | 12.70 | 13.10 | 12.80 | 13.10 | 13.70 | 12.75 |
| 2018-19 | 14.30 | 12.40 | 12.30 | 12.60 | 12.70 | 13.50 | 12.40 | 11.90 | 12.00 | 11.90 | 12.20 | 12.90 | 12.59 |
| 2019-20 | 12.70 | 12.30 | 12.80 | 13.60 | 12.80 | 14.10 | 13.70 | 13.80 | 14.10 | 14.50 | 14.90 | 14.70 | 13.67 |
| 2020-21 | 15.80 | 13.70 | 13.40 | 13.90 | 14.10 | 14.60 | 14.40 | 14.40 | 14.40 | 15.00 | 15.00 | 14.60 | 14.44 |
| 2021-22 | 15.40 | 14.20 | 14.80 | 15.70 | 16.80 | 17.10 | 15.60 | 15.60 | 16.20 | 16.90 | 17.50 | 17.80 | 16.13 |
| 2022-23[1] | 19.80 | 17.60 | 17.50 | 18.70 | 20.40 | 19.10 | 18.50 | | | | | | 18.80 |

[1] Preliminary.  [2] Weighted average by sales.   Source: Economic Research Service, U.S. Department of Agriculture (ERS-USDA)

# RICE

## Salient Statistics of Rice, Rough & Milled (Rough Equivalent) in the United States    In Millions of Cwt.

| Crop Year Beginning Aug. 1 | Stocks Aug. 1 | Production | Imports | Total Supply | Food | Brewers | Seed | Total | Residual | Exports | Total Disappearance | CCC Stocks July 31 | Put Under Price Support | Long | Medium | All Classes | Milled Long |
|---|---|---|---|---|---|---|---|---|---|---|---|---|---|---|---|---|---|
| 2013-14 | 36.4 | 190.0 | 23.1 | 249.5 | 120.7 | 4 | 3.6 | 124.4 | 4 | 93.3 | 217.7 | 0 | 36.0 | 6.50 | 6.50 | 6.50 | 10.34 |
| 2014-15 | 31.8 | 222.2 | 24.7 | 278.7 | 131.2 | 4 | 3.2 | 133.9 | 4 | 96.3 | 230.2 | 0 | 42.3 | 6.50 | 6.50 | 6.50 | 10.25 |
| 2015-16 | 48.5 | 193.1 | 24.1 | 264.9 | 107.7 | 4 | 3.9 | 112.7 | 4 | 106.6 | 219.3 | 0 | | 6.50 | 6.50 | 6.50 | 10.22 |
| 2016-17 | 46.5 | 224.1 | 23.5 | 294.1 | NA | 4 | NA | 133.2 | 4 | 114.8 | 248.0 | 0 | | 6.50 | 6.50 | 6.50 | 9.98 |
| 2017-18 | 46.0 | 178.2 | 26.9 | 251.8 | ---- | 4 | ---- | 135.4 | 4 | 87.1 | 222.4 | | | 6.50 | 6.50 | 6.50 | 10.01 |
| 2018-19 | 29.4 | 224.2 | 29.0 | 282.2 | ---- | 4 | ---- | 143.8 | 4 | 93.6 | 237.3 | | | 6.50 | 6.50 | 6.50 | 10.08 |
| 2019-20 | 44.9 | 184.7 | 37.3 | 267.3 | ---- | 4 | ---- | 144.4 | 4 | 94.2 | 238.6 | | | 7.00 | 7.00 | 7.00 | 11.09 |
| 2020-21 | 28.7 | 227.6 | 34.1 | 290.2 | ---- | 4 | ---- | 153.1 | 4 | 93.5 | 246.6 | | | 7.00 | 7.00 | 7.00 | 11.10 |
| 2021-22[1] | 43.7 | 191.8 | 37.8 | 273.0 | ---- | 4 | ---- | 151.1 | 4 | 82.2 | 233.3 | | | 7.00 | 7.00 | 7.00 | 11.06 |
| 2022-23[2] | 39.7 | 164.3 | 45.0 | 245.1 | ---- | 4 | ---- | 147.0 | 4 | 66.0 | 213.0 | | | 7.00 | 7.00 | 7.00 | |

[1] Preliminary.  [2] Forecast.  [3] Loan rate for each class of rice is the sum of the whole kernels' loan rate weighted by its milling yield (average 56%) and the broken kernels' loan rate weighted by its milling yield (average 12%).  [4] Included in Food.
*Source: Economic Research Service, U.S. Department of Agriculture (ERS-USDA)*

## Acreage, Yield, Production and Prices of Rice in the United States

| Crop Year Beginning Aug. 1 | Acreage Harvested Southern States (1,000 Acres) | California | United States | Yield Per Harvested Acre California (In Lbs.) | United States | Production Southern States (1,000 Cwt.) | California | United States | Value of Production ($1,000) | Wholesale Prices Arkansas[2] ($ Per Cwt.) | Houston[3] | Milled Rice, Average C.I.F. Rotterdam U.S. No. 2[4] ($ Per Metric Ton) | Thai "A"[5] | Thai "B"[5] |
|---|---|---|---|---|---|---|---|---|---|---|---|---|---|---|
| 2013-14 | 1,907 | 562 | 2,469 | 8,480 | 7,694 | 142,312 | 47,641 | 189,953 | 3,181,993 | 30.39 | 30.17 | ---- | ---- | ---- |
| 2014-15 | 2,491 | 442 | 2,933 | 8,580 | 7,576 | 184,279 | 37,936 | 222,215 | 3,075,618 | 29.87 | 26.52 | ---- | ---- | ---- |
| 2015-16 | 2,159 | 426 | 2,585 | 8,890 | 7,472 | 155,271 | 37,877 | 193,148 | 2,421,955 | 24.23 | 24.72 | ---- | ---- | ---- |
| 2016-17 | 2,561 | 536 | 3,097 | 8,840 | 7,237 | 176,751 | 47,394 | 224,145 | 2,384,690 | 22.51 | 22.51 | ---- | ---- | ---- |
| 2017-18 | 1,931 | 443 | 2,374 | 8,410 | 7,507 | 140,951 | 37,277 | 178,228 | 2,360,439 | 27.86 | 25.31 | ---- | ---- | ---- |
| 2018-19 | 2,411 | 504 | 2,915 | 8,620 | 7,692 | 180,786 | 43,425 | 224,211 | 2,898,996 | 30.69 | 26.56 | ---- | ---- | ---- |
| 2019-20 | 1,976 | 501 | 2,477 | 8,460 | 7,473 | 142,313 | 42,362 | 184,675 | 2,631,955 | 31.82 | 27.89 | ---- | ---- | ---- |
| 2020-21 | 2,472 | 514 | 2,986 | 8,720 | 7,619 | 182,773 | 44,810 | 227,583 | 3,314,161 | 32.37 | 30.21 | ---- | ---- | ---- |
| 2021-22 | 2,083 | 405 | 2,488 | 9,050 | 7,709 | 155,143 | 36,653 | 191,796 | 3,280,335 | 35.09 | 28.63 | ---- | ---- | ---- |
| 2022-23[1] | 1,922 | 255 | 2,177 | 8,700 | 7,549 | 142,134 | 22,185 | 164,319 | 3,101,998 | | | ---- | ---- | ---- |

[1] Preliminary.  [2] F.O.B. mills, Arkansas, medium.  [3] Houston, Texas (long grain).  [4] Milled, 4%, container, FAS.
[5] SWR, 100%, bulk.  NA = Not available.  *Source: Economic Research Service, U.S. Department of Agriculture (ERS-USDA)*

## U.S. Exports of Milled Rice, by Country of Destination    In Thousands of Metric Tons

| Trade Year Beginning October | Canada | Haiti | Iran | Ivory Coast | Jamaica | Mexico | Netherlands | Peru | Saudi Arabia | South Africa | Switzerland | United Kingdom | Total |
|---|---|---|---|---|---|---|---|---|---|---|---|---|---|
| 2012-13 | 231.6 | 365.0 | 125.7 | 14.9 | 2.7 | 885.8 | 4.6 | .3 | 126.2 | 2.6 | .6 | 21.4 | 3,848 |
| 2013-14 | 242.6 | 346.0 | .2 | 13.5 | 2.3 | 741.2 | 5.4 | 6.8 | 106.1 | 2.3 | .6 | 23.6 | 3,355 |
| 2014-15 | 219.2 | 392.1 | ---- | .1 | 2.6 | 837.4 | 5.3 | 9.0 | 111.9 | 1.6 | .6 | 30.6 | 3,971 |
| 2015-16 | 207.1 | 413.5 | 61.4 | 16.0 | 2.5 | 769.6 | 6.7 | 6.6 | 115.7 | .9 | .7 | 28.0 | 3,789 |
| 2016-17 | 212.6 | 478.0 | ---- | 17.2 | 3.1 | 962.0 | 6.0 | 8.7 | 130.1 | .8 | .6 | 34.0 | 3,986 |
| 2017-18 | 211.3 | 450.0 | ---- | 19.0 | 3.8 | 730.5 | 7.4 | .2 | 88.5 | .3 | .5 | 22.3 | 3,052 |
| 2018-19 | 238.4 | 459.0 | ---- | 1.2 | 4.0 | 861.4 | 5.8 | .2 | 110.4 | .6 | .6 | 18.7 | 3,600 |
| 2019-20 | 239.0 | 397.3 | ---- | 38.2 | 5.4 | 609.9 | 5.3 | .1 | 120.3 | .3 | .5 | 28.5 | 3,106 |
| 2020-21 | 226.4 | 437.0 | ---- | 51.7 | 5.8 | 856.1 | 7.4 | .1 | 12.6 | .5 | .7 | 29.6 | 3,730 |
| 2021-22[1] | 248.8 | 445.6 | | 3.2 | 5.0 | 513.0 | 11.6 | .1 | 85.0 | .4 | .2 | 23.1 | 2,772 |

[1] Preliminary.  *Source: Economic Research Service, U.S. Department of Agriculture (ERS-USDA)*

## Production of Rice (Rough) in the United States, by Type and Variety    In Thousands of Cwt.

| Year | Long Grain | Medium Grain | Short Grain | Total | Year | Long Grain | Medium Grain | Short Grain | Total |
|---|---|---|---|---|---|---|---|---|---|
| 2013 | 131,896 | 54,915 | 3,142 | 189,953 | 2018 | 163,956 | 57,339 | 2,916 | 224,211 |
| 2014 | 162,665 | 57,222 | 2,328 | 222,215 | 2019 | 125,610 | 57,098 | 2,396 | 184,675 |
| 2015 | 133,401 | 57,041 | 2,706 | 193,148 | 2020 | 170,784 | 53,920 | 2,810 | 227,583 |
| 2016 | 166,465 | 54,533 | 3,147 | 224,145 | 2021 | 144,639 | 44,494 | 2,663 | 191,796 |
| 2017 | 127,850 | 47,867 | 2,511 | 178,228 | 2022[1] | 131,659 | 30,527 | 2,163 | 164,319 |

[1] Preliminary.  *Source: National Agricultural Statistics Service, U.S. Department of Agriculture (NASS-USDA)*

# Rubber

Rubber is a natural or synthetic substance characterized by elasticity, water repellence, and electrical resistance. Pre-Columbian Native South Americans discovered many uses for rubber, such as containers, balls, shoes, and waterproofing for fabrics such as coats and capes. The Spaniards tried to duplicate these products for many years but were unsuccessful. The first commercial application of rubber began in 1791 when Samuel Peal patented a waterproofing cloth method by treating it with a rubber and turpentine solution. In 1839, Charles Goodyear revolutionized the rubber industry by discovering a process called vulcanization, which involved combining rubber and sulfur and heating the mixture.

Natural rubber is obtained from latex, a milky white fluid, from the Hevea Brasiliensis tree. The latex is gathered by cutting a chevron shape through the bark of the rubber tree. The latex is collected in a small cup, with approximately one fluid ounce per cutting. The cuttings are usually done every other day until the cuttings reach the ground. The tree is then allowed to renew itself before a new tapping is started. The collected latex is strained, diluted with water, and treated with acid to bind the rubber particles together. The rubber is then pressed between rollers to consolidate the rubber into slabs or thin sheets and is air-dried or smoke-dried for shipment.

During World War II, natural rubber supplies from the Far East were cut off, and the rubber shortage accelerated the development of synthetic rubber in the U.S. Synthetic rubber is produced by chemical reactions, condensation, or polymerization, of certain unsaturated hydrocarbons. Synthetic rubber is made of raw material derived from petroleum, coal, oil, natural gas, and acetylene and is almost identical to natural rubber in chemical and physical properties.

Natural rubber and Rubber Index futures are traded on the Osaka Mercantile Exchange (OME). The OME's natural rubber contract is based on the RSS3 ribbed smoked sheet No. 3. The OME's Rubber Index Futures Contract is based on a composite of 8 component grades from 6 rubber markets in the world. Rubber futures are also traded on the Shanghai Futures Exchange (SHFE), the Singapore Exchange (SGX), and the Tokyo Commodity Exchange (TOCOM).

**Prices** – Singapore SGX Rubber futures prices (Barchart.com symbol U6) on the nearest-futures chart in 2022 showed strength in early the year but then fell back and closed the year -20.2% yr/yr at $152.00 per metric ton.

**Supply** – World production of natural rubber in 2022 rose by +0.1% yr/yr to 14.022 million metric tons. The world's largest producers of natural rubber in 2022 were Thailand with 33.1% of world production, and Indonesia with a 22.3% share of world production.

**Trade** – World exports of natural rubber in 2021 rose by +1.4% yr/yr to 1.878 million metric tons. The world's largest exporter of natural rubber in 2021 was Thailand, with 63.2% of world exports. U.S. imports of natural dry rubber in 2021 rose by +23.3% yr/yr to 946,234 metric tons.

### World Production of Natural Rubber    In Thousands of Metric Tons

| Year | Brazil | China | Côte d'Ivoire | India | Indonesia | Liberia | Malaysia | Nigeria | Philippines | Sri Lanka | Thailand | Vietnam | World Total |
|---|---|---|---|---|---|---|---|---|---|---|---|---|---|
| 2012 | 177.1 | 802.3 | 256.6 | 900.0 | 3,012.3 | 78.3 | 923.0 | 148.1 | 443.0 | 150.6 | 4,139.4 | 877.1 | 12,705.1 |
| 2013 | 185.7 | 864.8 | 289.6 | 900.0 | 3,107.5 | 74.6 | 826.4 | 150.1 | 444.8 | 130.4 | 4,305.1 | 946.9 | 13,126.4 |
| 2014 | 192.4 | 840.2 | 316.1 | 940.0 | 3,153.2 | 47.5 | 668.6 | 148.9 | 453.1 | 109.2 | 4,566.3 | 961.1 | 13,385.0 |
| 2015 | 191.5 | 816.1 | 350.0 | 944.5 | 3,145.4 | 58.6 | 722.1 | 146.9 | 398.1 | 91.0 | 4,466.1 | 1,012.8 | 13,361.5 |
| 2016 | 189.8 | 815.9 | 453.0 | 950.6 | 3,307.1 | 60.5 | 673.5 | 146.3 | 362.6 | 79.1 | 4,519.0 | 1,035.3 | 13,613.3 |
| 2017 | 190.5 | 817.4 | 580.0 | 713.0 | 3,680.4 | 63.0 | 740.1 | 146.8 | 407.0 | 83.1 | 4,503.1 | 1,094.5 | 13,906.8 |
| 2018 | 199.7 | 824.1 | 624.1 | 660.0 | 3,630.4 | 75.4 | 603.3 | 148.7 | 423.4 | 82.6 | 4,813.5 | 1,137.7 | 14,234.1 |
| 2019 | 217.4 | 839.9 | 780.1 | 702.0 | 3,448.8 | 89.4 | 639.8 | 149.0 | 431.7 | 74.8 | 4,840.0 | 1,182.5 | 14,536.0 |
| 2020[1] | 225.6 | 687.6 | 936.1 | 687.6 | 3,037.3 | 86.5 | 514.7 | 149.5 | 422.4 | 78.2 | 4,703.2 | 1,226.1 | 14,009.8 |
| 2021[2] | 239.9 | 749.0 | 730.1 | 749.0 | 3,121.5 | 90.8 | 469.7 | 150.1 | 430.6 | 76.9 | 4,643.7 | 1,271.9 | 14,022.0 |

[1] Preliminary.   [2] Estimate.   Source: Food and Agricultural Organization of the United Nations (FAO-UN)

### World Imports of Natural Rubber    In Metric Tons

| Year | Brazil | Canada | China | European Union | Germany | Italy | Korea, South | Malaysia | Mexico | Pakistan | United Kingdom | United States | World Total |
|---|---|---|---|---|---|---|---|---|---|---|---|---|---|
| 2012 | 17,397 | 23,315 | 327,683 | 137,333 | 29,621 | 20,253 | 19,306 | 330,910 | 19,963 | 14,021 | 20,337 | 44,887 | 1,032,232 |
| 2013 | 17,849 | 22,309 | 345,330 | 164,192 | 32,169 | 20,894 | 20,130 | 344,581 | 19,318 | 14,023 | 28,656 | 45,939 | 1,094,300 |
| 2014 | 29,603 | 18,870 | 375,538 | 218,822 | 26,123 | 21,481 | 33,719 | 315,711 | 21,582 | 20,086 | 45,644 | 49,914 | 1,268,199 |
| 2015 | 28,048 | 18,802 | 386,157 | 145,989 | 18,092 | 21,065 | 34,398 | 318,300 | 21,796 | 14,223 | 38,546 | 50,278 | 1,196,131 |
| 2016 | 27,832 | 3,088 | 432,273 | 129,251 | 21,089 | 22,518 | 34,302 | 318,419 | 22,967 | 6,722 | 19,313 | 48,619 | 1,172,683 |
| 2017 | 28,549 | 2,768 | 501,351 | 134,852 | 18,580 | 21,556 | 32,686 | 323,121 | 24,000 | 10,095 | 14,388 | 54,724 | 1,267,024 |
| 2018 | 29,700 | 2,205 | 597,641 | 142,203 | 17,086 | 21,600 | 26,268 | 333,427 | 25,606 | 10,551 | 14,332 | 47,795 | 1,381,809 |
| 2019 | 30,088 | 1,293 | 560,346 | 132,472 | 14,837 | 20,008 | 24,172 | 312,006 | 31,479 | 8,755 | 13,341 | 47,384 | 1,310,089 |
| 2020[1] | 31,470 | 838 | 576,027 | 141,556 | 12,085 | 16,917 | 20,864 | 348,311 | 51,170 | 11,386 | 11,871 | 36,756 | 1,374,233 |
| 2021[2] | 36,183 | 1,997 | 555,696 | 175,874 | 16,876 | 21,445 | 21,018 | 337,255 | 60,484 | 18,211 | 16,662 | 54,597 | 1,417,392 |

[1] Preliminary.   [2] Estimate.   Source: Food and Agricultural Organization of the United Nations (FAO-UN)

# RUBBER

**World Exports of Natural Rubber**   In Metric Tons

| Year | Belgium | Cameroon | Hong Kong | Germany | Guatemala | India | Indonesia | Malaysia | Myanmar | Netherlands | Thailand | United States | World Total |
|---|---|---|---|---|---|---|---|---|---|---|---|---|---|
| 2012 | 37,031 | 4,826 | 1,675 | 7,332 | 23,301 | 4,499 | 7,620 | 31,748 | 50 | 2,288 | 949,103 | 7,909 | 1,151,861 |
| 2013 | 54,754 | 9,866 | 1,414 | 8,209 | 24,068 | 4,635 | 5,907 | 33,538 | 80 | 3,328 | 1,038,421 | 5,398 | 1,253,098 |
| 2014 | 80,932 | 7,169 | 1,802 | 5,982 | 42,899 | 815 | 5,410 | 32,370 | ---- | 12,967 | 1,057,520 | 6,470 | 1,348,083 |
| 2015 | 19,981 | 5,596 | 2,346 | 5,136 | 41,910 | 653 | 6,410 | 31,904 | ---- | 17,834 | 1,072,710 | 7,119 | 1,303,512 |
| 2016 | 37,912 | 6,241 | 1,692 | 6,070 | 40,242 | 2,148 | 6,067 | 30,375 | 410 | 20,240 | 1,240,189 | 6,045 | 1,522,245 |
| 2017 | 24,628 | 6,918 | 1,888 | 9,598 | 51,286 | 15,580 | 6,213 | 32,920 | 2,798 | 30,436 | 1,185,942 | 5,753 | 1,553,472 |
| 2018 | 20,076 | 10,849 | 1,970 | 11,030 | 52,390 | 535 | 5,154 | 27,019 | 12,859 | 30,667 | 1,298,800 | 5,176 | 1,784,597 |
| 2019 | 27,711 | 12,722 | 768 | 8,726 | 54,842 | 1,093 | 4,863 | 23,188 | 16,586 | 19,035 | 1,155,741 | 3,327 | 1,757,662 |
| 2020[1] | 21,819 | 9,334 | 239 | 6,487 | 60,126 | 6,550 | 5,208 | 19,644 | 8,170 | 17,342 | 1,147,585 | 3,518 | 1,852,709 |
| 2021[2] | 30,522 | 15,335 | 320 | 3,636 | 76,079 | 3,322 | 2,395 | 21,106 | 3,188 | 25,332 | 1,187,302 | 6,482 | 1,877,912 |

[1] Preliminary.   [2] Estimate.   *Source: Food and Agricultural Organization of the United Nations (FAO-UN)*

**World Imports of Natural Dry Rubber**   In Metric Tons

| Year | Brazil | Canada | China | European Union | France | Germany | Italy | Japan | Korea, South | Malaysia | Spain | United States | World Total |
|---|---|---|---|---|---|---|---|---|---|---|---|---|---|
| 2012 | 163,742 | 120,209 | 1,962,901 | 1,468,217 | 162,806 | 338,306 | 93,204 | 685,966 | 378,016 | 541,519 | 141,411 | 923,981 | 7,126,936 |
| 2013 | 205,903 | 109,375 | 2,241,937 | 1,440,785 | 159,935 | 342,548 | 97,455 | 711,490 | 376,217 | 660,136 | 143,491 | 881,396 | 7,494,684 |
| 2014 | 211,843 | 110,737 | 2,352,994 | 1,534,502 | 154,533 | 361,112 | 107,044 | 678,945 | 383,051 | 589,328 | 164,149 | 897,012 | 7,873,239 |
| 2015 | 191,039 | 113,698 | 2,460,397 | 1,588,344 | 161,967 | 353,750 | 115,197 | 677,837 | 367,806 | 639,001 | 169,108 | 899,721 | 8,169,952 |
| 2016 | 206,383 | 118,204 | 2,178,575 | 1,619,850 | 160,774 | 315,651 | 116,682 | 655,337 | 361,975 | 611,916 | 162,043 | 897,493 | 7,868,585 |
| 2017 | 196,052 | 125,100 | 2,409,917 | 1,663,256 | 167,182 | 292,603 | 122,666 | 477,288 | 364,758 | 789,885 | 183,887 | 917,585 | 8,204,930 |
| 2018 | 195,665 | 139,483 | 2,105,367 | 1,711,504 | 168,438 | 282,150 | 119,539 | 705,747 | 352,674 | 681,357 | 175,553 | 949,536 | 8,353,274 |
| 2019 | 195,287 | 141,174 | 1,998,757 | 1,672,325 | 156,893 | 247,256 | 115,854 | 727,558 | 341,110 | 770,694 | 183,639 | 962,455 | 8,259,775 |
| 2020[1] | 141,173 | 103,815 | 1,825,358 | 1,375,349 | 104,846 | 215,170 | 98,047 | 554,382 | 286,818 | 873,582 | 157,084 | 767,174 | 7,544,341 |
| 2021[2] | 197,817 | 133,319 | 1,928,931 | 1,718,640 | 139,116 | 262,563 | 118,813 | 692,090 | 327,688 | 870,047 | 186,860 | 946,234 | 8,515,929 |

[1] Preliminary.   [2] Estimate.   *Source: Food and Agricultural Organization of the United Nations (FAO-UN)*

**World Exports of Natural Dry Rubber**   In Metric Tons

| Year | Côte d'Ivoire | Germany | Guatemala | India | Indonesia | Liberia | Malaysia | Nigeria | Philippines | Sri Lanka | Thailand | Vietnam | World Total |
|---|---|---|---|---|---|---|---|---|---|---|---|---|---|
| 2012 | 267,368 | 112,745 | 64,267 | 8,893 | 2,436,819 | 70,606 | 739,426 | 56,847 | 38,614 | 35,313 | 2,049,683 | 799,489 | 7,055,019 |
| 2013 | 259,860 | 110,488 | 64,182 | 22,134 | 2,696,087 | 58,946 | 813,714 | 51,332 | 66,930 | 23,007 | 2,398,556 | 674,342 | 7,648,372 |
| 2014 | 352,543 | 148,976 | 65,355 | 2,171 | 2,618,061 | 67,688 | 689,352 | 38,760 | 87,162 | 15,415 | 2,351,795 | 918,574 | 7,930,414 |
| 2015 | 409,815 | 142,222 | 60,862 | 4,685 | 2,623,903 | 55,819 | 674,589 | 37,115 | 78,604 | 12,050 | 2,579,309 | 709,029 | 8,066,183 |
| 2016 | 492,322 | 98,908 | 57,302 | 5,882 | 2,572,097 | 66,393 | 611,588 | 33,292 | 68,788 | 15,529 | 2,356,971 | 585,250 | 7,656,891 |
| 2017 | 644,446 | 60,326 | 64,269 | 9,584 | 3,188,798 | 65,025 | 583,120 | 42,738 | 133,745 | 13,290 | 2,482,824 | 473,634 | 8,600,302 |
| 2018 | 557,764 | 53,822 | 66,110 | 5,516 | 2,806,801 | 76,148 | 611,896 | 40,775 | 111,178 | 15,983 | 2,226,029 | 559,636 | 7,969,487 |
| 2019 | 691,056 | 44,444 | 62,079 | 8,872 | 2,644,557 | 89,089 | 608,116 | 42,828 | 122,946 | 12,146 | 2,132,595 | 590,750 | 8,000,098 |
| 2020[1] | 847,427 | 40,533 | 60,779 | 5,919 | 2,274,882 | 74,190 | 544,907 | 32,993 | 144,608 | 13,693 | 1,506,110 | 382,768 | 6,938,860 |
| 2021[2] | 1,135,134 | 59,900 | 69,129 | 2,414 | 2,332,339 | 106,894 | 632,139 | 42,986 | 203,204 | 12,539 | 2,229,982 | 503,415 | 8,632,211 |

[1] Preliminary.   [2] Estimate.   *Source: Food and Agricultural Organization of the United Nations (FAO-UN)*

**U.S. Imports of Natural Rubber (Includes Latex & Guayule)**   In Metric Tons

| Year | Jan. | Feb. | Mar. | Apr. | May | June | July | Aug. | Sept. | Oct. | Nov. | Dec. | Total |
|---|---|---|---|---|---|---|---|---|---|---|---|---|---|
| 2011 | 82,559 | 83,695 | 100,449 | 94,540 | 104,094 | 82,569 | 92,187 | 95,040 | 68,872 | 90,280 | 79,167 | 75,984 | 1,049,435 |
| 2012 | 80,134 | 87,794 | 93,327 | 95,541 | 75,109 | 62,804 | 68,098 | 83,118 | 88,059 | 75,963 | 80,187 | 78,828 | 968,960 |
| 2013 | 75,848 | 66,517 | 84,667 | 80,380 | 72,054 | 82,234 | 77,067 | 72,617 | 76,176 | 76,111 | 88,195 | 76,234 | 928,100 |
| 2014 | 80,647 | 75,094 | 87,363 | 95,293 | 70,447 | 72,062 | 79,663 | 82,402 | 71,885 | 77,073 | 74,484 | 80,532 | 946,946 |
| 2015 | 84,504 | 57,323 | 86,017 | 81,059 | 102,381 | 78,643 | 83,734 | 79,336 | 83,083 | 77,489 | 73,360 | 65,115 | 952,042 |
| 2016 | 77,751 | 72,275 | 77,523 | 85,225 | 88,091 | 79,224 | 86,991 | 80,035 | 70,754 | 83,342 | 72,110 | 72,826 | 946,147 |
| 2017 | 78,217 | 71,901 | 88,085 | 85,883 | 64,955 | 97,920 | 82,746 | 79,584 | 82,898 | 80,086 | 71,825 | 88,396 | 972,495 |
| 2018 | 82,600 | 75,326 | 96,446 | 75,441 | 101,791 | 86,553 | 65,733 | 84,977 | 87,418 | 97,657 | 73,051 | 70,410 | 997,403 |
| 2019 | 103,581 | 64,889 | 102,213 | 91,161 | 84,602 | 88,177 | 64,568 | 93,991 | 78,237 | 72,177 | 96,745 | 69,546 | 1,009,887 |
| 2020[1] | 70,468 | 80,501 | 83,060 | 94,526 | 87,448 | 45,332 | 43,862 | 51,601 | 58,419 | 48,980 | 66,297 | | 796,900 |

[1] Preliminary.   *Source: Economic Research Service, U.S. Department of Agriculture (ERS-USDA)*

# Rye

Rye is a cereal grain and a member of the grass family. Hardy varieties of rye have been developed for winter planting. Rye is most widely grown in northern Europe and Asia. In the U.S., rye is used as an animal feed and as an ingredient in bread and some whiskeys. Bread using rye was developed in northern Europe in the Middle Ages, where bakers developed dark, hearty bread consisting of rye, oat, and barley flours. Those were crops that grew more readily in the wet and damp climate of northern Europe, as opposed to wheat, which fares better in the warmer and drier climates in central Europe. Modern rye bread is made with a mixture of white and rye flours. Coarsely ground rye flour is also used in pumpernickel bread and helps provide the dark color and coarse texture, along with molasses. The major producing states are North and South Dakota, Oklahoma, and Georgia. The crop year runs from June to May.

**Supply** – World rye production in 2022/23 marketing year is forecasted to fall by -3.9% yr/yr to 12.056 million metric tons.

The world's largest producers of rye are the European Union with 63.2% of world production, followed by Russia with 15.8%, Belarus with 6.2%, and Canada with 4.4%. U.S. production of rye accounts for only 2.6% of world production.

U.S. production of rye in 2022 rose by +25.4% to 12.302 million bushels, far below the production levels of over 20 million bushels seen from the late 1800s through the 1960s. U.S. production of rye posted a record low of 6.051million bushels in 2011. U.S. acreage harvested with rye in 2022/23 is expected to rise by +16.0% yr/yr to 341,000 acres. U.S. farmers in the late 1800s through the 1960s typically harvested more than 1 million acres of rye, showing how domestic planting of rye has dropped off sharply in the past several decades. Rye yield in 2022/23 is expected to rise by +8.1% yr/yr to 36.1 bushels per acre.

**Demand** – Total U.S. domestic usage of rye in 2021/22 fell by -7.2% yr/yr to 19.291 million bushels. The breakdown of 2021/22 domestic usage shows that 25.8% of rye was used for feed and residual, 25.8% for industry, 22.3% for seed, and 18.5% for food.

**Trade** – World exports of rye in the 2022/23 marketing year are expected to fall by -35.7% yr/yr to 396,000 metric tons, above the record low of 225,000 metric tons in 2008/09. The largest exporters will be Canada, with 44.2% of the world total at 175,000 metric tons, and the European Union with 37.9% at 150,000 metric tons. World imports of rye in 2022/23 are expected to fall by -23.5% to 470,000 metric tons. U.S. imports of rye in 2022/23 are expected to rise by +26.0% yr/yr to 330,000 metric tons.

## World Production of Rye    In Thousands of Metric Tons

| Crop Year | Argentina | Australia | Belarus | Canada | Chile | European Union | Kazakhstan | Norway | Russia | Turkey | Ukraine | United States | World Total |
|---|---|---|---|---|---|---|---|---|---|---|---|---|---|
| 2013-14 | 52 | 31 | 648 | 223 | 4 | 10,151 | 43 | 13 | 3,360 | 365 | 638 | 194 | 15,772 |
| 2014-15 | 97 | 30 | 867 | 218 | 5 | 8,864 | 61 | 38 | 3,279 | 300 | 475 | 183 | 14,469 |
| 2015-16 | 61 | 30 | 753 | 226 | 5 | 7,833 | 37 | 66 | 2,084 | 330 | 394 | 295 | 12,162 |
| 2016-17 | 79 | 30 | 651 | 436 | 5 | 7,405 | 41 | 23 | 2,538 | 300 | 394 | 339 | 12,333 |
| 2017-18 | 86 | 30 | 670 | 341 | 5 | 7,366 | 39 | 50 | 2,540 | 320 | 510 | 260 | 12,304 |
| 2018-19 | 87 | 31 | 503 | 236 | 5 | 6,173 | 23 | 9 | 1,914 | 320 | 396 | 214 | 10,000 |
| 2019-20 | 220 | 32 | 756 | 333 | 5 | 8,395 | 23 | 50 | 1,424 | 320 | 339 | 270 | 12,257 |
| 2020-21[1] | 135 | 32 | 1,051 | 488 | 5 | 8,968 | 30 | 50 | 2,376 | 320 | 459 | 293 | 14,299 |
| 2021-22[2] | 225 | 32 | 800 | 473 | 5 | 7,948 | 40 | 50 | 1,716 | 330 | 600 | 249 | 12,544 |
| 2022-23[3] | 160 | 32 | 750 | 520 | 5 | 7,615 | 30 | 50 | 1,900 | 320 | 285 | 312 | 12,056 |

[1] Preliminary.  [2] Estimate.  [3] Forecast.  Source: Foreign Agricultural Service, U.S. Department of Agriculture (FAS-USDA)

## World Imports and Exports of Rye    In Thousands of Metric Tons

| | Imports ||||||| Exports ||||||
|---|---|---|---|---|---|---|---|---|---|---|---|---|
| Crop Year | European Union | Japan | Korea, South | Norway | Russia | United States | World Total | Belarus | Canada | European Union | Russia | United States | World Total |
|---|---|---|---|---|---|---|---|---|---|---|---|---|---|
| 2013-14 | 77 | 37 | 8 | 22 | 5 | 234 | 425 | ---- | 118 | 169 | 74 | 7 | 420 |
| 2014-15 | 102 | 22 | 4 | 8 | 5 | 237 | 409 | ---- | 86 | 184 | 114 | 6 | 413 |
| 2015-16 | 51 | 16 | 5 | 1 | 8 | 222 | 335 | 20 | 98 | 161 | 48 | 5 | 353 |
| 2016-17 | 16 | 24 | 4 | 3 | 4 | 167 | 232 | 11 | 142 | 79 | 9 | 4 | 257 |
| 2017-18 | 65 | 21 | 3 | 4 | ---- | 224 | 363 | ---- | 193 | 91 | 71 | 4 | 398 |
| 2018-19 | 297 | 23 | 3 | 18 | ---- | 304 | 693 | ---- | 144 | 198 | 283 | 4 | 718 |
| 2019-20 | 4 | 19 | 4 | 9 | 90 | 302 | 447 | ---- | 163 | 262 | 1 | 5 | 439 |
| 2020-21[1] | 87 | 22 | 4 | 8 | 4 | 244 | 408 | 17 | 150 | 156 | 83 | 5 | 429 |
| 2021-22[2] | 258 | 13 | 4 | 6 | 1 | 262 | 614 | 10 | 149 | 159 | 125 | 5 | 616 |
| 2022-23[3] | 80 | 15 | 5 | 10 | 1 | 330 | 470 | 10 | 175 | 150 | 50 | 5 | 396 |

[1] Preliminary.  [2] Estimate.  [3] Forecast.  Source: Foreign Agricultural Service, U.S. Department of Agriculture (FAS-USDA)

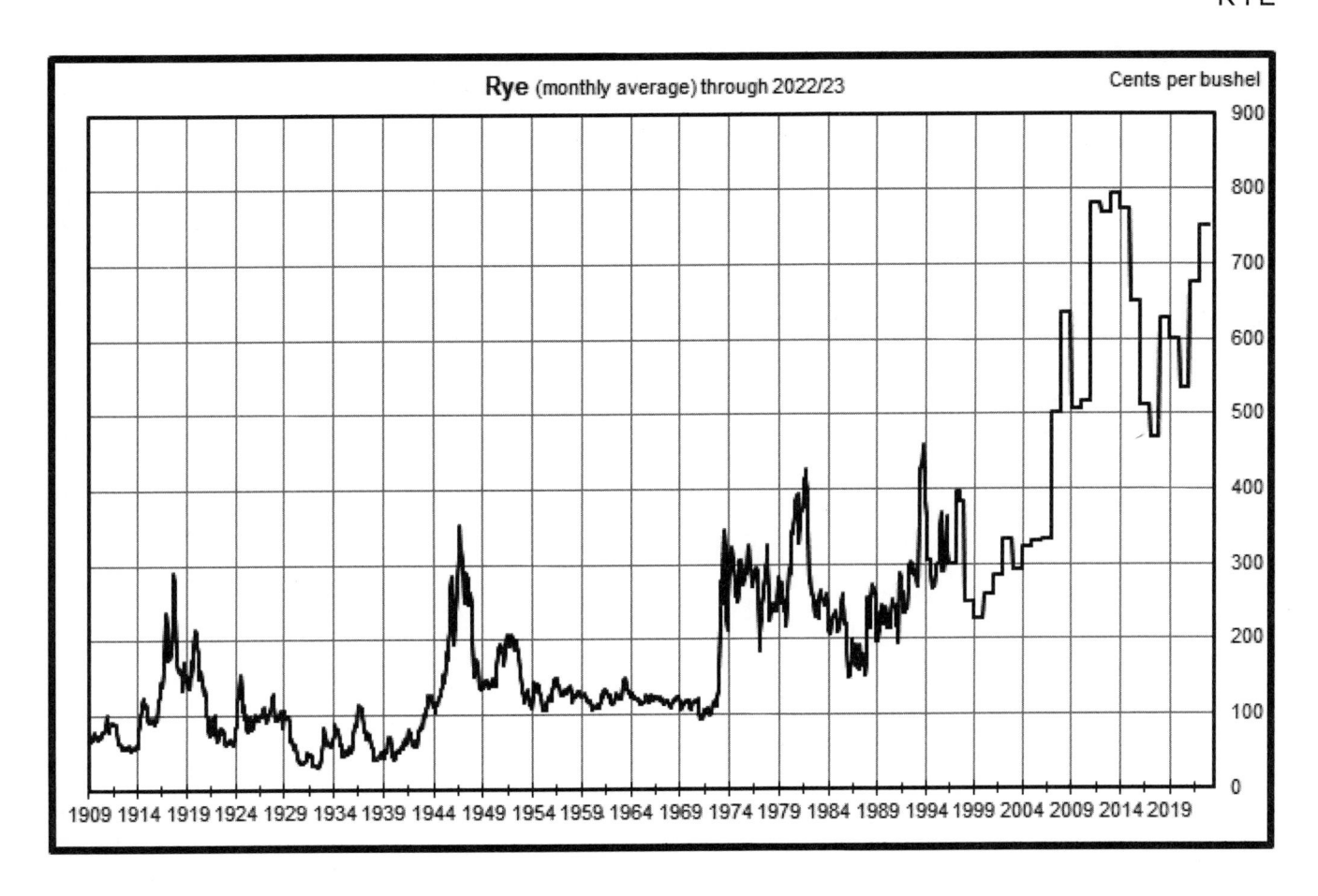

# RYE

**Rye** (monthly average) through 2022/23 — Cents per bushel

## Production of Rye in the United States   In Thousands of Bushels

| Year | Georgia | Minnesota | North Dakota | Oklahoma | Pennsylvania | Other States[2] | Total |
|---|---|---|---|---|---|---|---|
| 2013 | 1,080 | ---- | ---- | 1,600 | ---- | 4,946 | 7,626 |
| 2014 | 540 | ---- | ---- | 495 | ---- | 6,154 | 7,189 |
| 2015 | 420 | ---- | ---- | 2,040 | ---- | 9,156 | 11,616 |
| 2016 | 630 | ---- | ---- | 1,875 | ---- | 10,832 | 13,337 |
| 2017 | 475 | W | W | 1,080 | W | 8,697 | 10,252 |
| 2018 | 390 | W | W | 1,100 | W | 6,942 | 8,432 |
| 2019 | W | 702 | 2,565 | 1,485 | 364 | 4,826 | 10,622 |
| 2020 | W | 570 | 2,200 | 728 | 1,872 | 5,362 | 11,532 |
| 2021 | ---- | 484 | 1,152 | 1,250 | 600 | 5,502 | 9,808 |
| 2022[1] | ---- | 1,456 | 2,760 | 1,000 | 646 | 5,279 | 12,301 |

[1] Preliminary.  [2] Includes IL, KS, ME, MD, MI, MN, NE, NJ, NY, NC, ND, PA, SC, SD, TX, VA, and WI.  *Source: Agricultural Statistics Board, U.S. Department of Agriculture (ASB-USDA)*

## Salient Statistics of Rye in the United States   In Thousands of Bushels

| Crop Year Beginning June 1 | Stocks June 1 | Production | Imports | Total Supply | Food | Industry | Seed | Feed & Residual | Total | Exports | Total Disappearance | Planted 1,000 Acres | Harvested for Grain 1,000 Acres | Yield Per Harvested Acre (Bushels) |
|---|---|---|---|---|---|---|---|---|---|---|---|---|---|---|
| 2013-14 | 401 | 7,626 | 9,213 | 17,240 | 3,430 | 3,399 | 2,970 | 6,888 | 16,687 | 268 | 16,955 | 1,451 | 278 | 27.4 |
| 2014-15 | 285 | 7,189 | 9,319 | 16,793 | 3,450 | 3,173 | 3,200 | 6,141 | 15,964 | 240 | 16,204 | 1,434 | 258 | 27.9 |
| 2015-16 | 589 | 11,616 | 8,757 | 20,962 | 3,480 | 5,321 | 3,840 | 7,685 | 20,326 | 181 | 20,507 | 1,584 | 365 | 31.8 |
| 2016-17 | 455 | 13,337 | 6,586 | 20,378 | 3,500 | 5,727 | 4,110 | 6,168 | 19,505 | 175 | 19,680 | 1,891 | 411 | 32.5 |
| 2017-18 | 698 | 10,252 | 8,825 | 19,775 | 3,530 | 5,800 | 4,250 | 5,445 | 19,025 | 157 | 19,182 | 1,961 | 300 | 34.2 |
| 2018-19 | 593 | 8,432 | 11,964 | 20,989 | 3,550 | 6,000 | 3,860 | 7,011 | 20,421 | 149 | 20,570 | 2,011 | 273 | 30.9 |
| 2019-20 | 419 | 10,622 | 11,908 | 22,949 | 3,570 | 6,100 | 4,070 | 7,904 | 21,644 | 205 | 21,849 | 1,855 | 310 | 34.3 |
| 2020-21[1] | 1,100 | 11,532 | 9,615 | 22,247 | 3,590 | 6,200 | 4,510 | 6,506 | 20,806 | 188 | 20,994 | 1,253 | 330 | 34.9 |
| 2021-22[2] | 1,253 | 9,808 | 10,327 | 21,388 | 3,610 | 6,300 | 4,550 | 6,096 | 20,556 | 200 | 20,756 | 632 | 294 | 33.4 |
| 2022-23[3] | 632 | 12,301 | 13,000 | 25,933 | 3,630 | 6,400 | 4,430 | 10,493 | 24,953 | 200 | 25,153 | 780 | 341 | 36.1 |

[1] Preliminary.  [2] Estimate.  [3] Forecast.  *Source: Economic Research Service, U.S. Department of Agriculture (ERS-USDA)*

# Salt

Salt, also known as sodium chloride, is a chemical compound that is an essential element in the diet of humans, animals, and even many plants. Since prehistoric times, salt has been used to preserve foods and was commonly used in the religious rites of the Greeks, Romans, Hebrews, and Christians. Salt, in the form of salt cakes, served as money in ancient Ethiopia and Tibet. As long ago as 1450 BC, Egyptian art shows records of salt production.

The simplest method of obtaining salt is through the evaporation of saltwater from areas near oceans or seas. In most regions, rock salt is obtained from underground mining or by wells sunk into deposits. Salt is soluble in water, is slightly soluble in alcohol, but is insoluble in concentrated hydrochloric acid. In its crystalline form, salt is transparent and colorless, shining with an ice-like luster.

**Prices** – The price of salt in 2022 (FOB mine, vacuum, and open pan) rose by +4.5% yr/yr to $230.00 per metric ton a new record high.

**Supply** – World production of salt in 2022 fell by -1.4% yr/yr to 290.000 million metric tons. The world's largest salt producers were China with 22.1% and the India with 15.5% of world production. U.S. salt production in 2022 remained unchanged at 42.000 million metric tons.

**Demand** – U.S. consumption of salt in 2022 was unchanged yr/yr at 59.000 million metric tons, down from the 2015 record high of 65.600 million.

**Trade** – U.S. imports of salt for consumption in 2022 fell by -0.6% yr/yr to 18.000 million metric tons, below the 2015 record high of 21.600. The U.S. relied on imports for 30.5% of its salt consumption in 2022. U.S. exports of salt in 2022 fell by -34.0% yr/yr to 700,000 metric tons.

## World Production of All Salt    In Thousands of Metric Tons

| Year | Australia | Canada | China | France | Germany | India | Italy | Mexico | Poland | Spain | United Kingdom | United States | World Total |
|---|---|---|---|---|---|---|---|---|---|---|---|---|---|
| 2015 | 11,000 | 14,343 | 66,655 | 6,000 | 12,480 | 24,241 | 3,336 | 9,088 | 4,119 | 4,300 | 5,000 | 45,125 | 292,000 |
| 2016 | 12,000 | 14,000 | 67,000 | 6,000 | 12,890 | 25,000 | 3,035 | 9,000 | 4,170 | 4,300 | 5,100 | 41,795 | 284,000 |
| 2017 | 11,000 | 12,000 | 67,000 | 4,500 | 13,000 | 28,000 | 3,047 | 9,000 | 4,450 | 4,500 | 5,100 | 40,000 | 286,000 |
| 2018 | 12,000 | 12,000 | 58,000 | 5,700 | 14,000 | 29,000 | 3,000 | 9,000 | 4,400 | 4,200 | 5,100 | 41,000 | 286,000 |
| 2019 | 13,000 | 11,000 | 59,000 | 5,600 | 14,300 | 29,000 | 4,200 | 9,000 | 4,480 | 4,200 | 4,100 | 42,000 | 283,000 |
| 2020 | 11,000 | 10,000 | 63,000 | 5,400 | 15,300 | 29,000 | 1,540 | 9,000 | 3,780 | 4,200 | 4,700 | 41,000 | 280,000 |
| 2021[1] | 12,200 | 11,800 | 64,000 | 5,400 | 15,000 | 45,000 | 1,900 | 9,000 | 4,000 | 4,200 | 2,400 | 42,000 | 294,000 |
| 2022[2] | 13,000 | 11,000 | 64,000 | 5,500 | 15,000 | 45,000 | 2,000 | 9,000 | 4,000 | 4,200 | 2,800 | 42,000 | 290,000 |

[1] Preliminary.  [2] Estimate.  Source: U.S. Geological Survey (USGS)

## Salient Statistics of the Salt Industry in the United States    In Thousands of Metric Tons

| Year | Net Import Reliance As a % of Apparent Consumption | Average Value FOB Mine Vacuum & Open Pan ($ Per Ton) | Production Total | Production Open & Vacuum Pan | Production Solar | Production Rock | Production Brine | Sold or Used, Producers Open & Vacuum Pan | Sold or Used Rock | Sold or Used Brine | Total Salt | Imports Value[3] Million $ | Imports for Consumption | Exports Total | Exports To Canada | Apparent Consumption |
|---|---|---|---|---|---|---|---|---|---|---|---|---|---|---|---|---|
| 2015 | 33 | 188.87 | 45,100 | 4,190 | 3,590 | 20,400 | 16,900 | 4,220 | 18,200 | 17,000 | 42,800 | $2,360 | 21,600 | 830 | 699 | 63,600 |
| 2016 | 22 | 197.78 | 41,700 | 4,050 | 2,900 | 17,900 | 16,900 | 4,040 | 16,100 | 16,400 | 39,900 | $2,190 | 12,100 | 729 | 594 | 51,300 |
| 2017 | 23 | 211.71 | 39,900 | 4,490 | 3,340 | 16,500 | 15,600 | 4,500 | 15,500 | 15,500 | 38,700 | $2,390 | 12,600 | 1,130 | 971 | 50,200 |
| 2018 | 28 | 220.00 | 43,900 | 4,260 | 2,950 | 18,900 | 17,900 | 4,210 | 19,400 | 17,900 | 44,200 | $2,570 | 17,900 | 986 | 811 | 61,100 |
| 2019 | 28 | 215.00 | 45,000 | | | | | | | | 45,000 | | 18,700 | 1,020 | | 62,500 |
| 2020 | 25 | 215.00 | 43,000 | | | | | | | | 43,000 | | 15,800 | 1,250 | | 58,000 |
| 2021[1] | 29 | 220.00 | 42,000 | | | | | | | | 42,000 | | 18,100 | 1,060 | | 59,000 |
| 2022[2] | 29 | 230.00 | 42,000 | | | | | | | | 42,000 | | 18,000 | 700 | | 59,000 |

[1] Preliminary.  [2] Estimate.  [3] Values are f.o.b. mine or refinery & do not include cost of cooperage or containers.  Source: U.S. Geological Survey (USGS)

## Salt Sold or Used by Producers in the U.S. by Classes & Consumers or Uses    In Thousands of Metric Tons

| Year | Chemical[2] | Tanning Leather | Textile & Dyeing | Meat Packers[3] | Canning | Baking | Agricultural Distribution | Feed Dealers | Feed Manufacturers | Rubber | Paper Oil & Pulp | Metal Processing | Water Treatment | Grocery Stores | Water Conditioning Distrib. | Ice Control and/or Stabilization |
|---|---|---|---|---|---|---|---|---|---|---|---|---|---|---|---|---|
| 2011 | 18,530 | 42 | 49 | 260 | 195 | 162 | 375 | 1,170 | 438 | 5 | 322 | 67 | 44 | 312 | 706 | 493 | 19,560 |
| 2012 | 16,824 | 36 | 41 | 248 | 182 | 160 | 253 | 1,010 | 392 | 7 | 441 | 61 | 53 | 446 | 591 | 472 | 11,100 |
| 2013 | 17,990 | 38 | 39 | 258 | 179 | 162 | 351 | 913 | 516 | 5 | 409 | 66 | 42 | 472 | 665 | 627 | 20,340 |
| 2014 | 20,360 | 39 | 38 | 240 | 171 | 158 | 389 | 939 | 514 | 6 | 400 | 71 | 56 | 603 | 708 | 504 | 24,490 |
| 2015 | 19,430 | 38 | 39 | 275 | 175 | 181 | 306 | 849 | 336 | 3 | 302 | 69 | 46 | 723 | 707 | 440 | 22,760 |
| 2016 | 18,350 | 36 | 64 | 283 | 181 | 171 | 428 | 660 | 377 | 4 | 316 | 63 | 41 | 469 | 669 | 437 | 20,300 |
| 2017 | 17,050 | 33 | 30 | 257 | 177 | 177 | 470 | 708 | 458 | 3 | 275 | 62 | 34 | 471 | 537 | 447 | 19,520 |
| 2018[1] | 20,120 | 44 | 37 | 310 | 203 | 215 | 526 | 761 | 363 | 4 | 313 | 76 | 38 | 566 | 570 | 520 | 22,880 |

[1] Preliminary.  [2] Chloralkali producers and other chemical.  Source: U.S. Geological Survey (USGS)

# Sheep and Lambs

Sheep and lambs are raised for both their wool and meat. In countries that have high wool production, there is also demand for sheep and lamb meat due to the easy availability. Production levels have declined in New Zealand and Australia, but that has been counteracted by a substantial increase in China.

**Prices** – The average monthly wholesale price of slaughter lambs (choice) at San Angelo, Texas, in 2022 fell by -18.2% to 176.67 cents per pound.

**Supply** – World sheep and goat numbers in 2021 rose by +0.7% to 2.396 billion head, a new record high. The world's largest producers of sheep and goats are China with 13.3% of world production in 2021, India with 9.3%, Australia with 3.0%, Turkey with 2.4%, and the United Kingdom with 1.4%.

The number of sheep and lambs on U.S. farms in 2022 (Jan 1) was down by -2.0% yr/yr to 5.065 million head. U.S. states with the most sheep and lambs are Texas with 13.8% of the U.S. total, California with 11.4%, Colorado with 8.5%, Wyoming with 6.5%, and Utah with 5.3%.

### World Sheep and Goat Numbers in Specified Countries on January 1    In Thousands of Head

| Year | Argentina | Australia | China | India | Kazakhstan | New Zealand | Romania | Russia | South Africa | Spain | Turkey | United Kingdom | World Total |
|---|---|---|---|---|---|---|---|---|---|---|---|---|---|
| 2012 | 19,047 | 78,272 | 285,319 | 200,242 | 18,092 | 31,353 | 9,770 | 22,858 | 30,533 | 18,977 | 32,310 | 32,313 | 2,084,420 |
| 2013 | 18,950 | 79,098 | 289,520 | 197,800 | 17,633 | 30,867 | 10,100 | 24,180 | 30,556 | 18,729 | 35,783 | 32,954 | 2,127,171 |
| 2014 | 18,934 | 76,182 | 289,507 | 196,000 | 17,561 | 29,901 | 10,449 | 24,337 | 30,094 | 18,136 | 38,510 | 33,843 | 2,134,678 |
| 2015 | 19,580 | 74,510 | 304,072 | 205,085 | 18,016 | 29,196 | 10,935 | 24,683 | 29,810 | 19,533 | 41,485 | 33,438 | 2,186,505 |
| 2016 | 19,576 | 71,193 | 311,900 | 211,799 | 18,184 | 27,696 | 11,250 | 24,606 | 28,906 | 19,051 | 41,924 | 34,047 | 2,228,923 |
| 2017 | 19,610 | 75,725 | 302,463 | 215,913 | 18,329 | 27,625 | 11,359 | 24,717 | 28,164 | 19,023 | 41,329 | 34,936 | 2,254,708 |
| 2018 | 18,907 | 73,715 | 297,281 | 219,612 | 18,699 | 27,385 | 11,716 | 24,389 | 27,905 | 18,617 | 46,117 | 33,885 | 2,275,496 |
| 2019 | 19,413 | 69,653 | 300,857 | 223,145 | 19,156 | 26,915 | 11,954 | 23,129 | 27,336 | 18,138 | 48,481 | 33,691 | 2,342,385 |
| 2020[1] | 19,268 | 67,410 | 306,679 | 226,227 | 20,058 | 26,146 | 11,893 | 22,618 | 26,775 | 18,090 | 54,113 | 32,809 | 2,379,373 |
| 2021[2] | 17,629 | 71,981 | 319,820 | 223,033 | 20,877 | 25,850 | 11,580 | 21,660 | 26,615 | 17,671 | 57,519 | 33,068 | 2,396,135 |

[1] Preliminary.  [2] Forecast.  Source: Food and Agricultural Organization of the United Nations (FAO-UN)

### Salient Statistics of Sheep & Lambs in the United States (Average Live Weight)    In Thousands of Head

| Year | Inventory Jan. 1 Without New Crop Lambs | Inventory Jan. 1 With New Crop Lambs | Lamb Crop | Total Supply | Marketings[3] Sheep | Marketings[3] Lambs | Slaughter Farm | Slaughter Commercial | Slaughter Total[4] | Net Exports | Total Disappearance | Production (Live Weight) (Mil. Lbs.) | Farm Value Jan. 1 Total |
|---|---|---|---|---|---|---|---|---|---|---|---|---|---|
| 2013 | 5,360 | 5,467 | 3,370 | 8,837 | ---- | ---- | 94 | 2,319 | 2,412 | ---- | ---- | ---- | ---- |
| 2014 | 5,245 | 5,356 | 3,440 | 8,796 | ---- | ---- | 95 | 2,310 | 2,404 | ---- | ---- | ---- | ---- |
| 2015 | 5,280 | 5,385 | 3,290 | 8,675 | ---- | ---- | 95 | 2,224 | 2,319 | ---- | ---- | ---- | ---- |
| 2016 | 5,300 | 5,405 | 3,265 | 8,670 | ---- | ---- | 95 | 2,238 | 2,333 | ---- | ---- | ---- | ---- |
| 2017 | 5,250 | 5,356 | 3,230 | 8,586 | ---- | ---- | 96 | 2,178 | 2,274 | ---- | ---- | ---- | ---- |
| 2018 | 5,265 | 5,372 | 3,235 | 8,607 | ---- | ---- | 92 | 2,261 | 2,353 | ---- | ---- | ---- | ---- |
| 2019 | 5,230 | 5,338 | 3,230 | 8,568 | ---- | ---- | 92 | 2,322 | 2,413 | ---- | ---- | ---- | ---- |
| 2020 | 5,200 | 5,308 | 3,210 | 8,518 | ---- | ---- | 93 | 2,225 | 2,318 | ---- | ---- | ---- | ---- |
| 2021[1] | 5,170 | 5,277 | 3,160 | 8,437 | ---- | ---- | 92 | 2,263 | 2,355 | ---- | ---- | ---- | ---- |
| 2022[2] | 5,065 | 5,172 | 3,110 | 8,282 | ---- | ---- | 95 | 2,059 | 2,154 | ---- | ---- | ---- | ---- |

[1] Preliminary.  [2] Estimate.  [3] Excludes interfarm sales.  [4] Includes all commercial and farm.
Source: Economic Research Service, U.S. Department of Agriculture (ERS-USDA)

### Sheep and Lambs[3] on Farms in the United States on January 1    In Thousands of Head

| Year | California | Colorado | Idaho | Iowa | Minnesota | Montana | New Mexico | Ohio | Dakota | Texas | Utah | Wyoming | Total |
|---|---|---|---|---|---|---|---|---|---|---|---|---|---|
| 2015 | 600 | 420 | 260 | 175 | 130 | 215 | 90 | 121 | 255 | 720 | 290 | 345 | 5,280 |
| 2016 | 575 | 435 | 255 | 175 | 125 | 230 | 90 | 120 | 265 | 725 | 285 | 355 | 5,300 |
| 2017 | 600 | 420 | 250 | 175 | 130 | 230 | 97 | 117 | 250 | 710 | 275 | 360 | 5,250 |
| 2018 | 570 | 445 | 235 | 165 | 130 | 225 | 96 | 119 | 250 | 750 | 275 | 345 | 5,265 |
| 2019 | 550 | 420 | 220 | 153 | 125 | 215 | 100 | 121 | 255 | 750 | 290 | 350 | 5,230 |
| 2020 | 570 | 425 | 230 | 151 | 115 | 200 | 95 | 126 | 250 | 735 | 285 | 340 | 5,200 |
| 2021 | 555 | 445 | 230 | 160 | 113 | 200 | 85 | 126 | 245 | 730 | 285 | 340 | 5,170 |
| 2022 | 575 | 430 | 230 | 160 | 112 | 190 | 90 | 127 | 235 | 700 | 270 | 330 | 5,065 |
| 2023[1] | 550 | 415 | 220 | 162 | 115 | 190 | 85 | 125 | 250 | 675 | 280 | 335 | 5,020 |

[1] Preliminary.  [2] Includes sheep & lambs on feed for market and stock sheep & lambs.  Source: Economic Research Service, U.S. Department of Agriculture (ERS-USDA)

# SHEEP AND LAMBS

## Average Wholesale Price of Slaughter Lambs (Choice[2]) at San Angelo Texas  In Dollars Per Hundred Pounds (Cwt.)

| Year | Jan. | Feb. | Mar. | Apr. | May | June | July | Aug. | Sept. | Oct. | Nov. | Dec. | Average |
|---|---|---|---|---|---|---|---|---|---|---|---|---|---|
| 2014 | 165.00 | 168.38 | 154.88 | 150.97 | 135.17 | 160.83 | 150.23 | 152.94 | 164.90 | 159.25 | 162.00 | 166.83 | 157.62 |
| 2015 | 155.25 | 148.75 | 137.75 | 137.38 | 147.25 | 147.88 | 140.50 | 148.00 | 150.20 | 139.00 | 148.67 | 139.88 | 145.04 |
| 2016 | 139.00 | 134.07 | 127.45 | 136.56 | 136.40 | 135.50 | 130.66 | 139.90 | 142.00 | 130.50 | 126.13 | 139.00 | 134.76 |
| 2017 | 138.10 | 139.25 | 139.38 | 140.50 | 159.00 | 160.88 | 146.00 | 147.00 | 138.88 | 127.50 | 130.17 | 136.00 | 141.89 |
| 2018 | 130.88 | 133.75 | 135.50 | 149.05 | 155.63 | 159.91 | 157.29 | 145.58 | 140.98 | 136.58 | 134.35 | 131.98 | 142.62 |
| 2019 | 132.45 | 134.63 | 141.61 | 152.39 | 156.15 | 159.93 | 160.22 | 153.47 | 151.10 | 150.12 | 151.64 | 151.69 | 149.62 |
| 2020 | 153.52 | 161.27 | 163.15 | ---- | ---- | ---- | ---- | ---- | ---- | ---- | 167.50 | 159.78 | 161.04 |
| 2021 | 158.24 | 163.77 | 172.49 | 184.64 | 202.60 | 238.36 | 264.00 | 258.93 | 247.09 | 239.61 | 231.22 | 230.71 | 215.97 |
| 2022[1] | 234.84 | 228.78 | 225.00 | 219.25 | 213.76 | 210.33 | 167.54 | 132.81 | 117.20 | 119.29 | 124.23 | 129.28 | 176.86 |

[1] Preliminary.  Source: Economic Research Service, U.S. Department of Agriculture (ERS-USDA)

## Federally Inspected Slaughter of Sheep & Lambs in the United States  In Thousands of Head

| Year | Jan. | Feb. | Mar. | Apr. | May | June | July | Aug. | Sept. | Oct. | Nov. | Dec. | Total |
|---|---|---|---|---|---|---|---|---|---|---|---|---|---|
| 2014 | 166.9 | 155.4 | 176.5 | 204.0 | 176.5 | 175.3 | 188.9 | 161.4 | 172.7 | 186.8 | 157.1 | 182.8 | 2,104.6 |
| 2015 | 153.0 | 149.9 | 190.0 | 179.1 | 152.7 | 172.8 | 166.8 | 155.5 | 167.4 | 166.3 | 162.6 | 182.3 | 1,998.4 |
| 2016 | 144.4 | 159.9 | 187.5 | 169.7 | 166.7 | 174.0 | 152.4 | 173.3 | 170.1 | 163.0 | 169.6 | 178.9 | 2,009.5 |
| 2017 | 161.6 | 144.8 | 177.3 | 156.1 | 157.1 | 165.5 | 146.3 | 171.9 | 153.9 | 165.1 | 167.3 | 170.1 | 1,937.0 |
| 2018 | 161.9 | 146.0 | 185.2 | 163.3 | 177.8 | 158.8 | 158.0 | 174.1 | 148.1 | 176.1 | 174.1 | 176.2 | 1,999.6 |
| 2019 | 165.7 | 146.1 | 170.3 | 204.5 | 182.0 | 151.6 | 162.6 | 171.3 | 154.7 | 179.8 | 158.9 | 172.9 | 2,020.4 |
| 2020 | 161.3 | 142.6 | 165.0 | 154.1 | 166.6 | 166.7 | 163.9 | 148.6 | 154.4 | 151.0 | 152.2 | 168.5 | 1,894.9 |
| 2021 | 140.7 | 142.8 | 188.5 | 189.8 | 153.4 | 158.9 | 153.5 | 147.5 | 153.7 | 162.0 | 171.3 | 165.2 | 1,927.3 |
| 2022[1] | 133.3 | 121.5 | 163.2 | 167.5 | 138.3 | 147.4 | 132.9 | 155.3 | 146.8 | 142.5 | 155.6 | 154.4 | 1,758.7 |

[1] Preliminary.  Source: Economic Research Service, U.S. Department of Agriculture (ERS-USDA)

## Average Live Weight of Sheep & Lambs Slaughtered in the United States  In Pounds per Head

| Year | Jan. | Feb. | Mar. | Apr. | May | June | July | Aug. | Sept. | Oct. | Nov. | Dec. | Average |
|---|---|---|---|---|---|---|---|---|---|---|---|---|---|
| 2014 | 140 | 140 | 142 | 140 | 147 | 141 | 135 | 131 | 130 | 132 | 135 | 137 | 138 |
| 2015 | 144 | 144 | 142 | 142 | 145 | 142 | 141 | 137 | 132 | 131 | 134 | 135 | 139 |
| 2016 | 142 | 145 | 141 | 138 | 144 | 138 | 138 | 132 | 128 | 130 | 133 | 135 | 137 |
| 2017 | 141 | 144 | 143 | 133 | 134 | 136 | 135 | 134 | 131 | 131 | 136 | 138 | 136 |
| 2018 | 144 | 148 | 142 | 141 | 140 | 141 | 138 | 136 | 137 | 134 | 136 | 134 | 139 |
| 2019 | 138 | 138 | 142 | 134 | 132 | 135 | 131 | 129 | 125 | 127 | 128 | 134 | 132 |
| 2020 | 134 | 136 | 136 | 128 | 135 | 135 | 129 | 127 | 121 | 121 | 128 | 127 | 129 |
| 2021 | 134 | 136 | 135 | 126 | 125 | 125 | 119 | 119 | 119 | 124 | 122 | 126 | 126 |
| 2022[1] | 132 | 132 | 135 | 128 | 137 | 137 | 132 | 132 | 129 | 125 | 126 | 126 | 131 |

[1] Preliminary.  Source: Economic Research Service, U.S. Department of Agriculture (ERS-USDA)

## Federally Inspected Slaughter of Goats in the United States  In Thousands of Head

| Year | Jan. | Feb. | Mar. | Apr. | May | June | July | Aug. | Sept. | Oct. | Nov. | Dec. | Total |
|---|---|---|---|---|---|---|---|---|---|---|---|---|---|
| 2014 | 35.4 | 31.5 | 36.4 | 41.6 | 39.8 | 44.3 | 45.3 | 40.9 | 42.7 | 43.9 | 37.2 | 47.4 | 486.5 |
| 2015 | 34.9 | 28.3 | 38.2 | 35.5 | 33.8 | 40.1 | 38.5 | 37.2 | 40.4 | 36.5 | 36.2 | 41.7 | 441.3 |
| 2016 | 31.1 | 32.5 | 38.1 | 32.0 | 35.5 | 39.9 | 35.4 | 41.8 | 40.8 | 38.1 | 38.8 | 44.9 | 448.9 |
| 2017 | 36.9 | 32.2 | 36.8 | 38.1 | 45.1 | 42.9 | 38.9 | 43.9 | 41.7 | 43.2 | 42.4 | 46.7 | 488.8 |
| 2018 | 39.4 | 35.3 | 42.4 | 38.6 | 45.8 | 42.6 | 43.0 | 47.7 | 36.8 | 46.0 | 46.4 | 50.1 | 514.1 |
| 2019 | 42.9 | 36.6 | 41.0 | 48.1 | 49.3 | 40.0 | 47.7 | 48.2 | 44.4 | 48.9 | 46.3 | 52.2 | 545.6 |
| 2020 | 43.2 | 37.6 | 44.4 | 36.1 | 39.9 | 43.4 | 44.9 | 41.7 | 44.3 | 46.0 | 45.2 | 51.1 | 517.8 |
| 2021 | 38.0 | 31.4 | 41.9 | 38.9 | 36.4 | 39.8 | 41.8 | 43.8 | 42.3 | 44.4 | 45.8 | 49.1 | 493.6 |
| 2022[1] | 39.9 | 36.1 | 44.0 | 43.8 | 39.0 | 39.6 | 36.4 | 43.0 | 41.9 | 44.2 | 44.1 | 47.0 | 499.0 |

[1] Preliminary.  Source: Economic Research Service, U.S. Department of Agriculture (ERS-USDA)

## Cold Storage Holdings of Lamb and Mutton in the United States, on First of Month  In Thousands of Pounds

| Year | Jan. | Feb. | Mar. | Apr. | May | June | July | Aug. | Sept. | Oct. | Nov. | Dec. |
|---|---|---|---|---|---|---|---|---|---|---|---|---|
| 2014 | 24,508 | 25,658 | 26,191 | 28,076 | 26,536 | 25,208 | 31,119 | 33,968 | 40,157 | 39,693 | 38,686 | 31,366 |
| 2015 | 33,942 | 35,206 | 36,771 | 34,250 | 37,004 | 38,360 | 35,470 | 39,064 | 41,883 | 41,921 | 40,742 | 44,693 |
| 2016 | 41,452 | 47,111 | 40,051 | 40,648 | 39,787 | 44,816 | 39,518 | 40,979 | 36,563 | 32,736 | 29,439 | 21,876 |
| 2017 | 26,140 | 20,361 | 25,694 | 25,792 | 28,603 | 29,859 | 26,177 | 26,770 | 32,383 | 31,415 | 31,594 | 28,977 |
| 2018 | 26,714 | 26,790 | 28,280 | 28,615 | 33,992 | 35,591 | 38,678 | 42,129 | 39,386 | 40,466 | 39,321 | 37,859 |
| 2019 | 36,454 | 38,376 | 35,503 | 31,026 | 40,949 | 38,484 | 40,025 | 43,052 | 46,642 | 41,648 | 37,805 | 34,022 |
| 2020 | 34,752 | 36,856 | 37,379 | 37,575 | 40,790 | 48,023 | 46,524 | 44,712 | 39,466 | 30,668 | 25,731 | 25,917 |
| 2021 | 24,911 | 24,470 | 26,833 | 25,342 | 24,753 | 21,896 | 21,489 | 21,010 | 22,051 | 25,607 | 27,155 | 23,487 |
| 2022[1] | 22,124 | 21,856 | 22,224 | 24,006 | 24,414 | 22,192 | 22,813 | 25,589 | 29,161 | 31,364 | 28,652 | 29,682 |

[1] Preliminary.  Source: Economic Research Service, U.S. Department of Agriculture (ERS-USDA)

# Silk

Silk is a fine, tough, elastic fiber produced by caterpillars, commonly called silkworms. Silk is one of the oldest known textile fibers. Chinese tradition credits Lady Hsi-Ling-Shih, wife of the Emperor Huang Ti, with the discovery of the silkworm and the invention of the first silk reel. A group of ribbons, threads, and woven silk fragments were found in China dating back to 3000 BC. Also found, along the lower Yangzi River, were 7,000-year-old spinning tools, silk thread, and fabric fragments.

Silk filament was first woven into cloth in Ancient China. The Chinese successfully guarded this secret until 300AD, when Japan, and later India, learned the secret. In 550 AD, two Nestorian monks were sent to China to steal mulberry seeds and silkworm eggs, which they hid in their walking staffs, and then brought them back to Rome. By the 17th century, France was the silk center of the West. Unfortunately, the silkworm did not flourish in the English climate, nor has it ever flourished in the U.S.

Sericulture is the term for the raising of silkworms. The blind, flightless moth, Bombyx mori, lays more than 500 tiny eggs. After hatching, the tiny worms eat chopped mulberry leaves continuously until they are ready to spin their cocoons. After gathering the complete cocoons, the first step in silk manufacturing is to kill the insects inside the cocoons with heat. The cocoons are then placed in boiling water to loosen the gummy substance, sericin, holding the filament together. The filament is unwound, and then rewound in a process called reeling. Each cocoon's silk filament is between 600 and 900 meters long. Four different types of silk thread may be produced: organzine, crepe, tram, and thrown singles. During the last 30 years, despite the use of man-made fibers, world silk production has doubled.

**Supply** – World production of raw silk in 2019 fell – 0.1% yr/y to 173.162. China is the world's largest silk producer by far, with a 78.5% share of world production in 2019. Another key producer is India, with 17.3% of world production.

**Trade** – In 2020, the world's largest exporter of silk was China, with 54.8 % of world exports. In 2020, the world's largest importers of silk were India with 37.8% of world imports, Italy with 9.7%, and Japan with 2.9%.

## World Production of Raw Silk     In Metric Tons

| Year | Brazil | China | India | Iran | Japan | Korea, North | Korea, South | Kyrgyzstan | Thailand | Turkmenistan | Uzbekistan | Vietnam | World Total |
|---|---|---|---|---|---|---|---|---|---|---|---|---|---|
| 2011 | 515 | 104,000 | 20,410 | 120 | 42 | 400 | 1 | 50 | 655 | 4,500 | 940 | 1,059 | 130,556 |
| 2012 | 437 | 126,000 | 23,060 | 123 | 30 | 400 | 1 | 50 | 655 | 4,500 | 940 | 1,128 | 155,190 |
| 2013 | 433 | 130,001 | 23,679 | 123 | 30 | 400 | 1 | 50 | 680 | 4,500 | 980 | 954 | 159,694 |
| 2014 | 429 | 158,400 | 26,480 | 110 | 30 | ---- | 1 | 50 | 692 | 4,500 | 1,100 | 1,014 | 191,067 |
| 2015 | 600 | 170,000 | 28,708 | 120 | 30 | ---- | 1 | 50 | 698 | ---- | 1,200 | 450 | 204,643 |
| 2016 | 650 | 158,400 | 28,523 | 125 | 30 | ---- | 1 | 50 | 712 | ---- | 1,256 | 523 | 193,045 |
| 2017 | 600 | 142,000 | 30,348 | 120 | 20 | ---- | 1 | 50 | 680 | ---- | 1,200 | 520 | 178,313 |
| 2018 | 650 | 120,000 | 31,906 | 110 | 20 | ---- | 1 | 50 | 680 | ---- | 1,800 | 680 | 156,538 |
| 2019[1] | 469 | 68,600 | 35,261 | 227 | 16 | ---- | 1 | 50 | 700 | ---- | 2,037 | 795 | 108,796 |
| 2020[2] | 377 | 53,359 | 35,820 | 270 | 16 | ---- | 1 | 50 | 520 | ---- | 2,037 | 969 | 94,070 |

[1] Preliminary.  [2] Estimate.  NA = Not avaliable.  *Source: Food and Agricultural Organization of the United Nations (FAO-UN)*

## World Trade of Silk by Selected Countries     In Metric Tons

| | | | Imports | | | | | | Exports | | | |
|---|---|---|---|---|---|---|---|---|---|---|---|---|
| Year | France | Hong Kong | India | Italy | Japan | Korea, South | World Total | Brazil | China | Hong Kong | Japan | Korea, South | World Total |
| 2012 | 135 | ---- | 5,235 | 692 | 607 | 503 | 21,161 | ---- | 7,676 | 2 | 25 | 245 | 9,158 |
| 2013 | 248 | ---- | 3,609 | 676 | 570 | 410 | 24,917 | ---- | 6,690 | ---- | 18 | 118 | 8,454 |
| 2014 | 230 | ---- | 3,403 | 785 | 497 | 346 | 8,169 | ---- | 6,359 | ---- | 1 | 73 | 8,654 |
| 2015 | 185 | ---- | 3,454 | 733 | 391 | 313 | 7,644 | ---- | 6,695 | ---- | ---- | 17 | 9,193 |
| 2016 | 156 | ---- | 3,757 | 710 | 395 | 310 | 8,848 | ---- | 6,927 | ---- | ---- | 97 | 9,981 |
| 2017 | 185 | ---- | 4,003 | 607 | 456 | 271 | 8,128 | ---- | 5,936 | ---- | ---- | ---- | 10,612 |
| 2018 | 236 | ---- | 2,728 | 660 | 303 | 184 | 7,036 | ---- | 4,581 | ---- | ---- | ---- | 7,668 |
| 2019 | 131 | ---- | 3,264 | 911 | 292 | 138 | 7,701 | ---- | 4,305 | ---- | ---- | ---- | 8,834 |
| 2020 | 138 | ---- | 1,920 | 495 | 147 | 112 | 4,829 | ---- | 2,354 | ---- | ---- | ---- | 5,798 |
| 2021[1] | 115 | ---- | 2,031 | 520 | 185 | 94 | 5,413 | ---- | 1,863 | ---- | ---- | ---- | 5,003 |

[1] Preliminary.  *Source: Food and Agricultural Organization of the United Nations (FAO-UN)*

# Silver

Silver is a white, lustrous metallic element that conducts heat and electricity better than any other metal. In ancient times, many silver deposits were near the earth's surface. Before 2,500 BC, silver mines were worked in Asia Minor. Around 700 BC, ancient Greeks stamped a turtle on their first silver coins. Silver assumed a key role in the U.S. monetary system in 1792 when Congress based the currency on the silver dollar. However, the U.S. discontinued the use of silver in coinage in 1965. Today Mexico is the only country that uses silver in its circulating coinage.

Silver is the most malleable and ductile of all metals, apart from gold. Silver melts at about 962 degrees Celsius and boils at about 2212 degrees Celsius. Silver is not very chemically active, although tarnishing occurs when sulfur and sulfides attack silver, forming silver sulfide on the surface of the metal. Because silver is too soft in its pure form, a hardening agent, usually copper, is mixed into the silver. Copper is usually used as the hardening agent because it does not discolor the silver. The term "sterling silver" refers to silver that contains at least 925 parts of silver per thousand (92.5%) to 75 parts of copper (7.5%).

Silver is usually found combined with other elements in minerals and ores. In the U.S., silver is mined in conjunction with lead, copper, and zinc. In the U.S., Nevada, Idaho, Alaska, and Arizona are the leading silver-producing states. For industrial purposes, silver is used for photography, electrical appliances, glass, and as an antibacterial agent for the health industry.

Silver futures and options are traded at the CME Group and the London Metal Exchange (LME). Silver futures are traded on the Tokyo Commodity Exchange (TOCOM). The CME silver futures contract calls for the delivery of 5,000 troy ounces of silver (0.999 fineness) and is priced in terms of dollars and cents per troy ounce.

**Prices** – CME silver futures prices (Barchart.com symbol SI) rallied through Q1 of 2022 and posted a 1-1/2 year high of $27.32 per troy ounce in March. Russia's invasion of Ukraine in February sparked a surge of safe-haven demand for precious metals. Also, global supply concerns pushed silver prices higher as many countries stopped imports of Russian goods and commodities. In 2021, Russia was the world's fifth-largest silver producer. Silver prices trended lower into Q3 and posted a 2-1/2 year low in August of $17.32 per troy ounce. The Federal Reserve's aggressive 4.25 percentage point hike in interest rates in 2022 sparked a rally in the dollar to a 20-year high, which undercut silver prices. Also, other major central banks tightened their monetary policies, fueling concern that global industrial metals demand would decline as economic growth slowed. However, silver prices rebounded into year-end after China abruptly ended its Covid restrictions, which bolstered expectations the reopening of its economy would lead to an acceleration of Chinese economic growth and industrial metals demand. Silver prices finished 2022 up by +2.3% yr/yr at $23.86 per troy ounce.

**Supply** – World mine production of silver in 2022 rose by +4.0% yr/yr to 26,000 metric tons, down from the 2016 record high of 28,600. The world's largest mine producers in 2022 were Mexico with 24.2% of world production, China with 13.8%, Peru with 11.9%, Chile with 6.2%, Poland with 5.0%, Russia with 4.6%, and the U.S. with 4.2%. U.S. production of refined silver in 2021 fell by -8.1% yr/yr to 6,242 metric tons.

**Trade** – U.S. imports of silver bullion in 2021 fell by -9.9% yr/yr to a record 5,235 metric tons. The bulk of U.S. silver imports come from Mexico and Canada.

### World Mine Production of Silver    In Thousands of Kilograms (Metric Ton)

| Year | Australia | Bolivia | Canada[3] | Chile | China | Kazakhstan | Mexico | Peru | Poland | Russia | Sweden | United States | World Total[2] |
|---|---|---|---|---|---|---|---|---|---|---|---|---|---|
| 2013 | 1,735 | 1,287 | 640 | 1,174 | 3,673 | 584 | 5,821 | 3,674 | 1,393 | 2,176 | 341 | 1,050 | 26,700 |
| 2014 | 1,847 | 1,398 | 472 | 1,572 | 3,568 | 475 | 5,766 | 3,768 | 1,384 | 2,360 | 383 | 1,180 | 27,800 |
| 2015 | 1,430 | 1,306 | 371 | 1,504 | 3,568 | 370 | 5,592 | 4,102 | 1,407 | 2,297 | 480 | 1,090 | 27,400 |
| 2016 | 1,418 | 1,353 | 385 | 1,501 | 3,754 | 587 | 5,409 | 4,375 | 1,482 | 2,261 | 515 | 1,150 | 28,600 |
| 2017 | 1,120 | 1,196 | 368 | 1,319 | 3,601 | 461 | 6,109 | 4,304 | 1,490 | 1,373 | 488 | 1,030 | 26,700 |
| 2018 | 1,254 | 1,191 | 392 | 1,370 | 3,422 | 369 | 6,049 | 4,160 | 1,471 | 1,400 | 471 | 934 | 26,200 |
| 2019 | 1,325 | 1,153 | 350 | 1,309 | 3,443 | 422 | 5,840 | 3,860 | 1,249 | 1,407 | 424 | 981 | 25,700 |
| 2020 | 1,343 | 930 | 295 | 1,576 | 3,378 | 435 | 5,541 | 2,772 | 1,218 | 1,380 | 421 | 1,030 | 23,700 |
| 2021[1] | 1,360 | 1,290 | | 1,280 | 3,500 | 450 | 6,110 | 3,310 | 1,300 | 1,320 | | 1,020 | 25,000 |
| 2022[2] | 1,400 | 1,300 | | 1,600 | 3,600 | | 6,300 | 3,100 | 1,300 | 1,200 | | 1,100 | 26,000 |

[1] Preliminary.    [2] Estimate.    [3] Shipments.    *Source: U.S. Geological Survey (USGS)*

# SILVER

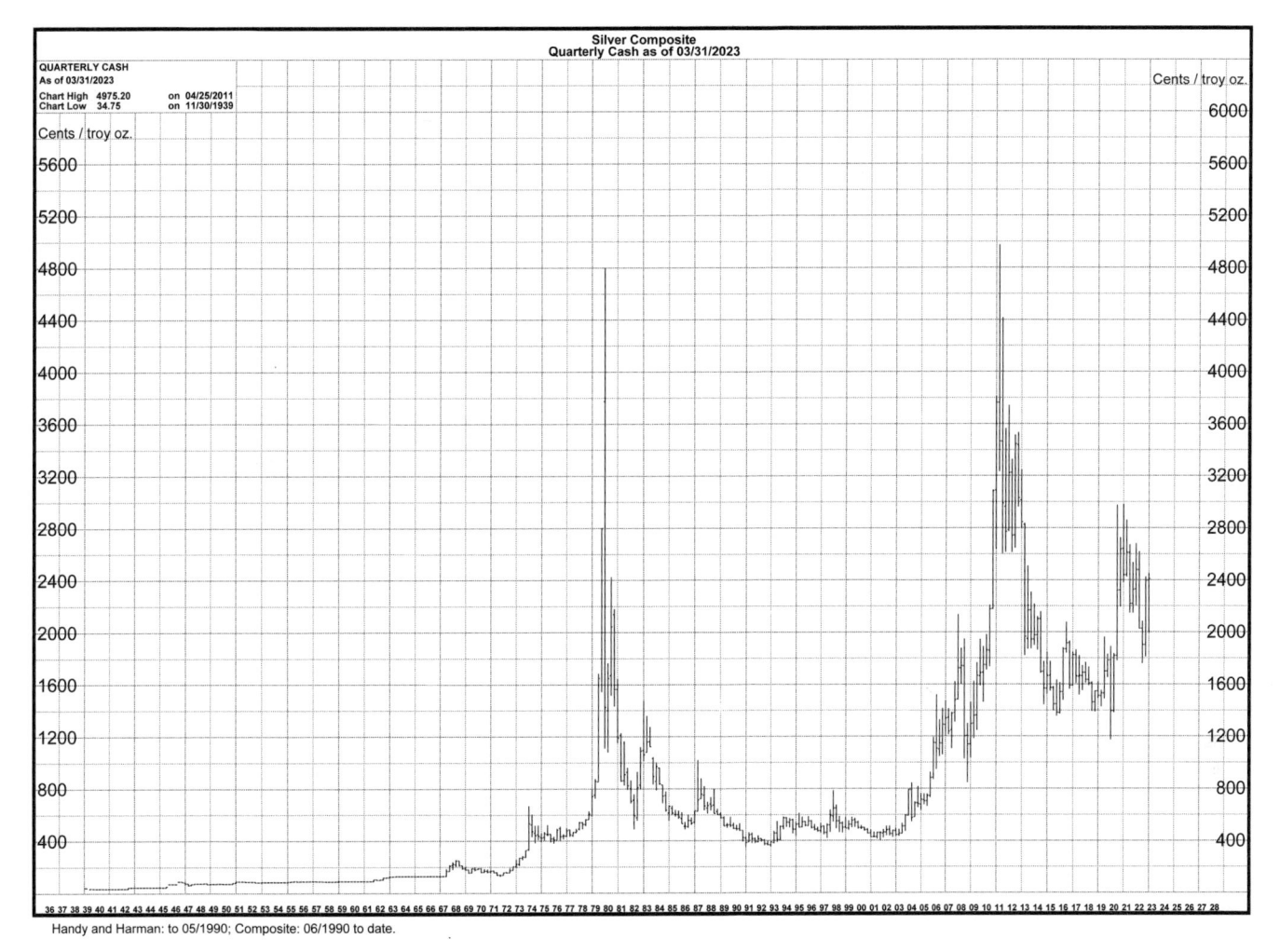

## Average Price of Silver in New York (Handy & Harman)   In Cents Per Troy Ounce (.999 Fine)

| Year | Jan. | Feb. | Mar. | Apr. | May | June | July | Aug. | Sept. | Oct. | Nov. | Dec. | Average |
|---|---|---|---|---|---|---|---|---|---|---|---|---|---|
| 2013 | 3,112 | 3,028 | 2,879 | 2,525 | 2,302 | 2,112 | 1,969 | 2,208 | 2,249 | 2,201 | 2,072 | 1,962 | 2,385 |
| 2014 | 1,988 | 2,087 | 2,072 | 1,974 | 1,934 | 1,989 | 2,092 | 1,974 | 1,837 | 1,716 | 1,597 | 1,629 | 1,907 |
| 2015 | 1,724 | 1,679 | 1,624 | 1,634 | 1,683 | 1,607 | 1,505 | 1,494 | 1,475 | 1,581 | 1,445 | 1,409 | 1,572 |
| 2016 | 1,411 | 1,517 | 1,546 | 1,636 | 1,695 | 1,729 | 1,999 | 1,959 | 1,933 | 1,764 | 1,741 | 1,645 | 1,715 |
| 2017 | 1,690 | 1,793 | 1,762 | 1,803 | 1,674 | 1,693 | 1,615 | 1,695 | 1,743 | 1,694 | 1,698 | 1,617 | 1,707 |
| 2018 | 1,713 | 1,658 | 1,647 | 1,665 | 1,649 | 1,654 | 1,572 | 1,499 | 1,427 | 1,460 | 1,435 | 1,477 | 1,571 |
| 2019 | 1,562 | 1,581 | 1,530 | 1,506 | 1,466 | 1,504 | 1,579 | 1,722 | 1,816 | 1,765 | 1,716 | 1,714 | 1,622 |
| 2020 | 1,797 | 1,788 | 1,489 | 1,506 | 1,630 | 1,771 | 2,065 | 2,700 | 2,574 | 2,423 | 2,408 | 2,497 | 2,054 |
| 2021 | 2,593 | 2,728 | 2,565 | 2,569 | 2,750 | 2,700 | 2,569 | 2,399 | 2,323 | 2,341 | 2,423 | 2,253 | 2,518 |
| 2022 | 2,313 | 2,352 | 2,528 | 2,452 | 2,187 | 2,151 | 1,910 | 1,968 | 1,889 | 1,943 |  |  | 2,169 |

*Source: American Metal Market (AMM)*

## Average Price of Silver in London (Spot Fix)   In Pence Per Troy Ounce (.999 Fine)

| Year | Jan. | Feb. | Mar. | Apr. | May | June | July | Aug. | Sept. | Oct. | Nov. | Dec. | Average |
|---|---|---|---|---|---|---|---|---|---|---|---|---|---|
| 2013 | 1,950 | 1,957 | 1,909 | 1,649 | 1,506 | 1,362 | 1,297 | 1,424 | 1,417 | 1,368 | 1,286 | 1,198 | 1,527 |
| 2014 | 1,207 | 1,260 | 1,247 | 1,178 | 1,148 | 1,176 | 1,225 | 1,182 | 1,127 | 1,068 | 1,012 | 1,042 | 1,156 |
| 2015 | 1,138 | 1,095 | 1,085 | 1,092 | 1,089 | 1,031 | 968 | 959 | 962 | 1,031 | 951 | 940 | 1,028 |
| 2016 | 981 | 1,060 | 1,085 | 1,143 | 1,167 | 1,216 | 1,521 | 1,495 | 1,470 | 1,430 | 1,399 | 1,319 | 1,274 |
| 2017 | 1,368 | 1,436 | 1,427 | 1,426 | 1,296 | 1,322 | 1,243 | 1,308 | 1,309 | 1,283 | 1,283 | 1,206 | 1,326 |
| 2018 | 1,239 | 1,188 | 1,179 | 1,183 | 1,225 | 1,245 | 1,194 | 1,164 | 1,093 | 1,122 | 1,113 | 1,167 | 1,176 |
| 2019 | 1,211 | 1,215 | 1,161 | 1,156 | 1,142 | 1,186 | 1,267 | 1,418 | 1,470 | 1,394 | 1,332 | 1,308 | 1,272 |
| 2020 | 1,374 | 1,381 | 1,205 | 1,213 | 1,326 | 1,414 | 1,628 | 2,056 | 1,987 | 1,868 | 1,822 | 1,857 | 1,594 |
| 2021 | 1,901 | 1,967 | 1,851 | 1,856 | 1,953 | 1,926 | 1,860 | 1,739 | 1,693 | 1,711 | 1,802 | 1,693 | 1,829 |
| 2022 | 1,707 | 1,738 | 1,921 | 1,898 | 1,757 | 1,747 | 1,592 | 1,644 | 1,669 | 1,719 |  |  | 1,449 |

*Source: American Metal Market (AMM)*

# SILVER

**SILVER 5,000 TROY OZ - COMEX**
Weekly Selected Futures as of 03/31/2023

WEEKLY SELECTED FUTURES
As of 03/31/2023
Chart High 3248.50 on 01/23/2013
Chart Low 1173.50 on 03/18/2020

Nearby Futures through Last Trading Day.

## Volume of Trading of Silver Futures in Chicago    In Thousands of Contracts

| Year | Jan. | Feb. | Mar. | Apr. | May | June | July | Aug. | Sept. | Oct. | Nov. | Dec. | Total |
|---|---|---|---|---|---|---|---|---|---|---|---|---|---|
| 2013 | 1,021.7 | 1,346.4 | 780.3 | 1,980.5 | 1,172.0 | 1,555.4 | 932.3 | 1,652.5 | 958.1 | 948.4 | 1,270.3 | 857.7 | 14,475.6 |
| 2014 | 915.0 | 1,498.8 | 973.7 | 1,388.9 | 883.1 | 1,459.4 | 957.2 | 1,216.7 | 990.8 | 1,013.7 | 1,435.1 | 964.7 | 13,697.2 |
| 2015 | 979.5 | 1,196.0 | 875.8 | 1,431.4 | 886.3 | 1,499.6 | 988.4 | 1,511.0 | 822.3 | 1,107.5 | 1,291.7 | 864.9 | 13,454.4 |
| 2016 | 960.5 | 1,694.2 | 1,212.5 | 1,974.1 | 1,183.6 | 1,828.3 | 1,458.7 | 1,939.3 | 1,290.1 | 1,327.6 | 2,214.4 | 1,135.5 | 18,218.7 |
| 2017 | 1,414.0 | 1,809.3 | 1,495.9 | 2,120.9 | 1,904.5 | 2,371.5 | 1,829.7 | 2,604.7 | 1,730.4 | 1,826.4 | 2,539.5 | 1,388.1 | 23,035.0 |
| 2018 | 2,186.6 | 2,155.7 | 1,842.3 | 2,625.8 | 1,702.2 | 2,486.3 | 1,582.4 | 2,364.1 | 1,648.3 | 1,793.5 | 2,299.1 | 1,300.6 | 23,987.1 |
| 2019 | 1,526.3 | 1,783.6 | 1,418.5 | 1,920.3 | 1,476.3 | 2,651.2 | 2,087.0 | 3,018.6 | 2,579.9 | 1,810.5 | 2,334.3 | 1,542.7 | 24,149.1 |
| 2020 | 2,012.7 | 2,515.3 | 2,275.1 | 1,357.8 | 1,210.9 | 1,846.7 | 2,623.6 | 4,633.8 | 2,183.5 | 1,645.6 | 2,139.7 | 1,682.0 | 26,126.8 |
| 2021 | 2,028.4 | 2,595.9 | 1,580.5 | 1,762.6 | 1,515.7 | 2,003.3 | 1,272.4 | 1,693.7 | 1,143.6 | 1,184.3 | 1,880.8 | 1,008.1 | 19,669.5 |
| 2022 | 1,289.2 | 1,601.7 | 1,440.7 | 1,488.9 | 1,204.0 | 1,596.9 | 1,206.2 | 1,570.9 | 1,358.8 | 1,346.7 | 1,849.0 | 1,123.7 | 17,076.5 |

Contract size = 5,000 oz.    Source: CME Group; Commodity Exchange (COMEX)

## Average Open Interest of Silver Futures in Chicago    In Contracts

| Year | Jan. | Feb. | Mar. | Apr. | May | June | July | Aug. | Sept. | Oct. | Nov. | Dec. |
|---|---|---|---|---|---|---|---|---|---|---|---|---|
| 2013 | 143,032 | 141,751 | 149,900 | 156,813 | 145,964 | 147,042 | 133,417 | 130,278 | 113,116 | 116,266 | 130,050 | 133,668 |
| 2014 | 137,682 | 145,743 | 141,847 | 157,064 | 152,154 | 161,079 | 161,447 | 161,613 | 168,883 | 172,012 | 169,706 | 148,854 |
| 2015 | 158,200 | 167,554 | 171,411 | 177,026 | 176,403 | 190,678 | 190,121 | 173,457 | 155,598 | 164,457 | 167,660 | 164,215 |
| 2016 | 161,725 | 167,337 | 170,875 | 190,935 | 203,017 | 203,311 | 217,206 | 207,634 | 197,360 | 192,183 | 177,922 | 161,707 |
| 2017 | 172,215 | 198,811 | 194,560 | 220,791 | 202,476 | 203,230 | 207,098 | 192,201 | 187,569 | 190,554 | 198,941 | 199,229 |
| 2018 | 197,597 | 198,883 | 207,295 | 218,714 | 199,496 | 220,429 | 212,471 | 233,201 | 206,398 | 201,730 | 211,615 | 175,572 |
| 2019 | 189,481 | 213,207 | 191,157 | 210,647 | 206,496 | 226,614 | 227,668 | 234,590 | 215,936 | 214,545 | 220,824 | 211,176 |
| 2020 | 233,640 | 228,860 | 169,311 | 140,127 | 145,645 | 175,076 | 179,905 | 192,625 | 159,633 | 157,366 | 157,744 | 161,855 |
| 2021 | 171,024 | 177,706 | 157,192 | 165,421 | 177,605 | 181,280 | 152,970 | 150,282 | 142,312 | 141,546 | 147,733 | 139,752 |
| 2022 | 146,589 | 154,885 | 158,420 | 153,584 | 143,515 | 145,143 | 144,032 | 141,012 | 133,857 | 133,475 | 135,170 | 125,910 |

Contract size = 5,000 oz.    Source: CME Group; Commodity Exchange (COMEX)

# SILVER

**Mine Production of Recoverable Silver in the United States**    In Metric Tons

| Year | Arizona | Idaho | Montana | Nevada | New Mexico | Other States | Total |
|---|---|---|---|---|---|---|---|
| 2013 | W | W | W | 255 | W | 791 | 1,050 |
| 2014 | W | W | W | 326 | W | 858 | 1,180 |
| 2015 | W | W | W | 296 | W | 777 | 1,070 |
| 2016 | 87 | W | W | 276 | W | 264 | 1,150 |
| 2017 | 79 | W | W | 265 | W | 173 | 1,030 |
| 2018 | 58 | W | W | 247 | W | 164 | 934 |
| 2019 | 65 | W | W | 190 | W | 186 | 981 |
| 2020 | 71 | W | W | 165 | W | 217 | 1,030 |
| 2021 | W | W | W | 167 | W | 841 | 1,008 |
| 2022[1] | W | W | W | 173 | W | 837 | 1,010 |

[1] Preliminary.    W = Withheld proprietary data; included in "Other States".    *Source: U.S. Geological Survey (USGS)*

**Production[2] of Refined Silver in the United States, from All Sources**    In Metric Tons

| Year | Jan. | Feb. | Mar. | Apr. | May | June | July | Aug. | Sept. | Oct. | Nov. | Dec. | Total |
|---|---|---|---|---|---|---|---|---|---|---|---|---|---|
| 2013 | 505 | 438 | 421 | 486 | 376 | 337 | 415 | 365 | 364 | 450 | 292 | 431 | 4,880 |
| 2014 | 431 | 334 | 348 | 399 | 450 | 418 | 458 | 386 | 506 | 456 | 430 | 474 | 5,080 |
| 2015 | 515 | 507 | 473 | 505 | 434 | 479 | 467 | 498 | 453 | 480 | 390 | 547 | 5,750 |
| 2016 | 496 | 476 | 581 | 507 | 496 | 429 | 455 | 575 | 545 | 503 | 475 | 481 | 6,020 |
| 2017 | 507 | 497 | 398 | 461 | 390 | 426 | 485 | 348 | 326 | 374 | 425 | 345 | 4,980 |
| 2018 | 480 | 380 | 317 | 357 | 458 | 304 | 395 | 424 | 383 | 392 | 382 | 412 | 4,684 |
| 2019 | 415 | 356 | 419 | 426 | 375 | 301 | 377 | 488 | 425 | 417 | 375 | 390 | 4,764 |
| 2020 | 398 | 322 | 380 | 470 | 444 | 606 | 1,076 | 543 | 746 | 578 | 643 | 590 | 6,796 |
| 2021 | 457 | 475 | 607 | 483 | 697 | 560 | 671 | 608 | 381 | 453 | 479 | 370 | 6,243 |
| 2022[1] | 372 | 302 | 373 | 475 | 460 | 429 | 422 | 357 | 363 | 352 | 385 | 503 | 4,792 |

[1] Preliminary.    [2] Includes U.S. mine production of recoverable silver plus imports of refined silver.    *Source: U.S. Geological Survey (USGS)*

**Mine Production of Recoverable Silver in the United States**    In Metric Tons

| Year | Jan. | Feb. | Mar. | Apr. | May | June | July | Aug. | Sept. | Oct. | Nov. | Dec. | Total |
|---|---|---|---|---|---|---|---|---|---|---|---|---|---|
| 2013 | 88.8 | 84.2 | 88.5 | 90.2 | 89.6 | 91.5 | 90.3 | 86.2 | 83.9 | 86.4 | 79.0 | 88.3 | 1,046.9 |
| 2014 | 95.5 | 86.2 | 95.5 | 94.2 | 102.0 | 90.8 | 106.0 | 101.0 | 103.0 | 103.0 | 105.0 | 110.0 | 1,180.0 |
| 2015 | 94.2 | 90.1 | 99.5 | 89.8 | 90.6 | 87.5 | 88.0 | 90.8 | 83.6 | 93.9 | 89.2 | 94.2 | 1,090.0 |
| 2016 | 94.0 | 95.4 | 98.0 | 92.2 | 93.8 | 90.6 | 91.0 | 104.0 | 98.5 | 100.0 | 94.6 | 96.1 | 1,150.0 |
| 2017 | 98.4 | 84.1 | 94.3 | 87.5 | 82.9 | 85.4 | 84.7 | 83.6 | 74.5 | 82.4 | 87.6 | 82.4 | 1,030.0 |
| 2018 | 75.1 | 67.6 | 69.7 | 73.7 | 76.5 | 79.4 | 73.6 | 80.1 | 78.7 | 87.2 | 80.0 | 88.3 | 934.0 |
| 2019 | 80.7 | 71.2 | 75.6 | 84.3 | 84.1 | 84.2 | 86.7 | 83.2 | 85.2 | 75.1 | 87.0 | 77.8 | 975.1 |
| 2020 | 80.1 | 77.1 | 77.1 | 70.5 | 75.9 | 75.3 | 88.2 | 87.3 | 86.2 | 88.5 | 86.1 | 93.5 | 985.8 |
| 2021 | 85.4 | 83.2 | 86.1 | 84.2 | 86.8 | 90.2 | 83.3 | 83.0 | 79.0 | 83.4 | 76.9 | 86.2 | 1,007.7 |
| 2022[1] | 81.7 | 84.1 | 88.9 | 86.3 | 83.9 | 80.5 | 87.2 | 86.6 | 81.5 | 81.8 | 79.3 | 87.8 | 1,009.6 |

[1] Preliminary.    *Source: U.S. Geological Survey (USGS)*

**Mine Production of Recoverable Silver in Nevada**    In Metric Tons

| Year | Jan. | Feb. | Mar. | Apr. | May | June | July | Aug. | Sept. | Oct. | Nov. | Dec. | Total |
|---|---|---|---|---|---|---|---|---|---|---|---|---|---|
| 2013 | 21.1 | 18.4 | 20.6 | 23.6 | 21.0 | 22.0 | 17.7 | 23.1 | 20.9 | 23.0 | 19.5 | 24.2 | 255.1 |
| 2014 | 25.0 | 23.9 | 26.5 | 24.9 | 29.2 | 28.3 | 29.1 | 29.1 | 28.3 | 29.9 | 29.6 | 31.1 | 326.0 |
| 2015 | 25.1 | 23.7 | 25.6 | 26.0 | 26.2 | 25.3 | 24.8 | 24.2 | 22.5 | 22.8 | 21.5 | 22.9 | 290.0 |
| 2016 | 22.1 | 20.7 | 21.6 | 22.6 | 22.9 | 22.0 | 23.5 | 24.3 | 23.6 | 23.9 | 24.5 | 25.8 | 276.0 |
| 2017 | 23.1 | 22.1 | 22.1 | 22.2 | 22.8 | 23.1 | 20.7 | 19.4 | 19.2 | 21.5 | 22.6 | 23.2 | 265.0 |
| 2018 | 18.8 | 18.4 | 19.6 | 19.4 | 18.9 | 19.2 | 19.9 | 20.3 | 20.4 | 22.8 | 21.7 | 23.7 | 247.0 |
| 2019 | 16.2 | 14.6 | 15.7 | 14.9 | 16.0 | 15.9 | 16.2 | 16.1 | 15.8 | 15.5 | 15.8 | 15.7 | 190.0 |
| 2020 | 12.2 | 12.4 | 12.5 | 12.3 | 12.5 | 12.8 | 12.2 | 12.3 | 12.5 | 12.0 | 12.6 | 12.7 | 165.0 |
| 2021 | 12.8 | 12.8 | 12.7 | 12.5 | 12.5 | 12.5 | 12.4 | 15.5 | 15.4 | 15.6 | 15.8 | 16.2 | 166.7 |
| 2022[1] | 14.4 | 13.6 | 14.8 | 13.7 | 14.2 | 14.1 | 14.5 | 15.0 | 14.7 | 14.5 | 14.8 | 14.8 | 173.1 |

[1] Preliminary.    *Source: U.S. Geological Survey (USGS)*

255

# SILVER

**U.S. Imports of Silver Bullion**   In Metric Tons

| Year | Jan. | Feb. | Mar. | Apr. | May | June | July | Aug. | Sept. | Oct. | Nov. | Dec. | Total |
|---|---|---|---|---|---|---|---|---|---|---|---|---|---|
| 2013 | 416.0 | 354.0 | 332.0 | 396.0 | 286.0 | 245.0 | 325.0 | 279.0 | 280.0 | 364.0 | 213.0 | 343.0 | 3,833.0 |
| 2014 | 335.0 | 248.0 | 252.0 | 305.0 | 348.0 | 327.0 | 352.0 | 285.0 | 403.0 | 353.0 | 325.0 | 364.0 | 3,900.0 |
| 2015 | 421.0 | 417.0 | 373.0 | 415.0 | 343.0 | 391.0 | 379.0 | 407.0 | 369.0 | 386.0 | 301.0 | 453.0 | 4,660.0 |
| 2016 | 402.0 | 381.0 | 483.0 | 415.0 | 402.0 | 338.0 | 364.0 | 471.0 | 446.0 | 403.0 | 380.0 | 385.0 | 4,870.0 |
| 2017 | 409.0 | 413.0 | 304.0 | 373.0 | 307.0 | 341.0 | 400.0 | 264.0 | 251.0 | 292.0 | 337.0 | 263.0 | 3,950.0 |
| 2018 | 405.0 | 312.0 | 247.0 | 283.0 | 381.0 | 225.0 | 321.0 | 344.0 | 304.0 | 305.0 | 302.0 | 324.0 | 3,750.0 |
| 2019 | 334.0 | 285.0 | 343.0 | 342.0 | 291.0 | 217.0 | 290.0 | 405.0 | 340.0 | 342.0 | 288.0 | 312.0 | 3,789.0 |
| 2020 | 318.0 | 245.0 | 303.0 | 399.0 | 368.0 | 531.0 | 988.0 | 456.0 | 660.0 | 489.0 | 557.0 | 496.0 | 5,810.0 |
| 2021 | 372.0 | 392.0 | 521.0 | 399.0 | 610.0 | 470.0 | 588.0 | 525.0 | 302.0 | 370.0 | 402.0 | 284.0 | 5,235.0 |
| 2022[1] | 290.0 | 218.0 | 284.0 | 389.0 | 376.0 | 348.0 | 335.0 | 270.0 | 281.0 | 270.0 | 306.0 | 415.0 | 3,782.0 |

[1] Preliminary.   Source: U.S. Geological Survey (USGS)


**Commodity Exchange Warehouse of Stocks of Silver, on First of Month**   In Thousands of Troy Ounces

| Year | Jan. 1 | Feb. 1 | Mar. 1 | Apr. 1 | May 1 | June 1 | July 1 | Aug. 1 | Sept. 1 | Oct. 1 | Nov. 1 | Dec. 1 |
|---|---|---|---|---|---|---|---|---|---|---|---|---|
| 2013 | 148,205 | 154,577 | 162,830 | 164,163 | 166,050 | 165,749 | 166,746 | 164,711 | 163,771 | 165,329 | 169,012 | 169,985 |
| 2014 | 173,927 | 179,297 | 182,831 | 179,791 | 174,483 | 175,267 | 175,517 | 175,317 | 179,292 | 182,194 | 181,185 | 177,008 |
| 2015 | 174,359 | 178,053 | 177,163 | 176,650 | 176,310 | 179,287 | 182,384 | 175,671 | 170,562 | 165,009 | 162,813 | 158,954 |
| 2016 | 160,671 | 158,266 | 154,261 | 154,999 | 151,780 | 153,898 | 151,481 | 154,090 | 162,921 | 173,354 | 173,583 | 178,616 |
| 2017 | 183,006 | 180,805 | 186,606 | 190,223 | 196,524 | 201,367 | 208,937 | 215,512 | 217,741 | 218,121 | 225,904 | 235,906 |
| 2018 | 244,724 | 246,977 | 251,320 | 260,510 | 262,948 | 270,519 | 275,911 | 286,599 | 295,357 | 289,725 | 290,258 | 295,015 |
| 2019 | 293,901 | 298,005 | 298,844 | 305,542 | 306,750 | 304,961 | 305,683 | 310,364 | 311,900 | 313,603 | 315,503 | 314,008 |
| 2020 | 317,166 | 321,312 | 324,302 | 321,002 | 316,635 | 311,570 | 321,179 | 334,509 | 344,970 | 375,203 | 381,797 | 388,052 |
| 2021 | 396,542 | 397,323 | 393,063 | 370,157 | 361,318 | 353,573 | 350,695 | 355,823 | 362,072 | 361,010 | 353,278 | 352,644 |
| 2022 | 355,704 | 354,059 | 346,810 | 340,970 | 333,532 | 337,178 | 336,855 | 336,774 | 327,803 | 313,060 | 301,160 | 297,539 |

Source: CME Group; Commodity Exchange (COMEX)


**U.S. Exports of Refined Silver**   In Kilograms

| Year | Australia | Canada | Germany | Hong Kong | India | Italy | Japan | Mexico | Singapore | Switzerland | United Arab Emirates | United Kingdom | Total |
|---|---|---|---|---|---|---|---|---|---|---|---|---|---|
| 2011 | 20,700 | 98,400 | 6,030 | 8,830 | ---- | 237 | 148,000 | 288,000 | 9,700 | 823 | 1,100 | 19,500 | 625,000 |
| 2012 | 27,800 | 79,200 | 16,900 | 5,670 | 19,100 | 115 | 86,200 | 250,000 | 4,010 | 12,100 | 270 | 320,000 | 837,000 |
| 2013 | 124,000 | 77,300 | 8,760 | 4,030 | 36,300 | 302 | ---- | 76,300 | 11,800 | 64 | 28 | 73 | 347,000 |
| 2014 | 55,300 | 200,000 | 1,190 | 1,330 | 1,180 | 3,410 | ---- | 62,400 | 9,820 | 1,090 | 198 | 1,550 | 346,000 |
| 2015 | 24,000 | 430,000 | 8,720 | 2,720 | 284,000 | 5,880 | ---- | 8,650 | 6,560 | 1,700 | ---- | 2,690 | 781,000 |
| 2016 | 18,800 | 136,000 | 10,400 | 1,050 | 39,300 | 1,460 | ---- | 7,330 | 6,120 | 3,300 | ---- | 1,590 | 237,000 |
| 2017 | 7,620 | 55,700 | 5,380 | 136 | 2,000 | 2,750 | 36 | 3,470 | 4,630 | ---- | 28 | 1,070 | 91,800 |
| 2018 | 3,160 | 18,900 | 6,460 | 529 | 398,000 | 6,890 | 25,700 | 10,800 | 7,770 | 6,600 | ---- | 65,100 | 558,000 |
| 2019 | 4,240 | 25,300 | 7,020 | 98 | 129,000 | 4,190 | 14 | 7,790 | 2,340 | 2,420 | 17 | 653 | 190,000 |
| 2020[1] | 2,640 | 99,700 | 3,810 | 114 | 450 | 63 | ---- | 9,460 | 4,490 | 80 | ---- | 1,370 | 130,000 |

[1] Preliminary.   Source: U.S. Geological Survey (USGS)


**U.S. Imports of Silver From Selected Countries**   In Kilograms

| | Ores and Concentrates | | | | Refined Bullion | | | | | | |
|---|---|---|---|---|---|---|---|---|---|---|---|
| Year | Canada | Mexico | Other Countries | Total | Canada | Korea, South | Mexico | Peru | Poland | United Kingdom | Total |
| 2011 | 84,200 | ---- | ---- | 84,200 | 1,260,000 | 207,000 | 2,100,000 | 29,600 | 780,000 | 20,500 | 5,250,000 |
| 2012 | 73,800 | 7,770 | ---- | 82,700 | 1,330,000 | 55,600 | 2,390,000 | 44,100 | 36,700 | 330 | 4,030,000 |
| 2013 | 26 | 10,700 | ---- | 10,700 | 1,600,000 | 36,300 | 2,010,000 | 38,300 | 55,500 | 20,700 | 3,830,000 |
| 2014 | ---- | ---- | 59 | 59 | 1,120,000 | 333,000 | 2,140,000 | 77,800 | 77,000 | 41,000 | 3,900,000 |
| 2015 | ---- | ---- | ---- | 253 | 1,920,000 | 159,000 | 1,980,000 | 90,300 | 234,000 | 3,000 | 4,660,000 |
| 2016 | 4,430 | 203 | [3] | 4,630 | 1,720,000 | 188,000 | 2,030,000 | 128,000 | 250,000 | 21,200 | 4,870,000 |
| 2017 | 5,940 | 803 | 90 | 6,840 | 1,170,000 | 126,000 | 1,780,000 | 136,000 | 175,000 | 54,600 | 3,950,000 |
| 2018 | 1,700 | 517 | ---- | 2,260 | 1,430,000 | 53,900 | 1,650,000 | 86,000 | 112,000 | 175 | 3,750,000 |
| 2019 | 5,460 | 1,750 | 77 | 7,290 | 1,160,000 | 18,900 | 1,980,000 | 31,900 | 186,000 | 1,070 | 3,790,000 |
| 2020[1] | 7,720 | 1,210 | [3] | 8,930 | 1,180,000 | 487,000 | 1,830,000 | 9,920 | 330,000 | 613,000 | 5,830,000 |

[1] Preliminary.   [3] Less than 1/2 unit..   Source: U.S. Geological Survey (USGS)

# Soybean Meal

Soybean meal is produced through processing and separating soybeans into oil and meal components. If the soybeans are of particularly good quality, then the processor can get more meal weight by including more hulls in the meal while still meeting a 48% protein minimum. Soybean meal can be further processed into soy flour and isolated soy protein, but the bulk of soybean meal is used as animal feed for poultry, hogs, and cattle. Soybean meal accounts for about two-thirds of the world's high-protein animal feed, followed by cottonseed and rapeseed meal, which together account for less than 20%. Soybean meal consumption has been moving to record highs in recent years. The soybean meal marketing year begins in October and ends in September. Soybean meal futures and options are traded at the CME Group. The CME soybean meal futures contract calls for the delivery of 100 tons of soybean meal produced by conditioning ground soybeans and reducing the oil content of the conditioned product and having a minimum of 48.0% protein, minimum of 0.5% fat, maximum of 3.5% fiber, and maximum of 12.0% moisture.

**Soybean crush** – The term soybean "crush" refers to both to the physical processing of soybeans and to the dollar-value premium received for processing soybeans into their component products of meal and oil. The conventional model says that processing 60 pounds (one bushel) of soybeans produces 11 pounds of soybean oil, 44 pounds of 48% protein soybean meal, 3 pounds of hulls, and 1 pound of waste. The Gross Processing Margin (GPM) or crush equals (0.22 times Soybean Meal Prices in dollars per ton) + (11 times Soybean Oil prices in cents/pound) – Soybean prices in $/bushel. A higher crush value will occur when the price of the meal and oil products are strong relative to soybeans, e.g., because of supply disruptions or because of an increase in demand for the products. When the crush value is high, companies will have a strong incentive to buy raw soybeans and boost the output of the products. That supply increase should eventually bring the crush value back into line with the long-term equilibrium.

**Prices** – CME soybean meal futures prices (Barchart.com symbol ZM) in 2022 rallied early in the year and then traded mostly sideways in a choppy range, finally closing the year up +16.2% yr/yr at $478.5 per short ton.

**Supply** – World soybean meal production in 2022/23 is expected to rise by +4.2% yr/yr to a new record high of 256.927 million metric tons. The world's largest soybean meal producers are expected to be China with 29.3% of world production in 2022/23, the U.S. with 18.7%, Brazil with 15.8%, and Argentina with 11.5%.

U.S. production of soybean meal in 2022/23 is expected to rise by +2.0% yr/yr to 52.839 million short tons, a new record high. U.S. soybean meal ending stocks in 2022/23 are expected to rise by +12.5% yr/yr to 350,000 short tons.

**Demand** – World consumption of soybean meal in 2022/23 is expected to rise by +3.5% yr/yr to 252.514 million metric tons, a new record high. China is expected to account for 29.6% of that consumption, the U.S. for 14.3%, and the European Union for 11.0%. U.S. consumption of soybean meal in 2022/23 is expected to rise by +1.9% yr/yr to 36.015 million metric tons, a new record high.

**Trade** – World exports of soybean meal in 2022/23 are expected to rise by +2.3% yr/yr to a new record high 69.735 million metric tons. Argentina is expected to account for 38.0% of total world exports, Brazil for 29.7%, and the U.S. for 17.8%. World imports of soybean meal in 2022/23 are expected to rise by +0.3% yr/yr to 65.451 million metric tons, a record high. U.S. exports of soybean meal in 2022/23 are expected to rise by +1.3% yr/yr to 13.700 million short tons. U.S. imports of soybean meal in 2022/23 are expected to fall by -7.6% yr/yr to 600,000 short tons.

### Supply and Distribution of Soybean Meal in the United States    In Thousands of Short Tons

| Crop Year Beginning Oct. 1 | For Stocks Oct. 1 | Production | Total Supply | Domestic | Exports | Total | Decatur 48% Protein Solvent | Decatur 44% Protein Solvent | Brazil FOB 45-46% Protein | Rotterdam CIF |
|---|---|---|---|---|---|---|---|---|---|---|
| 2013-14 | 275 | 40,685 | 41,343 | 29,547 | 11,546 | 41,093 | 489.94 | 540 | 500 | 533 |
| 2014-15 | 250 | 45,062 | 45,645 | 32,277 | 13,108 | 45,384 | 368.49 | 406 | 376 | 403 |
| 2015-16 | 260 | 44,672 | 45,336 | 33,118 | 11,954 | 45,072 | 324.56 | 358 | 335 | 351 |
| 2016-17 | 264 | 44,787 | 45,400 | 33,420 | 11,580 | 45,000 | 316.88 | 349 | 322 | 336 |
| 2017-18 | 401 | 49,226 | 50,121 | 35,497 | 14,057 | 49,554 | 345.02 | 380 | 368 | 382 |
| 2018-19 | 555 | 48,814 | 50,053 | 36,212 | 13,438 | 49,651 | 308.28 | 340 | 325 | 329 |
| 2019-20 | 402 | 51,100 | 52,142 | 37,967 | 13,834 | 51,801 | 299.50 | 330 | 328 | 338 |
| 2020-21[1] | 341 | 50,565 | 51,691 | 37,674 | 13,675 | 51,350 | 392.31 | 432 | 447 | 463 |
| 2021-22[2] | 341 | 51,814 | 52,804 | 38,970 | 13,524 | 52,493 | 439.81 | 484 | 476 | 520 |
| 2022-23[3] | 311 | 52,539 | 53,450 | 39,400 | 13,700 | 53,100 | 410.00 | 503 | 500 | 537 |

[1] Preliminary.  [2] Estimate.  [3] Forecast.    Source: Economic Research Service, U.S. Department of Agriculture (ERS-USDA)

# SOYBEAN MEAL

## World Production of Soybean Meal   In Thousands of Metric Tons

| Crop Year | Argentina | Bolivia | Brazil | China | European Union | India | Japan | Mexico | Paraguay | Russia | Taiwan | United States | World Total |
|---|---|---|---|---|---|---|---|---|---|---|---|---|---|
| 2013-14 | 15,100 | 52,572 | 2,360 | 28,042 | 3,640 | 3,800 | 2,800 | 3,429 | 4,575 | 4,150 | 26,774 | 4,200 | 186,806 |
| 2014-15 | 15,700 | 57,467 | 2,600 | 30,142 | 4,500 | 4,000 | 2,850 | 3,365 | 5,050 | 4,100 | 29,282 | 4,750 | 201,862 |
| 2015-16 | 16,470 | 62,663 | 2,900 | 30,567 | 4,460 | 4,150 | 3,125 | 3,440 | 5,700 | 4,180 | 30,037 | 5,565 | 213,874 |
| 2016-17 | 16,943 | 68,646 | 3,100 | 27,792 | 4,674 | 4,250 | 3,125 | 3,430 | 5,870 | 4,250 | 30,314 | 5,590 | 222,019 |
| 2017-18 | 17,311 | 70,105 | 3,200 | 27,717 | 4,739 | 4,450 | 3,235 | 3,520 | 6,150 | 4,280 | 32,237 | 5,830 | 228,804 |
| 2018-19 | 17,645 | 66,405 | 3,325 | 27,867 | 5,430 | 4,625 | 3,325 | 3,470 | 6,625 | 4,400 | 32,901 | 5,930 | 229,862 |
| 2019-20 | 18,500 | 71,507 | 3,450 | 28,267 | 5,770 | 4,960 | 3,400 | 3,580 | 6,650 | 4,840 | 34,444 | 6,080 | 240,721 |
| 2020-21 | 19,200 | 72,678 | 3,600 | 28,392 | 6,050 | 5,273 | 3,430 | 3,650 | 6,725 | 4,850 | 34,179 | 6,280 | 244,112 |
| 2021-22[1] | 19,550 | 68,872 | 3,725 | 28,142 | 7,022 | 5,655 | 3,525 | 3,700 | 6,875 | 4,833 | 35,349 | 6,130 | 243,966 |
| 2022-23[2] | 19,850 | 74,690 | 3,825 | 27,742 | 6,945 | 5,750 | 3,575 | 3,695 | 6,950 | 4,850 | 36,015 | 6,260 | 252,514 |

Crop year beginning October 1.   [1] Preliminary.   [2] Forecast.   Source: *Foreign Agricultural Service, U.S. Department of Agriculture (FAS-USDA)*

## World Exports of Soybean Meal   In Thousands of Metric Tons

| Crop Year | Argentina | Bolivia | Brazil | Canada | China | European Union | India | Korea, South | Norway | Paraguay | Russia | United States | World Total |
|---|---|---|---|---|---|---|---|---|---|---|---|---|---|
| 2013-14 | 24,972 | 1,608 | 13,948 | 241 | 2,017 | 296 | 3,252 | 179 | 153 | 2,428 | 526 | 10,504 | 60,867 |
| 2014-15 | 28,575 | 1,674 | 14,290 | 212 | 1,595 | 362 | 1,521 | 112 | 175 | 2,569 | 505 | 11,891 | 64,658 |
| 2015-16 | 30,333 | 1,726 | 15,407 | 335 | 1,909 | 304 | 409 | 76 | 198 | 2,552 | 480 | 10,843 | 65,814 |
| 2016-17 | 31,323 | 1,289 | 13,762 | 291 | 1,111 | 734 | 2,019 | 100 | 181 | 2,379 | 323 | 10,505 | 65,356 |
| 2017-18 | 26,265 | 1,653 | 16,033 | 357 | 1,198 | 770 | 1,863 | 41 | 182 | 2,625 | 384 | 12,717 | 65,763 |
| 2018-19 | 28,833 | 1,638 | 16,095 | 425 | 932 | 753 | 2,185 | 71 | 157 | 2,333 | 374 | 12,141 | 68,018 |
| 2019-20 | 27,461 | 1,723 | 17,499 | 329 | 1,012 | 874 | 886 | 44 | 202 | 2,138 | 557 | 12,549 | 67,592 |
| 2020-21 | 28,325 | 2,116 | 16,576 | 363 | 1,052 | 847 | 2,025 | 43 | 196 | 1,916 | 640 | 12,406 | 68,975 |
| 2021-22[1] | 26,589 | 1,750 | 20,207 | 406 | 484 | 770 | 660 | 51 | 200 | 1,300 | 700 | 12,269 | 68,190 |
| 2022-23[2] | 26,500 | 1,675 | 20,700 | 350 | 600 | 800 | 1,200 | 50 | 200 | 2,150 | 550 | 12,428 | 69,735 |

Crop year beginning October 1.   [1] Preliminary.   [2] Forecast.   Source: *Foreign Agricultural Service, U.S. Department of Agriculture (FAS-USDA)*

## World Imports of Soybean Meal   In Thousands of Metric Tons

| Crop Year | Algeria | European Union | Indonesia | Iran | Japan | Korea, South | Malaysia | Mexico | Peru | Philippines | Thailand | Vietnam | World Total |
|---|---|---|---|---|---|---|---|---|---|---|---|---|---|
| 2013-14 | 1,441 | 18,140 | 3,806 | 2,683 | 1,976 | 1,825 | 1,397 | 1,410 | 1,173 | 2,335 | 2,665 | 3,344 | 58,334 |
| 2014-15 | 1,132 | 19,623 | 3,844 | 1,948 | 1,699 | 1,751 | 1,465 | 1,795 | 1,145 | 2,204 | 3,068 | 4,311 | 61,255 |
| 2015-16 | 1,488 | 19,213 | 4,203 | 1,420 | 1,721 | 2,118 | 1,291 | 2,367 | 1,277 | 2,617 | 2,433 | 5,093 | 63,125 |
| 2016-17 | 1,242 | 17,353 | 4,255 | 1,623 | 1,621 | 1,764 | 1,427 | 2,064 | 1,327 | 2,660 | 2,782 | 4,580 | 61,626 |
| 2017-18 | 1,513 | 16,992 | 4,486 | 1,544 | 1,728 | 1,846 | 1,609 | 1,875 | 1,353 | 2,886 | 3,191 | 4,957 | 63,420 |
| 2018-19 | 1,374 | 17,197 | 4,449 | 2,542 | 1,596 | 1,855 | 1,278 | 1,887 | 1,345 | 2,897 | 2,889 | 5,063 | 63,640 |
| 2019-20 | 1,143 | 16,329 | 5,043 | 618 | 1,858 | 1,992 | 1,414 | 1,818 | 1,414 | 2,872 | 2,854 | 5,176 | 62,502 |
| 2020-21 | 396 | 16,513 | 5,336 | 2,018 | 1,839 | 1,727 | 1,263 | 1,854 | 1,560 | 2,707 | 2,687 | 5,052 | 64,071 |
| 2021-22[1] | 116 | 16,840 | 5,535 | 1,406 | 1,699 | 1,726 | 1,292 | 1,827 | 1,500 | 2,700 | 3,038 | 5,000 | 65,234 |
| 2022-23[2] | 250 | 16,700 | 5,750 | 1,700 | 1,850 | 1,875 | 1,350 | 1,850 | 1,525 | 2,800 | 2,800 | 5,300 | 65,451 |

Crop year beginning October 1.   [1] Preliminary.   [2] Forecast.   Source: *Foreign Agricultural Service, U.S. Department of Agriculture (FAS-USDA)*

## U.S. Exports of Soybean Cake & Meal by Country of Destination   In Thousands of Metric Tons

| Year | Algeria | Australia | Canada | Dominican Republic | Italy | Japan | Mexico | Netherlands | Philippines | Russia | Spain | Venezuela | Total |
|---|---|---|---|---|---|---|---|---|---|---|---|---|---|
| 2013 | 17.3 | 69.0 | 895.1 | 331.6 | 229.6 | 180.2 | 1,269.5 | 0.9 | 1,120.1 | 0.1 | 198.4 | 755.1 | 10,133 |
| 2014 | 3.0 | 0.1 | 971.6 | 374.4 | 253.0 | 211.0 | 1,593.3 | 1.6 | 1,104.3 | 15.0 | 267.0 | 842.6 | 10,281 |
| 2015 | 30.6 | 0.2 | 805.4 | 472.8 | 75.2 | 174.4 | 2,001.4 | 10.3 | 1,509.2 | ---- | 315.5 | 540.9 | 11,394 |
| 2016 | 27.3 | 0.5 | 755.9 | 506.2 | 0.4 | 158.4 | 2,130.3 | 1.1 | 1,847.2 | ---- | 0.0 | 311.9 | 10,539 |
| 2017 | 15.1 | 0.7 | 894.6 | 489.4 | 2.0 | 250.0 | 2,041.1 | 2.5 | 2,041.1 | ---- | 114.3 | 301.8 | 10,585 |
| 2018 | ---- | 0.6 | 979.9 | 491.5 | 125.1 | 330.7 | 1,760.3 | 4.5 | 2,156.7 | ---- | 354.7 | 182.8 | 12,852 |
| 2019 | ---- | 0.4 | 961.1 | 543.4 | 106.1 | 335.7 | 1,758.5 | 4.4 | 2,136.0 | ---- | 70.0 | 150.3 | 12,030 |
| 2020 | ---- | 30.5 | 1,121.2 | 456.5 | ---- | 226.3 | 1,770.4 | 3.0 | 2,429.9 | ---- | 224.3 | 244.4 | 12,748 |
| 2021 | 36.0 | 12.8 | 1,228.3 | 473.8 | 46.6 | 260.9 | 1,783.7 | 21.6 | 2,169.8 | ---- | 165.6 | 353.5 | 12,169 |
| 2022[1] | ---- | 0.5 | 1,131.5 | 433.3 | 0.2 | 278.6 | 1,560.0 | 51.0 | 1,846.9 | ---- | 1.6 | 418.7 | 10,741 |

[1] Preliminary.   Source: *Foreign Agricultural Service, U.S. Department of Agriculture (FAS-USDA)*

# SOYBEAN MEAL

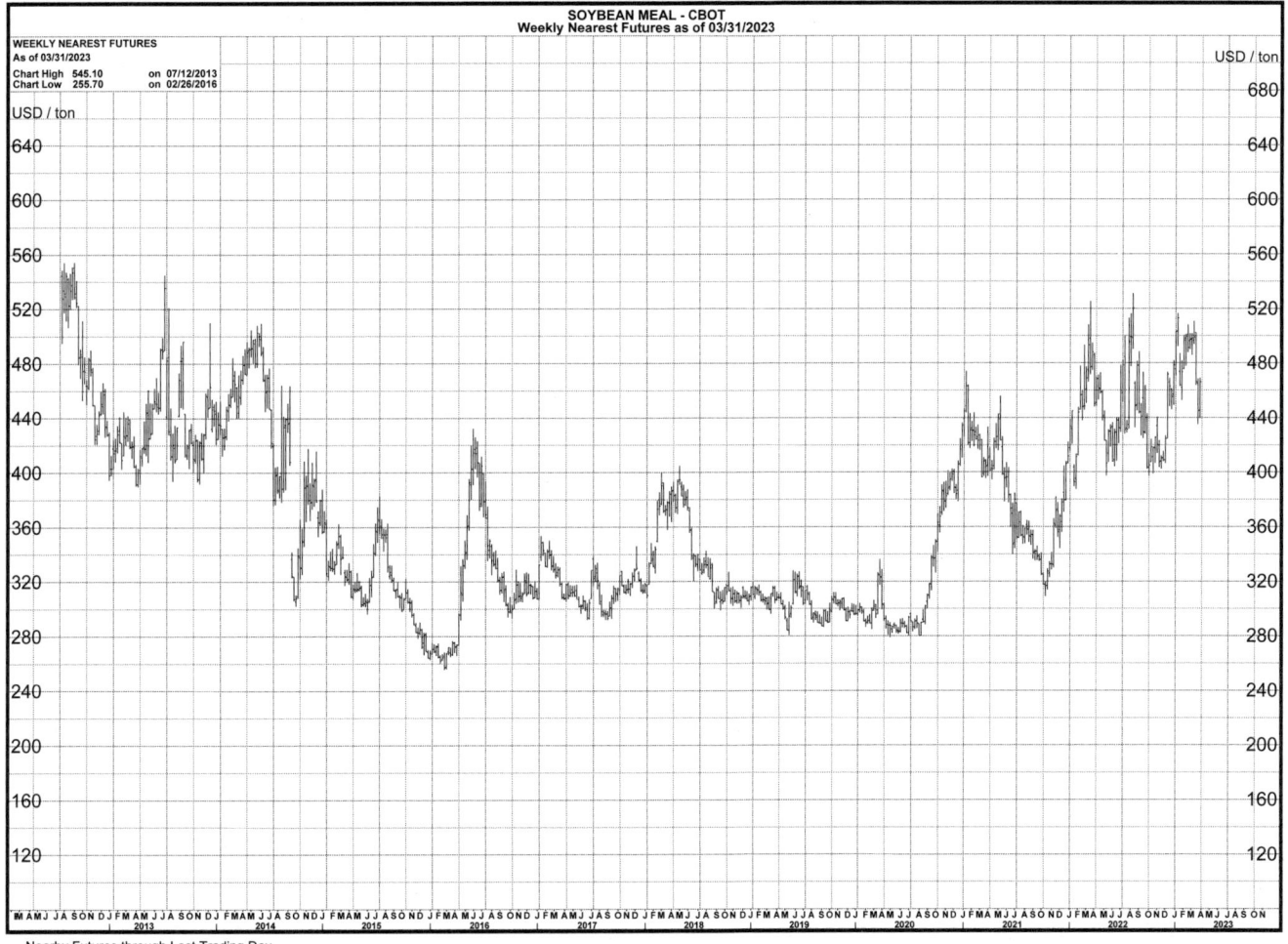

**SOYBEAN MEAL - CBOT**
Weekly Nearest Futures as of 03/31/2023

Chart High 545.10 on 07/12/2013
Chart Low 255.70 on 02/26/2016

Nearby Futures through Last Trading Day.

## Volume of Trading of Soybean Meal Futures in Chicago    In Thousands of Contracts

| Year | Jan. | Feb. | Mar. | Apr. | May | June | July | Aug. | Sept. | Oct. | Nov. | Dec. | Total |
|---|---|---|---|---|---|---|---|---|---|---|---|---|---|
| 2013 | 1,520.3 | 1,758.3 | 1,277.9 | 1,985.6 | 1,558.3 | 1,839.5 | 1,919.1 | 1,797.3 | 1,433.2 | 1,632.4 | 1,881.6 | 1,633.7 | 20,237.2 |
| 2014 | 1,519.1 | 1,918.1 | 1,409.7 | 1,711.2 | 1,138.3 | 1,811.9 | 1,703.3 | 1,664.5 | 1,613.9 | 2,456.8 | 2,070.8 | 1,619.9 | 20,637.4 |
| 2015 | 1,558.6 | 1,863.0 | 1,627.7 | 2,118.1 | 1,655.7 | 2,861.9 | 2,181.3 | 2,145.4 | 1,942.1 | 2,106.6 | 2,147.4 | 2,107.4 | 24,315.3 |
| 2016 | 1,547.6 | 2,055.5 | 1,696.5 | 3,289.2 | 2,564.1 | 2,971.6 | 2,027.7 | 1,880.0 | 1,738.5 | 1,967.8 | 2,156.9 | 2,058.7 | 25,953.9 |
| 2017 | 1,858.5 | 2,157.2 | 1,854.4 | 2,379.1 | 1,812.1 | 2,591.4 | 2,356.1 | 2,184.0 | 1,940.2 | 1,781.8 | 2,591.0 | 2,490.8 | 25,996.4 |
| 2018 | 2,482.4 | 3,466.9 | 2,294.9 | 3,361.6 | 2,275.4 | 3,268.2 | 2,417.4 | 2,725.2 | 2,329.5 | 2,641.3 | 2,470.2 | 2,105.7 | 31,838.9 |
| 2019 | 1,838.0 | 2,688.8 | 1,871.1 | 2,796.4 | 2,667.8 | 2,811.9 | 1,992.6 | 2,270.8 | 2,086.4 | 2,372.2 | 3,009.2 | 2,998.4 | 29,403.5 |
| 2020 | 2,241.9 | 3,323.9 | 2,982.5 | 2,240.4 | 1,489.6 | 2,759.8 | 2,252.5 | 2,244.2 | 2,847.2 | 2,570.3 | 2,454.8 | 2,507.8 | 29,914.8 |
| 2021 | 1,927.9 | 2,111.5 | 1,985.1 | 2,619.6 | 1,912.4 | 2,775.5 | 1,815.0 | 1,835.3 | 1,863.9 | 2,487.7 | 3,045.5 | 2,396.8 | 26,776.2 |
| 2022 | 2,273.1 | 2,792.1 | 1,850.2 | 2,095.5 | 1,733.7 | 2,590.0 | 2,179.7 | 2,450.5 | 2,438.0 | 2,267.8 | 2,633.3 | 2,787.5 | 28,091.6 |

Contract size = 100 tons.    Source: CME Group; Chicago Board of Trade (CBT)

## Average Open Interest of Soybean Meal Futures in Chicago    In Contracts

| Year | Jan. | Feb. | Mar. | Apr. | May | June | July | Aug. | Sept. | Oct. | Nov. | Dec. |
|---|---|---|---|---|---|---|---|---|---|---|---|---|
| 2013 | 248,644 | 287,037 | 281,914 | 262,103 | 264,520 | 305,549 | 285,970 | 266,192 | 267,963 | 272,131 | 279,717 | 274,139 |
| 2014 | 272,424 | 307,186 | 312,283 | 321,497 | 310,358 | 320,237 | 309,536 | 319,263 | 340,910 | 362,209 | 382,227 | 353,605 |
| 2015 | 347,095 | 363,919 | 341,479 | 342,428 | 352,507 | 402,421 | 400,309 | 385,239 | 379,936 | 401,497 | 422,294 | 415,217 |
| 2016 | 411,932 | 416,103 | 376,318 | 369,967 | 367,597 | 389,845 | 373,020 | 359,333 | 362,886 | 375,331 | 373,239 | 350,214 |
| 2017 | 356,312 | 382,823 | 366,137 | 377,335 | 379,196 | 399,940 | 353,194 | 370,584 | 381,819 | 380,034 | 403,480 | 409,863 |
| 2018 | 401,624 | 465,945 | 454,202 | 506,093 | 522,647 | 510,772 | 518,013 | 507,407 | 524,092 | 525,893 | 503,197 | 448,462 |
| 2019 | 449,026 | 460,468 | 453,985 | 454,723 | 493,991 | 477,710 | 441,846 | 445,260 | 442,094 | 419,844 | 429,417 | 446,866 |
| 2020 | 467,470 | 500,452 | 426,318 | 406,124 | 435,722 | 451,089 | 430,972 | 445,888 | 453,829 | 443,089 | 440,686 | 425,125 |
| 2021 | 412,016 | 412,107 | 410,079 | 412,143 | 410,456 | 399,884 | 370,032 | 361,063 | 362,051 | 426,818 | 443,775 | 388,644 |
| 2022 | 403,211 | 431,048 | 388,836 | 394,769 | 362,978 | 388,199 | 397,860 | 407,524 | 384,266 | 374,103 | 396,856 | 396,335 |

Contract size = 100 tons.    Source: CME Group; Chicago Board of Trade (CBT)

# SOYBEAN MEAL

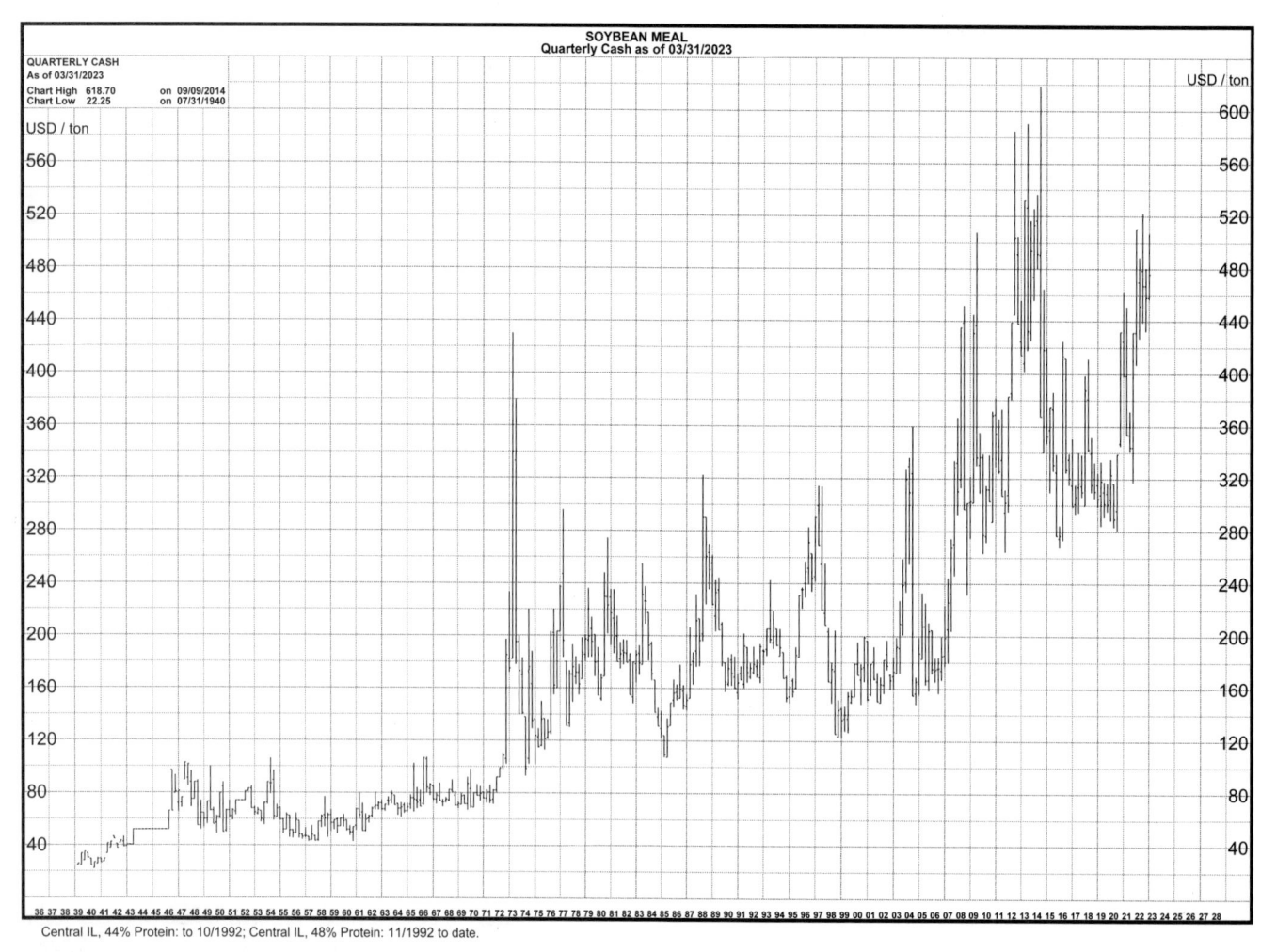

**Average Price of Soybean Meal (48% Solvent) in Decatur Illinois** — In Dollars Per Short Ton -- Bulk

| Crop Year | Oct. | Nov. | Dec. | Jan. | Feb. | Mar. | Apr. | May. | June | July | Aug. | Sept. | Average |
|---|---|---|---|---|---|---|---|---|---|---|---|---|---|
| 2013-14 | 443.63 | 451.13 | 498.10 | 479.54 | 509.25 | 495.71 | 514.01 | 519.38 | 501.72 | 450.79 | 490.32 | 525.72 | 489.94 |
| 2014-15 | 381.50 | 441.39 | 431.73 | 380.03 | 370.38 | 357.83 | 336.61 | 320.23 | 335.03 | 375.71 | 357.85 | 333.62 | 368.49 |
| 2015-16 | 327.97 | 308.60 | 289.78 | 279.56 | 273.61 | 276.22 | 303.81 | 376.35 | 408.57 | 371.49 | 340.80 | 337.95 | 324.56 |
| 2016-17 | 323.37 | 322.41 | 321.02 | 332.34 | 334.42 | 320.34 | 305.67 | 307.63 | 300.72 | 326.04 | 301.05 | 307.70 | 316.89 |
| 2017-18 | 315.23 | 313.52 | 319.22 | 322.60 | 362.85 | 379.85 | 385.84 | 393.55 | 355.71 | 341.08 | 332.50 | 318.32 | 345.02 |
| 2018-19 | 319.15 | 310.62 | 311.70 | 314.92 | 306.83 | 306.38 | 304.26 | 297.52 | 324.75 | 310.77 | 296.92 | 295.57 | 308.28 |
| 2019-20 | 309.48 | 303.13 | 299.59 | 300.11 | 295.28 | 312.38 | 295.40 | 288.56 | 288.66 | 291.25 | 290.18 | 319.99 | 299.50 |
| 2020-21 | 367.11 | 387.83 | 396.68 | 439.20 | 427.28 | 410.02 | 413.36 | 421.03 | 378.18 | 365.23 | 358.21 | 343.55 | 392.31 |
| 2021-22 | 325.43 | 358.73 | 399.53 | 421.21 | 460.45 | 493.98 | 475.36 | 441.28 | 445.93 | 467.87 | 510.90 | 473.94 | 439.55 |
| 2022-23 | 468.68 | 436.75 | 462.85 | 482.40 | 500.53 | | | | | | | | 470.24 |

*Source: Economic Research Service, U.S. Department of Agriculture (ERS-USDA)*

**Average Price of Soybean Meal (44% Solvent) in Decatur Illinois** — In Dollars Per Short Ton -- Bulk

| Crop Year | Oct. | Nov. | Dec. | Jan. | Feb. | Mar. | Apr. | May. | June | July | Aug. | Sept. | Average |
|---|---|---|---|---|---|---|---|---|---|---|---|---|---|
| 1992-93 | 168.6 | 170.9 | 176.4 | 175.6 | 167.5 | 172.4 | 175.6 | 181.7 | 181.3 | 217.6 | 206.9 | 186.5 | 181.8 |
| 1993-94 | 180.6 | 195.7 | 192.5 | 185.9 | 184.4 | 182.0 | 176.4 | 191.1 | 183.0 | 168.1 | 165.6 | 162.5 | 180.7 |
| 1994-95 | 156.4 | 150.9 | 145.4 | 145.1 | 149.4 | 145.7 | 151.0 | 148.1 | 149.1 | 160.1 | 157.5 | 171.8 | 152.5 |
| 1995-96 | 183.4 | 194.1 | 213.6 | 220.5 | 216.7 | 215.7 | 237.9 | 232.3 | 227.9 | 242.3 | 251.1 | 265.5 | 225.1 |
| 1996-97 | 238.0 | 242.7 | 240.9 | 240.7 | 253.6 | 270.4 | 277.7 | 296.0 | 275.9 | 261.5 | 261.6 | 265.7 | 260.4 |
| 1997-98 | 216.0 | 231.6 | 214.9 | 193.1 | 182.1 | 165.3 | 152.8 | 150.3 | 157.8 | 173.3 | 135.7 | 126.9 | 175.0 |
| 1998-99 | 129.4 | 139.3 | 139.6 | 131.0 | 124.4 | 127.2 | 128.6 | 127.0 | 131.7 | 125.7 | 135.9 | 144.1 | 132.0 |
| 1999-00 | 147.2 | 148.1 | 145.4 | 155.0 | 163.6 | 166.6 | 168.1 | 180.1 | 170.2 | 156.8 | 151.4 | 166.9 | 160.0 |
| 2000-01 | 166.0 | 173.7 | 187.9 | 175.6 | 158.3 | 149.1 | 149.7 | 155.6 | 163.1 | 183.9 | 170.6 | 163.5 | 166.4 |
| 2001-02 | 157.7 | 157.2 | 146.6 | Discontinued | | | | | | | | | 153.8 |

*Source: Economic Research Service, U.S. Department of Agriculture (ERS-USDA)*

# Soybean Oil

Soybean oil is the natural oil extracted from whole soybeans. Typically, about 19% of a soybean's weight can be extracted as crude soybean oil. The oil content of U.S. soybeans correlates directly with the temperatures and amount of sunshine during the soybean pod-filling stages. Edible products produced with soybean oil include cooking and salad oils, shortening, and margarine. Soybean oil is the most widely used cooking oil in the U.S. It accounts for 80% of margarine production and for more than 75% of total U.S. consumer vegetable fat and oil consumption. Soy oil is cholesterol-free and high in polyunsaturated fat. Soy oil is also used to produce inedible products such as paints, varnish, resins, and plastics. Of the edible vegetable oils, soy oil is the world's largest at about 32%, followed by palm oil and rapeseed oil. Soybean oil futures and options are traded at the CME Group.

**Prices** – CME soybean oil futures prices (Barchart.com symbol ZL) on the nearest-futures chart in 2022 closed the year up +13.3% yr/yr at 63.81 cents per pound.

**Supply** – World production of soybean oil in 2022/23 is expected to rise by +3.8% yr/yr to a new record high of 61.494 million metric tons. China will account for 27.7% of world soybean oil production, while the U.S. will account for 19.4%, Brazil for 16.4%, and Argentina for 12.2%. U.S. production of soybean oil in 2022/23 is expected to rise by +0.6% yr/yr to 26.310 billion pounds, a new record high.

**Demand** – World consumption of soybean oil in 2022/23 is expected to rise by +1.7% yr/yr to a new record high of 60.323 million metric tons. China will account for 29.3% of world consumption, while the U.S. will account for 19.5%, Brazil for 13.1%, and India for 8.3%. U.S. consumption of soybean oil in 2022/23 is expected to rise by +3.2% yr/yr to 25.600 billion pounds, a new record high.

**Trade** – World exports of soybean oil in 2021/22 are expected to rise by +1.1% yr/yr to 12.280 million metric tons, a record high. U.S. exports of soybean oil in 2021/23 are expected to fall by -54.9% yr/yr to 363,000 metric tons, the lowest level since 2003/04.

### World Production of Soybean Oil    In Thousands of Metric Tons

| Crop Year | Argentina | Bolivia | Brazil | China | European Union | India | Japan | Mexico | Paraguay | Russia | Taiwan | United States | World Total |
|---|---|---|---|---|---|---|---|---|---|---|---|---|---|
| 2013-14 | 6,785 | 415 | 7,074 | 12,347 | 2,489 | 1,566 | 389 | 720 | 669 | 591 | 343 | 9,131 | 45,293 |
| 2014-15 | 7,687 | 450 | 7,759 | 13,350 | 2,746 | 1,386 | 414 | 745 | 725 | 645 | 352 | 9,706 | 49,336 |
| 2015-16 | 8,433 | 470 | 7,627 | 14,605 | 2,841 | 990 | 445 | 785 | 725 | 717 | 352 | 9,956 | 51,675 |
| 2016-17 | 8,395 | 406 | 7,755 | 15,770 | 2,660 | 1,620 | 466 | 885 | 725 | 788 | 360 | 10,035 | 53,909 |
| 2017-18 | 7,236 | 490 | 8,485 | 16,128 | 2,755 | 1,386 | 468 | 1,005 | 755 | 824 | 355 | 10,783 | 55,279 |
| 2018-19 | 8,044 | 500 | 8,180 | 15,232 | 2,850 | 1,728 | 478 | 1,135 | 725 | 834 | 375 | 10,976 | 56,063 |
| 2019-20 | 7,700 | 482 | 8,998 | 16,397 | 2,964 | 1,512 | 468 | 1,110 | 665 | 834 | 370 | 11,299 | 58,519 |
| 2020-21[1] | 7,930 | 575 | 8,985 | 16,666 | 3,002 | 1,710 | 460 | 1,145 | 625 | 809 | 365 | 11,350 | 59,232 |
| 2021-22[2] | 7,664 | 471 | 9,673 | 15,680 | 2,926 | 1,712 | 504 | 1,171 | 418 | 862 | 374 | 11,858 | 59,259 |
| 2022-23[3] | 7,509 | 492 | 10,112 | 17,024 | 2,831 | 1,780 | 488 | 1,208 | 714 | 916 | 383 | 11,934 | 61,494 |

Crop year beginning October 1.    [1] Preliminary.    [2] Forecast.    *Source: Foreign Agricultural Service, U.S. Department of Agriculture (FAS-USDA)*

### World Consumption of Soybean Oil    In Thousands of Metric Tons

| Crop Year | Algeria | Argentina | Bangladesh | Brazil | China | Egypt | European Union | India | Iran | Korea, South | Mexico | United States | World Total |
|---|---|---|---|---|---|---|---|---|---|---|---|---|---|
| 2013-14 | 590 | 2,844 | 551 | 5,705 | 13,650 | 587 | 1,990 | 3,350 | 600 | 440 | 905 | 8,577 | 45,465 |
| 2014-15 | 640 | 2,401 | 673 | 6,215 | 14,200 | 752 | 2,040 | 4,100 | 660 | 435 | 961 | 8,599 | 47,729 |
| 2015-16 | 690 | 2,840 | 785 | 6,288 | 15,350 | 885 | 2,285 | 5,250 | 660 | 440 | 1,050 | 9,145 | 52,123 |
| 2016-17 | 715 | 3,085 | 1,006 | 6,570 | 16,350 | 660 | 1,955 | 5,150 | 650 | 450 | 1,140 | 9,010 | 53,583 |
| 2017-18 | 725 | 2,981 | 1,085 | 6,940 | 16,500 | 735 | 1,935 | 4,670 | 600 | 470 | 1,180 | 9,698 | 54,370 |
| 2018-19 | 755 | 2,624 | 1,159 | 7,165 | 15,850 | 910 | 2,255 | 4,750 | 615 | 505 | 1,240 | 10,376 | 55,120 |
| 2019-20 | 785 | 2,175 | 1,189 | 7,750 | 17,000 | 935 | 2,380 | 5,125 | 650 | 535 | 1,285 | 10,122 | 56,968 |
| 2020-21[1] | 825 | 2,042 | 1,205 | 7,950 | 17,600 | 1,085 | 2,430 | 4,950 | 725 | 580 | 1,300 | 10,575 | 58,416 |
| 2021-22[2] | 850 | 2,660 | 1,222 | 7,450 | 16,650 | 1,010 | 2,405 | 5,825 | 800 | 590 | 1,300 | 11,256 | 59,300 |
| 2022-23[3] | 890 | 2,340 | 1,250 | 7,900 | 17,650 | 1,025 | 2,330 | 4,980 | 850 | 610 | 1,335 | 11,748 | 60,323 |

Crop year beginning October 1.    [1] Preliminary.    [2] Forecast.    *Source: Foreign Agricultural Service, U.S. Department of Agriculture (FAS-USDA)*

# SOYBEAN OIL

### World Exports of Soybean Oil    In Thousands of Metric Tons

| Crop Year | Argentina | Bolivia | Brazil | Canada | European Union | Malaysia | Para-guay | Russia | South Africa | Ukraine | United States | Vietnam | World Total |
|---|---|---|---|---|---|---|---|---|---|---|---|---|---|
| 2013-14 | 4,087 | 371 | 1,378 | 92 | 766 | 157 | 641 | 332 | 94 | 118 | 852 | 91 | 9,441 |
| 2014-15 | 5,094 | 392 | 1,510 | 118 | 1,010 | 170 | 699 | 423 | 71 | 136 | 914 | 104 | 11,176 |
| 2015-16 | 5,698 | 444 | 1,550 | 151 | 915 | 148 | 702 | 431 | 64 | 152 | 1,017 | 17 | 11,824 |
| 2016-17 | 5,387 | 249 | 1,241 | 175 | 973 | 137 | 680 | 529 | 63 | 177 | 1,159 | 35 | 11,464 |
| 2017-18 | 4,164 | 380 | 1,511 | 157 | 1,074 | 124 | 691 | 568 | 48 | 192 | 1,108 | 40 | 10,771 |
| 2018-19 | 5,268 | 393 | 1,085 | 169 | 977 | 120 | 652 | 572 | 47 | 334 | 880 | 9 | 11,479 |
| 2019-20 | 5,404 | 408 | 1,156 | 144 | 909 | 118 | 631 | 641 | 52 | 338 | 1,287 | 9 | 12,372 |
| 2020-21[1] | 6,137 | 525 | 1,262 | 119 | 1,063 | 108 | 562 | 561 | 81 | 232 | 785 | 74 | 12,610 |
| 2021-22[2] | 4,873 | 400 | 2,409 | 153 | 969 | 120 | 380 | 480 | 70 | 235 | 804 | 75 | 12,150 |
| 2022-23[3] | 5,250 | 390 | 2,250 | 150 | 1,075 | 115 | 600 | 575 | 85 | 250 | 363 | 75 | 12,280 |

Crop year beginning October 1.    [1] Preliminary.    [2] Forecast.    Source: Foreign Agricultural Service, U.S. Department of Agriculture (FAS-USDA)

### World Imports of Soybean Oil    In Thousands of Metric Tons

| Crop Year | Algeria | Bangla-desh | China | Colom-bia | Egypt | European Union | India | Iran | Korea, South | Peru | Morocco | Vene-zuela | World Total |
|---|---|---|---|---|---|---|---|---|---|---|---|---|---|
| 2013-14 | 629 | 442 | 1,353 | 288 | 230 | 329 | 1,804 | 551 | 278 | 444 | 355 | 453 | 9,325 |
| 2014-15 | 631 | 508 | 773 | 304 | 498 | 253 | 2,815 | 421 | 257 | 432 | 395 | 461 | 10,152 |
| 2015-16 | 720 | 647 | 586 | 372 | 688 | 325 | 4,269 | 299 | 250 | 465 | 382 | 206 | 11,734 |
| 2016-17 | 674 | 826 | 711 | 352 | 246 | 306 | 3,534 | 291 | 306 | 497 | 449 | 268 | 11,245 |
| 2017-18 | 776 | 859 | 481 | 344 | 227 | 288 | 2,984 | 127 | 276 | 502 | 503 | 205 | 9,991 |
| 2018-19 | 899 | 1,017 | 783 | 343 | 277 | 419 | 3,000 | 346 | 328 | 536 | 539 | 43 | 10,978 |
| 2019-20 | 693 | 690 | 1,000 | 387 | 397 | 483 | 3,626 | 79 | 402 | 573 | 521 | 160 | 11,479 |
| 2020-21[1] | 632 | 665 | 1,231 | 285 | 428 | 492 | 3,246 | 570 | 407 | 507 | 594 | 193 | 11,712 |
| 2021-22[2] | 571 | 640 | 291 | 317 | 230 | 462 | 4,231 | 372 | 392 | 529 | 515 | 209 | 11,461 |
| 2022-23[3] | 575 | 750 | 1,000 | 335 | 350 | 500 | 3,150 | 375 | 420 | 550 | 570 | 210 | 11,346 |

Crop year beginning October 1.    [1] Preliminary.    [2] Forecast.    Source: Foreign Agricultural Service, U.S. Department of Agriculture (FAS-USDA)

### Supply and Distribution of Soybean Oil in the United States    In Millions of Pounds

| Crop Year | Beginning Stocks Oct. 1 | Pro-duction | Imports | Exports | Domestic Total | Biodiesel | Food & Other | Exports | Total Disap-pearance | Ending Stocks |
|---|---|---|---|---|---|---|---|---|---|---|
| 2013-14 | 1,655 | 20,130 | 165 | 21,950 | 18,908 | 5,010 | 13,948 | 1,877 | 20,785 | 1,165 |
| 2014-15 | 1,165 | 21,399 | 264 | 22,828 | 18,959 | 5,039 | 13,922 | 2,014 | 20,973 | 1,855 |
| 2015-16 | 1,855 | 21,950 | 288 | 24,093 | 20,163 | 5,670 | 14,493 | 2,243 | 22,406 | 1,687 |
| 2016-17 | 1,687 | 22,123 | 319 | 24,129 | 19,862 | 6,200 | 13,662 | 2,556 | 22,418 | 1,711 |
| 2017-18 | 1,711 | 23,772 | 335 | 25,819 | 21,380 | 7,134 | 14,247 | 2,443 | 23,823 | 1,995 |
| 2018-19 | 1,995 | 24,197 | 398 | 26,590 | 22,873 | 7,863 | 15,010 | 1,941 | 24,814 | 1,775 |
| 2019-20 | 1,775 | 24,911 | 320 | 27,007 | 22,317 | 8,658 | 13,660 | 2,837 | 25,154 | 1,853 |
| 2020-21 | 1,853 | 25,023 | 302 | 27,177 | 23,314 | 8,920 | 14,394 | 1,731 | 25,046 | 2,131 |
| 2021-22[1] | 2,131 | 26,155 | 303 | 28,590 | 24,825 | 10,348 | 14,477 | 1,773 | 26,599 | 1,991 |
| 2022-23[2] | 1,991 | 26,195 | 300 | 28,486 | 26,050 | 11,600 | 14,450 | 500 | 26,550 | 1,936 |

Crop year beginning October 1.    [1] Preliminary.    [2] Forecast.    Source: Economic Research Service, U.S. Department of Agriculture (ERS-USDA)

### U.S. Exports of Soybean Oil[2], by Country of Destination    In Metric Tons

| Crop Year | Canada | Ecuador | Ethiopia | Haiti | India | Mexico | Morocco | Pakistan | Panama | Peru | Turkey | Vene-zuela | Total |
|---|---|---|---|---|---|---|---|---|---|---|---|---|---|
| 2012-13 | 30,867 | 28 | ---- | 2,230 | 113,104 | 187,117 | 23,248 | 0 | 6,374 | 193 | 76 | 51,377 | 981,345 |
| 2013-14 | 31,755 | 13 | 390 | 1,576 | 22 | 189,759 | 29,702 | 0 | 4,139 | 42,121 | ---- | 18,988 | 852,074 |
| 2014-15 | 28,755 | 11 | 450 | 649 | 39 | 245,163 | 64,658 | 9,190 | 5,434 | 104,743 | ---- | 61,920 | 913,704 |
| 2015-16 | 15,647 | 6 | ---- | 2,687 | 51 | 235,554 | 50,521 | 11,165 | 6,054 | 75,355 | ---- | 50,055 | 1,017,200 |
| 2016-17 | 22,658 | 8 | ---- | 1,307 | 139 | 265,028 | 30,432 | 7,137 | 7,055 | 2 | 75 | 32,437 | 1,159,229 |
| 2017-18 | 21,213 | 9 | ---- | ---- | 105 | 166,657 | 11,798 | ---- | 7,723 | 93,051 | 17 | 48,345 | 1,108,143 |
| 2018-19 | 21,805 | 47 | ---- | 28 | 118 | 125,570 | ---- | 10,893 | 3,157 | 11,959 | ---- | 1,007 | 880,161 |
| 2019-20 | 31,613 | 31 | ---- | 2,645 | 103 | 128,945 | 82,900 | 12,975 | 2,304 | 26,437 | ---- | 59,037 | 1,286,703 |
| 2020-21 | 40,162 | 40 | ---- | 1,758 | 36,090 | 64,051 | ---- | ---- | 2,204 | 50,856 | ---- | 60,021 | 785,331 |
| 2021-22[1] | 72,214 | ---- | ---- | 5,536 | 192,637 | 91,764 | ---- | ---- | 2,122 | 18 | ---- | 59,118 | 804,421 |

Crop year beginning October 1.    [1] Preliminary.    [2] Crude & Refined oil combined as such.    Source: Foreign Agricultural Service, U.S. Department of Agriculture (FAS-USDA)

# SOYBEAN OIL

## CORN OIL
Quarterly Cash as of 03/31/2023

## Production of Soybean Oil in the United States — In Millions of Pounds

| Crop Year | Oct. | Nov. | Dec. | Jan. | Feb. | Mar. | Apr. | May | June | July | Aug. | Sept. | Total |
|---|---|---|---|---|---|---|---|---|---|---|---|---|---|
| 2013-14 | ---- | ---- | ---- | ---- | ---- | ---- | ---- | ---- | ---- | ---- | ---- | ---- | 20,130 |
| 2014-15 | ---- | ---- | ---- | ---- | ---- | ---- | ---- | ---- | ---- | ---- | ---- | ---- | 21,399 |
| 2015-16 | 1,962.9 | 1,901.9 | 1,929.0 | 1,864.9 | 1,795.9 | 1,943.5 | 1,840.3 | 1,876.2 | 1,787.2 | 1,789.4 | 1,642.5 | 1,616.6 | 21,950 |
| 2016-17 | 2,028.5 | 1,961.3 | 1,950.2 | 1,977.2 | 1,752.5 | 1,857.1 | 1,731.7 | 1,839.3 | 1,735.6 | 1,801.4 | 1,762.2 | 1,701.8 | 22,098 |
| 2017-18 | 2,016.9 | 1,977.0 | 2,015.3 | 1,995.6 | 1,889.8 | 2,079.1 | 1,964.9 | 1,966.5 | 1,936.9 | 2,043.3 | 1,945.0 | 1,936.9 | 23,767 |
| 2018-19 | 2,134.6 | 2,060.6 | 2,135.4 | 2,115.8 | 1,899.2 | 2,094.4 | 1,989.1 | 1,916.0 | 1,811.5 | 2,090.2 | 2,048.2 | 1,900.7 | 24,195 |
| 2019-20 | 2,150.0 | 1,999.6 | 2,110.9 | 2,154.4 | 1,999.5 | 2,201.1 | 2,099.5 | 2,057.6 | 2,035.3 | 2,123.2 | 2,012.8 | 1,967.6 | 24,911 |
| 2020-21 | 2,282.5 | 2,206.8 | 2,233.5 | 2,308.8 | 1,924.7 | 2,222.1 | 1,991.9 | 2,043.1 | 1,908.6 | 1,972.7 | 1,989.7 | 1,938.2 | 25,022 |
| 2021-22 | 2,347.6 | 2,235.4 | 2,324.2 | 2,277.4 | 2,064.2 | 2,277.5 | 2,143.1 | 2,158.8 | 2,068.6 | 2,158.0 | 2,095.6 | 1,993.0 | 26,143 |
| 2022-23[1] | 2,338.1 | 2,200.0 | 2,195.4 | 2,252.3 | | | | | | | | | 26,957 |

[1] Preliminary. *Source: Economic Research Service, U.S. Department of Agriculture (ERS-USDA)*

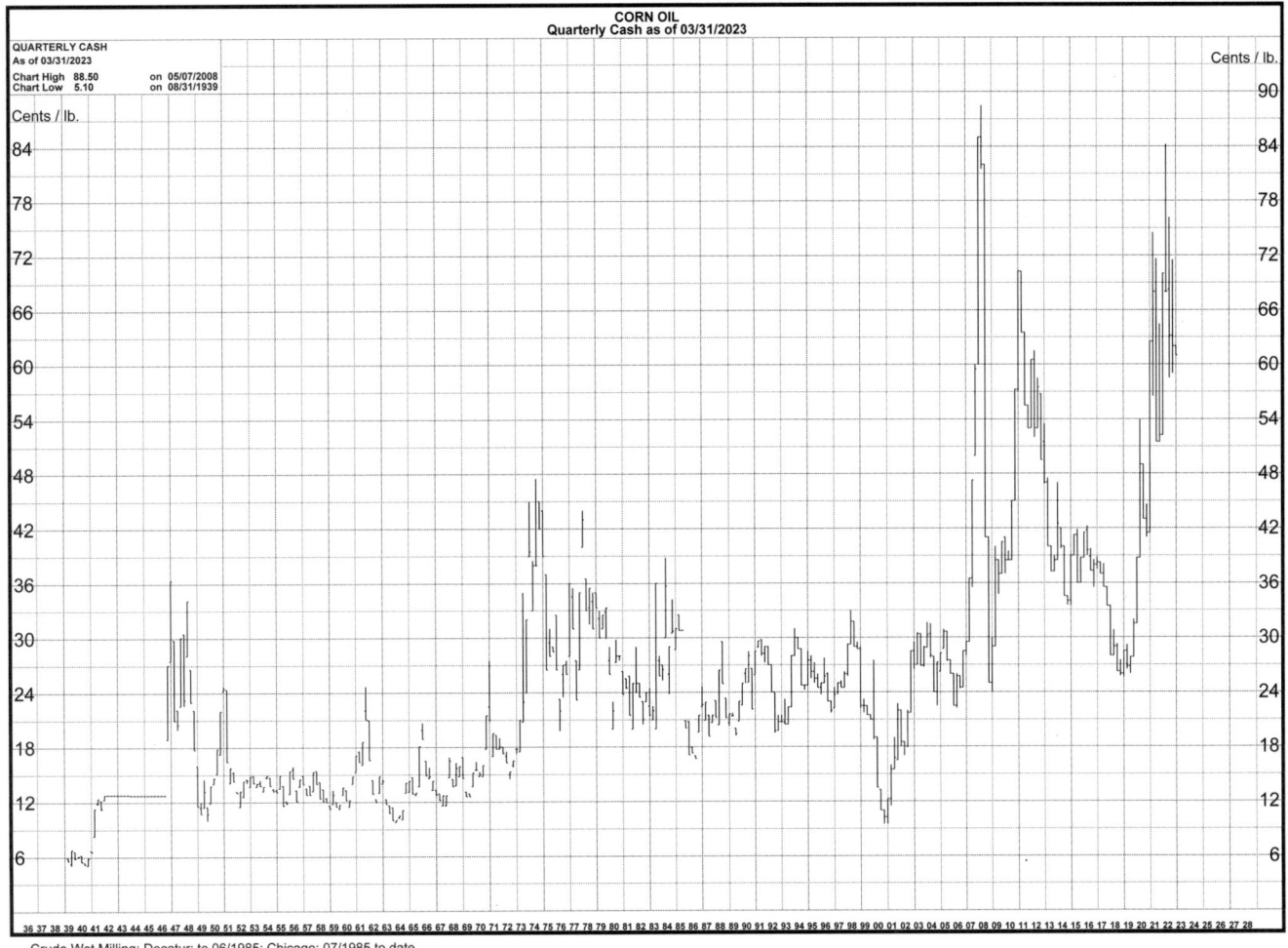

## U.S. Exports of Soybean Oil (Crude and Refined) — In Millions of Pounds

| Year | Jan. | Feb. | Mar. | Apr. | May | June | July | Aug. | Sept. | Oct. | Nov. | Dec. | Total |
|---|---|---|---|---|---|---|---|---|---|---|---|---|---|
| 2013 | 258.9 | 339.7 | 136.7 | 135.9 | 79.3 | 75.1 | 70.7 | 92.8 | 87.9 | 71.4 | 135.9 | 320.2 | 1,805 |
| 2014 | 267.2 | 277.5 | 195.5 | 92.6 | 45.8 | 79.7 | 198.0 | 119.0 | 75.6 | 159.2 | 231.4 | 236.2 | 1,978 |
| 2015 | 256.7 | 220.5 | 233.5 | 125.7 | 72.5 | 157.4 | 64.6 | 154.6 | 101.9 | 179.6 | 233.0 | 320.7 | 2,121 |
| 2016 | 168.0 | 114.6 | 233.1 | 126.2 | 103.8 | 158.4 | 281.8 | 93.1 | 227.2 | 241.0 | 236.7 | 235.5 | 2,219 |
| 2017 | 259.4 | 238.7 | 294.5 | 258.3 | 161.2 | 138.2 | 199.4 | 163.1 | 130.2 | 212.8 | 132.0 | 173.0 | 2,361 |
| 2018 | 180.7 | 181.1 | 201.5 | 212.3 | 431.4 | 228.3 | 174.7 | 197.6 | 121.7 | 146.1 | 215.8 | 170.5 | 2,462 |
| 2019 | 221.1 | 91.7 | 271.8 | 148.2 | 205.7 | 95.4 | 174.3 | 165.6 | 48.5 | 252.5 | 247.4 | 184.3 | 2,106 |
| 2020 | 125.1 | 396.2 | 320.8 | 230.2 | 357.8 | 167.7 | 164.6 | 201.7 | 180.1 | 184.0 | 177.2 | 235.0 | 2,740 |
| 2021 | 327.8 | 256.0 | 155.8 | 129.6 | 71.2 | 91.6 | 35.7 | 24.6 | 33.9 | 57.2 | 253.6 | 182.7 | 1,620 |
| 2022[1] | 284.4 | 235.6 | 266.4 | 168.1 | 73.9 | 73.2 | 118.2 | 57.1 | 45.1 | 23.1 | 23.4 | 34.7 | 1,403 |

[1] Preliminary. *Source: Bureau of the Census, U.S. Department of Commerce*

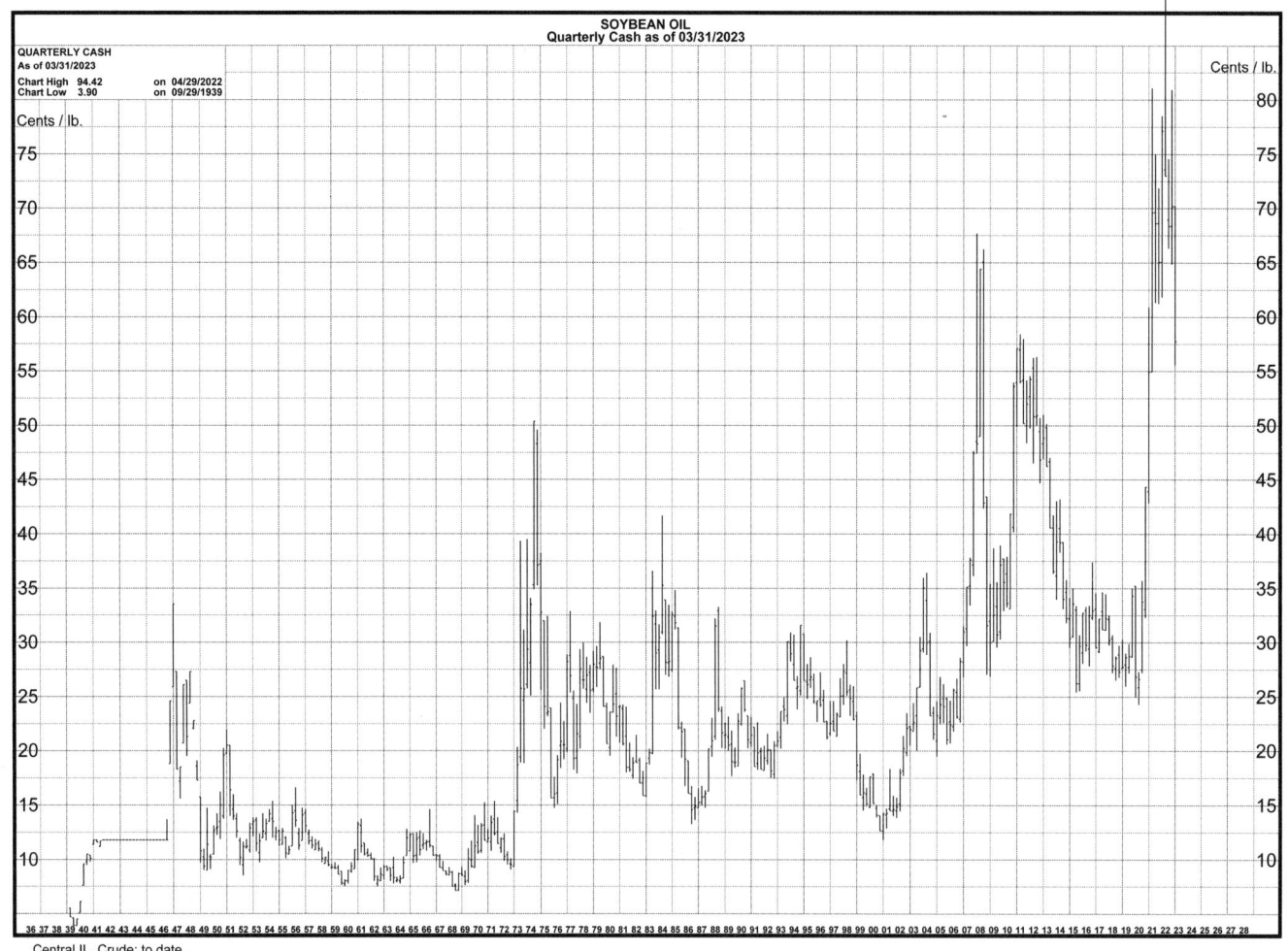

# SOYBEAN OIL

**SOYBEAN OIL Quarterly Cash as of 03/31/2023**

Chart High 94.42 on 04/29/2022
Chart Low 3.90 on 09/29/1939

Central IL, Crude: to date.

### Stocks of Soybean Oil (Crude and Refined) at Factories and Warehouses in the U.S.    In Millions of Pounds

| Crop Year | Oct. 1 | Nov. 1 | Dec. 1 | Jan. 1 | Feb. 1 | Mar. 1 | Apr. 1 | May 1 | June 1 | July 1 | Aug. 1 | Sept. 1 |
|---|---|---|---|---|---|---|---|---|---|---|---|---|
| 2013-14 | 1,655.0 | ---- | ---- | ---- | ---- | ---- | ---- | ---- | ---- | ---- | ---- | ---- |
| 2014-15 | 1,165.0 | ---- | ---- | ---- | ---- | ---- | ---- | ---- | ---- | ---- | ---- | ---- |
| 2015-16 | 1,854.8 | 1,940.4 | 1,965.9 | 1,972.5 | 2,110.8 | 2,280.2 | 2,324.9 | 2,420.0 | 2,466.1 | 2,424.1 | 2,214.3 | 1,985.7 |
| 2016-17 | 1,686.8 | 1,795.3 | 1,780.7 | 1,872.3 | 2,112.6 | 2,205.9 | 2,353.4 | 2,233.8 | 2,269.3 | 2,142.9 | 2,000.6 | 1,810.3 |
| 2017-18 | 1,711.0 | 1,626.2 | 1,690.6 | 1,950.7 | 2,239.8 | 2,425.4 | 2,444.5 | 2,688.8 | 2,374.1 | 2,304.8 | 2,383.6 | 2,214.8 |
| 2018-19 | 1,995.4 | 2,047.6 | 1,900.3 | 1,945.8 | 2,004.7 | 2,149.1 | 2,232.9 | 2,257.6 | 2,018.9 | 2,014.4 | 2,039.5 | 1,805.6 |
| 2019-20 | 1,775.3 | 1,821.0 | 1,880.4 | 2,134.1 | 2,355.9 | 2,376.8 | 2,326.6 | 2,600.6 | 2,445.4 | 2,270.8 | 2,123.2 | 1,945.1 |
| 2020-21 | 1,852.7 | 1,968.0 | 2,117.1 | 2,110.8 | 2,306.0 | 2,306.0 | 2,245.3 | 2,177.6 | 2,147.0 | 2,100.7 | 2,070.1 | 2,183.4 |
| 2021-22 | 2,131.2 | 2,386.3 | 2,406.0 | 2,465.9 | 2,499.9 | 2,566.1 | 2,433.7 | 2,424.2 | 2,384.4 | 2,315.5 | 2,228.2 | 2,103.7 |
| 2022-23[1] | 1,991.1 | 2,093.6 | 2,112.3 | 2,306.1 | | | | | | | | |

On First of Month.    [1] Preliminary.    *Source: Economic Research Service, U.S. Department of Agriculture (ERS-USDA)*

### Average Price of Crude Domestic Soybean Oil (in Tank Cars) F.O.B. Decatur    In Cents Per Pound

| Crop Year | Oct. | Nov. | Dec. | Jan. | Feb. | Mar. | Apr. | May | June | July | Aug. | Sept. | Average |
|---|---|---|---|---|---|---|---|---|---|---|---|---|---|
| 2013-14 | 39.66 | 39.58 | 37.63 | 34.95 | 37.11 | 40.82 | 41.87 | 40.68 | 39.84 | 37.60 | 35.04 | 33.99 | 38.23 |
| 2014-15 | 34.10 | 33.45 | 32.56 | 32.33 | 31.57 | 30.89 | 31.13 | 32.65 | 33.73 | 31.54 | 28.87 | 26.43 | 31.60 |
| 2015-16 | 27.14 | 26.42 | 29.72 | 28.89 | 29.79 | 30.86 | 32.45 | 30.76 | 30.35 | 28.75 | 31.21 | 31.99 | 29.86 |
| 2016-17 | 33.86 | 34.52 | 35.57 | 33.58 | 32.00 | 30.86 | 29.57 | 30.60 | 30.74 | 32.82 | 33.17 | 33.28 | 32.55 |
| 2017-18 | 32.35 | 33.43 | 32.27 | 31.61 | 30.63 | 30.28 | 29.70 | 29.40 | 28.30 | 27.21 | 27.60 | 27.73 | 30.04 |
| 2018-19 | 28.89 | 27.49 | 28.14 | 28.44 | 29.58 | 28.62 | 27.86 | 26.93 | 28.24 | 27.68 | 28.41 | 28.81 | 28.26 |
| 2019-20 | 30.14 | 30.62 | 32.27 | 33.04 | 30.26 | 27.04 | 25.69 | 25.27 | 26.61 | 28.71 | 32.13 | 34.20 | 29.67 |
| 2020-21 | 33.91 | 37.79 | 40.85 | 44.31 | 48.37 | 56.00 | 62.88 | 74.75 | 74.75 | 72.93 | 70.01 | 65.93 | 56.87 |
| 2021-22 | 70.42 | 66.46 | 63.69 | 65.70 | 70.91 | 76.41 | 83.85 | 87.39 | 80.30 | 67.75 | 72.34 | 70.63 | 72.99 |
| 2022-23[1] | 72.67 | 79.18 | 68.14 | 66.00 | 63.24 | | | | | | | | 69.85 |

[1] Preliminary.    *Source: Economic Research Service, U.S. Department of Agriculture (ERS-USDA)*

# SOYBEAN OIL

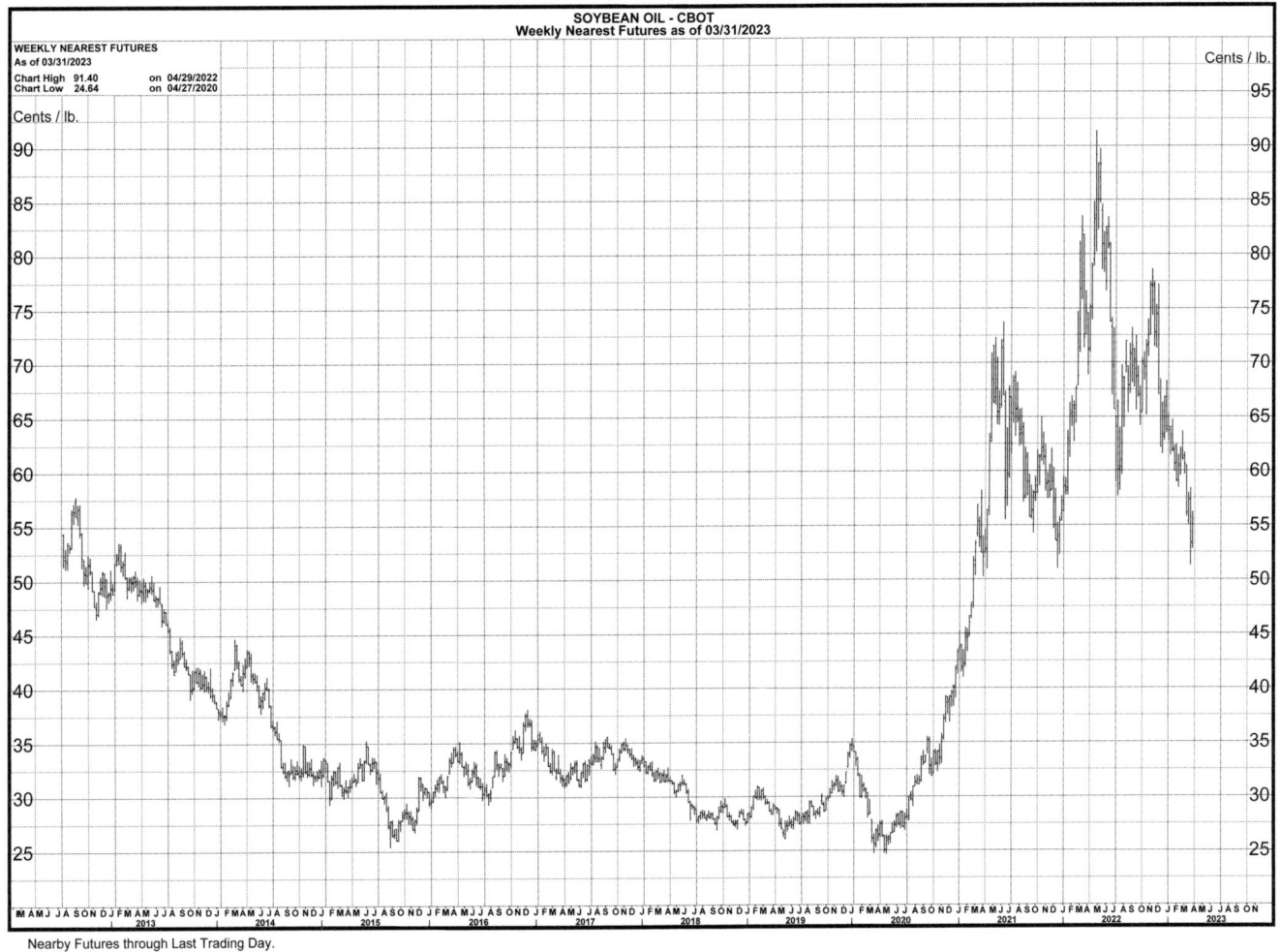

**SOYBEAN OIL - CBOT**
Weekly Nearest Futures as of 03/31/2023

As of 03/31/2023
Chart High 91.40 on 04/29/2022
Chart Low 24.64 on 04/27/2020

Nearby Futures through Last Trading Day.

## Volume of Trading of Soybean Oil Futures in Chicago    In Thousands of Contracts

| Year | Jan. | Feb. | Mar. | Apr. | May | June | July | Aug. | Sept. | Oct. | Nov. | Dec. | Total |
|---|---|---|---|---|---|---|---|---|---|---|---|---|---|
| 2013 | 2,043.6 | 2,403.6 | 1,465.9 | 2,453.7 | 1,831.6 | 2,213.7 | 1,918.7 | 1,850.1 | 1,560.5 | 1,908.5 | 2,263.2 | 1,892.7 | 23,806 |
| 2014 | 1,752.1 | 2,531.9 | 1,657.5 | 2,058.5 | 1,450.2 | 2,199.9 | 1,869.4 | 1,775.4 | 1,768.9 | 2,199.9 | 2,386.3 | 2,119.2 | 23,769 |
| 2015 | 1,985.3 | 2,348.9 | 1,683.5 | 2,527.2 | 2,042.6 | 3,236.5 | 2,358.9 | 2,412.7 | 2,190.7 | 2,519.5 | 2,667.4 | 2,924.0 | 28,897 |
| 2016 | 1,713.2 | 2,310.9 | 1,866.0 | 3,407.3 | 2,476.6 | 2,822.7 | 2,165.3 | 2,385.6 | 2,143.2 | 2,393.9 | 3,144.7 | 2,599.8 | 29,429 |
| 2017 | 2,001.6 | 2,737.6 | 2,421.6 | 2,639.6 | 1,882.5 | 2,952.5 | 2,467.6 | 2,721.7 | 2,451.3 | 2,125.4 | 3,128.1 | 2,702.9 | 30,232 |
| 2018 | 2,127.2 | 3,503.1 | 2,185.3 | 3,210.2 | 2,097.3 | 3,481.7 | 2,175.5 | 2,203.0 | 2,375.4 | 2,312.2 | 3,139.3 | 2,455.6 | 31,266 |
| 2019 | 1,975.0 | 2,890.1 | 2,023.1 | 3,012.6 | 2,405.6 | 2,762.6 | 2,231.8 | 2,651.3 | 2,527.4 | 2,759.0 | 3,242.7 | 3,213.2 | 31,694 |
| 2020 | 2,779.1 | 3,334.0 | 3,258.7 | 2,946.4 | 1,772.2 | 2,785.2 | 2,494.8 | 2,316.3 | 2,775.4 | 2,674.1 | 2,927.0 | 2,898.7 | 32,962 |
| 2021 | 2,635.6 | 2,586.4 | 3,100.9 | 3,056.4 | 2,282.9 | 3,949.3 | 2,278.4 | 2,464.7 | 2,472.5 | 2,437.2 | 2,813.6 | 2,597.6 | 32,675 |
| 2022 | 2,261.2 | 2,618.7 | 2,036.8 | 2,258.5 | 1,770.1 | 2,796.9 | 2,343.0 | 2,638.3 | 2,663.6 | 2,429.1 | 3,003.4 | 3,232.4 | 30,052 |

Contract size = 60,000 lbs.    Source: CME Group; Chicago Board of Trade (CBT)

## Average Open Interest of Soybean Oil Futures in Chicago    In Contracts

| Year | Jan. | Feb. | Mar. | Apr. | May | June | July | Aug. | Sept. | Oct. | Nov. | Dec. |
|---|---|---|---|---|---|---|---|---|---|---|---|---|
| 2013 | 313,467 | 327,562 | 329,956 | 353,044 | 351,425 | 357,052 | 340,600 | 308,032 | 291,005 | 314,235 | 333,607 | 344,607 |
| 2014 | 364,056 | 339,211 | 302,398 | 326,545 | 313,757 | 333,690 | 325,337 | 347,395 | 373,086 | 391,486 | 395,330 | 365,382 |
| 2015 | 370,576 | 385,819 | 367,203 | 383,502 | 394,773 | 410,233 | 372,932 | 390,494 | 413,151 | 420,227 | 448,872 | 412,621 |
| 2016 | 404,388 | 411,898 | 415,026 | 457,557 | 404,143 | 389,896 | 361,443 | 378,813 | 399,625 | 443,699 | 446,001 | 407,110 |
| 2017 | 391,377 | 386,979 | 385,217 | 423,805 | 412,142 | 414,657 | 398,719 | 416,321 | 438,439 | 440,831 | 469,775 | 467,647 |
| 2018 | 480,781 | 499,421 | 496,026 | 519,883 | 514,763 | 505,702 | 512,638 | 534,033 | 575,527 | 539,882 | 556,831 | 497,905 |
| 2019 | 492,981 | 507,871 | 480,036 | 483,650 | 535,026 | 472,080 | 435,429 | 466,176 | 498,072 | 496,430 | 536,756 | 521,342 |
| 2020 | 537,082 | 509,621 | 460,552 | 460,731 | 468,485 | 464,880 | 440,128 | 448,159 | 473,386 | 469,071 | 484,466 | 482,763 |
| 2021 | 469,161 | 490,193 | 491,039 | 501,302 | 501,643 | 523,176 | 468,859 | 431,637 | 389,345 | 408,042 | 425,305 | 391,390 |
| 2022 | 398,767 | 419,837 | 350,206 | 371,203 | 370,679 | 385,154 | 369,909 | 395,214 | 400,811 | 409,532 | 448,350 | 406,558 |

Contract size = 60,000 lbs.    Source: CME Group; Chicago Board of Trade (CBT)

# Soybeans

Soybean is the common name for the annual leguminous plant and its seed. The soybean is a member of the oilseed family and is not considered a grain. The soybean seeds are contained in pods, and are nearly spherical. The seeds are usually light yellow. The seeds contain 20% oil and 40% protein. Soybeans were an ancient food crop in China, Japan, and Korea and were only introduced to the U.S. in the early 1800s. Today, soybeans are the second-largest crop produced in the U.S. behind corn. Soybean production in the U.S. is concentrated in the Midwest and the lower Mississippi Valley. Soybean crops in the U.S. are planted in May or June and are harvested in autumn. Soybean plants usually reach maturity 100-150 days after planting, depending on growing conditions.

Soybeans are used to produce a wide variety of food products. The key value of soybeans lies in the relatively high protein content, which makes it an excellent source of protein without many of the negative factors of animal meat. Popular soy-based food products include whole soybeans (roasted for snacks or used in sauces, stews and soups), soy oil for cooking and baking, soy flour, protein concentrates, isolated soy protein (which contains up to 92% protein), soy milk and baby formula (as an alternative to dairy products), soy yogurt, soy cheese, soy nut butter, soy sprouts, tofu and tofu products (soybean curd), soy sauce (which is produced by a fermentation process), and meat alternatives (hamburgers, breakfast sausage, etc.).

The primary market for soybean futures is at the CME Group. The CME's soybean contract calls for the delivery of 5,000 bushels of No. 2 yellow soybeans (at contract par), No. 1 yellow soybeans (at 6 cents per bushel above the contract price), or No. 3 yellow soybeans (at 6 cents under the contract price). Soybean futures are also traded at exchanges in Brazil, Argentina, China, and Tokyo.

**Prices** – CME soybean futures prices (Barchart.com symbol ZS) posted the low for 2022 of $13.32 per bushel in January. Soybeans then soared to a 10-year high of $17.65 per bushel in February. Prices rallied due to drought in South America that undercut the crop prospects in Brazil, the world's biggest soybean producer and exporter, and in Argentina, the world's third biggest soybean producer. Also, Russia's invasion of Ukraine in February roiled global commodity markets and sharply reduced Ukraine's sunflower-oil exports, fueling increased demand for U.S. soybean oil. Soybean prices traded sideways within a $1 per bushel range into June when they jumped to a new 10-year high of $17.84 per bushel as a cold and wet spring delayed U.S soybean plantings. Soybean prices then came under pressure as beneficial summer weather boosted the prospects for the U.S. soybean crop. Also, a resurgence of Covid in China, the world's largest soybean importer, raised demand concern as the country's strict Covid Zero policy led to lockdowns and travel restrictions that shut down ports and curbed commodity demand. However, soybeans rallied by more than $3 per bushel from July into August as excessive heat in the central U.S. stressed soybean crops. Also, a surge in soybean oil prices underpinned soybeans when Congress extended a tax credit for biodiesel and renewable diesel through 2024. Soybean prices tumbled from mid-August into October on signs of a bumper U.S. soybean crop. In the August WASDE report, the USDA forecasted a record U.S. 2022/23 soybean crop at 4.531 billion bushels, above estimates of 4.473 billion bushels. Also, a soaring dollar made U.S. soybeans more expensive than South American supplies and weighed on U.S. export prospects after the dollar index rallied to a 20-year high in September. Soybean prices then stabilized and moved higher into year-end. Expectations of greater Chinese demand for soybeans pushed prices higher after it abruptly ended its Covid Zero policy in December. Also, excessive dryness in Argentina parched farms and delayed soybean planting. Soybean prices finished 2022 up sharply by +14.3% yr/yr at $15.19 per bushel.

**Supply** – World soybean production during the 2022/23 marketing year (Sep-Aug) is expected to rise by +8.4% yr/yr to a record 388.008 million metric tons. World soybean production has risen sharply from only 80 million metric tons back in the 1980s. The world's largest soybean producers in 2022/23 are expected to be Brazil with 39.4% of world production, the U.S. with 30.0%, Argentina with 11.7%, China with 5.2%, and India with 3.1%. Brazil's production has risen by almost eight-fold since 1980. China's soybean production has roughly doubled since 1980.

U.S. soybean production in 2022/23 is expected to fall by -4.2% yr/yr to 116.377 million metric tons. U.S. farmers are expected to harvest 86,336 million acres of soybeans in 2022/23, remaining unchanged since 2021/22 yr/yr, but still below the 2017/18 record high of 89.542 billion bushels. The average yield in 2022/23 is expected to fall by -3.7% yr/yr to 49.5 bushels per acre but remain below the 2016/17 record high of 51.9 bushels per acre. U.S. ending stocks for the 2022/23 marketing year are expected to fall by -19.7% yr/yr to 220.0 million bushels.

**Demand** – Total U.S. soybean distribution in 2022/23 is expected to fall by -1.1% yr/yr to 4.414 billion bushels. The distribution tables for U.S. soybeans for the 2022/23 marketing year show that 50.9% of U.S. soybean usage will go for crushed oil and meal products, 46.3% for exports, and 2.8% for seed, feed, and residual. The quantity of U.S. soybeans that will go for crushing is expected to rise by +1.9% yr/yr in 2022/23 to 2.245 billion bushels. The world soybean crush in 2022/23 is expected to rise by +4.2% yr/yr to a new record high of 327.323 million metric tons, which is about triple the level seen in 1993/94.

**Trade** – World exports of soybeans in 2022/23 are expected to rise by +8.9% to 167.532 million metric tons. The world's largest soybean exporters in 2022/23 are expected to be Brazil with 54.3% of world exports, the U.S. with 32.3%, Paraguay with 3.5%, Argentina with 3.4%, and Canada with 2.5%. Brazil's soybean exports have more than doubled in the past decade. U.S. soybean exports in 2021/22 fell by -10.4% yr/yr to 2.049 billion bushels.

World soybean imports in 2022/23 are expected to rise by +4.6% yr/yr to 164.318 million metric tons. The world's largest importers of soybeans in 2022/23 are expected to be China with 58.4% of world imports, the European Union with 8.8%, Mexico with 3.9%, and Egypt with 2.6%. China's imports in 2022/23 are expected to rise by +4.8% yr/yr to 96.000 million metric tons.

# SOYBEANS

## World Production of Soybeans   In Thousands of Metric Tons

| Crop Year[4] | Argentina | Bolivia | Brazil | Canada | China | European Union | India | Paraguay | Russia | Ukraine | United States | Uruguay | World Total |
|---|---|---|---|---|---|---|---|---|---|---|---|---|---|
| 2013-14 | 53,400 | 2,814 | 86,200 | 5,356 | 12,407 | 1,215 | 9,477 | 8,190 | 1,517 | 2,774 | 91,363 | 3,163 | 282,907 |
| 2014-15 | 61,450 | 3,106 | 97,100 | 6,045 | 12,686 | 1,839 | 8,711 | 8,856 | 2,362 | 3,900 | 106,905 | 3,109 | 321,415 |
| 2015-16 | 58,800 | 3,205 | 95,700 | 6,456 | 12,367 | 2,332 | 6,929 | 9,163 | 2,707 | 3,932 | 106,869 | 2,225 | 315,670 |
| 2016-17 | 55,000 | 2,671 | 114,900 | 6,597 | 13,596 | 2,465 | 10,992 | 10,340 | 3,134 | 4,286 | 116,931 | 3,295 | 350,473 |
| 2017-18 | 37,800 | 2,942 | 123,400 | 7,717 | 15,283 | 2,619 | 8,350 | 10,260 | 3,621 | 3,985 | 120,065 | 1,415 | 343,818 |
| 2018-19 | 55,300 | 2,991 | 120,500 | 7,417 | 15,967 | 2,737 | 10,930 | 8,510 | 4,027 | 4,831 | 120,515 | 3,045 | 362,660 |
| 2019-20 | 48,800 | 2,829 | 128,500 | 6,145 | 18,092 | 2,711 | 9,300 | 10,250 | 4,359 | 4,499 | 96,667 | 2,205 | 340,367 |
| 2020-21[1] | 46,200 | 3,318 | 139,500 | 6,359 | 19,602 | 2,600 | 10,450 | 9,900 | 4,307 | 3,000 | 114,749 | 1,785 | 368,522 |
| 2021-22[2] | 43,900 | 3,000 | 129,500 | 6,272 | 16,395 | 2,705 | 11,900 | 4,200 | 4,760 | 3,800 | 121,528 | 3,070 | 358,100 |
| 2022-23[3] | 45,500 | 3,100 | 153,000 | 6,543 | 20,328 | 2,465 | 12,000 | 10,000 | 5,500 | 3,600 | 116,377 | 2,300 | 388,008 |

[1] Preliminary.   [2] Estimate.   [3] Forecast.   [4] Spilt year includes Northern Hemisphere crops harvested in the late months of the first year shown combined with Southern Hemisphere crops harvested in the early months of the following year.   *Sources: Foreign Agricultural Service, U.S. Department of Agriculture (FAS-USDA)*

## World Crushings of Soybeans   In Thousands of Metric Tons

| Crop Year | Argentina | Bolivia | Brazil | China | European Union | India | Japan | Mexico | Paraguay | Russia | Taiwan | United States | World Total |
|---|---|---|---|---|---|---|---|---|---|---|---|---|---|
| 2013-14 | 36,173 | 2,250 | 36,861 | 68,900 | 13,100 | 8,700 | 1,969 | 4,030 | 3,550 | 3,300 | 1,925 | 47,192 | 243,122 |
| 2014-15 | 40,235 | 2,450 | 40,435 | 74,500 | 14,450 | 7,700 | 2,150 | 4,175 | 3,900 | 3,600 | 1,980 | 50,975 | 265,139 |
| 2015-16 | 43,267 | 2,550 | 39,747 | 81,500 | 14,950 | 5,500 | 2,283 | 4,400 | 3,900 | 4,000 | 1,980 | 51,335 | 275,849 |
| 2016-17 | 43,309 | 2,150 | 40,411 | 88,000 | 14,000 | 9,000 | 2,392 | 4,800 | 3,900 | 4,400 | 1,995 | 51,742 | 288,211 |
| 2017-18 | 36,933 | 2,600 | 44,205 | 90,000 | 14,500 | 7,700 | 2,400 | 5,450 | 4,000 | 4,600 | 2,000 | 55,926 | 295,445 |
| 2018-19 | 40,567 | 2,650 | 42,527 | 85,000 | 15,000 | 9,600 | 2,450 | 6,150 | 3,820 | 4,650 | 2,100 | 56,935 | 298,619 |
| 2019-20 | 38,770 | 2,550 | 46,742 | 91,500 | 15,600 | 8,400 | 2,400 | 6,000 | 3,500 | 4,650 | 2,080 | 58,910 | 312,301 |
| 2020-21[1] | 40,162 | 3,050 | 46,675 | 93,000 | 15,800 | 9,500 | 2,365 | 6,200 | 3,300 | 4,500 | 2,050 | 58,257 | 315,443 |
| 2021-22[2] | 38,825 | 2,500 | 50,250 | 87,500 | 15,400 | 9,500 | 2,581 | 6,350 | 2,200 | 4,800 | 2,100 | 59,978 | 314,194 |
| 2022-23[3] | 38,000 | 2,600 | 52,500 | 95,000 | 14,900 | 9,900 | 2,500 | 6,550 | 3,750 | 5,100 | 2,150 | 61,099 | 327,323 |

[1] Preliminary.   [2] Estimate.   [3] Forecast.   *Sources: Foreign Agricultural Service, U.S. Department of Agriculture (FAS-USDA)*

## World Exports of Soybeans   In Thousands of Metric Tons

| Crop Year | Argentina | Bolivia | Brazil | Canada | China | India | Paraguay | Russia | Serbia | Ukraine | United States | Uruguay | World Total |
|---|---|---|---|---|---|---|---|---|---|---|---|---|---|
| 2013-14 | 7,842 | 141 | 46,829 | 3,469 | 215 | 183 | 4,844 | 24 | 23 | 1,261 | 44,594 | 3,150 | 112,798 |
| 2014-15 | 10,575 | 8 | 50,612 | 3,855 | 143 | 234 | 4,576 | 313 | 136 | 2,422 | 50,136 | 3,113 | 126,443 |
| 2015-16 | 9,922 | 91 | 54,383 | 4,236 | 114 | 134 | 5,381 | 456 | 68 | 2,369 | 52,869 | 2,221 | 132,810 |
| 2016-17 | 7,025 | 13 | 63,137 | 4,592 | 114 | 268 | 6,129 | 375 | 186 | 2,904 | 58,964 | 3,199 | 147,664 |
| 2017-18 | 2,132 | 8 | 76,136 | 4,925 | 134 | 217 | 6,029 | 891 | 28 | 2,757 | 58,071 | 1,354 | 153,351 |
| 2018-19 | 9,104 | 13 | 74,887 | 5,258 | 116 | 165 | 4,901 | 797 | 143 | 2,531 | 47,721 | 2,967 | 149,187 |
| 2019-20 | 10,004 | 17 | 92,135 | 3,909 | 90 | 80 | 6,619 | 1,298 | 252 | 2,633 | 45,800 | 2,148 | 165,556 |
| 2020-21[1] | 5,195 | 111 | 81,650 | 4,706 | 70 | 32 | 6,330 | 1,355 | 143 | 1,466 | 61,665 | 1,774 | 164,994 |
| 2021-22[2] | 2,861 | 500 | 79,143 | 4,276 | 102 | 61 | 2,250 | 730 | 15 | 1,385 | 58,721 | 3,000 | 153,888 |
| 2022-23[3] | 5,700 | 100 | 91,000 | 4,200 | 100 | 150 | 5,800 | 1,450 | 130 | 1,800 | 54,159 | 2,225 | 167,532 |

[1] Preliminary.   [2] Estimate.   [3] Forecast.   *Sources: Foreign Agricultural Service, U.S. Department of Agriculture (FAS-USDA)*

## World Imports of Soybeans   In Thousands of Metric Tons

| Crop Year | China | Egypt | European Union | Indonesia | Japan | Korea, South | Mexico | Russia | Taiwan | Thailand | Turkey | Vietnam | World Total |
|---|---|---|---|---|---|---|---|---|---|---|---|---|---|
| 2013-14 | 70,364 | 1,694 | 13,293 | 2,241 | 2,894 | 1,271 | 3,842 | 2,048 | 2,335 | 1,798 | 1,750 | 1,564 | 113,305 |
| 2014-15 | 78,350 | 1,947 | 13,914 | 2,006 | 3,004 | 1,246 | 3,819 | 1,986 | 2,520 | 2,411 | 2,256 | 1,707 | 124,418 |
| 2015-16 | 83,230 | 1,575 | 15,120 | 2,274 | 3,186 | 1,249 | 4,126 | 2,336 | 2,476 | 2,798 | 2,376 | 1,362 | 133,713 |
| 2016-17 | 93,495 | 2,114 | 12,742 | 2,649 | 3,175 | 1,286 | 4,479 | 2,221 | 2,566 | 3,078 | 2,273 | 1,646 | 145,183 |
| 2017-18 | 94,093 | 3,255 | 13,915 | 2,483 | 3,256 | 1,256 | 5,134 | 2,237 | 2,666 | 2,482 | 2,872 | 1,824 | 154,110 |
| 2018-19 | 82,537 | 3,657 | 14,346 | 2,623 | 3,314 | 1,373 | 5,933 | 2,162 | 2,614 | 3,155 | 2,411 | 1,688 | 146,022 |
| 2019-20 | 98,532 | 4,896 | 15,017 | 2,636 | 3,325 | 1,291 | 5,743 | 2,047 | 2,708 | 3,831 | 3,148 | 1,875 | 165,124 |
| 2020-21[1] | 99,740 | 3,703 | 14,786 | 2,617 | 3,085 | 1,336 | 6,101 | 2,042 | 2,615 | 4,157 | 2,745 | 2,015 | 165,545 |
| 2021-22[2] | 91,566 | 4,870 | 14,549 | 2,307 | 3,455 | 1,268 | 5,956 | 1,850 | 2,750 | 3,243 | 2,949 | 1,900 | 157,127 |
| 2022-23[3] | 96,000 | 4,300 | 14,400 | 2,775 | 3,350 | 1,380 | 6,400 | 1,600 | 2,750 | 4,100 | 3,000 | 2,050 | 164,318 |

[1] Preliminary.   [2] Estimate.   [3] Forecast.   *Sources: Foreign Agricultural Service, U.S. Department of Agriculture (FAS-USDA)*

# SOYBEANS

## World Ending Stocks of Soybeans   In Thousands of Metric Tons

| Crop Year | Argentina | Bolivia | Brazil | Canada | China | European Union | India | Japan | Paraguay | Turkey | Ukraine | United States | World Total |
|---|---|---|---|---|---|---|---|---|---|---|---|---|---|
| 2013-14 | 21,677 | 139 | 20,790 | 237 | 13,967 | 1,260 | 600 | 256 | 298 | 379 | 265 | 2,504 | 64,092 |
| 2014-15 | 27,069 | 433 | 24,498 | 458 | 17,060 | 857 | 200 | 212 | 635 | 401 | 166 | 5,188 | 79,348 |
| 2015-16 | 27,156 | 635 | 23,803 | 380 | 16,643 | 1,559 | 338 | 259 | 423 | 328 | 113 | 5,354 | 79,126 |
| 2016-17 | 26,996 | 783 | 32,632 | 355 | 20,120 | 974 | 880 | 217 | 610 | 314 | 151 | 8,208 | 95,287 |
| 2017-18 | 23,734 | 700 | 33,031 | 651 | 22,553 | 1,111 | 339 | 235 | 697 | 515 | 76 | 11,923 | 99,881 |
| 2018-19 | 28,890 | 700 | 33,342 | 700 | 18,404 | 1,387 | 432 | 237 | 349 | 255 | 223 | 24,740 | 114,259 |
| 2019-20 | 26,650 | 663 | 20,419 | 621 | 24,612 | 1,721 | 472 | 299 | 330 | 428 | 92 | 14,276 | 94,732 |
| 2020-21[1] | 25,060 | 430 | 29,404 | 294 | 31,145 | 1,560 | 420 | 193 | 453 | 247 | 102 | 6,994 | 100,034 |
| 2021-22[2] | 23,903 | 107 | 26,805 | 428 | 31,404 | 1,553 | 1,114 | 250 | 178 | 222 | 717 | 7,468 | 98,215 |
| 2022-23[3] | 23,453 | 134 | 33,455 | 651 | 31,332 | 1,688 | 1,104 | 267 | 463 | 227 | 716 | 5,720 | 103,517 |

[1] Preliminary.   [2] Estimate.   [3] Forecast.   Sources: Foreign Agricultural Service, U.S. Department of Agriculture (FAS-USDA)

## Supply and Distribution of Soybeans in the United States   In Millions of Bushels

| Crop Year Beginning Sept. 1 | Stocks, Sept. 1 Farms | Mills, Elevators[3] | Total Stocks | Production | Imports | Total Supply | Crushings | Seed, Feed & Residual Use | Exports | Total Distribution | Ending Stocks |
|---|---|---|---|---|---|---|---|---|---|---|---|
| 2013-14 | 39.6 | 101.0 | 140.6 | 3,358 | 72 | 3,570 | 1,734 | 107 | 1,638 | 3,478 | 92 |
| 2014-15 | 21.3 | 70.7 | 92.0 | 3,927 | 33 | 4,052 | 1,873 | 146 | 1,842 | 3,862 | 191 |
| 2015-16 | 49.7 | 140.9 | 190.6 | 3,926 | 24 | 4,140 | 1,886 | 115 | 1,942 | 3,944 | 197 |
| 2016-17 | 41.6 | 155.2 | 196.7 | 4,296 | 22 | 4,515 | 1,901 | 146 | 2,166 | 4,214 | 302 |
| 2017-18 | 87.9 | 213.7 | 301.6 | 4,412 | 22 | 4,735 | 2,055 | 108 | 2,134 | 4,297 | 438 |
| 2018-19 | 101.0 | 337.1 | 438.1 | 4,428 | 14 | 4,880 | 2,092 | 127 | 1,752 | 3,971 | 909 |
| 2019-20 | 265.0 | 644.1 | 909.1 | 3,552 | 15 | 4,476 | 2,165 | 108 | 1,679 | 3,952 | 525 |
| 2020-21 | 141.2 | 383.3 | 524.5 | 4,216 | 20 | 4,761 | 2,141 | 97 | 2,266 | 4,504 | 257 |
| 2021-22[1] | 68.1 | 188.9 | 257.0 | 4,465 | 16 | 4,738 | 2,204 | 102 | 2,158 | 4,464 | 274 |
| 2022-23[2] | 62.9 | 211.5 | 274.4 | 4,276 | 15 | 4,566 | 2,220 | 120 | 2,015 | 4,355 | 210 |

[1] Preliminary.   [2] Estimate.   [3] Also warehouses.   Source: Economic Research Service, U.S. Department of Agriculture (ERS-USDA)

## Salient Statistics & Official Crop Production Reports of Soybeans in the United States   In Millions of Bushels

| Crop Year | Planted 1,000 Acres | Acreage Harvested 1,000 Acres | Yield Per Acre (Bu.) | Farm Price ($/Bu.) | Farm Value (Million Dollars) | Yield of Oil (Lbs. Per Bushel Crushed) | Yield of Meal (Lbs. Per Bushel Crushed) | Aug. 1 | Sept. 1 | Oct. 1 | Nov. 1 | Dec. 1 | Final |
|---|---|---|---|---|---|---|---|---|---|---|---|---|---|
| 2013-14 | 76,840 | 76,253 | 44.0 | 13.32 | 43,583 | ---- | ---- | 3,255,444 | 3,149,166 | NA | 3,257,746 | ---- | 3,357,984 |
| 2014-15 | 83,276 | 82,591 | 47.5 | 10.00 | 39,475 | ---- | ---- | 3,815,679 | 3,913,079 | 3,926,812 | 3,958,272 | ---- | 3,927,090 |
| 2015-16 | 82,650 | 81,732 | 48.0 | 9.18 | 35,192 | ---- | ---- | 3,916,448 | 3,935,277 | 3,887,721 | 3,981,337 | ---- | 3,926,339 |
| 2016-17 | 83,453 | 82,706 | 51.9 | 9.46 | 40,695 | ---- | ---- | 4,060,188 | 4,200,985 | 4,268,884 | 4,361,023 | ---- | 4,296,496 |
| 2017-18 | 90,162 | 89,542 | 49.3 | 9.38 | 41,309 | ---- | ---- | 4,381,053 | 4,431,043 | 4,430,621 | 4,425,279 | ---- | 4,411,633 |
| 2018-19 | 89,167 | 87,594 | 50.6 | 8.43 | 37,558 | ---- | ---- | 4,585,916 | 4,693,135 | 4,689,628 | 4,599,530 | ---- | 4,428,150 |
| 2019-20 | 76,100 | 74,939 | 47.4 | 8.52 | 30,526 | ---- | ---- | 3,680,217 | 3,632,651 | 3,550,281 | 3,549,977 | ---- | 3,551,908 |
| 2020-21 | 83,354 | 82,603 | 51.0 | 12.30 | 45,732 | ---- | ---- | 4,424,800 | 4,312,819 | 4,267,890 | 4,170,262 | ---- | 4,216,302 |
| 2021-22[1] | 87,195 | 86,332 | 51.4 | 14.23 | 57,479 | ---- | ---- | 4,338,853 | 4,373,927 | 4,448,043 | 4,424,942 | ---- | 4,465,382 |
| 2022-23[2] | 87,450 | 86,336 | 49.5 | 14.27 | | ---- | ---- | 4,530,561 | 4,378,194 | 4,312,949 | 4,345,524 | ---- | 4,276,123 |

[1] Preliminary.   [2] Forecast.   NA = Not available.   Source: National Agricultural Statistics Service, U.S. Department of Agriculture (NASS-USDA)

## Stocks of Soybeans in the United States   In Thousands of Bushels

| Year | On Farms Mar. 1 | June 1 | Sept. 1 | Dec. 1 | Off Farms Mar. 1 | June 1 | Sept. 1 | Dec. 1 | Total Stocks Mar. 1 | June 1 | Sept. 1 | Dec. 1 |
|---|---|---|---|---|---|---|---|---|---|---|---|---|
| 2013 | 456,700 | 171,100 | 39,550 | 955,000 | 541,320 | 263,564 | 101,007 | 1,198,621 | 998,020 | 434,664 | 140,557 | 2,153,621 |
| 2014 | 381,900 | 109,100 | 21,325 | 1,218,000 | 611,928 | 295,945 | 70,666 | 1,309,744 | 993,828 | 405,045 | 91,991 | 2,527,744 |
| 2015 | 609,200 | 246,300 | 49,700 | 1,308,500 | 717,399 | 380,768 | 140,910 | 1,405,577 | 1,326,599 | 627,068 | 190,610 | 2,714,077 |
| 2016 | 727,500 | 281,300 | 41,560 | 1,335,000 | 803,406 | 590,481 | 155,169 | 1,563,379 | 1,530,906 | 871,781 | 196,729 | 2,898,379 |
| 2017 | 668,500 | 332,500 | 87,900 | 1,485,000 | 1,070,433 | 633,356 | 213,695 | 1,675,679 | 1,738,933 | 965,856 | 301,595 | 3,160,679 |
| 2018 | 855,000 | 377,000 | 101,000 | 1,935,000 | 1,254,303 | 842,329 | 337,105 | 1,810,824 | 2,109,303 | 1,219,329 | 438,105 | 3,745,824 |
| 2019 | 1,270,000 | 730,000 | 265,000 | 1,519,500 | 1,457,069 | 1,053,080 | 644,052 | 1,732,988 | 2,727,069 | 1,783,080 | 909,052 | 3,252,488 |
| 2020 | 1,011,500 | 633,000 | 141,200 | 1,308,500 | 1,243,382 | 748,394 | 383,341 | 1,638,240 | 2,254,882 | 1,381,394 | 524,541 | 2,946,740 |
| 2021 | 594,000 | 219,900 | 68,100 | 1,522,000 | 967,684 | 549,140 | 188,879 | 1,614,524 | 1,561,684 | 769,040 | 256,979 | 3,136,524 |
| 2022[1] | 750,000 | 331,400 | 62,930 | 1,477,000 | 1,181,817 | 636,125 | 211,464 | 1,544,152 | 1,931,817 | 967,525 | 274,394 | 3,021,152 |

[1] Preliminary.   Source: National Agricultural Statistics Service, U.S. Department of Agriculture (NASS-USDA)

# SOYBEANS

## Commercial Stocks of Soybeans in the United States, on First of Month    In Millions of Bushels

| Year | Jan. | Feb. | Mar. | Apr. | May | June | July | Aug. | Sept. | Oct. | Nov. | Dec. |
|------|------|------|------|------|------|------|------|------|-------|------|------|------|
| 2005 | 26.5 | 21.5 | 19.5 | 16.0 | 14.8 | 12.1 | 11.5 | 8.8 | 5.4 | 17.0 | 36.7 | 36.1 |
| 2006 | 36.8 | 30.2 | 26.1 | 25.7 | 17.6 | 20.5 | 14.6 | 14.5 | 14.5 | 19.0 | 40.1 | 43.7 |
| 2007 | 42.0 | 36.5 | 37.3 | 34.3 | 29.7 | 27.4 | 26.6 | 24.6 | 25.5 | 32.0 | 54.0 | 61.3 |
| 2008 | 51.1 | 45.5 | 41.8 | 36.3 | 28.2 | 25.6 | 19.2 | 14.8 | 11.4 | 19.6 | 40.5 | 46.1 |
| 2009 | 44.6 | 36.8 | 27.0 | 15.6 | 13.9 | 11.8 | 10.0 | 5.8 | 5.9 | 24.7 | 40.5 | 44.3 |
| 2010 | 30.0 | 28.5 | 20.1 | 22.3 | 10.8 | 8.0 | 8.2 | 4.5 | 3.3 | 19.2 | 45.0 | 32.0 |
| 2011 | 32.6 | 23.2 | 16.0 | 11.3 | 10.2 | 5.9 | 6.2 | 5.7 | 4.6 | 9.8 | 49.4 | 50.7 |
| 2012 | 42.7 | 34.8 | 29.9 | 28.5 | 27.1 | 23.8 | 16.6 | 10.4 | 5.2 | 18.8 | 41.6 | 33.8 |
| 2013 | 25.2 | 20.3 | 16.1 | 10.0 | 6.4 | 6.6 | 4.1 | 2.9 | 2.1 | 27.2 | 36.9 | 35.5 |
| 2014 | 30.7 | 20.4 | 15.5 | 12.2 | 7.0 | 5.1 | 5.2 | 2.3 | ---- | ---- | ---- | ---- |

This report was discontinued as of August 26, 2014.    *Source: Livestock Division, U.S. Department of Agriculture (LD-USDA)*

## Production of Soybeans for Beans in the United States, by State    In Millions of Bushels

| Crop Year | Arkansas | Illinois | Indiana | Iowa | Kentucky | Michigan | Minnesota | Mississippi | Missouri | Nebraska | Ohio | Tennessee | Total |
|-----------|----------|----------|---------|------|----------|----------|-----------|-------------|----------|----------|------|-----------|-------|
| 2013-14 | 140.9 | 474.0 | 267.3 | 420.9 | 83.0 | 85.4 | 278.0 | 91.5 | 202.0 | 255.2 | 222.3 | 72.1 | 3,358.0 |
| 2014-15 | 158.4 | 547.1 | 301.9 | 498.3 | 83.1 | 86.7 | 301.7 | 113.9 | 259.9 | 287.8 | 246.2 | 74.1 | 3,927.1 |
| 2015-16 | 155.3 | 544.3 | 275.0 | 553.7 | 88.7 | 99.0 | 377.5 | 104.4 | 181.0 | 305.7 | 237.0 | 79.1 | 3,926.3 |
| 2016-17 | 145.2 | 593.0 | 323.7 | 566.4 | 89.0 | 104.0 | 389.5 | 97.0 | 271.5 | 314.2 | 263.8 | 73.4 | 4,296.5 |
| 2017-18 | 178.5 | 611.9 | 320.8 | 566.6 | 102.8 | 96.5 | 384.3 | 115.0 | 292.5 | 326.0 | 252.0 | 83.0 | 4,411.6 |
| 2018-19 | 162.1 | 666.8 | 342.7 | 550.5 | 98.4 | 109.7 | 374.9 | 118.3 | 257.2 | 324.2 | 281.1 | 76.0 | 4,428.2 |
| 2019-20 | 127.9 | 532.4 | 273.4 | 501.6 | 77.7 | 69.7 | 297.9 | 81.5 | 230.5 | 283.1 | 209.2 | 64.4 | 3,551.9 |
| 2020-21 | 144.2 | 615.0 | 338.1 | 506.0 | 101.2 | 105.1 | 369.0 | 111.2 | 296.3 | 299.3 | 270.6 | 81.0 | 4,216.3 |
| 2021-22 | 156.0 | 683.2 | 338.4 | 631.9 | 103.0 | 109.1 | 356.3 | 117.2 | 276.9 | 350.9 | 278.2 | 76.0 | 4,465.4 |
| 2022-23[1] | 167.0 | 684.8 | 344.0 | 591.2 | 98.9 | 102.6 | 369.0 | 127.7 | 290.4 | 285.0 | 279.4 | 74.5 | 4,276.1 |

[1] Preliminary.    *Source: Agricultural Statistics Board, U.S. Department of Agriculture (ASB-USDA)*

## U. S. Exports of Soybeans    In Millions of Bushels

| Crop Year | Sept. | Oct. | Nov. | Dec. | Jan. | Feb. | Mar. | Apr. | May | June | July | Aug. | Total |
|-----------|-------|------|------|------|------|------|------|------|-----|------|------|------|-------|
| 2013-14 | 55.3 | 290.1 | 331.5 | 255.0 | 259.0 | 198.7 | 117.0 | 42.9 | 32.2 | 22.2 | 19.2 | 16.4 | 1,639.5 |
| 2014-15 | 77.9 | 329.9 | 405.3 | 301.7 | 257.5 | 166.6 | 94.1 | 49.7 | 44.0 | 34.4 | 39.7 | 42.6 | 1,843.5 |
| 2015-16 | 86.4 | 369.0 | 336.3 | 250.1 | 218.1 | 207.5 | 95.8 | 52.3 | 33.8 | 36.8 | 98.5 | 152.6 | 1,937.1 |
| 2016-17 | 138.5 | 415.9 | 378.6 | 291.2 | 272.9 | 162.4 | 114.7 | 89.4 | 53.3 | 66.0 | 83.2 | 113.1 | 2,179.3 |
| 2017-18 | 170.6 | 347.1 | 332.1 | 237.2 | 211.9 | 154.9 | 119.1 | 79.7 | 110.0 | 119.7 | 126.0 | 123.8 | 2,131.9 |
| 2018-19 | 119.0 | 205.2 | 186.3 | 150.9 | 177.5 | 168.3 | 136.3 | 88.2 | 94.1 | 117.4 | 135.3 | 181.3 | 1,759.8 |
| 2019-20 | 143.4 | 216.7 | 250.9 | 208.0 | 195.6 | 101.4 | 94.5 | 79.5 | 72.3 | 66.1 | 81.5 | 173.1 | 1,683.0 |
| 2020-21 | 263.9 | 425.5 | 408.0 | 397.7 | 324.6 | 167.6 | 84.4 | 50.9 | 46.6 | 34.0 | 34.8 | 48.1 | 2,286.0 |
| 2021-22 | 77.2 | 395.2 | 389.0 | 291.9 | 235.0 | 139.4 | 117.1 | 134.5 | 88.7 | 83.5 | 85.4 | 12.2 | 2,049.1 |
| 2022-23[1] | 78.0 | 359.6 | 355.4 | 304.9 | 314.7 | | | | | | | | 3,390.5 |

[1] Preliminary.    *Source: Economic Research Service, U.S. Department of Agriculture (ERS-USDA)*

## Soybean Crushed (Factory Consumption) in the United States    In Millions of Bushels

| Crop Year | Sept. | Oct. | Nov. | Dec. | Jan. | Feb. | Mar. | Apr. | May | June | July | Aug. | Total |
|-----------|-------|------|------|------|------|------|------|------|-----|------|------|------|-------|
| 2013-14 | ---- | 675.8 | ---- | ---- | 457.0 | ---- | ---- | 422.0 | ---- | ---- | 285.6 | ---- | 1,733.9 |
| 2014-15 | ---- | 687.3 | ---- | ---- | 480.2 | ---- | ---- | 522.7 | ---- | 151.6 | 155.8 | 144.6 | 1,873.5 |
| 2015-16 | 134.6 | 170.1 | 165.8 | 167.0 | 160.5 | 154.6 | 166.4 | 158.2 | 160.9 | 154.1 | 153.5 | 140.6 | 1,886.3 |
| 2016-17 | 138.3 | 175.9 | 170.7 | 169.0 | 170.4 | 151.0 | 160.0 | 149.8 | 158.0 | 148.2 | 155.6 | 151.6 | 1,898.5 |
| 2017-18 | 145.4 | 175.9 | 173.3 | 176.3 | 174.7 | 165.0 | 182.2 | 171.6 | 172.5 | 169.6 | 178.9 | 169.9 | 2,055.3 |
| 2018-19 | 169.3 | 183.6 | 178.1 | 183.8 | 183.1 | 162.8 | 179.4 | 171.5 | 165.4 | 157.6 | 179.5 | 177.3 | 2,091.4 |
| 2019-20 | 162.3 | 187.2 | 174.6 | 184.7 | 188.8 | 175.3 | 192.2 | 183.4 | 179.6 | 177.3 | 184.5 | 174.7 | 2,164.6 |
| 2020-21 | 171.1 | 196.6 | 191.0 | 193.1 | 196.5 | 164.4 | 188.2 | 169.9 | 173.5 | 161.7 | 166.3 | 168.3 | 2,140.6 |
| 2021-22 | 164.2 | 196.9 | 190.6 | 198.2 | 194.3 | 174.4 | 192.9 | 180.9 | 180.9 | 174.1 | 181.3 | 175.1 | 2,203.8 |
| 2022-23[1] | 167.6 | 196.7 | 189.6 | 187.4 | 191.1 | | | | | | | | 2,237.8 |

[1] Preliminary.    *Source: Economic Research Service, U.S. Department of Agriculture (ERS-USDA)*

# SOYBEANS

**SOYBEANS - CBOT**
Weekly Nearest Futures as of 03/31/2023

Chart High 1784.00 on 06/09/2022
Chart Low 780.50 on 05/13/2019

Nearby Futures through Last Trading Day.

### Volume of Trading of Soybean Futures in Chicago    In Thousands of Contracts

| Year | Jan. | Feb. | Mar. | Apr. | May | June | July | Aug. | Sept. | Oct. | Nov. | Dec. | Total |
|---|---|---|---|---|---|---|---|---|---|---|---|---|---|
| 2013 | 3,628.0 | 4,568.4 | 3,193.0 | 4,516.5 | 3,522.9 | 3,644.1 | 3,328.3 | 4,132.9 | 3,442.2 | 5,288.6 | 3,401.3 | 4,054.9 | 46,721 |
| 2014 | 3,692.7 | 5,090.5 | 3,613.9 | 4,191.9 | 2,914.6 | 3,929.4 | 3,765.7 | 2,967.5 | 3,672.1 | 7,261.6 | 3,661.2 | 4,408.2 | 49,169 |
| 2015 | 3,570.3 | 4,867.3 | 4,011.2 | 5,029.8 | 3,422.5 | 6,284.1 | 4,425.8 | 4,256.8 | 3,693.6 | 6,251.6 | 3,314.6 | 4,967.4 | 54,095 |
| 2016 | 3,846.1 | 5,203.8 | 4,455.3 | 8,380.0 | 6,211.8 | 7,135.0 | 4,779.8 | 3,432.5 | 3,373.1 | 5,936.7 | 4,085.1 | 4,891.6 | 61,731 |
| 2017 | 3,760.7 | 5,197.1 | 3,837.0 | 4,612.5 | 3,781.0 | 5,251.6 | 5,287.5 | 4,132.3 | 3,629.0 | 6,075.2 | 3,726.4 | 5,213.9 | 54,504 |
| 2018 | 4,066.9 | 6,799.5 | 5,116.2 | 6,789.1 | 4,592.8 | 6,603.2 | 3,794.3 | 4,088.9 | 3,151.9 | 5,831.5 | 3,439.6 | 4,264.6 | 58,539 |
| 2019 | 3,245.1 | 4,692.8 | 3,351.5 | 4,801.5 | 5,096.2 | 5,784.5 | 3,820.6 | 3,771.8 | 3,445.3 | 6,913.2 | 3,416.5 | 4,994.4 | 53,333 |
| 2020 | 3,719.9 | 5,513.0 | 5,500.2 | 4,709.2 | 3,341.8 | 5,562.8 | 4,115.7 | 4,432.9 | 5,669.6 | 7,545.1 | 4,910.5 | 6,102.4 | 61,123 |
| 2021 | 5,400.5 | 5,117.7 | 4,344.1 | 5,529.0 | 3,784.8 | 5,600.8 | 3,301.1 | 3,328.9 | 3,105.6 | 5,388.3 | 3,633.7 | 4,790.0 | 53,324 |
| 2022 | 4,262.6 | 6,391.4 | 3,777.9 | 4,230.3 | 3,328.8 | 4,914.0 | 3,395.2 | 3,567.3 | 4,123.4 | 5,495.6 | 3,523.4 | 4,707.7 | 51,718 |

Contract size = 5,000 bu.    Source: *CME Group; Chicago Board of Trade (CBT)*

### Average Open Interest of Soybean Futures in Chicago    In Contracts

| Year | Jan. | Feb. | Mar. | Apr. | May | June | July | Aug. | Sept. | Oct. | Nov. | Dec. |
|---|---|---|---|---|---|---|---|---|---|---|---|---|
| 2013 | 549,767 | 615,897 | 589,572 | 565,212 | 565,761 | 596,479 | 517,022 | 535,645 | 615,389 | 626,484 | 582,859 | 625,222 |
| 2014 | 589,906 | 675,981 | 649,898 | 645,604 | 601,103 | 616,406 | 622,020 | 642,043 | 724,924 | 766,218 | 664,485 | 668,492 |
| 2015 | 644,320 | 698,627 | 708,314 | 746,322 | 698,151 | 722,449 | 663,522 | 653,707 | 675,762 | 701,419 | 673,127 | 681,902 |
| 2016 | 674,273 | 721,934 | 723,375 | 824,649 | 840,893 | 859,598 | 747,309 | 668,100 | 636,957 | 657,062 | 642,826 | 709,587 |
| 2017 | 681,161 | 736,942 | 691,919 | 729,828 | 654,509 | 695,963 | 648,861 | 645,305 | 666,063 | 723,614 | 712,476 | 747,181 |
| 2018 | 762,139 | 781,574 | 846,901 | 923,139 | 879,489 | 893,661 | 838,433 | 797,279 | 846,361 | 839,514 | 743,667 | 723,335 |
| 2019 | 683,830 | 706,877 | 693,239 | 767,901 | 763,593 | 734,373 | 658,702 | 636,025 | 675,040 | 736,987 | 753,829 | 807,431 |
| 2020 | 767,124 | 846,942 | 790,798 | 826,659 | 849,949 | 865,514 | 830,455 | 839,763 | 938,439 | 1,010,657 | 928,015 | 935,198 |
| 2021 | 935,234 | 905,458 | 857,961 | 873,376 | 806,462 | 773,210 | 680,714 | 667,051 | 667,573 | 712,214 | 658,746 | 654,705 |
| 2022 | 701,786 | 823,877 | 75,114 | 746,268 | 714,941 | 731,705 | 606,032 | 593,948 | 650,416 | 670,484 | 614,213 | 623,336 |

Contract size = 5,000 bu.    Source: *CME Group; Chicago Board of Trade (CBT)*

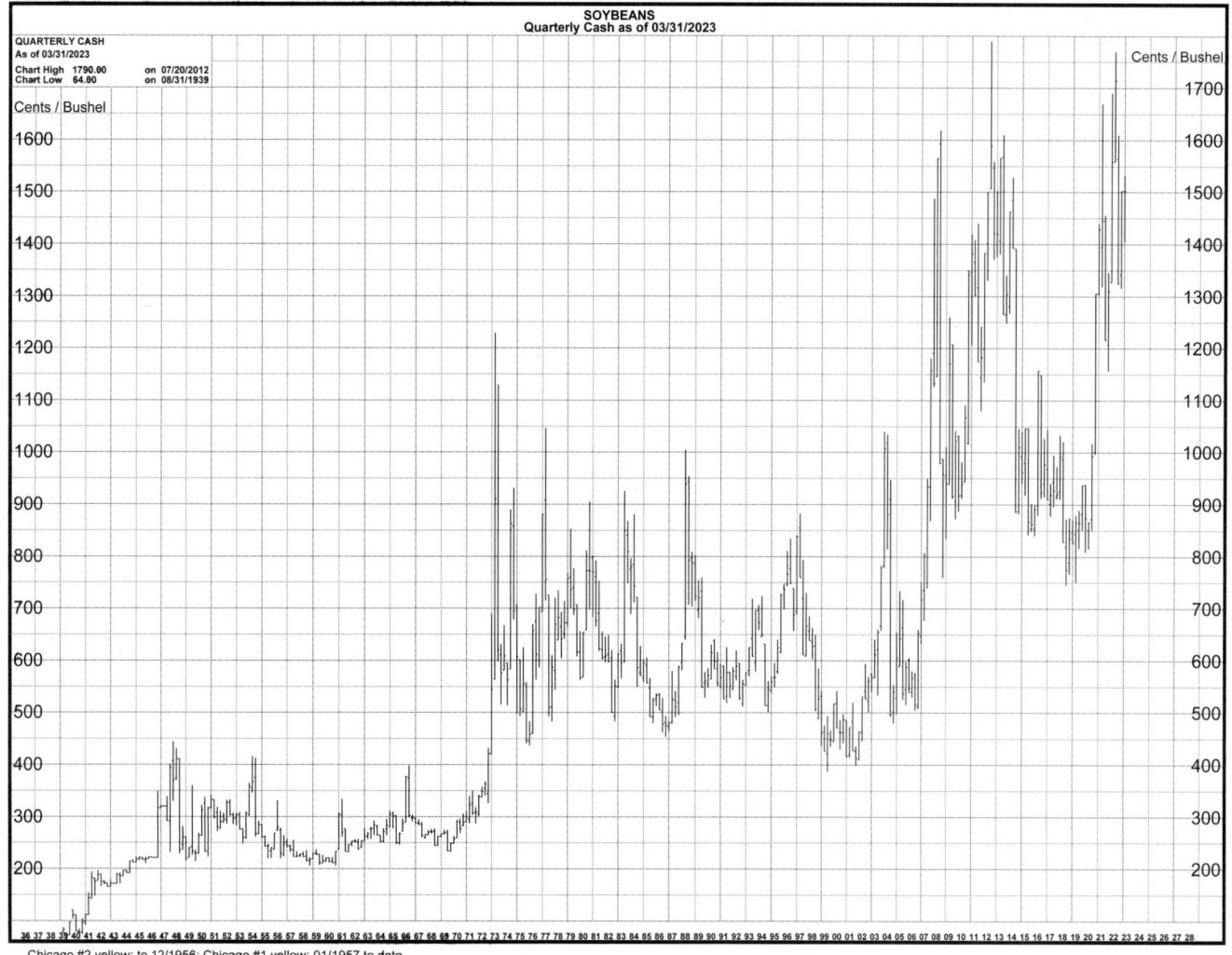

# SOYBEANS

## Average Price Received by Farmers for Soybeans in the United States — In Dollars Per Bushel

| Crop Year | Sept. | Oct. | Nov. | Dec. | Jan. | Feb. | Mar. | Apr. | May | June | July | Aug. | Average |
|---|---|---|---|---|---|---|---|---|---|---|---|---|---|
| 2013-14 | 13.30 | 12.50 | 12.70 | 13.00 | 12.90 | 13.20 | 13.70 | 14.30 | 14.40 | 14.30 | 13.10 | 12.40 | 13.32 |
| 2014-15 | 10.90 | 9.97 | 10.20 | 10.30 | 10.30 | 9.91 | 9.85 | 9.69 | 9.58 | 9.58 | 9.95 | 9.71 | 10.00 |
| 2015-16 | 9.05 | 8.81 | 8.68 | 8.76 | 8.71 | 8.51 | 8.56 | 9.01 | 9.76 | 10.20 | 10.20 | 9.93 | 9.18 |
| 2016-17 | 9.41 | 9.30 | 9.47 | 9.64 | 9.71 | 9.86 | 9.69 | 9.33 | 9.29 | 9.10 | 9.42 | 9.24 | 9.46 |
| 2017-18 | 9.35 | 9.18 | 9.22 | 9.30 | 9.30 | 9.50 | 9.81 | 9.85 | 9.84 | 9.55 | 9.08 | 8.59 | 9.38 |
| 2018-19 | 8.78 | 8.59 | 8.36 | 8.56 | 8.64 | 8.52 | 8.52 | 8.28 | 8.02 | 8.31 | 8.38 | 8.22 | 8.43 |
| 2019-20 | 8.35 | 8.60 | 8.59 | 8.70 | 8.84 | 8.60 | 8.47 | 8.35 | 8.28 | 8.34 | 8.50 | 8.66 | 8.52 |
| 2020-21 | 9.24 | 9.63 | 10.30 | 10.60 | 10.90 | 12.70 | 13.20 | 13.90 | 14.80 | 14.50 | 14.10 | 13.70 | 12.30 |
| 2021-22 | 12.20 | 11.90 | 12.10 | 12.50 | 12.90 | 14.70 | 15.40 | 15.80 | 16.10 | 16.40 | 15.50 | 15.30 | 14.23 |
| 2022-23[1] | 14.10 | 13.50 | 14.00 | 14.40 | 14.50 | 15.10 | | | | | | | 14.27 |

[1] Preliminary.   Source: Economic Research Service, U.S. Department of Agriculture (ERS-USDA)

## Average Cash Price of No. 1 Yellow Soybeans at Illinois Processor — In Cents Per Bushel

| Crop Year | Sept. | Oct. | Nov. | Dec. | Jan. | Feb. | Mar. | Apr. | May | June | July | Aug. | Average |
|---|---|---|---|---|---|---|---|---|---|---|---|---|---|
| 2001-02 | 469 | 430 | 441 | 438 | 437 | 440 | 464 | 471 | 492 | 519 | 575 | 567 | 479 |
| 2002-03 | 579 | 541 | 575 | 566 | 570 | 590 | 580 | 611 | 640 | 635 | 601 | 589 | 590 |
| 2003-04 | 639 | 729 | 763 | 772 | 823 | 872 | 975 | 992 | 958 | 890 | 809 | 641 | 822 |
| 2004-05 | 562 | 519 | 534 | 545 | 539 | 544 | 628 | 622 | 644 | 701 | 703 | 639 | 598 |
| 2005-06 | 565 | 553 | 574 | 592 | 576 | 575 | 569 | 562 | 581 | 576 | 577 | 542 | 570 |
| 2006-07 | 535 | 580 | 661 | 657 | 683 | 735 | 730 | 718 | 749 | 792 | 801 | 804 | 704 |
| 2007-08 | 907 | 944 | 1,032 | 1,123 | 1,216 | 1,335 | 1,312 | 1,292 | 1,324 | 1,499 | 1,516 | 1,288 | 1,232 |
| 2008-09 | 1,140 | 903 | 893 | 868 | 991 | 938 | 917 | 1,025 | 1,166 | 1,237 | 1,096 | 1,136 | 1,026 |
| 2009-10 | 1,012 | 978 | 1,009 | 1,033 | 984 | 944 | 949 | 975 | 955 | 955 | 1,030 | 1,066 | 991 |
| 2010-11[1] | 1,065 | 1,148 | 1,252 | 1,311 | 1,378 | 1,386 | 1,350 | 1,364 | 1,368 | 1,382 | 1,384 | 1,381 | 1,314 |

[1] Preliminary.   Source: Economic Research Service, U.S. Department of Agriculture (ERS-USDA)

# SOYBEANS

## Weekly Outstanding Export Sales and Cumulative Exports of U.S. Soybeans — In Thousands of Metric Tons

| Marketing Year 2021/2022 Week Ending | Weekly Exports | Accumulated Exports | Net Sales | Outstanding Sales | Marketing Year 2022/2023 Week Ending | Weekly Exports | Accumulated Exports | Net Sales | Outstanding Sales |
|---|---|---|---|---|---|---|---|---|---|
| Sep 02, 2021 | 13,826 | 13,826 | 3,277,758 | 21,011,415 | Sep 01, 2022 | 46,592 | 46,592 | 3,947,846 | 24,391,430 |
| Sep 09, 2021 | 244,431 | 258,257 | 1,264,245 | 22,031,229 | Sep 08, 2022 | 375,918 | 422,510 | 842,989 | 24,858,501 |
| Sep 16, 2021 | 274,446 | 532,703 | 902,896 | 22,659,679 | Sep 15, 2022 | 522,535 | 945,045 | 446,364 | 24,782,330 |
| Sep 23, 2021 | 442,439 | 975,142 | 1,007,578 | 23,224,818 | Sep 22, 2022 | 269,208 | 1,214,253 | 1,003,017 | 25,516,139 |
| Sep 30, 2021 | 869,532 | 1,844,674 | 971,226 | 23,326,512 | Sep 29, 2022 | 574,130 | 1,788,383 | 733,706 | 25,675,715 |
| Oct 07, 2021 | 1,713,814 | 3,558,488 | 1,147,834 | 22,760,532 | Oct 06, 2022 | 887,954 | 2,676,337 | 724,405 | 25,512,166 |
| Oct 14, 2021 | 2,080,011 | 5,638,499 | 2,751,109 | 23,431,630 | Oct 13, 2022 | 1,813,956 | 4,490,293 | 2,252,726 | 25,950,936 |
| Oct 21, 2021 | 2,292,320 | 7,930,819 | 1,069,926 | 22,209,236 | Oct 20, 2022 | 2,748,615 | 7,238,908 | 1,026,381 | 24,228,702 |
| Oct 28, 2021 | 2,650,461 | 10,581,280 | 1,863,912 | 21,422,687 | Oct 27, 2022 | 2,582,254 | 9,821,162 | 760,621 | 22,407,069 |
| Nov 04, 2021 | 3,631,691 | 14,212,971 | 1,219,393 | 19,010,389 | Nov 03, 2022 | 2,612,700 | 12,433,862 | 655,229 | 20,449,598 |
| Nov 11, 2021 | 2,277,318 | 16,490,289 | 1,315,805 | 18,048,876 | Nov 10, 2022 | 2,012,048 | 14,445,910 | 2,960,367 | 21,397,917 |
| Nov 18, 2021 | 2,252,978 | 18,743,267 | 1,564,459 | 17,360,357 | Nov 17, 2022 | 2,352,673 | 16,798,583 | 610,215 | 19,655,459 |
| Nov 25, 2021 | 2,327,104 | 21,070,371 | 1,063,405 | 16,096,658 | Nov 24, 2022 | 2,046,570 | 18,845,153 | 623,363 | 18,232,252 |
| Dec 02, 2021 | 2,368,983 | 23,439,354 | 1,572,957 | 15,300,632 | Dec 01, 2022 | 2,247,641 | 21,092,794 | 1,716,221 | 17,700,832 |
| Dec 09, 2021 | 1,918,211 | 25,357,565 | 1,308,569 | 14,690,990 | Dec 08, 2022 | 1,846,026 | 22,938,820 | 2,943,405 | 18,798,211 |
| Dec 16, 2021 | 1,789,785 | 27,147,350 | 746,584 | 13,647,789 | Dec 15, 2022 | 1,918,361 | 24,857,181 | 664,844 | 17,544,694 |
| Dec 23, 2021 | 1,723,421 | 28,870,771 | 524,023 | 12,448,391 | Dec 22, 2022 | 1,705,947 | 26,563,128 | 563,257 | 16,402,004 |
| Dec 30, 2021 | 1,742,808 | 30,613,579 | 382,669 | 11,088,252 | Dec 29, 2022 | 1,478,296 | 28,041,424 | 720,997 | 15,644,705 |
| Jan 06, 2022 | 1,020,128 | 31,633,707 | 735,598 | 10,803,722 | Jan 05, 2023 | 1,620,720 | 29,662,144 | 717,415 | 14,741,400 |
| Jan 13, 2022 | 1,804,625 | 33,438,332 | 671,001 | 9,670,098 | Jan 12, 2023 | 2,066,189 | 31,728,333 | 986,196 | 13,661,407 |
| Jan 20, 2022 | 1,594,116 | 35,032,448 | 1,025,545 | 9,101,527 | Jan 19, 2023 | 1,900,328 | 33,628,661 | 1,145,723 | 12,906,802 |
| Jan 27, 2022 | 1,262,916 | 36,295,364 | 1,029,525 | 8,868,136 | Jan 26, 2023 | 1,891,607 | 35,520,268 | 667,954 | 11,683,149 |
| Feb 03, 2022 | 1,301,447 | 37,596,811 | 1,596,208 | 9,162,897 | Feb 02, 2023 | 1,743,076 | 37,263,344 | 373,892 | 10,313,965 |
| Feb 10, 2022 | 1,168,442 | 38,765,253 | 1,317,229 | 9,311,684 | Feb 09, 2023 | 1,846,566 | 39,109,910 | 456,124 | 8,923,523 |
| Feb 17, 2022 | 1,260,085 | 40,025,338 | 1,232,513 | 9,284,112 | Feb 16, 2023 | 1,614,468 | 40,724,378 | 419,672 | 7,728,727 |
| Feb 24, 2022 | 750,961 | 40,776,299 | 857,029 | 9,390,180 | Feb 23, 2023 | 880,839 | 41,605,217 | 360,669 | 7,208,557 |
| Mar 03, 2022 | 834,852 | 41,611,151 | 2,204,290 | 10,759,618 | Mar 02, 2023 | | | | |
| Mar 10, 2022 | 714,324 | 42,325,475 | 1,253,181 | 11,298,475 | Mar 09, 2023 | | | | |
| Mar 17, 2022 | 549,224 | 42,874,699 | 412,213 | 11,161,464 | Mar 16, 2023 | | | | |
| Mar 24, 2022 | 614,184 | 43,488,883 | 1,249,803 | 11,797,083 | Mar 23, 2023 | | | | |
| Mar 31, 2022 | 832,798 | 44,321,681 | 800,746 | 11,765,031 | Mar 30, 2023 | | | | |
| Apr 07, 2022 | 806,538 | 45,128,219 | 548,913 | 11,507,406 | Apr 06, 2023 | | | | |
| Apr 14, 2022 | 889,017 | 46,017,236 | 460,244 | 11,078,633 | Apr 13, 2023 | | | | |
| Apr 21, 2022 | 710,878 | 46,728,114 | 481,317 | 10,849,072 | Apr 20, 2023 | | | | |
| Apr 28, 2022 | 563,689 | 47,291,803 | 734,613 | 11,019,996 | Apr 27, 2023 | | | | |
| May 05, 2022 | 471,736 | 47,763,539 | 143,699 | 10,691,959 | May 04, 2023 | | | | |
| May 12, 2022 | 957,153 | 48,720,692 | 752,689 | 10,487,495 | May 11, 2023 | | | | |
| May 19, 2022 | 473,505 | 49,194,197 | 210,840 | 10,224,830 | May 18, 2023 | | | | |
| May 26, 2022 | 406,344 | 49,600,541 | 111,557 | 9,930,043 | May 25, 2023 | | | | |
| Jun 02, 2022 | 476,544 | 50,008,669 | 429,945 | 9,883,444 | Jun 01, 2023 | | | | |
| Jun 09, 2022 | 708,669 | 50,717,338 | 317,157 | 9,491,932 | Jun 08, 2023 | | | | |
| Jun 16, 2022 | 494,055 | 51,142,868 | 29,348 | 9,027,225 | Jun 15, 2023 | | | | |
| Jun 23, 2022 | 517,693 | 51,660,561 | -120,175 | 8,389,357 | Jun 22, 2023 | | | | |
| Jun 30, 2022 | 504,880 | 52,101,382 | -160,035 | 7,724,442 | Jun 29, 2023 | | | | |
| Jul 07, 2022 | 440,944 | 52,473,540 | -362,885 | 6,920,613 | Jul 06, 2023 | | | | |
| Jul 14, 2022 | 499,879 | 52,973,419 | 203,465 | 6,624,199 | Jul 13, 2023 | | | | |
| Jul 21, 2022 | 395,394 | 53,368,813 | -58,596 | 6,170,209 | Jul 20, 2023 | | | | |
| Jul 28, 2022 | 527,605 | 53,896,418 | -11,005 | 5,631,599 | Jul 27, 2023 | | | | |
| Aug 04, 2022 | 894,474 | 54,790,892 | -66,710 | 4,670,415 | Aug 03, 2023 | | | | |
| Aug 11, 2022 | 691,092 | 55,481,984 | 96,892 | 4,076,215 | Aug 10, 2023 | | | | |
| Aug 18, 2022 | | 55,481,984 | | 4,076,215 | Aug 17, 2023 | | | | |
| Aug 25, 2022 | 1,282,779 | 56,764,763 | 222,910 | 3,016,346 | Aug 24, 2023 | | | | |
| Sep 01, 2022 | 424,085 | 57,188,848 | -112,470 | 2,479,791 | Aug 31, 2023 | | | | |

*Source: Foreign Agricultural Service, U.S. Department of Agriculture (FAS-USDA)*

# Stock Index Futures - U.S.

A stock index simply represents a basket of underlying stocks. Indexes can be either price-weighted or capitalization-weighted. In a price-weighted index, such as the Dow Jones Industrial Average, the individual stock prices are simply added up and then divided by a divisor, meaning that stocks with higher prices have a higher weighting in the index value. In a capitalization-weighted index, such as the Standard and Poor's 500 index, the weighting of each stock corresponds to the size of the company as determined by its capitalization (i.e., the total dollar value of its stock). Stock indexes cover a variety of different sectors. For example, the Dow Jones Industrial Average contains 30 blue-chip stocks that represent the industrial sector. The S&P 500 index includes 500 of the largest blue-chip U.S. companies. The NYSE index includes all the stocks that are traded at the New York Stock Exchange. The Nasdaq 100 includes the largest 100 companies that are traded on the Nasdaq Exchange. The most popular U.S. stock index futures contract is the E-mini S&P 500 futures contract, which is traded at the CME Group.

**Prices** – The S&P 500 index (Barchart.com symbol $SPX) posted an all-time high of 4818.62 in January 2022 on optimism that the easing of the Covid pandemic would bolster the global economy. However, stocks ratcheted lower the remainder of the year as soaring inflation prompted the Federal Reserve (Fed) to aggressively raise interest rates. As a result, the S&P 500 finished 2022 down by -19% yr/yr at 3839.50.

Stocks came under pressure in early 2022 after the Fed became concerned about mounting inflation pressures. Fed Chair Powell signaled at the January FOMC meeting that the Fed would begin raising interest rates at the March policy meeting.

Stocks fell further in February 2022 after Russia invaded Ukraine. The U.S. and its allies immediately imposed sanctions on Russian goods, which sent commodity prices soaring and sparked fears that inflation would undercut economic growth and corporate earnings.

Soaring inflation led to sharply higher interest rates through Q2 of 2022, which weighed on stocks. The U.S. CPI in June 2022 surged to a 41-year high of 9.1% yr/yr. The Fed began raising interest rates with a 25 basis point rate hike in March and then increased the pace to a 50 basis point rate hike in May and a 75 basis point hike in June. The 10-year T-note yield soared to an 11-year high of 3.497% in June.

Stocks staged a countertrend rally from June into August of 2022, on hopes that the strength of the U.S. economy would allow the Fed to navigate a soft landing. However, market sentiment soured as the Fed remained hawkish, and stocks sold off into October, with the S&P 500 falling to a 2-year low of 3491.58.

T-note yields surged as the FOMC raised the federal funds target range by 75 basis points for four consecutive meetings from June through November. The 10-year T-note yield climbed to a 15-year high of 4.335% in October.

The S&P 500 recovered into year-end as inflation eased and the Fed slowed the pace of its rate-hike regime. The FOMC, at its December meeting, raised the federal funds target range by 50 basis points to 4.25%-4.50%. Also, the economy held up well due to a strong labor market, with the U.S. December unemployment rate at a 54-year low of 3.5%. In addition, after contracting in the first half of 2022, U.S. GDP expanded at a 3.2% (q/q annualized) pace in Q3 and at a 2.7% pace in Q4-2022.

Earnings growth for the S&P 500 companies slowed throughout 2022. Quarterly S&P earnings growth in Q1-2022 slowed to +11.4% yr/yr from 32.1% in Q4-2021. S&P earnings growth then slowed further to 8.4% in Q2 and 4.4% in Q3. By Q4, earnings growth turned negative to -3.2% yr/yr. On a calendar year basis, S&P 500 earnings in 2022 slowed to +4.8% yr/yr from +52% in 2021.

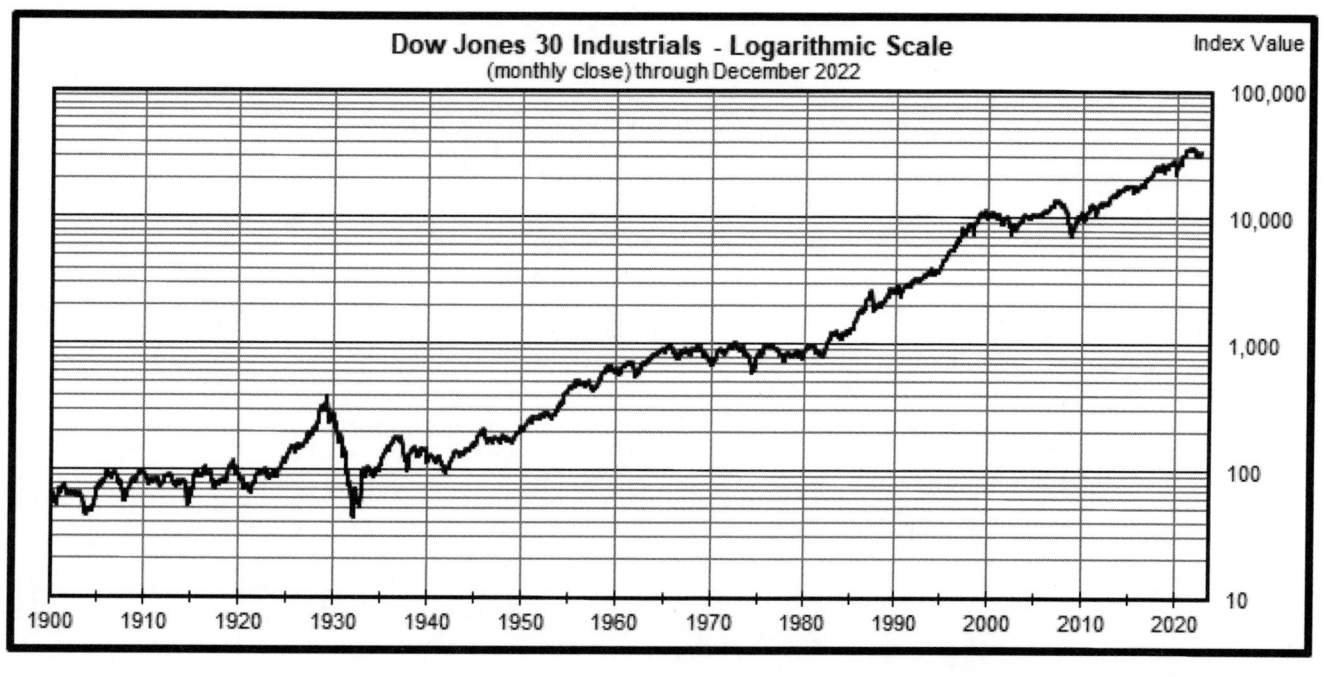

# STOCK INDEX FUTURES - U.S.

## Composite Index of Leading Indicators  (1992 = 100)

| Year | Jan. | Feb. | Mar. | Apr. | May | June | July | Aug. | Sept. | Oct. | Nov. | Dec. | Average |
|---|---|---|---|---|---|---|---|---|---|---|---|---|---|
| 2006 | 104.7 | 104.4 | 104.6 | 104.4 | 103.7 | 103.9 | 103.7 | 103.3 | 103.7 | 103.9 | 103.8 | 104.4 | 104.0 |
| 2007 | 104.0 | 103.7 | 104.1 | 103.9 | 104.0 | 103.9 | 104.6 | 103.6 | 103.7 | 103.2 | 102.8 | 102.6 | 103.7 |
| 2008 | 102.1 | 101.9 | 101.9 | 102.0 | 101.9 | 101.9 | 101.2 | 100.3 | 100.3 | 99.4 | 99.0 | 98.8 | 100.9 |
| 2009 | 98.8 | 98.3 | 98.1 | 99.2 | 100.6 | 101.3 | 102.5 | 103.1 | 104.2 | 104.7 | 105.8 | 106.2 | 101.9 |
| 2010 | 106.7 | 107.2 | 108.6 | 108.6 | 109.0 | 108.8 | 109.0 | 109.1 | 109.9 | 110.1 | 111.4 | 112.3 | 109.2 |
| 2011 | 91.8 | 92.7 | 93.7 | 93.7 | 94.2 | 94.2 | 94.4 | 93.7 | 93.2 | 93.8 | 94.1 | 92.2 | 93.5 |
| 2012 | 92.2 | 92.9 | 93.1 | 92.9 | 93.3 | 92.7 | 93.1 | 92.7 | 93.2 | 93.4 | 93.4 | 94.3 | 93.1 |
| 2013 | 94.8 | 95.3 | 95.1 | 95.8 | 96.0 | 96.1 | 96.5 | 97.2 | 98.2 | 98.5 | 99.4 | 113.8 | 98.1 |
| 2014 | 113.7 | 114.3 | 115.4 | 115.8 | 116.5 | 117.2 | 118.4 | 118.5 | 119.2 | 119.9 | 120.5 | 121.0 | 117.5 |
| 2015[1] | 121.2 | 120.9 | 121.2 | 121.9 | 122.9 | 123.6 | Discontinued | | | | | | 122.0 |

[1] Preliminary.  Source: The Conference Board

## Consumer Confidence, The Conference Board  (2004 = 100)

| Year | Jan. | Feb. | Mar. | Apr. | May | June | July | Aug. | Sept. | Oct. | Nov. | Dec. | Average |
|---|---|---|---|---|---|---|---|---|---|---|---|---|---|
| 2006 | 106.8 | 102.7 | 107.5 | 109.8 | 104.7 | 105.4 | 107.0 | 100.2 | 105.9 | 105.1 | 105.3 | 110.0 | 105.9 |
| 2007 | 110.2 | 111.2 | 108.2 | 106.3 | 108.5 | 105.3 | 111.9 | 105.6 | 99.5 | 95.2 | 87.8 | 90.6 | 103.4 |
| 2008 | 87.3 | 76.4 | 65.9 | 62.8 | 58.1 | 51.0 | 51.9 | 58.5 | 61.4 | 38.8 | 44.7 | 38.6 | 58.0 |
| 2009 | 37.4 | 25.3 | 26.9 | 40.8 | 54.8 | 49.3 | 47.4 | 54.5 | 53.4 | 48.7 | 50.6 | 53.6 | 45.2 |
| 2010 | 56.5 | 46.4 | 52.3 | 57.7 | 62.7 | 54.3 | 51.0 | 53.2 | 48.6 | 49.9 | 57.8 | 63.4 | 54.5 |
| 2011 | 64.8 | 72.0 | 63.8 | 66.0 | 61.7 | 57.6 | 59.2 | 45.2 | 46.4 | 40.9 | 55.2 | 64.8 | 58.1 |
| 2012 | 61.5 | 71.6 | 69.5 | 68.7 | 64.4 | 62.7 | 65.4 | 61.3 | 68.4 | 73.1 | 71.5 | 66.7 | 67.1 |
| 2013 | 58.4 | 68.0 | 61.9 | 69.0 | 74.3 | 82.1 | 81.0 | 81.8 | 80.2 | 72.4 | 72.0 | 77.5 | 73.2 |
| 2014 | 79.4 | 78.3 | 83.9 | 81.7 | 82.2 | 86.4 | 90.3 | 93.4 | 89.0 | 94.1 | 91.0 | 93.1 | 86.9 |
| 2015[1] | 103.8 | 98.8 | 101.4 | 94.3 | 94.6 | 101.4 | Discontinued | | | | | | 99.1 |

[1] Preliminary.  Source: The Conference Board (TCB) Copyrighted.

## Capacity Utilization Rates (Total Industry)  In Percent

| Year | Jan. | Feb. | Mar. | Apr. | May | June | July | Aug. | Sept. | Oct. | Nov. | Dec. | Average |
|---|---|---|---|---|---|---|---|---|---|---|---|---|---|
| 2013 | 77.1 | 77.4 | 77.6 | 77.5 | 77.4 | 77.5 | 77.1 | 77.6 | 77.9 | 77.7 | 77.9 | 78.1 | 77.6 |
| 2014 | 77.6 | 78.2 | 78.9 | 78.9 | 79.1 | 79.2 | 79.2 | 79.1 | 79.2 | 79.1 | 79.6 | 79.4 | 79.0 |
| 2015 | 78.8 | 78.4 | 78.1 | 77.7 | 77.3 | 76.9 | 77.3 | 77.2 | 76.9 | 76.6 | 76.1 | 75.7 | 77.3 |
| 2016 | 75.9 | 75.3 | 74.7 | 74.7 | 74.6 | 74.9 | 75.1 | 75.0 | 74.9 | 75.0 | 74.9 | 75.5 | 75.0 |
| 2017 | 75.5 | 75.2 | 75.7 | 76.4 | 76.5 | 76.6 | 76.5 | 76.2 | 76.1 | 77.3 | 77.6 | 77.9 | 76.5 |
| 2018 | 78.0 | 78.3 | 78.8 | 79.7 | 79.0 | 79.6 | 79.8 | 80.3 | 80.3 | 80.1 | 80.0 | 79.9 | 79.5 |
| 2019 | 79.4 | 78.9 | 78.9 | 78.5 | 78.5 | 78.5 | 78.1 | 78.5 | 78.2 | 77.5 | 77.7 | 77.4 | 78.3 |
| 2020 | 77.0 | 77.3 | 74.3 | 64.5 | 65.6 | 69.8 | 72.5 | 73.3 | 73.3 | 74.0 | 74.4 | 75.3 | 72.6 |
| 2021 | 76.4 | 74.2 | 76.3 | 76.6 | 77.3 | 77.7 | 78.2 | 78.2 | 77.4 | 78.6 | 79.0 | 78.7 | 77.4 |
| 2022[1] | 78.9 | 79.4 | 79.8 | 80.2 | 80.0 | 79.7 | 80.0 | 79.8 | 79.9 | 79.8 | 79.3 | 78.4 | 79.6 |

[1] Preliminary.  Source: Bureau of Economic Analysis, U.S. Department of Commerce (BEA)

## Manufacturers New Orders, Durable Goods  In Millions of Constant Dollars

| Year | Jan. | Feb. | Mar. | Apr. | May | June | July | Aug. | Sept. | Oct. | Nov. | Dec. | Average |
|---|---|---|---|---|---|---|---|---|---|---|---|---|---|
| 2013 | 216,919 | 229,202 | 211,757 | 220,286 | 231,193 | 240,895 | 215,452 | 221,749 | 231,395 | 224,605 | 238,295 | 230,735 | 226,040 |
| 2014 | 221,898 | 229,822 | 233,750 | 236,290 | 232,665 | 238,124 | 290,709 | 238,736 | 235,647 | 230,525 | 228,416 | 223,741 | 236,694 |
| 2015 | 226,806 | 219,304 | 230,337 | 226,960 | 220,679 | 233,102 | 231,512 | 227,210 | 221,142 | 227,110 | 225,927 | 220,920 | 225,917 |
| 2016 | 226,398 | 217,882 | 216,926 | 225,797 | 220,851 | 208,990 | 216,738 | 220,654 | 219,736 | 231,303 | 219,574 | 224,108 | 220,746 |
| 2017 | 223,049 | 222,023 | 228,253 | 228,086 | 227,201 | 243,829 | 224,989 | 229,906 | 242,818 | 235,856 | 238,976 | 245,755 | 232,562 |
| 2018 | 225,906 | 234,140 | 242,658 | 239,492 | 240,608 | 243,274 | 234,585 | 244,108 | 244,834 | 239,723 | 231,653 | 238,448 | 238,286 |
| 2019 | 229,028 | 223,455 | 233,044 | 223,929 | 217,479 | 219,553 | 225,239 | 224,546 | 221,949 | 222,975 | 212,779 | 215,324 | 222,442 |
| 2020 | 225,551 | 231,488 | 200,119 | 159,130 | 179,384 | 198,774 | 218,041 | 221,086 | 225,593 | 229,735 | 228,470 | 231,460 | 212,403 |
| 2021 | 237,284 | 237,479 | 241,392 | 236,566 | 241,545 | 245,826 | 246,741 | 250,577 | 246,849 | 250,503 | 254,074 | 256,464 | 245,442 |
| 2022[1] | 264,356 | 262,494 | 264,258 | 265,376 | 267,533 | 273,571 | 273,203 | 273,841 | 274,399 | 276,366 | 271,403 | 285,249 | 271,004 |

[1] Preliminary.  Source: Bureau of Economic Analysis, U.S. Department of Commerce (BEA)

## Corporate Profits After Tax -- Quarterly  In Billions of Dollars

| Year | First Quarter | Second Quarter | Third Quarter | Fourth Quarter | Total | Year | First Quarter | Second Quarter | Third Quarter | Fourth Quarter | Total |
|---|---|---|---|---|---|---|---|---|---|---|---|
| 2011 | 1,385.2 | 1,506.6 | 1,562.1 | 1,662.1 | 1,529.0 | 2017 | 1,791.4 | 1,803.7 | 1,845.1 | 1,884.6 | 1,831.2 |
| 2012 | 1,705.7 | 1,672.7 | 1,643.7 | 1,629.2 | 1,662.8 | 2018 | 1,968.3 | 1,972.7 | 2,028.4 | 2,087.6 | 2,014.3 |
| 2013 | 1,622.8 | 1,643.1 | 1,646.4 | 1,680.0 | 1,648.1 | 2019 | 2,051.0 | 2,115.3 | 2,130.0 | 2,122.7 | 2,104.7 |
| 2014 | 1,563.7 | 1,712.5 | 1,793.1 | 1,783.3 | 1,713.1 | 2020 | 1,965.9 | 1,746.1 | 2,154.3 | 2,018.5 | 1,971.2 |
| 2015 | 1,706.9 | 1,689.2 | 1,675.6 | 1,585.2 | 1,664.2 | 2021 | 2,237.4 | 2,401.7 | 2,456.4 | 2,435.9 | 2,382.8 |
| 2016 | 1,664.9 | 1,624.2 | 1,649.9 | 1,707.0 | 1,661.5 | 2022[1] | 2,374.6 | 2,522.6 | 2,543.0 | | 2,480.0 |

[1] Preliminary.  Source: Bureau of Economic Analysis, U.S. Department of Commerce (BEA)

# STOCK INDEX FUTURES - U.S.

### Change in Manufacturing and Trade Inventories    In Billions of Dollars

| Year | Jan. | Feb. | Mar. | Apr. | May | June | July | Aug. | Sept. | Oct. | Nov. | Dec. | Average |
|---|---|---|---|---|---|---|---|---|---|---|---|---|---|
| 2006 | 85.9 | -49.7 | 129.5 | 82.7 | 169.3 | 169.3 | 92.2 | 93.2 | 65.9 | 22.9 | 28.3 | 4.2 | 85.2 |
| 2007 | 37.8 | 43.6 | -17.0 | 59.5 | 68.1 | 55.0 | 75.6 | 62.7 | 87.7 | 23.8 | 53.3 | 96.3 | 53.4 |
| 2008 | 169.4 | 78.5 | 35.6 | 81.4 | 66.2 | 133.3 | 202.6 | 34.8 | -64.9 | -99.6 | | -250.0 | 35.2 |
| 2009 | -170.2 | -188.5 | -232.1 | -197.4 | -196.7 | -218.1 | -159.1 | -232.5 | -46.8 | 59.8 | 75.6 | -14.9 | -126.7 |
| 2010 | 27.9 | 104.4 | 95.5 | 95.3 | 54.9 | 136.3 | 173.2 | 139.3 | 179.6 | 190.5 | 63.3 | 173.4 | 119.5 |
| 2011 | 167.1 | 129.1 | 226.8 | 154.7 | 184.1 | 50.0 | 75.1 | 114.0 | -26.5 | 158.7 | 69.4 | 79.7 | 115.2 |
| 2012 | 139.9 | 118.4 | 47.8 | 46.5 | 56.8 | 27.0 | 128.1 | 85.0 | 118.2 | 60.8 | 37.4 | 33.6 | 75.0 |
| 2013 | 205.4 | 30.2 | -18.8 | 66.4 | -1.8 | 17.5 | 62.3 | 71.5 | 117.8 | 137.2 | 95.7 | 82.0 | 72.1 |
| 2014 | 65.6 | 74.8 | 82.9 | 124.5 | 104.5 | 64.6 | 70.8 | 32.9 | 54.1 | 52.7 | 20.9 | 15.3 | 63.6 |
| 2015[1] | -29.5 | 57.0 | 25.4 | 83.8 | 59.8 | Discontinued | | | | | | | 39.3 |

[1] Preliminary.    Source: Bureau of Economic Analysis, U.S. Department of Commerce (BEA)

### Productivity: Index of Output per Hour, All Persons, Nonfarm Business -- Quarterly    (1992 = 100)

| Year | First Quarter | Second Quarter | Third Quarter | Fourth Quarter | Total | Year | First Quarter | Second Quarter | Third Quarter | Fourth Quarter | Total |
|---|---|---|---|---|---|---|---|---|---|---|---|
| 2011 | 99.3 | 99.3 | 99.0 | 99.6 | 99.3 | 2017 | 103.6 | 103.5 | 104.6 | 105.0 | 104.2 |
| 2012 | 100.0 | 100.5 | 100.3 | 99.9 | 100.1 | 2018 | 105.3 | 105.7 | 106.1 | 105.9 | 105.8 |
| 2013 | 100.4 | 100.0 | 100.5 | 101.3 | 100.6 | 2019 | 106.8 | 107.5 | 108.1 | 108.7 | 107.8 |
| 2014 | 100.3 | 101.1 | 102.0 | 101.4 | 101.2 | 2020 | 108.6 | 113.0 | 114.8 | 113.7 | 112.5 |
| 2015 | 102.1 | 102.5 | 102.8 | 102.2 | 102.4 | 2021 | 114.7 | 115.4 | 114.5 | 115.3 | 115.0 |
| 2016 | 102.5 | 102.5 | 103.0 | 103.6 | 102.9 | 2022[1] | 113.5 | 112.5 | 112.8 | 113.3 | 113.0 |

[1] Preliminary.    Source: Bureau of Economic Analysis, U.S. Department of Commerce (BEA)

### Civilian Unemployment Rate - U3

| Year | Jan. | Feb. | Mar. | Apr. | May | June | July | Aug. | Sept. | Oct. | Nov. | Dec. | Average |
|---|---|---|---|---|---|---|---|---|---|---|---|---|---|
| 2013 | 7.9 | 7.7 | 7.5 | 7.5 | 7.5 | 7.5 | 7.3 | 7.2 | 7.2 | 7.2 | 7.0 | 6.7 | 7.4 |
| 2014 | 6.6 | 6.7 | 6.6 | 6.2 | 6.3 | 6.1 | 6.2 | 6.1 | 5.9 | 5.7 | 5.8 | 5.6 | 6.2 |
| 2015 | 5.7 | 5.5 | 5.4 | 5.4 | 5.5 | 5.3 | 5.2 | 5.1 | 5.0 | 5.0 | 5.0 | 5.0 | 5.3 |
| 2016 | 4.9 | 4.9 | 5.0 | 5.0 | 4.7 | 4.9 | 4.9 | 4.9 | 4.9 | 4.8 | 4.6 | 4.7 | 4.9 |
| 2017 | 4.8 | 4.7 | 4.5 | 4.4 | 4.3 | 4.4 | 4.3 | 4.4 | 4.2 | 4.1 | 4.1 | 4.1 | 4.4 |
| 2018 | 4.1 | 4.1 | 4.1 | 3.9 | 3.8 | 4.0 | 3.9 | 3.8 | 3.7 | 3.8 | 3.7 | 3.9 | 3.9 |
| 2019 | 4.0 | 3.8 | 3.8 | 3.6 | 3.6 | 3.7 | 3.7 | 3.7 | 3.5 | 3.6 | 3.5 | 3.5 | 3.7 |
| 2020 | 3.5 | 3.6 | 4.4 | 14.7 | 13.3 | 11.1 | 10.2 | 8.4 | 7.9 | 6.9 | 6.7 | 6.7 | 8.1 |
| 2021 | 6.3 | 6.2 | 6.0 | 6.1 | 5.8 | 5.9 | 5.4 | 5.2 | 4.7 | 4.6 | 4.2 | 3.9 | 5.4 |
| 2022[1] | 4.0 | 3.8 | 3.6 | 3.6 | 3.6 | 3.6 | 3.5 | 3.7 | 3.5 | 3.7 | 3.6 | 3.5 | 3.6 |

[1] Preliminary.    Source: Bureau of Economic Analysis, U.S. Department of Commerce (BEA)

**S&P 500 Index - Logarithmic Scale**
(monthly close) through December 2022

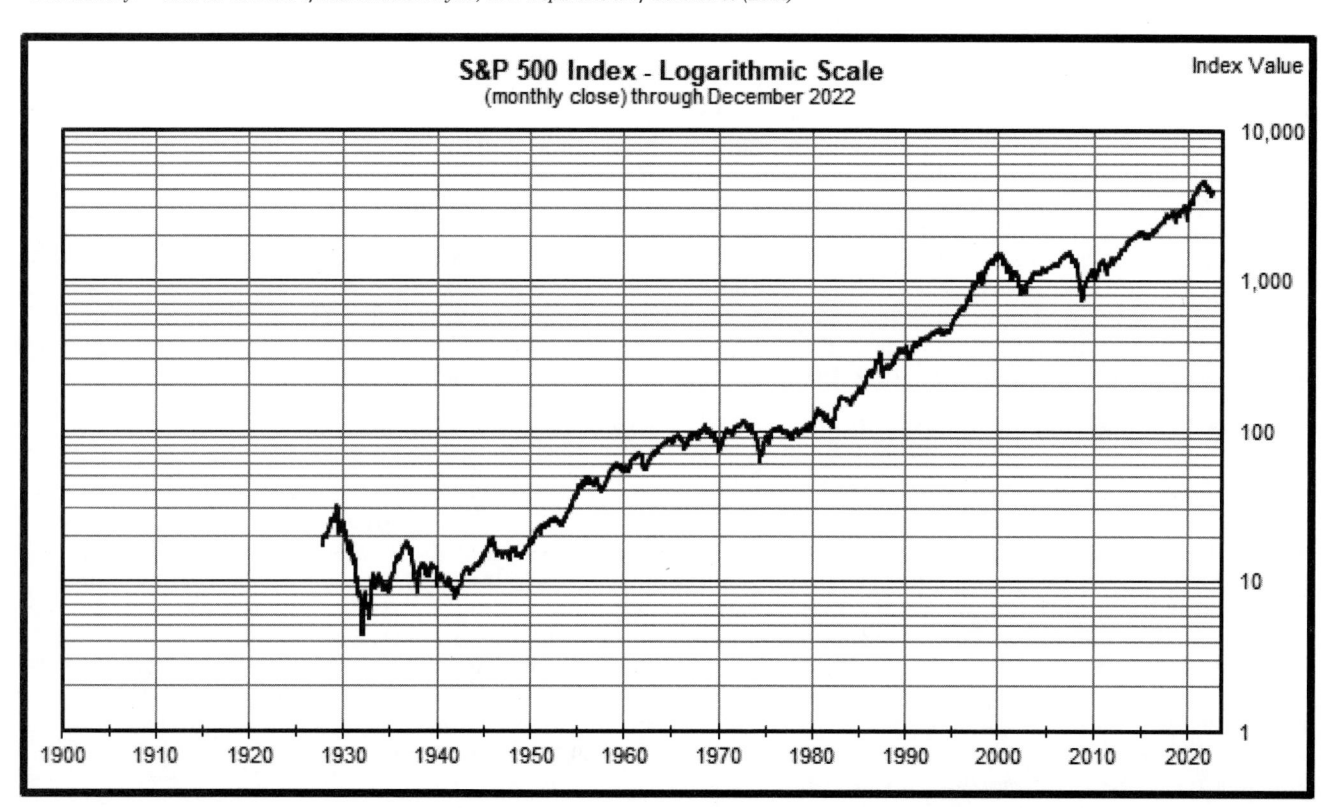

# STOCK INDEX FUTURES - U.S.

**DOW JONES INDUSTRIALS**
Weekly Cash as of 03/31/2023

Chart High 36952.65 on 01/05/2022
Chart Low 12035.09 on 06/04/2012

"Dow Jones", "The Dow", "Dow Jones Industrial Average" and "DJIA" are service marks of Dow Jones & Company, Inc.    Shaded areas indicate US recessions.

### Average Value of Dow Jones Industrials Index (30 Stocks)

| Year | Jan. | Feb. | Mar. | Apr. | May | June | July | Aug. | Sept. | Oct. | Nov. | Dec. | Average |
|---|---|---|---|---|---|---|---|---|---|---|---|---|---|
| 2013 | 13,615.3 | 13,967.3 | 14,418.3 | 14,675.9 | 15,172.2 | 15,035.8 | 15,390.2 | 15,195.3 | 15,269.8 | 15,289.8 | 15,870.8 | 16,095.8 | 14,999.7 |
| 2014 | 16,243.6 | 15,958.4 | 16,308.6 | 16,399.5 | 16,567.3 | 16,843.8 | 16,988.3 | 16,775.2 | 17,098.1 | 16,701.9 | 17,649.0 | 17,754.2 | 16,774.0 |
| 2015 | 17,542.3 | 17,945.4 | 17,931.7 | 17,970.5 | 18,124.7 | 17,927.2 | 17,795.0 | 17,061.6 | 16,340.0 | 17,182.3 | 17,723.8 | 17,542.9 | 17,590.6 |
| 2016 | 16,305.3 | 16,299.9 | 17,302.1 | 17,844.4 | 17,692.3 | 17,754.9 | 18,341.2 | 18,495.2 | 18,267.4 | 18,184.6 | 18,697.3 | 19,712.4 | 17,908.1 |
| 2017 | 19,908.2 | 20,424.1 | 20,823.1 | 20,684.7 | 20,936.8 | 21,317.8 | 21,581.3 | 21,914.1 | 22,173.4 | 23,036.2 | 23,557.9 | 24,545.4 | 21,741.9 |
| 2018 | 25,804.0 | 24,981.5 | 24,582.2 | 24,304.2 | 24,572.5 | 24,790.1 | 24,978.2 | 25,630.0 | 26,232.7 | 25,609.3 | 25,258.7 | 23,805.5 | 25,045.8 |
| 2019 | 24,157.8 | 25,605.5 | 25,722.6 | 26,401.6 | 25,744.8 | 26,160.1 | 27,089.2 | 26,057.8 | 26,900.2 | 26,736.8 | 27,797.1 | 28,167.0 | 26,378.4 |
| 2020 | 28,880.0 | 28,519.7 | 22,637.4 | 23,293.9 | 24,271.0 | 26,062.3 | 26,385.8 | 27,821.4 | 27,733.4 | 28,005.1 | 29,124.0 | 30,148.6 | 26,906.9 |
| 2021 | 30,821.4 | 31,283.9 | 32,373.3 | 33,803.3 | 34,270.3 | 34,289.9 | 34,798.8 | 35,244.0 | 34,688.4 | 35,055.5 | 35,848.6 | 35,641.3 | 34,009.9 |
| 2022 | 35,456.2 | 34,648.5 | 34,029.7 | 34,315.0 | 32,379.5 | 31,446.7 | 31,535.3 | 33,009.6 | 30,649.6 | 30,570.7 | 33,418.0 | 33,482.3 | 32,911.7 |

*Source: New York Stock Exchange (NYSE)*

### Volume of Trading of Mini Dow Jones Industrials Index Futures in Chicago    In Thousands of Contracts

| Year | Jan. | Feb. | Mar. | Apr. | May | June | July | Aug. | Sept. | Oct. | Nov. | Dec. | Total |
|---|---|---|---|---|---|---|---|---|---|---|---|---|---|
| 2013 | 2,143.3 | 2,525.2 | 3,044.9 | 3,417.8 | 3,212.1 | 4,386.6 | 2,492.1 | 2,820.5 | 2,934.8 | 3,480.8 | 2,494.0 | 2,496.7 | 35,448.8 |
| 2014 | 3,180.8 | 3,115.6 | 3,965.0 | 3,351.6 | 2,637.7 | 2,641.1 | 3,028.9 | 2,683.7 | 3,476.0 | 5,444.0 | 1,954.8 | 3,574.5 | 39,053.7 |
| 2015 | 4,146.7 | 2,343.8 | 3,126.0 | 2,988.1 | 2,558.3 | 3,546.6 | 3,063.7 | 4,651.2 | 4,649.7 | 3,226.2 | 2,566.1 | 3,734.5 | 40,601.1 |
| 2016 | 5,169.8 | 4,307.1 | 3,300.6 | 3,164.9 | 3,083.4 | 4,152.0 | 2,600.0 | 2,641.6 | 4,047.4 | 3,274.0 | 3,887.6 | 2,927.5 | 42,555.9 |
| 2017 | 2,515.6 | 2,343.6 | 3,891.9 | 2,722.0 | 2,564.0 | 3,465.6 | 2,132.3 | 2,858.2 | 2,672.1 | 2,144.2 | 2,707.7 | 2,849.1 | 32,866.3 |
| 2018 | 3,623.3 | 6,592.1 | 6,939.8 | 5,479.4 | 4,405.7 | 4,558.5 | 3,310.8 | 2,989.4 | 3,521.3 | 7,088.2 | 4,886.0 | 6,929.7 | 60,324.2 |
| 2019 | 4,900.8 | 3,651.9 | 4,927.9 | 3,353.4 | 5,889.6 | 4,224.5 | 3,566.3 | 5,763.7 | 3,868.9 | 3,924.5 | 2,713.2 | 3,593.0 | 50,377.7 |
| 2020 | 5,015.6 | 6,334.8 | 8,432.1 | 4,349.6 | 4,357.1 | 6,025.1 | 4,459.1 | 3,451.9 | 5,188.2 | 4,656.0 | 3,681.5 | 3,420.6 | 59,371.7 |
| 2021 | 3,761.1 | 3,493.0 | 5,203.9 | 2,927.1 | 3,438.6 | 3,440.8 | 3,244.2 | 2,973.8 | 4,520.8 | 3,651.7 | 3,527.1 | 4,222.6 | 44,404.7 |
| 2022 | 5,436.3 | 4,892.6 | 4,627.7 | 3,706.9 | 4,270.1 | 4,374.1 | 3,318.9 | 3,780.1 | 4,309.0 | 4,207.3 | 4,221.5 | 3,872.4 | 51,016.8 |

Contract value = $5.    *Source: Chicago Board of Trade (CBT)*

### Average Open Interest of Mini Dow Jones Industrials Index Futures in Chicago    In Contracts

| Year | Jan. | Feb. | Mar. | Apr. | May | June | July | Aug. | Sept. | Oct. | Nov. | Dec. |
|---|---|---|---|---|---|---|---|---|---|---|---|---|
| 2013 | 104,630 | 122,311 | 131,290 | 114,419 | 118,633 | 113,230 | 113,658 | 115,707 | 119,479 | 106,434 | 131,168 | 134,255 |
| 2014 | 127,534 | 114,491 | 134,383 | 119,028 | 127,150 | 131,818 | 124,601 | 115,822 | 140,265 | 119,716 | 139,521 | 135,980 |
| 2015 | 106,993 | 111,350 | 109,677 | 104,565 | 112,992 | 110,880 | 92,351 | 93,151 | 77,209 | 75,595 | 100,777 | 98,535 |
| 2016 | 65,416 | 62,194 | 83,643 | 117,857 | 119,596 | 122,482 | 120,095 | 144,885 | 135,208 | 120,288 | 127,896 | 140,802 |
| 2017 | 131,853 | 130,492 | 145,630 | 130,214 | 121,956 | 129,328 | 131,569 | 149,149 | 159,249 | 157,990 | 155,973 | 154,854 |
| 2018 | 153,793 | 126,347 | 118,343 | 100,414 | 102,356 | 96,326 | 87,601 | 100,558 | 112,896 | 95,850 | 80,908 | 80,929 |
| 2019 | 77,165 | 83,432 | 85,168 | 80,534 | 79,824 | 80,412 | 91,970 | 90,051 | 100,267 | 105,282 | 112,609 | 108,479 |
| 2020 | 102,791 | 102,595 | 75,348 | 60,895 | 71,735 | 79,524 | 78,506 | 90,866 | 76,430 | 91,547 | 94,005 | 94,361 |
| 2021 | 88,108 | 95,365 | 94,672 | 92,836 | 97,114 | 109,248 | 106,382 | 110,073 | 106,144 | 103,990 | 104,634 | 102,108 |
| 2022 | 94,070 | 81,108 | 74,789 | 74,225 | 83,020 | 77,368 | 69,484 | 77,446 | 72,973 | 69,519 | 76,463 | 83,216 |

Contract value = $5.    *Source: Chicago Board of Trade (CBT)*

# STOCK INDEX FUTURES - U.S.

**S&P 500 INDEX**
Weekly Cash as of 03/31/2023

WEEKLY CASH
As of 03/31/2023
Chart High 4818.62 on 01/04/2022
Chart Low 1266.74 on 06/04/2012

The S&P 500® Index is a trademark of The McGraw-Hill Companies, Inc. Shaded areas indicate US recessions.

## Average Value of Standard & Poor's 500 Index

| Year | Jan. | Feb. | Mar. | Apr. | May | June | July | Aug. | Sept. | Oct. | Nov. | Dec. | Average |
|---|---|---|---|---|---|---|---|---|---|---|---|---|---|
| 2013 | 1,480.4 | 1,512.3 | 1,550.8 | 1,570.7 | 1,639.8 | 1,618.8 | 1,668.7 | 1,670.1 | 1,687.2 | 1,720.1 | 1,783.5 | 1,807.8 | 1,642.5 |
| 2014 | 1,822.4 | 1,817.0 | 1,863.5 | 1,864.3 | 1,889.8 | 1,947.1 | 1,973.1 | 1,961.5 | 1,993.2 | 1,937.3 | 2,044.6 | 2,054.3 | 1,930.7 |
| 2015 | 2,028.2 | 2,082.2 | 2,080.0 | 2,094.9 | 2,111.9 | 2,099.3 | 2,094.1 | 2,039.9 | 1,944.4 | 2,024.8 | 2,080.6 | 2,054.1 | 2,061.2 |
| 2016 | 1,918.6 | 1,904.4 | 2,022.0 | 2,075.5 | 2,065.6 | 2,083.9 | 2,148.9 | 2,177.5 | 2,157.7 | 2,143.0 | 2,165.0 | 2,246.6 | 2,092.4 |
| 2017 | 2,275.1 | 2,329.9 | 2,366.8 | 2,359.3 | 2,395.4 | 2,434.0 | 2,454.1 | 2,456.2 | 2,492.8 | 2,557.0 | 2,593.6 | 2,664.3 | 2,448.2 |
| 2018 | 2,789.8 | 2,705.2 | 2,702.8 | 2,653.6 | 2,701.5 | 2,754.4 | 2,793.6 | 2,857.8 | 2,901.5 | 2,785.5 | 2,723.2 | 2,567.3 | 2,744.7 |
| 2019 | 2,607.4 | 2,754.9 | 2,804.0 | 2,903.8 | 2,854.7 | 2,890.2 | 2,996.1 | 2,897.5 | 2,982.2 | 2,977.7 | 3,104.9 | 3,176.8 | 2,912.5 |
| 2020 | 3,278.2 | 3,277.3 | 2,652.4 | 2,762.0 | 2,919.6 | 3,104.7 | 3,207.6 | 3,391.7 | 3,365.5 | 3,418.7 | 3,549.0 | 3,695.3 | 3,218.5 |
| 2021 | 3,793.8 | 3,883.4 | 3,910.5 | 4,141.2 | 4,167.9 | 4,238.5 | 4,363.7 | 4,454.2 | 4,445.5 | 4,460.7 | 4,667.4 | 4,674.8 | 4,266.8 |
| 2022 | 4,573.8 | 4,436.0 | 4,391.3 | 4,391.3 | 4,040.4 | 3,899.0 | 3,911.7 | 4,158.6 | 3,850.5 | 3,726.1 | 3,917.5 | 3,912.4 | 4,100.7 |

Source: Index and Option Market (IOM), division of the Chicago Mercantile Exchange (CME)

## Volume of Trading of E-mini S&P 500 Stock Index Futures in Chicago    In Thousands of Contracts

| Year | Jan. | Feb. | Mar. | Apr. | May | June | July | Aug. | Sept. | Oct. | Nov. | Dec. | Total |
|---|---|---|---|---|---|---|---|---|---|---|---|---|---|
| 2013 | 30,743 | 35,953 | 43,787 | 41,242 | 41,901 | 52,896 | 29,323 | 34,906 | 39,752 | 39,069 | 28,689 | 34,028 | 452,291 |
| 2014 | 33,770 | 33,265 | 43,038 | 34,460 | 27,653 | 33,330 | 33,263 | 28,020 | 40,843 | 54,465 | 22,223 | 40,690 | 425,020 |
| 2015 | 38,362 | 25,643 | 38,949 | 26,801 | 24,516 | 39,037 | 32,990 | 46,325 | 48,962 | 36,264 | 28,643 | 43,312 | 429,803 |
| 2016 | 47,987 | 42,532 | 44,628 | 34,639 | 33,049 | 48,583 | 31,172 | 33,429 | 49,729 | 32,532 | 38,250 | 36,148 | 472,679 |
| 2017 | 28,663 | 26,871 | 43,248 | 27,397 | 28,105 | 40,315 | 22,213 | 32,605 | 33,473 | 24,444 | 27,662 | 30,604 | 365,602 |
| 2018 | 29,153 | 42,946 | 47,450 | 35,694 | 28,915 | 35,955 | 23,295 | 25,086 | 33,325 | 53,156 | 37,153 | 53,071 | 445,199 |
| 2019 | 33,983 | 25,491 | 38,615 | 23,894 | 41,914 | 36,451 | 25,475 | 44,708 | 35,370 | 31,055 | 23,059 | 35,129 | 395,144 |
| 2020 | 37,026 | 46,041 | 78,873 | 38,201 | 35,313 | 52,930 | 35,600 | 26,785 | 50,101 | 36,020 | 31,134 | 34,203 | 502,227 |
| 2021 | 30,235 | 29,958 | 50,906 | 28,565 | 32,577 | 32,498 | 28,690 | 25,059 | 41,991 | 29,063 | 29,498 | 44,600 | 403,640 |
| 2022 | 41,943 | 36,439 | 43,282 | 32,288 | 42,556 | 48,010 | 34,151 | 38,653 | 59,775 | 48,152 | 36,343 | 42,202 | 503,794 |

Contract value = $50.    Source: Index and Option Market (IOM), division of the Chicago Mercantile Exchange (CME)

## Average Open Interest of E-mini S&P 500 Stock Index Futures in Chicago    In Thousands of Contracts

| Year | Jan. | Feb. | Mar. | Apr. | May | June | July | Aug. | Sept. | Oct. | Nov. | Dec. |
|---|---|---|---|---|---|---|---|---|---|---|---|---|
| 2013 | 2,872.7 | 3,117.0 | 3,199.6 | 3,038.9 | 3,279.6 | 3,245.5 | 2,778.0 | 2,910.8 | 2,954.2 | 2,717.7 | 2,848.0 | 2,973.0 |
| 2014 | 2,865.8 | 3,123.2 | 3,283.5 | 2,800.4 | 2,949.6 | 3,160.0 | 2,946.3 | 2,985.7 | 3,153.2 | 2,821.8 | 2,990.2 | 3,025.6 |
| 2015 | 2,724.4 | 2,820.5 | 3,000.4 | 2,707.2 | 2,776.2 | 2,863.5 | 2,672.8 | 2,893.6 | 3,179.8 | 2,921.9 | 2,889.2 | 2,801.6 |
| 2016 | 2,792.2 | 3,072.3 | 3,109.5 | 2,863.7 | 2,884.5 | 3,056.9 | 2,971.7 | 2,971.2 | 3,115.3 | 2,960.2 | 2,985.0 | 2,989.9 |
| 2017 | 2,833.2 | 2,991.5 | 3,112.3 | 2,905.0 | 3,049.8 | 3,062.1 | 2,924.0 | 3,192.3 | 3,279.6 | 3,104.8 | 3,293.9 | 3,348.8 |
| 2018 | 3,310.8 | 3,366.2 | 3,200.3 | 3,017.3 | 3,081.8 | 2,985.4 | 2,745.8 | 2,833.8 | 2,950.5 | 2,887.7 | 2,993.6 | 3,024.4 |
| 2019 | 2,669.4 | 2,643.7 | 2,620.1 | 2,604.3 | 2,667.3 | 2,721.3 | 2,617.6 | 2,585.9 | 2,677.3 | 2,532.7 | 2,772.7 | 2,940.4 |
| 2020 | 2,737.3 | 2,820.8 | 3,584.9 | 3,415.4 | 3,232.2 | 3,077.7 | 2,637.2 | 2,720.0 | 2,664.9 | 2,452.8 | 2,492.2 | 2,666.4 |
| 2021 | 2,598.9 | 2,648.0 | 2,742.6 | 2,663.0 | 2,692.8 | 2,774.1 | 2,645.6 | 2,724.5 | 2,701.4 | 2,411.4 | 2,447.6 | 2,455.4 |
| 2022 | 2,331.1 | 2,298.7 | 2,320.7 | 2,157.0 | 2,252.6 | 2,358.4 | 2,322.8 | 2,333.5 | 2,319.2 | 2,310.4 | 2,322.0 | 2,181.2 |

Contract value = $50.    Source: Index and Option Market (IOM), division of the Chicago Mercantile Exchange (CME)

# STOCK INDEX FUTURES - U.S.

**NASDAQ 100 Index**
Weekly Cash as of 03/31/2023

WEEKLY CASH
As of 03/31/2023
Chart High 16764.86 on 11/22/2021
Chart Low 2423.24 on 01/24/2012

The NASDAQ 100® Index is a trademark of The Nasdaq Stock Market, Inc.   Shaded areas indicate US recessions.

## Average Value of NASDAQ 100 Index

| Year | Jan. | Feb. | Mar. | Apr. | May | June | July | Aug. | Sept. | Oct. | Nov. | Dec. | Average |
|---|---|---|---|---|---|---|---|---|---|---|---|---|---|
| 2013 | 2,736.9 | 2,748.2 | 2,795.3 | 2,818.6 | 2,981.2 | 2,937.3 | 3,033.0 | 3,105.5 | 3,187.5 | 3,292.0 | 3,399.5 | 3,513.8 | 3,045.7 |
| 2014 | 3,557.9 | 3,615.0 | 3,661.1 | 3,554.5 | 3,621.1 | 3,792.1 | 3,926.7 | 3,979.4 | 4,070.3 | 3,964.6 | 4,221.1 | 4,260.8 | 3,852.0 |
| 2015 | 4,182.6 | 4,343.5 | 4,389.2 | 4,418.9 | 4,476.4 | 4,481.7 | 4,528.3 | 4,422.3 | 4,261.6 | 4,445.5 | 4,653.2 | 4,628.0 | 4,435.9 |
| 2016 | 4,259.3 | 4,129.6 | 4,377.1 | 4,491.9 | 4,379.4 | 4,427.0 | 4,592.6 | 4,785.7 | 4,813.3 | 4,845.3 | 4,791.8 | 4,886.3 | 4,564.9 |
| 2017 | 5,056.8 | 5,261.2 | 5,386.2 | 5,447.9 | 5,687.4 | 5,767.0 | 5,816.1 | 5,874.4 | 5,954.9 | 6,088.5 | 6,328.2 | 6,398.0 | 5,755.5 |
| 2018 | 6,790.5 | 6,704.4 | 6,844.9 | 6,606.9 | 6,875.9 | 7,159.6 | 7,296.6 | 7,453.1 | 7,528.0 | 7,171.6 | 6,855.0 | 6,498.0 | 6,982.0 |
| 2019 | 6,619.8 | 7,021.1 | 7,254.2 | 7,660.6 | 7,481.0 | 7,505.2 | 7,897.8 | 7,619.8 | 7,814.0 | 7,859.7 | 8,284.4 | 8,527.4 | 7,628.7 |
| 2020 | 9,031.2 | 9,297.5 | 7,835.4 | 8,437.0 | 9,208.0 | 9,898.7 | 10,658.3 | 11,406.5 | 11,330.8 | 11,605.0 | 11,893.3 | 12,622.1 | 10,268.6 |
| 2021 | 13,048.1 | 13,473.8 | 12,900.2 | 13,832.3 | 13,470.8 | 14,064.5 | 14,849.7 | 15,173.0 | 15,315.1 | 15,143.7 | 16,237.2 | 16,135.4 | 14,470.3 |
| 2022 | 15,207.2 | 14,428.7 | 14,151.3 | 13,964.7 | 12,375.0 | 11,916.7 | 12,140.2 | 13,090.4 | 11,841.0 | 11,212.4 | 11,458.1 | 11,365.2 | 12,762.6 |

*Source: Index and Option Market (IOM), division of the Chicago Mercantile Exchange (CME)*

## Volume of Trading of E-mini NASDAQ 100 Index Futures in Chicago   In Thousands of Contracts

| Year | Jan. | Feb. | Mar. | Apr. | May | June | July | Aug. | Sept. | Oct. | Nov. | Dec. | Total |
|---|---|---|---|---|---|---|---|---|---|---|---|---|---|
| 2013 | 4,420.0 | 4,365.7 | 4,911.6 | 5,226.0 | 4,549.5 | 6,411.2 | 4,222.9 | 4,686.9 | 5,210.9 | 6,077.2 | 4,280.9 | 5,030.3 | 59,393.1 |
| 2014 | 5,641.0 | 5,236.1 | 7,514.0 | 7,765.8 | 5,541.1 | 5,252.7 | 5,305.9 | 4,774.4 | 7,103.7 | 10,105.5 | 4,013.9 | 7,229.6 | 75,483.7 |
| 2015 | 6,833.3 | 3,985.2 | 6,094.0 | 4,617.1 | 3,880.7 | 5,542.4 | 5,100.7 | 7,432.1 | 7,310.1 | 5,782.1 | 4,431.2 | 6,301.3 | 67,310.3 |
| 2016 | 8,223.6 | 6,818.4 | 5,768.6 | 5,007.9 | 4,813.8 | 6,045.0 | 3,857.8 | 4,059.2 | 6,567.4 | 4,716.0 | 5,396.7 | 4,476.2 | 65,750.5 |
| 2017 | 3,626.6 | 3,403.0 | 5,698.7 | 4,376.9 | 5,129.1 | 9,012.5 | 5,528.7 | 7,491.5 | 6,785.4 | 5,498.9 | 6,481.7 | 6,526.1 | 69,559.1 |
| 2018 | 7,000.4 | 10,100.0 | 12,243.8 | 10,030.7 | 7,692.8 | 8,400.0 | 7,283.8 | 7,592.7 | 9,416.3 | 16,684.0 | 13,094.0 | 14,657.0 | 124,195.5 |
| 2019 | 10,846.1 | 7,708.1 | 10,799.4 | 8,157.1 | 12,812.9 | 9,468.0 | 7,921.1 | 13,397.1 | 9,556.8 | 9,475.4 | 6,734.3 | 8,204.2 | 115,080.5 |
| 2020 | 12,102.9 | 15,474.5 | 17,447.9 | 9,248.0 | 9,155.6 | 11,842.5 | 12,107.8 | 9,570.3 | 16,216.4 | 13,214.9 | 10,349.1 | 9,987.2 | 146,717.1 |
| 2021 | 10,203.8 | 10,836.7 | 15,925.4 | 10,569.4 | 10,578.8 | 10,625.7 | 10,561.6 | 10,480.8 | 13,332.1 | 11,194.4 | 11,829.1 | 14,268.4 | 140,406.3 |
| 2022 | 16,376.2 | 13,920.8 | 15,190.8 | 12,884.5 | 15,730.9 | 15,520.8 | 12,307.7 | 14,022.5 | 17,684.3 | 16,051.8 | 13,225.9 | 13,916.6 | 176,832.7 |

Contract value = $20.   *Source: Index and Option Market (IOM), division of the Chicago Mercantile Exchange (CME)*

## Average Open Interest of E-mini NASDAQ 100 Index Futures in Chicago   In Contracts

| Year | Jan. | Feb. | Mar. | Apr. | May | June | July | Aug. | Sept. | Oct. | Nov. | Dec. |
|---|---|---|---|---|---|---|---|---|---|---|---|---|
| 2013 | 313,000 | 337,571 | 376,894 | 365,878 | 419,450 | 381,375 | 361,111 | 391,874 | 393,462 | 380,763 | 406,143 | 439,961 |
| 2014 | 427,403 | 428,404 | 452,936 | 352,802 | 355,239 | 383,300 | 365,320 | 359,978 | 399,636 | 349,013 | 357,410 | 376,694 |
| 2015 | 314,070 | 325,766 | 352,413 | 335,425 | 322,640 | 342,629 | 327,815 | 337,292 | 287,155 | 285,539 | 348,170 | 334,859 |
| 2016 | 287,540 | 269,926 | 244,045 | 227,743 | 227,844 | 237,463 | 242,541 | 295,495 | 301,601 | 303,400 | 269,558 | 247,601 |
| 2017 | 224,988 | 233,695 | 249,237 | 256,682 | 273,541 | 324,978 | 286,106 | 295,726 | 292,471 | 278,159 | 286,310 | 306,756 |
| 2018 | 264,915 | 239,065 | 250,925 | 242,489 | 243,195 | 251,523 | 243,189 | 244,958 | 268,030 | 250,113 | 245,902 | 240,458 |
| 2019 | 212,112 | 217,827 | 217,867 | 206,137 | 217,691 | 222,946 | 218,856 | 200,522 | 213,935 | 214,090 | 228,363 | 224,543 |
| 2020 | 213,795 | 208,540 | 226,372 | 181,126 | 199,383 | 206,398 | 220,553 | 233,772 | 300,472 | 238,614 | 235,732 | 237,238 |
| 2021 | 230,761 | 237,554 | 243,141 | 216,397 | 233,224 | 243,498 | 229,947 | 229,064 | 238,682 | 235,924 | 258,832 | 236,222 |
| 2022 | 231,103 | 243,997 | 238,907 | 233,598 | 249,365 | 265,397 | 258,178 | 262,812 | 286,551 | 279,588 | 265,951 | 260,538 |

Contract value = $20.   *Source: Index and Option Market (IOM), division of the Chicago Mercantile Exchange (CME)*

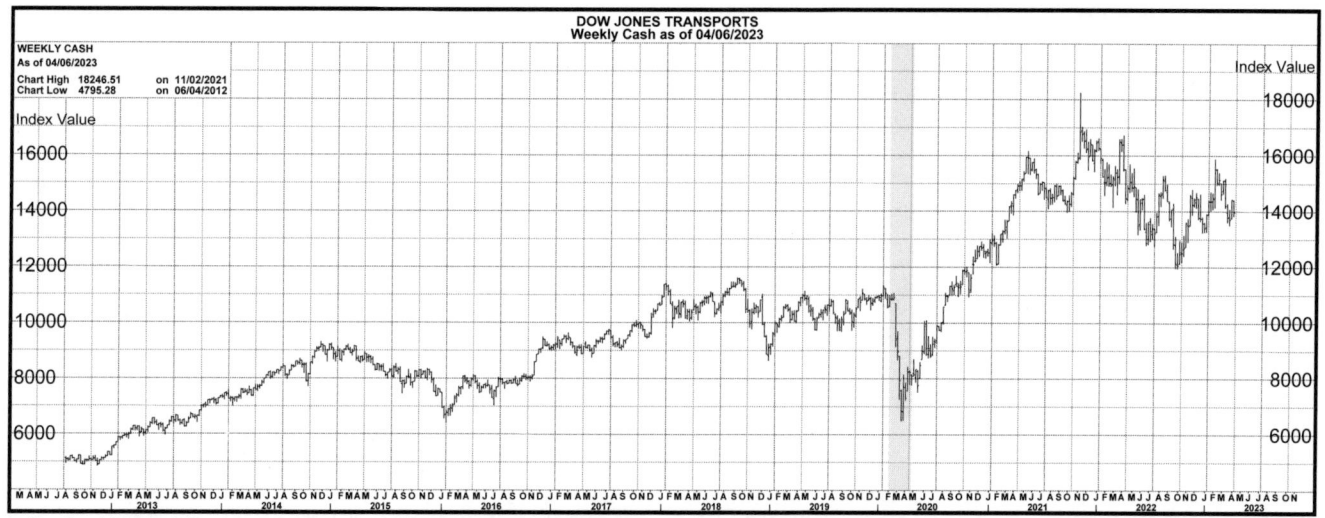

# STOCK INDEX FUTURES - U.S.

**DOW JONES TRANSPORTS**
Weekly Cash as of 04/06/2023

WEEKLY CASH
As of 04/06/2023
Chart High 18246.51 on 11/02/2021
Chart Low 4795.28 on 06/04/2012

"Dow Jones", "The Dow", "Dow Jones Industrial Average" and "DJIA" are service marks of Dow Jones & Company, Inc. Shaded areas indicate US recessions.

## Average Value of Dow Jones Transportation Index (20 Stocks)

| Year | Jan. | Feb. | Mar. | Apr. | May | June | July | Aug. | Sept. | Oct. | Nov. | Dec. | Average |
|------|------|------|------|------|-----|------|------|------|-------|------|------|------|---------|
| 2013 | 5,665.7 | 5,908.1 | 6,167.2 | 6,073.4 | 6,370.3 | 6,225.1 | 6,420.2 | 6,438.7 | 6,555.1 | 6,767.9 | 7,131.0 | 7,220.9 | 6,412.0 |
| 2014 | 7,361.9 | 7,235.3 | 7,512.0 | 7,587.8 | 7,854.6 | 8,135.4 | 8,308.7 | 8,272.8 | 8,534.2 | 8,308.9 | 9,033.8 | 9,025.7 | 8,097.6 |
| 2015 | 8,853.6 | 9,005.2 | 8,942.9 | 8,725.1 | 8,592.8 | 8,361.0 | 8,214.8 | 8,134.2 | 7,929.8 | 8,117.2 | 8,174.0 | 7,658.2 | 8,392.4 |
| 2016 | 6,871.7 | 7,133.1 | 7,771.2 | 7,919.7 | 7,700.9 | 7,615.7 | 7,817.1 | 7,845.3 | 7,913.3 | 8,054.3 | 8,622.5 | 9,207.6 | 7,872.7 |
| 2017 | 9,192.9 | 9,368.9 | 9,184.5 | 9,096.5 | 9,058.9 | 9,382.3 | 9,542.7 | 9,208.8 | 9,573.3 | 9,901.8 | 9,665.7 | 10,463.4 | 9,470.0 |
| 2018 | 11,106.0 | 10,471.7 | 10,477.7 | 10,427.8 | 10,631.9 | 10,795.0 | 10,663.5 | 11,220.3 | 11,443.3 | 10,604.3 | 10,507.1 | 9,544.1 | 10,657.7 |
| 2019 | 9,657.2 | 10,426.4 | 10,262.2 | 10,816.6 | 10,427.1 | 10,222.2 | 10,581.9 | 10,053.4 | 10,474.0 | 10,376.8 | 10,907.5 | 10,779.3 | 10,415.4 |
| 2020 | 10,994.0 | 10,617.1 | 7,941.0 | 8,002.8 | 8,307.7 | 9,249.4 | 9,600.0 | 10,829.0 | 11,292.7 | 11,603.4 | 12,095.7 | 12,568.9 | 10,258.5 |
| 2021 | 12,735.8 | 13,023.0 | 14,038.4 | 14,990.1 | 15,663.7 | 15,157.5 | 14,670.0 | 14,669.2 | 14,387.2 | 15,122.8 | 16,619.9 | 16,140.2 | 14,768.1 |
| 2022 | 15,726.6 | 15,199.7 | 15,843.7 | 14,977.0 | 14,343.4 | 13,546.7 | 13,553.1 | 14,658.3 | 13,081.5 | 12,877.0 | 14,079.7 | 13,802.1 | 14,307.4 |

*Source: New York Stock Exchange (NYSE)*

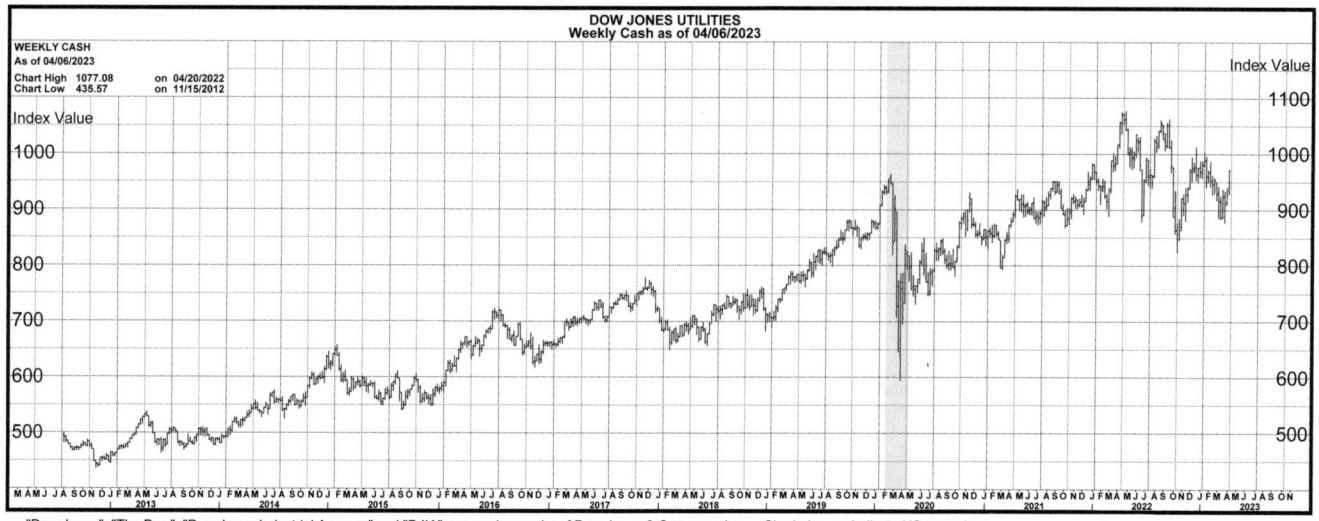

**DOW JONES UTILITIES**
Weekly Cash as of 04/06/2023

WEEKLY CASH
As of 04/06/2023
Chart High 1077.08 on 04/20/2022
Chart Low 435.57 on 11/15/2012

"Dow Jones", "The Dow", "Dow Jones Industrial Average" and "DJIA" are service marks of Dow Jones & Company, Inc. Shaded areas indicate US recessions.

## Average Value of Dow Jones Utilities Index (15 Stocks)

| Year | Jan. | Feb. | Mar. | Apr. | May | June | July | Aug. | Sept. | Oct. | Nov. | Dec. | Average |
|------|------|------|------|------|-----|------|------|------|-------|------|------|------|---------|
| 2013 | 463.6 | 474.7 | 493.1 | 522.2 | 511.0 | 481.1 | 496.7 | 490.3 | 480.7 | 492.3 | 499.5 | 485.4 | 490.9 |
| 2014 | 491.9 | 513.0 | 519.8 | 540.7 | 540.0 | 556.0 | 557.5 | 547.2 | 555.3 | 569.2 | 596.5 | 609.7 | 549.7 |
| 2015 | 634.5 | 610.4 | 582.6 | 589.7 | 584.5 | 564.1 | 570.8 | 587.1 | 558.1 | 588.0 | 566.9 | 567.7 | 583.7 |
| 2016 | 585.1 | 621.9 | 649.2 | 655.4 | 657.7 | 682.6 | 712.9 | 686.2 | 676.4 | 654.6 | 642.6 | 650.1 | 656.2 |
| 2017 | 658.2 | 674.0 | 696.8 | 703.8 | 705.4 | 726.4 | 712.0 | 738.2 | 736.9 | 740.9 | 760.2 | 742.3 | 716.3 |
| 2018 | 694.2 | 671.0 | 679.0 | 693.4 | 687.0 | 683.9 | 719.6 | 729.3 | 729.1 | 734.2 | 730.9 | 734.5 | 707.2 |
| 2019 | 708.6 | 741.2 | 773.2 | 776.7 | 784.7 | 810.1 | 820.1 | 829.5 | 859.4 | 867.4 | 848.0 | 863.5 | 806.9 |
| 2020 | 901.5 | 929.8 | 776.3 | 784.2 | 764.6 | 796.7 | 806.9 | 820.2 | 804.7 | 870.5 | 888.6 | 856.6 | 833.4 |
| 2021 | 853.3 | 850.3 | 844.0 | 907.2 | 904.6 | 896.8 | 900.3 | 932.9 | 913.7 | 899.7 | 914.1 | 945.8 | 896.9 |
| 2022 | 950.4 | 929.1 | 991.7 | 1,049.9 | 1,001.9 | 961.5 | 969.7 | 1,032.7 | 999.3 | 880.6 | 932.0 | 975.8 | 972.9 |

*Source: New York Stock Exchange (NYSE)*

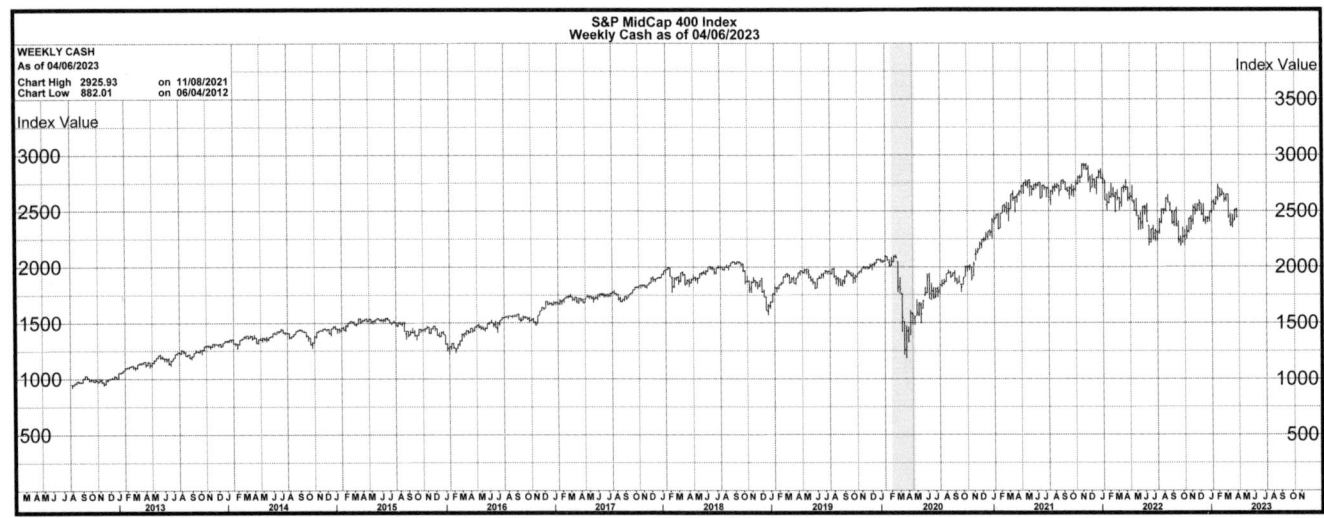

# STOCK INDEX FUTURES - U.S.

## Average Value of Standard & Poor's MidCap 400 Index

| Year | Jan. | Feb. | Mar. | Apr. | May | June | July | Aug. | Sept. | Oct. | Nov. | Dec. | Average |
|---|---|---|---|---|---|---|---|---|---|---|---|---|---|
| 2013 | 1,070.4 | 1,104.0 | 1,132.3 | 1,133.9 | 1,188.1 | 1,163.1 | 1,214.3 | 1,221.6 | 1,230.2 | 1,270.6 | 1,297.6 | 1,311.4 | 1,194.8 |
| 2014 | 1,333.5 | 1,333.4 | 1,373.9 | 1,355.0 | 1,361.6 | 1,410.5 | 1,413.6 | 1,402.5 | 1,415.2 | 1,351.5 | 1,435.2 | 1,438.2 | 1,385.3 |
| 2015 | 1,440.1 | 1,493.5 | 1,509.4 | 1,527.7 | 1,525.0 | 1,528.8 | 1,499.9 | 1,463.3 | 1,399.8 | 1,427.8 | 1,449.2 | 1,413.6 | 1,473.2 |
| 2016 | 1,299.3 | 1,296.5 | 1,408.0 | 1,456.5 | 1,458.3 | 1,489.2 | 1,534.0 | 1,559.7 | 1,546.7 | 1,526.0 | 1,571.6 | 1,668.8 | 1,484.5 |
| 2017 | 1,684.1 | 1,720.7 | 1,715.5 | 1,715.7 | 1,724.7 | 1,749.1 | 1,763.1 | 1,722.3 | 1,754.8 | 1,822.3 | 1,845.6 | 1,892.9 | 1,759.2 |
| 2018 | 1,959.7 | 1,876.7 | 1,902.7 | 1,886.0 | 1,930.2 | 1,981.1 | 1,988.5 | 2,016.0 | 2,032.4 | 1,892.6 | 1,859.1 | 1,715.6 | 1,920.0 |
| 2019 | 1,765.3 | 1,892.3 | 1,888.8 | 1,951.4 | 1,898.0 | 1,902.8 | 1,956.5 | 1,876.9 | 1,935.3 | 1,923.8 | 1,997.6 | 2,035.0 | 1,918.6 |
| 2020 | 2,062.5 | 2,034.1 | 1,520.6 | 1,523.4 | 1,656.9 | 1,804.9 | 1,820.0 | 1,931.5 | 1,867.7 | 1,963.4 | 2,108.2 | 2,265.3 | 1,879.9 |
| 2021 | 2,409.4 | 2,501.1 | 2,580.6 | 2,700.1 | 2,709.4 | 2,708.2 | 2,670.8 | 2,714.3 | 2,697.9 | 2,737.2 | 2,867.5 | 2,770.5 | 2,672.3 |
| 2022 | 2,714.1 | 2,646.6 | 2,649.9 | 2,618.4 | 2,449.0 | 2,364.7 | 2,354.1 | 23,536.6 | 2,356.3 | 2,322.6 | 2,486.0 | 2,463.3 | 4,246.8 |

Source: Index and Option Market (IOM), division of the Chicago Mercantile Exchange (CME)

## Volume of Trading of E-mini S&P 400 Index Futures in Chicago    In Contracts

| Year | Jan. | Feb. | Mar. | Apr. | May | June | July | Aug. | Sept. | Oct. | Nov. | Dec. | Total |
|---|---|---|---|---|---|---|---|---|---|---|---|---|---|
| 2012 | 408,514 | 411,301 | 751,336 | 513,459 | 613,049 | 820,825 | 494,705 | 410,688 | 615,845 | 453,404 | 431,072 | 612,709 | 6,536,907 |
| 2013 | 309,335 | 334,867 | 582,358 | 434,406 | 403,614 | 726,068 | 369,807 | 400,705 | 622,836 | 478,458 | 338,633 | 600,460 | 5,601,547 |
| 2014 | 369,537 | 360,548 | 604,474 | 385,135 | 334,222 | 500,963 | 343,309 | 283,606 | 618,774 | 648,830 | 242,848 | 593,469 | 5,285,715 |
| 2015 | 414,909 | 332,866 | 599,168 | 325,498 | 293,658 | 554,697 | 369,498 | 498,662 | 649,465 | 402,087 | 332,728 | 607,797 | 5,381,033 |
| 2016 | 529,519 | 442,219 | 633,841 | 325,445 | 347,829 | 654,024 | 305,479 | 313,218 | 626,528 | 336,632 | 352,772 | 538,251 | 5,405,757 |
| 2017 | 356,153 | 255,217 | 592,956 | 327,303 | 308,302 | 537,053 | 246,470 | 308,005 | 431,674 | 229,221 | 282,517 | 457,169 | 4,332,040 |
| 2018 | 316,880 | 430,453 | 590,759 | 332,663 | 294,698 | 498,591 | 268,791 | 227,276 | 481,588 | 531,815 | 363,033 | 614,553 | 4,951,100 |
| 2019 | 300,487 | 282,789 | 506,895 | 226,763 | 307,568 | 431,823 | 276,230 | 328,178 | 448,052 | 278,563 | 214,891 | 505,898 | 4,108,137 |
| 2020 | 331,980 | 370,629 | 776,538 | 235,431 | 224,250 | 549,761 | 278,221 | 239,926 | 497,873 | 286,787 | 252,149 | 488,901 | 4,532,446 |
| 2021 | 275,491 | 187,703 | 358,524 | 193,589 | 213,736 | 343,645 | 216,569 | 192,521 | 377,878 | 252,718 | 285,053 | 431,447 | 3,328,874 |

Contract value = $20.    Source: Index and Option Market (IOM), division of the Chicago Mercantile Exchange (CME)

## Civilian Unemployment Rate - U6

| Year | Jan. | Feb. | Mar. | Apr. | May | June | July | Aug. | Sept. | Oct. | Nov. | Dec. | Average |
|---|---|---|---|---|---|---|---|---|---|---|---|---|---|
| 2013 | 14.4 | 14.3 | 13.8 | 13.9 | 13.8 | 14.3 | 14.0 | 13.6 | 13.6 | 13.7 | 13.1 | 13.1 | 13.8 |
| 2014 | 12.7 | 12.6 | 12.7 | 12.3 | 12.2 | 12.1 | 12.2 | 12.0 | 11.7 | 11.5 | 11.4 | 11.2 | 12.1 |
| 2015 | 11.3 | 11.0 | 10.9 | 10.8 | 10.8 | 10.5 | 10.4 | 10.3 | 10.0 | 9.8 | 9.9 | 9.9 | 10.5 |
| 2016 | 9.9 | 9.7 | 9.8 | 9.7 | 9.7 | 9.6 | 9.7 | 9.7 | 9.7 | 9.5 | 9.3 | 9.2 | 9.6 |
| 2017 | 9.4 | 9.2 | 8.9 | 8.6 | 8.4 | 8.6 | 8.6 | 8.6 | 8.3 | 7.9 | 8.0 | 8.1 | 8.6 |
| 2018 | 8.2 | 8.2 | 8.0 | 7.8 | 7.6 | 7.8 | 7.5 | 7.4 | 7.5 | 7.4 | 7.6 | 7.6 | 7.7 |
| 2019 | 8.1 | 7.3 | 7.3 | 7.3 | 7.1 | 7.2 | 7.0 | 7.2 | 6.9 | 7.0 | 6.9 | 6.7 | 7.2 |
| 2020 | 6.9 | 7.0 | 8.7 | 22.8 | 21.2 | 18.0 | 16.5 | 14.2 | 12.8 | 12.1 | 12.0 | 11.7 | 13.7 |
| 2021 | 11.1 | 11.1 | 10.7 | 10.4 | 10.2 | 9.8 | 9.2 | 8.8 | 8.5 | 8.3 | 7.8 | 7.3 | 9.4 |
| 2022/1 | 7.1 | 7.2 | 6.9 | 7.0 | 7.1 | 6.7 | 6.7 | 7.0 | 6.7 | 6.8 | 6.7 | 6.5 | 6.9 |

The U6 unemployment rate counts not only people without work seeking full-time employment (the more familiar U-3 rate), but also counts "marginally attached workers and those working part-time for economic reasons." Note that some of these part-time workers counted as employed by U-3 could be working as little as an hour a week. And the "marginally attached workers" include those who have gotten discouraged and stopped looking, but still want to work. The age considered for this calculation is 16 years and over.

[1] Preliminary.    Source: Bureau of Economic Analysis, U.S. Department of Commerce (BEA)

# Stock Index Futures - WorldWide

**World stocks** – World stock markets in 2022 closed lower as inflation and higher interest rates took their toll. Also, Russia's invasion of Ukraine in early 2022 caused an energy crisis in Europe and pushed world oil and gas prices higher, thus undercutting the global economy. The MSCI World Index, a benchmark for large companies based in 23 developed countries, fell by -19.5%, reversing most of the +20.1% gain seen in 2021.

**Small-Capitalization Stocks** – The MSCI World Small-Cap Index, which tracks companies with market caps between $200 million and $1.5 billion, fell by -20.1% in 2022, more than reversing the +14.4% gain seen in 2021. The MSCI World Small-Cap Index in 2022 slightly underperformed the -19.5% decline in the large-cap MSCI World Index. Small caps in 2022 under-performed the large-caps for the second straight year and have now underperformed large-caps in four of the last five years.

**World Industry Groups** – All but one of the ten MSCI industry groups fell in 2022. The Energy sector was the only sector with a gain, rising +41.1% and adding to 2021's gain of +35.1%. The ranked returns of the other sectors are as follows: Health Care (-6.6%), Utilities (-7.0%), Consumer Staples (-8.0%), Financials (-12.4%), Materials (-13.7%), Industrials (-14.6%), Information Technology (-31.3%), Consumer Discretionary (-34.0%), and Telecom (-37.6%).

**Emerging markets** – The MSCI Emerging Markets Free Index, which tracks companies based in 26 emerging countries, fell by -22.4% in 2022, adding to the -4.6% decline seen in 2021. The -22.4% decline in emerging market stocks seen in 2022 was just mildly worse than the -19.5% decline seen in the MSCI World Index.

**G7** – The G7 stock markets in 2022 all closed lower except for the UK. The UK FTSE 100 index closed slightly higher by +0.9% in 2022. The U.S. S&P 500 index showed the largest decline, falling -19.4%. The ranked returns of the other G-7 countries were as follows: Canada's Toronto Composite index (-8.7%), Japan's Nikkei Index (-9.4%), French CAC-40 (-9.5%), German Dax index (-12.3%), and Italy's MIB index (-13.3%).

**North America** – In North America, the U.S. S&P 500 index in 2022 showed the largest decline by falling -19.4%. Canada's Toronto Composite index fell by -8.7%, and Mexico's Bolsa index fell by -9.0%.

**Latin America** – The Latin American stock markets in 2022 closed mixed. The ranked returns in 2022 were as follows: Argentina's Merval Index +142.0%, Chile's Stock Market Select Index +22.1%, Brazil's Bovespa Index +4.7%, Ecuador's Guayaqui Bolsa Index +4.2%, Peru's Lima General Index +1.0%, Colombia's General Index -8.9%, and Jamaica's Stock Exchange Index -10.2%.

**Europe** – European stocks in 2022 showed weakness due to rising interest rates and the energy crisis caused by the Russian invasion of Ukraine. The Euro Stoxx 50 index in 2022 fell by -4.4%, giving back some of the +22.8% gain seen in 2021. The ranked European returns in 2022 were as follows: UK FTSE 100 index +0.9%, Spanish IBEX 35 index -5.6%, French CAC-40 index -9.5%, German Dax index -12.3%, and Italian MIB index -13.3%.

**Asia** – The Asian-Pacific stock markets in 2022 closed mostly lower. The MSCI Far East Index in 2022 fell by -14.8%, more than reversing the small +1.5% gain seen in 2021. The ranked returns for the Asian-Pacific stock markets in 2022 were as follows: India's Mumbai Sensex 30 index +4.4%, Singapore's Straights Times Index +4.1%, Indonesia's Jakarta Composite Index +4.1%, Thailand's Stock Exchange index +0.7%, Malaysia's Kuala Lumpur Composite index -4.6%, Australia's All-Ordinaries Index -7.2%, Philippines' Composite index -7.8%, Japan's Nikkei 225 Index -9.4%, Pakistan's 100 Index -9.4%, New Zealand's Exchange 50 Index -12.0%, China's Shanghai Composite Index -15.1%, Hong Kong's Hang Seng -15.5%, Taiwan's TAIEX Index -22.4%, South Korea's Composite Index -24.9%, and Vietnam's Stock Index -32.8%.

# STOCK INDEX FUTURES - WORLDWIDE

## Comparison of International Indices   (2010=100)

| Year | Jan. | Feb. | Mar. | Apr. | May | June | July | Aug. | Sept. | Oct. | Nov. | Dec. | Average |
|---|---|---|---|---|---|---|---|---|---|---|---|---|---|
| **United States** | | | | | | | | | | | | | |
| 2015 | 177.3 | 181.3 | 181.2 | 181.6 | 183.1 | 181.1 | 179.8 | 172.4 | 165.1 | 173.6 | 179.1 | 177.3 | 177.7 |
| 2016 | 164.8 | 164.7 | 174.8 | 180.3 | 178.8 | 179.4 | 185.3 | 186.9 | 184.6 | 183.7 | 188.9 | 199.2 | 180.9 |
| 2017 | 201.2 | 206.4 | 210.4 | 209.0 | 211.6 | 215.4 | 218.1 | 221.4 | 224.0 | 232.8 | 238.0 | 248.0 | 219.7 |
| 2018 | 260.7 | 252.4 | 248.4 | 245.6 | 248.3 | 250.5 | 252.4 | 259.0 | 265.1 | 258.8 | 255.2 | 240.5 | 253.1 |
| 2019 | 244.1 | 258.7 | 259.9 | 266.8 | 260.1 | 264.3 | 273.7 | 263.3 | 271.8 | 270.2 | 280.9 | 284.6 | 266.5 |
| 2020 | 291.8 | 288.2 | 228.7 | 235.4 | 245.2 | 263.3 | 266.6 | 281.1 | 280.2 | 283.0 | 294.3 | 304.6 | 271.9 |
| 2021 | 311.4 | 316.1 | 327.1 | 341.6 | 346.3 | 346.5 | 351.6 | 356.1 | 350.5 | 354.2 | 362.2 | 360.1 | 343.6 |
| 2022 | 358.3 | 350.1 | 343.8 | 346.7 | 327.2 | 317.7 | 318.6 | 333.5 | 309.7 | 308.9 | 337.7 | 338.3 | 332.6 |
| **Canada** | | | | | | | | | | | | | |
| 2015 | 119.8 | 125.5 | 123.6 | 126.7 | 125.3 | 122.9 | 119.6 | 116.1 | 111.6 | 113.9 | 111.2 | 108.6 | 118.7 |
| 2016 | 102.4 | 104.6 | 110.9 | 113.1 | 114.7 | 116.3 | 119.7 | 121.6 | 121.2 | 121.9 | 122.8 | 126.4 | 116.3 |
| 2017 | 128.3 | 129.6 | 128.5 | 129.6 | 128.3 | 126.8 | 125.5 | 125.2 | 126.6 | 131.1 | 132.8 | 133.3 | 128.8 |
| 2018 | 134.8 | 127.8 | 128.3 | 127.4 | 132.2 | 134.6 | 136.1 | 135.3 | 133.6 | 127.9 | 125.4 | 120.5 | 130.3 |
| 2019 | 124.5 | 131.0 | 133.5 | 136.4 | 135.2 | 135.2 | 136.8 | 134.6 | 138.2 | 135.9 | 140.2 | 141.0 | 135.2 |
| 2020 | 144.0 | 145.3 | 114.0 | 116.6 | 123.5 | 128.2 | 132.1 | 137.4 | 134.5 | 134.4 | 138.7 | 145.1 | 132.8 |
| 2021 | 147.7 | 151.2 | 154.6 | 158.8 | 161.1 | 166.6 | 167.0 | 169.5 | 169.9 | 172.1 | 177.6 | 173.3 | 164.1 |
| 2022 | 174.2 | 175.9 | 179.1 | 178.8 | Discontinued | ---- | ---- | ---- | ---- | ---- | ---- | ---- | ---- |
| **France** | | | | | | | | | | | | | |
| 2015 | 117.0 | 127.2 | 133.4 | 138.0 | 135.0 | 131.5 | 132.2 | 130.4 | 120.8 | 125.8 | 131.0 | 124.5 | 128.9 |
| 2016 | 115.8 | 111.7 | 118.1 | 118.6 | 116.7 | 114.6 | 115.2 | 118.1 | 118.7 | 120.0 | 120.2 | 127.1 | 117.9 |
| 2017 | 129.8 | 129.3 | 133.6 | 137.0 | 142.8 | 140.5 | 138.1 | 136.7 | 139.0 | 143.8 | 144.0 | 143.4 | 138.2 |
| 2018 | 146.3 | 140.3 | 138.8 | 142.6 | 147.8 | 144.3 | 144.3 | 145.1 | 143.6 | 138.0 | 134.3 | 128.0 | 141.1 |
| 2019 | 128.7 | 136.6 | 141.8 | 147.1 | 143.0 | 144.6 | 148.9 | 142.8 | 135.2 | 150.1 | 157.2 | 157.8 | 144.5 |
| 2020 | 160.1 | 158.0 | 119.6 | 118.1 | 119.9 | 132.3 | 133.4 | 132.4 | 131.7 | 129.2 | 142.4 | 148.0 | 135.4 |
| 2021 | 149.1 | 152.0 | 159.1 | 166.0 | 169.6 | 175.4 | 173.9 | 180.0 | 177.1 | 177.5 | 187.1 | 186.7 | 171.1 |
| 2022 | 190.1 | 184.7 | 172.2 | 175.0 | 169.2 | 163.8 | 162.7 | 171.7 | 160.6 | 160.9 | 174.9 | 176.1 | 171.8 |
| **Germany** | | | | | | | | | | | | | |
| 2015 | 163.8 | 177.4 | 190.5 | 193.2 | 187.5 | 181.6 | 182.4 | 174.8 | 160.9 | 165.2 | 177.6 | 172.5 | 177.3 |
| 2016 | 158.8 | 150.2 | 159.4 | 162.0 | 161.8 | 159.3 | 161.0 | 170.2 | 169.8 | 171.7 | 171.2 | 181.3 | 164.7 |
| 2017 | 187.8 | 189.8 | 194.7 | 197.7 | 204.6 | 205.4 | 200.4 | 196.4 | 201.7 | 210.3 | 212.7 | 211.4 | 201.1 |
| 2018 | 214.5 | 201.4 | 196.6 | 200.6 | 208.7 | 204.7 | 203.3 | 201.4 | 196.9 | 188.4 | 183.6 | 175.1 | 197.9 |
| 2019 | 177.3 | 182.3 | 186.6 | 195.0 | 195.2 | 196.6 | 200.5 | 189.4 | 198.6 | 202.6 | 213.4 | 213.2 | 195.9 |
| 2020 | 216.1 | 215.5 | 162.2 | 167.7 | 177.7 | 199.0 | 205.9 | 208.2 | 209.5 | 203.7 | 209.5 | 217.0 | 199.3 |
| 2021 | 223.4 | 225.5 | 234.5 | 246.3 | 247.4 | 252.4 | 251.7 | 255.6 | 251.9 | 248.9 | 257.6 | 251.9 | 245.6 |
| 2022 | 254.2 | 244.0 | 226.5 | 229.0 | 226.1 | 219.8 | 209.8 | 217.4 | 205.1 | 204.8 | 227.4 | 229.0 | 224.4 |
| **Italy** | | | | | | | | | | | | | |
| 2013 | 82.6 | 77.9 | 75.1 | 75.3 | 81.8 | 76.1 | 75.5 | 80.8 | 83.1 | 89.4 | 89.9 | 86.9 | 81.2 |
| 2014 | 92.8 | 95.1 | 98.9 | 102.8 | 100.4 | 103.9 | 99.4 | 94.4 | 99.1 | 91.7 | 92.1 | 91.2 | 96.8 |
| 2015 | 92.0 | 101.1 | 107.9 | 111.5 | 110.8 | 109.1 | 109.2 | 108.3 | 102.2 | 105.3 | 105.6 | 10.2 | 97.8 |
| 2016 | 91.9 | 81.1 | 87.3 | 85.9 | 84.8 | 80.4 | 78.0 | 79.0 | 79.0 | 79.8 | 78.7 | 88.2 | 82.8 |
| 2017 | 92.0 | 89.7 | 94.3 | 95.9 | 101.0 | 99.1 | 101.1 | 103.1 | 105.4 | 106.8 | 106.7 | 105.8 | 100.1 |
| 2018 | 110.5 | 107.4 | 106.6 | 111.2 | 111.0 | 103.7 | 103.6 | 99.6 | 99.7 | 92.5 | 90.5 | 89.1 | 102.1 |
| 2019 | 91.6 | 95.0 | 99.5 | 103.3 | 98.4 | 98.5 | 103.7 | 98.4 | 103.9 | 105.0 | 111.1 | 110.8 | 101.6 |
| 2020 | 113.0 | 115.0 | 83.5 | 81.2 | 82.6 | 92.2 | 94.8 | 94.3 | 92.2 | Discontinued | | ---- | 94.3 |
| **Japan** | | | | | | | | | | | | | |
| 2015 | 172.6 | 180.4 | 191.8 | 197.5 | 199.5 | 203.8 | 203.5 | 199.0 | 179.3 | 183.6 | 195.6 | 191.8 | 191.5 |
| 2016 | 172.9 | 163.3 | 168.8 | 165.3 | 166.0 | 160.5 | 161.5 | 165.7 | 167.2 | 170.3 | 176.7 | 190.5 | 169.1 |
| 2017 | 191.8 | 191.7 | 193.2 | 187.2 | 197.1 | 200.3 | 200.3 | 196.5 | 199.1 | 212.5 | 225.0 | 227.5 | 201.8 |
| 2018 | 236.9 | 219.7 | 213.7 | 218.5 | 225.7 | 225.4 | 222.9 | 224.7 | 231.4 | 226.7 | 219.5 | 210.1 | 222.9 |
| 2019 | 204.4 | 211.0 | 213.9 | 219.4 | 212.0 | 210.4 | 215.7 | 206.1 | 215.6 | 221.8 | 232.6 | 236.4 | 216.6 |
| 2020 | 236.2 | 231.6 | 189.6 | 191.9 | 205.2 | 224.7 | 225.1 | 228.8 | 232.8 | 234.4 | 253.6 | 267.5 | 226.8 |
| 2021 | 281.5 | 294.2 | 292.9 | 294.0 | 284.9 | 289.2 | 280.9 | 276.7 | 298.6 | 285.6 | 293.4 | 284.9 | 288.1 |
| 2022 | 278.8 | 270.4 | 265.6 | 270.2 | 266.3 | 269.3 | 269.6 | 283.2 | 273.9 | 269.6 | 278.8 | 271.9 | 272.3 |

Not Seasonally Adjusted.   Source: *Economic and Statistics Administration, U.S. Department of Commerce (ESA)*

# STOCK INDEX FUTURES - WORLDWIDE

**DAX Index (FDAX)** — Weekly Cash as of 03/31/2023
WEEKLY CASH As of 03/31/2023
Chart High 16290.2 on 11/18/2021
Chart Low 5914.4 on 06/05/2012

DAX® is Deutsche Börse's blue chip index for the German stock market. It comprises the 30 largest and most actively traded German companies. Shaded areas indicate German recessions.

## Average Value of Deutscher Aktienindex (DAX)

| Year | Jan. | Feb. | Mar. | Apr. | May | June | July | Aug. | Sept. | Oct. | Nov. | Dec. | Average |
|------|------|------|------|------|-----|------|------|------|-------|------|------|------|---------|
| 2013 | 7,747.6 | 7,666.7 | 7,913.9 | 7,723.1 | 8,317.4 | 8,089.2 | 8,161.8 | 8,332.5 | 8,497.8 | 8,800.5 | 9,170.6 | 9,235.0 | 8,304.7 |
| 2014 | 9,516.8 | 9,509.5 | 9,339.9 | 9,490.0 | 9,709.5 | 9,927.4 | 9,751.8 | 9,273.1 | 9,638.7 | 8,971.9 | 9,490.3 | 9,812.3 | 9,535.9 |
| 2015 | 10,133.6 | 10,977.1 | 11,784.9 | 11,956.3 | 11,599.1 | 11,236.3 | 11,288.1 | 10,818.0 | 9,953.3 | 10,222.3 | 10,986.3 | 10,673.0 | 10,969.0 |
| 2016 | 9,827.1 | 9,291.4 | 9,859.9 | 10,023.2 | 10,010.6 | 9,859.2 | 9,960.5 | 10,530.3 | 10,504.5 | 10,624.2 | 10,595.5 | 11,214.9 | 10,191.8 |
| 2017 | 11,620.1 | 11,745.4 | 12,047.6 | 12,232.6 | 12,661.1 | 12,710.6 | 12,397.5 | 12,153.8 | 12,479.5 | 13,012.1 | 13,159.4 | 13,079.9 | 12,441.6 |
| 2018 | 13,270.7 | 12,459.4 | 12,165.9 | 12,411.6 | 12,911.2 | 12,667.6 | 12,581.7 | 12,458.9 | 12,185.2 | 11,659.1 | 11,359.6 | 10,834.5 | 12,247.1 |
| 2019 | 10,968.9 | 11,280.8 | 11,542.6 | 12,068.0 | 12,079.6 | 12,164.2 | 12,406.9 | 11,719.8 | 12,285.3 | 12,538.2 | 13,200.8 | 13,193.3 | 12,120.7 |
| 2020 | 13,370.5 | 13,330.6 | 10,034.3 | 10,374.5 | 10,993.7 | 12,313.7 | 12,741.0 | 12,882.4 | 12,960.9 | 12,603.1 | 12,960.7 | 13,426.0 | 12,332.6 |
| 2021 | 13,823.3 | 13,951.2 | 14,508.1 | 15,236.4 | 15,305.8 | 15,619.0 | 15,573.5 | 15,816.1 | 15,584.5 | 15,401.9 | 15,938.8 | 15,587.8 | 15,195.5 |
| 2022 | 15,726.9 | 15,094.5 | 14,012.7 | 14,167.0 | 13,991.9 | 13,601.0 | 12,981.4 | 13,449.6 | 12,692.6 | 12,673.5 | 14,068.9 | 14,168.9 | 13,885.7 |

*Source: EUREX*

**FTSE 100 INDEX** — Weekly Cash as of 06/29/2018
WEEKLY CASH As of 06/29/2018
Chart High 7903.5 on 05/22/2018
Chart Low 5229.8 on 06/01/2012

The FTSE 100 Index covers 100 of the largest companies traded on the LSE. Shaded areas indicate United Kingdom recessions.

## Average Value of FTSE 100 Stock Index

| Year | Jan. | Feb. | Mar. | Apr. | May | June | July | Aug. | Sept. | Oct. | Nov. | Dec. | Average |
|------|------|------|------|------|-----|------|------|------|-------|------|------|------|---------|
| 2009 | 4,281.85 | 4,074.38 | 3,760.23 | 4,046.33 | 4,393.78 | 4,349.25 | 4,374.50 | 4,755.63 | 5,033.13 | 5,161.18 | 5,242.29 | 5,309.54 | 4,565.17 |
| 2010 | 5,411.65 | 5,231.92 | 5,621.03 | 5,720.73 | 5,238.81 | 5,139.26 | 5,158.39 | 5,276.00 | 5,514.67 | 5,687.17 | 5,735.84 | 5,874.87 | 5,467.53 |
| 2011 | 5,971.31 | 6,021.12 | 5,858.24 | 6,007.85 | 5,937.95 | 5,792.18 | 5,909.81 | 5,271.31 | 5,228.50 | 5,408.62 | 5,402.52 | 5,480.08 | 5,690.79 |
| 2012 | 5,694.45 | 5,893.35 | 5,875.40 | 5,725.58 | 5,461.45 | 5,480.44 | 5,636.47 | 5,796.96 | 5,805.45 | 5,831.81 | 5,787.52 | 5,922.72 | 5,742.63 |
| 2013 | 6,161.87 | 6,316.35 | 6,435.58 | 6,361.01 | 6,647.35 | 6,299.43 | 6,517.86 | 6,521.48 | 6,552.36 | 6,571.95 | 6,694.32 | 6,572.98 | 6,471.05 |
| 2014 | 6,714.51 | 6,690.79 | 6,631.69 | 6,651.96 | 6,834.80 | 6,804.31 | 6,772.02 | 6,712.21 | 6,777.75 | 6,408.63 | 6,644.12 | 6,542.62 | 6,682.12 |
| 2015 | 6,612.63 | 6,878.54 | 6,884.51 | 7,012.39 | 6,981.68 | 6,783.17 | 6,646.60 | 6,455.96 | 6,087.34 | 6,340.81 | 6,306.91 | 6,162.31 | 6,596.07 |
| 2016 | 5,922.67 | 5,881.74 | 6,155.24 | 6,271.90 | 6,164.88 | 6,175.30 | 6,655.88 | 6,821.69 | 6,813.75 | 7,011.20 | 6,803.33 | 6,961.04 | 6,469.89 |
| 2017 | 7,211.36 | 7,240.42 | 7,359.53 | 7,263.60 | 7,422.66 | 7,463.97 | 7,395.85 | 7,409.18 | 7,334.65 | 7,508.18 | 7,441.23 | 7,481.74 | 7,377.70 |
| 2018 | 7,695.65 | 7,255.90 | 7,090.09 | 7,288.22 | 7,690.22 | 7,656.93 | Discontinued | | ---- | ---- | ---- | ---- | 7,446.17 |

*Source: Euronext LIFFE*

# STOCK INDEX FUTURES - WORLDWIDE

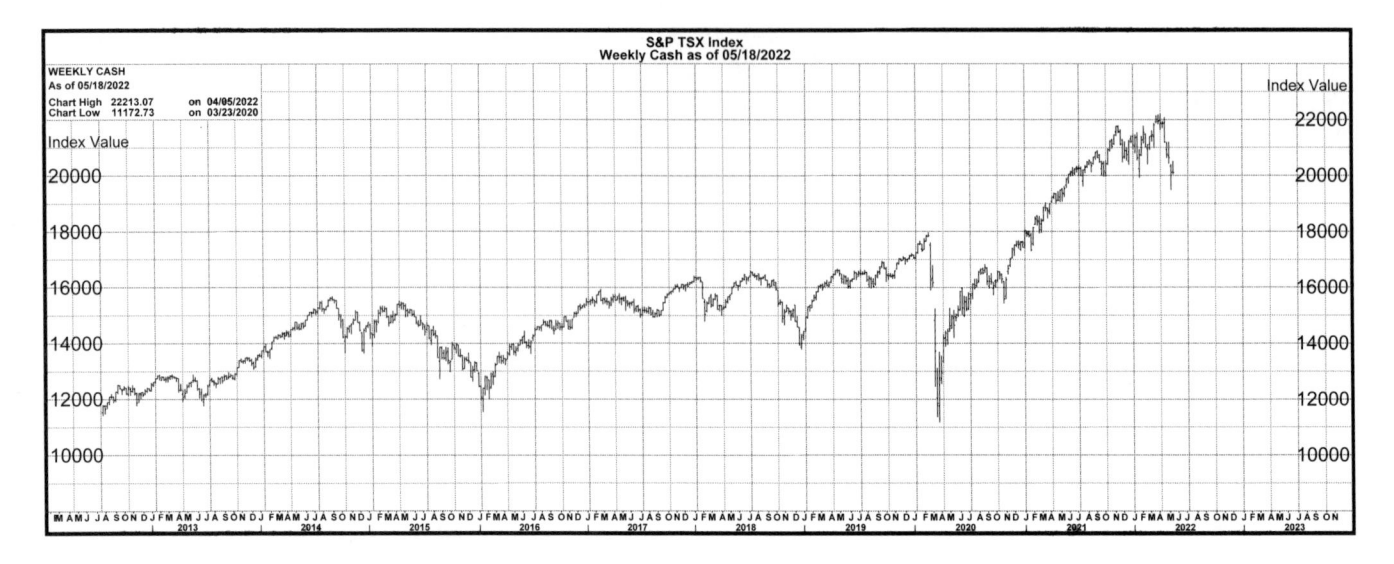

### Average Value of S&P TSX Index

| Year | Jan. | Feb. | Mar. | Apr. | May | June | July | Aug. | Sept. | Oct. | Nov. | Dec. | Average |
|---|---|---|---|---|---|---|---|---|---|---|---|---|---|
| 2013 | 12,668.8 | 12,737.0 | 12,777.3 | 12,299.2 | 12,585.1 | 12,221.4 | 12,479.7 | 12,622.7 | 12,818.9 | 13,057.7 | 13,396.1 | 13,339.2 | 12,750.3 |
| 2014 | 13,728.1 | 13,964.5 | 14,281.4 | 14,440.5 | 14,635.7 | 14,960.5 | 15,268.3 | 15,389.4 | 15,353.5 | 14,460.8 | 14,824.8 | 14,330.5 | 14,636.5 |
| 2015 | 14,460.9 | 15,155.0 | 14,921.6 | 15,299.3 | 15,127.2 | 14,835.9 | 14,436.4 | 14,010.4 | 13,477.6 | 13,751.9 | 13,424.2 | 13,115.1 | 14,334.6 |
| 2016 | 12,361.0 | 12,632.4 | 13,382.1 | 13,650.4 | 13,851.9 | 14,042.4 | 14,445.8 | 14,680.8 | 14,634.0 | 14,718.2 | 14,821.9 | 15,254.5 | 14,039.6 |
| 2017 | 15,486.6 | 15,639.7 | 15,515.3 | 15,642.3 | 15,486.8 | 15,308.8 | 15,153.5 | 15,108.9 | 15,284.5 | 15,826.0 | 16,032.6 | 16,092.8 | 15,548.2 |
| 2018 | 16,272.5 | 15,430.6 | 15,490.4 | 15,380.4 | 15,964.4 | 16,253.3 | 16,432.6 | 16,332.4 | 16,125.6 | 15,441.2 | 15,144.0 | 14,546.8 | 15,734.5 |
| 2019 | 15,031.9 | 15,811.2 | 16,119.6 | 16,470.4 | 16,316.8 | 16,322.6 | 16,515.0 | 16,243.1 | 16,683.3 | 16,403.2 | 16,926.0 | 17,020.0 | 16,321.9 |
| 2020 | 17,382.0 | 17,542.7 | 13,757.1 | 14,071.5 | 14,903.8 | 15,480.9 | 15,942.5 | 16,584.3 | 16,234.7 | 16,226.7 | 16,743.6 | 17,521.0 | 16,032.6 |
| 2021 | 17,830.7 | 18,250.1 | 18,658.1 | 19,168.9 | 19,442.9 | 20,110.1 | 20,165.3 | 20,462.6 | 20,510.9 | 20,777.6 | 21,439.1 | 20,917.4 | 19,811.1 |
| 2022 | 21,033.2 | 21,232.4 | 21,626.3 | 21,586.5 | Discontinued | | ---- | ---- | ---- | ---- | ---- | ---- | 21,369.6 |

*Source: Toronto Stock Exchange*

The CAC 40® is a free float market capitalization weighted index that reflects the performance of the 40 largest and most actively traded shares listed on Euronext Paris, and is the most widely used indicator of the Paris stock market. Shaded areas indicate French recessions.

### Average Value of CAC 40 Index

| Year | Jan. | Feb. | Mar. | Apr. | May | June | July | Aug. | Sept. | Oct. | Nov. | Dec. | Average |
|---|---|---|---|---|---|---|---|---|---|---|---|---|---|
| 2013 | 3,734.0 | 3,679.4 | 3,786.4 | 3,735.1 | 3,968.7 | 3,792.5 | 3,876.6 | 4,046.3 | 4,117.7 | 4,228.0 | 4,279.9 | 4,161.4 | 3,950.5 |
| 2014 | 4,248.4 | 4,301.1 | 4,338.1 | 4,437.3 | 4,484.8 | 4,522.0 | 4,362.0 | 4,249.6 | 4,425.3 | 4,129.8 | 4,261.0 | 4,262.2 | 4,335.1 |
| 2015 | 4,384.2 | 4,768.5 | 5,000.7 | 5,173.4 | 5,058.2 | 4,927.9 | 4,956.2 | 4,887.1 | 4,526.6 | 4,715.6 | 4,910.3 | 4,665.7 | 4,831.2 |
| 2016 | 4,340.1 | 4,184.8 | 4,427.5 | 4,445.2 | 4,373.5 | 4,293.9 | 4,317.6 | 4,425.4 | 4,448.6 | 4,497.6 | 4,504.3 | 4,764.5 | 4,418.6 |
| 2017 | 4,863.6 | 4,846.7 | 5,008.4 | 5,134.6 | 5,352.0 | 5,263.8 | 5,175.0 | 5,122.7 | 5,208.8 | 5,389.8 | 5,398.0 | 5,373.0 | 5,178.0 |
| 2018 | 5,483.0 | 5,257.8 | 5,200.6 | 5,345.3 | 5,537.6 | 5,408.3 | 5,409.4 | 5,438.3 | 5,381.7 | 5,170.1 | 5,035.1 | 4,798.2 | 5,288.8 |
| 2019 | 4,822.7 | 5,118.2 | 5,315.3 | 5,511.4 | 5,360.8 | 5,420.3 | 5,578.7 | 5,351.9 | 5,067.5 | 5,623.6 | 5,892.8 | 5,915.3 | 5,414.9 |
| 2020 | 6,001.1 | 5,923.3 | 4,481.8 | 4,425.2 | 4,492.5 | 4,958.3 | 4,999.9 | 4,962.6 | 4,937.4 | 4,843.4 | 5,335.7 | 5,546.8 | 5,075.7 |
| 2021 | 5,589.5 | 5,697.5 | 5,962.0 | 6,220.1 | 6,358.0 | 6,574.4 | 6,517.7 | 6,746.1 | 6,637.7 | 6,651.9 | 7,012.9 | 6,998.9 | 6,413.9 |
| 2022 | 7,125.2 | 6,920.8 | 6,452.0 | 6,558.0 | 6,341.9 | 6,139.3 | 6,096.0 | 6,435.9 | 6,017.4 | 6,030.4 | 6,556.7 | 6,600.2 | 6,439.5 |

*Source: Euronext Paris*

# STOCK INDEX FUTURES - WORLDWIDE

**HANG SENG INDEX**
Weekly Cash as of 03/31/2023

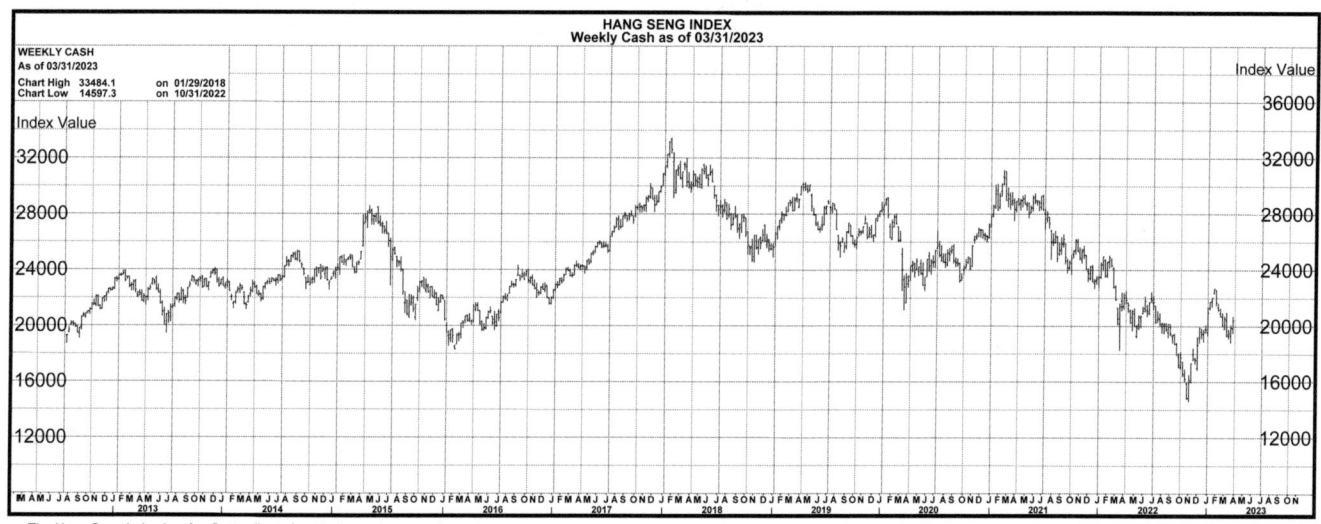

WEEKLY CASH
As of 03/31/2023
Chart High 33484.1 on 01/29/2018
Chart Low 14597.3 on 10/31/2022

The Hang Seng Index is a freefloat-adjusted market capitalization-weighted stock market index in Hong Kong. The Index was created by Hong Kong banker Stanley Kwan in 1969.

## Average Value of Hang Seng Index

| Year | Jan. | Feb. | Mar. | Apr. | May | June | July | Aug. | Sept. | Oct. | Nov. | Dec. | Average |
|---|---|---|---|---|---|---|---|---|---|---|---|---|---|
| 2013 | 23,470.7 | 23,148.3 | 22,518.0 | 22,054.3 | 22,933.1 | 21,063.9 | 21,298.5 | 22,009.5 | 22,932.7 | 23,102.2 | 23,304.5 | 23,370.8 | 22,600.5 |
| 2014 | 22,725.2 | 22,188.3 | 21,980.8 | 22,598.5 | 22,584.9 | 23,144.9 | 23,760.0 | 24,812.1 | 24,341.8 | 23,301.2 | 23,779.1 | 23,386.2 | 23,216.9 |
| 2015 | 24,209.9 | 24,670.4 | 24,306.8 | 27,451.5 | 27,656.2 | 27,009.0 | 25,032.2 | 23,223.2 | 21,365.1 | 22,649.3 | 22,509.5 | 21,910.2 | 24,332.8 |
| 2016 | 19,733.6 | 19,134.5 | 20,299.8 | 20,986.5 | 20,174.0 | 20,646.4 | 21,497.8 | 22,663.9 | 23,543.0 | 23,406.1 | 22,618.9 | 22,229.6 | 21,411.2 |
| 2017 | 22,814.5 | 23,725.3 | 24,029.6 | 24,262.7 | 25,189.4 | 25,828.2 | 26,326.0 | 27,532.4 | 27,790.9 | 28,394.4 | 29,213.7 | 29,109.6 | 26,184.7 |
| 2018 | 31,831.9 | 30,969.3 | 30,898.1 | 30,376.0 | 30,698.7 | 30,070.3 | 28,466.1 | 27,925.8 | 27,275.6 | 25,705.4 | 26,081.0 | 26,075.6 | 28,864.5 |
| 2019 | 26,711.6 | 28,392.4 | 28,900.0 | 29,882.0 | 28,132.3 | 27,718.0 | 28,465.3 | 25,987.1 | 26,474.3 | 26,458.2 | 26,979.0 | 27,264.3 | 27,613.7 |
| 2020 | 28,214.4 | 27,214.7 | 24,107.0 | 24,008.8 | 23,807.6 | 24,478.4 | 25,316.2 | 25,100.2 | 24,253.2 | 24,440.4 | 26,119.8 | 26,524.8 | 25,298.8 |
| 2021 | 28,662.9 | 29,869.8 | 28,836.3 | 28,875.1 | 28,537.1 | 28,850.2 | 27,252.4 | 25,928.8 | 25,223.4 | 25,304.4 | 24,912.9 | 23,481.2 | 27,144.5 |
| 2022 | 23,974.5 | 24,154.5 | 21,338.2 | 21,118.5 | 20,382.3 | 21,516.5 | 20,947.7 | 19,901.8 | 18,563.5 | 16,390.9 | 17,177.2 | 19,419.6 | 20,407.1 |

*Source: Hong Kong Futures Exchange*

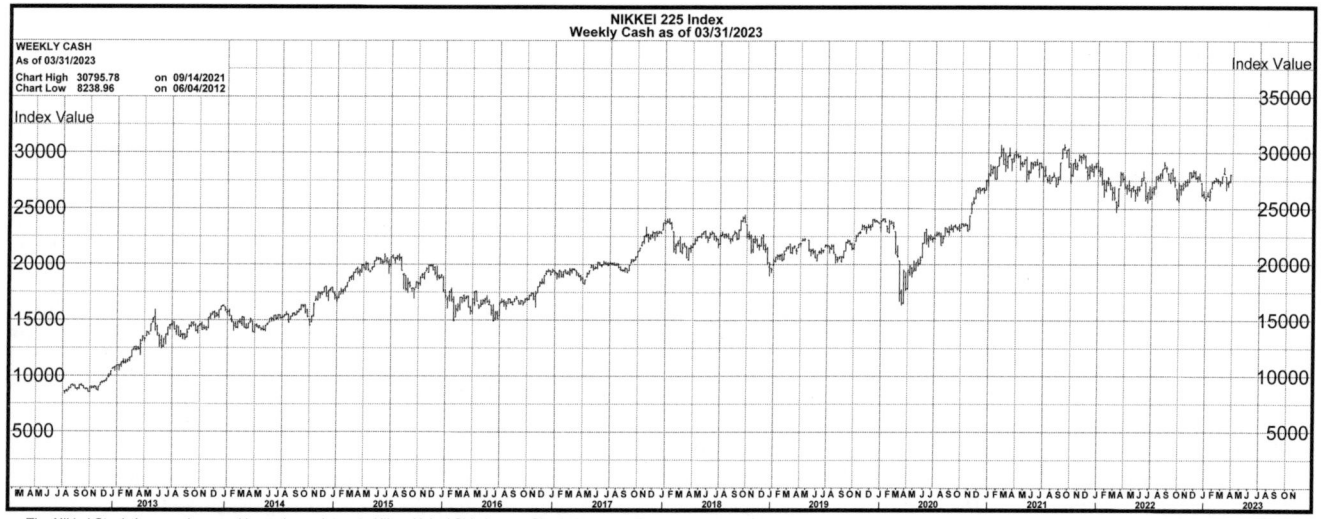

**NIKKEI 225 Index**
Weekly Cash as of 03/31/2023

WEEKLY CASH
As of 03/31/2023
Chart High 30795.78 on 09/14/2021
Chart Low 8238.96 on 06/04/2012

The Nikkei Stock Average is owned by and proprietary to Nihon Keisai Shimbun. Shaded areas indicate Japan recessions.

## Average Value of Nikkei 225 Index

| Year | Jan. | Feb. | Mar. | Apr. | May | June | July | Aug. | Sept. | Oct. | Nov. | Dec. | Average |
|---|---|---|---|---|---|---|---|---|---|---|---|---|---|
| 2013 | 10,750.9 | 11,327.3 | 12,254.7 | 13,224.1 | 14,494.3 | 13,106.6 | 14,317.5 | 13,726.7 | 14,372.1 | 14,329.0 | 14,931.7 | 15,655.2 | 13,540.8 |
| 2014 | 15,578.3 | 14,617.6 | 14,694.8 | 14,475.3 | 14,343.2 | 15,131.8 | 15,379.3 | 15,358.7 | 15,948.5 | 15,394.1 | 17,179.0 | 17,541.7 | 15,470.2 |
| 2015 | 17,274.4 | 18,053.2 | 19,197.6 | 19,767.9 | 19,974.2 | 20,403.8 | 20,372.6 | 19,919.1 | 17,944.2 | 18,374.1 | 19,581.8 | 19,202.6 | 19,172.1 |
| 2016 | 17,302.3 | 16,347.0 | 16,897.3 | 16,543.5 | 16,612.7 | 16,068.8 | 16,168.3 | 16,586.1 | 16,737.0 | 17,044.5 | 17,689.5 | 19,066.0 | 16,921.9 |
| 2017 | 19,194.1 | 19,188.7 | 19,340.2 | 18,736.4 | 19,726.8 | 20,045.6 | 20,044.9 | 19,670.2 | 19,924.4 | 21,267.5 | 22,525.2 | 22,769.9 | 20,202.8 |
| 2018 | 23,712.2 | 21,991.7 | 21,395.5 | 21,868.8 | 22,590.1 | 22,562.9 | 22,309.1 | 22,494.1 | 23,159.3 | 22,690.8 | 21,967.9 | 21,032.4 | 22,314.6 |
| 2019 | 20,460.5 | 21,123.6 | 21,414.9 | 21,964.9 | 21,218.4 | 21,060.2 | 21,593.7 | 20,629.7 | 21,585.5 | 22,197.5 | 23,278.1 | 23,660.4 | 21,682.3 |
| 2020 | 23,642.9 | 23,181.9 | 18,974.0 | 19,208.4 | 20,543.3 | 22,486.9 | 22,529.5 | 22,901.5 | 23,307.0 | 23,464.1 | 25,384.9 | 26,773.0 | 22,699.8 |
| 2021 | 28,175.4 | 29,443.6 | 29,315.3 | 29,426.8 | 28,517.1 | 28,943.2 | 28,118.2 | 27,692.7 | 29,893.6 | 28,586.2 | 29,370.6 | 28,514.2 | 28,833.1 |
| 2022 | 27,904.0 | 27,066.5 | 26,584.1 | 27,043.3 | 26,653.8 | 26,958.4 | 26,986.7 | 28,351.7 | 27,419.0 | 26,983.2 | 27,903.3 | 27,214.7 | 27,255.7 |

*Source: Singapore Exchange*

# Sugar

The white crystalline substance called "sugar" is the organic chemical compound sucrose, one of several related compounds, all known as sugars. These include glucose, dextrose, fructose, and lactose. All sugars are members of the larger group of compounds called carbohydrates and are characterized by a sweet taste. Sucrose is considered a double sugar because it is composed of one molecule of glucose and one molecule of fructose. While sucrose is common in many plants, it occurs in the highest concentration in sugarcane (Saccharum officinarum) and sugar beets (Beta vulgaris). Sugarcane is about 7 to 18 percent sugar by weight, while sugar beets are 8 to 22 percent.

Sugarcane is a member of the grass family and is a perennial. Sugarcane is cultivated in tropical and subtropical regions around the world roughly between the Tropics of Cancer and Capricorn. It grows best in hot, wet climates where there is heavy rainfall followed by a dry season. The largest cane producers are Florida, Louisiana, Texas, and Hawaii. On a commercial basis, sugarcane is not grown from seeds but from cuttings or pieces of the stalk.

Sugar beets, which are produced in temperate or colder climates, are annuals grown from seeds. Sugar beets do best with moderate temperatures and evenly distributed rainfall. The beets are planted in the spring and harvested in the fall. The sugar is contained in the root of the beet, but the sugars from beets and cane are identical. Sugar beet production takes place mostly in Europe, the U.S., China, and Japan. The largest sugar beet producing states are Minnesota, Idaho, North Dakota, and Michigan. Sugar beets are refined to yield white sugar, and very little raw sugar is produced.

Sugar beets and sugarcane are produced in over 100 countries around the world. Of all the sugar produced, about 25% is processed from sugar beets, and the remaining 75% is from sugar cane. The trend has been that the production of sugar from cane is increasing relative to that produced from beets. The significance of this in that sugarcane is a perennial plant while the sugar beet is an annual, and due to the longer production cycle, sugarcane production and the sugar processed from that cane, may not be quite as responsive to changes in price.

Sugar futures are traded at the ICE Futures U.S. exchange, the Bolsa de Mercadorias & Futuros (BM&F), Kansai Commodities Exchange (KANEX), the Tokyo Grain Exchange (TGE), and the ICE Futures Europe exchange.

Raw sugar is traded on the ICE Futures U.S. exchange, while white sugar is traded on the ICE Futures Europe exchange. The most actively traded contract is the No. 11 (World) sugar contract at the ICE exchange. The No. 11 contract calls for the delivery of 112,000 pounds (50 long tons) of raw cane centrifugal sugar from any of 28 foreign countries of origin and the United States. The ICE exchange also trades the No. 14 sugar contract (Domestic), which calls for the delivery of raw centrifugal cane sugar in the United States. Futures on white sugar are traded on the London International Financial Futures Exchange and call for the delivery of 50 metric tons of white beet sugar, cane crystal sugar, or refined sugar of any origin from the crop current at the time of delivery.

**Prices** – ICE World No. 11 sugar futures prices (Barchart.com symbol SB) traded sideways to higher into Q2 of 2022. Russia's invasion of Ukraine in February roiled global commodity markets and sent crude prices soaring to a 14-year high, supporting sugar prices. Strength in oil prices benefits ethanol prices and pressures Brazil's sugar mills to divert more cane crushing toward ethanol production rather than sugar, thus curbing sugar supplies. Sugar also found support after India, the world's second-largest sugar producer, said it was considering restrictions on sugar exports to prevent domestic prices from surging. Sugar prices tumbled to a 1-1/2-year low of 17.20 cents per pound in August. A rebound in sugar production in Thailand, the world's second-biggest sugar exporter, weighed on prices after Thailand's 2021/22 sugar cane output was forecast to jump +35% yr/yr to a 3-year high of 90 MMT. Also, India said in July that it would allow its sugar mills to export more sugar than previously permitted to prevent contract defaults. India's 2021/22 sugar exports jumped +57% y/y to a record 11 MMT. Sugar prices then traded sideways into October. Weakness in the Brazilian real weighed on sugar prices after the real dropped to a 1-year low against the dollar in November. A weaker real encourages export selling by Brazil's sugar producers. Also, the International Sugar Organization (ISO) on Nov 22 projected that global 2022/23 sugar production would climb +5.5% y/y to a record high of 182.1 MMT. Also, ISO projected that the 2022/23 global sugar market would have a surplus of +6.2 MMT. However, sugar prices pushed higher into year-end after India said it would limit its 2022/23 sugar exports to 9 MMT to safeguard domestic supplies. Sugar prices finished 2022 up +6.1% yr/yr at 20.04 cents per pound.

**Supply** – World production of centrifugal (raw) sugar in the 2022/23 marketing year (Oct 1 to Sep 30) is expected to rise by +1.6% yr/yr to 183.150 million metric tons, a forecasted record high. The world's largest sugar producers in 2022/23 are expected to be Brazil with 20.8% of world production, India with 19.5%, and the European Union with 8.8%. U.S. sugar production in 2022/23 is expected to fall by -0.6% yr/yr to 8.241 million metric tons. U.S. production of cane sugar in 2022/23 is expected to rise by +5.0% yr/yr to 4.199 million short tons, and beet sugar production is expected to fall by -2.1% yr/yr to 5.048 million short tons. World ending stocks in 2021/22 fell by -11.6% yr/yr to 44.488 million metric tons, moderately below the 2018/19 record high of 52.871 million metric tons.

**Demand** – World domestic consumption of centrifugal (raw) sugar in 2021/22 remained unchanged from 2020/21 at 174.477 million metric tons. U.S. domestic disappearance (consumption) of sugar in 2021/22 was down by -0.1% yr/yr at 12.340 million short tons.

**Trade** – World exports of centrifugal sugar in 2022/23 are expected to rise by +2.1% yr/yr to 69.252 million metric tons. The world's largest sugar exporters in 2022/23 are expected to be Brazil at 40.7% of total world exports, Thailand at 15.9%, and India at 13.6%.

U.S. sugar exports in 2021/22 fell by -32.7% yr/yr at 35,000 short tons, which is far down from the 3-decade high of 422,000 seen in 2006/07. U.S. sugar imports in 2022/23 are expected to fall by -5.6% yr/yr to 3.123 million metric tons.

# SUGAR

**World Production, Supply & Stocks/Consumption Ratio of Sugar**    In 1000's of Metric Tons (Raw Value)

| Marketing Year | Beginning Stocks | Production | Imports | Total Supply | Exports | Domestic Consumption | Ending Stocks | Stocks As a % of Consumption |
|---|---|---|---|---|---|---|---|---|
| 2013-14 | 42,288 | 175,971 | 51,450 | 269,709 | 57,951 | 166,960 | 44,798 | 26.8 |
| 2014-15 | 44,798 | 177,582 | 50,248 | 272,648 | 55,033 | 168,839 | 48,756 | 28.9 |
| 2015-16 | 48,756 | 164,972 | 54,629 | 268,310 | 54,187 | 170,034 | 44,422 | 26.1 |
| 2016-17 | 44,422 | 172,143 | 55,418 | 272,643 | 60,047 | 171,388 | 42,012 | 24.5 |
| 2017-18 | 42,012 | 194,222 | 55,621 | 291,855 | 65,868 | 173,813 | 51,574 | 29.7 |
| 2018-19 | 51,574 | 179,158 | 53,320 | 284,052 | 58,140 | 173,171 | 52,871 | 30.5 |
| 2019-20 | 52,871 | 166,559 | 53,804 | 273,234 | 53,424 | 170,869 | 47,702 | 27.9 |
| 2020-21[1] | 47,702 | 180,239 | 58,863 | 286,804 | 63,509 | 174,476 | 50,354 | 28.9 |
| 2021-22[2] | 50,354 | 180,348 | 55,843 | 286,545 | 67,842 | 174,477 | 44,488 | 25.5 |
| 2022-23[3] | 44,488 | 183,150 | 57,396 | 285,034 | 69,252 | | | |

[1] Preliminary.   [2] Estimate.   [3] Forecast.   Source: Foreign Agricultural Service, U.S. Department of Agriculture (FAS-USDA)

**World Production of Sugar (Centrifugal Sugar-Raw Value)**    In Thousands of Metric Tons

| Year | Australia | Brazil | China | Cuba | European Union | India | Indonesia | Mexico | Pakistan | Thailand | United States | Ukraine | World Total |
|---|---|---|---|---|---|---|---|---|---|---|---|---|---|
| 2013-14 | 4,380 | 37,800 | 14,263 | 1,650 | 16,020 | 26,605 | 2,300 | 6,382 | 5,630 | 11,333 | 1,196 | 7,676 | 175,971 |
| 2014-15 | 4,700 | 35,950 | 11,000 | 1,850 | 18,449 | 30,460 | 2,100 | 6,344 | 5,164 | 10,793 | 1,728 | 7,853 | 177,582 |
| 2015-16 | 4,900 | 34,650 | 9,050 | 1,625 | 14,283 | 27,385 | 2,025 | 6,484 | 5,265 | 9,743 | 1,638 | 8,155 | 164,972 |
| 2016-17 | 5,100 | 39,150 | 9,300 | 1,800 | 15,505 | 22,200 | 2,050 | 6,314 | 6,825 | 10,033 | 2,156 | 8,137 | 172,143 |
| 2017-18 | 4,480 | 38,870 | 10,300 | 1,100 | 19,508 | 34,309 | 2,100 | 6,371 | 7,225 | 14,710 | 2,180 | 8,430 | 194,222 |
| 2018-19 | 4,725 | 29,500 | 10,760 | 1,300 | 16,750 | 34,300 | 2,200 | 6,812 | 5,270 | 14,581 | 1,753 | 8,164 | 179,158 |
| 2019-20 | 4,285 | 30,300 | 10,400 | 1,200 | 17,040 | 28,900 | 2,250 | 5,596 | 5,340 | 8,294 | 1,638 | 7,392 | 166,559 |
| 2020-21[1] | 4,335 | 42,050 | 10,600 | 850 | 15,216 | 33,760 | 2,130 | 6,058 | 6,505 | 7,587 | 1,240 | 8,376 | 180,239 |
| 2021-22[2] | 4,120 | 35,450 | 9,600 | 475 | 16,479 | 36,880 | 2,300 | 6,556 | 7,140 | 10,157 | 1,415 | 8,287 | 180,348 |
| 2022-23[3] | 4,350 | 38,050 | 10,000 | 460 | 16,150 | 35,800 | 2,400 | 6,254 | 7,060 | 10,500 | 1,092 | 8,241 | 183,150 |

[1] Preliminary.   [2] Estimate.   [3] Forecast.   Source: Foreign Agricultural Service, U.S. Department of Agriculture (FAS-USDA)

**World Stocks of Centrifugal Sugar at Beginning of Marketing Year**    In Thousands of Metric Tons (Raw Value)

| Year | Australia | Brazil | China | Cuba | European Union | India | Indonesia | Iran | Mexico | Philippines | Russia | United States | World Total |
|---|---|---|---|---|---|---|---|---|---|---|---|---|---|
| 2013-14 | 83 | 10 | 6,793 | 170 | 3,836 | 9,373 | 879 | 700 | 1,548 | 942 | 395 | 1,958 | 42,288 |
| 2014-15 | 111 | 350 | 9,977 | 140 | 3,066 | 8,227 | 1,299 | 700 | 881 | 1,032 | 370 | 1,642 | 44,798 |
| 2015-16 | 140 | 950 | 10,390 | 180 | 4,151 | 10,607 | 949 | 400 | 860 | 997 | 100 | 1,647 | 48,756 |
| 2016-17 | 230 | 750 | 9,591 | 115 | 791 | 9,294 | 1,098 | 460 | 1,099 | 1,168 | 150 | 1,863 | 44,422 |
| 2017-18 | 220 | 850 | 7,811 | 125 | 1,776 | 6,570 | 1,743 | 535 | 1,062 | 1,167 | 350 | 1,702 | 42,012 |
| 2018-19 | 130 | 920 | 6,567 | 110 | 1,547 | 14,214 | 1,793 | 480 | 1,479 | 1,067 | 440 | 1,822 | 51,574 |
| 2019-20 | 137 | 220 | 5,408 | 127 | 1,260 | 17,614 | 2,300 | 485 | 1,239 | 1,234 | 550 | 1,618 | 52,871 |
| 2020-21[1] | 38 | 590 | 4,027 | 110 | 2,076 | 14,614 | 1,941 | 430 | 910 | 1,289 | 609 | 1,468 | 47,702 |
| 2021-22[2] | 135 | 340 | 5,374 | 95 | 1,106 | 13,213 | 2,653 | 565 | 1,116 | 1,196 | 565 | 1,547 | 50,354 |
| 2022-23[3] | 294 | 340 | 5,385 | 75 | 1,245 | 9,439 | 2,370 | 490 | 1,022 | 931 | 624 | 1,646 | 44,488 |

[1] Preliminary.   [2] Estimate.   [3] Forecast.   Source: Foreign Agricultural Service, U.S. Department of Agriculture (FAS-USDA)

**Centrifugal Sugar (Raw Value) Imported into Selected Countries**    In Thousands of Metric Tons

| Year | Algeria | Canada | China | European Union | Indonesia | Iran | Japan | Korea, South | Malaysia | Nigeria | Russia | United States | World Total |
|---|---|---|---|---|---|---|---|---|---|---|---|---|---|
| 2013-14 | 1,854 | 1,007 | 4,275 | 3,262 | 3,570 | 1,629 | 1,360 | 1,909 | 1,897 | 1,470 | 1,020 | 3,395 | 51,450 |
| 2014-15 | 1,844 | 1,184 | 5,058 | 2,918 | 2,950 | 266 | 1,360 | 1,882 | 2,063 | 1,465 | 1,100 | 3,223 | 50,248 |
| 2015-16 | 1,921 | 1,229 | 6,116 | 3,055 | 3,724 | 822 | 1,275 | 1,900 | 2,009 | 1,470 | 750 | 3,031 | 54,629 |
| 2016-17 | 2,135 | 1,139 | 4,600 | 2,908 | 4,781 | 962 | 1,232 | 1,757 | 1,893 | 1,820 | 327 | 2,943 | 55,418 |
| 2017-18 | 2,261 | 1,238 | 4,350 | 1,612 | 4,325 | 203 | 1,240 | 1,864 | 2,002 | 1,870 | 274 | 2,972 | 55,621 |
| 2018-19 | 2,328 | 1,268 | 4,086 | 2,374 | 5,362 | 935 | 1,187 | 1,999 | 2,139 | 1,870 | 562 | 2,785 | 53,320 |
| 2019-20 | 2,468 | 1,245 | 3,808 | 2,235 | 4,758 | 1,111 | 1,142 | 1,926 | 1,966 | 1,890 | 604 | 3,778 | 53,804 |
| 2020-21[1] | 2,258 | 1,389 | 6,379 | 1,792 | 6,124 | 1,421 | 1,051 | 1,934 | 2,142 | 1,880 | 584 | 2,922 | 58,863 |
| 2021-22[2] | 2,246 | 1,319 | 5,380 | 2,000 | 5,466 | 789 | 1,004 | 1,983 | 1,954 | 1,930 | 860 | 3,307 | 55,843 |
| 2022-23[3] | 2,202 | 1,470 | 4,400 | 2,000 | 5,700 | 815 | 1,037 | 1,995 | 2,165 | 1,950 | 365 | 3,123 | 57,396 |

[1] Preliminary.   [2] Estimate.   [3] Forecast.   Source: Foreign Agricultural Service, U.S. Department of Agriculture (FAS-USDA)

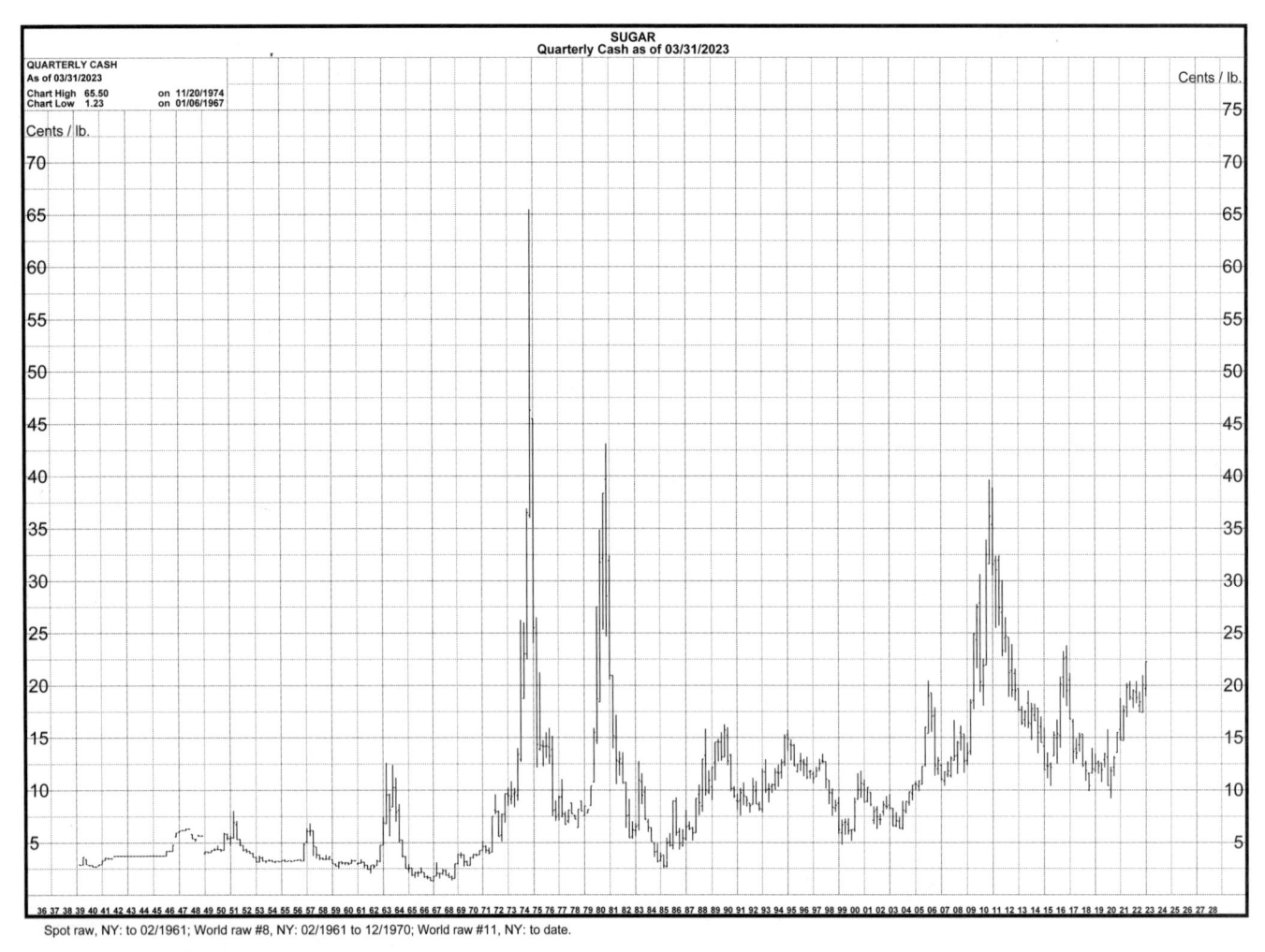

# SUGAR

**SUGAR**
Quarterly Cash as of 03/31/2023

QUARTERLY CASH
As of 03/31/2023
Chart High 65.50 on 11/20/1974
Chart Low 1.23 on 01/06/1967

Spot raw, NY: to 02/1961; World raw #8, NY: 02/1961 to 12/1970; World raw #11, NY: to date.

## Centrifugal Sugar (Raw Value) Exported From Selected Countries — In Thousands of Metric Tons

| Year | Australia | Brazil | Colombia | Cuba | Dominican Republic | European Union | Guatemala | India | Mauritius | South Africa | Swaziland | Thailand | World Total |
|---|---|---|---|---|---|---|---|---|---|---|---|---|---|
| 2013-14 | 3,242 | 26,200 | 900 | 957 | 208 | 412 | 1,552 | 2,100 | 2,806 | 416 | 868 | 7,200 | 57,951 |
| 2014-15 | 3,561 | 23,950 | 835 | 915 | 186 | 641 | 1,582 | 2,340 | 2,580 | 457 | 772 | 8,252 | 55,033 |
| 2015-16 | 3,700 | 24,350 | 584 | 1,112 | 186 | 665 | 1,548 | 2,029 | 3,800 | 463 | 305 | 7,055 | 54,187 |
| 2016-17 | 4,000 | 28,500 | 695 | 1,160 | 185 | 587 | 1,987 | 1,978 | 2,125 | 474 | 218 | 7,016 | 60,047 |
| 2017-18 | 3,600 | 28,200 | 732 | 557 | 184 | 519 | 4,349 | 1,881 | 2,236 | 390 | 768 | 10,907 | 65,868 |
| 2018-19 | 3,735 | 19,600 | 801 | 636 | 185 | 582 | 2,411 | 2,125 | 4,700 | 347 | 1,041 | 10,612 | 58,140 |
| 2019-20 | 3,600 | 19,280 | 778 | 690 | 212 | 778 | 1,459 | 1,858 | 5,800 | 396 | 1,451 | 6,695 | 53,424 |
| 2020-21[1] | 3,400 | 32,150 | 669 | 378 | 215 | 634 | 1,278 | 1,395 | 8,406 | 369 | 1,007 | 3,739 | 63,509 |
| 2021-22[2] | 3,120 | 25,950 | 710 | 117 | 220 | 524 | 1,340 | 1,740 | 11,730 | 324 | 595 | 10,000 | 67,842 |
| 2022-23[3] | 3,570 | 28,200 | 730 | 117 | 190 | 545 | 1,300 | 1,750 | 9,390 | 325 | 600 | 11,000 | 69,252 |

[1] Preliminary. [2] Estimate. [3] Forecast. *Source: Foreign Agricultural Service, U.S. Department of Agriculture (FAS-USDA)*

## Average Wholesale Price of Refined Beet Sugar[2]--Midwest Market — In Cents Per Pound

| Year | Jan. | Feb. | Mar. | Apr. | May | June | July | Aug. | Sept. | Oct. | Nov. | Dec. | Average |
|---|---|---|---|---|---|---|---|---|---|---|---|---|---|
| 2013 | 30.50 | 28.50 | 27.60 | 26.63 | 26.30 | 26.50 | 26.00 | 25.50 | 26.25 | 27.38 | 28.00 | 27.50 | 47.22 |
| 2014 | 26.50 | 26.25 | 26.50 | 29.75 | 31.60 | 35.00 | 36.00 | 36.60 | 37.50 | 36.60 | 36.00 | 36.00 | 32.86 |
| 2015 | 36.00 | 35.25 | 35.13 | 35.50 | 34.30 | 34.00 | 33.80 | 33.13 | 33.00 | 32.40 | 32.00 | 32.00 | 33.88 |
| 2016 | 32.00 | 31.00 | 31.00 | 30.50 | 30.00 | 29.75 | 29.00 | 28.50 | 28.50 | 28.50 | 28.50 | 28.50 | 29.65 |
| 2017 | 28.50 | 28.63 | 29.10 | 29.50 | 29.50 | 30.70 | 31.88 | 32.13 | 32.90 | 33.50 | 34.63 | 35.00 | 31.33 |
| 2018 | 35.25 | 36.00 | 36.00 | 36.00 | 36.00 | 36.00 | 36.00 | 36.00 | 36.00 | 33.38 | 34.90 | 35.00 | 35.54 |
| 2019 | 35.00 | 35.00 | 35.00 | 35.00 | 35.00 | 35.00 | 35.00 | 35.00 | 35.00 | 35.00 | 40.40 | 43.25 | 36.14 |
| 2020 | 44.00 | 44.00 | 44.00 | 44.00 | 44.00 | 44.00 | 44.00 | 44.00 | 44.00 | 36.50 | 36.50 | 36.50 | 42.13 |
| 2021 | 36.50 | 36.50 | 36.50 | 36.50 | 36.50 | 36.50 | 37.20 | 39.00 | 39.00 | 39.00 | 39.00 | 39.00 | 37.60 |
| 2022[1] | 39.00 | 41.00 | 42.00 | 42.00 | NQ | NQ | 70.00 | 70.00 | 70.00 | 55.25 | 58.00 | NQ | 54.14 |

[1] Preliminary. [2] These are f.o.b. basis prices in bulk, not delivered prices. *Source: Economic Research Service, U.S. Department of Agriculture (ERS)*

# SUGAR

## Average Price of World Raw Sugar[1]   In Cents Per Pound

| Year | Jan. | Feb. | Mar. | Apr. | May | June | July | Aug. | Sept. | Oct. | Nov. | Dec. | Average |
|---|---|---|---|---|---|---|---|---|---|---|---|---|---|
| 2013 | 18.37 | 18.28 | 18.33 | 17.71 | 17.08 | 16.79 | 16.38 | 16.44 | 17.33 | 18.81 | 17.58 | 16.41 | 17.46 |
| 2014 | 15.42 | 16.28 | 17.58 | 17.01 | 17.50 | 17.22 | 17.18 | 15.89 | 14.60 | 16.48 | 15.89 | 14.99 | 16.34 |
| 2015 | 15.06 | 14.52 | 12.84 | 12.93 | 12.70 | 11.75 | 11.88 | 10.67 | 11.32 | 14.14 | 14.89 | 15.00 | 13.14 |
| 2016 | 14.29 | 13.31 | 15.43 | 15.00 | 16.68 | 19.34 | 19.69 | 20.01 | 21.30 | 22.92 | 20.81 | 18.83 | 18.13 |
| 2017 | 20.54 | 20.40 | 18.06 | 16.32 | 15.66 | 13.53 | 14.11 | 13.80 | 13.92 | 14.23 | 14.66 | 14.43 | 15.81 |
| 2018 | 13.99 | 13.56 | 12.83 | 11.82 | 11.85 | 12.06 | 11.17 | 10.46 | 10.78 | 13.18 | 12.78 | 12.55 | 12.25 |
| 2019 | 12.70 | 12.94 | 12.47 | 12.55 | 11.82 | 12.44 | 12.15 | 11.56 | 11.16 | 12.46 | 12.69 | 13.34 | 12.36 |
| 2020 | 14.18 | 15.07 | 11.81 | 10.07 | 10.65 | 11.83 | 11.92 | 12.81 | 12.42 | 14.29 | 14.93 | 14.67 | 12.89 |
| 2021 | 15.94 | 16.97 | 15.81 | 16.17 | 17.20 | 17.21 | 17.73 | 19.38 | 19.28 | 19.62 | 19.75 | 19.17 | 17.85 |
| 2022[1] | 18.46 | 18.20 | 19.11 | 19.68 | 19.27 | 18.80 | 18.35 | 18.06 | 18.19 | 18.30 | 19.40 | 20.02 | 18.82 |

[1] Contract No. 11, f.o.b. stowed Caribbean port, including Brazil, bulk spot price.   [2] Preliminary.   Source: Economic Research Service, U.S. Department of Agriculture (ERS-USDA)

## Average Price of Raw Sugar in New York (C.I.F., Duty/Free Paid, Contract #12 & #14)   In Cents Per Pound

| Year | Jan. | Feb. | Mar. | Apr. | May | June | July | Aug. | Sept. | Oct. | Nov. | Dec. | Average |
|---|---|---|---|---|---|---|---|---|---|---|---|---|---|
| 2013 | 21.20 | 20.72 | 20.82 | 20.38 | 19.51 | 19.31 | 19.22 | 20.97 | 21.05 | 21.82 | 20.61 | 19.95 | 20.46 |
| 2014 | 20.27 | 21.65 | 22.03 | 24.33 | 24.66 | 25.65 | 24.78 | 25.64 | 25.36 | 26.41 | 24.26 | 24.81 | 24.15 |
| 2015 | 25.24 | 24.62 | 24.07 | 24.39 | 24.61 | 24.76 | 24.67 | 24.50 | 24.21 | 25.04 | 26.63 | 25.83 | 24.88 |
| 2016 | 25.76 | 25.50 | 26.32 | 27.90 | 27.26 | 27.68 | 28.15 | 28.54 | 28.16 | 28.57 | 28.76 | 29.24 | 27.65 |
| 2017 | 29.44 | 30.59 | 29.95 | 28.72 | 28.41 | 27.83 | 26.77 | 25.11 | 26.90 | 27.09 | 27.28 | 26.93 | 27.92 |
| 2018 | 26.60 | 25.83 | 24.73 | 24.92 | 24.59 | 25.72 | 25.56 | 25.60 | 25.40 | 25.21 | 25.04 | 25.23 | 25.37 |
| 2019 | 25.57 | 25.90 | 26.23 | 26.95 | 26.33 | 26.49 | 25.66 | 25.80 | 25.65 | 26.07 | 27.21 | 26.01 | 26.16 |
| 2020 | 25.90 | 26.71 | 27.09 | 26.02 | 25.85 | 25.95 | 26.59 | 27.39 | 26.85 | 27.55 | 29.33 | 28.42 | 26.97 |
| 2021 | 28.79 | 29.72 | 30.48 | 31.24 | 32.42 | 33.05 | 35.77 | 34.50 | 35.72 | 37.06 | 37.12 | 36.71 | 33.55 |
| 2022[1] | 35.48 | 35.43 | 36.33 | 36.66 | 36.38 | 36.15 | 34.83 | 35.63 | 34.97 | 34.70 | 35.94 | 36.51 | 35.75 |

[1] Preliminary.   Source: Economic Research Service, U.S. Department of Agriculture (ERS-USDA)

## Supply and Utilization of Sugar (Cane and Beet) in the United States   In Thousands of Short Tons (Raw Value)

| | Supply | | | | | | | | Utilization | | | | | |
|---|---|---|---|---|---|---|---|---|---|---|---|---|---|---|
| | Production | | | Offshore Receipts | | | | | | Net Changes in Invisible Stocks | Refining Loss Adjustment | Domestic Disappearance | | |
| Year | Cane | Beet | Total | Foreign | Territories | Total | Beginning Stocks | Total Supply | Total Use | Exports | | | In Polyhydric Alcohol[4] | Total | Per Capita Pounds |
| 2013-14 | 3,667 | 4,794 | 8,462 | 3,742 | 0 | 3,742 | 2,158 | 14,362 | 12,552 | 306 | 0 | 0 | 346 | 11,819 | 68.0 |
| 2014-15 | 3,763 | 4,893 | 8,656 | 3,553 | 0 | 3,553 | 1,810 | 14,019 | 12,204 | 185 | 0 | 0 | 28 | 11,888 | 68.2 |
| 2015-16 | 3,870 | 5,119 | 8,989 | 3,341 | 0 | 3,341 | 1,815 | 14,145 | 12,091 | 74 | -33 | 0 | 22 | 11,881 | 69.3 |
| 2016-17 | 3,867 | 5,103 | 8,970 | 3,244 | 0 | 3,244 | 2,054 | 14,267 | 12,391 | 95 | 38 | 0 | 29 | 12,102 | 69.8 |
| 2017-18 | 4,014 | 5,279 | 9,293 | 3,277 | 0 | 3,277 | 1,876 | 14,445 | 12,438 | 170 | 82 | 0 | 28 | 12,048 | 69.3 |
| 2018-19 | 4,060 | 4,939 | 8,999 | 3,070 | 0 | 3,070 | 2,008 | 14,077 | 12,294 | 35 | 28 | 0 | 27 | 12,106 | 68.7 |
| 2019-20 | 3,798 | 4,351 | 8,149 | 4,165 | 0 | 4,165 | 1,783 | 14,097 | 12,479 | 61 | 74 | 0 | 20 | 12,246 | 68.4 |
| 2020-21[1] | 4,141 | 5,092 | 9,233 | 3,221 | 0 | 3,221 | 1,618 | 14,071 | 12,367 | 49 | 40 | 0 | 27 | 12,161 | 69.0 |
| 2021-22[2] | 4,000 | 5,155 | 9,156 | 3,646 | 0 | 3,646 | 1,704 | 14,507 | 12,688 | 29 | 81 | 0 | 27 | 12,470 | |
| 2022-23[3] | 4,199 | 5,048 | 9,248 | 3,330 | 0 | 3,330 | 1,820 | 14,460 | 12,740 | 35 | | 0 | 25 | 12,600 | |

[1] Preliminary.   [2] Estimate.   [3] Forecast.   [4] Includes feed use.   Source: Economic Research Service, U.S. Department of Agriculture (ERS-USDA)

## Sugarcane for Sugar & Seed and Production of Cane Sugar and Molasses in the United States

| | | | | | | | | | Farm Value | | Sugar Production | | | |
| | Acreage Harvested (1,000 Acres) | Yield of Cane Per Havested Acre Net Tons | Production for Sugar | Production for Seed | Total | Sugar Yield Per Acre (Short Tons) | Farm Price ($ Per Ton) | of Cane Used for Sugar | of Cane Used for Sugar & Seed | Raw Value Total (1,000 Tons) | Per Ton of Cane (In Lbs.) | Refined Basis (1,000 Tons) | Molasses Made Edible | Total[3] |
| Year | | | 1,000 Tons | | | | | 1,000 Dollars | | | | | 1,000 Gallons | |
| 2013 | 910.8 | 33.8 | 29,023 | 1,738 | 30,761 | 4.27 | 31.4 | 910,377 | 962,807 | 3,667 | ---- | ---- | ---- | ---- |
| 2014 | 868.5 | 35.0 | 28,895 | 1,529 | 30,424 | 4.57 | 34.7 | 1,002,138 | 1,054,657 | 3,764 | ---- | ---- | ---- | ---- |
| 2015 | 874.7 | 36.7 | 30,555 | 1,567 | 32,122 | 4.64 | 31.2 | 953,328 | 1,000,620 | 3,857 | ---- | ---- | ---- | ---- |
| 2016 | 903.1 | 35.6 | 30,371 | 1,747 | 32,118 | 4.52 | 32.6 | 990,209 | 1,043,953 | 3,856 | ---- | ---- | ---- | ---- |
| 2017 | 904.1 | 36.8 | 31,182 | 2,056 | 33,238 | 4.72 | 31.0 | 1,025,524 | | 4,017 | ---- | ---- | ---- | ---- |
| 2018 | 899.7 | 38.4 | 32,934 | 1,608 | 34,542 | 4.69 | 33.4 | 1,154,907 | | 4,029 | ---- | ---- | ---- | ---- |
| 2019 | 913.2 | 35.0 | 30,287 | 1,650 | 31,937 | 4.36 | 38.3 | 1,223,686 | | 3,790 | ---- | ---- | ---- | ---- |
| 2020 | 947.6 | 38.1 | 34,338 | 1,762 | 36,100 | 4.65 | 40.9 | 1,476,508 | | 4,199 | ---- | ---- | ---- | ---- |
| 2021[1] | 935.2 | 35.1 | 32,838 | 1,797 | 32,838 | 4.43 | 46.9 | 1,540,497 | | 3,938 | ---- | ---- | ---- | ---- |
| 2022[2] | 930.2 | 37.3 | 34,671 | | | 4.74 | | | | 4,219 | ---- | ---- | ---- | ---- |

[1] Preliminary.   [2] Estimate.   [3] Excludes edible molasses.   Source: Economic Research Service, U.S. Department of Agriculture (ERS-USDA)

# SUGAR

## U.S. Sugar Beets, Beet Sugar, Pulp & Molasses Produced from Sugar Beets and Raw Sugar Spot Prices

| Year of Harvest | Acreage Planted (1,000 Acres) | Acreage Harvested (1,000 Acres) | Yield Per Harvested Acre (Sh. Tons) | Production (1,000 Tons) | Sugar Yield Per Acre (Sh. Tons) | Price[3] (Dollars) | Farm Value (1,000 $) | Sugar Production Equivalent Raw Value[4] (1,000 Short Tons) | Refined Basis (1,000 Short Tons) | World[5] Refined #5 (Cents/Lb) | CSCE #11 World (Cents/Lb) | CSCE N.Y. Duty Paid (Cents/Lb) | Wholesale List Price HFCS (42%) Midwest |
|---|---|---|---|---|---|---|---|---|---|---|---|---|---|
| 2013 | 1,198 | 1,154 | 28.4 | 32,789 | 4.15 | 46.90 | 1,536,422 | 4,794 | ---- | 22.17 | 17.46 | 20.46 | 35.86 |
| 2014 | 1,163 | 1,146 | 27.3 | 31,285 | 4.27 | 46.00 | 1,440,068 | 4,893 | ---- | 20.05 | 16.34 | 24.15 | 29.96 |
| 2015 | 1,160 | 1,145 | 30.9 | 35,359 | 4.47 | 47.20 | 1,669,310 | 5,119 | ---- | 16.94 | 13.14 | 24.88 | 32.75 |
| 2016 | 1,163 | 1,126 | 32.8 | 36,920 | 4.53 | 35.70 | 1,318,267 | 5,103 | ---- | 22.63 | 18.13 | 27.65 | 37.68 |
| 2017 | 1,132 | 1,114 | 31.7 | 35,317 | 4.74 | 41.20 | 1,456,165 | 5,279 | ---- | 19.62 | 15.81 | 27.92 | 39.79 |
| 2018 | 1,113 | 1,095 | 30.3 | 33,145 | 4.50 | 35.60 | 1,183,562 | 4,939 | ---- | 15.56 | 12.25 | 25.37 | 39.32 |
| 2019 | 1,133 | 980 | 29.2 | 28,650 | 4.44 | 38.30 | 1,098,421 | 4,351 | ---- | 15.18 | 12.36 | 26.16 | 41.23 |
| 2020 | 1,162 | 1,142 | 29.4 | 33,610 | 4.46 | 50.50 | 1,696,742 | 5,092 | ---- | 17.02 | 12.89 | 26.97 | 42.53 |
| 2021[1] | 1,160 | 1,108 | 33.2 | 36,751 | 4.65 | 52.70 | 1,936,497 | 5,155 | ---- | 21.40 | 17.85 | 33.55 | 42.53 |
| 2022[2] | 1,160 | 1,137 | 28.6 | 33,462 | 4.44 | | | 5,048 | ---- | 24.17 | 18.82 | 35.75 | 43.67 |

[1] Preliminary. [2] Estimate. [3] Includes support payments, but excludes Gov't. sugar beet payments. [4] Refined sugar multiplied by factor of 1.07. [5] F.O.B. Europe. *Source: Economic Research Service, U.S. Department of Agriculture (ERS-USDA)*

## Sugar Deliveries and Stocks in the United States    In Thousands of Short Tons (Raw Value)

| Year | Quota Allocation | Actual Imports | Cane Sugar Refineries Deliveries | Beet Sugar Factories Deliveries | Importers of Direct Consumption Sugar | Mainland Cane Sugar Mills[3] | Total Deliveries | Total Domestic Consumption | Cane Sugar Refineries | Beet Sugar Factories | CCC | Refiners' Raw | Mainland Cane Mills | Total |
|---|---|---|---|---|---|---|---|---|---|---|---|---|---|---|
| 2013 | ---- | ---- | 5,849 | 4,777 | 949 | ---- | 11,575 | 12,124 | 388 | 2,013 | 0 | 574 | 1,646 | 4,621 |
| 2014 | ---- | ---- | 6,069 | 4,875 | 760 | ---- | 11,704 | 11,831 | 572 | 1,603 | 0 | 592 | 1,714 | 4,481 |
| 2015 | ---- | ---- | 6,285 | 4,614 | 1,034 | ---- | 11,933 | 12,067 | 351 | 1,589 | 0 | 556 | 1,634 | 4,130 |
| 2016 | ---- | ---- | 6,386 | 4,809 | 921 | ---- | 12,115 | 12,287 | 413 | 1,889 | 0 | 322 | 1,336 | 3,960 |
| 2017 | ---- | ---- | 5,976 | 5,425 | 682 | ---- | 12,083 | 12,232 | 325 | 2,041 | 0 | 362 | 1,623 | 4,351 |
| 2018 | ---- | ---- | 6,219 | 5,121 | 705 | ---- | 12,045 | 12,184 | 316 | 1,716 | 0 | 538 | 1,529 | 4,099 |
| 2019 | ---- | ---- | 6,317 | 5,099 | 645 | ---- | 12,062 | 12,185 | 288 | 1,889 | 0 | 528 | 1,673 | 4,378 |
| 2020 | ---- | ---- | 6,593 | 4,387 | 1,201 | ---- | 12,182 | 12,276 | 326 | 1,454 | 0 | 565 | 1,510 | 3,855 |
| 2021[1] | ---- | ---- | 6,235 | 5,043 | 1,147 | ---- | 12,424 | 12,546 | 339 | 1,760 | 0 | 560 | 1,422 | 4,081 |
| 2022[2] | ---- | ---- | 6,458 | 5,286 | 679 | ---- | 12,423 | 12,526 | 327 | 1,744 | 0 | 483 | 1,524 | 4,077 |

[1] Preliminary. [2] Estimate. [3] Sugar for direct consumption only. [4] Refined. *Source: Economic Research Service, U.S. Department of Agriculture (ERS-USDA)*

## Sugar, Refined--Deliveries to End User in the United States    In Thousands of Short Tons

| Year | Bakery & Cereal Products | Beverages | Confectionery[2] | Hotels, Restar. & Institutions | Ice Cream & Dairy Products | Canned, Bottled & Frozen Foods | All Other Food Uses | Retail Grocers[3] | Wholesale Grocers[4] | Non-food Uses | Non-Industrial Uses | Industrial Uses | Total Deliveries |
|---|---|---|---|---|---|---|---|---|---|---|---|---|---|
| 2013 | 2,296 | 547 | 1,149 | 112 | 678 | 399 | 760 | 1,109 | 2,427 | 117 | 4,040 | 5,947 | 9,987 |
| 2014 | 2,435 | 598 | 1,142 | 118 | 756 | 434 | 853 | 1,193 | 2,151 | 118 | 3,965 | 6,336 | 10,300 |
| 2015 | 2,391 | 755 | 1,172 | 103 | 764 | 473 | 791 | 1,230 | 2,086 | 162 | 3,832 | 6,509 | 10,341 |
| 2016 | 2,517 | 695 | 1,156 | 92 | 764 | 433 | 880 | 1,303 | 2,248 | 179 | 4,100 | 6,625 | 10,725 |
| 2017 | 2,519 | 680 | 1,171 | 105 | 753 | 420 | 1,048 | 1,250 | 2,206 | 137 | 4,055 | 6,729 | 10,784 |
| 2018 | 2,468 | 725 | 1,222 | 91 | 812 | 375 | 1,147 | 1,224 | 2,175 | 138 | 3,825 | 6,887 | 10,713 |
| 2019 | 2,526 | 725 | 1,189 | 83 | 760 | 409 | 1,160 | 1,237 | 2,264 | 127 | 3,875 | 6,896 | 10,771 |
| 2020 | 2,421 | 620 | 993 | 90 | 766 | 430 | 1,016 | 1,311 | 2,244 | 143 | 3,951 | 6,389 | 10,340 |
| 2021 | 2,476 | 746 | 1,039 | 132 | 822 | 399 | 1,076 | 1,227 | 2,271 | 126 | 3,943 | 6,683 | 10,627 |
| 2022[1] | 2,592 | 837 | 1,189 | 94 | 835 | 394 | 963 | 2,434 | 1,283 | 119 | 4,120 | 6,929 | 11,049 |

[1] Preliminary. [2] And related products. [3] Chain stores, supermarkets. [4] Jobbers, sugar dealers. *Source: Economic Research Service, U.S. Department of Agriculture (ERS-USDA)*

## Deliveries[1] of All Sugar by Primary Distributors in the United States, by Quarters    In Thousands of Short Tons

| Year | First Quarter | Second Quarter | Third Quarter | Fourth Quarter | Total | Year | First Quarter | Second Quarter | Third Quarter | Fourth Quarter | Total |
|---|---|---|---|---|---|---|---|---|---|---|---|
| 2011 | 2,649 | 2,809 | 3,131 | 2,781 | 11,370 | 2017 | 2,869 | 3,130 | 3,161 | 3,073 | 12,232 |
| 2012 | 2,663 | 2,915 | 2,954 | 2,873 | 11,405 | 2018 | 2,926 | 2,964 | 3,223 | 3,071 | 12,184 |
| 2013 | 2,720 | 2,954 | 3,222 | 3,229 | 12,124 | 2019 | 2,935 | 3,059 | 3,166 | 3,024 | 12,185 |
| 2014 | 2,742 | 3,053 | 3,189 | 2,847 | 11,831 | 2020 | 3,119 | 2,964 | 3,241 | 2,951 | 12,276 |
| 2015 | 2,861 | 3,070 | 3,274 | 2,862 | 12,067 | 2021 | 2,958 | 3,185 | 3,184 | 3,220 | 12,546 |
| 2016 | 2,992 | 2,946 | 3,250 | 3,098 | 12,287 | 2022[2] | 3,016 | 3,181 | 3,160 | 3,168 | 12,525 |

[1] Includes for domestic consumption and for export. [2] Preliminary. *Source: Economic Research Service, U.S. Department of Agriculture (ERS-USDA)*

# SUGAR

## Volume of Trading of World Sugar #11 Futures in New York   In Thousands of Contracts

| Year | Jan. | Feb. | Mar. | Apr. | May | June | July | Aug. | Sept. | Oct. | Nov. | Dec. | Total |
|---|---|---|---|---|---|---|---|---|---|---|---|---|---|
| 2013 | 2,368.0 | 3,038.0 | 2,039.9 | 3,086.2 | 1,908.9 | 3,974.1 | 2,037.0 | 2,117.1 | 3,791.9 | 2,279.9 | 1,559.9 | 1,612.7 | 29,814 |
| 2014 | 2,461.6 | 4,157.3 | 2,477.4 | 2,857.3 | 1,906.5 | 3,370.3 | 1,981.4 | 1,853.3 | 3,657.9 | 1,651.3 | 1,574.3 | 1,448.0 | 29,397 |
| 2015 | 2,547.7 | 3,635.6 | 2,790.0 | 3,850.9 | 2,274.2 | 3,789.2 | 2,260.8 | 2,315.0 | 4,329.7 | 2,600.5 | 2,303.8 | 1,697.0 | 34,394 |
| 2016 | 3,182.7 | 3,772.8 | 2,652.9 | 3,517.9 | 2,596.7 | 4,210.0 | 1,738.1 | 2,008.6 | 3,963.5 | 1,721.8 | 1,964.4 | 1,786.0 | 33,115 |
| 2017 | 2,494.1 | 3,269.3 | 2,773.6 | 3,294.8 | 2,484.6 | 3,515.7 | 1,859.0 | 2,291.5 | 3,359.1 | 1,665.9 | 2,055.1 | 1,898.4 | 30,961 |
| 2018 | 3,212.7 | 3,692.3 | 2,839.4 | 4,157.9 | 3,195.2 | 3,984.1 | 2,003.6 | 2,836.6 | 4,144.2 | 3,216.5 | 2,129.3 | 1,599.2 | 37,011 |
| 2019 | 3,371.9 | 3,497.8 | 3,015.9 | 4,319.7 | 3,170.8 | 4,020.9 | 2,198.2 | 2,495.6 | 4,812.1 | 2,059.5 | 2,308.6 | 2,417.1 | 37,688 |
| 2020 | 4,764.5 | 5,033.4 | 4,650.2 | 3,940.6 | 2,903.6 | 3,812.2 | 2,238.7 | 2,418.5 | 3,936.7 | 2,522.3 | 2,033.8 | 1,694.8 | 39,949 |
| 2021 | 2,570.6 | 3,512.8 | 2,629.1 | 3,537.5 | 2,092.9 | 3,337.2 | 2,070.3 | 2,307.4 | 3,439.3 | 1,815.9 | 1,900.6 | 1,789.1 | 31,003 |
| 2022 | 2,360.9 | 3,011.4 | 2,788.3 | 3,305.4 | 2,088.8 | 3,260.4 | 2,071.4 | 2,084.2 | 3,562.5 | 2,118.0 | 2,595.5 | 2,028.4 | 31,275 |

Contract size = 112,000 lbs.   Source: ICE Futures U.S. (ICE)

## Average Open Interest of World Sugar #11 Futures in New York   In Contracts

| Year | Jan. | Feb. | Mar. | Apr. | May | June | July | Aug. | Sept. | Oct. | Nov. | Dec. |
|---|---|---|---|---|---|---|---|---|---|---|---|---|
| 2013 | 796,708 | 824,203 | 804,682 | 852,113 | 846,873 | 901,021 | 848,276 | 878,813 | 870,124 | 818,823 | 803,346 | 810,753 |
| 2014 | 834,655 | 838,471 | 787,473 | 792,420 | 809,219 | 870,191 | 842,551 | 885,193 | 851,724 | 766,320 | 811,959 | 828,791 |
| 2015 | 824,778 | 848,192 | 862,965 | 876,247 | 853,458 | 885,602 | 805,457 | 837,922 | 790,609 | 766,704 | 838,992 | 861,944 |
| 2016 | 870,944 | 830,246 | 795,043 | 820,305 | 841,639 | 894,893 | 837,385 | 880,629 | 885,571 | 841,889 | 837,131 | 818,873 |
| 2017 | 828,436 | 824,169 | 778,676 | 791,551 | 790,116 | 833,483 | 768,669 | 812,524 | 773,437 | 700,720 | 709,575 | 752,794 |
| 2018 | 844,185 | 891,797 | 915,120 | 1,003,293 | 1,012,957 | 977,622 | 973,446 | 1,041,981 | 871,673 | 774,976 | 791,152 | 840,548 |
| 2019 | 905,607 | 889,863 | 889,788 | 890,306 | 997,302 | 947,567 | 903,584 | 1,036,573 | 1,012,939 | 913,104 | 968,649 | 1,002,550 |
| 2020 | 1,084,021 | 1,222,255 | 1,073,698 | 991,547 | 960,551 | 970,496 | 942,507 | 1,026,601 | 1,009,797 | 992,075 | 1,065,231 | 1,059,590 |
| 2021 | 1,099,067 | 1,102,368 | 1,040,251 | 1,030,890 | 1,019,569 | 978,263 | 936,320 | 1,027,094 | 979,906 | 881,092 | 902,347 | 867,312 |
| 2022 | 880,822 | 887,549 | 822,512 | 883,294 | 824,490 | 795,711 | 711,378 | 752,195 | 739,528 | 706,106 | 819,550 | 911,523 |

Contract size = 112,000 lbs.   Source: ICE Futures U.S. (ICE)

# Sulfur

Sulfur (atomic symbol S) is an odorless, tasteless, light yellow, nonmetallic element. As early as 2000 BC, Egyptians used sulfur compounds to bleach fabric. The Chinese used sulfur as an essential component when they developed gunpowder in the 13th century.

Sulfur is widely found in both its free and combined states. Free sulfur is found mixed with gypsum and pumice stone in volcanic regions. Sulfur dioxide is an air pollutant that is released by the burning of fossil fuels. The most important use of sulfur is for the production of sulfur compounds. Sulfur is used in skin ointments, matches, dyes, gunpowder, and phosphoric acid.

**Supply** – World production of all forms of sulfur in 2022 rose by +0.7% yr/yr to 82.000 million metric tons, a new record high. The world's largest producers of sulfur in 2022 were China with 22.0% of the world's production, the U.S. with 10.5%, Russia with 8.9%, Saudi Arabia with 8.5%, and Canada with 6.0%. U.S. production of sulfur in 2022 rose by +6.6% yr/yr to 8.600 million metric tons.

**Demand** – U.S. consumption of all forms of sulfur in 2022 was up by +3.5% at 9.800 million metric tons. U.S. consumption of elemental sulfur in 2020 rose by +6.3% yr/yr to 8.240 million metric tons. U.S. consumption of sulfuric acid in 2020 rose +8.3% yr/yr to 7.010 million metric tons.

**Trade** – U.S. exports of recovered sulfur in 2020 fell by -40.5% yr/yr to 1.310 million metric tons. U.S. imports of recovered sulfur in 2020 rose by +21.2% yr/yr to 1.850 million metric tons.

## World Production of Sulfur (All Forms)   In Thousands of Metric Tons

| Year | Canada | China | France | Germany | Kazakh-stan | Japan | Mexico | Poland | Russia | Saudi Arabia | Spain | United States | World Total |
|---|---|---|---|---|---|---|---|---|---|---|---|---|---|
| 2015 | 5,745 | 17,290 | 400 | 1,012 | 3,362 | 3,120 | 858 | 1,202 | 6,951 | 4,900 | ---- | 9,540 | 77,800 |
| 2016 | 5,381 | 17,000 | 400 | 930 | 3,518 | 3,151 | 673 | 1,196 | 7,072 | 6,000 | ---- | 9,740 | 78,900 |
| 2017 | 5,327 | 17,440 | 400 | 866 | 3,372 | 3,514 | 551 | 1,236 | 7,297 | 6,500 | ---- | 9,630 | 79,600 |
| 2018 | 5,333 | 17,500 | 400 | 674 | 3,408 | 3,510 | 443 | 1,190 | 7,561 | 6,500 | ---- | 9,670 | 79,600 |
| 2019 | 6,938 | 17,500 | 400 | 670 | 3,400 | 3,500 | 365 | 1,190 | 7,560 | 6,500 | ---- | 8,710 | 80,000 |
| 2020 | 4,900 | 17,300 |  | 633 | 3,040 | 4,480 |  | 992 | 7,530 | 6,500 | ---- | 7,890 | 79,800 |
| 2021[1] | 4,880 | 18,800 |  | 592 | 3,150 | 4,600 |  | 995 | 7,530 | 7,000 | ---- | 8,070 | 81,400 |
| 2022[2] | 4,900 | 18,000 |  | 600 | 3,200 | 4,600 |  | 1,000 | 7,300 | 7,000 | ---- | 8,600 | 82,000 |

[1] Preliminary.   [2] Estimate.   Source: U.S. Geological Survey (USGS)

## Salient Statistics of Sulfur in the United States   In Thousands of Metric Tons (Sulfur Content)

| | Production of | | | | | | | | | | Apparent | Sales Value of Shipments | | |
|---|---|---|---|---|---|---|---|---|---|---|---|---|---|---|
| | Elemental Sulfur | | | | | By- | Other | | | | Con- | F.O.B. Mine/Plant | | |
| | Native - Sulfur[3] | Recovered | | | Total | product | Sulf. Acid | Imports | Exports | Producer | sumption | | | |
| Year | Frasch | Petroleum & Coke | Natural Gas | Total | Elemental Sulfur | Sulfuric Acid[4] | Com-pounds | Sulfuric Acid[4] | Sulfuric Acid[4] | Stocks, Dec. 31[5] | (All Forms) | Frasch | Recovered | Average Total |
| 2015 | ---- | 7,910 | 984 | 8,890 | 646 | ---- | 9,540 | 3,540 | 177 | 138 | 11,000 | ---- | ---- | 87.62 |
| 2016 | ---- | 8,290 | 781 | 9,070 | 673 | ---- | 9,740 | 3,220 | 180 | 142 | 10,500 | ---- | ---- | 37.88 |
| 2017 | ---- | 8,410 | 662 | 9,070 | 560 | ---- | 9,630 | 2,920 | 246 | 124 | 10,100 | ---- | ---- | 46.39 |
| 2018 | ---- | 8,378 | 626 | 9,005 | 672 | ---- | 9,670 | 3,050 | 342 | 118 | 10,400 | ---- | ---- | 81.16 |
| 2019 | ---- | 7,788 | 341 | 8,128 | 596 | ---- | 8,710 | 2,970 | 220 | 124 | 9,240 | ---- | ---- | 51.10 |
| 2020 | ---- | 7,029 | 276 | 7,303 | 581 | ---- | 7,890 |  | 349 | 109 | 9,950 | ---- | ---- | 24.40 |
| 2021[1] | ---- | 6,915 | 551 | 7,464 | 600 | ---- | 8,070 |  | 395 | 113 | 9,470 | ---- | ---- | 92.30 |
| 2022[2] | ---- | 7,500 | 503 | 8,004 | 600 | ---- | 8,600 |  | 609 | 120 | 9,800 | ---- | ---- | 150.00 |

[1] Preliminary.   [2] Estimate.   [3] Or sulfur ore; Withheld included in natural gas.   [4] Basis 100% H2SO4, sulfur equivalent.   [5] Frasch & recovered.
W = Withheld proprietary data.   Source: U.S. Geological Survey (USGS)

## Sulfur Consumption & Foreign Trade of the United States   In Thousands of Metric Tons (Sulfur Content)

| | Consumption | | | Sulfuric Acid Sold or Used, by End Use[2] | | | | | | Foreign Trade | | | | |
|---|---|---|---|---|---|---|---|---|---|---|---|---|---|---|
| | Native | Rec- | Total | Pulpmills | Inorganic | Synthetic | Phosph- | Petro- | | Exports | | | Imports | | |
| | Sulfur | overed | Elemental | & Paper | Chem- | Rubber | atic | leum | | Re- | Value | | Re- | Value |
| Year | (Frasch) | Sulfur | Form | Products | icals[3] | & Plastic | Fertilizers | Refining[4] | Frasch | Frasch | covered | $1,000 | Frasch | covered | $1,000 |
| 2013 | ---- | ---- | 9,810 | 7,780 | 168 | 101 | 70 | 5,270 | 1,270 | ---- | 1,770 | 235,000 | ---- | 2,990 | 202,000 |
| 2014 | ---- | ---- | 9,450 | 6,410 | 129 | 74 | 6 | 4,810 | 410 | ---- | 2,010 | 315,000 | ---- | 2,370 | 134,000 |
| 2015 | ---- | ---- | 9,310 | 6,320 | 124 | 128 | 6 | 4,610 | 428 | ---- | 1,850 | 284,000 | ---- | 2,240 | 136,000 |
| 2016 | ---- | ---- | 8,840 | 7,550 | 119 | 79 | 6 | 5,820 | 387 | ---- | 2,060 | 214,000 | ---- | 1,820 | 79,800 |
| 2017 | ---- | ---- | 8,630 | 6,650 | 125 | 90 | 7 | 5,010 | 347 | ---- | 2,340 | 251,000 | ---- | 1,850 | 110,000 |
| 2018 | ---- | ---- | 8,860 | 6,790 | 139 | 107 | 12 | 5,070 | 338 | ---- | 2,390 | 299,000 | ---- | 2,230 | 205,000 |
| 2019 | ---- | ---- | 7,750 | 6,470 | 133 | 70 | 11 | 4,850 | 337 | ---- | 2,200 | 173,000 | ---- | 1,840 | 137,000 |
| 2020[1] | ---- | ---- | 8,240 | 7,010 | 129 | 66 | 9 | 5,440 | 336 | ---- | 1,310 | 93,300 | ---- | 2,230 | 121,000 |

[1] Preliminary.   [2] Sulfur equivalent.   [3] Including inorganic pigments, paints & allied products, and other inorganic chemicals & products.
[4] Including other petroleum and coal products.   W = Withheld proprietary data.   NA = Not available.   Source: U.S. Geological Survey (USGS)

# Sunflowerseed, Meal and Oil

Sunflowers are native to South and North America but are now grown almost worldwide. Sunflower oil accounts for approximately 14% of the world's production of seed oils. Sunflower varieties that are commercially grown contain from 39% to 49% oil in the seed. Sunflower crops produce about 50 bushels of seed per acre on average, which yields approximately 50 gallons of oil.

Sunflower oil accounts for around 80% of the value of the sunflower crop. Refined sunflower oil is edible and used primarily as a salad and cooking oil and in margarine. Crude sunflower oil is used industrially for making soaps, candles, varnishes, and detergents. Sunflower oil contains 93% of the energy of U.S. No. 2 diesel fuel and is being explored as a potential alternate fuel source in diesel engines. Sunflower meal is used in livestock feed, and when fed to poultry, increases the yield of eggs. Sunflower seeds are also used for birdfeed and as a snack for humans.

**Prices** – The average monthly price received by U.S. farmers for sunflower seeds in the first four months of the 2022/23 marketing year (Sep/Aug) fell by -12.5% to $30.03 per hundred pounds.

**Supply** – World sunflower seed production in 2022/23 is expected to fall by -10.9% yr/yr to 51.072 million metric tons. The world's largest sunflower seed producers are forecasted to be Russia with 32.3% of world production, Ukraine with 19.6%, European Union with 18.6%, Argentina with 9.0%, China with 5.2%, Turkey with 3.7%, the U.S. with 2.5%, and Kazakhstan with 2.2%.

U.S. production of sunflower seeds in 2022/23 is expected to rise by +47.7% yr/yr to 1.276 million metric tons. U.S. farmers are expected to harvest 1.607 million acres of sunflowers in 2022/23, up +29.2% yr/yr. U.S sunflower seed yield in 2022/23 is expected to be 17.50 hundred pounds per acre, up +14.4% yr/yr.

**Demand** – Total U.S. disappearance of sunflower seeds in 2022/23 is expected to rise by +29.6% yr/yr to 1.578 million metric tons, of which 46.1% will go to non-oil and seed use, 40.1% to exports, and 3.4% to crushing for oil and meal.

**Trade** – World sunflower seed exports in 2022/23 are expected to rise by +38.0% yr/yr to 5.395 million metric tons, a new record high. The world's largest exporters will be Ukraine, accounting for 45.4% of world exports, the European Union with 11.1%, Moldova with 6.5%, China with 6.5%, and Kazakhstan with 5.2%. World sunflower seed imports in 2022/23 are expected to rise by +41.1% yr/yr to 5.339 million metric tons, a new record high. The world's largest importers will be European Union with 53.4% of world imports and Turkey with 23.4%.

## World Production of Sunflowerseed    In Thousands of Metric Tons

| Crop Year | Argentina | China | European Union | India | Kazakhstan | Pakistan | Russia | Serbia | South Africa | Turkey | Ukraine | United States | World Total |
|---|---|---|---|---|---|---|---|---|---|---|---|---|---|
| 2013-14 | 2,065 | 2,448 | 9,054 | 580 | 573 | 193 | 9,842 | 425 | 832 | 1,400 | 11,600 | 917 | 41,568 |
| 2014-15 | 3,160 | 2,582 | 8,974 | 383 | 513 | 169 | 8,374 | 525 | 661 | 1,200 | 10,200 | 1,004 | 39,284 |
| 2015-16 | 3,000 | 2,872 | 7,721 | 323 | 534 | 86 | 9,173 | 450 | 755 | 1,100 | 11,900 | 1,327 | 40,750 |
| 2016-17 | 3,547 | 3,201 | 8,651 | 318 | 755 | 106 | 10,858 | 650 | 874 | 1,320 | 15,200 | 1,203 | 48,393 |
| 2017-18 | 3,538 | 3,149 | 10,128 | 230 | 903 | 147 | 10,362 | 540 | 862 | 1,550 | 13,700 | 970 | 48,010 |
| 2018-19 | 3,825 | 2,494 | 9,505 | 172 | 848 | 133 | 12,710 | 680 | 678 | 1,800 | 15,000 | 956 | 50,659 |
| 2019-20 | 3,235 | 2,664 | 9,474 | 140 | 839 | 105 | 15,305 | 660 | 789 | 1,750 | 16,500 | 887 | 54,160 |
| 2020-21 | 3,430 | 2,570 | 8,898 | 185 | 844 | 87 | 13,269 | 675 | 678 | 1,560 | 14,100 | 1,353 | 49,196 |
| 2021-22[1] | 4,050 | 2,424 | 10,249 | 190 | 1,032 | 141 | 15,572 | 600 | 846 | 1,750 | 17,500 | 864 | 57,314 |
| 2022-23[2] | 4,600 | 2,650 | 9,475 | 215 | 1,100 | 135 | 16,500 | 600 | 850 | 1,900 | 10,000 | 1,276 | 51,072 |

[1] Preliminary.  [2] Forecast.  Source: Economic Research Service, U.S. Department of Agriculture (ERS-USDA)

## World Exports of Sunflowerseed    In Thousands of Metric Tons

| Crop Year | Argentina | Canada | China | European Union | Israel | Kazakhstan | Moldova | Russia | Serbia | Turkey | Ukraine | United States | World Total |
|---|---|---|---|---|---|---|---|---|---|---|---|---|---|
| 2013-14 | 74 | 49 | 202 | 712 | 3 | 146 | 322 | 135 | 106 | 57 | 70 | 120 | 2,010 |
| 2014-15 | 63 | 34 | 244 | 518 | 3 | 118 | 339 | 61 | 77 | 41 | 45 | 116 | 1,675 |
| 2015-16 | 308 | 29 | 286 | 424 | 3 | 168 | 369 | 107 | 134 | 109 | 83 | 99 | 2,132 |
| 2016-17 | 77 | 18 | 365 | 421 | 2 | 275 | 604 | 368 | 127 | 126 | 191 | 90 | 2,683 |
| 2017-18 | 63 | 17 | 480 | 705 | 1 | 321 | 674 | 98 | 112 | 148 | 39 | 79 | 2,756 |
| 2018-19 | 148 | 27 | 452 | 680 | 1 | 451 | 629 | 363 | 162 | 116 | 105 | 64 | 3,213 |
| 2019-20 | 212 | 38 | 500 | 528 | 1 | 318 | 479 | 1,253 | 140 | 99 | 53 | 45 | 3,687 |
| 2020-21 | 176 | 51 | 475 | 624 | 1 | 266 | 273 | 554 | 82 | 123 | 191 | 59 | 2,900 |
| 2021-22[1] | 156 | 43 | 438 | 396 | 1 | 224 | 524 | 235 | 84 | 118 | 1,622 | 50 | 3,910 |
| 2022-23[2] | 250 | 50 | 350 | 600 | 1 | 280 | 350 | 800 | 70 | 125 | 2,450 | 54 | 5,395 |

[1] Preliminary.  [2] Forecast.  Source: Economic Research Service, U.S. Department of Agriculture (ERS-USDA)

# SUNFLOWERSEED, MEAL AND OIL

## World Imports of Sunflowerseed     In Thousands of Metric Tons

| Crop Year | Belarus | Canada | Egypt | European Union | Iran | Mexico | Moldova | Morocco | Pakistan | Russia | Turkey | United States | World Total |
|---|---|---|---|---|---|---|---|---|---|---|---|---|---|
| 2013-14 | 13 | 25 | 43 | 319 | 42 | 18 | 2 | 1 | 197 | 35 | 597 | 65 | 1,702 |
| 2014-15 | 19 | 30 | 57 | 266 | 69 | 19 | 3 | 38 | 178 | 88 | 462 | 75 | 1,624 |
| 2015-16 | 25 | 22 | 63 | 622 | 120 | 21 | 6 | 15 | 94 | 121 | 483 | 72 | 2,111 |
| 2016-17 | 53 | 29 | 62 | 699 | 160 | 28 | 4 | 8 | 40 | 107 | 656 | 80 | 2,455 |
| 2017-18 | 27 | 22 | 102 | 521 | 66 | 27 | 3 | 19 | 45 | 47 | 770 | 97 | 2,383 |
| 2018-19 | 56 | 24 | 90 | 555 | 47 | 25 | 5 | 2 | 4 | 52 | 1,116 | 115 | 2,890 |
| 2019-20 | 58 | 26 | 76 | 976 | 31 | 20 | 4 | 11 | 5 | 56 | 1,178 | 181 | 3,343 |
| 2020-21 | 19 | 36 | 66 | 779 | 42 | 22 | 5 | 40 | 5 | 70 | 907 | 170 | 2,735 |
| 2021-22[1] | 50 | 37 | 44 | 1,794 | 45 | 30 | 88 | 4 | 5 | 75 | 669 | 175 | 3,784 |
| 2022-23[2] | 135 | 25 | 50 | 2,850 | 30 | 25 | 15 | 15 | 5 | 55 | 1,250 | 168 | 5,339 |

[1] Preliminary.  [2] Forecast.  Source: Economic Research Service, U.S. Department of Agriculture (ERS-USDA)

## World Production of Sunflowerseed Oil     In Thousands of Metric Tons

| Crop Year | Argentina | Burma | China | European Union | India | Pakistan | Russia | Serbia | South Africa | Turkey | Ukraine | United States | World Total |
|---|---|---|---|---|---|---|---|---|---|---|---|---|---|
| 2013-14 | 934 | 112 | 466 | 3,196 | 179 | 148 | 3,785 | 123 | 347 | 774 | 4,759 | 195 | 15,647 |
| 2014-15 | 1,153 | 131 | 466 | 3,232 | 121 | 132 | 3,428 | 161 | 298 | 677 | 4,429 | 146 | 14,974 |
| 2015-16 | 1,170 | 131 | 502 | 3,042 | 105 | 68 | 3,552 | 153 | 335 | 587 | 5,010 | 205 | 15,469 |
| 2016-17 | 1,335 | 131 | 609 | 3,335 | 105 | 38 | 4,171 | 191 | 348 | 761 | 6,351 | 211 | 18,300 |
| 2017-18 | 1,385 | 131 | 645 | 3,755 | 75 | 44 | 4,192 | 212 | 352 | 881 | 5,913 | 197 | 18,578 |
| 2018-19 | 1,425 | 131 | 466 | 3,671 | 58 | 48 | 4,935 | 212 | 272 | 1,066 | 6,364 | 201 | 19,603 |
| 2019-20 | 1,160 | 131 | 430 | 3,645 | 45 | 36 | 5,699 | 225 | 306 | 1,086 | 7,390 | 163 | 21,109 |
| 2020-21 | 1,350 | 131 | 430 | 3,460 | 62 | 29 | 5,121 | 225 | 300 | 1,044 | 5,913 | 212 | 19,031 |
| 2021-22[1] | 1,503 | 131 | 556 | 4,394 | 60 | 53 | 5,823 | 221 | 348 | 923 | 4,644 | 189 | 19,841 |
| 2022-23[2] | 1,609 | 131 | 538 | 4,605 | 64 | 48 | 6,195 | 225 | 344 | 1,219 | 4,085 | 265 | 20,355 |

[1] Preliminary.  [2] Forecast.  Source: Economic Research Service, U.S. Department of Agriculture (ERS-USDA)

## World Production of Sunflowerseed Meal     In Thousands of Metric Tons

| Crop Year | Argentina | Burma | China | European Union | India | Kazakhstan | Pakistan | Russia | South Africa | Turkey | Ukraine | United States | World Total |
|---|---|---|---|---|---|---|---|---|---|---|---|---|---|
| 2013-14 | 963 | 110 | 709 | 4,108 | 238 | 144 | 155 | 3,571 | 356 | 990 | 4,646 | 240 | 16,841 |
| 2014-15 | 1,147 | 128 | 709 | 4,131 | 156 | 135 | 137 | 3,407 | 302 | 866 | 4,254 | 179 | 16,177 |
| 2015-16 | 1,180 | 128 | 763 | 3,888 | 135 | 135 | 71 | 3,530 | 340 | 743 | 4,811 | 252 | 16,602 |
| 2016-17 | 1,350 | 128 | 927 | 4,263 | 135 | 176 | 40 | 4,146 | 353 | 963 | 6,030 | 259 | 19,493 |
| 2017-18 | 1,400 | 128 | 981 | 4,801 | 97 | 217 | 46 | 4,167 | 357 | 1,114 | 5,679 | 242 | 20,016 |
| 2018-19 | 1,435 | 128 | 709 | 4,696 | 75 | 155 | 50 | 4,911 | 275 | 1,348 | 6,112 | 247 | 20,940 |
| 2019-20 | 1,170 | 128 | 654 | 4,663 | 58 | 215 | 35 | 5,672 | 310 | 1,361 | 6,455 | 198 | 21,709 |
| 2020-21 | 1,335 | 128 | 654 | 4,432 | 80 | 225 | 29 | 5,096 | 305 | 1,306 | 5,679 | 257 | 20,262 |
| 2021-22[1] | 1,514 | 128 | 845 | 5,621 | 78 | 369 | 52 | 5,795 | 353 | 1,156 | 4,460 | 230 | 21,432 |
| 2022-23[2] | 1,621 | 128 | 818 | 5,891 | 91 | 368 | 48 | 6,165 | 350 | 1,524 | 3,924 | 322 | 22,120 |

[1] Preliminary.  [2] Forecast.  Source: Economic Research Service, U.S. Department of Agriculture (ERS-USDA)

## Sunflowerseed Statistics in the United States     In Thousands of Metric Tons

| Crop Year Beginning Sept. 1 | Acres Harvested (1,000) | Harvested Yield Per CWT | Farm Price ($/Metric Ton) | Value of Production (Million $) | Stocks, Sept. 1 | Production | Imports | Total Supply | Crush | Exports | Non-Oil Use & Seed | Total Disappearance |
|---|---|---|---|---|---|---|---|---|---|---|---|---|
| 2013-14 | 1,465 | 13.80 | 472 | 443.3 | 154 | 917 | 65 | 1,136 | 120 | 463 | 462 | 1,136 |
| 2014-15 | 1,510 | 14.69 | 478 | 497.8 | 91 | 1,004 | 75 | 1,170 | 116 | 366 | 580 | 1,170 |
| 2015-16 | 1,799 | 16.25 | 432 | 574.2 | 108 | 1,327 | 72 | 1,507 | 99 | 495 | 726 | 1,507 |
| 2016-17 | 1,532 | 17.31 | 384 | 464.0 | 187 | 1,203 | 80 | 1,470 | 90 | 508 | 605 | 1,470 |
| 2017-18 | 1,334 | 16.03 | 379 | 375.1 | 267 | 970 | 97 | 1,334 | 79 | 475 | 605 | 1,334 |
| 2018-19 | 1,217 | 17.31 | 384 | 370.4 | 175 | 956 | 115 | 1,246 | 64 | 485 | 567 | 1,246 |
| 2019-20 | 1,254 | 15.60 | 430 | 386.3 | 130 | 887 | 181 | 1,198 | 45 | 389 | 676 | 1,198 |
| 2020-21 | 1,666 | 17.90 | 470 | 632.0 | 88 | 1,353 | 170 | 1,611 | 59 | 504 | 869 | 1,611 |
| 2021-22[1] | 1,244 | 15.30 | 699 | 594.9 | 179 | 864 | 175 | 1,218 | 50 | 450 | 584 | 1,218 |
| 2022-23[2] | 1,607 | 17.50 | | | 134 | 1,276 | 168 | 1,578 | 54 | 632 | 728 | 1,578 |

[1] Preliminary.  [2] Forecast.  Source: Economic Research Service, U.S. Department of Agriculture (ERS-USDA)

# SUNFLOWERSEED, MEAL AND OIL

**Sunflower Oil Statistics in the United States**  In Thousands of Metric Tons

| Crop Year Beginning Sept. 1 | Stocks, Oct. 1 | Production | Imports | Total Supply | Exports | Domestic Use | Total Disappearance | Price $ Per Metric Ton (Crude Mpls.) |
|---|---|---|---|---|---|---|---|---|
| 2013-14 | 23 | 195 | 35 | 253 | 37 | 193 | 230 | 1,305 |
| 2014-15 | 23 | 146 | 80 | 249 | 29 | 197 | 226 | 1,449 |
| 2015-16 | 23 | 205 | 42 | 270 | 39 | 197 | 236 | 1,309 |
| 2016-17 | 34 | 211 | 54 | 299 | 32 | 226 | 258 | 1,182 |
| 2017-18 | 41 | 197 | 73 | 311 | 40 | 238 | 278 | 1,205 |
| 2018-19 | 33 | 201 | 60 | 294 | 55 | 220 | 275 | 1,173 |
| 2019-20 | 19 | 163 | 169 | 351 | 40 | 289 | 329 | 1,430 |
| 2020-21 | 22 | 212 | 134 | 368 | 45 | 297 | 342 | 1,543 |
| 2021-22[1] | 26 | 189 | 204 | 419 | 56 | 340 | 396 | 2,530 |
| 2022-23[2] | 23 | 265 | 125 | 413 | 45 | 345 | 390 | 2,012 |

[1] Preliminary.  [2] Forecast.  Source: Economic Research Service, U.S. Department of Agriculture (ERS-USDA)

**Sunflower Meal Statistics in the United States**  In Thousands of Metric Tons

| Crop Year Beginning Sept. 1 | Stocks, Oct. 1 | Production | Imports | Total Supply | Exports | Domestic Use | Total Disappearance | Price USD Per Metric Ton 28% Protein |
|---|---|---|---|---|---|---|---|---|
| 2013-14 | 5 | 240 | 11 | 256 | 8 | 243 | 256 | 270 |
| 2014-15 | 5 | 179 | 20 | 204 | 7 | 192 | 204 | 224 |
| 2015-16 | 5 | 252 | 21 | 278 | 12 | 261 | 278 | 175 |
| 2016-17 | 5 | 259 | 11 | 275 | 5 | 265 | 275 | 161 |
| 2017-18 | 5 | 242 | 1 | 248 | 6 | 237 | 248 | 190 |
| 2018-19 | 5 | 247 | 2 | 254 | 15 | 234 | 254 | 182 |
| 2019-20 | 5 | 198 | 2 | 205 | 20 | 180 | 205 | 201 |
| 2020-21 | 5 | 257 | 4 | 266 | 28 | 233 | 266 | 270 |
| 2021-22[1] | 5 | 230 | 14 | 249 | 28 | 216 | 249 | 308 |
| 2022-23[2] | 5 | 322 | 9 | 336 | 18 | 313 | 336 | 308 |

[1] Preliminary.  [2] Forecast.  Source: Economic Research Service, U.S. Department of Agriculture (ERS-USDA)

**Average Price Received by Farmers for Sunflower[2] in the United States**  In Dollars Per Hundred Pounds (Cwt.)

| Crop Year | Sept. | Oct. | Nov. | Dec. | Jan. | Feb. | Mar. | Apr. | May | June | July | Aug. | Average |
|---|---|---|---|---|---|---|---|---|---|---|---|---|---|
| 2013-14 | 22.60 | 23.00 | 20.70 | 18.80 | 19.60 | 22.80 | 21.60 | 22.30 | 24.10 | 22.80 | 22.10 | 22.40 | 21.90 |
| 2014-15 | 20.20 | 21.70 | 20.30 | 19.70 | 19.10 | 21.50 | 22.50 | 23.20 | 26.40 | 25.40 | 26.40 | 24.20 | 22.55 |
| 2015-16 | 25.20 | 18.40 | 18.30 | 19.30 | 20.10 | 20.40 | 21.10 | 20.90 | 19.50 | 20.10 | 19.00 | 19.60 | 20.16 |
| 2016-17 | 17.90 | 17.00 | 16.40 | 17.20 | 17.20 | 17.60 | 17.40 | 17.90 | 17.30 | 17.60 | 17.90 | 19.10 | 17.54 |
| 2017-18 | 17.40 | 16.80 | 16.60 | 17.00 | 17.60 | 17.70 | 17.30 | 18.00 | 17.90 | 17.70 | 17.40 | 16.90 | 17.36 |
| 2018-19 | 16.70 | 16.70 | 17.00 | 16.90 | 17.30 | 18.00 | 17.80 | 17.60 | 18.30 | 17.90 | 18.00 | 17.80 | 17.50 |
| 2019-20 | 18.50 | 17.50 | 17.70 | 17.80 | 19.50 | 20.40 | 20.90 | 20.30 | 20.50 | 21.70 | 23.70 | 25.80 | 20.36 |
| 2020-21 | 23.70 | 19.10 | 18.90 | 19.20 | 19.50 | 21.40 | 21.50 | 23.70 | 26.40 | 28.40 | 28.00 | 29.40 | 23.27 |
| 2021-22 | 30.70 | 30.50 | 30.30 | 31.60 | 31.00 | 32.20 | 33.90 | 37.10 | 40.20 | 40.20 | 36.20 | 37.80 | 34.31 |
| 2022-23[1] | 32.90 | 29.30 | 28.40 | 29.50 | 28.50 | 30.80 | | | | | | | 29.90 |

[1] Preliminary.  [2] KS, MN, ND and SD average.  Source: Economic Research Service, U.S. Department of Agriculture (ERS-USDA)

**Average Price of Crude Sunflower Oil at Minneapolis**  In Cents Per Pound

| Crop Year | Sept. | Oct. | Nov. | Dec. | Jan. | Feb. | Mar. | Apr. | May | June | July | Aug. | Average |
|---|---|---|---|---|---|---|---|---|---|---|---|---|---|
| 2013-14 | 63.75 | 60.50 | 57.40 | 57.00 | 57.00 | 57.00 | 58.00 | 59.00 | 59.00 | 57.50 | 61.00 | 63.00 | 59.18 |
| 2014-15 | 63.00 | 63.00 | 61.75 | 58.00 | 63.00 | 65.63 | 65.56 | 65.50 | 65.00 | 69.75 | 73.40 | 75.00 | 65.72 |
| 2015-16 | 75.00 | 72.00 | 64.50 | 62.00 | 58.00 | 54.25 | 53.80 | 53.80 | 54.00 | 54.20 | 55.20 | 56.00 | 59.40 |
| 2016-17 | 56.00 | 56.00 | 56.00 | 56.00 | 56.00 | 55.00 | 52.00 | 51.00 | 50.50 | 50.80 | 51.25 | 52.75 | 53.61 |
| 2017-18 | 55.20 | 56.00 | 55.50 | 54.80 | 55.50 | 55.00 | 54.00 | 54.00 | 54.00 | 54.00 | 54.00 | 54.00 | 54.67 |
| 2018-19 | 54.00 | 54.00 | 52.80 | 53.50 | 53.50 | 53.00 | 53.20 | 54.00 | 53.40 | 51.00 | 52.50 | 53.40 | 53.19 |
| 2019-20 | 55.00 | 56.00 | 56.00 | 76.00 | 70.00 | 70.00 | 76.00 | 76.00 | 74.00 | 56.00 | 56.40 | 57.00 | 64.87 |
| 2020-21 | 57.00 | 57.00 | NA | NA | NA | NA | NA | 83.00 | 83.00 | NA | NA | NA | 70.00 |
| 2021-22 | 129.00 | 129.00 | 125.00 | 125.00 | 123.13 | 115.33 | 129.00 | 120.40 | 113.50 | 97.75 | 78.20 | 92.00 | 114.78 |
| 2022-23[1] | 88.40 | 93.75 | 106.00 | 92.30 | 85.75 | 81.25 | | | | | | | 91.24 |

[1] Preliminary.  Source: Economic Research Service, U.S. Department of Agriculture (ERS-USDA)

# SUNFLOWERSEED, MEAL AND OIL

## Average Price of Sunflower Meal (26% protein) in the United States   In Cents Per Pound

| Crop Year | Sept. | Oct. | Nov. | Dec. | Jan. | Feb. | Mar. | Apr. | May | June | July | Aug. | Average |
|---|---|---|---|---|---|---|---|---|---|---|---|---|---|
| 2013-14 | 218.13 | 236.25 | 246.88 | 277.50 | 283.75 | 285.00 | 271.25 | 267.50 | 265.00 | 250.00 | 192.50 | 151.25 | 245.42 |
| 2014-15 | 139.50 | 162.50 | 208.13 | 245.00 | 247.50 | 225.63 | 202.50 | 202.50 | 192.50 | 180.50 | 214.38 | 222.50 | 203.60 |
| 2015-16 | 216.00 | 212.50 | 187.50 | 163.13 | 156.88 | 131.88 | 120.00 | 109.38 | 149.50 | 165.63 | 151.88 | 141.00 | 158.77 |
| 2016-17 | 148.75 | 148.75 | 140.50 | 145.00 | 159.00 | 161.88 | 155.00 | 147.50 | 144.00 | 140.00 | 130.63 | 134.50 | 146.29 |
| 2017-18 | 134.38 | 153.00 | 165.00 | 185.00 | 178.00 | 185.63 | 187.50 | 191.88 | 201.50 | 175.63 | 155.50 | 153.13 | 172.18 |
| 2018-19 | 150.63 | 164.00 | 171.25 | 187.50 | 190.50 | 187.50 | 189.38 | 166.50 | 141.25 | 143.13 | 142.00 | 144.38 | 164.84 |
| 2019-20 | 142.50 | 169.00 | 166.88 | 180.00 | 185.00 | 188.13 | 180.00 | 183.75 | 180.63 | 187.50 | 202.50 | 217.50 | 181.95 |
| 2020-21 | 211.50 | 211.25 | 213.13 | 252.50 | 280.63 | 291.88 | 279.50 | 258.13 | 265.00 | 252.50 | 206.25 | 219.50 | 245.15 |
| 2021-22 | 221.25 | 222.50 | 256.50 | 289.17 | 301.25 | 320.00 | 333.33 | 321.00 | 285.63 | 281.88 | 268.50 | 255.00 | 279.67 |
| 2022-23[1] | 225.00 | NA | NA | 200.00 | 355.00 | 336.25 | | | | | | | 279.06 |

[1] Preliminary.   Source: Economic Research Service, U.S. Department of Agriculture (ERS-USDA)

## Production of Sunflower in the United States   In Thousands of Pounds

| Crop Year | California | Colorado | Kansas | Minnesota | Nebraska | North Dakota | Oklahoma | South Dakota | Texas | Total |
|---|---|---|---|---|---|---|---|---|---|---|
| 2013 | 75,150 | 45,600 | 82,000 | 69,250 | 32,975 | 600,560 | 5,180 | 996,800 | 114,250 | 2,021,765 |
| 2014 | 61,925 | 95,700 | 91,540 | 87,870 | 47,375 | 847,420 | 3,200 | 876,620 | 137,400 | 2,219,050 |
| 2015 | 44,720 | 85,200 | 135,560 | 166,050 | 79,410 | 1,068,800 | 6,600 | 1,230,040 | 107,350 | 2,923,730 |
| 2016 | 61,875 | 90,500 | 82,660 | 113,550 | 58,150 | 1,137,450 | ---- | 1,057,050 | 50,400 | 2,651,635 |
| 2017 | 51,305 | 86,200 | 84,520 | 68,475 | 61,800 | 704,250 | ---- | 1,020,000 | 61,200 | 2,137,750 |
| 2018 | 76,500 | 61,950 | 74,250 | 113,835 | 47,380 | 739,400 | ---- | 966,150 | 27,580 | 2,107,045 |
| 2019 | 70,680 | 59,400 | 53,925 | 102,630 | 44,850 | 740,700 | ---- | 831,600 | 39,650 | 1,943,435 |
| 2020 | 57,170 | 46,110 | 120,540 | 137,640 | 54,180 | 1,338,250 | ---- | 1,167,020 | 79,980 | 2,982,890 |
| 2021 | 49,850 | 47,195 | 52,800 | 94,220 | 34,550 | 761,900 | ---- | 817,800 | 46,970 | 1,902,985 |
| 2022[1] | 30,200 | 31,135 | 45,750 | 174,790 | 46,405 | 1,340,510 | ---- | 1,082,400 | 61,350 | 2,812,540 |

[1] Preliminary.   Source: Economic Research Service, U.S. Department of Agriculture (ERS-USDA)

## Production of Sunflower Oil in the United States   In Thousands of Pounds

| Crop Year | California | Colorado | Kansas | Minnesota | Nebraska | North Dakota | Oklahoma | South Dakota | Texas | Total |
|---|---|---|---|---|---|---|---|---|---|---|
| 2013 | 72,150 | 29,600 | 58,000 | 51,200 | 19,975 | 504,000 | 3,480 | 820,800 | 78,000 | 1,637,205 |
| 2014 | 57,200 | 44,800 | 57,540 | 65,250 | 29,000 | 683,400 | 2,100 | 668,000 | 56,800 | 1,664,090 |
| 2015 | 42,900 | 68,400 | 80,560 | 123,750 | 42,660 | 889,350 | 4,800 | 1,048,000 | 82,650 | 2,383,870 |
| 2016 | 60,075 | 68,400 | 57,540 | 96,000 | 37,800 | 1,055,300 | ---- | 960,300 | 33,600 | 2,369,015 |
| 2017 | 49,875 | 73,000 | 65,000 | 64,350 | 37,050 | 628,650 | ---- | 848,000 | 45,600 | 1,847,525 |
| 2018 | 74,100 | 53,900 | 61,500 | 99,000 | 34,080 | 665,000 | ---- | 878,400 | 21,280 | 1,887,260 |
| 2019 | 68,600 | 44,000 | 49,000 | 94,350 | 33,800 | 660,000 | ---- | 782,000 | 33,800 | 1,765,550 |
| 2020 | 55,250 | 26,560 | 76,440 | 128,640 | 40,950 | 1,184,400 | ---- | 1,064,000 | 41,100 | 2,617,340 |
| 2021 | 48,950 | 36,270 | 38,400 | 89,040 | 28,050 | 715,500 | ---- | 744,000 | 37,950 | 1,738,160 |
| 2022[1] | 29,450 | 22,360 | 36,400 | 158,790 | 41,400 | 1,225,500 | ---- | 1,009,200 | 48,750 | 2,571,850 |

[1] Preliminary.   Source: Economic Research Service, U.S. Department of Agriculture (ERS-USDA)

## Production of Sunflower Oil in the United States   In Thousands of Pounds

| Crop Year | California | Colorado | Kansas | Minnesota | Nebraska | North Dakota | Oklahoma | South Dakota | Texas | Total |
|---|---|---|---|---|---|---|---|---|---|---|
| 2013 | 3,000 | 16,000 | 24,000 | 18,050 | 13,000 | 96,560 | 1,700 | 176,000 | 36,250 | 384,560 |
| 2014 | 4,725 | 20,900 | 34,000 | 22,620 | 18,375 | 164,020 | 1,100 | 208,620 | 80,600 | 554,960 |
| 2015 | 1,820 | 16,800 | 55,000 | 42,300 | 36,750 | 179,450 | 1,800 | 181,240 | 24,700 | 539,860 |
| 2016 | 1,800 | 22,100 | 25,120 | 17,550 | 20,350 | 82,150 | ---- | 96,750 | 16,800 | 282,620 |
| 2017 | 1,430 | 13,200 | 19,520 | 4,125 | 24,750 | 75,600 | ---- | 136,000 | 15,600 | 290,225 |
| 2018 | 2,400 | 8,050 | 12,750 | 14,835 | 13,300 | 74,400 | ---- | 87,750 | 6,300 | 219,785 |
| 2019 | 2,080 | 15,400 | 9,125 | 8,280 | 11,050 | 89,100 | ---- | 49,600 | 5,850 | 190,485 |
| 2020 | 1,920 | 19,550 | 26,100 | 9,000 | 13,230 | 153,850 | ---- | 103,020 | 38,880 | 365,550 |
| 2021 | 900 | 10,925 | 14,400 | 5,180 | 6,500 | 46,400 | ---- | 73,800 | 9,020 | 167,125 |
| 2022[1] | 750 | 8,775 | 9,350 | 16,000 | 5,005 | 115,010 | ---- | 73,200 | 12,600 | 240,690 |

[1] Preliminary.   Source: Economic Research Service, U.S. Department of Agriculture (ERS-USDA)

# Tallow and Greases

Tallow and grease are derived from processing (rendering) the fat of cattle. Tallow is used to produce both edible and inedible products. Edible tallow products include margarine, cooking oil, and baking products. Inedible tallow products include soap, candles, and lubricants. Production of tallow and greases is directly related to the number of cattle produced. Those countries that are the leading cattle producers are also the largest producers of tallow. The American Fats and Oils Association provides specifications for a variety of different types of tallow and grease, including edible tallow, lard (edible), top white tallow, all beef packer tallow, extra fancy tallow, fancy tallow, bleachable fancy tallow, prime tallow, choice white grease, and yellow grease. The specifications include such characteristics as the melting point, color, density, moisture content, insoluble impurities, and others.

**Prices** – The monthly average wholesale price of tallow (inedible, No. 1 Packers-Prime, delivered to Chicago) in 2022 rose by +30.7% yr/yr to 75.36 cents per pound, a new record high.

**Supply** – World production of tallow and greases (edible and inedible) in 2021 rose by +1.6% yr/yr to 11.157 million metric tons. The world's largest producer of tallow and greases by far is the U.S., with 41.3% of world production, followed by Brazil, far behind with 8.4%, Australia with 4.4%, and Canada with 2.9%. U.S. production of edible tallow in 2022 fell by -3.1% yr/yr to 2.292 billion pounds.

**Demand** – U.S. consumption of inedible tallow and greases in 2011 fell by 0.9% yr/yr to 1.560 billion pounds, of which virtually all went for animal feed. U.S. consumption of edible tallow in 2022 rose by +3.5% yr/yr to 2.209 billion, a new record high. U.S. per capita consumption of edible tallow in 2010 rose from 0.7 pounds per person to 3.4 pounds per person yr/yr, down from the 2000 and 2004 record high of 4.0 pounds.

**Trade** – U.S. exports of inedible tallow and grease in 2011 fell by -3.2% yr/yr to 752.990 million pounds and accounted for 48.3% of total U.S. supply. U.S. exports of edible tallow in 2022 fell by -38.8% yr/yr to 153 million pounds and accounted for 6.5% of U.S. supply.

### World Production of Tallow and Greases (Edible and Inedible)   In Thousands of Metric Tons

| Year | Argentina | Australia | Brazil | Canada | France | Germany | Korea, South | Nether- lands | New Zealand | Russia | United Kingdom | United States | World Total |
|---|---|---|---|---|---|---|---|---|---|---|---|---|---|
| 2012 | 160 | 494 | 587 | 242 | 198 | 131 | 18 | 106 | 166 | 199 | 139 | 4,488 | 9,190 |
| 2013 | 175 | 548 | 654 | 241 | 191 | 130 | 21 | 103 | 169 | 207 | 138 | 4,457 | 9,319 |
| 2014 | 167 | 601 | 635 | 248 | 192 | 131 | 20 | 101 | 167 | 213 | 142 | 4,225 | 9,189 |
| 2015 | 171 | 605 | 707 | 238 | 196 | 132 | 20 | 105 | 176 | 219 | 145 | 4,205 | 9,298 |
| 2016 | 167 | 507 | 717 | 248 | 198 | 132 | 19 | 108 | 165 | 226 | 147 | 4,432 | 9,451 |
| 2017 | 212 | 543 | 941 | 296 | 234 | 161 | 30 | 116 | 172 | 243 | 180 | 4,652 | 10,995 |
| 2018 | 226 | 581 | 974 | 308 | 238 | 160 | 31 | 120 | 177 | 250 | 181 | 4,670 | 11,208 |
| 2019 | 232 | 264 | 978 | 317 | 235 | 160 | 31 | 115 | 177 | 255 | 185 | 4,722 | 11,210 |
| 2020[1] | 235 | 511 | 961 | 312 | 235 | 157 | 32 | 118 | 178 | 260 | 188 | 4,552 | 10,983 |
| 2021[2] | 225 | 491 | 942 | 325 | 234 | 152 | 33 | 116 | 190 | 259 | 183 | 4,613 | 11,158 |

[1] Preliminary.   [2] Forecast.   Source: Foreign Agricultural Service, U.S. Department of Agriculture (FAS-USDA)

### Salient Statistics of Tallow and Greases (Inedible) in the United States   In Millions of Pounds

| | Supply | | | | Consumption | | | Wholesale Prices, Cents Per Lb. | |
|---|---|---|---|---|---|---|---|---|---|
| Year | Production | Stocks, Jan. 1 | Total | Exports | Soap | Feed | Total | Edible, (Loose) Chicago | Inedible, Chicago No. 1 |
| 2006 | 6,460 | 309 | 6,769 | 730 | W | 2,585 | 2,585 | 18.6 | 16.9 |
| 2007 | 6,369 | 291 | 6,661 | 795 | W | 2,385 | 2,385 | 30.7 | 27.8 |
| 2008 | 6,224 | 350 | 6,573 | 703 | W | 2,095 | 2,095 | 38.0 | 34.2 |
| 2009 | 5,878 | 315 | 6,193 | 727 | W | 1,770 | 1,770 | 27.5 | 25.2 |
| 2010 | 5,887 | 286 | 6,174 | 778 | W | 1,574 | 1,574 | 35.1 | 33.3 |
| 2011 | 3,654 | 281 | 3,934 | 753 | W | 1,560 | 1,560 | 53.2 | 49.6 |
| 2012[1] | NA | NA | NA | NA | NA | NA | NA | 47.8 | 43.8 |
| 2013[2] | NA | NA | NA | NA | NA | NA | NA | 42.6 | 40.4 |
| 2014[2] | ---- | ---- | ---- | ---- | ---- | ---- | ---- | 38.7 | 36.7 |
| 2015[2] | ---- | ---- | ---- | ---- | ---- | ---- | ---- | 28.4 | 26.9 |

[1] Preliminary.   [2] Forecast.   Source: Foreign Agricultural Service, U.S. Department of Agriculture (FAS-USDA)

# TALLOW AND GREASES

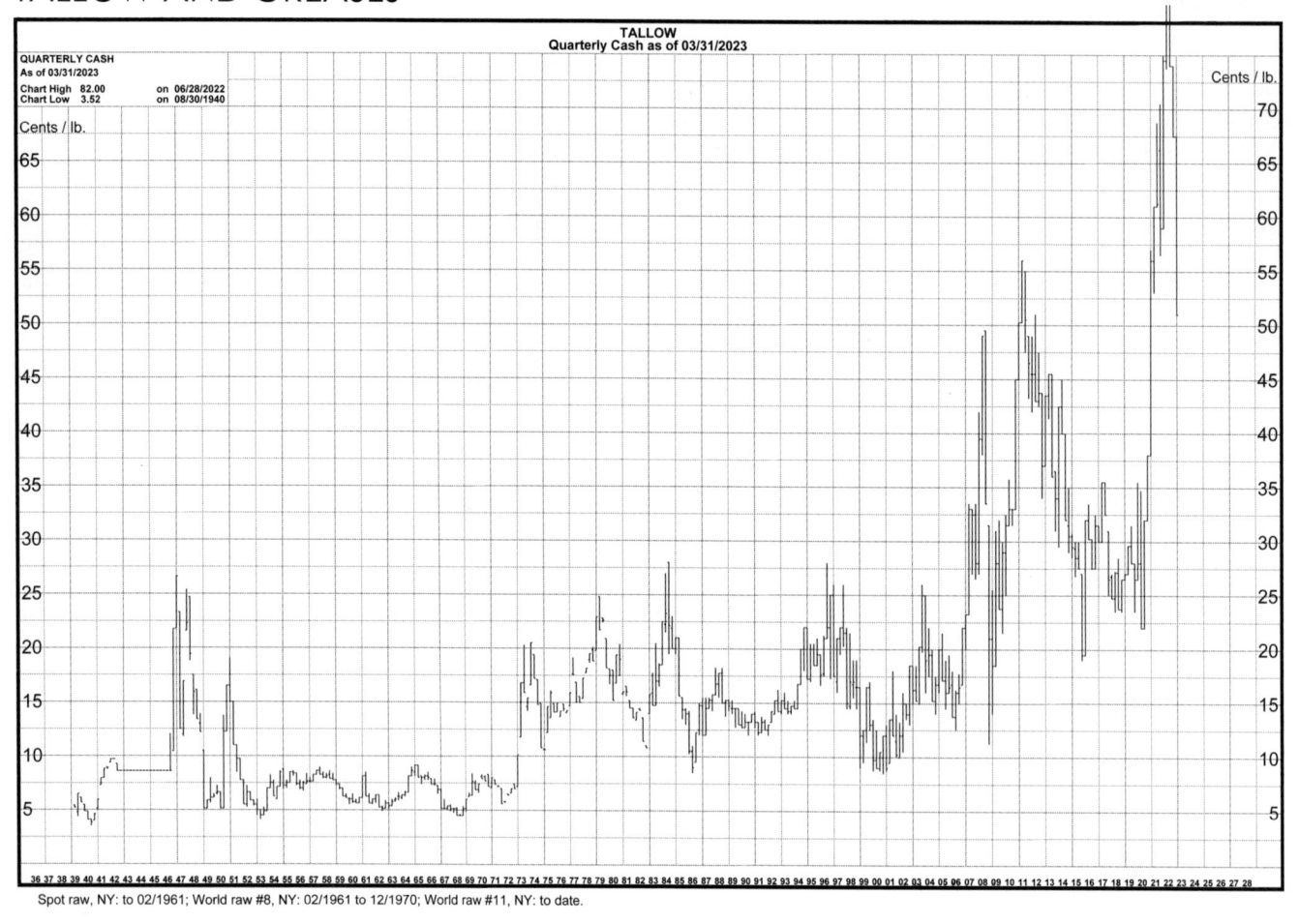

## Supply and Disappearance of Edible Tallow in the United States   In Millions of Pounds, Rendered Basis

| Year | Stocks, Jan. 1 | Production | Total Supply | Domestic Disappearance | Exports | Total Disappearance | Direct Use | Baking or Frying Fats | Per Capita (Lbs.) |
|---|---|---|---|---|---|---|---|---|---|
| 2013 | 30 | 2,043 | 2,122 | 1,935 | 157 | 2,092 | ---- | ---- | ---- |
| 2014 | 30 | 1,922 | 2,004 | 1,884 | 90 | 1,974 | ---- | ---- | ---- |
| 2015 | 30 | 1,928 | 2,003 | 1,830 | 143 | 1,973 | ---- | ---- | ---- |
| 2016 | 30 | 2,143 | 2,235 | 1,929 | 265 | 2,194 | ---- | ---- | ---- |
| 2017 | 41 | 2,053 | 2,159 | 1,945 | 181 | 2,126 | ---- | ---- | ---- |
| 2018 | 33 | 2,233 | 2,302 | 2,010 | 260 | 2,270 | ---- | ---- | ---- |
| 2019 | 32 | 2,252 | 2,298 | 2,012 | 268 | 2,280 | ---- | ---- | ---- |
| 2020 | 18 | 2,202 | 2,244 | 2,007 | 227 | 2,234 | ---- | ---- | ---- |
| 2021[1] | 10 | 2,365 | 2,406 | 2,135 | 250 | 2,385 | ---- | ---- | ---- |
| 2022[2] | 21 | 2,292 | 2,385 | 2,209 | 153 | 2,362 | ---- | ---- | ---- |

[1] Preliminary.   [2] Forecast.   W = Withheld.   Sources: Economic Research Service, U.S. Department of Agriculture (ERS-USDA); Bureau of the Census, U.S. Department of Commerce

## Average Wholesale Price of Tallow, Inedible, No. 1 Packers (Prime), Delivered, Chicago   In Cents Per Pound

| Year | Jan. | Feb. | Mar. | Apr. | May | June | July | Aug. | Sept. | Oct. | Nov. | Dec. | Average |
|---|---|---|---|---|---|---|---|---|---|---|---|---|---|
| 2013 | 40.00 | 40.00 | 42.42 | 43.06 | 41.67 | 45.00 | 45.39 | 42.74 | 40.53 | 33.37 | 35.14 | 35.14 | 40.37 |
| 2014 | 31.95 | 31.61 | 38.52 | 42.60 | 44.57 | 42.04 | 39.96 | 39.85 | 34.90 | 29.51 | 32.47 | 32.09 | 36.67 |
| 2015 | 28.77 | 28.84 | 30.42 | 28.22 | 28.64 | 29.72 | 28.50 | 29.21 | 28.71 | 22.41 | 19.48 | 19.50 | 26.87 |
| 2016 | 23.14 | 26.50 | 29.64 | 32.93 | 32.67 | 31.34 | 29.04 | 27.50 | 27.50 | 27.90 | 31.49 | 31.64 | 29.27 |
| 2017 | 31.35 | 31.11 | 30.11 | 30.33 | 33.49 | 35.40 | 35.50 | 35.37 | 33.96 | 27.83 | 26.36 | 26.50 | 31.44 |
| 2018 | 26.38 | 25.00 | 25.59 | 24.61 | 24.20 | 26.35 | 28.05 | 27.88 | 25.20 | 23.76 | 25.85 | 26.50 | 25.78 |
| 2019 | 26.50 | 26.50 | 26.52 | 28.14 | 28.69 | 29.63 | 30.65 | 31.32 | 28.26 | 26.29 | 23.77 | 25.56 | 27.65 |
| 2020 | 30.57 | 34.67 | 31.57 | 30.95 | 33.94 | 25.14 | 23.50 | 30.33 | 31.58 | 32.10 | 32.50 | 35.80 | 31.05 |
| 2021 | 40.45 | 44.22 | 51.04 | 54.02 | 55.05 | 58.92 | 61.95 | 66.77 | 65.51 | 69.08 | 67.05 | 57.69 | 57.65 |
| 2022[1] | 66.65 | 71.08 | 74.11 | 74.94 | 80.50 | 81.33 | 80.32 | 81.00 | 77.40 | 74.00 | 74.00 | 68.93 | 75.36 |

[1] Preliminary.   Sources: Economic Research Service, U.S. Department of Agriculture (ERS-USDA)

# Tea

Tea is the common name for a family of mostly woody flowering plants. The tea family contains about 600 species placed in 28 genera and they are distributed throughout the tropical and subtropical areas, with most species occurring in eastern Asia and South America. The tea plant is native to Southeast Asia. There are more than 3,000 varieties of tea, each with its own distinct character, and each is generally named for the area in which it is grown. Tea may have been consumed in China as long ago as 2700 BC and certainly since 1000 BC. In 2737 BC, the Chinese Emperor Shen Nung, according to Chinese mythology, was a scholar and herbalist. While his servant boiled drinking water, a leaf from the wild tea tree he was sitting under dropped into the water, and Shen Nung decided to try the brew. Today, half the world's population drinks tea. Tea is the world's most popular beverage next to water.

Tea is a healthful drink and contains antioxidants, fluoride, niacin, folic acid, and as much vitamin C as a lemon. The average 5 ounce cup of brewed tea contains approximately 40 to 60 milligrams of caffeine (compared to 80 to 115 mg in brewed coffee). Decaffeinated tea has been available since the 1980s. Herbal tea contains no true tea leaves but is actually brewed from a collection of herbs and spices.

Tea grows mainly between the tropic of Cancer and the tropic of Capricorn, requiring 40 to 50 inches of rain per year and a temperature ideally between 50 to 86 degrees Fahrenheit. The bushes must be pruned every four to five years to rejuvenate the bush and keep it at a convenient height for the pickers to access. A tea bush can produce tea for 50 to 70 years, but after 50 years, the yield declines.

The two key factors in determining different varieties of tea are the production process (sorting, withering, rolling, fermentation, and drying methods) and the growing conditions (geographical region, growing altitude, and soil type). Black tea, often referred to as fully fermented tea, is produced by allowing picked tea leaves to wither and ferment for up to 24 hours. After fermenting, the leaves are fired, which stops oxidation. Green tea, or unfermented tea, is produced by immediately and completely drying the leaves and omitting the oxidization process, thus allowing the tea to remain green in color.

**Supply** – World production of tea in 2020 rose by +2.0% to 6.257 million metric tons, a new record high. The world's largest producers of tea in 2020 were China with 47.7% of world production, India with 22.8%, Kenya with 9.1%, Argentina with 5.4%, Sri Lanka with 4.5%, and Turkey with 4.1%.

**Trade** – U.S. tea imports in 2022 rose by +17.4% to 223,852 metric tons. World tea imports in 2021 rose by +0.2% to 1.931 million metric tons. The world's largest tea importers were Pakistan with 13.5% of total world imports, Russia with 8.0%, the U.S. with 6.0%, and the United Kingdom with 5.6%. World exports of tea in 2021 fell by -5.4% yr/yr to 2.053 million metric tons. The world's largest exporters of tea in 2021 were Kenya with 27.1% of world exports, China with 18.7%, Sri Lanka with 13.8%, and India with 9.6%.

### World Tea Production, in Major Producing Countries    In Metric Tons

| Year | Argentina | Bangladesh | China | India | Indonesia | Iran | Japan | Kenya | Malawi | Sri Lanka | Turkey | Ex-USSR[2] | World Total |
|---|---|---|---|---|---|---|---|---|---|---|---|---|---|
| 2014 | 82,632 | 63,780 | 2,110,770 | 1,207,310 | 154,369 | 72,277 | 83,600 | 445,105 | 45,480 | 338,032 | 226,800 | 2,496 | 5,493,989 |
| 2015 | 82,492 | 66,101 | 2,291,405 | 1,233,140 | 132,615 | 196,957 | 79,500 | 399,100 | 47,877 | 317,967 | 239,028 | 2,925 | 5,761,926 |
| 2016 | 382,618 | 64,500 | 2,326,018 | 1,250,490 | 144,015 | 121,771 | 80,200 | 473,000 | 48,887 | 292,574 | 243,000 | 4,465 | 6,108,836 |
| 2017 | 366,159 | 81,850 | 2,473,843 | 1,325,050 | 146,251 | 100,580 | 82,000 | 439,857 | 47,415 | 307,720 | 234,000 | 3,629 | 6,299,415 |
| 2018 | 369,613 | 78,150 | 2,625,138 | 1,338,630 | 140,237 | 99,245 | 86,300 | 492,990 | 48,060 | 303,840 | 270,000 | 3,073 | 6,650,602 |
| 2019 | 375,115 | 90,685 | 2,791,837 | 1,390,080 | 128,724 | 90,832 | 81,700 | 458,850 | 48,121 | 300,120 | 261,000 | 3,227 | 6,761,711 |
| 2020[1] | 335,225 | 89,931 | 2,984,341 | 1,424,662 | 138,323 | 84,683 | 69,800 | 569,500 | 47,865 | 278,489 | 255,183 | 3,674 | 7,024,042 |

[1] Preliminary.  [2] Mostly Georgia and Azerbaijan.  Sources: Foreign Agricultural Service, U.S. Department of Agriculture (FAS-USDA); Food and Agriculture Organization of the United Nations (FAO-UN)

### World Exports of Tea from Producing Countries    In Metric Tons

| Year | Argentina | Bangladesh | Brazil | China | India | Indonesia | Kenya | Malawi | Papua New Guinea | Sri Lanka | Vietnam | Zimbabwe | World Total |
|---|---|---|---|---|---|---|---|---|---|---|---|---|---|
| 2015 | 76,029 | 574 | 399 | 331,751 | 235,132 | 61,915 | 298,557 | 38,785 | 1,303 | 304,835 | 125,185 | 13,959 | 1,849,293 |
| 2016 | 78,177 | 721 | 367 | 336,618 | 230,456 | 51,317 | 481,076 | 43,656 | 896 | 286,760 | 136,362 | 11,083 | 2,040,835 |
| 2017 | 74,921 | 2,149 | 297 | 367,550 | 261,419 | 51,357 | 467,024 | 41,273 | 938 | 286,863 | 146,441 | 13,396 | 2,133,983 |
| 2018 | 72,619 | 949 | 227 | 380,860 | 262,423 | 49,030 | 500,591 | 47,625 | 711 | 164,709 | 77,234 | 14,229 | 2,028,119 |
| 2019 | 75,322 | 880 | 305 | 385,783 | 258,051 | 42,491 | 475,997 | 46,944 | 345 | 289,586 | 134,933 | 14,534 | 2,168,354 |
| 2020[1] | 65,978 | 2,225 | 235 | 361,799 | 210,486 | 45,265 | 575,509 | 46,923 | 305 | 285,087 | 126,449 | 12,138 | 2,171,401 |
| 2021[2] | 64,201 | 869 | 182 | 384,097 | 197,240 | 42,640 | 556,552 | 36,798 | 269 | 282,986 | 82,470 | 11,569 | 2,053,405 |

[1] Preliminary.  [2] Estimate.  Source: Food and Agriculture Organization of the United Nations (FAO-UN)

### Imports of Tea in the United States    In Metric Tons

| Year | Jan. | Feb. | Mar. | Apr. | May | June | July | Aug. | Sept. | Oct. | Nov. | Dec. | Total |
|---|---|---|---|---|---|---|---|---|---|---|---|---|---|
| 2017 | 14,923 | 12,784 | 16,132 | 18,980 | 21,458 | 19,263 | 20,082 | 19,684 | 18,930 | 12,874 | 13,657 | 13,349 | 202,116 |
| 2018 | 15,231 | 11,716 | 11,611 | 17,712 | 20,164 | 18,202 | 17,370 | 18,866 | 17,850 | 13,205 | 13,993 | 12,314 | 188,234 |
| 2019 | 14,523 | 14,128 | 16,810 | 18,058 | 19,626 | 17,829 | 20,574 | 18,243 | 15,784 | 15,231 | 15,738 | 14,250 | 200,796 |
| 2020 | 16,085 | 11,457 | 17,037 | 17,600 | 18,745 | 16,861 | 15,970 | 17,250 | 17,458 | 15,650 | 15,075 | 14,861 | 194,048 |
| 2021 | 15,114 | 14,923 | 16,339 | 16,174 | 20,623 | 16,345 | 19,321 | 18,667 | 7,080 | 13,502 | 16,140 | 16,514 | 190,741 |
| 2022[1] | 14,660 | 14,130 | 19,271 | 20,913 | 21,339 | 17,806 | 22,263 | 19,965 | 23,101 | 15,008 | 16,742 | 13,914 | 219,112 |

[1] Preliminary.  Source: Foreign Agricultural Service, U.S. Department of Agriculture (FAS-USDA)

# Thorium

**World Production of Monazite Concentrate**  In Metric Tons (gross weight)

| Year | Brazil | India | Madagascar | Malaysia | Nigeria | Thailand | United States | Vietnam | World Total |
|---|---|---|---|---|---|---|---|---|---|
| 2011 | 290 | 3,000 | ---- | 571 | ---- | 5,100 | ---- | 360 | 9,320 |
| 2012 | 2,700 | 3,000 | ---- | 113 | ---- | 200 | ---- | 370 | 6,380 |
| 2013 | 600 | 3,000 | ---- | 261 | ---- | 210 | ---- | 180 | 4,250 |
| 2014 | ---- | 3,000 | ---- | 372 | 104 | 3,200 | ---- | ---- | 6,680 |
| 2015 | 1,625 | 3,000 | ---- | 499 | 80 | 1,300 | ---- | 460 | 6,960 |
| 2016 | 4,525 | 2,500 | ---- | 220 | ---- | 2,600 | ---- | 400 | 10,200 |
| 2017 | 2,900 | 3,000 | ---- | 380 | 55 | 2,200 | ---- | 360 | 8,900 |
| 2018 | 2,000 | 5,000 | 16,000 | 50 | 50 | 1,700 | 500 | 1,500 | 26,800 |
| 2019[1] | 1,200 | 5,000 | 21,000 | 90 | 54 | 3,200 | 1,700 | 2,200 | 34,400 |
| 2020[2] | 1,200 | 5,000 | 25,000 | 160 | 210 | 6,000 | 960 | 1,200 | 83,700 |

[1] Preliminary.  [2] Estimate.  *Source: U.S. Geological Survey (USGS)*

**Salient U.S. Thorium Statistics**  In Metric Tons (gross weight)

| Year | Exports: Thorium Ore, including Monazite | Exports: Metal, Waste and Scrap | Exports: Compounds | Imports for Consumption: Thorium Ore, including Monazite | Imports for Consumption: Compounds | Shipments from Gov't stockpile excesses | Consumption Reported Non-energy applications | Prices: Nitrate[3] | Prices: Oxide, 99.9% purity[3] | Prices: Compounds: France | Prices: Compounds: India | Net Import Reliance as a % of Apparent Consumption |
|---|---|---|---|---|---|---|---|---|---|---|---|---|
| 2013 | ---- | ---- | 1.010 | ---- | 2.830 | ---- | ---- | ---- | ---- | ---- | $65.00 | 100 |
| 2014 | ---- | ---- | 14.800 | ---- | 11.000 | ---- | ---- | ---- | ---- | ---- | $65.00 | 100 |
| 2015 | ---- | ---- | 2.700 | ---- | 2.740 | ---- | ---- | ---- | ---- | ---- | $63.00 | 100 |
| 2016 | ---- | ---- | 64.000 | 16.000 | 3.120 | ---- | ---- | ---- | ---- | ---- | $65.00 | 100 |
| 2017 | ---- | ---- | 89.000 | ---- | 8.510 | ---- | ---- | ---- | ---- | ---- | $73.00 | 100 |
| 2018 | 521.000 | ---- | 21.000 | 1.000 | 9.000 | ---- | ---- | ---- | ---- | ---- | $72.00 | 100 |
| 2019 | 1,680.000 | ---- | 154.000 | ---- | 3.970 | ---- | ---- | ---- | ---- | ---- | $72.00 | 100 |
| 2020 | 958.000 | ---- | 60.000 | 3.000 | 1.920 | ---- | ---- | ---- | ---- | ---- | NA | 100 |
| 2021[1] | W | ---- | 46.000 | 16.000 | 5.790 | ---- | ---- | ---- | ---- | ---- | NA | 100 |
| 2022[2] | W | ---- | 31.000 | ---- | 2.900 | ---- | ---- | ---- | ---- | ---- | NA | 100 |

[1] Preliminary.  [2] Estimate.  [3] Free on board port of entry, duty paid, thorium oxide basis.  *Source: U.S. Geological Survey (USGS)*

**U.S. Foreign Trade in Thorium and Thorium-Bearing Materials**  In Metric Tons (gross weight)

| Year | Exports: Thorium Ore, including Monazite | Exports: Metals | Exports: Compounds | Exports: Thorium Ore, including Monazite: Value (USD) | Exports: Metals: Value (USD) | Exports: Compounds: Value (USD) | Imports: Thorium Ore, including Monazite | Imports: Compounds | Imports: Thorium Ore, including Monazite: Value (USD) | Imports: Compounds: Value (USD) |
|---|---|---|---|---|---|---|---|---|---|---|
| 2013 | ---- | ---- | 1.010 | ---- | ---- | $523,000 | ---- | 2.830 | ---- | $184,000 |
| 2014 | ---- | ---- | 14.800 | ---- | ---- | $1,970,000 | ---- | 11.000 | ---- | $761,000 |
| 2015 | ---- | ---- | 2.700 | ---- | ---- | $779,000 | ---- | 2.740 | ---- | $216,000 |
| 2016 | ---- | ---- | 64.000 | ---- | ---- | $1,790,000 | 16.000 | 3.120 | ---- | $284,000 |
| 2017 | ---- | ---- | 89.000 | ---- | ---- | $1,340,000 | ---- | 8.510 | ---- | $731,000 |
| 2018 | 521.000 | ---- | 21.000 | ---- | ---- | $1,150,000 | 1.000 | 9.000 | ---- | $567,000 |
| 2019 | 1,680.000 | ---- | 154.000 | ---- | ---- | $9,380,000 | ---- | 3.970 | ---- | $213,000 |
| 2020 | 958.000 | ---- | 60.000 | ---- | ---- | $817,000 | 3.000 | 1.920 | ---- | $55,400 |
| 2021 | W | ---- | 46.000 | ---- | ---- | ---- | 16.000 | 5.790 | ---- | ---- |
| 2022[1] | W | ---- | 31.000 | ---- | ---- | ---- | ---- | 2.900 | ---- | ---- |

[1] Preliminary.  [2] Based on manufacture of 2,205 gas mantles per kilogram ThO2.  *Source: U.S. Geological Survey (USGS)*

# Tin

Tin (atomic symbol Sn) is a silvery-white, lustrous gray metallic element. Tin is soft, pliable and has a highly crystalline structure. When a tin bar is bent or broken, a crackling sound called a "tin cry" is produced due to the breaking of the tin crystals. People have been using tin for at least 5,500 years. Tin has been found in the tombs of ancient Egyptians. In ancient times, tin and lead were considered different forms of the same metal. Tin was exported to Europe in large quantities from Cornwall, England, during the Roman period, from approximately 2100 BC to 1500 BC. Cornwall was one of the world's leading sources of tin for much of its known history and into the late 1800s.

The principal ore of tin is the mineral cassiterite, which is found in Malaya, Bolivia, Indonesia, Thailand, and Nigeria. About 80% of the world's tin deposits occur in unconsolidated placer deposits in riverbeds and valleys, or on the seafloor, with only about 20% occurring as primary hard-rock lodes. Tin deposits are generally small and are usually allied with granite. Tin is also recovered as a by-product of mining tungsten, tantalum, and lead. After extraction, tin ore is ground and washed to remove impurities, roasted to oxidize the sulfides of iron and copper, washed a second time, and then reduced by carbon in a reverberatory furnace. Electrolysis may also be used to purify tin.

Pure tin, rarely used by itself, was used as currency in the form of tin blocks and was considered legal tender for taxes in Phuket, Thailand, until 1932. Tin is used in the manufacture of coatings for steel containers used to preserve food and beverages. Tin is also used in solder alloys, electroplating, ceramics, and in plastic. The world's major tin research and development laboratory, ITRI Ltd, is funded by companies that produce and consume tin. The research efforts have focused on possible new uses for tin that would take advantage of tin's relative non-toxicity to replace other metals in various products. Some of the replacements could be lead-free solders, antimony-free flame-retardant chemicals, and lead-free shotgun pellets. No tin is currently mined in the U.S.

Tin futures and options trade on the London Metal Exchange (LME). Tin has traded on the LME since 1877, and the standard tin contract began in 1912. The futures contract calls for the delivery of 5 metric tons of tin ingots of at least 99.85% purity. The contract trades in terms of U.S. dollars per metric ton.

**Prices** – The average monthly price of tin (straights) in New York in 2022 fell by -3.1% yr/yr to $19.45 per pound. The average monthly price of ex-dock tin in New York in 2022 fell by -4.1% yr/yr to a record $15.26 per pound.

**Supply** – World mine production of tin in 2022 rose by +1.6% yr/yr to 310,000 metric tons, slightly below the 2018 record high of 318,000 metric tons. The world's largest mine producers of tin in 2022 were China with 30.6% of world production, Indonesia with 23.9%, Burma with 10.0%, Peru with 9.4%, and Congo with 6.5%. World smelter production of tin in 2019 fell by -6.7% yr/yr to 349,000 metric tons, the lowest since 2012. The world's largest producers of smelted tin are China, with 47.6% of world production in 2019, Indonesia with 21.9%, and Malaysia with 7.0%. The U.S. does not mine tin, and therefore its supply consists only of scrap and imports. U.S. tin recovery in 2021 fell by -3.6% yr/yr to 5,350 metric tons.

**Demand** – U.S. consumption of tin (pig) in 2022 fell by -2.8% yr/yr to 18,502 metric tons. The breakdown of U.S. consumption of tin by finished products in 2020 shows that the largest consuming industry of tin is chemicals with 24.8% of consumption, tin plate with 22.4%, followed by solder with 8.8%, and bronze and brass with 6.3%.

**Trade** – U.S. imports of unwrought tin metal in 2022 fell by -10.8% yr/yr to 34,000 metric tons. The largest sources of U.S. imports in 2016 were Indonesia with 26.6%, Malaysia with 23.5%, and Bolivia with 19.2%. U.S. exports of tin in 2022 rose by +8.5% yr/yr to 1,400 metric tons.

## World Mine Production of Tin    In Metric Tons (Contained Tin)

| Year | Australia | Bolivia | Brazil | Burma | China | Congo | Indonesia | Malaysia | Nigeria | Peru | Rwanda | Vietnam | World Total |
|---|---|---|---|---|---|---|---|---|---|---|---|---|---|
| 2013 | 6,472 | 19,282 | 16,830 | 17,000 | 97,000 | 4,500 | 59,412 | 3,697 | 2,600 | 23,668 | 3,100 | 5,400 | 260,000 |
| 2014 | 6,900 | 19,802 | 25,534 | 30,000 | 104,000 | 6,500 | 51,801 | 3,777 | 2,800 | 23,105 | 4,200 | 5,400 | 285,000 |
| 2015 | 7,000 | 20,000 | 25,000 | 34,271 | 110,156 | 6,400 | 52,000 | 3,800 | 2,500 | 19,511 | 2,000 | 5,400 | 289,000 |
| 2016 | 6,640 | 17,000 | 25,000 | 54,000 | 92,000 | 5,500 | 52,000 | 4,000 | 2,290 | 18,800 | 2,200 | 5,500 | 288,000 |
| 2017 | 7,200 | 18,500 | 18,000 | 47,000 | 93,000 | 9,500 | 83,000 | 3,810 | 5,960 | 17,800 | 2,860 | 4,560 | 313,000 |
| 2018 | 6,870 | 16,900 | 17,100 | 54,600 | 90,000 | 7,400 | 85,000 | 4,300 | 7,800 | 18,600 | 2,400 | 4,560 | 318,000 |
| 2019 | 7,740 | 17,000 | 14,000 | 42,000 | 84,500 | 12,200 | 77,500 | 3,610 | 5,800 | 19,900 | 2,300 | 5,500 | 296,000 |
| 2020 | 8,120 | 14,700 | 16,900 | 29,000 | 84,000 | 17,300 | 53,000 | 2,960 | 5,000 | 20,600 | 1,800 | 5,400 | 264,000 |
| 2021[1] | 8,772 | 19,628 | 15,517 | 36,900 | 90,000 | 16,700 | 70,000 | 5,000 | 1,600 | 26,995 | 2,000 | 5,400 | 305,000 |
| 2022[2] | 9,700 | 18,000 | 18,000 | 31,000 | 95,000 | 20,000 | 74,000 | 5,000 | 1,700 | 29,000 | 2,200 | 5,200 | 310,000 |

[1] Preliminary.    [2] Estimate.    *Source: U.S. Geological Survey (USGS)*

# TIN

## World Smelter Production of Primary Tin   In Metric Tons

| Year | Australia | Belgium | Bolivia | Brazil | China | Indonesia | Japan | Malaysia | Peru | Russia | Thailand | United States | World Total |
|---|---|---|---|---|---|---|---|---|---|---|---|---|---|
| 2010 | 400 | 9,900 | 15,003 | 9,348 | 150,000 | 51,418 | 841 | 38,771 | 36,451 | 1,381 | 20,000 | 11,100 | 348,000 |
| 2011 | 400 | 10,000 | 14,295 | 9,632 | 156,000 | 43,832 | 947 | 40,281 | 32,290 | 726 | 20,000 | 11,000 | 344,000 |
| 2012 | 400 | 11,400 | 14,626 | 12,205 | 148,000 | 51,400 | 1,133 | 37,823 | 24,811 | 700 | 19,996 | 11,200 | 342,000 |
| 2013 | 400 | 12,000 | 14,862 | 14,721 | 159,000 | 54,800 | 1,786 | 32,699 | 24,181 | 550 | 19,088 | 10,600 | 353,000 |
| 2014 | 400 | 9,810 | 15,439 | 22,334 | 187,000 | 69,800 | 1,746 | 34,971 | 24,462 | 550 | 16,494 | 10,100 | 401,000 |
| 2015 | 400 | 8,860 | 15,464 | 16,531 | 167,200 | 67,400 | 1,688 | 30,209 | 20,396 | 550 | 10,616 | 10,100 | 357,000 |
| 2016 | 400 | 8,540 | 16,810 | 12,542 | 182,500 | 66,900 | 1,620 | 26,758 | 19,390 | ---- | 10,807 | 9,960 | 365,000 |
| 2017 | ---- | 9,700 | 16,648 | 13,796 | 178,400 | 80,000 | 1,624 | 27,200 | 17,906 | ---- | 10,588 | 10,000 | 373,000 |
| 2018 | ---- | 9,330 | 15,611 | 12,900 | 182,000 | 81,427 | 1,650 | 27,197 | 18,255 | ---- | 10,721 | 9,900 | 374,000 |
| 2019[1] | ---- | 9,300 | 14,000 | 11,927 | 166,000 | 76,389 | 1,547 | 24,320 | 19,555 | ---- | 9,600 | 10,500 | 349,000 |

[1] Preliminary.   Source: U.S. Geological Survey (USGS)

## United States Foreign Trade of Tin   In Metric Tons

Imports for Consumption — Concentrates[2] (Ore) / Unwrought Tin Metal

| Year | Exports (Metal) | Total All Ore | Bolivia | Peru | Total All Metal | Bolivia | Brazil | China | Indonesia | Malaysia | Singapore | Thailand | United Kingdom |
|---|---|---|---|---|---|---|---|---|---|---|---|---|---|
| 2013 | 5,870 | ---- | ---- | ---- | 34,900 | 6,510 | 3,100 | 1,610 | 5,560 | 4,190 | 101 | 2,380 | ---- |
| 2014 | 5,700 | ---- | ---- | ---- | 35,600 | 4,570 | 3,030 | 3,470 | 8,140 | 6,050 | 375 | 291 | ---- |
| 2015 | 3,350 | ---- | ---- | ---- | 33,600 | 6,260 | 2,950 | 1,230 | 5,210 | 9,990 | 225 | 20 | 2 |
| 2016 | 1,150 | ---- | ---- | ---- | 32,200 | 6,170 | 2,120 | 229 | 8,580 | 7,560 | 176 | 392 | ---- |
| 2017 | 1,560 | ---- | ---- | ---- | 34,300 | | | | | | | | |
| 2018 | 941 | ---- | ---- | ---- | 36,800 | | | | | | | | |
| 2019 | 1,300 | ---- | ---- | ---- | 34,100 | | | | | | | | |
| 2020 | 519 | ---- | ---- | ---- | 31,600 | | | | | | | | |
| 2021 | 1,290 | ---- | ---- | ---- | 38,100 | | | | | | | | |
| 2022[1] | 1,400 | ---- | ---- | ---- | 34,000 | | | | | | | | |

[1] Preliminary.   [2] Tin content.   [4] Less than 1/2 unit.   Source: U.S. Geological Survey (USGS)

## Consumption (Total) of Tin (Pig) in the United States   In Metric Tons

| Year | Jan. | Feb. | Mar. | Apr. | May | June | July | Aug. | Sept. | Oct. | Nov. | Dec. | Total |
|---|---|---|---|---|---|---|---|---|---|---|---|---|---|
| 2013 | 2,959 | 2,970 | 3,009 | 2,989 | 2,970 | 2,949 | 2,099 | 2,140 | 2,079 | 2,069 | 2,026 | 2,047 | 30,306 |
| 2014 | 1,819 | 1,818 | 1,878 | 1,938 | 2,164 | 2,212 | 2,202 | 2,202 | 2,212 | 2,182 | 2,193 | 2,143 | 24,963 |
| 2015 | 2,183 | 2,181 | 2,211 | 2,241 | 2,211 | 2,271 | 2,251 | 2,261 | 2,261 | 2,231 | 2,161 | 2,191 | 26,590 |
| 2016 | 2,239 | 2,239 | 2,179 | 2,179 | 2,189 | 2,209 | 2,189 | 2,239 | 2,209 | 2,197 | 2,165 | 2,127 | 26,360 |
| 2017 | 2,137 | 2,127 | 2,155 | 2,165 | 2,194 | 2,176 | 2,166 | 2,195 | 2,158 | 2,187 | 2,061 | 1,804 | 25,525 |
| 2018 | 1,870 | 1,832 | 1,835 | 1,874 | 1,856 | 1,843 | 1,823 | 1,859 | 1,838 | 1,809 | 1,827 | 1,949 | 22,215 |
| 2019 | 1,874 | 1,884 | 1,857 | 1,834 | 1,875 | 1,947 | 1,854 | 1,908 | 1,826 | 1,875 | 1,855 | 1,805 | 22,394 |
| 2020 | 1,880 | 1,910 | 1,937 | 1,951 | 1,925 | 1,921 | 1,913 | 1,932 | 1,920 | 1,972 | 1,924 | 1,904 | 23,089 |
| 2021 | 1,878 | 1,859 | 1,541 | 1,564 | 1,539 | 1,491 | 1,560 | 1,495 | 1,529 | 1,560 | 1,508 | 1,518 | 19,042 |
| 2022[1] | 1,551 | 1,542 | 1,548 | 1,539 | 1,556 | 1,544 | 1,525 | 1,526 | 1,565 | 1,522 | 1,471 | 1,472 | 18,361 |

[1] Preliminary.   Source: U.S. Geological Survey (USGS)

## Tin Stocks (Pig-Industrial) in the United States, on First of Month   In Metric Tons

| Year | Jan. | Feb. | Mar. | Apr. | May | June | July | Aug. | Sept. | Oct. | Nov. | Dec. |
|---|---|---|---|---|---|---|---|---|---|---|---|---|
| 2013 | 6,470 | 6,670 | 6,640 | 6,590 | 6,640 | 7,110 | 6,660 | 6,670 | 6,680 | 6,580 | 6,570 | 6,480 |
| 2014 | 6,520 | 6,540 | 6,560 | 6,570 | 6,490 | 6,800 | 6,800 | 6,770 | 6,740 | 7,360 | 7,060 | 6,970 |
| 2015 | 7,010 | 6,860 | 6,910 | 6,960 | 6,910 | 6,910 | 7,360 | 6,970 | 6,900 | 7,510 | 6,930 | 6,940 |
| 2016 | 6,420 | 6,420 | 6,400 | 6,350 | 6,380 | 6,310 | 6,220 | 6,220 | 6,210 | 6,320 | 6,480 | 6,510 |
| 2017 | 6,490 | 6,550 | 6,570 | 6,580 | 6,480 | 6,540 | 6,520 | 6,580 | 6,590 | 6,560 | 6,550 | 6,570 |
| 2018 | 6,300 | 6,330 | 6,300 | 6,430 | 6,280 | 6,360 | 6,400 | 6,310 | 6,400 | 5,180 | 5,610 | 5,610 |
| 2019 | 5,140 | 5,350 | 4,700 | 5,880 | 5,540 | 5,390 | 5,350 | 4,790 | 5,910 | 4,840 | 4,820 | 5,940 |
| 2020 | 6,540 | 6,560 | 5,110 | 5,110 | 5,090 | 5,080 | 5,070 | 5,090 | 5,100 | 5,060 | 5,100 | 5,150 |
| 2021 | 5,240 | 5,150 | 4,540 | 4,550 | 4,540 | 4,500 | 4,460 | 4,440 | 4,530 | 4,510 | 4,530 | 4,550 |
| 2022[1] | 5,040 | 5,060 | 4,940 | 4,750 | 4,710 | 4,770 | 4,740 | 4,700 | 4,740 | 4,770 | 4,710 | 5,020 |

[1] Preliminary.   Source: U.S. Geological Survey (USGS)

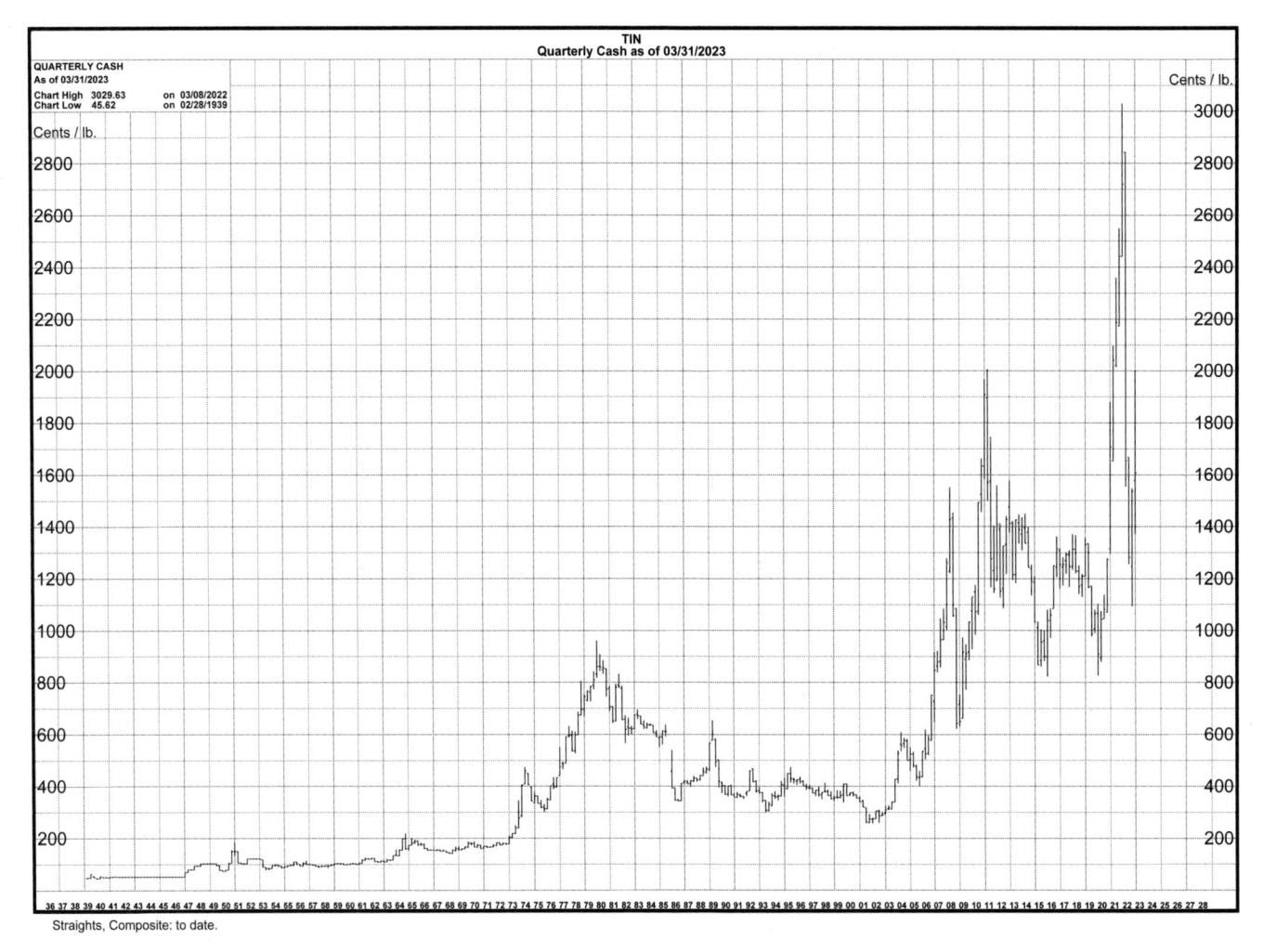

# TIN

**TIN**
Quarterly Cash as of 03/31/2023

QUARTERLY CASH
As of 03/31/2023
Chart High 3029.63 on 03/08/2022
Chart Low 45.62 on 02/28/1939

Straights, Composite: to date.

## Average Price of Ex-Dock Tin in New York[1]    In Cents Per Pound

| Year | Jan. | Feb. | Mar. | Apr. | May | June | July | Aug. | Sept. | Oct. | Nov. | Dec. | Average |
|---|---|---|---|---|---|---|---|---|---|---|---|---|---|
| 2013 | 1,147.61 | 1,132.62 | 1,088.32 | 1,016.82 | 968.64 | 946.60 | 914.64 | 1,008.50 | 1,062.18 | 1,076.08 | 1,064.68 | 1,061.89 | 1,040.71 |
| 2014 | 1,026.81 | 1,061.00 | 1,074.64 | 1,088.65 | 1,083.18 | 1,059.89 | 1,041.12 | 1,037.98 | 983.57 | 929.95 | 931.02 | 925.65 | 1,020.29 |
| 2015 | 910.45 | 857.51 | 818.81 | 754.37 | 745.34 | 721.70 | NQ | NQ | NQ | 733.84 | 694.41 | 693.59 | 770.00 |
| 2016 | 653.01 | 737.23 | 797.61 | 798.88 | 786.39 | 796.12 | 834.14 | 861.60 | 913.95 | 940.57 | 987.73 | 990.44 | 841.47 |
| 2017 | 965.02 | 907.96 | 925.11 | 931.47 | 943.03 | 920.97 | 946.70 | 959.93 | 971.40 | 953.69 | 913.47 | 907.11 | 937.15 |
| 2018 | 965.23 | 1,009.51 | 987.72 | 993.12 | 974.52 | 962.92 | 918.93 | 900.01 | 887.62 | 891.53 | 893.21 | 898.89 | 940.27 |
| 2019 | 955.87 | 993.47 | 1,001.46 | 964.84 | 910.96 | 893.74 | 838.94 | 773.46 | 786.32 | 777.06 | 767.10 | 799.46 | 871.89 |
| 2020 | 795.91 | 769.10 | 719.07 | 709.11 | 724.63 | 785.65 | 815.13 | 824.32 | 836.15 | 846.26 | 864.00 | 923.79 | 801.09 |
| 2021 | 1,033.85 | 1,257.16 | 1,312.26 | 1,373.28 | 1,569.40 | 1,624.10 | 1,717.85 | 1,773.89 | 1,762.79 | 1,867.24 | 1,904.74 | 1,902.07 | 1,591.55 |
| 2022 | 1,999.52 | 2,106.62 | 2,121.54 | 2,062.23 | 1,751.30 | 1,559.91 | 1,232.29 | 1,203.14 | 1,059.67 | 980.36 | 1,048.41 | 1,187.81 | 1,526.07 |

Source: American Metal Market (AMM)

## Average Price of Tin (Straights) in New York    In Cents Per Pound

| Year | Jan. | Feb. | Mar. | Apr. | May | June | July | Aug. | Sept. | Oct. | Nov. | Dec. | Average |
|---|---|---|---|---|---|---|---|---|---|---|---|---|---|
| 2013 | 1,502.64 | 1,480.17 | 1,422.82 | 1,328.61 | 1,265.73 | 1,252.58 | 1,200.86 | 1,321.68 | 1,391.23 | 1,413.19 | 1,392.13 | 1,391.85 | 1,363.62 |
| 2014 | 1,345.40 | 1,388.75 | 1,406.24 | 1,423.40 | 1,416.15 | 1,388.17 | 1,365.31 | 1,362.21 | 1,289.78 | 1,219.57 | 1,223.03 | 1,211.06 | 1,336.59 |
| 2015 | 1,193.00 | 1,125.26 | 1,076.19 | 989.76 | 978.73 | 930.77 | 924.68 | 933.28 | 945.21 | 973.65 | 908.21 | 909.01 | 990.65 |
| 2016 | 854.30 | 965.15 | 1,050.78 | 1,056.03 | 1,037.46 | 1,051.94 | 1,105.23 | 1,143.75 | 1,208.97 | 1,246.19 | 1,309.82 | 1,314.74 | 1,112.03 |
| 2017 | 1,282.89 | 1,205.68 | 1,232.26 | 1,233.41 | 1,251.83 | 1,218.85 | 1,253.86 | 1,272.12 | 1,289.49 | 1,263.32 | 1,212.57 | 1,207.57 | 1,243.65 |
| 2018 | 1,282.77 | 1,342.47 | 1,316.42 | 1,321.32 | 1,294.62 | 1,280.95 | 1,223.25 | 1,191.67 | 1,175.96 | 1,185.53 | 1,182.02 | 1,194.59 | 1,249.30 |
| 2019 | 1,268.38 | 1,318.36 | 1,326.39 | 1,276.72 | 1,210.19 | 1,189.98 | 1,114.63 | 1,027.78 | 1,043.50 | 1,029.41 | 1,012.80 | 1,062.75 | 1,156.74 |
| 2020 | 1,055.81 | 1,021.78 | 948.04 | 927.43 | 954.67 | 1,043.95 | 1,083.14 | 1,094.94 | 1,112.98 | 1,126.95 | 1,148.39 | 1,225.20 | 1,061.94 |
| 2021 | 1,359.06 | 1,631.58 | 1,677.78 | 1,751.49 | 1,997.51 | 2,015.16 | 2,109.25 | 2,169.18 | 2,163.01 | 2,338.82 | 2,427.84 | 2,446.77 | 2,007.29 |
| 2022 | 2,583.94 | 2,726.97 | 2,724.88 | 2,666.46 | 2,231.75 | 1,977.19 | 1,574.54 | 1,528.93 | 1,310.29 | 1,202.25 | 1,317.47 | 1,497.94 | 1,945.22 |

Source: U.S. Geological Survey (USGS)

# TIN

## Tin Plate Production & Tin Recovered in the United States   In Metric Tons

| | ------ Tin Content of Tinplate Produced ------ | | | | ------------------------ Tin Recovered from Scrap by Form of Recovery ------------------------ | | | | | | | | |
|---|---|---|---|---|---|---|---|---|---|---|---|---|---|
| | ------ Tinplate (All Forms) ------ | | | | | | | | | | | | |
| Year | Tinplate Waste ----- Gross Weight ----- | | Tin Content (Met. Ton) | Tin per Tonne of Plate (Kilograms) | Tin Metal | Bronze & Brass | Solder | Type Metal | Babbitt | Anti-monial Lead | Chemical Com-pounds | Misc.[2] | Grand Total |
| 2013 | 20,800 | 1,090,000 | 6,030 | 5.5 | ---- | ---- | ---- | ---- | ---- | ---- | ---- | ---- | ---- |
| 2014 | 32,900 | 1,030,000 | 5,680 | 5.5 | ---- | ---- | ---- | ---- | ---- | ---- | ---- | ---- | ---- |
| 2015 | 43,800 | 812,000 | 4,650 | 5.7 | ---- | ---- | ---- | ---- | ---- | ---- | ---- | ---- | ---- |
| 2016 | 29,800 | 623,000 | 7,840 | 12.6 | ---- | ---- | ---- | ---- | ---- | ---- | ---- | ---- | ---- |
| 2017 | 27,700 | 496,000 | 5,340 | 10.8 | ---- | ---- | ---- | ---- | ---- | ---- | ---- | ---- | ---- |
| 2018 | NA | 487,000 | 4,600 | 9.3 | ---- | ---- | ---- | ---- | ---- | ---- | ---- | ---- | ---- |
| 2019 | NA | 437,000 | 4,690 | 10.7 | ---- | ---- | ---- | ---- | ---- | ---- | ---- | ---- | ---- |
| 2020 | ---- | 518,000 | 5,550 | 10.8 | ---- | ---- | ---- | ---- | ---- | ---- | ---- | ---- | ---- |
| 2021 | ---- | 470,000 | 5,350 | 11.4 | ---- | ---- | ---- | ---- | ---- | ---- | ---- | ---- | ---- |
| 2022[1] | ---- | 460,000 | 5,100 | 11.2 | ---- | ---- | ---- | ---- | ---- | ---- | ---- | ---- | ---- |

[1] Preliminary.   [2] Includes foil, terne metal, cable lead, and items indicated by symbol "W".   W = Withheld.   NA = Not available.
Source: U.S. Geological Survey (USGS)

## Consumption of Primary and Secondary Tin in the United States   In Metric Tons

| Year | Net Import Reliance as a % of Apparent Consump | Stocks, Jan. 1[2] | Net Receipts | | | | Available Supply | Stocks, Dec. 31 (Total Available Less Total Processed) | Total Pro-cessed | Consumed in Manu-facturing Products |
|---|---|---|---|---|---|---|---|---|---|---|
| | | | Primary | Secondary | Scrap | Total | | | | |
| 2013 | 75 | 7,110 | 25,600 | 2,620 | 1,970 | 30,100 | 37,300 | 6,820 | 30,400 | 30,400 |
| 2014 | 76 | 5,530 | 24,000 | 1,250 | 2,450 | 27,700 | 33,200 | 5,350 | 27,800 | 27,500 |
| 2015 | 76 | 5,330 | 24,200 | 1,180 | 2,140 | 27,500 | 32,800 | 5,700 | 27,100 | 26,800 |
| 2016 | 76 | 7,090 | 22,600 | 1,140 | 2,040 | 25,800 | 31,200 | 5,480 | 25,700 | 25,400 |
| 2017 | 76 | 6,370 | 23,100 | 1,230 | 2,210 | 26,500 | 32,100 | 5,320 | 26,800 | 26,400 |
| 2018 | 77 | 6,660 | 28,100 | 2,890 | 2,210 | 33,200 | 42,300 | 9,230 | 33,000 | 32,700 |
| 2019 | 76 | 10,100 | 28,400 | 2,460 | 2,150 | 33,000 | 41,700 | 8,590 | 33,100 | 32,700 |
| 2020 | 76 | 10,300 | 28,000 | 2,460 | 972 | 31,400 | 40,000 | 9,010 | 31,000 | 30,400 |
| 2021[1] | 81 | 10,400 | | | | | | | | |
| 2022[1] | 77 | 8,900 | | | | | | | | |

[1] Preliminary.   [2] Includes tin in transit in the U.S.   NA = Not available.   Source: U.S. Geological Survey (USGS)

## Consumption of Tin in the United States, by Finished Products   In Metric Tons (Contained Tin)

| Year | Tin-plate[2] | Solder | Babbitt | Bronze & Brass | Tinning | Chem-icals[3] | Tin Powder | Bar Tin & Anodes | White Metal | Other | Total |
|---|---|---|---|---|---|---|---|---|---|---|---|
| 2011 | 6,230 | 4,100 | 315 | 3,810 | 552 | 9,990 | W | W | W | 757 | 28,500 |
| 2012 | 6,090 | 4,930 | 281 | 2,460 | 467 | 9,860 | W | W | W | 726 | 27,800 |
| 2013 | 6,030 | 5,940 | 820 | 2,380 | 511 | 6,790 | W | W | W | 807 | 30,400 |
| 2014 | 5,940 | 4,860 | 282 | 1,720 | 514 | 5,420 | W | W | W | 4,780 | 27,500 |
| 2015 | 5,880 | 4,400 | 312 | 1,750 | 463 | 5,410 | W | W | W | 6,090 | 26,800 |
| 2016 | 4,660 | 4,220 | 289 | 1,720 | 405 | 5,320 | W | W | W | 6,190 | 25,400 |
| 2017 | 5,440 | 2,520 | 265 | 1,880 | 337 | 5,450 | W | W | W | 7,440 | 26,400 |
| 2018 | 5,760 | 4,170 | 403 | 2,260 | 427 | 7,150 | W | W | W | 8,740 | 32,700 |
| 2019 | 5,820 | 3,740 | 318 | 1,840 | 423 | 7,290 | W | W | W | 8,540 | 32,700 |
| 2020[1] | 6,810 | 2,660 | 227 | 1,910 | 314 | 7,540 | W | W | W | 6,650 | 30,400 |

[1] Preliminary.   [2] Includes small quantity of secondary pig tin and tin acquired in chemicals.   [3] Including tin oxide.
W = Withheld proprietary data.   Source: U.S. Geological Survey (USGS)

## Salient Statistics of Recycling Tin in the United States

| Year | New Scrap[1] | Old Scrap[2] | Recycled Metal[3] | Apparent Supply | Percent Recycled | New Scrap[1] | Old Scrap[2] | Recycled Metal[3] | Apparent Supply |
|---|---|---|---|---|---|---|---|---|---|
| | ------------------------ In Metric Tons ------------------------ | | | | | ---------------- Value in Thousands of Dollars ---------------- | | | |
| 2013 | 2,150 | 10,600 | 12,700 | 45,100 | 28.0 | 49,300 | 243,000 | 292,000 | 1,050,000 |
| 2014 | 2,060 | 10,600 | 12,600 | 44,900 | 27.0 | 46,400 | 238,000 | 285,000 | 1,040,000 |
| 2015 | 1,120 | 10,100 | 11,200 | 43,800 | 25.0 | 18,700 | 168,000 | 186,000 | 722,000 |
| 2016 | 8,770 | 9,960 | 18,700 | 50,900 | 37.0 | 162,000 | 184,000 | 346,000 | 942,000 |
| 2017 | 8,080 | 10,000 | 18,100 | 52,400 | 35.0 | 167,000 | 207,000 | 374,000 | 1,080,000 |
| 2018 | 8,110 | 9,890 | 18,000 | 54,800 | 33.0 | 167,000 | 204,000 | 371,000 | 1,130,000 |
| 2019 | 8,120 | 10,100 | 18,600 | 52,800 | 35.0 | 155,000 | 201,000 | 356,000 | 1,010,000 |
| 2020 | 7,990 | 9,550 | 17,500 | 49,200 | 36.0 | 141,000 | 168,000 | 309,000 | 866,000 |

[1] Scrap that results from the manufacturing process.   [2] Scrap that results from consumer products.   [3] Metal recovered from new plus old scrap.
Source: U.S. Geological Survey (USGS)

# Titanium

Titanium (atomic symbol Ti) is a silver-white, metallic element used primarily to make light, strong alloys. It ranks ninth in abundance among the elements in the crust of the earth, but it is never found in its pure state. It occurs as an oxide in various minerals. It was first discovered in 1791 by Rev. William Gregor and was first isolated as a basic element in 1910. Titanium was named after the mythological Greek god Titan for its strength.

Titanium is extremely brittle when cold but is malleable and ductile at low heat, making it easy to fabricate. Due to its strength, low weight, and resistance to corrosion, titanium is used in metallic alloys and as a substitute for aluminum. It is used extensively in the aerospace industry, in desalinization plants, construction, medical implants, paints, pigments, and lacquers.

**Supply** – World production of titanium ilmenite concentrates in 2022 remained unchanged yr/yr at 8.900 million metric tons. The world's largest producers of titanium ilmenite concentrates are China with 38.2% of world production in 2022, Australia with 7.4%, Norway with 4.8%, and Ukraine and India both with 2.2%. World production of titanium rutile concentrates in 2022 fell by -4.5% yr/yr to 590,000 metric tons. The world's largest producers of titanium rutile concentrates are Australia with 32.2% of world production in 2022, followed by Sierra Leone with 22.0%, South Africa with 16.1, and Ukraine with 9.7%.

**Demand** – U.S. consumption of titanium dioxide pigment in 2022 rose by +9.7% yr/yr to 940,000 metric tons, remaining below 2004's record high of 1.170 million metric tons.

**Trade** – U.S. imports of titanium dioxide pigment in 2022 rose by +3.6% yr/yr to 260,000 metric tons. U.S. imports of ilmenite in 2019 rose by +2.8% yr/yr to 726,000 metric tons.

## World Produciton of Titanium Illmenite Concentrates   In Thousands of Metric Tons

| Year | Australia[2] | Brazil | China | Egypt | India | Malaysia | Norway | Ukraine | United States | Vietnam | World Total | Titaniferous Slag[4] Canada | Africa |
|---|---|---|---|---|---|---|---|---|---|---|---|---|---|
| 2013 | 1,562 | 78 | 3,850 | 20 | 436 | 16 | 826 | 670 | 300 | 1,026 | 10,400 | 900 | 1,170 |
| 2014 | 1,250 | 136 | 4,240 | ---- | 663 | 8 | 864 | 450 | 200 | 558 | 10,400 | 900 | 1,100 |
| 2015 | 1,156 | 133 | 3,910 | ---- | 552 | 6 | 630 | 350 | 300 | 238 | 9,440 | 700 | 94 |
| 2016 | 1,400 | 106 | 3,800 | ---- | 618 | 4 | 590 | 350 | 100 | 211 | 9,800 | 700 | 800 |
| 2017 | 1,500 | 67 | 3,830 | ---- | 517 | 6 | 670 | 392 | 100 | 226 | 10,100 | 880 | 1,000 |
| 2018 | 1,400 | 110 | 4,200 | ---- | 172 | 14 | 590 | 745 | 100 | 235 | 10,300 | 700 | 950 |
| 2019 | 1,000 | 41 | 4,600 | ---- | 291 | 2 | 640 | 819 | 100 | 217 | 10,600 | 800 | 903 |
| 2020 | 800 | 57 | 5,100 | ---- | 290 | 3 | 740 | 773 | 100 | 230 | 11,100 | 700 | 820 |
| 2021 | 600 | 33 | 3,400 | ---- | 204 | | 468 | 316 | 100 | 122 | 8,900 | 430 | 900 |
| 2022[1] | 660 | 32 | 3,400 | ---- | 200 | | 430 | 200 | 100 | 160 | 8,900 | 470 | 900 |

[1] Preliminary.   [2] Includes leucoxene.   [3] Approximately 10% of total production is ilmenite. Beginning in 1988, 25% of Norway's ilmenite production was used to produce slag containing 75% TiO2.   NA = Not available.   *Source: U.S. Geological Survey (USGS)*

## Salient Statistics of Titanium in the United States   In Metric Tons

| Year | Titanium Dioxide Pigment Production | Imports[3] | Apparent Consumption | Ilmenite Imports[3] | Consumption | Titanium Slag Imports[3] | Consumption | Rutile[4] Imports[3] | Consumption | Exports Ores & Concentrates | Scrap | Dioxide & Pigments | Ingots, Billets, Etc. |
|---|---|---|---|---|---|---|---|---|---|---|---|---|---|
| 2013 | 1,280,000 | 213,000 | 826,000 | 389,000 | ---- | 681,000 | ---- | 406,000 | ---- | 11,500 | 4,700 | 624,000 | 12,500 |
| 2014 | 1,260,000 | 224,000 | 802,000 | 355,000 | ---- | 678,000 | ---- | 342,500 | ---- | 2,240 | 4,610 | 685,000 | 11,500 |
| 2015 | 1,220,000 | 221,000 | 792,000 | 649,000 | ---- | 399,000 | ---- | 394,000 | ---- | 2,040 | 6,860 | 649,000 | 10,400 |
| 2016 | 1,240,000 | 247,000 | 840,000 | 592,000 | ---- | 402,000 | ---- | 349,700 | ---- | 7,330 | 9,720 | 651,000 | 10,100 |
| 2017 | 1,260,000 | 240,000 | 870,000 | 748,000 | ---- | 479,000 | ---- | 334,100 | ---- | 8,940 | 9,450 | 634,000 | 10,900 |
| 2018 | 1,150,000 | 268,000 | 890,000 | 706,000 | ---- | 500,000 | ---- | 260,100 | ---- | 51,400 | 11,900 | 528,000 | 11,300 |
| 2019 | 1,000,000 | 226,000 | 825,000 | 726,000 | ---- | 473,000 | ---- | 342,300 | ---- | 12,200 | 15,000 | 401,000 | 12,100 |
| 2020 | 1,000,000 | 262,000 | 876,000 | 481,000 | ---- | 435,000 | ---- | 158,128 | ---- | 28,800 | 14,100 | 386,000 | 8,040 |
| 2021[1] | 1,100,000 | 251,000 | 857,000 | | ---- | | ---- | | ---- | | | 494,000 | |
| 2022[2] | 1,100,000 | 260,000 | 940,000 | | ---- | | ---- | | ---- | | | 420,000 | |

[1] Preliminary.   [2] Estimate.   [3] For consumption.   [4] Natural and synthetic.   W = Withheld.   *Source: U.S. Geological Survey (USGS)*

# TITANIUM

## World Production of Titanium Rutile Concentrates   In Metric Tons

| Year | Australia | Brazil | India | Madagascar | Malaysia | Mozambique | Sierra Leone | South Africa | Sri Lanka | Ukraine | United States | World Total |
|---|---|---|---|---|---|---|---|---|---|---|---|---|
| 2015 | 320,000 | 3,300 | 16,400 | 3,300 | 198 | 5,981 | 126,022 | 95,000 | 1,808 | 90,000 | W | 751,000 |
| 2016 | 300,000 | 270 | 16,200 | 5,400 | 3,810 | 7,781 | 143,000 | 120,000 | 2,237 | 100,000 | W | 799,000 |
| 2017 | 300,000 | 1,000 | 14,100 | 8,100 | 5,266 | 9,137 | 168,000 | 110,000 | 2,174 | 100,000 | W | 818,000 |
| 2018 | 200,000 | 2,000 | 11,000 | 5,070 | 5,070 | 8,830 | 121,500 | 110,000 | 2,319 | 106,858 | W | 679,000 |
| 2019 | 200,000 | 600 | 12,000 | 5,947 | 5,947 | 8,264 | 137,200 | 105,000 | 1,959 | 100,000 | W | 667,000 |
| 2020 | 190,000 | 226 | 12,000 | 8,000 | 5,136 | 5,958 | 120,200 | 95,000 | 1,311 | 100,000 | W | 632,000 |
| 2021 | 190,000 |  | 12,000 | 10,000 |  | 8,000 | 123,000 | 95,000 |  | 95,000 | W | 618,000 |
| 2022[1] | 190,000 |  | 11,000 |  |  | 8,000 | 130,000 | 95,000 |  | 57,000 | W | 590,000 |

[1] Preliminary.   Source: U.S. Geological Survey (USGS)

## World Production of Titanium Sponge Metal & U.S. Consumption of Titanium Concentrates

| | Production of Titanium (In Metric Tons) Sponge Metal[2] | | | | | | U.S. Consumption of Titanium Concentrates, by Products (In Metric Tons) | | | | | | |
|---|---|---|---|---|---|---|---|---|---|---|---|---|---|
| | | | | | | | Ilmenite (TiO$_2$ Content) | | | Rutile (TiO$_2$ Content) | | | |
| Year | China | Japan | Russia | United Kingdom | United States | Total | Pigments | Misc. | Total | Welding Rod Coatings | Pigments | Misc. | Total |
| 2014 | 110,000 | 25,000 | 42,000 | ---- | W | 194,000 | NA | NA | 1,430,000 | ---- | ---- | ---- | ---- |
| 2015 | 62,000 | 42,000 | 40,000 | ---- | W | 160,000 | NA | NA | 1,390,000 | ---- | ---- | ---- | ---- |
| 2016 | 60,000 | 54,000 | 38,000 | ---- | W | 170,000 | NA | NA | 1,390,000 | ---- | ---- | ---- | ---- |
| 2017 | 72,000 | 51,000 | 40,000 | ---- | W | 181,000 | NA | NA | 1,410,000 | ---- | ---- | ---- | ---- |
| 2018 | 70,000 | 52,000 | 40,000 | ---- | W | 180,000 | NA | NA | 1,290,000 | ---- | ---- | ---- | ---- |
| 2019 | 85,000 | 49,000 | 44,000 | ---- | W | 200,000 | NA | NA | 1,250,000 | ---- | ---- | ---- | ---- |
| 2020 | 123,000 | 49,200 | 31,000 | ---- | W | 230,000 | | | | ---- | ---- | ---- | ---- |
| 2021[1] | 120,000 | 35,000 | 27,000 | ---- | W | 210,000 | | | | ---- | ---- | ---- | ---- |

[1] Preliminary.   [2] Unconsolidated metal in various forms.   [4] Included in Pigments.   NA = Not available.   W = Withheld.
Source: U.S. Geological Survey (USGS)

## Average Prices of Titanium in the United States

| Year | Ilmenite FOB Australian Ports[2] | Slag, 85% TiO2 FOB Richards Bay, South Africa | Rutile Large Lots Bulk, FOB U.S. East Coast[3] | Rutile Bagged FOB Australian Ports | Avg. Price of Grade A Titanium Sponge, FOB Shipping Point | Titanium Metal Sponge | Titanium Dioxide Pigments FOB US Plants Anatase | Titanium Dioxide Pigments FOB US Plants Rutile |
|---|---|---|---|---|---|---|---|---|
| | Dollars Per Metric Ton | | | | | Dollars Per Pound | | |
| 2013 | $230 - $300 | $405 - $455 | $1,100-$1,400 | $1,200-$1,500 | ---- | $3.20 - $6.23 | ---- | ---- |
| 2014 | $150 - $165 | $690 - $835 | $820 - $950 | $840 - $1,000 | ---- | $4.07 - $5.96 | ---- | ---- |
| 2015 | $100 - $120 | $630 - $751 | $790 - $890 | $800 - $840 | ---- | $3.32 - $5.36 | ---- | ---- |
| 2016 | $100 - $110 | $674 - $676 | $710 - $770 | $770 - $850 | ---- | $5.03 - $5.42 | ---- | ---- |
| 2017 | $160 - $185 | $600 - $690 | $710 - $770 | $770 - $850 | ---- | $6.88 - $11.26 | ---- | ---- |
| 2018 | ---- | $770 - $790 | $1,000 - $1,050 | $1,045 - $1,350 | ---- | $9.50 - $10.81 | ---- | ---- |
| 2019 | ---- | $805 - $955 | $1,100 - $1,200 | $1,250 - $1,300 | ---- | $10.60 | ---- | ---- |
| 2020[1] | ---- | $540-$1,010 | $1,150 - $1,200 | $1,300 - $1,350 | ---- | $11.50 | ---- | ---- |

[1] Preliminary.   NA = Not available.   Source: U.S. Geological Survey (USGS)

## Average Price of Titanium[1] in United States   In Dollars Per Pound

| Year | Jan. | Feb. | Mar. | Apr. | May | June | July | Aug. | Sept. | Oct. | Nov. | Dec. | Average |
|---|---|---|---|---|---|---|---|---|---|---|---|---|---|
| 2017 | 8.16 | 8.25 | 8.25 | 8.25 | 8.25 | 8.25 | 8.25 | 8.25 | 8.25 | 8.09 | 8.02 | 8.02 | 8.19 |
| 2018 | 8.02 | 8.02 | 8.02 | 8.10 | 8.12 | 8.12 | 8.12 | 8.12 | 8.12 | 8.30 | 8.38 | 8.38 | 8.15 |
| 2019 | 9.11 | 9.40 | 9.40 | 9.38 | 9.38 | 9.38 | 9.92 | 10.12 | 10.12 | 10.12 | 10.13 | 10.13 | 9.72 |
| 2020 | 10.13 | 10.13 | 10.13 | 10.13 | 10.13 | 9.53 | 9.25 | 9.25 | 9.25 | 9.25 | 9.25 | 9.25 | 9.64 |
| 2021 | 8.38 | 8.38 | 8.38 | 8.00 | 8.00 | 8.00 | 8.25 | 8.25 | 8.25 | 8.25 | 8.25 | 8.25 | 8.22 |
| 2022 | 8.25 | 8.25 | 8.25 | 11.50 | 11.50 | 11.50 | 13.25 | 13.25 | 13.25 | 15.75 | 15.75 | 15.75 | 12.19 |

[1] Ingot, 6Al - 4V.   Source: American Metal Market (AMM)

## Average Price of Titanium[1] in United States   In Dollars Per Pound

| Year | Jan. | Feb. | Mar. | Apr. | May | June | July | Aug. | Sept. | Oct. | Nov. | Dec. | Average |
|---|---|---|---|---|---|---|---|---|---|---|---|---|---|
| 2017 | 26.40 | 28.50 | 28.50 | 28.02 | 28.00 | 28.00 | 28.80 | 29.00 | 29.00 | 29.00 | 29.00 | 29.00 | 28.44 |
| 2018 | 29.00 | 29.00 | 29.00 | 30.43 | 31.00 | 31.00 | 29.48 | 29.00 | 29.00 | 29.70 | 30.00 | 30.00 | 29.72 |
| 2019 | 32.50 | 33.50 | 33.50 | 33.50 | 33.50 | 33.50 | 33.50 | 33.50 | 33.50 | 32.80 | 32.50 | 32.50 | 33.19 |
| 2020 | 32.50 | 32.50 | 32.50 | 32.50 | 32.50 | 29.09 | 27.50 | 27.50 | 27.50 | 27.50 | 27.50 | 27.50 | 29.72 |
| 2021 | 27.50 | 27.50 | 27.50 | 27.50 | 27.50 | 27.50 | 27.50 | 27.50 | 27.50 | 27.50 | 27.50 | 27.50 | 27.50 |
| 2022 | 27.50 | 27.50 | 27.50 | 30.50 | 30.50 | 30.50 | 31.00 | 31.00 | 31.00 | 31.00 | 31.00 | 31.00 | 30.00 |

[1] Plate, Alloy.   Source: American Metal Market (AMM)

# Tobacco

Tobacco is a member of the nightshade family. It is commercially grown for its leaves and stems, which are rolled into cigars, shredded for use in cigarettes and pipes, processed for chewing, or ground into snuff. Christopher Columbus introduced tobacco cultivation and use to Spain after observing natives from the Americas smoking loosely rolled tobacco-stuffed tobacco leaves.

Tobacco is cured, or dried, after harvesting and then aged to improve its flavor. The four common methods of curing are: air cured, fire cured, sun cured, and flue cured. Flue curing is the fastest method of curing and requires only about a week compared with up to 10 weeks for other methods. Cured tobacco is tied into small bundles of about 20 leaves and aged one to three years.

Virginia tobacco is by far the most popular type used in pipe tobacco since it is the mildest of all blending tobaccos. Approximately 60% of the U.S. tobacco crop is Virginia-type tobacco. Burley tobacco is the next most popular tobacco. It is air-cured, burns slowly and provides a relatively cool smoke. Other tobacco varieties include Perique, Kentucky, Oriental, and Latakia.

**Prices** – U.S. tobacco farm prices in 2021 rose by +1.9% to 214.6 cents per pound.

**Supply** – World production of leaf tobacco in 2020 fell by -8.9% yr/yr to 5.886 million metric tons, the smallest production since 1980. The world's largest producers of tobacco are China, with 36.3% of world production, followed at a distance by India with 12.9%, Brazil with 11.9%, Indonesia with 3.4%, Zimbabwe with 3.5%, and the U.S. with 3.0%.

U.S. production in 2020 fell by -16.8% yr/yr to 176,635 metric tons, which was a new record low. Tobacco in the U.S. is grown primarily in the mid-Atlantic States. Specifically, in 2022, the largest tobacco-producing states in the U.S. were North Carolina with 51.9% of U.S. production, Kentucky with 23.4%, Tennessee with 7.0%, Virginia with 6.3%, Pennsylvania with 2.9%, and both Georgia and South Carolina with 2.8%.

U.S. production of flue-cured tobacco (type 11-14), the most popular tobacco type grown in the U.S., fell by -9.2% yr/yr to 284.700 million pounds in 2022. The second most popular type is Class A light air-cured (type 31-32), which saw U.S. production in 2022 fell by -22.0% yr/yr to 65.680 million pounds. Total U.S. production of tobacco in 2022 fell by -6.4% yr/yr to 447.367 million pounds, which is less than one-third of the almost 3-decade high of 1.787 billion pounds posted in 1997.

U.S. farmers have sharply reduced the planting acreage for tobacco. In 2022, harvested tobacco acreage fell by -7.8% yr/yr to 201.800 acres, which was far below the 25-year high of 836,230 posted in 1997. Yield in 2022 rose by +1.6% to 2,217 pounds per acre, moderately below the 15-year high of 2,323 pounds per acre posted in 2009. The farm value of the U.S. tobacco crop in 2021 rose by +30.7% yr/yr to $1.026 billion.

**Trade** – U.S. tobacco exports in 2022 fell by -18.2% yr/yr to 185.3 million pounds, which was a new record low.

## World Production of Leaf Tobacco    In Metric Tons

| Year | Brazil | Canada | China | Greece | India | Indonesia | Italy | Japan | Pakistan | Turkey | United States | Zimbabwe | World Total |
|---|---|---|---|---|---|---|---|---|---|---|---|---|---|
| 2012 | 810,550 | 30,723 | 3,408,142 | 24,000 | 820,000 | 260,800 | 50,620 | 19,700 | 97,878 | 73,285 | 336,245 | 139,179 | 7,498,392 |
| 2013 | 850,673 | 28,620 | 3,375,400 | 26,690 | 765,154 | 260,200 | 49,770 | 19,800 | 108,307 | 93,158 | 328,210 | 147,068 | 7,514,156 |
| 2014 | 862,396 | 27,744 | 2,997,050 | 40,940 | 719,420 | 196,300 | 53,925 | 20,000 | 129,878 | 74,696 | 397,533 | 184,003 | 7,211,873 |
| 2015 | 867,355 | 27,525 | 2,678,604 | 37,031 | 738,029 | 193,790 | 51,406 | 18,700 | 120,022 | 75,000 | 326,210 | 171,083 | 6,719,594 |
| 2016 | 677,472 | 27,963 | 2,575,371 | 37,865 | 747,977 | 126,728 | 48,470 | 17,900 | 115,574 | 74,238 | 285,180 | 168,974 | 6,240,911 |
| 2017 | 865,620 | 27,744 | 2,392,335 | 32,712 | 744,410 | 181,142 | 56,398 | 19,000 | 100,015 | 93,666 | 322,120 | 110,816 | 6,269,352 |
| 2018 | 756,232 | 27,744 | 2,242,083 | 22,730 | 747,277 | 195,482 | 49,530 | 16,998 | 106,727 | 75,276 | 241,870 | 239,906 | 6,053,397 |
| 2019 | 769,801 | 27,817 | 2,612,693 | 22,530 | 758,892 | 269,803 | 41,860 | 16,798 | 104,355 | 70,000 | 212,260 | 184,584 | 6,527,388 |
| 2020[1] | 702,208 | 27,768 | 2,135,277 | 20,870 | 766,373 | 261,017 | 37,830 | 13,748 | 132,872 | 76,540 | 169,130 | 203,488 | 5,813,280 |
| 2021[2] | 744,161 | 27,776 | 2,128,877 | 19,370 | 757,514 | 237,115 | 41,010 | 14,237 | 167,862 | 73,000 | 216,800 | 162,370 | 5,888,764 |

[1] Preliminary.  [2] Estimate.  Source: Food and Agriculture Organization of the United Nations (FAO-UN)

## World Imports of Leaf Tobacco    In Metric Tons

| Year | Belgium | China | Egypt | France | Germany | Indonesia | Netherlands | Poland | Republic of Korea | Russia | Turkey | United States | World Total |
|---|---|---|---|---|---|---|---|---|---|---|---|---|---|
| 2012 | 114,592 | 180,306 | 52,292 | 117,236 | 173,253 | 137,426 | 151,815 | 89,338 | 54,546 | 250,324 | 60,697 | 219,159 | 2,637,129 |
| 2013 | 104,165 | 174,593 | 16,915 | 113,865 | 165,412 | 121,218 | 127,185 | 88,299 | 59,503 | 241,616 | 61,099 | 199,731 | 2,502,941 |
| 2014 | 167,586 | 199,041 | 63,508 | 97,874 | 164,534 | 95,732 | 90,466 | 96,119 | 48,910 | 210,741 | 66,252 | 164,221 | 2,444,884 |
| 2015 | 181,372 | 179,371 | 71,704 | 75,251 | 183,277 | 75,353 | 104,020 | 115,230 | 44,110 | 202,614 | 67,445 | 152,614 | 2,356,763 |
| 2016 | 185,399 | 162,383 | 40,939 | 64,425 | 159,119 | 81,502 | 87,847 | 111,011 | 60,826 | 194,190 | 73,459 | 153,767 | 2,303,344 |
| 2017 | 233,557 | 171,942 | 29,654 | 59,710 | 181,922 | 168,060 | 78,685 | 126,939 | 60,092 | 154,313 | 74,577 | 134,908 | 2,451,453 |
| 2018 | 264,024 | 156,281 | 57,418 | 57,708 | 158,168 | 121,390 | 81,550 | 137,084 | 52,611 | 151,503 | 83,178 | 135,647 | 2,457,795 |
| 2019 | 236,243 | 184,244 | 86,491 | 46,758 | 150,392 | 102,648 | 94,192 | 137,901 | 47,230 | 158,403 | 87,316 | 132,855 | 2,369,003 |
| 2020[1] | 204,883 | 108,708 | 68,707 | 45,896 | 136,327 | 110,275 | 83,464 | 143,039 | 52,772 | 150,787 | 93,829 | 108,315 | 2,137,577 |
| 2021[2] | 184,595 | 173,737 | 16,051 | 55,559 | 153,297 | 116,931 | 86,957 | 135,412 | 44,145 | 143,807 | 74,418 | 129,829 | 2,181,753 |

[1] Preliminary.  [2] Estimate.  Source: Food and Agriculture Organization of the United Nations (FAO-UN)

# TOBACCO

## World Exports of Leaf Tobacco    In Metric Tons

| Year | Argentina | Belgium | Brazil | China | India | Italy | Malawi | Mozambique | Tanzania | Turkey | United States | Zimbabwe | World Total |
|---|---|---|---|---|---|---|---|---|---|---|---|---|---|
| 2012 | 89,122 | 85,536 | 624,699 | 212,369 | 234,221 | 76,654 | 141,009 | 55,570 | 107,593 | 75,680 | 165,039 | 131,853 | 2,641,523 |
| 2013 | 70,053 | 73,348 | 609,927 | 199,967 | 253,934 | 69,083 | 135,676 | 60,708 | 69,449 | 57,512 | 171,844 | 147,873 | 2,597,396 |
| 2014 | 54,607 | 105,205 | 460,525 | 159,760 | 215,656 | 61,500 | 154,708 | 58,607 | 76,525 | 67,895 | 158,767 | 141,559 | 2,385,145 |
| 2015 | 44,232 | 164,510 | 497,956 | 154,708 | 205,610 | 58,601 | 126,235 | 67,671 | 65,682 | 54,153 | 110,127 | 148,268 | 2,333,294 |
| 2016 | 90,948 | 161,656 | 466,300 | 173,582 | 217,859 | 64,521 | 150,104 | 82,559 | 74,341 | 50,742 | 173,908 | 155,191 | 2,496,396 |
| 2017 | 83,656 | 186,541 | 442,921 | 206,710 | 191,006 | 68,059 | 150,533 | 69,555 | 48,280 | 48,899 | 159,276 | 157,337 | 2,460,431 |
| 2018 | 61,804 | 223,938 | 440,755 | 187,114 | 194,280 | 74,136 | 139,844 | 66,326 | 72,236 | 60,625 | 151,479 | 171,281 | 2,442,708 |
| 2019 | 52,674 | 229,522 | 530,168 | 194,641 | 185,946 | 67,478 | 136,411 | 90,463 | 42,581 | 46,665 | 104,696 | 173,559 | 2,437,089 |
| 2020[1] | 56,431 | 219,956 | 485,115 | 186,066 | 176,700 | 59,254 | 112,439 | 60,936 | 42,558 | 48,243 | 97,785 | 177,606 | 2,245,569 |
| 2021[2] | 32,709 | 204,736 | 434,178 | 192,154 | 190,184 | 59,822 | 108,120 | 53,322 | 37,705 | 51,689 | 105,453 | 177,171 | 2,224,456 |

[1] Preliminary.  [2] Estimate.    Source: Food and Agriculture Organization of the United Nations (FAO-UN)

## Production of Tobacco in the United States, by States    In Thousands of Pounds

| Year | Georgia | Kentucky | North Carolina | Ohio | Pennsylvania | South Carolina | Tennessee | Virginia | Total |
|---|---|---|---|---|---|---|---|---|---|
| 2013 | 22,400 | 187,240 | 362,660 | 4,620 | 21,260 | 24,650 | 44,570 | 52,613 | 723,579 |
| 2014 | 34,500 | 214,280 | 453,860 | 4,300 | 22,250 | 33,180 | 52,155 | 57,651 | 876,415 |
| 2015 | 32,400 | 149,830 | 380,250 | 3,610 | 18,090 | 26,000 | 48,770 | 55,655 | 719,171 |
| 2016 | 28,350 | 136,280 | 331,800 | ---- | 20,460 | 24,700 | 35,690 | 51,440 | 628,720 |
| 2017 | 26,250 | 183,300 | 360,040 | ---- | 18,990 | 25,200 | 43,000 | 53,381 | 710,161 |
| 2018 | 23,750 | 134,370 | 251,925 | ---- | 17,400 | 22,140 | 39,610 | 44,046 | 533,241 |
| 2019 | 18,900 | 123,390 | 234,700 | ---- | 14,300 | 15,770 | 30,490 | 30,406 | 467,956 |
| 2020 | 19,355 | 102,395 | 178,727 | ---- | 13,440 | 6,600 | 27,940 | 24,420 | 372,877 |
| 2021 | 14,400 | 117,060 | 252,400 | ---- | 14,020 | 13,680 | 31,950 | 34,463 | 477,973 |
| 2022[1] | 12,600 | 104,880 | 232,320 | ---- | 13,050 | 12,600 | 31,170 | 28,345 | 447,367 |

[1] Preliminary.    Source: Agricultural Statistics Board, U.S. Department of Agriculture (ASB-USDA)

## Salient Statistics of Tobacco in the United States

| Year | Acres Harvested 1,000 Acres | Yield Per Acre Pounds | Production Million Pounds | Farm Price cents Lb. | Farm Value Million $ | Tobacco (June-July) Exports[2] Million Pounds | Imports[3] Million Pounds | U.S. Exports of Cigarettes In Millions | Cigars & Cheroots In Millions | All Tobacco | Smoking Tobacco[4] | Stocks of Tobacco[5] All Tobacco | Fire Cured[6] | Cigar Filler[7] | Maryland |
|---|---|---|---|---|---|---|---|---|---|---|---|---|---|---|---|
| 2013 | 355.7 | 2,034 | 724 | 217.7 | 1,575 | ---- | ---- | ---- | ---- | ---- | ---- | ---- | ---- | ---- | ---- |
| 2014 | 378.4 | 2,316 | 876 | 209.4 | 1,835 | ---- | ---- | ---- | ---- | ---- | ---- | ---- | ---- | ---- | ---- |
| 2015 | 328.7 | 2,188 | 719 | 200.3 | 1,441 | ---- | ---- | ---- | ---- | ---- | ---- | ---- | ---- | ---- | ---- |
| 2016 | 319.7 | 1,967 | 629 | 200.7 | 1,262 | ---- | ---- | ---- | ---- | ---- | ---- | ---- | ---- | ---- | ---- |
| 2017 | 321.5 | 2,209 | 710 | 205.8 | 1,462 | ---- | ---- | ---- | ---- | ---- | ---- | ---- | ---- | ---- | ---- |
| 2018 | 291.4 | 1,830 | 533 | 205.1 | 1,093 | ---- | ---- | ---- | ---- | ---- | ---- | ---- | ---- | ---- | ---- |
| 2019 | 227.1 | 2,060 | 468 | 200.9 | 940 | ---- | ---- | ---- | ---- | ---- | ---- | ---- | ---- | ---- | ---- |
| 2020 | 191.1 | 1,951 | 373 | 210.5 | 785 | ---- | ---- | ---- | ---- | ---- | ---- | ---- | ---- | ---- | ---- |
| 2021 | 218.9 | 2,183 | 478 | 214.6 | 1,026 | ---- | ---- | ---- | ---- | ---- | ---- | ---- | ---- | ---- | ---- |
| 2022[1] | 201.8 | 2,217 | 447 | | | ---- | ---- | ---- | ---- | ---- | ---- | ---- | ---- | ---- | ---- |

[1] Preliminary.   [2] Domestic.   [3] For consumption.   [4] In bulk.   [5] Flue-cured and cigar wrapper, year beginning July 1; for all other types, October 1.
[6] Kentucky-Tennessee types 22-23.   [7] Types 41-46.   Source: Economic Research Service, U.S. Department of Agriculture (ERS-USDA)

## Tobacco Production in the United States, by Types    In Thousands of Pounds (Farm-Sale Weight)

| Year | Class 1, Flue-cured (11-14) | Class 2, Fire-cured (21-23) | Class 3A, Light air-cured (31-32) | Class 3B, Dark air-cured (35-37) | Total Cigar types (41-61) | US Total |
|---|---|---|---|---|---|---|
| 2013 | 454,350 | 50,388 | 197,165 | 13,790 | 7,886 | 723,579 |
| 2014 | 572,880 | 59,146 | 217,860 | 17,490 | 9,039 | 876,415 |
| 2015 | 489,475 | 56,125 | 148,195 | 17,050 | 8,326 | 719,171 |
| 2016 | 431,450 | 39,520 | 143,890 | 10,020 | 3,840 | 628,720 |
| 2017 | 460,650 | 59,531 | 165,460 | 20,200 | 4,320 | 710,161 |
| 2018 | 338,690 | 58,926 | 103,515 | 26,590 | 5,520 | 533,241 |
| 2019 | 297,170 | 45,766 | 92,830 | 24,390 | 5,500 | 467,956 |
| 2020 | 227,555 | 37,335 | 80,332 | 21,215 | 5,520 | 372,877 |
| 2021 | 313,430 | 48,102 | 84,256 | 25,165 | 6,250 | 477,973 |
| 2022[1] | 284,700 | 50,295 | 65,680 | 24,600 | 9,250 | 447,367 |

[1] Preliminary.    Source: Agricultural Statistics Board, U.S. Department of Agriculture (ASB-USDA)

# TOBACCO

## U.S. Exports of Unmanufactured Tobacco   In Millions of Pounds (Declared Weight)

| Year | Australia | Belgium-Luxem. | Denmark | France | Germany | Italy | Japan | Netherlands | Sweden | Switzerland | Thailand | United Kingdom | Total U.S. Exports |
|---|---|---|---|---|---|---|---|---|---|---|---|---|---|
| 2013 | .3 | 3.8 | .7 | 6.5 | 20.1 | 1.5 | .0 | 25.0 | .5 | 62.2 | 2.7 | 1.4 | 349.9 |
| 2014 | .1 | 9.8 | 1.2 | 9.8 | 14.4 | .5 | .0 | 14.3 | .4 | 63.5 | 3.2 | 3.2 | 330.2 |
| 2015 | .1 | 10.9 | 1.1 | 5.2 | 15.2 | .6 | .0 | 7.9 | .4 | 89.7 | 1.8 | 1.0 | 343.0 |
| 2016 | .0 | 20.5 | .9 | 2.0 | 11.9 | 6.3 | .2 | 8.5 | .3 | 79.5 | .6 | 1.1 | 362.2 |
| 2017 |  | 14.6 | .9 | 1.2 | 6.6 | 7.2 | .3 | 7.5 | .4 | 76.6 |  | 1.0 | 317.8 |
| 2018 |  | 13.8 | .9 | 2.9 | 5.5 | 8.6 | .2 | 9.4 | .1 | 70.4 |  | 1.2 | 326.9 |
| 2019 | .1 | 12.2 | .7 | .9 | 2.2 | 12.2 | .1 | 2.6 | .1 | 58.2 |  | 1.4 | 222.5 |
| 2020 | .0 | 11.1 | .7 | 1.3 | 2.6 | 4.6 | .1 | 3.9 | .3 | 34.2 |  |  | 206.3 |
| 2021 |  | 7.0 | .7 | 2.7 | 1.1 | 1.1 | .9 | 2.4 | .4 | 39.2 |  | .0 | 226.5 |
| 2022[1] | .0 | 13.7 | .6 | 3.1 | 1.0 | 1.6 | .0 | 2.8 |  | 31.1 |  | .0 | 185.3 |

[1] Preliminary.   Source: Economic Research Service, U.S. Department of Agriculture (ERS-USDA)

## U.S. Salient Statistics for Flue-Cured Tobacco (Types 11-14) in the United States   In Millions of Pounds

| Crop Year | Acres Harvested 1,000 | Yield Per Acre Pounds | Marketings | Stocks Oct. 1 | Total Supply | Exports | Domestic Disappearance | Total Disappearance | Farm Price cents/Lb. | Placed Under Gov't Loan (Mil. Lb.) | Price Support Level (cents)/Lb. | Loan Stocks Nov. 30 | Uncommitted |
|---|---|---|---|---|---|---|---|---|---|---|---|---|---|
| 2013-14 | 228.8 | 1,986 | ---- | ---- | ---- | ---- | ---- | ---- | ---- | ---- | ---- | ---- | ---- |
| 2014-15 | 245.3 | 2,335 | ---- | ---- | ---- | ---- | ---- | ---- | ---- | ---- | ---- | ---- | ---- |
| 2015-16 | 220.0 | 2,225 | ---- | ---- | ---- | ---- | ---- | ---- | ---- | ---- | ---- | ---- | ---- |
| 2016-17 | 213.5 | 2,021 | ---- | ---- | ---- | ---- | ---- | ---- | ---- | ---- | ---- | ---- | ---- |
| 2017-18 | 209.5 | 2,199 | ---- | ---- | ---- | ---- | ---- | ---- | ---- | ---- | ---- | ---- | ---- |
| 2018-19 | 197.8 | 1,712 | ---- | ---- | ---- | ---- | ---- | ---- | ---- | ---- | ---- | ---- | ---- |
| 2019-20 | 149.3 | 1,990 | ---- | ---- | ---- | ---- | ---- | ---- | ---- | ---- | ---- | ---- | ---- |
| 2020-21 | 124.1 | 1,834 | ---- | ---- | ---- | ---- | ---- | ---- | ---- | ---- | ---- | ---- | ---- |
| 2021-22[1] | 150.1 | 2,088 | ---- | ---- | ---- | ---- | ---- | ---- | ---- | ---- | ---- | ---- | ---- |
| 2022-23[2] | 140.5 | 2,026 | ---- | ---- | ---- | ---- | ---- | ---- | ---- | ---- | ---- | ---- | ---- |

[1] Preliminary.   [2] Estimate.   NA = Not available.   Source: Economic Research Service, U.S. Department of Agriculture (ERS-USDA)

## Salient Statistics for Burley Tobacco (Type 31) in the United States   In Millions of Pounds

| Crop Year | Acres Harvested 1,000 | Yield Per Acre Pounds | Marketings | Stocks Oct. 1 | Total Supply | Exports | Domestic Disappearance | Total Disappearance | Farm Price cents/Lb. | Gross Sales[3] | Price Support Level cents/Lb. | Loan Stocks Nov. 30 | Uncommitted |
|---|---|---|---|---|---|---|---|---|---|---|---|---|---|
| 2013-14 | 99.0 | 1,944 | ---- | ---- | ---- | ---- | ---- | ---- | ---- | ---- | ---- | ---- | ---- |
| 2014-15 | 101.5 | 2,100 | ---- | ---- | ---- | ---- | ---- | ---- | ---- | ---- | ---- | ---- | ---- |
| 2015-16 | 78.9 | 1,834 | ---- | ---- | ---- | ---- | ---- | ---- | ---- | ---- | ---- | ---- | ---- |
| 2016-17 | 80.0 | 1,747 | ---- | ---- | ---- | ---- | ---- | ---- | ---- | ---- | ---- | ---- | ---- |
| 2017-18 | 81.5 | 1,977 | ---- | ---- | ---- | ---- | ---- | ---- | ---- | ---- | ---- | ---- | ---- |
| 2018-19 | 61.1 | 1,645 | ---- | ---- | ---- | ---- | ---- | ---- | ---- | ---- | ---- | ---- | ---- |
| 2019-20 | 48.6 | 1,910 | ---- | ---- | ---- | ---- | ---- | ---- | ---- | ---- | ---- | ---- | ---- |
| 2020-21 | 41.0 | 1,959 | ---- | ---- | ---- | ---- | ---- | ---- | ---- | ---- | ---- | ---- | ---- |
| 2021-22[1] | 41.0 | 2,055 | ---- | ---- | ---- | ---- | ---- | ---- | ---- | ---- | ---- | ---- | ---- |
| 2022-23[2] | 34.9 | 1,885 | ---- | ---- | ---- | ---- | ---- | ---- | ---- | ---- | ---- | ---- | ---- |

[1] Preliminary.   [2] Estimate.   [3] Before Christmas holidays.   NA = Not available.
Source: Economic Research Service, U.S. Department of Agriculture (ERS-USDA)

## Exports of Tobacco from the United States (Quantity and Value)   In Metric Tons

| Year | Flue-Cured | Value 1,000 USD | Burley | Value 1,000 USD | Total | Value 1,000 USD | Manufactured | Value 1,000 USD |
|---|---|---|---|---|---|---|---|---|
| 2013 | 78,079 | 650,887 | 32,124 | 265,809 | 158,728 | 1,137,947 | 21,930 | 485,412 |
| 2014 | 76,239 | 645,462 | 25,441 | 217,329 | 149,758 | 1,085,958 | 18,111 | 426,981 |
| 2015 | 77,942 | 657,188 | 26,100 | 226,807 | 155,578 | 1,108,756 | 21,880 | 423,179 |
| 2016 | 88,283 | 707,889 | 20,202 | 166,246 | 164,276 | 1,085,439 | 18,620 | 408,341 |
| 2017 | 77,830 | 643,791 | 16,335 | 139,327 | 144,136 | 1,010,325 | 16,321 | 197,428 |
| 2018 | 81,873 | 670,927 | 19,888 | 165,051 | 148,259 | 1,049,085 | 14,540 | 184,761 |
| 2019 | 52,250 | 427,691 | 10,098 | 85,776 | 100,924 | 732,495 | 12,711 | 210,520 |
| 2020 | 36,848 | 290,318 | 9,602 | 78,211 | 93,595 | 665,805 | 14,216 | 213,011 |
| 2021[1] | 53,301 | 442,388 | 3,202 | 28,223 | 102,748 | 827,318 | 15,454 | 201,883 |
| 2022[2] | 43,076 | 363,648 | 3,693 | 32,307 | 84,051 | 676,510 | 12,543 | 190,738 |

[1] Preliminary.   [2] Forecast.   Source: Foreign Agricultural Service, U.S. Department of Agriculture (FAS-USDA)

# Tungsten

Tungsten (atomic symbol W) is a grayish-white, lustrous, metallic element. The atomic symbol for tungsten is W because of its former name of Wolfram. Tungsten has the highest melting point of any metal at about 3410 degrees Celsius and boils at about 5660 degrees Celsius. In 1781, the Swedish chemist Carl Wilhelm Scheele discovered tungsten.

Tungsten is never found in nature but is instead found in the minerals wolframite, scheelite, huebnertite, and ferberite. Tungsten has excellent corrosion resistance qualities and is resistant to most mineral acids. Tungsten is used as filaments in incandescent lamps, electron and television tubes, alloys of steel, spark plugs, electrical contact points, cutting tools, and in the chemical and tanning industries.

**Prices** – The average monthly price of tungsten at U.S. ports in 2022 rose by +18.1% yr/yr to $341.65 per short ton, below the 2012 record high of $375.16.

**Supply** – World concentrate production of tungsten in 2022 rose by +0.2% yr/yr to 84,000 metric tons. The world's largest producer of tungsten by far is China, with 71,000 metric tons of production in 2022, which was 84.5% of total world production. Russia is the next largest producer at 2.7%, with a small production level of 2,300 metric tons.

**Trade** – The U.S. in 2022 relied on imports for more than 50% of its tungsten consumption. U.S. imports for consumption in 2022 rose by +25.8% yr/yr to 2,000 metric tons. U.S. exports in 2022 rose by +36.1% yr/yr to 600 metric tons.

### World Concentrate Production of Tungsten    In Metric Tons (Contained Tungsten[3])

| Year | Austria | Bolivia | Brazil | Burma | Canada | China | Korea, North | Mongolia | Portugal | Russia | Rwanda | Thailand | Total |
|---|---|---|---|---|---|---|---|---|---|---|---|---|---|
| 2013 | 850 | 1,253 | 494 | 235 | 2,128 | 65,000 | 65 | 274 | 692 | 4,191 | 1,100 | 140 | 79,400 |
| 2014 | 819 | 1,252 | 510 | 247 | 2,344 | 65,000 | 70 | 557 | 671 | 3,775 | 1,000 | 99 | 82,600 |
| 2015 | 861 | 1,460 | 432 | 144 | 1,600 | 67,000 | 70 | 351 | 474 | 3,262 | 850 | 35 | 83,700 |
| 2016 | 954 | 1,110 | 323 | 182 | ---- | 64,000 | 50 | 732 | 549 | 2,672 | 820 | 33 | 78,400 |
| 2017 | 975 | 994 | 411 | 216 | ---- | 67,000 | 310 | 510 | 669 | 2,144 | 720 | 65 | 81,400 |
| 2018 | 936 | 1,365 | 400 | 77 | ---- | 65,000 | 1,410 | 1,938 | 715 | 2,234 | 920 | 69 | 82,200 |
| 2019 | 892 | 1,064 | 400 | 82 | ---- | 69,000 | 1,130 | 1,900 | 518 | 2,200 | 900 | 40 | 83,800 |
| 2020 | 890 | 1,350 | | | ---- | 66,000 | 410 | 1,900 | 550 | 2,400 | 860 | | 78,400 |
| 2021[1] | 900 | 1,563 | | | ---- | 71,000 | 400 | | 502 | 2,300 | 1,340 | | 83,800 |
| 2022[2] | 900 | 1,400 | | | ---- | 71,000 | | | 500 | 2,300 | 1,100 | | 84,000 |

[1] Preliminary.  [2] Estimate.  [3] Conversion Factors: $WO_3$ to W, multiply by 0.7931; 60% $WO_3$ to W, multiply by 0.4758.
*Source: U.S. Geological Survey (USGS)*

### Salient Statistics of Tungsten in the United States    In Metric Tons (Contained Tungsten)

| Year | Net Import Reliance as a % Apparent Consumption | Total Consumption | Steel Tool | Stainless & Heat Assisting | Alloy Steel[3] | Super-alloys | Cutting & Wear Resistant Materials | Products Made From Metal Powder | Miscellaneous | Chemical and Ceramic | Exports | Imports for Consumption | Stocks, Dec. 31 Concentrates Consumers | Producers |
|---|---|---|---|---|---|---|---|---|---|---|---|---|---|---|
| 2013 | 41 | W | W | 86 | W | W | 6,260 | W | ---- | 88 | 1,050 | 3,690 | W | W |
| 2014 | >25 | W | W | 82 | W | W | 6,880 | W | ---- | 88 | 1,230 | 4,080 | W | W |
| 2015 | >25 | W | W | 205 | W | W | 6,310 | W | ---- | 88 | 398 | 3,970 | W | W |
| 2016 | >25 | W | W | 94 | W | W | 5,760 | W | ---- | 88 | 183 | 3,580 | W | W |
| 2017 | >50 | W | W | 87 | W | W | 6,550 | W | ---- | 88 | 532 | 3,920 | W | W |
| 2018 | >50 | W | W | 84 | W | W | 6,950 | W | ---- | 88 | 284 | 4,050 | W | W |
| 2019 | >50 | W | W | 82 | W | W | 6,940 | W | ---- | 88 | 583 | 2,760 | W | W |
| 2020 | >50 | W | W | | W | W | | W | ---- | | 480 | 2,020 | W | W |
| 2021[1] | >50 | W | W | | W | W | | W | ---- | | 441 | 1,590 | W | W |
| 2022[2] | >50 | W | W | | W | W | | W | ---- | | 600 | 2,000 | W | W |

[1] Preliminary.  [2] Estimate.  [3] Other than tool.  [4] Included with stainless & heat assisting.  W = Withheld.
*Source: U.S. Geological Survey (USGS)*

### Average Price of Tungsten at U.S. Ports (Including Duty)    In Dollars Per Short Ton

| Year | Jan. | Feb. | Mar. | Apr. | May | June | July | Aug. | Sept. | Oct. | Nov. | Dec. | Average |
|---|---|---|---|---|---|---|---|---|---|---|---|---|---|
| 2015 | 293.18 | 281.80 | 272.64 | 254.20 | 243.45 | 228.50 | 222.95 | 207.90 | 188.81 | 184.77 | 173.33 | 176.28 | 227.32 |
| 2016 | 171.79 | 167.74 | 175.43 | 189.52 | 217.82 | 212.75 | 188.69 | 191.74 | 190.00 | 192.45 | 198.89 | 191.39 | 190.68 |
| 2017 | 194.33 | 200.30 | 211.83 | 211.18 | 217.80 | 221.68 | 222.76 | 252.28 | 310.60 | 286.02 | 280.68 | 296.79 | 242.19 |
| 2018 | 311.96 | 321.62 | 327.93 | 327.55 | 338.02 | 349.36 | 341.50 | 307.52 | 282.50 | 283.48 | 285.00 | 281.31 | 313.15 |
| 2019 | 268.80 | 266.25 | 276.14 | 275.95 | 273.00 | 257.50 | 222.13 | 205.50 | 202.50 | 228.75 | 235.00 | 239.38 | 245.91 |
| 2020 | 240.00 | 242.50 | 242.50 | 236.88 | 219.00 | 215.00 | 208.50 | 208.75 | 220.88 | 219.90 | 222.50 | 228.13 | 225.38 |
| 2021 | 239.50 | 255.00 | 270.88 | 274.00 | 274.00 | 276.50 | 291.60 | 312.25 | 313.75 | 319.50 | 322.50 | 322.50 | 289.33 |
| 2022 | 330.63 | 339.75 | 348.75 | 351.70 | 347.88 | 347.00 | 343.50 | 342.50 | 339.50 | 337.50 | 336.25 | 334.80 | 341.65 |

U.S. Spot Quotations, 65% $WO_3$, Basis C.I.F.    *Source: U.S. Geological Survey (USGS)*

# Turkeys

During the past three decades, the turkey industry has experienced tremendous growth in the U.S. Turkey production has more than tripled since 1970, with a current value of over $7 billion. Turkey was not a popular dish in Europe until a roast turkey was eaten on June 27, 1570, at the wedding feast of Charles XI of France and Elizabeth of Austria. The King was so impressed with the birds that the turkey subsequently became a popular dish at banquets held by French nobility.

The most popular turkey product continues to be the whole bird, with strong demand at Thanksgiving and Christmas. The primary breeders maintain and develop the quality stock, concentrating on growth and conformation in males and fecundity in females, as well as characteristics important to general health and welfare. Turkey producers include large companies that produce turkeys all year round, and relatively small companies and farmers who produce turkeys primarily for the seasonal Thanksgiving market.

**Prices** – The average monthly price received by farmers for turkeys in the U.S. in 2022 rose by +29.0% yr/yr to 106.3 cents per pound, which was a new record high.

**Supply** – World production of turkeys in 2018 rose by +0.4% yr/yr to 5.901 million metric tons. World production of turkeys has grown by more than 2.5 times since 1980, when production was 2.090 million metric tons. The U.S. is the world's largest producer of turkeys by far, with 2.666 million metric tons of production in 2018, accounting for a hefty 45.2% of world production. The value of U.S. turkey production in the U.S. in 2021 was $5.891 billion.

**Demand** – U.S. per-capita consumption of turkeys in 2023 is expected to rise by +6.8% at 15.7 pounds per person per year.

### World Production of Turkey Meat   In Thousands of Metric Tons (Ready-to-Cook-Equivalents)

| Year | Brazil | Canada | Chile | France | Germany | Italy | Morocco | Poland | Spain | Tunisia | United Kingdom | United States | World Total |
|---|---|---|---|---|---|---|---|---|---|---|---|---|---|
| 2012 | 510.0 | 160.7 | 103.1 | 387.1 | 464.2 | 321.6 | 70.0 | 129.0 | 173.7 | 60.6 | 196.0 | 2,706.7 | 5,842.8 |
| 2013 | 520.0 | 168.2 | 98.1 | 340.4 | 458.1 | 310.6 | 75.0 | 128.5 | 156.9 | 63.8 | 187.0 | 2,633.3 | 5,670.1 |
| 2014 | 470.0 | 167.9 | 96.8 | 377.9 | 469.1 | 309.9 | 78.0 | 145.0 | 158.5 | 70.9 | 172.0 | 2,610.7 | 5,665.5 |
| 2015 | 480.0 | 171.6 | 103.6 | 352.6 | 464.8 | 313.0 | 90.0 | 162.4 | 170.7 | 69.6 | 181.0 | 2,552.2 | 5,697.7 |
| 2016 | 528.9 | 183.4 | 110.7 | 394.0 | 483.3 | 331.9 | 90.0 | 179.1 | 191.7 | 73.5 | 166.0 | 2,713.0 | 6,025.4 |
| 2017 | 546.2 | 171.2 | 76.9 | 374.8 | 465.6 | 308.6 | 90.0 | 172.2 | 197.9 | 79.0 | 147.0 | 2,712.7 | 5,884.2 |
| 2018 | 548.6 | 168.6 | 95.1 | 331.0 | 467.0 | 300.1 | 100.0 | 376.6 | 210.4 | 82.6 | 157.0 | 2,666.3 | 6,037.3 |
| 2019 | 551.2 | 165.0 | 84.4 | 317.0 | 471.0 | 300.7 | 107.0 | 385.6 | 212.8 | 82.3 | 175.1 | 2,644.3 | 6,020.0 |
| 2020[1] | 561.8 | 158.3 | 72.2 | 321.0 | 476.0 | 313.3 | 100.0 | 406.8 | 226.0 | 85.5 | 174.0 | 2,610.5 | 6,029.2 |
| 2021[2] | 572.6 | 158.9 | 71.6 | 295.0 | 441.0 | 297.8 | 115.0 | 363.2 | 224.8 | 88.7 | 128.8 | 2,526.6 | 5,792.4 |

[1] Preliminary.  [2] Forecast.  Source: Food and Agriculture Organization of the United Nations (FAO-UN)

### World Exports of Turkey Meat   In Thousands of Metric Tons (Ready-to-Cook-Equivalents)

| Year | Brazil | Canada | Chile | France | Germany | Hungary | Italy | Netherlands | Poland | Spain | United Kingdom | United States | World Total |
|---|---|---|---|---|---|---|---|---|---|---|---|---|---|
| 2012 | 94.2 | 22.4 | 20.3 | 87.3 | 96.5 | 42.8 | 52.2 | 31.8 | 117.1 | 25.2 | 46.6 | 332.2 | 1,050.9 |
| 2013 | 92.1 | 23.6 | 19.1 | 75.2 | 102.7 | 36.3 | 58.3 | 41.1 | 108.9 | 30.5 | 54.3 | 310.2 | 1,032.5 |
| 2014 | 79.6 | 23.3 | 24.7 | 76.2 | 106.5 | 38.5 | 59.2 | 37.9 | 119.7 | 33.9 | 41.9 | 329.0 | 1,057.9 |
| 2015 | 83.5 | 21.2 | 35.9 | 69.8 | 98.7 | 36.9 | 60.7 | 34.3 | 146.6 | 37.6 | 29.8 | 201.7 | 942.0 |
| 2016 | 93.4 | 25.8 | 37.1 | 72.1 | 102.7 | 39.9 | 68.5 | 25.0 | 153.0 | 44.9 | 28.7 | 216.5 | 1,002.4 |
| 2017 | 72.4 | 22.8 | 13.2 | 77.6 | 109.2 | 33.8 | 65.3 | 21.6 | 140.7 | 50.6 | 27.0 | 231.4 | 962.0 |
| 2018 | 62.7 | 19.2 | 25.8 | 67.9 | 101.0 | 34.2 | 64.6 | 23.6 | 153.3 | 48.2 | 23.7 | 219.3 | 935.6 |
| 2019 | 35.0 | 20.3 | 25.3 | 58.4 | 100.7 | 33.2 | 57.8 | 23.4 | 169.6 | 47.7 | 22.2 | 242.4 | 927.2 |
| 2020[1] | 38.2 | 24.7 | 24.5 | 53.0 | 95.5 | 27.7 | 58.6 | 19.5 | 168.2 | 46.8 | 15.7 | 213.8 | 871.3 |
| 2021[2] | 41.8 | 26.6 | 22.5 | 50.3 | 96.6 | 34.3 | 58.9 | 27.4 | 153.8 | 52.8 | 11.5 | 216.2 | 890.5 |

[1] Preliminary.  [2] Forecast.  Source: Food and Agriculture Organization of the United Nations (FAO-UN)

### World Imports of Turkey Meat   In Thousands of Metric Tons (Ready-to-Cook-Equivalents)

| Year | Austria | Belgium | Benin | China | France | Germany | Mexico | Netherlands | Portugal | South Africa | Spain | United Kingdom | World Total |
|---|---|---|---|---|---|---|---|---|---|---|---|---|---|
| 2012 | 38.9 | 38.2 | 62.9 | 65.8 | 29.4 | 107.8 | 157.5 | 30.4 | 15.7 | 32.5 | 27.9 | 29.3 | 971.5 |
| 2013 | 38.3 | 38.6 | 67.8 | 54.0 | 33.2 | 108.9 | 154.1 | 26.4 | 20.2 | 35.2 | 24.9 | 28.4 | 908.0 |
| 2014 | 38.9 | 34.7 | 61.6 | 34.6 | 29.8 | 110.1 | 153.7 | 26.2 | 24.7 | 24.3 | 30.2 | 31.8 | 1,000.8 |
| 2015 | 35.4 | 31.7 | 57.8 | 20.3 | 29.8 | 116.7 | 126.4 | 18.8 | 27.9 | 10.6 | 33.2 | 32.8 | 948.8 |
| 2016 | 34.6 | 40.1 | 47.0 | 50.3 | 29.7 | 114.8 | 156.9 | 20.3 | 29.6 | 31.4 | 42.8 | 35.4 | 1,031.2 |
| 2017 | 31.5 | 35.5 | 41.8 | 12.3 | 28.6 | 117.8 | 161.8 | 22.3 | 25.4 | 32.2 | 37.3 | 41.1 | 937.6 |
| 2018 | 29.2 | 32.3 | 42.0 | 13.2 | 29.3 | 121.1 | 156.3 | 21.8 | 23.3 | 26.3 | 37.4 | 41.0 | 916.2 |
| 2019 | 25.6 | 39.7 | 42.9 | 22.7 | 28.6 | 113.6 | 150.2 | 22.7 | 25.0 | 27.8 | 46.0 | 33.2 | 918.4 |
| 2020[1] | 25.4 | 37.7 | 40.0 | 30.9 | 28.9 | 106.1 | 131.2 | 23.7 | 24.0 | 24.6 | 43.5 | 25.3 | 871.6 |
| 2021[2] | 26.2 | 31.4 | 50.7 | 19.6 | 31.6 | 95.9 | 154.6 | 27.4 | 22.8 | 25.3 | 34.5 | 23.7 | 888.2 |

[1] Preliminary.  [2] Forecast.  Source: Food and Agriculture Organization of the United Nations (FAO-UN)

# TURKEYS

## Salient Statistics of Turkeys in the United States

| Year | Poults Placed[3] --- In Thousands --- | Number Raised[4] | Liveweight Produced Mil Lbs | Price cents Per Lb. | Value of Production Million $ | Ready-to-Cook Basis Production | Beginning Stocks | Exports | Consumption Total | Per Capita Lbs. | Production Costs Feed - Liveweight Basis - | Total | Wholesale Ready-to-Cook Production Costs | 3-Region Weighted Avg Price[5] |
|---|---|---|---|---|---|---|---|---|---|---|---|---|---|---|
| 2012 | 283,550 | 253,500 | 7,561.9 | 71.9 | 5,452.1 | 5,967 | 210,787 | 797 | 5,028 | 16.0 | ---- | ---- | ---- | ---- |
| 2013 | 260,571 | 240,000 | 7,277.5 | 66.4 | 4,839.6 | 5,806 | 296,479 | 741 | 5,068 | 16.0 | ---- | ---- | ---- | ---- |
| 2014 | 267,153 | 237,500 | 7,217.0 | 73.2 | 5,304.5 | 5,756 | 237,407 | 775 | 5,052 | 15.8 | ---- | ---- | ---- | ---- |
| 2015 | 257,999 | 233,100 | 7,038.1 | 81.1 | 5,707.9 | 5,627 | 193,429 | 529 | 5,136 | 16.0 | ---- | ---- | ---- | ---- |
| 2016 | 270,711 | 241,418 | 7,487.0 | 82.5 | 6,184.2 | 5,981 | 201,011 | 569 | 5,386 | 16.6 | ---- | ---- | ---- | ---- |
| 2017 | 270,561 | 245,200 | 7,544.4 | 64.5 | 4,873.7 | 5,981 | 278,741 | 622 | | 16.5 | ---- | ---- | ---- | ---- |
| 2018 | 267,489 | 238,000 | 7,422.9 | 51.0 | 3,785.7 | 5,878 | 309,625 | 611 | | 16.2 | ---- | ---- | ---- | ---- |
| 2019 | 261,185 | 228,500 | 7,468.0 | 57.9 | 4,324.0 | 5,818 | 302,763 | 639 | | 16.0 | ---- | ---- | ---- | ---- |
| 2020[1] | 252,046 | 224,000 | 7,320.1 | 70.9 | 5,189.9 | 5,743 | 232,652 | 571 | | 15.8 | ---- | ---- | ---- | ---- |
| 2021[2] | 246,433 | | | 83.1 | | 5,592 | 223,024 | 561 | | 15.3 | ---- | ---- | ---- | ---- |

[1] Preliminary. [2] Estimate. [3] Poults placed for slaughter by hatcheries. [4] Turkeys place August 1-July 31. [5] Regions include central, eastern and western. Central region receives twice the weight of the other regions in calculating the average.
*Source: Economic Research Service, U.S. Department of Agriculture (ERS-USDA)*

## Turkey-Feed Price Ratio in the United States   In Pounds[2]

| Year | Jan. | Feb. | Mar. | Apr. | May | June | July | Aug. | Sept. | Oct. | Nov. | Dec. | Average |
|---|---|---|---|---|---|---|---|---|---|---|---|---|---|
| 2012 | 4.8 | 4.7 | 4.8 | 5.0 | 5.0 | 5.1 | 4.4 | 4.3 | 4.8 | 4.9 | 4.7 | 4.3 | 4.7 |
| 2013 | 4.0 | 3.9 | 4.1 | 4.2 | 4.1 | 4.1 | 4.3 | 4.6 | 5.0 | 5.8 | 5.3 | 5.5 | 4.6 |
| 2014 | 5.2 | 5.4 | 5.3 | 5.1 | 5.4 | 5.6 | 6.2 | 6.8 | 7.6 | 8.3 | 8.1 | 7.1 | 6.3 |
| 2015 | 6.3 | 6.6 | 6.8 | 7.1 | 7.9 | 8.4 | 8.5 | 9.4 | 10.0 | 10.6 | 10.2 | 9.8 | 8.5 |
| 2016 | 8.7 | 9.0 | 9.0 | 9.2 | 8.8 | 8.9 | 9.3 | 9.5 | 10.3 | 9.9 | 9.3 | 8.4 | 9.2 |
| 2017 | 7.6 | 7.3 | 7.5 | 7.5 | 7.7 | 7.4 | 7.3 | 7.2 | 6.9 | 7.1 | 6.5 | 6.0 | 7.2 |
| 2018 | 5.7 | 5.5 | 5.2 | 5.2 | 5.1 | 5.3 | 5.7 | 5.8 | 5.9 | 5.7 | 6.0 | 5.5 | 5.6 |
| 2019 | 5.6 | 5.8 | 5.3 | 6.3 | 6.1 | 6.1 | 6.2 | 6.6 | 7.0 | 7.0 | 7.5 | 6.9 | 6.4 |
| 2020 | 6.7 | 7.0 | 7.4 | 7.9 | 8.3 | 8.5 | 8.7 | 8.7 | 8.6 | 8.2 | 7.3 | 6.9 | 7.9 |
| 2021[1] | 6.7 | 6.0 | 6.0 | 5.8 | 5.6 | 5.8 | 5.9 | 6.1 | 7.2 | 7.4 | 6.3 | 6.1 | 6.2 |

[1] Preliminary. [2] Pounds of feed equal in value to one pound of turkey, liveweight.   *Source: Economic Research Service, U.S. Department of Agriculture (ERS-USDA)*

## Average Price Received by Farmers for Turkeys in the United States (Liveweight)   In Cents Per Pound

| Year | Jan. | Feb. | Mar. | Apr. | May | June | July | Aug. | Sept. | Oct. | Nov. | Dec. | Average |
|---|---|---|---|---|---|---|---|---|---|---|---|---|---|
| 2012 | 65.7 | 65.0 | 69.0 | 73.7 | 72.7 | 73.9 | 72.9 | 74.4 | 76.2 | 76.9 | 75.1 | 67.4 | 71.9 |
| 2013 | 62.9 | 62.7 | 65.0 | 66.2 | 64.9 | 65.7 | 67.7 | 67.4 | 67.9 | 72.4 | 65.6 | 68.7 | 66.4 |
| 2014 | 64.5 | 66.4 | 68.3 | 68.7 | 72.6 | 72.8 | 74.0 | 75.6 | 77.5 | 82.2 | 82.1 | 73.4 | 73.2 |
| 2015 | 66.2 | 66.9 | 68.3 | 70.2 | 75.9 | 81.2 | 84.8 | 89.7 | 92.5 | 97.2 | 92.2 | 88.6 | 81.1 |
| 2016 | 78.9 | 79.4 | 78.9 | 83.2 | 83.1 | 86.5 | 86.6 | 84.3 | 87.8 | 85.2 | 81.5 | 74.4 | 82.5 |
| 2017 | 68.9 | 67.2 | 69.0 | 66.6 | 68.6 | 65.8 | 67.8 | 64.7 | 62.3 | 62.7 | 57.7 | 52.9 | 64.5 |
| 2018 | 50.8 | 50.6 | 49.9 | 50.0 | 49.8 | 50.8 | 51.9 | 51.7 | 53.1 | 51.1 | 53.0 | 49.8 | 51.0 |
| 2019 | 50.9 | 52.8 | 53.2 | 55.6 | 53.3 | 56.1 | 57.6 | 59.2 | 62.2 | 63.9 | 67.1 | 62.4 | 57.9 |
| 2020 | 62.5 | 64.4 | 66.4 | 67.7 | 70.1 | 71.4 | 73.7 | 73.5 | 77.6 | 78.4 | 73.4 | 72.1 | 70.9 |
| 2021[1] | 72.3 | 73.7 | 75.5 | 77.6 | 80.9 | 83.9 | 84.1 | 88.6 | 96.9 | 94.8 | 84.7 | 83.9 | 83.1 |

[1] Preliminary.   *Source: Economic Research Service, U.S. Department of Agriculture (ERS-USDA)*

## Average Wholesale Price of Turkeys[1] (Hens, 8-16 Lbs.) in New York   In Cents Per Pound

| Year | Jan. | Feb. | Mar. | Apr. | May | June | July | Aug. | Sept. | Oct. | Nov. | Dec. | Average |
|---|---|---|---|---|---|---|---|---|---|---|---|---|---|
| 2012 | 98.35 | 100.15 | 103.70 | 106.89 | 107.77 | 106.00 | 106.43 | 108.53 | 110.54 | 110.27 | 108.86 | 99.08 | 105.55 |
| 2013 | 96.27 | 95.00 | 96.58 | 97.30 | 97.59 | 98.18 | 99.09 | 99.28 | 101.22 | 106.75 | 105.64 | 103.83 | 99.73 |
| 2014 | 99.78 | 99.88 | 102.34 | 103.52 | 106.15 | 107.18 | 108.56 | 109.15 | 112.79 | 116.20 | 118.78 | 106.79 | 107.59 |
| 2015 | 99.12 | 99.12 | 100.57 | 104.06 | 108.82 | 112.53 | 120.86 | 126.62 | 131.65 | 135.68 | 130.63 | 123.96 | 116.14 |
| 2016 | 114.71 | 114.77 | 114.73 | 116.17 | 116.00 | 117.21 | 119.45 | 118.95 | 123.57 | 121.84 | 122.54 | 105.33 | 117.11 |
| 2017 | 99.81 | 100.56 | 100.90 | 99.25 | 99.44 | 98.54 | 97.61 | 96.38 | 96.59 | 94.97 | 88.76 | 80.16 | 96.08 |
| 2018 | 79.10 | 79.64 | 79.31 | 79.50 | 79.31 | 79.98 | 79.11 | 80.03 | 82.09 | 82.00 | 82.24 | 79.85 | 80.18 |
| 2019 | 80.96 | 83.50 | 83.90 | 84.31 | 84.74 | 87.38 | 88.26 | 90.43 | 93.76 | 96.88 | 99.24 | 97.17 | 89.21 |
| 2020 | 95.45 | 97.25 | 99.63 | 101.78 | 103.92 | 105.39 | 109.56 | 110.90 | 113.48 | 115.74 | 112.97 | 112.20 | 106.52 |
| 2021[1] | 108.76 | 109.66 | 111.99 | 113.55 | 118.15 | 121.40 | 122.00 | 129.33 | 136.30 | 135.13 | 135.32 | 129.87 | 122.62 |

[1] Ready-to-cook. [2] Preliminary.   *Source: Economic Research Service, U.S. Department of Agriculture (ERS-USDA)*

# TURKEYS

### Per Capita Consumption of Turkeys in the United States    In Pounds

| Year | First Quarter | Second Quarter | Third Quarter | Fourth Quarter | Total | Year | First Quarter | Second Quarter | Third Quarter | Fourth Quarter | Total |
|---|---|---|---|---|---|---|---|---|---|---|---|
| 2011 | 3.5 | 3.5 | 4.0 | 5.0 | 16.1 | 2017 | 3.7 | 3.7 | 4.0 | 5.0 | 16.5 |
| 2012 | 3.5 | 3.6 | 4.1 | 4.9 | 16.0 | 2018 | 3.5 | 3.8 | 3.9 | 4.9 | 16.2 |
| 2013 | 3.7 | 3.6 | 4.0 | 4.8 | 16.0 | 2019 | 3.5 | 3.7 | 4.0 | 4.9 | 16.0 |
| 2014 | 3.4 | 3.5 | 3.9 | 5.0 | 15.8 | 2020 | 3.6 | 3.5 | 3.9 | 4.7 | 15.8 |
| 2015 | 3.5 | 3.6 | 3.9 | 4.9 | 16.0 | 2021[1] | 3.4 | 3.6 | 3.8 | 4.4 | 15.3 |
| 2016 | 3.6 | 3.9 | 4.2 | 4.9 | 16.6 | 2022[2] | 3.4 | 3.6 | 3.9 | | 15.3 |

[1] Preliminary.   [2] Estimate.   Source: Economic Research Service, U.S. Department of Agriculture (ERS-USDA)

### Certified Federally Inspected Turkey Slaughter in the U.S. (Ready-to-Cook Weights)    In Thousands of Pounds

| Year | Jan. | Feb. | Mar. | Apr. | May | June | July | Aug. | Sept. | Oct. | Nov. | Dec. | Total |
|---|---|---|---|---|---|---|---|---|---|---|---|---|---|
| 2012 | 474,530 | 464,839 | 499,864 | 475,184 | 516,910 | 504,083 | 494,852 | 526,318 | 450,670 | 576,265 | 512,931 | 438,521 | 5,934,967 |
| 2013 | 522,128 | 458,794 | 470,052 | 502,276 | 505,780 | 471,529 | 512,059 | 482,373 | 438,111 | 514,181 | 477,015 | 420,380 | 5,774,678 |
| 2014 | 451,344 | 419,636 | 454,990 | 468,525 | 469,331 | 484,245 | 497,961 | 480,569 | 490,385 | 558,196 | 478,421 | 472,065 | 5,725,668 |
| 2015 | 489,634 | 431,503 | 498,992 | 493,905 | 432,442 | 455,913 | 446,207 | 447,301 | 450,088 | 522,359 | 466,917 | 458,298 | 5,593,559 |
| 2016 | 472,415 | 451,760 | 500,407 | 482,346 | 496,204 | 532,226 | 476,204 | 535,290 | 492,914 | 514,928 | 511,897 | 475,553 | 5,942,144 |
| 2017 | 495,763 | 454,965 | 526,631 | 433,274 | 520,061 | 519,205 | 581,127 | 673,714 | 581,261 | 686,143 | 642,370 | 573,273 | 6,687,787 |
| 2018 | 633,654 | 571,596 | 598,038 | 597,493 | 633,247 | 603,743 | 604,483 | 644,881 | 531,593 | 710,416 | 619,092 | 558,969 | 7,307,205 |
| 2019 | 637,240 | 570,119 | 596,483 | 601,863 | 611,273 | 590,011 | 610,283 | 622,416 | 573,499 | 681,966 | 583,138 | 557,236 | 7,235,527 |
| 2020 | 641,354 | 556,414 | 631,105 | 548,888 | 531,730 | 622,960 | 630,187 | 590,712 | 587,725 | 647,572 | 569,190 | 584,075 | 7,141,912 |
| 2021[1] | 556,549 | 522,972 | 649,318 | 571,606 | 561,687 | 605,013 | 571,231 | 588,402 | 585,139 | 601,443 | 564,684 | 530,205 | 6,908,249 |

[1] Preliminary.   Source: Economic Research Service, U.S. Department of Agriculture (ERS-USDA)

### Storage Stocks of Turkeys (Frozen) in the United States on First of Month    In Thousands of Pounds

| Year | Jan. | Feb. | Mar. | Apr. | May | June | July | Aug. | Sept. | Oct. | Nov. | Dec. |
|---|---|---|---|---|---|---|---|---|---|---|---|---|
| 2012 | 210,787 | 297,736 | 349,577 | 375,268 | 438,384 | 498,419 | 547,091 | 547,465 | 547,766 | 521,810 | 453,378 | 255,191 |
| 2013 | 296,479 | 360,018 | 394,755 | 401,246 | 457,575 | 521,556 | 566,475 | 581,357 | 580,069 | 541,183 | 434,493 | 221,221 |
| 2014 | 237,407 | 275,787 | 310,756 | 336,383 | 375,013 | 422,502 | 462,586 | 489,758 | 494,786 | 484,547 | 390,654 | 187,563 |
| 2015 | 193,429 | 280,400 | 321,337 | 345,578 | 394,415 | 441,388 | 462,020 | 494,037 | 477,579 | 449,622 | 351,828 | 190,268 |
| 2016 | 201,011 | 289,746 | 341,094 | 368,073 | 398,719 | 454,147 | 504,385 | 530,278 | 532,579 | 511,199 | 400,355 | 236,862 |
| 2017 | 278,741 | 339,493 | 378,370 | 428,752 | 471,484 | 529,904 | 565,123 | 595,623 | 600,013 | 569,963 | 460,856 | 288,536 |
| 2018 | 309,625 | 375,188 | 427,618 | 462,985 | 493,844 | 536,026 | 561,858 | 594,927 | 606,359 | 564,746 | 445,059 | 274,166 |
| 2019 | 302,763 | 390,972 | 452,174 | 470,335 | 471,592 | 494,439 | 538,714 | 557,031 | 563,076 | 528,394 | 393,008 | 221,996 |
| 2020 | 232,652 | 301,623 | 340,709 | 387,503 | 417,981 | 420,129 | 474,786 | 522,325 | 533,285 | 501,131 | 376,347 | 192,559 |
| 2021[1] | 223,024 | 301,409 | 320,144 | 350,588 | 362,510 | 390,655 | 405,996 | 435,479 | 428,055 | 414,128 | 301,999 | 139,670 |

[1] Preliminary.   Source: Economic Research Service, U.S. Department of Agriculture (ERS-USDA)

### Average Retail Price of Turkeys (Whole frozen) in the United States    In U.S. Dollars Per Pound

| Year | Jan. | Feb. | Mar. | Apr. | May | June | July | Aug. | Sept. | Oct. | Nov. | Dec. | Average |
|---|---|---|---|---|---|---|---|---|---|---|---|---|---|
| 2011 | 1.459 | 1.526 | 1.572 | 1.562 | 1.596 | 1.581 | 1.603 | 1.641 | 1.676 | 1.673 | 1.541 | 1.574 | 1.584 |
| 2012 | 1.671 | 1.671 | 1.812 | 1.791 | 1.608 | 1.557 | 1.561 | 1.586 | 1.621 | 1.661 | 1.488 | 1.433 | 1.622 |
| 2013 | 1.579 | 1.591 | 1.593 | 1.649 | 1.654 | 1.595 | 1.624 | 1.663 | 1.819 | NA | 1.721 | 1.650 | 1.649 |
| 2014 | 1.713 | 1.699 | 1.733 | 1.610 | 1.602 | 1.606 | 1.641 | 1.604 | 1.584 | 1.667 | 1.425 | 1.331 | 1.601 |
| 2015 | 1.445 | 1.480 | 1.503 | 1.487 | 1.527 | 1.541 | 1.568 | 1.546 | 1.538 | 1.558 | 1.424 | 1.448 | 1.505 |
| 2016 | 1.528 | 1.494 | 1.509 | 1.488 | 1.527 | 1.515 | 1.586 | 1.622 | 1.649 | 1.692 | 1.527 | 1.495 | 1.553 |
| 2017 | 1.581 | 1.570 | 1.585 | 1.567 | 1.532 | 1.576 | 1.622 | 1.615 | 1.623 | 1.656 | 1.556 | 1.502 | 1.582 |
| 2018 | 1.399 | 1.435 | 1.512 | 1.483 | 1.526 | 1.529 | 1.585 | 1.567 | 1.578 | 1.582 | 1.400 | 1.413 | 1.501 |
| 2019 | 1.455 | 1.488 | 1.521 | 1.543 | 1.560 | 1.574 | 1.531 | 1.562 | 1.604 | 1.601 | 1.412 | 1.389 | 1.520 |
| 2020[1] | 1.580 | 1.639 | ---- | ---- | ---- | ---- | ---- | ---- | ---- | ---- | ---- | ---- | 1.610 |

[1] Preliminary.   Source: Economic Research Service, U.S. Department of Agriculture (ERS-USDA)

# Uranium

Uranium (atomic symbol U) is a chemically reactive, radioactive, steel-gray, metallic element and is the main fuel used in nuclear reactors. Uranium is the heaviest of all the natural elements. Traces of uranium have been found in archeological artifacts dating back to 79 AD. Uranium was discovered in pitchblende by German chemist Martin Heinrich Klaproth in 1789. Klaproth named it uranium after the recently discovered planet Uranus. French physicist Antoine Henri Becquerel discovered the radioactive properties of uranium in 1896 when he produced an image on a photographic plate covered with a light-absorbing substance. Following Becquerel's experiments, investigations of radioactivity led to the discovery of radium (atomic symbol Ra) and to new concepts of atomic organization.

Uranium is mainly used as fuel in nuclear power plants. Demand for uranium concentrates is directly linked to the level of electricity generated by nuclear power plants. Uranium ores are widely distributed throughout the world and are primarily found in Canada, DRC (formerly Zaire), and the U.S. Uranium is obtained from primary mine production and secondary sources. Two Canadian companies, Cameco and Cogema Resources, are the primary producers of uranium from deposits in the Athabasca Basin of northern Saskatchewan. Secondary sources of uranium include excess inventories from utilities and other fuel cycle participants, used reactor fuel, and dismantled Russian nuclear weapons.

**Supply** – World production of uranium oxide (U308) concentrate in 2017, the last available year of data, fell by -4.7% yr/yr to 57,083 metric tons, down from the previous year's record high. The world's largest uranium producers in 2017 were Kazakhstan with 41.0% of world production, Canada with 23.0%, Australia with 10.3%, Namibia with 7.4%, and Niger with 6.0%.

**Trade** – U.S. imports of uranium in 2021 rose by +4.3% yr/yr to 41.300 million pounds. The record high of 66.100 million pounds was posted in 2004. The U.S. has generally been forced to import more uranium as domestic production steadily declined. U.S. exports of uranium in 2021 fell by -24.2% yr/yr to 7.500 million pounds.

## Uranium Industry Statistics in the United States — In Millions of Pounds $U_3O_8$

| Year | Production Mine | Production Concentrate | Concentrate Shipments | Exploration | Mining | Milling | Processing | Total[1] | Deliveries to U.S. Utilities[2] | Avg Price Delivered Uranium $/lb $U_3O_8$ | Imports | Avg Price Delivered Uranium Imports $/lb $U_3O_8$ | Exports |
|---|---|---|---|---|---|---|---|---|---|---|---|---|---|
| 2012 | 4.3 | 4.146 | 3.911 | 161 | 462 | W | W | 1,196 | 57.5 | 54.99 | 56.2 | 51.44 | 18.0 |
| 2013 | 4.6 | 4.659 | 4.655 | 149 | 392 | W | W | 1,156 | 57.4 | 51.99 | 57.4 | 48.27 | 18.9 |
| 2014 | 4.9 | 4.891 | 4.593 | 86 | 246 | W | W | 787 | 53.3 | 46.16 | 56.5 | 44.03 | 20.0 |
| 2015 | 3.7 | 3.343 | 4.023 | 58 | 251 | W | W | 625 | 56.5 | 44.13 | 64.2 | 42.95 | 25.7 |
| 2016 | 2.5 | 2.917 | 3.018 | 38 | 255 | W | W | 560 | 50.6 | 42.43 | 50.7 | 40.45 | 17.2 |
| 2017 | 1.2 | 2.443 | 2.277 | 50 | 136 | W | W | 424 | 43.0 | 38.80 | 42.1 | 37.09 | 14.0 |
| 2018 | .7 | 1.466 | 1.489 | 27 | 110 | W | W | 372 | 40.3 | 38.81 | 41.5 | 35.73 | 13.9 |
| 2019 | .2 | 0.174 | 0.190 | 40 | 48 | W | W | 265 | 48.3 | 35.59 | 42.9 | 34.77 | 11.7 |
| 2020 | W | 0.008 | W | W | W | W | W | 225 | 48.9 | 33.27 | 39.6 | 33.79 | 9.9 |
| 2021 | .0 | 0.015 | W | 42 | 32 | ---- | 52 | 207 | 46.7 | 33.91 | 41.3 | 33.26 | 7.5 |

[1] From suppliers under domestic purchases. Source: Energy Information Administration, U.S. Department of Energy (EIA-DOE)

## Commercial and U.S. Government Stocks of Uranium, End of Year — In Millions of Pounds $U_3O_8$ Equivalent

| Year | Utility Natural Uranium | Utility Enriched Uranium[1] | Domestic Supplier Natural Uranium | Domestic Supplier Enriched Uranium[1] | Total Commercial Stocks | DOE Owned & USEC Held Natural Uranium | DOE Owned & USEC Held Enriched Uranium[1] |
|---|---|---|---|---|---|---|---|
| 2012 | 45.0 | 52.6 | W | 23.3 | 120.9 | W | W |
| 2013 | 56.5 | 56.6 | W | 21.3 | 134.4 | W | W |
| 2014 | 59.9 | 54.2 | W | 18.7 | 132.7 | W | W |
| 2015 | 68.8 | 52.4 | W | 14.3 | 135.5 | W | W |
| 2016 | 74.4 | 53.6 | W | 16.7 | 144.6 | W | W |
| 2017 | 71.2 | 52.6 | W | 17.8 | 141.7 | W | W |
| 2018 | 62.6 | 48.6 | W | 19.3 | 130.5 | W | W |
| 2019 | 64.7 | 48.4 | W | 17.5 | 130.7 | W | W |
| 2020 | 59.7 | 47.2 | W | 24.2 | 131.0 | W | W |
| 2021 | 56.1 | 52.4 | W | 33.2 | 141.7 | W | W |

[1] Includes amount reported as $UF_6$ at enrichment suppliers. DOE = Department of Energy  USEC = U.S. Energy Commission
Source: Energy Information Administration, U.S. Department of Energy (EIA-DOE)

# URANIUM

## World Production of Uranium Oxide (U3O8) Concentrate   In Metric Tons (Uranium Content)

| Year | Australia | Canada | China | Czech Republic | Kazakh-stan | Namibia | Niger | Russia | South Africa | United States | Ukraine | Uzbeki-stan | World Total |
|---|---|---|---|---|---|---|---|---|---|---|---|---|---|
| 2014 | 5,001 | 9,134 | 1,500 | 193 | 23,127 | 3,255 | 4,156 | 2,990 | 393 | 926 | 1,919 | 2,400 | 54,282 |
| 2015 | 5,654 | 11,709 | 1,616 | 155 | 23,800 | 2,993 | 4,115 | 3,055 | 322 | 1,200 | 1,256 | 2,385 | 56,451 |
| 2016 | 6,315 | 14,039 | 1,616 | 138 | 24,575 | 3,654 | 3,478 | 3,004 | 490 | 1,005 | 1,125 | 2,404 | 59,934 |
| 2017 | 5,882 | 13,116 | 1,885 | 70 | 23,391 | 4,224 | 3,485 | 2,917 | 308 | 550 | 940 | 2,404 | 57,225 |
| 2018 | 6,517 | 7,001 | 1,885 | ---- | 21,705 | 5,525 | 2,910 | 2,904 | 346 | 1,180 | 582 | 2,404 | 50,978 |
| 2019 | 6,613 | 6,938 | 1,885 | ---- | 22,808 | 5,476 | 2,982 | 2,911 | 346 | 801 | 58 | 3,500 | 51,158 |
| 2020[1] | 6,203 | 3,885 | 1,885 | ---- | 19,477 | 5,413 | 2,992 | 2,846 | 250 | 744 | 6 | 3,500 | 44,101 |
| 2021[2] | 4,192 | 4,693 | 1,885 | ---- |  | 5,753 |  |  | 385 | 455 | 8 | 3,500 | 17,986 |

[1] Preliminary.  [2] Estimate.  Source: Food and Agriculture Organization of the United Nations (FAO-UN)

## Total Production of Uranium Concentrate in the United States, by Quarters   In Pounds $U_3O_8$

| Year | First Quarter | Second Quarter | Third Quarter | Fourth Quarter | Total | Year | First Quarter | Second Quarter | Third Quarter | Fourth Quarter | Total |
|---|---|---|---|---|---|---|---|---|---|---|---|
| 2011 | 1,063,047 | 1,189,083 | 846,624 | 892,013 | 3,990,767 | 2017 | 450,215 | 726,375 | 643,212 | 622,987 | 2,442,789 |
| 2012 | 1,078,404 | 1,061,289 | 1,048,018 | 957,936 | 4,145,647 | 2018 | 226,780 | 365,421 | 528,870 | 345,425 | 1,466,496 |
| 2013 | 1,147,031 | 1,394,232 | 1,171,278 | 946,301 | 4,658,842 | 2019 | 58,481 | 44,569 | 32,211 | 38,614 | 173,875 |
| 2014 | 1,242,179 | 1,095,011 | 1,468,608 | 1,085,534 | 4,891,332 | 2020 | 8,098 | W | W | W | 8,098 |
| 2015 | 1,154,408 | 789,980 | 774,541 | 624,278 | 3,343,207 | 2021[1] | W | W | 5,297 | 9,978 | 15,275 |
| 2016 | 626,522 | 745,306 | 818,783 | 725,947 | 2,916,558 | 2022[2] | 9,946 | 6,042 | 3,245 |  | 19,233 |

[1] Preliminary.  [2] Estimate.  Source: Energy Information Administration, U.S. Department of Energy (EIA-DOE)

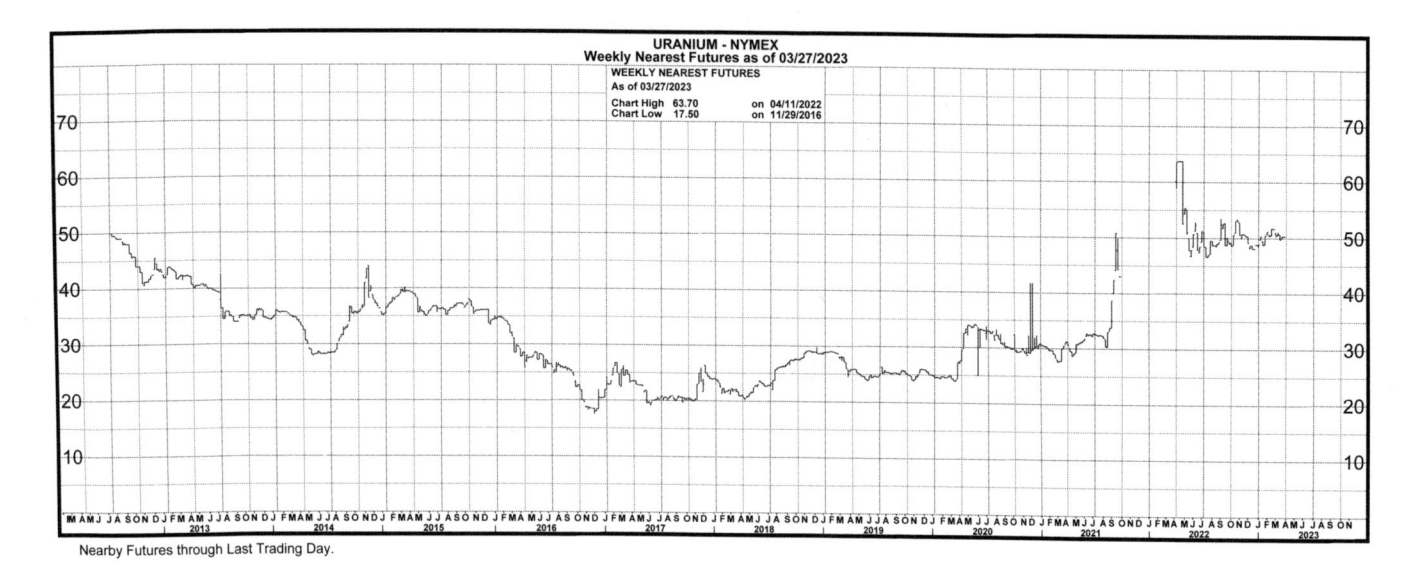

**URANIUM - NYMEX Weekly Nearest Futures as of 03/27/2023**
Chart High 63.70 on 04/11/2022
Chart Low 17.50 on 11/29/2016
Nearby Futures through Last Trading Day.

## Volume of Trading of Uranium Futures   In Contracts

| Year | Jan. | Feb. | Mar. | Apr. | May | June | July | Aug. | Sept. | Oct. | Nov. | Dec. | Total |
|---|---|---|---|---|---|---|---|---|---|---|---|---|---|
| 2016 | 400 | 400 | 3,119 | 1,120 | 1,054 | 400 | ---- | ---- | 200 | 600 | 2 | 288 | 7,583 |
| 2017 | 370 | 1,180 | 744 | 200 | 915 | 530 | 286 | 232 | 17 | ---- | 978 | 941 | 6,393 |
| 2018 | 650 | 35 | 200 | 27 | 100 | 431 | 521 | 190 | 1,298 | 827 | 2,169 | 714 | 7,162 |
| 2019 | 1,558 | 1,000 | 3,117 | 1,000 | 1,175 | 1,234 | 300 | ---- | 1,217 | ---- | ---- | 20 | 10,621 |
| 2020 | 9 | 1,200 | 621 | 5 | 1 | 18 | ---- | ---- | ---- | 1 | ---- | ---- | 1,855 |
| 2021 | ---- | ---- | 400 | ---- | 460 | 5 | 120 | 120 | 25 | 53 | ---- | ---- | 1,183 |
| 2022 | 6 | ---- | ---- | ---- | ---- | ---- | ---- | ---- | ---- | ---- | ---- | ---- | 6 |

Contract size = 250 pounds of $U_3O_8$.   Source: CME Group; New York Mercantile Exchange (NYMEX)

## Average Open Interest of Uranium Futures   In Contracts

| Year | Jan. | Feb. | Mar. | Apr. | May | June | July | Aug. | Sept. | Oct. | Nov. | Dec. |
|---|---|---|---|---|---|---|---|---|---|---|---|---|
| 2016 | 4,238 | 17,036 | 5,899 | 7,102 | 6,882 | 6,195 | 5,376 | 4,851 | 4,837 | 4,980 | 4,708 | 4,323 |
| 2017 | 4,100 | 4,447 | 4,768 | 4,348 | 4,565 | 4,808 | 4,447 | 4,288 | 4,236 | 4,191 | 3,785 | 3,810 |
| 2018 | 3,707 | 2,952 | 2,926 | 2,764 | 2,719 | 2,628 | 2,499 | 3,026 | 3,420 | 4,636 | 4,619 | 4,097 |
| 2019 | 3,854 | 3,322 | 3,218 | 3,611 | 3,003 | 2,688 | 2,699 | 2,718 | 2,406 | 2,406 | 2,403 | 2,343 |
| 2020 | 1,809 | 1,702 | 1,281 | 344 | 333 | 320 | 318 | 310 | 302 | 303 | 303 | 302 |
| 2021 | 300 | 300 | 683 | 700 | 907 | 1,160 | 1,222 | 1,211 | 930 | 800 | 800 | 800 |
| 2022 | 800 | 800 | 800 | 800 | 800 | 800 | 800 | 800 | 800 | 800 | 800 | 800 |

Contract size = 250 pounds of $U_3O_8$.   Source: CME Group; New York Mercantile Exchange (NYMEX)

# URANIUM

## Uranium Industry Statistics in the United States   In Millions of Pounds U$_3$O$_8$

| Year | Total Operable Units[2,3] Number | Net Summer Capacity of Operable Units[3,4] Million Kilowatts | Nuclear Electricity Net Generation Million Kilowatthours | Nuclear Share of Electricity Net Gen. Percent | Capacity Factor Percent | Year | Total Operable Units[2,3] Number | Net Summer Capacity of Operable Units[3,4] Million Kilowatts | Nuclear Electricity Net Generation Million Kilowatthours | Nuclear Share of Electricity Net Gen. Percent | Capacity Factor Percent |
|---|---|---|---|---|---|---|---|---|---|---|---|
| 2009 | 104.0 | 101.0 | 798,855 | 20.2 | 90.3 | 2016 | 99.0 | 99.5 | 805,325 | 19.9 | 92.3 |
| 2010 | 104.0 | 101.2 | 806,968 | 19.6 | 91.1 | 2017 | 99.0 | 99.6 | 804,950 | 20.0 | 92.2 |
| 2011 | 104.0 | 101.4 | 790,204 | 19.3 | 89.1 | 2018 | 98.0 | 99.5 | 807,078 | 19.4 | 92.5 |
| 2012 | 104.0 | 101.9 | 769,331 | 19.0 | 86.1 | 2019 | 96.0 | 98.8 | 809,412 | 19.7 | 93.4 |
| 2013 | 100.0 | 99.2 | 789,016 | 19.4 | 89.9 | 2020 | 94.0 | 97.2 | 789,878 | 19.8 | 92.4 |
| 2014 | 99.0 | 99.1 | 797,167 | 19.5 | 91.7 | 2021 | 93.0 | 95.8 | 778,187 | 19.1 | 92.7 |
| 2015 | 99.0 | 98.6 | 797,177 | 19.6 | 92.3 | 2022[1] | 92.0 | 95.1 | 771,537 | 18.3 | 92.7 |

[1] Preliminary.   [2] Total of nuclear generating units holding full-power licenses, or equivalent permission to operate, at end of period.
[3] At end of period.   [4] Beginning in 2011, monthly capacity values are estimated in two steps: 1) uprates and derates reported on Form EIA-860M are added to specific months; and 2) the difference between the resulting year-end capacity and final capacity is allocated to the month of January. purchases.   Source: Energy Information Administration, U.S. Department of Energy (EIA-DOE)

## Nuclear Electricity Net Generation   In Million Kilowatthours

| Year | Jan. | Feb. | Mar. | Apr. | May | June | July | Aug. | Sept. | Oct. | Nov. | Dec. | Total |
|---|---|---|---|---|---|---|---|---|---|---|---|---|---|
| 2013 | 71,406 | 61,483 | 62,947 | 56,767 | 62,848 | 66,430 | 70,539 | 71,344 | 65,799 | 63,184 | 64,975 | 71,294 | 789,016 |
| 2014 | 73,163 | 62,639 | 62,397 | 56,385 | 62,947 | 68,138 | 71,940 | 71,129 | 67,535 | 62,391 | 65,140 | 73,363 | 797,167 |
| 2015 | 74,270 | 63,462 | 64,547 | 59,757 | 65,833 | 68,546 | 71,412 | 72,415 | 66,466 | 60,571 | 60,264 | 69,634 | 797,177 |
| 2016 | 72,525 | 65,638 | 66,149 | 62,365 | 66,576 | 67,175 | 70,349 | 71,526 | 65,448 | 60,733 | 65,179 | 71,662 | 805,325 |
| 2017 | 73,121 | 63,560 | 65,093 | 56,743 | 61,313 | 67,011 | 71,314 | 72,384 | 68,098 | 65,995 | 66,618 | 73,700 | 804,950 |
| 2018 | 74,649 | 64,790 | 67,033 | 59,133 | 67,320 | 69,688 | 72,456 | 72,282 | 64,725 | 59,397 | 63,948 | 71,657 | 807,078 |
| 2019 | 73,701 | 64,715 | 65,080 | 60,581 | 67,124 | 68,805 | 72,199 | 71,911 | 66,064 | 62,033 | 64,125 | 73,074 | 809,412 |
| 2020 | 74,170 | 65,911 | 63,997 | 59,170 | 64,338 | 67,205 | 69,385 | 68,982 | 65,727 | 59,362 | 61,760 | 69,871 | 789,878 |
| 2021 | 71,732 | 62,954 | 63,708 | 57,092 | 63,394 | 66,070 | 68,832 | 69,471 | 64,520 | 56,945 | 62,749 | 70,720 | 778,187 |
| 2022[1] | 70,577 | 61,852 | 63,154 | 55,290 | 63,382 | 65,715 | 68,857 | 68,897 | 63,733 | 58,945 | 62,041 | 69,094 | 771,537 |

[1] Preliminary.   Source: Energy Information Administration, U.S. Department of Energy (EIA-DOE)

## Nuclear Share of Electricity Net Generation   In Percent

| Year | Jan. | Feb. | Mar. | Apr. | May | June | July | Aug. | Sept. | Oct. | Nov. | Dec. | Average |
|---|---|---|---|---|---|---|---|---|---|---|---|---|---|
| 2013 | 20.5 | 19.9 | 19.3 | 19.0 | 19.5 | 18.6 | 17.9 | 18.5 | 19.3 | 20.1 | 20.7 | 20.2 | 19.4 |
| 2014 | 19.4 | 19.3 | 18.8 | 18.9 | 19.4 | 19.0 | 18.6 | 18.5 | 19.9 | 19.8 | 20.5 | 21.7 | 19.5 |
| 2015 | 20.6 | 19.0 | 19.9 | 20.3 | 20.4 | 18.9 | 17.8 | 18.5 | 19.0 | 19.4 | 20.0 | 21.5 | 19.6 |
| 2016 | 20.6 | 20.9 | 21.7 | 21.3 | 21.0 | 18.2 | 17.1 | 17.4 | 18.6 | 19.4 | 21.9 | 20.8 | 19.9 |
| 2017 | 21.3 | 21.9 | 20.5 | 19.3 | 19.0 | 18.7 | 17.6 | 18.8 | 20.3 | 20.6 | 21.5 | 20.9 | 20.0 |
| 2018 | 19.9 | 21.2 | 20.9 | 19.6 | 19.8 | 18.7 | 17.6 | 17.7 | 18.1 | 18.2 | 19.8 | 21.2 | 19.4 |
| 2019 | 20.5 | 20.5 | 19.9 | 20.4 | 20.3 | 19.5 | 17.6 | 17.9 | 18.3 | 19.4 | 20.3 | 21.6 | 19.7 |
| 2020 | 21.7 | 20.6 | 20.7 | 21.2 | 21.1 | 19.1 | 16.9 | 17.3 | 19.7 | 18.9 | 20.5 | 20.3 | 19.8 |
| 2021 | 20.5 | 19.4 | 20.5 | 19.5 | 19.8 | 17.7 | 17.0 | 16.8 | 18.6 | 17.9 | 20.0 | 21.0 | 19.1 |
| 2022[1] | 18.7 | 18.9 | 19.4 | 18.2 | 18.5 | 17.3 | 16.2 | 16.7 | 18.2 | 18.8 | 19.2 | 19.0 | 18.3 |

[1] Preliminary.   Source: Energy Information Administration, U.S. Department of Energy (EIA-DOE)

## Capacity Factor   In Percent

| Year | Jan. | Feb. | Mar. | Apr. | May | June | July | Aug. | Sept. | Oct. | Nov. | Dec. | Average |
|---|---|---|---|---|---|---|---|---|---|---|---|---|---|
| 2013 | 93.9 | 90.3 | 83.4 | 77.6 | 83.3 | 93.1 | 95.6 | 96.7 | 92.2 | 85.7 | 91.0 | 96.6 | 89.9 |
| 2014 | 99.1 | 94.0 | 84.5 | 78.8 | 85.2 | 95.4 | 97.5 | 96.4 | 94.6 | 84.5 | 91.3 | 99.6 | 91.7 |
| 2015 | 101.3 | 95.8 | 88.0 | 84.3 | 89.8 | 96.4 | 97.3 | 98.6 | 93.6 | 82.5 | 84.8 | 94.9 | 92.3 |
| 2016 | 98.5 | 95.3 | 89.9 | 88.1 | 90.5 | 94.2 | 94.5 | 96.1 | 90.9 | 81.7 | 90.9 | 96.7 | 92.3 |
| 2017 | 98.7 | 94.9 | 87.8 | 79.1 | 82.7 | 93.4 | 96.2 | 97.6 | 94.9 | 89.0 | 92.9 | 99.4 | 92.2 |
| 2018 | 100.7 | 96.7 | 90.4 | 82.4 | 90.8 | 97.1 | 97.7 | 97.5 | 90.4 | 80.5 | 89.4 | 96.9 | 92.5 |
| 2019 | 99.6 | 96.8 | 88.0 | 84.5 | 90.8 | 96.6 | 98.1 | 97.7 | 93.1 | 85.0 | 90.8 | 100.1 | 93.4 |
| 2020 | 101.6 | 96.5 | 87.7 | 83.9 | 89.1 | 96.2 | 96.1 | 95.5 | 94.0 | 82.2 | 88.9 | 97.3 | 92.4 |
| 2021 | 99.9 | 97.0 | 88.7 | 82.1 | 89.2 | 96.0 | 96.8 | 97.7 | 93.8 | 80.1 | 91.2 | 99.5 | 92.7 |
| 2022[1] | 99.3 | 96.4 | 88.9 | 80.4 | 89.2 | 96.3 | 97.7 | 97.7 | 93.4 | 83.6 | 90.9 | 98.0 | 92.7 |

[1] Preliminary.   [2] Beginning in 2008, capacity factor data are calculated using a new methodology.   Source: Energy Information Administration, U.S. Department of Energy (EIA-DOE)

# Vanadium

Vanadium (atomic symbol V) is a silvery-white, soft, ductile, metallic element. Discovered in 1801, but mistaken for chromium, vanadium was rediscovered in 1830 by Swedish chemist Nils Sefstrom, who named the element in honor of the Scandinavian goddess Vanadis.

Never found in the pure state, vanadium is found in about 65 different minerals such as carnotite, roscoelite, vanadinite, and patronite, as well as in phosphate rock, certain iron ores, some crude oils, and meteorites. Vanadium is one of the hardest of all metals. It melts at about 1890 degrees Celsius and boils at about 3380 degrees Celsius.

Vanadium has good structural strength and is used as an alloying agent with iron, steel, and titanium. It is used in aerospace applications, transmission gears, photography as a reducing agent, and as a drying agent in various paints.

**Prices** – The price of vanadium in 2021 rose by +22.3% yr/yr to $8.17 per pound, remaining well below the record high of $16.28 per pound posted in 2005.

**Supply** – Virtually all (99%) vanadium is produced from ores, concentrates, and slag, with the remainder coming from petroleum residues, ash, and spent catalysts. World production in 2022 from ore, concentrates, and slag fell by -4.8% yr/yr to a record high 100,000 metric tons. The world's largest producer of vanadium from ores, concentrates, and slag in 2022 was China, with 70,000 metric tons of production, which was 70.0% of total world production. The two other major producers were Russia, with 17,000 metric tons of production and 17.0% of world production, and South Africa, with 9,100 metric tons of production and 9.1% of world production.

**Trade** – U.S. exports of vanadium in 2021 were in the forms of vanadium pent-oxide and anhydride at 17 metric tons (down -66.0% yr/yr), ferro-vanadium at 173 metric tons (up +723.8% yr/yr), and oxides and hydroxides at 35 metric tons (down -31.4% yr/yr). U.S. imports of vanadium in 2021 were in the forms of ferro-vanadium at 2,170 metric tons (up +59.6% yr/yr), vanadium pent-oxide at 1,740 metric tons (up +4.2% yr/yr), ore, slag, and residues at 1,800 metric tons (up +8.4% yr/yr), and oxides and hydroxides at 69 metric tons (up +3.0% yr/yr).

## World Production of Vanadium — In Metric Tons (Contained Vanadium)

| Year | Australia | China[3] | Kazakhstan | Russia | South Africa | Total[4] | Japan[5] | United States[6] | Total | World Total |
|------|-----------|----------|------------|--------|--------------|----------|----------|------------------|-------|-------------|
| 2013 | ---- | 45,000 | 14,400 | 21,397 | 591 | 81,400 | 580 | ---- | 580 | 81,000 |
| 2014 | 578 | 48,000 | 15,100 | 21,600 | ---- | 85,300 | 580 | ---- | 580 | 82,700 |
| 2015 | 3,250 | 45,000 | 16,000 | 17,788 | ---- | 82,000 | 600 | ---- | 600 | 79,400 |
| 2016 | 4,460 | 41,000 | 16,000 | 8,160 | ---- | 69,600 | ---- | ---- | ---- | ---- |
| 2017 | 5,206 | 55,900 | 18,636 | 7,959 | ---- | 87,700 | ---- | ---- | ---- | ---- |
| 2018 | 5,500 | 59,500 | 17,052 | 7,700 | ---- | 89,800 | ---- | ---- | ---- | ---- |
| 2019 | 5,923 | 60,000 | 18,380 | 8,030 | 460 | 92,800 | ---- | ---- | ---- | ---- |
| 2020 | 6,622 | 70,200 | 19,533 | 8,584 | 17 | 105,000 | ---- | ---- | ---- | ---- |
| 2021[1] | 5,780 | 70,300 | 20,100 | 8,800 | ---- | 105,000 | ---- | ---- | ---- | ---- |
| 2022[2] | 6,200 | 70,000 | 17,000 | 9,100 | ---- | 100,000 | ---- | ---- | ---- | ---- |

[1] Preliminary. [2] Estimate. [3] In vanadiferous slag product. [4] Excludes U.S. production. [5] In vanadium pentoxide product. [6] In vanadium pentoxide and ferrovanadium products. Source: U.S. Geological Survey (USGS)

## Salient Statistics of Vanadium in the United States — In Metric Tons (Contained Vanadium)

| Year | Consumer & Producer Stocks, Dec. 31 | Tool Steel | Cast Irons | High Strength, Low Alloy | Stainless & Heat Resisting | Super-alloys | Carbon | Full Alloy | Total | Average $ Per Lb. V₂O₅ | Vanadium Pent-oxide, Anhydride | Oxides & Hydr- oxides | Ferro- Vana- dium | Ores, Slag, Residues | Vanadium Pent-oxide, Anhydride | Oxides & Hydr- oxides | Ferro- Vana- dium |
|------|------|------|------|------|------|------|------|------|------|------|------|------|------|------|------|------|------|
| 2013 | 220 | 161 | W | W | 61 | 9 | 671 | 1,510 | 3,980 | 6.04 | 90 | 407 | 299 | 2,340 | 2,040 | 205 | 3,710 |
| 2014 | 225 | W | W | W | 61 | 8 | 710 | 1,540 | 4,070 | 5.61 | 171 | 231 | 253 | 3,450 | 3,410 | 104 | 3,230 |
| 2015 | W | W | W | W | 61 | 9 | 743 | 1,460 | 3,930 | 4.16 | 303 | 66 | 122 | 4,600 | 2,870 | 94 | 1,980 |
| 2016 | W | W | W | W | 61 | 10 | 718 | 1,460 | 3,830 | 3.38 | 5 | 81 | 394 | 5,030 | 2,460 | 660 | 1,590 |
| 2017 | W | W | W | W | 62 | 9 | 755 | 1,260 | 3,880 | 7.61 | 126 | 148 | 229 | 4,530 | 3,400 | 148 | 2,810 |
| 2018 | W | W | W | W | 63 | W | 798 | 1,270 | 5,640 | 16.40 | 563 | 53 | 575 | 2,810 | 4,600 | 98 | 2,970 |
| 2019 | W | W | W | W | 63 | W | 763 | 1,260 | 4,840 | 12.17 | 423 | 750 | 295 | 2,120 | 3,620 | 105 | 2,280 |
| 2020 | W | W | W | W | 88 | W | 1,100 | 1,760 | 7,920 | 6.68 | 50 | 51 | 21 | 1,550 | 1,670 | 67 | 1,360 |
| 2021[1] | W | W | W | W | 88 | W | 1,460 | 1,770 | 8,030 | 8.17 | 17 | 35 | 173 | 1,680 | 1,740 | 69 | 2,170 |
| 2022[2] | | | | | | | | | | 9.20 | 170 | 400 | 220 | 1,800 | 1,500 | 100 | 2,700 |

[1] Preliminary. [2] Estimate. W = Withheld. Source: U.S. Geological Survey (USGS)

# Vegetables

Vegetables are the edible products of herbaceous plants, which are plants with soft stems. Vegetables are grouped according to the edible part of each plant, including leaves (e.g., lettuce), stalks (celery), roots (carrot), tubers (potato), bulbs (onion), fruits (tomato), seeds (pea), and flowers (broccoli). Each of these groups contributes to the human diet in its own way. Fleshy roots are high in energy value and good sources of the vitamin B group, seeds are relatively high in carbohydrates and proteins, while leaves, stalks, and fruits are excellent sources of minerals, vitamins, water, and roughage. Vegetables are an important food for the maintenance of health and prevention of disease. Higher intakes of vegetables have been shown to lower the risks of cancer and coronary heart disease.

Vegetables are best consumed fresh in their raw state to derive the maximum benefits from their nutrients. While canned and frozen vegetables are often thought to be inferior to fresh vegetables, they are sometimes nutritionally superior to fresh produce because they are usually processed immediately after harvest when nutrient content is at its peak. When cooking vegetables, aluminum utensils should not be used, because aluminum is a soft metal that is affected by food acids and alkalis. Scientific evidence shows that tiny particles of aluminum from foods cooked in aluminum utensils enter the stomach and can injure the sensitive lining of the stomach.

**Prices** – The monthly average index of fresh vegetable prices received by growers in the U.S. in 2022 rose by +54.3% yr/yr to 365.8.

**Demand** – The leading vegetable in terms of U.S. per capita consumption in 2019 was the potato with 118.8 pounds of consumption, tomatoes with 88.3 pounds, lettuce with 25.0 pounds, onions with 22.1 pounds, and sweet corn with 18.9 pounds. Total U.S. per capita vegetable consumption in 2019 was 409.2 pounds.

### Index of Prices Received by Growers for Fresh Vegetables in the United States   (1990-92=100)

| Year | Jan. | Feb. | Mar. | Apr. | May | June | July | Aug. | Sept. | Oct. | Nov. | Dec. | Average |
|---|---|---|---|---|---|---|---|---|---|---|---|---|---|
| 2013 | 240.8 | 182.0 | 236.8 | 201.0 | 211.6 | 195.8 | 175.1 | 229.1 | 188.8 | 222.2 | 218.5 | 177.0 | 206.6 |
| 2014 | 197.0 | 193.3 | 197.1 | 200.2 | 195.9 | 214.6 | 197.3 | 184.7 | 191.0 | 219.6 | 249.1 | 229.0 | 205.7 |
| 2015 | 253.2 | 197.1 | 200.5 | 211.0 | 230.2 | 213.5 | 209.9 | 206.2 | 235.1 | 229.4 | 228.3 | 284.0 | 224.9 |
| 2016 | 343.7 | 266.3 | 222.6 | 209.1 | 240.2 | 226.3 | 225.4 | 184.8 | 217.0 | 205.8 | 179.7 | 182.3 | 225.3 |
| 2017 | 185.1 | 223.6 | 244.6 | 332.3 | 266.8 | 228.1 | 211.8 | 185.4 | 209.9 | 262.3 | 268.3 | 239.8 | 238.2 |
| 2018 | 252.3 | 160.8 | 247.0 | 183.7 | 235.5 | 189.5 | 173.9 | 197.7 | 190.2 | 221.6 | 317.8 | 432.9 | 233.6 |
| 2019 | 295.9 | 238.4 | 289.4 | 242.7 | 262.1 | 272.2 | 277.6 | 205.5 | 191.6 | 287.8 | 296.1 | 265.2 | 260.4 |
| 2020 | 350.0 | 208.0 | 203.3 | 200.8 | 220.9 | 256.9 | 220.3 | 213.4 | 276.9 | 381.3 | 342.6 | 254.0 | 260.7 |
| 2021 | 283.8 | 218.8 | 197.5 | 172.4 | 188.0 | 184.5 | 175.8 | 191.7 | 251.1 | 323.5 | 366.7 | 291.6 | 237.1 |
| 2022[1] | 275.7 | 237.5 | 394.0 | 251.1 | 262.4 | 249.0 | 277.4 | 226.8 | 336.2 | 509.7 | 729.6 | 640.6 | 365.8 |

[1] Preliminary.   Not seasonally adjusted.   Source: National Agricultural Statistics Service, U.S. Department of Agriculture (NASS-USDA)

### Producer Price Index of Canned[2] Processed Vegetables in the United States   (1982 = 100)

| Year | Jan. | Feb. | Mar. | Apr. | May | June | July | Aug. | Sept. | Oct. | Nov. | Dec. | Average |
|---|---|---|---|---|---|---|---|---|---|---|---|---|---|
| 2013 | 173.9 | 174.1 | 173.9 | 174.6 | 174.0 | 173.7 | 173.9 | 174.1 | 174.0 | 173.9 | 173.6 | 173.6 | 173.9 |
| 2014 | 173.2 | 173.4 | 173.0 | 172.4 | 172.3 | 172.9 | 173.0 | 173.7 | 174.2 | 174.6 | 174.7 | 174.8 | 173.5 |
| 2015 | 175.7 | 176.3 | 179.4 | 175.0 | 174.9 | 177.0 | 176.2 | 172.6 | 172.1 | 172.3 | 172.6 | 168.8 | 174.4 |
| 2016 | 166.7 | 168.4 | 165.4 | 166.6 | 167.3 | 166.0 | 165.9 | 166.2 | 165.9 | 165.4 | 165.4 | 165.5 | 166.2 |
| 2017 | 164.2 | 164.6 | 163.6 | 165.4 | 166.4 | 165.7 | 165.6 | 166.4 | 165.5 | 165.8 | 167.6 | 167.4 | 165.7 |
| 2018 | 167.4 | 170.2 | 168.8 | 169.1 | 168.6 | 169.5 | 168.5 | 170.8 | 171.5 | 173.4 | 175.7 | 177.4 | 170.9 |
| 2019 | 176.5 | 176.5 | 176.8 | 176.0 | 175.2 | 175.7 | 175.9 | 177.2 | 178.0 | 178.8 | 180.4 | 181.8 | 177.4 |
| 2020 | 183.3 | 182.7 | 183.3 | 184.4 | 185.0 | 183.8 | 183.3 | 182.0 | 184.2 | 184.3 | 185.4 | 185.4 | 183.9 |
| 2021 | 185.9 | 186.0 | 186.6 | 186.6 | 187.1 | 185.3 | 186.8 | 188.0 | 190.8 | 194.0 | 193.9 | 195.6 | 188.9 |
| 2022[1] | 197.7 | 199.5 | 203.8 | 206.6 | 214.4 | 217.2 | 223.2 | 227.1 | 233.2 | 235.1 | 241.9 | 243.2 | 220.3 |

[1] Preliminary.   [2] Includes canned vegetables and juices, including hominy and mushrooms.   Not seasonally adjusted.   Source: Bureau of Labor Statistics, U.S. Department of Labor (BLS)

### Producer Price Index of Frozen Processed Vegetables in the United States   (1982 = 100)

| Year | Jan. | Feb. | Mar. | Apr. | May | June | July | Aug. | Sept. | Oct. | Nov. | Dec. | Average |
|---|---|---|---|---|---|---|---|---|---|---|---|---|---|
| 2013 | 194.0 | 194.5 | 194.4 | 194.4 | 194.6 | 194.6 | 194.6 | 192.4 | 192.5 | 192.3 | 192.4 | 192.3 | 193.6 |
| 2014 | 192.2 | 192.3 | 192.3 | 192.4 | 192.4 | 192.3 | 192.3 | 192.9 | 193.2 | 193.5 | 193.5 | 193.5 | 192.7 |
| 2015 | 193.8 | 193.1 | 193.2 | 193.3 | 193.5 | 193.3 | 193.3 | 193.1 | 195.9 | 195.8 | 195.3 | 195.3 | 194.1 |
| 2016 | 195.2 | 195.2 | 195.2 | 195.2 | 195.3 | 195.4 | 195.5 | 195.3 | 195.3 | 195.6 | 196.0 | 196.0 | 195.4 |
| 2017 | 198.6 | 199.5 | 199.6 | 199.5 | 199.6 | 199.6 | 202.7 | 202.7 | 204.3 | 205.7 | 205.7 | 206.8 | 202.0 |
| 2018 | 208.0 | 208.1 | 209.3 | 209.5 | 209.6 | 210.3 | 211.5 | 211.5 | 213.6 | 213.9 | 213.5 | 211.5 | 210.9 |
| 2019 | 211.6 | 211.9 | 212.1 | 212.1 | 212.1 | 212.2 | 212.2 | 214.7 | 214.4 | 215.2 | 215.2 | 215.9 | 213.3 |
| 2020 | 216.4 | 216.1 | 216.2 | 216.4 | 216.3 | 216.3 | 216.4 | 216.8 | 218.8 | 219.0 | 219.0 | 220.0 | 217.3 |
| 2021 | 220.0 | 220.1 | 218.6 | 219.0 | 220.1 | 220.3 | 220.3 | 220.4 | 222.3 | 222.8 | 223.7 | 224.2 | 221.0 |
| 2022[1] | 227.4 | 229.0 | 231.1 | 234.0 | 246.2 | 249.1 | 249.3 | 254.3 | 271.7 | 274.3 | 280.1 | 280.2 | 252.2 |

[1] Preliminary.   Not seasonally adjusted.   Source: Bureau of Labor Statistics, U.S. Department of Labor (BLS)

# VEGETABLES

**Per Capita Use of Selected Commercially Produced Fresh and Processing Vegetables and Melons in the United States**   In Pounds, farm weight basis

| Crop | 2010 | 2011 | 2012 | 2013 | 2014 | 2015 | 2016 | 2017 | 2018[10] | 2019[11] |
|---|---|---|---|---|---|---|---|---|---|---|
| Asparagus, All | 1.6 | 1.6 | 1.7 | 1.6 | 1.8 | 1.6 | 1.8 | 1.8 | 1.9 | 1.9 |
| Fresh | 1.4 | 1.4 | 1.4 | 1.4 | 1.7 | 1.5 | 1.6 | 1.6 | 1.8 | 1.8 |
| Canning | 0.1 | 0.1 | 0.1 | 0.1 | 0.1 | 0.1 | 0.1 | 0.1 | 0.1 | 0.1 |
| Freezing | 0.1 | 0.1 | 0.1 | 0.1 | 0.1 | 0.1 | 0.2 | 0.1 | 0.1 | 0.1 |
| Snap beans, All | 7.5 | 6.4 | 6.5 | 6.6 | 6.0 | 6.4 | 6.9 | 6.6 | 6.3 | 6.6 |
| Fresh | 1.9 | 1.7 | 1.6 | 1.6 | 1.5 | 1.6 | 1.7 | 1.6 | 1.6 | 1.8 |
| Canning | 3.7 | 3.2 | 2.9 | 2.9 | 2.8 | 3.0 | 3.2 | 3.1 | 2.9 | 2.9 |
| Freezing | 2.0 | 1.5 | 1.9 | 2.1 | 1.8 | 1.9 | 2.0 | 1.9 | 1.8 | 1.9 |
| Broccoli, All [1] | 8.4 | 8.6 | 8.9 | 9.4 | 9.2 | 10.0 | 10.1 | 9.5 | 8.4 | 8.8 |
| Fresh | 6.0 | 6.0 | 6.3 | 6.9 | 6.7 | 7.4 | 7.5 | 7.1 | 5.9 | 6.1 |
| Freezing | 2.5 | 2.7 | 2.6 | 2.5 | 2.6 | 2.6 | 2.6 | 2.4 | 2.5 | 2.6 |
| Cabbage, All | 8.5 | 7.6 | 7.4 | 7.9 | 7.6 | 7.2 | 7.0 | 7.5 | 6.4 | 7.1 |
| Fresh | 7.5 | 6.6 | 6.3 | 6.9 | 6.7 | 6.3 | 5.9 | 6.2 | 5.7 | 6.5 |
| Canning (kraut) | 1.0 | 1.0 | 1.2 | 1.0 | 0.9 | 0.9 | 1.0 | 1.3 | 0.8 | 0.7 |
| Carrots, All [2] | 10.0 | 9.9 | 9.9 | 10.5 | 10.4 | 10.9 | 10.8 | 10.9 | 15.6 | 16.6 |
| Fresh | 7.8 | 7.5 | 8.0 | 8.0 | 8.5 | 8.8 | 7.8 | 7.4 | 12.2 | 13.6 |
| Canning | 0.8 | 0.8 | 0.8 | 0.8 | 0.7 | 0.7 | 1.1 | 1.1 | 1.0 | 1.2 |
| Freezing | 1.5 | 1.6 | 1.2 | 1.7 | 1.2 | 1.4 | 1.9 | 2.4 | 2.4 | 1.8 |
| Cauliflower, All [1] | 1.7 | 1.7 | 1.5 | 1.7 | 1.6 | 1.9 | 2.1 | 2.9 | 3.1 | 3.7 |
| Fresh | 1.3 | 1.2 | 1.2 | 1.3 | 1.3 | 1.6 | 1.7 | 2.4 | 2.5 | 3.0 |
| Freezing | 0.4 | 0.4 | 0.3 | 0.3 | 0.4 | 0.3 | 0.4 | 0.5 | 0.6 | 0.7 |
| Celery | 6.1 | 6.0 | 6.0 | 5.5 | 5.5 | 5.1 | 5.0 | 4.7 | 4.9 | 5.3 |
| Sweet Corn, All [3] | 24.7 | 23.8 | 24.3 | 21.7 | 21.1 | 22.0 | 19.6 | 20.3 | 19.9 | 18.9 |
| Fresh | 9.3 | 8.2 | 8.7 | 8.9 | 7.7 | 8.6 | 7.1 | 7.2 | 6.8 | 6.8 |
| Canning | 6.9 | 5.8 | 5.9 | 5.8 | 5.8 | 5.3 | 5.0 | 5.1 | 5.2 | 5.3 |
| Freezing | 8.6 | 9.8 | 9.8 | 7.0 | 7.7 | 8.0 | 7.5 | 8.1 | 7.9 | 6.9 |
| Cucumbers, All | 10.5 | 9.2 | 10.1 | 10.6 | 11.3 | 11.0 | 11.1 | 11.1 | 11.3 | 11.4 |
| Fresh | 6.7 | 6.4 | 7.1 | 7.3 | 7.4 | 7.6 | 8.1 | 7.4 | 8.0 | 8.0 |
| Pickling | 3.7 | 2.8 | 3.0 | 3.2 | 3.9 | 3.4 | 3.0 | 3.7 | 3.3 | 3.4 |
| Melons | 26.4 | 25.5 | ----- | ----- | ----- | ----- | ----- | ----- | ----- | ----- |
| Watermelon | 15.7 | 14.8 | ----- | ----- | ----- | ----- | ----- | ----- | ----- | ----- |
| Cantaloupe | 8.6 | 8.7 | ----- | ----- | ----- | ----- | ----- | ----- | ----- | ----- |
| Honeydew | 1.5 | 1.5 | ----- | ----- | ----- | ----- | ----- | ----- | ----- | ----- |
| Other | 0.6 | 0.5 | ----- | ----- | ----- | ----- | ----- | ----- | ----- | ----- |
| Lettuce, All | 27.9 | 27.6 | 27.9 | 25.5 | 25.3 | 25.5 | 31.4 | 30.4 | 24.5 | 25.0 |
| Head lettuce | 15.9 | 15.8 | 16.0 | 14.1 | 14.5 | 13.6 | 16.9 | 15.3 | 12.3 | 12.7 |
| Romaine & Leaf | 12.0 | 11.7 | 11.9 | 11.4 | 10.8 | 11.9 | 14.5 | 15.1 | 12.1 | 12.3 |
| Onions, All | 20.9 | 20.4 | 20.7 | 19.6 | 19.4 | 19.7 | 24.5 | 26.5 | 21.1 | 22.1 |
| Fresh | 19.6 | 19.1 | 19.3 | 18.5 | 18.4 | 18.3 | 22.8 | 25.1 | 20.5 | 20.4 |
| Dehydrating | 1.3 | 1.2 | 1.4 | 1.1 | 1.1 | 1.4 | 1.7 | 1.4 | 0.6 | 1.7 |
| Green Peas, All [4] | 2.6 | 2.4 | 2.7 | 2.4 | 2.3 | 2.3 | 1.8 | 2.0 | 1.9 | 1.9 |
| Canning | 1.1 | 0.8 | 0.8 | 0.9 | 0.7 | 0.8 | 0.8 | 0.7 | 0.6 | 0.7 |
| Freezing | 1.5 | 1.6 | 1.9 | 1.5 | 1.6 | 1.5 | 1.0 | 1.3 | 1.3 | 1.3 |
| Peppers, All | 11.2 | 11.4 | 11.7 | 10.9 | 11.6 | 11.6 | 12.0 | 12.2 | 12.0 | 12.2 |
| Bell Peppers, All | 10.3 | 10.6 | 10.8 | 10.0 | 10.7 | 10.7 | 11.1 | 11.3 | 11.2 | 11.3 |
| Chile Peppers, All | 0.8 | 0.8 | 0.9 | 0.9 | 0.9 | 0.9 | 1.0 | 0.9 | 0.9 | 0.9 |
| Tomatoes, All | 91.3 | 86.8 | 87.4 | 86.3 | 88.0 | 76.9 | 81.5 | 78.0 | 85.9 | 88.3 |
| Fresh | 20.6 | 21.0 | 20.8 | 20.3 | 20.6 | 20.6 | 20.3 | 20.1 | 20.3 | 20.3 |
| Canning | 70.8 | 65.8 | 66.6 | 66.0 | 67.4 | 56.3 | 61.2 | 57.9 | 65.6 | 68.0 |
| Other, Fresh [5] | 18.3 | 18.8 | 19.3 | 18.8 | 20.5 | 18.3 | 23.9 | 24.5 | 23.4 | 23.4 |
| Other, Canning [6] | 2.5 | 2.6 | 2.7 | 2.7 | 2.6 | 2.9 | 3.0 | 3.0 | 3.3 | 3.2 |
| Other, Freezing [7] | 4.5 | 4.3 | 4.5 | 4.3 | 4.6 | 4.7 | 4.6 | 4.7 | 6.1 | 4.3 |
| Subtotal, All [8] | 262.7 | 253.8 | 258.2 | 251.1 | 254.5 | 242.9 | 262.0 | 261.8 | 261.4 | 267.6 |
| Fresh | 144.7 | 142.2 | 144.8 | 141.2 | 142.6 | 141.9 | 155.9 | 157.1 | 149.2 | 153.3 |
| Canning | 97.1 | 89.6 | 91.1 | 90.3 | 92.1 | 80.6 | 86.0 | 83.3 | 89.6 | 92.6 |
| Freezing | 20.9 | 22.0 | 22.3 | 19.6 | 19.9 | 20.5 | 20.2 | 21.4 | 22.6 | 21.6 |
| Potatoes, All | 113.8 | 110.5 | 114.9 | 113.6 | 113.1 | 115.4 | 110.2 | 117.8 | 116.0 | 118.8 |
| Fresh | 36.8 | 34.1 | 34.6 | 34.6 | 33.6 | 34.2 | 33.7 | 34.9 | 33.0 | 34.1 |
| Processing | 77.0 | 76.4 | 80.3 | 79.0 | 79.5 | 81.2 | 76.5 | 82.9 | 83.0 | 84.7 |
| Sweet Potatoes | 6.3 | 7.1 | 6.9 | 6.3 | 7.5 | 7.6 | 7.2 | 8.0 | 5.6 | 7.9 |
| Mushrooms | 3.7 | 3.8 | 4.0 | 3.8 | 3.8 | 3.9 | 4.0 | 4.0 | 3.9 | 3.8 |
| Dry Peas & Lentils [9] | 1.6 | 1.1 | 0.9 | 1.0 | 0.8 | 1.2 | 4.0 | 3.4 | 4.8 | 4.2 |
| Dry Edible Beans | 6.7 | 5.1 | 5.9 | 5.5 | 5.6 | 7.2 | 6.7 | 7.7 | 8.9 | 6.9 |
| Total, All Items | 394.9 | 381.4 | 390.8 | 381.3 | 385.3 | 378.2 | 394.1 | 402.7 | 400.6 | 409.2 |

[1] All production for processing broccoli and cauliflower is for freezing.   [2] Industry allocation suggests that 27 percent of processing carrot production is for canning and 73 percent is for freezing.   [3] On-cob basis.   [4] In-shell basis.   [5] Includes artichokes, brussels sprouts, eggplant, endive/escarole, garlic, radishes, green limas, squash, and spinach. In 2000, okra, pumpkins, kale, collards, turnip greens and mustard greens added.   [6] Includes beets, green limas (1992-2003), spinach, and miscellaneous imports (1990-2001).   [7] Includes green limas, spinach, and miscellaneous freezing vegetables.   [8] Fresh, canning, and freezing data do not sum to the total because onions for dehydrating are included in the total.   [9] Production from new areas in upper midwest added in 1998. A portion of this is likely for feed use.   [10] Preliminary.   [11] Forecast.   NA = Not available.   *Source: Economic Research Service, U.S. Department of Agriculture (ERS-USDA)*

# VEGETABLES

**Average Price Received by Growers for Broccoli in the United States — In Dollars per Cwt**

| Year | Jan. | Feb. | Mar. | Apr. | May | June | July | Aug. | Sept. | Oct. | Nov. | Dec. | Season Average |
|---|---|---|---|---|---|---|---|---|---|---|---|---|---|
| 2013 | 80.40 | 38.10 | 30.60 | NA | NA | NA | NA | NA | NA | NA | NA | NA | 43.20 |
| 2014 | NA | NA | NA | 40.10 | 48.00 | 49.60 | 31.80 | 47.10 | 53.40 | 34.60 | 45.00 | 33.10 | 40.70 |
| 2015 | 67.30 | 29.90 | 47.80 | 50.60 | 54.50 | 34.70 | 38.20 | 49.90 | 57.10 | 58.10 | 65.10 | 84.70 | 49.10 |
| 2016 | 50.80 | 26.80 | 30.90 | 39.30 | 48.10 | 49.30 | 41.60 | 28.00 | 36.60 | 37.70 | 35.90 | 34.80 | 37.70 |
| 2017 | 55.70 | 54.10 | 70.90 | 95.60 | 82.60 | 50.50 | 51.00 | 62.10 | 82.10 | 66.60 | 54.80 | 40.30 | 45.40 |
| 2018 | 45.00 | 28.50 | 46.80 | 39.70 | 56.90 | 46.80 | 37.60 | 53.90 | 51.40 | 56.50 | 70.70 | 85.50 | 42.80 |
| 2019 | 56.20 | 50.60 | 62.40 | 50.00 | 77.90 | 51.10 | 40.20 | 43.60 | 71.60 | 77.40 | 57.50 | 38.10 | 56.38 |
| 2020 | 99.00 | 41.00 | 79.60 | 53.80 | 46.00 | 118.00 | 54.20 | 48.10 | 102.00 | 64.50 | 106.00 | 71.60 | 73.65 |
| 2021 | 56.10 | 36.90 | 52.10 | 41.70 | 37.90 | 39.90 | 49.40 | 50.10 | 99.70 | 128.00 | 116.00 | 90.70 | 66.54 |
| 2022[1] | 91.00 | 61.00 | 58.00 | 59.00 | 50.60 | 58.20 | 70.30 | 51.40 | 98.80 | 137.00 | 181.00 | 205.00 | 93.44 |

[1] Preliminary. NA = Not available. *Source: National Agricultural Statistics Service, U.S. Department of Agriculture (NASS-USDA)*

**Average Price Received by Growers for Carrots in the United States — In Dollars per Cwt**

| Year | Jan. | Feb. | Mar. | Apr. | May | June | July | Aug. | Sept. | Oct. | Nov. | Dec. | Season Average |
|---|---|---|---|---|---|---|---|---|---|---|---|---|---|
| 2013 | 28.20 | 28.50 | 30.80 | NA | NA | NA | NA | NA | NA | NA | NA | NA | 28.60 |
| 2014 | NA | NA | NA | 28.20 | 27.20 | 25.50 | 25.10 | 23.00 | 21.50 | 26.90 | 28.00 | 33.40 | 27.10 |
| 2015 | 33.80 | 33.00 | 32.20 | 31.80 | 31.40 | 30.60 | 29.90 | 30.20 | 30.40 | 31.30 | 31.00 | 32.90 | 30.50 |
| 2016 | 34.40 | 35.80 | 34.90 | 38.60 | 39.30 | 31.80 | 29.90 | 29.30 | 28.90 | 28.90 | 28.90 | 27.90 | 24.80 |
| 2017 | 28.60 | 28.40 | 28.00 | 27.80 | 27.80 | 25.70 | 25.90 | 28.90 | 30.80 | 24.20 | 31.30 | 31.30 | 22.50 |
| 2018 | 31.40 | 31.00 | 27.90 | 27.30 | 27.70 | 26.70 | 27.10 | 25.80 | 26.30 | 26.60 | 26.50 | 26.40 | 22.20 |
| 2019 | 26.50 | 26.30 | 29.00 | 28.10 | 28.10 | 28.20 | 28.60 | 28.50 | 28.80 | 29.30 | 29.70 | 29.90 | 28.42 |
| 2020 | 50.90 | 49.70 | 57.50 | 47.50 | 47.00 | 48.30 | 49.30 | 48.30 | 46.10 | 45.10 | 42.30 | 42.60 | 47.88 |
| 2021 | 43.10 | 42.90 | 42.00 | 44.60 | 46.10 | 46.00 | 45.30 | 42.10 | 45.10 | 40.50 | 40.50 | 40.50 | 43.23 |
| 2022[1] | 44.50 | 50.70 | 50.20 | 50.20 | 50.20 | 45.50 | 42.60 | 38.70 | 40.20 | 48.30 | 49.70 | 50.00 | 46.73 |

[1] Preliminary. NA = Not available. *Source: National Agricultural Statistics Service, U.S. Department of Agriculture (NASS-USDA)*

**Average Price Received by Growers for Cauliflower in the United States — In Dollars per Cwt**

| Year | Jan. | Feb. | Mar. | Apr. | May | June | July | Aug. | Sept. | Oct. | Nov. | Dec. | Season Average |
|---|---|---|---|---|---|---|---|---|---|---|---|---|---|
| 2013 | 69.90 | 43.30 | 46.00 | NA | NA | NA | NA | NA | NA | NA | NA | NA | 44.50 |
| 2014 | NA | NA | NA | 65.80 | 79.10 | 66.30 | 43.10 | 31.80 | 64.70 | 43.20 | 67.60 | 84.80 | 50.10 |
| 2015 | 58.40 | 40.10 | 85.10 | 87.80 | 108.00 | 49.60 | 31.10 | 42.80 | 55.50 | 68.60 | 121.00 | 184.00 | 61.50 |
| 2016 | 59.10 | 45.30 | 39.80 | 53.70 | 82.00 | 62.20 | 41.00 | 39.10 | 42.70 | 42.80 | 42.40 | 81.10 | 55.70 |
| 2017 | 56.70 | 65.00 | 134.00 | 136.00 | 70.60 | 55.60 | 44.90 | 35.60 | 49.90 | 56.00 | 73.20 | 90.10 | 45.90 |
| 2018 | 47.80 | 42.90 | 87.60 | 60.80 | 78.60 | 35.50 | 38.40 | 39.80 | 45.30 | 46.40 | 95.50 | 74.80 | 45.80 |
| 2019 | 79.00 | 105.00 | 99.70 | 67.00 | 112.00 | 47.50 | 65.40 | 57.70 | 65.20 | 111.00 | 92.20 | 41.90 | 78.63 |
| 2020 | 97.00 | 70.40 | 102.00 | 72.00 | 43.30 | 79.90 | 40.90 | 32.00 | 40.30 | 45.80 | 95.90 | 101.00 | 68.38 |
| 2021 | 43.20 | 46.30 | 69.60 | 52.60 | 48.80 | 35.00 | 42.30 | 38.10 | 51.30 | 78.80 | 52.70 | 50.80 | 50.79 |
| 2022[1] | 99.10 | 60.50 | 94.20 | 59.80 | 50.40 | 42.70 | 42.60 | 39.90 | 83.60 | 101.00 | 263.00 | 200.00 | 94.73 |

[1] Preliminary. NA = Not available. *Source: National Agricultural Statistics Service, U.S. Department of Agriculture (NASS-USDA)*

**Average Price Received by Growers for Celery in the United States — In Dollars per Cwt**

| Year | Jan. | Feb. | Mar. | Apr. | May | June | July | Aug. | Sept. | Oct. | Nov. | Dec. | Season Average |
|---|---|---|---|---|---|---|---|---|---|---|---|---|---|
| 2013 | 39.70 | 47.00 | 29.20 | NA | NA | NA | NA | NA | NA | NA | NA | NA | 25.40 |
| 2014 | NA | NA | NA | 15.50 | 15.80 | 14.50 | 20.60 | 18.70 | 17.90 | 16.90 | 26.60 | 28.70 | 17.10 |
| 2015 | 19.40 | 14.60 | 14.00 | 18.60 | 26.80 | 17.60 | 17.10 | 23.50 | 22.70 | 28.00 | 40.60 | 59.80 | 24.80 |
| 2016 | 67.20 | 29.90 | 18.80 | 20.00 | 26.20 | 18.80 | 17.70 | 16.40 | 15.80 | 18.60 | 26.60 | 17.30 | 18.10 |
| 2017 | 17.50 | 15.60 | 24.50 | 39.30 | 79.90 | 42.40 | 27.70 | 17.70 | 17.30 | 19.20 | 29.60 | 23.60 | 20.10 |
| 2018 | 20.80 | 19.20 | 25.20 | 30.70 | 27.10 | 24.70 | 21.10 | 16.80 | 18.60 | 20.20 | 30.50 | 46.60 | 25.00 |
| 2019 | 52.10 | 70.90 | 96.00 | 113.00 | 109.00 | 88.80 | 26.60 | 23.30 | 26.30 | 29.90 | 35.60 | 27.40 | 58.24 |
| 2020 | 45.90 | 33.90 | 55.70 | 49.60 | 45.10 | 46.80 | 58.70 | 40.50 | 35.00 | 36.90 | 49.80 | 55.10 | 46.08 |
| 2021 | 112.00 | 47.80 | 31.10 | 28.70 | 31.70 | 35.70 | 36.60 | 33.10 | 35.20 | 43.70 | 54.50 | 44.30 | 44.53 |
| 2022[1] | 51.70 | 49.90 | 64.90 | 46.90 | 97.50 | 61.40 | 52.60 | 40.60 | 40.60 | 50.70 | 97.40 | 191.00 | 70.43 |

[1] Preliminary. NA = Not available. *Source: National Agricultural Statistics Service, U.S. Department of Agriculture (NASS-USDA)*

# VEGETABLES

**Average Price Received by Growers for Sweet Corn in the United States    In Dollars per Cwt**

| Year | Jan. | Feb. | Mar. | Apr. | May | June | July | Aug. | Sept. | Oct. | Nov. | Dec. | Season Average |
|---|---|---|---|---|---|---|---|---|---|---|---|---|---|
| 2013 | 30.40 | 36.70 | 33.30 | NA | NA | NA | NA | NA | NA | NA | NA | NA | 24.10 |
| 2014 | NA | NA | NA | 26.00 | 25.40 | 32.00 | 37.70 | 29.00 | 23.10 | 42.20 | 40.70 | 41.40 | 23.90 |
| 2015 | 39.80 | 40.00 | 31.70 | 29.60 | 26.80 | 27.70 | 33.70 | 29.50 | 32.30 | 47.90 | 24.40 | 26.00 | 21.80 |
| 2016 | 43.80 | 58.70 | 67.50 | 34.30 | 26.20 | 25.40 | 29.50 | 23.60 | 28.20 | 33.60 | 37.40 | 37.50 | 20.70 |
| 2017 | 30.90 | 35.70 | 26.20 | 30.80 | 29.80 | 34.30 | 30.70 | 26.80 | 21.30 | 32.50 | 54.70 | 34.10 | 29.10 |
| 2018 | 35.40 | 24.70 | 26.90 | 32.60 | 28.30 | 27.10 | 26.20 | 24.40 | 30.50 | 30.50 | 45.80 | 31.70 | 30.34 |
| 2019 | 35.70 | 47.90 | 26.60 | 34.80 | 30.50 | 31.20 | 35.90 | 51.80 | NA | NA | 34.30 | 30.50 | 35.92 |
| 2020 | 52.70 | 38.20 | 28.60 | 28.20 | 33.20 | 75.90 | 54.30 | 33.30 | 49.60 | 61.20 | 35.60 | 72.90 | 46.98 |
| 2021 | 97.40 | 77.40 | 47.00 | 34.40 | 28.40 | 26.30 | 25.80 | 21.90 | 24.30 | 52.10 | 66.50 | 48.20 | 45.81 |
| 2022[1] | 43.50 | 48.60 | 45.60 | 40.50 | 37.70 | 31.10 | 64.70 | 48.60 | 44.20 | 42.60 | 55.00 | 56.30 | 46.53 |

[1] Preliminary.   NA = Not available.   *Source: National Agricultural Statistics Service, U.S. Department of Agriculture (NASS-USDA)*

**Average Price Received by Growers for Head Lettuce in the United States    In Dollars per Cwt**

| Year | Jan. | Feb. | Mar. | Apr. | May | June | July | Aug. | Sept. | Oct. | Nov. | Dec. | Season Average |
|---|---|---|---|---|---|---|---|---|---|---|---|---|---|
| 2013 | 44.80 | 31.70 | 46.90 | NA | NA | NA | NA | NA | NA | NA | NA | NA | 26.70 |
| 2014 | NA | NA | NA | 18.20 | 26.10 | 35.30 | 29.00 | 29.60 | 32.90 | 33.40 | 49.10 | 15.90 | 24.40 |
| 2015 | 38.20 | 15.20 | 19.10 | 23.10 | 25.10 | 30.30 | 18.80 | 35.70 | 48.90 | 34.40 | 60.10 | 51.90 | 29.10 |
| 2016 | 42.00 | 20.90 | 15.40 | 20.80 | 32.50 | 25.90 | 26.00 | 20.70 | 20.80 | 20.60 | 26.60 | 30.20 | 26.70 |
| 2017 | 29.10 | 51.40 | 49.60 | 82.50 | 26.10 | 22.80 | 25.60 | 24.70 | 31.70 | 42.20 | 23.00 | 30.50 | 35.90 |
| 2018 | 26.00 | 27.00 | 46.70 | 25.50 | 28.90 | 25.90 | 20.90 | 27.80 | 25.90 | 28.60 | 76.70 | 74.80 | 30.10 |
| 2019 | 33.80 | 37.60 | 52.40 | 28.10 | 19.70 | 41.00 | 41.50 | 22.70 | 22.90 | 39.20 | 65.30 | 49.00 | 37.77 |
| 2020 | 80.50 | 20.60 | 27.40 | 22.30 | 20.80 | 24.50 | 25.00 | 18.60 | 38.60 | 48.60 | 58.30 | 21.20 | 33.87 |
| 2021 | 21.80 | 15.80 | 21.40 | 16.10 | 14.70 | 17.60 | 19.90 | 19.30 | 31.90 | 74.90 | 63.00 | 22.50 | 28.24 |
| 2022[1] | 21.10 | 22.10 | 68.70 | 28.70 | 22.10 | 23.30 | 24.80 | 37.90 | 50.30 | 126.00 | 181.00 | 142.00 | 62.33 |

[1] Preliminary.   NA = Not available.   *Source: National Agricultural Statistics Service, U.S. Department of Agriculture (NASS-USDA)*

**Average Price Received by Growers for Tomatoes in the United States    In Dollars per Cwt**

| Year | Jan. | Feb. | Mar. | Apr. | May | June | July | Aug. | Sept. | Oct. | Nov. | Dec. | Season Average |
|---|---|---|---|---|---|---|---|---|---|---|---|---|---|
| 2013 | 34.10 | 37.70 | 53.50 | NA | NA | NA | NA | NA | NA | NA | NA | NA | 44.60 |
| 2014 | NA | NA | NA | 45.20 | 39.10 | 57.60 | 27.00 | 33.20 | 34.70 | 54.60 | 71.80 | 66.70 | 41.50 |
| 2015 | 34.80 | 49.40 | 44.20 | 45.20 | 24.00 | 33.50 | 41.30 | 36.30 | 35.80 | 41.80 | 39.30 | 42.50 | 46.30 |
| 2016 | 108.00 | 88.30 | 70.90 | 38.60 | 30.40 | 32.00 | 30.40 | 28.10 | 34.50 | 37.50 | 42.80 | 29.40 | 42.50 |
| 2017 | 28.40 | 28.50 | 30.20 | 32.90 | 62.80 | 43.90 | 28.20 | 30.10 | 37.20 | 42.40 | 62.40 | 80.20 | 37.30 |
| 2018 | 47.90 | 34.40 | 40.00 | 25.70 | 35.40 | 28.30 | 15.30 | 29.90 | 29.00 | 39.60 | 55.50 | 57.20 | 36.52 |
| 2019 | 53.30 | 45.40 | 52.20 | 43.40 | 36.20 | 36.10 | 32.10 | 34.20 | 33.00 | 40.90 | 54.40 | 112.00 | 47.77 |
| 2020 | 130.00 | 84.70 | 57.60 | 65.00 | 87.00 | 57.10 | 47.70 | 44.60 | 48.00 | 86.50 | 82.60 | 73.50 | 72.03 |
| 2021 | 95.40 | 46.20 | 47.20 | 37.10 | 58.30 | 41.80 | 35.30 | 42.60 | 55.40 | 94.60 | 70.70 | 48.60 | 56.10 |
| 2022[1] | 52.20 | 51.40 | 45.70 | 53.80 | 68.90 | 45.80 | 40.40 | 55.40 | 60.00 | 107.00 | 131.00 | 92.30 | 66.99 |

[1] Preliminary.   NA = Not available.   *Source: National Agricultural Statistics Service, U.S. Department of Agriculture (NASS-USDA)*

**Average Price Received by Growers for Asparagus in the United States    In Dollars per Cwt**

| Year | Jan. | Feb. | Mar. | Apr. | May | June | July | Aug. | Sept. | Oct. | Nov. | Dec. | Season Average |
|---|---|---|---|---|---|---|---|---|---|---|---|---|---|
| 2013 | NQ | NQ | NQ | NA | NA | NA | NA | NA | NA | NA | NA | NA | 131.00 |
| 2014 | NA | NA | NA | 116.00 | 131.00 | 115.00 | NA | NA | NA | NA | NA | NA | 106.00 |
| 2015 | NA | NA | 113.00 | 143.00 | 133.00 | 71.30 | NA | NA | NA | NA | NA | NA | 116.00 |
| 2016 | NA | 115.00 | 103.00 | 125.00 | 122.00 | 134.00 | NA | NA | NA | NA | NA | NA | 110.00 |
| 2017 | NA | NA | 96.60 | 126.00 | 119.00 | 90.50 | NA | NA | NA | NA | NA | NA | 120.00 |
| 2018 | NA | NA | 165.00 | 105.00 | 107.00 | 87.60 | NA | NA | NA | NA | NA | NA | 113.00 |
| 2019 | NA | NA | NA | 119.00 | 121.00 | 96.40 | NA | NA | NA | NA | NA | NA | 112.13 |
| 2020 | NA | NA | NA | 284.00 | 262.00 | 211.00 | NA | NA | NA | NA | NA | NA | 252.33 |
| 2021 | NA | NA | NA | 226.00 | 206.00 | 201.00 | NA | NA | NA | NA | NA | NA | 211.00 |
| 2022[1] | NA | NA | NA | NA | 225.00 | 219.00 | NA | NA | NA | NA | NA | NA | 222.00 |

[1] Preliminary.   NA = Not available.   *Source: National Agricultural Statistics Service, U.S. Department of Agriculture (NASS-USDA)*

# VEGETABLES

**Average Price Received by Growers for Cantaloupes in the United States**   In Dollars per Cwt

| Year | Jan. | Feb. | Mar. | Apr. | May | June | July | Aug. | Sept. | Oct. | Nov. | Dec. | Season Average |
|---|---|---|---|---|---|---|---|---|---|---|---|---|---|
| 2013 | NQ | NQ | NQ | NQ | NA | NA | NA | NA | NA | NA | NA | NA | NA |
| 2014 | NA | NA | NA | NA | 20.50 | 24.70 | 19.20 | 21.70 | 21.40 | 36.10 | 31.90 | 21.30 | 22.10 |
| 2015 | NA | NA | NA | NA | 17.30 | 17.70 | 26.20 | 25.70 | 27.70 | 22.30 | NQ | NQ | 19.50 |
| 2016 | NA | NA | NA | NA | 23.80 | 17.50 | 20.60 | 16.30 | 18.50 | 22.70 | 21.50 | NQ | 17.20 |
| 2017 | NA | NA | NA | NA | 22.80 | 26.80 | 34.90 | 23.30 | 24.10 | 29.50 | 29.60 | NQ | 19.20 |
| 2018 | NA | NA | NA | NA | 23.20 | 20.40 | 16.60 | 16.90 | 20.00 | 27.60 | 35.00 | 39.00 | 22.70 |
| 2019 | NA | NA | NA | NA | 12.80 | 21.40 | 21.80 | 21.80 | 25.90 | 26.00 | 24.30 | NQ | 22.00 |
| 2020 | NA | NA | NA | NA | 31.90 | 26.90 | 29.70 | 20.00 | 27.10 | 26.30 | 22.60 | NQ | 26.36 |
| 2021 | NA | NA | NA | 32.60 | 26.90 | 29.00 | 22.30 | 24.10 | 22.90 | 32.20 | 51.40 | NQ | 30.18 |
| 2022[1] | NA | NA | NA | 37.30 | 34.20 | 25.70 | 35.70 | 24.60 | 30.50 | 37.60 | 50.00 | NQ | 34.45 |

[1] Preliminary.   NA = Not available.   Source: National Agricultural Statistics Service, U.S. Department of Agriculture (NASS-USDA)

**Average Price Received by Growers for Cucumbers in the United States**   In Dollars per Cwt

| Year | Jan. | Feb. | Mar. | Apr. | May | June | July | Aug. | Sept. | Oct. | Nov. | Dec. | Season Average |
|---|---|---|---|---|---|---|---|---|---|---|---|---|---|
| 2013 | 21.70 | NQ | NQ | NQ | NA | NA | NA | NA | NA | NA | NA | NA | 26.80 |
| 2014 | NA | NA | NA | 26.20 | 40.00 | 25.50 | 21.30 | 29.90 | 24.10 | 37.00 | 24.80 | 34.20 | 24.40 |
| 2015 | 30.60 | 27.60 | 40.80 | 24.00 | 23.40 | 36.30 | 25.30 | 28.90 | 33.00 | W | 29.30 | 38.40 | 26.10 |
| 2016 | 35.00 | NA | 48.70 | 26.20 | 36.10 | 24.40 | 21.00 | 19.90 | 20.60 | W | 25.90 | 18.70 | 25.90 |
| 2017 | 39.20 | NA | 37.80 | 34.30 | 33.40 | 36.70 | 20.30 | 16.00 | 17.50 | 41.90 | 34.50 | 29.90 | 29.50 |
| 2018 | 41.10 | NA | 33.40 | 32.70 | 43.50 | 35.40 | 20.50 | 17.80 | 19.10 | 42.60 | 37.50 | 36.70 | 32.75 |
| 2019 | 37.40 | NA | 33.30 | 29.20 | 26.30 | 30.40 | 23.60 | 18.80 | 24.00 | 39.60 | 31.10 | 41.50 | 30.47 |
| 2020 | NA | NA | NA | 23.40 | 27.20 | 29.60 | 25.30 | 33.50 | 37.70 | 25.00 | 31.80 | 26.70 | 28.91 |
| 2021 | NA | NA | 27.70 | 39.50 | 28.60 | 20.30 | 27.40 | 23.20 | 24.50 | 30.80 | 27.90 | 21.80 | 27.17 |
| 2022[1] | NA | NA | 43.30 | 45.40 | 28.30 | 22.00 | 29.30 | 27.00 | 24.30 | 49.80 | 43.00 | 28.00 | 34.04 |

[1] Preliminary.   NA = Not available.   Source: National Agricultural Statistics Service, U.S. Department of Agriculture (NASS-USDA)

**Average Price Received by Growers for Celery in the United States**   In Dollars per Cwt

| Year | Jan. | Feb. | Mar. | Apr. | May | June | July | Aug. | Sept. | Oct. | Nov. | Dec. | Season Average |
|---|---|---|---|---|---|---|---|---|---|---|---|---|---|
| 2013 | 58.00 | 60.30 | 113.00 | NA | NA | NA | NA | NA | NA | NA | NA | NA | 68.90 |
| 2014 | NA | NA | NA | 52.30 | 74.20 | 48.60 | 83.50 | 77.20 | 85.70 | 63.10 | 62.00 | 68.10 | 60.20 |
| 2015 | 40.80 | 53.90 | 60.50 | 54.80 | 85.30 | W | W | W | W | W | 72.80 | 118.00 | 59.40 |
| 2016 | 95.90 | 125.00 | 95.20 | 42.80 | 46.40 | W | 107.00 | 75.00 | 85.30 | 89.90 | 78.40 | 50.60 | 60.20 |
| 2017 | 36.50 | 54.90 | 59.90 | 67.10 | 74.10 | W | W | 93.80 | 64.70 | W | 72.30 | 69.50 | 55.60 |
| 2018 | 101.00 | 61.50 | 45.90 | 66.50 | 64.50 | W | W | W | W | W | 99.00 | 62.80 | 71.60 |
| 2019 | 57.90 | 55.90 | 30.40 | 60.00 | 58.50 | W | 60.60 | W | W | W | 99.10 | 89.30 | 63.96 |
| 2020 | 62.80 | 48.40 | 43.20 | 45.30 | 49.50 | 84.10 | W | 58.70 | 46.70 | 78.40 | 77.70 | 86.80 | 61.96 |
| 2021 | 75.70 | 54.00 | 36.50 | 56.10 | 43.80 | 42.10 | 51.20 | 47.80 | 65.10 | 75.10 | 80.40 | 43.40 | 55.93 |
| 2022[1] | 70.00 | 74.80 | 50.10 | 48.80 | 65.40 | 63.60 | 51.10 | 55.30 | 57.90 | 112.00 | 125.00 | 79.10 | 71.09 |

[1] Preliminary.   NA = Not available.   W = Withheld.   Source: National Agricultural Statistics Service, U.S. Department of Agriculture (NASS-USDA)

**Cold Storage Stocks of Frozen Asparagus in the United States, on First of Month**   In Thousands of Pounds

| Year | Jan. | Feb. | Mar. | Apr. | May | June | July | Aug. | Sept. | Oct. | Nov. | Dec. |
|---|---|---|---|---|---|---|---|---|---|---|---|---|
| 2013 | 8,304 | 7,087 | 6,515 | 5,517 | 4,648 | 6,476 | 9,900 | 9,695 | 9,432 | 9,378 | 9,307 | 9,576 |
| 2014 | 9,758 | 9,701 | 9,497 | 9,038 | 7,946 | 10,252 | 15,185 | 15,656 | 16,324 | 16,916 | 14,873 | 14,572 |
| 2015 | 13,603 | 12,620 | 11,115 | 10,608 | 10,084 | 13,037 | 14,457 | 14,209 | 14,270 | 13,283 | 12,579 | 12,883 |
| 2016 | 11,926 | 12,144 | 11,225 | 10,877 | 10,290 | 12,246 | 14,490 | 13,429 | 12,697 | 12,328 | 12,089 | 12,133 |
| 2017 | 11,395 | 10,780 | 10,273 | 9,243 | 9,012 | 9,781 | 11,137 | 11,395 | 12,102 | 11,928 | 10,893 | 9,914 |
| 2018 | 10,188 | 9,690 | 8,119 | 6,989 | 6,036 | 7,767 | 10,855 | 10,971 | 10,120 | 9,358 | 8,933 | 8,364 |
| 2019 | 8,106 | 7,694 | 7,136 | 6,419 | 5,714 | 5,807 | 7,220 | 7,297 | 6,454 | 6,372 | 6,344 | 6,257 |
| 2020 | 6,002 | 5,936 | 4,893 | 4,610 | 4,298 | 5,090 | 8,393 | 7,666 | 7,179 | 6,435 | 5,933 | 5,591 |
| 2021 | 5,293 | 4,531 | 4,151 | 4,192 | 3,928 | 5,420 | 9,778 | 8,470 | 7,553 | 7,093 | 6,412 | 6,316 |
| 2022[1] | 5,451 | 4,831 | 4,807 | 4,505 | 4,196 | 7,629 | 11,689 | 10,803 | 10,305 | 9,254 | 8,821 | 8,348 |

[1] Preliminary.   Source: Economic Research Service, U.S. Department of Agriculture (ERS-USDA)

# VEGETABLES

## Frozen Vegetables: January 1 and July 1 Cold Storage Holdings in the United States  In Thousands of Pounds

| Crop | 2018 July 1 | 2019 Jan. 1 | 2019 July 1 | 2020 Jan. 1 | 2020 July 1 | 2021 Jan. 1 | 2021 July 1 | 2022 Jan. 1 | 2022 July 1 | 2023[1] Jan. 1 |
|---|---|---|---|---|---|---|---|---|---|---|
| Asparagus | 10,855 | 8,106 | 7,220 | 6,002 | 8,393 | 5,293 | 9,778 | 5,451 | 11,665 | 7,668 |
| Lima Beans | 33,421 | 38,647 | 14,441 | 33,509 | 14,576 | 21,497 | 7,107 | 28,305 | 13,906 | 22,228 |
| Green Beans, Reg. Cut | 81,164 | 152,495 | 82,556 | 155,713 | 68,409 | 204,173 | 90,561 | 182,212 | 83,694 | 197,366 |
| Green Beans, Fr. Style | 11,184 | 13,747 | 9,879 | 14,887 | 9,697 | 13,061 | 7,610 | 14,285 | 9,198 | 16,921 |
| Broccoli, Spears | 45,339 | 26,691 | 43,927 | 41,991 | 47,273 | 34,491 | 42,749 | 36,795 | 51,498 | 30,310 |
| Broccoli, Chopped & Cut | 34,532 | 37,761 | 32,061 | 34,048 | 31,362 | 36,427 | 35,964 | 25,773 | 22,531 | 21,670 |
| Brussels sprouts | 17,361 | 15,680 | 12,774 | 13,254 | 9,613 | 8,016 | 12,709 | 11,881 | 12,420 | 13,967 |
| Carrots, Diced | 84,708 | 125,994 | 100,442 | 173,673 | 100,000 | 152,684 | 88,092 | 174,895 | 106,120 | 168,251 |
| Carrots, Other | 94,449 | 110,822 | 64,844 | 98,720 | 59,108 | 112,189 | 80,049 | 85,334 | 69,052 | 80,509 |
| Cauliflower | 25,340 | 29,760 | 18,926 | 24,382 | 27,252 | 30,408 | 31,042 | 24,638 | 22,366 | 24,090 |
| Corn, Cut | 240,908 | 475,712 | 240,636 | 567,306 | 270,432 | 597,036 | 264,952 | 612,730 | 282,728 | 593,790 |
| Corn, Cob | 79,134 | 269,689 | 137,539 | 275,612 | 106,869 | 272,573 | 78,876 | 300,426 | 165,902 | 316,250 |
| Mixed vegetables | 56,417 | 53,845 | 47,214 | 41,323 | 45,371 | 50,758 | 61,610 | 47,821 | 55,423 | 44,316 |
| Okra | 30,181 | 44,156 | 28,658 | 48,906 | 33,460 | 33,817 | 19,240 | 34,970 | 19,650 | 30,463 |
| Onion Rings | 17,976 | 17,160 | 15,146 | 14,918 | 14,144 | 14,203 | 11,103 | 12,859 | 17,585 | 23,522 |
| Onions, Other | 60,160 | 51,663 | 72,312 | 51,024 | 73,559 | 60,448 | 60,812 | 38,086 | 35,573 | 41,718 |
| Blackeye Peas | 1,293 | 1,479 | 1,413 | 1,227 | 2,168 | 1,779 | 2,645 | 2,497 | 1,421 | 1,891 |
| Green Peas | 284,008 | 207,808 | 233,194 | 212,684 | 232,490 | 243,072 | 231,790 | 207,468 | 164,500 | 232,097 |
| Peas and Carrots Mixed | 6,754 | 7,262 | 9,098 | 9,058 | 8,779 | 7,809 | 7,890 | 6,605 | 5,759 | 6,850 |
| Spinach | 57,896 | 30,994 | 41,009 | 33,492 | 58,434 | 53,278 | 64,854 | 49,212 | 58,802 | 39,805 |
| Squash, Summer/Zucchini | 44,881 | 60,482 | 40,456 | 56,884 | 37,204 | 56,841 | 40,641 | 57,436 | 40,275 | 53,927 |
| Southern greens | 10,996 | 12,174 | 12,907 | 10,908 | 11,380 | 15,577 | 15,559 | 17,082 | 11,005 | 15,787 |
| Other Vegetables | 377,555 | 582,039 | 355,236 | 435,111 | 373,489 | 460,079 | 323,050 | 401,496 | 38,631 | 392,617 |
| Total | 1,706,512 | 2,374,166 | 1,621,888 | 2,354,632 | 1,643,462 | 2,485,509 | 1,588,683 | 2,378,257 | 1,569,704 | 2,376,013 |
| Potatoes, French Fries | 941,336 | 944,230 | 945,264 | 948,850 | 868,583 | 917,398 | 912,824 | 864,148 | 989,728 | 999,180 |
| Potatoes, Other Frozen | 270,621 | 230,329 | 239,233 | 207,080 | 216,545 | 204,660 | 201,477 | 199,872 | 237,963 | 220,267 |
| Potatoes, Total | 1,211,957 | 1,174,559 | 1,184,497 | 1,155,930 | 1,085,128 | 1,122,058 | 1,114,301 | 1,064,020 | 1,227,691 | 1,219,447 |
| Grand Total | 2,918,469 | 3,548,725 | 2,806,385 | 3,510,562 | 2,728,590 | 3,607,567 | 2,702,984 | 3,442,277 | 2,797,395 | 3,595,460 |

## Cold Storage Stocks of Frozen Limas in the United States, on First of Month  In Thousands of Pounds

| Year | Jan. | Feb. | Mar. | Apr. | May | June | July | Aug. | Sept. | Oct. | Nov. | Dec. |
|---|---|---|---|---|---|---|---|---|---|---|---|---|
| 2013 | 57,819 | 55,077 | 49,776 | 43,163 | 38,938 | 31,743 | 29,717 | 26,868 | 28,225 | 52,301 | 69,060 | 63,264 |
| 2014 | 60,262 | 58,462 | 54,696 | 51,382 | 43,074 | 39,818 | 34,333 | 31,632 | 35,991 | 52,979 | 73,497 | 69,543 |
| 2015 | 64,530 | 58,804 | 53,249 | 51,849 | 47,874 | 42,782 | 41,133 | 37,376 | 44,819 | 62,195 | 66,999 | 59,313 |
| 2016 | 57,841 | 53,533 | 50,432 | 47,576 | 46,603 | 42,577 | 40,193 | 37,743 | 45,577 | 61,184 | 66,795 | 59,516 |
| 2017 | 55,895 | 51,451 | 48,414 | 44,371 | 40,852 | 39,116 | 36,817 | 33,753 | 33,807 | 48,322 | 63,786 | 56,226 |
| 2018 | 54,024 | 49,217 | 45,506 | 42,318 | 37,826 | 36,355 | 33,421 | 29,161 | 33,072 | 44,301 | 47,691 | 42,601 |
| 2019 | 38,647 | 34,443 | 29,861 | 26,059 | 18,879 | 17,010 | 14,441 | 11,091 | 15,153 | 31,086 | 39,771 | 35,701 |
| 2020 | 33,509 | 30,762 | 27,080 | 24,133 | 21,005 | 18,479 | 14,576 | 11,083 | 15,256 | 24,571 | 27,107 | 25,544 |
| 2021 | 21,497 | 19,938 | 16,728 | 12,506 | 9,807 | 8,062 | 7,107 | 5,626 | 8,734 | 28,637 | 33,454 | 32,965 |
| 2022[1] | 28,305 | 24,657 | 22,524 | 18,570 | 17,853 | 16,192 | 13,751 | 11,704 | 13,258 | 20,637 | 28,050 | 26,335 |

[1] Preliminary.  Source: Economic Research Service, U.S. Department of Agriculture (ERS-USDA)

## Cold Storage Stocks of Frozen Green Beans[2] in the United States, on First of Month  In Thousands of Pounds

| Year | Jan. | Feb. | Mar. | Apr. | May | June | July | Aug. | Sept. | Oct. | Nov. | Dec. |
|---|---|---|---|---|---|---|---|---|---|---|---|---|
| 2013 | 252,309 | 203,122 | 201,608 | 179,446 | 164,526 | 152,338 | 143,931 | 166,636 | 237,400 | 252,315 | 224,385 | 200,790 |
| 2014 | 181,073 | 162,305 | 149,444 | 139,195 | 125,882 | 109,855 | 96,376 | 147,470 | 225,135 | 253,066 | 235,830 | 205,861 |
| 2015 | 182,136 | 161,510 | 153,916 | 135,211 | 123,221 | 119,151 | 113,449 | 155,410 | 226,850 | 255,661 | 243,986 | 225,001 |
| 2016 | 199,994 | 180,082 | 158,534 | 142,228 | 136,727 | 131,014 | 122,127 | 169,238 | 242,529 | 265,200 | 263,320 | 233,980 |
| 2017 | 209,496 | 190,073 | 174,009 | 159,278 | 144,992 | 132,483 | 115,498 | 138,593 | 196,016 | 238,830 | 230,850 | 216,052 |
| 2018 | 191,291 | 172,503 | 155,853 | 128,304 | 109,337 | 93,324 | 81,164 | 115,005 | 173,836 | 202,123 | 190,921 | 173,687 |
| 2019 | 152,495 | 143,960 | 130,780 | 117,427 | 110,140 | 87,598 | 82,556 | 125,225 | 163,225 | 203,481 | 185,412 | 173,403 |
| 2020 | 155,713 | 142,537 | 126,346 | 107,604 | 91,905 | 76,783 | 68,409 | 125,541 | 197,217 | 252,835 | 240,075 | 219,751 |
| 2021 | 204,173 | 176,731 | 156,314 | 139,827 | 120,531 | 100,787 | 90,561 | 128,013 | 178,850 | 230,704 | 214,727 | 200,020 |
| 2022[1] | 182,212 | 166,098 | 145,791 | 131,105 | 111,740 | 97,078 | 84,672 | 112,994 | 177,436 | 232,590 | 243,963 | 222,148 |

[1] Preliminary.  [2] Regular cut.  Source: Economic Research Service, U.S. Department of Agriculture (ERS-USDA)

# VEGETABLES

### Cold Storage Stocks of Frozen Green Beans[2] in the United States, on First of Month    In Thousands of Pounds

| Year | Jan. | Feb. | Mar. | Apr. | May | June | July | Aug. | Sept. | Oct. | Nov. | Dec. |
|---|---|---|---|---|---|---|---|---|---|---|---|---|
| 2013 | 15,761 | 14,313 | 14,331 | 12,910 | 11,732 | 8,587 | 8,749 | 13,128 | 20,760 | 20,563 | 17,647 | 15,421 |
| 2014 | 14,248 | 13,479 | 11,607 | 11,680 | 10,675 | 8,790 | 8,194 | 15,306 | 18,840 | 20,852 | 18,439 | 16,975 |
| 2015 | 14,754 | 13,214 | 10,323 | 10,177 | 8,250 | 7,246 | 8,025 | 12,653 | 12,695 | 19,787 | 19,142 | 16,305 |
| 2016 | 15,279 | 14,378 | 14,121 | 13,331 | 12,092 | 10,477 | 9,912 | 13,009 | 18,951 | 20,521 | 18,876 | 16,312 |
| 2017 | 14,482 | 14,324 | 13,321 | 12,838 | 11,522 | 9,874 | 8,923 | 12,355 | 16,478 | 18,836 | 18,222 | 16,302 |
| 2018 | 15,187 | 14,738 | 13,923 | 13,402 | 12,230 | 10,651 | 11,184 | 12,886 | 14,413 | 15,847 | 15,328 | 13,793 |
| 2019 | 13,747 | 12,622 | 12,025 | 11,534 | 11,471 | 10,112 | 9,879 | 16,571 | 21,160 | 20,285 | 19,950 | 17,134 |
| 2020 | 14,887 | 14,569 | 13,264 | 12,967 | 11,788 | 10,857 | 9,697 | 11,301 | 14,283 | 16,864 | 15,253 | 14,809 |
| 2021 | 13,061 | 13,044 | 11,790 | 10,384 | 9,310 | 8,696 | 7,610 | 11,259 | 14,740 | 19,400 | 22,686 | 20,254 |
| 2022[1] | 14,285 | 12,214 | 11,611 | 11,113 | 9,620 | 8,928 | 9,100 | 11,912 | 17,281 | 20,345 | 19,300 | 17,710 |

[1] Preliminary.   [2] French style.   Source: Economic Research Service, U.S. Department of Agriculture (ERS-USDA)


### Cold Storage Stocks of Frozen Broccoli[2] in the United States, on First of Month    In Thousands of Pounds

| Year | Jan. | Feb. | Mar. | Apr. | May | June | July | Aug. | Sept. | Oct. | Nov. | Dec. |
|---|---|---|---|---|---|---|---|---|---|---|---|---|
| 2013 | 27,652 | 26,693 | 23,701 | 23,110 | 27,768 | 27,359 | 27,359 | 24,656 | 20,776 | 21,245 | 21,604 | 22,365 |
| 2014 | 21,705 | 19,728 | 20,956 | 23,558 | 30,509 | 34,882 | 34,093 | 34,054 | 32,216 | 30,285 | 30,697 | 29,339 |
| 2015 | 27,108 | 25,796 | 27,826 | 29,124 | 29,731 | 29,475 | 27,821 | 26,272 | 27,564 | 28,387 | 26,873 | 27,317 |
| 2016 | 25,023 | 24,480 | 26,498 | 26,783 | 33,170 | 29,783 | 27,727 | 28,986 | 27,355 | 25,951 | 25,119 | 24,068 |
| 2017 | 21,870 | 24,405 | 26,382 | 32,156 | 31,070 | 30,890 | 30,877 | 28,038 | 27,541 | 24,817 | 26,515 | 22,921 |
| 2018 | 23,877 | 25,814 | 29,513 | 31,806 | 34,494 | 38,616 | 45,339 | 44,166 | 44,250 | 37,705 | 35,174 | 30,802 |
| 2019 | 26,691 | 26,337 | 28,628 | 34,710 | 40,829 | 39,849 | 43,927 | 45,936 | 48,278 | 47,694 | 46,109 | 43,369 |
| 2020 | 41,991 | 41,480 | 45,744 | 49,290 | 50,584 | 51,904 | 47,273 | 46,002 | 40,460 | 39,828 | 39,271 | 33,879 |
| 2021 | 34,491 | 30,236 | 31,453 | 31,548 | 39,376 | 43,656 | 42,749 | 45,550 | 43,612 | 41,671 | 41,144 | 38,682 |
| 2022[1] | 36,795 | 34,637 | 40,894 | 46,183 | 48,863 | 45,821 | 50,925 | 45,454 | 44,894 | 42,333 | 39,107 | 31,660 |

[1] Preliminary.   [2] Spears.   Source: Economic Research Service, U.S. Department of Agriculture (ERS-USDA)


### Cold Storage Stocks of Frozen Broccoli[2] in the United States, on First of Month    In Thousands of Pounds

| Year | Jan. | Feb. | Mar. | Apr. | May | June | July | Aug. | Sept. | Oct. | Nov. | Dec. |
|---|---|---|---|---|---|---|---|---|---|---|---|---|
| 2013 | 52,022 | 48,011 | 46,544 | 41,799 | 44,958 | 41,581 | 41,353 | 43,215 | 46,830 | 43,243 | 39,861 | 34,655 |
| 2014 | 34,836 | 34,253 | 33,570 | 31,421 | 30,447 | 32,993 | 33,394 | 38,547 | 41,970 | 41,131 | 43,775 | 37,347 |
| 2015 | 36,143 | 34,751 | 38,107 | 37,416 | 39,532 | 39,932 | 42,211 | 41,556 | 50,159 | 50,323 | 44,935 | 41,373 |
| 2016 | 39,398 | 38,275 | 35,525 | 34,633 | 35,389 | 34,273 | 37,574 | 40,191 | 44,837 | 41,996 | 41,969 | 41,462 |
| 2017 | 42,915 | 46,006 | 43,333 | 40,864 | 39,286 | 36,102 | 31,521 | 34,386 | 39,995 | 37,178 | 34,739 | 33,388 |
| 2018 | 32,738 | 30,206 | 31,302 | 33,530 | 36,759 | 35,108 | 34,532 | 38,981 | 41,735 | 43,080 | 41,796 | 39,422 |
| 2019 | 37,761 | 36,913 | 39,476 | 37,688 | 35,876 | 32,798 | 32,061 | 36,520 | 43,555 | 45,550 | 39,750 | 37,303 |
| 2020 | 34,048 | 34,106 | 33,750 | 32,692 | 31,544 | 32,163 | 31,362 | 29,903 | 29,956 | 32,250 | 37,907 | 35,867 |
| 2021 | 36,427 | 33,513 | 33,034 | 31,411 | 36,950 | 34,205 | 35,964 | 32,986 | 32,830 | 28,362 | 27,209 | 24,422 |
| 2022[1] | 25,773 | 22,924 | 22,135 | 22,577 | 22,377 | 22,217 | 22,519 | 21,727 | 20,724 | 23,630 | 23,030 | 22,352 |

[1] Preliminary.   [2] Chopped & cut.   Source: Economic Research Service, U.S. Department of Agriculture (ERS-USDA)


### Cold Storage Stocks of Frozen Brussel Sprouts in the United States, on First of Month    In Thousands of Pounds

| Year | Jan. | Feb. | Mar. | Apr. | May | June | July | Aug. | Sept. | Oct. | Nov. | Dec. |
|---|---|---|---|---|---|---|---|---|---|---|---|---|
| 2013 | 13,663 | 13,883 | 13,534 | 12,244 | 11,373 | 11,119 | 10,675 | 9,532 | 8,058 | 7,594 | 7,117 | 9,258 |
| 2014 | 13,612 | 15,327 | 15,343 | 14,071 | 14,283 | 13,452 | 12,480 | 10,911 | 10,142 | 9,798 | 12,149 | 13,585 |
| 2015 | 15,960 | 15,090 | 14,120 | 13,448 | 13,170 | 13,658 | 14,691 | 13,401 | 12,241 | 12,352 | 14,338 | 16,636 |
| 2016 | 19,843 | 18,028 | 16,367 | 14,363 | 13,801 | 13,785 | 13,061 | 13,569 | 12,265 | 11,564 | 15,110 | 18,241 |
| 2017 | 22,021 | 23,187 | 22,721 | 20,508 | 19,588 | 18,428 | 16,253 | 14,379 | 14,101 | 13,415 | 16,126 | 17,219 |
| 2018 | 21,878 | 21,121 | 20,636 | 20,900 | 20,736 | 19,317 | 17,361 | 17,102 | 15,536 | 13,257 | 13,410 | 13,940 |
| 2019 | 15,680 | 15,728 | 13,164 | 12,916 | 13,341 | 12,501 | 12,774 | 12,930 | 12,823 | 12,237 | 12,982 | 12,505 |
| 2020 | 13,254 | 13,256 | 11,691 | 9,494 | 9,172 | 10,074 | 9,613 | 10,118 | 10,037 | 9,947 | 9,355 | 8,640 |
| 2021 | 8,016 | 9,276 | 11,028 | 12,199 | 12,726 | 12,672 | 12,709 | 12,879 | 12,781 | 12,368 | 11,711 | 12,336 |
| 2022[1] | 11,881 | 12,709 | 11,743 | 12,629 | 11,620 | 11,876 | 12,466 | 12,902 | 14,323 | 15,334 | 14,632 | 13,184 |

[1] Preliminary.   Source: Economic Research Service, U.S. Department of Agriculture (ERS-USDA)

# VEGETABLES

### Cold Storage Stocks of Frozen Carrots[2] in the United States, on First of Month   In Thousands of Pounds

| Year | Jan. | Feb. | Mar. | Apr. | May | June | July | Aug. | Sept. | Oct. | Nov. | Dec. |
|---|---|---|---|---|---|---|---|---|---|---|---|---|
| 2013 | 170,186 | 153,103 | 143,728 | 141,134 | 130,094 | 120,599 | 109,846 | 92,114 | 79,840 | 75,125 | 123,044 | 153,748 |
| 2014 | 157,220 | 153,372 | 143,648 | 130,512 | 114,796 | 109,991 | 97,279 | 81,749 | 74,944 | 71,990 | 130,075 | 173,870 |
| 2015 | 168,289 | 155,485 | 144,853 | 134,587 | 121,669 | 115,221 | 99,334 | 87,345 | 84,143 | 83,391 | 148,160 | 172,525 |
| 2016 | 161,755 | 159,472 | 148,175 | 142,072 | 129,994 | 116,769 | 99,573 | 95,109 | 83,701 | 85,034 | 125,903 | 173,404 |
| 2017 | 161,641 | 145,245 | 127,999 | 119,945 | 114,784 | 107,957 | 97,296 | 86,068 | 79,758 | 75,024 | 109,489 | 152,316 |
| 2018 | 142,941 | 128,815 | 121,470 | 114,872 | 108,053 | 98,881 | 84,708 | 65,564 | 53,967 | 48,927 | 86,070 | 129,184 |
| 2019 | 125,994 | 120,219 | 116,148 | 109,514 | 105,619 | 110,909 | 100,442 | 84,444 | 72,505 | 62,579 | 113,835 | 171,712 |
| 2020 | 173,673 | 169,269 | 156,725 | 139,078 | 129,593 | 118,912 | 100,000 | 84,686 | 69,085 | 57,589 | 103,313 | 142,673 |
| 2021 | 152,684 | 137,414 | 132,324 | 115,552 | 107,679 | 97,098 | 88,092 | 72,849 | 60,728 | 55,855 | 101,665 | 160,063 |
| 2022[1] | 174,895 | 166,403 | 157,749 | 148,342 | 137,032 | 126,488 | 106,780 | 89,137 | 78,133 | 67,319 | 115,722 | 158,821 |

[1] Preliminary.   [2] Diced.   *Source: Economic Research Service, U.S. Department of Agriculture (ERS-USDA)*

### Cold Storage Stocks of Frozen Carrots[2] in the United States, on First of Month   In Thousands of Pounds

| Year | Jan. | Feb. | Mar. | Apr. | May | June | July | Aug. | Sept. | Oct. | Nov. | Dec. |
|---|---|---|---|---|---|---|---|---|---|---|---|---|
| 2013 | 173,980 | 154,606 | 143,605 | 132,941 | 123,435 | 113,051 | 108,905 | 97,698 | 101,655 | 113,138 | 155,412 | 170,679 |
| 2014 | 160,585 | 146,956 | 134,187 | 121,009 | 118,973 | 114,263 | 102,942 | 97,360 | 103,813 | 130,307 | 171,014 | 195,425 |
| 2015 | 180,493 | 155,156 | 138,003 | 120,999 | 117,545 | 102,967 | 88,645 | 83,838 | 79,673 | 106,742 | 157,115 | 173,385 |
| 2016 | 166,317 | 163,079 | 154,349 | 144,494 | 141,373 | 132,722 | 119,896 | 109,006 | 113,894 | 117,326 | 163,522 | 197,013 |
| 2017 | 191,102 | 171,689 | 157,377 | 152,193 | 143,200 | 129,246 | 112,691 | 100,623 | 106,683 | 118,442 | 144,425 | 160,556 |
| 2018 | 164,466 | 149,233 | 136,166 | 125,914 | 119,288 | 104,184 | 94,449 | 87,118 | 84,641 | 96,342 | 105,654 | 113,794 |
| 2019 | 110,822 | 100,107 | 93,262 | 87,761 | 77,125 | 73,787 | 64,844 | 57,293 | 53,727 | 67,712 | 86,019 | 105,246 |
| 2020 | 98,720 | 93,213 | 81,789 | 72,680 | 69,704 | 67,242 | 59,108 | 55,115 | 54,034 | 76,293 | 97,060 | 115,016 |
| 2021 | 112,189 | 103,845 | 97,456 | 96,316 | 95,033 | 93,905 | 80,049 | 73,240 | 64,594 | 58,234 | 81,048 | 93,261 |
| 2022[1] | 85,334 | 81,678 | 75,903 | 75,476 | 77,886 | 76,253 | 69,031 | 65,757 | 58,003 | 52,283 | 65,854 | 81,790 |

[1] Preliminary.   [2] Other.   *Source: Economic Research Service, U.S. Department of Agriculture (ERS-USDA)*

### Cold Storage Stocks of Frozen Cauliflower in the United States, on First of Month   In Thousands of Pounds

| Year | Jan. | Feb. | Mar. | Apr. | May | June | July | Aug. | Sept. | Oct. | Nov. | Dec. |
|---|---|---|---|---|---|---|---|---|---|---|---|---|
| 2013 | 26,249 | 25,515 | 24,983 | 23,370 | 21,609 | 21,895 | 21,738 | 21,030 | 16,866 | 18,745 | 23,242 | 26,758 |
| 2014 | 23,139 | 21,680 | 21,139 | 18,386 | 17,768 | 18,035 | 16,497 | 15,461 | 14,427 | 15,581 | 22,014 | 21,897 |
| 2015 | 20,567 | 20,172 | 18,289 | 17,903 | 17,761 | 17,424 | 18,203 | 16,963 | 15,146 | 14,226 | 24,622 | 24,833 |
| 2016 | 26,448 | 25,971 | 24,669 | 23,833 | 23,236 | 23,443 | 22,634 | 21,690 | 18,853 | 19,651 | 26,266 | 26,986 |
| 2017 | 27,325 | 28,913 | 28,826 | 29,002 | 27,679 | 27,497 | 28,013 | 28,703 | 26,193 | 25,043 | 33,584 | 32,655 |
| 2018 | 34,083 | 34,901 | 36,257 | 35,212 | 32,896 | 30,354 | 25,340 | 24,701 | 24,088 | 23,258 | 30,422 | 28,645 |
| 2019 | 29,760 | 28,000 | 26,134 | 24,059 | 23,981 | 18,478 | 18,926 | 19,682 | 18,565 | 19,684 | 21,973 | 23,324 |
| 2020 | 24,382 | 26,212 | 29,012 | 29,567 | 28,132 | 30,131 | 27,252 | 28,570 | 28,218 | 28,301 | 32,386 | 31,667 |
| 2021 | 30,408 | 30,165 | 28,788 | 27,276 | 29,590 | 29,136 | 31,042 | 29,242 | 25,502 | 25,035 | 25,854 | 23,925 |
| 2022[1] | 24,638 | 23,079 | 21,792 | 19,532 | 20,094 | 22,289 | 22,305 | 22,468 | 22,011 | 21,338 | 22,233 | 23,246 |

[1] Preliminary.   *Source: Economic Research Service, U.S. Department of Agriculture (ERS-USDA)*

### Cold Storage Stocks of Frozen Sweet Corn[2] in the United States, on First of Month   In Thousands of Pounds

| Year | Jan. | Feb. | Mar. | Apr. | May | June | July | Aug. | Sept. | Oct. | Nov. | Dec. |
|---|---|---|---|---|---|---|---|---|---|---|---|---|
| 2013 | 465,827 | 450,464 | 410,588 | 369,771 | 330,335 | 282,126 | 249,147 | 226,862 | 397,483 | 585,455 | 630,849 | 581,072 |
| 2014 | 550,708 | 492,643 | 460,752 | 397,092 | 345,504 | 296,765 | 250,726 | 273,738 | 462,352 | 596,616 | 631,669 | 576,419 |
| 2015 | 529,586 | 464,026 | 431,593 | 395,330 | 348,564 | 313,388 | 262,028 | 287,729 | 446,215 | 621,237 | 640,668 | 582,672 |
| 2016 | 520,804 | 488,940 | 479,571 | 412,766 | 381,312 | 339,900 | 289,897 | 301,633 | 464,716 | 587,865 | 600,062 | 552,697 |
| 2017 | 522,396 | 463,549 | 414,754 | 371,774 | 316,608 | 275,307 | 220,012 | 216,938 | 377,400 | 519,847 | 568,117 | 521,589 |
| 2018 | 479,654 | 446,194 | 403,945 | 356,223 | 312,151 | 276,599 | 240,908 | 257,797 | 443,885 | 558,378 | 592,617 | 530,696 |
| 2019 | 475,712 | 433,018 | 394,400 | 351,796 | 295,948 | 259,917 | 240,636 | 250,720 | 461,516 | 662,567 | 674,400 | 637,174 |
| 2020 | 567,306 | 510,508 | 451,650 | 418,608 | 372,483 | 316,418 | 270,432 | 261,628 | 428,745 | 648,159 | 694,618 | 644,835 |
| 2021 | 597,036 | 564,162 | 511,718 | 449,689 | 389,300 | 325,593 | 264,952 | 275,274 | 452,627 | 675,517 | 722,281 | 666,265 |
| 2022[1] | 612,730 | 568,673 | 515,485 | 435,525 | 414,658 | 355,657 | 282,762 | 260,024 | 408,006 | 654,728 | 688,599 | 651,364 |

[1] Preliminary.   [2] Cut.   *Source: Economic Research Service, U.S. Department of Agriculture (ERS-USDA)*

# VEGETABLES

### Cold Storage Stocks of Frozen Sweet Corn[2] in the United States, on First of Month   In Thousands of Pounds

| Year | Jan. | Feb. | Mar. | Apr. | May | June | July | Aug. | Sept. | Oct. | Nov. | Dec. |
|---|---|---|---|---|---|---|---|---|---|---|---|---|
| 2013 | 235,766 | 219,301 | 202,672 | 173,684 | 150,267 | 123,501 | 100,019 | 83,647 | 151,447 | 244,077 | 271,819 | 251,382 |
| 2014 | 238,575 | 225,426 | 200,562 | 174,569 | 156,311 | 121,262 | 101,087 | 108,477 | 175,199 | 258,604 | 268,087 | 240,784 |
| 2015 | 223,053 | 206,000 | 175,910 | 156,425 | 132,387 | 110,912 | 88,817 | 112,873 | 165,657 | 239,922 | 244,687 | 229,113 |
| 2016 | 220,295 | 216,834 | 198,513 | 164,351 | 135,956 | 112,977 | 91,597 | 97,354 | 177,551 | 223,337 | 250,261 | 227,305 |
| 2017 | 207,064 | 197,123 | 177,461 | 150,107 | 128,032 | 101,904 | 73,922 | 74,754 | 181,921 | 278,137 | 297,466 | 286,139 |
| 2018 | 257,185 | 231,840 | 207,582 | 176,477 | 142,645 | 107,713 | 79,134 | 105,145 | 208,224 | 276,776 | 307,075 | 288,300 |
| 2019 | 269,689 | 242,621 | 226,032 | 202,924 | 169,151 | 149,776 | 137,539 | 137,583 | 246,139 | 332,852 | 345,723 | 307,982 |
| 2020 | 275,612 | 246,556 | 216,990 | 191,158 | 177,364 | 133,697 | 106,869 | 128,561 | 207,408 | 290,645 | 317,958 | 306,616 |
| 2021 | 272,573 | 234,201 | 207,331 | 169,892 | 132,944 | 112,487 | 78,876 | 91,040 | 194,189 | 307,591 | 357,651 | 327,096 |
| 2022[1] | 300,426 | 272,063 | 239,377 | 220,008 | 193,655 | 172,037 | 161,681 | 164,793 | 280,245 | 334,702 | 367,932 | 332,755 |

[1] Preliminary.   [2] Cob.   Source: Economic Research Service, U.S. Department of Agriculture (ERS-USDA)

### Cold Storage Stocks of Mixed Vegetables in the United States, on First of Month   In Thousands of Pounds

| Year | Jan. | Feb. | Mar. | Apr. | May | June | July | Aug. | Sept. | Oct. | Nov. | Dec. |
|---|---|---|---|---|---|---|---|---|---|---|---|---|
| 2013 | 43,340 | 46,003 | 44,219 | 40,716 | 44,956 | 44,713 | 46,674 | 47,610 | 51,082 | 51,341 | 48,420 | 51,988 |
| 2014 | 50,977 | 56,257 | 54,208 | 47,594 | 48,023 | 47,670 | 49,422 | 52,108 | 58,514 | 60,248 | 62,359 | 59,702 |
| 2015 | 53,082 | 55,851 | 56,039 | 57,851 | 59,040 | 58,132 | 58,099 | 56,960 | 60,109 | 62,186 | 58,359 | 55,274 |
| 2016 | 55,067 | 56,725 | 55,364 | 57,650 | 59,996 | 61,403 | 60,593 | 66,007 | 65,596 | 65,498 | 62,944 | 61,384 |
| 2017 | 62,424 | 68,538 | 68,978 | 72,412 | 73,221 | 69,127 | 69,734 | 67,369 | 72,540 | 74,115 | 71,407 | 68,516 |
| 2018 | 57,762 | 59,410 | 60,105 | 53,310 | 52,886 | 54,013 | 56,417 | 60,139 | 66,995 | 63,700 | 60,301 | 56,423 |
| 2019 | 53,845 | 52,405 | 54,958 | 53,253 | 55,753 | 48,189 | 47,214 | 52,260 | 50,131 | 47,185 | 50,241 | 41,737 |
| 2020 | 41,323 | 42,714 | 45,978 | 41,802 | 44,271 | 44,150 | 45,371 | 46,385 | 51,430 | 55,198 | 52,011 | 48,504 |
| 2021 | 50,758 | 51,609 | 55,592 | 52,793 | 56,307 | 56,589 | 61,610 | 59,752 | 64,928 | 66,635 | 57,398 | 51,599 |
| 2022[1] | 47,821 | 45,533 | 44,307 | 42,537 | 47,473 | 50,865 | 53,742 | 48,908 | 48,795 | 60,713 | 52,232 | 45,326 |

[1] Preliminary.   Source: Economic Research Service, U.S. Department of Agriculture (ERS-USDA)

### Cold Storage Stocks of Frozen Okra in the United States, on First of Month   In Thousands of Pounds

| Year | Jan. | Feb. | Mar. | Apr. | May | June | July | Aug. | Sept. | Oct. | Nov. | Dec. |
|---|---|---|---|---|---|---|---|---|---|---|---|---|
| 2013 | 23,643 | 19,951 | 14,701 | 10,579 | 9,713 | 11,107 | 17,750 | 23,728 | 26,156 | 25,739 | 28,318 | 26,182 |
| 2014 | 21,405 | 14,964 | 10,651 | 7,129 | 7,353 | 7,670 | 14,800 | 26,511 | 36,605 | 46,743 | 48,448 | 44,192 |
| 2015 | 39,375 | 34,631 | 29,153 | 23,998 | 19,361 | 16,410 | 16,337 | 31,938 | 48,184 | 66,862 | 70,851 | 63,695 |
| 2016 | 56,080 | 46,590 | 38,266 | 27,614 | 18,995 | 15,574 | 27,167 | 40,280 | 46,536 | 51,893 | 45,379 | 38,372 |
| 2017 | 33,964 | 27,901 | 22,677 | 15,482 | 12,582 | 13,608 | 24,246 | 35,802 | 38,821 | 41,607 | 35,675 | 30,451 |
| 2018 | 27,190 | 20,870 | 16,743 | 14,666 | 13,443 | 12,632 | 30,181 | 41,318 | 50,058 | 54,779 | 55,093 | 48,631 |
| 2019 | 44,156 | 37,915 | 31,855 | 21,396 | 16,652 | 17,388 | 28,658 | 43,014 | 56,509 | 58,883 | 57,568 | 52,782 |
| 2020 | 48,906 | 43,036 | 35,209 | 27,603 | 25,797 | 26,520 | 33,460 | 39,287 | 41,001 | 41,934 | 40,734 | 38,120 |
| 2021 | 33,817 | 28,637 | 25,641 | 20,088 | 15,071 | 13,626 | 19,240 | 29,431 | 35,977 | 39,183 | 39,815 | 39,424 |
| 2022[1] | 34,970 | 31,655 | 28,607 | 21,228 | 18,517 | 13,545 | 19,222 | 28,371 | 33,950 | 37,250 | 38,050 | 35,990 |

[1] Preliminary.   Source: Economic Research Service, U.S. Department of Agriculture (ERS-USDA)

### Cold Storage Stocks of Frozen Blackeye Peas in the United States, on First of Month   In Thousands of Pounds

| Year | Jan. | Feb. | Mar. | Apr. | May | June | July | Aug. | Sept. | Oct. | Nov. | Dec. |
|---|---|---|---|---|---|---|---|---|---|---|---|---|
| 2013 | 1,597 | 1,650 | 1,455 | 1,987 | 1,415 | 1,647 | 1,693 | 1,787 | 2,430 | 3,004 | 2,249 | 1,540 |
| 2014 | 1,386 | 1,925 | 1,620 | 2,072 | 1,684 | 2,145 | 1,655 | 1,830 | 1,484 | 1,784 | 1,870 | 1,929 |
| 2015 | 1,565 | 1,969 | 1,846 | 1,822 | 2,364 | 2,816 | 2,869 | 2,975 | 2,121 | 2,330 | 2,159 | 2,493 |
| 2016 | 2,434 | 2,245 | 2,249 | 2,222 | 1,740 | 1,674 | 1,377 | 1,511 | 1,332 | 1,650 | 1,243 | 1,629 |
| 2017 | 1,600 | 1,806 | 1,758 | 1,440 | 1,477 | 1,308 | 1,804 | 1,728 | 1,900 | 2,048 | 2,015 | 1,564 |
| 2018 | 1,484 | 1,606 | 1,655 | 1,512 | 1,357 | 1,407 | 1,293 | 2,089 | 2,009 | 2,000 | 2,037 | 1,790 |
| 2019 | 1,479 | 1,497 | 1,394 | 1,712 | 1,495 | 1,373 | 1,413 | 1,615 | 1,655 | 1,930 | 1,904 | 1,332 |
| 2020 | 1,227 | 1,187 | 1,135 | 1,338 | 1,499 | 1,749 | 2,168 | 1,589 | 1,759 | 1,723 | 1,261 | 1,623 |
| 2021 | 1,779 | 1,345 | 1,375 | 2,623 | 3,253 | 2,909 | 2,645 | 2,318 | 2,692 | 2,300 | 2,118 | 3,512 |
| 2022[1] | 2,497 | 2,076 | 1,830 | 1,518 | 1,465 | 1,411 | 1,397 | 1,498 | 1,855 | 1,401 | 1,275 | 1,400 |

[1] Preliminary.   Source: Economic Research Service, U.S. Department of Agriculture (ERS-USDA)

# VEGETABLES

### Cold Storage Stocks of Frozen Green Peas in the United States, on First of Month   In Thousands of Pounds

| Year | Jan. | Feb. | Mar. | Apr. | May | June | July | Aug. | Sept. | Oct. | Nov. | Dec. |
|---|---|---|---|---|---|---|---|---|---|---|---|---|
| 2013 | 219,559 | 195,388 | 165,683 | 138,449 | 112,263 | 99,542 | 240,208 | 392,588 | 349,572 | 305,131 | 285,313 | 256,457 |
| 2014 | 228,586 | 192,134 | 168,608 | 136,081 | 111,179 | 95,529 | 284,293 | 427,634 | 395,401 | 354,716 | 314,577 | 285,406 |
| 2015 | 243,251 | 205,887 | 189,997 | 154,385 | 127,621 | 127,985 | 314,155 | 414,632 | 397,020 | 372,987 | 335,536 | 308,934 |
| 2016 | 274,778 | 251,096 | 225,590 | 195,128 | 166,005 | 173,146 | 360,749 | 455,262 | 437,827 | 401,126 | 361,786 | 343,397 |
| 2017 | 323,820 | 294,248 | 267,497 | 238,263 | 205,494 | 191,203 | 322,460 | 428,002 | 410,645 | 381,666 | 342,202 | 305,457 |
| 2018 | 277,206 | 247,040 | 223,679 | 198,966 | 190,125 | 177,152 | 284,008 | 341,193 | 319,549 | 303,905 | 268,892 | 244,288 |
| 2019 | 207,808 | 188,769 | 174,792 | 147,662 | 132,510 | 121,763 | 233,194 | 385,001 | 352,447 | 309,511 | 277,596 | 250,797 |
| 2020 | 212,684 | 185,946 | 154,812 | 135,690 | 112,569 | 90,073 | 232,490 | 341,429 | 342,432 | 309,867 | 279,854 | 259,458 |
| 2021 | 243,072 | 206,560 | 180,490 | 156,380 | 138,486 | 125,457 | 231,790 | 320,166 | 309,734 | 282,403 | 263,263 | 240,454 |
| 2022[1] | 207,468 | 181,801 | 165,547 | 130,025 | 115,849 | 99,425 | 167,215 | 334,539 | 303,787 | 289,483 | 260,744 | 251,800 |

[1] Preliminary.   Source: Economic Research Service, U.S. Department of Agriculture (ERS-USDA)


### Cold Storage Stocks of Frozen Peas & Carrots in the United States, on First of Month   In Thousands of Pounds

| Year | Jan. | Feb. | Mar. | Apr. | May | June | July | Aug. | Sept. | Oct. | Nov. | Dec. |
|---|---|---|---|---|---|---|---|---|---|---|---|---|
| 2013 | 7,178 | 7,660 | 7,539 | 6,546 | 7,376 | 6,382 | 6,951 | 6,862 | 6,948 | 6,476 | 6,675 | 6,726 |
| 2014 | 6,250 | 6,051 | 7,608 | 7,234 | 7,106 | 6,494 | 7,274 | 7,813 | 7,840 | 7,703 | 7,483 | 7,525 |
| 2015 | 7,671 | 7,299 | 7,326 | 7,315 | 6,964 | 7,459 | 7,580 | 7,637 | 8,292 | 8,225 | 8,135 | 7,751 |
| 2016 | 7,052 | 7,409 | 7,783 | 8,168 | 8,970 | 8,308 | 8,348 | 8,125 | 8,462 | 8,570 | 8,046 | 6,640 |
| 2017 | 6,884 | 7,052 | 7,082 | 7,843 | 8,829 | 8,820 | 8,989 | 8,965 | 8,685 | 8,985 | 9,184 | 8,819 |
| 2018 | 7,914 | 7,454 | 8,135 | 7,410 | 8,083 | 7,758 | 6,754 | 7,424 | 7,605 | 6,947 | 7,457 | 6,928 |
| 2019 | 7,262 | 7,826 | 7,391 | 8,001 | 7,954 | 8,436 | 9,098 | 9,953 | 9,545 | 8,515 | 8,423 | 8,567 |
| 2020 | 9,058 | 10,076 | 10,364 | 9,479 | 10,361 | 9,129 | 8,779 | 8,490 | 8,965 | 7,877 | 7,778 | 7,420 |
| 2021 | 7,809 | 9,101 | 8,613 | 9,350 | 9,409 | 8,253 | 7,890 | 8,659 | 8,190 | 7,173 | 6,324 | 6,356 |
| 2022[1] | 6,605 | 6,462 | 6,036 | 5,387 | 5,935 | 6,575 | 5,662 | 6,440 | 6,198 | 6,465 | 7,093 | 6,685 |

[1] Preliminary.   Source: Economic Research Service, U.S. Department of Agriculture (ERS-USDA)


### Cold Storage Stocks of Other Frozen Vegetables in the United States, on First of Month   In Thousands of lbs

| Year | Jan. | Feb. | Mar. | Apr. | May | June | July | Aug. | Sept. | Oct. | Nov. | Dec. |
|---|---|---|---|---|---|---|---|---|---|---|---|---|
| 2013 | 387,366 | 363,899 | 352,909 | 350,651 | 349,274 | 301,871 | 298,588 | 310,171 | 369,266 | 436,882 | 455,362 | 433,678 |
| 2014 | 425,010 | 371,053 | 366,772 | 359,294 | 311,776 | 285,450 | 281,639 | 310,021 | 348,093 | 402,271 | 415,446 | 392,454 |
| 2015 | 381,070 | 357,718 | 335,823 | 327,915 | 319,475 | 307,475 | 302,891 | 321,753 | 364,047 | 397,496 | 407,400 | 391,876 |
| 2016 | 391,886 | 368,774 | 346,407 | 326,102 | 322,249 | 328,465 | 331,768 | 340,474 | 405,041 | 441,482 | 476,689 | 463,852 |
| 2017 | 453,978 | 447,244 | 447,065 | 451,698 | 416,977 | 385,932 | 397,044 | 418,221 | 518,807 | 618,682 | 660,094 | 646,967 |
| 2018 | 626,616 | 563,016 | 504,878 | 461,985 | 406,018 | 376,945 | 377,555 | 422,205 | 502,853 | 569,778 | 623,597 | 603,165 |
| 2019 | 582,039 | 535,862 | 510,354 | 476,131 | 440,646 | 377,702 | 355,236 | 354,953 | 384,582 | 423,955 | 458,115 | 455,499 |
| 2020 | 435,111 | 406,680 | 402,718 | 386,470 | 381,515 | 366,163 | 373,489 | 363,933 | 686,604 | 449,473 | 499,198 | 477,272 |
| 2021 | 460,079 | 434,674 | 400,757 | 372,563 | 357,090 | 342,259 | 323,050 | 323,858 | 338,441 | 376,810 | 419,162 | 424,223 |
| 2022[1] | 401,496 | 358,563 | 337,398 | 320,872 | 315,329 | 310,075 | 302,060 | 307,282 | 329,977 | 364,602 | 390,779 | 395,983 |

[1] Preliminary.   Source: Economic Research Service, U.S. Department of Agriculture (ERS-USDA)


### Cold Storage Stocks of Total Frozen Vegetables in the United States, on First of Month   In Millions of Pounds

| Year | Jan. | Feb. | Mar. | Apr. | May | June | July | Aug. | Sept. | Oct. | Nov. | Dec. |
|---|---|---|---|---|---|---|---|---|---|---|---|---|
| 2013 | 2,366.0 | 2,203.9 | 2,046.3 | 1,874.4 | 1,760.8 | 1,581.4 | 1,646.3 | 1,763.7 | 2,090.0 | 2,431.0 | 2,578.5 | 2,480.2 |
| 2014 | 2,360.4 | 2,157.4 | 2,025.0 | 1,842.1 | 1,660.2 | 1,519.9 | 1,607.9 | 1,863.8 | 2,232.8 | 2,530.6 | 2,663.6 | 2,546.8 |
| 2015 | 2,359.3 | 2,144.9 | 1,995.5 | 1,850.1 | 1,714.1 | 1,620.7 | 1,697.1 | 1,889.1 | 2,222.9 | 2,570.1 | 2,688.7 | 2,580.2 |
| 2016 | 2,423.8 | 2,302.3 | 2,169.7 | 1,973.7 | 1,861.4 | 1,769.2 | 1,855.6 | 2,028.6 | 2,413.9 | 2,626.6 | 2,757.7 | 2,695.1 |
| 2017 | 2,570.3 | 2,407.5 | 2,256.6 | 2,125.7 | 1,954.2 | 1,803.6 | 1,814.2 | 1,938.1 | 2,366.1 | 2,731.8 | 2,866.1 | 2,788.6 |
| 2018 | 2,626.0 | 2,412.9 | 2,221.9 | 2,018.1 | 1,838.3 | 1,682.5 | 1,706.5 | 1,867.7 | 2,276.2 | 2,544.6 | 2,669.9 | 2,548.1 |
| 2019 | 2,374.2 | 2,193.7 | 2,064.7 | 1,902.1 | 1,738.6 | 1,575.7 | 1,621.9 | 1,821.9 | 2,191.6 | 2,530.1 | 2,615.7 | 2,555.2 |
| 2020 | 2,354.6 | 2,184.6 | 2,018.9 | 1,869.7 | 1,759.6 | 1,598.3 | 1,643.5 | 1,781.1 | 2,122.9 | 2,531.8 | 2,693.5 | 2,616.5 |
| 2021 | 2,485.5 | 2,283.8 | 2,102.0 | 1,889.7 | 1,750.9 | 1,610.8 | 1,588.7 | 1,716.8 | 2,039.4 | 2,437.8 | 2,613.5 | 2,554.0 |
| 2022[1] | 2,378.3 | 2,183.0 | 2,011.9 | 1,821.5 | 1,738.9 | 1,614.2 | 1,562.2 | 1,712.4 | 2,032.7 | 2,429.9 | 2,552.0 | 2,491.9 |

[1] Preliminary.   Source: Economic Research Service, U.S. Department of Agriculture (ERS-USDA)

# Wheat

Wheat is a cereal grass. Wheat was a wild grass before humans started to cultivate it for larger-scale food production. It has been grown in temperate regions and cultivated for food since prehistoric times. Wheat is believed to have originated in southwestern Asia. Archeological research indicates that wheat was grown as a crop in the Nile Valley about 5,000 BC. Wheat is not native to the U.S. and was first grown here in 1602 near the Massachusetts coast. The common types of wheat grown in the U.S. are spring and winter wheat. Wheat planted in the spring for summer or autumn harvest is mostly red wheat. Wheat planted in the fall or winter for spring harvest is mostly white wheat. Winter wheat accounts for nearly three-fourths of total U.S. production. Wheat is used mainly for human consumption and supplies about 20% of the food calories for the world's population. The primary use for wheat is flour, but it is also used for brewing and distilling, and for making oil, gluten, straw for livestock bedding, livestock feed, hay or silage, newsprint, and other products.

Wheat futures and options are traded at the CME Group, the Mercado a Termino de Buenos Aires (MAT), Sydney Futures Exchange (SFE), London International Financial Futures and Options Exchange (LIFFE), Marche a Terme International de France (MATIF), Budapest Commodity Exchange (BCE), the Kansas City Board of Trade (KCBT), and the Minneapolis Grain Exchange (MGE). The CME's wheat futures contract calls for the delivery of soft red wheat (No. 1 and 2), hard red winter wheat (No. 1 and 2), dark northern spring wheat (No. 1 and 2), No.1 northern spring at 3 cents/bushel premium, or No. 2 northern spring at par.

**Prices** – CME wheat futures prices (Barchart.com symbol ZW) surged in early 2022 to a record high of $14.25 per bushel in March 2022. Wheat prices soared after Russia invaded Ukraine, and wheat exports from both countries were sharply reduced. The war closed major Black Sea ports in Ukraine, and the subsequent sanctions against Russia reduced demand for its wheat exports. Ukraine and Russia together account for a quarter of the global wheat trade. Wheat prices also garnered support from drought concerns in the Great Plains that parched the U.S. 2022 winter wheat crop, which was the smallest since 1963. In addition, the USDA in its May WASDE reported that 2022/23 global wheat ending stocks fell to a 6-year low of 267 MMT. Wheat prices remained above $10 per bushel into June after India, the world's second-largest wheat producer said it was banning wheat exports to ensure adequate domestic supplies. Wheat prices retreated below $10 per bushel into Q3 2022 and posted a 1-year low of $7.26 per bushel in August after Turkey brokered a plan with Russia to allow Ukraine to resume wheat exports at several of its Black Sea ports. Also, a rally in the dollar index to a 20-year high in September made U.S. wheat supplies less competitive in the global market. In the October WASDE report, the USDA cut its U.S. 2022/23 wheat export estimate to 775 million bushels, the lowest in 50 years. Wheat prices rebounded into October as Russia intensified its war in Ukraine, stoking fears it would not extend a Ukraine export deal. However, wheat prices dropped to a 1-year low of $7.03 per bushel in December after the Russia-Ukraine export agreement allowing safe passage of grain exports from Ukraine's Black Sea ports was extended. Wheat prices recovered into year-end after a record cold snap in the U.S. threatened the U.S. winter wheat crop. Wheat prices finished 2022 up +2.7% yr/yr at $7.92 per bushel.

**Supply** – World wheat production in the 2022/23 marketing year is forecasted to rise by +0.3% yr/yr to 781.312 million metric tons, a new record high. The world's largest wheat producers in 2022/23 are expected to be China with 17.6% of world production, the European Union with 17.2%, India with 13.2%, Russia with 11.6%, and the U.S. with 5.7%. China's wheat production in 2022/23 is expected to rise by +0.6% yr/yr to a record 137.723 million metric tons. India's wheat production in 2022/23 is expected to fall by -6.0% yr/yr to 103.00 million metric tons. The world land area harvested with wheat in 2022/23 is expected to fall -1.0% yr/yr to 220.0 million hectares (1 hectare equals 10,000 square meters or 2.471 acres). The world wheat yield in 2022/23 is expected to rise by +1.1% yr/yr to 3.55 million metric tons, forecasted to be a record high from the 2019/29 high record of 3.53 million metric tons.

U.S. wheat production in 2022/23 is expected to rise by +0.2% yr/yr to 1.649 billion bushels. The U.S. winter wheat crop in 2022 fell by -13.6% yr/yr to 1.103 billion bushels, which was well below the record winter wheat crop of 2.097 billion bushels seen in 1981. U.S. production of durum wheat in 2022 rose by +1599.9% yr/yr to 639.981 million bushels. U.S. production of other spring wheat in 2022 rose by +45.7% yr/yr to 482.190 million bushels. The largest U.S. producing states of winter wheat in 2022 was Kansas with 22.1% of U.S. production, Washington with 11.1%, Oklahoma with 6.2%, Idaho with 5.8%, and Montana with 5.4%. U.S. farmers planted 45.738 million acres of wheat in 2022, down by -2.1% yr/yr. The U.S. wheat yield in 2022/23 is expected to be up by +5.0% yr/yr at 46.5 bushels per acre.

**Demand** – World wheat utilization in 2022/23 is forecasted to fall by -0.3% yr/yr to 789.7 million metric tons, falling below the record high of 792.5 million metric tons in 2021/22. U.S. consumption of wheat in 2022/23 is expected to fall by -0.7% yr/yr to 1.118 billion bushels, which would be below the 2012/13 record high of 1.389 billion bushels. The wheat usage breakdown in 2022/23 is expected to be 86.8% for food, 7.2% for feed and residuals, and 6.1% for seed.

**Trade** – World trade in wheat in 2022/23 is expected to rise by +4.5% yr/yr to a record 211.6 million metric tons. U.S. exports of wheat in 2022/23 are expected to rise by +3.1% yr/yr to 825.0 million bushels. U.S. imports of wheat in 2022/23 are expected to rise by +15.5% yr/yr to 110.0 million bushels.

# WHEAT

**World Production of Wheat**  In Thousands of Metric Tons

| Crop Year | Australia | Canada | China | European Union | India | Iran | Kazakh-stan | Pakistan | Russia | Turkey | Ukraine | United States | World Total |
|---|---|---|---|---|---|---|---|---|---|---|---|---|---|
| 2013-14 | 25,303 | 37,589 | 123,639 | 144,583 | 93,506 | 14,000 | 13,941 | 24,211 | 52,091 | 18,750 | 22,278 | 58,105 | 716,738 |
| 2014-15 | 23,743 | 29,442 | 128,235 | 156,912 | 95,850 | 13,000 | 12,996 | 25,979 | 59,080 | 15,250 | 24,750 | 55,147 | 730,255 |
| 2015-16 | 22,275 | 27,647 | 132,555 | 160,480 | 86,527 | 14,500 | 13,748 | 25,086 | 61,044 | 19,500 | 27,274 | 56,117 | 737,958 |
| 2016-17 | 31,819 | 32,140 | 133,188 | 130,986 | 87,000 | 14,500 | 14,985 | 25,633 | 72,529 | 17,250 | 26,791 | 62,832 | 756,144 |
| 2017-18 | 20,941 | 30,377 | 134,241 | 136,681 | 98,510 | 12,700 | 14,802 | 26,674 | 85,167 | 21,000 | 26,981 | 47,380 | 761,564 |
| 2018-19 | 17,598 | 32,352 | 131,441 | 123,124 | 99,870 | 14,500 | 13,947 | 25,076 | 71,685 | 19,000 | 25,057 | 51,306 | 730,920 |
| 2019-20 | 14,480 | 32,670 | 133,600 | 138,799 | 103,600 | 15,550 | 11,452 | 24,349 | 73,610 | 17,500 | 29,171 | 52,581 | 761,507 |
| 2020-21[1] | 31,923 | 35,437 | 134,250 | 126,684 | 107,860 | 15,000 | 14,256 | 25,248 | 85,352 | 18,250 | 25,420 | 49,751 | 774,547 |
| 2021-22[2] | 36,347 | 22,296 | 136,946 | 138,216 | 109,586 | 12,000 | 11,814 | 27,464 | 75,158 | 16,000 | 33,007 | 44,804 | 779,314 |
| 2022-23[3] | 36,600 | 33,824 | 137,723 | 134,700 | 103,000 | 13,200 | 14,000 | 26,400 | 91,000 | 17,250 | 21,000 | 44,902 | 781,312 |

[1] Preliminary.  [2] Estimate.  [3] Forecast.  *Source: Foreign Agricultural Service, U.S. Department of Agriculture (FAS-USDA)*

**World Consumption of Wheat**  In Thousands of Metric Tons

| Crop Year | Australia | Brazil | China | Egypt | European Union | India | Iran | Pakistan | Russia | Turkey | Ukraine | United States | World Total |
|---|---|---|---|---|---|---|---|---|---|---|---|---|---|
| 2013-14 | 6,950 | 11,400 | 117,500 | 18,500 | 116,300 | 93,848 | 16,250 | 24,100 | 34,100 | 17,750 | 11,500 | 34,260 | 690,107 |
| 2014-15 | 7,200 | 10,700 | 118,000 | 19,100 | 124,677 | 93,102 | 16,400 | 24,500 | 35,500 | 17,500 | 11,500 | 31,328 | 701,066 |
| 2015-16 | 7,125 | 11,100 | 117,500 | 19,200 | 129,850 | 88,548 | 16,100 | 24,400 | 37,000 | 17,700 | 12,200 | 31,943 | 712,793 |
| 2016-17 | 7,450 | 11,800 | 119,000 | 19,400 | 112,100 | 97,234 | 16,250 | 24,500 | 40,000 | 17,000 | 10,300 | 31,865 | 733,837 |
| 2017-18 | 8,475 | 11,800 | 121,000 | 19,800 | 113,500 | 95,677 | 15,900 | 25,000 | 43,000 | 18,300 | 9,800 | 29,245 | 740,590 |
| 2018-19 | 9,200 | 11,900 | 125,000 | 20,100 | 106,300 | 95,629 | 16,100 | 25,400 | 40,500 | 18,800 | 8,800 | 29,986 | 732,206 |
| 2019-20 | 8,000 | 11,900 | 126,000 | 20,300 | 107,250 | 95,403 | 17,200 | 25,500 | 40,000 | 20,000 | 8,300 | 30,437 | 740,365 |
| 2020-21[1] | 8,025 | 11,800 | 150,000 | 20,500 | 104,750 | 102,217 | 17,400 | 26,300 | 42,500 | 20,600 | 8,700 | 30,412 | 774,019 |
| 2021-22[2] | 8,525 | 11,750 | 148,000 | 20,500 | 108,250 | 109,882 | 18,200 | 27,700 | 42,750 | 20,200 | 10,000 | 29,607 | 788,408 |
| 2022-23[3] | 8,550 | 11,700 | 144,000 | 20,600 | 108,250 | 104,075 | 17,800 | 29,200 | 45,000 | 20,500 | 9,200 | 30,644 | 783,163 |

[1] Preliminary.  [2] Estimate.  [3] Forecast.  *Source: Foreign Agricultural Service, U.S. Department of Agriculture (FAS-USDA)*

**World Exports of Wheat**  In Thousands of Metric Tons

| Crop Year | Argentina | Australia | Brazil | Canada | European Union | Kazakh-stan | Mexico | Russia | Turkey | Ukraine | United States | Uruguay | World Total |
|---|---|---|---|---|---|---|---|---|---|---|---|---|---|
| 2013-14 | 2,250 | 18,615 | 80 | 23,268 | 32,035 | 8,100 | 1,322 | 18,609 | 4,449 | 9,755 | 32,012 | 1,384 | 165,935 |
| 2014-15 | 5,301 | 16,591 | 1,691 | 24,170 | 35,455 | 5,539 | 1,104 | 22,800 | 4,090 | 11,269 | 23,523 | 624 | 164,253 |
| 2015-16 | 9,600 | 16,119 | 1,059 | 22,091 | 34,760 | 7,414 | 1,568 | 25,546 | 5,878 | 17,431 | 21,168 | 692 | 172,972 |
| 2016-17 | 13,825 | 22,644 | 619 | 20,218 | 28,366 | 7,409 | 1,119 | 27,815 | 6,699 | 18,107 | 28,600 | 246 | 186,783 |
| 2017-18 | 12,730 | 13,849 | 230 | 22,000 | 24,895 | 9,000 | 1,147 | 41,447 | 6,698 | 17,775 | 24,658 | 44 | 185,432 |
| 2018-19 | 12,188 | 9,006 | 602 | 24,404 | 24,686 | 8,296 | 526 | 35,863 | 6,814 | 16,019 | 25,503 | 325 | 176,200 |
| 2019-20 | 12,785 | 9,136 | 425 | 24,142 | 39,788 | 6,986 | 1,168 | 34,485 | 6,534 | 21,016 | 26,373 | 279 | 193,969 |
| 2020-21[1] | 11,531 | 23,773 | 925 | 26,429 | 29,736 | 8,194 | 612 | 39,100 | 6,469 | 16,851 | 27,048 | 534 | 203,326 |
| 2021-22[2] | 15,975 | 27,532 | 3,070 | 15,134 | 31,915 | 8,098 | 924 | 33,000 | 6,714 | 18,844 | 21,782 | 450 | 202,553 |
| 2022-23[3] | 7,500 | 27,500 | 3,500 | 26,000 | 36,500 | 9,000 | 900 | 43,000 | 6,750 | 13,000 | 21,092 | 500 | 211,621 |

[1] Preliminary.  [2] Estimate.  [3] Forecast.  *Source: Foreign Agricultural Service, U.S. Department of Agriculture (FAS-USDA)*

**World Imports of Wheat**  In Thousands of Metric Tons

| Crop Year | Algeria | Brazil | Egypt | European Union | Indonesia | Iran | Japan | Korea, South | Mexico | Nigeria | Philip-pines | Turkey | World Total |
|---|---|---|---|---|---|---|---|---|---|---|---|---|---|
| 2013-14 | 7,484 | 7,066 | 10,150 | 3,976 | 7,391 | 4,850 | 6,123 | 4,288 | 4,639 | 4,580 | 3,476 | 4,070 | 158,953 |
| 2014-15 | 7,257 | 5,374 | 11,300 | 5,977 | 7,477 | 6,315 | 5,878 | 3,942 | 4,471 | 4,244 | 5,054 | 5,841 | 159,410 |
| 2015-16 | 8,153 | 6,745 | 11,925 | 6,928 | 10,045 | 3,500 | 5,715 | 4,420 | 4,805 | 4,410 | 4,919 | 4,087 | 170,020 |
| 2016-17 | 8,414 | 7,349 | 11,181 | 6,287 | 10,190 | 1,200 | 5,911 | 4,667 | 5,370 | 4,972 | 5,708 | 4,732 | 183,477 |
| 2017-18 | 8,172 | 7,021 | 12,407 | 6,060 | 10,763 | 200 | 5,876 | 4,269 | 5,245 | 5,162 | 6,059 | 6,222 | 183,994 |
| 2018-19 | 7,515 | 7,020 | 12,354 | 5,763 | 10,934 | 180 | 5,726 | 3,908 | 4,861 | 4,659 | 7,570 | 6,395 | 174,168 |
| 2019-20 | 7,145 | 7,029 | 12,811 | 5,551 | 10,586 | 2,000 | 5,683 | 3,941 | 5,080 | 5,338 | 7,065 | 10,851 | 188,358 |
| 2020-21[1] | 7,680 | 6,395 | 12,149 | 5,390 | 9,995 | 2,200 | 5,493 | 3,889 | 4,724 | 6,586 | 6,113 | 8,081 | 194,683 |
| 2021-22[2] | 8,286 | 6,392 | 11,256 | 4,612 | 11,229 | 7,300 | 5,605 | 5,099 | 5,326 | 6,187 | 6,865 | 9,421 | 198,473 |
| 2022-23[3] | 8,200 | 5,600 | 11,000 | 8,000 | 11,000 | 5,000 | 5,750 | 5,000 | 5,000 | 6,100 | 6,500 | 10,000 | 205,046 |

[1] Preliminary.  [2] Estimate.  [3] Forecast.  *Source: Foreign Agricultural Service, U.S. Department of Agriculture (FAS-USDA)*

# WHEAT

## World Ending Stocks of Wheat    In Thousands of Metric Tons

| Crop Year | Australia | Canada | China | Egypt | European Union | India | Iran | Kazakh-stan | Morocco | Russia | Ukraine | United States | World Total |
|---|---|---|---|---|---|---|---|---|---|---|---|---|---|
| 2013-14 | 4,555 | 10,398 | 66,324 | 4,135 | 13,976 | 17,830 | 7,751 | 2,027 | 4,513 | 5,177 | 3,670 | 16,065 | 200,795 |
| 2014-15 | 4,665 | 7,101 | 77,682 | 4,353 | 16,733 | 17,220 | 9,466 | 3,284 | 4,417 | 6,287 | 5,678 | 20,477 | 225,141 |
| 2015-16 | 3,858 | 5,178 | 95,484 | 4,709 | 19,531 | 14,540 | 11,166 | 2,790 | 6,974 | 5,604 | 3,348 | 26,552 | 247,354 |
| 2016-17 | 5,750 | 6,931 | 113,334 | 4,125 | 13,551 | 9,800 | 10,416 | 3,537 | 4,926 | 10,823 | 1,773 | 32,131 | 266,355 |
| 2017-18 | 4,549 | 6,732 | 129,508 | 4,401 | 17,897 | 13,230 | 6,766 | 2,581 | 5,133 | 12,010 | 1,238 | 29,907 | 285,891 |
| 2018-19 | 4,440 | 6,041 | 138,088 | 4,015 | 15,798 | 16,992 | 4,936 | 1,713 | 5,423 | 7,778 | 1,555 | 29,386 | 282,573 |
| 2019-20 | 2,678 | 5,499 | 150,015 | 4,318 | 13,110 | 24,700 | 4,786 | 663 | 3,611 | 7,228 | 1,504 | 27,985 | 298,104 |
| 2020-21[1] | 3,001 | 5,953 | 144,120 | 4,162 | 10,698 | 27,800 | 4,336 | 1,475 | 1,147 | 11,380 | 1,505 | 23,001 | 289,989 |
| 2021-22[2] | 3,501 | 3,673 | 141,759 | 3,618 | 13,361 | 19,500 | 5,086 | 1,491 | 2,075 | 11,088 | 5,811 | 19,008 | 276,815 |
| 2022-23[3] | 4,251 | 3,547 | 144,082 | 3,418 | 11,311 | 12,625 | 5,086 | 1,641 | 1,600 | 14,388 | 4,711 | 15,440 | 268,389 |

[1] Preliminary.  [2] Estimate.  [3] Forecast.  Source: Foreign Agricultural Service, U.S. Department of Agriculture (FAS-USDA)

## World Supply and Demand of Wheat    In Millions of Metric Tons/Hectares

| Crop Year | Area Harvested | Yield | Production | World Trade | Utilization Total | Ending Stocks | Stocks as a % of Utilization |
|---|---|---|---|---|---|---|---|
| 2013-14 | 220.0 | 3.26 | 716.7 | 165.9 | 697.1 | 200.8 | 28.8 |
| 2014-15 | 221.3 | 3.30 | 730.3 | 164.3 | 705.9 | 225.1 | 31.9 |
| 2015-16 | 224.0 | 3.30 | 738.0 | 173.0 | 715.7 | 247.4 | 34.6 |
| 2016-17 | 222.3 | 3.40 | 756.1 | 186.8 | 737.1 | 266.4 | 36.1 |
| 2017-18 | 218.1 | 3.49 | 761.6 | 185.4 | 742.0 | 285.9 | 38.5 |
| 2018-19 | 215.4 | 3.39 | 730.9 | 176.2 | 734.2 | 282.6 | 38.5 |
| 2019-20 | 215.5 | 3.53 | 761.5 | 194.0 | 746.0 | 298.1 | 40.0 |
| 2020-21[1] | 220.5 | 3.51 | 774.5 | 203.3 | 782.7 | 290.0 | 37.1 |
| 2021-22[2] | 222.1 | 3.51 | 779.3 | 202.6 | 792.5 | 276.8 | 34.9 |
| 2022-23[3] | 220.0 | 3.55 | 781.3 | 211.6 | 789.7 | 268.4 | 34.0 |

[1] Preliminary.  [2] Estimate.  [3] Forecast.  Source: Foreign Agricultural Service, U.S. Department of Agriculture (FAS-USDA)

## Salient Statistics of Wheat in the United States

| Crop Year | Planting Intentions (1,000 Acres) | Winter (1,000 Acres) | Spring (1,000 Acres) | All (1,000 Acres) | Average All Yield Per Acre in Bushels | Value of Production $1,000 | Domestic Exports[2] (Mil Bu) | Imports[3] (Mil Bu) | Per Capita[4] Flour (Lbs) | Per Capita[4] Cereal (Lbs) |
|---|---|---|---|---|---|---|---|---|---|---|
| 2013-14 | 56,236 | 32,650 | 12,672 | 45,332 | 47.1 | 14,604,442 | 1,176.2 | 172.5 | 135.0 | ---- |
| 2014-15 | 56,841 | 32,299 | 14,086 | 46,385 | 43.7 | 11,914,954 | 864.3 | 151.2 | ---- | ---- |
| 2015-16 | 54,999 | 32,346 | 14,972 | 47,318 | 43.6 | 10,018,323 | 777.8 | 112.8 | ---- | ---- |
| 2016-17 | 50,116 | 20,235 | 13,613 | 43,848 | 52.7 | 9,179,190 | 1,050.9 | 118.0 | ---- | ---- |
| 2017-18 | 46,052 | 25,301 | 12,254 | 37,555 | 46.3 | 8,255,119 | 905.9 | 158.0 | ---- | ---- |
| 2018-19 | 47,815 | 24,742 | 14,870 | 39,612 | 47.6 | 9,661,916 | 937.1 | 134.6 | ---- | ---- |
| 2019-20 | 45,485 | 24,592 | 12,802 | 37,394 | 51.7 | 8,919,117 | 969.0 | 103.8 | ---- | ---- |
| 2020-21 | 44,450 | 23,029 | 13,760 | 36,789 | 49.7 | 9,389,104 | 993.9 | 100.1 | ---- | ---- |
| 2021-22 | 46,740 | 25,464 | 11,699 | 37,145 | 44.3 | 12,208,186 | 800.4 | 95.2 | ---- | ---- |
| 2022-23[1] | 45,738 | 23,459 | 12,021 | 35,480 | 46.5 | 14,595,696 | 825.0 | 110.0 | ---- | ---- |

[1] Preliminary.  [2] Includes flour milled from imported wheat.  [3] Total wheat, flour & other products.  [4] Civilian only.  [5] Year beginning June.
Source: Economic Research Service, U.S. Department of Agriculture (ERS-USDA)

## Supply and Distribution of Wheat in the United States    In Millions of Bushels

| Crop Year Beginning June 1 | Stocks, June 1 On Farms | Stocks, June 1 Mills, Elevators[3] | Total Stocks | Production | Imports[4] | Total Supply | Food | Seed | Feed & Residual[5] | Total | Exports[4] | Total Disappearance |
|---|---|---|---|---|---|---|---|---|---|---|---|---|
| 2013-14 | 120.2 | 597.7 | 717.9 | 2,135.0 | 172.5 | 3,025.3 | 955.1 | 75.6 | 228.2 | 1,258.8 | 1,176.2 | 2,435.1 |
| 2014-15 | 97.0 | 493.3 | 590.3 | 2,026.3 | 151.2 | 2,767.8 | 958.3 | 79.4 | 113.4 | 1,151.1 | 864.3 | 2,015.4 |
| 2015-16 | 155.2 | 597.2 | 752.4 | 2,061.9 | 112.8 | 2,927.1 | 957.2 | 67.2 | 149.4 | 1,173.8 | 777.8 | 1,951.5 |
| 2016-17 | 197.2 | 778.4 | 975.6 | 2,308.7 | 118.0 | 3,402.3 | 948.9 | 61.3 | 160.7 | 1,170.8 | 1,050.9 | 2,221.7 |
| 2017-18 | 191.8 | 988.8 | 1,180.6 | 1,739.6 | 158.0 | 3,079.5 | 964.2 | 63.4 | 47.2 | 1,074.7 | 905.9 | 1,980.7 |
| 2018-19 | 130.5 | 968.4 | 1,098.9 | 1,885.2 | 134.6 | 3,118.6 | 954.4 | 59.5 | 87.9 | 1,101.8 | 937.1 | 2,038.9 |
| 2019-20 | 206.5 | 873.2 | 1,079.8 | 1,932.0 | 103.8 | 3,115.6 | 961.6 | 60.0 | 96.7 | 1,118.3 | 969.0 | 2,087.3 |
| 2020-21 | 228.6 | 799.7 | 1,028.3 | 1,828.0 | 100.1 | 2,956.4 | 960.5 | 63.8 | 93.2 | 1,117.4 | 993.9 | 2,111.3 |
| 2021-22[1] | 141.7 | 703.5 | 845.2 | 1,646.3 | 95.2 | 2,586.1 | 971.5 | 60.0 | 94.3 | 1,125.8 | 800.4 | 1,926.1 |
| 2022-23[2] | 93.0 | 605.5 | 698.4 | 1,649.9 | 110.0 | 2,552.9 | 970.0 | 68.0 | 80.0 | 1,118.0 | 825.0 | 1,943.0 |

[1] Preliminary.  [2] Estimate.  [3] Also warehouses and all off-farm storage not otherwise designated, including flour mills.  [4] Imports & exports are for wheat, including flour & other products in terms of wheat.  [5] Mostly feed use.
Source: Economic Research Service, U.S. Department of Agriculture (ERS-USDA)

# WHEAT

## Stocks, Production and Exports of Wheat in the United States, by Class     In Millions of Bushels

|  | Hard Spring | | | Durum[2] | | | Hard Winter | | | Soft Red Winter | | | White | | |
|---|---|---|---|---|---|---|---|---|---|---|---|---|---|---|---|
| Crop Year | Stocks June 1 | Production | Exports[3] | Stocks June 1 | Production | Exports[3] | Stocks June 1 | Production | Exports[3] | Stocks June 1 | Production | Exports[3] | Stocks June 1 | Production | Exports[3] |
| 2013-14 | 165 | 491 | 246 | 23 | 58 | 32 | 343 | 747 | 446 | 124 | 568 | 283 | 63 | 271 | 170 |
| 2014-15 | 169 | 556 | 274 | 22 | 54 | 37 | 237 | 739 | 272 | 113 | 455 | 134 | 50 | 224 | 147 |
| 2015-16 | 212 | 568 | 254 | 26 | 84 | 29 | 294 | 830 | 227 | 154 | 359 | 120 | 67 | 221 | 147 |
| 2016-17 | 272 | 491 | 319 | 28 | 104 | 25 | 446 | 1,082 | 453 | 157 | 345 | 91 | 74 | 286 | 163 |
| 2017-18 | 235 | 384 | 229 | 36 | 55 | 18 | 589 | 750 | 373 | 215 | 293 | 91 | 105 | 259 | 195 |
| 2018-19 | 191 | 587 | 259 | 35 | 78 | 22 | 581 | 662 | 332 | 205 | 286 | 128 | 87 | 272 | 197 |
| 2019-20 | 263 | 520 | 269 | 55 | 54 | 42 | 516 | 845 | 378 | 158 | 240 | 92 | 88 | 273 | 188 |
| 2020-21 | 280 | 531 | 286 | 42 | 69 | 28 | 506 | 659 | 340 | 105 | 266 | 69 | 95 | 303 | 270 |
| 2021-22 | 235 | 297 | 209 | 27 | 38 | 14 | 428 | 750 | 317 | 85 | 361 | 112 | 70 | 201 | 148 |
| 2022-23[1] | 146 | 446 | 230 | 24 | 64 | 20 | 376 | 531 | 220 | 99 | 337 | 125 | 54 | 272 | 180 |

[1] Preliminary.   [2] Includes "Red Durum."   [3] Includes four made from U.S. wheat & shipments to territories.
*Source: Economic Research Service, U.S. Department of Agriculture (ERS-USDA)*

## Seeded Acreage, Yield and Production of all Wheat in the United States

|  | Seed Acreage - 1,000 Acres | | | | Yield Per Harvested Acre (Bushels) | | | | Production (Million Bushels) | | | |
|---|---|---|---|---|---|---|---|---|---|---|---|---|
| Year | Winter | Other Spring | Durum | All | Winter | Other Spring | Durum | All | Winter | Other Spring | Durum | All |
| 2013 | 43,230 | 11,606 | 1,400 | 56,236 | 47.3 | 47.1 | 43.3 | 47.1 | 1,542.9 | 534.1 | 58.0 | 2,135.0 |
| 2014 | 42,409 | 13,025 | 1,407 | 56,841 | 42.6 | 46.7 | 40.2 | 43.7 | 1,377.2 | 595.0 | 54.1 | 2,026.3 |
| 2015 | 39,681 | 13,367 | 1,951 | 54,999 | 42.5 | 46.3 | 43.5 | 43.6 | 1,374.7 | 603.2 | 84.0 | 2,061.9 |
| 2016 | 36,149 | 11,555 | 2,412 | 50,116 | 55.3 | 47.3 | 44.0 | 52.7 | 1,672.6 | 532.2 | 103.9 | 2,308.7 |
| 2017 | 32,726 | 11,019 | 2,307 | 46,052 | 50.2 | 41.0 | 26.0 | 46.3 | 1,270.3 | 415.9 | 54.8 | 1,739.6 |
| 2018 | 32,542 | 13,200 | 2,073 | 47,815 | 47.9 | 48.3 | 39.5 | 47.6 | 1,183.9 | 623.2 | 78.0 | 1,885.2 |
| 2019 | 31,474 | 12,670 | 1,341 | 45,485 | 53.6 | 48.3 | 45.8 | 51.7 | 1,317.0 | 561.1 | 54.0 | 1,932.0 |
| 2020 | 30,450 | 12,310 | 1,690 | 44,450 | 50.9 | 48.6 | 41.5 | 49.7 | 1,171.4 | 587.5 | 69.1 | 1,828.0 |
| 2021 | 33,678 | 11,420 | 1,642 | 46,740 | 50.2 | 32.6 | 24.7 | 44.3 | 1,277.8 | 330.9 | 37.6 | 1,646.3 |
| 2022[1] | 33,271 | 10,835 | 1,632 | 45,738 | 47.0 | 46.2 | 40.5 | 46.5 | 1,103.7 | 482.2 | 64.0 | 1,649.9 |

[1] Preliminary.   *Source: Economic Research Service, U.S. Department of Agriculture (ERS-USDA)*

## Production of Winter Wheat in the United States, by State     In Thousands of Bushels

| Year | Colorado | Idaho | Illinois | Kansas | Missouri | Montana | Nebraska | Ohio | Oklahoma | Oregon | Texas | Washington | Total |
|---|---|---|---|---|---|---|---|---|---|---|---|---|---|
| 2013 | 40,750 | 63,640 | 56,280 | 321,100 | 56,145 | 81,700 | 39,900 | 44,800 | 105,400 | 48,360 | 68,150 | 115,230 | 1,542,902 |
| 2014 | 89,300 | 58,400 | 44,890 | 246,400 | 42,920 | 91,840 | 71,050 | 40,330 | 47,600 | 40,700 | 67,500 | 85,280 | 1,377,216 |
| 2015 | 81,030 | 58,220 | 33,800 | 321,900 | 32,330 | 91,020 | 45,980 | 32,160 | 98,800 | 34,545 | 106,500 | 89,040 | 1,374,690 |
| 2016 | 105,120 | 66,740 | 34,780 | 467,400 | 39,900 | 105,350 | 70,740 | 44,800 | 136,500 | 35,500 | 89,600 | 130,260 | 1,672,582 |
| 2017 | 86,860 | 53,600 | 35,720 | 333,600 | 36,720 | 66,780 | 46,920 | 34,040 | 98,600 | 43,470 | 68,150 | 120,450 | 1,270,282 |
| 2018 | 70,200 | 61,200 | 36,960 | 277,400 | 30,680 | 78,500 | 49,490 | 33,750 | 70,000 | 46,565 | 56,000 | 125,400 | 1,183,939 |
| 2019 | 98,000 | 59,160 | 36,850 | 348,400 | 24,570 | 95,000 | 55,290 | 21,560 | 110,000 | 49,640 | 71,400 | 119,000 | 1,316,963 |
| 2020 | 41,040 | 66,660 | 35,360 | 281,250 | 22,940 | 75,990 | 34,030 | 34,790 | 104,000 | 46,400 | 61,500 | 133,000 | 1,171,397 |
| 2021 | 69,560 | 45,440 | 48,190 | 364,000 | 31,850 | 53,630 | 41,160 | 43,775 | 115,050 | 31,725 | 74,000 | 70,980 | 1,277,755 |
| 2022[1] | 35,750 | 63,900 | 44,240 | 244,200 | 24,600 | 59,400 | 26,240 | 36,735 | 68,600 | 48,960 | 39,000 | 122,400 | 1,103,707 |

[1] Preliminary.   *Source: Crop Reporting Board, U.S. Department of Agriculture (CRB-USDA)*

## Official Winter Wheat Crop Production Reports in the United States     In Thousands of Bushels

| Crop Year | May 1 | June 1 | July 1 | August 1 | September 1 | Current December | Final |
|---|---|---|---|---|---|---|---|
| 2013-14 | 1,485,757 | 1,509,142 | 1,543,095 | 1,542,605 | ---- | ---- | 1,542,902 |
| 2014-15 | 1,402,505 | 1,381,060 | 1,367,432 | 1,396,742 | ---- | ---- | 1,377,216 |
| 2015-16 | 1,471,802 | 1,505,072 | 1,455,516 | 1,438,278 | ---- | ---- | 1,374,690 |
| 2016-17 | 1,427,084 | 1,506,626 | 1,627,664 | 1,657,440 | ---- | ---- | 1,672,582 |
| 2017-18 | 1,246,392 | 1,250,192 | 1,279,363 | 1,287,133 | ---- | ---- | 1,270,282 |
| 2018-19 | 1,191,542 | 1,197,716 | 1,192,585 | 1,189,199 | ---- | ---- | 1,183,939 |
| 2019-20 | 1,268,461 | 1,274,451 | 1,290,626 | 1,326,223 | ---- | ---- | 1,316,963 |
| 2020-21 | 1,254,600 | 1,265,700 | 1,217,784 | 1,198,362 | ---- | ---- | 1,171,397 |
| 2021-22 | 1,282,925 | 1,309,000 | 1,364,205 | 1,318,735 | ---- | ---- | 1,277,755 |
| 2022-23[1] | 1,173,547 | 1,181,632 | 1,200,691 | 1,197,650 | ---- | ---- | 1,103,707 |

[1] Preliminary.   *Source: Crop Reporting Board, U.S. Department of Agriculture (CRB-USDA)*

# WHEAT

## Production of All Spring Wheat in the United States, by State    In Thousands of Bushels

| | | | | | | | | | | | | | |
|---|---|---|---|---|---|---|---|---|---|---|---|---|---|
| | ---------------------- Durum Wheat ---------------------- | | | | | | ---------------------------------- Other Spring Wheat ---------------------------------- | | | | | | |
| Year | Arizona | California | Montana | North Dakota | South Dakota | Total | Idaho | Minnesota | Montana | North Dakota | Oregon | South Dakota | Washington | Total |
| 2013 | 7,548 | 4,900 | 15,260 | 42,720 | 115 | 81,501 | 39,270 | 66,120 | 104,710 | 235,290 | 5,544 | 51,260 | 30,300 | 534,101 |
| 2014 | 8,436 | 3,150 | 15,225 | 29,453 | 168 | 57,976 | 34,580 | 64,900 | 104,300 | 291,650 | 3,744 | 71,680 | 23,180 | 595,038 |
| 2015 | 15,150 | 6,695 | 13,330 | 28,223 | 180 | 54,056 | 30,450 | 85,800 | 78,740 | 319,200 | 4,650 | 60,480 | 22,860 | 603,240 |
| 2016 | 9,408 | 4,042 | 18,755 | 42,463 | 246 | 84,009 | 34,365 | 74,340 | 75,960 | 269,100 | 4,437 | 47,250 | 27,030 | 532,227 |
| 2017 | 8,989 | 2,484 | 31,365 | 58,118 | 231 | 103,914 | 35,275 | 75,710 | 48,090 | 270,050 | 4,599 | 20,770 | 22,050 | 415,851 |
| 2018 | 7,738 | 3,515 | 12,560 | 28,920 | 108 | 54,777 | 42,275 | 92,630 | 95,880 | 318,010 | 5,025 | 40,530 | 27,810 | 623,232 |
| 2019 | 3,640 | 2,244 | 23,250 | 42,463 | 84 | 77,985 | 39,160 | 79,800 | 101,010 | 291,550 | ---- | 25,370 | 24,205 | 561,095 |
| 2020 | 4,851 | 1,479 | 21,715 | 25,925 | ---- | 53,959 | 45,045 | 72,080 | 125,780 | 275,870 | ---- | 35,485 | 33,245 | 587,505 |
| 2021 | 5,310 | 2,200 | 26,910 | 35,100 | ---- | 69,141 | 30,555 | 55,680 | 37,060 | 174,535 | ---- | 16,820 | 16,200 | 330,850 |
| 2022[1] | 9,576 | 3,850 | 10,160 | 19,680 | ---- | 37,259 | 29,160 | 73,810 | 61,000 | 263,000 | ---- | 33,600 | 21,620 | 482,190 |

[1] Preliminary.    Source: Crop Reporting Board, U.S. Department of Agriculture (CRB-USDA)

## Stocks of All Wheat in the United States    In Thousands of Bushels

| | On Farms | | | | Off Farms | | | | Total Stocks | | | |
|---|---|---|---|---|---|---|---|---|---|---|---|---|
| Year | Mar. 1 | June 1 | Sept. 1 | Dec. 1 | Mar. 1 | June 1 | Sept. 1 | Dec. 1 | Mar. 1 | June 1 | Sept. 1 | Dec. 1 |
| 2013 | 236,970 | 120,150 | 555,000 | 398,400 | 997,860 | 597,739 | 1,314,637 | 1,076,451 | 1,234,830 | 717,889 | 1,869,637 | 1,474,851 |
| 2014 | 237,530 | 96,995 | 713,450 | 472,800 | 819,435 | 493,288 | 1,193,770 | 1,056,830 | 1,056,965 | 590,283 | 1,907,220 | 1,529,630 |
| 2015 | 278,710 | 155,170 | 650,200 | 503,450 | 861,697 | 597,224 | 1,446,889 | 1,242,457 | 1,140,407 | 752,394 | 2,097,089 | 1,745,907 |
| 2016 | 319,800 | 197,210 | 728,200 | 571,280 | 1,051,862 | 778,393 | 1,816,830 | 1,506,042 | 1,371,662 | 975,603 | 2,545,030 | 2,077,322 |
| 2017 | 349,500 | 191,755 | 491,800 | 394,080 | 1,309,175 | 988,847 | 1,774,275 | 1,479,335 | 1,658,675 | 1,180,602 | 2,266,075 | 1,873,415 |
| 2018 | 259,310 | 130,475 | 632,700 | 504,280 | 1,236,131 | 968,414 | 1,757,071 | 1,505,205 | 1,495,441 | 1,098,889 | 2,389,771 | 2,009,485 |
| 2019 | 367,870 | 206,545 | 734,500 | 519,470 | 1,225,201 | 873,216 | 1,611,025 | 1,321,305 | 1,593,071 | 1,079,761 | 2,345,525 | 1,840,775 |
| 2020 | 338,690 | 228,585 | 705,050 | 483,470 | 1,076,724 | 799,699 | 1,452,775 | 1,219,220 | 1,415,414 | 1,028,284 | 2,157,825 | 1,702,690 |
| 2021 | 283,920 | 141,655 | 419,190 | 273,290 | 1,026,870 | 703,496 | 1,354,347 | 1,103,873 | 1,310,790 | 845,151 | 1,773,537 | 1,377,163 |
| 2022[1] | 174,410 | 92,965 | 591,130 | 361,900 | 854,758 | 605,466 | 1,186,719 | 949,930 | 1,029,168 | 698,431 | 1,777,849 | 1,311,830 |

[1] Preliminary.    Source: National Agricultural Statistics Service, U.S. Department of Agriculture (NASS-USDA)

## Stocks of Durum Wheat in the United States    In Thousands of Bushels

| | On Farms | | | | Off Farms | | | | Total Stocks | | | |
|---|---|---|---|---|---|---|---|---|---|---|---|---|
| Year | Mar. 1 | June 1 | Sept. 1 | Dec. 1 | Mar. 1 | June 1 | Sept. 1 | Dec. 1 | Mar. 1 | June 1 | Sept. 1 | Dec. 1 |
| 2013 | 21,400 | 13,600 | 42,900 | 32,800 | 21,088 | 9,450 | 23,465 | 21,175 | 42,488 | 23,050 | 66,365 | 53,975 |
| 2014 | 20,700 | 12,800 | 38,700 | 23,900 | 17,430 | 8,724 | 19,121 | 20,147 | 38,130 | 21,524 | 57,821 | 44,047 |
| 2015 | 16,200 | 10,250 | 44,900 | 35,700 | 21,454 | 15,406 | 29,146 | 24,787 | 37,654 | 25,656 | 74,046 | 60,487 |
| 2016 | 17,700 | 12,190 | 65,500 | 49,200 | 24,785 | 15,609 | 26,386 | 23,696 | 42,485 | 27,799 | 91,886 | 72,896 |
| 2017 | 32,400 | 18,350 | 33,400 | 30,700 | 20,584 | 17,953 | 32,756 | 25,351 | 52,984 | 36,303 | 66,156 | 56,051 |
| 2018 | 25,800 | 14,950 | 51,800 | 46,700 | 23,740 | 19,996 | 38,260 | 36,830 | 49,540 | 34,946 | 90,060 | 83,530 |
| 2019 | 40,600 | 26,050 | 49,600 | 33,200 | 33,789 | 28,920 | 38,773 | 31,187 | 74,389 | 54,970 | 88,373 | 64,387 |
| 2020 | 23,500 | 17,700 | 43,500 | 39,000 | 27,898 | 24,230 | 27,517 | 22,639 | 51,398 | 41,930 | 71,017 | 61,639 |
| 2021 | 22,600 | 13,500 | 21,000 | 16,900 | 19,592 | 13,843 | 25,010 | 25,086 | 42,192 | 27,343 | 46,010 | 41,986 |
| 2022[1] | 12,600 | 9,290 | 31,500 | 25,900 | 17,713 | 14,449 | 22,259 | 22,166 | 30,313 | 23,739 | 53,759 | 48,066 |

[1] Preliminary.    Source: National Agricultural Statistics Service, U.S. Department of Agriculture (NASS-USDA)

## Wheat Supply and Distribution in Canada, Australia and Argentina    In Millions of Metric Tons

| | ------ Canada (Year Beginning Aug. 1) ------ | | | | | ------ Australia (Year Beginning Oct. 1) ------ | | | | | ----- Argentina (Year Beginning Dec. 1) ----- | | | | |
|---|---|---|---|---|---|---|---|---|---|---|---|---|---|---|---|
| | --------- Supply --------- | | | | | --------- Supply --------- | | | | | --------- Supply --------- | | | | |
| Crop Year | Stocks Aug. 1 | New Crop | Total Supply | - Disappearance - Domestic | Exports[3] | Stocks Oct. 1 | New Crop | Total Supply | - Disappearance - Domestic | Exports[3] | Stocks Dec. 1 | New Crop | Total Supply | - Disappearance - Domestic | Exports[3] |
| 2013-14 | 5.1 | 37.6 | 42.7 | 9.5 | 23.3 | 4.7 | 25.3 | 30.0 | 7.0 | 18.6 | 0.3 | 10.5 | 10.8 | 6.1 | 2.3 |
| 2014-15 | 10.4 | 29.4 | 39.8 | 9.1 | 24.2 | 4.6 | 23.7 | 28.3 | 7.2 | 16.6 | 2.5 | 13.9 | 16.4 | 6.4 | 5.3 |
| 2015-16 | 7.1 | 27.6 | 34.7 | 8.0 | 22.1 | 4.7 | 22.3 | 26.9 | 7.1 | 16.1 | 4.8 | 11.3 | 16.1 | 5.7 | 9.6 |
| 2016-17 | 5.2 | 32.1 | 37.3 | 10.7 | 20.2 | 3.9 | 31.8 | 35.7 | 7.5 | 22.6 | 0.8 | 18.4 | 19.2 | 5.2 | 13.8 |
| 2017-18 | 6.9 | 30.4 | 37.3 | 9.0 | 22.0 | 5.8 | 20.9 | 26.7 | 8.5 | 13.8 | 0.2 | 18.5 | 18.7 | 5.6 | 12.7 |
| 2018-19 | 6.7 | 32.4 | 39.1 | 9.1 | 24.4 | 4.5 | 17.6 | 22.1 | 9.2 | 9.0 | 0.5 | 19.5 | 20.0 | 6.1 | 12.2 |
| 2019-20 | 6.0 | 32.7 | 38.7 | 9.8 | 24.1 | 4.4 | 14.5 | 18.9 | 8.0 | 9.1 | 1.7 | 19.8 | 21.5 | 6.3 | 12.8 |
| 2020-21 | 5.5 | 35.4 | 40.9 | 9.1 | 26.4 | 2.7 | 31.9 | 34.6 | 8.0 | 23.8 | 2.5 | 17.6 | 20.1 | 6.3 | 11.5 |
| 2021-22[1] | 6.0 | 22.3 | 28.2 | 10.0 | 15.1 | 3.0 | 36.3 | 39.3 | 8.5 | 27.5 | 2.3 | 22.2 | 24.5 | 6.2 | 16.0 |
| 2022-23[2] | 3.7 | 33.8 | 37.5 | 8.6 | 26.0 | 3.5 | 36.6 | 40.1 | 8.6 | 27.5 | 2.4 | 12.5 | 14.9 | 6.2 | 7.5 |

[1] Preliminary.    [2] Forecast.    [3] Including flour.    Source: Foreign Agricultural Service, U.S. Department of Agriculture (FAS-USDA)

# WHEAT

## Quarterly Supply and Disappearance of Wheat in the United States    In Millions of Bushels

| Crop Year Beginning June 1 | Beginning Stocks | Production | Imports[3] | Total Supply | Food | Seed | Feed & Residual | Total | Exports[3] | Total Disappearance | Total Stocks | Gov't Owned[4] | Privately Owned[5] |
|---|---|---|---|---|---|---|---|---|---|---|---|---|---|
| 2012-13 | 742.6 | 2,252.3 | 124.3 | 3,119.2 | 950.8 | 73.1 | 365.3 | 1,389.3 | 1,012.1 | 2,401.4 | 717.9 | ---- | ---- |
| June-Aug. | 742.6 | 2,252.3 | 25.5 | 3,020.4 | 237.6 | 1.4 | 402.7 | 641.7 | 263.7 | 905.3 | 2,115.1 | ---- | ---- |
| Sept.-Nov. | 2,115.1 | ---- | 32.9 | 2,148.0 | 246.6 | 55.4 | -22.4 | 279.6 | 197.9 | 477.5 | 1,670.6 | ---- | ---- |
| Dec.-Feb. | 1,670.6 | ---- | 34.7 | 1,705.3 | 229.0 | 1.4 | 4.9 | 235.3 | 235.2 | 470.4 | 1,234.8 | ---- | ---- |
| Mar.-May | 1,234.8 | ---- | 31.2 | 1,266.0 | 237.6 | 15.0 | -19.9 | 232.8 | 315.4 | 548.1 | 717.9 | ---- | ---- |
| 2013-14 | 717.9 | 2,135.0 | 172.5 | 3,025.3 | 955.1 | 75.6 | 228.2 | 1,258.8 | 1,176.2 | 2,435.1 | 590.3 | ---- | ---- |
| June-Aug. | 717.9 | 2,135.0 | 35.7 | 2,888.5 | 234.8 | 4.1 | 422.4 | 661.4 | 357.5 | 1,018.9 | 1,869.6 | ---- | ---- |
| Sept.-Nov. | 1,869.6 | ---- | 48.0 | 1,917.7 | 249.3 | 52.7 | -168.0 | 134.0 | 308.8 | 442.8 | 1,474.9 | ---- | ---- |
| Dec.-Feb. | 1,474.9 | ---- | 42.0 | 1,516.9 | 231.1 | 1.9 | -0.8 | 232.2 | 227.7 | 459.9 | 1,057.0 | ---- | ---- |
| Mar.-May | 1,057.0 | ---- | 46.7 | 1,103.7 | 239.9 | 16.8 | -25.4 | 231.3 | 282.1 | 513.4 | 590.3 | ---- | ---- |
| 2014-15 | 590.3 | 2,026.3 | 151.2 | 2,767.8 | 958.3 | 79.4 | 113.4 | 1,151.1 | 864.3 | 2,015.4 | 752.4 | ---- | ---- |
| June-Aug. | 590.3 | 2,026.3 | 44.2 | 2,660.8 | 238.9 | 6.4 | 255.7 | 501.0 | 252.5 | 753.5 | 1,907.2 | ---- | ---- |
| Sept.-Nov. | 1,907.2 | ---- | 34.6 | 1,941.8 | 248.2 | 48.8 | -92.6 | 204.4 | 207.7 | 412.1 | 1,529.6 | ---- | ---- |
| Dec.-Feb. | 1,529.6 | ---- | 36.7 | 1,566.4 | 230.8 | 2.1 | 7.9 | 240.9 | 185.1 | 426.0 | 1,140.4 | ---- | ---- |
| Mar.-May | 1,140.4 | ---- | 35.8 | 1,176.2 | 240.3 | 22.1 | -57.6 | 204.8 | 219.0 | 423.8 | 752.4 | ---- | ---- |
| 2015-16 | 752.4 | 2,061.9 | 112.8 | 2,927.1 | 957.1 | 67.2 | 149.5 | 1,173.8 | 777.8 | 1,951.5 | 975.6 | ---- | ---- |
| June-Aug. | 752.4 | 2,061.9 | 26.5 | 2,840.9 | 240.2 | 1.0 | 297.8 | 539.0 | 204.8 | 743.8 | 2,097.1 | ---- | ---- |
| Sept.-Nov. | 2,097.1 | ---- | 27.0 | 2,124.1 | 248.7 | 44.2 | -107.2 | 185.8 | 192.4 | 378.2 | 1,745.9 | ---- | ---- |
| Dec.-Feb. | 1,745.9 | ---- | 34.4 | 1,780.3 | 229.5 | 1.7 | 2.2 | 233.5 | 175.2 | 408.6 | 1,371.7 | ---- | ---- |
| Mar.-May | 1,371.7 | ---- | 24.9 | 1,396.5 | 238.6 | 20.3 | -43.4 | 215.5 | 205.5 | 420.9 | 975.6 | ---- | ---- |
| 2016-17 | 975.6 | 2,308.7 | 118.0 | 3,402.3 | 948.9 | 61.3 | 160.7 | 1,170.8 | 1,050.9 | 2,221.7 | 1,180.6 | ---- | ---- |
| June-Aug. | 975.6 | 2,308.7 | 32.6 | 3,316.9 | 237.6 | 0.6 | 265.7 | 504.0 | 267.9 | 771.9 | 2,545.0 | ---- | ---- |
| Sept.-Nov. | 2,545.0 | ---- | 29.5 | 2,574.5 | 245.5 | 40.6 | -30.2 | 255.8 | 239.3 | 495.2 | 2,079.4 | ---- | ---- |
| Dec.-Feb. | 2,079.4 | ---- | 24.6 | 2,104.0 | 227.9 | 1.3 | -13.0 | 216.2 | 229.1 | 445.3 | 1,658.7 | ---- | ---- |
| Mar.-May | 1,658.7 | ---- | 31.3 | 1,689.9 | 237.9 | 18.7 | -61.8 | 194.8 | 314.5 | 509.3 | 1,180.6 | ---- | ---- |
| 2017-18 | 1,180.6 | 1,740.9 | 158.0 | 3,079.5 | 964.2 | 63.4 | 47.2 | 1,074.7 | 905.9 | 1,980.7 | 1,098.9 | ---- | ---- |
| June-Aug. | 1,180.6 | 1,740.9 | 42.0 | 2,963.6 | 238.8 | 0.9 | 164.8 | 404.4 | 292.4 | 696.8 | 2,266.8 | ---- | ---- |
| Sept.-Nov. | 2,266.8 | ---- | 35.9 | 2,302.7 | 250.6 | 40.1 | -54.7 | 235.9 | 193.3 | 429.2 | 1,873.5 | ---- | ---- |
| Dec.-Feb. | 1,873.5 | ---- | 37.8 | 1,911.3 | 232.9 | 1.8 | -19.5 | 215.1 | 200.8 | 415.9 | 1,495.4 | ---- | ---- |
| Mar.-May | 1,495.4 | ---- | 42.2 | 1,537.7 | 242.0 | 20.6 | -43.3 | 219.3 | 219.5 | 438.8 | 1,098.9 | ---- | ---- |
| 2018-19 | 1,098.9 | 1,885.2 | 134.6 | 3,118.6 | 954.4 | 59.5 | 87.9 | 1,101.8 | 937.1 | 2,038.9 | 1,079.8 | ---- | ---- |
| June-Aug. | 1,098.9 | 1,885.2 | 40.9 | 3,024.9 | 239.2 | 2.1 | 189.2 | 430.5 | 204.6 | 635.2 | 2,389.8 | ---- | ---- |
| Sept.-Nov. | 2,389.8 | ---- | 31.2 | 2,421.0 | 246.5 | 37.6 | -75.1 | 209.0 | 202.5 | 411.5 | 2,009.5 | ---- | ---- |
| Dec.-Feb. | 2,009.5 | ---- | 32.1 | 2,041.5 | 229.1 | 2.8 | -27.4 | 204.6 | 243.9 | 448.5 | 1,593.1 | ---- | ---- |
| Mar.-May | 1,593.1 | ---- | 30.4 | 1,623.4 | 239.5 | 17.0 | 1.1 | 257.7 | 286.0 | 543.7 | 1,079.8 | ---- | ---- |
| 2019-20 | 1,079.8 | 1,932.0 | 103.8 | 3,115.6 | 961.6 | 60.0 | 96.7 | 1,118.3 | 969.0 | 2,087.3 | 1,028.3 | ---- | ---- |
| June-Aug. | 1,079.8 | 1,932.0 | 23.2 | 3,035.0 | 238.2 | 3.6 | 195.7 | 437.5 | 251.9 | 689.4 | 2,345.5 | ---- | ---- |
| Sept.-Nov. | 2,345.5 | ---- | 22.5 | 2,368.0 | 247.0 | 37.3 | 9.6 | 293.8 | 233.4 | 527.2 | 1,840.8 | ---- | ---- |
| Dec.-Feb. | 1,840.8 | ---- | 28.3 | 1,869.1 | 236.1 | 2.0 | -21.2 | 216.9 | 236.8 | 453.7 | 1,415.4 | ---- | ---- |
| Mar.-May | 1,415.4 | ---- | 29.9 | 1,445.3 | 240.4 | 17.1 | -87.3 | 170.1 | 246.9 | 417.0 | 1,028.3 | ---- | ---- |
| 2020-21 | 1,028.3 | 1,828.0 | 100.1 | 2,956.4 | 960.5 | 63.8 | 93.2 | 1,117.4 | 993.9 | 2,111.3 | 845.2 | ---- | ---- |
| June-Aug. | 1,028.3 | 1,828.0 | 29.7 | 2,886.0 | 240.9 | 2.2 | 213.4 | 456.5 | 271.7 | 728.2 | 2,157.8 | ---- | ---- |
| Sept.-Nov. | 2,157.8 | ---- | 27.8 | 2,185.6 | 249.3 | 42.0 | -45.6 | 245.7 | 237.3 | 482.9 | 1,702.7 | ---- | ---- |
| Dec.-Feb. | 1,702.7 | ---- | 21.9 | 1,724.6 | 231.6 | 1.0 | -30.4 | 202.2 | 211.5 | 413.8 | 1,310.8 | ---- | ---- |
| Mar.-May | 1,310.8 | ---- | 20.7 | 1,331.5 | 238.8 | 18.5 | -44.3 | 213.0 | 273.4 | 486.4 | 845.2 | ---- | ---- |
| 2021-22[1] | 845.2 | 1,646.3 | 95.2 | 2,586.6 | 971.5 | 57.7 | 58.6 | 1,087.8 | 800.4 | 1,888.2 | 698.4 | ---- | ---- |
| June-Aug. | 845.2 | 1,646.3 | 25.2 | 2,516.6 | 237.1 | 0.9 | 254.8 | 492.9 | 250.3 | 743.1 | 1,773.5 | ---- | ---- |
| Sept.-Nov. | 1,773.5 | ---- | 23.6 | 1,797.1 | 248.7 | 40.1 | -55.6 | 233.3 | 186.7 | 420.0 | 1,377.2 | ---- | ---- |
| Dec.-Feb. | 1,377.2 | ---- | 21.4 | 1,398.6 | 236.6 | 2.6 | -51.2 | 188.0 | 181.4 | 369.4 | 1,029.2 | ---- | ---- |
| Mar.-May | 1,029.2 | ---- | 25.0 | 1,054.1 | 249.1 | 14.1 | -89.5 | 173.7 | 182.0 | 355.7 | 698.4 | ---- | ---- |
| 2022-23[2] | 698.4 | 1,649.9 | 120.0 | 2,468.3 | 977.0 | 69.0 | 80.0 | 1,126.0 | 775.0 | 1,901.0 | 567.3 | ---- | ---- |
| June-Aug. | 698.4 | 1,649.9 | 33.0 | 2,381.3 | 247.8 | 4.7 | 139.5 | 392.0 | 211.4 | 603.4 | 1,777.8 | ---- | ---- |
| Sept.-Nov. | 1,777.8 | ---- | 27.4 | 1,805.2 | 251.0 | 45.0 | 13.5 | 309.5 | 215.6 | 525.0 | 1,280.2 | ---- | ---- |

[1] Preliminary.  [2] Forecast.  [3] Imports & exports include flour and other products expressed in wheat equivalent.  [4] Uncommitted, Government only.  [5] Includes total loans.  [6] Includes alcoholic beverages.  Source: Economic Research Service, U.S. Department of Agriculture (ERS-USDA)

333

# WHEAT

## Exports of Wheat (Only)[2] from the United States   In Thousands of Bushels

| Crop Year | June | July | Aug. | Sept. | Oct. | Nov. | Dec. | Jan. | Feb. | Mar. | Apr. | May | Total |
|---|---|---|---|---|---|---|---|---|---|---|---|---|---|
| 2013-14 | 94,904 | 114,879 | 142,197 | 151,935 | 87,681 | 64,108 | 73,735 | 80,725 | 68,543 | 77,859 | 102,988 | 95,876 | 1,155,431 |
| 2014-15 | 77,912 | 73,314 | 95,989 | 97,967 | 58,258 | 45,692 | 59,967 | 51,471 | 68,363 | 74,564 | 74,102 | 64,539 | 842,136 |
| 2015-16 | 59,531 | 60,229 | 79,422 | 90,351 | 44,850 | 50,968 | 62,994 | 51,899 | 54,281 | 70,087 | 65,495 | 63,676 | 753,784 |
| 2016-17 | 83,009 | 75,485 | 103,642 | 103,742 | 63,389 | 65,452 | 80,095 | 60,537 | 82,555 | 98,116 | 98,509 | 112,397 | 1,026,928 |
| 2017-18 | 109,687 | 87,501 | 89,362 | 86,496 | 48,308 | 54,448 | 72,945 | 64,994 | 58,101 | 76,469 | 72,031 | 66,140 | 886,482 |
| 2018-19 | 57,363 | 65,546 | 76,856 | 66,047 | 70,998 | 60,225 | 84,023 | 72,254 | 82,437 | 74,980 | 101,249 | 104,930 | 916,907 |
| 2019-20 | 83,335 | 68,853 | 94,857 | 79,901 | 83,641 | 64,645 | 80,808 | 70,543 | 80,660 | 66,051 | 91,275 | 84,125 | 948,693 |
| 2020-21 | 83,699 | 88,446 | 94,222 | 98,699 | 63,899 | 69,498 | 69,076 | 73,081 | 64,838 | 83,106 | 93,696 | 91,289 | 973,550 |
| 2021-22 | 68,781 | 80,972 | 95,700 | 85,740 | 45,835 | 50,380 | 45,465 | 63,509 | 68,184 | 62,939 | 64,358 | 49,999 | 781,863 |
| 2022-23[1] | 58,529 | 55,710 | 92,445 | 112,072 | 50,865 | 48,420 | 39,680 | | | | | | 784,662 |

[1] Preliminary.  [2] Grains.  Source: Economic Research Service, U.S. Department of Agriculture (ERS-USDA)

## Wheat Government Loan Program Data in the United States   Loan Rates--Cents Per Bushel

|  |  |  | Farm Loan Prices |  |  |  |  |  |  | Stocks, May 31 |  |  |  |
|---|---|---|---|---|---|---|---|---|---|---|---|---|---|
|  |  |  | Corn Belt | Central & Southern Plains | Northern Plains | Pacific | Placed | % of | Acquired by CCC | Total | Total CCC | Outstanding CCC | Farmer- |
| Crop Year Beginning June 1 | National Average[3] | Target Rate[4] | (Soft Red Winter) | (Hard Winter) | (Spring & Durum) | Northwest (White) | Under Loan | Pro- duction | Under Program | Stocks May 31 | Stocks May 31 | Loans | Owned Reserve | "Free" |
|  |  |  |  |  |  |  | In Millions of Bushels |  |  |  |  |  |  |
| 2010-11 | 294 | 417 | ---- | ---- | ---- | ---- | 67 | 3.0 | 0 | 862 | 0 | ---- | ---- | ---- |
| 2011-12 | 294 | 417 | ---- | ---- | ---- | ---- | 36 | 1.8 | 0 | 743 | 0 | ---- | ---- | ---- |
| 2012-13 | 294 | 417 | ---- | ---- | ---- | ---- | 28 | 1.2 | 0 | 718 | 0 | ---- | ---- | ---- |
| 2013-14 | 294 | 417 | ---- | ---- | ---- | ---- | 25 | 1.2 | 0 | 590 | 0 | ---- | ---- | ---- |
| 2014-15 | 294 | 550 | ---- | ---- | ---- | ---- | 43 | 2.1 | 0 | 752 | 0 | ---- | ---- | ---- |
| 2015-16 | 294 | 550 | ---- | ---- | ---- | ---- | 81 | 3.9 | 0 | 976 | 0 | ---- | ---- | ---- |
| 2016-17 | 294 | 550 | ---- | ---- | ---- | ---- | 151 | 6.5 | 0.25 | 1,181 | 0 | ---- | ---- | ---- |
| 2017-18 | 294 | 550 | ---- | ---- | ---- | ---- | 45 | 2.6 | 0 | 1,099 | 0 | ---- | ---- | ---- |
| 2018-19[1] | 294 | 550 | ---- | ---- | ---- | ---- | 65 | 5.9 | 0 | 1,080 | 0 | ---- | ---- | ---- |
| 2019-20[2] | 338 | 550 | ---- | ---- | ---- | ---- | 69 | 3.6 | 0 | 1,028 | 0 | ---- | ---- | ---- |

[1] Preliminary.  [2] Estimate.  [3] The national average loan rate at the farm as a percentage of the parity-priced wheat at the beginning of the marketing year.  [4] 1996-97 through 2001-02 marketing year, target prices not applicable.  NA = Not avaliable.
Source: Agricultural Marketing Service, U.S. Department of Agriculture (AMS-USDA)

## United States Wheat and Wheat Flour Imports and Exports   In Thousands of Bushels

|  | Imports |  |  |  |  | Exports |  |  |  |  |  |
|---|---|---|---|---|---|---|---|---|---|---|---|
|  | Wheat |  |  |  |  |  |  |  |  | Export |  |
| Crop Year Beginning June 1 | Suitable for Milling | Wheat Unfit for Human Consump. | Grain | Flour & Products[2] | Total | P.L. 480 | Foreign Donations Sec. 416 | Aid[3] | Total con- cessional | CCC Export Credit | Enhance- ment Program | Total U.S. Wheat |
|  |  | -- Wheat Equivalent -- |  |  |  | In Thousands of Metric Tons |  |  |  |  |  |  |
| 2013-14 | 141,665 | ---- | 141,665 | 30,802 | 172,467 | ---- | ---- | ---- | ---- | ---- | ---- | ---- |
| 2014-15 | 116,973 | ---- | 116,973 | 34,276 | 151,249 | ---- | ---- | ---- | ---- | ---- | ---- | ---- |
| 2015-16 | 76,433 | ---- | 76,433 | 36,292 | 112,725 | ---- | ---- | ---- | ---- | ---- | ---- | ---- |
| 2016-17 | 83,849 | ---- | 83,849 | 34,291 | 118,140 | ---- | ---- | ---- | ---- | ---- | ---- | ---- |
| 2017-18 | 120,746 | ---- | 120,746 | 37,238 | 157,984 | ---- | ---- | ---- | ---- | ---- | ---- | ---- |
| 2018-19 | 97,657 | ---- | 97,657 | 36,975 | 134,633 | ---- | ---- | ---- | ---- | ---- | ---- | ---- |
| 2019-20[1] | 65,345 | ---- | 65,345 | 39,664 | 105,009 | ---- | ---- | ---- | ---- | ---- | ---- | ---- |

[1] Preliminary.  [2] Includes macaroni, semolina & similar products.  [3] Shipment mostly under the Commodity Import Program, financed with foreign aid funds.  NA = Not available.  Source: Economic Research Service, U.S. Department of Agriculture (ERS-USDA)

## Comparative Average Cash Wheat Prices   In Dollars Per Bushel

|  |  |  | -- Minneapolis -- |  |  |  |  |  | Export Prices[2] (U.S. $ Per Metric Ton) |  |  |  |  |
|---|---|---|---|---|---|---|---|---|---|---|---|---|---|
|  |  | No 1 Hard Red |  | No 1 |  | No 1 | No 2 |  |  | Canada |  |  | Rotterdam |
| Crop Year June to May | Received by U.S. Farmers | No. 2 Ordinary Soft Red Winter, Chicago | No 2 Protein, Kansas City | Dark Soft Red Northern Winter, Spring St. Louis 14% | No 1 Hard Amber Durum | Soft White, Portland, Oregon | Western White Pacific Northwest | No 2 Soft White, Toledo | Aust- ralian Standard White | Vancouver No 1 CWRS 13 1/2% | Argen- tina F.O.B. B.A. | U.S. Gulf No. 2 Hard Winter | C.I.F. U.S. No 2 Hard Winter |
| 2015-16 | 4.89 | 4.90 | 5.58 | 4.60 | 6.34 | ---- | 5.38 | ---- | 4.99 | 218 | 232 | 209 | 187 | ---- |
| 2016-17 | 3.89 | 4.06 | 4.60 | 4.14 | 6.28 | ---- | 4.79 | ---- | 4.09 | 195 | 216 | 191 | 157 | ---- |
| 2017-18 | 4.72 | 4.46 | 5.58 | 4.58 | 7.62 | ---- | 5.35 | ---- | 4.49 | 227 | 260 | 198 | 188 | ---- |
| 2018-19 | 5.16 | 4.90 | 6.10 | 5.12 | 6.79 | ---- | 6.09 | ---- | 4.96 | 278 | 253 | 235 | 212 | ---- |
| 2019-20 | 4.58 | 5.28 | 5.66 | 5.46 | 6.39 | ---- | 5.99 | ---- | 5.34 | 247 | 240 | 231 | 205 | ---- |
| 2020-21 | 5.05 | 6.01 | 6.55 | 6.24 | 7.09 | ---- | 6.44 | ---- | 5.96 | 250 | 272 | 260 | 245 | ---- |
| 2021-22 | 7.63 | 8.18 | 10.00 | 8.36 | 11.36 | ---- | 10.40 | ---- | 8.18 | 329 | 406 | 332 | 339 | ---- |
| 2022-23[1] | 9.10 | 8.17 | 11.01 | 8.14 | 11.42 | ---- | 9.34 | ---- | 8.16 | 361 | 393 | 421 | 374 | ---- |

[1] Preliminary.  [2] Calendar year.  NA = Not available.  Source: Economic Research Service, U.S. Department of Agriculture (ERS-USDA)

# WHEAT

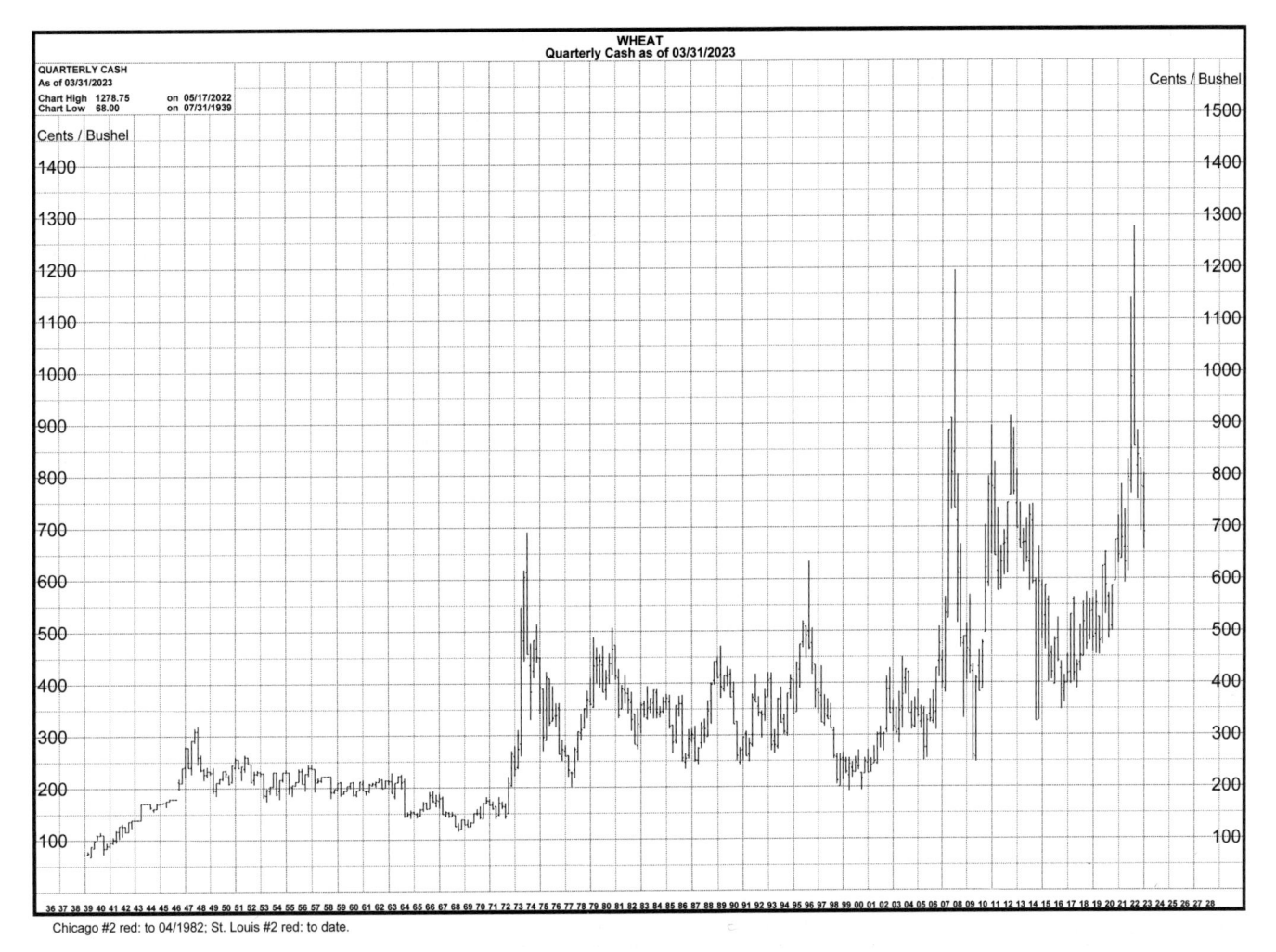

**WHEAT**
Quarterly Cash as of 03/31/2023

QUARTERLY CASH
As of 03/31/2023
Chart High 1278.75 on 05/17/2022
Chart Low 68.00 on 07/31/1939

Chicago #2 red: to 04/1982; St. Louis #2 red: to date.

## Average Price of No. 2 Soft Red Winter (30 Days) Wheat in Chicago — In Dollars Per Bushel

| Crop Year | June | July | Aug. | Sept. | Oct. | Nov. | Dec. | Jan. | Feb. | Mar. | Apr. | May | Average |
|---|---|---|---|---|---|---|---|---|---|---|---|---|---|
| 2013-14 | 6.94 | 6.60 | 6.26 | 6.41 | 6.77 | 6.46 | 6.23 | 5.86 | 6.08 | 6.91 | 6.91 | 6.86 | 6.52 |
| 2014-15 | 5.87 | 5.30 | 5.34 | 4.82 | 5.04 | 5.43 | 6.21 | 5.56 | 5.19 | 5.07 | 5.02 | 4.87 | 5.31 |
| 2015-16 | 5.17 | 5.40 | 5.00 | 4.86 | 5.02 | 4.98 | 4.83 | 4.75 | 4.69 | 4.70 | 4.71 | 4.65 | 4.90 |
| 2016-17 | 4.70 | 4.12 | 3.99 | 3.76 | 3.82 | 3.88 | 3.94 | 4.16 | 4.26 | 4.06 | 3.93 | 4.08 | 4.06 |
| 2017-18 | 4.41 | 4.96 | 4.12 | 4.23 | 4.22 | 4.13 | 4.12 | 4.27 | 4.55 | 4.69 | 4.74 | 5.08 | 4.46 |
| 2018-19 | 4.92 | 4.98 | 5.32 | 4.81 | 4.88 | 5.01 | 5.24 | 5.20 | 4.97 | 4.46 | 4.43 | 4.57 | 4.90 |
| 2019-20 | 5.27 | 5.12 | 4.78 | 4.76 | 5.05 | 5.15 | 5.42 | 5.86 | 5.76 | 5.47 | 5.51 | 5.22 | 5.28 |
| 2020-21 | 5.08 | 5.25 | 5.12 | 5.37 | 5.94 | 5.89 | 5.93 | 6.57 | 6.54 | 6.41 | 6.84 | 7.21 | 6.01 |
| 2021-22 | 6.79 | 6.67 | 7.05 | 6.78 | 7.35 | 7.97 | 7.83 | 7.69 | 8.02 | 10.91 | 10.15 | 10.99 | 8.18 |
| 2022-23[1] | 9.69 | 7.71 | 7.63 | 8.31 | 8.34 | 7.95 | 7.58 | ---- | 7.49 | | | | 8.17 |

[1] Preliminary. *Source: Economic Research Service, U.S. Department of Agriculture (ERS-USDA)*

## Average Price of No. 1 Hard Red Winter (Ordinary Protein) Wheat in Kansas City — In Dollars Per Bushel

| Crop Year | June | July | Aug. | Sept. | Oct. | Nov. | Dec. | Jan. | Feb. | Mar. | Apr. | May | Average |
|---|---|---|---|---|---|---|---|---|---|---|---|---|---|
| 2013-14 | 8.32 | 8.14 | 8.12 | 8.00 | 8.70 | 8.44 | 8.03 | 7.56 | 8.04 | 8.87 | 8.81 | 9.01 | 8.34 |
| 2014-15 | 8.23 | 7.61 | 7.33 | 7.11 | 7.35 | 7.20 | 7.54 | 6.75 | 6.44 | 6.46 | 6.22 | 6.18 | 7.04 |
| 2015-16 | 6.40 | 6.27 | 5.70 | 5.44 | 5.62 | 5.55 | 5.60 | 5.46 | 5.28 | 5.34 | 5.22 | 5.08 | 5.58 |
| 2016-17 | 5.04 | 4.24 | 4.15 | 4.24 | 4.40 | 4.64 | 4.56 | 4.91 | 5.04 | 4.80 | 4.37 | 4.80 | 4.60 |
| 2017-18 | 5.24 | 5.65 | 4.80 | 5.07 | 5.11 | 5.30 | 5.38 | 5.73 | 5.93 | 6.05 | 6.09 | 6.56 | 5.58 |
| 2018-19 | 6.35 | 6.20 | 6.61 | 6.03 | 6.11 | 6.18 | 6.36 | 6.26 | 6.02 | 5.94 | 5.61 | 5.50 | 6.10 |
| 2019-20 | 6.06 | 5.56 | 5.11 | 5.00 | 5.24 | 5.54 | 5.72 | 5.92 | 6.59 | 5.74 | 5.83 | 5.63 | 5.66 |
| 2020-21 | 5.44 | 5.45 | 5.24 | 5.70 | 6.34 | 6.48 | 6.61 | 7.33 | 7.37 | 6.94 | 7.52 | 8.12 | 6.55 |
| 2021-22 | 7.42 | 7.20 | 8.07 | 8.05 | 8.56 | 9.56 | 10.52 | 10.03 | 9.91 | 12.35 | 13.81 | 14.50 | 10.00 |
| 2022-23[1] | 12.50 | 10.11 | 10.18 | 10.75 | 11.41 | 11.73 | 10.40 | 9.99 | 10.29 | | | | 10.82 |

[1] Preliminary. *Source: Economic Research Service, U.S. Department of Agriculture (ERS-USDA)*

# WHEAT

## Average Price Received by Farmers for All Wheat in the United States    In Dollars Per Bushel

| Crop Year | June | July | Aug. | Sept. | Oct. | Nov. | Dec. | Jan. | Feb. | Mar. | Apr. | May | Average |
|---|---|---|---|---|---|---|---|---|---|---|---|---|---|
| 2013-14 | 7.37 | 6.95 | 6.88 | 6.80 | 6.94 | 6.85 | 6.73 | 6.65 | 6.50 | 6.74 | 6.82 | 7.08 | 6.86 |
| 2014-15 | 6.49 | 6.15 | 5.97 | 5.71 | 5.71 | 6.04 | 6.14 | 6.15 | 5.89 | 5.70 | 5.56 | 5.33 | 5.90 |
| 2015-16 | 5.42 | 5.23 | 4.84 | 4.72 | 4.86 | 4.86 | 4.75 | 4.82 | 4.61 | 4.40 | 4.46 | 4.45 | 4.79 |
| 2016-17 | 4.20 | 3.75 | 3.68 | 3.48 | 3.68 | 3.88 | 3.90 | 4.01 | 4.16 | 4.37 | 4.16 | 4.05 | 3.94 |
| 2017-18 | 4.37 | 4.77 | 4.84 | 4.65 | 4.64 | 4.72 | 4.50 | 4.65 | 4.92 | 5.10 | 5.28 | 5.39 | 4.82 |
| 2018-19 | 5.17 | 5.00 | 5.31 | 5.15 | 5.22 | 5.23 | 5.28 | 5.28 | 5.33 | 5.19 | 4.93 | 4.78 | 5.16 |
| 2019-20 | 4.81 | 4.52 | 4.34 | 4.26 | 4.45 | 4.39 | 4.64 | 4.88 | 4.88 | 4.86 | 4.85 | 4.76 | 4.64 |
| 2020-21 | 4.57 | 4.54 | 4.54 | 4.73 | 4.98 | 5.24 | 5.46 | 5.48 | 5.83 | 5.86 | 6.04 | 6.46 | 5.31 |
| 2021-22 | 6.23 | 6.26 | 7.14 | 7.75 | 7.92 | 8.52 | 8.59 | 8.48 | 9.16 | 9.94 | 10.20 | 10.90 | 8.42 |
| 2022-23[1] | 9.55 | 8.69 | 8.55 | 8.85 | 9.21 | 9.16 | 8.98 | 8.82 | 8.53 | | | | 8.93 |

[1] Preliminary.    Source: Economic Research Service, U.S. Department of Agriculture (ERS-USDA)

## Average Farm Prices of Winter Wheat in the United States    In Dollars Per Bushel

| Crop Year | June | July | Aug. | Sept. | Oct. | Nov. | Dec. | Jan. | Feb. | Mar. | Apr. | May | Average |
|---|---|---|---|---|---|---|---|---|---|---|---|---|---|
| 2013-14 | 7.18 | 6.85 | 6.81 | 6.80 | 7.07 | 6.96 | 6.84 | 6.72 | 6.58 | 6.92 | 7.07 | 7.26 | 6.92 |
| 2014-15 | 6.34 | 5.99 | 5.90 | 5.69 | 5.65 | 5.87 | 6.14 | 6.02 | 5.70 | 5.55 | 5.50 | 5.19 | 5.80 |
| 2015-16 | 5.20 | 5.15 | 4.80 | 4.64 | 4.76 | 4.66 | 4.57 | 4.63 | 4.47 | 4.28 | 4.31 | 4.28 | 4.65 |
| 2016-17 | 3.97 | 3.56 | 3.41 | 3.25 | 3.37 | 3.41 | 3.40 | 3.53 | 3.77 | 3.82 | 3.70 | 3.77 | 3.58 |
| 2017-18 | 4.11 | 4.56 | 4.27 | 4.11 | 4.17 | 4.07 | 3.89 | 4.15 | 4.63 | 4.73 | 4.90 | 5.05 | 4.39 |
| 2018-19 | 5.05 | 4.92 | 5.24 | 5.14 | 5.22 | 5.20 | 5.24 | 5.25 | 5.40 | 5.16 | 4.86 | 4.74 | 5.12 |
| 2019-20 | 4.77 | 4.48 | 4.28 | 4.19 | 4.35 | 4.35 | 4.58 | 4.86 | 4.98 | 4.84 | 4.88 | 4.83 | 4.62 |
| 2020-21 | 4.44 | 4.53 | 4.51 | 4.68 | 4.97 | 5.33 | 5.60 | 5.55 | 5.96 | 6.05 | 6.20 | 6.55 | 5.36 |
| 2021-22 | 6.10 | 6.10 | 6.78 | 7.18 | 7.23 | 7.78 | 7.79 | 7.70 | 8.51 | 9.52 | 9.84 | 10.50 | 7.92 |
| 2022-23[1] | 9.14 | 8.34 | 8.43 | 8.73 | 9.14 | 8.92 | 8.44 | 8.32 | 8.33 | | | | 8.64 |

[1] Preliminary.    Source: Economic Research Service, U.S. Department of Agriculture (ERS-USDA)

## Average Farm Prices of Durum Wheat in the United States    In Dollars Per Bushel

| Crop Year | June | July | Aug. | Sept. | Oct. | Nov. | Dec. | Jan. | Feb. | Mar. | Apr. | May | Average |
|---|---|---|---|---|---|---|---|---|---|---|---|---|---|
| 2013-14 | 8.51 | 8.32 | 7.73 | 7.84 | 7.03 | 6.72 | 6.90 | 7.01 | 6.43 | 6.69 | 6.80 | 7.21 | 7.27 |
| 2014-15 | 7.96 | 8.13 | 8.03 | 8.25 | 8.48 | 11.00 | 10.70 | 9.89 | 10.10 | 9.50 | 7.79 | 8.02 | 8.99 |
| 2015-16 | 9.16 | 8.74 | 7.28 | 6.36 | 6.57 | 6.97 | 6.93 | 6.60 | 6.08 | 6.03 | 6.24 | 6.57 | 6.96 |
| 2016-17 | 6.50 | 6.47 | 5.66 | 5.61 | 5.51 | 6.00 | 6.07 | 5.90 | 5.71 | 5.72 | 5.90 | 5.82 | 5.91 |
| 2017-18 | 6.69 | 6.30 | 6.89 | 6.31 | 6.41 | 6.55 | 6.25 | 6.05 | 6.19 | 5.66 | 5.41 | 6.02 | 6.23 |
| 2018-19 | 6.33 | 5.79 | 5.05 | 5.00 | 4.99 | 4.72 | 4.83 | 4.86 | 4.72 | 5.05 | 4.85 | 4.92 | 5.09 |
| 2019-20 | 5.58 | 5.53 | 4.67 | 4.64 | 4.54 | 4.17 | 4.44 | 4.72 | 4.96 | 5.46 | 5.26 | 5.27 | 4.94 |
| 2020-21 | 6.52 | 6.01 | 5.59 | 5.66 | 5.66 | 5.83 | 5.87 | 5.88 | 6.37 | 6.00 | 6.46 | 7.15 | 6.08 |
| 2021-22 | 7.14 | 7.69 | 9.98 | 13.80 | 14.00 | 14.00 | 12.70 | 14.90 | 15.90 | 15.30 | 15.50 | 14.30 | 12.93 |
| 2022-23[1] | 12.00 | 12.70 | 10.80 | 9.92 | 10.20 | 10.40 | 11.20 | 10.60 | 9.34 | | | | 10.80 |

[1] Preliminary.    Source: Economic Research Service, U.S. Department of Agriculture (ERS-USDA)

## Average Farm Prices of Other Spring Wheat in the United States    In Dollars Per Bushel

| Crop Year | June | July | Aug. | Sept. | Oct. | Nov. | Dec. | Jan. | Feb. | Mar. | Apr. | May | Average |
|---|---|---|---|---|---|---|---|---|---|---|---|---|---|
| 2013-14 | 7.72 | 7.30 | 6.97 | 6.71 | 6.66 | 6.70 | 6.55 | 6.48 | 6.40 | 6.56 | 6.61 | 6.85 | 6.79 |
| 2014-15 | 6.60 | 6.23 | 5.93 | 5.51 | 5.57 | 5.73 | 5.80 | 5.84 | 5.55 | 5.53 | 5.51 | 5.29 | 5.76 |
| 2015-16 | 5.20 | 5.15 | 4.71 | 4.68 | 4.78 | 4.91 | 4.80 | 4.81 | 4.56 | 4.47 | 4.55 | 4.64 | 4.77 |
| 2016-17 | 4.61 | 4.48 | 4.26 | 4.22 | 4.38 | 4.48 | 4.66 | 4.74 | 4.83 | 4.86 | 4.83 | 4.81 | 4.60 |
| 2017-18 | 5.35 | 6.09 | 5.86 | 5.62 | 5.56 | 5.78 | 5.62 | 5.72 | 5.66 | 5.74 | 5.78 | 5.84 | 5.72 |
| 2018-19 | 5.66 | 5.41 | 5.41 | 5.16 | 5.26 | 5.33 | 5.36 | 5.37 | 5.30 | 5.23 | 5.03 | 4.86 | 5.28 |
| 2019-20 | 4.79 | 4.64 | 4.43 | 4.35 | 4.70 | 4.53 | 4.79 | 4.92 | 4.74 | 4.82 | 4.72 | 4.51 | 4.66 |
| 2020-21 | 4.47 | 4.36 | 4.51 | 4.73 | 4.91 | 5.03 | 5.17 | 5.34 | 5.62 | 5.64 | 5.86 | 6.31 | 5.16 |
| 2021-22 | 6.63 | 70.35 | 7.88 | 7.93 | 8.73 | 8.84 | 8.75 | 8.53 | 9.16 | 9.85 | 10.20 | 11.00 | 13.99 |
| 2022-23[1] | 10.90 | 10.00 | 8.71 | 8.93 | 9.15 | 9.24 | 9.13 | 9.06 | 8.70 | | | | 9.31 |

[1] Preliminary.    Source: Economic Research Service, U.S. Department of Agriculture (ERS-USDA)

# WHEAT

**WHEAT, CHICAGO - CBOT**
Weekly Nearest Futures as of 03/31/2023

Nearby Futures through Last Trading Day.

## Volume of Trading of Wheat Futures in Chicago   In Thousands of Contracts

| Year | Jan. | Feb. | Mar. | Apr. | May | June | July | Aug. | Sept. | Oct. | Nov. | Dec. | Total |
|---|---|---|---|---|---|---|---|---|---|---|---|---|---|
| 2013 | 2,006.5 | 2,679.0 | 1,937.3 | 2,888.9 | 1,872.7 | 2,488.8 | 1,872.6 | 2,487.0 | 1,323.5 | 1,741.4 | 2,312.0 | 1,235.7 | 24,845.5 |
| 2014 | 1,888.8 | 2,681.9 | 2,375.1 | 2,605.2 | 2,389.1 | 3,028.9 | 2,210.8 | 3,064.6 | 1,804.6 | 1,793.2 | 2,387.5 | 1,962.5 | 28,192.3 |
| 2015 | 1,787.2 | 2,612.3 | 2,394.8 | 3,074.8 | 2,433.3 | 4,087.8 | 2,753.5 | 2,961.6 | 1,919.4 | 2,322.0 | 3,144.4 | 1,611.0 | 31,102.0 |
| 2016 | 1,820.7 | 3,224.7 | 2,084.5 | 3,611.5 | 2,355.1 | 3,693.2 | 2,353.2 | 3,410.3 | 1,457.6 | 2,200.7 | 3,270.0 | 1,578.1 | 31,059.7 |
| 2017 | 2,384.5 | 3,190.9 | 2,293.9 | 3,293.2 | 2,515.3 | 4,132.5 | 3,121.2 | 3,381.6 | 1,891.5 | 2,200.8 | 3,692.9 | 1,619.4 | 33,717.8 |
| 2018 | 2,699.7 | 3,731.2 | 3,045.3 | 3,473.5 | 3,416.5 | 4,219.7 | 2,990.5 | 4,177.6 | 2,082.6 | 2,407.8 | 3,073.7 | 1,486.9 | 36,805.2 |
| 2019 | 1,924.5 | 3,438.2 | 2,584.2 | 3,062.6 | 2,879.6 | 3,497.9 | 2,271.6 | 2,877.3 | 1,539.8 | 1,952.4 | 2,614.6 | 1,764.3 | 30,407.1 |
| 2020 | 2,524.0 | 3,404.0 | 3,342.7 | 2,699.6 | 1,870.2 | 3,369.4 | 2,600.7 | 3,292.5 | 2,253.8 | 2,749.4 | 3,199.5 | 2,059.6 | 33,365.3 |
| 2021 | 2,440.7 | 2,906.9 | 2,091.4 | 3,652.5 | 2,182.5 | 3,304.4 | 2,284.4 | 3,153.6 | 1,656.9 | 1,725.1 | 2,997.8 | 1,580.8 | 29,977.0 |
| 2022 | 1,946.1 | 3,141.5 | 2,930.8 | 1,788.5 | 1,826.2 | 2,581.7 | 1,811.1 | 2,374.2 | 1,842.9 | 1,797.4 | 2,543.6 | 1,371.4 | 25,955.4 |

Contract size = 5,000 bu.   *Source: CME Group; Chicago Board of Trade (CBT)*

## Average Open Interest of Wheat Futures in Chicago   In Contracts

| Year | Jan. | Feb. | Mar. | Apr. | May | June | July | Aug. | Sept. | Oct. | Nov. | Dec. |
|---|---|---|---|---|---|---|---|---|---|---|---|---|
| 2013 | 463,359 | 470,154 | 457,785 | 436,052 | 410,871 | 414,728 | 404,821 | 399,943 | 358,054 | 366,743 | 394,264 | 396,016 |
| 2014 | 429,507 | 413,808 | 350,290 | 371,767 | 371,689 | 389,610 | 407,989 | 417,932 | 400,815 | 419,886 | 403,348 | 372,284 |
| 2015 | 382,618 | 415,559 | 426,147 | 453,404 | 444,906 | 432,352 | 402,961 | 406,381 | 372,538 | 377,775 | 381,822 | 351,546 |
| 2016 | 396,301 | 436,358 | 430,193 | 437,750 | 404,026 | 411,893 | 457,192 | 456,866 | 460,023 | 483,899 | 494,269 | 445,295 |
| 2017 | 473,794 | 458,494 | 463,099 | 508,045 | 445,294 | 441,396 | 430,971 | 452,301 | 433,612 | 486,843 | 551,386 | 521,674 |
| 2018 | 546,304 | 499,112 | 481,428 | 477,365 | 489,652 | 514,394 | 472,514 | 483,532 | 460,995 | 500,521 | 493,664 | 435,278 |
| 2019 | 450,353 | 467,963 | 494,051 | 479,684 | 469,294 | 412,885 | 371,636 | 380,149 | 358,914 | 396,981 | 392,793 | 385,505 |
| 2020 | 476,950 | 499,412 | 397,950 | 364,502 | 368,140 | 405,629 | 387,116 | 380,385 | 380,499 | 430,462 | 434,387 | 388,969 |
| 2021 | 434,655 | 438,308 | 419,004 | 430,490 | 411,472 | 394,468 | 341,669 | 385,714 | 361,253 | 391,152 | 412,390 | 358,848 |
| 2022 | 377,141 | 389,613 | 344,266 | 335,989 | 321,534 | 321,360 | 294,737 | 313,672 | 289,571 | 310,501 | 342,221 | 332,531 |

Contract size = 5,000 bu.   *Source: CME Group; Chicago Board of Trade (CBT)*

# WHEAT

### Average Price of No. 1 Dark Northern Spring (13% Protein) Wheat in Minneapolis    In Dollars Per Bushel

| Crop Year | June | July | Aug. | Sept. | Oct. | Nov. | Dec. | Jan. | Feb. | Mar. | Apr. | May | Average |
|---|---|---|---|---|---|---|---|---|---|---|---|---|---|
| 2013-14 | 9.08 | 8.56 | 8.10 | 7.91 | 8.62 | 8.22 | 8.22 | 8.52 | 8.42 | 9.22 | 8.39 | 8.75 | 8.50 |
| 2014-15 | 8.32 | 8.04 | 7.57 | 7.02 | 7.14 | 7.52 | 7.41 | 6.82 | 6.78 | 6.79 | 6.40 | 6.44 | 7.19 |
| 2015-16 | 6.50 | 6.33 | 5.72 | 5.88 | 6.23 | 6.30 | 5.94 | 5.82 | 5.69 | 5.66 | 5.98 | 5.85 | 5.99 |
| 2016-17 | 5.86 | 5.50 | 5.61 | 5.40 | 6.28 | 6.26 | 6.28 | 6.47 | 6.22 | 6.08 | 5.86 | 6.38 | 6.02 |
| 2017-18 | 7.26 | 8.24 | 7.43 | 6.84 | 7.07 | 7.16 | 6.94 | 7.10 | 6.91 | 7.24 | 7.28 | 7.35 | 7.24 |
| 2018-19 | 6.84 | 6.62 | 6.70 | 6.52 | 6.76 | 6.94 | 6.60 | 6.72 | 7.14 | 7.26 | 6.34 | 6.27 | 6.73 |
| 2019-20 | 6.63 | 6.18 | 5.76 | 6.12 | 6.36 | 6.84 | 6.60 | 6.57 | 6.36 | 6.54 | 6.33 | 5.29 | 6.30 |
| 2020-21 | 6.47 | 6.18 | 5.80 | 6.37 | 6.74 | ---- | ---- | 7.37 | 7.32 | 7.33 | 8.10 | 8.80 | 7.05 |
| 2021-22 | 8.59 | 9.65 | 10.47 | ---- | 11.65 | 11.96 | 11.44 | ---- | ---- | ---- | 12.60 | ---- | 10.91 |
| 2022-23[1] | 11.49 | 10.55 | 10.51 | ---- | ---- | ---- | 10.82 | ---- | 10.33 | | | | 10.74 |

[1] Preliminary.    Source: Economic Research Service, U.S. Department of Agriculture (ERS-USDA)

### Average Price of No. 1 Dark Northern Spring (14% Protein) Wheat in Minneapolis    In Dollars Per Bushel

| Crop Year | June | July | Aug. | Sept. | Oct. | Nov. | Dec. | Jan. | Feb. | Mar. | Apr. | May | Average |
|---|---|---|---|---|---|---|---|---|---|---|---|---|---|
| 2013-14 | 9.18 | 8.57 | 8.36 | 8.22 | 8.78 | 8.40 | 8.64 | 9.32 | 9.03 | 9.64 | 8.72 | 8.95 | 8.82 |
| 2014-15 | 9.00 | 8.66 | 8.18 | 8.48 | 8.12 | 8.50 | 8.22 | 7.37 | 7.51 | 7.91 | 7.39 | 7.62 | 8.08 |
| 2015-16 | 7.56 | 7.12 | 6.16 | 6.15 | 6.44 | 6.49 | 6.25 | 6.05 | 5.93 | 5.84 | 6.11 | 6.02 | 6.34 |
| 2016-17 | 6.11 | 5.74 | 5.87 | 5.62 | 6.48 | 6.32 | 6.64 | 6.75 | 6.58 | 6.33 | 6.34 | 6.60 | 6.28 |
| 2017-18 | 7.66 | 8.64 | 7.64 | 7.18 | 7.36 | 7.66 | 7.40 | 7.41 | 7.68 | 7.58 | 7.57 | 7.66 | 7.62 |
| 2018-19 | 7.14 | 6.86 | 6.72 | 6.48 | 6.76 | 7.02 | 6.77 | 6.79 | 7.17 | 7.19 | 6.33 | 6.23 | 6.79 |
| 2019-20 | 6.59 | 6.22 | 5.90 | 6.24 | 6.54 | 6.98 | 6.76 | 5.82 | 6.54 | 6.58 | 6.22 | 6.32 | 6.39 |
| 2020-21 | 6.66 | 6.16 | 6.20 | 6.73 | 6.82 | 6.87 | 6.84 | 7.40 | 7.41 | 7.40 | 8.00 | 8.61 | 7.09 |
| 2021-22 | 9.01 | 10.16 | 10.40 | 10.20 | 11.09 | 11.55 | 11.78 | 11.08 | 11.20 | 12.23 | 13.23 | 14.40 | 11.36 |
| 2022-23[1] | 13.21 | 10.85 | 10.56 | 10.67 | 11.36 | 11.90 | 11.37 | 11.13 | 10.69 | | | | 11.30 |

[1] Preliminary.    Source: Economic Research Service, U.S. Department of Agriculture (ERS-USDA)

### Average Price of No. 2 Soft Red Winter Wheat in Toledo, OH    In Dollars Per Bushel

| Crop Year | June | July | Aug. | Sept. | Oct. | Nov. | Dec. | Jan. | Feb. | Mar. | Apr. | May | Average |
|---|---|---|---|---|---|---|---|---|---|---|---|---|---|
| 2013-14 | 6.75 | 6.50 | 6.32 | 6.32 | 6.61 | 6.29 | 6.01 | 5.60 | 5.91 | 6.73 | 6.78 | 6.74 | 6.38 |
| 2014-15 | 5.89 | 5.41 | 4.65 | 3.65 | 5.13 | 5.44 | 6.19 | 5.54 | 4.45 | 5.17 | 5.08 | 4.92 | 5.13 |
| 2015-16 | 5.22 | 5.58 | 5.20 | 5.04 | 5.25 | 5.16 | 4.97 | 4.93 | 4.69 | 4.61 | 4.63 | 4.61 | 4.99 |
| 2016-17 | 4.69 | 4.22 | 4.03 | 3.72 | 3.90 | 3.92 | 3.80 | 4.09 | 4.28 | 4.14 | 4.08 | 4.19 | 4.09 |
| 2017-18 | 4.44 | 4.94 | 4.20 | 4.27 | 4.24 | 4.18 | 4.04 | 4.22 | 4.54 | 4.75 | 4.85 | 5.24 | 4.49 |
| 2018-19 | 5.15 | 5.20 | 5.48 | 5.04 | 5.04 | 5.00 | 5.14 | 5.12 | 4.95 | 4.48 | 4.43 | 4.50 | 4.96 |
| 2019-20 | 5.42 | 5.28 | 4.99 | 4.99 | 5.26 | 5.31 | 5.54 | 5.78 | 5.62 | 5.41 | 5.35 | 5.07 | 5.34 |
| 2020-21 | 4.95 | 5.28 | 5.14 | 5.43 | 5.93 | 5.79 | 5.95 | 6.50 | 6.47 | 6.32 | 6.71 | 7.09 | 5.96 |
| 2021-22 | 6.74 | 6.70 | 7.27 | 6.89 | 7.30 | 7.89 | 7.74 | 7.56 | 7.83 | 10.73 | 10.37 | 11.18 | 8.18 |
| 2022-23[1] | 9.94 | 7.88 | 7.63 | 8.29 | 8.36 | 7.86 | 7.19 | 7.16 | 7.23 | | | | 7.95 |

[1] Preliminary.    Source: Economic Research Service, U.S. Department of Agriculture (ERS-USDA)

### Average Price of No. 1 Soft White Wheat in Portland, OR    In Dollars Per Bushel

| Crop Year | June | July | Aug. | Sept. | Oct. | Nov. | Dec. | Jan. | Feb. | Mar. | Apr. | May | Average |
|---|---|---|---|---|---|---|---|---|---|---|---|---|---|
| 2013-14 | ---- | 7.23 | 7.32 | 7.17 | 7.27 | 7.04 | 6.97 | 6.78 | 7.20 | 7.55 | 7.65 | 7.65 | 7.26 |
| 2014-15 | 6.99 | 6.69 | 6.88 | 6.75 | 6.79 | 7.00 | 7.19 | 6.52 | 6.49 | 6.36 | 6.23 | 5.94 | 6.65 |
| 2015-16 | ---- | ---- | 5.55 | 5.38 | 5.49 | 5.37 | ---- | 5.31 | 5.30 | ---- | 5.33 | 5.34 | 5.38 |
| 2016-17 | 5.46 | 5.07 | 4.89 | 4.77 | 4.65 | 4.64 | 4.57 | 4.63 | 4.74 | 4.70 | 4.61 | 4.77 | 4.79 |
| 2017-18 | 4.91 | 5.40 | 5.13 | 5.19 | 5.30 | 5.26 | 5.22 | 5.30 | 5.39 | 5.64 | 5.63 | 5.79 | 5.35 |
| 2018-19 | 5.92 | 5.88 | 6.18 | 5.98 | 6.11 | 6.25 | 6.23 | 6.29 | 6.36 | 6.10 | 5.94 | 5.83 | 6.09 |
| 2019-20 | 5.94 | 5.96 | 5.76 | 5.83 | 5.99 | 5.96 | 5.96 | 6.22 | 6.24 | 6.02 | 6.06 | 5.94 | 5.99 |
| 2020-21 | 5.87 | 5.79 | 5.39 | 5.26 | ---- | 6.21 | 6.26 | 6.60 | 7.28 | 7.35 | ---- | 8.40 | 6.44 |
| 2021-22 | 8.44 | 8.36 | 9.90 | 10.69 | 10.43 | 10.83 | 10.79 | 10.78 | 10.88 | 11.44 | 11.00 | 11.26 | 10.40 |
| 2022-23[1] | 11.09 | 9.29 | 8.85 | 9.37 | 9.11 | 9.01 | 8.63 | 8.36 | 8.47 | | | | 9.13 |

[1] Preliminary.    Source: Economic Research Service, U.S. Department of Agriculture (ERS-USDA)

# WHEAT

## Average Producer Price Index of Wheat Flour (Spring[2])    June 1983 = 100

| Crop Year | Jan. | Feb. | Mar. | Apr. | May | June | July | Aug. | Sept. | Oct. | Nov. | Dec. | Average |
|---|---|---|---|---|---|---|---|---|---|---|---|---|---|
| 2012 | 206.8 | 216.4 | 219.2 | 219.7 | 214.3 | 214.4 | 231.2 | 226.5 | 232.0 | 232.4 | 236.4 | 233.8 | 223.6 |
| 2013 | 231.0 | 223.5 | 219.6 | 220.6 | 229.1 | 230.2 | 226.0 | 219.8 | 218.4 | 225.5 | 220.1 | 218.4 | 223.5 |
| 2014 | 223.3 | 224.9 | 235.6 | 229.5 | 234.8 | 225.5 | 225.7 | 218.8 | 231.5 | 225.3 | 225.6 | 230.5 | 227.6 |
| 2015 | 213.4 | 214.5 | 214.5 | 210.5 | 212.2 | 216.1 | 214.3 | 193.5 | 189.1 | 192.6 | 191.2 | 196.3 | 204.9 |
| 2016 | 194.3 | 192.1 | 193.5 | 193.4 | 195.2 | 195.1 | 186.3 | 183.8 | 183.8 | 187.9 | 186.4 | 186.2 | 189.8 |
| 2017 | 188.9 | 189.2 | 184.5 | 181.1 | 187.4 | 194.5 | 215.4 | 197.9 | 194.0 | 193.1 | 197.1 | 193.1 | 193.0 |
| 2018 | 194.8 | 193.0 | 196.0 | 196.4 | 197.0 | 197.9 | 193.3 | 196.5 | 191.8 | 193.1 | 193.8 | 193.5 | 194.8 |
| 2019 | 192.4 | 193.5 | 191.8 | 190.4 | 188.1 | 194.3 | 192.4 | 185.2 | 182.9 | 191.0 | 192.1 | 192.3 | 190.5 |
| 2020 | 195.6 | 193.3 | 192.7 | 193.4 | 191.3 | 192.4 | 192.2 | 189.5 | 191.8 | 193.7 | 196.8 | 196.3 | 193.3 |
| 2021[1] | 204.9 | 203.7 | 208.0 | 206.0 | 219.8 | 219.0 | 230.6 | 246.7 | 246.7 | 256.7 | 261.8 | 260.8 | 230.4 |

[1] Preliminary.    [2] Standard patent.    Source: Bureau of Labor Statistics, U.S. Department of Commerce (BLS) (0212-0301)

## United States Wheat Flour Exports (Grain Equivalent[2])    In Thousands of Bushels

| Crop Year | June | July | Aug. | Sept. | Oct. | Nov. | Dec. | Jan. | Feb. | Mar. | Apr. | May | Total |
|---|---|---|---|---|---|---|---|---|---|---|---|---|---|
| 2013-14 | 1,626 | 975 | 836 | 1,005 | 1,218 | 986 | 1,173 | 955 | 807 | 954 | 1,141 | 1,140 | 12,816 |
| 2014-15 | 955 | 1,214 | 1,067 | 1,301 | 1,182 | 1,430 | 1,096 | 1,057 | 1,283 | 1,524 | 1,062 | 1,315 | 14,486 |
| 2015-16 | 1,222 | 1,225 | 1,208 | 1,431 | 1,466 | 1,491 | 1,521 | 1,457 | 1,085 | 1,685 | 1,303 | 1,467 | 16,562 |
| 2016-17 | 1,711 | 1,338 | 1,399 | 1,672 | 1,872 | 1,774 | 1,469 | 1,624 | 1,430 | 1,288 | 1,191 | 1,574 | 18,344 |
| 2017-18 | 1,463 | 1,438 | 1,664 | 915 | 716 | 873 | 1,072 | 935 | 1,136 | 1,162 | 1,094 | 1,367 | 13,833 |
| 2018-19 | 1,371 | 945 | 1,097 | 1,016 | 1,624 | 1,191 | 1,250 | 1,282 | 1,267 | 1,172 | 1,167 | 1,105 | 14,485 |
| 2019-20 | 1,057 | 1,198 | 1,284 | 1,227 | 1,327 | 1,141 | 993 | 1,142 | 1,163 | 1,265 | 1,291 | 1,168 | 14,255 |
| 2020-21 | 1,214 | 1,128 | 1,220 | 1,110 | 1,116 | 1,228 | 1,084 | 983 | 879 | 1,259 | 1,188 | 1,100 | 13,510 |
| 2021-22 | 1,000 | 959 | 1,055 | 1,054 | 927 | 1,031 | 1,027 | 914 | 945 | 1,059 | 1,059 | 1,003 | 12,031 |
| 2022-23[1] | 951 | 983 | 1,056 | 911 | 870 | 789 | 687 | 627 | | | | | 10,311 |

[1] Preliminary.    [2] Includes meal, groats and durum.    Source: Economic Research Service, U.S. Department of Agriculture (ERS-USDA)

## Supply and Distribution of Wheat Flour in the United States

| Year | Wheat Ground 1,000 Bu. | Milfeed Production 1,000 Tons | Flour Production[3] | Flour & Product Imports[2] | Total Supply | Exports Flour | Exports Products | Domestic Disappearance | Total Population July 1 Millions | Per Capita Disappearance Pounds |
|---|---|---|---|---|---|---|---|---|---|---|
| 2013 | 919,830 | 6,367 | 424,550 | 12,281 | 436,831 | 5,274 | 3,755 | 427,803 | 316.8 | 135.0 |
| 2014 | 921,264 | 6,423 | 424,949 | 13,859 | 438,808 | 5,303 | 3,664 | 429,841 | 319.2 | 134.7 |
| 2015 | 923,641 | 6,641 | 424,910 | 14,753 | 439,663 | 6,376 | 3,567 | 429,720 | 323.0 | 133.0 |
| 2016 | 914,635 | 6,559 | 423,846 | 15,038 | 438,884 | 7,368 | 2,973 | 428,543 | 323.1 | 132.6 |
| 2017 | 917,816 | 6,447 | 426,399 | 14,843 | 441,242 | 6,212 | 2,777 | 432,253 | 325.1 | 132.9 |
| 2018 | 918,373 | 6,458 | 426,871 | 15,552 | 442,423 | 5,693 | 2,723 | 434,008 | 326.9 | 132.8 |
| 2019 | 912,609 | 6,485 | 422,277 | 15,692 | 437,969 | 5,867 | 2,600 | 429,502 | 328.5 | 130.8 |
| 2020 | 917,978 | 6,547 | 425,797 | 19,068 | 444,865 | 5,791 | 3,183 | 435,890 | 331.2 | 131.6 |
| 2021 | 913,380 | 6,639 | 421,176 | 16,201 | 437,377 | 5,097 | 3,073 | 429,207 | 332.3 | 129.2 |
| 2022[1] | 928,615 | 6,732 | 430,284 | 19,655 | 449,939 | 4,473 | 2,877 | 442,589 | 333.5 | 132.7 |

[1] Preliminary.    [2] Commercial production of wheat flour, whole wheat, industrial and durum flour and farina reported by Bureau of Census.
Source: Economic Research Service, U.S. Department of Agriculture (ERS-USDA)

## Wheat and Flour Price Relationships at Milling Centers in the United States    In Dollars

| Crop Year | At Kansas City - Cost of Wheat to Produce 100 lb. Flour[1] | At Kansas City - Bakery Flour 100 lb. Flour[2] | At Kansas City - By-Products Obtained 100 lb. Flour[3] | At Kansas City - Total Products Actual | At Kansas City - Total Products Over Cost of Wheat | At Minneapolis - Cost of Wheat to Produce 100 lb. Flour[1] | At Minneapolis - Bakery Flour 100 lb. Flour[2] | At Minneapolis - By-Products Obtained 100 lb. Flour[3] | At Minneapolis - Total Products Actual | At Minneapolis - Total Products Over Cost of Wheat |
|---|---|---|---|---|---|---|---|---|---|---|
| 2014-15 | 16.16 | 17.24 | 1.91 | 19.15 | 2.99 | 19.35 | 18.75 | 1.86 | 20.61 | 1.37 |
| 2015-16 | 13.16 | 14.00 | 1.61 | 15.61 | 2.45 | 14.00 | 14.34 | 1.28 | 15.62 | 1.17 |
| 2016-17 | 12.74 | 13.14 | 1.35 | 14.49 | 1.75 | 14.32 | 14.51 | .65 | 15.16 | .84 |
| 2017-18 | 15.33 | 15.51 | 1.79 | 17.31 | 1.97 | 17.38 | 17.24 | .73 | 17.96 | .59 |
| 2018-19 | 14.41 | 15.40 | 1.96 | 17.37 | 2.96 | 15.57 | 15.28 | .79 | 16.06 | .48 |
| 2019-20 | 14.11 | 14.31 | 2.07 | 16.38 | 2.26 | 14.58 | 14.63 | .91 | 15.55 | .96 |
| 2020-21 | 15.76 | 15.78 | 2.69 | 18.47 | 2.71 | 16.17 | 15.40 | 1.08 | 16.48 | .31 |
| 2021-22 | 24.41 | 23.63 | 3.28 | 26.91 | 2.50 | 24.42 | 23.22 | 1.38 | 24.60 | .18 |
| 2022-23 | 24.64 | 23.18 | 4.24 | 27.42 | 2.78 | 24.42 | 23.22 | 1.38 | 24.60 | .18 |
| June-Aug. | 25.01 | 24.27 | 3.65 | 27.91 | 2.90 | 22.48 | 21.50 | 1.44 | 22.94 | .46 |
| Sept.-Nov. | 25.38 | 23.58 | 4.66 | 28.24 | 2.87 | 24.95 | 23.63 | 1.33 | 24.96 | .01 |

[1] Based on 73% extraction rate, cost of 2.28 bushels: At Kansas City, No. 1 hard winter 13% protein; and at Minneapolis, No. 1 dark northern spring, 14% protein.    [2] quoted as mid-month bakers' standard patent at Kansas City and spring standard patent at Minneapolis, bulk basis.    [3] Assumed 50-50 millfeed distribution between bran and shorts or middlings, bulk basis.    Source: Agricultural Marketing Service, U.S. Department of Agriculture

# WHEAT

## Weekly Outstanding Export Sales and Cumulative Exports of U.S. Wheat    In Thousands of Metric Tons

| Marketing Year 2021/2022 Week Ending | Weekly Exports | Accumulated Exports | Net Sales | Outstanding Sales | Marketing Year 2022/2023 Week Ending | Weekly Exports | Accumulated Exports | Net Sales | Outstanding Sales |
|---|---|---|---|---|---|---|---|---|---|
| Jun 03, 2021 | 136,257 | 136,257 | 1,163,059 | 5,376,191 | Jun 02, 2022 | 212,022 | 212,022 | 450,955 | 4,346,835 |
| Jun 10, 2021 | 298,589 | 434,846 | 287,137 | 5,364,739 | Jun 09, 2022 | 370,137 | 582,159 | 236,857 | 4,213,555 |
| Jun 17, 2021 | 590,830 | 1,025,676 | 374,147 | 5,148,056 | Jun 16, 2022 | 336,344 | 918,503 | 477,776 | 4,354,987 |
| Jun 24, 2021 | 135,996 | 1,161,672 | 226,331 | 5,238,391 | Jun 23, 2022 | 241,395 | 1,159,898 | 496,719 | 4,610,311 |
| Jul 01, 2021 | 385,080 | 1,546,752 | 290,836 | 5,144,147 | Jun 30, 2022 | 287,056 | 1,446,954 | 286,385 | 4,609,640 |
| Jul 08, 2021 | 365,910 | 1,912,662 | 424,691 | 5,202,928 | Jul 07, 2022 | 269,985 | 1,716,939 | 1,017,156 | 5,356,811 |
| Jul 15, 2021 | 470,988 | 2,383,650 | 473,166 | 5,205,106 | Jul 14, 2022 | 141,803 | 1,858,742 | 511,086 | 5,726,094 |
| Jul 22, 2021 | 344,965 | 2,728,615 | 515,168 | 5,375,309 | Jul 21, 2022 | 345,842 | 2,204,584 | 411,989 | 5,792,241 |
| Jul 29, 2021 | 387,164 | 3,115,779 | 308,275 | 5,296,420 | Jul 28, 2022 | 288,415 | 2,492,999 | 249,923 | 5,753,749 |
| Aug 05, 2021 | 627,929 | 3,743,708 | 293,119 | 4,961,610 | Aug 04, 2022 | 615,250 | 3,108,249 | 359,165 | 5,497,664 |
| Aug 12, 2021 | 591,757 | 4,335,465 | 306,678 | 4,676,531 | Aug 11, 2022 | 349,630 | 3,457,879 | 207,152 | 5,355,186 |
| Aug 19, 2021 | 675,753 | 5,011,218 | 115,964 | 4,116,742 | Aug 18, 2022 |  | 3,457,879 |  | 5,355,186 |
| Aug 26, 2021 | 417,091 | 5,428,309 | 295,303 | 3,994,954 | Aug 25, 2022 | 1,147,211 | 4,605,090 | 999,538 | 5,207,513 |
| Sep 02, 2021 | 390,079 | 5,818,388 | 388,384 | 3,993,259 | Sep 01, 2022 | 546,611 | 5,151,701 | 192,625 | 4,853,527 |
| Sep 09, 2021 | 514,110 | 6,332,498 | 617,115 | 4,096,264 | Sep 08, 2022 | 676,767 | 5,828,468 | 217,336 | 4,394,096 |
| Sep 16, 2021 | 507,804 | 6,840,302 | 355,805 | 3,944,265 | Sep 15, 2022 | 678,196 | 6,506,664 | 183,467 | 3,899,367 |
| Sep 23, 2021 | 368,865 | 7,209,167 | 290,124 | 3,865,524 | Sep 22, 2022 | 620,679 | 7,127,343 | 279,793 | 3,558,481 |
| Sep 30, 2021 | 543,444 | 7,752,611 | 333,218 | 3,655,298 | Sep 29, 2022 | 629,766 | 7,757,109 | 229,400 | 3,158,115 |
| Oct 07, 2021 | 458,882 | 8,211,493 | 567,598 | 3,764,014 | Oct 06, 2022 | 560,497 | 8,317,606 | 211,823 | 2,809,441 |
| Oct 14, 2021 | 160,174 | 8,371,667 | 362,374 | 3,966,214 | Oct 13, 2022 | 242,584 | 8,560,190 | 163,128 | 2,729,985 |
| Oct 21, 2021 | 185,559 | 8,557,226 | 269,265 | 4,049,920 | Oct 20, 2022 | 136,762 | 8,696,952 | 533,220 | 3,126,443 |
| Oct 28, 2021 | 136,373 | 8,693,599 | 400,102 | 4,313,649 | Oct 27, 2022 | 118,125 | 8,815,077 | 348,054 | 3,356,372 |
| Nov 04, 2021 | 250,739 | 8,944,338 | 266,679 | 4,329,589 | Nov 03, 2022 | 151,524 | 8,966,601 | 322,501 | 3,527,349 |
| Nov 11, 2021 | 310,881 | 9,255,219 | 399,100 | 4,417,808 | Nov 10, 2022 | 118,572 | 9,085,173 | 290,299 | 3,699,076 |
| Nov 18, 2021 | 199,166 | 9,454,385 | 567,487 | 4,786,129 | Nov 17, 2022 | 138,382 | 9,223,555 | 511,769 | 4,072,463 |
| Nov 25, 2021 | 370,097 | 9,824,482 | 78,600 | 4,494,632 | Nov 24, 2022 | 271,230 | 9,494,785 | 155,534 | 3,956,767 |
| Dec 02, 2021 | 213,415 | 10,037,897 | 239,898 | 4,521,115 | Dec 01, 2022 | 257,445 | 9,752,230 | 189,858 | 3,889,180 |
| Dec 09, 2021 | 274,383 | 10,312,280 | 650,587 | 4,897,319 | Dec 08, 2022 | 255,918 | 10,008,148 | 468,962 | 4,102,224 |
| Dec 16, 2021 | 190,359 | 10,502,639 | 425,397 | 5,132,357 | Dec 15, 2022 | 235,346 | 10,243,494 | 334,207 | 4,201,085 |
| Dec 23, 2021 | 335,045 | 10,837,684 | 199,523 | 4,996,835 | Dec 22, 2022 | 337,074 | 10,580,568 | 478,122 | 4,342,133 |
| Dec 30, 2021 | 210,877 | 11,048,561 | 48,569 | 4,834,527 | Dec 29, 2022 | 81,488 | 10,662,056 | 47,142 | 4,307,787 |
| Jan 06, 2022 | 258,415 | 11,306,976 | 264,435 | 4,840,547 | Jan 05, 2023 | 193,620 | 10,855,676 | 90,803 | 4,204,970 |
| Jan 13, 2022 | 391,370 | 11,698,346 | 380,645 | 4,829,822 | Jan 12, 2023 | 308,908 | 11,164,584 | 473,124 | 4,369,186 |
| Jan 20, 2022 | 360,866 | 12,059,212 | 676,681 | 5,145,637 | Jan 19, 2023 | 264,248 | 11,428,832 | 500,429 | 4,605,367 |
| Jan 27, 2022 | 383,560 | 12,442,772 | 57,459 | 4,819,536 | Jan 26, 2023 | 496,170 | 11,925,002 | 136,383 | 4,245,580 |
| Feb 03, 2022 | 380,935 | 12,823,707 | 84,767 | 4,523,368 | Feb 02, 2023 | 538,149 | 12,463,151 | 131,389 | 3,838,820 |
| Feb 10, 2022 | 411,635 | 13,235,342 | 118,060 | 4,229,793 | Feb 09, 2023 | 500,140 | 12,963,291 | 209,847 | 3,548,527 |
| Feb 17, 2022 | 546,616 | 13,781,958 | 516,926 | 4,200,103 | Feb 16, 2023 | 338,033 | 13,301,324 | 338,828 | 3,549,322 |
| Feb 24, 2022 | 364,776 | 14,146,734 | 299,967 | 4,135,294 | Feb 23, 2023 | 610,016 | 13,911,340 | 284,115 | 3,223,421 |
| Mar 03, 2022 | 384,467 | 14,531,201 | 307,213 | 4,058,040 | Mar 02, 2023 |  |  |  |  |
| Mar 10, 2022 | 249,466 | 14,780,667 | 145,930 | 3,954,504 | Mar 09, 2023 |  |  |  |  |
| Mar 17, 2022 | 366,053 | 15,146,720 | 155,654 | 3,744,105 | Mar 16, 2023 |  |  |  |  |
| Mar 24, 2022 | 349,209 | 15,495,929 | 94,987 | 3,489,883 | Mar 23, 2023 |  |  |  |  |
| Mar 31, 2022 | 309,754 | 15,805,683 | 156,255 | 3,336,384 | Mar 30, 2023 |  |  |  |  |
| Apr 07, 2022 | 340,372 | 16,146,055 | 96,141 | 3,092,153 | Apr 06, 2023 |  |  |  |  |
| Apr 14, 2022 | 504,002 | 16,650,057 | 26,347 | 2,614,498 | Apr 13, 2023 |  |  |  |  |
| Apr 21, 2022 | 246,017 | 16,896,074 | 32,324 | 2,400,805 | Apr 20, 2023 |  |  |  |  |
| Apr 28, 2022 | 377,403 | 17,273,477 | 118,757 | 2,142,159 | Apr 27, 2023 |  |  |  |  |
| May 05, 2022 | 240,306 | 17,513,783 | 14,108 | 1,915,961 | May 04, 2023 |  |  |  |  |
| May 12, 2022 | 345,363 | 17,859,146 | 8,515 | 1,579,113 | May 11, 2023 |  |  |  |  |
| May 19, 2022 | 298,245 | 18,157,391 | -2,317 | 1,278,551 | May 18, 2023 |  |  |  |  |
| May 26, 2022 | 372,662 | 18,530,053 | 712 | 906,601 | May 25, 2023 |  |  |  |  |
| Jun 02, 2022 | 138,801 | 18,668,854 | -27,480 | 740,320 | Jun 01, 2023 |  |  |  |  |

*Source: Foreign Agricultural Service, U.S. Department of Agriculture (FAS-USDA)*

# Wool

Wool is light, warm, absorbs moisture, and is resistant to fire. Wool is also used for insulation in houses, for carpets and furnishing, and for bedding. Sheep are sheared once a year and produce about 4.3 kg of "greasy" wool per year.

Greasy wool is wool that has not been washed or cleaned. Wool fineness is determined by fiber diameter, which is measured in microns (one-millionth of a meter). Fine wool is softer, lightweight, and produces fine clothing. Merino sheep produce the finest wool.

**Prices** – Average monthly wool prices at U.S. mills in 2022 fell by -9.7% yr/yr to $3.48 per pound. The value of U.S. wool production in 2021 fell by -0.5% yr/yr to $38.177 million, still below the 2011 record high of $48.925 million.

**Supply** – World production of wool has been falling in the past decade due to the increased use of polyester fabrics. Greasy wool world production in 2021 rose by +4.6% yr/yr to 1.763 million metric tons. The world's largest producers of greasy wool in 2021 were China with 20.2% of world production, followed by Australia with 19.8%, and New Zealand with 7.1%. U.S. wool production of 10.184 metric tons in 2021 accounted for only 0.6% of world production.

**Trade** – U.S. exports of domestic wool in 2021 rose by +31.5% yr/yr to 4.970 million pounds. U.S. imports in 2021 fell by -2.7% to 2.996 million pounds, a record low.

## World Production of Wool, Greasy   In Metric Tons

| Year | Argentina | Australia | China | Kazakhstan | New Zealand | Pakistan | Romania | Russia | South Africa | United Kingdom | United States | Uruguay | World Total |
|---|---|---|---|---|---|---|---|---|---|---|---|---|---|
| 2012 | 42,000 | 351,919 | 437,119 | 38,437 | 165,000 | 43,000 | 19,713 | 55,253 | 39,904 | 68,000 | 12,428 | 36,000 | 2,018,893 |
| 2013 | 44,000 | 358,854 | 471,111 | 37,638 | 159,548 | 43,600 | 20,719 | 54,651 | 43,902 | 68,000 | 12,247 | 36,224 | 2,075,578 |
| 2014 | 45,988 | 350,546 | 459,564 | 37,779 | 152,480 | 44,100 | ---- | 56,409 | 45,200 | 67,426 | 12,111 | 35,755 | 2,026,704 |
| 2015 | 46,000 | 363,824 | 413,134 | 38,025 | 147,731 | 44,600 | ---- | 55,644 | 49,788 | 68,390 | 12,270 | 31,000 | 1,983,479 |
| 2016 | 42,700 | 354,991 | 411,642 | 38,518 | 153,253 | 45,100 | ---- | 56,006 | 46,297 | 68,791 | 11,816 | 25,672 | 1,975,118 |
| 2017 | 42,400 | 376,967 | 410,523 | 38,980 | 150,680 | 45,700 | ---- | 56,733 | 45,524 | 68,904 | 11,204 | 25,497 | 1,990,551 |
| 2018 | 40,424 | 385,945 | 356,608 | 39,166 | 145,217 | 45,452 | ---- | 55,471 | 45,190 | 68,947 | 11,068 | 26,634 | 1,829,982 |
| 2019 | 42,000 | 328,608 | 341,120 | 39,492 | 139,622 | 43,538 | ---- | 50,211 | 44,683 | 69,621 | 10,891 | 26,557 | 1,742,027 |
| 2020[1] | 40,677 | 283,794 | 333,624 | 40,210 | 133,836 | 43,449 | ---- | 51,660 | 43,217 | 70,021 | 10,489 | 24,720 | 1,686,205 |
| 2021[2] | 39,742 | 348,608 | 356,216 | 41,199 | 125,772 | 43,328 | ---- | 47,838 | 42,406 | 70,448 | 10,184 | 23,376 | 1,763,309 |

[1] Preliminary.  [2] Estimate.  NA = Not avaliable.  *Source: Food and Agriculture Organization of the United Nations (FAO-UN)*

## Salient Statistics of Wool in the United States

| Year | Sheep & Lambs Shorn[4] -1,000's- | Weight per Fleece -In Lbs.- | Shorn Wool Production 1,000 Lbs. | Price per Lb. | Value of Production -$1,000- | Shorn Wool Support Cents Per Lb. | Shorn Wool Payment Rate | Total Wool Production | Domestic Production | Domestic Wool Exports | Dutiable Imports for Consumption[3] (48's & Finer) | Total New Supply[2] | Duty Free Raw Imports (Not Finer than 46's) | Mill Consumption Apparel | Carpet |
|---|---|---|---|---|---|---|---|---|---|---|---|---|---|---|---|
| 2015 | 3,675 | 7.40 | 27,015 | 145.0 | 39,205 | 115 | 40.0 | 27,015 | 14,300 | 7,847 | 3,980 | 13,718 | 3,321 | ---- | ---- |
| 2016 | 3,585 | 7.30 | 26,050 | 145.0 | 37,721 | 115 | 40.0 | 26,050 | 13,800 | 7,826 | 3,909 | 12,015 | 2,178 | ---- | ---- |
| 2017 | 3,435 | 7.20 | 24,810 | 148.0 | 36,774 | 115 | 40.0 | 24,810 | 13,100 | 11,002 | 3,396 | 7,779 | 2,285 | ---- | ---- |
| 2018 | 3,372 | 7.20 | 24,400 | 175.0 | 42,772 | 115 | 40.0 | 24,400 | 12,883 | 10,421 | 3,116 | 6,033 | 2,348 | ---- | ---- |
| 2019 | 3,320 | 7.20 | 24,010 | 189.0 | 45,364 | | | | | 6,895 | 4,790 | | 2,714 | ---- | ---- |
| 2020 | 3,275 | 7.10 | 23,124 | 166.0 | 38,387 | | | | | 3,781 | 3,079 | | 2,857 | ---- | ---- |
| 2021 | 3,195 | 7.00 | 22,451 | 170.0 | 38,177 | | | | | 4,970 | 2,996 | | 3,683 | ---- | ---- |
| 2022[1] | 3,170 | 7.00 | 22,224 | 153.0 | 33,907 | | | | | | | | | ---- | ---- |

[1] Preliminary.  [2] Production minus exports plus imports; stocks not taken into consideration.  [3] Apparel wool includes all dutiable wool; carpet wool includes all duty-free wool.  [4] Includes sheep shorn at commercial feeding yards.
*Source: Economic Research Service, U.S. Department of Agriculture (ERS-USDA)*

## Shorn Wool Prices   In Dollars Per Pound

| | US Farm Price Shorn Wool Greasy Basis[1] | Australian Offering Price, Clean[2] | | | | | | Graded Territory Shorn Wool, Clean Basis[4] | | | | |
|---|---|---|---|---|---|---|---|---|---|---|---|---|
| Year | cents/Lb | Grade 70's type 61 | Grade 64's type 63 | Grade 62's type 64 | Grade 60/62's type 64A | Grade 58's-56's 433-34 | Market Indicator[3] Cents/Kg. | 62's Staple 3"& up | 60's Staple 3"& up | 58's Staple 3 1/4"& up | 56's Staple 3 1/4"& up | 54's Staple 3 1/2"& up |
| 2014 | 146.0 | 5.03 | 4.89 | 4.91 | 4.80 | 3.39 | 1,046 | 4.17 | 3.44 | 3.00 | 2.47 | 2.21 |
| 2015 | 145.0 | 4.71 | 4.50 | 4.54 | 4.38 | 3.58 | 1,198 | 3.58 | 3.15 | 3.04 | 2.63 | 2.39 |
| 2016 | 145.0 | 5.19 | 4.89 | 4.98 | 4.79 | 3.69 | 1,293 | 3.94 | 3.22 | 3.21 | 2.43 | 2.36 |
| 2017 | 148.0 | 6.67 | 5.50 | 5.84 | 5.13 | 3.80 | 1,540 | 4.36 | 3.57 | 3.24 | 2.36 | NA |
| 2018 | 175.0 | 7.70 | 7.23 | 7.37 | 7.04 | 4.62 | 1,908 | 6.04 | 4.85 | 4.43 | 4.18 | NA |
| 2019 | 189.0 | 6.60 | 6.50 | 6.47 | 6.53 | 4.29 | 1,740 | 5.75 | 5.04 | 3.90 | 3.54 | NA |
| 2020 | 166.0 | 4.59 | 4.35 | 4.28 | 3.39 | 2.83 | 1,227 | 3.08 | 2.30 | 1.83 | 1.45 | NA |
| 2021 | 170.0 | 5.73 | 4.80 | 4.51 | NA | 2.82 | 1,334 | 3.85 | 3.16 | NA | NA | NA |

[1] Annual weighted average.  [2] F.O.B. Australian Wool Corporation South Carolina warehouse in bond.  [3] Index of prices of all wool sold in Australia for the crop year July-June.  [4] Wool principally produced in Texas and the Rocky Mountain States.
*Source: Economic Research Service, U.S. Department of Agriculture (ERS-USDA)*

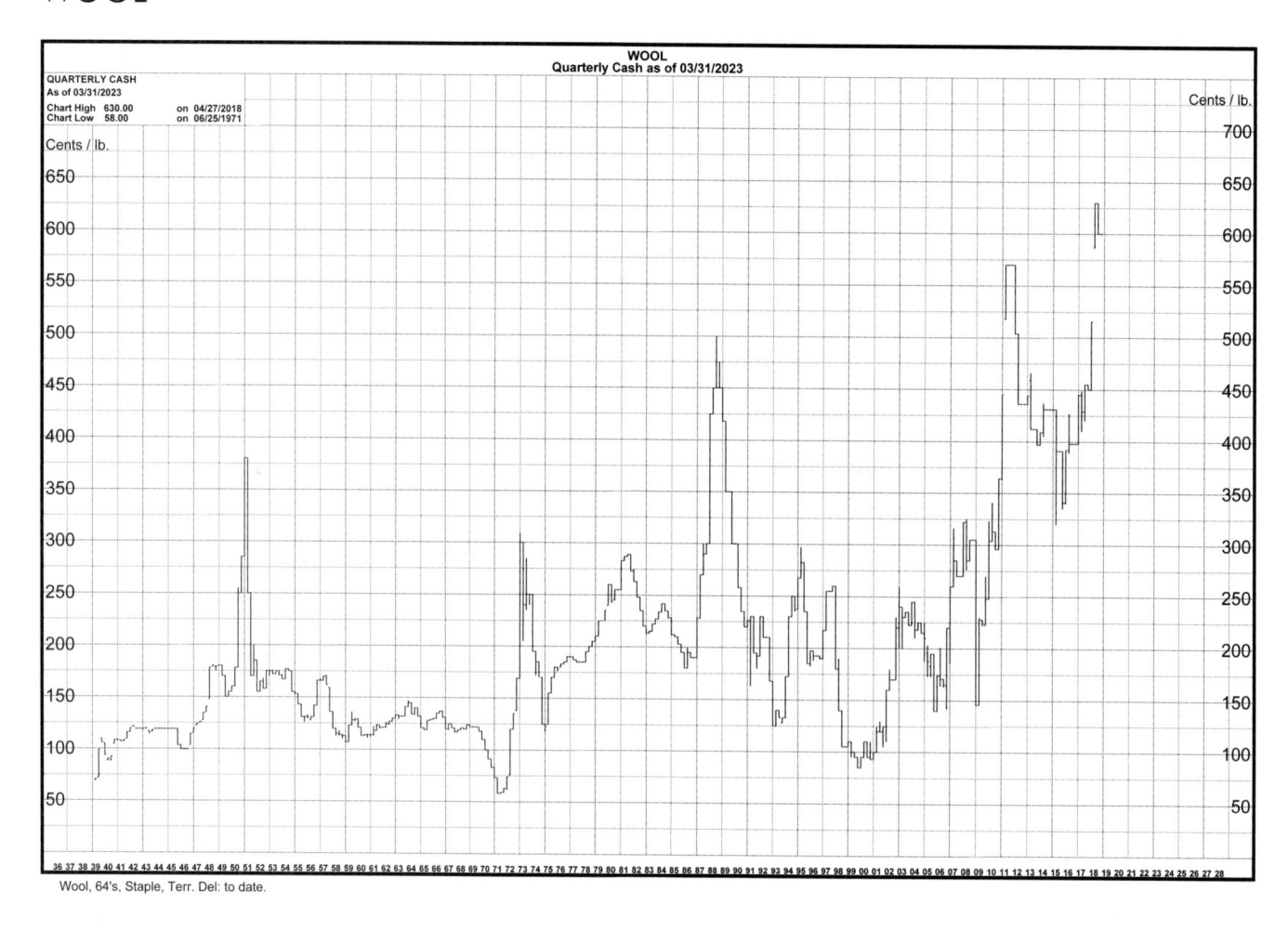

# WOOL

## Average Wool Prices[1] of Australian 64's, Type 62, Duty Paid at U.S. Mills   In Dollars Per Pound

| Year | Jan. | Feb. | Mar. | Apr. | May | June | July | Aug. | Sept. | Oct. | Nov. | Dec. | Average |
|------|------|------|------|------|-----|------|------|------|-------|------|------|------|---------|
| 2013 | 5.87 | 5.95 | 5.84 | 5.38 | 5.17 | 5.09 | 4.71 | 4.67 | 4.79 | 5.45 | 5.37 | 4.89 | 5.27 |
| 2014 | 5.18 | 5.06 | 4.86 | 4.92 | 5.04 | 4.98 | 5.02 | 4.86 | 4.79 | 4.71 | 4.68 | 4.56 | 4.89 |
| 2015 | 4.34 | 4.27 | 4.21 | 4.34 | 4.90 | 5.17 | 4.64 | 4.62 | 4.30 | 4.28 | 4.43 | 4.55 | 4.50 |
| 2016 | 4.53 | 4.65 | 4.72 | 4.89 | 4.80 | 4.86 | 5.17 | 5.23 | 5.06 | 4.99 | 4.90 | 4.94 | 4.90 |
| 2017 | 5.14 | 5.16 | 5.28 | 5.10 | 5.23 | 5.40 | 5.48 | 5.97 | 5.77 | 5.70 | 5.81 | 5.96 | 5.50 |
| 2018 | 6.60 | 6.86 | 6.85 | 6.92 | 7.26 | 7.95 | 7.67 | 7.70 | 7.47 | 7.23 | 7.08 | 7.17 | 7.23 |
| 2019 | 7.38 | 7.72 | 7.54 | 7.45 | 7.11 | 6.82 | 6.60 | 5.34 | 5.36 | 5.44 | 5.53 | 5.50 | 6.48 |
| 2020 | 5.66 | 5.88 | 4.88 | 4.32 | 4.00 | 4.06 | 3.98 | 3.52 | 3.30 | 3.74 | 4.10 | 4.19 | 4.30 |
| 2021 | 4.36 | 4.61 | 4.68 | 4.57 | 4.62 | 4.76 | 4.61 | 4.35 | 4.37 | 4.32 | 4.48 | 4.42 | 4.51 |
| 2022 | 4.57 | 4.60 | 4.54 | 4.50 | 4.47 | 4.70 | 4.53 | 4.31 | 4.14 | 4.01 | 4.04 | 4.40 | 4.40 |

[1] Raw, clean basis.   Source: Economic Research Service, U.S. Department of Agriculture (ERS-USDA)

## United States Imports[2] of Unmanufactured Wool (Clean Yield)   In Thousands of Pounds

| Year | Jan. | Feb. | Mar. | Apr. | May | June | July | Aug. | Sept. | Oct. | Nov. | Dec. | Total |
|------|------|------|------|------|-----|------|------|------|-------|------|------|------|-------|
| 2013 | 457.3 | 251.4 | 358.7 | 819.7 | 909.1 | 891.0 | 796.5 | 889.8 | 437.1 | 919.6 | 458.2 | 430.8 | 7,619.2 |
| 2014 | 597.6 | 379.1 | 348.3 | 583.8 | 868.5 | 553.2 | 707.7 | 718.8 | 544.0 | 967.5 | 403.5 | 420.5 | 7,092.5 |
| 2015 | 504.8 | 800.1 | 420.0 | 657.0 | 765.2 | 585.8 | 681.5 | 619.8 | 404.9 | 664.2 | 527.1 | 655.5 | 7,285.9 |
| 2016 | 564.6 | 321.8 | 600.5 | 942.4 | 514.6 | 746.8 | 419.2 | 229.9 | 330.1 | 300.3 | 488.1 | 568.8 | 6,027.1 |
| 2017 | 488.1 | 490.8 | 747.9 | 706.3 | 427.9 | 552.7 | 341.0 | 627.6 | 486.6 | 357.7 | 283.0 | 171.7 | 5,681.3 |
| 2018 | 279.8 | 281.0 | 485.3 | 624.8 | 416.8 | 383.4 | 629.0 | 591.4 | 550.5 | 443.1 | 449.3 | 328.9 | 5,463.3 |
| 2019 | 271.8 | 784.0 | 1,158.3 | 787.8 | 1,241.1 | 590.6 | 380.1 | 497.4 | 254.9 | 622.1 | 667.5 | 248.0 | 7,503.6 |
| 2020 | 623.4 | 299.1 | 933.0 | 650.5 | 281.2 | 291.1 | 296.1 | 368.7 | 963.7 | 483.9 | 397.0 | 348.8 | 5,936.5 |
| 2021 | 547.3 | 289.9 | 486.0 | 795.3 | 307.9 | 1,025.5 | 550.2 | 286.6 | 821.0 | 457.0 | 814.8 | 296.6 | 6,678.1 |
| 2022[1] | 444.5 | 325.9 | 424.0 | 590.1 | 609.0 | 860.9 | 521.3 | 514.6 | 335.9 | 491.8 | 473.8 | 613.4 | 6,205.2 |

[1] Preliminary.   [2] Data are imports for consumption.   Source: Economic Research Service, U.S. Department of Agriculture (ERS-USDA)

# Zinc

Zinc (atomic symbol Zn) is a bluish-white metallic element that is the 24th most abundant element in the earth's crust. Zinc is never found in its pure state but rather in zinc oxide, zinc silicate, zinc carbonate, zinc sulfide, and also in minerals such as zincite, hemimorphite, smithsonite, franklinite, and sphalerite. Zinc is used as a protective coating for other metals, such as iron and steel, in a process known as galvanizing. Zinc is used as an alloy with copper to make brass, and also as an alloy with aluminum and magnesium. There are, however, a number of substitutes for zinc in chemicals, electronics, and pigments. For example, for aluminum, steel and plastics can substitute for galvanized aluminum sheets. Aluminum alloys can also replace brass. Zinc is used as the negative electrode in dry cell (flashlight) batteries and also in the zinc-mercuric-oxide battery cell, which is the round, flat battery typically used in watches, cameras, and other electronic devices. Zinc is also used in medicine as an antiseptic ointment.

Zinc futures and options are traded on the London Metals Exchange (LME). The LME zinc futures contract calls for the delivery of 25 metric tons of at least 99.995% purity zinc ingots (slabs and plates). The contract trades in terms of U.S. dollars per metric ton. Zinc first started trading on the LME in 1915.

**Prices** – Zinc prices in 2022 rose by +30.7% yr/yr to a monthly average of 191.06 cents per pound, a new record high from the 2006 record of 158.44 cents per pound.

**Supply** – World smelter production of zinc in 2020 rose by +1.5% yr/yr at 13.800 million metric tons and matched the record high from 2016. The world's largest producer of zinc in 2020 was China, with 46.6% of world smelter production, followed by Canada with 4.9%, Japan with 3.6%, Spain with 3.6%, and Australia with 3.2%. China's record-high production of 6.425 million metric tons in 2020 was more than ten times its production level of 550,000 metric tons seen in 1990.

U.S. smelter production in 2020 rose by +56.5% yr/yr to 180,000 metric tons. U.S. mine production of recoverable zinc in 2021 rose by +3.3% yr/yr to 714,500 metric tons. U.S. production in 2019 of slab zinc on a primary basis fell by -1/1% yr/yr at 99,900 metric tons, while secondary production was unchanged yr/yr at 15,000 metric tons.

**Demand** – U.S. consumption of slab zinc in 2022 rose by +0.2% yr/yr to 910,000 metric tons. U.S. consumption of refined zinc in 2021 rose by +6.3% yr/yr to 904,200 metric tons, still below the 2014 record high of 965,000. The breakdown of consumption by industries for 2020 showed that 88.2% of slab zinc consumption was for galvanizers, 7.5% for brass products, and the rest for other miscellaneous industries. The consumption breakdown by grades for 2020 showed that 38.3% was for re-melt and other, 3.2% was for special high grade, 18.2% was for high grade, and 11.7% was for prime western.

**Trade** – The U.S. in 2022 relied on imports for 76% of its consumption of zinc, up sharply from the 35% average seen in the 1990s. U.S. imports for consumption of slab zinc fell by -0.3% yr/yr at 700,000 metric tons in 2022. The breakdown of imports in 2022 shows that zinc is imported as blocks, pigs and slabs (715,964 metric tons); ores (4.829 metric tons); dust, powder, and flakes (208 metric tons); dross, ashes, and fume (272 metric tons); and sheets, plates, other (26,600 metric tons).

### Salient Statistics of Zinc in the United States — In Metric Tons

| Year | Slab Zinc Production Primary | Slab Zinc Production Secondary | Mine Production Recovered | Imports for Consumption Slab Zinc | Imports for Consumption Ore (Zinc Content) | Exports Slab Zinc | Exports Ore (Zinc Content) | Consumption Slab Zinc | Consumption Consumed as Ore | Consumption All Classes[3] | Net Import Reliance As a % of Apparent Consump | High-Grade, Price -Cents/Lb.- |
|---|---|---|---|---|---|---|---|---|---|---|---|---|
| 2013 | 106,000 | 127,000 | 784,000 | 713,000 | 2,550 | 11,500 | 669,000 | 935,000 | ---- | ---- | 75 | 95.60 |
| 2014 | 110,000 | 70,000 | 831,000 | 805,000 | 2 | 19,800 | 644,000 | 965,000 | ---- | ---- | 81 | 107.10 |
| 2015 | 124,000 | 48,000 | 825,000 | 771,000 | ---- | 13,000 | 708,000 | 931,000 | ---- | ---- | 81 | 95.50 |
| 2016 | 111,000 | 15,000 | 805,000 | 713,000 | ---- | 47,000 | 597,000 | 792,000 | ---- | ---- | 84 | 101.40 |
| 2017 | 117,000 | 15,000 | 774,000 | 729,000 | ---- | 33,000 | 682,000 | 829,000 | ---- | ---- | 84 | 139.30 |
| 2018 | 101,000 | 15,000 | 824,000 | 775,000 | ---- | 23,000 | 806,000 | 868,000 | ---- | ---- | 87 | 141.00 |
| 2019 | 99,900 | 15,000 | 753,000 | 830,000 | ---- | 5,000 | 792,000 | 939,000 | ---- | ---- | 88 | 124.10 |
| 2020 | 110,000 | 70,000 | 723,000 | 700,000 | ---- | 2,000 | 546,000 | 878,000 | ---- | ---- | 79 | 110.80 |
| 2021[1] | 110,000 | 110,000 | 704,000 | 702,000 | ---- | 13,200 | 644,000 | 908,000 | ---- | ---- | 76 | 145.80 |
| 2022[2] |  |  | 770,000 | 700,000 | ---- | 10,000 | 660,000 | 910,000 | ---- | ---- | 76 | 190.00 |

[1] Preliminary.  [2] Estimate.  [3] Based on apparent consumption of slab zinc plus zinc content of ores and concentrates and secondary materials used to make zinc dust and chemicals.  Source: U.S. Geological Survey (USGS)

# ZINC

## World Smelter Production of Zinc[3]   In Thousands of Metric Tons

| Year | Australia | Belgium | Canada | China | France | Germany | Italy | Japan | Kazakhstan | Mexico | Spain | United States | World Total |
|---|---|---|---|---|---|---|---|---|---|---|---|---|---|
| 2012 | 498.3 | 250.0 | 648.6 | 4,890.0 | 161.0 | 169.4 | 100.0 | 571.0 | 319.8 | 323.6 | 489.5 | 261.0 | 12,600 |
| 2013 | 498.3 | 252.0 | 651.6 | 5,310.0 | 152.0 | 166.0 | 267.6 | 587.3 | 320.2 | 322.8 | 490.5 | 233.0 | 13,200 |
| 2014 | 481.6 | 262.0 | 649.2 | 5,610.0 | 171.0 | 168.0 | 155.0 | 583.0 | 324.9 | 320.9 | 491.3 | 180.0 | 13,500 |
| 2015 | 489.0 | 260.0 | 683.1 | 5,910.0 | 169.0 | 169.0 | 158.2 | 566.6 | 323.8 | 326.6 | 493.8 | 172.0 | 13,700 |
| 2016 | 464.0 | 236.0 | 691.0 | 6,196.0 | 149.0 | 168.0 | 189.0 | 534.0 | 326.0 | 321.0 | 495.0 | 126.0 | 13,800 |
| 2017 | 462.0 | 249.0 | 598.0 | 6,144.0 | 166.0 | 174.0 | 186.0 | 524.0 | 331.0 | 327.0 | 500.0 | 132.0 | 13,700 |
| 2018 | 490.0 | 275.0 | 620.0 | 5,607.0 | 155.0 | 180.0 | 195.0 | 521.0 | 318.0 | 336.0 | 505.0 | 116.0 | 13,200 |
| 2019 | 436.0 | 270.0 | 655.0 | 6,162.0 | 150.0 | 180.0 | 188.0 | 527.0 | 318.0 | 389.0 | 508.0 | 115.0 | 13,600 |
| 2020[1] | 447.0 | 270.0 | 682.0 | 6,342.0 | 166.0 | 161.0 | 181.0 | 501.0 | 311.0 | 363.0 | 511.0 | 180.0 | 13,800 |
| 2021[2] | 463.0 | 270.0 | 641.0 | 6,408.0 | 168.0 | 160.0 | 181.0 | 517.0 | 327.0 | 357.0 | 510.0 | 220.0 | 13,400 |

[1] Preliminary.   [2] Estimate.   [3] Secondary metal included.   *Source: U.S. Geological Survey (USGS)*

## Consumption (Reported) of Slab Zinc in the United States, by Industries and Grades   In Metric Tons

| | | ---------- By Industries ---------- | | | | | ---------- By Grades ---------- | | | |
|---|---|---|---|---|---|---|---|---|---|---|
| Year | Total | Galvanizers | Brass Products | Zinc-Base Alloy[3] | Zinc Oxide | Other | Special High Grade | High Grade | Remelt and Other | Prime Western |
| 2012 | 806,000 | 685,000 | 49,700 | 44,700 | ---- | 26,500 | 255,000 | 138,000 | 357,455 | 55,300 |
| 2013 | 428,000 | 369,000 | 24,900 | 24,200 | ---- | 9,660 | 105,000 | 85,200 | 208,038 | 30,300 |
| 2014 | 403,000 | 340,000 | 25,600 | 33,000 | ---- | 4,460 | 101,000 | 97,900 | 182,185 | 21,200 |
| 2015 | 433,000 | 367,000 | 27,400 | 34,300 | ---- | 4,710 | 126,000 | 78,200 | 210,260 | 18,800 |
| 2016 | 462,000 | 397,000 | 26,900 | 34,000 | ---- | 4,190 | 136,000 | 78,200 | 227,337 | 21,100 |
| 2017 | 536,000 | 469,000 | 29,000 | 33,900 | ---- | 4,540 | 189,000 | 89,200 | 238,328 | 20,200 |
| 2018 | 509,000 | 450,000 | 21,100 | 34,000 | ---- | 4,490 | 187,000 | 93,100 | 210,161 | 19,100 |
| 2019 | 562,000 | 477,000 | 30,400 | 49,800 | ---- | 4,830 | 206,000 | 107,000 | 231,175 | 17,100 |
| 2020[1] | 535,000 | 472,000 | 40,300 | 19,900 | ---- | 2,560 | 17,000 | 97,200 | 205,000 | 62,600 |
| 2021[2] | 430,000 | 372,000 | 36,300 | 19,400 | ---- | 2,840 | 135,000 | 77,500 | 205,000 | 12,300 |

[1] Preliminary.   [2] Estimated.   [3] Die casters.   [4] Included in other.   W = Withheld.   NA = Not applicable.   *Source: U.S. Geological Survey (USGS)*

## United States Foreign Trade of Zinc   In Metric Tons

| | ---------- Imports for Consumption ---------- | | | | | | ---------- Zinc Ore & Manufactures Exported ---------- | | | | | |
|---|---|---|---|---|---|---|---|---|---|---|---|---|
| | | | | | | | Blocks, Pigs, Anodes, etc. | | Wrought & Alloys | | | |
| Year | Ores[3] | Blocks, Pigs, Slabs | Sheets, Plates, Other | Waste & Scrap | Dross, Ashes, Fume | Dust, Powder & Flakes | Unwrought | Unwrought Alloys | Sheets, Plates & Strips | Angles, Bars, Rods, etc. | Waste & Scrap | Dust (Blue Powder) | Zinc Ore & Concentrates |
| 2013 | 2,550 | 713,000 | 3,570 | 21,000 | 13,000 | 24,500 | 11,500 | 23,200 | 6,500 | 8,580 | 87,500 | 10,700 | 670,000 |
| 2014 | 2 | 805,000 | 4,090 | 24,900 | 8,590 | 31,700 | 19,800 | 27,100 | 6,710 | 10,000 | 71,400 | 10,400 | 644,000 |
| 2015 | 22 | 771,000 | 3,680 | 18,000 | 5,610 | 29,100 | 12,700 | 19,700 | 8,010 | 15,400 | 55,200 | 12,300 | 708,000 |
| 2016 | 60 | 713,000 | 3,650 | 11,300 | 3,770 | 27,800 | 49,792 | 16,194 | 6,960 | 8,101 | 30,091 | 12,753 | 604,000 |
| 2017 | 6,780 | 730,000 | 3,690 | 11,100 | 6,350 | 27,100 | 32,700 | 14,500 | 7,670 | 9,110 | 33,600 | 12,800 | 688,000 |
| 2018 | 31,000 | 774,700 | 5,410 | 12,900 | 4,300 | 26,600 | 23,300 | 21,800 | 7,170 | 10,600 | 40,400 | 13,500 | 789,790 |
| 2019 | 10,000 | 829,500 | 19 | 272 | 1,250 | 12,900 | 21,800 | 10,600 | 8,300 | 7,170 | 179 | 40,400 | 868,500 |
| 2020 | 3,171,000 | 700,400 | 4,300 | 115,000 | 26,600 | 272 | 10,600 | 7,170 | 23,900 | 8,300 | 60,200 | 179 | 548,190 |
| 2021[1] | 13,426,000 | 701,700 | 1,250 | 208 | 12,900 | 115,000 | 7,170 | 8,300 | 13,500 | 23,900 | 281 | 60,200 | 701,700 |
| 2022[2] | 4,868,000 | 762,300 | 26,600 | 98,800 | 272 | 208 | 8,300 | 23,900 | 40,400 | 13,500 | 1,000 | 281 | 762,300 |

[1] Preliminary.   [2] Estimate.   [3] Zinc content.   *Source: U.S. Geological Survey (USGS)*

## Mine Production of Recoverable Zinc in the United States   In Thousands of Metric Tons

| Year | Jan. | Feb. | Mar. | Apr. | May | June | July | Aug. | Sept. | Oct. | Nov. | Dec. | Total |
|---|---|---|---|---|---|---|---|---|---|---|---|---|---|
| 2013 | 64.1 | 54.5 | 56.0 | 63.2 | 65.8 | 61.3 | 61.7 | 67.2 | 66.7 | 68.0 | 68.8 | 68.7 | 761.0 |
| 2014 | 67.9 | 67.8 | 70.6 | 69.5 | 63.3 | 61.2 | 64.6 | 65.6 | 66.4 | 63.2 | 71.3 | 75.0 | 803.0 |
| 2015 | 67.3 | 63.6 | 72.4 | 68.5 | 74.5 | 70.4 | 62.5 | 65.9 | 58.4 | 58.9 | 59.6 | 56.9 | 781.0 |
| 2016 | 54.3 | 55.9 | 68.6 | 66.8 | 67.1 | 68.9 | 59.0 | 67.1 | 66.0 | 68.6 | 54.2 | 52.6 | 777.0 |
| 2017 | 58.2 | 50.5 | 60.0 | 62.3 | 53.7 | 53.4 | 64.9 | 71.3 | 62.9 | 73.7 | 72.2 | 62.5 | 748.0 |
| 2018 | 63.9 | 55.5 | 51.9 | 65.7 | 69.5 | 74.9 | 74.7 | 68.3 | 70.5 | 79.1 | 56.5 | 77.0 | 807.5 |
| 2019 | 71.6 | 43.3 | 46.1 | 73.2 | 67.7 | 70.3 | 70.4 | 65.1 | 66.1 | 57.8 | 50.3 | 57.2 | 739.1 |
| 2020 | 56.0 | 58.8 | 60.1 | 38.2 | 47.0 | 47.6 | 57.9 | 75.0 | 59.9 | 59.9 | 59.5 | 71.5 | 691.4 |
| 2021 | 71.6 | 51.2 | 61.3 | 56.1 | 65.8 | 69.1 | 56.9 | 65.7 | 50.3 | 56.3 | 46.7 | 63.5 | 714.5 |
| 2022[1] | 49.7 | 60.9 | 69.7 | 65.4 | 63.0 | 64.4 | 71.1 | 75.0 | 62.7 | 54.0 | 45.4 | 63.5 | 744.8 |

[1] Preliminary.   *Source: U.S. Geological Survey (USGS)*

# ZINC

**Mine Production of Zinc Content of Concentrate in the United States**   In Thousands of Metric Tons

| Year | Jan. | Feb. | Mar. | Apr. | May | June | July | Aug. | Sept. | Oct. | Nov. | Dec. | Total |
|---|---|---|---|---|---|---|---|---|---|---|---|---|---|
| 2013 | 66.4 | 56.4 | 57.8 | 65.4 | 68.1 | 63.5 | 63.8 | 69.5 | 69.0 | 70.4 | 71.3 | 71.1 | 788.0 |
| 2014 | 70.2 | 70.2 | 73.0 | 71.9 | 65.5 | 63.4 | 66.9 | 67.9 | 68.7 | 65.5 | 73.7 | 77.5 | 832.0 |
| 2015 | 69.5 | 65.8 | 74.9 | 70.9 | 76.9 | 72.8 | 64.7 | 68.2 | 60.5 | 60.9 | 61.7 | 58.9 | 808.0 |
| 2016 | 58.9 | 57.8 | 71.0 | 69.1 | 69.4 | 71.3 | 61.0 | 69.3 | 68.3 | 71.0 | 56.0 | 54.4 | 803.0 |
| 2017 | 60.1 | 52.2 | 62.1 | 64.3 | 55.6 | 55.2 | 67.0 | 73.8 | 65.0 | 76.2 | 74.7 | 64.6 | 774.0 |
| 2018 | 66.0 | 57.4 | 53.7 | 68.0 | 71.9 | 77.5 | 77.3 | 70.7 | 71.7 | 81.9 | 58.4 | 79.6 | 834.1 |
| 2019 | 74.0 | 44.9 | 47.6 | 75.5 | 69.7 | 71.8 | 72.5 | 67.1 | 68.1 | 59.6 | 51.7 | 58.9 | 761.4 |
| 2020 | 57.7 | 60.6 | 61.9 | 39.4 | 48.5 | 49.1 | 59.7 | 77.3 | 61.7 | 61.7 | 61.2 | 73.6 | 712.4 |
| 2021 | 73.8 | 52.3 | 62.6 | 57.3 | 57.3 | 70.6 | 58.2 | 67.2 | 51.5 | 57.6 | 47.7 | 64.9 | 721.0 |
| 2022[1] | 50.8 | 62.3 | 71.2 | 66.8 | 64.4 | 65.9 | 72.7 | 76.7 | 64.1 | 55.3 | 46.4 | 64.9 | 761.5 |

[1] Preliminary.   Source: U.S. Geological Survey (USGS)


**Smelter Production of Refined Zinc in the United States**   In Thousands of Metric Tons

| Year | Jan. | Feb. | Mar. | Apr. | May | June | July | Aug. | Sept. | Oct. | Nov. | Dec. | Total |
|---|---|---|---|---|---|---|---|---|---|---|---|---|---|
| 2013 | 22.7 | 18.5 | 18.5 | 20.2 | 19.7 | 19.7 | 20.3 | 19.8 | 19.8 | 19.8 | 18.3 | 18.3 | 229.0 |
| 2014 | 18.3 | 18.0 | 18.0 | 18.0 | 17.1 | 17.1 | 12.1 | 11.0 | 10.5 | 13.6 | 13.8 | 15.7 | 180.0 |
| 2015 | 15.0 | 14.6 | 14.6 | 14.0 | 15.2 | 14.8 | 15.1 | 13.7 | 13.5 | 12.7 | 14.4 | 13.5 | 172.0 |
| 2016 | ---- | 10.6 | 10.6 | 10.6 | 10.6 | 10.6 | 10.6 | 9.6 | 9.6 | 9.6 | 11.3 | 11.3 | 126.0 |
| 2017 | 10.6 | 10.9 | 10.9 | 10.9 | 11.3 | 11.3 | 11.3 | 9.9 | 9.9 | 9.9 | 9.9 | 9.9 | 132.0 |
| 2018 | 11.3 | 6.1 | 11.3 | 10.9 | 10.6 | 10.6 | 11.5 | 9.3 | 8.9 | 9.9 | 9.9 | 9.9 | 120.2 |
| 2019 | 8.4 | 8.6 | 8.6 | 8.6 | 8.6 | 8.6 | 8.6 | 9.9 | 9.9 | 9.9 | 9.9 | 9.9 | 109.5 |
| 2020 | 9.9 | 9.9 | 9.9 | 9.9 | 9.9 | 12.0 | 14.0 | 14.0 | 15.0 | 15.0 | 15.0 | 18.0 | 152.5 |
| 2021 | 18.0 | 18.0 | 18.0 | 18.0 | 18.0 | 18.0 | 18.0 | 18.0 | 18.0 | 18.0 | 18.0 | 18.0 | 216.0 |
| 2022[1] | 18.0 | 18.0 | 18.0 | 18.0 | 18.0 | 18.0 | 8.0 | 18.0 | 18.0 | 18.0 | 18.0 | 18.0 | 206.0 |

[1] Preliminary.   Reported zinc content in both zinc and lead concentrates. Includes zinc metal used to manufacture zinc oxide.
Source: U.S. Geological Survey (USGS)


**Imports of Refined Zinc in the United States**   In Thousands of Metric Tons

| Year | Jan. | Feb. | Mar. | Apr. | May | June | July | Aug. | Sept. | Oct. | Nov. | Dec. | Total |
|---|---|---|---|---|---|---|---|---|---|---|---|---|---|
| 2013 | 55.3 | 57.1 | 57.3 | 75.7 | 57.8 | 58.1 | 55.7 | 118.0 | 66.6 | 59.5 | 50.5 | 62.5 | 717.0 |
| 2014 | 88.7 | 48.5 | 52.1 | 70.4 | 99.9 | 52.4 | 58.7 | 81.8 | 64.1 | 57.6 | 66.3 | 65.8 | 805.0 |
| 2015 | 58.9 | 47.5 | 60.8 | 60.0 | 103.0 | 78.9 | 52.3 | 84.7 | 56.2 | 56.1 | 56.3 | 56.2 | 771.0 |
| 2016 | 54.1 | 52.0 | 54.8 | 53.1 | 85.5 | 51.8 | 61.3 | 58.8 | 64.2 | 60.7 | 62.7 | 53.8 | 713.0 |
| 2017 | 97.0 | 52.2 | 89.3 | 68.4 | 54.6 | 56.9 | 45.1 | 47.9 | 49.6 | 58.0 | 44.2 | 66.6 | 730.0 |
| 2018 | 57.4 | 57.2 | 67.2 | 79.9 | 64.5 | 62.6 | 58.6 | 69.0 | 64.4 | 77.4 | 57.2 | 59.3 | 774.7 |
| 2019 | 74.4 | 60.2 | 69.2 | 66.4 | 68.2 | 67.5 | 71.4 | 63.1 | 81.5 | 68.2 | 61.1 | 78.3 | 829.5 |
| 2020 | 69.5 | 50.9 | 73.4 | 64.7 | 61.8 | 46.8 | 66.0 | 56.4 | 46.7 | 59.0 | 54.3 | 50.9 | 700.4 |
| 2021 | 57.5 | 55.8 | 57.2 | 54.9 | 50.9 | 62.5 | 53.8 | 77.2 | 62.0 | 64.6 | 55.9 | 49.4 | 701.7 |
| 2022[1] | 57.5 | 46.7 | 56.0 | 62.8 | 57.6 | 82.6 | 48.3 | 67.7 | 45.4 | 65.9 | 65.8 | 106.0 | 762.3 |

[1] Preliminary.   Source: U.S. Geological Survey (USGS)


**Exports of Refined Zinc in the United States**   In Thousands of Metric Tons

| Year | Jan. | Feb. | Mar. | Apr. | May | June | July | Aug. | Sept. | Oct. | Nov. | Dec. | Total |
|---|---|---|---|---|---|---|---|---|---|---|---|---|---|
| 2013 | 0.4 | 1.5 | 1.6 | 2.4 | 1.5 | 1.1 | 0.9 | 0.3 | 1.3 | 0.3 | 0.3 | 0.1 | 11.5 |
| 2014 | 1.1 | 4.0 | 0.9 | 1.7 | 1.5 | 0.3 | 0.2 | 0.5 | 2.4 | 8.8 | 0.8 | 2.3 | 19.8 |
| 2015 | 0.7 | 1.2 | 1.7 | 0.1 | 2.1 | 1.3 | 1.2 | 0.2 | 0.2 | 2.6 | 0.3 | 1.1 | 12.7 |
| 2016 | 10.5 | 21.4 | 2.3 | 7.1 | 0.5 | 2.0 | 2.1 | 1.0 | 1.1 | 1.3 | 0.4 | 0.2 | 49.8 |
| 2017 | 2.1 | 5.4 | 4.1 | 2.6 | 1.6 | 2.9 | 4.2 | 1.1 | 2.0 | 1.5 | 3.6 | 1.8 | 32.7 |
| 2018 | 1.7 | 0.5 | 0.4 | 0.3 | 3.3 | 4.3 | 1.9 | 2.2 | 1.8 | 1.4 | 2.1 | 3.6 | 23.2 |
| 2019 | 1.4 | 0.3 | 0.3 | 0.3 | 0.4 | 0.2 | 0.2 | 0.3 | 0.3 | 0.3 | 0.3 | 0.3 | 4.6 |
| 2020 | 0.5 | 0.2 | 0.4 | 0.2 | 0.1 | 0.1 | 0.2 | 0.1 | 0.1 | 0.3 | 0.2 | 0.2 | 2.5 |
| 2021 | 0.3 | 0.2 | 1.8 | 0.2 | 0.1 | 0.6 | 0.2 | 0.3 | 0.3 | 0.8 | 4.9 | 3.7 | 13.4 |
| 2022[1] | 2.0 | 2.8 | 0.4 | 0.2 | 0.2 | 0.2 | 0.3 | 1.0 | 0.3 | 0.3 | 0.3 | 0.6 | 8.6 |

[1] Preliminary.   Source: U.S. Geological Survey (USGS)

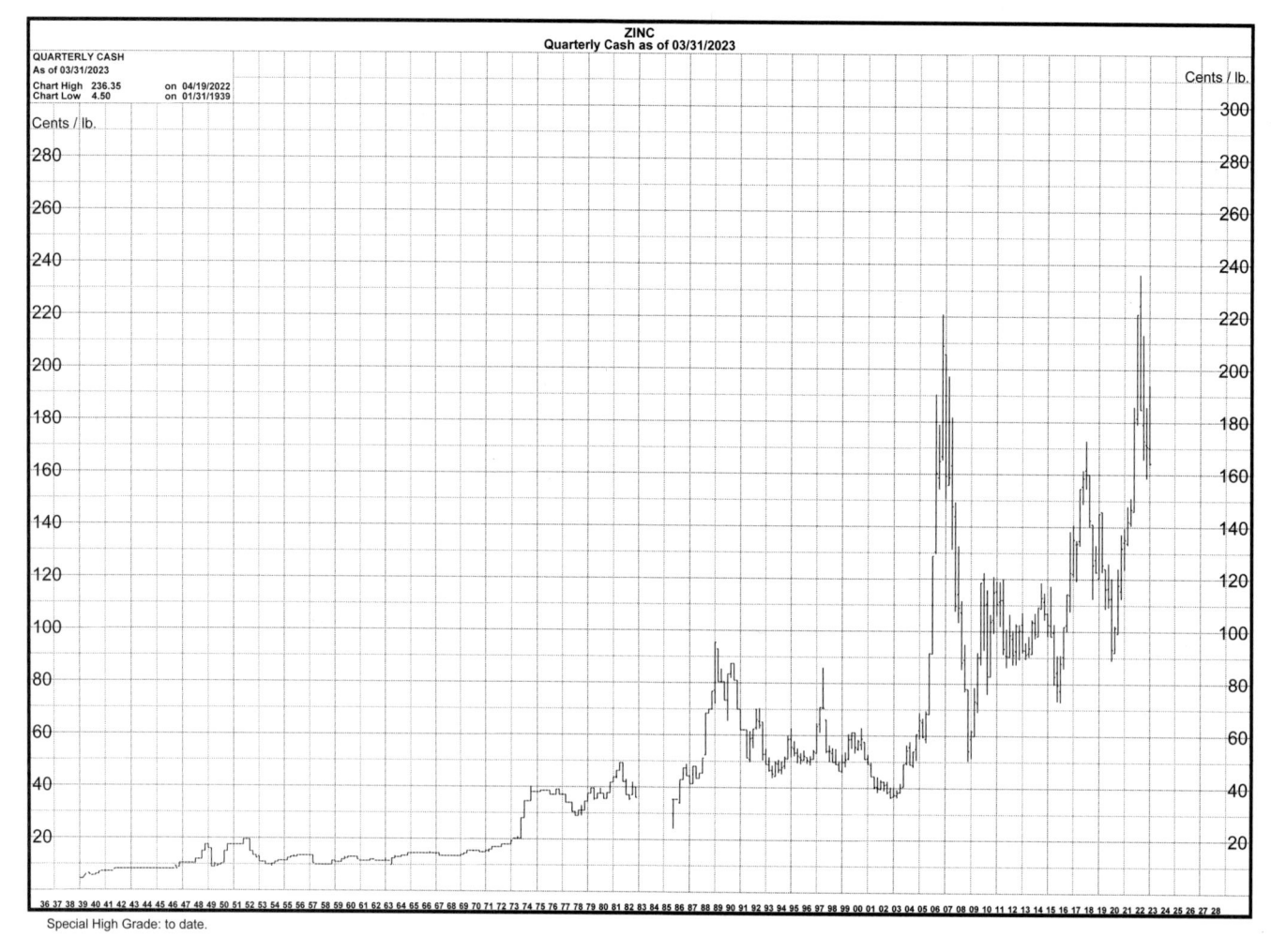

# ZINC

## Average Price of Zinc, Prime Western Slab (Delivered U.S. Basis)   In Cents Per Pound

| Year | Jan. | Feb. | Mar. | Apr. | May | June | July | Aug. | Sept. | Oct. | Nov. | Dec. | Average |
|---|---|---|---|---|---|---|---|---|---|---|---|---|---|
| 2013 | 100.21 | 104.53 | 95.62 | 92.04 | 91.25 | 91.88 | 92.18 | 95.47 | 93.11 | 93.86 | 93.40 | 98.17 | 95.14 |
| 2014 | 101.35 | 101.41 | 100.58 | 101.54 | 102.75 | 105.78 | 113.91 | 114.56 | 112.82 | 112.02 | 111.17 | 107.09 | 107.08 |
| 2015 | 104.08 | 103.48 | 100.33 | 108.09 | 112.42 | 102.59 | 98.49 | 89.77 | 85.54 | 86.07 | 79.26 | 76.02 | 95.51 |
| 2016 | 75.65 | 84.61 | 88.64 | 90.59 | 91.48 | 98.21 | 105.64 | 110.08 | 110.30 | 111.42 | 122.23 | 127.26 | 101.34 |
| 2017 | 129.14 | 135.58 | 134.68 | 128.04 | 126.96 | 125.45 | 135.06 | 144.21 | 150.02 | 157.19 | 155.18 | 153.34 | 139.57 |
| 2018 | 164.74 | 169.02 | 157.64 | 153.85 | 147.33 | 149.04 | 129.11 | 122.68 | 119.08 | 129.99 | 126.18 | 127.68 | 141.36 |
| 2019 | 124.85 | 131.63 | 138.27 | 142.02 | 133.68 | 126.46 | 119.18 | 111.66 | 113.84 | 119.36 | 119.36 | 111.58 | 124.32 |
| 2020 | 115.12 | 104.53 | 94.90 | 94.38 | 97.53 | 99.89 | 106.60 | 117.67 | 119.37 | 118.98 | 129.02 | 134.63 | 111.05 |
| 2021 | 131.28 | 132.62 | 134.98 | 136.38 | 143.11 | 142.29 | 141.98 | 144.28 | 147.63 | 164.78 | 164.25 | 171.16 | 146.23 |
| 2022 | 183.79 | 187.33 | 204.60 | 228.46 | 205.14 | 206.62 | 178.44 | 201.35 | 179.40 | 171.19 | 169.55 | 176.80 | 191.06 |

*Source: American Metal Market (AMM)*

## Consumption of Refined Zinc in the United States   In Thousands of Metric Tons

| Year | Jan. | Feb. | Mar. | Apr. | May | June | July | Aug. | Sept. | Oct. | Nov. | Dec. | Total |
|---|---|---|---|---|---|---|---|---|---|---|---|---|---|
| 2013 | 77.6 | 77.1 | 77.3 | 98.4 | 78.9 | 76.7 | 75.2 | 138.0 | 85.1 | 78.9 | 68.5 | 80.7 | 934.0 |
| 2014 | 106.0 | 62.4 | 69.2 | 86.7 | 116.0 | 69.3 | 70.6 | 92.3 | 72.2 | 62.4 | 79.3 | 79.2 | 965.0 |
| 2015 | 73.2 | 60.9 | 73.8 | 73.9 | 116.0 | 92.5 | 66.2 | 98.2 | 69.5 | 66.3 | 70.4 | 68.5 | 931.0 |
| 2016 | ---- | 41.2 | 63.2 | 56.7 | 95.5 | 60.3 | 69.8 | 67.4 | 72.7 | 68.9 | 73.5 | 64.8 | 789.0 |
| 2017 | 106.0 | 57.8 | 96.1 | 76.7 | 64.3 | 65.3 | 52.1 | 56.7 | 57.6 | 66.5 | 50.5 | 74.8 | 829.0 |
| 2018 | 66.9 | 62.9 | 78.0 | 90.5 | 71.8 | 68.9 | 68.3 | 76.1 | 71.6 | 86.0 | 65.1 | 65.6 | 871.7 |
| 2019 | 81.5 | 67.9 | 77.5 | 74.7 | 76.4 | 75.8 | 79.8 | 72.8 | 91.1 | 77.8 | 70.7 | 88.0 | 934.0 |
| 2020 | 79.0 | 60.6 | 82.9 | 74.4 | 71.6 | 58.7 | 79.7 | 70.3 | 61.6 | 73.7 | 69.1 | 68.7 | 850.3 |
| 2021 | 75.2 | 73.5 | 73.4 | 72.7 | 68.8 | 79.9 | 71.6 | 94.9 | 79.7 | 81.8 | 69.0 | 63.7 | 904.2 |
| 2022[1] | 73.5 | 61.9 | 73.6 | 80.5 | 75.4 | 100.0 | 66.0 | 84.8 | 63.1 | 83.6 | 83.4 | 123.0 | 968.8 |

[1] Preliminary.   *Source: U.S. Geological Survey (USGS)*

```
R
332.644 C649 2023

The cmdty yearbook
Central REFERENCE
07/23
```
DISCARD